Organizational Behavior

Organizational Behavior

EDITION

16

Stephen P. Robbins
—San Diego State University

Timothy A. Judge
—University of Notre Dame

PEARSON

Boston   Columbus   Indianapolis   New York   San Francisco   Upper Saddle River
Amsterdam   Cape Town   Dubai   London   Madrid   Milan   Munich   Paris   Montreal   Toronto
Delhi   Mexico City   São Paulo   Sydney   Hong Kong   Seoul   Singapore   Taipei   Tokyo

Editor in Chief: Stephanie Wall
Senior Acquisitions Editor: Kris Ellis-Levy
Program Manager: Sarah Holle
Editorial Assistant: Bernard Ollila
Director of Marketing: Maggie Moylan
Senior Marketing Manager: Erin Gardner
Marketing Assistant: Gianna Sandri
Project Manager Team Lead: Judy Leale
Program Manager Team Lead: Ashley Santora
Project Manager: Kelly Warsak
Operations Specialist: Nancy Maneri
Creative Director: Jayne Conte
Cover Designer: Bruce Kenselaar
Cover Art: © Bule Sky Studio/Shutterstock

VP, Director of Digital Strategy & Assessment: Paul Gentile
Digital Editor: Brian Surette
Digital Development Manager: Robin Lazrus
Digital Project Manager: Alana Coles
MyLab Production Manager: Joan Waxman
Full-Service Project Management: Christian Holdener/S4Carlisle Publishing Services
Composition: S4Carlisle Publishing Services
Printer/Binder: Courier/Kendallville
Cover Printer: Lehigh-Phoenix Color/Hagerstown
Text Font: ITC New Baskerville Std

Library of Congress Cataloging-in-Publication Data
Robbins, Stephen P.,
   Organizational behavior / Stephen P . Robbins, San Diego State University Timothy A . Judge, University of Notre Dame.—Edition 16.
      pages cm
   Includes indexes.
   ISBN 978-0-13-350764-5
1. Organizational behavior. I. Judge, Tim. II. Title.

HD58.7.R62 2015
658.3—dc23

2013022717

10 9 8 7 6 5 4 3 2 1

ISBN 10:   0-13-350764-5
ISBN 13: 978-0-13-350764-5

Brief Contents

Contents

2   The Individual

4 *Emotions and Moods* 88

3 The Group

12 *Leadership* 330

15 *Foundations of Organization Structure* 430

4   The Organization System

16   *Organizational Culture* 462

17 *Human Resource Policies and Practices* 496

About the Authors

Stephen P. Robbins

Education

Ph.D., University of Arizona

Professional Experience

Academic Positions: Professor, San Diego State University, Southern Illinois University at Edwardsville, University of Baltimore, Concordia University in Montreal, and University of Nebraska at Omaha.

Research: Research interests have focused on conflict, power, and politics in organizations; behavioral decision making; and the development of effective interpersonal skills.

Books Published: World's best-selling author of textbooks in both management and organizational behavior. His books have sold more than 5 million copies and have been translated into 20 languages; editions have been adapted for Canada, Australia, South Africa, and India, such as these:

- *Essentials of Organizational Behavior,* 12th ed. (Prentice Hall, 2014)
- *Management,* 12th ed. with Mary Coulter (Prentice Hall, 2014)
- *Fundamentals of Human Resource Management,* 10th ed., with David DeCenzo (Wiley, 2010)
- *Prentice Hall's Self-Assessment Library 3.4* (Prentice Hall, 2010)
- *Fundamentals of Management,* 8th ed., with David DeCenzo and Mary Coulter (Prentice Hall, 2013)
- *Supervision Today!* 7th ed., with David DeCenzo and Robert Wolter (Prentice Hall, 2013)
- *Training in Interpersonal Skills: TIPS for Managing People at Work,* 6th ed., with Phillip Hunsaker (Prentice Hall, 2012)
- *Managing Today!* 2nd ed. (Prentice Hall, 2000)
- *Organization Theory,* 3rd ed. (Prentice Hall, 1990)
- *The Truth About Managing People,* 2nd ed. (Financial Times/Prentice Hall, 2008)
- *Decide and Conquer: Make Winning Decisions and Take Control of Your Life* (Financial Times/Prentice Hall, 2004).

Other Interests

In his "other life," Dr. Robbins actively participates in masters' track competition. After turning 50 in 1993, he won 18 national championships and 12 world titles. He is the current world record holder at 100 meters (12.37 seconds) and 200 meters (25.20 seconds) for men 65 and over.

Timothy A. Judge

Education

Ph.D., University of Illinois at Urbana-Champaign

Professional Experience

Academic Positions: Franklin D. Schurz Chair, Department of Management, Mendoza College of Business, University of Notre Dame; Visiting Distinguished Adjunct Professor of King Abdulaziz University, Saudi Arabia; Visiting Professor, Division of Psychology & Language Sciences, University College London; Matherly-McKethan Eminent Scholar in Management, Warrington College of Business Administration, University of Florida; Stanley M. Howe Professor in Leadership, Henry B. Tippie College of Business, University of Iowa; Associate Professor (with tenure), Department of Human Resource Studies, School of Industrial and Labor Relations, Cornell University; Lecturer, Charles University, Czech Republic, and Comenius University, Slovakia; Instructor, Industrial/Organizational Psychology, Department of Psychology, University of Illinois at Urbana-Champaign.

Research: Dr. Judge's primary research interests are in (1) personality, moods, and emotions; (2) job attitudes; (3) leadership and influence behaviors; and (4) careers (person–organization fit, career success). Dr. Judge has published more than 145 articles on these and other major topics in journals such as *Journal of Organizational Behavior, Personnel Psychology, Academy of Management Journal, Journal of Applied Psychology, European Journal of Personality,* and *European Journal of Work and Organizational Psychology.*

Fellowship: Dr. Judge is a fellow of the American Psychological Association, the Academy of Management, the Society for Industrial and Organizational Psychology, and the American Psychological Society.

Awards: In 1995, Dr. Judge received the Ernest J. McCormick Award for Distinguished Early Career Contributions from the Society for Industrial and Organizational Psychology. In 2001, he received the Larry L. Cummings Award for mid-career contributions from the Organizational Behavior Division of the Academy of Management. In 2007, he received the Professional Practice Award from the Institute of Industrial and Labor Relations, University of Illinois. In 2008, he received the University of Florida Doctoral Mentoring Award. And in 2012, he received the Editorial Board of the *European Journal of Work and Organizational Psychology* (EJWOP) best paper of the year award.

Other Books Published: H. G. Heneman III, T. A. Judge, and J. D. Kammeyer-Mueller, *Staffing Organizations,* 7th ed. (Madison, WI: Mendota House/Irwin, 2012)

Other Interests

Although he cannot keep up (literally!) with Dr. Robbins' accomplishments on the track, Dr. Judge enjoys golf, cooking and baking, literature (he's a particular fan of Thomas Hardy and is a member of the Thomas Hardy Society), and keeping up with his three children, who range in age from 24 to 10.

Preface

Welcome to the sixteenth edition of *Organizational Behavior!* Long considered the standard for all organizational behavior textbooks, this edition continues its tradition of making current, relevant research come alive for students. While maintaining its hallmark features—clear writing style, cutting-edge content, and engaging pedagogy—the sixteenth edition has been updated to reflect the most recent research within the field of organizational behavior. This is one of the most comprehensive and thorough revisions of *Organizational Behavior* we've undertaken, and while we've preserved the core material, we're confident that this edition reflects the most important research and topical issues facing organizations, managers, and employees.

Key Changes to the Sixteenth Edition

- *NEW* The **most substantial updating ever.** The following features are completely rewritten and contain new content:
  - *Opening Vignette*
  - *OB Poll*
  - *glOBalization!*
  - *Myth or Science?*
- *NEW* The following features are either completely rewritten with **new content or are substantially revised and updated**:
  - *An Ethical Choice*
  - *Point/Counterpoint*
- *NEW* **Global OB icon** makes it easy to identify throughout the text where the latest global OB research has been woven into the content.
- *NEW* **Photos and captions** throughout the text have been updated to help engage students in the concepts being covered.
- *NEW* The **Summary** and **Implications for Managers** sections are now separate features, making it easier for students to focus on and recognize practical ways to apply the chapter's material on the job.
- *NEW* The following end of chapter material is either completely rewritten with **new content or substantially revised and updated**:
  - *Case Incidents*
  - *Ethical Dilemmas*
- *NEW* **Assisted Graded Questions** that students can complete and submit via MyManagementLab® are provided for each chapter.

Chapter-by-Chapter Changes
Chapter 1: What Is Organizational Behavior?
- Entirely new *Opening Vignette* (Got Your Degree? Great, Go Flip Burgers)
- New *glOBalization!* (Suicide by Economic Crisis)
- New *Myth or Science?* ("Management by Walking Around Is the Most Effective Management")
- New *OB Poll* (Percentage of Men and Women Working)

- New *Experiential Exercise* (Intoxicated Workplaces)
- New *An Ethical Choice* (Vacation Deficit Disorder)
- New *Case Incident* (Apple Goes Global)
- New/Updated *Point/Counterpoint* (Lost in Translation?)
- New Exhibit (Employment Options)
- New section (Implications for Managers) with how-to tips on applying the chapter to worklife
- Major new section (Enhancing Well-Being at Work)
- New research on the importance of interpersonal skills
- Updated discussion in Challenges and Opportunities for OB and Responding to Economic Pressures
- New section (Adapting to Differing Cultural and Regulatory Norms)
- Updated section with new research on Improving Customer Service
- Updated business examples in Creating a Positive Work Environment

Chapter 2: Diversity in Organizations

- Entirely new *Opening Vignette* (Dynamics of Diversity)
- New *glOBalization!* (Worldwide Talent Search for Women)
- New *OB Poll* (Gender Pay Gap: Narrowing But Still There)
- New *Myth or Science?* ("Bald Is Better")
- New *An Ethical Choice* (Affirmative Action for Unemployed Veterans)
- New *Point/Counterpoint* (Affirmative Action Should Be Abolished)
- Updated *Ethical Dilemma* (Board Quotas)
- New section (Implications for Managers) with how-to tips on applying the chapter to worklife
- New research on the composition and fitness of the aging workforce
- New research and discussion on the representation of gender equality at work
- New research in Race and Ethnicity
- Updated/new major section (Sexual Orientation and Gender Identity)
- Major new section (Cultural Identity)
- New/updated *Case Incident 1* (Levitating IQs)
- New/updated *Case Incident 2* (The Treasure Trove of the Aging Workforce)
- New research in Attracting, Selecting, Developing, and Retaining Diverse Employees

Chapter 3: Attitudes and Job Satisfaction

- Entirely new *Opening Vignette* (Micro-Entrepreneurs)
- New *glOBalization!* (Exodus Phenomenon)
- New *OB Poll* (Happy Places)
- New *Myth or Science?* ("Happy Workers Means Happy Profits")
- Updated *Point/Counterpoint* (Employer–Employee Loyalty Is an Outdated Concept)
- New section (Implications for Managers) with how-to tips on applying the chapter to worklife
- Updated/New *Ethical Dilemma* (Bounty Hunters)
- New *An Ethical Choice* (Are Employers Responsible for Workplace Incivilities?)
- New *Case Incident 1* (The Pursuit of Happiness: Flexibility)
- Updated *Case Incident 2* (Job Crafting)
- New research on the relationship between job satisfaction and turnover
- New research in What Are the Major Job Attitudes? and Are These Job Attitudes Really All That Distinct?

- New research and discussion in Perceived Organizational Support
- New research and discussion in Employee Engagement
- New Exhibit (Worst Jobs of 2013)
- New research in Does Behavior Always Follow from Attitudes? and What Causes Job Satisfaction?

Chapter 4: Emotions and Moods

- Entirely new *Opening Vignette* (Affective Computing: Reading Your Mind)
- New *glOBalization!* (Creating Highly Productive Teams Across the Cultural Emotional Barrier)
- New *OB Poll* (Emotional States)
- New *Myth or Science?* ("Smile, and the Work World Smiles With You")
- New Exhibit (Time of Day Effects on Mood of Americans as Rated from Twitter Postings)
- New Exhibit (Day-of-Week Mood Effects Across Four Cultures)
- New research and discussion on moods and energy
- New section (Implications for Managers) with how-to tips on applying the chapter to worklife
- New research and discussion on the role of emotions on ethical decisions
- New research on gender and emotions
- New research on surface acting and well-being
- Major new section (Emotion Regulation)
- New research and discussion on transformational leadership and emotional display
- New research and discussion on anger and workplace outcomes
- Updated *Experiential Exercise* (Who Can Catch a Liar?)
- Updated *Ethical Dilemma* (Happiness Coaches for Employees)
- New *Point/Counterpoint* (Sometimes Blowing Your Top Is a Good Thing)
- New *An Ethical Choice* (Should Managers Use Emotional Intelligence (EI) Tests?)
- Updated *Case Incident 1* (Is It Okay to Cry at Work?)
- Updated *Case Incident 2* (Can You Read Emotions from Faces?)

Chapter 5: Personality and Values

- Entirely new *Opening Vignette* (A Fresh Personality)
- New *glOBalization!* (Is the Personality Profile of an Entrepreneur the Same Across the United States, the United Kingdom, and Germany?)
- New *OB Poll* (Does Business School Make You Narcissistic?)
- New *Myth or Science?* ("We Can Accurately Judge Individuals' Personalities a Few Seconds after Meeting Them")
- Introduces concepts related to dispositional self- and other-orientation
- New material regarding vocational choices
- New discussion of values and reactions to violations of employee values
- New section (Implications for Managers) with how-to tips on applying the chapter to worklife
- Updated information on personality and expatriate success
- Updated *Point/Counterpoint* (Millennials Are More Narcissistic)
- New *An Ethical Choice* (Do You Have a Cheating Personality?)
- New *Ethical Dilemma* (Generational Values and "Staying Put")
- Major new section (The Dark Triad)
- Major new section (Personality Needs the Situation!)

- New Exhibit (Trait Activation Theory: Jobs in Which Certain Big Five Traits Are More Relevant)
- Major new section (Approach–Avoidance)
- New research and discussion in Proactive Personality
- Major new section (Personality and Situations)
- New *Case Incident 1* (On the Costs of Being Nice)
- New *Case Incident 2* (The Power of Quiet)
- Updated research in The GLOBE Framework for Assessing Cultures
- Updated discussion in Terminal and Instrumental Values

Chapter 6: Perception and Individual Decision Making

- Entirely new *Opening Vignette* (The Pricetag for Creativity: $30 Million. The Return: Priceless)
- New *glOBalization!* (Does Multicultural Experience Make for Better Decisions?)
- New *OB Poll* (Is Innovation More Talk than Show?)
- New *Myth or Science?* ("All Stereotypes Are Negative")
- Major new section (Creativity, Creative Decision Making, and Innovation in Organizations)
- New Exhibit (Three-Stage Model of Creativity in Organizations)
- New research and discussion in Three Ethical Decision Criteria
- New research on the availability bias
- New research and discussion on Escalation of Commitment
- New section (Implications for Managers) with how-to tips on applying the chapter to worklife
- New research and discussion in The Rational Model, Bounded Rationality, and Intuition
- New *Point/Counterpoint* (Stereotypes Are Dying)
- New *Ethical Dilemma* (Deciding to Cheat)
- New *An Ethical Choice* (Choosing to Lie)
- New *Case Incident 2* (The Youngest Billionaire)

Chapter 7: Motivation Concepts

- Entirely new *Opening Vignette* (An Engaging Proposition)
- New *glOBalization!* (Autonomy Needs Around the Globe)
- New *OB Poll* (Asking for a Raise: Business Executives, 2012)
- New *Myth or Science?* ("Helping Others and Being a Good Citizen Is Good for Your Career")
- New section (Implications for Managers) with how-to tips on applying the chapter to worklife
- New research on social loafing
- New research on extrinsic rewards
- New research and discussion on goal pursuit and accomplishment
- New section (Implications for Managers) with how-to tips on applying the chapter to worklife
- New/Updated section (Equity Theory/Organizational Justice)
- New *Point/Counterpoint* (Goals Get You to Where You Want to Be)
- New *An Ethical Choice* (Motivated by Big Brother)
- New *Case Incident 1* (Equity and Executive Pay)
- New *Case Incident 2* (Sleeping on the Job)
- New *Experiential Exercise* (Organizational Justice Task)
- New *Ethical Dilemma* (Grade Inflation)

Chapter 8: Motivation: From Concepts to Applications

- Entirely new *Opening Vignette* (Telecommuting? No. Extra Maternity Leave? Yes)
- New *glOBalization!* (Outcry Over Executive Pay Is Heard Everywhere)
- New *OB Poll* (Who Works from Home?)
- New *Myth or Science?* ("Money Can't Buy Happiness")
- Major new section (Relational Job Design)
- New research on flextime
- New research on job sharing
- New research and discussion on telecommuting
- New research on employee involvement and participative management
- New section (Implications for Managers) with how-to tips on applying the chapter to worklife
- New research and discussion on pay strategies
- Updated section (Merit-Based Pay)
- New research in Bonuses and Profit-Sharing Plans
- New *Experiential Exercise* (Applying the Job Characteristics Model)
- New *Ethical Dilemma* (Inmates for Hire)
- New *An Ethical Choice* (Sweatshops and Worker Safety)
- New *Point/Counterpoint* ("Face-Time" Matters)
- New *Case Incident 1* (Motivation for Leisure)
- Updated *Case Incident 2* (Attaching the Carrot to the Stick)

Chapter 9: Foundations of Group Behavior

- Entirely new *Opening Vignette* (Bulls and Bears, But What About Women?)
- New *glOBalization!* (Making Global Virtual Teams Effective)
- New *OB Poll* (Most People Report Drinking with Co-Workers Is Acceptable)
- New/Updated *Myth or Science?* ("Americans Are More Biased than Asians")
- Major new section: Faultlines
- Major new section: Status and Stigmatization
- New research and discussion in Deviant Workplace Behavior
- New research and discussion on psychological contracts
- New section (Implications for Managers) with how-to tips on applying the chapter to worklife
- New *Point/Counterpoint* (People Are More Creative when They Work Alone)
- New/Updated *An Ethical Choice* (Using Peer Pressure as an Influence Tactic)
- New/Updated *Ethical Dilemma* (Is Social Loafing Unethical?)
- New/Updated *Experiential Exercise* (Surviving the Wild: Join a Group or Go It Alone?)
- New *Case Incident 1* (The Calamities of Consensus)
- Updated *Case Incident 2* (Investing in the Herd)

Chapter 10: Understanding Work Teams

- Entirely new *Opening Vignette* (Slaying Teamwork)
- New *glOBalization!* (Developing Team Members' Trust Across Cultures)
- New *OB Poll* (The Challenge of the Virtual Team)
- New *Myth or Science?* ("Team Members Who Are 'Hot' Should Make the Play")
- Major new section (Multiteam Systems)
- Review of research on team decision-making strategies
- New perspectives on creativity in teams
- New material on team proactivity
- Presents new literature on work teams in international contexts

- New section (Implications for Managers) with how-to tips on applying the chapter to worklife
- New *Point/Counterpoint* (To Get the Most Out of Teams, Empower Them)
- New *Experiential Exercise* (Composing the "Perfect" Team)
- New/Updated *An Ethical Choice* (Virtual Teams Leave a Smaller Carbon Footprint)
- New/Updated *Ethical Dilemma* (It's Easy to Be Unethical When Everyone Else Is)
- New *Case Incident 1* (Tongue-Tied in Teams)
- Updated *Case Incident 2* (Multicultural Multinational Teams)

Chapter 11: Communication

- Entirely new *Opening Vignette* (Communication Incompatibility)
- New *glOBalization!* (Multinational Firms Adopt English as Global Language Strategy)
- New *OB Poll* (Do You Use Social-Networking Sites to Research Job Candidates?)
- New *Myth or Science?* ("Today, Writing Skills Are More Important than Speaking Skills")
- New Exhibit (E-mail Traffic at Work by Days of the Week)
- New research and discussion in Choosing Communication Methods
- New research and discussion in A Cultural Guide
- New sections in Oral Communication (Meetings and Telephone)
- New sections in Written Communication (Letters, PowerPoint, E-mail, and Social Media)
- New section in Written Communication to include new internet platforms
- New material on instant messaging and text messaging
- New research on nonverbal communication and information security
- New section (Implications for Managers) with how-to tips on applying the chapter to worklife
- New *Point/Counterpoint* (Social Media Presence)
- New *An Ethical Choice* (Using Employees in Organizational Social Media Strategy)
- Updated *Case Incident 1* (Using Social Media to Your Advantage)
- New *Case Incident 2* (PowerPoint Purgatory)

Chapter 12: Leadership

- Entirely new *Opening Vignette* (The Right Stuff: Jeff Bezos of Amazon)
- New *glOBalization!* (Leaders Broaden Their Span of Control in Multinational Organizations)
- New *OB Poll* (How Are You Developing Your Leadership Skills?)
- New *Myth or Science?* ("Top Leaders Feel the Most Stress")
- New research and discussion in Charismatic Leadership
- New research and discussion in Transformational Leadership
- New research in Authentic Leadership
- Major new section (Ethical Leadership)
- New research in Trust as a Process
- New research on mentoring
- New discussion on selecting and training leaders
- New section (Implications for Managers) with how-to tips on applying the chapter to worklife
- New *Experiential Exercise* (What Is Leadership?)

- New/Updated *Ethical Dilemma* (Undercover Leaders)
- New *An Ethical Choice* (Holding Leaders Ethically Accountable)
- Updated *Case Incident 1* (Leadership Mettle Forged in Battle)
- New *Case Incident 2* (Leadership by Algorithm)
- Updated *Point/Counterpoint* (Heroes Are Made, Not Born)

Chapter 13: Power and Politics

- Entirely new *Opening Vignette* (From Power to Prison)
- New *glOBalization!* (Power, Gender, and Sexual Harassment in France)
- New *OB Poll* (Importance of Organizational Politics)
- New *Myth or Science?* (Powerful Leaders Keep Their (Fr)Enemies Close)
- Major new section (How Power Affects People)
- Major new section (Drawing Your Power Map)
- New exhibit (Your Power Map)
- New research and discussion in Sexual Harassment
- New section (Implications for Managers) with how-to tips on applying the chapter to worklife
- New *Point/Counterpoint* (Everyone Wants Power)
- New *Ethical Dilemma* (How Much Should You Defer to Those in Power?)
- New *Case Incident 2* (Barry's Peer Becomes His Boss)

Chapter 14: Conflict and Negotiation

- Entirely new *Opening Vignette* (Jamie Dimon and the London Whale)
- New *glOBalization!* (Trust Is an Issue)
- New *OB Poll* (Men Ask More)
- New *Myth or Science?* ("Teams Negotiate Better in Collectivistic Cultures")
- Major new section (Types and Loci of Conflict)
- New section (Culture in Negotiations)
- New section (Gender Differences in Negotiation)
- New research and discussion in Personality Traits in Negotiation
- New research and discussion in Moods/Emotions in Negotiation
- New section (Implications for Managers) with how-to tips on applying the chapter to worklife
- New *Point/Counterpoint* (Pro Sports Strikes Are Caused by Greedy Owners)
- New *An Ethical Choice* (Using Empathy to Negotiate More Ethically)
- New *Ethical Dilemma* (The Lowball Applicant)
- New *Case Incident* (Choosing Your Battles)
- New *Case Incident 2* (Twinkies, Rubber Rooms, and Collective Bargaining)

Chapter 15: Foundations of Organization Structure

- Entirely new *Opening Vignette* (Heard But Not Seen—The Virtual Assistant)
- New *glOBalization!* (The World Is My Corporate Headquarters)
- New *OB Poll* (The Incredible Shrinking Office)
- New *Myth or Science?* ("Employees Can Work Just as Well from Home")
- Discussion of the latest trends in job specialization
- New examples of international company responses to regional adaptation
- New research and discussion on centralization/decentralization
- Updated information on the simple structure
- New research and discussion on virtual and boundaryless organization structures
- New research and discussion on downsizing and organizational strategy

- New section (Implications for Managers) with how-to tips on applying the chapter to worklife
- New *Point/Counterpoint* (The End of Management)
- New *An Ethical Choice* (Ethical Concerns of Deskless Workplaces)
- New *Case Incident 1* (Creative Deviance: Bucking the Hierarchy?)
- New *Case Incident 2* (Boeing Dreamliner: Engineering Nightmare or Organizational Disaster?)
- Updated *Ethical Dilemma* (Directing the Directors)

Chapter 16: Organizational Culture

- Entirely new *Opening Vignette* (A Culture Out of this World: Mars Inc.)
- New *glOBalization!* (Creating a Multinational Organizational Culture)
- New *OB Poll* (Job Is Not as Good as Advertised)
- New *Myth or Science?* ("An Organization's Culture Is Forever")
- New discussion in A Definition of Organizational Culture
- Major new section (The Ethical Dimension of Culture)
- Major new section (Culture and Innovation)
- New research in Culture as a Liability
- New research in Keeping a Culture Alive
- New research and discussion in Rituals and Symbols
- New research in Creating an Ethical Organizational Culture
- New research in Emphasizing Vitality and Growth and Achieving a Spiritual Organization
- New research and discussion in Global Implications
- New section (Implications for Managers) with how-to tips on applying the chapter to worklife
- New *An Ethical Choice* (A Culture of Compassion)
- Updated *Ethical Dilemma* (A Bankrupt Culture)
- Updated *Case Incident 1* (Mergers Don't Always Lead to Culture Clashes)
- Updated *Case Incident 2* (Did Toyota's Culture Cause Its Problems?)

Chapter 17: Human Resource Policies and Practices

- Entirely new *Opening Vignette* (Laszlo Bock Is A Real People Person)
- New *glOBalization!* (Perceptions of Fairness in Selection Methods)
- New *OB Poll* (Interview Derailment)
- New *Myth or Science?* ("Work–Family Policies Make Good Business Sense")
- New section (Recruitment Practices)
- New research and discussion in Selection Practices
- New research in Initial Selection
- New research and discussion in Application Forms and Background Checks
- New research in Written Tests
- New research and discussion on work sample tests and interviews
- New research on job training
- Major new section (The Leadership Role of HR)
- New section (Implications for Managers) with how-to tips on applying the chapter to worklife
- Updated *Point/Counterpoint* (Social Media Is a Great Source of New Hires)
- New *An Ethical Choice* (HIV/AIDS and the Multinational Organization)
- Updated *Ethical Dilemma* (Credit Checking)
- Updated *Case Incident 1* (The End of the Performance Appraisal?)
- New *Case Incident 2* (You May Be Supporting Slavery)

Chapter 18: Organizational Change and Stress Management

- Entirely new *Opening Vignette* (Stress and the Work-More Economy)
- New *glOBalization!* (The State of Perpetual Change: Globalization)
- New *OB Poll* (Many Employees Feel Extreme Stress)
- New *Myth or Science?* ("When You're Working Hard, Sleep Is Optional")
- New research in Forces for Change
- New research in Planned Change
- Major new section (Organizational Change and Stress)
- New research in Work Stress and Its Management
- New section (Implications for Managers) with how-to tips on applying the chapter to worklife
- New *Experiential Exercise* (Strategizing Change)
- New *An Ethical Choice* (Manager and Employee Stress during Organizational Change)
- Updated *Case Incident 1* (Starbucks Returns to Its Roots)
- New *Case Incident 2* (When Companies Fail to Change)

Teaching and Learning Support

Instructor Supplements

At **www.pearsonhighered.com/irc**, instructors can access a variety of digital resources available with this text in downloadable format. Registration is easy; contact your Pearson Sales Representative, who will assign you your login and password information. As a registered faculty member, you can download resource files and receive immediate access and instructions for installing course management content on your campus server.

If you need assistance, our dedicated technical support team is ready to help with the media supplements that accompany this text. Visit **247pearsoned.custhelp.com** for answers to frequently asked questions and toll-free user support phone numbers.

- **Instructor's Manual**—Has been completely updated to align with the changes made in the text. For each chapter, the following are covered: Learning Objective, Chapter Outlines, Class Exercises, Teaching Notes, Short Answer Questions, Additional Cases and Questions.
- **Test Item File**—Revised and updated to include questions that require students to apply the knowledge that they've read about in the text through Learning Objectives and Learning Outcomes. Questions are also tagged to reflect the new AACSB Learning Standards.
- **TestGen** Test Generating Software—Test management software that contains all material from the Test Item File. This software is completely user-friendly and allows instructors to view, edit, and add test questions with just a few mouse clicks. All of our TestGens are converted for use in multiple course management systems and are available for download from www.pearsonhighered.com/irc.
- **PowerPoint Presentation**—A ready-to-use PowerPoint slideshow designed for classroom presentation. Use it as is, or edit content to fit your individual classroom needs.

Video Library

Videos illustrating the most important subject topics are available in two formats:

- DVD–available for in classroom use by instructors, includes videos mapped to Pearson textbooks.
- MyLab–available for instructors and students, provides round the clock instant access to videos and corresponding assessment and simulations for Pearson textbooks.

Contact your local Pearson representative to request access to either format.

Course Management Systems

BlackBoard and WebCT Course Cartridges are available for download from www.pearsonhighered.com/irc. These standard course cartridges contain the Instructor's Manual, TestGen, Instructor PowerPoints.

CourseSmart eTextbooks Online

CourseSmart eTextbooks were developed for students looking to save money on required or recommended textbooks. Students simply select their eText by title or author and purchase immediate access to the content for the duration of the course using any major credit card. With CourseSmart eText, students can search for specific keywords or page numbers, make notes online, print reading assignments that incorporate lecture notes, and bookmark important passages for later review. For more information, or to purchase a CourseSmart eTextbook, visit www.coursesmart.com.

Pearson's Self-Assessment Library (S.A.L.)

A hallmark of the Robbins series, S.A.L. is a unique learning tool that allows you to assess your knowledge, beliefs, feelings, and actions in regard to a wide range of personal skills, abilities, and interests. Self-assessments have been integrated into each chapter, including a self-assessment at the beginning of each chapter. S.A.L. helps students better understand their interpersonal and behavioral skills as they relate to the theoretical concepts presented in each chapter. *Ask your Pearson Representative for more details.*

Highlights

- **69 research-based self-assessments**—All 69 instruments of our collection are from sources such as *Journal of Social Behavior and Personality, Harvard Business Review, Organizational Behavior: Experiences and Cases, Journal of Experimental Education, Journal of Applied Measurement,* and more.
- **Work–life and career focused**—All self-assessments are focused to help individuals better manage their work lives or careers. Organized in four parts, these instruments offer you one source from which to learn more about yourself.
- **Save feature**—Students can take the self-assessments an unlimited number of times, and they can save and print their scores for class discussion.
- **Scoring key**—The key to the self-assessments has been edited by Steve Robbins to allow students to quickly make sense of the results of their score.
- **Instructor's manual**—An *Instructor's Manual* guides instructors in interpreting self-assessments and helps facilitate better classroom discussion.

Acknowledgments

Getting this book into your hands was a team effort. It took faculty reviewers and a talented group of designers and production specialists, editorial personnel, and marketing and sales staff.

The sixteenth edition was peer reviewed by many experts in the field. Their comments, compliments, and suggestions have significantly improved the final product. The authors would also like to extend their sincerest thanks to the following instructors: Pam DeLotell, Kaplan University; Phil Roth, Clemson University; Jody Tolan, MBA, Lecturer, Management and Organization, University of Southern California Marshall School of Business; Holly A. Schroth, University of California, Berkeley; Jon C. Tomlinson, Ph.D., University of Northwestern Ohio; Andrew Johnson, Santa Clara University; Dr. Alan Goldman, Professor of Management, Faculty Director, W. P. Carey School of Business, Arizona State University West; Dr. Edward F. Lisoski, Angelo State University; E. Anne Christo-Baker, Purdue University North Central; and Dr. Josh Plaskoff, Kelley School of Business—IUPUI.

The authors wish to thank Lori Ehrman Tinkey of the University of Notre Dame and Brent A. Scott of Michigan State University for help with several key aspects of this revision.

We owe a debt of gratitude to all those at Pearson Education who have supported this text over the past 30 years and who have worked so hard on the development of this latest edition. On the development and editorial side, we want to thank Kris Ellis-Levy, Senior Acquisitions Editor; Ashley Santora, Program Manager Team Lead; and Elisa Adams, Development Editor. On the design and production side, Judy Leale, Project Manager Team Lead, did an outstanding job, as did Kelly Warsak, Project Manager, and Nancy Moudry, Photo Development Editor. Last but not least, we would like to thank Erin Gardner, Senior Marketing Manager; Maggie Moylan, Director of Marketing; and their sales staff, who have been selling this book over its many editions. Thank you for the attention you've given to this book.

What Is Organizational Behavior?

When you see this icon, visit **www.mymanagementlab.com** for activities that are applied, personalized, and offer immediate feedback.

Source: AP Photo/Greg M. Cooper.

GOT YOUR DEGREE? GREAT, GO FLIP BURGERS

Alison Parker has all the right stuff: a recent college degree and a strong résumé that includes prestigious internships with a member of Congress and with the National Park Service. With this solid start, Alison should have enjoyed a great career launch, but instead she's working a part-time, temporary job and living with her parents.

Why? Despite her best efforts, Alison has received no job offers, at least not the kind she wants. "I didn't anticipate that a year out I would be barely making any money at all," she says.

Melissa Jenkins, shown in the photo with her mom Diana Jenkins, had to move back in with her parents after graduating without a job in hand.

Alison and Melissa are not alone. According to a study by the Center for College Affordability and Productivity, almost half—48 percent—of U.S. degree holders are in positions classified as requiring less than a four-year college education. Many of these graduates are in service industries, working as retail salespeople, cashiers, wait staff, taxi drivers, and, yes, fast-food burger flippers.

There's no denying this is a big problem. Student loans have topped $1 trillion, and recent college grads are feeling the heat of their first payments on balances averaging $25,250. As a result, seniors like Jianna Lieberman have downgraded their aspirations even before testing the job market. "I can't imagine settling down, traveling, pretty much anything but working until I get rid of this burden," she says, knowing that she will be lucky to land that first "real" job after graduation.

Chances are that Jianna will have to join Melissa Jenkins as a member of the "boomerang generation" of 53 percent of 18- to 24-year-olds who move back home. And with 41 percent of the decline in U.S. full-time jobs hitting under-25-year-olds, Jianna may have to settle for part-time work like Alison's. If she is lucky enough to land a full-time position, her usable income may be lower next year, because weekly earnings after inflation fell 6 percent among 18-to-24-year-olds from 2007 to 2011.

At first glance, then, the situation is dismal. Some blame the economy. Some, like student A. J. Fofanah, blame their own choices. "I feel like I didn't do as much research as I should have," he says. But as is the case with many issues involving people, a deeper look suggests we need a broader perspective. Overall, a college degree puts you in a better position for higher pay and lower unemployment. In fact, the difference is significantly in your favor: the jobless rate is currently 3.9 percent for workers who have a college degree or higher, versus 8 percent for people with only a high school certificate, and the earnings differential for those with a degree reveals even greater

LEARNING OBJECTIVES

After studying this chapter, you should be able to:

1 Demonstrate the importance of interpersonal skills in the workplace.

2 Describe the manager's functions, roles, and skills.

3 Define *organizational behavior* (*OB*).

4 Show the value to OB of systematic study.

5 Identify the major behavioral science disciplines that contribute to OB.

6 Demonstrate why few absolutes apply to OB.

7 Identify the challenges and opportunities managers have in applying OB concepts.

8 Compare the three levels of analysis in this book's OB model.

advantages. Also, as we will explore in this chapter, there is a worldwide shortage of skilled workers. Microsoft, for instance, reports more than 6,000 open jobs in the United States, a 15 percent increase over the year before.

Understanding yourself, your aspirations, your labor market prospects, and the organizations you might call home has never been more complicated. Because of this, individuals who excel at analyzing themselves, their environments, and their organizations are primed to excel at work as never before. Jean Pierre Salendres, a junior at Columbia, is majoring in international diplomacy for this reason. "Maybe something more practical lands you a job," he says.

Statistics tell a story, and we will employ data to better understand the challenges people face in the work world. We will also use statistics and research to help you see the paths toward excelling—in any environment. For instance, there are many things you can do to differentiate yourself from other candidates for employment—attend a business boot camp, work on your "soft" skills like interpersonal communication and good habits of personal responsibility, and understand who counts in the organization structure. For now, the moral of this story is, don't believe everything you read. Or, to put it another way, don't believe *anything* you read, but do believe *everything* you read, taken as a whole.

Sources: P. Coy, "The Solutions Are Out There," *Bloomberg Businessweek* (September 10–September 16, 2012), pp. 62–69; M. Dorning, "The Young and the Wageless," *Bloomberg Businessweek* (June 25–July 1, 2012), pp. 2730; M. Korn, "The Business of Boot Camps," *The Wall Street Journal* (March 7, 2013), p. B7; B. Smith, "How to Reduce America's Talent Deficit," *The Wall Street Journal* (October 19, 2012), p. A13; J. S. Lublin, "How to Prove You're a Keeper to a New CEO," *The Wall Street Journal* (March 6, 2013), p. B8; M. V. Rafter, "Benefits of the Boomerang," *The Wall Street Journal* (October 22, 2012), p. R6; and M. Trumbull, "Have Degree, Driving Cab: Nearly Half of College Grads Are Overqualified," *The Christian Science Monitor* (January 28, 2013), www.csmonitor.com/Business/2013/0128/Have-degree-driving-cab-Nearly-half-of-college-grads-are-overqualified.

The details of the chapter-opening story might be disheartening to read, but they accurately reflect some of the problems faced by the contemporary workforce. The story also highlights several issues of interest to organizational behavior researchers, including motivation, emotions, personality, and communication. Through the course of this book, you'll learn how all these elements can be studied systematically.

You've probably made many observations about people's behavior in your life. In a way, you are already proficient at seeing some of the major themes in organizational behavior. At the same time, you probably have not had the tools to make these observations systematically. This is where organizational behavior comes into play. And, as we'll learn, it is much more than common sense, intuition, and soothsaying.

To see how far common sense gets you, try the following from the Self-Assessment Library.

How Much Do I Know About Organizational Behavior?

In the Self-Assessment Library (available in MyManagementLab), take assessment IV.G.1 (How Much Do I Know About OB?) and answer the following questions:

1. How did you score? Are you surprised by your score?
2. How much of effective management do you think is common sense? Did your score on the test change your answer to this question?

The Importance of Interpersonal Skills

1 Demonstrate the importance of interpersonal skills in the workplace.

Until the late 1980s, business school curricula emphasized the technical aspects of management, focusing on economics, accounting, finance, and quantitative techniques. Course work in human behavior and people skills received relatively less attention. Over the past three decades, however, business school faculty have come to realize the significant role understanding human behavior plays in determining a manager's effectiveness; required courses on people skills have been added to many curricula. As the director of leadership at MIT's Sloan School of Management put it, "M.B.A. students may get by on their technical and quantitative skills the first couple of years out of school. But soon, leadership and communication skills come to the fore in distinguishing the managers whose careers really take off."[1]

Developing managers' interpersonal skills also helps organizations attract and keep high-performing employees. Regardless of labor market conditions, outstanding employees are always in short supply. Companies known as good places to work—such as Starbucks, Adobe Systems, Cisco, Whole Foods, Google, American Express, Amgen, Pfizer, and Marriott—have a big advantage. A recent survey of hundreds of workplaces, and more than 200,000 respondents, showed the social relationships among co-workers and supervisors were strongly related to overall job satisfaction. Positive social relationships also were associated with lower stress at work and lower intentions to quit.[2] Having managers with good interpersonal skills is likely to make the workplace more pleasant, and research indicates that employees who know how to relate to their managers well with supportive dialogue and proactivity will find their ideas are endorsed more often, further improving workplace satisfaction.[3] Creating a pleasant workplace also appears to make good economic sense. Companies with reputations as good places to work (such as *Forbes'* "100 Best Companies to Work For in America") have been found to generate superior financial performance.[4] Partially for these reasons, universities have begun to incorporate social entrepreneurship education into their curriculum in order to train future leaders to address social issues within their organizations with interpersonal skills.[5] This is especially important because there is a growing awareness of the need for understanding the means and outcomes of corporate social responsibility.[6]

We have come to understand that in today's competitive and demanding workplace, managers can't succeed on their technical skills alone. They also have to have good people skills. This book has been written to help both managers and potential managers develop those people skills.

Photo 1-1 IBM Chief Executive Virginia Rometty has the interpersonal skills required to succeed in management. Communication and leadership skills distinguish managers, such as Rometty, who rise to the top of their profession. Shown here at a meeting in Beijing, she is an innovative leader capable of driving IBM's entrepreneurial culture.

Source: © Li Tao/Xinhua Press/Corbis.

What Managers Do

2   Describe the manager's functions, roles, and skills.

manager   *An individual who achieves goals through other people.*

organization   *A consciously coordinated social unit, composed of two or more people, that functions on a relatively continuous basis to achieve a common goal or set of goals.*

Let's begin by briefly defining the terms *manager* and *organization*—the place where managers work. Then let's look at the manager's job; specifically, what do managers do?

Managers get things done through other people. They make decisions, allocate resources, and direct the activities of others to attain goals. Managers do their work in an **organization**, which is a consciously coordinated social unit, composed of two or more people, that functions on a relatively continuous basis to achieve a common goal or set of goals. By this definition, manufacturing and service firms are organizations, and so are schools, hospitals, churches, military units, retail stores, police departments, and local, state, and federal government agencies. The people who oversee the activities of others and who are responsible for attaining goals in these organizations are managers (sometimes called *administrators*, especially in not-for-profit organizations).

Management Functions

In the early part of the twentieth century, French industrialist Henri Fayol wrote that all managers perform five management functions: planning, organizing, commanding, coordinating, and controlling.[7] Today, we have condensed these to four: planning, organizing, leading, and controlling.

Because organizations exist to achieve goals, someone has to define those goals and the means for achieving them; management is that someone. The **planning** function encompasses defining an organization's goals, establishing an overall strategy for achieving those goals, and developing a comprehensive set of

planning   *A process that includes defining goals, establishing strategy, and developing plans to coordinate activities.*

plans to integrate and coordinate activities. Evidence indicates this function increases the most as managers move from lower-level to mid-level management.[8]

Managers are also responsible for designing an organization's structure. We call this function **organizing**. It includes determining what tasks are to be done, who is to do them, how the tasks are to be grouped, who reports to whom, and where decisions are to be made.

Every organization contains people, and it is management's job to direct and coordinate those people. This is the **leading** function. When managers motivate employees, direct their activities, select the most effective communication channels, or resolve conflicts among members, they're engaging in leading.

To ensure things are going as they should, management must monitor the organization's performance and compare it with previously set goals. If there are any significant deviations, it is management's job to get the organization back on track. This monitoring, comparing, and potential correcting is the **controlling** function.

So, using the functional approach, the answer to the question "What do managers do?" is that they plan, organize, lead, and control.

organizing   *Determining what tasks are to be done, who is to do them, how the tasks are to be grouped, who reports to whom, and where decisions are to be made.*

leading   *A function that includes motivating employees, directing others, selecting the most effective communication channels, and resolving conflicts.*

controlling   *Monitoring activities to ensure they are being accomplished as planned and correcting any significant deviations.*

Management Roles

In the late 1960s, Henry Mintzberg, then a graduate student at MIT, undertook a careful study of five executives to determine what they did on their jobs. On the basis of his observations, Mintzberg concluded that managers perform ten different, highly interrelated roles—or sets of behaviors.[9] As shown in Exhibit 1-1, these ten roles are primarily (1) interpersonal, (2) informational, or (3) decisional.

Exhibit **1-1**	Minztberg's Managerial Roles
Role	**Description**
Interpersonal	
Figurehead	Symbolic head; required to perform a number of routine duties of a legal or social nature
Leader	Responsible for the motivation and direction of employees
Liaison	Maintains a network of outside contacts who provide favors and information
Informational	
Monitor	Receives a wide variety of information; serves as nerve center of internal and external information of the organization
Disseminator	Transmits information received from outsiders or from other employees to members of the organization
Spokesperson	Transmits information to outsiders on organization's plans, policies, actions, and results; serves as expert on organization's industry
Decisional	
Entrepreneur	Searches organization and its environment for opportunities and initiates projects to bring about change
Disturbance handler	Responsible for corrective action when organization faces important, unexpected disturbances
Resource allocator	Makes or approves significant organizational decisions
Negotiator	Responsible for representing the organization at major negotiations

Source: Adapted from *The Nature of Managerial Work* by H. Mintzberg. Copyright © 1973 by H. Mintzberg. MINTZBERG, HENRY, THE NATURE OF MANAGERIAL WORK, 1st Edition, © 1980, pp. 92–93. Reprinted with permission of Pearson Education, Inc., Upper Saddle River, NJ.

Interpersonal Roles   All managers are required to perform duties that are ceremonial and symbolic in nature. For instance, when the president of a college hands out diplomas at commencement or a factory supervisor gives a group of high school students a tour of the plant, he or she is acting in a *figurehead* role. All managers also have a *leadership* role. This role includes hiring, training, motivating, and disciplining employees. The third role within the interpersonal grouping is the *liaison* role, or contacting others who provide the manager with information. The sales manager who obtains information from the quality-control manager in his or her own company has an internal liaison relationship. When that sales manager has contacts with other sales executives through a marketing trade association, he or she has an outside liaison relationship.

Informational Roles   All managers, to some degree, collect information from outside organizations and institutions, typically by scanning the news media (including the Internet) and talking with other people to learn of changes in the public's tastes, what competitors may be planning, and the like. Mintzberg called this the *monitor* role. Managers also act as a conduit to transmit information to organizational members. This is the *disseminator* role. In addition, managers perform a *spokesperson* role when they represent the organization to outsiders.

Decisional Roles   Mintzberg identified four roles that require making choices. In the *entrepreneur* role, managers initiate and oversee new projects that will improve their organization's performance. As *disturbance handlers*, managers take corrective action in response to unforeseen problems. As *resource allocators*, managers are responsible for allocating human, physical, and monetary resources. Finally, managers perform a *negotiator* role, in which they discuss issues and bargain with other units to gain advantages for their own unit.

Management Skills

Still another way of considering what managers do is to look at the skills or competencies they need to achieve their goals. Researchers have identified a number of skills that differentiate effective from ineffective managers.[10]

Technical Skills   Technical skills encompass the ability to apply specialized knowledge or expertise. When you think of the skills of professionals such as civil engineers or oral surgeons, you typically focus on the technical skills they have learned through extensive formal education. Of course, professionals don't have a monopoly on technical skills, and not all technical skills have to be learned in schools or other formal training programs. All jobs require some specialized expertise, and many people develop their technical skills on the job.

technical skills *The ability to apply specialized knowledge or expertise.*

Human Skills   The ability to understand, communicate with, motivate, and support other people, both individually and in groups, defines **human skills**. Many people are technically proficient but poor listeners, unable to understand the needs of others, or weak at managing conflicts. Because managers get things done through other people, they must have good human skills.

human skills *The ability to work with, understand, and motivate other people, both individually and in groups.*

Conceptual Skills   Managers must have the mental ability to analyze and diagnose complex situations. These tasks require **conceptual skills**. Decision making, for instance, requires managers to identify problems, develop alternative solutions to correct those problems, evaluate those alternative solutions, and select the best one. After they have selected a course of action, managers must be able to organize a plan of action and then execute it. The ability to integrate new ideas with existing processes and innovate on the job are also crucial conceptual skills for today's managers.

conceptual skills *The mental ability to analyze and diagnose complex situations.*

Effective versus Successful Managerial Activities

Fred Luthans and his associates looked at what managers do from a somewhat different perspective.[11] They asked, "Do managers who move up the quickest in an organization do the same activities and with the same emphasis as managers who do the best job?" You might think the answer is yes, but that's not always the case.

Luthans and his associates studied more than 450 managers. All engaged in four managerial activities:

1. **Traditional management.**   Decision making, planning, and controlling.
2. **Communication.**   Exchanging routine information and processing paperwork.
3. **Human resource management.**   Motivating, disciplining, managing conflict, staffing, and training.
4. **Networking.**   Socializing, politicking, and interacting with outsiders.

When you see this icon, Global OB issues are being discussed in the paragraph.

The "average" manager spent 32 percent of his or her time in traditional management activities, 29 percent communicating, 20 percent in human resource management activities, and 19 percent networking. However, the time and effort different *individual* managers spent on those activities varied a great deal. As shown in Exhibit 1-2, among managers who were *successful* (defined in terms of speed of promotion within their organization), networking made the largest relative contribution to success, and human resource management activities made the least relative contribution. Among *effective* managers (defined in terms of quantity and quality of their performance and the satisfaction and commitment of employees), communication made the largest relative contribution and networking the least. More recent studies in Australia, Israel, Italy, Japan, and the United States confirm the link between networking and social relationships and success within an organization.[12] And the connection between communication and effective managers is also clear. A study of 410 U.S. managers indicates those who seek information from colleagues and employees—even if it's negative—and who explain their decisions are the most effective.[13]

This research offers important insights. Successful managers give almost the opposite emphases to traditional management, communication, human

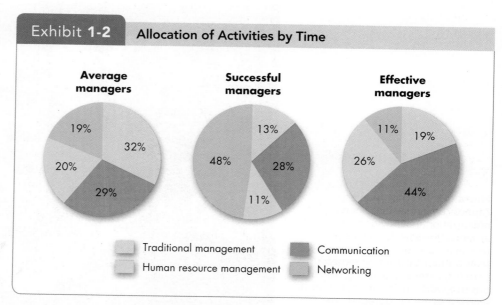

Source: Based on F. Luthans, R. M. Hodgetts, and S. A. Rosenkrantz, *Real Managers* (Cambridge, MA: Ballinger, 1988).

resource management, and networking as do effective managers. This finding challenges the historical assumption that promotions are based on performance, and it illustrates the importance of networking and political skills in getting ahead in organizations.

A Review of the Manager's Job

One common thread runs through the functions, roles, skills, activities, and approaches to management: Each recognizes the paramount importance of managing people, whether it is called "the leading function," "interpersonal roles," "human skills," or "human resource management, communication, and networking activities." It's clear managers must develop their people skills to be effective and successful.

Enter Organizational Behavior

3   Define *organizational behavior (OB)*.

organizational behavior (OB)   *A field of study that investigates the impact that individuals, groups, and structure have on behavior within organizations, for the purpose of applying such knowledge toward improving an organization's effectiveness.*

We've made the case for the importance of people skills. But neither this book nor the discipline on which it is based is called "people skills." The term that is widely used to describe the discipline is *organizational behavior*.

Organizational behavior (often abbreviated OB) is a field of study that investigates the impact individuals, groups, and structure have on behavior within organizations, for the purpose of applying such knowledge toward improving an organization's effectiveness. That's a mouthful, so let's break it down.

Organizational behavior is a field of study, meaning that it is a distinct area of expertise with a common body of knowledge. What does it study? It studies three determinants of behavior in organizations: individuals, groups, and structure. In addition, OB applies the knowledge gained about individuals, groups,

Photo 1-2 Internet retailer Zappos.com understands how organizational behavior affects an organization's performance. The firm maintains good employee relationships by offering generous benefits, extensive training, and a positive work environment in which employees are encouraged "to create fun and a little weirdness."

and the effect of structure on behavior in order to make organizations work more effectively.

To sum up our definition, OB is the study of what people do in an organization and how their behavior affects the organization's performance. And because OB is concerned specifically with employment-related situations, it emphasizes behavior as related to concerns such as jobs, work, absenteeism, employment turnover, productivity, human performance, and management. Although debate exists about the relative importance of each, OB includes the core topics:

- Motivation
- Leader behavior and power
- Interpersonal communication
- Group structure and processes
- Attitude development and perception
- Change processes
- Conflict and negotiation
- Work design[14]

Complementing Intuition with Systematic Study

4 Show the value to OB of systematic study.

Each of us is a student of behavior. Whether you've explicitly thought about it before, you've been "reading" people almost all your life, watching their actions and trying to interpret what you see or predict what people might do under different conditions. Unfortunately, the casual or commonsense approach to reading others can often lead to erroneous predictions. However, you can improve your predictive ability by supplementing intuition with a more systematic approach.

The systematic approach in this book will uncover important facts and relationships and provide a base from which to make more accurate predictions of behavior. Underlying this systematic approach is the belief that behavior is not random. Rather, we can identify fundamental consistencies underlying the behavior of all individuals and modify them to reflect individual differences.

These fundamental consistencies are very important. Why? Because they allow predictability. Behavior is generally predictable, and the *systematic study* of behavior is a means to making reasonably accurate predictions. When we use the term **systematic study**, we mean looking at relationships, attempting to attribute causes and effects, and basing our conclusions on scientific evidence—that is, on data gathered under controlled conditions and measured and interpreted in a reasonably rigorous manner. (See Appendix A for a basic review of research methods used in studies of organizational behavior.)

systematic study *Looking at relationships, attempting to attribute causes and effects, and drawing conclusions based on scientific evidence.*

evidence-based management (EBM) *The basing of managerial decisions on the best available scientific evidence.*

Evidence-based management (EBM) complements systematic study by basing managerial decisions on the best available scientific evidence. For example, we want doctors to make decisions about patient care based on the latest available evidence, and EBM argues that managers should do the same, becoming more scientific in how they think about management problems. A manager might pose a managerial question, search for the best available evidence, and apply the relevant information to the question or case at hand. You might think it difficult to argue against this (what manager would say decisions shouldn't be based on evidence?), but the vast majority of management

"Management by Walking Around Is the Most Effective Management"

This is mostly false, but with a caveat. Management by walking around (MBWA) is an organizational principle made famous with the 1982 publication of *In Search of Excellence* and based upon a 1970s initiative by Hewlett-Packard—in other words, it's a dinosaur. But the idea of requiring managers at all levels of the organization to wander around their departments to observe, converse, and hear from employees continues as a common business practice. Many companies expecting managers and executives to do regular "floor time" have claimed benefits from employee engagement to deeper management understanding of company issues. While MBWA sounds helpful, though, it is not a panacea or cure-all. The limitations of MBWA are threefold: available hours, focus, and application.

1. **Available hours.** Managers are tasked with planning, organizing, coordinating, and controlling, yet even CEOs—the managers who should be the most in control of their time—report 53 percent of their average 55-hour workweek is spent in meetings. We've yet to see a meeting conducted while touring the plant!

2. **Focus.** MBWA turns management's focus toward the concerns of employees. This is good, but only to a degree. As noted by Jeff Weiner, CEO of LinkedIn, this is a problem. "Part of the key to time management is carving out time to think, as opposed to constantly reacting. And during that thinking time, you're not only thinking strategically, thinking proactively, thinking longer-term, but you're literally thinking about what is urgent versus important." Weiner and other CEOs argue that meetings distract them from their purpose, especially internal company interactions.

3. **Application.** The principle behind MBWA is that the more managers know their employees, the more effective those managers will be. This is not always (or even often) true. As we'll learn in Chapter 6, knowing something (or thinking you know) should not always lead us to *acting* on only that information. For example, a 30-minute test to determine personality traits and reactions to scenarios recently resulted in a 20 percent reduction in attrition for a Xerox call center, even though managers had previously been diligent in seeking information on candidates through interviews. There is no substitute for good, objective data.

Based on the need for managers to dedicate their efforts to administering and growing businesses, and given the proven effectiveness of objective performance measures, it seems the time for MBWA is gone. Yet there is one caveat. We certainly don't argue that managers should refrain from knowing their employees, or that a stroll through on the work floor is a bad idea. Rather, we find the regular, intentional interactions of MBWA do not, in themselves, make an effective management tool.

Sources: H. Mintzberg, "The Manager's Job," *Harvard Business Review* (March–April 1990), pp. 1–13; R. E. Silverman, "Where's the Boss? Trapped in a Meeting," *The Wall Street Journal* (February 14, 2012), p. B1, B9; and J. Walker, "Meet the New Boss: Big Data," *The Wall Street Journal* (September 20, 2012), p. B1.

---

decisions are still made "on the fly," with little or systematic study of available evidence.[15]

intuition   *A gut feeling not necessarily supported by research.*

Systematic study and EBM add to **intuition**, or those "gut feelings" about what makes others (and ourselves) "tick." Of course, the things you have come to believe in an unsystematic way are not necessarily incorrect. Jack Welch (former CEO of GE) noted, "The trick, of course, is to know when to go with your gut." But if we make *all* decisions with intuition or gut instinct, we're likely working with incomplete information—like making an investment decision with only half the data about the potential for risk and reward.

Relying on intuition is made worse because we tend to overestimate the accuracy of what we think we know. Surveys of human resource managers have also shown many managers hold "commonsense" opinions regarding effective management that have been flatly refuted by empirical evidence.

We find a similar problem in chasing the business and popular media for management wisdom. The business press tends to be dominated by fads. As a writer for *The New Yorker* put it, "Every few years, new companies succeed, and they are scrutinized for the underlying truths they might reveal. But often there is no underlying truth; the companies just happened to be in the right place at the right time."[16] Although we try to avoid it, we might also fall into this trap. It's not that the business press stories are all wrong; it's that without a systematic approach, it's hard to separate the wheat from the chaff.

Big Data

It is good news for the future of business that researchers, the media, and company leaders have identified the potential of data-driven management and decision-making. While "big data"—the extensive use of statistical compilation and analysis—has been applied to many areas of business, increasingly it is applied to making effective decisions (which we cover in Chapter 6) and managing human resources (covered in Chapter 17). Online retailers may have been the first to notice and act upon information on customer preferences newly available through the internet shopping experience, information far superior to data gathered in simple store transactions. This enabled online retailers to create more targeted marketing strategies than ever before. The bookselling industry is a case in point: Before online selling, brick-and-mortar bookstores could collect data about book sales only to make their projections about consumer interests and trends. With the advent of Amazon, suddenly a vast array of information about consumer preferences became available for tracking: what customers bought, what they looked at, how they navigated the site, and what they were influenced by (such as promotions, reviews, and page presentation). The challenge for Amazon then was to identify which statistics were *persistent,* giving relatively constant outcomes over time, and *predictive,* showing steady causality between certain inputs and outcomes. The company used these statistics to develop algorithms that let it forecast which books customers would like to read next. Amazon then could base its wholesale purchase decisions on the feedback customers provided, both through these passive methods and through solicited recommendations for upcoming titles, by which Amazon could continuously perfect its algorithms.

The success of Amazon has revolutionized bookselling—and even retail industries—and has served as a model for innovative online retailers. It also illustrates what big data can do for other businesses that can capitalize on the wealth of data available through virtually any internet connection, from Facebook posts to sensor readings to GPS signals from cell phones. Savvy businesses use big data to manage people as well as technology. A recent study of 330 companies found that the data-driven companies were 5 percent more productive and 6 percent more profitable than their competitors. These may seem like small percentage gains, but they represent a big impact on economic strength and measurable increases in stock market evaluations for these companies, which are in the top third of their industries.[17] Another study of 8,000 firms in 20 countries confirms that constant measuring against targets for productivity and other criteria is a hallmark of well-run companies.[18]

The use of big data for managerial practices is a relatively new area but one that holds convincing promise. In dealing with people, leaders often rely on hunches and estimate the influence of information that they've heard most recently, that has been frequently repeated, or that is of personal relevance. Obviously, this is not always the best evidence because all managers (all people) have natural biases. A manager who uses data to define objectives, develop theories of causality, and test those theories can find which employee activities are relevant to the objectives.[19]

We're not advising that you throw your intuition, or all the business press, out the window. Nor are we arguing that research is always right. Researchers make mistakes, too. What we are advising is to use evidence as much as possible to inform your intuition and experience. That is the promise of OB.

Disciplines That Contribute to the OB Field

5 Identify the major behavioral science disciplines that contribute to OB.

Organizational behavior is an applied behavioral science built on contributions from a number of behavioral disciplines, mainly psychology and social psychology, sociology, and anthropology. Psychology's contributions have been mainly at the individual or micro level of analysis, while the other disciplines have contributed to our understanding of macro concepts such as group processes and organization. Exhibit 1-3 is an overview of the major contributions to the study of organizational behavior.

psychology *The science that seeks to measure, explain, and sometimes change the behavior of humans and other animals.*

Psychology

Psychology seeks to measure, explain, and sometimes change the behavior of humans and other animals. Those who have contributed and continue to add

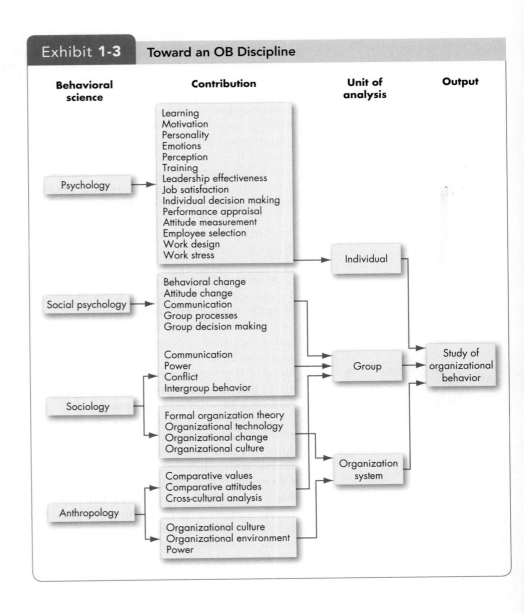

Exhibit 1-3   Toward an OB Discipline

to the knowledge of OB are learning theorists, personality theorists, counseling psychologists, and, most important, industrial and organizational psychologists.

Early industrial/organizational psychologists studied the problems of fatigue, boredom, and other working conditions that could impede efficient work performance. More recently, their contributions have expanded to include learning, perception, personality, emotions, training, leadership effectiveness, needs and motivational forces, job satisfaction, decision-making processes, performance appraisals, attitude measurement, employee-selection techniques, work design, and job stress.

Social Psychology

social psychology *An area of psychology that blends concepts from psychology and sociology and that focuses on the influence of people on one another.*

Social psychology, generally considered a branch of psychology, blends concepts from both psychology and sociology to focus on peoples' influence on one another. One major study area is *change*—how to implement it and how to reduce barriers to its acceptance. Social psychologists also contribute to measuring, understanding, and changing attitudes; identifying communication patterns; and building trust. Finally, they have made important contributions to our study of group behavior, power, and conflict.

Sociology

sociology *The study of people in relation to their social environment or culture.*

While psychology focuses on the individual, **sociology** studies people in relation to their social environment or culture. Sociologists have contributed to OB through their study of group behavior in organizations, particularly formal and complex organizations. Perhaps most important, sociologists have studied organizational culture, formal organization theory and structure, organizational technology, communications, power, and conflict.

Anthropology

anthropology *The study of societies to learn about human beings and their activities.*

Anthropology is the study of societies to learn about human beings and their activities. Anthropologists' work on cultures and environments has helped us understand differences in fundamental values, attitudes, and behavior between people in different countries and within different organizations. Much of our current understanding of organizational culture, organizational environments, and differences among national cultures is a result of the work of anthropologists or those using their methods.

There Are Few Absolutes in OB

6 Demonstrate why few absolutes apply to OB.

Laws in the physical sciences—chemistry, astronomy, physics—are consistent and apply in a wide range of situations. They allow scientists to generalize about the pull of gravity or to be confident about sending astronauts into space to repair satellites. But as a noted behavioral researcher observed, "God gave all the easy problems to the physicists." Human beings are complex, and few, if any, simple and universal principles explain organizational behavior. Because we are not alike, our ability to make simple, accurate, and sweeping generalizations is limited. Two people often act very differently in the same situation, and the same person's behavior changes in different situations. Not everyone is motivated by money, and people may behave differently at a religious service than they do at a party.

contingency variables *Situational factors: variables that moderate the relationship between two or more variables.*

That doesn't mean, of course, that we can't offer reasonably accurate explanations of human behavior or make valid predictions. It does mean that OB concepts must reflect situational, or contingency, conditions. We can say *x* leads to *y*, but only under conditions specified in *z*—the **contingency variables**. The science of OB was developed by applying general concepts to a particular situation, person, or group. For example, OB scholars would avoid stating that everyone likes complex and challenging work (the general concept). Why? Because not everyone wants a challenging job. Some people prefer routine over varied, or simple over complex. A job attractive to one person may not be to another; its appeal is contingent on the person who holds it.

As you proceed through this book, you'll encounter a wealth of research-based theories about how people behave in organizations. But don't expect to find a lot of straightforward cause-and-effect relationships. There aren't many! Organizational behavior theories mirror the subject matter with which they deal, and people are complex and complicated.

Challenges and Opportunities for OB

7 Identify the challenges and opportunities managers have in applying OB concepts.

Understanding organizational behavior has never been more important for managers. Take a quick look at the dramatic changes in organizations. The typical employee is getting older; more women and people of color are in the workplace; corporate downsizing and the heavy use of temporary workers are severing the bonds of loyalty that tied many employees to their employers; and global competition requires employees to become more flexible and cope with rapid change. The global recession has brought to the forefront the challenges of working with and managing people during uncertain times.

As a result of these changes and others such as the rising use of technology, employment options have adapted to include new opportunities for workers. Exhibit 1-4 details some of the types of options individuals may find offered to them by organizations or for which they would like to negotiate. Under each heading in the exhibit, you will find a grouping of options from which to choose—or combine. For instance, at one point in your career you may find yourself employed full-time in an office in a localized, nonunion setting with a salary and bonus compensation package, while at another point you may wish to negotiate for a flex-time, virtual position and choose to work from overseas for a combination of salary and extra paid time off.

In short, today's challenges bring opportunities for managers to use OB concepts. In this section, we review some of the most critical issues confronting managers for which OB offers solutions—or at least meaningful insights toward solutions.

Responding to Economic Pressures

When the U.S. economy plunged into a deep and prolonged recession in 2008, virtually all other large economies around the world followed suit. Layoffs and job losses were widespread, and those who survived the ax were often asked to accept pay cuts. When times are bad, managers are on the front lines with employees who must be fired, who are asked to make do with less, and who worry about their futures. The difference between good and bad management can be the difference between profit and loss or, ultimately, between survival and failure.

Managing employees well when times are tough is just as hard as when times are good—if not harder. But the OB approaches sometimes differ. In good times, understanding how to reward, satisfy, and retain employees is at a premium. In bad times, issues like stress, decision making, and coping come to the fore.

Exhibit 1-4   Employment Options

Categories of Employment	Types of Employment	Places of Employment	Conditions of Employment	Compensation for Employment
Employed	Full-time	Anchored (office/cubicle)	Local	Salary
Underemployed/ underutilized	Part-time	Floating (shared space)	Expatriate	Hourly
Re-employed	Flex-time	Virtual	Short-term assignee	Overtime
Unemployed/jobless	Job share	Flexible	Flexpatriate	Bonus
Entrepreneur	Contingent	Work from home	International business traveler	Contract
Retired	Independent contractor		Visa employee	Time off
Job seeking	Temporary		Union/nonunion employee	Benefits
Furloughed	Reduced hours			
Laid off	Intern			

Employed—working for a for-profit or nonprofit company, organization, or for an individual, either for money and/or benefits, with established expectations for performance and compensation

Underemployed/underutilized—working in a position or with responsibilities that are below one's educational or experience attainment level, or working less than full-time when one wants full-time employment

Re-employed—refers to either employees who were dismissed by a company and rehired by the same company, or to employees who left the workforce (were unemployed) and found new employment

Unemployed/jobless—currently not working; may be job seeking, either with or without government benefits/assistance, either with or without severance pay from previous job, either new to the workforce or terminated from previous employment, either short-term unemployed (months) or long-term/chronic unemployed (years)

Entrepreneur—one who runs his or her own business, either as a sole worker or as the founder of a company with employees

Retired—one who has ended his or her career in a profession, either voluntarily by choice or involuntarily by an employer's mandate

Job seeking—currently unemployed; actively looking for a job, either with or without government benefits from previous job or from disability/need, either with or without severance pay from previous job, either new to the workforce or terminated from previous employment

Furloughed—similar to a layoff; an employer-required work stoppage, temporary (weeks up to a month, usually); pay is often suspended during this time, though the person retains employment status with the company

Laid off—can be a temporary employer-required work stoppage, usually without pay, but is more often a permanent termination from the company in which the employee is recognized to be not at fault

Full-time—hours for full-time employment are established by companies, generally more than 30 hours per week in a set schedule, sometimes with salary pay and sometimes with hourly pay, often with a benefit package greater than that for the part-time employment category

Part-time—hours for full-time employment are established by companies, generally less than 30 hours per week in a set schedule, often with hourly pay, often with a benefit package less than that for the full-time employment category

Flex-time—an arrangement where the employee and employer create nonstandard working hours, which may be a temporary or permanent schedule; may be an expectation for a number of hours worked per week

Job share—an arrangement where two or more employees fill one job, generally by splitting the hours of a full time position that do not overlap

Contingent—the workforce of outsourced workers (including professional service firms, specialized experts, and business consultants), these employees are paid hourly or by the job and do not generally receive any company benefits and are not considered as part of the company; contingent workers may be also temporary employees or independent contractors

Independent contractor—an entrepreneur in essence, but often a specialist professional who does not aspire to create a business but who provides services or goods to a company

Temporary—individuals who may be employed directly by the organization or through an employment agency/temporary agency; their hours may be fixed per week or vary, they do not generally receive any company benefits, and are not considered as part of the company; they are employed either for a short duration or as a trial for an organization's position openings

Reduced-hours—reduction in the normal employee's work schedule by the employer, sometimes as a measure to retain employees/reduce layoffs in economic downturns as in Germany's *Kurzarbeit* program, which provides government subsidies to keep workers on the job at reduced hours; employees are only paid for the time they work

Intern—short-term employment, often with an established term, designed to provide practical training to a pre-professional, either with or without pay

Anchored—an employee with an assigned office, cubicle, or desk space

Floating—an employee with a shared space workplace and no assigned working area

Virtual—an employee who works through the Internet and is not connected with any office location

Flexible—an employee who is connected with an office location but may work from anywhere

Work from home—an employee who is set up by the company to work from an office at home

Local—employees who work in one established location

Expatriate—employees who are on extended international work assignments with the expectation that they will return (repatriate) after an established term, usually a year or more; either sent by corporate request or out of self-initiated interest

Short-term assignee—employees on international assignments longer than business trips yet shorter than typical corporate expatriate assignments, usually 3 to 12 months

Flexpatriate—employees who travel for brief assignments across cultural or national borders, usually 1 to 2 months

International business traveler—employees who take multiple short international business trips for 1 to 3 weeks

(continued)

| Exhibit **1-4** | **Employment Options (continued)** |

Visa employee—an employee working outside of his or her country of residence who must have a work visa for employment in the current country

Union/nonunion employee—an employee who is a member of a labor union, often by trade, and subject to its protections and provisions, which then negotiates with management on certain working condition issues, or an employee who works for a nonunion facility or who sometimes elects to stay out of membership in a unionized facility

Salary—employee compensation based on a full-time workweek, where the hours are generally not kept on a time clock but where it is understood that the employee will work according to job needs

Hourly—employee compensation for each hour worked, often recorded on time sheets or by time clocks

Overtime—for hourly employees, compensation for hours worked that are greater than the standard workweek and paid at an hourly rate determined by law

Bonus—compensation in addition to standard pay, usually linked to individual or organizational performance

Contract—prenegotiated compensation for project work, usually according to a schedule as the work progresses

Time off —either paid or unpaid; negotiated time off according to the employment contract (including vacation time, sick leave, and personal days) and/or given by management as compensation for time worked

Benefits—generally stated in the employment contract or the Human Resources Employee Handbook; potentially include health insurance plans, savings plans, retirement plans, discounts, and other options available to employees at various types of employment

Sources: J. R. Anderson Jr., et al., "Action Items: 42 Trends Affecting Benefits, Compensation, Training, Staffing and Technology," *HR Magazine* (January 2013) p. 33; M. Dewhurst, B. Hancock, and D. Ellsworth, "Redesigning Knowledge Work," *Harvard Business Review* (January–February 2013), pp. 58–64; E. Frauenheim, "Creating a New Contingent Culture," *Workforce Management* (August 2012), pp. 34–39; N. Koeppen, "State Job Aid Takes Pressure off Germany," *The Wall Street Journal* (February 1, 2013), p. A8; and M. A. Shaffer, M. L. Kraimer, Y.-P. Chen, and M. C. Bolino, "Choices, Challenges, and Career Consequences of Global Work Experiences: A Review and Future Agenda," *Journal of Management* (July 2012), pp. 1282–1327.

Responding to Globalization

Organizations are no longer constrained by national borders. Burger King is owned by a British firm, and McDonald's sells hamburgers in more than 100 companies in six continents. ExxonMobil, a so-called U.S. company, reported that less than 6 percent of their 2011 earnings were from gas and natural products sales in the United States. New employees at Finland-based phone maker Nokia are increasingly being recruited from India, China, and other developing countries—non-Finns now outnumber Finns at their renowned research center in Helsinki. And all major automobile makers now manufacture cars outside their borders; Honda builds cars in Ohio, Ford in Brazil, Volkswagen in Mexico, and both Mercedes and BMW in South Africa.

The world has become a global village. In the process, the manager's job has changed.

Increased Foreign Assignments   If you're a manager, you are increasingly likely to find yourself in a foreign assignment—transferred to your employer's operating division or subsidiary in another country. Once there, you'll have to manage a workforce very different in needs, aspirations, and attitudes from those you are used to back home.

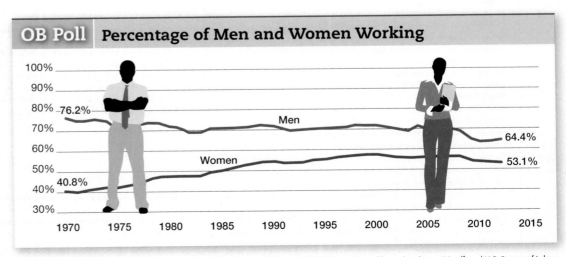

OB Poll   Percentage of Men and Women Working

Sources: Based on U.S. Bureau of Labor Statistics, "Household Data Annual Averages" (2012), http://www.bls.gov/cps/cpsaat03.pdf; and U.S. Bureau of Labor Statistics, "Women in the Labor Force: A Datebook," *BLS Report 1040* (February 2013), Table 2, pp. 11–12.

Working with People from Different Cultures   Even in your own country, you'll find yourself working with bosses, peers, and other employees born and raised in different cultures. What motivates you may not motivate them. Or your communication style may be straightforward and open, which others may find uncomfortable and threatening. To work effectively with people from different cultures, you need to understand how their culture, geography, and religion have shaped them and how to adapt your management style to their differences.

Managers at global companies such as IBM, Disney, and Coca-Cola have come to realize that economic values are not universally transferable. Management practices need to be modified to reflect the values of the different countries in which an organization operates.

Overseeing Movement of Jobs to Countries with Low-Cost Labor   It is increasingly difficult for managers in advanced nations, where minimum wages are typically $6 or more an hour, to compete against firms that rely on workers from China and other developing nations where labor is available for 30 cents an hour. It's not by chance that many in the United States wear clothes made in China, work on computers whose microchips came from Taiwan, and watch movies filmed in Canada. In a global economy, jobs tend to flow where lower costs give businesses a comparative advantage, though labor groups, politicians, and local community leaders see the exporting of jobs as undermining the job market at home. Managers face the difficult task of balancing the interests of their organizations with their responsibilities to the communities in which they operate.

Adapting to Differing Cultural and Regulatory Norms   "Going global" for a business is not as simple as typing in an overseas e-mail address, shipping goods off to a foreign port, or building facilities in other countries. To be successful, managers need to know the cultural practices of the workforce in each country where they do business. For instance, in some countries a large percentage of the workforce enjoys long holidays. There will be country and local regulations to consider, too. Managers of subsidiaries abroad need to be aware of the unique financial and legal regulations applying to "guest companies" or else risk violating

Photo 1-3 Guy Woolaert, senior vice president and chief technical officer of The Coca-Cola Company, has worked effectively with people from many cultures. He learned from his 20 years of assignments abroad in Europe, the Pacific, and other geographic regions how to adapt his management style to reflect the values of different countries.

Source: Robin Nelson/ZUMA Press/Newscom.

them, which can have economic and even political consequences. Such violations can have implications for their operations in that country and also for political relations between countries. As well, managers need to be cognizant of differences in regulations for their competitors in that country; many times, the laws will give national companies significant financial advantages over foreign subsidiaries.

Managing Workforce Diversity

One of the most important challenges for organizations is *workforce diversity*, the concept that organizations are becoming more heterogeneous in terms of gender, age, race, ethnicity, sexual orientation, and inclusion of other diverse groups. Whereas globalization focuses on differences among people *from* different countries, workforce diversity addresses differences among people *within* given countries.

workforce diversity *The concept that organizations are becoming more heterogeneous in terms of gender, age, race, ethnicity, sexual orientation, and inclusion of other diverse groups.*

Workforce diversity acknowledges a workforce of women and men, many racial and ethnic groups, individuals with a variety of physical or psychological abilities, and people who differ in age and sexual orientation. Managing this diversity is a global concern. For example, most European countries have experienced dramatic growth in immigration from the Middle East. Argentina and Venezuela host a significant number of migrants from other South American countries, and nations from India to Iraq to Indonesia find great cultural diversity within their borders.

The most significant change in the U.S. labor force during the last half of the twentieth century was the rapid increase in the number of female workers. In 1950, for instance, only 29.6 percent of the workforce was female.[20] By 2010, it was 46.7 percent. The first half of the twenty-first century will be notable for changes in racial and ethnic composition and an aging baby boom generation. By 2020, Hispanics will grow from 14.8 percent of the workforce in 2010 to 18.6 percent, blacks will increase from 11.6 to 12 percent, and Asians from 4.7 to 5.7 percent. Meanwhile, in the near term the labor force will be aging. The 55-and-older age group, 19.5 percent of the labor force in 2010, will increase to 25.2 percent by 2020.[21]

Though we have more to say about workforce diversity in the next chapter, suffice it to say here that it presents great opportunities and poses challenging questions for managers and employees in all countries. How can we leverage differences within groups for competitive advantage? Should we treat all employees alike? Should we recognize individual and cultural differences? How can we foster cultural awareness in employees without lapsing into political correctness? What are the legal requirements in each country? Does diversity even matter?

Improving Customer Service

Service employees include technical support representatives, fast-food counter workers, sales clerks, nurses, automobile repair technicians, consultants, financial planners, and flight attendants. The shared characteristic of their jobs is substantial interaction with an organization's customers. OB can help managers increase the success of these interactions by showing how employee attitudes and behavior influence customer satisfaction.

Many an organization has failed because its employees failed to please customers. Management needs to create a customer-responsive culture. OB can provide considerable guidance in helping managers create such cultures—in which employees are friendly and courteous, accessible, knowledgeable, prompt in responding to customer needs, and willing to do what's necessary to please the customer.[22]

Improving People Skills

As you proceed through the chapters of this book, we'll present relevant concepts and theories that can help you explain and predict the behavior of people

Photo 1-4 A Whole Foods Market customer learns how to grind flour with the help of the store's cooking coach, whose job is to provide information about cooking ingredients, methods, and techniques. The coaches embody the best of the retailer's customer-responsive culture of serving people with competency, efficiency, knowledge, and flair.

Source: The Washington Post/Getty Images.

at work. You'll also gain insights into specific people skills that you can use on the job. For instance, you'll learn ways to design motivating jobs, techniques for improving your listening skills, and how to create more effective teams.

Working in Networked Organizations

Networked organizations allow people to communicate and work together even though they may be thousands of miles apart. Independent contractors can telecommute via computer to workplaces around the globe and change employers as the demand for their services changes. Software programmers, graphic designers, systems analysts, technical writers, photo researchers, book and media editors, and medical transcribers are just a few examples of people who can work from home or other nonoffice locations.

The manager's job is different in a networked organization. Motivating and leading people and making collaborative decisions online requires different techniques than when individuals are physically present in a single location. As more employees do their jobs by linking to others through networks, managers must develop new skills. OB can provide valuable insights to help with honing those skills.

Enhancing Employee Well-Being at Work

The typical employee in the 1960s or 1970s showed up at a specified workplace Monday through Friday and worked for clearly defined 8- or 9-hour chunks of time. That's no longer true for a large segment of today's workforce. Employees are increasingly complaining that the line between work and nonwork time has become blurred, creating personal conflicts and stress. At the same time, today's workplace presents opportunities for workers to create and structure their own roles. And even if employees work at home or from half a continent away, managers need to consider their well-being at work.

One of the biggest challenges to maintaining employee well-being is the new reality that many workers never get away from the virtual workplace. Communication technology allows many technical and professional employees to do their work at home, in their cars, or on the beach in Tahiti—but it also means many feel like they never really get a break. Another challenge is that organizations are asking employees to put in longer hours. According to a recent study, one in four employees show signs of burnout, partially as a result of longer work hours, and two in three report high stress levels and fatigue.[23] This may actually be an underestimate because workers report maintaining "always on" access for their managers through e-mail and texting. Finally, employee well-being is challenged by heavy outside commitments. Millions of single-parent households and employees with dependent parents have even more significant challenges in balancing work and family responsibilities, for instance.

As a result of their increased responsibilities in and out of the workplace, employees want more time off. Recent studies suggest employees want jobs that give them flexibility in their work schedules so they can better manage work–life conflicts.[24] In fact, 56 percent of men and women in a recent study reported that work–life balance was their definition of career success, more than money, recognition, and autonomy.[25] Most college and university students say attaining a balance between personal life and work is a primary career goal; they want a life as well as a job. Organizations that don't help their people achieve work–life balance will find it increasingly difficult to attract and retain the most capable and motivated employees.

As you'll see in later chapters, the field of OB offers a number of suggestions to guide managers in designing workplaces and jobs that can help employees deal with work–life conflicts.

Creating a Positive Work Environment

Although competitive pressures on most organizations are stronger than ever, some organizations are trying to realize a competitive advantage by fostering a positive work environment. Sometimes they do this by creating pleasing physical environments with attractive modern workstations, workplace "perks" such as Google's free lunches, or a shared commitment to environmental sustainability initiatives such as recycling.[26] But, more often, employees perceive a work environment as positive or negative in terms of their work experiences with other employees, rather than in the quality of its physical surroundings. Jeff Immelt and Jim McNerney, both disciples of Jack Welch, have tried to maintain high-performance expectations (a characteristic of GE's culture) while fostering a positive work environment in their organizations (GE and Boeing). "In

Photo 1-5 Dr. Orit Wimpfheimer performs her job by linking to others through networks. A radiologist who works from her home office near Jerusalem, Israel, she analyzes test results from hospitals in the United States. Networked organizations use e-mail, the Internet, and videoconferencing for communication and collaboration.

this time of turmoil and cynicism about business, you need to be passionate, positive leaders," Mr. Immelt recently told his top managers.

A real growth area in OB research is **positive organizational scholarship** (also called *positive organizational behavior*), which studies how organizations develop human strengths, foster vitality and resilience, and unlock potential. Researchers in this area say too much of OB research and management practice has been targeted toward identifying what's wrong with organizations and their employees. In response, they try to study what's *good* about them.[27] Some key independent variables in positive OB research are engagement, hope, optimism, and resilience in the face of strain.

positive organizational scholarship
An area of OB research that concerns how organizations develop human strength, foster vitality and resilience, and unlock potential.

Positive organizational scholars have studied a concept called "reflected best-self"—asking employees to think about when they were at their "personal best" in order to understand how to exploit their strengths. The idea is that we all have things at which we are unusually good, yet too often we focus on addressing our limitations and too rarely think about how to exploit our strengths.[28]

Although positive organizational scholarship does not deny the value of the negative (such as critical feedback), it does challenge researchers to look at OB through a new lens and pushes organizations to exploit employees' strengths rather than dwell on their limitations.

Improving Ethical Behavior

In an organizational world characterized by cutbacks, expectations of increasing productivity, and tough competition, it's not surprising many employees feel pressured to cut corners, break rules, and engage in other questionable practices.

Increasingly they face **ethical dilemmas and ethical choices**, in which they are required to identify right and wrong conduct. Should they "blow the whistle" if they uncover illegal activities in their company? Do they follow orders with which they don't personally agree? Should they give an inflated performance evaluation to an employee they like, knowing it could save that employee's job? Do they "play politics" to advance their career?

ethical dilemmas and ethical choices   *Situations in which individuals are required to define right and wrong conduct.*

What constitutes good ethical behavior has never been clearly defined, and, in recent years, the line differentiating right from wrong has blurred. Employees see people all around them engaging in unethical practices—elected officials pad expense accounts or take bribes; corporate executives inflate profits so they can cash in lucrative stock options; and university administrators look the other way when winning coaches encourage scholarship athletes to take easy courses. When caught, these people give excuses such as "Everyone does it" or "You have to seize every advantage nowadays." Determining the ethically correct way to behave is especially difficult in a global economy because different cultures have different perspectives on certain ethical issues.[29] Fair treatment of employees in an economic downturn varies considerably across cultures, for instance. As we'll see in Chapter 2, perceptions of religious, ethnic, and gender diversity differ across countries. Is it any wonder employees are expressing decreased confidence in management and increasing uncertainty about what is appropriate ethical behavior in their organizations?[30]

Managers and their organizations are responding to the problem of unethical behavior in a number of ways.[31] They're writing and distributing codes of ethics to guide employees through dilemmas. They're offering seminars, workshops, and other training programs to try to improve ethical behaviors. They're providing in-house advisors who can be contacted, in many cases anonymously, for assistance in dealing with issues, and they're creating protection mechanisms for employees who reveal internal unethical practices.

Today's manager must create an ethically healthy climate for his or her employees, where they can do their work productively with minimal ambiguity about right versus wrong behaviors. Companies that promote a strong ethical

Vacation Deficit Disorder

Do you work to live, or live to work? Those of us who think it's a choice might be wrong. No matter what employee vacation accrual balance sheets indicate, in many cases workers will end this year with a week of unused time. Or more. Consider Ken Waltz, a director for Alexian Brothers Health System. He has 500 hours (approximately 3 months) in banked time off and no plans to spend it, choosing work over time with his two sons. "You're on call 24/7 and these days, you'd better step up or step out," he says, referring to today's leaner workforce, "It's not just me—it's upper management. . . . It's everybody."

Jane Himmel, a senior manager for Palmer House Hilton, agrees. She took 5 of her allotted 22 days off in 2012, but didn't consider even those days a break because she chose to monitor her e-mail constantly. "If I don't keep up with it, it's just insane when I get back," she says. Almost a full one-third of 1,000 respondents in a study by Kelton Research agreed, citing workload as a reason for not using allotted vacation days. In 2011, 65 percent of U.S. workers had unused vacation days, and experts believe the percentage is increasing. Much of the reason is attributable to the economy; one person is often doing the work of three, and many fear they may lose their jobs if they take vacation. But the cost of nonstop working can be high. There are ethical choices here, for the employer and for the employee.

It would be easy to assume employers prefer employees to work without breaks, but that's not always the case. Many states require employers to compensate departing employees financially for accrued vacation time, and most companies say they recognize the benefits of a refreshed workforce. As a result, they often encourage their employees to take their vacations through periodic "use it or lose it" e-mail reminders. Yet, employers are also expecting workers to do more with less, in the form of fewer co-workers to help get the job done, putting implicit or explicit pressure on them to use all available resources—chiefly their time—to meet manager expectations.

Research indicates employees are more likely to respond to the direct pressure of management than to the indirect benevolence of corporate policy. Thus, policy or not, many employees do not take their allotted vacation time due to direct or indirect pressure from their manager. While it is easy to dismiss these pressures, in today's economy there is always a ready line of replacement, and many employees will do everything possible to keep in their manager's good graces, including foregoing vacation time.

The downside, of course, is the risk of burnout. Foregoing vacation time can wear you down emotionally, leading to exhaustion, negative feelings about your work, and a reduced feeling of accomplishment. You may find you are absent more often, contemplate leaving your job, and grow less likely to want to help anyone (including your managers). Here are some choices you can make to prevent a downward spiral:

1. **Recognize your feelings.** According to a recent report by ComPsych Corp. on 2,000 employees, two in three identified high levels of stress, out-of-control feelings, and extreme fatigue. We solve few problems without first recognizing them.

2. **Identify your tendency for burnout.** Research on 2,089 employees found that burnout is especially acute for newcomers and job changers. If you have recently made a career change, it can help you to know any increase in symptoms should level off after 2 years. But keep in mind that each individual experiences stress differently.

3. **Talk about your stressors.** Thomas Donohoe, a researcher on work–life balance, recommends talking with trusted friends or family. On the job, appropriately discussing your stress factors can help you reduce job overload.

4. **Build in high physical activity.** Recent research found an increase in job burnout (and depression) was strongest for employees who did not engage in regular physical activity, while it was almost negligible for employees who did engage in regular high physical activity. Physical activity distracts the mind from stressors, enhances feelings of mastery and self-efficacy, and builds physiological resilience to stress.

5. **Take brief breaks throughout your day.** For office employees, the current expert suggestion is to spend at least 1 to 2 minutes standing up every hour to combat the effects of all-day sitting. Donohoe also suggests snack breaks, walks, or small naps to recharge.

6. **Take your vacation!** Studies suggest that recovery from stress can happen only if employees are (a) physically away from work and (b) not occupied by work-related duties. That means log off your e-mail accounts, shut off your phone, and put down your pen for the duration of the vacation. As much as possible, remove yourself from the work environment physically and mentally.

With work only a thumb swipe away and performance demands high, it is not always easy to look beyond the next deadline. But to maximize your long-term productivity and avoid stress, burnout, and illness—all of which are ultimately harmful to employer aims and employee careers alike—you should not succumb to vacation deficit disorder. Educate your managers. Your employer should thank you for it.

Sources: B. B. Dunford, A. J. Shipp, R. W. Boss, I. Angermeier, and A. D. Boss, "Is Burnout Static or Dynamic? A Career Transition Perspective of Employee Burnout Trajectories," *Journal of Applied Psychology* 97, no. 3 (2012), pp. 637–650; E. J. Hirst, "Burnout on the Rise," *Chicago Tribune* (October 29, 2012), pp. 3-1, 3-4; B. M. Rubin, "Rough Economy Means No Vacation," *Chicago Tribune* (September 3, 2012), p. 4; and S. Toker and M. Biron, "Job Burnout and Depression: Unraveling Their Temporal Relationship and Considering the Role of Physical Activity," *Journal of Applied Psychology* 97, no. 3 (2012), pp. 699–710.

mission, encourage employees to behave with integrity, and provide strong leadership can influence employee decisions to behave ethically.[32] In upcoming chapters, we'll discuss the actions managers can take to create an ethically healthy climate and help employees sort through ambiguous situations. We'll also present ethical-dilemma exercises at the end of each chapter that allow you to think through ethical issues and assess how you would handle them.

Coming Attractions: Developing an OB Model

8 Compare the three levels of analysis in this book's OB model.

We conclude this chapter by presenting a general model that defines the field of OB, stakes out its parameters, and identifies inputs, processes, and outcomes. The result will be "coming attractions" of the topics in the remainder of this book.

An Overview

model *An abstraction of reality. A simplified representation of some real-world phenomenon.*

A **model** is an abstraction of reality, a simplified representation of some real-world phenomenon. Exhibit 1-5 presents the skeleton on which we will construct our OB model. It proposes three types of variables (inputs, processes, and outcomes) at three levels of analysis (individual, group, and organizational). The model proceeds from left to right, with inputs leading to processes and processes leading to outcomes. Notice that the model also shows that outcomes can influence inputs in the future.

Inputs

input *Variables that lead to processes.*

Inputs are the variables like personality, group structure, and organizational culture that lead to processes. These variables set the stage for what will occur in an organization later. Many are determined in advance of the employment relationship. For example, individual diversity characteristics, personality, and values

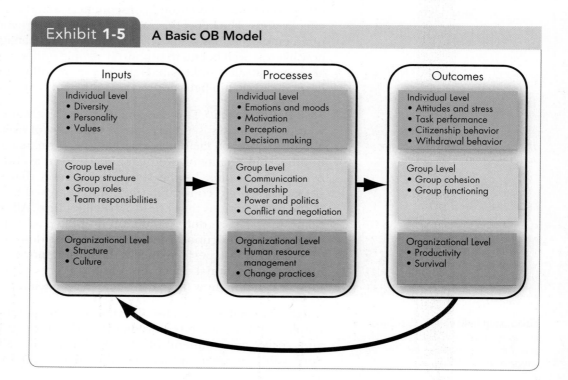

Exhibit 1-5   A Basic OB Model

Inputs	Processes	Outcomes
Individual Level • Diversity • Personality • Values	**Individual Level** • Emotions and moods • Motivation • Perception • Decision making	**Individual Level** • Attitudes and stress • Task performance • Citizenship behavior • Withdrawal behavior
Group Level • Group structure • Group roles • Team responsibilities	**Group Level** • Communication • Leadership • Power and politics • Conflict and negotiation	**Group Level** • Group cohesion • Group functioning
Organizational Level • Structure • Culture	**Organizational Level** • Human resource management • Change practices	**Organizational Level** • Productivity • Survival

are shaped by a combination of an individual's genetic inheritance and childhood environment. Group structure, roles, and team responsibilities are typically assigned immediately before or after a group is formed. Finally, organizational structure and culture are usually the result of years of development and change as the organization adapts to its environment and builds up customs and norms.

Processes

processes *Actions that individuals, groups, and organizations engage in as a result of inputs and that lead to certain outcomes.*

If inputs are like the nouns in organizational behavior, processes are like verbs. **Processes** are actions that individuals, groups, and organizations engage in as a result of inputs and that lead to certain outcomes. At the individual level, processes include emotions and moods, motivation, perception, and decision making. At the group level, they include communication, leadership, power and politics, and conflict and negotiation. Finally, at the organizational level, processes include human resource management and change practices.

Outcomes

outcomes *Key factors that are affected by some other variables.*

Outcomes are the key variables that you want to explain or predict, and that are affected by some other variables. What are the primary outcomes in OB? Scholars have emphasized individual-level outcomes like attitudes and satisfaction, task performance, citizenship behavior, and withdrawal behavior. At the group level, cohesion and functioning are the dependent variables. Finally, at the organizational level, we look at overall profitability and survival. Because these outcomes will be covered in all the chapters, we'll briefly discuss each here so you can understand what the "goal" of OB will be.

attitudes *Evaluations employees make about objects, people, or events.*

stress *An unpleasant psychological process that occurs in response to environmental pressures.*

Attitudes and Stress   Employee **attitudes** are the evaluations employees make, ranging from positive to negative, about objects, people, or events. For example, the statement, "I really think my job is great," is a positive job attitude, and "My job is boring and tedious" is a negative job attitude. **Stress** is an unpleasant psychological process that occurs in response to environmental pressures.

Some people might think that influencing employee attitudes and stress is purely soft stuff and not the business of serious managers, but as we will show, attitudes often have behavioral consequences that directly relate to organizational effectiveness. The belief that satisfied employees are more productive than dissatisfied employees has been a basic tenet among managers for years, though only now has research begun to support it. Ample evidence shows that employees who are more satisfied and treated fairly are more willing to engage in the above-and-beyond citizenship behavior so vital in the contemporary business environment.

task performance *The combination of effectiveness and efficiency at doing your core job tasks.*

Task Performance   The combination of effectiveness and efficiency at doing your core job tasks is a reflection of your level of **task performance**. If we think about the job of a factory worker, task performance could be measured by the number and quality of products produced in an hour. The task performance of a teacher would be the level of education that students obtain. The task performance of a consultant might be measured by the timeliness and quality of the presentations they offer to the client firm. All these types of performance relate to the core duties and responsibilities of a job and are often directly related to the functions listed on a formal job description.

Obviously task performance is the most important human output contributing to organizational effectiveness, so in every chapter we devote considerable time to detailing how task performance is affected by the topic in question.

citizenship behavior *Discretionary behavior that contributes to the psychological and social environment of the workplace.*

Citizenship Behavior   The discretionary behavior that is not part of an employee's formal job requirements, and that contributes to the psychological and social environment of the workplace, is called **citizenship behavior**. Successful organizations need employees who will do more than their usual job duties—who will provide performance *beyond* expectations. In today's dynamic workplace, where tasks are increasingly performed by teams and flexibility is critical, employees who engage in "good citizenship" behaviors help others on their team, volunteer for extra work, avoid unnecessary conflicts, respect the spirit as well as the letter of rules and regulations, and gracefully tolerate occasional work-related impositions and nuisances.

Organizations want and need employees who will do things that aren't in any job description. Evidence indicates organizations that have such employees outperform those that don't. As a result, OB is concerned with citizenship behavior as an outcome variable.

Withdrawal Behavior   We've already mentioned behavior that goes above and beyond task requirements, but what about behavior that in some way is below task requirements? **Withdrawal behavior** is the set of actions that employees take to separate themselves from the organization. There are many forms of withdrawal, ranging from showing up late or failing to attend meetings to absenteeism and turnover.

withdrawal behavior *The set of actions employees take to separate themselves from the organization.*

Employee withdrawal can have a very negative effect on an organization. The cost of employee turnover alone has been estimated to run into the thousands of dollars, even for entry-level positions. Absenteeism also costs organizations significant amounts of money and time every year. For instance, a recent survey found the average direct cost to U.S. employers of unscheduled absences is 8.7 percent of payroll.[33] In Sweden, an average of 10 percent of the country's workforce is on sick leave at any given time.[34]

It's obviously difficult for an organization to operate smoothly and attain its objectives if employees fail to report to their jobs. The workflow is disrupted, and important decisions may be delayed. In organizations that rely heavily on assembly-line production, absenteeism can be considerably more than a disruption; it can drastically reduce the quality of output or even shut down the facility. Levels of absenteeism beyond the normal range have a direct impact on any organization's effectiveness and efficiency. A high rate of turnover can also disrupt the efficient running of an organization when knowledgeable and

Photo 1-6 Task performance is one of the primary individual-level outcomes in organizational behavior and the most important human output contributing to organizational effectiveness. For these women who install wiring in car doors at a GM plant, task performance is measured by the number and quality of the work they produce.

Source: AP Photo/Mark Duncan.

experienced personnel leave and replacements must be found to assume positions of responsibility.

All organizations, of course, have some turnover. The U.S. national turnover rate averages about 3 percent per month, about a 36 percent turnover per year. This average varies a lot by occupation, of course; the monthly turnover rate for government jobs is less than 1 percent, versus 5 to 7 percent in the construction industry.[35] If the "right" people are leaving the organization—the marginal and submarginal employees—turnover can actually be positive. It can create an opportunity to replace an underperforming individual with someone who has higher skills or motivation, open up increased opportunities for promotions, and bring new and fresh ideas to the organization.[36] In today's changing world of work, reasonable levels of employee-initiated turnover improve organizational flexibility and employee independence, and they can lessen the need for management-initiated layoffs.

So why do employees withdraw from work? As we will show later in the book, reasons include negative job attitudes, emotions and moods, and negative interactions with co-workers and supervisors.

group cohesion *The extent to which members of a group support and validate one another while at work.*

Group Cohesion   Although many outcomes in our model can be conceptualized as individual level phenomena, some relate to how groups operate. **Group cohesion** is the extent to which members of a group support and validate one another at work. In other words, a cohesive group is one that sticks together. When employees trust one another, seek common goals, and work together to achieve these common ends, the group is cohesive; when employees are divided among themselves in terms of what they want to achieve and have little loyalty to one another, the group is not cohesive.

There is ample evidence showing that cohesive groups are more effective.[37] These results are found both for groups that are studied in highly controlled laboratory settings and also for work teams observed in field settings. This fits with our intuitive sense that people tend to work harder in groups that have a common purpose. Companies attempt to increase cohesion in a variety of ways ranging from brief icebreaker sessions to social events like picnics, parties, and outdoor adventure-team retreats. Throughout the book we will try to assess whether these specific efforts are likely to result in increases in group cohesiveness. We'll also consider ways that picking the right people to be on the team in the first place might be an effective way to enhance cohesion.

group functioning *The quantity and quality of a work group's output.*

Group Functioning   In the same way that positive job attitudes can be associated with higher levels of task performance, group cohesion should lead to positive group functioning. **Group functioning** refers to the quantity and quality of a group's work output. In the same way that the performance of a sports team is more than the sum of individual players' performance, group functioning in work organizations is more than the sum of individual task performances.

What does it mean to say that a group is functioning effectively? In some organizations, an effective group is one that stays focused on a core task and achieves its ends as specified. Other organizations look for teams that are able to work together collaboratively to provide excellent customer service. Still others put more of a premium on group creativity and the flexibility to adapt to changing situations. In each case, different types of activities will be required to get the most from the team.

productivity *The combination of the effectiveness and efficiency of an organization.*

effectiveness *The degree to which an organization meets the needs of its clientele or customers.*

efficiency *The degree to which an organization can achieve its ends at a low cost.*

Productivity   The highest level of analysis in organizational behavior is the organization as a whole. An organization is productive if it achieves its goals by transforming inputs into outputs at the lowest cost. Thus **productivity** requires both **effectiveness** and **efficiency**.

A hospital is *effective* when it successfully meets the needs of its clientele. It is *efficient* when it can do so at a low cost. If a hospital manages to achieve higher output from its present staff by reducing the average number of days a patient is confined to bed or increasing the number of staff–patient contacts per day, we say the hospital has gained productive efficiency. A business firm is effective when it attains its sales or market share goals, but its productivity also depends on achieving those goals efficiently. Popular measures of organizational efficiency include return on investment, profit per dollar of sales, and output per hour of labor.

Service organizations must include customer needs and requirements in assessing their effectiveness. Why? Because a clear chain of cause and effect runs from employee attitudes and behavior to customer attitudes and behavior to a service organization's productivity. Sears has carefully documented this chain.[38] The company's management found that a 5 percent improvement in employee attitudes leads to a 1.3 percent increase in customer satisfaction, which in turn translates into a 0.5 percent improvement in revenue growth. By training employees to improve the employee–customer interaction, Sears was able to improve customer satisfaction by 4 percent over a 12-month period, generating an estimated $200 million in additional revenues.

organizational survival *The degree to which an organization is able to exist and grow over the long term.*

Survival The final outcome we will consider is **organizational survival**, which is simply evidence that the organization is able to exist and grow over the long term. The survival of an organization depends not just on how productive the organization is, but also on how well it fits with its environment. A company that is very productively making goods and services of little value to the market is unlikely to survive for long, so survival factors in things like perceiving the market successfully, making good decisions about how and when to pursue opportunities, and engaging in successful change management to adapt to new business conditions.

Having reviewed the input, process, and outcome model, we're going to change the figure up a little bit by grouping topics together based on whether we study them at the individual, group, or organizational level. As you can see in Exhibit 1-6, we will deal with inputs, processes, and outcomes at all three levels of

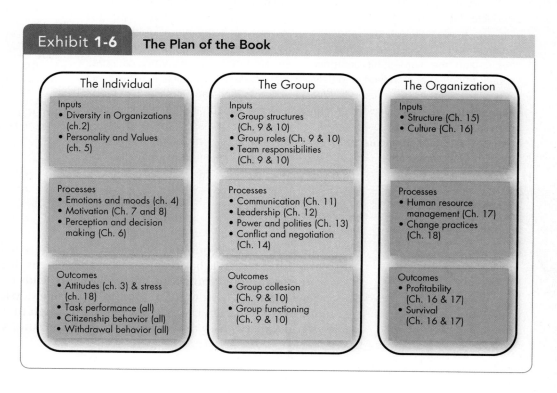

Exhibit 1-6 The Plan of the Book

The Individual

Inputs
- Diversity in Organizations (ch. 2)
- Personality and Values (ch. 5)

Processes
- Emotions and moods (ch. 4)
- Motivation (Ch. 7 and 8)
- Perception and decision making (Ch. 6)

Outcomes
- Attitudes (ch. 3) & stress (ch. 18)
- Task performance (all)
- Citizenship behavior (all)
- Withdrawal behavior (all)

The Group

Inputs
- Group structures (Ch. 9 & 10)
- Group roles (Ch. 9 & 10)
- Team responsibilities (Ch. 9 & 10)

Processes
- Communication (Ch. 11)
- Leadership (Ch. 12)
- Power and politics (Ch. 13)
- Conflict and negotiation (Ch. 14)

Outcomes
- Group cohesion (Ch. 9 & 10)
- Group functioning (Ch. 9 & 10)

The Organization

Inputs
- Structure (Ch. 15)
- Culture (Ch. 16)

Processes
- Human resource management (Ch. 17)
- Change practices (Ch. 18)

Outcomes
- Profitability (Ch. 16 & 17)
- Survival (Ch. 16 & 17)

Suicide by Economic Crisis

The tragedy of Dimitris Christoulas is all too familiar in recent European history, and indeed in all industrialized nations affected by the ongoing global economic crisis. As the retired pharmacist wrote before he fatally shot himself in 2012, "[the] government has annihilated all traces for my survival, which was based on a very dignified pension that I alone paid for 35 years with no help from the state . . . I see no other solution than this dignified end to my life, so I don't find myself fishing through garbage cans for my sustenance." Christoulas took his life in public outside the Greek Parliament, but many others have silently slipped away, sharing his sentiment. European newspapers have dubbed these cases "death by economic crisis," and they are on the rise.

The World Health Organization, which records trends in mortality rates for Europe, has reported that the long-term decline in suicides reversed in 2007 and is now increasing dramatically. Though up-to-date data are not available due to the lag time in reporting, the hardest-hit groups appear to be men and small-business entrepreneurs, and the hardest-hit countries appear to be Greece, Ireland, and Italy. Greek government statistics indicate a 24 percent increase in suicides among men from 2007 to 2009, while Ireland reported a 16 percent increase among men in the same time period. Suicides attributed to economic hardship motives in Italy increased 52 percent from 2005 to 2010.

The link between economic crises and suicide is well established in research built upon the work of several early prominent social scientists. While a link between economic conditions and suicide was hypothesized in as early as 1822, Durkheim's 1897 study was a foundational work proving strong social forces behind suicide motivation. Later in 1954, Henry and Short predicted that suicide rates will rise during periods of economic crisis as a result of frustration/aggression from status hierarchy changes. Soon after, in 1966, Ginsberg found that, whenever rewards fall short of aspirations as perceived by an individual in a society, suicides increase. Although the three schools of thought did not agree on all points, they definitively proved a link strong between economic turmoil and suicide rates.

Contemporary research in sociology and psychology has focused on the reasons that hard economic times appear to correlate with suicide. Early results suggest that countries that responded to economic downturns with austerity measures experienced the highest suicide rate increases, while countries that relied on stimulus initiatives did not experience an increase. This raises concerns about the United Kingdom, Spain, Portugal, and Cyprus, which are under austerity measures due to the economic downturn but have not yet reported increases in suicide rates.

For those countries with reported increases in suicide rates, efforts to heighten societal support have been found helpful. In some regions, communities and charities have provided assistance by setting up suicide prevention numbers and raising money for free mental health services, for instance. These may seem to be small measures, but the emerging research indicates that an individual's feeling of societal support has an even stronger affect upon suicidal intention than his or her hardship circumstances.

Troubling as it is, this body of research shows how important work is to individuals' identities—when work is lost, many individuals' self-worth appears to be lost with it.

Sources: A. E. Cha, "'Economic Suicides' Shake Europe as Financial Crisis Takes Toll on Mental Health," *Washington Post* (August 14, 2012), http://articles.washingtonpost.com/2012-08-14/business/35491624_1_double-suicide-mental-health-financial-crisis; B. Y. Lester, "Learning from Durkheim and Beyond: The Economy and Suicide," *Suicide and Life-Threatening Behavior* (Spring 2001), pp. 15–31; M. McKee, M. Karanikolos, P. Belcher, and D. Stuckler, "Austerity: A Failed Experiment on the People of Europe," *Clinical Medicine* 12, no. 4 (2012), pp. 346–350; C. von Hoffman, "Suicide Rate Jumps amid European Financial Crisis," *MoneyWatch* (April 5, 2012), www.cbsnews.com/8301-505123_162-57409506/suicide-rate-jumps-amid-european-financial-crisis/; and A. Yur'yev, A. Vaernik, P. Vaernik, et al., "Employment Status Influences Suicide Mortality in Europe," *International Journal of Social Psychiatry* (January 2012), pp. 62–68.

analysis, but we group the chapters as shown here to correspond with the typical ways that research has been done in these areas. It is easier to understand one unified presentation about how personality leads to motivation, which leads to performance, than to jump around levels of analysis. Because each level builds on the one that precedes it, after going through them in sequence you will have a good idea of how the human side of organizations functions.

Summary

Managers need to develop their interpersonal, or people, skills to be effective in their jobs. Organizational behavior (OB) investigates the impact that individuals, groups, and structure have on behavior within an organization, and it applies that knowledge to make organizations work more effectively. Specifically, OB focuses on how to improve productivity; reduce absenteeism, turnover, and deviant workplace behavior; and increase organizational citizenship behavior and job satisfaction.

Implications for Managers

- Resist the inclination to rely on generalizations; some provide valid insights into human behavior, but many are erroneous.
- Use metrics and situational variables rather than "hunches" to explain cause-and-effect relationships.
- Work on your interpersonal skills to increase your leadership potential.
- Improve your technical skills and conceptual skills through training and staying current with organizational behavior trends like big data.
- Organizational behavior can improve your employees' work quality and productivity by showing you how to empower your employees, design and implement change programs, improve customer service, and help your employees balance work–life conflicts.

Lost in Translation?

Walk into your nearest major bookstore. You'll undoubtedly find a large selection of books devoted to management and managing. Consider the following recent titles:

- *Hardcore Leadership: 11 Master Lessons from My Airborne Ranger Uncle's "Final Jump"* (CreateSpace, 2013)
- *Half-Naked Interview* (Amazon Digital, 2013)
- *Fu*k Jobs!: How to Create a Passive Income Stream and Never Work Again* (CreateSpace, 2013)
- *The Chimp Paradox: The Mind Management Program to Help You Achieve Success, Confidence, and Happiness* (Tarcher, 2013)
- *Four Dead Kings at Work* (SlimBooks, 2013)
- *Monopoly, Money, and You: How to Profit from the Game's Secrets of Success* (McGraw-Hill, 2013)
- *The Tao of Rice and Tigers: Taoist Leadership in the 21st Century* (Publius Press, 2013)
- *Nothing to Lose, Everything to Gain: How I Went from Gang Member to Multimillionaire Entrepreneur* (Portfolio Trade, 2013)
- *Ninja Innovation: The Ten Killer Strategies of the World's Most Successful Businesses* (William Morrow, 2013)
- *Giraffes of Technology: The Making of the Twenty-First-Century Leader* (CreateSpace, 2013)

Popular books on organizational behavior often have cute titles and are fun to read, but they make the job of managing people seem much simpler than it is. Most are based on the author's opinions rather than substantive research, and it is doubtful that one person's experience translates into effective management practice for everyone. Why do we waste our time on "fluff" when, with a little effort, we can access knowledge produced from thousands of scientific studies on human behavior in organizations?

Organizational behavior is a complex subject. Few, if any, simple statements about human behavior are generalizable to all people in all situations. Should you really try to apply leadership insights you got from a book about Geronimo or Tony Soprano to managing software engineers in the twenty-first century?

Organizations are always looking for leaders, and managers and manager-wannabes are continually looking for ways to hone their leadership skills. Publishers respond to this demand by offering hundreds of titles that promise insights into managing people. Books like these can provide people with the secrets to management that others know about. Moreover, isn't it better to learn about management from people in the trenches, as opposed to the latest esoteric musings from the "Ivory Tower"? Many of the most important insights we gain from life aren't necessarily the product of careful empirical research studies.

It is true there are some bad books out there. But do they outnumber the esoteric research studies published every year? For example, a couple of recent management and organizational behavior studies were published in 2013 with the following titles:

- *Market Segmentation, Service Quality, and Overall Satisfaction: Self-Organizing Map and Structural Equation Modeling Methods*
- *The Effects of Performance Rating, Leader–Member Exchange, Perceived Utility, and Organizational Justice on Performance Appraisal Satisfaction: Applying a Moral Judgment Perspective*
- *Nonlinear Moderating Effect of Tenure on Organizational Identification (OID) and the Subsequent Role of OID in Fostering Readiness for Change*
- *Examining the Influence of Modularity and Knowledge Management (KM) on Dynamic Capabilities*

We don't mean to poke fun at these studies. Rather, our point is that you can't judge a book by its cover any more than you can a research study by its title.

There is no one right way to learn the science and art of managing people in organizations. The most enlightened managers are those who gather insights from multiple sources: their own experience, research findings, observations of others, and, yes, business press books, too. If great management were produced by carefully gleaning results from research studies, academicians would make the best managers. How often do we see that?

Research and academics have an important role to play in understanding effective management. But it isn't fair to condemn all business books by citing the worst (or, at least, the worse-sounding ones).

END-OF-CHAPTER REVIEW

MyManagementLab

Go to **mymanagementlab.com** to complete the problems marked with this icon. ★

QUESTIONS FOR REVIEW

1-1 What is the importance of interpersonal skills?

1-2 What do managers do in terms of functions, roles, and skills?

1-3 What is organizational behavior (OB)?

1-4 Why is it important to complement intuition with systematic study?

1-5 What are the major behavioral science disciplines that contribute to OB?

1-6 Why are there few absolutes in OB?

1-7 What are the challenges and opportunities for managers in using OB concepts?

1-8 What are the three levels of analysis in this book's OB model?

EXPERIENTIAL EXERCISE Intoxicated Workplaces

Purpose

Devising a substance abuse policy is one thing, but developing a plan to enforce it is another. This exercise will help students determine whether a policy is even needed and, if so, develop a statement and a system of implementation.

Time Required

Approximately 40 minutes.

Participants and Roles

Divide the class into groups of approximately four members each. These separate groups should each come up with (a) a one-to-two paragraph corporate statement and (b) a comprehensive plan for ensuring adherence to the policy.

Background

Substance abuse is pervasive and costs businesses more than $100 billion annually in workers' compensation and medical costs, absenteeism, lost productivity, and employee turnover. According to the National Institute on Drug Abuse, "nearly 75 percent of all adult illicit drug users are employed, as are most binge and heavy alcohol users." Many companies have written substance abuse policies, but some may not be effective or may even pose a liability risk for the firm.

Research indicates the problem with adherence to substance abuse policies is not a lack of understanding the violations, but one of enforcement. Supervisors can play a key role, but research indicates that many times supervisors are ill equipped at identifying abuse, are afraid of invading employees' privacy, and would rather do nothing than do the wrong thing.

Each group will decide whether substance abuse policies are needed and, if so, create a policy statement and action plan.

The Task, Part A: The Plan

1-9. Identify the scope of the problem. Take a poll: Does everyone see this as a problem? To what extent? Are some types of impairment worse than others? Break down your answer in terms of each of the reported incident rates (drunk once per year, high once per year, etc.). Does the type of employment (manufacturing, lab work, office work) change the tolerance level?

1-10. Identify the risks. For each type of work listed in part 1, write down the risks to the worker and to the company of having impaired workers on the job in terms of (a) physical safety risks to the company and employees, (b) liability risks, and (c) damage to the company culture.

1-11. Consider the implications. Note the potential consequences of not developing a substance abuse policy for (a) the workers, (b) the managers, and (c) the company. What are the pros and cons of not formalizing a policy? Conversely, what are the pros and cons of creating a policy?

1-12. Decide. Will you develop a policy? If so, draft a one- to two-paragraph company statement. If not, list the reasons having a policy may be detrimental to the company.

The Task, Part B: The Implementation Plan

1-13. Develop tolerance thresholds for noncompliance with the policy.

1-14. Decide whether data will be needed to measure compliance. Will you require regular drug and alcohol screenings, periodic screenings, on-request screenings for suspected violations, or no screenings for employees (which means supervisors act upon observations instead)? Identify the type of data that will satisfy your policy (onsite or offsite testing).

1-15. On what level of the organization should responsibility for enforcement be assigned? Does management need to observe and voice suspicions, and if so, can a manager accuse any employee, or just those who work for him or her? If employees can initiate inquiries about co-workers or managers, will they do so anonymously or in person?

1-16. How will you equip those assigned as enforcement agents to detect substance abuse? Record what your training methods will be, and include frequency and type of training for each level of the organization.

1-17. What proactive steps will you take to raise awareness of the substance abuse issue, your new policy, and your implementation plan?

Sources: National Institute on Drug Abuse website, http://www.drugabuse.gov/publications/drugfacts/workplace-resources, accessed July 31, 2013; and Nationwide Medical Review website, http://www.drugfreeworkplace.com/employers/drug-free-workplace.php#drugnworkplace, accessed July 31, 2013.

ETHICAL DILEMMA Jekyll and Hyde

Let's assume you have been offered a job by Jekyll Corporation, a company in the consumer products industry. The job is in your chosen career path.

Jekyll Corporation has offered you a position that would begin 2 weeks after you graduate. The job responsibilities are appealing to you, make good use of your training, and are intrinsically interesting. The company seems well positioned financially, and you have met the individual who would be your supervisor, who assures you that the future prospects for your position and career are bright. Several other graduates of your program work at Jekyll Corporation, and they speak quite positively of the company and promise to socialize and network with you once you start.

As a company, Jekyll Corporation promotes itself as a fair-trade and sustainable organization. Fair trade is a trading partnership—based on dialogue, transparency, and respect—that seeks greater equity in international trade. It contributes to sustainable development by offering better trading conditions to, and securing the rights of, local producers and businesses. Fair-trade organizations are actively engaged in supporting producers and sustainable environmental farming practices, and fair-trade practices prohibit child or forced labor.

Yesterday, Gabriel Utterson—a human resources manager at Jekyll Corporation—called you to discuss initial terms of the offer, which seemed reasonable and standard for the industry. However, one aspect was not mentioned, your starting salary. Gabriel said Jekyll is an internally transparent organization—there are no secrets. While the

firm very much wants to hire you, there are limits to what it can afford to offer, and before it makes a formal offer, it was reasonable to ask what you would expect. Gabriel wanted you to think about this and call back tomorrow.

Before calling Gabriel, you thought long and hard about what it would take to accept Jekyll Corporation's offer. You have a number in mind, which may or may not be the same number you give Gabriel. What starting salary would it take for you to accept Jekyll Corporation's offer?

Questions

1-18. What starting salary will you give Gabriel? What salary represents the minimum offer you would accept? If these two numbers are different, why? Does giving Gabriel a different number than your "internal" number violate Jekyll Corporation's transparent culture? Why or why not?

1-19. Assume you've received another offer, this one from Hyde Associates. Like the Jekyll job, this position is on your chosen career path and in the consumer products industry. Assume, however, that you've read in the news that *"Hyde Associates has been criticized for unsustainable manufacturing practices that may be harmful to the environment. It has further been criticized for unfair trade practices and for employing underage children.* Would that change whether you'd be willing to take the job? Why or why not?

⭐**1-20.** These scenarios are based on studies of corporate social responsibility (CSR) practices that show consumers generally charge a kind of rent to companies that do not practice CSR. In other words, they generally expect a substantial discount in order to buy a product from Hyde rather than from Jekyll. For example, if Jekyll and Hyde sold coffee, people would pay a premium of $1.40 to buy coffee from Jekyll and demand a discount of $2.40 to buy Hyde coffee. Do you think this preference translates into job choice decisions? Why or why not?

CASE INCIDENT 1   Apple Goes Global

It wasn't long ago that products from Apple, perhaps the most recognizable name in electronics manufacturing around the world, were made entirely in America. This is not so anymore. Now, almost all of the approximately 70 million iPhones, 30 million iPads, and 59 million other Apple products sold yearly are manufactured overseas. This change represents more than 20,000 jobs directly lost by U.S. workers, not to mention more than 700,000 other jobs and business given to foreign companies in Asia, Europe, and elsewhere. The loss is not temporary. As the late Steven P. Jobs, Apple's iconic co-founder, told President Obama, "Those jobs aren't coming back."

At first glance, the transfer of jobs from one workforce to another would seem to hinge on a difference in wages, but Apple shows this is an oversimplification. In fact, paying U.S. wages would add only $65 to each iPhone's expense, while Apple's profits average hundreds of dollars per phone. Rather, and of more concern, Apple's leaders believe the intrinsic characteristics of the labor force available to them in China—which they identify as flexibility, diligence, and industrial skills—are superior to those of the U.S. labor force. Apple executives tell stories of shorter lead times and faster manufacturing processes in China that are becoming the stuff of company legend. "The speed and flexibility is breathtaking," one executive said. "There's no American plant that can match that." Another said, "We shouldn't be criticized for using Chinese workers. The U.S. has stopped producing people with the skills we need."

Because Apple is one of the most imitated companies in the world, this perception of an overseas advantage might suggest that the U.S. workforce needs to be better led, better trained, more effectively managed, and more motivated to be proactive and flexible. If U.S. (and western European) workers are less motivated and less adaptable, it's hard to imagine that does not spell trouble for the future of the American workforce. Perhaps, though, Apple's switch from "100% Made in the U.S.A." to "10% Made in the U.S.A." represents the natural growth pattern of a company going global. At this point, the iPhone is largely designed in the United States (where Apple has 43,000 employees); parts are made in South Korea, Taiwan, Singapore, Malaysia, Japan, Europe, and elsewhere; and products are assembled in China. The future of at least 247 suppliers worldwide depends on Apple's approximately $30.1 billion in orders per quarter.

As maker of some of the most cutting-edge, revered products in the electronics marketplace, perhaps Apple serves not as a failure of one country to hold onto a company completely, but as one of the best examples of global ingenuity.

Questions

1-21. What are the pros and cons for local and overseas labor forces of Apple's going global? What are the potential political implications for country relationships?

⭐ 1-22. Do you think Apple is justified in drawing the observations and conclusions expressed in the case? Why or why not? Do you think it is good or harmful to the company that its executives have voiced these opinions?

1-23. How could managers use increased worker flexibility and diligence to increase the competitiveness of their manufacturing sites? What would you recommend?

Sources: C. Duhigg and K. Bradsher, "How U.S. Lost Out on iPhone Work," *The New York Times* (January 22, 2013), pp. A1, A22–A23; H. Gao, "How the Apple Confrontation Divides China," *The Atlantic* (April 8, 2013), www.theatlantic.com/china/archive/2013/04/how-the-apple-confrontation-divides-china/274764/; and A. Satariano, "Apple Slowdown Threatens $30 Billion Global Supplier Web," *Bloomberg,* www.bloomberg.com/news/2013-04-18/apple-slowdown-threatens-30-billion-global-supplier-web-tech.html.

CASE INCIDENT 2 Era of the Disposable Worker?

The great global recession has claimed many victims. In many countries, unemployment is at near-historic highs, and even those who have managed to keep their jobs have often been asked to accept reduced work hours or pay cuts. Another consequence of the current business and economic environment is an increase in the number of individuals employed on a temporary or contingent basis.

The statistics on U.S. temporary workers are grim. Many, like single mother Tammy Smith, have no health insurance, no retirement benefits, no vacation, no severance, and no access to unemployment insurance. Increases in layoffs mean that many jobs formerly considered safe have become "temporary" in the sense that they could disappear at any time with little warning. Forecasts suggest that the next 5 to 10 years will be similar, with small pay increases, worse working conditions, and low levels of job security. As Peter Cappelli of the University of Pennsylvania's Wharton School notes, "Employers are trying to get rid of all fixed costs. First they did it with employment benefits. Now they're doing it with the jobs themselves. Everything is variable."

We might suppose these corporate actions are largely taking place in an era of diminishing profitability. However, data from the financial sector is not consistent with this explanation. Among *Fortune* 500 companies, 2009 saw the second-largest jump in corporate earnings in the list's 56-year history. Moreover, many of these gains do not appear to be the result of increases in revenue. Rather, they reflect dramatic decreases in labor costs. One equity market researcher noted, "The largest part of the gain came from lower payrolls rather than the sluggish rise in sales . . ." Wages also rose only slightly during this period of rapidly increasing corporate profitability.

Some observers suggest the very nature of corporate profit monitoring is to blame for the discrepancy between corporate profitability and outcomes for workers. Some have noted that teachers whose evaluations are based on standardized test scores tend to "teach to the test," to the detriment of other areas of learning. In the same way, when a company is judged primarily by the single metric of a stock price, executives naturally try their best to increase this number, possibly to the detriment of other concerns like employee well-being or corporate culture. On the other hand, others defend corporate actions that increase the degree to which they can treat labor flexibly, noting that in an increasingly competitive global marketplace, it might be necessary to sacrifice some jobs to save the organization as a whole.

The issues of how executives make decisions about workforce allocation, how job security and corporate loyalty influence employee behavior, and how emotional reactions come to surround these issues are all core components of organizational behavior research.

Questions

1-24. To what extent can individual business decisions (as opposed to economic forces) explain deterioration in working conditions for many workers?

1-25. Do business organizations have a responsibility to ensure that employees have secure jobs with good working conditions, or is their primary responsibility to shareholders?

1-26. What alternative measures of organizational performance, besides share prices, do you think might change the focus of business leaders?

Sources: Based on P. Coy, M. Conlin, and M. Herbst, "The Disposable Worker," *Bloomberg Businessweek* (January 7, 2010), www.businessweek.com; S. Tully, "Fortune 500: Profits Bounce Back," *Fortune* (May 3, 2010), pp. 140–144; and D. Ariely, "You Are What You Measure," *Harvard Business Review* (June 2010), p. 38.

MyManagementLab

Go to **mymanagementlab.com** for Auto-graded writing questions as well as the following Assisted-graded writing questions:

1-27. Now that you've read the chapter and Case Incident 1, if you were an Apple manager whose employees were losing their jobs to overseas workers, what would you advise your teams to do in order to find re-employment in their professions? What types of training—basic, technical, interpersonal, problem-solving—would you recommend?

1-28. In relation to Case Incident 2, what do you think the likely impact of the growth of temporary employment relationships will be for employee attitudes and behaviors? How would you develop a measurement system to evaluate the impact of corporate downsizing and temporary job assignments on employees?

1-29. MyManagementLab Only—comprehensive writing assignment for this chapter.

2

Diversity in Organizations

MyManagementLab®

⭐ **Improve Your Grade!**

When you see this icon, visit **www.mymanagementlab.com** for activities that are applied, personalized, and offer immediate feedback.

DYNAMICS OF DIVERSITY

At first glance, the case of Ellen Pao and Alphonse "Buddy" Fletcher is a modern story of achievement in diversity. Pao, the daughter of Chinese immigrants, and her husband Fletcher, the son of a Navy veteran and a public school administrator, are successful beyond most people's wildest dreams. She has been a partner at one of the leading U.S. venture capital firms, and his career as a hedge fund manager has made him one of the country's richest African Americans. Pao and Fletcher hold five Ivy League degrees between them, divide their time between one of Manhattan's most famous apartment buildings and a 1,100-acre Connecticut estate, and drive a Bentley (actually, the chauffeur does the driving). What might they have to complain about?

Discrimination, they say. Despite the couple's achievements, both Pao and Fletcher have filed lawsuits that allege they have suffered sexual and racial discrimination. There are higher stakes here than just money. If they win, they will have helped set an important precedence against discrimination at top organizational levels. But they have already risked public embarrassment, financial ruin, and discomfort in their own home.

By all accounts, Ellen Pao and Buddy Fletcher were an unlikely couple, not only because of their different ethnic backgrounds. First, though Pao had not been known for her cultural identity, Fletcher had actively supported civil rights causes through establishing multi-million-dollar fellowships by the time they met. Second, Pao had not been involved in discrimination lawsuits, while Fletcher had both sued employers for racial discrimination and been sued for sexual harassment by two of his employees. Third, their personalities were notably different. Pao was the nerdy, quiet type whom Harvard law school classmate Rebecca Eisenberg described as "one of the least objectionable people on earth." Fletcher, on the other hand, was political and outgoing; Harvard classmate Roy Niederhoffer described his popularity as "almost unmatched." And fourth, they were living different lifestyles. Pao was a heterosexual divorcée, while Fletcher had been living with his boyfriend, Hobart "Bo" Fowlkes, for many years when he and Pao met. Yet Pao and Fletcher married four months later, and their daughter Matilda was born soon after.

Less than four years later, Pao filed a headline-grabbing lawsuit against her employer Kleiner Perkins Caufield & Bye, claiming she was sexually harassed and discriminated against by two other senior partners. Her chief allegations are against a man with whom she'd previously had a mutual relationship, and she also claims companywide gender discrimination. Meanwhile, her husband filed an equally newsworthy racial discrimination lawsuit against their posh Manhattan building after his ability to pay $4.5 million for an extra two-bedroom space was questioned.

LEARNING OBJECTIVES

After studying this chapter, you should be able to:

1 Describe the two major forms of workforce diversity.

2 Recognize stereotypes and understand how they function in organizational settings.

3 Identify the key biographical characteristics and describe how they are relevant to OB.

4 Define *intellectual ability* and demonstrate its relevance to OB.

5 Contrast intellectual and physical ability.

6 Describe how organizations manage diversity effectively.

If Pao wins, she may be awarded a large monetary settlement and a judgment that helps women compete fairly at the top levels of organizations. A win for Fletcher would help signal the end of discrimination in upper levels of society. As a result of the filings, there has already been an impact on the couple's professional and private lives. Pao has left her job, been forced to discuss details of private incidences publicly, and become a recognized face in national media. The media has also placed close scrutiny on Fletcher, who has faced major losses as a result of his building's skepticism about his financial holdings; he has filed bankruptcy for part of his firm. The lawsuit also puts him and Pao at odds with neighbors in their building. No matter what the outcome of the lawsuits, these cases highlight the high stakes nature of managing diversity in organizations.

Sources: S. Andrews, "Sex, Lies, and Lawsuits," *Vanity Fair* (March 1, 2013), www.vanityfair.com/society/2013/03/buddy-fletcher-ellen-pao; A. Lashinsky and K. Benner, "The Odd Couple," *Fortune* (November 12, 2012), pp. 106–116; and D. Primack, "Ellen Pao Has Landed . . . at Reddit," *CNN Money* (April 11, 2013), http://finance.fortune.cnn.com/2013/04/11/ellen-pao-has-landed-at-reddit/.

Ellen Pao and Buddy Fletcher illustrate the complexity of diversity in society in general and in organizations in particular. In this chapter, we look at how organizations work to maximize the potential contributions of a diverse workforce. We also show how demographic characteristics such as ethnicity and individual differences in the form of ability affect employee performance and satisfaction.

But first check out the following Self-Assessment Library, where you can assess your views on one of the characteristics we'll discuss in this chapter: age.

SELF-ASSESSMENT LIBRARY

What's My Attitude Toward Older People?

In the Self-Assessment Library (available in MyManagementLab), take assessment IV.C.1 (What's My Attitude Toward Older People?) and answer the following questions:

1. Are you surprised by your results?
2. How do your results compare to those of others?

Diversity

1 Describe the two major forms of workforce diversity.

We aren't all the same. This is obvious enough, but managers sometimes forget they need to recognize and capitalize on differences to get the most from their employees. Effective diversity management increases an organization's access to the widest possible pool of skills, abilities, and ideas. Managers also need to recognize that differences among people can lead to miscommunication, misunderstanding, and conflict. In this chapter, we'll learn about how individual characteristics like age, gender, race, ethnicity, and abilities can influence

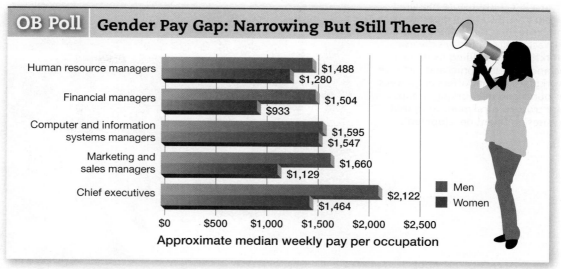

OB Poll | **Gender Pay Gap: Narrowing But Still There**

Approximate median weekly pay per occupation

- Human resource managers: Men $1,488; Women $1,280
- Financial managers: Men $1,504; Women $933
- Computer and information systems managers: Men $1,595; Women $1,547
- Marketing and sales managers: Men $1,660; Women $1,129
- Chief executives: Men $2,122; Women $1,464

Source: Bureau of Labor Statistics, www.bls.gov/cps/cpswom2011.pdf.

employee performance. We'll also see how managers can develop awareness about these characteristics and manage a diverse workforce effectively.

Demographic Characteristics of the U.S. Workforce

In the past, OB textbooks noted that rapid change was about to occur as the predominantly white, male managerial workforce gave way to a gender-balanced, multiethnic workforce. Today, that change is no longer happening: It has happened, and it is increasingly reflected in the makeup of managerial and professional jobs. Compared to 1976, women today are much more likely to be employed full-time, have more education, and earn wages comparable to those of men.[1] In addition, over the past 50 years the earnings gap between Whites and other racial and ethnic groups has decreased significantly; past differences between Whites and Asians have disappeared or been reversed.[2] Workers over the age of 55 are an increasingly large portion of the workforce as well. This permanent shift toward a diverse workforce means organizations need to make diversity management a central component of their policies and practices. At the same time, however, differences in wages across genders and racial and ethnic groups persist, and executive positions in *Fortune* 500 corporations continue to be held by white males in numbers far beyond their representation in the workforce in general.

A survey by the Society for Human Resources Management shows some major employer concerns and opportunities resulting from the demographic makeup of the U.S. workforce.[3] The aging of the workforce was consistently the most significant concern of HR managers. The loss of skills resulting from the retirement of many Baby Boomers, increased medical costs due to an aging workforce, and many employees' needs to care for elderly relatives topped the list of issues. Other issues include developing multilingual training materials and providing work–life benefits for dual-career couples.

Levels of Diversity

Although much has been said about diversity in age, race, gender, ethnicity, religion, and disability status, experts now recognize that these demographic characteristics are just the tip of the iceberg.[4] Demographics mostly reflect **surface-level diversity**, not thoughts and feelings, and can lead employees to

surface-level diversity *Differences in easily perceived characteristics, such as gender, race, ethnicity, age, or disability, that do not necessarily reflect the ways people think or feel but that may activate certain stereotypes.*

Photo 2-1 Target store manager Jerald Bryant (center) motivating his team reflects demographic characteristics of today's diverse workforce. In building its gender-balanced, multiethnic, and inclusive workplace, Target offers employees resource and networking groups and cross-cultural mentoring that focuses on talent development.

Source: © ZUMA Press, Inc./Alamy.

deep-level diversity *Differences in values, personality, and work preferences that become progressively more important for determining similarity as people get to know one another better.*

perceive one another through stereotypes and assumptions. However, evidence has shown that as people get to know one another, they become less concerned about demographic differences if they see themselves as sharing more important characteristics, such as personality and values, that represent **deep-level diversity**.[5]

To understand this difference between surface- and deep-level diversity, consider a few examples. Luis and Carol are co-workers who seem to have little in common at first glance. Luis is a young, recently hired male college graduate with a business degree, raised in a Spanish-speaking neighborhood in Miami. Carol is an older, long-tenured woman raised in rural Kansas, who achieved her current level in the organization by starting as a high school graduate and working her way through the hierarchy. At first, these co-workers may experience some differences in communication based on their surface-level differences in education, ethnicity, regional background, and gender. However, as they get to know one another, they may find they are both deeply committed to their families, share a common way of thinking about important work problems, like to work collaboratively, and are interested in international assignments in the future. These deep-level similarities will overshadow the more superficial differences between them, and research suggests they will work well together.

On the other hand, Steve and Dave are two unmarried, White, male college graduates from Oregon who recently started working together. Superficially, they seem well matched. But Steve is highly introverted, prefers to avoid risks, solicits the opinions of others before making decisions, and likes the office quiet. Dave is extroverted, risk-seeking, and assertive and likes a busy, active, and energetic work environment. Their surface-level similarity will not necessarily lead to positive interactions because they have such fundamental, deep-level differences. It will be a challenge for them to collaborate regularly at work, and they'll have to make some compromises to get things done together.

Affirmative Action for Unemployed Veterans

Unemployed veterans, take heart: Walmart wants YOU. In a historic move, the retailing giant vows to hire any returning U.S. veteran who applies. Projections are that Walmart will extend job offers to 100,000 veterans from 2013 to 2018. Other businesses are launching similar initiatives, such as JPMorgan Chase's 100,000 Jobs Mission, which aims to hire that many veterans by 2020. Is this an ethical choice all businesses should be emulating, or a form of reverse discrimination?

Few people would disagree there is a need to address the plight of returning soldiers in America. As a rule, veterans say employers don't want them. "There are a lot of companies that say they want veterans, but that conflicts with the unemployment numbers," said Hakan Jackson, a former technician in the Air Force. He's right: Unemployment rates remain higher for veterans. The suicide rate for veterans is also sharply higher than for active-duty soldiers, and the "hopelessness of unemployment almost certainly plays a role," reports Georgette Mosbacher, CEO of the Borghese cosmetics company and board member of the Intrepid Fallen Heroes Fund. Veterans need jobs. But is affirmative action justified,

or are these former soldiers not competing well in the job market?

According to some veterans, the returning solders are not competitive in the marketplace. Erik Sewell, an Iraq war veteran, suggested the reason the veteran unemployment rate is poor is partly that vets often don't market their strengths well or showcase their transferable skills to potential employers. Bryson DeTrent, a 12-year veteran of the National Guard, observed that one of the key reasons vets haven't found jobs is that they aren't working hard at it, preferring to collect unemployment instead. However, he also found that companies are reluctant to hire veterans, especially National Guard members, fearing these employees may later be recalled to duty. Employers also worry that veterans may suffer from post-traumatic stress disorder (PTSD), though some managers report that veterans' work ethic, team outlook, and receptivity to training are greater than among the general populace.

Sometimes, affirmative action is needed to give an unfairly disadvantaged workforce segment an opportunity to succeed, whether it is done through percentage quotas, number quotas, or hiring all prospective employees from the desired groups. But any

affirmative action program risks including underqualified individuals from the target group while excluding qualified individuals from other workforce segments, creating reverse discrimination. Resources are always scarce, and there are only so many jobs to go around. If a manager must choose between a qualified civilian candidate and a qualified veteran, the manager might favor the veteran without discrimination. But if a manager must choose an underqualified veteran candidate over a qualified civilian candidate due to an affirmative action policy, the manager is forced to discriminate against the qualified candidate. Managers must balance the ethics of affirmative action against the responsibility of strengthening their workforces for the good of their organizations.

Sources: D. C. Baldridge and M. L. Swift, "Withholding Requests for Disability Accommodation: The Role of Individual Differences and Disability Attributes," *Journal of Management* (March 2013), pp. 743–762; G. Mosbacher, "Wal-Mart Wants You!" *The Wall Street Journal* (February 1, 2013), p. A11; B. Yerbak and C. V. Jackson, "Battling to Get More Vets in the Work Force," *Chicago Tribune* (October 28, 2012), http://articles.chicagotribune.com/2012-10-28/business/ct-biz-1028-vets--20121028_1_train-veterans-unemployment-rate-war-zone; and "Veterans Unemployment Drops But Remains High," *HR Magazine* (February 2013), p. 16.

Throughout this book, we will encounter differences between deep- and surface-level diversity in various contexts. Individual differences in personality and culture shape preferences for rewards, communication styles, reactions to leaders, negotiation styles, and many other aspects of behavior in organizations.

Discrimination

2 Recognize stereotypes and understand how they function in organizational settings.

Although diversity does present many opportunities for organizations, effective diversity management also means working to eliminate unfair **discrimination**. To discriminate is to note a difference between things, which in itself isn't necessarily bad. Noticing one employee is more qualified is necessary for making hiring decisions; noticing another is taking on leadership responsibilities exceptionally well is necessary for making promotion decisions. Usually

discrimination *Noting of a difference between things; often we refer to unfair discrimination, which means making judgments about individuals based on stereotypes regarding their demographic group.*

when we talk about discrimination, though, we mean allowing our behavior to be influenced by stereotypes about *groups* of people. Rather than looking at individual characteristics, unfair discrimination assumes everyone in a group is the same. This discrimination is often very harmful to organizations and employees.

Exhibit 2-1 provides definitions and examples of some forms of discrimination in organizations. Although many of these actions are prohibited by law, and therefore aren't part of almost any organization's official policies, thousands of cases of employment discrimination are documented every year, and many more go unreported. As discrimination has increasingly come under both legal scrutiny and social disapproval, most overt forms have faded, which may have resulted in an increase in more covert forms like incivility or exclusion.[6]

As you can see, discrimination can occur in many ways, and its effects can be just as varied depending on the organizational context and the personal biases of its members. Some forms, like exclusion or incivility, are especially hard to root out because they are impossible to observe and may occur simply because the actor isn't aware of the effects of his or her actions. Whether intentional or not, discrimination can lead to serious negative consequences for employers, including reduced productivity and citizenship behavior, negative conflicts, and increased turnover. Unfair discrimination also leaves qualified job candidates out of initial hiring and promotions. Even if an employment discrimination lawsuit is never filed, a strong business case can be made for aggressively working to eliminate unfair discrimination.

Exhibit 2-1	Forms of Discrimination	
Type of Discrimination	**Definition**	**Examples from Organizations**
Discriminatory policies or practices	Actions taken by representatives of the organization that deny equal opportunity to perform or unequal rewards for performance.	Older workers may be targeted for layoffs because they are highly paid and have lucrative benefits.
Sexual harassment	Unwanted sexual advances and other verbal or physical conduct of a sexual nature that create a hostile or offensive work environment.	Salespeople at one company went on company-paid visits to strip clubs, brought strippers into the office to celebrate promotions, and fostered pervasive sexual rumors.
Intimidation	Overt threats or bullying directed at members of specific groups of employees.	African-American employees at some companies have found nooses hanging over their work stations.
Mockery and insults	Jokes or negative stereotypes; sometimes the result of jokes taken too far.	Arab-Americans have been asked at work whether they were carrying bombs or were members of terrorist organizations.
Exclusion	Exclusion of certain people from job opportunities, social events, discussions, or informal mentoring; can occur unintentionally.	Many women in finance claim they are assigned to marginal job roles or are given light workloads that don't lead to promotion.
Incivility	Disrespectful treatment, including behaving in an aggressive manner, interrupting the person, or ignoring his or her opinions.	Female lawyers note that male attorneys frequently cut them off or do not adequately address their comments.

Sources: J. Levitz and P. Shishkin, "More Workers Cite Age Bias after Layoffs," *The Wall Street Journal* (March 11, 2009), pp. D1–D2; W. M. Bulkeley, "A Data-Storage Titan Confronts Bias Claims," *The Wall Street Journal* (September 12, 2007), pp. A1, A16; D. Walker, "Incident with Noose Stirs Old Memories," *McClatchy-Tribune Business News* (June 29, 2008); D. Solis, "Racial Horror Stories Keep EEOC Busy," *Knight-Ridder Tribune Business News*, July 30, 2005, p. 1; H. Ibish and A. Stewart, *Report on Hate Crimes and Discrimination Against Arab Americans: The Post-September 11 Backlash, September 11, 2001–October 11, 2001* (Washington, DC: American-Arab Anti-Discrimination Committee, 2003); A. Raghavan, "Wall Street's Disappearing Women," *Forbes* (March 16, 2009), pp. 72–78; and L. M. Cortina, "Unseen Injustice: Incivility as Modern Discrimination in Organizations," *Academy of Management Review* 33, no. 1 (2008), pp. 55–75.

Diversity is a broad term, and the phrase workplace diversity can refer to any characteristic that makes people different from one another. The following section covers some important surface-level characteristics that differentiate members of the workforce.

Biographical Characteristics

3 Identify the key biographical characteristics and describe how they are relevant to OB.

biographical characteristics
Personal characteristics—such as age, gender, race, and length of tenure—that are objective and easily obtained from personnel records. These characteristics are representative of surface-level diversity.

Biographical characteristics such as age, gender, race, disability, and length of service are some of the most obvious ways employees differ. As discussed in Chapter 1, this textbook is essentially concerned with finding and analyzing the variables that affect employee productivity, absence, turnover, deviance, citizenship, and satisfaction (refer back to Exhibit 1-4). Many organizational concepts—motivation, say, or power and politics or organizational culture—are hard to assess. Let's begin, then, by looking at factors that are easily definable and readily available—data that can be obtained, for the most part, from an employee's human resources (HR) file. Variations in these surface-level characteristics may be the basis for discrimination against classes of employees, so it is worth knowing how closely related they actually are to important work outcomes. Many are not as important as people believe, and far more variation occurs *within* groups sharing biographical characteristics than between them.

Bald Is Better

This is true, at least for men: What you wear (or don't wear) on your head matters. A recent study showed that observers believe a male's shaved head indicates greater masculinity, dominance, and leadership potential than longer or thinning hair. Thinning hair was perceived as the least powerful look, and other studies have agreed that male-pattern baldness (where some hair remains) is not considered advantageous. But why is this?

In some respects, the reported youthful advantage of a shaved head is counterintuitive. Because we have more hair when we are young, and our culture considers youthfulness a sign of capability (if you doubt this, see the sections on aging in this chapter), it would make more sense for a hairless head to be a distinct disadvantage. Yet culture has influenced this perception, loading the media with images of powerful men who are intentionally bald with shaved heads—military heroes, winning athletes, action heroes. No wonder the study participants declared the men with shaved heads were an inch taller and 13 percent stronger than the same men with hair.

A shaved head has become the hallmark of some important CEOs, notably Jeff Bezos of Amazon, Dan Akerson of General Motors, and Steve Ballmer of Microsoft. Men who have shaved their heads report it can give them a business advantage, whether or not it makes them look older (which is debatable). According to psychologist Caroline Keating, just as older silver-back gorillas are "typically the powerful actors in their social groups," so it is in the office, where baldness may "signal who is in charge and potentially dangerous." Research professor Michael Cunningham agrees, adding that baldness "is nature's way of telling the rest of the world you are a survivor." Men with shaved heads convey aggressiveness, competitiveness, and independence, he adds. Will you join the 13 percent of men who shave their heads? Time will tell.

Sources: J. Misener, "Men With Shaved Heads Appear More Dominant, Study Finds," *The Huffington Post* (October 1, 2012), www.huffingtonpost.com/2012/10/01/bald-men-dominant-shaved-heads-study_n_1930489.html; A. E. Mannes, "Shorn Scalps and Perceptions of Male Dominance," *Social Psychological and Personality Science*, doi: 10.1177/1948550612449490; and R. E. Silverman, "Bald Is Powerful," *The Wall Street Journal* (October 3, 2012), pp. B1, B6.

Age

The relationship between age and job performance is likely to be an issue of increasing importance during the next decade for many reasons. For one, the workforce is aging worldwide. The civilian participation rate for U.S. workers over age 59, for example, has increased from approximately 22 percent in 2002 to 29 percent in 2012, and 93 percent of the growth in the labor force from 2006 to 2016 will be from workers over age 54.[7] For another, U.S. legislation has, for all intents and purposes, outlawed mandatory retirement. Most workers today no longer have to retire at age 70, and 62 percent of those aged 45 to 60 plan to delay retirement.[8]

Employers express mixed feelings about the older worker.[9] They see a number of positive qualities older workers bring to their jobs, such as experience, judgment, a strong work ethic, and commitment to quality. But older workers are also perceived as lacking flexibility and resisting new technology. And when organizations are actively seeking individuals who are adaptable and open to change, the negatives associated with age clearly hinder the initial hiring of older workers and increase the likelihood they will be let go during cutbacks.

Now let's take a look at the evidence. What effect does age actually have on turnover, absenteeism, productivity, and satisfaction? The older you get, the less likely you are to quit your job. That conclusion is based on studies of the age–turnover relationship.[10] Of course, this shouldn't be too surprising. As workers get older, they have fewer alternative job opportunities as their skills have become more specialized to certain types of work. Their long tenure also tends to provide them with higher wage rates, longer paid vacations, and more attractive pension benefits.

It's tempting to assume that age impacts absenteeism. Most studies show that older employees have lower rates of avoidable absence versus younger employees and equal rates of unavoidable absence, such as sickness absence.[11] In general, the older working population is healthier than you might expect. Recent research indicates that, worldwide, older workers do not have more psychological problems or day-to-day physical health problems than younger workers.[12]

Many believe productivity declines with age. It is often assumed that skills like speed, agility, strength, and coordination decay over time and that prolonged job boredom and lack of intellectual stimulation contribute to reduced productivity. The evidence, however, contradicts those assumptions. Reviews of the research find that age and job task performance are unrelated and that older workers are more likely to engage in citizenship behavior.[13]

Our final concern is the relationship between age and job satisfaction, where the evidence is mixed. A review of more than 800 studies found that older workers tend to be more satisfied with their work, report better relationships with co-workers, and are more committed to their employing organizations.[14] Other studies, however, have found a U-shaped relationship. Several explanations could clear up these results, the most plausible being that these studies are intermixing professional and nonprofessional employees. When we separate the two types, satisfaction tends to continually increase among professionals as they age, whereas it falls among nonprofessionals during middle age and then rises again in the later years.

What are the effects of discrimination against individuals on the basis of age? One large-scale study of more than 8,000 employees in 128 companies found that an organizational climate favoring age discrimination was associated with lower levels of commitment to the company. This lower commitment was, in turn, related to lower levels of organizational performance.[15] Such results suggest that combating age discrimination may be associated with higher levels of organizational performance.

Photo 2-2 At Publix Supermarkets, older employees are an integral part of the workforce, with one in five employees over the age of 50. Publix actively recruits older workers and values their work ethic, maturity, and variety of skills, experience, and knowledge they bring to their jobs and share with younger employees.

Source: Newscom.

Sex

Few issues initiate more debates, misconceptions, and unsupported opinions than whether women perform as well on jobs as men do.

The best place to begin to consider this is with the recognition that few, if any, important differences between men and women affect job performance. In fact, a recent meta-analysis of job performance studies found that women scored slightly higher than men on performance measures (although, pertinent to our discussion on discrimination, men were rated as having higher promotion potential).[16] There are no consistent male–female differences in problem-solving ability, analytical skills, competitive drive, motivation, sociability, or learning ability.[17]

Unfortunately, sex roles still affect our perceptions. For example, while women earn 60 percent of the bachelor's degrees in the United States,[18] one recent study found that science professors still view their female undergraduate students as less competent than males with the same accomplishments and skills.[19] Female students are prone to accept occupational stereotypes, unfortunately, and often perceive a lack of fit between themselves and traditionally male roles.[20] In the hiring realm, modern research indicates that managers are still influenced by gender bias when selecting candidates for certain positions.[21] And a new study reported that once on the job, men and women may be offered a similar number of developmental experiences, but females are less likely to be assigned challenging positions by men, assignments that may have helped them achieve higher organizational positions.[22] Women who succeed in traditionally male domains are perceived as less likable, more hostile, and less desirable as supervisors,[23] but women at the top have been reporting that this perception is changing and can be countered by effective interpersonal skills.[24] Research also suggests that women believe sex-based discrimination is more prevalent than do male employees, and these beliefs are especially pronounced among women who work with a large proportion of men.[25]

It is worth asking what the implications of sex discrimination are for individuals. Notably, women still earn less money than men for the same positions,[26] even in traditionally female roles ("the glass escalator" means men receive faster

Worldwide Talent Search for Women

In looking to fill the worldwide skills gap, global companies are scouring the earth in search of top talent. What they are finding is a wealth of potential among women in emerging markets such as Brazil, Russia, India, China, and the United Arab Emirates. These women are educated: according to researcher Sylvia Ann Hewlett, they are "surprisingly well-qualified, out-achieving men in tertiary [college] education." They are ambitious: in India, 83 percent of women ages 31 to 63 consider themselves highly ambitious, for example. And they are available to work: with stipulations.

While multinational corporations might seek to standardize recruitment strategies, company policies, and expectations for employee performance, increasing evidence suggests this standardization will not be successful with the female workforce worldwide. Recruitment of candidates for assignments in their home countries, for instance, is most successful when the companies are tuned into the specific needs and incentive points unique to women in those cultures. Ceree T. Eberly, chief people officer and senior vice president for Coca-Cola, concluded from her experience in China, Latin America, and Europe, "We have to reflect the local market."

A Western company's family leave provision might not be acceptable in India, where women tend to stay home longer after the birth of a child, as noted by Saundarya Rajesh, president of Avtar Career Creators. The benefit may not be sufficient for a female employee in China as well, but for a different reason: the cultural expectation that adult children will serve as primary caregivers for their elderly parents. For out-of-country assignments, some obstacles for women are expensive Visa applications with long wait times and the cultural expectation that the "trailing" spouse should out-earn his wife.

Family leave policies are not the only areas where a "one size fits all" approach may prove ineffective. For example, a standardized dress code will mean different clothing in Saudi Arabia, where women must wear black head scarves, than in Europe. Even the nearly universal practice of a handshake between businesspeople is a hardship for women in cultures that do not allow women to touch men outside their families.

Companies should adapt their expectations of employee performance as well, according to Eberly. Time with family is highly valued in emerging market countries, so companies should establish boundaries such as limiting weekend e-mail and travel. In other cases, sensitivity to cultural values could save a worker from the perils of traveling dangerous streets alone at night. In cultures where women are forbidden to live on their own, single females must live with their families even if their jobs are far away. "Many very high-level women in Dubai have horrendous commutes because they have to live with their family of origin," explained Hewlett. Safety is an issue: in Brazil, for example, 62 percent of women indicated commuting to and from work without incident is a challenge.

Savvy companies keen to tap the new candidate pool of women need to be ready to recruit, but they must also foresee the challenges of developing and retaining these uniquely equipped individuals. Mentoring programs, active women's groups, and flexible working arrangements can go a long way toward bridging the gap.

Sources: K. Gurchiek, "The Global Battle for Female Talent," *HR Magazine* (June 2012), pp. 48–52; E. Nickmeyer, "Saudis Push Young People, Including Women, Into Jobs," *The Wall Street Journal* (January 31, 2012), p. A11; S. A. Hewlett and R. Rashid, "The Battle for Female Talent in Emerging Markets," *Harvard Business Review* (May 2010), pp. 101–106; and K. Rose, "Muslims on Wall Street, Bridging Two Traditions," *The New York Times* (April 15, 2012), pp. B1, B6.

promotions in many female-dominated occupations).[27] In a recent study, experienced managers allocated 71 percent of available pay raise funds for male employees, leaving only 29 percent for females.[28] Working mothers also face "maternal wall bias" by employers, which limits their professional opportunities, and both men and women face discrimination for their family caregiving roles.[29] Research has shown that workers who experience the worst form of overt discrimination, sexual harassment, have higher levels of psychological stress, and these feelings in turn are related to lower levels of organizational commitment and job satisfaction, and higher intentions to leave.[30] As with age discrimination, the evidence suggests that combating sex discrimination may be associated with better performance for the organization as a whole, partially since employees who are discriminated against are more likely to leave.

Research continues to underline that although the reasons for employee turnover are complex, it is detrimental to organizational performance, particularly for intellectual positions, for managerial employees, in the United States, and in medium-size firms.[31]

Race and Ethnicity

Race is a controversial issue. Evidence suggests that some people find interacting with other racial groups uncomfortable unless there are clear behavioral scripts to guide their behavior.[32]

In the United States, the Bureau of the Census classifies individuals according to seven broad racial categories: American Indian and Alaska Native, Asian, Black or African American, Native Hawaiian and Other Pacific Islander, Some Other Race, White, and Two or More Races. An ethnicity distinction is also made between native English speakers and Hispanics: Hispanics can be of any race. We define *race* as the biological heritage people use to identify themselves; *ethnicity* is the additional set of cultural characteristics that often overlaps with race. These definitions allow each individual to define his or her race and ethnicity.

Race and ethnicity have been studied as they relate to employment outcomes such as hiring decisions, performance evaluations, pay, and workplace discrimination. Most research has concentrated on the differences in outcomes and attitudes between Whites and African Americans, with little study of issues relevant to Asian, Native American, and Hispanic populations. Doing justice to all this research isn't possible here, so let's summarize a few points.

First, in employment settings, individuals tend to slightly favor colleagues of their own race in performance evaluations, promotion decisions, and pay raises, although such differences are not found consistently, especially when highly structured methods of decision making are employed.[33] Second, African Americans and Hispanics perceive discrimination to be more prevalent in the workplace.[34] Third, African Americans generally fare worse than Whites in employment decisions. They receive lower ratings in employment interviews, receive lower job performance ratings, are paid less, and are promoted less frequently.[35] Yet there are no statistically significant differences between African Americans and Whites in observed absence rates, applied social skills at work, or accident rates. African Americans and Hispanics also have higher turnover rates than Whites. Some industries have remained less racially diverse than others. For instance, U.S. advertising and media organizations suffer a lack of racial diversity in their management ranks even though their client base is increasingly ethnically diverse.[36]

Most research shows that members of racial and ethnic minorities report higher levels of discrimination in the workplace.[37] As we discussed before, discrimination—for any reason—leads to increased turnover, which is detrimental to organizational performance. While better representation of all racial groups in organizations remains a goal, recent research indicates that an individual of minority status is much less likely to leave their organization if there is a feeling of inclusiveness (a positive diversity climate).[38] Some research suggests that having a positive climate for diversity overall can also lead to increased sales.[39]

Disability

With the passage of the Americans with Disabilities Act (ADA) in 1990, the representation of individuals with disabilities in the U.S. workforce rapidly increased.[40] According to the ADA, employers are required to make reasonable accommodations so their workplaces will be accessible to individuals with physical or mental disabilities. The U.S. Equal Employment Opportunity Commission classifies a person as *disabled* who has any physical or mental impairment that substantially limits one or more major life activities. Examples include missing limbs, seizure

Photo 2-3 Microsoft views employees with disabilities as valuable assets because they help ensure that the firm's products meet all customer needs. At Microsoft's Accessibility Lab, employees like Kelly Ford, who is blind, can experience assistive technologies and ergonomic hardware designs that enable them to be more productive.

Source: AP Photo/Ted S. Warren.

disorder, Down syndrome, deafness, schizophrenia, alcoholism, diabetes, and chronic back pain. These conditions share almost no common features, so there's no generalization about how each condition is related to employment. Some jobs obviously cannot be accommodated to some disabilities—the law and common-sense recognize that a blind person could not be a bus driver, for instance. One of the most controversial aspects of the ADA is the provision that requires employers to make reasonable accommodations for people with psychiatric disabilities.[41] Due to negative employer biases, many who suffer from mental illnesses are reluctant to disclose their status, which compounds the problem. However, continuing technology advancements have greatly increased the scope of available jobs for those with disabilities, providing new and diverse opportunities.

The impact of disabilities on employment outcomes has been explored from a variety of perspectives. On the one hand, a review of the evidence suggests workers with disabilities receive higher performance evaluations. However, this same review found that despite their higher performance, individuals with disabilities tend to encounter lower performance expectations and are less likely to be hired.[42] These negative effects are much stronger for individuals with mental disabilities, and there is some evidence to suggest mental disabilities may impair performance more than physical disabilities: Individuals with such common mental health issues as depression and anxiety are significantly more likely to be absent from work.[43]

Though individuals with disabilities continue to experience discrimination, they are sometimes given preferential treatment in the workplace. When disability status is randomly manipulated among hypothetical candidates, disabled individuals are rated as having superior personal qualities like dependability and potency.[44]

Other Biographical Characteristics: Tenure, Religion, Sexual Orientation and Gender Identity, and Cultural Identity

The last set of biographical characteristics we'll look at includes tenure, religion, sexual orientation and gender identity, and cultural identity.

Tenure   Except for gender and racial differences, few issues are more subject to misconceptions and speculations than the impact of seniority on job performance.

Extensive reviews have been conducted of the seniority–productivity relationship.[45] If we define *seniority* as time on a particular job, the most recent evidence demonstrates a positive relationship between seniority and job productivity. So *tenure*, expressed as work experience, appears to be a good predictor of employee productivity.

The research relating tenure to absence is quite straightforward. Studies consistently show seniority to be negatively related to absenteeism.[46] Tenure is also a potent variable in explaining turnover. The longer a person is in a job, the less likely he or she is to quit.[47] Moreover, consistent with research suggesting past behavior is the best predictor of future behavior, evidence indicates tenure at an employee's previous job is a powerful predictor of that employee's future turnover.[48]

Evidence indicates tenure and job satisfaction are positively related.[49] In fact, when age and tenure are treated separately, tenure appears a more consistent and stable predictor of job satisfaction than age.

Religion   Not only do religious and nonreligious people question each other's belief systems; often people of different religious faiths conflict. U.S. federal law prohibits employers from discriminating against employees based on their religion, with very few exceptions. However, that doesn't mean religion is a nonissue in OB.

Perhaps the greatest religious diversity issue in the United States today revolves around Islam. There are nearly 2 million Muslims in the United States, and across the world Islam is one of the most popular religions. There are a wide variety of perspectives on Islam. Research has shown that job applicants in Muslim-identified religious attire who applied for hypothetical retail jobs in the United States had shorter, more interpersonally negative interviews than applicants who did not wear Muslim-identified attire.[50]

Faith can be an employment issue when religious beliefs prohibit or encourage certain behaviors. Based on their religious beliefs, some pharmacists refuse to hand out RU-486, the "morning after" abortion pill. Many Christians do not believe they should work on Sundays, and many conservative Jews believe they should not work on Saturdays. Religious individuals may also believe they have an obligation to express their beliefs in the workplace, and those who do not share those beliefs may object. Perhaps as a result of different perceptions of religion's role in the workplace, religious discrimination claims have been a growing source of discrimination claims in the United States.

Sexual Orientation and Gender Identity   While much has changed, the full acceptance and accommodation of gay, lesbian, bisexual, and transgender employees remains a work in progress. A recent Harvard University study investigated this issue with a field experiment. The researcher sent fictitious but realistic résumés in applications to 1,700 actual entry-level job openings. These applications were identical with one exception: Half mentioned involvement in gay organizations during college, and the other half did not. The applications without the mention received 60 percent more callbacks than the ones with it.[51] For states and municipalities that do protect against discrimination based on sexual orientation, roughly as many sexual orientation discrimination claims are filed as for sex and race discrimination.[52]

Federal law does not prohibit discrimination against employees based on sexual orientation, though 21 states and more than 160 municipalities do. Recent developments suggest, however, that we may be on the cusp of change.

The federal government has prohibited discrimination against government employees based on sexual orientation. The Equal Employment Opportunity Commission (EEOC), the federal agency responsible for enforcing employment discrimination laws, has recently held that sex-stereotyping against lesbian, gay, and bisexual individuals represents gender discrimination enforceable under the Civil Rights Act of 1964.[53] Finally, pending federal legislation against discrimination based on sexual orientation—the Employment Non-Discrimination Act (ENDA)—continues to receive more and more support in Congress.[54]

Even in the absence of federal legislation, many organizations have implemented policies and procedures protecting employees on the basis of sexual orientation. Some have been legendary for their conservative cultures. IBM, famous for at one time requiring all employees to wear white shirts and ties, has adopted many policies to facilitate the acceptance and productivity of gay and transgender employees. Ted Childs, its vice president, says, "IBM ensures that people who are gay, lesbian, bisexual or transgender feel safe, welcomed and valued within the global walls of our business . . . The contributions that are made by [gay and transgender] IBMers accrue directly to our bottom line and ensure the success of our business."[55] Raytheon, builder of Tomahawk cruise missiles and other defense systems, offers domestic-partner benefits, supports a wide array of gay rights groups, and wants to be an employer of choice for gays. The firm believes these policies give it an advantage in the ever-competitive market for engineers and scientists.

IBM and Raytheon are not alone. Surveys indicate that more than 90 percent of the *Fortune* 500, for example, have policies that cover sexual orientation. Ken Disken, senior vice president of defense contractor Lockheed Martin, justifies the firm's policies as follows: "Lockheed Martin is committed to providing the most supportive and inclusive environment for all employees. Ensuring a positive, respectful workplace and robust set of benefits for everyone is critical to retaining employees and helping them develop to their fullest potential."[56]

As for gender identity, companies are increasingly putting in place policies to govern how their organizations treat called transgender employees. In 2001, only eight companies in the *Fortune* 500 had policies on gender identity. By 2013, that number had swelled to roughly half.

Among the *Fortune* 1000, some companies do not currently have domestic-partner benefits or nondiscrimination clauses for gay employees. Among these are ExxonMobil, Gannett, Goodrich, H. J. Heinz, Kohl's, Liberty Mutual, Lowe's, Nestlé, The New York Stock Exchange (NYSE), Philip Morris, RadioShack, Sherwin Williams, SYSCO, TRW, Tyson Foods, and *The Washington Post*.[57] Recently, the National Football League (NFL) acquired some unwanted publicity when it was revealed that during the NFL combine, when college players are assessed before the draft, several NFL teams inquired about players' relationships with women seemingly to ascertain the players' sexual orientation.

Thus, while times have certainly changed, sexual orientation and gender identity remain individual differences that receive very different treatment under our laws and are accepted quite differently in different organizations.

Cultural Identity   We have seen that people define themselves in terms of race and ethnicity. Many carry a strong cultural identity as well, a link with the culture of family ancestry or youth that lasts a lifetime, no matter where the individual may live in the world. People choose their cultural identity, and they also choose how closely they observe the norms of that culture. Cultural norms influence the workplace, sometimes resulting in clashes. Organizations must adapt.

Workplace practices that coincided with the norms of a person's cultural identity were commonplace years ago when societies were less mobile. People looked for work near home, managers shared the cultural identity of their employees, and organizations established holidays, observances, practices, and customs that suited the majority. Workers who struck out for other locales either looked for groups and organizations that shared their cultural identity, or they adapted their practices to the norms of their new employers. Organizations were generally not expected to accommodate each individual's preferences.

Thanks to global integration and changing labor markets, however, global companies do well to understand and respect the cultural identities of their employees, both as groups and as individuals. A U.S. company looking to do business in, say, Latin America, needs to understand that employees in those cultures expect long summer holidays. A company that provides incentives to work during this culturally established break will find resistance among employees is great.

National labor markets are changing for many reasons, many economic. In Italy, for example, guaranteed jobs, pensions, and benefits used to be the norm. Thus, while older workers hold solid contracts providing benefits for life, the crippled economy has meant younger workers are able to find only temporary jobs despite attaining higher education levels than their parents. The financial provision that was part of the cultural identity of Italy's citizens is now creating a generational divide.[58]

A company seeking to be sensitive to the cultural identities of its employees should look beyond accommodating its majority groups and instead create as much of an individualized approach to practices and norms as possible.

Ability

We've so far covered surface characteristics unlikely, on their own, to directly relate to job performance. Now we turn to deep-level abilities that *are* closely related to job performance. Contrary to what we were taught in grade school, we weren't all created equal in our abilities. Most people are to the left or the right of the median on some normally distributed ability curve. For example, regardless of how motivated you are, you may not be able to act as Scarlett Johansson, play basketball as well as LeBron James, or write as well as Stephen King. Of course, just because we aren't all equal in abilities does not imply that some individuals are inherently inferior. Everyone has strengths and weaknesses that make him or her relatively superior or inferior to others in performing certain tasks or activities. From management's standpoint, the issue is not whether people differ in terms of their abilities. They clearly do. The issue is using the knowledge that people differ to increase the likelihood an employee will perform his or her job well.

ability   *An individual's capacity to perform the various tasks in a job.*

What does *ability* mean? As we use the term, **ability** is an individual's current capacity to perform the various tasks in a job. Overall abilities are essentially made up of two sets of factors: intellectual and physical.

Intellectual Abilities

4   Define *intellectual ability* and demonstrate its relevance to OB.

intellectual abilities   *The capacity to do mental activities—thinking, reasoning, and problem solving.*

Intellectual abilities are abilities needed to perform mental activities—thinking, reasoning, and problem solving. Most societies place a high value on intelligence, and for good reason. Smart people generally earn more money and attain higher levels of education. They are also more likely to emerge as leaders of groups. However, while people aren't consistently capable of correctly assessing their cognitive ability,[59] the origins, influence factors, and testing of intelligence quotient (IQ) are controversial.[60] IQ tests are designed to ascertain a person's general intellectual abilities. So, too, are popular college admission tests, such as the SAT and ACT and graduate admission tests in business (GMAT), law (LSAT), and medicine (MCAT). Testing firms don't claim their tests assess intelligence, but experts know they do.[61] The seven most frequently cited dimensions making up intellectual abilities are number aptitude, verbal comprehension, perceptual speed, inductive reasoning, deductive reasoning, spatial visualization, and memory.[62] Exhibit 2-2 describes these dimensions.

Intelligence dimensions are positively related, so if you score high on verbal comprehension, for example, you're more likely to also score high on spatial visualization. The correlations aren't perfect, meaning people do have specific abilities that predict important work-related outcomes when considered individually.[63] However, they are high enough that researchers also recognize a general factor of intelligence, **general mental ability (GMA)**. Evidence strongly supports the idea that the structures and measures of intellectual abilities generalize across cultures. Thus, someone in Venezuela or Sudan does not have a different set of mental abilities than a U.S. or Czech worker. There is some evidence that IQ scores vary to some degree across cultures, but those differences are much smaller when we take into account educational and economic differences.[64]

Jobs differ in the demands they place on intellectual abilities. Research consistently indicates a correlation between cognitive ability and task performance.[65] The more complex a job in terms of information-processing demands, the more general intelligence and verbal abilities will be necessary to perform successfully.[66] Where employee behavior is highly routine and there are few or no opportunities to exercise discretion, a high IQ is not as important to performing well. However, that does not mean people with high IQs cannot have an impact on traditionally less complex jobs.

It might surprise you that the intelligence test most widely used in hiring decisions takes only 12 minutes to complete. It's the Wonderlic Cognitive Ability Test. There are different forms, and each has 50 questions. Here are a few examples:

- When rope is selling at $0.10 a foot, how many feet can you buy for $0.60?
- Assume the first two statements are true. Is the final one:
    1. True.
    2. False.
    3. Not certain.
        a. The boy plays baseball.
        b. All baseball players wear hats.
        c. The boy wears a hat.

general mental ability (GMA)
An overall factor of intelligence, as suggested by the positive correlations among specific intellectual ability dimensions.

Exhibit **2-2**	Dimensions of Intellectual Ability	
Dimension	**Description**	**Job Example**
Number aptitude	Ability to do speedy and accurate arithmetic	Accountant: Computing the sales tax on a set of items
Verbal comprehension	Ability to understand what is read or heard and the relationship of words to each other	Plant manager: Following corporate policies on hiring
Perceptual speed	Ability to identify visual similarities and differences quickly and accurately	Fire investigator: Identifying clues to support a charge of arson
Inductive reasoning	Ability to identify a logical sequence in a problem and then solve the problem	Market researcher: Forecasting demand for a product in the next time period
Deductive reasoning	Ability to use logic and assess the implications of an argument	Supervisor: Choosing between two different suggestions offered by employees
Spatial visualization	Ability to imagine how an object would look if its position in space were changed	Interior decorator: Redecorating an office
Memory	Ability to retain and recall past experiences	Salesperson: Remembering the names of customers

The Wonderlic measures both speed (almost nobody has time to answer every question) and power (questions get harder as you go along), so the average score is pretty low—about 21 of 50. And because it is able to provide valid information cheaply (for $5 to $10 per applicant), more companies are using the Wonderlic in hiring decisions. The Factory Card & Party Outlet, with 182 stores nationwide, uses it. So do Subway, Peoples Flowers, Security Alarm, Workforce Employment Solutions, and many others. Most of these companies don't give up other hiring tools, such as application forms or interviews. Rather, they add the Wonderlic for its ability to provide valid data on applicants' intelligence levels.

While intelligence is a big help in performing a job well, it doesn't make people happier or more satisfied with their jobs. The correlation between intelligence and job satisfaction is about zero. Why? Research suggests that although intelligent people perform better and tend to have more interesting jobs, they are also more critical when evaluating their job conditions. Thus, smart people have it better, but they also expect more.[67]

Physical Abilities

5 Contrast intellectual and physical ability.

physical abilities *The capacity to do tasks that demand stamina, dexterity, strength, and similar characteristics.*

Though the changing nature of work suggests intellectual abilities are increasingly important for many jobs, **physical abilities** have been and will remain valuable. Research on hundreds of jobs has identified nine basic abilities needed in the performance of physical tasks.[68] These are described in Exhibit 2-3. Individuals differ in the extent to which they have each of these abilities. Not surprisingly, there is also little relationship among them: a high score on one is no assurance of a high score on others. High employee performance is likely to be achieved when management has ascertained the extent to which a job requires each of the nine abilities and then ensures that employees in that job have those abilities.

The Role of Disabilities

The importance of ability at work obviously creates problems when we attempt to formulate workplace policies that recognize diversity in terms of disability

---

Exhibit 2-3   **Nine Basic Physical Abilities**

Strength Factors

1. Dynamic strength	Ability to exert muscular force repeatedly or continuously over time
2. Trunk strength	Ability to exert muscular strength using the trunk (particularly abdominal) muscles
3. Static strength	Ability to exert force against external objects
4. Explosive strength	Ability to expend a maximum of energy in one or a series of explosive acts

Flexibility Factors

5. Extent flexibility	Ability to move the trunk and back muscles as far as possible
6. Dynamic flexibility	Ability to make rapid, repeated flexing movements

Other Factors

7. Body coordination	Ability to coordinate the simultaneous actions of different parts of the body
8. Balance	Ability to maintain equilibrium despite forces pulling off balance
9. Stamina	Ability to continue maximum effort requiring prolonged effort over time

status. As we have noted, recognizing that individuals have different abilities that can be taken into account when making hiring decisions is not problematic. However, it is discriminatory to make blanket assumptions about people on the basis of a disability. It is also possible to make accommodations for disabilities.

Implementing Diversity Management Strategies

diversity management   *The process and programs by which managers make everyone more aware of and sensitive to the needs and differences of others.*

Having discussed a variety of ways in which people differ, we now look at how a manager can and should manage these differences. **Diversity management** makes everyone more aware of and sensitive to the needs and differences of others. This definition highlights the fact that diversity programs include and are meant for everyone. Diversity is much more likely to be successful when we see it as everyone's business than if we believe it helps only certain groups of employees.

Attracting, Selecting, Developing, and Retaining Diverse Employees

One method of enhancing workforce diversity is to target recruiting messages to specific demographic groups underrepresented in the workforce. This means placing advertisements in publications geared toward specific demographic groups; recruiting at colleges, universities, and other institutions with significant numbers of underrepresented minorities; and forming partnerships with associations like the Society for Women Engineers or the Graduate Minority Business Association.

Research has shown that women and minorities do have greater interest in employers that make special efforts to highlight a commitment to diversity in their recruiting materials. Diversity advertisements that fail to show women and minorities in positions of organizational leadership send a negative message about the diversity climate at an organization.[69] Of course, in order to show the pictures, organizations must have diversity in their management ranks. Some companies have been actively working toward recruiting less-represented groups. Google, for instance, has been making sure female candidates meet other women during interviews and offering family benefits that may appeal to them.[70] Etsy, an online retailer, hosts engineering classes, provides grants for aspiring women coders, then hires the best.[71] McKinsey & Co., Bain & Co., Boston Consulting Group, and Goldman Sachs group have similarly been actively recruiting women who left the workforce to start families by offering phase-in programs and other benefits.[72]

The selection process is one of the most important places to apply diversity efforts. Managers who hire need to value fairness and objectivity in selecting employees and focus on the productive potential of new recruits. When managers use a well-defined protocol for assessing applicant talent and the organization clearly prioritizes nondiscrimination policies, qualifications become far more important in determining who gets hired than demographic characteristics.[73]

Similarity in personality appears to affect career advancement. Those whose personality traits are similar to those of their co-workers are more likely to be promoted than those whose personalities are different.[74] There's an important qualifier to these results: In collectivistic cultures, similarity to supervisors is more important for predicting advancement, whereas in individualistic cultures, similarity to peers is more important.

As we mentioned before, individuals who are demographically different from their co-workers may be more likely to feel low commitment and to turn over, but a positive diversity climate can be helpful. Many diversity training programs are available to employers, and research efforts are focusing on identifying the most effective initiatives. It seems that the best programs are inclusive in their design and implementation.[75] What we know is that a positive diversity climate should be the goal. All workers appear to prefer an organization that values diversity.

Diversity in Groups

Most contemporary workplaces require extensive work in group settings. When people work in groups, they need to establish a common way of looking at and accomplishing the major tasks, and they need to communicate with one another often. If they feel little sense of membership and cohesion in their groups, all these group attributes are likely to suffer.

Does diversity help or hurt group performance? The answer is "yes." In some cases, diversity in traits can hurt team performance, whereas in others it can facilitate it.[76] Whether diverse or homogeneous teams are more effective depends on the characteristic of interest. Demographic diversity (in gender, race, and ethnicity) does not appear to either help or hurt team performance in general. On the other hand, teams of individuals who are highly intelligent, conscientious, and interested in working in team settings are more effective. Thus, diversity on these variables is likely to be a bad thing—it makes little sense to try to form teams that mix in members who are lower in intelligence, conscientiousness, and uninterested in teamwork. In other cases, differences can be a strength. Groups of individuals with different types of expertise and education are more effective than homogeneous groups. Similarly, a group made entirely of assertive people who want to be in charge, or a group whose members all prefer to follow the lead of others, will be less effective than a group that mixes leaders and followers.

Regardless of the composition of the group, differences can be leveraged to achieve superior performance. The most important way is to emphasize the higher-level similarities among members.[77] In other words, groups of diverse individuals will be much more effective if leaders can show how members have a common interest in the group's success. Evidence also shows transformational leaders (who emphasize higher-order goals and values in their leadership style) are more effective in managing diverse teams.[78]

Effective Diversity Programs

6 Describe how organizations manage diversity effectively.

Organizations use a variety of efforts to capitalize on diversity, including the recruiting and selection policies we have already discussed, as well as training and development practices. Effective, comprehensive workforce programs encouraging diversity have three distinct components. First, they teach managers about the legal framework for equal employment opportunity and encourage fair treatment of all people regardless of their demographic characteristics. Second, they teach managers how a diverse workforce will be better able to serve a diverse market of customers and clients. Third, they foster personal development practices that bring out the skills and abilities of all workers, acknowledging how differences in perspective can be a valuable way to improve performance for everyone.[79]

Much concern about diversity has to do with fair treatment.[80] Most negative reactions to employment discrimination are based on the idea that discriminatory treatment is unfair. Regardless of race or gender, people are generally in favor of diversity-oriented programs, including affirmative action, if they believe the policies ensure everyone a fair opportunity to show their skills and abilities.

Photo 2-4 Developing the talents of women is a strategic imperative for business success at Nissan Motor Company in Japan. The company helps women develop their careers at the firm's manufacturing plants and car dealerships by providing skill-development training programs and one-on-one counseling services of career advisors.

A major study of the consequences of diversity programs came to what might seem a surprising conclusion.[81] Organizations that provided diversity training were not consistently more likely to have women and minorities in upper management positions than organizations that did not. On closer examination though, these results are not surprising. Experts have long known that one-shot training sessions without strategies to encourage effective diversity management back on the job are not likely to be very effective. Some diversity programs are truly effective in improving representation in management. They include strategies to measure the representation of women and minorities in managerial positions, and they hold managers accountable for achieving more demographically diverse management teams. Researchers also suggest that diversity experiences are more likely to lead to positive adaptation for all parties if (1) the diversity experience undermines stereotypical attitudes, (2) if the perceiver is motivated and able to consider a new perspective on others, (3) if the perceiver engages in stereotype suppression and generative thought in response to the diversity experience, and (4) if the positive experience of stereotype undermining is repeated frequently.[82] Diversity programs based on these principles are likely to be more effective than traditional classroom learning.

Organizational leaders should examine their workforce to determine whether target groups have been underutilized. If groups of employees are not proportionally represented in top management, managers should look for any hidden barriers to advancement. They can often improve recruiting practices, make selection systems more transparent, and provide training for those employees who have not had adequate exposure to certain material in the past. The organization should also clearly communicate its policies to employees so they can understand how and why certain practices are followed. Communications should focus as much as possible on qualifications and job performance; emphasizing certain groups as needing more assistance could well backfire. A case study of the multinational Finnish company TRANSCO found it was possible to develop a consistent global philosophy for diversity management. However, differences in legal and cultural factors across nations forced TRANSCO to develop unique policies to match the cultural and legal frameworks of each country in which it operated.[83]

Photo 2-5 Employees of Grow Financial Credit Union in Tampa, Florida, enjoy a lunch-hour program on women executives and their careers sponsored by the firm's diversity committee. Fostering diversity is part of Grow's corporate culture that begins with employee orientation and includes ongoing events that reflect Grow's diverse employee mix.

Source: Cherie Diez/ZUMA Press/Newscom.

Summary

This chapter looked at diversity from many perspectives. We paid particular attention to three variables—biographical characteristics, ability, and diversity programs. Diversity management must be an ongoing commitment that crosses all levels of the organization. Policies to improve the climate for diversity can be effective, so long as they are designed to acknowledge all employees' perspectives.

Implications for Managers

- Understand your organization's anti-discrimination policies thoroughly and share them with your employees.
- Assess and challenge your stereotype beliefs to increase your objectivity.
- Look beyond readily observable biographical characteristics and consider the individual's capabilities before making management decisions.
- Fully evaluate what accommodations person with disabilities will need and then fine-tune a job to that person's abilities.
- Seek to understand and respect the unique biographical characteristics of your employees; a fair but individualistic approach yields the best performance.

Affirmative Action Should Be Abolished

POINT

COUNTERPOINT

Michigan had it right when it banned preferential treatment of applicants for public university admissions in 2006, and the Supreme Court should use that case and the *Fisher v. University of Texas* case to confirm that affirmative action—whether for university admissions processes or in any other sphere—is a poor organizational choice. The practice, now outlawed in Arizona, California, Florida, Nebraska, New Hampshire, Oklahoma, and Washington, raises the percentage of minority individuals but does not create a positive diversity climate. Here's why:

- Affirmative action lowers the standards for everyone by shifting the criteria for admission from performance standards to quotas based on race or other nonperformance attributes. Performance standards for the organization are then effectively lowered. Groups not helped by the initiative will be resentful, and qualified members of the protected minority may be as well.

- Research indicates that minority students are not helped by school admission initiatives. In fact, a large-scale study showed that minority law students who attended schools best matched to their LSAT scores performed better than those who went to higher-ranked schools than their scores would warrant without affirmative action. Similarly, employees who are mismatched to their positions—who have poor *person-organization fit*—underperform and are generally less satisfied in their jobs.

- U.S. businesses and laws do support diversity, and indicators show that U.S. workers generally consider it important. But they value fairness more. In fact, though recently aimed at creating diversity, affirmative action was enacted to ensure fairness to the disadvantaged. Now that experience and research have proven a culture of inclusivity is more important for diversity than headcount, organizations should focus on the fairness of objective standards. Affirmative action is even unfair to its highest-performing beneficiaries, who suffer from the misperception that their success is due only to its advantages.

Affirmative action has run its course to increase diversity, and it's time to create true equality by focusing on merit-based achievements.

Affirmative action was enacted to ensure equality, and it's still needed today. When the United States was considering the issue for black minorities back in 1965, President Lyndon B. Johnson said, "You do not take a person who, for years, has been hobbled by chains and liberate him, bring him up to the starting line of a race and then say, 'You are free to compete with all the others,' and still justly believe that you have been completely fair." Dr. Martin Luther agreed that, in order to create equal opportunity, proactive measures are needed as long as some people remain at a disadvantage. Therefore, what we should be asking is: are minority groups faring as well as majority groups in the United States? No, not by any indicator. Minority groups test lower in academics, are underrepresented in management and leadership roles, and have a smaller presence in the professional ranks.

Affirmative action continues to benefit the community. Consider the following:

- Affirmative action programs have given all workers access to training and promotion opportunities through the establishment of merit-based norms.

- Affirmative action policies work. The percentages of minorities in universities, management, and the professions have increased in the years since it was adopted.

- Diversity has contributed to the college and workplace experience. As research shows, understanding and tolerance are increased when members of different people groups work together. Classrooms with a diverse student body help raise future leaders from minority and sometimes economically disadvantaged groups, which helps them become integrated into U.S. society.

To be certain, fairness is in the eye of the beholder. Affirmative action provides opportunity, but then it is up to the individual to meet the expectations schools or employers. As blogger Berneta Haynes wrote, "I'm not ashamed to admit that without affirmative action, I'm not certain I would be on the precipice of the law career that I'm at right now. As an African-American woman from a poor family, I have little doubt that affirmative action helped me get into college, earn a degree, and enroll in law school." Her underprivileged status earned her an opportunity to succeed, but is that different from anyone else using his or her social status to get a foot in the door?

If anything about affirmative action is changed through Supreme Court rulings, it should be only to expand the program until the statistics of minority-group achievements fully match those of the long-overpriveleged majority.

Sources: B. Haynes, "Affirmative Action Helped Me," *Inside Higher Ed* (March 12, 2013), www.insidehighered.com/views/2013/03/12/affirmative-action-helped-me-and-benefits-society-essay; L. Hurley, "Supreme Court Agrees to Hear Michigan Affirmative Action Case," *Reuters* (March 25, 2013), www.reuters.com/article/2013/03/25/us-usa-court-affirmative-idUSBRE9200GM20130325; D. Leonhardt, "Rethinking Affirmative Action," *The New York Times* (October 13, 2012), www.nytimes.com/2012/10/14/sunday-review/rethinking-affirmative-action.html?pagewanted=all; and M. Sherman, "Supreme Court to Hear Affirmative Action Case," *Huffington Post* (March 25, 2013), www.huffingtonpost.com/2013/03/25/supreme-court-affirmative-action_n_2948200.html.

END-OF-CHAPTER REVIEW

MyManagementLab

Go to **mymanagementlab.com** to complete the problems marked with this icon. ⭐

QUESTIONS FOR REVIEW

2-1 What are the two major forms of workforce diversity?

2-2 What are stereotypes and how do they function in organizational settings?

2-3 What are the key biographical characteristics and how are they relevant to OB?

2-4 What is *intellectual ability* and how is it relevant to OB?

2-5 How can you contrast intellectual and physical ability?

2-6 How do organizations manage diversity effectively?

EXPERIENTIAL EXERCISE **Feeling Excluded**

This six-step exercise takes approximately 20 minutes.

Individual Work (Steps 1 and 2)

2-7. All participants are asked to recall a time when they have felt uncomfortable or targeted because of their demographic status. Ideally, situations at work should be used, but if no work situations come to mind, any situation will work. Encourage students to use any demographic characteristic they think is most appropriate, so they can write about feeling excluded on the basis of race, ethnicity, gender, age, disability status, religion, or any other characteristic. They should briefly describe the situation, what precipitated the event, how they felt at the time, how they reacted, and how they believe the other party could have made the situation better.

2-8. The instructor asks the students to then think about a time when they might have either deliberately or accidentally done something that made someone else feel excluded or targeted because of their demographic status. Once again, they should briefly describe the situation, what precipitated the event, how they felt at the time, how the other person reacted, and how they could have made the situation better.

Small Groups (Steps 3 and 4)

2-9. Once everyone has written their descriptions, divide the class into small groups of not more than four people. If at all possible, try to compose groups that are somewhat demographically diverse, to avoid intergroup conflicts in the class review discussion. Students should be encouraged to discuss their situations and consider how their experiences were similar or different.

2-10. After reading through everyone's reactions, each group should develop a short list of principles for how they personally can avoid excluding or targeting people in the future. Encourage them to be as specific as possible, and also ask each group to find solutions that work for everyone. Solutions should focus on both avoiding these situations in the first place and resolving them when they do occur.

Class Review (Steps 5 and 6)

2-11. Members of each group are invited to provide a very brief summary of the major principles of how they've felt excluded or targeted, and then to describe their groups' collective decisions regarding how these situations can be minimized in the future.

2-12. The instructor should lead a discussion on how companies might be able to develop comprehensive policies that will encourage people to be sensitive in their interactions with one another.

ETHICAL DILEMMA **Board Quotas**

That women are underrepresented on boards of directors is an understatement. In the United States, only 16 percent of board members among the *Fortune* 500 are women. Among the 100 largest companies in Great Britain, women hold approximately 12 percent of board seats, a representation that has changed little over the past 5 years. In the European Union (EU) more generally, only 9.7 percent of the directors of the 300 largest companies are women. In China and India, the figure is roughly half that.

In response to such underrepresentation, many countries have enacted laws and guidelines. French law stipulates that corporate boards must be 20 percent female by 2014. A 2011 official British government report recommended that women make up at least 25 percent of the boards of the largest British companies. Belgium, Spain, the Netherlands, Norway, Iceland, and Italy have similar "pink quotas" in place, and Sweden is recommending 50 percent representation.

Questions

2-13. Given that women participate in the labor force in roughly the same proportion as men, why do you think women occupy so few seats on boards of directors?

2-14. Do you agree with the quotas established in many countries? Why or why not?

2-15. Beyond legal remedies, what do you think can be done to increase women's representations on boards of directors?

Sources: J. Werdigier, "In Britain, a Push for More Women on Boards of Large Companies," *The New York Times* (February 25, 2011), p. B3; J. Galbreath, "Are There Gender-Related Influences on Corporate Sustainability? A Study of Women on Boards of Directors," *Journal of Management & Organization* 17, no. 1 (2011), pp. 17–38; and J. S. Lublin, "'Pink Quotas' Alter Europe's Boards," *The Wall Street Journal* (September 12, 2012), p. B8.

CASE INCIDENT 1 Levitating IQs

Given that a substantial amount of intellectual ability is inherited, it might surprise you to learn that intelligence test scores have been rising dramatically for about a century. On an IQ scale where 100 is the average, scores have been rising about 3 points per decade, meaning if your grandparent scored 100, the average score for your generation would be around 115. That's a pretty big difference—about a standard deviation, meaning someone from your grandparent's generation whose score was at the 84th percentile would be only average (50th percentile) by today's norms. But don't think for a minute that we are necessarily smarter.

James Flynn is a New Zealand researcher and trained political philosopher credited with first documenting the rising scores. He reported the results in 1984, when he found that almost everyone who took a well-validated IQ test in the 1970s did better than those who took one in the 1940s. His findings became known as the Flynn effect. Now Flynn is saying that though the scores continue to rise, it would "probably be better to say that we are "more modern" than "smarter." The fact is that we're not getting better at everything, he reported recently. A modern mind simply takes a scientific approach to problems, with abstract classification, logic, and imaginative hypothetical reasoning. The prescientific mind was utilitarian, on the other hand, and concentrated on the uses for things.

This change in our mental processes may actually have a greater impact on the rising scores than better educational opportunities do. Flynn reports that our ability to do puzzles, identify similarities, and process nonverbal symbols and visual images has increased, but not our ability to calculate arithmetic. Adults today have broader vocabularies and possess greater general information than in previous generations, but children do not, compared to children in previous generations. The Flynn effect has been shown to be valid in most countries in which it has been tested, even in less-developed countries. Recently, Flynn reported a strong rise in scores in Kenya and Saudi Arabia, but a slower rise in Sudan and Brazil.

Before you chide your elders for what you think must be a differential in your favor, however, consider your future. IQ is not static throughout a person's lifetime, and it might just be a use-it-or-lose-it proposition. In general, verbal intelligence rises until middle age then slowly declines—but at different rates across individuals. Someone with a high IQ will have a much slower decline than a person with lower IQ; in his or her 80s and 90s, the high scorer's verbal intelligence will about equal that of his or her teen years. Unfortunately for your elders, and maybe for you too, the reverse is true for analytical intelligence: It peaks in adolescence.

Despite the strong heritability of IQ, researchers continue to pursue mechanisms that might raise IQ scores, chief among them the pursuit of finer educational systems for youth and adult alike. Factors like regular physical exercise and brain exercises (even videogames) seem to boost brain power, at least temporarily. Other recent research in neuroscience has had difficulty pinpointing physical mechanisms that can boost IQ, although researchers propose that a focus on brain chemicals like dopamine may lead, in time, to drugs that can do so chemically.

Questions

⭐ **2-16.** Do you believe people are really getting smarter? Why or why not?

2-17. How do you reconcile Flynn's recent description of the modern mind with the General Social Survey's findings that U.S. adults perform poorly on scientific questions and aren't knowledgeable about scientific method?

2-18. If the Flynn effect is real, does this undermine the theory that IQ is mostly inherited? Why or why not?

Sources: Based on S. Begley, "Sex, Race, and IQ: Off Limits?" *Newsweek* (April 20, 2009), www.newsweek.com; B. Caplan, "The Intelligence Boom," *The Wall Street Journal* (October 10, 2012), p. A17; J. R. Flynn, "Are We *Really* Getting Smarter?" *The Wall Street Journal* (September 22–23, 2012), p. C3; M. A. Mingroni, "Resolving the IQ Paradox: Heterosis as a Cause of the Flynn Effect and Other Trends," *Psychological Review* (July 2007), pp. 806–829; and S. Begley, "Can You Build a Better Brain?" *Newsweek* (January 10, 2011), www.newsweek.com.

CASE INCIDENT 2 The Treasure Trove of the Aging Workforce

Over the past century, the average age of the workforce has continually increased as medical science has continued to enhance longevity and vitality. Recent medical research is exploring techniques that could extend human life to 100 years or more. As we discussed in the chapter, many individuals will work past the previous established ages of retirement, and the fastest-growing segment of the workforce is individuals over the age of 55.

Unfortunately, older workers face a variety of discriminatory attitudes in the workplace. Researchers scanned more than 100 publications on age discrimination to determine what types of age stereotypes were most prevalent across studies. They found that stereotypes inferred that older workers are lower performers. Research, on the other hand, indicates they are not, and organizations are realizing the benefits of this needed employee group.

Dale Sweere, a human resources director for engineering firm Stanley Consultants, is one of the growing number of management professionals actively recruiting the older workforce. Sweere says older workers "typically hit the ground running much quicker and they fit into the organization well." They bring to the job a higher skill level earned through years of experience, remember the organization's history, and know the aging customer base.

Tell that to the older worker who is unemployed. Older workers have long been sought by government contractors, financial firms, and consultants, according to Cornelia Gamlem, president of consulting firm GEMS Group Ltd., and she actively recruits them. However, the Bureau of Labor Statistics reports that the average job search for an unemployed worker over age 55 is 56 weeks, versus 38 weeks for the rest of the unemployed population. The reason might be that unemployed older job-seekers are actually preselecting themselves right out of potential jobs. They report assuming that employers will consider them overqualified and requiring of higher salaries, greater health care, and more training than the jobs warrant. Faced with the possibility of rejection, they do not always pursue position opportunities they might otherwise consider.

To be sure, there is age discrimination in organizations. It is the responsibility of companies to ensure that employees are treated fairly regardless of age. Many of the techniques to limit age discrimination come down to fundamentally sound management practices relevant for all employees: set clear expectations for performance, deal with problems directly, communicate with workers frequently, and follow clear policies and procedures consistently. In particular, management professionals note that clarity and consistency can help ensure all employees are treated equally regardless of age.

As we've seen, older workers should also take some responsibility for ending age discrimination. Older unemployed job-seekers need to stay current in their training, with technology, and on the latest trends. For employees interested in positions that are not as demanding as their former careers, clear communication of skills and salary/benefit expectations can go a long way toward establishing a fit in the mind of the potential employer. Finally, individuals who are knowledgeable about the older-worker stereotypes can show employers how that outdated viewpoint is wrong.

Questions

2-19. What changes in employment relationships are likely to occur as the population ages?

⭐ 2-20. Do you think increasing age diversity will create new challenges for managers? What types of challenges do you expect will be most profound?

2-21. How can organizations cope with differences related to age discrimination in the workplace? How can older employees help?

Sources: Based on S. Giegerich, "Older Job-Seekers Must Take Charge, Adapt," *Chicago Tribune* (September 10, 2012), pp. 2–3; T. Lytle, "Benefits for Older Workers," *HR Magazine* (March 2012), pp. 53–58; D. Stipp, "The Anti-Aging Revolution," *Fortune* (June 14, 2010), pp. 124–130; R. A. Posthuma and M. A. Campion, "Age Stereotypes in the Workplace: Common Stereotypes, Moderators, and Future Research Directions," *Journal of Management* 35 (2009), pp. 158–188; and H. Perlowski, "With an Aging Workforce, a Rising Risk of Discrimination Claims," *Workforce Management Online* (July 2008), www.workforce.com.

MyManagementLab

Go to **mymanagementlab.com** for Auto-graded writing questions as well as the following Assisted-graded writing questions:

2-22. In relation to this chapter's Ethical Dilemma, one recent study found no link between female representation on boards of directors and these companies' corporate sustainability or environmental policies. The study's author expressed surprise at the findings. Do the findings surprise you? Why or why not?

2-23. Now that you've read the chapter and Case Incident 2, what types of policies do you think might lead to charges of age discrimination, and how can they be changed to eliminate these problems?

2-24. MyManagementLab Only—comprehensive writing assignment for this chapter.

3

Attitudes and Job Satisfaction

Source: © Steve Rhodes/Demotix/Corbis.

MICRO-ENTREPRENEURS

There are full-time workers, part-timers, contract workers, and now, in the newly minted "distributed workforce," there's the person you hired solely to race your contract to a client. Meet the "micro-entrepreneurs," individuals employed so briefly, and so anonymously, that you may never meet them. How can this happen?

Micro-entrepreneurs use apps they load onto their personal phones (with location capabilities) to view potential jobs and click on the ones they want. Once selected, often based on proximity to the job, they complete their task, and their temporary employers send the agency an electronic payment (plus a 20 percent service fee) with an evaluation of the work done. Originally, these jobs were mainly of the errand and fix-it variety, but intellectual work opportunities are opening up because the business model has potential.

Is the effort worth it?

It depends on whom you ask. According to Brad Stone of *Bloomberg Businessweek*, who spent three days as a micro-entrepreneur with almost a dozen employers, not really. "My three-day haul won't feed my family," he observed in counting his roughly $67/day earnings through TaskRabbit, Postmates, and Cherry. Rob Coneybeer, managing director of Shasta Ventures, which invests in distributed workforce sites, disagrees. He says these sites are trying to establish a market "where people end up getting paid more per hour than they would have otherwise and find it easier to do jobs they are good at." TaskRabbit founder Leah Busque says thousands of people make up to $60,000 per year through her site, though bloggers report that winning bids to work isn't always easy. Venture capitalists have invested $38 million in TaskRabbit alone, however, and millions more at similar sites. And according to Google's chief economist Hal Varian, "Improving the efficiency of finding jobs is a really big deal, even if it's sporadic work."

App-based micro work is not limited to the United States. Blogger James McAloon commented, "The local task culture is spreading. I have helped launch Servango in the U.K. and it is proving very popular. People are able to find tasks to complete which are from a variety of sectors. Not to mention we help people advertise their services and skills to the people around them so there is always a great local option. It is about making the local service and talent sharing environment more efficient."

It remains to be seen whether micro-entrepreneurship is a viable long-term business model or just a backup employment plan during lean economic years. The answer may lie in the attitudes and level of job satisfaction for these workers. Many are happy with the opportunity to work in their desired fields. Blogger Meghan says, "Sure, the tasks are not the most exciting and some task posters do try to mislead you," she wrote, "but overall my

LEARNING OBJECTIVES

After studying this chapter, you should be able to:

1 Contrast the three components of an attitude.

2 Summarize the relationship between attitudes and behavior.

3 Compare and contrast the major job attitudes.

4 Define *job satisfaction* and show how we can measure it.

5 Summarize the main causes of job satisfaction.

6 Identify four employee responses to dissatisfaction.

experience as a TaskRabbit has taught me a lot about communication, respect, and hard work. This kind of life might not be glamorous, but I can look back on my work week and feel proud that I found a way to make ends meet. . . . I just hope it's not forever!"

_____

Sources: Postmates company website, www.postmates.com; K. Ryssdal, "Unemployed or Underemployed? There's an App for That," *Marketplace Tech* (September 12, 2012), www.marketplace.org/; B. Stone, "My Life as a Task Rabbit," *Bloomberg Businessweek* (September 13, 2012), www.businessweek.com/articles/2012-09-13/my-life-as-a-taskrabbit#p1; TaskRabbit company website, www.taskrabbit.com; Servango company website, www.servango.com; and WeGoLook company website, www.WeGoLook.com.

As you can see from the opening example, sometimes attitude is everything when it comes to making the most of unique job opportunities such as those that micro-entrepreneurial work apps provide. In this chapter, we look at attitudes, their link to behavior, and how employees' satisfaction or dissatisfaction with their jobs affects the workplace.

What are your attitudes toward your job? Use the following Self-Assessment Library to determine your level of satisfaction with your current or past jobs.

SELF-ASSESSMENT LIBRARY

How Satisfied Am I with My Job?

In the Self-Assessment Library (available in MyManagementLab), take assessment I.B.3 (How Satisfied Am I with My Job?) and then answer the following questions. If you currently do not have a job, answer the questions for your most recent job.

1. How does your job satisfaction compare to that of others in your class who have taken the assessment?
2. Why do you think your satisfaction is higher or lower than average?

Attitudes

1 Contrast the three components of an attitude.

attitudes *Evaluative statements or judgments concerning objects, people, or events.*

cognitive component *The opinion or belief segment of an attitude.*

Attitudes are evaluative statements—either favorable or unfavorable—about objects, people, or events. They reflect how we feel about something. When you say "I like my job," you are expressing your attitude about work.

Attitudes are complex. If you ask people about their attitude toward religion, Lady Gaga, or the organization they work for, you may get a simple response, but the underlying reasons are probably complicated. In order to fully understand attitudes, we must consider their fundamental properties or components.

What Are the Main Components of Attitudes?

Typically, researchers have assumed that attitudes have three components: cognition, affect, and behavior.[1] Let's look at each.

The statement "My pay is low" is the **cognitive component** of an attitude—a description of or belief in the way things are. It sets the stage for the more

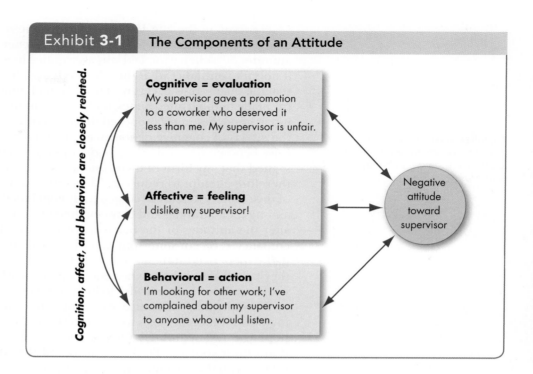

Exhibit **3-1**   The Components of an Attitude

Cognition, affect, and behavior are closely related.

Cognitive = evaluation
My supervisor gave a promotion to a coworker who deserved it less than me. My supervisor is unfair.

Affective = feeling
I dislike my supervisor!

Behavioral = action
I'm looking for other work; I've complained about my supervisor to anyone who would listen.

Negative attitude toward supervisor

affective component   *The emotional or feeling segment of an attitude.*

behavioral component   *An intention to behave in a certain way toward someone or something.*

critical part of an attitude—its **affective component**. Affect is the emotional or feeling segment of an attitude and is reflected in the statement "I am angry over how little I'm paid." Finally, affect can lead to behavioral outcomes. The **behavioral component** of an attitude describes an intention to behave in a certain way toward someone or something—to continue the example, "I'm going to look for another job that pays better."

Viewing attitudes as having three components—cognition, affect, and behavior—is helpful in understanding their complexity and the potential relationship between attitudes and behavior. Keep in mind that these components are closely related, and cognition and affect in particular are inseparable in many ways. For example, imagine you realized that someone has just treated you unfairly. Aren't you likely to have feelings about that, occurring virtually instantaneously with the realization? Thus, cognition and affect are intertwined.

Exhibit 3-1 illustrates how the three components of an attitude are related. In this example, an employee didn't get a promotion he thought he deserved; a coworker got it instead. The employee's attitude toward his supervisor is illustrated as follows: The employee thought he deserved the promotion (cognition), he strongly dislikes his supervisor (affect), and he has complained and taken action (behavior). As we've noted, although we often think cognition causes affect, which then causes behavior, in reality these components are difficult to separate.

In organizations, attitudes are important for their behavioral component. If workers believe, for example, that supervisors, auditors, bosses, and time-and-motion engineers are all in conspiracy to make employees work harder for the same or less money, it makes sense to try to understand how these attitudes formed, how they relate to actual job behavior, and how they might be changed.

Does Behavior Always Follow from Attitudes?

2   Summarize the relationship between attitudes and behavior.

Early research on attitudes assumed they were causally related to behavior—that is, the attitudes people hold determine what they do. Common sense, too, suggests a relationship. Isn't it logical that people watch television programs they like, or that employees try to avoid assignments they find distasteful?

cognitive dissonance   *Any incompatibility between two or more attitudes or between behavior and attitudes.*

However, in the late 1960s, a review of the research challenged this assumed effect of attitudes on behavior.[2] One researcher—Leon Festinger—argued that attitudes *follow* behavior. Did you ever notice how people change what they say so it doesn't contradict what they do? Perhaps a friend of yours consistently argued that the quality of U.S. cars isn't up to that of imports until his dad gave him a new car made in the United States, and then he argued that U.S. cars have always been just as good. Festinger proposed that cases of attitude following behavior illustrate the effects of **cognitive dissonance**,[3] any incompatibility an individual might perceive between two or more attitudes or between behavior and attitudes. Festinger argued that any form of inconsistency is uncomfortable and that individuals will therefore attempt to reduce it. They will seek a stable state, which is a minimum of dissonance. Research has generally concluded that people do seek consistency among their attitudes and between their attitudes and their behavior.[4] They either alter the attitudes or the behavior, or they develop a rationalization for the discrepancy. A recent study found, for instance, that the attitudes of employees who had experienced difficult, emotionally challenging work events improved after they talked about their experiences with co-workers. Social sharing helped these workers adjust their attitudes to behavioral expectations.[5]

No individual, of course, can completely avoid dissonance. You know cheating on your income tax is wrong, but you fudge the numbers a bit every year and hope you're not audited. Or you tell your children to floss their teeth, but you don't do it yourself. Festinger proposed that the desire to reduce dissonance depends on three factors, including the *importance* of the elements creating it and the degree of *influence* we believe we have over them. Individuals will be more motivated to reduce dissonance when the attitudes are important or when they believe the dissonance is due to something they can control. The third factor is the *rewards* of dissonance; high rewards accompanying high dissonance tend to reduce the tension inherent in the dissonance (the dissonance is less distressing if accompanied by something good, such as a higher pay raise than expected).

Although Festinger argued that attitudes follow behavior, other researchers asked whether there was any relationship at all. More recent research shows that attitudes predict future behavior and confirmed Festinger's idea that "moderating variables" can strengthen the link.[6]

Photo 3-1 Westin Hotels strives for consistency between employee attitudes and behavior through a global wellness program to help employees improve their health. Shown here is Westin's Executive Chef Frank Tujague, whose cooking demonstrations give employees direct experience with healthy ingredients and cooking techniques.

Moderating Variables   The most powerful moderators of the attitudes relationship are the *importance* of the attitude, its *correspondence to behavior,* its *accessibility,* the presence of *social pressures,* and whether a person has *direct experience* with the attitude.[7]

Important attitudes reflect our fundamental values, self-interest, or identification with individuals or groups we value. These attitudes tend to show a strong relationship to our behavior.

Specific attitudes tend to predict specific behaviors, whereas general attitudes tend to best predict general behaviors. For instance, asking someone about her intention to stay with an organization for the next six months is likely to better predict turnover for that person than asking her how satisfied she is with her job overall. On the other hand, overall job satisfaction would better predict a general behavior, such as whether the individual was engaged in her work or motivated to contribute to her organization.[8]

Attitudes that our memories can easily access are more likely to predict our behavior. Interestingly, you're more likely to remember attitudes you frequently express. So the more you talk about your attitude on a subject, the more likely you are to remember it, and the more likely it is to shape your behavior. Discrepancies between attitudes and behaviors tend to occur when social pressures to behave in certain ways hold exceptional power, as in most organizations. Finally, the attitude–behavior relationship is likely to be much stronger if an attitude refers to something with which we have direct personal experience.

An Ethical Choice

Are Employers Responsible for Workplace Incivilities?

Workplace incivility is sadly commonplace. Research suggests that 86 percent of U.S. employees experience some form of incivility yearly, ranging from a boss who unleashes a string of expletives to a co-worker who scrawls threatening messages in the break room.

Few employees bring such incidents to their human resources departments, though stress can increase their number and incivility can even lead to violence. When people do complain, some employers do nothing, as at Emerson Electric when CEO David Farr's habitual swearing went unchecked and even his apology was vulgar. Other responses can be limited by applicable law. When female co-workers complained that public notes written by truck driver Kevin Grosso were vulgar, offensive, and threatening, he was dismissed, but later the National Labor Review Board determined the termination was unlawful.

In Europe, bullying claims "seek to redress what are deemed attacks on the dignity of workers and degradation of employees as people," says attorney Roselyn Sands. Perhaps all countries need tighter guidelines for workplace incivilities, but ethical questions will always remain at the individual and organizational level. And it is true, of course, that a person can be perhaps wrongly accused of incivility for simply expressing disagreement or engaging in a mundane conflict. Each individual must determine the right response to a perceived offense and consider the organizational culture before deciding whether to report the problem. A culture tolerant of workplace incivility may lead a perpetrator to counterproductive work behaviors or violence. An overly vigilant culture will suppress the free expression of ideas and willingness to disagree. The balance lies in between.

The organization that promotes a culture of civility will hear from its employees and react before the situation escalates. The ethical choice for employers is to create a code of conduct fostering respect for employees, recruit on personality traits, test for conflict management styles, initiate role modeling, and train leaders in workplace civility. Organizations need to decide what is uncivil in advance of, rather in reaction to, such episodes.

Sources: J. R. Hagerty, "Emerson CEO Raises Eyebrows by Unleashing His Salty Tongue," *The Wall Street Journal* (February 19, 2013), pp. B1, B8; D. M. Owens, "Incivility Rising," *HR Magazine* (February 2012), p. 33; M. K. Shoss, R. Eisenberger, S. L. D. Restubog, and T. J. Zagenczyk, "Blaming the Organization for Abusive Supervision: The Roles of Perceived Organizational Support and Supervisor's Organizational Embodiment," *Journal of Applied Psychology* 98 (2013), pp. 158–168; and A. Smith, "Bullying Claims: Bigger Deal in Europe," *HR Magazine* (January 2013), p. 16.

What Are the Major Job Attitudes?

3 Compare and contrast the major job attitudes.

We each have thousands of attitudes, but OB focuses our attention on a very limited number of work-related attitudes. These tap positive or negative evaluations that employees hold about aspects of their work environments. Most of the research in OB has looked at three attitudes: job satisfaction, job involvement, and organizational commitment.[9] A few other important attitudes are perceived organizational support and employee engagement; we'll also briefly discuss these.

Job Satisfaction   When people speak of employee attitudes, they usually mean **job satisfaction**, which describes a positive feeling about a job, resulting from an evaluation of its characteristics. A person with a high level of job satisfaction holds positive feelings about his or her job, while a person with a low level holds negative feelings. Because OB researchers give job satisfaction high importance, we'll review this attitude in detail later in the chapter.

job satisfaction   *A positive feeling about one's job resulting from an evaluation of its characteristics.*

Job Involvement   Related to job satisfaction is **job involvement**,[10] which measures the degree to which people identify psychologically with their jobs and consider their perceived performance levels important to self-worth.[11] Employees with a high level of job involvement strongly identify with and really care about the kind of work they do. Another closely related concept is **psychological empowerment**, employees' beliefs in the degree to which they influence their work environment, their competencies, the meaningfulness of their job, and their perceived autonomy.[12] One study of nursing managers in Singapore found that good leaders empower their employees by fostering their self-perception of competence—through involving them in decisions, making them feel their work is important, and giving them discretion to "do their own thing."[13] Another study found, however, that for teachers in India, the self-perception of competence does not affect innovative behavior, which would be a desired outcome. This research suggests that empowerment initiatives need to be tailored to the culture and desired behavioral outcomes.[14]

job involvement   *The degree to which a person identifies with a job, actively participates in it, and considers performance important to self-worth.*

psychological empowerment   *Employees' belief in the degree to which they affect their work environment, their competence, the meaningfulness of their job, and their perceived autonomy in their work.*

High levels of both job involvement and psychological empowerment are positively related to organizational citizenship (known as OCB, this is discretionary behavior that is not part of an employee's formal job requirements but contributes to the psychological and social environment of the workplace) and job performance.[15]

Organizational Commitment   In **organizational commitment**, an employee identifies with a particular organization and its goals and wishes to remain a member. Most research has focused on emotional attachment to an organization and belief in its values as the "gold standard" for employee commitment.[16]

organizational commitment   *The degree to which an employee identifies with a particular organization and its goals and wishes to maintain membership in the organization.*

A positive relationship appears to exist between organizational commitment and job productivity, but it is a modest one.[17] A review of 27 studies suggested the relationship between commitment and performance is strongest for new employees and considerably weaker for more experienced employees.[18] Interestingly, research indicates that employees who feel their employers fail to keep promises to them feel less committed, and these reductions in commitment, in turn, lead to lower levels of creative performance.[19] And, as with job involvement, the research evidence demonstrates negative relationships between organizational commitment and both absenteeism and turnover.[20]

Theoretical models propose that employees who are committed will be less likely to engage in work withdrawal even if they are dissatisfied because they have a sense of organizational loyalty or attachment. On the other hand, employees who are not committed, who feel less loyal to the organization, will tend to show lower levels of attendance at work across the board. Research

glOBalization!

Exodus Phenomenon

The recent Kelly Global Workforce report on 170,000 employees in 30 countries paints a picture of dissatisfied employees everywhere, with two-thirds expressing the intention to leave their companies for other organizations and more than one-third entertaining the idea of quitting. But a closer look at variations from country to country is surprising. In Brazil and Mexico, for instance, 56 percent of respondents to a Mercer survey of 30,000 employees at different companies reported seriously considering leaving their organizations, versus just 28 percent in the Netherlands. The United States was somewhat in between, at 32 percent.

If U.S. statistics are indicative, almost a quarter of high-potential employees are taking the next step and actually looking for new jobs, a significant increase over the 13 percent who did so in 2005. Even more distressing, employers are not likely to get an opportunity to address employees' concerns: more than one-third of the individuals contemplating quitting report they are not likely to tell their employers they are thinking of leaving. For many reasons, especially lack of job engagement, these individuals are likely to contribute to an upward trend in expensive organizational turnover.

Perhaps the most disturbing statistic from an organizational behavior perspective is the one-quarter of workers in each country who don't plan to quit but who are more negative about their work than the potential quit group.

As Pete Foley, a principal at Mercer, says, this "signals to us we have a fairly big group . . . of apathetic, disaffected, [mentally] checked-out employees." It is the express role of organizational behavior experts to determine what companies can do to alleviate this problem. This chapter offers some suggestions.

Sources: "Acquisition and Retention in the War for Talent," *Kelly Global Workforce Index Report* (April 2012), www.kellyocg.com/uploadedFiles/Content/Knowledge/Kelly_Global_Workforce_Index_Content/Acquisition%20and%20Retention%20in%20the%20War%20for%20Talent%20Report.pdf; K. Gurchiek, "Engagement Erosion Plagues Employers Worldwide," *HR Magazine* (June 2012), p. 17; and G. Kranz, "Keeping the Keepers," *Workforce Management* (April 2012), pp. 34–37.

confirms this theoretical proposition.[21] It does appear that even if employees are not currently happy with their work, they are willing to make sacrifices for the organization if they are committed enough.

perceived organizational support (POS) *The degree to which employees believe an organization values their contribution and cares about their well-being.*

Perceived Organizational Support   Perceived organizational support (POS) is the degree to which employees believe the organization values their contributions and cares about their well-being. An excellent example has been related often by R&D engineer John Greene. When Greene was diagnosed with leukemia, CEO Marc Benioff and 350 fellow Salesforce.com employees covered all out-of-pocket costs for his care, staying in touch with him throughout his recovery. No doubt stories like this are part of the reason Salesforce.com is on *Fortune*'s 100 Best Companies to Work For list.[22] Research shows that people perceive their organization as supportive when rewards are deemed fair, when employees have a voice in decisions, and when they see their supervisors as supportive.[23] Employees with strong POS perceptions have been found more likely to have higher levels of organizational citizenship behaviors, lower levels of tardiness, and better customer service.[24] This seems to hold true mainly in countries where the power distance, the degree to which people in a country accept that power in institutions and organizations is distributed unequally, is lower. In these countries, like the United States, people are more likely to view work as an exchange than as a moral obligation. This isn't to say POS can't be a predictor anywhere on a situation-specific basis. Though little cross-cultural research has been done, one study found POS predicted only the job performance and citizenship behaviors of untraditional or low power-distance Chinese employees—in short, those more likely to think of work as an exchange rather than a moral obligation.[25]

Photo 3-2 Employees waving to guests at Hong Kong Disneyland are committed to the company and its goal of giving visitors a magical and memorable experience. Through careful hiring and extensive training, Disney ensures that employees identify with its priority of pleasing customers by serving them as special guests.

Source: AP Photo/Hong Kong Disneyland, Matt Stroshane, HO.

employee engagement *An individual's involvement with, satisfaction with, and enthusiasm for the work he or she does.*

Employee Engagement   A new concept is **employee engagement**, an individual's involvement with, satisfaction with, and enthusiasm for, the work he or she does. To evaluate this, we might ask employees whether they have access to resources and the opportunities to learn new skills, whether they feel their work is important and meaningful, and whether their interactions with co-workers and supervisors are rewarding.[26] Highly engaged employees have a passion for their work and feel a deep connection to their company; disengaged employees have essentially checked out—putting time but not energy or attention into their work. Engagement becomes a real concern for most organizations because surveys indicate that few employees—between 17 percent and 29 percent—are highly engaged by their work. A study of nearly 8,000 business units in 36 companies found that those whose employees reported high-average levels of engagement produced higher levels of customer satisfaction, were more productive, brought in higher profits, and experienced lower levels of turnover and accidents than at other companies.[27] Molson Coors, for example, found engaged employees were five times less likely to have safety incidents, and when one did occur it was much less serious and less costly for the engaged employee than for a disengaged one ($63 per incident versus $392). Caterpillar set out to increase employee engagement and recorded a resulting 80 percent drop in grievances and a 34 percent increase in highly satisfied customers.[28]

Such promising findings have earned employee engagement a following in many business organizations and management consulting firms. However, the concept is relatively new and still generates active debate about its usefulness. Part of the reason for this is the difficulty of identifying what creates job engagement. For instance, the top two reasons for job engagement that participants gave in a recent study were (1) having a good manager they enjoy working for and (2) feeling appreciated by their supervisor. Because both factors relate to a good manager–employee relationship, it would be easy to conclude that "the people make the place" and that this proves the case for job engagement. Yet, in this same study, individuals ranked "liking and respecting my co-workers" lower on the list, below career advancement concerns.[29]

One review of the job engagement literature concluded, "The meaning of employee engagement is ambiguous among both academic researchers and among practitioners who use it in conversations with clients." Another reviewer called engagement "an umbrella term for whatever one wants it to be."[30] More recent research has set out to clarify the dimensions of employee engagement. For instance, a study in Australia found that emotional intelligence is linked to job satisfaction and well-being, and to employee engagement.[31] Another recent study suggested that engagement fluctuates partially due to daily challenge-seeking and demands.[32] This work has demonstrated that engagement is distinct from job satisfaction and job involvement and incrementally predicts job behaviors after we take these traditional job attitudes into account.

SELF-ASSESSMENT LIBRARY

Am I Engaged?

In the Self-Assessment Library (available in MyManagementLab), take assessment IV.B.1 (Am I Engaged?). (Note: If you do not currently have a job, answer the questions for your most recent job.)

Are These Job Attitudes Really All That Distinct?   You might wonder whether the preceding job attitudes are really distinct. If people feel deeply engaged by their job (high job involvement), isn't it probable they like it, too (high job satisfaction)? Won't people who think their organization is supportive (high perceived organizational support) also feel committed to it (strong organizational commitment)? Evidence suggests these attitudes *are* highly related, perhaps to a troubling degree.

There is some distinctiveness among attitudes, but they overlap greatly for various reasons, including the employee's personality. If you as a manager know someone's level of job satisfaction, you know most of what you need to know about how that person sees the organization. Recent research suggests that managers tend to identify their employees as belonging to one of four distinct categories: enthusiastic stayers, reluctant stayers, enthusiastic leavers (planning to leave), and reluctant leavers (not planning to leave but should leave).[33]

Job Satisfaction

4   Define *job satisfaction* and show how we can measure it.

We have already discussed job satisfaction briefly. Now let's dissect the concept more carefully. How do we measure job satisfaction? What causes an employee to have a high level of job satisfaction? How do dissatisfied and satisfied employees affect an organization? Before you answer, a look at the list of worst jobs (Exhibit 3-2) may give you some indications.

Measuring Job Satisfaction

Our definition of job satisfaction—a positive feeling about a job resulting from an evaluation of its characteristics—is clearly broad. Yet that breadth is appropriate. A job is more than just shuffling papers, writing programming code, waiting on customers, or driving a truck. Jobs require interacting with co-workers and bosses, following organizational rules and policies, meeting performance standards, living with less than ideal working conditions, and the like.[34] An employee's assessment of his satisfaction with the job is thus a complex summation of many discrete elements. How, then, do we measure it?

Two approaches are popular. The single global rating is a response to one question, such as "All things considered, how satisfied are you with your job?" Respondents circle a number between 1 and 5 on a scale from "highly satisfied" to "highly dissatisfied." The second method, the summation of job facets, is

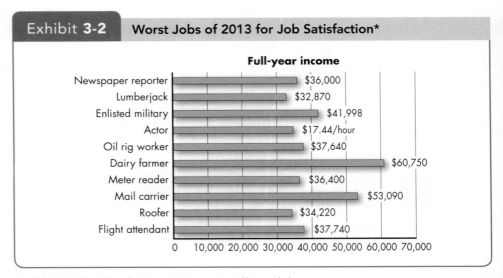

Exhibit 3-2 Worst Jobs of 2013 for Job Satisfaction*

Full-year income

Newspaper reporter	$36,000
Lumberjack	$32,870
Enlisted military	$41,998
Actor	$17.44/hour
Oil rig worker	$37,640
Dairy farmer	$60,750
Meter reader	$36,400
Mail carrier	$53,090
Roofer	$34,220
Flight attendant	$37,740

*Based on physical demands, work environment, income, stress, and hiring outlook.
Sources: L. Weber, "Best and Worst Jobs," *The Wall Street Journal* (April 11, 2012) in the CareerCast.com Jobs Rated report, p. B6; and K. Kensing, "The Worst Jobs of 2013," CareerCast.com (2013), http://www.careercast.com/jobs-rated/worst-jobs-2013.

more sophisticated. It identifies key elements in a job such as the nature of the work, supervision, present pay, promotion opportunities, and relationships with co-workers.[35] Respondents rate these on a standardized scale, and researchers add the ratings to create an overall job satisfaction score.

Is one of these approaches superior? Intuitively, summing up responses to a number of job factors seems likely to achieve a more accurate evaluation of job satisfaction. Research, however, doesn't support the intuition.[36] This is one of those rare instances in which simplicity seems to work as well as complexity, making one method essentially as valid as the other. The best explanation is that the concept of job satisfaction is so broad a single question captures its essence. The summation of job facets may also leave out some important data. Both methods are helpful. The single global rating method isn't very time consuming, thus freeing time for other tasks, and the summation of job facets helps managers zero in on problems and deal with them faster and more accurately.

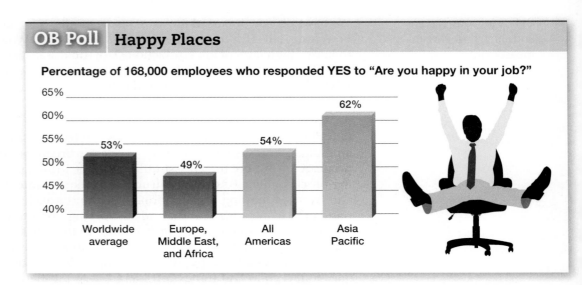

OB Poll | **Happy Places**

Percentage of 168,000 employees who responded YES to "Are you happy in your job?"

Category	Percentage
Worldwide average	53%
Europe, Middle East, and Africa	49%
All Americas	54%
Asia Pacific	62%

Sources: Statista (2013), http://www.statista.com/statistics/224508/employee-job-satisfaction-worldwide/; Kelly Services Group (2012), http://www.kellyocg.com/uploadedFiles/Content/Knowledge/Kelly_Global_Workforce_Index_Content/Acquisition%20and%20Retention%20in%20the%20War%20for%20Talent%20Report.pdf

How Satisfied Are People in Their Jobs?

Are most people satisfied with their jobs? The answer seems to be a qualified "yes" in the United States and most other developed countries. Independent studies conducted among U.S. workers over the past 30 years generally indicate more workers are satisfied with their jobs than not. Thus it shouldn't surprise you that recent research found that average job satisfaction levels were consistently high from 1972 to 2006.[37] But a caution is in order. Recent data show a dramatic drop-off in average job satisfaction levels during the economic contraction that started in late 2007, so much so that only about half of workers report being satisfied with their jobs now.[38]

Research also shows satisfaction levels vary a lot, depending on which facet of job satisfaction you're talking about. As shown in Exhibit 3-3, people have typically been more satisfied with their jobs overall, with the work itself, and with their supervisors and co-workers than they have been with their pay and with promotion opportunities. It's not really clear why people dislike their pay and promotion possibilities more than other aspects of their jobs.[39]

Although job satisfaction appears relevant across cultures, that doesn't mean there are no cultural differences in job satisfaction. Evidence suggests employees in Western cultures have higher levels of job satisfaction than those in Eastern cultures.[40] Exhibit 3-4 provides the results of a global study of job satisfaction levels of workers in 15 countries. As the exhibit shows, the highest levels appear in Mexico and Switzerland. Do employees in these cultures have better jobs? Or are they simply more positive (and less self-critical)? Conversely, the lowest score in the study was for South Korea. There is a lack of autonomy in the South Korean culture and businesses tend to be rigidly hierarchical in structure. Does this make for low job satisfaction?[41] It is difficult to discern all of the factors in the scores, but considering if and how businesses are responding to changes brought on by globalization may give us clues. The South Korean culture, for instance, is in the midst of a clash between traditional and contemporary influences. Businesses that adhere to Confucian values of respect

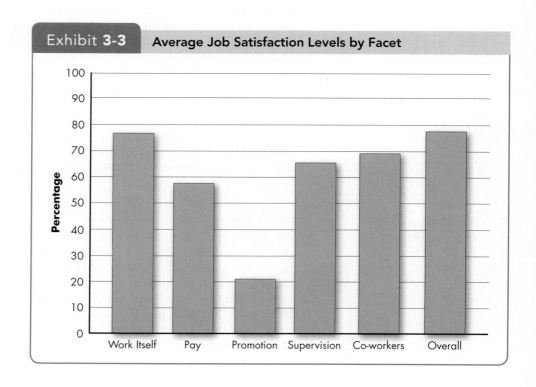

Exhibit 3-3   **Average Job Satisfaction Levels by Facet**

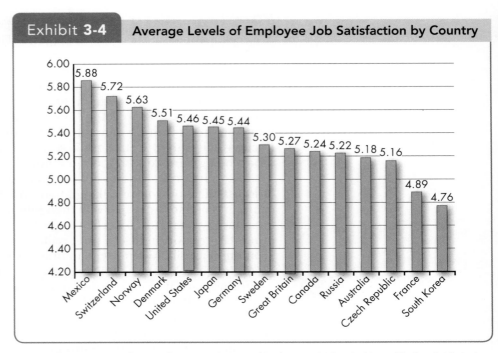

Exhibit 3-4   Average Levels of Employee Job Satisfaction by Country

Mexico 5.88, Switzerland 5.72, Norway 5.63, Denmark 5.51, United States 5.46, Japan 5.45, Germany 5.44, Sweden 5.30, Great Britain 5.27, Canada 5.24, Russia 5.22, Australia 5.18, Czech Republic 5.16, France 4.89, South Korea 4.76

Source: Based on J. H. Westover, "The Impact of Comparative State-Directed Development on Working Conditions and Employee Satisfaction," *Journal of Management & Organization* (July 2012), pp. 537–554.

for elders and authority by maintaining centralized decision-making cannot always compete well with the needed decentralized decision-making processes for globalization.[42] Another factor may be the amount of exposure the culture is getting to diverse ways of life. South Korea has the highest percentage of wireless internet broadband subscriptions of any country (100 percent, or 100 subscriptions per every 100 people), which indicates that people have access to worldwide contemporary business practices. South Korean employees may therefore know about autonomy, merit-based rewards, and benefits for workers in other countries that are unavailable to them. In contrast, Mexico, which has one of the highest job satisfaction scores, has the lowest percentage of internet subscriptions (7.7 percent).[43] The higher job satisfaction rate in Mexico could still indicate there are better jobs for their workers, or that employees are more satisfied in lesser jobs because there is not as much opportunity for exposure to outside contemporary influences. As you can see, higher job satisfaction may somewhat reflect employee acceptance of the culture's business practices, whether the practices are traditional or cutting-edge contemporary. There are also many other potential contributing factors.

What Causes Job Satisfaction?

5 Summarize the main causes of job satisfaction.

Think about the best job you've ever had. What made it so? Chances are you liked the work you did and the people with whom you worked. Interesting jobs that provide training, variety, independence, and control satisfy most employees.[44] A recent European study indicated that job satisfaction is positively correlated with life satisfaction, in that your attitudes and experiences in life spill over into your job approaches and experiences.[45] Interdependence, feedback, social support, and interaction with co-workers outside the workplace are strongly related to job satisfaction, even after accounting for characteristics of the work itself.[46]

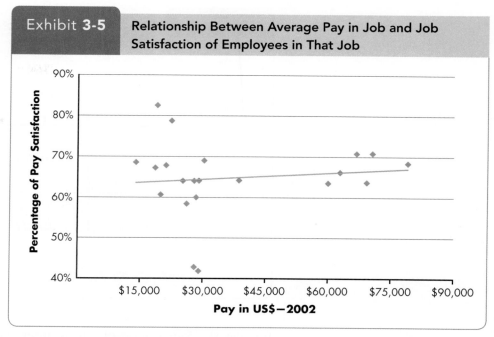

Exhibit 3-5   Relationship Between Average Pay in Job and Job Satisfaction of Employees in That Job

Source: T. A. Judge, R. F. Piccolo, N. P. Podsakoff, J. C. Shaw, and B. L. Rich, "Can Happiness Be 'Earned'? The Relationship Between Pay and Job Satisfaction," working paper, University of Florida, 2005.

You've probably noticed that pay comes up often when people discuss job satisfaction. For people who are poor or who live in poor countries, pay does correlate with job satisfaction and overall happiness. But once an individual reaches a level of comfortable living (in the United States, that occurs at about $40,000 a year, depending on the region and family size), the relationship between pay and job satisfaction virtually disappears. People who earn $80,000 are, on average, no happier with their jobs than those who earn closer to $40,000. Take a look at Exhibit 3-5. It shows the relationship between the average pay for a job and the average level of job satisfaction. As you can see, there isn't much of a relationship there. One researcher even found no significant difference when he compared the overall well-being of the richest people on the *Forbes* 400 list with that of Maasai herders in East Africa.[47]

Money does motivate people, as we will discover in Chapter 6. But what motivates us is not necessarily the same as what makes us happy. A recent study found that people who work for companies with fewer than 100 employees, who supervise others, whose jobs include caregiving, who work in a skilled trade, and who aren't in their 40s are more likely to be happy in their jobs.[48] Job satisfaction is not just about job conditions. Personality also plays a role. Research has shown that people who have positive **core self-evaluations (CSEs)**—who believe in their inner worth and basic competence—are more satisfied with their jobs than those with negative core self-evaluations.

core self-evaluations (CSEs)
Bottom-line conclusions individuals have about their capabilities, competence, and worth as a person.

The Impact of Satisfied and Dissatisfied Employees on the Workplace

6   Identify four employee responses to dissatisfaction.

What happens when employees like their jobs, and when they dislike their jobs? One theoretical model—the exit–voice–loyalty–neglect framework—is helpful in understanding the consequences of dissatisfaction. Exhibit 3-6 illustrates the

Exhibit 3-6   Responses to Dissatisfaction

	Constructive	Destructive
Active	VOICE	EXIT
Passive	LOYALTY	NEGLECT

framework's four responses, which differ along two dimensions: constructive/destructive and active/passive. The responses are as follows:[49]

exit   *Dissatisfaction expressed through behavior directed toward leaving the organization.*

- **Exit.**   The **exit** response directs behavior toward leaving the organization, including looking for a new position as well as resigning. Researchers study individual terminations and *collective turnover*, the total loss to the organization of employee knowledge, skills, abilities, and other characteristics.[50]

voice   *Dissatisfaction expressed through active and constructive attempts to improve conditions.*

- **Voice.**   The **voice** response includes actively and constructively attempting to improve conditions, including suggesting improvements, discussing problems with superiors, and undertaking some forms of union activity.

loyalty   *Dissatisfaction expressed by passively waiting for conditions to improve.*

- **Loyalty.**   The **loyalty** response means passively but optimistically waiting for conditions to improve, including speaking up for the organization in the face of external criticism and trusting the organization and its management to "do the right thing."

neglect   *Dissatisfaction expressed through allowing conditions to worsen.*

- **Neglect.**   The **neglect** response passively allows conditions to worsen and includes chronic absenteeism or lateness, reduced effort, and increased error rate.

Exit and neglect behaviors encompass our performance variables—productivity, absenteeism, and turnover. But this model expands employee response to include voice and loyalty—constructive behaviors that allow individuals to tolerate unpleasant situations or revive satisfactory working conditions. It helps us understand situations, such as we sometimes find among unionized workers, for whom low job satisfaction is coupled with low turnover.[51] Union members often express dissatisfaction through the grievance procedure or formal contract negotiations. These voice mechanisms allow them to continue in their jobs while convincing themselves they are acting to improve the situation.

As helpful as this framework is, it's quite general. We now discuss more specific outcomes of job satisfaction and dissatisfaction in the workplace.

Job Satisfaction and Job Performance   As several studies have concluded, happy workers are more likely to be productive workers. Some researchers used to believe the relationship between job satisfaction and job performance was a myth. But a review of 300 studies suggested the correlation is quite strong.[52] As we move from the individual to the organizational level, we also find support for the satisfaction–performance relationship.[53] When we gather satisfaction and

"Happy Workers Means Happy Profits"

There are exceptions, of course, but this is basically true. A glance at the top 25 of *Fortune*'s Best Companies to Work For reveals a list of recognizable profit leaders: Google, SAS, Edward Jones, and REI, to name a few. However, all happiness is not created equal.

An employee who is happy because his dog just had puppies isn't necessarily going to work harder that day, for instance. In the same way, some employer happiness-inducers seem unrelated to profit increases, such as Google's bowling alley and Irish pub, Facebook's free chocolate lunches, and Salesforce.com's off-the-charts parties. Profit is not about the established benefits, either, though they're important. Employees can appreciate Marriott's hotel discounts, for example, and research indicates employees highly value paid time off, a defined-contribution retirement plan such as a 401(k), and lower health premiums. But many companies offer their employees these benefits and are nowhere near the *Fortune* 500.

It turns out that the value of happiness in the profit equation is in the level of employee engagement. As Julie Gebauer, a managing director for Towers Watson, says, "It's not just about making them happy—that's not a business issue. Engagement is." Job engagement "represents employees' commitment . . . and the level of discretionary effort they are willing to put forth at work," writes Jack in the Box's Senior VP Mark Blankenship. Happy employees with higher job engagement are willing to work hard, make customers happy, and stay with the company—three factors that affect the bottom line in a big way with productivity gains and reduced turnover costs. And many of the Best Companies to Work For report great stock performance. A recent review of 300 studies even revealed that turnover rates resulting from poor attitudes or low engagement led to poorer organizational performance.

So the moral of the story seems to be, treat others as we want to be treated. Pass the chocolate.

Sources: M. H. Blankenship, "Happier Employees + Happier Customers = More Profit," *HR Magazine* (July 2012), pp. 36–38; A. Edmans, "The Link Between Job Satisfaction and Firm Value, with Implications for Corporate Social Responsibility," *Academy of Management Perspectives* (November 2012), pp. 1–19; "Getting Them to Stay," *Workforce Management* (February 2013), p. 19; J. K. Harter et al., "Causal Impact of Employee Work Perceptions on the Bottom Line of Organizations," *Perspectives on Psychological Science* (July 2010), pp. 378–389; T.-Y. Park and J. D. Shaw, "Turnover Rates and Organizational Performance: A Meta-Analysis," *Journal of Applied Psychology* (March 2013), pp. 268–309; and J. Waggoner, "Do Happy Workers Mean Higher Profit?" *USA Today* (February 20, 2013), pp. B1–B2.

productivity data for the organization as a whole, we find organizations with more satisfied employees tend to be more effective than organizations with fewer.

Job Satisfaction and OCB   It seems logical to assume job satisfaction should be a major determinant of an employee's organizational citizenship behavior (OCB), discussed in Chapter 1.[54] Satisfied employees would seem more likely to talk positively about the organization, help others, and go beyond the normal expectations in their job, perhaps because they want to reciprocate their positive experiences. Consistent with this thinking, evidence suggests job satisfaction *is* moderately correlated with OCB; people who are more satisfied with their jobs are more likely to engage in OCB.[55] Why? Fairness perceptions help explain the relationship.[56] Those who feel their co-workers support them are more likely to engage in helpful behaviors, whereas those who have antagonistic relationships with co-workers are less likely to do so.[57] Individuals with certain personality traits are also more satisfied with their work, which in turn leads them to engage in more OCBs.[58] Finally, research shows that when people are in a good mood, they are more likely to engage in OCBs.[59]

Job Satisfaction and Customer Satisfaction   As we noted in Chapter 1, employees in service jobs often interact with customers. Because service organization managers should be concerned with pleasing those customers, it is reasonable to ask, Is employee satisfaction related to positive customer outcomes? For frontline employees who have regular customer contact, the answer is "yes." Satisfied employees increase customer satisfaction and loyalty.[60]

A number of companies are acting on this evidence. The first core value of online retailer Zappos, "Deliver WOW through service," seems fairly obvious,

Photo 3-3 Employee engagement is high at Baptist Health of South Florida, where employees share a serious commitment to patient care and are passionate about the work they do. Looking at an EKG readout, hospital employees Yaima Millan and Marvin Rosete feel their work is meaningful and can make a difference in patients' lives.

Source: AP Photo/Wilfredo Lee.

but the way in which Zappos does it is not. Employees are encouraged to "create fun and a little weirdness" and are given unusual discretion in making customers satisfied; they are encouraged to use their imaginations, like sending flowers to disgruntled customers. Zappos offers a $2,000 bribe to quit the company after training (to weed out the half-hearted).[61]

Job Satisfaction and Absenteeism   We find a consistent negative relationship between satisfaction and absenteeism, but it is moderate to weak.[62] While it certainly makes sense that dissatisfied employees are more likely to miss work, other factors affect the relationship. Organizations that provide liberal sick leave benefits are encouraging all their employees—including those who are highly satisfied—to take days off. You can find work satisfying yet still want to enjoy a 3-day weekend if those days come free with no penalties. When numerous alternative jobs are available, dissatisfied employees have high absence rates, but when there are few they have the same (low) rate of absence as satisfied employees.[63]

Job Satisfaction and Turnover   The relationship between job satisfaction and turnover is stronger than between satisfaction and absenteeism.[64] Recent research suggests that managers looking to determine who might be likely to leave should focus on employees' job satisfaction levels over time, because levels do change. A pattern of lowered job satisfaction is a predictor of possible intent to leave. Job satisfaction has an environmental connection too. If the climate within employee's immediate workplace is one of low job satisfaction, there will be a "contagion effect." This research suggests managers should consider the job satisfaction patterns of co-workers when assigning new workers to a new area for this reason.[65]

The satisfaction–turnover relationship also is affected by alternative job prospects. If an employee is presented with an unsolicited job offer, job dissatisfaction is less predictive of turnover because the employee is more likely leaving in response to "pull" (the lure of the other job) than "push" (the unattractiveness of the current job). Similarly, job dissatisfaction is more likely to translate into turnover when employment opportunities are plentiful because employees

Photo 3-4 Service firms like Air Canada understand that satisfied employees increase customer satisfaction and loyalty. As frontline employees who have regular customer contact, the airline's ticket agents are friendly, upbeat, and responsive while greeting passengers and helping them with luggage check-in and seat assignments.

Source: Bloomberg via Getty Images.

perceive it is easy to move. Also, when employees have high "human capital" (high education, high ability), job dissatisfaction is more likely to translate into turnover because they have, or perceive, many available alternatives.[66] Finally, employees' embeddedness in their jobs and communities can help lower the probability of turnover, particularly in collectivist cultures.[67]

Job Satisfaction and Workplace Deviance   Job dissatisfaction and antagonistic relationships with co-workers predict a variety of behaviors organizations find undesirable, including unionization attempts, substance abuse, stealing at work, undue socializing, and tardiness. Researchers argue these behaviors are indicators of a broader syndrome called *deviant behavior in the workplace* (or *counterproductive behavior* or *employee withdrawal*).[68] If employees don't like their work environment, they'll respond somehow, though it is not always easy to forecast exactly *how*. One worker might quit. Another might use work time to surf the Internet or take work supplies home for personal use. In short, workers who don't like their jobs "get even" in various ways—and because those ways can be quite creative, controlling only one behavior, such as with an absence control policy, leaves the root cause untouched. To effectively control the undesirable consequences of job dissatisfaction, employers should attack the source of the problem—the dissatisfaction—rather than try to control the different responses.

Managers Often "Don't Get It"   Given the evidence we've just reviewed, it should come as no surprise that job satisfaction can affect the bottom line. One study by a management consulting firm separated large organizations into high morale (more than 70 percent of employees expressed overall job satisfaction) and medium or low morale (fewer than 70 percent). The stock prices of companies in the high-morale group grew 19.4 percent, compared with 10 percent for the medium- or low-morale group. Despite these results, many managers are unconcerned about employee job satisfaction. Still others overestimate how satisfied employees are with their jobs, so they don't think there's a problem when there is. In one study of 262 large employers, 86 percent of senior managers believed their organization treated its employees well, but only 55 percent of employees agreed. Another study found 55 percent of managers thought morale was good in their organization, compared to only 38 percent of employees.[69]

Regular surveys can reduce gaps between what managers *think* employees feel and what they *really* feel. This can impact the bottom line in small franchise sites as well as in large companies. For instance, Jonathan McDaniel, manager of a KFC restaurant in Houston, surveys his employees every 3 months. Some results led him to make changes, such as giving employees greater say about which workdays they have off. However, McDaniel believes the process itself is valuable. "They really love giving their opinions," he says. "That's the most important part of it—that they have a voice and that they're heard." Surveys are no panacea, but if job attitudes are as important as we believe, organizations need to find out where they can be improved.[70]

Summary

Managers should be interested in their employees' attitudes because attitudes give warnings of potential problems and influence behavior. Creating a satisfied workforce is hardly a guarantee of successful organizational performance, but evidence strongly suggests that whatever managers can do to improve employee attitudes will likely result in heightened organizational effectiveness all the way to high customer satisfaction—and profits.

Implications for Managers

- Pay attention to your employees' job satisfaction levels as determinants of their performance, turnover, absenteeism, and withdrawal behaviors.
- Measure employee job attitudes objectively and at regular intervals in order to determine how employees are reacting to their work.
- To raise employee satisfaction, evaluate the fit between the employee's work interests and on the intrinsic parts of his/her job to create work that is challenging and interesting to the individual.
- Consider the fact that high pay alone is unlikely to create a satisfying work environment.

Employer–Employee Loyalty Is an Outdated Concept

POINT

The word *loyalty* is horribly outdated. Long gone are the days when an employer would keep an employee for life, as are the days when an employee would work for a single company for his or her entire career.

Workplace guru Linda Gratton says, "Loyalty is dead—killed off through shortening contracts, outsourcing, automation and multiple careers. Faced with what could be 50 years of work, who honestly wants to spend that much time with one company? Serial monogamy is the order of the day." Everyone agrees; in a recent study, only 59 percent of employers reported they felt very loyal to their employees, while a mere 32 percent believed their employers were loyal to them.

The commitment on each side of the equation is weak. For example, Renault ended the 31-year career of employee Michel Balthazard (and two others) on false charges of espionage. When the wrongness of the charges became public, Renault halfheartedly offered the employees their jobs back and a lame apology: "Renault thanks them for the quality of their work at the group and wishes them every success in the future."

As for employee's loyalty to their employers, that is worth little nowadays. One manager with Deloitte says the current employee attitude is, "I'm leaving, I had a great experience, and I'm taking that with me." There just isn't an expectation of loyalty. In fact, only 9 percent of recent college graduates would stay with an employer for more than a year if they didn't like the job, research showed.

The sooner we see the employment experience for what it is (mostly transactional, mostly short to medium term), the better off we'll be. The workplace is no place for fantasies.

COUNTERPOINT

There are employers and employees who show little regard for each other. That each side can be uncaring or cavalier is hardly a revelation. No doubt such cynical attitudes are as old as the employment relationship itself.

But is that the norm? And is it desirable? The answer to both these questions is "no."

Says management guru Tom Peters, "Bottom line: loyalty matters. A lot. Yesterday. Today. Tomorrow." University of Michigan's Dave Ulrich says, "Leaders who encourage loyalty want employees who are not only committed to and engaged in their work but who also find meaning from it."

It is true that the employer–employee relationship has changed. For example, (largely) gone are the days when employers provide guaranteed payout pensions to which employees contribute nothing. But is that such a bad thing? There is a big difference between asking employees to contribute to their pension plans and abandoning plans altogether (or firing without cause).

Moreover, it's not that loyalty is dead, but rather that employers are loyal to a different kind of employee. Gone are the days when an employer would refuse to fire a long-tenured but incompetent employee. But is that the kind of loyalty most employees expect today anyway? Companies are loyal to employees who do their jobs well, and that too is as it should be. Constantly training new employees wears down morale and profitability.

In short, employees still expect certain standards of decency and loyalty from their employers, and employers want engaged, committed employees in return. That is a good thing—and not so different from yesterday. Says workplace psychologist Binna Kandola, "Workplaces may have changed but loyalty is not dead—the bonds between people are too strong."

Sources: "If You Started a Job and You Didn't Like It, How Long Would You Stay?" *USA Today* (June 11, 2012), p. 1B; O. Gough and S. Arkani, "The Impact of the Shifting Pensions Landscape on the Psychological Contract," *Personnel Review* 40, no. 2 (2011), pp. 173–184; "Loyalty Gap Widens," *USA Today* (May 16, 2012), p. 1B; P. Korkki, "The Shifting Definition of Worker Loyalty," *The New York Times* (April 24, 2011), p. BU8; and "Is Workplace Loyalty an Outmoded Concept?" *Financial Times* (March 8, 2011), www.ft.com/.

END-OF-CHAPTER REVIEW

MyManagementLab

Go to **mymanagementlab.com** to complete the problems marked with this icon. ⭐

QUESTIONS FOR REVIEW

3-1 What are the main components of attitudes? Are these components related or unrelated?

3-2 Does behavior always follow from attitudes? Why or why not? Discuss the factors that affect whether behavior follows from attitudes.

3-3 What are the major job attitudes? In what ways are these attitudes alike? What is unique about each?

3-4 How do we measure job satisfaction?

3-5 What causes job satisfaction? For most people, is pay or the work itself more important?

⭐3-6 What outcomes does job satisfaction influence? What implications does this have for management?

EXPERIENTIAL EXERCISE   What Factors Are Most Important to Your Job Satisfaction?

Most of us probably want a job we think will satisfy us. But because no job is perfect, we often have to trade off job attributes. One job may pay well but provide limited opportunities for advancement or skill development. Another may offer work we enjoy but have poor benefits. The following is a list of 21 job factors or attributes:

- Autonomy and independence.
- Benefits.
- Career advancement opportunities.
- Career development opportunities.
- Compensation/pay.
- Communication between employees and management.
- Contribution of work to organization's business goals.
- Feeling safe in the work environment.
- Flexibility to balance life and work issues.
- Job security.
- Job-specific training.
- Management recognition of employee job performance.
- Meaningfulness of job.
- Networking.

- Opportunities to use skills/abilities.
- Organization's commitment to professional development.
- Overall corporate culture.
- Relationship with co-workers.
- Relationship with immediate supervisor.
- The work itself.
- The variety of work.

On a sheet of paper, rank-order these from top to bottom so number 1 is the job factor you think is most important to your job satisfaction, number 2 is the second most important, and so on.

Next, gather in teams of three or four people and try the following:

- Appoint a spokesperson who will take notes and report to the class your group's answers to the following questions.

    3-7. Averaging across all members in your group, generate a list of the top five job factors.

    3-8. Did most people in your group seem to value the same job factors? Why or why not?

    3-9. Your instructor will provide you the results of a study of a random sample of 600 employees conducted by the Society for Human Resource Management (SHRM). How do your group's rankings compare with the SHRM results?

3-10. The chapter says pay doesn't correlate all that well with job satisfaction, but in the SHRM survey, people say it is relatively important. Can your group suggest a reason for the apparent discrepancy?

3-11. Now examine your own list again. Does your list agree with the group list? Does your list agree with the SHRM study?

ETHICAL DILEMMA Bounty Hunters

His SUV carefully obscured behind a row of trees, Rick Raymond, private investigator, was on another case. His goal was not to catch an unfaithful spouse or petty criminal in action. Instead, at the request of the man's employer, Raymond was tracking an Orlando repairman to see whether he was sick as he claimed today, and as he had claimed to be several times recently.

As we have seen, absenteeism is a huge problem for organizations that has left them desperate for solutions. One solution is to investigate. When an employee calls in sick an abnormal number of times, the employer may hire a P.I. to follow the employee and photograph or videotape his or her activity outside the house. Private investigators also are used to ascertain whether individuals filing injury claims (and drawing worker's compensation benefits) are, in fact, injured.

Hiring private investigators to follow employees is legal. So is monitoring employees' social media presence when they are "out ill" and questioning co-workers and friends. But one problem for employers is that sick-leave policies are different for every company and sometimes for different divisions within one company, leaving the interpretation up to administrators or employees. Some plans, for instance, allow employees to give unused sick leave to other employees, to accumulate it from year to year, and/or to receive compensation for it. Some policies conflict with union rules. Some administrators allow sick leave to be used for other purposes, which can backfire on the employee when there is a change in administration. These situations all present ethical problems for management.

If it seems the best sick leave policy might be no policy, think again: New York recently joined the list of cities requiring paid sick leave. Others include Portland, Seattle, San Francisco, Long Beach, and Washington, DC. Other regions are sure to follow. But despite these efforts at standardization, ethical questions will remain for developing and administering the best company policies.

Many consider paid sick leave an act of fairness. "This is not a significant increase in expense, and it has a huge impact on the quality of life that the employees have," Massachusetts State Senator Daniel Wolf said. "This will make an absolute difference in the lives of people."

Questions

3-12. If you had reason to believe someone was lying about an absence from work, do you think it would be appropriate to investigate? If so, by what methods?

3-13. If excessive absenteeism is a real problem in an organization, are there alternatives to surveillance? If so, what are they, and do they have any limitations of their own?

3-14. How might an organization help to curb sick leave abuse through its policies? How might administrators help or hinder effective implementation of those policies?

Sources: E. Applebaum, "Business Attitudes Toward Paid Sick Leave Are Changing," *U.S. News and World Report* (March 6, 2013), www.usnews.com/opinion/blogs/economic-intelligence/2013/03/06/business-attitudes-toward-paid-sick-leave-are-changing; D. Levine, "Oracle Enlists Private Eyes to Find HP CEO," *Reuters* (November 9, 2010), http://in.reuters.com/; M. Woolhouse, "Support Grows for Legislation Requiring Paid Sick Leave," *Boston Globe* (April 15, 2013), www.bostonglobe.com/business/2013/04/14/proposal-mandate-paid-sick-days-gaining-momentum/8whRYPA3yNN8TgZgIrEFLL/story.html; and E. Spitznagel, "The Sick-Day Bounty Hunters," *Bloomberg Businessweek* (December 6, 2010), pp. 93–95.

CASE INCIDENT 1 The Pursuit of Happiness: Flexibility

The management team at Learner's Edge, an online continuing education company, decided to adopt a ROWE (results-only work environment) policy, developed by Best Buy employees and summarized in its slogan, "Work whenever you want, wherever you want, as long as the work gets done." Kyle Pederson was one of only three Learner's Edge employees who showed up the first day of the experiment. And the second day, and the third.

"For almost a month, everyone cleared out," Pederson said. "It was just me, my co-founder and our executive director all wondering, 'What on earth have we done?'"

Clearly, they were testing the outer limits of workplace flexibility, from which even Best Buy pulled back when it recently canceled the program. But while Best Buy reported continuing financial woes as one reason for canceling their ROWE program, employers like Learner's Edge report "better work, higher productivity" after the initial phase of the program in their companies. Employees have learned the ways they work best. In fact, some of Pederson's employees have returned to the office, while others gather at Starbucks or over dinner . . . whatever gets the work done.

Suntell president and chief operating officer, Veronica Wooten, whose risk management software firm adopted the ROWE program a few years ago, is also a fan of the flexible workplace. "We made the transition, and started letting go and letting people make their own decisions," Wooten says. Her company's customer base increased 20 percent, meetings were reduced by 50 percent, and expenses decreased 12 percent (Wooten used the savings to give everyone a raise).

It seems that everyone should be happy with this degree of job flexibility, from the night-owl employee to the board of directors. But happiness, like job satisfaction, is a complex construct.

Employees worldwide do seem to increasingly value flexible work environments, with roughly two of three workers of all ages wanting to work from home, at least occasionally. Eighty percent of the U.S. female labor force finds a flexible work schedule very or extremely important, 58 percent rate work–life balance as their number-one goal, and flexibility is the single most important part of that balance for them. Southeast Asian employees are most interested in flexibility, while workers in North America, Europe, and the Australia/New Zealand region place flexibility in their top three wants.

Yet research correlates job satisfaction most strongly with the nature of the work itself, not where it is performed. Thus, while as employees we say we want flexibility, what actually makes us satisfied is often something else. Then there are the costs of such work arrangements. Employers like Yahoo!'s Marissa Mayer are concerned that flexible workers will become detached from the organization, communicate less, be less available, and lose the benefits of teamwork. Employees have similar concerns: Will out of sight mean out of mind? International research suggests that employee and employer happiness depends on correctly motivating the individual. For ROWE or any flexible arrangement to work, companies need to create clear job descriptions, set attainable goals, and rely on strong metrics to indicate productivity. Managers need to foster close connections and communicate meaningfully to keep flexible workers engaged in the company, its culture, and its processes. And employees need to get the work done, no matter where and when they do it.

Questions

✪ **3-15.** Do you think only certain individuals are attracted to flexible work arrangements (FWAs)? Why or why not?

3-16. What characteristics of FWAs might contribute to increased levels of job satisfaction?

3-17. How do you see FWAs affecting a company's bottom line?

Sources: "2013 Women's Research Reveals How to Make Women Happy (In the Workplace)," Accenture, www.accenture.com/us-en/pages/insight-what-means-have-all.aspx (March 1, 2013); L. Belkin, "Is ROWE the Future of Work? Or an Unworkable Fantasy?" *The Huffington Post Business* (April 17, 2013), www.huffingtonpost.com/2013/04/15/rowe-future-work_n_3084426.html; R. R. Hastings, "Full Engagement Lacking Around World," *Society for Human Resources Management* (January 3, 2011), www.shrm.org/hrdisciplines/employeerelations/articles/Pages/FullEngagementLacking.aspx; A. McGrory-Dixon, "Workplace Flexibility, Equity Important for Millennials," *Benefits Pro* (April 19, 2013), www.benefitspro.com/2013/04/19/workplace-flexibility-equity-important-for-millenn; and F. Origo and L. Pagani, "Workplace Flexibility and Job Satisfaction: Some Evidence from Europe," *International Journal of Manpower* 29 (2008), pp. 539–566.

CASE INCIDENT 2 Job Crafting

Consider for a moment a midlevel manager, Fatima, who seems to be doing well. She's consistently making her required benchmarks and goals, she has built successful relationships with colleagues, and senior management has identified her as having "high potential." But she isn't happy with her work. She'd be much more interested in understanding how her organization can use social media in marketing efforts at all levels of the organization. Ideally, she'd like to quit and find something that better suits her passions, but in the current economic environment this may not be an option. So she has decided to proactively reconfigure her current job.

Fatima is part of a movement toward job "crafting," which is the process of deliberately reorganizing your job so that it better fits your motives, strengths, and passions. The process of job crafting can start with creating diagrams of day-to-day activities with a coach. Then you and the coach can collaboratively identify which tasks fit with your personal passions and which tend to drain motivation and satisfaction. Next you and your coach can work together to imagine ways to emphasize preferred activities and de-emphasize those that are less interesting. Many people engaged in job crafting find that upon deeper consideration, they have more control over their work than they thought.

So how did Fatima craft her job? She first noticed that she was spending too much of her time monitoring her team's performance and answering team questions and not enough time working on the creative projects that inspire her. She then considered how to modify her relationship with the team so that these activities incorporated her passion for social media strategies, with team activities more centered around developing new marketing. She also identified members of her team who might be able to help her implement these new strategies and directed her interactions with these individuals toward her new goals. As a result, not only has her engagement in her work increased, but she has also developed new ideas that are being recognized and advanced within the organization. In sum, she has found that by actively and creatively examining her work, she has been able to craft her current job into one that is truly satisfying.

As you may have noted, Fatima exhibited a proactive personality—she was eager to develop her own options and find her own resources. Proactive individuals are often self-empowered and are, therefore, more open to seeking workable solutions when they are not satisfied. Research would lead us to believe Fatima will be successful in her customized job. In fact, it is quite possible her employer never would have helped her craft a better job had she not sought help and that her proactivity is responsible for her success. To the extent possible, then, all employees should feel encouraged to be proactive in creating their best work situations.

Questions

3-18. Why do you think many people are in jobs that are not satisfying? Do organizations help people craft satisfying and motivating jobs, and if not, why not?

✪ **3-19.** Think about how you might reorient yourself to your own job. Are the principles of job crafting described here relevant to your work? Why or why not?

3-20. Are there any potential drawbacks to the job crafting approach? How can these concerns be minimized?

Sources: A. B. Bakker, M. Tims, and D. Derks, "Proactive Personality and Job Performance: The Role of Job Crafting and Work Engagement," *Human Relations* (October 2012), pp. 1359–1378; A. Wrzesniewski, J. M. Berg, and J. E. Dutton, "Turn the Job You Have into the Job You Want," *Harvard Business Review* (June 2010), pp. 114–117; A. Wrzesniewski and J. E. Dutton, "Crafting a Job: Revisioning Employees as Active Crafters of Their Work," *Academy of Management Review* 26 (2010), pp. 179–201; and J. Caplan, "Hate Your Job? Here's How to Reshape It," *Time* (December 4, 2009), www.time.com.

MyManagementLab

Go to **mymanagementlab.com** for Auto-graded writing questions as well as the following Assisted-graded writing questions:

3-21. Based on your reading from the chapter and Case Incident 1, how might increased job satisfaction from FWAs relate to employee job performance, citizenship behavior, and turnover?

3-22. In consideration of Case Incident 2, some contend that job crafting sounds good in principle but is not necessarily available to everyone. What types of jobs are probably not good candidates for job crafting activities?

3-23. MyManagementLab Only—comprehensive writing assignment for this chapter.

4

Emotions and Moods

MyManagementLab®
⭐ **Improve Your Grade!**

When you see this icon, visit **www.mymanagementlab.com** for activities that are applied, personalized, and offer immediate feedback.

AFFECTIVE COMPUTING: READING YOUR MIND

I magine you're sitting in a plastic chair in a dim basement classroom. The only sound is the instructor's voice in the dullest instructional film you have ever seen. You start to stare. Suddenly, your ear bud crackles to life. "I see you are feeling bored," a computer says, and the video switches to today's high-energy management lesson. Is this the classroom of the future?

Thanks to affective computing, which allows computers to read emotions from facial expressions, middle-school classrooms have already tested this kind of technology. Researchers hope it can soon be used to tell whether students in online classes are bored and need more challenging questions, for instance, or confused and need more help. The potential ranges far beyond education to limitless applications for managing people in organizations. The Massachusetts Institute of Technology (MIT) Media Lab is currently programming computers to use 24 facial points to infer an emotion, for instance. What if computers could be made emotionally intelligent, to help a person get past frustration into productivity? What if managers could automatically receive reports on virtual employees' emotions? What if sensors could help employees stay well by providing feedback on their emotional reactions to stress?

Affective computing can provide managers with in-the-moment help. At MIT's lab, a tiny traffic light, visible only to the wearer, flashes yellow when a listener's face indicates lack of engagement in the conversation and red for complete disengagement. These cues could help a manager delivering important safety information to an employee, for instance. The MIT team has also developed wristbands that sense emotional states and activity levels. These could help managers work with employees who are on the Asperger's or autism spectrum. "With this technology in the future, we'll be able to understand things . . . that we weren't able to see before, things that calm them, things that stress them," said Rosalind Picard, the team's director.

With this possibility comes responsibility, of course. There are obvious ethical issues that will only grow with the technology's increasing sophistication. Employees may not want computers to read their emotions either for their managers or for automatic feedback. "We want to have some control over how we display ourselves to others," said Nick Bostrom of the University of Oxford's Future of Humanity Institute.

There are also limits to affective computing's ability to interpret emotions correctly, particularly across cultures. Work is progressing in Egypt and other countries, but "if we don't have enough samples, across cultures and age ranges, the machine won't be able to discriminate these subtle expressions," said Rana el Kaliouby of the MIT lab. Organizations will eventually have to decide when it is appropriate to read employees' emotions, as well as which emotions. In the meantime, according to affective computing experts,

LEARNING OBJECTIVES

After studying this chapter, you should be able to:

1 Differentiate between emotions and moods.

2 Discuss whether emotions are rational and what functions they serve.

3 Identify the sources of emotions and moods.

4 Show the impact emotional labor has on employees.

5 Describe affective events theory and its applications.

6 Contrast the evidence for and against the existence of emotional intelligence.

7 Identify strategies for emotion regulation and their likely effects.

8 Apply concepts about emotions and moods to specific OB issues.

people are still the best readers of emotions from facial cues. Perhaps there is an opportunity to get to know your employees before the cameras roll.

Sources: "Affective Computing," MIT webpage, http://affect.media.mit.edu/; "Affective Computing and Intelligent Interaction 2013," IEEE Computer Society Annual Conference webpage, www.acii2013.org/; and K. Weintraub, "But How Do You Really Feel? Someday the Computer May Know," *The New York Times* (October 16, 2012), p. D3.

W hether or not your employer has a sensor trained on you to gauge your emotions, your emotions do matter to the workplace. It might surprise you that, until recently, the field of OB has given the topic of emotions little attention.[1] Why? We offer two possible explanations.

First is the *myth of rationality*.[2] Until very recently, the protocol of the work world kept a damper on emotions. A well-run organization didn't allow employees to express frustration, fear, anger, love, hate, joy, grief, or similar feelings thought to be the antithesis of rationality. Although researchers and managers knew emotions were an inseparable part of everyday life, they tried to create organizations that were emotion-free. Of course, that wasn't possible.

The second explanation is that many believed emotions of any kind were disruptive.[3] Researchers looked at strong negative emotions—especially anger—that interfered with an employee's ability to work effectively. They rarely viewed emotions as constructive or contributing to enhanced performance.

Certainly some emotions, particularly exhibited at the wrong time, can hinder performance. But employees do bring their emotions to work every day, and no study of OB would be comprehensive without considering their role in workplace behavior.

SELF-ASSESSMENT LIBRARY

How Are You Feeling Right Now?

In the Self-Assessment Library (available in MyManagementLab), take assessment IV.D.1 (How Are You Feeling Right Now?) and answer the following questions.

1. What was higher—your positive mood score or negative mood score? How do these scores compare with those of your classmates?
2. Did your score surprise you? Why or why not?
3. What sorts of things influence your positive moods, your negative moods?

What Are Emotions and Moods?

1 Differentiate between emotions and moods.

affect *A broad range of feelings that people experience.*

emotions *Intense feelings that are directed at someone or something.*

In our analysis, we'll need three terms that are closely intertwined: *affect, emotions,* and *moods.*

Affect is a generic term that covers a broad range of feelings people experience, including both emotions and moods.[4] **Emotions** are intense feelings directed at someone or something.[5] **Moods** are less intense feelings than emotions and often (though not always) arise without a specific event acting as a stimulus.[6]

moods *Feelings that tend to be less intense than emotions and that lack a contextual stimulus.*

Most experts believe emotions are more fleeting than moods.[7] For example, if someone is rude to you, you'll feel angry. That intense emotion probably comes and goes fairly quickly, maybe even in a matter of seconds. When you're in a bad mood, though, you can feel bad for several hours.

Emotions are reactions to a person (seeing a friend at work may make you feel glad) or an event (dealing with a rude client may make you feel frustrated). You show your emotions when you're "happy about something, angry at someone, afraid of something."[8] Moods, in contrast, aren't usually directed at a person or an event. But emotions can turn into moods when you lose focus on the event or object that started the feeling. And, by the same token, good or bad moods can make you more emotional in response to an event. So when a colleague criticizes how you spoke to a client, you might show emotion (anger) toward a specific object (your colleague). But as the specific emotion dissipates, you might just feel generally dispirited. You can't attribute this feeling to any single event; you're just not your normal self. You might then overreact to other events. This affect state describes a mood. Exhibit 4-1 shows the relationships among affect, emotions, and mood.

First, as the exhibit shows, *affect* is a broad term that encompasses emotions and moods. Second, there are differences between emotions and moods. Some of these differences—that emotions are more likely to be caused by a specific event and emotions are more fleeting than moods—we just discussed. Other differences are subtler. For example, unlike moods, emotions like anger and disgust tend to be more clearly revealed by facial expressions. Also, some researchers speculate that emotions may be more action-oriented—they may lead us to some immediate action—while moods may be more cognitive, meaning they may cause us to think or brood for a while.[9]

Finally, the exhibit shows that emotions and moods are closely connected and can influence each other. Getting your dream job may generate the emotion of joy, which can put you in a good mood for several days. Similarly, if you're in a good or bad mood, it might make you experience a more intense positive or negative emotion than otherwise. In a bad mood, you might blow up in response to a co-worker's comment that would normally have generated only a mild reaction.

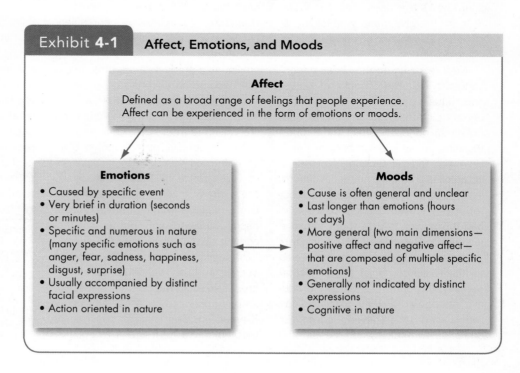

Exhibit 4-1   Affect, Emotions, and Moods

Affect
Defined as a broad range of feelings that people experience. Affect can be experienced in the form of emotions or moods.

Emotions
- Caused by specific event
- Very brief in duration (seconds or minutes)
- Specific and numerous in nature (many specific emotions such as anger, fear, sadness, happiness, disgust, surprise)
- Usually accompanied by distinct facial expressions
- Action oriented in nature

Moods
- Cause is often general and unclear
- Last longer than emotions (hours or days)
- More general (two main dimensions—positive affect and negative affect—that are composed of multiple specific emotions)
- Generally not indicated by distinct expressions
- Cognitive in nature

Affect, emotions, and moods are separable in theory; in practice the distinction isn't always crystal-clear. In some areas, researchers have studied mostly moods, in other areas mainly emotions. So, when we review the OB topics on emotions and moods, you may see more information about emotions in one area and about moods in another. This is simply the state of the research.

The Basic Emotions

How many emotions are there? There are dozens, including anger, contempt, enthusiasm, envy, fear, frustration, disappointment, embarrassment, disgust, happiness, hate, hope, jealousy, joy, love, pride, surprise, and sadness. Numerous researchers have tried to limit them to a fundamental set.[10] But some argue that it makes no sense to think in terms of "basic" emotions because even emotions we rarely experience, such as shock, can have a powerful effect on us.[11]

As the complexity of affective computing programming we discussed at the beginning of the chapter shows, psychologists try to identify basic emotions by studying facial expressions but have found the process difficult.[12] One problem is that some emotions are too complex to be easily represented on our faces. Cultures also have norms that govern emotional expression, so the way

"Smile, and the Work World Smiles with You"

It is true that a smile is used as social currency in most organizations to create a positive atmosphere, and it usually creates an unconscious reflexive return smile. However, anyone who has ever smiled at an angry manager knows this doesn't always work. In truth, the giving and withholding of smiles is an unconscious power play of office politics.

New research on the "boss effect" suggests that the amount of power and status a person feels over another person dictates who will smile. Subordinates generally smile more often than their bosses smile back at them. However, the perception of power is complex and varies by national culture: in a recent study, Chinese workers reflexively smiled only at bosses who had the power to give them negative job evaluations, while U.S. participants smiled most to managers perceived to have higher social power. Other researchers found that when individuals felt powerful, they usually didn't return even a high-ranking individual's smile. Conversely, when people felt

powerless, they returned everyone's smiles.

While we think of smiling as a choice, smiling (or concealing a smile) is often unconscious. Researchers are finding that social pressure affects neurobiology. "It shapes your neural architecture," said cognitive neuroscientist Sook-Lei Liew. Smile reactions are, therefore, partially involuntary; when smiling is a product of our attitudes, it can become an unconscious process. Thus, "Your feelings about power and status seem to dictate how much you are willing to return a smile to another person," cognitive neuroscientist Evan Carr affirmed.

The science of smiling transcends the expression of emotion. While an angry manager may not smile back, a happy manager might not as well, according to the "boss effect" research. "The relationship of what we show on our face and how we feel is a very loose one," said Arvid Kappas, a professor of emotion research at Jacobs University Bremen in Germany. This suggests that, when we want to display positive

emotions to others, we should do more than smile, such as when service representatives try to create happy moods in their customers with excited voice pitch, encouraging gestures, and energetic body movement.

The science of smiling is an area of current research, but it is clear already that knowing about the "boss effect" suggests many practical applications. For one, managers and employees can be made more aware of ingrained tendencies toward others and, through careful self-observation, change their habits. Comprehensive displays of positive emotion using voice inflection, gestures, and word choice may also be more helpful in building good business relationships than the simple smile.

Sources: R. L. Hotz, "Too Important to Smile Back: The 'Boss Effect,'" *The Wall Street Journal* (October 16, 2012), p. D2; E. Kim and D. J. Yoon, "Why Does Service with a Smile Make Employees Happy? A Social Interaction Model," *Journal of Applied Psychology* 97 (2012), pp. 1059–1967; and K. Weintraub, "But How Do You Really Feel? Someday the Computer May Know," *The New York Times* (October 16, 2012), p. D3.

we *experience* an emotion isn't always the same as the way we *show* it. People in the United States and the Middle East recognize a smile as indicating happiness, but in the Middle East a smile is also more likely to be seen as a sign of sexual attraction, so women have learned not to smile at men. In collectivist countries, people are more likely to believe another's emotional displays have something to do with the relationship between them, while people in individualistic cultures don't think others' emotional expressions are directed at them. French retail clerks, for example, are infamous for being surly toward customers. German shoppers have reportedly been turned off by Walmart's friendly greeters and helpful staff.[13]

It's unlikely psychologists or philosophers will ever completely agree on a set of basic emotions, or even on whether there is such a thing. Still, many researchers agree on six essentially universal emotions—anger, fear, sadness, happiness, disgust, and surprise.[14] Some even plot them along a continuum: happiness—surprise—fear—sadness—anger—disgust.[15] The closer two emotions are to each other on this continuum, the more likely people will confuse them. We sometimes mistake happiness for surprise, but rarely do we confuse happiness and disgust. In addition, as we'll see later on, cultural factors can also influence interpretations.

The Basic Moods: Positive and Negative Affect

One way to classify emotions is to ask whether they are positive or negative.[16] Positive emotions—such as joy and gratitude—express a favorable evaluation or feeling. Negative emotions—such as anger or guilt—express the opposite. Keep in mind that emotions can't be neutral. Being neutral is being nonemotional.[17]

When we group emotions into positive and negative categories, they become mood states because we are now looking at them more generally instead of isolating one particular emotion. In Exhibit 4-2, excited is a pure marker of high positive affect, while boredom is a pure marker of low negative affect. Nervous is a pure marker of high negative affect; relaxed is a pure marker of low positive affect. Finally, some emotions—such as contentment (a mixture of high positive affect and low positive affect) and sadness (a mixture of low negative affect and high negative affect)—are in between. You'll notice this model does not include all emotions. Some, such as surprise, don't fit well because they're not as clearly positive or negative.

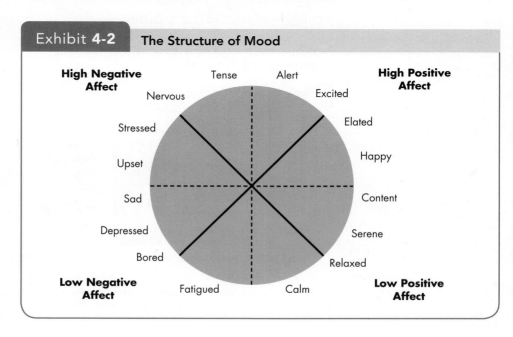

Exhibit 4-2   The Structure of Mood

positive affect *A mood dimension that consists of specific positive emotions such as excitement, self-assurance, and cheerfulness at the high end and boredom, sluggishness, and tiredness at the low end.*

negative affect *A mood dimension that consists of emotions such as nervousness, stress, and anxiety at the high end and relaxation, tranquility, and poise at the low end.*

positivity offset *The tendency of most individuals to experience a mildly positive mood at zero input (when nothing in particular is going on).*

So, we can think of **positive affect** as a mood dimension consisting of positive emotions such as excitement, alertness, and elation at the high end and contentedness, calmness, and serenity at the low end. **Negative affect** is a mood dimension consisting of nervousness, stress, and anxiety at the high end and boredom, depression, and fatigue at the low end. (*Note:* Positive and negative affect *are* moods. We're using these labels, rather than *positive mood* and *negative mood*, because that's how researchers label them.)

Negative emotions are likely to become negative moods. People think about events that created strong negative emotions five times as long as they do about events that created strong positive ones.[18] So, we should expect people to recall negative experiences more readily than positive ones. Perhaps one reason is that, for most of us, negative experiences also are more unusual. Indeed, research finds a **positivity offset**, meaning that at zero input (when nothing in particular is going on), most individuals experience a mildly positive mood.[19] So for most people, positive moods are somewhat more common than negative moods. The positivity offset also appears to operate at work. One study of customer-service representatives in a British call center (a job where it's probably difficult to feel positive) revealed people reported experiencing positive moods 58 percent of the time.[20]

Does the degree to which people experience these positive and negative emotions vary across cultures? Yes. In China, people report experiencing fewer positive and negative emotions than people in other cultures, and the emotions they experience are less intense. Compared with Mainland Chinese, Taiwanese are more like U.S. workers in their experience of emotions: On average, they report more positive and fewer negative emotions than their Chinese counterparts.[21] People in most cultures appear to experience certain positive and negative emotions, but the frequency and intensity varies to some degree. Despite these differences, people from all over the world interpret negative and positive emotions in much the same way. We all view negative emotions, such as hate, terror, and rage, as dangerous and destructive, and we desire positive emotions, such as joy, love, and happiness. However, some cultures value certain emotions more than others. U.S. culture values enthusiasm, while the Chinese consider negative emotions more useful and constructive than do people in the United

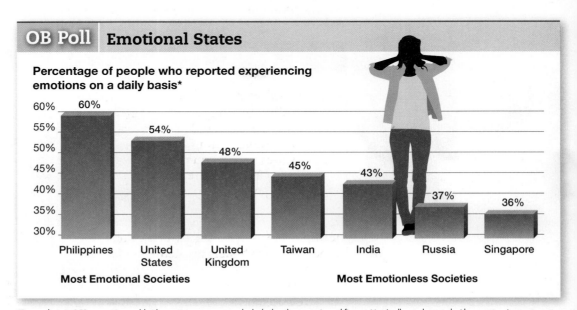

OB Poll   Emotional States

Percentage of people who reported experiencing emotions on a daily basis*

60%	54%	48%	45%	43%	37%	36%
Philippines	United States	United Kingdom	Taiwan	India	Russia	Singapore

Most Emotional Societies   **Most Emotionless Societies**

*Respondents in 150+ countries worldwide over two years were asked whether they experienced five positive (well-rested, treated with respect, enjoyment, smiling and laughing, learning or doing something interesting) and five negative emotions (anger, stress, sadness, physical pain, worry) daily.
Source: J. Clifton, "Singapore Ranks as Least Emotional Country in the World," *Gallup* (November 21, 2012), http://www.gallup.com/poll/158882/singapore-ranks-least-emotional-country-world.aspx.

States. Recent research has suggested that negative affect actually has many benefits. Visualizing the worst-case scenario often allows people to accept present circumstances and cope, for instance.[22] Negative affect can allow managers to think more critically and fairly, other research indicates.[23] Pride is generally a positive emotion in Western individualistic cultures such as the United States, but Eastern cultures such as China and Japan view pride as undesirable.[24]

The Function of Emotions

2 Discuss whether emotions are rational and what functions they serve.

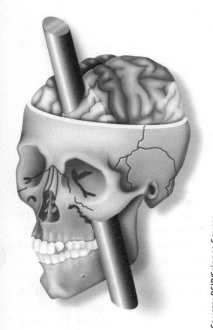

Source: BSIP/Science Source.

Photo 4-1 By studying brain injuries, such as the injury experienced by Phineas Gage whose skull is illustrated here, researchers discovered an important link between emotions and rational thinking. They learned that our emotions provide us with valuable information that helps our thinking process.

Do Emotions Make Us Irrational?   How often have you heard someone say, "Oh, you're just being emotional"? You might have been offended. The famous astronomer Carl Sagan once wrote, "Where we have strong emotions, we're liable to fool ourselves." These observations suggest rationality and emotion are in conflict and that if you exhibit emotion you are likely to act irrationally. One team of authors argues that displaying emotions such as sadness to the point of crying is so toxic to a career that we should leave the room rather than allow others to witness it.[25] These perspectives suggest the demonstration or even experience of emotions can make us seem weak, brittle, or irrational. However, research is increasingly showing that emotions are actually critical to rational thinking. There has been evidence of such a link for a long time.

Consider Phineas Gage, a railroad worker in Vermont. One September day in 1848, a 3-foot 7-inch iron bar flew into his lower-left jaw and out through the top of his skull from an explosive charge. Remarkably, Gage survived his injury, was able to read and speak, and performed well above average on cognitive ability tests. However, he completely lost his ability to experience emotion. Gage's inability to express emotion eventually took away his ability to reason. As a result, he often behaved erratically and against his self-interests. Gage drifted from job to job, eventually joining a circus. In commenting on Gage's condition, one expert noted, "Reason may not be as pure as most of us think it is or wish it were . . . emotions and feelings may not be intruders in the bastion of reason at all: they may be enmeshed in its networks, for worse *and* for better."[26]

The example of Phineas Gage and many other brain injury studies show we must have the ability to experience emotions to be rational. Why? Because our emotions provide important information about how we understand the world around us. For instance, a recent study indicated that individuals in a negative mood are better able to discern truthful from accurate information than people in a happy mood.[27] Would we really want a manager to make a decision about firing an employee without regarding either his or the employee's emotions? The key to good decision making is to employ both thinking *and* feeling in our decisions.

Do Emotions Make Us Ethical?   A growing body of research has begun to examine the relationship between emotions and moral attitudes.[28] It was previously believed that, like decision making in general, most ethical decision making was based on higher-order cognitive processes, but research on moral emotions increasingly questions this perspective. Examples of moral emotions include sympathy for the suffering of others, guilt about our own immoral behavior, anger about injustice done to others, contempt for those who behave unethically, and disgust at violations of moral norms. Numerous studies suggest that these reactions are largely based on feelings rather than on cold cognition. However, we see our moral boundaries as logical and reasonable, not as emotional. Our beliefs are actually shaped by our groups, which influence our perceptions of others, resulting in unconscious responses and a feeling that shared emotions are "right." Unfortunately, this feeling allows us sometimes to justify purely emotional reactions as "ethical."[29] In work and in life, our moral judgments therefore have more to do with emotions than with cognitions, yet we tend to think the opposite, especially when those judgments are shared by fellow members of our in-group.

You can think about this research in your own life to see how the emotional model of ethics operates. Consider the massive earthquake that struck Japan in 2011. When you heard about it, did you feel emotionally upset about the suffering of others, or did you make more of a rational calculation about their unfortunate situation? Consider a time when you have done something that hurt someone else. Did you feel angry or upset with yourself? Or think about a time when you have seen someone else treated unfairly. Did you feel contempt for the person acting unfairly, or did you engage in a cool rational calculation of the justice of the situation? Most people who think about these situations do have at least some sense of an emotional stirring that might prompt them to engage in ethical actions like donating money to help others, apologizing and attempting to make amends, or intervening on behalf of those who have been mistreated. In sum, we can conclude that people who are behaving ethically are at least partially making decisions based on their emotions and feelings, and this emotional reaction will often be a good thing.

Sources of Emotions and Moods

3 Identify the sources of emotions and moods.

Have you ever said, "I got up on the wrong side of the bed today"? Have you ever snapped at a co-worker or family member for no particular reason? If you have, it probably makes you wonder where emotions and moods come from. Here we discuss some of the primary influences.

Personality Moods and emotions have a trait component: Most people have built-in tendencies to experience certain moods and emotions more frequently than others do. People also experience the same emotions with different intensities. Contrast Microsoft CEO Steven Ballmer to Facebook's Mark Zuckerberg, for instance. Ballmer is easily moved to emote; software engineer Mark Lucovsky reported that when he told Ballmer he was leaving Microsoft for Google, Ballmer threw a chair against a wall and said of Google's CEO, "I'm going to f—ing bury that guy."[30] Zuckerman, conversely, is notably distant and unemotional. Ballmer and Zuckerman probably differ in **affect intensity**, or how strongly they experience their emotions.[31] Affectively intense people experience both positive and negative emotions more deeply: when they're sad, they're really sad, and when they're happy, they're really happy.

affect intensity *Individual differences in the strength with which individuals experience their emotions.*

What's My Affect Intensity?

In the Self-Assessment Library (available in MyManagementLab), take assessment IV.D.2 (What's My Affect Intensity?).

Time of the Day Are you a morning person? Or do you feel best later in the day? People do vary in their moods by time of day. However, research suggests most of us actually follow the same pattern, and the nature of this pattern may surprise you. Levels of positive affect tend to peak in the late morning (10 A.M.–noon) and then remain at that level until early evening (around 7 P.M.).[32] Starting about 12 hours after waking, positive affect begins to drop until midnight, and then, for those who remain awake, the drop accelerates until positive mood picks up again after sunrise.[33] As for negative affect, most research suggests it fluctuates less than positive affect,[34] but the general trend is for it to increase over the course of a day, so that it is lowest early in the morning and highest late in the evening.[35]

Recently, a fascinating study assessed mood by analyzing 509 million Twitter messages from 2.4 million individuals across 84 countries.[36] The researchers assessed mood by noting the presence of words connoting positive affect (happy, enthused,

Exhibit **4-3**	Time of Day Effects on Mood of U.S. Adults as Rated from Twitter Postings

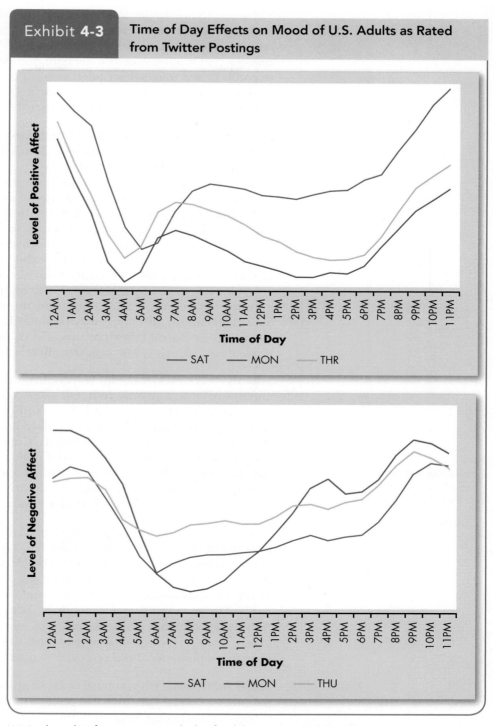

Note: Based on analysis of U.S. Twitter postings and coding of words that represent positive feelings (delight, enthusiasm) and negative feelings (fear, guilt). Lines represent percent of total words in Twitter post that convey these moods.
Sources: Based on S. A. Golder and M. W. Macy, "Diurnal and Seasonal Mood Vary with Work, Sleep, and Daylength Across Diverse Cultures," *Science* 333 (2011), pp. 1878–1881; A. Elejalde-Ruiz, "Seize the day," *Chicago Tribune* (September 5, 2012), downloaded June 20, 2013 from http://articles.chicagotribune.com/.

excited) and negative (sad, angry, anxious) affect. You can see these trends in the positive affect part of Exhibit 4-3. Daily fluctuations in mood tended to follow a similar pattern in most countries. Specifically, regardless of the day of the week, positive affect increased after sunrise, tended to peak mid-morning, remained stable until roughly 7 P.M., and then tended to increase again until the midnight drop.

These results are similar to what we reported above from previous research. A major difference, though, was what happens in the evening. As we noted earlier, most research suggests that positive affect tends to drop after 7 P.M., whereas this study suggests that it *increases* before the midnight decline. We'll have to wait for further research to see which description is accurate. The negative affect trends in this study were more consistent with past research, showing that negative affect is lowest in the morning and tends to increase over the course of the day and evening.

Day of the Week   Are people in their best moods on the weekends? In most cultures that is true—for example, U.S. adults tend to experience their highest positive affect on Friday, Saturday, and Sunday, and their lowest on Monday.[37] As shown in Exhibit 4-4, again based on the study of over 500 million Twitter messages, that tends to be true in several other cultures as well. For Germans and Chinese, positive affect is highest from Friday to Sunday and lowest on Monday. The same pattern even seems to hold in countries—such as many Muslim countries—where the weekend occurs on different days. This isn't the case in all cultures, however. As the exhibit shows, in Japan, positive affect is higher on Monday than on either Friday or Saturday.

As for negative affect, Monday is the highest negative-affect day across most cultures. However, in many countries, negative affect is lower on Friday and Saturday than on Sunday. It may be that while Sunday is enjoyable as a day off (and thus we have higher positive affect), we also get a bit stressed about the week ahead (which is why negative affect is higher).

Weather   When do you think you would be in a better mood—when it's 70 degrees and sunny, or on a gloomy, cold, rainy day? Many people believe their mood is tied to the weather. However, a fairly large and detailed body of evidence conducted by multiple researchers suggests weather has little effect on mood, at least for most people.[38] One expert concluded, "Contrary to the prevailing cultural view, these data indicate that people do not report a better mood on bright and sunny days (or, conversely, a worse mood on dark and rainy days)."[39] **Illusory correlation**, which occurs when we associate two events that in reality have no connection, explains why people tend to *think* nice weather improves their mood.

illusory correlation *The tendency of people to associate two events when in reality there is no connection.*

Stress   As you might imagine, stressful daily events at work (a nasty e-mail, an impending deadline, the loss of a big sale, a reprimand from the boss) negatively affect moods. The effects of stress also build over time. As the authors of one study note, "a constant diet of even low-level stressful events has the potential to cause workers to experience gradually increasing levels of strain over time."[40] Mounting levels of stress can worsen our moods, and we experience more negative emotions. Although sometimes we thrive on stress, most of us find stress takes a toll on our mood. Recent research also suggests that when situations are overly emotionally charged, we have a natural response to disengage, to literally look away.[41]

Social Activities   Do you tend to be happiest when out with friends? For most people, social activities increase positive mood and have little effect on negative mood. But do people in positive moods seek out social interactions, or do social interactions cause people to be in good moods? It seems both are true.[42] Does the *type* of social activity matter? Indeed it does. Research suggests activities that are physical (skiing or hiking with friends), informal (going to a party), or epicurean (eating with others) are more strongly associated with increases in positive mood than events that are formal (attending a meeting) or sedentary (watching TV with friends).[43]

Sleep   U.S. adults report sleeping less than adults a generation ago.[44] According to researchers and public health specialists, a large portion of the

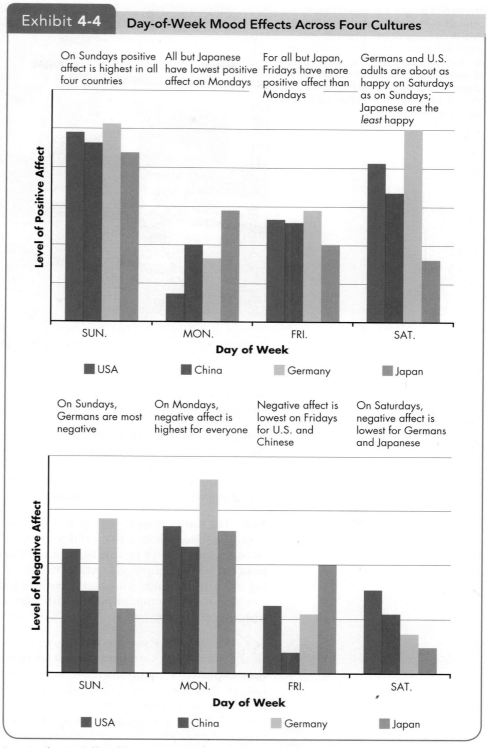

| Exhibit **4-4** | Day-of-Week Mood Effects Across Four Cultures |

On Sundays positive affect is highest in all four countries

All but Japanese have lowest positive affect on Mondays

For all but Japan, Fridays have more positive affect than Mondays

Germans and U.S. adults are about as happy on Saturdays as on Sundays; Japanese are the *least* happy

Level of Positive Affect

SUN.   MON.   FRI.   SAT.

Day of Week

■ USA   ■ China   ■ Germany   ■ Japan

On Sundays, Germans are most negative

On Mondays, negative affect is highest for everyone

Negative affect is lowest on Fridays for U.S. and Chinese

On Saturdays, negative affect is lowest for Germans and Japanese

Level of Negative Affect

SUN.   MON.   FRI.   SAT.

Day of Week

■ USA   ■ China   ■ Germany   ■ Japan

Source: Based on S. A. Golder and M. W. Macy, "Diurnal and Seasonal Mood Vary with Work, Sleep, and Daylength Across Diverse Cultures," *Science* 333 (2011), pp. 1878–1881; A. Elejalde-Ruiz, "Seize the Day," *Chicago Tribune* (September 5, 2012), downloaded June 20, 2013 from http://articles.chicagotribune.com/.

U.S. workforce suffers from sleep deprivation: 41 million workers are able to sleep less than six hours per night. Sleep quality affects mood, and increased fatigue puts workers at health risks of disease, injury, and depression.[45] One reason is that poor or reduced sleep impairs decision making and makes it

Photo 4-2 Blizzard Entertainment believes that exercise and social activities increase positive moods and result in happier, healthier, and more productive employees. The developer of entertainment software offers employees yoga classes, a sand volleyball court, basketball court, bike track, and fitness center.

Source: Ang Veneras/ZUMAPRESS/Newscom.

difficult to control emotions.[46] A recent study suggests poor sleep also impairs job satisfaction because people feel fatigued, irritable, and less alert.[47]

Exercise   You often hear people should exercise to improve their mood. Does "sweat therapy" really work? It appears so. Research consistently shows exercise enhances peoples' positive mood.[48] While not terribly strong overall, the effects are strongest for those who are depressed. So exercise may help put you in a better mood, but don't expect miracles.

Age   Do young people experience more extreme positive emotions (so-called youthful exuberance) than older people? If you answered "yes," you were wrong. One study of people ages 18 to 94 revealed that negative emotions seem to occur less as people get older. Periods of highly positive moods lasted longer for older individuals, and bad moods faded more quickly.[49] The study implies emotional experience improves with age; as we get older, we experience fewer negative emotions.

Sex   Many believe women are more emotional than men. Is there any truth to this? Evidence does confirm women are more emotionally expressive than men;[50] they experience emotions more intensely, they tend to "hold onto" emotions longer than men, and they display more frequent expressions of both positive and negative emotions, except anger.[51] Evidence from a study of participants from 37 different countries found that men consistently report higher levels of powerful emotions like anger, whereas women report more powerless emotions like sadness and fear. Thus, there are some sex differences in the experience and expression of emotions.[52]

People also tend to attribute men's and women's emotions in ways that might be based on stereotypes of what typical emotional reactions are. One study showed that experimental participants who read about emotional expressions interpreted women's reactions as being dispositional (related to personality), whereas men's reactions were interpreted as being due to the situation around them.[53] For example, a picture of a sad woman led observers to believe she was acting consistently with an emotional personality type, whereas a picture of a sad man was more likely to be attributed to his having a bad day. Another study showed that participants were faster at detecting angry expressions on male faces and happy expressions on female faces; neutral faces in men were attributed as more angry and neutral faces in women were interpreted as happy.[54]

Emotional Labor

4 Show the impact emotional labor has on employees.

emotional labor *A situation in which an employee expresses organizationally desired emotions during interpersonal transactions at work.*

emotional dissonance *Inconsistencies between the emotions people feel and the emotions they project.*

If you've ever had a job in retail sales or waited on tables in a restaurant, you know the importance of projecting a friendly demeanor and smiling. Even though there were days when you didn't feel cheerful, you knew management expected you to be upbeat when dealing with customers. So you faked it. Every employee expends physical and mental labor by putting body and mind, respectively, into the job. But jobs also require **emotional labor**, an employee's expression of organizationally desired emotions during interpersonal transactions at work.

The concept of emotional labor emerged from studies of service jobs. We expect flight attendants to be cheerful, funeral directors to be sad, and doctors emotionally neutral. But emotional labor is relevant to almost every job. At the least your managers expect you to be courteous, not hostile, in your interactions with co-workers. The true challenge arises when employees have to project one emotion while feeling another. This disparity is **emotional dissonance**, and it can take a heavy toll. Bottled-up feelings of frustration, anger, and resentment can eventually lead to emotional exhaustion and burnout. Emotional dissonance is like cognitive dissonance discussed in the previous chapter, except that emotional dissonance concerns feelings rather than thinking. It's from the increasing importance of emotional labor as a key component of effective job performance that we have come to understand the relevance of emotion within the field of OB.

Emotional labor creates dilemmas for employees. There are people with whom you have to work that you just plain don't like. Maybe you consider their personality abrasive. Maybe you know they've said negative things about you

Photo 4-3 Employees of this Apple store in Tokyo, Japan, greet customers with enthusiasm and excitement as they wait in line for the store to open on the day the iPad mini went on sale. Employees' smiles and high fives are expressions of emotional labor that Apple requires and considers appropriate for their jobs.

Source: © Aflo Co. Ltd./Alamy.

behind your back. Regardless, your job requires you to interact with these people on a regular basis. So you're forced to feign friendliness.

It can help you, on the job especially, if you separate emotions into *felt* or *displayed emotions*.[55] **Felt emotions** are an individual's actual emotions. In contrast, **displayed emotions** are those that the organization requires workers to show and considers appropriate in a given job. They're not innate; they're learned. Similarly, most of us know we're expected to act sad at funerals, regardless of whether we consider the person's death a loss, and to appear happy at weddings even if we don't feel like celebrating.

Research suggests that at U.S. workplaces, it is expected that we should typically display positive emotions like happiness and excitement and suppress negative emotions like fear, anger, disgust, and contempt.[56] Effective managers have learned to be serious when giving an employee a negative performance evaluation and to hide their anger when they've been passed over for promotion. A salesperson who hasn't learned to smile and appear friendly, despite his or her true feelings at the moment, typically won't last long in the job. The way we experience an emotion isn't always the same as the way we show it.

Displaying fake emotions requires us to suppress real ones. **Surface acting** is hiding inner feelings and hiding emotional expressions in response to display rules. A worker who smiles at a customer even when he doesn't feel like it is surface acting. **Deep acting** is trying to modify our true inner feelings based on display rules. A health care provider trying to genuinely feel more empathy for her patients is deep acting.[57] Surface acting deals with *displayed* emotions, and deep acting deals with *felt* emotions. Research in the Netherlands and Belgium indicated that surface acting is stressful to employees, while *mindfulness* (learning to objectively evaluate our emotional situation in the moment) is beneficial to employee well-being.[58] Displaying emotions we don't really feel is exhausting, so it is important to give employees who engage in surface displays a chance to relax and recharge. A study that looked at how cheerleading instructors spent their breaks from teaching found those who used the time to rest and relax were more effective after their breaks.[59] Instructors who did chores during their breaks were only about as effective after their break as they were before. Another study found that in hospital work groups where there were heavy emotional display demands, burnout was higher than in other hospital work groups.[60]

felt emotions   *An individual's actual emotions.*

displayed emotions   *Emotions that are organizationally required and considered appropriate in a given job.*

surface acting   *Hiding one's inner feelings and forgoing emotional expressions in response to display rules.*

deep acting   *Trying to modify one's true inner feelings based on display rules.*

Affective Events Theory

5   Describe affective events theory and its applications.

affective events theory (AET)   *A model that suggests that workplace events cause emotional reactions on the part of employees, which then influence workplace attitudes and behaviors.*

We've seen that emotions and moods are an important part of our lives and our work lives. But how do they influence our job performance and satisfaction? A model called **affective events theory (AET)** demonstrates that employees react emotionally to things that happen to them at work, and this reaction influences their job performance and satisfaction.[61]

Exhibit 4-5 summarizes AET. The theory begins by recognizing that emotions are a response to an event in the work environment. The work environment includes everything surrounding the job—the variety of tasks and degree of autonomy, job demands, and requirements for expressing emotional labor. This environment creates work events that can be hassles, uplifting events, or both. Examples of hassles are colleagues who refuse to carry their share of work, conflicting directions from different managers, and excessive time pressures. Uplifting events include meeting a goal, getting support from a colleague, and receiving recognition for an accomplishment.[62]

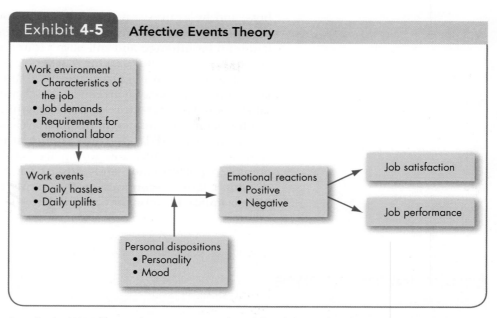

Exhibit **4-5**   **Affective Events Theory**

Source: Based on N. M. Ashkanasy and C. S. Daus, "Emotion in the Workplace: The New Challenge for Managers," *Academy of Management Executive* (February 2002), p. 77.

These work events trigger positive or negative emotional reactions, to which employees' personalities and moods predispose them to respond with greater or lesser intensity. People who score low on emotional stability are more likely to react strongly to negative events. And our emotional response to a given event can change depending on mood. Finally, emotions influence a number of performance and satisfaction variables, such as organizational citizenship behavior, organizational commitment, level of effort, intention to quit, and workplace deviance.

Tests of affective events theory suggest the following:

1. An emotional episode is actually a series of emotional experiences, precipitated by a single event and containing elements of both emotions and mood cycles.
2. Current emotions influence job satisfaction at any given time, along with the history of emotions surrounding the event.
3. Because moods and emotions fluctuate over time, their effect on performance also fluctuates.
4. Emotion-driven behaviors are typically short in duration and of high variability.
5. Because emotions, even positive ones, tend to be incompatible with behaviors required to do a job, they typically have a negative influence on job performance.[63]

Consider an example.[64] Say you work as an aeronautical engineer for Boeing. Because of the downturn in demand for commercial jets, you've just learned the company is considering laying off 10,000 employees, possibly including you. This event is likely to make you feel negative emotions, especially fear that you might lose your primary source of income. And because you're prone to worry a lot and obsess about problems, this event increases your feelings of insecurity. Your worry is increased because you (1) didn't take the risk voluntarily, (2) don't trust your employer, (3) realize the risk is in the hands of people whose perspectives might not favor you, and (4) see no benefit if you act out.[65] The layoff also sets in motion a series of smaller events that create an episode: You talk with your boss, and he assures you your job is safe; you hear rumors your department is high on the list to be eliminated; and you run into a former colleague who was laid off 6 months ago and still hasn't found work. These events, in turn, create emotional ups and downs. One day, you're feeling upbeat that you'll survive the cuts. The next, you might be depressed and anxious. These emotional swings take your attention away from your work and lower your job performance and satisfaction. Finally, your response is magnified because this is the fourth-largest layoff Boeing has initiated in the past 3 years.

In summary, AET offers two important messages.[66] First, emotions provide valuable insights into how workplace hassles and uplifting events influence employee performance and satisfaction. Second, employees and managers shouldn't ignore emotions or the events that cause them, even when they appear minor, because they accumulate.

Emotional Intelligence

6 Contrast the evidence for and against the existence of emotional intelligence.

emotional intelligence (EI) *The ability to detect and to manage emotional cues and information.*

Diane is an office manager. Her awareness of her own and others' emotions is almost nil. She's moody and unable to generate much enthusiasm or interest in her employees. She doesn't understand why employees get upset with her. She often overreacts to problems and chooses the most ineffectual responses to emotional situations.[67] Diane has low emotional intelligence. **Emotional intelligence (EI)** is a person's ability to (1) perceive emotions in the self and others, (2) understand the meaning of these emotions, and (3) regulate one's emotions accordingly in a cascading model, as shown in Exhibit 4-6. People who know their own emotions and are good at reading emotional cues—for instance, knowing why they're angry and how to express themselves without violating norms—are most likely to be effective.[68]

Several studies suggest EI plays an important role in job performance. One study that used functional magnetic resonance imaging (fMRI) technology found executive MBA students who performed best on a strategic decision-making task were more likely to incorporate emotion centers of the brain into their choice process. The students also de-emphasized the use of the more cognitive parts of their brains.[69] Another study looked at the successes and failures of

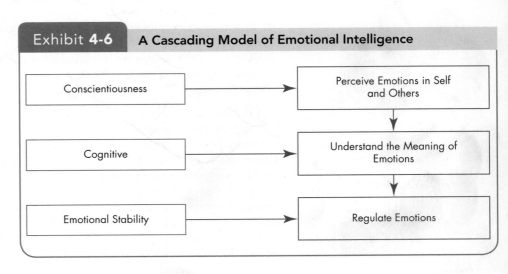

Exhibit 4-6   A Cascading Model of Emotional Intelligence

Conscientiousness → Perceive Emotions in Self and Others

Cognitive → Understand the Meaning of Emotions

Emotional Stability → Regulate Emotions

11 U.S. presidents—from Franklin Roosevelt to Bill Clinton—and evaluated them on six qualities: communication, organization, political skill, vision, cognitive style, and emotional intelligence. The key quality that differentiated the successful (such as Roosevelt, Kennedy, and Reagan) from the unsuccessful (such as Johnson, Carter, and Nixon) was emotional intelligence.[70] One simulation study also showed that students who were good at identifying and distinguishing among their own feelings were able to make more profitable investment decisions.[71]

EI has been a controversial concept in OB, with supporters and detractors. In the following sections, we review the arguments for and against its viability.

The Case for EI

The arguments in favor of EI include its intuitive appeal, the fact that it predicts criteria that matter, and the idea that it is biologically based.

Intuitive Appeal   Intuition suggests people who can detect emotions in others, control their own emotions, and handle social interactions well have a powerful leg up in the business world. One company's promotional materials for an EI measure claimed, "EI accounts for more than 85 percent of star performance in top leaders."[72]

EI Predicts Criteria That Matter   Evidence suggests a high level of EI means a person will perform well on the job. For example, one study found EI predicted the performance of employees in a cigarette factory in China.[73] A review of studies indicated that, overall, EI was weakly but consistently positively correlated with job performance, even after researchers took cognitive ability, conscientiousness, and neuroticism into account.[74]

EI Is Biologically Based   In one study, people with damage to the brain area that governs emotional processing (part of the prefrontal cortex) scored no lower on standard measures of intelligence than people without similar damage.

Photo 4-4 These new employees of a government ward office in the city of Daejeon, South Korea, practice smiling during their training on how to be kind public employees. Researchers of emotion regulation study the strategy of surface acting, or "putting on a face," as an appropriate response in modifying emotions in a given situation.

Source: Yonhap News/YNA/Newscom.

Nevertheless, they scored significantly lower on EI tests and were impaired in normal decision making. This study suggests EI is neurologically based in a way that's unrelated to standard measures of intelligence.[75] There is also evidence EI is genetically influenced, further supporting the idea that it measures a real underlying biological factor.[76]

The Case Against EI

For all its supporters, EI has just as many critics who say it is vague and impossible to measure, and they question its validity.

EI Researchers Do Not Agree on Definitions   To many researchers, it's not clear what EI is, because researchers use different definitions of it.[77] Some have focused on tests with right and wrong answers from which we can infer someone's ability to recognize and control emotions. This is the ability-based perspective on EI. Other researchers have viewed emotional intelligence as a broad variety of ideas that we can measure by self-reports and that are connected primarily by the fact

---

An Ethical Choice

Should Managers Use Emotional Intelligence (EI) Tests?

As we discussed in this chapter, the concept of emotional intelligence has raised some debate. One of the topic questions for managers is whether to use EI tests in the selection process. Here are some ethical considerations:

- There is no commonly accepted test. For instance, researchers have recently used the Mayer–Salovey–Caruso Emotional Intelligence Test (MSCEIT), the Trait Emotional Intelligence Questionnaire, and the newly developed Situational Judgment Test of Emotional Intelligence (SJT of EI) in studies. Researchers feel EI tests may need to be culturally specific because emotional displays vary by culture; thus, the interpretation of emotional cues differs. A recent study in India comparing the emotional intelligence scores for Indian and North American executives using the Emotional Competence Inventory (ECI-2) test found the results similar but not the same, suggesting the need for modification.

- Applicants may react negatively to taking an EI test in general, or to

parts of it. The face recognition test, for example, may seem culturally biased to some if the subject photos are not diverse. Also, participants who score high on EI tests tend to consider them fair; applicants who score lower may not perceive the tests to be fair and can thus consider the hiring organizations unfavorably—even if they score well on other assessments.

- EI tests may not be predictive of performance for all types of jobs. In a study of 600 Romanian participants, results indicated that EI was valid for salespeople, public servants, and CEOs of public hospitals, but these were all roles requiring significant social interaction. EI tests may need to be tailored for each position category or not be used when the position description does not warrant.

- It remains somewhat unclear what EI tests are actually measuring. They may reflect personality or intelligence, in which case other measures might be better.

- There is not enough research on how emotional intelligence affects,

for instance, counterproductive work behaviors. It may not be prudent to test and select applicants who are rated high on EI when we aren't yet certain that everything about EI leads to desired workplace outcomes.

These concerns suggest EI tests should be avoided in hiring decisions. However, because research has indicated that emotional intelligence does predict job performance to some degree, managers should not be too hasty to dismiss the tests. Rather, those wishing to use EI in hiring decisions should be aware of these issues to make informed and ethical decisions about not only whom to hire, but how.

Sources: D. Iliescu, A. Ilie, D. Ispas, and A. Ion, "Emotional Intelligence in Personnel Selection: Applicant Reactions, Criterion, and Incremental Validity," *International Journal of Selection and Assessment* (September 2012), pp. 347–358; R. Sharma, "Measuring Social and Emotional Intelligence Competencies in the Indian Context," *Cross Cultural Management* 19 (2012), pp. 30–47; and S. Sharma, M. Gangopadhyay, E. Austin, and M. K. Mandal, "Development and Validation of a Situational Judgment Test of Emotional Intelligence," *International Journal of Selection and Assessment* (March 2013), pp. 57–73.

that none of them are the same as cognitive intelligence. Not only are these two definitions different, but the measures used by each perspective are barely correlated with one another.[78]

EI Can't Be Measured   Many critics have raised questions about measuring EI. Because EI is a form of intelligence, they argue, there must be right and wrong answers for it on tests. Some tests do have right and wrong answers, although the validity of some questions is doubtful. One measure asks you to associate feelings with colors, as if purple always makes us feel cool and not warm. Other measures are self-reported, such as "I'm good at 'reading' other people," and have no right or wrong answers. The measures of EI are diverse, and researchers have not subjected them to as much rigorous study as they have measures of personality and general intelligence.[79]

EI Is Nothing but Personality with a Different Label   Some critics argue that because EI is so closely related to intelligence and personality, once you control for these factors, it has nothing unique to offer. There is some foundation to this argument. EI appears to be correlated with measures of personality, especially emotional stability.[80] If this is true, then biological markers like brain activity and heritability are attributable to other well-known and much better researched psychological constructs. To some extent, researchers have resolved this issue by noting that EI is a construct partially determined by traits like cognitive intelligence, conscientiousness, and neuroticism, so it makes sense that EI is correlated with these characteristics.[81]

Although the field is progressing in its understanding of EI, many questions have not been answered. EI is wildly popular among consulting firms and in the popular press, but it's still difficult to validate this construct with the research literature.

Emotion Regulation

Have you ever tried to cheer yourself up when you're feeling down, or calm yourself when you're feeling angry? If so, you have engaged in *emotion regulation,* which is part of the EI literature but is increasingly being studied as an independent concept.[82] The central idea behind emotion regulation is to identify and modify the emotions you feel. Recent research suggests that emotion management ability is a strong predictor of task performance for some jobs and organizational citizenship behaviors.[83]

Researchers of emotion regulation often study the strategies people may employ to change their emotions. One strategy we have discussed in this chapter is surface acting, or literally "putting on a face" of appropriate response to a given situation. Surface acting doesn't change the emotions, though, so the regulation effect is minimal. Perhaps due to the costs of expressing what we don't feel, a recent study suggested that individuals who vary their surface-acting response may have lower job satisfaction and higher levels of work withdrawal than those who consistently use surface acting.[84] Deep acting, another strategy we have covered, is less psychologically costly than surface acting because the employee is actually trying to experience the emotion. Deep acting, though less "false" than surface acting, still may be difficult because it represents acting nonetheless.

Organizational behavior researchers are therefore looking to understand strategies people may employ that yield the results of acting, like showing appropriate emotions, but mitigate the effects of acting, like emotional exhaustion and workplace withdrawal. The goal is to give employees and managers tools to monitor and modify their emotional responses to workplace situations.

Although the research is ongoing, studies indicate that effective emotion regulation techniques include acknowledging rather than suppressing our emotional responses to situations, and re-evaluating events after they occur.[85] A recent study illustrates the potentially powerful effect of cognitive reappraisal. Of the Israeli participants who were shown anger-inducing information on the Israeli-Palestinian conflict, those who were primed to reappraise the situation showed more willingness to consider conciliatory measures toward Palestine and less support for aggressive tactics than the control group, not only immediately after the study but up to 5 months later. This suggests that cognitive reappraisal techniques may allow people to change their emotional responses, even when the subject matter is as highly emotionally charged as the Israeli-Palestinian conflict.[86]

Another technique with potential for emotion regulation is venting. Research shows that the open expression of emotions can be helpful to the individual, as opposed to keeping emotions "bottled up." Caution must be exercised, though, because venting, or expressing your frustration outwardly, touches other people. In fact, whether venting emotions helps the "venter" feel better depends very much upon the listener's response. If the listener doesn't respond (many refuse to respond to venting), the venter actually feels worse. If the listener responds with expressions of support or validation, the venter feels better. Therefore, if we are going to vent to a co-worker, we need to choose someone who will respond sympathetically. Venting to the perceived offender rarely improves things and can result in heightening the negative emotions.[87]

As you might suspect, not everyone is equally good at regulating his or her emotions. Individuals who are higher in the personality trait of neuroticism have more trouble doing so and often find their moods are beyond their ability to control. Individuals who have lower levels of self-esteem are also less likely to try to improve their sad moods, perhaps because they are less likely than others to feel they deserve to be in a good mood.[88]

While it might seem in some ways desirable to regulate your emotions, research suggests there is a downside to trying to change the way you feel. Changing your emotions takes effort, and as we noted when discussing emotional labor, this effort can be exhausting. Sometimes attempts to change an emotion actually make the emotion stronger; for example, trying to talk yourself out of being afraid can make you focus more on what scares you, which makes you more afraid.[89] From another perspective, research suggests that avoiding negative emotional experiences is less likely to lead to positive moods than does seeking out positive emotional experiences.[90] For example, you're more likely to experience a positive mood if you have a pleasant conversation with a friend than if you avoid an unpleasant conversation with a hostile co-worker.

While emotion regulation techniques can help us cope with difficult workplace situations, research indicates that the effect varies. A recent study in Taiwan found that participants who worked for abusive supervisors reported emotional exhaustion and work withdrawal tendencies, but to different degrees based on the emotion regulation strategies they employed. This suggests that more research on the application of techniques needs to be done to help employees.[91] Thus, while there is much promise in emotion regulation techniques, the best route to a positive workplace is to recruit positive-minded individuals and to train leaders to manage their moods, job attitudes, and performance.[92] The best leaders manage emotions as much as they do tasks and activities.

What's My Emotional Intelligence Score?

In the Self-Assessment Library (available in MyManagementLab), take assessment I.E.1 (What's My Emotional Intelligence Score?).

OB Applications of Emotions and Moods

7 Identify strategies for emotion regulation and their likely effects.

In this section, we assess how an understanding of emotions and moods can improve our ability to explain and predict the selection process in organizations, decision making, creativity, motivation, leadership, interpersonal conflict, negotiation, customer service, job attitudes, and deviant workplace behaviors. We also look at how managers can influence our moods.

Selection

One implication from the evidence on EI to date is that employers should consider it a factor in hiring employees, especially for jobs that demand a high degree of social interaction. In fact, more employers *are* starting to use EI measures to hire people. A study of U.S. Air Force recruiters showed that top-performing recruiters exhibited high levels of EI. Using these findings, the Air Force revamped its selection criteria. A follow-up investigation found future hires who had high EI scores were 2.6 times more successful than those who didn't. At L'Oreal, salespersons selected on EI scores outsold those hired using the company's old selection procedure. On an annual basis, salespeople selected for their emotional competence sold $91,370 more than other salespeople did, for a net revenue increase of $2,558,360.[93]

Photo 4-5 A leader of high emotional intelligence, Starbucks CEO Howard Schultz bounds on stage before addressing 10,000 Starbucks managers at the firm's Global Leadership Conference. Schultz's optimism, excitement, and enthusiasm energize employees and motivate them to accept his vision of the company's future.

Source: Bloomberg via Getty Images.

Decision Making

As you will see in Chapter 6, traditional approaches to the study of decision making in organizations have emphasized rationality. But OB researchers are increasingly finding that moods and emotions have important effects on decision making.

Positive moods and emotions seem to help people make sound decisions. People in good moods or experiencing positive emotions are more likely than others to use heuristics, or rules of thumb,[94] to help make good decisions quickly. Positive emotions also enhance problem-solving skills, so positive people find better solutions to problems.[95]

OB researchers continue to debate the role of negative emotions and moods in decision making. Although one often-cited study suggested depressed people reach more accurate judgments,[96] more recent evidence hints they make poorer decisions. Why? Because depressed people are slower at processing information and tend to weigh all possible options rather than the most likely ones.[97] They search for the perfect solution, when there rarely is one.

Creativity

People in good moods tend to be more creative than people in bad moods.[98] They produce more ideas and more options, and others think their ideas are original.[99] It seems people experiencing positive moods or emotions are more flexible and open in their thinking, which may explain why they're more creative.[100] Supervisors should actively try to keep employees happy because doing so creates more good moods (employees like their leaders to encourage them and provide positive feedback on a job well done), which in turn leads people to be more creative.[101]

Some researchers, however, do not believe a positive mood makes people more creative. They argue that when people are in positive moods, they may relax ("If I'm in a good mood, things must be going okay, and I must not need to think of new ideas") and not engage in the critical thinking necessary for some forms of creativity.[102] The answer may lie in thinking of moods somewhat differently. Rather than looking at positive or negative affect, it's possible to conceptualize moods as active feelings like anger, fear, or elation and contrast these with deactivating moods like sorrow, depression, or serenity. All the activating moods, whether positive *or* negative, seem to lead to more creativity, whereas deactivating moods lead to less.[103] As well, we discussed earlier that other factors such as fatigue may boost creativity. A study of 428 students found they performed best on a creative problem-solving task when they were fatigued, suggesting that tiredness may free the mind to consider novel solutions.[104]

Motivation

Several studies have highlighted the importance of moods and emotions on motivation. One study set two groups of people to solving word puzzles. The first group saw a funny video clip intended to put them in a good mood first. The other group was not shown the clip and started working on the puzzles right away. The results? The positive-mood group reported higher expectations of being able to solve the puzzles, worked harder at them, and did solve more as a result.[105]

Another study found that giving people performance feedback—whether real or fake—influenced their mood, which then influenced their motivation.[106] So, a cycle can exist in which positive moods cause people to be more creative, which leads to positive feedback from those observing their work. This positive feedback further reinforces the positive mood, which may make people perform even better, and so on.

Another study looked at the moods of insurance sales agents in Taiwan.[107] Agents in a good mood were found to be more helpful toward their co-workers and also felt better about themselves. These factors in turn led to superior performance in the form of higher sales and better supervisor reports of performance.

Leadership

Effective leaders rely on emotional appeals to help convey their messages. In fact, the expression of emotion in speeches is often the critical element that makes us accept or reject a leader's message. Politicians, as a case in point, have learned to show enthusiasm when talking about their chances of winning an election, even when polls suggest otherwise.

Recent research has focused on the effects of transformational leaders, whom we can think of for now as extraordinary leaders (until we cover the topic more thoroughly in Chapter 12). Transformational leaders realize the effect emotion has on their followers and often freely share emotions. A study with Taiwanese military participants indicates that by sharing emotions, transformational leaders inspire positive emotions in their followers that lead to higher task performance.[108]

Corporate executives know emotional content is critical if employees are to buy into their vision of the company's future and accept change. When higher-ups offer new visions, especially with vague or distant goals, it is often difficult for employees to accept the changes they'll bring. By arousing emotions and linking them to an appealing vision, leaders increase the likelihood that managers and employees alike will accept change.[109] Leaders who focus on inspirational goals also generate greater optimism and enthusiasm in employees, leading to more positive social interactions with co-workers and customers.[110]

Negotiation

Negotiation is an emotional process; however, we often say a skilled negotiator has a "poker face." The founder of Britain's Poker Channel, Crispin Nieboer, stated, "It is a game of bluff and there is fantastic human emotion and tension, seeing who can bluff the longest."[111] Several studies have shown that a negotiator who feigns anger has an advantage over the opponent. Why? Because when a negotiator shows anger, the opponent concludes the negotiator has conceded all he or she can and so gives in.[112] Anger should be used selectively in negotiation: angry negotiators who have less information or less power than their opponents have significantly worse outcomes.[113] It appears that a powerful, better-informed individual will be less willing to share information or meet an angry opponent halfway.

Displaying a negative emotion (such as anger) can be effective, but feeling bad about your performance appears to impair future negotiations. Individuals who do poorly in a negotiation experience negative emotions, develop negative perceptions of their counterpart, and are less willing to share information or be cooperative in future negotiations.[114] Interestingly, then, while moods and emotions have benefits at work, in negotiation—unless we're putting up a false front like feigning anger—emotions may impair negotiator performance. A 2005 study found people who suffered damage to the emotional centers of their brains (the same part that was injured in Phineas Gage) may be the *best* negotiators because they're not likely to overcorrect when faced with negative outcomes.[115]

Customer Service

A worker's emotional state influences customer service, which influences levels of repeat business and of customer satisfaction.[116] Providing high-quality customer service makes demands on employees because it often puts them in a state of emotional dissonance. Long-term emotional dissonance is a predictor for job burnout, declines in job performance, and lower job satisfaction.[117]

emotional contagion *The process by which peoples' emotions are caused by the emotions of others.*

Employees' emotions can transfer to the customer. Studies indicate a matching effect between employee and customer emotions called **emotional contagion**—the "catching" of emotions from others.[118] How does it work? The primary explanation is that when someone experiences positive emotions and laughs and smiles at you, you tend to respond positively. Emotional contagion is important because customers who catch the positive moods or emotions of employees shop longer. But are negative emotions and moods contagious, too? Absolutely. When an employee feels unfairly treated by a customer, for example, it's harder for him to display the positive emotions his organization expects of him.[119]

Job Attitudes

Ever hear the advice "Never take your work home with you," meaning you should forget about work once you go home? That's easier said than done. Several studies have shown people who had a good day at work tend to be in a better mood at home that evening, and vice versa.[120] People who have a stressful day at work also have trouble relaxing after they get off work.[121] One study had married couples describing their moods when responding to timed cell phone surveys through the course of the day. As most married readers might suspect, if one member of the couple was in a negative mood during the workday, that mood spilled over to the spouse at night.[122] In other words, if you've had a bad day at work, your spouse is likely to have an unpleasant evening. Even though people do emotionally take their work home with them, however, by the next day the effect is usually gone.[123]

Deviant Workplace Behaviors

Anyone who has spent much time in an organization realizes people often behave in ways that violate established norms and threaten the organization, its members, or both. As we saw in Chapter 1, these actions are called *workplace deviant behaviors*.[124] Many can be traced to negative emotions.

For instance, envy is an emotion that occurs when you resent someone for having something you don't have but strongly desire—such as a better work assignment, larger office, or higher salary. It can lead to malicious deviant behaviors. An envious employee could backstab another employee, negatively distort others' successes, and positively distort his own accomplishments.[125] Angry people look for other people to blame for their bad mood, interpret other people's behavior as hostile, and have trouble considering others' point of view.[126] It's not hard to see how these thought processes, too, can lead directly to verbal or physical aggression.

Evidence suggests people who feel negative emotions are more likely than others to engage in short-term deviant behavior at work such as gossiping or searching the Internet.[127] Of concern, a recent study with Pakistani telecommunications and IT participants found that anger correlated with more aggressive counterproductive behaviors such as abuse against others and production deviance, while sadness did not. Interestingly, neither anger nor sadness predicted workplace withdrawal, which suggests that managers need to take employee expressions of anger seriously because employees may stay with an organization and continue to act aggressively toward others.[128] Once aggression starts, it's likely that other people will become angry and aggressive, so the stage is set for a serious escalation of negative behavior.

Safety and Injury at Work

Research relating negative affectivity to increased injuries at work suggests employers might improve health and safety (and reduce costs) by ensuring workers aren't engaged in potentially dangerous activities when they're in a bad mood. Bad moods can contribute to injury at work in several ways.[129] Individuals in negative moods tend to be more anxious, which can make them less able to cope effectively with hazards. A person who is always fearful will be more pessimistic about the effectiveness of safety precautions because she feels she'll just get hurt anyway, or she might panic or freeze up when confronted with a threatening situation. Negative moods also make people more distractable, and distractions can obviously lead to careless behaviors.

How Managers Can Influence Moods

8 Apply concepts about emotions and moods to specific OB issues.

You can usually improve a friend's mood by sharing a funny video clip, giving the person a small bag of candy, or even offering a pleasant beverage.[130] But what can companies do to improve employees' moods? Managers can use humor and give their employees small tokens of appreciation for work well done. Also, when leaders themselves are in good moods, group members are more positive; as a result, they cooperate better.[131] But what about when leaders are sad?

glOBalization!

Creating Highly Productive Teams Across the Cultural Emotional Barrier

The best teams are emotionally intelligent; each member's emotions are discerned and respectfully considered by the leaders and by the rest of the group. Across cultures, however, this is often easier said than done. Our environments dictate the norms for displaying emotions, resulting in a cultural emotional barrier whenever members from different parts of the world interact.

Research on cultures has focused on Eastern versus Western global comparisons to describe differing belief and value systems. Eastern countries tend to be more collectivistic, whereas Western countries are more individualistic. These distinctions have a profound effect on the emotional dynamics of work teams.

It is easy to see how misunderstandings can lead to ineffective group dynamics. A member of an Eastern culture, for instance, will tend to focus on the good of the team over his or her personal success. He or she will likely value harmony and

cooperation and may consider any emotional display of anger, disagreement, or contempt to be inappropriate. A group of Eastern members, therefore, will achieve high team productivity in a very different manner from a team of Western members, who value freedom of expression, directness, and other ways of showing individuality. The Western members may be more comfortable working independently than the Eastern members and be more accepting of emotional displays of frustration or enthusiasm. The Eastern members may look for a balance of negative and positive experiences, while the Western members may tally only the positive experiences.

These are generalizations, of course. Any examination of cultures will look for similarities between people. Yet just as individuals' emotional expressions will vary by personality and experience, so are we and our emotions influenced by our cultures. Knowing where someone's emotions are "coming from" can

be an important step toward understanding and thus working well with your teammates. For a team to be highly productive, members need to become emotionally sensitive to the viewpoints of others, and leaders need to learn culturally appropriate emotional responses to motivate team members. Through better understanding of cultures and emotions, multicultural teams can capitalize on the strengths that each individual viewpoint can contribute to organizational goals.

Sources: G. M. Fisk, and J. P. Friesen, "Perceptions of Leader Emotion Regulation and LMX as Predictors of Followers' Job Satisfaction and Organizational Citizenship Behaviors," *Leadership Quarterly* (February 2012), pp. 1–12; E. J. Hartel and X.-Y. Liu, "How Emotional Climate in Teams Affects Workplace Effectiveness in Individualistic and Collectivistic Contexts," *Journal of Management & Organization* (July 2012), pp. 573–585; and V. A. Visser et al., "How Leader Displays of Happiness and Sadness Influence Follower Performance: Emotional Contagion and Creative versus Analytical Performance," *Leadership Quarterly* (February 2013), pp. 172–188.

A recent study on emotional contagion found that leader displays of sadness increase the analytic performance of followers, perhaps because leaders are less engaged with them when sad. However, this study also indicated that leaders are perceived as more effective when they share positive emotions, and followers are more creative in a positive emotional environment.[132]

Selecting positive team members can have a contagion effect because positive moods transmit from team member to team member. One study of professional cricket teams found players' happy moods affected the moods of their team members and positively influenced their performance.[133] It makes sense, then, for managers to select team members predisposed to positive moods.

Summary

Emotions and moods are similar in that both are affective in nature. But they're also different—moods are more general and less contextual than emotions. And events do matter. The time of day and day of the week, stressful events, social activities, and sleep patterns are some of the factors that influence emotions and moods. Emotions and moods have proven relevant for virtually every OB topic we study, and they have implications for managerial practice.

Implications for Managers

- To foster effective decision making, creativity, and motivation in employees, model positive emotions and moods as much as is authentically possible.
- Provide positive feedback to increase the positivity of employees.
- In the service sector, encourage positive displays of emotion, which make customers feel more positive and thus improve customer service interactions and negotiations.
- Regulate your intense emotional responses to an event by recognizing the legitimacy of the emotion and being careful to vent only to a supportive listener who is not involved in the event.
- Be careful not to ignore co-workers' and employees' emotions; do not assess others' behavior as if it were completely rational. As one consultant aptly put it, "You can't divorce emotions from the workplace because you can't divorce emotions from people."[134] Managers who understand the role of emotions and moods will significantly improve their ability to explain and predict their co-workers' and employees' behavior.

Sometimes Blowing Your Top Is a Good Thing

POINT

Anger is discussed throughout this chapter for a reason: It's an important emotion. However, what about our responses to feeling anger? Work cultures teach us to avoid showing any anger at all, lest we be seen as poor service providers or, worse, unprofessional or even deviant or violent. While, of course, there *are* times when the expression of anger is harmful or unprofessional, we've taken this view so far that we now teach people to suppress perfectly normal emotions. It is inappropriate to ask people to behave in abnormal ways, and there is even more evidence about the organizational and personal costs of emotion suppression.

Emerging research shows that suppressing anger takes a terrible toll on individuals. One Stanford University study showed, for example, that when individuals were asked to wear a poker face during the showing of the atomic bombings of Japan during World War II, they were much more stressful conversation partners once the video was over. Other research shows that college students who suppress emotions like anger have more trouble making friends and are more likely to be depressed and that employees who suppress anger feel more stressed by work.

There is a better way. One recent study showed that even when employees displayed anger deemed inappropriate by co-workers, if co-workers responded supportively to the anger (for example, by listening to the angry employee), favorable responses such as constructive work changes were the result.

Yes, managers must work to maintain a positive, respectful, and nonviolent culture. However, asking employees to suppress their anger not only is an ineffective and costly strategy, it ultimately may backfire if appropriate ways to express and release anger are blocked.

COUNTERPOINT

Yes, anger is a common emotion. But it's also a toxic one. The experience of anger and its close correlate, hostility, is linked to many counterproductive behaviors in organizations. That is why many organizations have developed anger management programs—to blunt the harmful effects of anger in the workplace.

The Bureau of Labor Statistics estimates that 16 percent of fatal workplace injuries resulted from workplace violence. Do we think the individuals who committed these acts were feeling joyful and contented?

To reduce anger in the workplace, many companies develop policies that govern conduct such as yelling, shouting profanities, and making hostile gestures. Others institute anger management programs. For example, one organization conducted mandatory in-house workshops that showed individuals how to deal with conflicts in the workplace before they boil over. The director who instituted the training said it "gave people specific tools for opening a dialogue to work things out." MTS Systems, an Eden Prairie, Minnesota, engineering firm, engages an outside consulting firm to conduct anger management programs for its organization. Typically, MTS holds an 8-hour seminar that discusses sources of anger, conflict resolution techniques, and organizational policies. This is followed by one-on-one sessions with individual employees that focus on cognitive behavioral techniques to manage their anger. The outside trainer charges $7,000–$10,000 for the seminar and one-on-one sessions. "You want people to get better at communicating with each other," says MTS manager Karen Borre.

In the end, everyone wins when organizations seek to diminish both the experience and also the expression of anger at work. The work environment is less threatening and stressful to employees and customers. Employees are likely to feel safer. And the angry employee is often helped as well.

Sources: B. Carey, "The Benefits of Blowing Your Top," *The New York Times* (July 6, 2010), p. D1; R. Y. Cheung and I. J. Park, "Anger Suppression, Interdependent Self-Construal, and Depression Among Asian American and European American College Students," *Cultural Diversity and Ethnic Minority Psychology* 16, no. 4 (2010), pp. 517–525; D. Geddes and L. T. Stickney, "The Trouble with Sanctions: Organizational Responses to Deviant Anger Displays at Work," *Human Relations* 64, no. 2 (2011), pp. 201–230; and J. Fairley, "Taking Control of Anger Management," *Workforce Management* (October 2010), p. 10.

END-OF-CHAPTER REVIEW

MyManagementLab

Go to mymanagementlab.com to complete the problems marked with this icon. ⭐

QUESTIONS FOR REVIEW

4-1 What is the difference between emotions and moods? What are the basic emotions and moods?

4-2 Are emotions rational? What functions do they serve?

4-3 What are the sources of emotions and moods?

4-4 What impact does emotional labor have on employees?

4-5 What is affective events theory? What are its applications?

4-6 What is the evidence for and against the existence of emotional intelligence?

4-7 What are some strategies for emotion regulation and their likely effects?

4-8 How do you apply concepts about emotions and moods to specific OB issues?

EXPERIENTIAL EXERCISE   Who Can Catch a Liar?

We mentioned earlier in the chapter that emotion researchers are highly interested in facial expressions as a window into individuals' emotional worlds. Research has also studied whether people can tell someone is lying based on signs of guilt or nervousness in their facial expressions. Let's see who is good at catching liars, but first consider this: How good you are at detecting lies by others is related to your own mood. You are actually less likely to correctly detect a lie if you are in a happy mood. *Hint:* If you are in a negative mood, concentrate mostly on the message itself (does it seem plausible?); if you are in a positive mood, read the nonverbal cues (such as fidgety or calm behavior) more.

Split up into teams and follow these instructions.

4-9. Randomly choose someone to be the team organizer. Have this person write down on a piece of paper "T" for truth and "L" for lie. If there are, say, six people in the group (other than the organizer), then three people will get a slip with a "T" and three a slip with an "L."

It's important that all team members keep what's on their paper a secret.

4-10. Each team member who holds a T slip needs to come up with a true statement, and each team member who holds an L slip needs to come up with a false statement. Try not to make the statement so outrageous that no one would believe it (for example, "I have flown to the moon").

4-11. The organizer will have each member make his or her statement. Group members should then examine the person making the statement closely to try to determine whether he or she is telling the truth or lying. Once each person has made his or her statement, the organizer will ask for a vote and record the tallies.

4-12. Each person should now indicate whether the statement was the truth or a lie.

4-13. How good was your group at catching the liars? Were some people good liars? What did you look for to determine whether someone was lying?

Source: Based on M.-A. Reinard and N. Schwartz, "The Influence of Affective States on the Presence of Lie Detection," *Journal of Experimental Psychology* 18 (2012), pp. 377–389.

ETHICAL DILEMMA Happiness Coaches for Employees

We know there is considerable spillover from personal unhappiness to negative emotions at work. Moreover, those who experience negative emotions in life and at work are more likely to engage in counterproductive behaviors with customers, clients, or fellow employees.

Increasingly, organizations such as American Express, UBS, and KPMG are turning to happiness coaches to address this spillover from personal unhappiness to work emotions and behaviors.

Srikumar Rao is a former college professor who has the nickname, "the happiness guru." Rao teaches people to analyze negative emotions to prevent them from becoming overwhelming. If your job is restructured, for example, Rao suggests avoiding negative thoughts and feelings about it. Instead, he advises, tell yourself it could turn out well in the long run, and there is no way to know at present.

Beyond reframing the emotional impact of work situations, some happiness coaches attack the negative emotional spillover from life to work (and from work to life). A working mother found that a happiness talk by Shawn Actor helped her stop focusing on her stressed-out life and instead look for chances to smile, laugh, and be grateful.

In some cases, the claims made by happiness coaches seem a bit trite. Jim Smith, who labels himself "The Executive Happiness Coach," asks: "What if I told you that there are secrets nobody told you as a kid—or as an adult, for that matter—that can unlock for you all sorts of positive emotional experiences? What if the only thing that gets in the way of you feeling more happiness is—YOU?! What if you can change your experience of the world by shifting a few simple things in your life, and then practicing them until they become second nature?"

If employees leave their experiences with a happiness coach feeling happier about their jobs and their lives, is that not better for everyone? Says one individual, Ivelisse Rivera, who felt she benefited from a happiness coach, "If I assume a negative attitude and complain all the time, whoever is working with me is going to feel the same way."

But what if you can't afford a happiness coach and your employer doesn't want to foot the bill? Recent research suggests a do-it-yourself opportunity to increase your good mood at home. The key is to lend a helping hand. If you help others at work, you may find that later at home, after you've had a chance to relax and reflect, your mood will be improved.

Questions

4-14. Do you think happiness coaches are effective? How might you assess their effectiveness?

4-15. Would you welcome happiness training in your workplace? Why or why not?

4-16. Under what circumstances—if any—is it ethically appropriate for a supervisor to suggest a happiness coach for a subordinate?

Sources: S. Shellenbarger, "Thinking Happy Thoughts at Work," *The Wall Street Journal* (January 27, 2010), p. D2; S. Sharma and D. Chatterjee, "Cos Are Keenly Listening to 'Happiness Coach,'" *Economic Times* (July 16, 2010), http://articles.economictimes.indiatimes.com; J. Smith, *The Executive Happiness Coach*, www.lifewithhappiness.com/ (downloaded May 3, 2011); and S. Sonnentag and A. M. Grant, "Doing Good at Work Feels Good at Home, But Not Right Way: When and Why Perceived Prosocial Impact Predicts Positive Affect," *Personnel Psychology* 65 (2012), pp. 495–530.

CASE INCIDENT 1 Is It Okay to Cry at Work?

As this chapter has shown, emotions are an inevitable part of people's behavior at work. At the same time, it's not entirely clear that we've reached a point where people feel comfortable expressing *all* emotions at work. The reason might be that business culture and etiquette remain poorly suited to handling overt emotional displays. The question is: Can organizations become more intelligent about emotional management? Is it ever appropriate to yell, laugh, or cry at work?

Some people are skeptical about the virtues of more emotional displays at the workplace. As the chapter notes, emotions are automatic physiological responses to the environment, and as such, they can be difficult to control appropriately. One 22-year-old customer service representative named Laura who was the subject of a case study noted that fear and anger were routinely used as methods to control employees, and employees deeply resented this use of emotions to manipulate them. In another case, the chairman of a major television network made a practice of screaming at employees whenever anything went wrong, leading to badly hurt feelings and a lack of loyalty to the organization. Like Laura, workers at this organization were hesitant to show their true reactions to these emotional outbursts for fear of being branded as "weak" or "ineffectual." It might seem like these individuals worked in heavily emotional workplaces, but in fact, only a narrow range of emotions was deemed acceptable. Anger appears to be more acceptable than sadness in many organizations, and anger can have serious maladaptive consequences. Many people find their negative reaction to hearing an angry outburst lasts, making it difficult for them to concentrate at work, while those who yell can seem to indicate a lack of emotional intelligence.

Others believe organizations that recognize and work with emotions effectively are more creative, satisfying, and productive. For example, Laura noted that if she could express her hurt feelings without fear, she would be much more satisfied with her work. In other words, the problem with Laura's organization was not that emotions were displayed, but that emotional displays were handled poorly. Others note that the use of emotional knowledge—like being able to read and understand the reactions of others—is crucial for workers ranging from salespeople and customer service agents all the way to managers and executives. One survey even found that 88 percent of workers feel being sensitive to the emotions of others is an asset. Management consultant Erika Anderson notes, "Crying at

work is transformative and can open the door to change." The question then is, Can organizations take specific steps to become better at allowing emotional displays without opening a Pandora's Box of outbursts?

Questions

4-17. What factors do you think make some organizations ineffective at managing emotions?

4-18. Do you think the strategic use and display of emotions serve to protect employees, or does covering your true emotions at work lead to more problems than it solves?

⊛ **4-19.** Have you ever worked where emotions were used as part of a management style? Describe the advantages and disadvantages of this approach in your experience.

4-20. Research shows that acts of co-workers (37 percent) and management (22 percent) cause more negative emotions for employees than do acts of customers (7 percent).[135] What can Laura's company do to change its emotional climate?

Sources: E. Bernstein, "Why People Have Big Explosions for Very Small Reasons," *The Wall Street Journal* (October 16, 2012), pp. D1, D2; A. Kreamer, "Go Ahead—Cry at Work," *Time* (April 4, 2010), www .time.com; J. S. Lerner and K. Shonk, "How Anger Poisons Decision Making," *Harvard Business Review* (September 2010), p. 26; S. Shellenbarger, "When the Boss Is a Screamer," *The Wall Street Journal* (August 15, 2012), pp. D1–D2; and J. Perrone and M. H. Vickers, "Emotions as Strategic Game in a Hostile Workplace: An Exemplar Case," *Employee Responsibilities and Rights Journal* 16, no. 3 (2004), pp. 167–178.

CASE INCIDENT 2 Can You Read Emotions from Faces?

We mentioned previously that some researchers—psychologist Paul Ekman may be the best known—have studied whether facial expressions reveal true emotions. These researchers have distinguished real smiles (so-called Duchenne smiles, named after French physician Guillaume Duchenne) from "fake" smiles. Duchenne found genuine smiles raised not only the corners of the mouth (easily faked) but also cheek and eye muscles (much more difficult to fake). So, one way to determine whether someone is genuinely happy or amused is to look at the muscles around the upper cheeks and eyes—if the person's eyes are smiling or twinkling, the smile is genuine. Ekman and his associates have developed similar methods to detect other emotions, such as anger, disgust, and distress. According to Ekman, the key to identifying real emotions is to focus on micro-expressions, or those facial muscles we cannot easily manipulate. Recent research indicates that people cannot accurately infer emotions in others from their facial expressions.

Dan Hill has used these techniques to study the facial expressions of CEOs and found they vary dramatically

not only in their Duchenne smiles but also in the degree to which they display positive versus negative facial expressions. The accompanying table shows Hill's analysis of the facial expressions of some prominent male executives:

Jeff Bezos, Amazon	51% positive
Warren Buffet, Berkshire Hathaway	69% positive
Michael Dell, Dell Computers	47% positive
Larry Ellison, Oracle	0% positive
Bill Gates, Microsoft	73% positive
Phil Knight, Nike	67% positive
Donald Trump, The Trump Organization	16% positive

It's interesting to note that these individuals, all of whom are successful in various ways, have such different levels of positive facial expressions. It also raises the question: Is a smile from Larry Ellison worth more than a smile from Bill Gates?

Questions

4-21. Most research suggests we are not very good at detecting fake emotions, and we think we're much better at it than we are. Do you believe training would improve your ability to detect emotional displays in others?

4-22. Do you think the information in this case could help you tell whether someone's smile is genuine?

4-23. Is your own impression of the facial expressions of the eight business leaders consistent with what the researcher found? If not, why do you think your views might be at odds with his?

✪ **4-24.** Assuming you could become better at detecting the real emotions in facial expressions, do you think it would help your career? Why or why not?

Sources: Based on P. Ekman, *Telling Lies: Clues to Deceit in the Marketplace, Politics, and Marriage* (New York: W. W. Norton & Co., 2009); D. Jones, "It's Written All Over Their Faces," *USA Today* (February 25, 2008), pp. 1B–2B; N. O. Rule and N. Ambady, "The Face of Success," *Psychological Science* 19, no. 2 (2008), pp. 109–111; and R. Reisenzein, M. Studtmann, and G. Horstmann, "Coherence between Emotion and Facial Expression: Evidence from Laboratory Experiments," *Emotion Review* (January 2013), pp. 16–23.

MyManagementLab

Go to **mymanagementlab.com** for Auto-graded writing questions as well as the following Assisted-graded writing questions:

4-25. In relation to the Ethical Dilemma, some argue that happiness coaches are a way for organizations to avoid solving real work problems—a diversion, if you will. How might we make this determination?

4-26. Concerning Case Incident 2, one research study found people's ratings of the positive affect displayed in CEO's faces had very little correlation to their company's profits. Does that suggest to you that Hill's analysis is immaterial?

4-27. MyManagementLab Only—comprehensive writing assignment for this chapter.

5

Personality and Values

A FRESH PERSONALITY

Matthew Corrin is CEO of Freshii, a rapidly expanding chain of restaurants that feature fresh ingredients from organic and local farms. "Healthy casual" is the niche Corrin claims to have created with his company.

Corrin started Freshii in Canada where he was born and raised. Today, the company has more U.S. than Canadian restaurants; is headquartered in Chicago; and has expanded into Austria, China, Columbia, Switzerland, and the United Arab Emirates.

Corrin started Freshii from his parents' house when he was 23; now 32, he runs a company whose annual revenues approach $100 million. His unusual personality may explain much of his early and rapid success. Corrin is known for his outsized ambitions; in fact, he intends to have 1,000 restaurants in the next few years and wants to create a "global, iconic brand" as ubiquitous as Starbucks. Asked to describe his philosophy in hiring managers, Corrin commented, "Merely 'good' managers need not apply. You will only fit into our organization if you're a 'super-achiever.'"

Corrin is also known for his hard-driving ways. He demands the best from others—"failure is not an option," he says—and is not afraid to do what it takes to succeed. He says: "I think the traditional restaurant mantra is, 'If you build it, they will come.' I think that is just so old school. So our philosophy is build it and then guerilla market the hell out of it to make them come."

Finally, Corrin might be described as somewhat narcissistic. He expects those around him to adapt to his personality. When asked what he looks for in potential employees and operators of his franchises, Corrin says, "I need to want them to be my friends." He also enjoys being the center of attention and likes being recognized. In fact, some might even label him a media hog. He loves rubbing elbows with celebrities: Ryan Seacrest and Ashton Kutcher attended one of Freshii's grand openings in New York.

Recently, Corrin appeared on a TV episode of *Undercover Boss Canada* where, to avoid being recognized, he donned a beard and a wig, wore a "fat suit," and worked in a Freshii restaurant slicing tomatoes. When he cut his finger, one of his employees offered to help him by dumping salt into the cut. Corrin grimaced in obvious pain as the blood poured from the salted wound, but the employee kept her job.

Sources: D. Eng, "Freshii's Fresh Take on Fast Food," *Fortune* (April 11, 2013), http://money.cnn .com/2013/04/11/news/companies/freshii-matthew-corrin.pr.fortune/index.html; M. Brandau, "Freshii CEO Discusses Move into China," *Restaurant News* (January 3, 2013), http://nrn.com/ international/freshii-ceo-discusses-move-china; "Freshii CEO: How 'Undercover Boss' Changed My Business" *Business Insider* (March 7, 2013), www.bullfax.com/?q=node-freshii-ceo-how-undercover-boss-changed-my-business; and K. Martonik, "Freshii CEO Matthew Corrin on Undercover Boss," *Fransmart Blog* (March 14, 2013), http://fransmart.com/blog/55/Freshii-CEO-Matthew-Corrin-on-Undercover-Boss.html.

LEARNING OBJECTIVES

After studying this chapter, you should be able to:

1 Describe personality, the way it is measured, and the factors that shape it.

2 Describe the Myers-Briggs Type Indicator personality framework and its strengths and weaknesses.

3 Identify the key traits in the Big Five personality model.

4 Demonstrate how the Big Five traits predict behavior at work.

5 Describe how the situation affects whether personality predicts behavior.

6 Contrast terminal and instrumental values.

7 Compare generational differences in values.

8 Identify Hofstede's five value dimensions of national culture.

As the story of Matthew Corrin indicates, we all have different personalities. In the first half of this chapter, we review the research on personality and its relationship to behavior. People also differ in their values. In the latter half of the chapter, we look at how values shape many of our work-related behaviors.

Although we focus much of our discussion on the Big Five personality traits, they are not the only traits that describe people. One of the others we'll discuss is narcissism. Check out the Self-Assessment Library to see how you score on narcissism. (Remember: Be honest!)

SELF-ASSESSMENT LIBRARY

Am I a Narcissist?

In the Self-Assessment Library (available in MyManagementLab), take assessment IV.A.1 (Am I a Narcissist?) and answer the following questions.

1. How did you score? Did your scores surprise you? Why or why not?
2. On which facet of narcissism did you score highest? Lowest?
3. Do you think this measure is accurate? Why or why not?

Personality

1 Describe personality, the way it is measured, and the factors that shape it.

Why are some people quiet and passive, while others are loud and aggressive? Are certain personality types better adapted than others for certain job types? Before we can answer these questions, we need to address a more basic one: What is personality?

What Is Personality?

When we speak of someone's personality, we don't mean the person has charm or is constantly smiling. As organizational behaviorists, we are describing a dynamic concept of the growth and development of a person's personality.

Defining Personality   The definition of *personality* we most frequently use was produced by Gordon Allport nearly 70 years ago. Allport said personality is "the dynamic organization within the individual of those psychophysical systems that determine his unique adjustments to his environment."[1] For our purposes, you should think of **personality** as the sum total of ways in which an individual reacts to and interacts with others. We most often describe it in terms of the measurable traits a person exhibits.

personality *The sum total of ways in which an individual reacts to and interacts with others.*

Measuring Personality   The most important reason managers need to know how to measure personality is that research has shown personality tests are useful in hiring decisions and help managers forecast who is best for a job.[2] The most common means of measuring personality is through self-report surveys in which individuals evaluate themselves on a series of factors, such as "I worry a lot about the future." Though self-report measures work when well constructed, the respondent might lie or practice impression management to create a good impression. When people know their personality scores are going to be used for hiring decisions, they rate themselves as about half a standard deviation more conscientious and emotionally stable than if they are taking the test to learn more about themselves.[3] Another problem is accuracy; a candidate who is in a bad mood when taking the survey may have inaccurate scores.

Observer-ratings surveys provide an independent assessment of personality. Here, a co-worker or another observer does the rating (sometimes with the subject's knowledge and sometimes not). Though the results of self-report surveys and observer-ratings surveys are strongly correlated, research suggests observer-ratings surveys better predict success on the job.[4] However, each can tell us something unique about an individual's behavior. An analysis of a large number of observer-reported personality studies shows that a combination of self-reports and observer-reports predicts performance better than any one type of information. The implication is clear: Use both observer ratings and self-report ratings of personality when making important employment decisions.

Personality Determinants   An early debate in personality research centered on whether an individual's personality is the result of heredity or environment. Personality appears to be a result of both; however, research tends to support the importance of heredity over the environment.

Heredity refers to factors determined at conception. Physical stature, facial features, gender, temperament, muscle composition and reflexes, energy level, and biological rhythms are generally considered to be either completely or substantially influenced by parentage—by your biological parents' biological, physiological, and inherent psychological makeup. The heredity approach argues that the ultimate explanation of an individual's personality is the molecular structure of the genes, located in the chromosomes.

Researchers in many different countries have studied thousands of sets of identical twins who were separated at birth and raised apart.[5] If heredity played little or no part in determining personality, you would expect to find few similarities between separated twins. Researchers have found, however, that genetics accounts for about 50 percent of the personality similarities between twins and more than 30 percent of the similarities in occupational and leisure interests. One set of twins separated for 39 years and raised 45 miles apart were found to drive the same model and color car. They chain-smoked the same brand of cigarette, owned dogs with the same name, and regularly vacationed within three blocks of each other in a beach community 1,500 miles away.

Interestingly, twin studies have suggested parents don't add much to our personality development. The personalities of identical twins raised in different households are more similar to each other than to the personalities of siblings with whom the twins were raised. Ironically, the most important contribution our parents may make to our personalities is giving us their genes!

This is not to suggest that personality never changes. People's scores on dependability tend to increase over time, as when young adults start families and establish careers. However, strong individual differences in dependability remain; everyone tends to change by about the same amount, so their rank order stays roughly the same.[6] An analogy to intelligence may make this clearer. Children become smarter as they age, so nearly everyone is smarter at age 20 than at age 10. Still, if Keisha is smarter than Blake at age 10, she is likely to be smarter at age 20, too. Research has shown that personality is more changeable in adolescence and more stable among adults.[7]

Early work on personality tried to identify and label enduring characteristics that describe an individual's behavior, including shy, aggressive, submissive, lazy, ambitious, loyal, and timid. When someone exhibits these characteristics in a large number of situations, we call them **personality traits** of that person.[8] The consistency over time and frequency of expression in diverse situations indicates how important the trait is for the individual.

heredity   *Factors determined at conception; one's biological, physiological, and inherent psychological makeup.*

personality traits   *Enduring characteristics that describe an individual's behavior.*

Photo 5-1 Personality traits used to describe Richard Branson, chairman of Virgin Group, include energetic, charismatic, decisive, ambitious, adaptable, courageous, and industrious. These traits helped Branson, shown here with his daughter, build one of the most recognized and respected global brands in travel, entertainment, and lifestyle.

Source: Eric Best/Landmark Media Landmark Media/Newscom.

Early efforts to identify and classify the primary traits that govern behavior[9] often produced long lists that were difficult to generalize from and provided little practical guidance to organizational decision makers. Two exceptions are the Myers-Briggs Type Indicator and the Big Five Model, now the dominant frameworks.

The Myers-Briggs Type Indicator

2 Describe the Myers-Briggs Type Indicator personality framework and its strengths and weaknesses.

Myers-Briggs Type Indicator (MBTI) *A personality test that taps four characteristics and classifies people into 1 of 16 personality types.*

The **Myers-Briggs Type Indicator (MBTI)** is the most widely used personality-assessment instrument in the world.[10] It is a 100-question personality test that asks people how they usually feel or act in situations. Respondents are classified as extraverted or introverted (E or I), sensing or intuitive (S or N), thinking or feeling (T or F), and judging or perceiving (J or P):

- **Extraverted (E) versus Introverted (I).** Extraverted individuals are outgoing, sociable, and assertive. Introverts are quiet and shy.
- **Sensing (S) versus Intuitive (N).** Sensing types are practical and prefer routine and order. They focus on details. Intuitives rely on unconscious processes and look at the "big picture."
- **Thinking (T) versus Feeling (F).** Thinking types use reason and logic to handle problems. Feeling types rely on their personal values and emotions.
- **Judging (J) versus Perceiving (P).** Judging types want control and prefer order and structure. Perceiving types are flexible and spontaneous.

These classifications describe 16 personality types by identifying one trait from each of the four pairs. For example, Introverted/Intuitive/Thinking/Judging people (INTJs) are visionaries with original minds and great drive. They are skeptical, critical, independent, determined, and often stubborn. ESTJs are organizers. They are realistic, logical, analytical, and decisive, perfect for business or mechanics. The ENTP type is innovative, individualistic, versatile, and attracted to entrepreneurial ideas. This person tends to be resourceful in solving challenging problems but may neglect routine assignments.

The MBTI has been widely used by organizations including Apple Computer, AT&T, Citigroup, GE, 3M Co.; many hospitals and educational institutions; and even the U.S. Armed Forces. Evidence is mixed about its validity as a measure of personality, however; most of the evidence is against it.[11] One problem is that the model forces a person into one type or another; that is, you're either introverted or extraverted. There is no in-between, though people can be both extraverted and introverted to some degree. The MBTI can be a valuable tool for increasing self-awareness and providing career guidance, but because results tend to be unrelated to job performance, managers probably shouldn't use it as a selection test for job candidates.

The Big Five Personality Model

3 Identify the key traits in the Big Five personality model.

Big Five Model *A personality assessment model that taps five basic dimensions.*

extraversion *A personality dimension describing someone who is sociable, gregarious, and assertive.*

agreeableness *A personality dimension that describes someone who is good natured, cooperative, and trusting.*

conscientiousness *A personality dimension that describes someone who is responsible, dependable, persistent, and organized.*

emotional stability *A personality dimension that characterizes someone as calm, self-confident, secure (positive) versus nervous, depressed, and insecure (negative).*

openness to experience *A personality dimension that characterizes someone in terms of imagination, sensitivity, and curiosity.*

The MBTI may lack strong supporting evidence, but an impressive body of research supports the **Big Five Model**—that five basic dimensions underlie all others and encompass most of the significant variation in human personality.[12] Moreover, test scores of these traits do a very good job of predicting how people behave in a variety of real-life situations.[13] These are the Big Five factors:

- **Extraversion.**   The **extraversion** dimension captures our comfort level with relationships. Extraverts tend to be gregarious, assertive, and sociable. Introverts tend to be reserved, timid, and quiet.
- **Agreeableness.**   The **agreeableness** dimension refers to an individual's propensity to defer to others. Highly agreeable people are cooperative, warm, and trusting. People who score low on agreeableness are cold, disagreeable, and antagonistic.
- **Conscientiousness.**   The **conscientiousness** dimension is a measure of reliability. A highly conscientious person is responsible, organized, dependable, and persistent. Those who score low on this dimension are easily distracted, disorganized, and unreliable.
- **Emotional stability.**   The **emotional stability** dimension—often labeled by its converse, neuroticism—taps a person's ability to withstand stress. People with positive emotional stability tend to be calm, self-confident, and secure. Those with high negative scores tend to be nervous, anxious, depressed, and insecure.
- **Openness to experience.**   The **openness to experience** dimension addresses range of interests and fascination with novelty. Extremely open people are creative, curious, and artistically sensitive. Those at the other end of the category are conventional and find comfort in the familiar.

How Do the Big Five Traits Predict Behavior at Work?   Research has found relationships between these personality dimensions and job performance.[14] As the authors of the most-cited review observed, "The preponderance of evidence shows that individuals who are dependable, reliable, careful, thorough, able to plan, organized, hardworking, persistent, and achievement-oriented tend to have higher job performance in most if not all occupations."[15] Employees who score higher in conscientiousness develop higher levels of job knowledge, probably because highly conscientious people learn more (a review of 138 studies revealed conscientiousness was related to GPA).[16] Higher levels of job knowledge contribute to higher levels of job performance. Conscientious individuals who are more interested in learning than in just performing on the job are also exceptionally good at maintaining performance in the face of negative feedback.[17] There can be "too much of a good thing," however, as extremely conscientious individuals typically do not perform better than those who are simply above average in conscientiousness.[18]

Photo 5-2 Angela Ahrendts, CEO of British fashion house Burberry Group, scores high on the Big Five Model personality dimensions. She is sociable, agreeable, conscientious, emotionally stable, and open to experiences—factors that have contributed to her high job performance and career success in revitalizing the Burberry brand.

Source: Felipe Trueba Garcia/ZUMApress/Newscom.

Conscientiousness is important to organizational success. As Exhibit 5-1 shows, a study of the personality scores of 313 CEO candidates in private equity companies (of whom 225 were hired; their company's performance later correlated with their personality scores) found conscientiousness—in the form of persistence, attention to detail, and setting of high standards—was more important than other traits.

Interestingly, conscientious people live longer; they take better care of themselves and engage in fewer risky behaviors like smoking, drinking and drugs, and risky sexual or driving behavior.[19] They don't adapt as well to changing contexts, however. They are generally performance oriented and may have trouble learning complex skills early in the training process because their focus is on performing well rather than on learning. Finally, they are often less creative than less conscientious people, especially artistically.[20]

Although conscientiousness is most consistently related to job performance, the other Big Five traits also have some bearing. Let's look at them one at a time. Exhibit 5-2 summarizes.

Of the Big Five traits, emotional stability is most strongly related to life satisfaction, job satisfaction, and low stress levels. High scorers are more likely to be positive and optimistic and experience fewer negative emotions; they are generally happier than low scorers. Low scorers are hypervigilant (looking for problems or impending signs of danger) and are vulnerable to the physical and psychological effects of stress.

4 Demonstrate how the Big Five traits predict behavior at work.

Exhibit 5-1	Traits That Matter Most to Business Success at Buyout Companies
Most Important	**Less Important**
Persistence	Strong oral communication
Attention to detail	Teamwork
Efficiency	Flexibility/adaptability
Analytical skills	Enthusiasm
Setting high standards	Listening skills

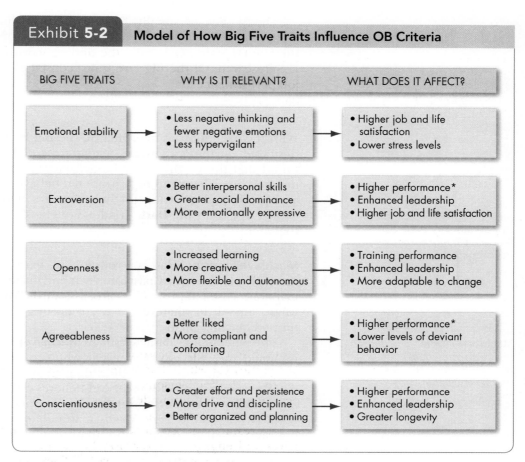

Exhibit 5-2	Model of How Big Five Traits Influence OB Criteria

BIG FIVE TRAITS	WHY IS IT RELEVANT?	WHAT DOES IT AFFECT?
Emotional stability	• Less negative thinking and fewer negative emotions • Less hypervigilant	• Higher job and life satisfaction • Lower stress levels
Extroversion	• Better interpersonal skills • Greater social dominance • More emotionally expressive	• Higher performance* • Enhanced leadership • Higher job and life satisfaction
Openness	• Increased learning • More creative • More flexible and autonomous	• Training performance • Enhanced leadership • More adaptable to change
Agreeableness	• Better liked • More compliant and conforming	• Higher performance* • Lower levels of deviant behavior
Conscientiousness	• Greater effort and persistence • More drive and discipline • Better organized and planning	• Higher performance • Enhanced leadership • Greater longevity

*In jobs requiring significant teamwork or frequent interpersonal interactions.

Extraverts tend to be happier in their jobs and in their lives. They experience more positive emotions than do introverts, and they express these feelings. Extraverts also tend to perform better in jobs with significant interpersonal interaction: They usually have more social skills and friends. Finally, extraversion is a relatively strong predictor of leadership emergence in groups; extraverts are more socially dominant, "take charge" people, usually more assertive than introverts.[21] Extraverts are more impulsive than introverts; they are more likely to be absent from work and engage in risky behavior such as unprotected sex, drinking, and other sensation-seeking acts.[22] One study also found extraverts were more likely than introverts to lie during job interviews.[23]

High scorers for openness to experience are more creative in science and art than low scorers. Because creativity is important to leadership, open people are more likely to be effective leaders—and more comfortable with ambiguity. They cope better with organizational change and are more adaptable in varying contexts. Recent evidence suggests they are susceptible to workplace accidents.[24]

You might expect agreeable people to be happier than disagreeable people. They are, but only slightly. When people choose romantic partners, friends, or organizational team members, agreeable individuals are usually first choice. Agreeable individuals are better liked than disagreeable people; they tend to do better in interpersonally oriented jobs such as customer service. Agreeable people also are more compliant and rule abiding, less likely to get into accidents, and more satisfied in their jobs. They contribute to organizational performance by engaging in citizenship behavior[25] and are less likely to engage in organizational deviance. Agreeableness is associated with lower levels of career success (especially earnings).

The Big Five personality factors appear in almost all cross-cultural studies,[26] including China, Israel, Germany, Japan, Spain, Nigeria, Norway, Pakistan, and the United States. Generally, the findings corroborate what has been found in U.S. research: Of the Big Five traits, conscientiousness is the best predictor of job performance.

The Dark Triad

With the exception of neuroticism, the Big Five traits are what we call socially desirable, meaning we would be glad to score high on them. Researchers have found that three other socially *undesirable* traits, which we all have in varying degrees, are relevant to organizational behavior: Machiavellianism, narcissism, and psychopathy. Owing to their negative nature, researchers have labeled these three traits the **Dark Triad**—though, of course, they do not always occur together.[27]

Dark Triad   *A constellation of negative personality traits consisting of Machiavellianism, narcissism, and psychopathy.*

Machiavellianism   Hao is a young bank manager in Shanghai. He's received three promotions in the past four years and makes no apologies for the aggressive tactics he's used to propel his career upward. "My name means clever, and that's what I am—I do whatever I have to do to get ahead," he says. Hao would be termed Machiavellian.

The personality characteristic of **Machiavellianism** (often abbreviated *Mach*) is named after Niccolo Machiavelli, who wrote in the sixteenth century on how to gain and use power. An individual high in Machiavellianism is pragmatic, maintains emotional distance, and believes ends can justify means. "If it works, use it" is consistent with a high-Mach perspective. A considerable amount of research has found high Machs manipulate more, win more, are persuaded less, and persuade others more than do low Machs.[28] They are more likely to act aggressively and engage in other counterproductive work behaviors as well. A recent review of the literature revealed that Machiavellianism does not significantly predict overall job performance.[29] High-Mach employees, by manipulating others to their advantage, win in the short term, but they lose those gains in the long term because they are not well-liked.

The effects of Machiavellianism depend somewhat on the context. The reason, in part, is that individuals' personalities affect the situations they choose. One study showed that high-Mach job seekers were less positively affected by knowing an organization engaged in a high level of corporate social responsibility (CSR).[30] Another study found that Machs' ethical leadership behaviors were less likely to translate into followers' work engagement because followers "see through" these behaviors and realize it is a case of surface acting.[31]

Machiavellianism   *The degree to which an individual is pragmatic, maintains emotional distance, and believes that ends can justify means.*

Narcissism   Sabrina likes to be the center of attention. She often looks at herself in the mirror, has extravagant dreams, and considers herself a person of many talents. Sabrina is a narcissist. The trait is named for the Greek myth of Narcissus, a youth so vain and proud he fell in love with his own image. In psychology, **narcissism** describes a person who has a grandiose sense of self-importance, requires excessive admiration, has a sense of entitlement, and is arrogant. Evidence suggests narcissists are more charismatic than others.[32] Both leaders and managers tend to score higher on narcissism, suggesting that a certain self-centeredness is needed to succeed. Narcissists also reported higher levels of work motivation, job engagement, and life satisfaction than others. A study of Norwegian bank employees found that those scoring high on narcissism enjoyed their work more.[33] Some evidence suggests that narcissists are more adaptable and make better business decisions than others when the decision is complex.[34]

narcissism   *The tendency to be arrogant, have a grandiose sense of self-importance, require excessive admiration, and have a sense of entitlement.*

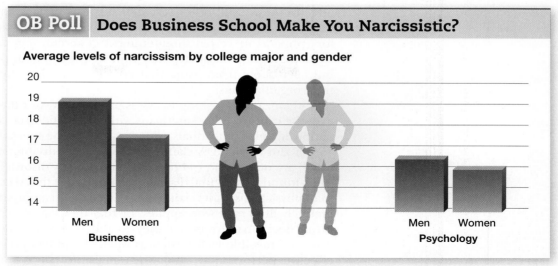

OB Poll Does Business School Make You Narcissistic?

Average levels of narcissism by college major and gender

Source: Based on J. W. Westerman, J. Z. Bergman, S. M. Bergman, and J. P. Daly, "Are Universities Creating Millennial Narcissistic Employees? An Empirical Examination of Narcissism in Business Students and Its Implications," *Journal of Management Education* 36 (2012), pp. 5–32.

While narcissism seems to have little relationship with job performance, it is fairly strongly related to increased counterproductive work behaviors and is linked to other negative outcomes. A study found that while narcissists thought they were *better* leaders than their colleagues, their supervisors rated them as *worse*. In highly ethical contexts, narcissistic leaders are likely to be perceived as ineffective and unethical.[35]

Special attention has been paid to the narcissism of CEOs. An Oracle executive described that company's CEO Larry Ellison as follows: "The difference between God and Larry is that God does not believe he is Larry."[36] A study of narcissistic CEOs revealed that they make more acquisitions, pay higher premiums for those acquisitions, respond less clearly to objective measures of performance, and respond to media praise by making even more acquisitions.[37] Research using data compiled over 100 years has shown that narcissistic CEOs of baseball organizations generate higher levels of manager turnover, although members of external organizations see them as more influential.[38]

Narcissism and its effects are not confined to CEOs or celebrities. Narcissists are more likely to post self-promoting material on their Facebook pages.[39] Like the effects of Machiavellianism, those of narcissism vary by context. A study of Swiss Air Force officers found that narcissists were particularly likely to be irritated by feeling under-benefited, meaning that when narcissists don't get what they want, they are more stressed by that than others.[40]

Psychopathy Psychopathy is part of the Dark Triad, but in organizational behavior, it does not connote insanity. In the OB context, **psychopathy** is defined as a lack of concern for others, and a lack of guilt or remorse when their actions cause harm.[41] Measures of psychopathy attempt to assess the person's motivation to comply with social norms; willingness to use deceit to obtain desired ends and the effectiveness of those efforts; impulsivity; and disregard, that is, lack of empathic concern, for others.

The literature is not consistent about whether psychopathy or other aberrant personality traits are important to work behavior. One review found little correlation between measures of psychopathy and job performance or counterproductive work behaviors. A recent study found that antisocial personality, which is closely related to psychopathy, was positively related to advancement in the organization but unrelated to other aspects of career success and

psychopathy *The tendency for a lack of concern for others and a lack of guilt or remorse when their actions cause harm.*

effectiveness.[42] Still other research suggests that psychopathy is related to the use of hard influence tactics (threats, manipulation) and bullying work behavior (physical or verbal threatening).[43] The cunning displayed by people who score high on psychopathy may thus help them gain power in an organization but keep them from using that power toward healthy ends for themselves or their organizations.

Organizations wishing to assess psychopathy or other aberrant traits need to exercise caution. The Americans with Disabilities Act (ADA) prohibits discrimination against individuals with "a physical or mental impairment." Roughly 15 percent of all ADA claims involve mental disabilities, the most common of which are depression (44 percent) and anxiety disorders (18 percent). A recent study found that mental disability claims under the ADA fared only slightly worse than physical disability claims. This does not mean organizations must hire every mentally ill person who applies, or that they cannot consider mental illness in hiring decisions. However, if they do, the ADA places specific guidelines on when it is a permissible factor, such as when the illness prevents or severely restricts effective performance, and when it cannot be reasonably accommodated.[44] Given the relative newness of research on the Dark Triad, using psychopathology in employment decisions may carry more risks for now than rewards.

Approach–Avoidance

approach–avoidance framework
The framework by which individuals react to stimuli, whereby approach motivation is attraction to positive stimuli and avoidance motivation is our aversion to negative stimuli.

The MBTI, the Big Five, and the Dark Triad are not the only theoretical frameworks for personality. Recently, the **approach-avoidance framework** has cast personality traits as motivations. Approach and avoidance motivation represent the degree to which we react to stimuli; approach motivation is our attraction to positive stimuli and avoidance motivation our aversion to negative stimuli.

The approach–avoidance framework thus organizes traits and may help explain how they predict work behavior. One study showed, for instance, that approach and avoidance motivation can help explain how core self-evaluations affect job satisfaction.[45] The framework also addresses our multiple motives when we act. For example, competitive pressures tend to invoke both approach motivation (people work harder to win) and avoidance motivation (people are distracted and demotivated by fear of losing). The way an individual performs depends on which of these motivations dominates.[46] Another study found that when newcomers joined IT companies in India, they received support from their supervisor (who helped the newcomer by doing a special favor), but also verbal aggression (the supervisor made fun of new ideas). The support provoked approach behavior (the newcomer asked the supervisor for feedback on performance). The aggression provoked avoidance behavior (the newcomer avoided speaking with the supervisor unless absolutely necessary). The net effect on performance depended on which of these dominated.[47]

While the approach–avoidance framework has provided some important insights into behavior in organizations, there are several unresolved issues. First, is the framework simply a way of categorizing positive and negative traits, such as conscientiousness and neuroticism? Second, what traits fit into the framework? Nearly all the traits reviewed in this book do—including the Big Five, the Dark Triad, and others—yet these traits are quite different. Do we gain enough from aggregating them to make up for possibly missing other insights into behavior that are unique to each? Further research and evaluation are needed.

Other Personality Traits Relevant to OB

The Big Five traits have proven highly relevant to OB, and the Dark Triad promises to be the subject of much future research, but they don't exhaust the range of traits that can describe someone's personality. Now we'll look at other, more specific, attributes that are powerful predictors of behavior in organizations: core self-evaluation, self-monitoring, and proactive personality.

core self-evaluation (CSE) *Bottom-line conclusions individuals have about their capabilities, competence, and worth as a person.*

Core Self-Evaluation   People who have positive **core self-evaluations (CSE)** like themselves and see themselves as effective, capable, and in control of their environment. Those with negative core self-evaluations tend to dislike themselves, question their capabilities, and view themselves as powerless over their environment.[48] We discussed in Chapter 3 that core self-evaluations relate to job satisfaction because people positive on this trait see more challenge in their jobs and actually attain more complex jobs.

People with positive core self-evaluations perform better than others because they set more ambitious goals, are more committed to their goals, and persist longer in attempting to reach them. One study of life insurance agents found core self-evaluations were critical predictors of performance. In fact, this study showed the majority of successful salespersons did have positive core self-evaluations.[49] Ninety percent of life insurance sales calls end in rejection, so an agent has to believe in him- or herself to persist. People who have high core self-evaluations provide better customer service, are more popular co-workers, and have careers that begin on better footing and ascend more rapidly over time.[50] They perform especially well if they feel their work provides meaning and is helpful to others.[51]

What happens when someone thinks he is capable but is actually incompetent? One study of *Fortune* 500 CEOs showed that many are overconfident, and their perceived infallibility often causes them to make bad decisions.[52] Teddy Forstmann, chair of the sports marketing giant IMG, said of himself, "I know God gave me an unusual brain. I can't deny that. I have a God-given talent for seeing potential."[53] People like Forstmann may be *over*confident, but those with lower CSE may sell themselves short and be less happy and effective than they could be because of it. If people decide they can't do something, they may not try, thus reinforcing their self-doubts.

Photo 5-3 Blake Mycoskie, founder of TOMS Shoes, has the personality trait of positive core self-evaluation. Confident, capable, and effective, he saw children in Argentina who suffered from injuries to their feet because they had no shoes and decided to do something about it by starting a company that gives shoes to children in need.

Source: WireImage/Getty Images.

"We Can Accurately Judge Individuals' Personalities a Few Seconds After Meeting Them"

Surprisingly, this statement appears to be true.

Research indicates that individuals can accurately appraise others' personalities only a few seconds after first meeting them. This "zero acquaintance" approach shows that regardless of the way in which people first meet someone, whether in person or online, their first judgments about the other's personality have validity. In one study, for example, individuals were asked to introduce themselves in, on average, 7.4 seconds. Observers' ratings of those individuals' extraversion were significantly correlated with the individuals' self-reported extraversion.

While some factors make these first impressions, or "thin slices," more accurate, they have only a modest effect. For example, some traits like extraversion are easier to perceive than others upon initial acquaintance, but less obvious traits like self-esteem and emotional stability are also often judged fairly accurately by others. Even being forced to make intuitive, quick judgments rather than deliberate evaluations does not seem to undermine the accuracy of the appraisals.

The moderate accuracy of "thin slices" helps to explain the moderate validity of employment interviews, which we discuss in Chapter 17. Specifically, research shows that interviewers make up their minds about candidates within 2 minutes of first meeting them. While this is hardly an ideal way to make important employment decisions, the research on personality also shows that these judgments do have some level of validity.

Source: S. Hirschmüller, B. Egloff, S. Nestler, and D. Mitja, "The Dual Lens Model: A Comprehensive Framework for Understanding Self–Other Agreement of Personality Judgments at Zero Acquaintance," _Journal of Personality and Social Psychology_ 104 (2013), pp. 335–353.

Self-Monitoring   Joyce is always in trouble at work. Although she's competent, hardworking, and productive, she is rated no better than average in performance reviews, and she seems to have made a career of irritating her bosses. Joyce's problem is that she's politically inept. She's unable to adjust her behavior to fit changing situations. As she said, "I'm true to myself. I don't remake myself to please others." Joyce is a low self-monitor.

Self-monitoring describes an individual's ability to adjust his or her behavior to external, situational factors.[54] High self-monitors show considerable adaptability in adjusting their behavior to external situational factors. They are highly sensitive to external cues and can behave differently in varying situations, sometimes presenting striking contradictions between their public persona and their private self. Low self-monitors like Joyce can't disguise themselves in that way. They tend to display their true dispositions and attitudes in every situation; hence, there is high behavioral consistency between who they are and what they do.

Evidence indicates high self-monitors pay closer attention to the behavior of others and are more capable of conforming than are low self-monitors.[55] They also receive better performance ratings, are more likely to emerge as leaders, and show less commitment to their organizations.[56] In addition, high self-monitor managers tend to be more mobile in their careers, receive more promotions (both internal and cross-organizational), and are more likely to occupy central positions in organizations.[57]

Proactive Personality   Did you ever notice that some people actively take the initiative to improve their current circumstances or create new ones? These are proactive personalities.[58] Those with a **proactive personality** identify opportunities, show initiative, take action, and persevere until meaningful change occurs, compared to others who passively react to situations. Not

self-monitoring   _A personality trait that measures an individual's ability to adjust his or her behavior to external, situational factors._

proactive personality   _People who identify opportunities, show initiative, take action, and persevere until meaningful change occurs._

surprisingly, proactive individuals have many desirable behaviors that organizations covet. They also have higher levels of job performance and career success.[59]

Are there downsides to having a proactive personality? A recent study of 231 Flemish unemployed individuals found that proactive personality was negatively related to persistence in job searching; proactive individuals abandoned their job searches sooner. However, it may be that proactivity includes knowing when to step back and reconsider alternatives in the face of failure.[60]

Proactive personality may be important for work teams. One study of 95 R&D teams in 33 Chinese companies revealed that teams with high-average levels of proactive personality were more innovative.[61] Like other traits, proactive personality is affected by the context. One study of bank branch teams in China found that if a team's leader was not proactive, the benefits of the team's proactively will lie dormant or, worse, be suppressed by the leader.[62]

In short, while proactive personality may be important to individual and team performance, like all traits it may have downsides, and its effectiveness may depend on the context.

Personality and Situations

5 Describe how the situation affects whether personality predicts behavior.

Earlier we discussed how research shows that heredity is more important than the environment in developing our personalities. The environment is not irrelevant, though. Some personality traits like the Big Five tend to be effective to almost any environment or situation. For example, research indicates that

glOBalization!

Is the Personality Profile of an Entrepreneur the Same Across the United States, the United Kingdom, and Germany?

What is an entrepreneurial personality? Some recent research has provided some answers, and some interesting insights into how well this profile translates across regions and countries. The personality profile of an entrepreneur is well represented in one study by a constellation of the Big Five traits, with high scores on extraversion, conscientiousness, and openness, and low scores on agreeableness and neuroticism.

Another recent study suggests there are more differences *within* than *between* countries on the entrepreneurial personality. This study constructed a personality profile of the entrepreneurial personality from the Big Five traits and then analyzed large samples of individuals from the United States, the United Kingdom, and Germany.

In Germany, individuals in Berlin and Hamburg scored the highest on the entrepreneurial personality profile. In the United Kingdom, East England and London scored highest. In the United States, there were differences across both cities and states. Of the 15 largest U.S. cities, Miami-Ft. Lauderdale, Seattle-Tacoma, and Atlanta scored highest on the entrepreneurial personality profile. Among the states, Colorado, Utah, and the District of Columbia scored highest.

Within each country, the study found that the entrepreneurial personality profile correlated with the region or city's level of entrepreneurial activity, as measured by the percentage of the population trying to start new businesses, the proportion of businesses less than 3.5 years old, and the number of individuals who were self-employed.

These results suggest there is an entrepreneurial personality profile; it correlates with actual entrepreneurial activity across countries; and within each country, regional and metropolitan differences exist in both the personality profile and entrepreneurial activity.

Of course, one limitation of these results is that they consider only three Western locations. It would be interesting to see whether the same pattern holds in other parts of the world.

Source: Based on M. Obschonka, E. Schmitt-Rodermund, R. K. Silbereisen, S. D. Gosling, and J. Potter, "The Regional Distribution and Correlates of an Entrepreneurship-Prone Personality Profile in the United States, Germany, and the United Kingdom: A Socioecological Perspective," *Journal of Personality and Social Psychology* (2013), doi: 10.1037/a0032275.

conscientiousness is helpful to the performance of most jobs, and extraversion is related to emergence as a leader in most situations.

Increasingly, we are learning that the effect of particular traits on organizational behavior depends on the situation. Two theoretical frameworks help explain how this works.

Situation Strength   Imagine you are in a meeting with your department. How likely are you to walk out in the middle of the meeting, shout at someone, turn your back on the group, or fall asleep? Probably highly unlikely. Now consider that you are working from home. You might work in your pajamas, listen to loud music, or take a catnap.

situation-strength theory   *A theory indicating that the way personality translates into behavior depends on the strength of the situation.*

Situation strength theory proposes that the way personality translates into behavior depends on the strength of the situation. By *situation strength*, we mean the degree to which norms, cues, or standards dictate appropriate behavior. Strong situations pressure us to exhibit the right behavior, clearly show us what that behavior is, and discourage the wrong behavior. In weak situations, conversely, "anything goes," and thus we are freer to express our personality in behavior. Thus, research suggests that personality traits better predict behavior in weak situations than in strong ones.

Researchers have analyzed situation strength in organizations in terms of four elements:[63]

1. *Clarity*, or the degree to which cues about work duties and responsibilities are available and clear. Jobs high in clarity produce strong situations because individuals can readily determine what to do, thus increasing the chances that everyone behaves similarly. For example, the job of janitor probably provides higher clarity about what needs to be done than the job of nanny.
2. *Consistency*, or the extent to which cues regarding work duties and responsibilities are compatible with one another. Jobs with high consistency represent strong situations because all the cues point toward the same desired behavior. The job of acute care nurse, for example, probably has higher consistency than the job of manager.
3. *Constraints*, or the extent to which individuals' freedom to decide or act is limited by forces outside their control. Jobs with many constraints represent strong situations because an individual has limited individual discretion. Bank examiner, for example, is probably a job with stronger constraints than forest ranger.
4. *Consequences*, or the degree to which decisions or actions have important implications for the organization or its members, clients, supplies, and so on. Jobs with important consequences represent strong situations because the environment is probably heavily structured to guard against mistakes. A surgeon's job, for example, has higher consequences than a foreign-language teacher's.

Some researchers have speculated that organizations are, by definition, strong situations because they impose rules, norms, and standards that govern behavior. These constraints are usually appropriate. For example, we would not want an employee to feel free to engage in sexual harassment, to follow questionable accounting procedures, or to come to work only when the mood strikes.

But that does not mean it is always desirable for organizations to create strong situations for their employees. First, jobs with myriad rules and tightly controlled processes can be dull or demotivating. Imagine that all work was executed with an assembly-line approach. Most of us prefer having some freedom to decide how to do our work. Second, people do differ, so what works well for one person might work poorly for another. Third, strong situations might suppress the creativity, initiative, and discretion prized by some cultures.

One recent study, for example, found that in weak organizational situations, employees were more likely to behave proactively in accordance with their values.[64] Finally, work is increasingly complex and interrelated globally. Creating strong rules to govern complex, interrelated, and culturally diverse systems might be not only difficult but unwise. Managers need to recognize the role of situation strength in the workplace and find the appropriate balance.

Trait Activation Theory Another important theoretical framework toward understanding situational activators for personality is **trait activation theory (TAT)**. TAT predicts that some situations, events, or interventions "activate" a trait more than others. For example, a commission-based compensation plan would likely activate individual differences in extraversion because extraversion is more reward-sensitive, than, say, openness. Conversely, in jobs that allow expression of individual creativity, individual differences in openness may better predict creative behavior than individual differences in extraversion would. See Exhibit 5-3 for specific examples.

A recent study found that people learning online responded differently when their behavior was being electronically monitored. Those who had high fear of failure had higher evaluation apprehension than others and learned significantly less. In this case, a feature of the environment (electronic monitoring) activated a trait (fear of failing), and the combination of the two meant lowered job performance.[65] TAT can also work in a positive way. A recent study applying TAT found that individual differences in the tendency to behave prosocially mattered more when co-workers were not supportive. In other words, in a supportive environment, everyone behaves prosocially, but in an environment that is not so nice, whether an individual has the personality to behave prosocially makes a major difference.[66]

Together, situation strength and trait activation theories show that the debate over nature versus nurture might best be framed as nature *and* nurture. Not only does each affect behavior, but they interact with one another. Put another way, personality affects work behavior and the situation affects work behavior, but when the situation is right, the power of personality to predict behavior is even higher.

trait activation theory (TAT)
A theory that predicts that some situations, events, or interventions "activate" a trait more than others.

Exhibit 5-3   Trait Activation Theory: Jobs in Which Certain Big Five Traits Are More Relevant

Detail Orientation Required	Social Skills Required	Competitive Work	Innovation Required	Dealing with Angry People	Time Pressure (Deadlines)
Jobs scoring high (the traits listed here should predict behavior in these jobs)					
Air traffic controller	Clergy	Coach/scout	Actor	Correctional officer	Broadcast news analyst
Accountant	Therapist	Financial manager	Systems analyst	Telemarketer	
Legal secretary	Concierge	Sales representative	Advertising writer	Flight attendant	Editor
					Airline pilot
Jobs scoring low (the traits listed here should not predict behavior in these jobs)					
Forester	Software engineer	Postal clerk	Court reporter	Composer	Skincare specialist
Masseuse	Pump operator	Historian	Archivist	Biologist	Mathematician
Model	Broadcast technician	Nuclear reactor operator	Medical technician	Statistician	Fitness trainer
Jobs that score high activate these traits (make them more relevant to predicting behavior)					
Conscientiousness (+)	Extraversion (+) Agreeableness (+)	Extraversion (+) Agreeableness (−)	Openness (+)	Extraversion (+) Agreeableness (+) Neuroticism (−)	Conscientiousness (+) Neuroticism (−)

Note: A plus (+) sign means individuals who score high on this trait should do better in this job. A minus (−) sign means individuals who score low on this trait should do better in this job.

Having discussed personality traits—the enduring characteristics that describe a person's behavior—we now turn to values. Values are often very specific and describe belief systems rather than behavioral tendencies. Some beliefs or values say little about a person's personality, and we don't always act consistently with our values.

Values

6 Contrast terminal and instrumental values.

values *Basic convictions that a specific mode of conduct or end-state of existence is personally or socially preferable to an opposite or converse mode of conduct or end-state of existence.*

value system *A hierarchy based on a ranking of an individual's values in terms of their intensity.*

Is capital punishment right or wrong? Is a desire for power good or bad? The answers to these questions are value-laden.

Values represent basic convictions that "a specific mode of conduct or end-state of existence is personally or socially preferable to an opposite or converse mode of conduct or end-state of existence."[67] Values contain a judgmental element because they carry an individual's ideas about what is right, good, or desirable. They have both content and intensity attributes. The content attribute says a mode of conduct or end-state of existence is *important*. The intensity attribute specifies *how important* it is. When we rank values in terms of intensity, we obtain that person's **value system**. We all have a hierarchy of values according to the relative importance we assign to values such as freedom, pleasure, self-respect, honesty, obedience, and equality.

Values tend to be relatively stable and enduring.[68] Many of the values we hold are established in our early years—by parents, teachers, friends, and others. As children, we are told certain behaviors or outcomes are *always* desirable or *always* undesirable, with few gray areas. You were never taught to be just a little bit honest or a little bit responsible, for example. It is this absolute, black-or-white characteristic of values that ensures their stability and endurance. If we question our values, they may change, but more often they are reinforced. There is also evidence linking personality to values, implying our values may be partly determined by genetically transmitted traits.[69]

The Importance and Organization of Values

Values lay the foundation for our understanding of people's attitudes and motivation and influence our perceptions. We enter an organization with preconceived notions of what "ought" and "ought not" to be. These notions are not value-free; on the contrary, they contain our interpretations of right and wrong and our preference for certain behaviors or outcomes over others. Values cloud objectivity and rationality; they influence attitudes and behavior.[70]

Suppose you enter an organization with the view that allocating pay on the basis of performance is right, while allocating pay on the basis of seniority is wrong. How will you react if you find the organization you've just joined rewards seniority and not performance? You're likely to be disappointed—this can lead to job dissatisfaction and a decision not to exert a high level of effort because "It's probably not going to lead to more money anyway." Would your attitudes and behavior be different if your values aligned with the organization's pay policies? Most likely.

terminal values *Desirable end-states of existence; the goals a person would like to achieve during his or her lifetime.*

instrumental values *Preferable modes of behavior or means of achieving one's terminal values.*

Terminal versus Instrumental Values How can we organize values? One researcher—Milton Rokeach—argued that we can separate them into two categories. One set, called **terminal values**, refers to desirable end-states. These are the goals a person would like to achieve during his or her lifetime. The other set, called **instrumental values**, refers to preferred modes of behavior, or means of achieving the terminal values. Some examples of terminal values are: prosperity and economic success, freedom, health and well-being, world peace, and meaning in life. Examples of instrumental values are autonomy and self-reliance, personal discipline, kindness, and goal-orientation. Each of us places value on both the ends (terminal values) and the means (instrumental values); a balance between the two is important, as well as an understanding of the means to get there. Which terminal and instrumental values are especially key vary by the person.

Generational Values

7 Compare generational differences in values.

Contemporary Work Cohorts Researchers have integrated several recent analyses of work values into groups that attempt to capture the unique values of different cohorts or generations in the U.S. workforce.[71] Exhibit 5-4 segments employees by the era during which they entered the workforce. Because most people start work between the ages of 18 and 23, the eras also correlate closely with employee age.

Boomers (*Baby Boomers*) are a large cohort born after World War II when veterans returned to their families and times were good. Boomers entered the workforce from the mid-1960s through the mid-1980s. They brought with them the "hippie ethic" and distrust of authority. But they place a great deal of emphasis on achievement and material success. Pragmatists who believe ends can justify means work hard and want to enjoy the fruits of their labors. Boomers see the organizations that employ them merely as vehicles for their careers. Terminal values such as a sense of accomplishment and social recognition rank high with them.

The lives of *Xers* (*Generation Xers*) have been shaped by globalization, two-career parents, MTV, AIDS, and computers. Xers value flexibility, life options, and the achievement of job satisfaction. Family and relationships are very important. Xers are skeptical, particularly of authority. They also enjoy team-oriented work. In search of balance in their lives, Xers are less willing to make personal sacrifices for the sake of their employer than previous generations were. They rate high on true friendship, happiness, and pleasure.

The most recent entrants to the workforce, the *Millennials* grew up during prosperous times. They have high expectations and seek meaning in their work. Millennials have life goals more oriented toward becoming rich (81 percent) and famous (51 percent) than do Generation Xers (62 percent and 29 percent, respectively), but they also see themselves as socially responsible. At ease with diversity, Millennials are the first generation to take technology for granted. More than other generations, they tend to be questioning, electronically networked, and entrepreneurial. At the same time, some have described Millennials as entitled and needy. They may clash with other generations over work attire and communication. They also like feedback. An Ernst & Young survey found that 85 percent of Millennials want "frequent and candid performance feedback," compared to only half of Boomers.[72]

| Exhibit 5-4 | Dominant Work Values in Today's Workforce |

Cohort	Entered the Workforce	Approximate Current Age	Dominant Work Values
Boomers	1965–1985	Mid-40s to mid-60s	Success, achievement, ambition, dislike of authority; loyalty to career
Xers	1985–2000	Late 20s to early 40s	Work/life balance, team-oriented, dislike of rules; loyalty to relationships
Millennials	2000 to present	Under 30	Confident, financial success, self-reliant but team-oriented; loyalty to both self and relationships

Photo 5-4 eBay's young employees rank their employer as one of the best places to work for Millennials. They value eBay's culture of fun, flexibility, and diversity, and they appreciate working for a firm that gives them job responsibility quickly, recognizes their achievements, and offers learning experiences that can advance their careers.

Do You Have a Cheating Personality?

Stories of widespread cheating have been on the rise, leading many experts to conclude that the incidence of cheating is increasing. Recently a major cheating scandal was uncovered at Harvard University, where more than 125 students (roughly half of whom were eventually expelled) were found to be involved in an organized cheating scheme. Harvard administrators took the scandal seriously—maybe too seriously. In 2013, the *Boston Globe* reported that administrators had secretly downloaded university e-mails in an effort to get to the bottom of the scandal, including the e-mail accounts of 16 deans.

Like most complex behaviors, cheating in school, at work, and in life is a product of the person and the situation. As for the person, research reveals that certain traits are related to the tendency to cheat, including high levels of narcissism, low levels of conscientiousness and agreeableness, and high levels of competitiveness. One study of business students found that narcissism

was especially likely to translate into cheating for the very religious.

As for the situation, experts find cheating increases when it is easier to cheat (such as on take-home exams), when there is greater pressure to cheat, and when clear standards are lacking or are not reinforced (such as when an organization's sexual harassment policy is not communicated to employees). Surveys reveal, for example, that most employees have never read their organization's policies on ethical conduct.

How can this research help inform you as a student and employee?

1. Recognize situations that are more likely to provoke pressures to cheat. Being explicit and open with yourself about your response to these pressures should keep you from succumbing to a moral blind spot, in which you engage in behavior without considering its ethical undertones.

2. If you score high on certain traits that predispose you to cheat, this

does not mean you are destined to cheat. However, you should realize that you may be more susceptible and therefore need to be especially wary about placing yourself in situations where there is pressure or opportunity to cheat.

Sources: M. J. Cooper, and C. Pullig, "I'm Number One! Does Narcissism Impair Ethical Judgment Even for the Highly Religious?" *Journal of Business Ethics* 112 (2013), pp. 167–176; H. E. Hershfield, T. R. Cohen, and L. Thompson, "Short Horizons and Tempting Situations: Lack of Continuity to our Future Selves Leads to Unethical Decision Making and Behavior," *Organizational Behavior and Human Decision Processes* 117 (2012), pp. 298–310; M. Carmichael, "Secret E-mail Searches on Harvard Cheating Scandal Broader Than Initially Described," *Boston Globe* (April 2, 2013), www.boston.com/metrodesk/2013/04/02/secret-mail-searches-harvard-cheating-scandal-broader-than-initially-described/Mgz0mc8hSk3IgWGjxLwsJP/story.html; P. E. Mudrack, J. M. Bloodgood, and W. H. Turnley, "Some Ethical Implications of Individual Competitiveness," *Journal of Business Ethics* 108 (2012), pp. 347–359; and R. Pérez-Peña, "Studies Find More Students Cheating, with High Achievers No Exception," *The New York Times* (September 8, 2012), p. A13.

Though it is fascinating to think about generational values, remember these classifications lack solid research support. Early research was plagued by methodological problems that made it difficult to assess whether differences actually exist. Recent reviews suggest many of the generalizations are either overblown or incorrect.[73] Studies that have found differences across generations often do not support popular conceptions of how generations differ. One study that used an appropriate longitudinal design did find the value placed on leisure has increased over generations from the Baby Boomers to the Millennials and work centrality has declined, but it did not find that Millennials had more altruistic work values as expected.[74] Generational classifications may help us understand our own and other generations better, but we must also appreciate their limits.

Linking an Individual's Personality and Values to the Workplace

Thirty years ago, organizations were concerned only with personality because their primary focus was to match individuals to specific jobs. That concern has expanded to include how well the individual's personality *and* values match the organization. Why? Because managers today are less interested in an applicant's ability to perform a *specific* job than with his or her *flexibility* to meet changing situations and commitment to the organization.

We'll now discuss person–job fit and person–organization fit in more detail.

Person–Job Fit

personality–job fit theory   *A theory that identifies six personality types and proposes that the fit between personality type and occupational environment determines satisfaction and turnover.*

The effort to match job requirements with personality characteristics is best articulated in John Holland's **personality–job fit theory**.[75] Holland presents six personality types and proposes that satisfaction and the propensity to leave a position depend on how well individuals match their personalities to a job. Exhibit 5-5 describes the six types, their personality characteristics, and examples of the congruent occupations for each.

Holland developed the Vocational Preference Inventory questionnaire, which contains 160 occupational titles. Respondents indicate which they like or dislike, and their answers form personality profiles. Research supports the

Exhibit 5-5	Holland's Typology of Personality and Congruent Occupations

Type	Personality Characteristics	Congruent Occupations
Realistic: Prefers physical activities that require skill, strength, and coordination	Shy, genuine, persistent, stable, conforming, practical	Mechanic, drill press operator, assembly-line worker, farmer
Investigative: Prefers activities that involve thinking, organizing, and understanding	Analytical, original, curious, independent	Biologist, economist, mathematician, news reporter
Social: Prefers activities that involve helping and developing others	Sociable, friendly, cooperative, understanding	Social worker, teacher, counselor, clinical psychologist
Conventional: Prefers rule-regulated, orderly, and unambiguous activities	Conforming, efficient, practical, unimaginative, inflexible	Accountant, corporate manager, bank teller, file clerk
Enterprising: Prefers verbal activities in which there are opportunities to influence others and attain power	Self-confident, ambitious, energetic, domineering	Lawyer, real estate agent, public relations specialist, small business manager
Artistic: Prefers ambiguous and unsystematic activities that allow creative expression	Imaginative, disorderly, idealistic, emotional, impractical	Painter, musician, writer, interior decorator

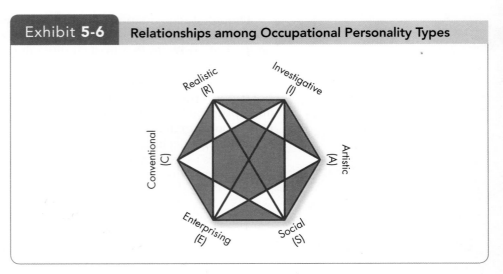

Exhibit 5-6   Relationships among Occupational Personality Types

resulting hexagonal diagram shown in Exhibit 5-6, even after taking personality into account.[76] The closer two fields or orientations are in the hexagon, the more compatible they are. Adjacent categories are quite similar, whereas diagonally opposite ones are highly dissimilar.

What does all this mean? The theory argues that satisfaction is highest and turnover lowest when personality and occupation are in agreement. A realistic person in a realistic job is in a more congruent situation than a realistic person in an investigative job. A realistic person in a social job is in the most incongruent situation possible. The key point of this model is that people in jobs congruent with their personality should be more satisfied and less likely to voluntarily resign than people in incongruent jobs.

Person–Organization Fit

We've noted that researchers have looked at matching people to organizations as well as to jobs. If an organization faces a dynamic and changing environment and needs employees able to readily change tasks and move easily between teams, it's more important that employees' personalities fit with the overall organization's culture than with the characteristics of any specific job.

The *person–organization fit* essentially argues that people are attracted to and selected by organizations that match their values, and they leave organizations that are not compatible with their personalities.[77] Using the Big Five terminology, for instance, we could expect that people high on extraversion fit well with aggressive and team-oriented cultures, that people high on agreeableness match up better with a supportive organizational climate than one focused on aggressiveness, and that people high on openness to experience fit better in organizations that emphasize innovation rather than standardization.[78] Following these guidelines at the time of hiring should identify new employees who fit better with the organization's culture, which should, in turn, result in higher employee satisfaction and reduced turnover. Research on person–organization fit has also looked at whether people's values match the organization's culture. This match predicts job satisfaction, commitment to the organization, and low turnover.[79] Some research found that person-organization fit was more important in predicting turnover in a collectivistic nation (India) than in a more individualistic nation (the United States).[80]

International Values

8 Identify Hofstede's five value dimensions of national culture.

power distance *A national culture attribute that describes the extent to which a society accepts that power in institutions and organizations is distributed unequally.*

individualism *A national culture attribute that describes the degree to which people prefer to act as individuals rather than as members of groups.*

collectivism *A national culture attribute that describes a tight social framework in which people expect others in groups of which they are a part to look after them and protect them.*

masculinity *A national culture attribute that describes the extent to which the culture favors traditional masculine work roles of achievement, power, and control. Societal values are characterized by assertiveness and materialism.*

femininity *A national culture attribute that indicates little differentiation between male and female roles; a high rating indicates that women are treated as the equals of men in all aspects of the society.*

uncertainty avoidance *A national culture attribute that describes the extent to which a society feels threatened by uncertain and ambiguous situations and tries to avoid them.*

long-term orientation *A national culture attribute that emphasizes the future, thrift, and persistence.*

short-term orientation *A national culture attribute that emphasizes the past and present, respect for tradition, and fulfillment of social obligations.*

One of the most widely referenced approaches for analyzing variations among cultures was done in the late 1970s by Geert Hofstede.[81] Hofstede surveyed more than 116,000 IBM employees in 40 countries about their work-related values and found that managers and employees vary on five value dimensions of national culture:

- **Power distance.** **Power distance** describes the degree to which people in a country accept that power in institutions and organizations is distributed unequally. A high rating on power distance means that large inequalities of power and wealth exist and are tolerated in the culture, as in a class or caste system that discourages upward mobility. A low power distance rating characterizes societies that stress equality and opportunity.
- **Individualism versus collectivism.** **Individualism** is the degree to which people prefer to act as individuals rather than as members of groups and believe in individual rights above all else. **Collectivism** emphasizes a tight social framework in which people expect others in groups of which they are a part to look after them and protect them.
- **Masculinity versus femininity.** Hofstede's construct of **masculinity** is the degree to which the culture favors traditional masculine roles such as achievement, power, and control, as opposed to viewing men and women as equals. A high masculinity rating indicates the culture has separate roles for men and women, with men dominating the society. A high **femininity** rating means the culture sees little differentiation between male and female roles and treats women as the equals of men in all respects.
- **Uncertainty avoidance.** The degree to which people in a country prefer structured over unstructured situations defines their **uncertainty avoidance**. In cultures that score high on uncertainty avoidance, people have an increased level of anxiety about uncertainty and ambiguity and use laws and controls to reduce uncertainty. People in cultures low on uncertainty avoidance are more accepting of ambiguity, are less rule oriented, take more risks, and more readily accept change.
- **Long-term versus short-term orientation.** This newest addition to Hofstede's typology measures a society's devotion to traditional values. People in a culture with **long-term orientation** look to the future and value thrift, persistence, and tradition. In a **short-term orientation**, people value the here and now; they accept change more readily and don't see commitments as impediments to change.

How do different countries score on Hofstede's dimensions? Exhibit 5-7 shows the ratings for the countries for which data are available. For example, power distance is higher in Malaysia than in any other country. The United States is very individualistic; in fact, it's the most individualistic nation of all (closely followed by Australia and Great Britain). The United States also tends to be short term in orientation and low in power distance (people in the United States tend not to accept built-in class differences between people). It is also relatively low on uncertainty avoidance, meaning most adults are relatively tolerant of uncertainty and ambiguity. The United States scores relatively high on masculinity; most people emphasize traditional gender roles (at least relative to countries such as Denmark, Finland, Norway, and Sweden).

You'll notice regional differences. Western and northern nations such as Canada and the Netherlands tend to be more individualistic. Poorer countries such as Mexico and the Philippines tend to be higher on power distance. South

Exhibit **5-7**	Hofstede's Cultural Values by Nation

Country	Power Distance		Individualism versus Collectivism		Masculinity versus Femininity		Uncertainty Avoidance		Long- versus Short-Term Orientation	
	Index	Rank	Index	Rank	Index	Rank	Index	Rank	Index	Rank
Argentina	49	35–36	46	22–23	56	20–21	86	10–15		
Australia	36	41	90	2	61	16	51	37	31	22–24
Austria	11	53	55	18	79	2	70	24–25	31	22–24
Belgium	65	20	75	8	54	22	94	5–6	38	18
Brazil	69	14	38	26–27	49	27	76	21–22	65	6
Canada	39	39	80	4–5	52	24	48	41–42	23	30
Chile	63	24–25	23	38	28	46	86	10–15		
Colombia	67	17	13	49	64	11–12	80	20		
Costa Rica	35	42–44	15	46	21	48–49	86	10–15		
Denmark	18	51	74	9	16	50	23	51	46	10
Ecuador	78	8–9	8	52	63	13–14	67	28		
El Salvador	66	18–19	19	42	40	40	94	5–6		
Finland	33	46	63	17	26	47	59	31–32	41	14
France	68	15–16	71	10–11	43	35–36	86	10–15	39	17
Germany	35	42–44	67	15	66	9–10	65	29	31	22–24
Great Britain	35	42–44	89	3	66	9–10	35	47–48	25	28–29
Greece	60	27–28	35	30	57	18–19	112	1		
Guatemala	95	2–3	6	53	37	43	101	3		
Hong Kong	68	15–16	25	37	57	18–19	29	49–50	96	2
India	77	10–11	48	21	56	20–21	40	45	61	7
Indonesia	78	8–9	14	47–48	46	30–31	48	41–42		
Iran	58	29–30	41	24	43	35–36	59	31–32		
Ireland	28	49	70	12	68	7–8	35	47–48	43	13
Israel	13	52	54	19	47	29	81	19		
Italy	50	34	76	7	70	4–5	75	23	34	19
Jamaica	45	37	39	25	68	7–8	13	52		
Japan	54	33	46	22–23	95	1	92	7	80	4
Korea (South)	60	27–28	18	43	39	41	85	16–17	75	5
Malaysia	104	1	26	36	50	25–26	36	46		
Mexico	81	5–6	30	32	69	6	82	18		
The Netherlands	38	40	80	4–5	14	51	53	35	44	11–12
New Zealand	22	50	79	6	58	17	49	39–40	30	25–26
Norway	31	47–48	69	13	8	52	50	38	44	11–12
Pakistan	55	32	14	47–48	50	25–26	70	24–25	0	34
Panama	95	2–3	11	51	44	34	86	10–15		
Peru	64	21–23	16	45	42	37–38	87	9		
Philippines	94	4	32	31	64	11–12	44	44	19	31–32
Portugal	63	24–25	27	33–35	31	45	104	2	30	25–26
Singapore	74	13	20	39–41	48	28	8	53	48	9
South Africa	49	35–36	65	16	63	13–14	49	39–40		
Spain	57	31	51	20	42	37–38	86	10–15	19	31–32
Sweden	31	47–48	71	10–11	5	53	29	49–50	33	20
Switzerland	34	45	68	14	70	4–5	58	33	40	15–16
Taiwan	58	29–30	17	44	45	32–33	69	26	87	3
Thailand	64	21–23	20	39–41	34	44	64	30	56	8
Turkey	66	18–19	37	28	45	32–33	85	16–17		
United States	40	38	91	1	62	15	46	43	29	27
Uruguay	61	26	36	29	38	42	100	4		
Venezuela	81	5–6	12	50	73	3	76	21–22		
Yugoslavia	76	12	27	33–35	21	48–49	88	8		
Regions:										
Arab countries	80	7	38	26–27	53	23	68	27		
East Africa	64	21–23	27	33–35	41	39	52	36	25	28–29
West Africa	77	10–11	20	39–41	46	30–31	54	34	16	33

Scores range from 0 = extremely low on dimension to 100 = extremely high.

Note: 1 = highest rank. LTO ranks: 1 = China; 15–16 = Bangladesh; 21 = Poland; 34 = lowest.

Source: Copyright Geert Hofstede BV, hofstede@bart.nl. Reprinted with permission.

American nations tend to be higher than other countries on uncertainty avoidance, and Asian countries tend to have a long-term orientation.

Hofstede's culture dimensions have been enormously influential on OB researchers and managers. Nevertheless, his research has been criticized. First, although the data have since been updated, the original work is more than 30 years old and was based on a single company (IBM). A lot has happened on the world scene since then. Some of the most obvious changes include the fall of the Soviet Union, the transformation of central and eastern Europe, the end of apartheid in South Africa, the rise of China as a global power, and the advent of a worldwide recession. Second, few researchers have read the details of Hofstede's methodology closely and are therefore unaware of the many decisions and judgment calls he had to make (for example, reducing the number of cultural values to just five). Despite these concerns, Hofstede has been one of the most widely cited social scientists ever, and his framework has left a lasting mark on OB.

Recent research across 598 studies with more than 200,000 respondents has investigated the relationship of Hofstede's cultural values and a variety of organizational criteria at both the individual and national level of analysis.[82] Overall, the five original culture dimensions were equally strong predictors of relevant outcomes, meaning researchers and practicing managers need to think about culture holistically and not just focus on one or two dimensions. The researchers also found that measuring individual scores resulted in much better predictions of most outcomes than assigning all people in a country the same cultural values. In sum, this research suggests that Hofstede's value framework may be a valuable way of thinking about differences among people, but we should be cautious about assuming all people from a country have the same values.

The GLOBE Framework for Assessing Cultures   Begun in 1993, the Global Leadership and Organizational Behavior Effectiveness (GLOBE) research program is an ongoing cross-cultural investigation of leadership and national culture. Using data from 825 organizations in 62 countries, the GLOBE team identified nine dimensions on which national cultures differ.[83] Some—such as power distance, individualism/collectivism, uncertainty avoidance, gender differentiation (similar to masculinity versus femininity), and future orientation (similar to long-term versus short-term

Photo 5-5 According to Hofstede's framework for assessing cultures, Asian countries have a strong collectivist culture that fosters relationships where everyone takes responsibility for group members. This helps explain the behavior of the employees shown here working at a department store outlet in Busan, South Korea.

Source: Yonhap News/YNA/Newscom.

orientation)—resemble the Hofstede dimensions. The main difference is that the GLOBE framework added dimensions, such as humane orientation (the degree to which a society rewards individuals for being altruistic, generous, and kind to others) and performance orientation (the degree to which a society encourages and rewards group members for performance improvement and excellence).

Which framework is better? That's hard to say, and each has its adherents. We give more emphasis to Hofstede's dimensions here because they have stood the test of time and the GLOBE study confirmed them. For example, a review of the organizational commitment literature shows that both the Hofstede and GLOBE individualism/collectivism dimensions operated similarly. Specifically, both frameworks showed that organizational commitment (which we discussed in Chapter 3) tends to be lower in individualistic countries.[84] This study shows that too often, we make false choices—both frameworks have a great deal in common, and each has something to offer.

Summary

Personality matters to organizational behavior. It does not explain all behavior, but it sets the stage. Emerging theory and research reveal how personality matters more in some situations than others. The Big Five has been a particularly important advancement, though the Dark Triad and other traits matter as well. Moreover, every trait has advantages and disadvantages for work behavior. There is no perfect constellation of traits that is ideal in every situation. Personality can help you to understand why people (including yourself!) act, think, and feel the way we do, and the astute manager can put that understanding to use by taking care to place employees in situations that best fit their personality.

Why is it important to know an individual's values? Values often underlie and explain attitudes, behaviors, and perceptions. So knowledge of an individual's value system can provide insight into what makes the person "tick."

Implications for Managers

- As a manager, you are more likely to appreciate, evaluate positively, and allocate rewards to employees who fit in, and your employees are more likely to be satisfied if they perceive they do fit in. Plan to objectively consider your employees' performance accordingly.
- Consider screening job candidates for high conscientiousness—as well as the other Big Five traits, depending on the criteria your organization finds most important. Other traits, such as core self-evaluation or narcissism, may be relevant in certain situations.
- You need to evaluate your employees' jobs, their work groups, and your organization to determine the optimal personality fit.
- Take into account employees' situational factors when evaluating their observable personality traits, and lower the situation strength, to better ascertain personality characteristics.
- Although the MBTI has been widely criticized, it may have a place in organizations. You may consider the results helpful for training and development; the results can also help employees better understand themselves, help team members better understand each other, open up communication in work groups, and possibly reduce conflicts.

Millennials Are More Narcissistic

| POINT | COUNTERPOINT |

POINT

Those in college today have many good qualities: they are more technologically savvy, more socially tolerant, and more balanced in their work and family priorities than previous generations. Thus, those poised to enter the workforce today do so with some important virtues. Humility, however, is not one of them.

Several large-scale, longitudinal studies found that those graduating from college today are more likely than those from previous generations to have seemingly inflated views of themselves. Compared to previous generations, more U.S. college students now rate themselves as above average on attributes such as academic ability, leadership, public speaking ability, and writing ability. College graduates today are more likely to agree they would be "very good" spouses (56 percent, compared to 37 percent among 1980 graduates), parents (54 percent, 36 percent among 1980 graduates), and workers (65 percent, compared to 49 percent among 1980 graduates).

Studies measuring narcissism suggest that scores are rising, especially among younger generations. For example, by presenting a choice between two statements—"I try not to be a show-off" versus "I will usually show off if I get the chance"—psychologists have found that narcissism has been growing since the early 1980s.

Another recent study found that compared to Baby Boomers and Generation X, students entering college today are more likely to emphasize extrinsic values (money, image, fame) and less likely to value intrinsic ones (concern for others, charity, jobs that contribute to society).

It doesn't paint a pretty picture, but data do not lie: The sooner we admit it, the sooner we can begin to address the problem in families, in education, and at work.

COUNTERPOINT

"THE YOUTH OF TODAY ARE LOST!" This argument is like a broken record that seems to play over and over: Every generation tends to think the new generation is without values, and the new generation thinks the older one is hopelessly judgmental and out of touch. Didn't the supposed "Me generation" occur a generation ago? Let's send the broken record to the recycling bin and review the evidence.

Another study offered an interesting explanation for why people *think* Millennials are more narcissistic. Specifically, young people in general are more self-focused, but as people age, they become more "other" focused. So we think young people are different when in fact they're just the way older folks were when they were younger. As these authors conclude, "Every generation is Generation Me." Our level of narcissism appears to be one of the many things that change as we get older.

In fact, this raises an important point: Values change over time as we age, but we should not confuse that change with generational effects. One large-scale review of the literature revealed that during college years, we place more weight on intrinsic values, and as we progress in our careers and start families, extrinsic values increase in importance.

Other research has found that people think the generations differ in their values much more than they in fact do. One study found that of 15 work values, in every case the perceived differences among Baby Boomers, Generation Xers, and Millennials were greater than the actual ones.

More broadly, narcissistic folks exist in every generation. We need to be careful when generalizing about entire groups (whether one sex, one race, one culture, or one generation). While generalizations have caused no small amount of trouble, we still like to simplify the world, sometimes for good reason. In this case, however, the good reason isn't there, especially considering the latest evidence.

Sources: J. M. Twenge, W. K. Campbell, and E. C. Freeman, "Generational Differences in Young Adults' Life Goals, Concern for Others, and Civic Orientation, 1966–2009," *Journal of Personality and Social Psychology* 102 (2012), pp. 1045–1062; J. Jin and J. Rounds, "Stability and Change in Work Values: A Meta-Analysis of Longitudinal Studies," *Journal of Vocational Behavior* 80 (2012), pp. 326–339; and S. W. Lester, R. L. Standifer, N. J. Schultz, and J. M. Windsor, "Actual Versus Perceived Generational Differences at Work: An Empirical Examination," *Journal of Leadership & Organizational Studies* 19 (2012), pp. 341–354.

END-OF-CHAPTER REVIEW

MyManagementLab

Go to **mymanagementlab.com** to complete the problems marked with this icon. ⊛

QUESTIONS FOR REVIEW

5-1 What is personality? How do we typically measure it? What factors determine personality?

5-2 What is the Myers-Briggs Type Indicator (MBTI), and what are its strengths and weaknesses?

5-3 What are the key traits in the Big Five personality model?

5-4 How do the Big Five traits predict behavior at work?

5-5 How does the situation or environment affect the degree to which personality predicts behavior?

5-6 What is the difference between terminal and instrumental values?

5-7 Do values differ across generations? How so?

5-8 What are Hofstede's five value dimensions of national culture?

EXPERIENTIAL EXERCISE What Organizational Culture Do You Prefer?

The Organizational Culture Profile (OCP) can help assess whether an individual's values match the organization's.[85] The OCP helps individuals sort their characteristics in terms of importance, which indicates what a person values.

5-9. Working on your own, complete the OCP found at www.jstor.org/stable/256404.

- Your instructor may ask you the following questions individually or as a group of three or four students (with a spokesperson appointed to speak to the class for each group):

5-10. What were your most preferred and least preferred values? Do you think your most preferred and least preferred values are similar to those of other class or group members?

5-11. Do you think there are generational differences in the most preferred and least preferred values?

5-12. Research has shown that individuals tend to be happier, and perform better, when their OCP values match those of their employer. How important do you think a "values match" is when you're deciding where you want to work?

ETHICAL DILEMMA Generational Values and "Staying Put"

Those who have been in the workforce for many years often lament the "job hopping" that occurs with those who are more recent entrants into the workforce. Younger individuals tend to see such an attitude as old-fashioned and may resent the implication that they have an ethical obligation to remain with their employer for life—or even a long time.

Lifelong commitment to one employer is a thing of the past. The Bureau of Labor Statistics reports that today, only 28 percent of women and 30 percent of men remain with their employer for 10 or more years, compared to 50 percent for both genders in 1973. Compensation research firm PayScale found that the average Millennial changes jobs every 2 years.

While those of previous generations cite this as evidence of job hopping, some of this movement is employer-driven. Lifetime job security is long gone for most positions. So are benefit packages that keep employees secure, such as rock-solid pensions and perpetual health benefits. But does a generational shift in values also explain the drop?

Some experts say yes. They argue that Millennials emphasize the present over the future and place a great value on lifestyle. Similarly, some argue that, rather than career planning and promises of long-term career prospects, Millennials need more feedback and reassurance. According to Neil Howe, the individual credited with coining the term *Millennial generation*, Millennials expect "the perfect employer who will be their ally and take care of them." For example, 1-800-Flowers.com instituted a program that provides frequent performance feedback because a large share of its workforce is from the Millennial generation.

According to Pew Research, 66 percent of Millennials say they want to switch careers some time in their life, while 62 percent of Generation X members and 84 percent of Baby Boomers say they would prefer to stay at their current job for the rest of their lives.

Andrew Leavitt, a 26-year-old who changed jobs a year after graduating college, said, "I mean, what kind of millennial would work for the same company for their whole life?"

These values don't sit well with some employers. "We prefer long tenured employees who have stuck with us and been loyal," says Dave Foster, CEO of AvreaFoster, an advertising agency in Dallas. "It appears that a lot of Millennials don't think that one path is the answer. This is a problem because the commitment isn't there."

Questions

✪ **5-13.** In your experience, do younger individuals differ from older individuals in terms of how long they plan to remain with a given firm?

5-14. Do you think you should feel free to "job surf"—purposely move from job to job as soon as the desire strikes? Do you think employers have a right to ask about "job surfing" plans when they interview you?

5-15. If you had an interview with Dave Foster or someone with his views of Millennials, how might you combat his preconceptions?

Sources: Bureau of Labor Statistics, *Employee Tenure Summary* (September 18, 2012), U.S. Department of Labor, www.bls.gov/news.release/tenure.nr0.htm; T. Hsu, "Millennials Change Jobs Every 2 Years on Average," *Chicago Tribune* (September 3, 2012), p. 2-1; L. Kwoh, "Firms Bow to Generation Y's Demands," *The Wall Street Journal* (August 22, 2012), p. B6; E. Frauenheim, "Deal or Not Deal? 'Employee Value Proposition' Evolves," *Workforce Management* (November 2012), pp. 16–17; T. S. Collins, "Millennials Take on the Workforce," *SHIFT Magazine* (May 3, 2011), downloaded April 29, 2013, from www.smudailymustang.com; and T. Henneman, "Talkin' About Their Generations: The Workforce of the '50s and Today," *Workforce Management* (April 2012), pp. 24–25.

CASE INCIDENT 1   On the Costs of Being Nice

Agreeable people tend to be kinder and more accommodating in social situations, which you might think could add to their success in life. However, one downside of agreeableness is potentially lower earnings. Recent research has shown the answer to this and other puzzles; some of them may surprise you.

First, and perhaps most obvious, agreeable individuals are less adept at a type of negotiation called distributive bargaining. As we discuss in Chapter 14, distributive bargaining is less about creating win–win solutions and more about claiming as large of a share of the pie as possible. Because salary negotiations are generally distributive, agreeable individuals often negotiate lower salaries for themselves than they might otherwise get. Perhaps because of this impaired ability to negotiate distributively, agreeable individuals have lower credit scores.

Second, agreeable individuals may choose to work in industries or occupations that earn lower salaries, such as the "caring" industries of education or health care. Agreeable individuals are also attracted to jobs both in the public sector and in nonprofit organizations.

Third, the earnings of agreeable individuals also may be reduced by their lower drive to emerge as leaders and by their tendency to engage in lower degrees of proactive task behaviors, such as coming up with ways to increase organizational effectiveness.

While being agreeable certainly doesn't appear to help one's pay, it does provide other benefits. Agreeable individuals are better liked at work, are more likely to help others at work, and generally are happier at work and in life.

Nice guys—and gals—may finish last in terms of earnings, but wages themselves do not define a happy life, and on that front, agreeable individuals have the advantage.

Questions

⊗ **5-16.** Do you think employers must choose between agreeable employees and top performers? Why or why not?

5-17. Often, the effects of personality depend on the situation. Can you think of some job situations in which agreeableness is an important virtue, and some in which it is harmful to job performance?

5-18. In some research we've conducted, we've found that the negative effect of agreeableness on earnings is stronger for men than for women (that is, being agreeable hurt men's earnings more than women's). Why do you think this might be the case?

Sources: T. A. Judge, B. A. Livingston, and C. Hurst, "Do Nice Guys—and Gals—Really Finish Last? The Joint Effects of Sex and Agreeableness on Income," *Journal of Personality and Social Psychology* 102 (2012), pp. 390–407; J. B. Bernerth, S. G. Taylor, H. J. Walker, and D. S. Whitman, "An Empirical Investigation of Dispositional Antecedents and Performance-Related Outcomes of Credit Scores," *Journal of Applied Psychology* 97 (2012), pp. 469–478; J. Carpenter, D. Doverspike, and R. F. Miguel, "Public Service Motivation as a Predictor of Attraction to the Public Sector," *Journal of Vocational Behavior* 80 (2012), pp. 509–523; and A. Neal, G. Yeo, A. Koy, and T. Xiao, "Predicting the Form and Direction of Work Role Performance from the Big 5 Model of Personality Traits," *Journal of Organizational Behavior* 33 (2012), pp. 175–192.

CASE INCIDENT 2   The Power of Quiet

If someone labeled you an "introvert" how would it make you feel?

Judging from research on social desirability, most of us would prefer to be labeled extroverts. Normal distributions being what they are, however, half the world is more introverted than average. Earlier in the chapter we discussed the upside of introversion, but in many ways, it's an extrovert's world. So says Susan Cain, in her bestselling book *Quiet*.

In the book, Cain makes three arguments:

1. **We see ourselves as extraverts.**   Introversion is generally seen as undesirable, partly because extraverts like being in charge and are more apt to shape environments to fit their wishes. "Many of the most important institutions of contemporary life are designed for those who enjoy group projects and high levels of stimulation."

2. **Introversion is driven underground.**   Thanks to social norms and structures, introverts often are forced to be "closet introverts"—acting according to an extraverted ideal, even if that is not their personality at heart. Think about it. If someone comments, "You're awfully quiet," they nearly always assume an underlying problem, as if not being quiet is the norm.

3. **Extraversion is not all it's cracked up to be.**   Because introversion is suppressed, we cause the introverts of the world distress and fail to capitalize on the many virtues of introversion. We may overlook the quiet, thoughtful introvert when choosing a leader, we may quell creativity by doing most of our work in groups, and we may mistake appearance for reality ("Don't mistake assertiveness or eloquence for good ideas," Cain writes). Society may unwittingly push people to take risks more than is warranted, to act before they think, and to focus on short-term rewards above all else.

Cain is not anti-extravert. She simply thinks we should encourage people to be who they truly are, and that means valuing extraversion *and* introversion. She concludes, "The next time you see a person with a composed face and soft voice, remember that inside her mind she might be solving an equation, composing a sonnet, designing a hat. She might, that is, be deploying the powers of quiet."

Questions

5-19. Would you classify yourself as introverted or extraverted? How would people who know you describe you?

5-20. Would you prefer to be more introverted, or more extraverted, than you are? Why?

5-21. Do you agree with Cain's arguments? Why or why not?

Source: Based on S. Cain, *Quiet: The Power of Introverts in a World That Can't Stop Talking* (New York: Random House/Broadway Paperbacks, 2013).

MyManagementLab

Go to **mymanagementlab.com** for Auto-graded writing questions as well as the following Assisted-graded writing questions:

5-22. What do you feel are the pros and cons of extraversion and introversion for your work life? Can you increase desirable traits?

5-23. The study cited in the Ethical Dilemma found that Millennials change jobs every 2 years while the average tenure for Baby Boomers was 7 years and for Generation X, 5. Because people change jobs less often as they age, do you think these statistics may have more to do with age than generational values?

5-24. MyManagementLab Only—comprehensive writing assignment for this chapter.

Perception and Individual Decision Making

THE PRICETAG FOR CREATIVITY: $30 MILLION. THE RETURN: PRICELESS

Nicholas D'Aloisio is not your average London teen. Yahoo! recently purchased his app Summly for $30 million, and at age 17, he is the youngest member of the *Forbes* "30 Under 30" Games & Apps innovators. Personable and engaging, D'Aloisio is also perhaps not your average techie. He is the ideal entrepreneur, able to turn his creativity into innovative decision making and use his natural charisma to bring his ideas to the global marketplace. D'Aloisio's rare combination of creativity and personality makes him priceless in the high-stakes Silicon Valley marketplace.

D'Aloisio showed creative talent early, like many innovators. His mother Diane, a London lawyer, said, "I remember him creating 3D models on his computer as a 10-year-old . . . we always knew Nicholas was technical and talented." D'Aloisio has always sought the cutting edge of his field and has been quick to apply his creativity to designing new products. When Apple launched its App Store in 2008, he wanted to work with the new platform even before Apple was ready. "I went into an Apple store with my dad and we asked one of the assistants how we did this [make an app], and they didn't know what we were talking about," he said.

D'Aloisio taught himself basic programming while he waited for the public release of the app development process. In August 2008, he launched a starter app, FingerMill, a treadmill for fingers. It made money the first day, providing early encouragement. D'Aloisio said, "So as a 12-year-old I was like, 'This is awesome.'" He continued to innovate, even though some efforts were less successful. "But every time I did an app I learned more."

D'Aloisio's learning, experience, and creativity led him to perceive a need for an innovative product that would meet a consumer need. At school in 2011, D'Aloisio was "using Twitter a lot on my phone, and was realizing there was a massive gap between the link on the tweet and the full story. If you could come up with a summary layer to show in Twitter, that would be awesome." He developed an algorithm app called Trimit to condense news articles into the space of an iPhone screen with an engaging design. "It helps publishers reach out to a younger audience," D'Aloisio says. "There is a generation of skimmers. It's not that they don't want to read in-depth content, but they want to evaluate what the content is before they commit time."

D'Aloisio went from technological innovator to marketable commodity when his personality helped win him investors, including billionaire Li Ka Shing of Hong Kong, actors Ashton Kutcher and Stephen Fry, Wendi Murdoch (wife of media mogul Rupert Murdoch), and Yoko Ono. Zynga Inc. and SRI International R&D helped bring the new version of Trimit, called Summly, online in November 2012. Then the young innovator caught the attention of CEO Marissa Mayer, who was searching for spokespeople to boost Yahoo!'s tech image.

LEARNING OBJECTIVES

After studying this chapter, you should be able to:

1 Define *perception*, and explain the factors that influence it.

2 Explain attribution theory, and list the three determinants of attribution.

3 Identify the shortcuts individuals use in making judgments about others.

4 Explain the link between perception and decision making.

5 Contrast the rational model of decision making with bounded rationality and intuition.

6 Describe the common decision biases or errors.

7 Explain how individual differences and organizational constraints affect decision making.

8 Contrast the three ethical decision criteria.

9 Define *creativity*, and describe the three-stage model of creativity.

It seems Mayer wanted D'Aloisio's creativity and perceptive decision-making skills more than his latest innovation, because Yahoo! bought Summly in March 2013 with plans to shut it down immediately. What Yahoo! gets is D'Aloisio's presence, at least for a while, and only if Mayer makes an exception to Yahoo!'s ban on working from home—because D'Aloisio has high school to finish and then an Oxford philosophy degree to pursue. The $30 million teen is noncommittal. He thinks he will work for Yahoo! a few years but said, "I have no limits on time. I want to go in with open eyes and try to innovate."

Sources: A. Efrati, "At 17, App Builder Rockets to Riches from Yahoo Deal," *The Wall Street Journal* (March 26, 2013), P. B1; E. Samer, "Summly Creator Nick D'Aloisio: 'I Try to Maintain a Level of Humbleness,'" *The Guardian* (March 29, 2013), www.guardian.co.uk/technology/2013/mar/29/summly-creator-nick-daloisio-interview; and B. Stetler, "He Has Millions and a New Job at Yahoo. And Soon He'll Be 18," *The New York Times* (March 26, 2013), pp. A1, A3.

The case of Nicholas D'Aloisio illustrates how important—and perhaps rare—an individual's creativity can be to an organization. The interpersonal skills of some innovators like D'Aloisio, who is described as humble and charismatic, can help bring ideas to the marketplace. As we will see later in the chapter, the creativity of individuals can lead to true innovation that solves problems. To better understand, we first explore our perceptions and how they affect our decision-making process. In the following Self-Assessment Library, consider one perception—that of appropriate gender roles.

SELF-ASSESSMENT LIBRARY

What Are My Gender Role Perceptions?

In the Self-Assessment Library (available in MyManagementLab), take assessment IV.C.2 (What Are My Gender Role Perceptions?) and answer the following questions.

1. Did you score as high as you thought you would?
2. Do you think a problem with measures like this is that people aren't honest in responding?
3. If others, such as friends, classmates, and family members, rated you, would they rate you differently? Why or why not?
4. Research has shown that people's gender role perceptions are becoming less traditional over time. Why do you suppose this is so?

What Is Perception?

1 Define *perception,* and explain the factors that influence it.

Perception is a process by which individuals organize and interpret sensory impressions in order to give meaning to their environment. What we perceive can be substantially different from objective reality. Perception is important to OB because people's behavior is based on their perception of what reality is, not on reality itself. *The world as it is perceived is the world that is behaviorally important.*

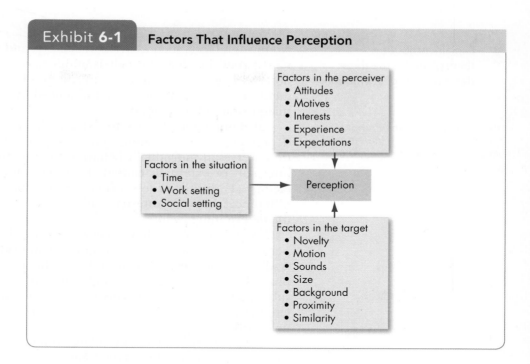

Exhibit 6-1 | **Factors That Influence Perception**

perception *A process by which individuals organize and interpret their sensory impressions in order to give meaning to their environment.*

Factors That Influence Perception

A number of factors shape and sometimes distort perception. These factors can reside in the *perceiver;* in the object, or *target,* being perceived; or in the *situation* in which the perception is made (see Exhibit 6-1).

When you look at a target, your interpretation of what you see is influenced by your personal characteristics—attitudes, personality, motives, interests, past experiences, and expectations. For instance, if you expect police officers to be authoritative, you may perceive them as such, regardless of their actual traits.

Characteristics of the target also affect what we perceive. Loud people are more likely to be noticed than quiet ones. So, too, are extremely attractive or unattractive individuals. Because we don't look at targets in isolation, the relationship of a target to its background influences perception, as does our tendency to group close things and similar things together. We often perceive women, men, Whites, African Americans, Asians, or members of any other group that has clearly distinguishable characteristics as alike in other, unrelated ways as well.

Context matters too. The time at which we see an object or event can influence our attention, as can location, light, heat, or situational factors. For instance, at a club on Saturday night you may not notice someone "decked out." Yet that same person so attired for your Monday morning management class would certainly catch your attention. Neither the perceiver nor the target has changed between Saturday night and Monday morning, but the situation is different.

Person Perception: Making Judgments About Others

Now we turn to the application of perception concepts most relevant to OB—*person perception,* or the perceptions people form about each other.

Attribution Theory

attribution theory *An attempt to determine whether an individual's behavior is internally or externally caused.*

Nonliving objects such as desks, machines, and buildings are subject to laws of nature, but they have no beliefs, motives, or intentions. People do. When we observe people, we attempt to explain their behavior. Our perception and judgment of a person's actions are influenced by the assumptions we make about that person's state of mind.

Attribution theory tries to explain the ways we judge people differently, depending on the meaning we attribute to a behavior.[1] It suggests that when we observe an individual's behavior, we attempt to determine whether it was internally or externally caused. That determination depends largely on three factors: (1) distinctiveness, (2) consensus, and (3) consistency. Let's clarify the differences between internal and external causation, and then we'll discuss the determining factors.

Internally caused behaviors are those an observer believes to be under the personal behavioral control of another individual. *Externally* caused behavior is what we imagine the situation forced the individual to do. If one of your employees is late for work, you might attribute that to his overnight partying and subsequent oversleeping. This is an internal attribution. But if you attribute lateness to an automobile accident that tied up traffic, you are making an external attribution.

Now let's discuss the three determining factors. *Distinctiveness* refers to whether an individual displays different behaviors in different situations. Is the employee who arrives late today also one who regularly "blows off" commitments? What we want to know is whether this behavior is unusual. If it is, we are likely to give it an external attribution. If it's not, we will probably judge the behavior to be internal.

If everyone who faces a similar situation responds in the same way, we can say the behavior shows *consensus*. The behavior of our tardy employee meets this criterion if all employees who took the same route were also late. From an attribution perspective, if consensus is high, you would probably give an external attribution to the employee's tardiness, whereas if other employees who took the same route made it to work on time, you would attribute his lateness to an internal cause.

Finally, an observer looks for *consistency* in a person's actions. Does the person respond the same way over time? Coming in 10 minutes late for work is not perceived in the same way for an employee who hasn't been late for several months as it is for an employee who is late three times a week. The more consistent the behavior, the more we are inclined to attribute it to internal causes.

Exhibit 6-2 summarizes the key elements in attribution theory. It tells us, for instance, that if an employee, Katelyn, generally performs at about the same level on related tasks as she does on her current task (low distinctiveness), other employees frequently perform differently—better or worse—than Katelyn on that task (low consensus), and Katelyn's performance on this current task is consistent over time (high consistency), anyone judging Katelyn's work will likely hold her primarily responsible for her task performance (internal attribution).

One of the findings from attribution theory research is that errors or biases distort attributions. When we make judgments about the behavior of other people, we tend to underestimate the influence of external factors and overestimate the influence of internal or personal factors.[2] This **fundamental attribution error** can explain why a sales manager is prone to attribute the poor performance of her sales agents to laziness rather than to a competitor's innovative product line. Individuals and organizations also tend to attribute their own successes to internal factors such as ability or effort, while blaming failure on external factors such as bad luck or unproductive co-workers. People also tend to attribute ambiguous information as relatively flattering, accept positive feedback,

fundamental attribution error *The tendency to underestimate the influence of external factors and overestimate the influence of internal factors when making judgments about the behavior of others.*

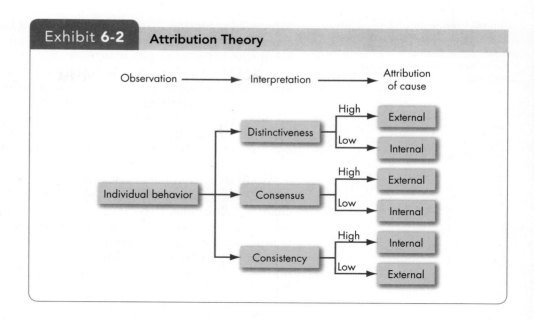

Exhibit **6-2**   **Attribution Theory**

self-serving bias *The tendency for individuals to attribute their own successes to internal factors and put the blame for failures on external factors.*

and reject negative feedback. This is **self-serving bias**.[3] Researchers asked one group of people, "If someone sues you and you win the case, should he pay your legal costs?" Eighty-five percent responded "yes." Another group was asked, "If you sue someone and lose the case, should you pay his costs?" Only 44 percent answered "yes."[4]

The evidence on cultural differences in perception is mixed, but most suggests there *are* differences across cultures in the attributions people make.[5] One study found Korean managers were less prone to self-serving bias—they tended to accept responsibility for group failure "because I was not a capable leader" instead of attributing failure to group members.[6] On the other hand, Asian managers are more likely to blame institutions or whole organizations, whereas Western observers believe individual managers should get blame or praise.[7] That probably explains why U.S. newspapers feature the names of individual executives when firms do poorly, whereas Asian media cover how the firm as a whole has failed. This tendency to make group-based attributions also explains why individuals from Asian cultures are more likely to make group-based stereotypes.[8] Attribution theory was developed based on experiments with U.S. and western European workers. But these studies suggest caution in making attribution theory predictions in non-Western societies, especially in countries with strong collectivist traditions.

Differences in attribution tendencies don't mean the basic concepts of attribution completely differ across cultures, though. Self-serving biases may be less common in East Asian cultures, but evidence suggests they still operate across cultures.[9] Studies indicate Chinese managers assess blame for mistakes using the same distinctiveness, consensus, and consistency cues Western managers use.[10] They also become angry and punish those deemed responsible for failure, a reaction shown in many studies of Western managers. This means the basic process of attribution applies across cultures, but that it takes more evidence for Asian managers to conclude someone else should be blamed.

Common Shortcuts in Judging Others

3 Identify the shortcuts individuals use in making judgments about others.

The shortcuts for judging others often allow us to make accurate perceptions rapidly and provide valid data for making predictions. However, they can and do sometimes result in significant distortions.

selective perception *The tendency to selectively interpret what one sees on the basis of one's interests, background, experience, and attitudes.*

Selective Perception   Any characteristic that makes a person, an object, or an event stand out will increase the probability we will perceive it. Why? Because it is impossible for us to assimilate everything we see; we can take in only certain stimuli. Thus, you are more likely to notice cars like your own, and your boss may reprimand some people and not others doing the same thing. Because we can't observe everything going on about us, we use **selective perception**. But we don't choose randomly: We select according to our interests, background, experience, and attitudes. Selective perception allows us to speed-read others, but not without the risk of drawing an inaccurate picture. Seeing what we want to see, we can draw unwarranted conclusions from an ambiguous situation.

We find an example of selective perception in financial analysis. From 2007 to 2009, the U.S. stock market lost roughly half its value. Yet during that time, analysts' sell ratings (typically, analysts rate a company's stock with three recommendations: buy, sell, or hold) actually *decreased* slightly. There are several reasons analysts are reluctant to put sell ratings on stocks; one is selective perception. When prices are going down, analysts often attend to the past (saying the stock is a bargain relative to its prior price), rather than the future (the downward trend may continue). As one money manager noted, "Each time the market went down was a new opportunity to buy the stock even cheaper."[11] True, but it shows the dangers of selective perception: By looking only at the past price, analysts were relying on a false reference point and failing to recognize that what has fallen can fall further still.

halo effect *The tendency to draw a general impression about an individual on the basis of a single characteristic.*

Halo Effect   When we draw an impression about an individual on the basis of a single characteristic, such as intelligence, sociability, or appearance, a **halo effect** is operating.[12] If you're a critic of President Obama, try listing ten things you admire about him. If you're an admirer, try listing ten things you dislike about him. No matter which describes you, odds are you won't find this an easy exercise! That's the halo effect: Our general views contaminate our specific ones.

The halo effect was confirmed in a classic study in which subjects were given a list of traits such as intelligent, skillful, practical, industrious, determined, and warm and asked to evaluate the person to whom those traits applied.[13] Subjects judged the person to be wise, humorous, popular, and imaginative. When the same list substituted "cold" for "warm," a completely different picture emerged. Clearly, the subjects were allowing a single trait to influence their overall impression of the person they were judging.

contrast effect *Evaluation of a person's characteristics that is affected by comparisons with other people recently encountered who rank higher or lower on the same characteristics.*

Contrast Effects   An old adage among entertainers is "Never follow an act that has kids or animals in it." Why? Audiences love children and animals so much that you'll look bad in comparison. This example demonstrates how a **contrast effect** can distort perceptions. We don't evaluate a person in isolation. Our reaction is influenced by other recent encounters.

In a series of job interviews, for instance, interviewers can make distortions in any given candidate's evaluation as a result of his or her place in the interview schedule. A candidate is likely to receive a more favorable evaluation if preceded by mediocre applicants and a less favorable evaluation if preceded by strong applicants.

stereotyping *Judging someone on the basis of one's perception of the group to which that person belongs.*

Stereotyping   When we judge someone on the basis of our perception of the group to which he or she belongs, we are **stereotyping**.[14]

We deal with the unmanageable number of stimuli of our complex world by using *heuristics* or stereotypes to make decisions quickly. For example, it does make sense to assume that Allison from finance will be able to help you figure out a forecasting problem. The problem occurs when we generalize inaccurately

Photo 6-1 These young women are taking a running test for a police officer job in Peshawar, Pakistan. Women in many countries report that it's difficult for them to enter the profession because gender stereotyping inaccurately generalizes that women lack the mental, physical, and emotional strength required to do police work.

Source: Pakistan Press International Photo/Newscom.

or too much. In organizations, we frequently hear comments that represent stereotypes based on gender, age, race, religion, ethnicity, and even weight (see Chapter 2):[15] "Men aren't interested in child care," "Older workers can't learn new skills," "Asian immigrants are hardworking and conscientious." Research suggests stereotypes operate emotionally and often below the level of conscious awareness, making them particularly hard to challenge and change.[16]

Stereotypes can be deeply ingrained and powerful enough to influence life-and-death decisions. One study, controlling for a wide array of factors (such as aggravating or mitigating circumstances), showed that the degree to which black defendants in murder trials looked "stereotypically black" essentially doubled their odds of receiving a death sentence if convicted.[17] Another study found that students who read scenarios describing leaders tended to assign higher scores for leadership potential and effective leadership to Whites than to minorities even though the content of the scenarios was equivalent, supporting the idea of a stereotype of Whites as better leaders.[18]

One problem of stereotypes is that they *are* widespread generalizations, though they may not contain a shred of truth when applied to a particular person or situation. We have to monitor ourselves to make sure we're not unfairly applying a stereotype in our evaluations and decisions. Stereotypes are an example of the warning, "The more useful, the more danger from misuse."

Specific Applications of Shortcuts in Organizations

People in organizations are always judging each other. Managers must appraise their employees' performances. We evaluate how much effort our co-workers are putting into their jobs. Team members immediately "size up" a new person. In many cases, our judgments have important consequences for the organization. Let's look at the most obvious applications.

Employment Interview   Few people are hired without an interview. But interviewers make perceptual judgments that are often inaccurate[19] and draw early impressions that quickly become entrenched. Research shows we form

"All Stereotypes Are Negative"

This statement is false. Positive stereotypes exist just as much as negative ones.

A study of Princeton University students shows, for example, that even today we believe Germans are better workers, Italians and African Americans are more loyal, Jews and Chinese are more intelligent, and Japanese and English are more courteous. What is surprising is that positive stereotypes are not always positive.

Men are commonly believed to have higher math ability than women. One study shows that when this stereotype is activated before men take a math test, their performance on the test actually goes down. Another study found that the belief that white men are better at science and math than women or minorities caused white men to leave science, technology, engineering, and math majors. Finally, a study used basketball to illustrate the complexity of stereotypes. Researchers provided evidence to one group of undergraduates that Whites were better free throw shooters than Blacks. Another group was provided evidence that Blacks were better free throw shooters than Whites. A third group was given

no stereotypic information. The undergraduates in all three groups then shot free throws while observers watched. The people who performed the worst were those in the negative stereotype condition (Black undergraduates who were told Whites were better and White undergraduates who were told Blacks were better). However, the positive stereotype group (Black undergraduates who were told Blacks were better and White undergraduates who were told Whites were better) also did not perform well. The best performance was turned in by those in the no stereotypic information group. In short, we are more likely to "choke" when we identify with positive stereotypes because they induce pressure to perform at the stereotypical level.

Choking is not the only negative thing about positive stereotypes. Research revealed that when women or Asian Americans heard positive stereotypes about themselves ("women are nurturing"; "Asians are good at math"), they felt depersonalized and reacted negatively to the individual expressing the positive stereotype. Another study showed that positive stereotypes about African Americans actually

solidified other, negative stereotypes because any stereotype tends to reinforce group-based differences, whether positive or negative.

Stereotypes are understandable. To function, we need shortcuts. This shortcut, however, runs both ways. Because stereotypes are socially learned, we need to be vigilant about not accepting or propagating them among our co-workers and peers.

Sources: A. C. Kay, M. V. Day, M. P. Zanna, and A. D. Nussbaum, "The Insidious (and Ironic) Effects of Positive Stereotypes," *Journal of Experimental Social Psychology* 49 (2013), pp. 287–291; J. O. Sly and S. Cheryan, "When Compliments Fail to Flatter: American Individualism and Responses to Positive Stereotypes," *Journal of Personality and Social Psychology* 104 (2013), pp. 87–102; M. J. Tagler, "Choking Under the Pressure of a Positive Stereotype: Gender Identification and Self-Consciousness Moderate Men's Math Test Performance," *Journal of Social Psychology* 152 (2012), pp. 401–416; M. A. Beasley and M. J. Fischer, "Why They Leave: The Impact of Stereotype Threat on the Attrition of Women and Minorities from Science, Math and Engineering Majors," *Social Psychology of Education* 15 (2012), pp. 427–448; and A. Krendl, I. Gainsburg, and N. Ambady, "The Effects of Stereotypes and Observer Pressure on Athletic Performance," *Journal of Sport & Exercise Psychology* 34 (2012), pp. 3–15.

impressions of others within a tenth of a second, based on our first glance.[20] Recent research indicates that our individual intuition about a job candidate is not reliable in predicting job performance, but that collecting input from multiple independent evaluators can be predictive.[21] Most interviewers' decisions change very little after the first 4 or 5 minutes of an interview. As a result, information elicited early in the interview carries greater weight than does information elicited later, and a "good applicant" is probably characterized more by the absence of unfavorable characteristics than by the presence of favorable ones.

self-fulfilling prophecy *A situation in which a person inaccurately perceives a second person, and the resulting expectations cause the second person to behave in ways consistent with the original perception.*

Performance Expectations People attempt to validate their perceptions of reality even when these are faulty.[22] The terms **self-fulfilling prophecy** and *Pygmalion effect* describe how an individual's behavior is determined by others' expectations. If a manager expects big things from her people, they're not likely to let her down. Similarly, if she expects only minimal performance, they'll likely meet those low expectations. Expectations become reality. The self-fulfilling prophecy has been found to affect the performance of students, soldiers, and even accountants.[23]

Performance Evaluation   We'll discuss performance evaluations in Chapter 17, but note that they very much depend on the perceptual process.[24] An employee's future is closely tied to the appraisal—promotion, pay raises, and continuation of employment are among the outcomes. Although the appraisal can be objective (for example, a sales-person is appraised on how many dollars of sales he generates in his territory), many jobs are evaluated subjectively. Subjective evaluations, though often necessary, are problematic because of the errors we've discussed—selective perception, contrast effects, halo effects, and so on. Sometimes performance ratings say as much about the evaluator as they do about the employee!

The Link Between Perception and Individual Decision Making

4 Explain the link between perception and decision making.

decisions *Choices made from among two or more alternatives.*

problem *A discrepancy between the current state of affairs and some desired state.*

Individuals make **decisions**, choices from among two or more alternatives. Top managers determine their organization's goals, what products or services to offer, how best to finance operations, or where to locate a new manufacturing plant. Middle- and lower-level managers set production schedules, select new employees, and decide how to allocate pay raises. Organizations have begun empowering their nonmanagerial employees with decision-making authority historically reserved for managers alone. Individual decision making is thus an important part of organizational behavior. But the way individuals make decisions and the quality of their choices are largely influenced by their perceptions.

Decision making occurs as a reaction to a **problem**.[25] That is, a discrepancy exists between the current state of affairs and some desired state, requiring us to consider alternative courses of action. If your car breaks down and you rely on it to get to work, you have a problem that requires a decision on your part. Unfortunately, most problems don't come neatly labeled "problem." One person's *problem* is another person's *satisfactory state of affairs*. One manager may view her division's 2 percent decline in quarterly sales to be a serious problem requiring immediate action on her part. Her counterpart in another division, who also had a 2 percent sales decrease, might consider that quite acceptable. So awareness that a problem exists and that a decision might or might not be needed is a perceptual issue.

Every decision requires us to interpret and evaluate information. We typically receive data from multiple sources we need to screen, process, and interpret. Which data are relevant to the decision, and which are not? Our perceptions will answer that question. We also need to develop alternatives and evaluate their strengths and weaknesses. Again, our perceptual process will affect the final outcome. Throughout the decision-making process, perceptual errors often surface that can bias analyses and conclusions.

Photo 6-2 Vanessa Cunningham is the leader of a pilot program planning team at Cummins that is turning individual cubicle workspaces into new collaborative work areas shown here. She uses employee feedback about their perceptions of the old versus new work areas in making decisions about the company's future office design.

Decision Making in Organizations

5 Contrast the rational model of decision making with bounded rationality and intuition.

Business schools train students to follow rational decision-making models. While models have merit, they don't always describe how people make decisions. OB improves the way we make decisions in organizations by addressing the decision-making errors people commit in addition to the perception errors we've discussed. Next we describe these errors, beginning with a brief overview of the rational decision-making model.

The Rational Model, Bounded Rationality, and Intuition

In OB, there are generally accepted constructs of decision making each of us employs to make determinations: rational decision making, bounded rationality, and intuition. Though their processes outwardly make sense, they may not lead to the most accurate (or best) decisions. More importantly, there are times when one strategy may lead to a better outcome than another in a given situation.

rational *Characterized by making consistent, value-maximizing choices within specified constraints.*

rational decision-making model *A decision-making model that describes how individuals should behave in order to maximize some outcome.*

Rational Decision Making   We often think the best decision maker is **rational** and makes consistent, value-maximizing choices within specified constraints.[26] These decisions follow a six-step **rational decision-making model**.[27] The six steps are listed in Exhibit 6-3.

Exhibit **6-3**	Steps in the Rational Decision-Making Model

1. Define the problem.
2. Identify the decision criteria.
3. Allocate weights to the criteria.
4. Develop the alternatives.
5. Evaluate the alternatives.
6. Select the best alternative.

The rational decision-making model assumes that the decision maker has complete information, is able to identify all the relevant options in an unbiased manner, and chooses the option with the highest utility.[28] Most decisions don't follow the rational model; people are usually content to find an acceptable or reasonable solution to a problem rather than an optimal one. Choices tend to be limited to the neighborhood of the problem symptom and the current alternative. As one expert in decision making put it, "Most significant decisions are made by judgment, rather than by a defined prescriptive model."[29] People are remarkably unaware of making suboptimal decisions.[30]

Bounded Rationality   Our limited information-processing capability makes it impossible to assimilate all the information necessary to optimize.[31] Most people respond to a complex problem by reducing it to a level they can readily understand. Many problems don't have an optimal solution because they are too complicated to fit the rational decision-making model, so people *satisfice;* they seek solutions that are satisfactory and sufficient.

When you considered which college to attend, did you look at every viable alternative? Did you carefully identify all the criteria that were important in your decision? Did you evaluate each alternative against the criteria in order to find the optimal college? The answers are probably "no." Don't feel bad; few people make their college choice this way. Instead of optimizing, you probably satisficed.

Because the human mind cannot formulate and solve complex problems with full rationality, we operate within the confines of **bounded rationality**. We construct simplified models that extract the essential features from problems without capturing all their complexity.[32] We can then behave rationally within the limits of the simple model.

How does bounded rationality work for the typical individual? Once we've identified a problem, we begin to search for criteria and alternatives. The criteria are unlikely to be exhaustive. We identify alternatives that are highly visible and that usually represent familiar criteria and tried-and-true solutions. Next, we begin reviewing the alternatives, focusing on choices that differ little from

bounded rationality   *A process of making decisions by constructing simplified models that extract the essential features from problems without capturing all their complexity.*

Photo 6-3 Isao Moriyasu is president of DeNA, a Japanese Internet firm focused on social game platforms and social games. Shown here with the firm's new "comm" app, Moriyasu operates within the confines of bounded rationality in making complex decisions about acquiring other firms, expanding globally, and rapidly developing new services.

the current state until we identify one that is "good enough"—that meets an acceptable level of performance. Thus ends our search. So the solution represents a satisficing choice—the first *acceptable* one we encounter—rather than an optimal one.

Satisficing is not always bad—a simple process may frequently be more sensible than the traditional rational decision-making model.[33] To use the rational model, you need to gather a great deal of information about all the options, compute applicable weights, and then calculate values across a huge number of criteria. All these processes can cost time, energy, and money. If there are many unknown weights and preferences, the fully rational model may not be any more accurate than a best guess. Sometimes a fast-and-frugal process of solving problems might be your best option. Returning to your college choice, would it be best to fly around the country to visit dozens of potential campuses and pay application fees for all? That depends: Can you know what type of college is best for you when in high school, or is there a lot of unknown information about how your interests are going to develop? It might be smarter to satisfice by finding a few colleges that match most of your preferences and then focus your attention on differentiating between those.

intuitive decision making *An unconscious process created out of distilled experience.*

Intuition Perhaps the least rational way of making decisions is **intuitive decision making**, an unconscious process created from distilled experience.[34] Intuitive decision making occurs outside conscious thought; relies on holistic associations, or links between disparate pieces of information; is fast; and is *affectively charged,* meaning it engages the emotions.[35]

While intuition isn't rational, it isn't necessarily wrong. Nor does it always contradict rational analysis; the two can complement each other. Nor is intuition superstition, or the product of some magical or paranormal sixth sense. Intuition is complex and based on years of experience and learning.

Does intuition help effective decision making? Researchers are divided, but most experts are skeptical, in part because intuition is hard to measure and analyze. Probably the best advice from one expert is: "Intuition can be very useful as a way of setting up a hypothesis but is unacceptable as 'proof,'" Use hunches derived from your experience to speculate, yes, but always make sure to test those hunches with objective data and rational, dispassionate analysis.[36]

Common Biases and Errors in Decision Making

6 Describe the common decision biases or errors.

Decision makers engage in bounded rationality, but they also allow systematic biases and errors to creep into their judgments.[37] To minimize effort and avoid trade-offs, people tend to rely too heavily on experience, impulses, gut feelings, and convenient rules of thumb. Shortcuts can be helpful; however, they can distort rationality. Following are the most common biases in decision making. Exhibit 6-4 provides some suggestions for how to avoid falling into these biases and errors.

Overconfidence Bias Recent research continues to conclude that we tend to be overconfident about our abilities and about the abilities of others; also, that we are usually not aware of this bias.[38] It's been said that "no problem in judgment and decision making is more prevalent and more potentially catastrophic than overconfidence."[39] When we're given factual questions and asked to judge the probability that our answers are correct, we tend to be overly optimistic. When people say they're 90 percent confident about the range a certain number might take, their estimated ranges contain the correct answer only about 50 percent of the time—and experts are no more accurate in setting up confidence intervals than are novices.[40]

Exhibit 6-4	Reducing Biases and Errors

Focus on Goals. Without goals, you can't be rational, you don't know what information you need, you don't know which information is relevant and which is irrelevant, you'll find it difficult to choose between alternatives, and you're far more likely to experience regret over the choices you make. Clear goals make decision making easier and help you eliminate options that are inconsistent with your interests.

Look for Information That Disconfirms Your Beliefs. One of the most effective means for counteracting overconfidence and the confirmation and hindsight biases is to actively look for information that contradicts your beliefs and assumptions. When we overtly consider various ways we could be wrong, we challenge our tendencies to think we're smarter than we actually are.

Don't Try to Create Meaning out of Random Events. The educated mind has been trained to look for cause-and-effect relationships. When something happens, we ask why. And when we can't find reasons, we often invent them. You have to accept that there are events in life that are outside your control. Ask yourself if patterns can be meaningfully explained or whether they are merely coincidence. Don't attempt to create meaning out of coincidence.

Increase Your Options. No matter how many options you've identified, your final choice can be no better than the best of the option set you've selected. This argues for increasing your decision alternatives and for using creativity in developing a wide range of diverse choices. The more alternatives you can generate, and the more diverse those alternatives, the greater your chance of finding an outstanding one.

Source: S. P. Robbins, *Decide & Conquer: Making Winning Decisions and Taking Control of Your Life* (Upper Saddle River, NJ: Financial Times/Prentice Hall, 2004), pp. 164–168.

Individuals whose intellectual and interpersonal abilities are *weakest* are most likely to overestimate their performance and ability.[41] There's also a negative relationship between entrepreneurs' optimism and performance of their new ventures: the more optimistic, the less successful.[42] The tendency to be too confident about their ideas might keep some from planning how to avoid problems that arise.

Investor overconfidence operates in a variety of ways.[43] Finance professor Terrance Odean says, "People think they know more than they do, and it costs them." Investors, especially novices, overestimate not just their skill in processing information, but also the quality of the information they're working with. Test your own confidence level with investments: compare the long-term returns of your stock market picks relative to index funds. You'll find an overall index performs as well as, or better than, hand-picked stocks. The main reason many people resist index funds is that they think they're better at picking stocks than the average person, but most investors will only do as well as or only slightly better than the market.

Anchoring Bias   **Anchoring bias** is a tendency to fixate on initial information and fail to adequately adjust for subsequent information.[44] As we discussed earlier in the chapter in relationship to employment interviews, our mind appears to give a disproportionate amount of emphasis to the first information it receives. Anchors are widely used by people in professions in which persuasion skills are important—advertising, management, politics, real estate, and law. Assume two pilots—Jason and Glenda—have been laid off, and after an extensive search their best offers are from Delta Airlines. Each would earn the average annual pay of Delta's narrow-body jet pilots: $126,000. Jason was previously a pilot for Pinnacle, a regional airline where the average annual salary is $82,000. Glenda

anchoring bias   *A tendency to fixate on initial information, from which one then fails to adequately adjust for subsequent information.*

was a pilot for FedEx, where the average annual salary is $200,000. Which pilot is most likely to accept, or be happiest with, Delta's offer? Obviously Jason, because he is anchored by the lower salary.[45]

Any time a negotiation takes place, so does anchoring. When a prospective employer asks how much you made in your prior job, your answer typically anchors the employer's offer. (Remember this when you negotiate your salary, but set the anchor only as high as you truthfully can.) The more precise your anchor, the smaller the adjustment. Some research suggests people think of making an adjustment after an anchor is set as rounding off a number: If you suggest a salary of $55,000, your boss will consider $50,000 to $60,000 a reasonable range for negotiation, but if you mention $55,650, your boss is more likely to consider $55,000 to $56,000 the range of likely values.[46]

Confirmation Bias   The rational decision-making process assumes we objectively gather information. But we don't. We *selectively* gather it. **Confirmation bias** represents a case of selective perception: we seek out information that reaffirms our past choices, and we discount information that contradicts them.[47] We also tend to accept at face value information that confirms our preconceived views, while we are skeptical of information that challenges them. Therefore, the information we gather is typically biased toward supporting views we already hold. We even tend to seek sources most likely to tell us what we want to hear, and we give too much weight to supporting information and too little to contradictory. We are most prone to confirmation bias when we believe we have good information and strongly hold our opinions. Fortunately, those who feel there is a strong need to be accurate in making a decision are less prone to confirmation bias.

Availability Bias   More people fear flying than fear driving in a car. But if flying on a commercial airline were as dangerous as driving, the equivalent of two 747s filled to capacity would crash every week, killing all aboard. Because the media give more attention to air accidents, we tend to overstate the risk of flying and understate the risk of driving.

Availability bias is our tendency to base judgments on information readily available. Recent research indicates that a combination of readily available information and our previous direct experience with similar information is particularly impactful to our decision making. Events that evoke emotions, that are particularly vivid, or that are more recent tend to be more available in our memory, leading us to overestimate the chances of unlikely events such as being in an airplane crash, suffering complications from medical treatment, or getting fired.[48] Availability bias can also explain why managers give more weight in performance appraisals to recent employee behaviors than to behaviors of 6 or 9 months earlier, or why credit-rating agencies such as Moody's or Standard & Poor's may issue overly positive ratings by relying on information presented by debt issuers, who have an incentive to offer data favorable to their case.[49]

Escalation of Commitment   Another distortion that creeps into decisions is a tendency to escalate commitment, often for increasingly nonrational reasons.[50] **Escalation of commitment** refers to our staying with a decision even if there is clear evidence it's wrong. Consider a friend who has been dating someone for several years. Although he admits things aren't going too well, he says he is still going to marry her. His justification: "I have a lot invested in the relationship!"

When is escalation most likely to occur? Evidence indicates it occurs when individuals view themselves as responsible for the outcome. The fear of personal failure even biases the way we search for and evaluate information so that we

confirmation bias   *The tendency to seek out information that reaffirms past choices and to discount information that contradicts past judgments.*

availability bias   *The tendency for people to base their judgments on information that is readily available to them.*

escalation of commitment   *An increased commitment to a previous decision in spite of negative information.*

choose only information that supports our dedication. We might, for example, weight opinions in favor of reinvestment as more credible than opinions for divestment.[51]

A recent meta-analysis revealed some interesting findings about what causes us to escalate our commitment after initial failure. First, it doesn't appear to matter whether we chose the failing course of action or it was assigned to us—we feel responsible and escalate in either case. Second, the sharing of decision authority—such as when others review the choice we made—can lead to higher escalation because the original decision is more public (thus individuals feel a stronger need to justify the original decision by continuing). Finally, awareness of sunk costs associated with the decision reduces escalation when individuals feel responsible (they now have an "escape clause").[52]

Randomness Error   Most of us like to think we have some control over our world. Our tendency to believe we can predict the outcome of random events is the **randomness error**.

randomness error   *The tendency of individuals to believe that they can predict the outcome of random events.*

Decision making suffers when we try to create meaning in random events, particularly when we turn imaginary patterns into superstitions.[53] These can be completely contrived ("I never make important decisions on Friday the 13th") or they can evolve from a reinforced past pattern of behavior (Tiger Woods often wears a red shirt during a golf tournament's final round because he won many junior tournaments wearing red shirts). Decisions based on random occurrences can handicap us when they affect our judgment or bias our major decisions.

Risk Aversion   Mathematically, we should find a 50–50 flip of the coin for $100 to be worth as much as a sure promise of $50. After all, the expected value of the gamble over a number of trials is $50. However, nearly everyone but committed gamblers would rather have the sure thing than a risky prospect.[54] For many people, a 50–50 flip of a coin even for $200 might not be worth as much as a sure promise of $50, even though the gamble is mathematically worth twice as much! This tendency to prefer a sure thing over a risky outcome is **risk aversion**.

risk aversion   *The tendency to prefer a sure gain of a moderate amount over a riskier outcome, even if the riskier outcome might have a higher expected payoff.*

Risk aversion has important implications. To offset the risks inherent in a commission-based wage, companies pay commissioned employees considerably more than they do those on straight salaries. Risk-averse employees will stick with the established way of doing their jobs, rather than taking a chance on innovative methods. Sticking with a strategy that has worked in the past minimizes risk, but it will lead to stagnation. Ambitious people with power that can be taken away (most managers) appear to be especially risk averse, perhaps because they don't want to lose on a gamble everything they've worked so hard to achieve.[55] CEOs at risk of termination are exceptionally risk averse, even when a riskier investment strategy is in their firms' best interests.[56]

Risk preference is sometimes reversed: People prefer to take chances when trying to prevent a negative outcome.[57] They would rather take a 50–50 gamble on losing $100 than accept the certain loss of $50. Thus they will risk losing a lot of money at trial rather than settle out of court. Trying to cover up wrongdoing instead of admitting a mistake, despite the risk of truly catastrophic press coverage or even jail time, is another example. Stressful situations can make risk preferences stronger. People will more likely engage in risk-seeking behavior for negative outcomes, and risk-averse behavior for positive outcomes, when under stress.[58]

hindsight bias   *The tendency to believe falsely, after an outcome of an event is actually known, that one would have accurately predicted that outcome.*

Hindsight Bias   **Hindsight bias** is the tendency to believe falsely, after the outcome is known, that we would have accurately predicted it.[59] When we have feedback on the outcome, we seem good at concluding it was obvious.

For instance, the home video rental industry collapsed as online distribution outlets ate away at the market.[60] Hollywood Video declared bankruptcy in May 2010 and began liquidating its assets; Blockbuster filed for bankruptcy in September 2010. Some have suggested that if these organizations had leveraged their brand and distribution resources effectively, developed web-based delivery sooner, as Netflix did, and added low-cost distribution in grocery and convenience stores, which Redbox offers, they could have avoided failure. While that seems obvious now in hindsight, tempting us to think we would have predicted it, many experts with good information failed to predict these two major trends that would upend the industry.

After the fact, it is easy to see that a combination of automated and mail-order distribution would outperform the traditional brick-and-mortar movie rental business. Similarly, in the recent housing bubble, former Merrill Lynch CEO John Thain—and other Wall Street executives—missed what now seems obvious—that housing prices were inflated, too many risky loans were being made, and the values of many "securities" were based on fragile assumptions. Though criticisms of decision makers may have merit, as Malcolm Gladwell, author of *Blink* and *The Tipping Point,* writes, "What is clear in hindsight is rarely clear before the fact."[61]

Hindsight bias reduces our ability to learn from the past. It lets us think we're better predictors than we are and can make us falsely confident. If your actual predictive accuracy is only 40 percent but you think it's 90, you're likely to be less skeptical about your predictive skills.

SELF-ASSESSMENT LIBRARY

Am I a Deliberate Decision Maker?

In the Self-Assessment Library (available in MyManagementLab), take assessment IV.A.2 (Am I a Deliberate Decision Maker?). Would it be better to be a more deliberate decision maker? Why or why not?

Influences on Decision Making: Individual Differences and Organizational Constraints

We turn here to factors that influence how people make decisions and the degree to which they are susceptible to errors and biases. We discuss individual differences and organizational constraints.

Individual Differences

7 Explain how individual differences and organizational constraints affect decision making.

As we discussed, decision making in practice is characterized by bounded rationality, common biases and errors, and the use of intuition. Individual differences also create deviations from the rational model. In this section, we look at the differences in turn.

Personality   Research on personality and decision making suggests personality influences our decisions. Let's look at conscientiousness and self-esteem (both discussed in Chapter 5).

Specific facets of conscientiousness—rather than the broad trait itself—may affect escalation of commitment,[62] particularly the conscientiousness facets of achievement-striving and dutifulness. First, research suggested that achievement-striving people were more likely to escalate their commitment, whereas dutiful people were less likely. Why? Generally, achievement-oriented people hate to fail, so they escalate their commitment, hoping to forestall failure. Dutiful people, however, are more inclined to do what they see as best for the organization. Second, achievement-striving individuals appear more susceptible to hindsight bias, perhaps because they have a need to justify their actions.[63] We don't have evidence yet on whether dutiful people are immune to this bias.

People with high self-esteem are strongly motivated to maintain it, so they use the self-serving bias to preserve it. They blame others for their failures while taking credit for successes.[64]

Gender   Research on rumination offers insights into gender differences in decision making.[65] *Rumination* refers to reflecting at length. In terms of decision making, it means overthinking problems. Twenty years of study finds women spend more time than men analyzing the past, present, and future. They're more likely to overanalyze problems before making a decision and to rehash a decision once made. This can lead to careful consideration of problems and choices. However, it can make problems harder to solve, increase regret over past decisions, and increase depression. Women are nearly twice as likely as men to develop depression.[66]

Why women ruminate more than men is not clear. One view is that parents encourage and reinforce the expression of sadness and anxiety more in girls than in boys. Another theory is that women, more than men, base their self-esteem and well-being on what others think of them. A third idea is that women are more empathetic and more affected by events in others' lives, so they have more to ruminate about.

By age 11, girls ruminate more than boys. But the gender difference seems to lessen with age. Differences are largest during young adulthood and smallest after age 65, when both men and women ruminate the least.[67]

Mental Ability   We know people with higher levels of mental ability are able to process information more quickly, solve problems more accurately, and learn faster, so you might expect them also to be less susceptible to common decision errors. However, mental ability appears to help people avoid only some of these.[68] Smart people are just as likely to fall prey to anchoring, overconfidence, and escalation of commitment, probably because just being smart doesn't alert you to the possibility you're too confident or emotionally defensive. It's not that intelligence never matters. Once warned about decision-making errors, more intelligent people learn more quickly to avoid them. They are also better able to avoid logical errors like false syllogisms or incorrect interpretation of data.

Cultural Differences   The rational model makes no acknowledgment of cultural differences, nor does the bulk of OB research literature on decision making. But Indonesians, for instance, don't necessarily make decisions the same way Australians do. Therefore, we need to recognize that the cultural background of a decision maker can significantly influence the selection of problems, the depth of analysis, the importance placed on logic and rationality, and whether organizational decisions should be made autocratically by an individual manager or collectively in groups.[69]

Cultures differ in time orientation, the importance of rationality, belief in the ability of people to solve problems, and preference for collective decision making. Differences in time orientation help us understand why managers in Egypt make decisions at a much slower and more deliberate pace than their U.S. counterparts. While rationality is valued in North America, that's not true elsewhere. A North American manager might make an important decision intuitively but know it's important to appear to proceed in a rational fashion because rationality is highly valued in the West. In countries such as Iran, where rationality is not as paramount as other factors, efforts to appear rational are not necessary.

Some cultures emphasize solving problems, while others focus on accepting situations as they are. The United States falls in the first category; Thailand and Indonesia are examples of the second. Because problem-solving managers believe they can and should change situations to their benefit, U.S. managers might identify a problem long before their Thai or Indonesian counterparts would choose to recognize it as such. Decision making by Japanese managers is much more group-oriented than in the United States. The Japanese value conformity and cooperation, so before Japanese CEOs make an important decision, they collect a large amount of information to use in consensus-forming group decisions. There are probably important cultural differences in decision making, but unfortunately not much research yet to identify them.

glOBalization!

Does Multicultural Experience Make for Better Decisions?

Does living in multiple cultures or countries improve decision making? One recent three-part study looked at the effect of multicultural identity on individual creativity and career success. The researchers defined multicultural identity as a strong identification with the culture in both the host country where the subject currently lives and the home country where the person grew up. One finding was that European MBA students with multicultural identities were more creative on three different tasks. Another was that multicultural U.S. MBA students had higher levels of innovation, measured in terms of the new ventures they started and novel products or services they created. The third part of the study showed that Israeli managers with multicultural identities were rated as higher performers and more promotable than Israeli managers who scored low on the multicultural identity measure. All three parts revealed that the reason multiculturals were more creative and effective was "integrative complexity"—the degree to which they approached problems from multiple points of view (the researchers measured this by asking participants to describe a problem and having independent evaluators rate their responses).

A second study focused on the effect of multicultural identities on intergroup biases, or the degree to which individuals hold stereotypes or prejudices about those outside the group with which they identify. For this study, researchers conducted six studies of Caucasian American, Asian American, and Israeli college students. In all six studies, those who had multicultural identities were less likely to endorse stereotypical beliefs against members outside their ethnic group, even though in three of the studies, multiculturalism was manipulated by the researchers. In two studies, for instance, they first showed some respondents a 20-minute PowerPoint presentation with pictures, music, and movie trailers from both U.S. and Chinese cultures and others a similar presentation with content from only U.S. or only Chinese culture. They also manipulated Israeli multicultural identity by asking Israeli students to think and write about a multicultural experience. Even when multicultural identity was manipulated, it reduced intergroup biases.

Thus, it seems that multiculturalism does make for better decisions, at least as far as creativity and lack of bias are concerned.

Sources: C. T. Tadmor, Y. Hong, M. M. Chao, F. Wiruchnipawan, and W. Wang, "Multicultural Experiences Reduce Intergroup Bias Through Epistemic Unfreezing," *Journal of Personality and Social Psychology* 103 (2012), pp. 750–772; and C. T. Tadmor, A. D. Galinsky, and W. W. Maddux, "Getting the Most Out of Living Abroad: Biculturalism and Integrative Complexity as Key Drivers of Creative and Professional Success," *Journal of Personality and Social Psychology* 103 (2012), pp. 520–542.

Organizational Constraints

Organizations can constrain decision makers, creating deviations from the rational model. For instance, managers shape decisions to reflect the organization's performance evaluation and reward system, to comply with formal regulations, and to meet organizationally imposed time constraints. Precedent can also limit decisions.

Performance Evaluation   Managers are influenced by the criteria on which they are evaluated. If a division manager believes the manufacturing plants under his responsibility are operating best when he hears nothing negative, we would find his plant managers spending a good part of their time ensuring that negative information doesn't reach him.

Reward System   The organization's reward system influences decision makers by suggesting which choices have better personal payoffs. If the organization rewards risk aversion, managers are more likely to make conservative decisions. From the 1930s through the mid-1980s, General Motors consistently gave promotions and bonuses to managers who kept a low profile and avoided controversy. These executives became adept at dodging tough issues and passing controversial decisions on to committees.

Formal Regulations   David, a shift manager at a Taco Bell restaurant in San Antonio, Texas, describes constraints he faces on his job: "I've got rules and regulations covering almost every decision I make—from how to make a burrito to how often I need to clean the restrooms. My job doesn't come with much freedom of choice." David's situation is not unique. All but the smallest organizations create rules and policies to program decisions and get individuals to act in the intended manner. In doing so, they limit decision choices.

System-Imposed Time Constraints   Almost all important decisions come with explicit deadlines. A report on new-product development may have to be ready for executive committee review by the first of the month. Such conditions often

Photo 6-4 Manager Kely Guardado (center) prepares hamburgers alongside employees at a Five Guys Burger and Fries restaurant. Decision choices of Five Guys crew members are limited because workers are required to follow rules and regulations for food preparation that meet the firm's high standards of quality, safety, and service.

make it difficult, if not impossible, for managers to gather all the information before making a final choice.

Historical Precedents   Decisions aren't made in a vacuum; they have a context. Individual decisions are points in a stream of choice; those made in the past are like ghosts that haunt and constrain current choices. It's common knowledge that the largest determinant of the size of any given year's budget is last year's budget.[70] Choices made today are largely a result of choices made over the years.

What About Ethics in Decision Making?

8   Contrast the three ethical decision criteria.

Ethical considerations should be an important criterion in all organizational decision making. In this section, we present three ways to frame decisions ethically.[71] Managers also need to understand the important role creativity should play in the decision process; the best managers employ strategies to increase the creative potential of their employees and harvest the ideas for organizational application.

Three Ethical Decision Criteria

utilitarianism   *A system in which decisions are made to provide the greatest good for the greatest number.*

The first ethical yardstick is **utilitarianism**, which proposes making decisions solely on the basis of their *outcomes*, ideally to provide the greatest good for the greatest number. This view dominates business decision making. It is consistent with goals such as efficiency, productivity, and high profits.

Another ethical criterion is to make decisions consistent with fundamental liberties and privileges, as set forth in documents such as the Bill of Rights. An emphasis on *rights* in decision making means respecting and protecting the basic rights of individuals, such as the right to privacy, free speech, and due process. This criterion protects **whistle-blowers** when they reveal an organization's unethical practices to the press or government agencies, using their right to free speech.

whistle-blowers   *Individuals who report unethical practices by their employer to outsiders.*

A third criterion is to impose and enforce rules fairly and impartially to ensure *justice* or an equitable distribution of benefits and costs. Union members typically favor this view. It justifies paying people the same wage for a given job regardless of performance differences and using seniority as the primary determination in layoff decisions.

Each criterion has advantages and liabilities. A focus on utilitarianism promotes efficiency and productivity, but it can sideline the rights of some individuals, particularly those with minority representation. The use of rights protects individuals from injury and is consistent with freedom and privacy, but it can create a legalistic environment that hinders productivity and efficiency. A focus on justice protects the interests of the underrepresented and less powerful, but it can encourage a sense of entitlement that reduces risk taking, innovation, and productivity.

Decision makers, particularly in for-profit organizations, feel comfortable with utilitarianism. The "best interests" of the organization and its stockholders can justify a lot of questionable actions, such as large layoffs. But many critics feel this perspective needs to change. Public concern about individual rights and social justice suggests managers should develop ethical standards based on nonutilitarian criteria. This presents a challenge because satisfying individual rights and social justice creates far more ambiguities than utilitarian effects on efficiency and profits. However, while raising prices, selling products with questionable effects on consumer health, closing down inefficient plants, laying off large numbers of employees, and moving production overseas to cut costs can be justified in utilitarian terms, there may no longer be a single measure by which good decisions are judged.

behavioral ethics *Analyzing how people actually behave when confronted with ethical dilemmas.*

Increasingly, researchers are turning to **behavioral ethics**—an area of study that analyzes how people behave when confronted with ethical dilemmas. Their research tells us that while ethical standards exist collectively (society and organizations) and individually (personal ethics), individuals do not always follow ethical standards promulgated by their organizations, and we sometimes violate our own standards. Our ethical behavior varies widely from one situation to the next.

How might we increase ethical decision-making in organizations? First, sociologist James Q. Wilson promulgated the *broken windows theory*—the idea that decayed and disorderly urban environments may facilitate criminal behavior because they signal antisocial norms. Although controversial, the theory does fit with behavioral ethics research showing that seemingly superficial aspects of the environment—such as lighting, outward displays of wealth and status, and cleanliness—can affect ethical behavior in organizations.[72] Managers must first realize that ethical behavior can be affected by signals; for example, if signs of status and money are everywhere, an employee may perceive those, rather than ethical standards, to be of the highest importance. Second, managers should encourage conversations about moral issues; they may serve as a reminder and increase ethical decision making. One study found that simply asking business school students to think of an ethical situation had powerful effects when they were making ethical choices later.[73] Finally, we should be aware of our own moral "blind spots"—the tendency to see ourselves as more moral than we are and others as less moral than they are. Although smart people can be just as susceptible to moral blind spots as others, an environment that encourages open discussions and does not penalize people for coming forward is key to overcoming blind spots and increasing the ethicality of decision making.[74]

Behavioral ethics research stresses the importance of culture to ethical decision making. There are few global standards for ethical decision making,[75] as contrasts between Asia and the West illustrate. What is ethical in one culture may be unethical in another. For example, because bribery is more common in countries such as China, a Canadian working in China might face a dilemma: Should I pay a bribe to secure business if it is an accepted part of that country's culture? Although some companies like IBM explicitly address this issue, many do not. Without sensitivity to cultural differences in defining ethical conduct, organizations may encourage unethical conduct without even knowing it.

Creativity, Creative Decision Making, and Innovation in Organizations

9 Define *creativity*, and describe the three-stage model of creativity.

creativity *The ability to produce novel and useful ideas.*

Although the rational decision-making model will often improve decisions, a decision maker also needs **creativity**, the ability to produce novel and useful ideas. These ideas are different from what's been done before but are appropriate for the problem.

Creativity allows the decision maker to fully appraise and understand problems, including seeing problems others can't see. For this reason, French cosmetics company L'Oréal puts its managers through creative exercises such as cooking or making music, and the University of Chicago requires MBA students to make short movies about their experiences.

Choosing to Lie

Mark Twain wrote, "The wise thing is for us diligently to train ourselves to lie thoughtfully." Not everyone agrees that lying is wrong. But we probably agree that people do lie, including each of us, to varying degrees. And most of us probably agree that if we lied less, organizations and society would be better off. So how might that be done? Research conducted by behavioral scientists suggests some steps to recovery.

1. **Stop lying to ourselves.** We lie to ourselves about how much we lie. Specifically, many studies reveal that we deem ourselves much less likely to lie than we judge others to be. At a collective level, this is impossible—everyone can't be below above average in their propensity to lie. So step 1 is to admit the truth: We underestimate the degree to which we lie, we overestimate our morality compared to

others, and we tend to engage in what Bazerman and Tenbrunsel call "moral hypocrisy"—we think we're more moral than we are.

2. **Trust, but verify.** A recent study showed that lying is learned at a very young age. When a toy was placed out of view, an experimenter told young children not to look at the toy and went out of sight. More than 80 percent of the children looked at the toy. When asked whether they had looked, 25 percent of 2-1/2 year-olds lied, compared to 90 percent of 4 year-olds. Why do we learn to lie? Because we often get away with it. Negotiation research shows that we are more likely to lie in the future when our lies have succeeded or gone undetected in the past. Managers need to identify areas where lying is costly and find ways to shine a light on it when it occurs.

3. **Reward honesty.** "The most difficult thing is to recognize that sometimes we too are blinded by our own incentives," writes Dan Ariely, "because we don't see how our conflicts of interest work on us." So if we want more honesty, we have to provide greater incentives for the truth, and more disincentives for lying and cheating.

Sources: Based on D. Ariely, *The Honest Truth About Dishonesty: How We Lie to Everyone—and Especially Ourselves* (New York: Harper, 2012); K. Canavan, "Even Nice People Cheat Sometimes," *The Wall Street Journal* (August 8, 2012), p. 4B; M. H. Bazerman and Ann E. Tenbrunsel, *Blind Spots: Why We Fail to Do What's Right and What to Do About It* (Princeton, NJ: Princeton University Press, 2012); A. D. Evans and K. Lee, "Emergence of Lying in Very Young Children," *Developmental Psychology* (2013); and L. Zhou Y. Sung, and D. Zhang, "Deception Performance in Online Group Negotiation and Decision Making: The Effects of Deception Experience and Deception Skill," *Group Decision and Negotiation* 22 (2013), pp. 153–172.

three-stage model of creativity *The proposition that creativity involves three stages: causes (creative potential and creative environment), creative behavior, and creative outcomes (innovation).*

Although all aspects of organizational behavior have complexities, that is especially true for creativity. To simplify, Exhibit 6-5 provides a **three-stage model of creativity** in organizations. The core of the model is *creative behavior*, which has both *causes* (predictors of creative behavior) and *effects* (outcomes of creative behavior). In this section, we discuss the three stages of creativity, starting with the center, creative behavior.

Creative Behavior

Creative behavior occurs in four steps, each of which leads to the next:

problem formulation *The stage of creative behavior which involved identifying problem or opportunity that requires a solution that is as yet unknown.*

1. **Problem formulation.**   Any act of creativity begins with a problem that the behavior is designed to solve. Thus, **problem formulation** is defined as the stage of creative behavior in which we identify a problem or opportunity that requires a solution as yet unknown. For example, artist/entrepreneur Marshall Carbee and businessperson John Bennett founded Eco Safety Products after discovering that even paints declared safe by the Environmental Protection Agency (EPA) emit hazardous chemical compounds. Thus, Bennett's development of artist-safe soy-based paint began with identifying a safety problem with paints currently on the market.[76]

information gathering *The stage of creative behavior when possible solutions to a problem incubate in individual's mind.*

2. **Information gathering.**   Given a problem, the solution is rarely directly at hand. We need time to learn more and to process that learning. Thus, **information gathering** is the stage of creative behavior when possible

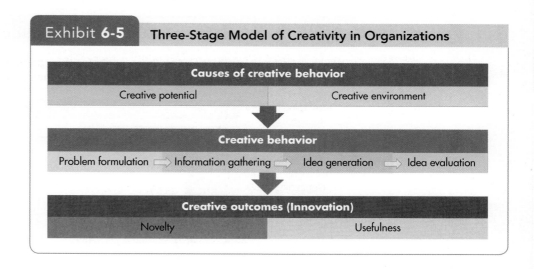

Exhibit 6-5   Three-Stage Model of Creativity in Organizations

Causes of creative behavior

Creative potential | Creative environment

Creative behavior

Problem formulation ⇒ Information gathering ⇒ Idea generation ⇒ Idea evaluation

Creative outcomes (Innovation)

Novelty | Usefulness

solutions to a problem incubate in an individual's mind. Niklas Laninge of Hoa's Tool Shop, a Stockholm-based company that helps organizations become more innovative, argues that creative information gathering means thinking beyond usual routines and comfort zones. For example, have lunch with someone outside your field to discuss the problem. "It's so easy, and you're forced to speak about your business and the things that you want to accomplish in new terms. You can't use buzzwords because people don't know what you mean," Laninge says.[77]

3. **Idea generation.**   Once we have collected the relevant information, it is time to translate knowledge into ideas. Thus, **idea generation** is the process of creative behavior in which we develop possible solutions to a problem from relevant information and knowledge. Increasingly, idea generation is collaborative. For example, when NASA engineers developed the idea for landing a spacecraft on Mars, they did so collaboratively. Before coming up with the Curiosity—an SUV-sized rover that lands on Mars from a sky crane— the team spent three days scribbling potential ideas on whiteboards.[78]

4. **Idea evaluation.**   Finally, it's time to choose from the ideas we have generated. Thus, **idea evaluation** is the process of creative behavior in which we evaluate potential solutions to identify the best one. Sometimes the method of choosing can be innovative. When Dallas Mavericks owner Mark Cuban was unhappy with the team's uniforms, he asked fans to help design and choose the best uniform. Cuban said, "What's the best way to come up with creative ideas? You ask for them. So we are going to crowd source the design and colors of our uniforms."[79] Generally, you want those who evaluate ideas to be different from those who generate them, to eliminate the obvious biases.

Causes of Creative Behavior

Having defined creative behavior, the main stage in the three-stage model, we now look back to the causes of creativity: creative potential and creative environment.

Creative Potential   Is there such a thing as a creative personality? Indeed. While creative genius—whether in science (Albert Einstein), art (Pablo Picasso), or business (Steve Jobs)—is scarce, most people have some of the characteristics shared by exceptionally creative people. The more of these characteristics we have, the higher our creative potential.

idea generation   *The process of creative behavior that involves developing possible solutions to a problem from relevant information and knowledge.*

idea evaluation   *The process of creative behavior involving the evaluation of potential solutions to problems to identify the best one.*

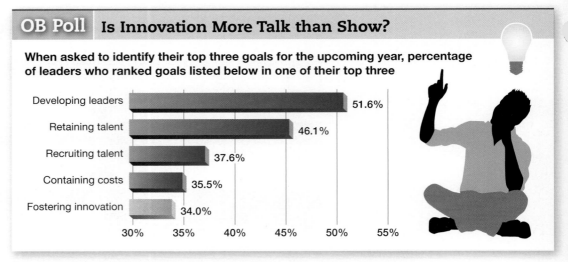

OB Poll | **Is Innovation More Talk than Show?**

When asked to identify their top three goals for the upcoming year, percentage of leaders who ranked goals listed below in one of their top three

Developing leaders — 51.6%
Retaining talent — 46.1%
Recruiting talent — 37.6%
Containing costs — 35.5%
Fostering innovation — 34.0%

Source: Based on T. Henneman, "Bright Ideas," *Workforce Management* (January 2013), pp. 18–25.

Intelligence is related to creativity. Smart people are more creative because they are better at solving complex problems. However, intelligent individuals may also be more creative because they have greater "working memory", that is, they can recall more information that is related to the task at hand.[80]

The Big Five personality trait of openness to experience (see Chapter 5) correlates with creativity, probably because open individuals are less conformist in action and more divergent in thinking.[81] Other traits of creative people include proactive personality, self-confidence, risk taking, tolerance for ambiguity, and perseverance.[82]

Expertise is the foundation for all creative work and thus is the single most important predictor of creative potential. Film writer, producer, and director Quentin Tarantino spent his youth working in a video rental store, where he built up an encyclopedic knowledge of movies. The potential for creativity is enhanced when individuals have abilities, knowledge, proficiencies, and similar expertise to their field of endeavor. You wouldn't expect someone with minimal knowledge of programming to be very creative as a software engineer.

Creative Environment   Most of us have creative potential we can learn to apply, but as important as creative potential is, by itself it is not enough. We need to be in an environment where creative potential can be realized. What environmental factors affect whether creative potential translates into creative behaviors?

First and perhaps most important is *motivation*. If you aren't motivated to be creative, it is unlikely you will be. A review of 26 studies revealed that intrinsic motivation, or the desire to work on something because it's interesting, exciting, satisfying, and challenging (discussed in more detail in the next chapter), correlates fairly strongly with creative outcomes. This link is true regardless of whether we are talking about student creativity or employee creativity.[83]

It is also valuable to work in an environment that rewards and recognizes creative work. The organization should foster the free flow of ideas, including providing fair and constructive judgment. Freedom from excessive rules encourages creativity; employees should have the freedom to decide what work is to be done and how to do it. One study of 385 employees working for several drug companies in China revealed that both structural empowerment (in which the structure of the work unit allows sufficient employee freedom) and psychological empowerment (which lets the individual feel personally empowered) were related to employee creativity.[84]

What is the role of culture? A recent nation-level study suggests that countries scoring high on Hofstede's culture dimension of individuality (discussed in Chapter 5) are more creative.[85] Western countries like the United States, Italy, and Belgium score high on individuality, and South American and Eastern countries like China, Colombia, and Pakistan score low; does this mean Western cultures are more creative? Some evidence suggests this is true. One study compared the creative projects of German and Chinese college students, some of whom were studying in their homeland, and some of whom were studying abroad. An independent panel of Chinese and German judges determined that the German students were most creative and that Asian German students were more creative than domestic Chinese students. This suggested that the German culture was more creative.[86] However, even if some cultures are more creative on average, there is always strong variation within cultures. Put another way, there are millions of Chinese more creative than their U.S. counterparts.

Good leadership matters to creativity too. A recent study of more than 100 teams working in a large bank revealed that when the leader behaved in a punitive, unsupportive manner, the teams were less creative.[87] On the other hand, when leaders are encouraging in tone, run their units in a transparent fashion, and encourage the development of their employees, the individuals they supervise are more creative.[88]

As we will learn in Chapter 10, more work today is being done in teams, and many people believe diversity will increase team creativity. Past research, unfortunately, has suggested that diverse teams are not more creative. More recently, however, one study of Dutch teams revealed that when team members were explicitly asked to understand and consider the point of view of the other team members (an exercise called perspective-taking), diverse teams *were* more creative than those with less diversity.[89] A study of 68 Chinese teams reported that diversity was positively related to team creativity only when the team's leader was inspirational and instilled members with confidence.[90] Another study in a multinational drug company found that teams from diverse business functions were more creative when they shared knowledge of each other's areas of expertise.[91] Collectively, these studies show that diverse teams *can* be more creative, but only under certain conditions.

Creative Outcomes (Innovation)

The final stage in our model of creativity is the outcome. Creative behavior does not always produce a creative or innovative outcome. An employee might generate a creative idea and never share it. Management might reject a creative solution. Teams might squelch creative behaviors by isolating those who propose different ideas. One study showed that most people have a bias against accepting creative ideas because ideas create uncertainty. When people feel uncertain, their ability to see any idea as creative is blocked.[92]

We can define *creative outcomes* as ideas or solutions judged to be novel and useful by relevant stakeholders. Novelty itself does not generate a creative outcome if it isn't useful. Thus, "off-the-wall" solutions are creative only if they help solve the problem. The usefulness of the solution might be self-evident (the iPad), or it might be considered successful by stakeholders before the actual success can be known.[93]

An organization may harvest many creative ideas from its employees and call itself innovative. However, as one expert recently stated, "Ideas are useless unless used." Soft skills help translate ideas into results. One researcher found that among employees of a large agribusiness company, creative ideas were most likely to be implemented when the individual was motivated to translate the idea into practice—and when he or she had strong networking ability.[94] Another important factor is organizational climate; a study of health care teams found that team creativity translated into innovation only when the climate actively supported innovation.[95] These studies highlight an important fact: Creative ideas do not implement themselves; translating them into creative outcomes is a social process that requires utilizing other concepts addressed in this book, including power and politics, leadership, and motivation.

SELF-ASSESSMENT LIBRARY

How Creative Am I?

In the Self-Assessment Library (available in MyManagementLab), take assessment I.A.5 (How Creative Am I?).

Summary

Individuals base their behavior not on the way their external environment actually is, but rather on the way they see it or believe it to be. An understanding of the way people make decisions can help us explain and predict behavior, but few important decisions are simple or unambiguous enough for the rational model's assumptions to apply. We find individuals looking for solutions that satisfice rather than optimize, injecting biases and prejudices into the decision process, and relying on intuition. Managers should encourage creativity in employees and teams to create a route to innovative decision-making.

Implications for Managers

- To influence productivity, assess how your employees perceive their jobs. Clue into employee absenteeism, turnover, and job satisfaction levels for indicators of their perception. Discuss their perceptions about fairness, compensation, and other abstract measures with them to clear up any perceptual distortions.
- Adjust your decision-making approach to the national culture you're operating in and to the criteria your organization values. If you're in a country that doesn't value rationality, don't feel compelled to follow the decision-making model or to try to make your decisions appear rational. Adjust your decision approach to ensure compatibility with the organizational culture.
- Be aware of biases. Then try to minimize their impact. Exhibit 6-4 offers some suggestions.
- Combine rational analysis with intuition. These are not conflicting approaches to decision making. By using both, you can actually improve your decision making effectiveness.
- Try to enhance your creativity. Actively look for novel solutions to problems, attempt to see problems in new ways, use analogies, and hire creative talent. Try to remove work and organizational barriers that might impede your creativity.

Stereotypes Are Dying

POINT

In the *Myth or Science?* feature in this chapter, we discussed the harmful effects of stereotypes, even positive ones. Fortunately, stereotypes are dying a slow but inexorable death. Whether they are about women, racial or ethnic minorities, or gays, each passing year brings evidence that stereotypes are losing their hold—thanks to the progress of society, but also thanks to younger individuals replacing older ones in the workforce. Younger people are less likely to endorse stereotypes across the board.

In the 1930s, when asked whether African Americans were "superstitious," 84 percent agreed; 75 percent endorsed a stereotype that African Americans were "lazy." Thankfully, those stereotypes are nearly gone. Results vary by study, but today between 0 and 10 percent of individuals agree with those stereotypes. These results show that racism still exists, but they also show it is waning.

Even when people endorse stereotypes, their consensus has weakened dramatically over time. For example, if forced to choose ten adjectives to describe a group of people, at one time people converged on a few (often incorrect) traits. Today, their lists will vary dramatically by person.

There is another factor at play here: the media. Media reports are not a good source of scientific information, yet to listen to them, you'd think stereotypes were as alive as ever. Fortunately, that's not the case, but when stereotypes fade, it's not newsworthy. Someday soon, stereotypic thinking will be as retrograde as outright acts of racism or sexism. We should count ourselves lucky to live in societies and work in organizations where such thinking and behavior are viewed quite negatively.

COUNTERPOINT

Unfortunately, stereotypes are alive and well. It is our ability to easily see them that causes us to believe they are disappearing.

Research shows that when individuals hold both positive and negative stereotypes, they bury the negative stereotypes when communicating with others. Why? Because they intuitively know that expressing these stereotypes may make them look bad to others, and research shows this is the case—when someone communicates a negative stereotype, listeners think less of the communicator, *even when they agree*. This doesn't mean negative stereotypes reverse themselves over time.

So, we cannot take expressed stereotypes, or the lack thereof, at face value. A prejudice unexpressed is no less a prejudice. Moreover, we know that over time, people conceal negative stereotypes in favor of emphasizing the positive ones. This tendency to "accentuate the positive, hide the negative" has been found to increase when individuals were communicating publicly (to a casual acquaintance) rather than privately (to a close friend).

If stereotypes really are waning, why would only negative stereotypes have declined over time? Because people in 2014 are better than those in 1964 or 1984? No, if people have positive stereotypes, they also have negative ones. Nowadays, it's just the positive ones they're willing to admit.

For example, nearly half (48.9 percent) of individuals describe Italians as "passionate"—and that has remained stable over time—whereas only 1.5 percent now describe them as "cowardly"—and that has declined greatly over time. We think this is progress, but it's less than it seems. All stereotypes are undesirable, positive stereotypes beget negative ones, and the negative ones haven't gone away; they've just been driven underground. We know from research that when such prejudices are concealed, they are harder to change. If a view is never addressed openly, it can never be argued against.

Time and the entrance of younger individuals into society and organizations have not eliminated or necessarily even reduced stereotypes. Ironically, even the assertion that younger workers are less likely to hold stereotypes than older ones relies on a stereotype (that older people are more likely to be prejudiced)! We need look no further for proof of their existence.

Sources: J. L. Skorinko and S. A. Sinclair, "Perspective Taking Can Increase Stereotyping: The Role of Apparent Stereotype Confirmation," *Journal of Experimental Social Psychology* 49 (2013), pp. 10–18; and H. B. Bergsieker, L. M. Leslie, V. S. Constantine, and S. T. Fiske, "Stereotyping by Omission: Eliminate the Negative, Accentuate the Positive," *Journal of Personality and Social Psychology* 102 (2012), pp. 1214–1238.

END-OF-CHAPTER REVIEW

MyManagementLab

Go to **mymanagementlab.com** to complete the problems marked with this icon. ⭐

QUESTIONS FOR REVIEW

6-1 What is perception, and what factors influence our perception?

6-2 What is attribution theory? What are the three determinants of attribution? What are the implications of attribution theory for explaining organizational behavior?

6-3 What shortcuts do people frequently use in making judgments about others?

6-4 What is the link between perception and decision making? How does one affect the other?

6-5 What is the rational model of decision making? How is it different from bounded rationality and intuition?

6-6 What are some common decision biases or errors people make?

6-7 How do individual differences and organizational constraints influence decision making?

⭐ 6-8 What are the three ethical decision criteria, and how do they differ?

6-9 What is creativity, and what is the three-stage model of creativity?

EXPERIENTIAL EXERCISE Biases in Decision Making

Step 1
Answer each of the following problems.

6-10. *Fortune* magazine ranked the following 10 corporations among the 500 largest U.S.–based firms according to revenue for 2013:
Group A: McDonald's, Visa, Amazon, Target, Coca-Cola
Group B: Berkshire Hathaway, General Electric, Valero, McKesson, Hewlett-Packard
Which group would you say had the larger revenue—A or B? By what percentage—10 percent, 50 percent, 100 percent?

6-11. The best student in your introductory MBA class this past semester writes poetry and is rather shy and small in stature. What was the student's undergraduate major—Chinese studies or psychology?

6-12. Which of the following causes more deaths in the United States each year?
a. Stomach cancer
b. Motor vehicle accidents

6-13. Which would you choose?
a. A sure gain of $240
b. A 25 percent chance of winning $1,000 and a 75 percent chance of winning nothing

6-14. Which would you choose?
a. A sure loss of $750
b. A 75 percent chance of losing $1,000 and a 25 percent chance of losing nothing

6-15. Which would you choose?
a. A sure loss of $3,000
b. An 80 percent chance of losing $4,000 and a 20 percent chance of losing nothing

Step 2
Break into groups of three to five students. Compare your answers. Explain why you chose the answers you did.

Step 3
Your instructor will give you the correct answers to each question. Now discuss the accuracy of your decisions, the biases evident in them, and ways you might improve your decision making to make it more accurate.

Sources: These problems are based on examples provided in M. H. Bazerman, *Judgment in Managerial Decision Making*, 3rd ed. (New York: Wiley, 1994); *Fortune* 500 2013 list, http://money.cnn.com/magazines/fortune/fortune500/2013/full_list/index.html?iid=F500_sp_full, accessed May 28, 2013.

ETHICAL DILEMMA Deciding to Cheat

We all have cheated at something. We could assume that deciding to cheat is a product of cold hard calculus: Is the benefit of cheating worth the cost? We're actually learning, however, that like many decisions, cheating is less rational than expected. Insight from research suggests ways in which organizations can stem cheating and other unethical behavior.

1. **Cheating happens away from the cash.** Duke Professor Dan Ariely finds that people steal more when they are a couple of steps removed from the cash. For example, the John F. Kenney Center for the Performing Arts' gift shop was hemorrhaging money, but the reason was that volunteers were helping themselves to merchandise, not the cash drawer. Similarly, when researchers put six packs of Coke and six $1 bills in dorm fridges, every Coke was gone within 72 hours, but none of the cash.

2. **Cheating is contagious.** When we see others cheat, we are more likely to do it ourselves. A study of high school students in upper middle class communities revealed that among the 93 percent who admitted to cheating, the top reason was the pervasiveness of cheating by others. A recent study of accounting undergraduates revealed that cheating was most likely among students who reported having recently seen cheating and having friends who cheated.

3. **Moods affect cheating.** Research shows that people cheat more when they are angry or tired. This insight reveals another positive dividend of trying to reduce negative moods at work, as we discussed in Chapter 4.

4. **Incentives matter.** Studies suggest that high-stakes outcomes create cheating as an inevitable consequence. Coaches, CEOs, and political leaders should still be held accountable, but it is helpful to understand circumstances in which expectations may seem attainable only by cheating.

Questions

6-16. Do you know classmates who have cheated in school? Have you ever cheated?

6-17. The authors of one study noted that people feel they don't need to be objective in evaluating potential cheaters when there are disclosures of unethical behavior. Do you agree? Why or why not?

6-18. Do you think that if we admitted it to ourselves when we cheated, we would be less likely to cheat in the future? Why or why not?

Sources: R. A. Bernardi, C. A. Banzhoff, A. M. Martino, and K. J. Savasta, "Challenges to Academic Integrity: Identifying the Factors Associated with the Cheating Chain," *Accounting Education* 21 (2012), pp. 247–263; M. K. Galloway, "Cheating in Advantaged High Schools: Prevalence, Justifications, and Possibilities for Change," *Ethics & Behavior* 22 (2012), pp. 378–399; and M. H. Bazerman and A. E. Tenbrunsel, *Blind Spots: Why We Fail to Do What's Right and What to Do about It* (Princeton, NJ: Princeton University Press, 2012).

CASE INCIDENT 1 Computerized Decision Making

Computerized decision making has taken off in recent years. Some have blamed the worldwide financial crisis on excessive reliance on these computerized decision-making models. Lending officers who previously made individualized decisions about creditworthiness through personal judgment were replaced by computerized statistical models, resulting in mechanistic decision making. Large numbers of decisions were tied to a common set of assumptions, and when those assumptions proved to be wrong, the entire credit system fell apart and the economy faltered.

Use of computerized systems like Twitter and apps for information sharing may be leading to information overload. Eric Kessler from Pace University's Lubin School of Business notes, "What starts driving decisions is the urgent rather than the important." Researchers are finding that people who use too much information actually make worse decisions than people with less information, or they get so swamped in information that they are unable to reach a decision at all.

Computer decision models present certain advantages. Computers can amass and compile enormous amounts of data to spot patterns a human observer would never see. Computers are not prone to emotional decision making or the heuristics and biases we discussed in this chapter. Finally, computerized decision-making systems are generally faster than human beings.

Computer decision-making systems have certain faults that might severely constrain their usefulness, however: They are not capable of intuition or creative thought. As scholar Amar Bhidé notes, "An innovator cannot simply rely on historical patterns in placing bets on future opportunities." People are much more likely to spot opportunities that lie just beyond what the data can tell us directly. Also, groups of people working in collaboration can discuss and question assumptions and conclusions.

Computers cannot consider whether their programming makes sense or adapt automatically when values change. There are computerized aids for almost any decision to be made; each of the tools from simple lists to complex statistical models needs to be considered in light of the application. Managers who use computerized decision making need to take great care in determining exactly what type of output will truly meet their informational needs so they—not their machines—can make the best organizational decisions.

Questions

6-19. What are specific advantages of using computerized decision making? How can computers be better decision makers than humans?

6-20. What are weaknesses of using computers as decision tools? Are computers likely to have specific problems in making decisions that people wouldn't have?

6-21. Are there advantages to completely disconnecting from the wired world when possible? What can you do to retain your ability to focus and process information deeply?

Sources: Based on S. Begley, "I Can't Think!" *Newsweek* (March 7, 2011), www.newsweek.com; A. Bhidé, "The Judgment Deficit" *Harvard Business Review* (September 2010), pp. 44–53; T. H. Davenport and J. H. Snabe, "How Fast and Flexible Do You Want Your Information, Really?" *Sloan Management Review* 52 (Spring 2011), pp. 57–62; and S. M. Sarif and S. B. Zaibon, "Decisional Guidance for Computerised Personal Decision Aid (ComPDA)," *Proceedings of Knowledge Management International Conference* (July 2012), pp. 532–537.

CASE INCIDENT 2 The Youngest Billionaire

Picture this. The billionaire owner and founder stands in the conference room trying on bras while the CEO stands behind her, adjusting the straps. The floor is littered with underwear. The owner takes off one bra and puts on another. Five executives in the conference room barely blink.

Welcome to Sara Blakely's company, Spanx. In just a few years, Spanx has become to slimming underwear what Jello is to gelatin and Kleenex is to facial tissue: So dominant is the brand that its name is synonymous with the category.

At 42, Blakely is not the youngest billionaire in the world. However, she is the youngest female self-made billionaire. Like many stories of entrepreneurial success, hers is part gritty determination, part inspiration, and part circumstance. The grit was easy to see early on. As a child growing up in Clearwater Beach, Florida, she lured friends into doing her chores by setting up a competition. At 16, Blakely was so intent on success that she listened to self-help guru Wayne Dyer's recordings incessantly. Friends refused to ride in her car. "No! She's going to make us listen to that motivational crap!" Blakely recalls they said.

After twice failing to get into law school, Blakely started her first business in 1990, running a kids' club at the Clearwater Beach Hilton. It worked until the Hilton's general manager found out. Later, while working full-time in sales, Blakely began learning how to start a business. Her inspiration for Spanx came while she was cold-calling customers as a sales manager for an office supply company. She hated pantyhose. "It's Florida, it's hot, I'm carrying copy machines," she noted.

At the Georgia Tech library, Blakely researched every pantyhose patent ever filed. She wrote her patent application by following a textbook she read in Barnes & Noble. Then she worked on marketing, manufacturing, and financing, treating each as its own project. After numerous rejections, she finally found mill owners in North Carolina willing to finance the manufacturing. "At the end of the day, the guy ended up just wanting to help me," Blakely said. "He didn't even believe in the idea."

For a time, Blakely relied on stores like Neiman Marcus to set up her table and on word-of-mouth to get the news out to the public. Her big break came when she sent samples to Oprah Winfrey's stylist. Harpo Productions called to say that Winfrey would name Spanx her favorite product of the year and warned Blakely to get her website ready. She didn't have a website.

Billions of dollars in sales later, Blakely has no plans to slow down. Spanx is sold in 54 countries, and Blakely wants to double international sales in 3 years. She says: "The biggest risk in life is not risking. Every risk you take in life is in direct proportion to the reward. If I'm afraid of something, it's the next thing I have to go do. That's just the way I've been."

Questions

6-22. How much of Blakely's success is due to her personality and effort and how much to serendipity (being in the right place at the right time)? Does attribution theory help you answer this question? Why or why not?

6-23. Does hindsight bias affect the factors to which you might attribute Blakely's success? Why or why not?

✪ **6-24.** Use the three-stage model of creativity to analyze Blakely's decision making. What can you learn from her story that might help you be more creative in the future?

Sources: Based on J. Mulkerrins, "All Spanx to Sara," *Daily Mail* (April 6, 2013), downloaded May 7, 2013, from www.dailymail.co.uk/home/; C. O'Connor, "American Booty," *Forbes* (March 26, 2012), pp. 172–178; and R. Tulshyan, "Spanx's Sara Blakely: Turning $5,000 into $1 Billion with Panties," *CNN.com* (December 5, 2012), downloaded on May 7, 2013, from http://edition.cnn.com/.

MyManagementLab

Go to **mymanagementlab.com** for Auto-graded writing questions as well as the following Assisted-graded writing questions:

6-25. In relation to Case Incident 1, do you think computer decision-making systems can effectively take ethical issues into account? What is the role of human decision makers in creating ethical choices?

6-26. Consider Case Incident 2, the chapter-opening story, and the chapter. Do you think creativity is "born" (inherent in the individual) or "made" (a product of opportunity and reinforcement)? Compare what we know of the lives of Nicholoas D'Aloisio and Sara Blakely with those of other creative individuals you know personally.

6-27. MyManagementLab Only—comprehensive writing assignment for this chapter.

Motivation Concepts

AN ENGAGING PROPOSITION

lthough the economy continues to show signs of improvement and hiring is picking up, many challenges lie ahead for organizations to keep their employees interested and engaged. While more than four of five U.S. employees say they're satisfied with their jobs, when it comes to motivation and engagement, the picture is not so rosy. Fatigued and frustrated as a result of a "work more but reward less" economy, 63 percent of U.S. workers say they're not fully engaged in their work. It's not just a problem for the United States: A Gallup poll found that only 15 percent of German workers reported being engaged with their jobs.

Their reasons? A global study revealed that 43 percent of employees believe their supervisors don't remove obstacles that get in the way of performing well. And only 26 percent of those workers say their managers include them in decisions that directly affect them. Another factor, according to Jason Corsello, vice president of corporate strategy and marketing at Cornerstone OnDemand Inc., a human resources software vendor, is lack of opportunities for career growth. "If individuals don't get what they need, eventually they could wind up leaving," says Corsello.

Faced with budget restrictions, some organizations are finding creative ways to engage their employees. At Minnesota Bank and Trust, CEO Kate Kelly, second from left in the photo, formed an "employee event committee" that ultimately led to lawn bowling, miniature golf outings, and a surprise shopping trip to buy Secret Santa gifts for co-workers. Says Kelly, "There is a noticeable difference in the mood here after an event. You don't have to spend a lot of money." Beyond boosting morale and mood, Kelly notes that while her bank grew from 20 to 33 employees in four years, only three workers have left since 2008.

Sources: D. Depass, "Employers Focus on Engaging Workers," *South Bend Tribune* (May 6, 2012), p. E1; R. R. Hastings, "Employees 'Moderately' Engaged in Work" *HR Magazine* (March 2012), p. 107; G. Kranz, "As Career Development Lags, Employees Are Going Places" *Workforce Management* (February 2013), p. 10; and G. Kranz, "A Broken Engagement?" *Workforce Management* (September 2012), p. 10.

LEARNING OBJECTIVES

After studying this chapter, you should be able to:

1 Describe the three key elements of motivation.

2 Evaluate the applicability of early theories of motivation.

3 Apply the predictions of self-determination theory to intrinsic and extrinsic rewards.

4 Identify the implications of employee job engagement for management.

5 Describe goal-setting theory, self-efficacy theory, and reinforcement theory.

6 Demonstrate how organizational justice is a refinement of equity theory.

7 Apply the key tenets of expectancy theory to motivating employees.

8 Compare contemporary theories of motivation.

otivating employees is one of the most important, and one of the most challenging, aspects of management. As we will see, there is no shortage of advice about how to do it.

Motivation is not simply about working hard—it also reflects your view of your own abilities. Try a self-assessment of your confidence in your ability to succeed.

Motivation is one of the most frequently researched topics in OB.[1] A Gallup poll revealed one reason—added to the majority of U.S. employees who are not actively engaged in their work, another portion (17 percent) are actively disengaged.[2] In another survey, 69 percent of workers reported wasting time at work every day, and nearly a quarter said they waste between 30 and 60 minutes each day. How? Usually by surfing the Internet (checking the news and visiting social network sites was cited) and chatting with coworkers.[3]

In this chapter, we'll review the basics of motivation, assess motivation theories, and provide an integrative model that fits theories together.

How Confident Am I in My Abilities to Succeed?

In the Self-Assessment Library (available in MyManagementLab), take assessment IV.A.3 (How Confident Am I in My Abilities to Succeed?) and answer the following questions.

1. How did you score relative to other class members? Does that surprise you?
2. Do you think self-confidence is critical to success? Can a person be too confident?

Defining Motivation

1 Describe the three key elements of motivation.

motivation *The processes that account for an individual's intensity, direction, and persistence of effort toward attaining a goal.*

Some individuals seem driven to succeed. The same student who struggles to read a textbook for more than 20 minutes may devour a *Harry Potter* book in a day. The difference is the situation. As we analyze the concept of motivation, keep in mind that the level of motivation varies both between individuals and within individuals at different times.

We define **motivation** as the processes that account for an individual's *intensity*, *direction*, and *persistence* of effort toward attaining a goal.[4] While general motivation is concerned with effort toward *any* goal, we'll narrow the focus to *organizational* goals toward work-related behavior.

Intensity describes how hard a person tries. This is the element most of us focus on when we talk about motivation. However, high intensity is unlikely to lead to favorable job-performance outcomes unless the effort is channeled in a *direction* that benefits the organization. Therefore, we consider the quality of effort as well as its intensity. Effort directed toward, and consistent with, the organization's goals is the kind of effort we should be seeking. Finally, motivation has a *persistence* dimension. This measures how long a person can maintain effort. Motivated individuals stay with a task long enough to achieve their goals.

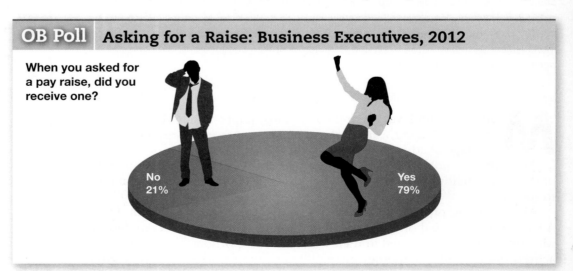

OB Poll | **Asking for a Raise: Business Executives, 2012**

When you asked for a pay raise, did you receive one?

No 21%

Yes 79%

Note: Survey of 3,900 executives from 31 countries.

Source: Based on Accenture, "The Path Forward" (2012), http://www.accenture.com/SiteCollectionDocuments/PDF/Accenture-IWD-Research-Deck-2012-FINAL.pdf#zoom=50, p. 36.

Early Theories of Motivation

2 Evaluate the applicability of early theories of motivation.

Four theories of employee motivation formulated during the 1950s, although now of questionable validity, are probably the best known. We discuss more valid explanations later, but these four represent a foundation, and practicing managers still use their terminology.

Hierarchy of Needs Theory

hierarchy of needs *Abraham Maslow's hierarchy of five needs—physiological, safety, social, esteem, and self-actualization—in which, as each need is substantially satisfied, the next need becomes dominant.*

The best-known theory of motivation is Abraham Maslow's **hierarchy of needs**.[5] Maslow hypothesized that within every human being, there exists a hierarchy of five needs:

1. **Physiological.**   Includes hunger, thirst, shelter, sex, and other bodily needs.
2. **Safety.**   Security and protection from physical and emotional harm.
3. **Social.**   Affection, belongingness, acceptance, and friendship.
4. **Esteem.**   Internal factors such as self-respect, autonomy, and achievement, and external factors such as status, recognition, and attention.
5. **Self-actualization.**   Drive to become what we are capable of becoming; includes growth, achieving our potential, and self-fulfillment.

Although no need is ever fully gratified, a substantially satisfied need no longer motivates. Thus, as each need becomes substantially satisfied, the next one becomes dominant. So if you want to motivate someone, according to Maslow, you need to understand what level of the hierarchy that person is currently on and focus on satisfying needs at or above that level, moving up the steps in Exhibit 7-1.

lower-order needs *Needs that are satisfied externally, such as physiological and safety needs.*

self-actualization *The drive to become what a person is capable of becoming.*

higher-order needs *Needs that are satisfied internally, such as social, esteem, and self-actualization needs.*

Maslow separated the five needs into higher and lower orders. Physiological and safety needs, where people start, are **lower-order needs**, and social, esteem, and **self-actualization** are **higher-order needs**. Higher-order needs are satisfied internally (within the person), whereas lower-order needs are predominantly satisfied externally (by rewards such as pay, union contracts, and tenure).

The hierarchy, if it applies at all, aligns with U.S. culture. In Japan, Greece, and Mexico, where uncertainty-avoidance characteristics are strong, security needs would be on top of the hierarchy. Countries that score high on nurturing characteristics—Denmark, Sweden, Norway, the Netherlands, and Finland—would have social needs and self-actualization on top.[6] Group work will motivate employees more when the country's culture scores high on the nurturing criterion.

Exhibit **7-1**	Maslow's Hierarchy of Needs

Self-actualization
Esteem
Social
Safety
Physiological

Source: A. H. Maslow, *Motivation and Personality,* 3rd ed., R. D. Frager and J. Fadiman (eds.). © 1997. Adapted by permission of Pearson Education, Inc., Upper Saddle River, New Jersey.

Maslow's theory has received wide recognition, particularly among practicing managers. It is intuitively logical and easy to understand. Unfortunately, however, research does not validate it. Maslow provided no empirical substantiation, and several studies that sought to validate it found no support for it.[7] But old theories, especially intuitively logical ones, die hard.

Some researchers have attempted to revive components of the need hierarchy concept, using principles from evolutionary psychology.[8] They propose that lower-level needs are the chief concern of immature animals or those with primitive nervous systems, whereas higher needs are more frequently observed in mature animals with more developed nervous systems. They also note distinct underlying biological systems for different types of needs. Time will tell whether these revisions to Maslow's hierarchy will be useful to practicing managers.

Theory X and Theory Y

Douglas McGregor proposed two distinct views of human beings: one basically negative, labeled Theory X, and the other basically positive, labeled Theory Y.[9] After studying managers' dealings with employees, McGregor concluded that the managers' views of the nature of human beings are based on certain assumptions that mold the managers' behavior toward the employees.

Theory X   *The assumption that employees dislike work, are lazy, dislike responsibility, and must be coerced to perform.*

Under **Theory X**, managers believe employees inherently dislike work and must therefore be directed or even coerced into performing it. Under **Theory Y**, in contrast, managers assume employees can view work as being as natural as rest or play, and therefore the average person can learn to accept, and even seek, responsibility.

Theory Y   *The assumption that employees like work, are creative, seek responsibility, and can exercise self-direction.*

To understand more fully, think in terms of Maslow's hierarchy. Theory Y assumes higher-order needs dominate individuals. McGregor himself believed Theory Y assumptions were more valid than Theory X. Therefore, he proposed such ideas as participative decision making, responsible and challenging jobs, and good group relations to maximize an employee's job motivation.

Unfortunately, no evidence confirms that *either* set of assumptions is valid or that acting on Theory Y assumptions will lead to more motivated workers. OB theories need empirical support before we can accept them. Theory X and Theory Y lack such support as much as does the hierarchy of needs theory.

Two-Factor Theory

Believing an individual's relationship to work is basic, and that the attitude toward work can determine success or failure, psychologist Frederick Herzberg wondered, "What do people want from their jobs?" He asked people to describe, in detail, situations in which they felt exceptionally *good* or *bad* about their jobs. The responses differed significantly and led Hertzberg to his **two-factor theory**—also called *motivation-hygiene theory*.[10]

two-factor theory   *A theory that relates intrinsic factors to job satisfaction and associates extrinsic factors with dissatisfaction. Also called motivation-hygiene theory.*

As shown in Exhibit 7-2, intrinsic factors such as advancement, recognition, responsibility, and achievement seem related to job satisfaction. Respondents who felt good about their work tended to attribute these factors to themselves, while dissatisfied respondents tended to cite extrinsic factors, such as supervision, pay, company policies, and working conditions.

To Hertzberg, the data suggest that the opposite of satisfaction is not dissatisfaction, as was traditionally believed. Removing dissatisfying characteristics from a job does not necessarily make the job satisfying. As illustrated in Exhibit 7-3, Herzberg proposed a dual continuum: The opposite of "satisfaction" is "no satisfaction," and the opposite of "dissatisfaction" is "no dissatisfaction."

According to Herzberg, the factors that lead to job satisfaction are separate and distinct from those that lead to job dissatisfaction. Therefore, managers who seek to eliminate factors that can create job dissatisfaction may bring about

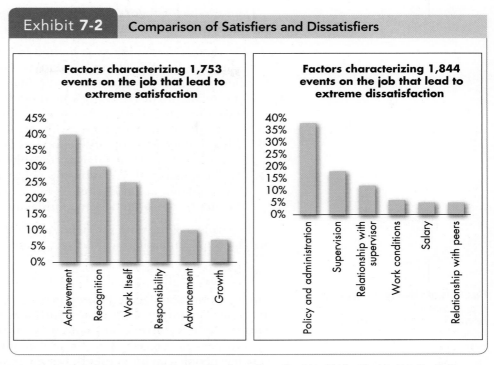

Source: Based on Harvard Business Review. "Comparison of Satisfiers and Dissatisfiers." An exhibit from One More Time: How Do You Motivate Employees? by Frederick Herzberg, January 2003. Copyright © 2003 by the Harvard Business School Publishing Corporation. All rights reserved.

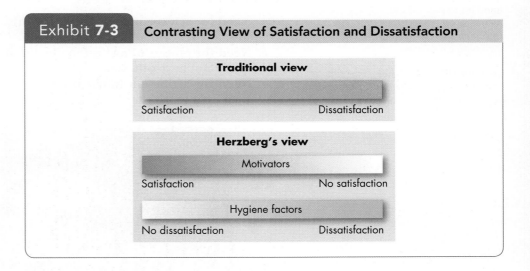

peace, but not necessarily motivation. They will be placating rather than motivating their workers. As a result, Herzberg characterized conditions such as quality of supervision, pay, company policies, physical working conditions, relationships with others, and job security as **hygiene factors**. When they're adequate, people will not be dissatisfied; neither will they be satisfied. If we want to *motivate* people on their jobs, Herzberg suggested emphasizing factors associated with the work itself or with outcomes directly derived from it, such as promotional opportunities, personal growth opportunities, recognition, responsibility, and achievement. These are the characteristics people find intrinsically rewarding.

hygiene factors *Factors—such as company policy and administration, supervision, and salary—that, when adequate in a job, placate workers. When these factors are adequate, people will not be dissatisfied.*

The two-factor theory has not been well supported in the literature, and it has many detractors.[11] Criticisms include the following:

1. Herzberg's methodology is limited because it relies on self-reports. When things are going well, people tend to take credit. If things do not go well, they blame failure on the extrinsic environment.
2. The reliability of Herzberg's methodology is questionable. Raters have to make interpretations, so they may contaminate the findings by interpreting one response in one manner while treating a similar response differently.
3. No overall measure of satisfaction was utilized. A person may dislike part of a job yet still think the job is acceptable overall.
4. Herzberg assumed a relationship between satisfaction and productivity, but he looked only at satisfaction. To make his research relevant, we must assume a strong relationship between satisfaction and productivity.

Regardless of the criticisms, Herzberg's theory has been widely read, and few managers are unfamiliar with its recommendations.

McClelland's Theory of Needs

You have one beanbag and five targets set up in front of you, each farther away than the last. Target A sits almost within arm's reach. If you hit it, you get $2. Target B is a bit farther out, but about 80 percent of the people who try can hit it. It pays $4. Target C pays $8, and about half the people who try can hit it. Very few people can hit Target D, but the payoff is $16 for those who do. Finally, Target E pays $32, but it's almost impossible to achieve. Which would you try for? If you selected C, you're likely to be a high achiever. Why? Read on.

McClelland's theory of needs was developed by David McClelland and his associates.[12] It looks at three needs:

- **Need for achievement (nAch)** is the drive to excel, to achieve in relationship to a set of standards.
- **Need for power (nPow)** is the need to make others behave in a way they would not have otherwise.
- **Need for affiliation (nAff)** is the desire for friendly and close interpersonal relationships.

McClelland's theory of needs *A theory that states achievement, power, and affiliation are three important needs that help explain motivation.*

need for achievement (nAch) *The drive to excel, to achieve in relationship to a set of standards, and to strive to succeed.*

need for power (nPow) *The need to make others behave in a way in which they would not have behaved otherwise.*

need for affiliation (nAff) *The desire for friendly and close interpersonal relationships.*

Photo 7-1 Entrepreneur Fred DeLuca is a high achiever motivated by work that demands a high degree of personal responsibility. He co-founded a subway restaurant in 1968 at the age of 17 to help finance his college education and built the company into the world's largest fast-food franchise with almost 40,000 shops in 102 countries.

Source: ERIC PIERMONT/AFP/Getty Images/Newscom.

McClelland and subsequent researchers focused most of their attention on nAch. High achievers perform best when they perceive their probability of success as 0.5—that is, a 50–50 chance. They dislike gambling with high odds because they get no achievement satisfaction from success that comes by pure chance. Similarly, they dislike low odds (high probability of success) because then there is no challenge to their skills. They like to set goals that require stretching themselves a little.

Relying on an extensive amount of research, we can predict some relationships between achievement need and job performance. First, when jobs have a high degree of personal responsibility and feedback and an intermediate degree of risk, high achievers are strongly motivated. They are successful in entrepreneurial activities such as running their own businesses, for example, and managing self-contained units within large organizations.[13] Second, a high need to achieve does not necessarily make someone a good manager, especially in large organizations. People with a high achievement need are interested in how well they do personally, and not in influencing others to do well. High-nAch salespeople do not necessarily make good sales managers, and the good general manager in a large organization does not typically have a high need to achieve.[14] Third, needs for affiliation and power tend to be closely related to managerial success. The best managers are high in their need for power and low in their need for affiliation.[15] In fact, a high power motive may be a requirement for managerial effectiveness.[16]

The view that a high achievement need acts as an internal motivator presupposes two cultural characteristics—willingness to accept a moderate degree of risk (which excludes countries with strong uncertainty-avoidance characteristics) and concern with performance (which applies to countries with strong achievement characteristics). This combination is found in Anglo-American countries such as the United States, Canada, and Great Britain[17] and much less in Chile and Portugal.

Among the early theories of motivation, McClelland's has had the best research support. Unfortunately, it has less practical effect than the others. Because McClelland argued that the three needs are subconscious—we may rank high on them but not know it—measuring them is not easy. In the most common approach, a trained expert presents pictures to individuals, asks them to tell a story about each, and then scores their responses in terms of the three needs. However, the process is time consuming and expensive, and few organizations have been willing to invest in measuring McClelland's concept.

Contemporary Theories of Motivation

Early theories of motivation either have not held up under close examination or have fallen out of favor. In contrast, contemporary theories have one thing in common: Each has a reasonable degree of valid supporting documentation. This doesn't mean they are unquestionably right. We call them "contemporary theories" because they represent the current state of thinking in explaining employee motivation.

Self-Determination Theory

3 Apply the predictions of self-determination theory to intrinsic and extrinsic rewards.

"It's strange," said Marcia. "I started work at the Humane Society as a volunteer. I put in 15 hours a week helping people adopt pets. And I loved coming to work. Then, 3 months ago, they hired me full-time at $11 an hour. I'm doing the same work I did before. But I'm not finding it nearly as much fun."

self-determination theory *A theory of motivation that is concerned with the beneficial effects of intrinsic motivation and the harmful effects of extrinsic motivation.*

cognitive evaluation theory *A version of self-determination theory which holds that allocating extrinsic rewards for behavior that had been previously intrinsically rewarding tends to decrease the overall level of motivation if the rewards are seen as controlling.*

Does Marcia's reaction seem counterintuitive? There's an explanation for it. It's called **self-determination theory**, which proposes that people prefer to feel they have control over their actions, so anything that makes a previously enjoyed task feel more like an obligation than a freely chosen activity will undermine motivation.[18] Much research on self-determination theory in OB has focused on **cognitive evaluation theory**, which hypothesizes that extrinsic rewards will reduce intrinsic interest in a task. When people are paid for work, it feels less like something they *want* to do and more like something they *have* to do. Self-determination theory also proposes that in addition to being driven by a need for autonomy, people seek ways to achieve competence and positive connections to others. A large number of studies support self-determination theory.[19] Its major implications relate to work rewards.

When organizations use extrinsic rewards as payoffs for superior performance, employees feel they are doing a good job less because of their own intrinsic desire to excel than because that's what the organization wants. Eliminating extrinsic rewards can also shift an individual's perception of why she works on a task from an external to an internal explanation. If you're reading a novel a week because your English literature instructor requires you to, you can attribute your reading behavior to an external source. However, if you find yourself continuing to read a novel a week after the course is over, your natural inclination is to say, "I must enjoy reading novels because I'm still reading one a week."

Studies examining how extrinsic rewards increase motivation for creative tasks suggest we might need to place cognitive evaluation theory's predictions into a broader context.[20] Goal-setting is more effective in improving motivation, for instance, when we provide rewards for achieving the goals. The original authors of self-determination theory acknowledge that extrinsic rewards such as verbal praise and feedback about competence can improve intrinsic motivation under specific circumstances. Deadlines and specific work standards do, too, if people believe they are in control of their behavior.[21] Making extrinsic rewards specifically contingent on creative performance, rather than more broadly on routine performance, can enhance rather than undermine creativity. Again, like deadlines and specific work standards, the benefits of extrinsic rewards for creativity seem to hold only if individuals have control over the task or the reward.[22] These findings are consistent with the central theme of self-determination theory: Rewards and deadlines diminish motivation if people see them as coercive or controlling.

What does self-determination theory suggest for providing rewards? If a senior sales representative really enjoys making the deal, a commission indicates she's been doing a good job and increases her sense of competence by providing feedback that could improve intrinsic motivation. On the other hand, if a computer programmer values writing code because she likes to solve problems, a reward for working to an externally imposed standard she does not accept, such as writing a certain number of lines of code every day, could feel coercive, and her intrinsic motivation would suffer. She would be less interested in the task and might reduce her effort.

self-concordance *The degree to which peoples' reasons for pursuing goals are consistent with their interests and core values.*

A recent outgrowth of self-determination theory is **self-concordance**, which considers how strongly peoples' reasons for pursuing goals are consistent with their interests and core values. If individuals pursue goals because of intrinsic interest, they are more likely to attain goals and are happy even if they do not. Why? Because the process of striving toward them is fun. In contrast, people who pursue goals for extrinsic reasons (money, status, or other benefits) are less likely to attain goals and less happy even when they do. Why? Because the goals are less meaningful to them.[23] OB research suggests that people who pursue work goals for intrinsic reasons are more satisfied with their jobs, feel they fit into their organizations better, and may perform better.[24] Research also suggests that in cases where people do *not* enjoy their work for intrinsic reasons, those who work because they feel obligated to do so can still perform well, though they experience higher levels of strain as a result.[25]

What does all this mean? For individuals, it means choose your job for reasons other than extrinsic rewards. For organizations, it means managers should provide intrinsic as well as extrinsic incentives. They need to make the work interesting, provide recognition, and support employee growth and development. Employees who feel what they do is within their control and a result of free choice are likely to be more motivated by their work and committed to their employers.[26]

Job Engagement

4 Identify the implications of employee job engagement for management.

When nurse Melissa Jones comes to work, it seems that everything else in her life goes away, and she becomes completely absorbed in what she is doing. Her emotions, her thoughts, and her behavior are all directed toward patient care. In fact, she can get so caught up in her work that she isn't even aware of how long she's been there. As a result of this total commitment, she is more effective in providing patient care and feels uplifted by her time at work.

job engagement *The investment of an employee's physical, cognitive, and emotional energies into job performance.*

Melissa has a high level of **job engagement**, the investment of an employee's physical, cognitive, and emotional energies into job performance.[27] Practicing managers and scholars have become interested in facilitating job engagement, believing something deeper than liking a job or finding it interesting drives performance. Studies attempt to measure this deeper level of commitment.

The Gallup organization has been using 12 questions to assess the extent to which employee engagement is linked to positive work outcomes for millions of employees over the past 30 years.[28] There are far more engaged employees in highly successful than in average organizations, and groups with more engaged employees have higher levels of productivity, fewer safety incidents, and lower turnover. Academic studies have also found positive outcomes.

glOBalization!

Autonomy Needs Around the Globe

Much of the research we have presented on self-determination needs, such as autonomy, competence, and relatedness, has been conducted in the United States and Canada, two countries that place a high value on personal independence and freedom of choice. But more recent research has moved beyond these countries to examine the importance of self-determination needs in other cultures.

Some research does suggest universal needs, while other studies find that different cultures see needs differently. In a survey of 40 nations, collectivistic countries valued social order, obedience, and respect for tradition more; within cultures, individuals who value autonomy tended to put less value on social connectedness.

Another study found that although Asians were lower than non-Asians in their levels of satisfaction for autonomy and competence needs, need satisfaction predicted overall feelings of well-being similarly across countries, including the United States, Australia, Mexico, Venezuela, the Philippines, Malaysia, China, and Japan. Although cultural differences arise, it appears that people across cultures are happier when they perceive that their self-determination needs are being fulfilled.

Sources: A. T. Church et al., "Need Satisfaction and Well-Being: Testing Self-Determination Theory in Eight Cultures," *Journal of Cross-Cultural Psychology* 8 (2013), pp. 507–534; and C. Vauclair, K. Hanke, R. Fischer, and J. Fontaine, "The Structure of Human Values at the Culture Level: A Meta-Analytical Replication of Schwartz's Value Orientations Using the Rokeach Value Survey," *Journal of Cross-Cultural Psychology* 42, no. 2 (2011), pp. 186–205.

One examined multiple business units for their level of engagement and found a positive relationship with a variety of practical outcomes.[29] Another reviewed 91 distinct investigations and found higher levels of engagement associated with task performance and citizenship behavior.[30]

What makes people more likely to be engaged in their jobs? One key is the degree to which an employee believes it is meaningful to engage in work. This is partially determined by job characteristics and access to sufficient resources to work effectively.[31] Another factor is a match between the individual's values and those of the organization.[32] Leadership behaviors that inspire workers to a greater sense of mission also increase employee engagement.[33]

One of the critiques of engagement is that the construct is partially redundant with job attitudes like satisfaction or stress.[34] However, engagement questionnaires usually assess motivation and absorption in a task, quite unlike job satisfaction questionnaires. Engagement may also predict important work outcomes better than traditional job attitudes.[35] Other critics note there may be a "dark side" to engagement, as evidenced by positive relationships between engagement and work–family conflict.[36] Individuals might grow so engaged in their work roles that family responsibilities become an unwelcome intrusion. Further research exploring how engagement relates to these negative outcomes may help clarify whether some highly engaged employees might be getting "too much of a good thing."

Myth or Science?

"Helping Others and Being a Good Citizen Is Good for Your Career"

We would be likely to think that we should encourage employee motivation toward organizational citizenship behavior (OCB), and that helping others would be a benefit to their careers. We would also likely believe that our own OCB would yield us career benefits. Surprisingly, there is some evidence that this statement is false, at least in certain organizations. Why?

In some organizations, employees are evaluated more on *how* their work gets done. If they possess the requisite knowledge and skills, or if they demonstrate the right behaviors on the job (for example, always greeting customers with a smile), they are determined by management to be motivated, "good" performers. In these organizations, actions targeted toward task performance goals and actions targeted toward "citizenship" goals (for example, helping a co-worker in need) are evaluated positively, which then motivates employees to continue their OCB. Employees' careers benefit as a result of their helpfulness toward co-workers.

However, in other organizations, employees are evaluated more on *what* gets done. Here, employees are determined to be "good" performers if they meet objective goals such as billing clients a certain number of hours or reaching a certain sales volume. When managers overlook employee OCB, frown on helpful behaviors, or create an overly competitive organizational culture, employees become unmotivated to continue their helpful actions. Employees who still engage in OCB can find their careers are hindered when they take time away from core tasks to be helpful.

The upshot? There may be a trade-off between being a good performer and being a good citizen. In organizations that focus more on behaviors, following your motivation to be a good citizen can help to accomplish your career goals. However, in organizations that focus more on objective outcomes, you may need to consider the cost.

Sources: D. M. Bergeron, "The Potential Paradox of Organizational Citizenship Behavior: Good Citizens at What Cost?" *Academy of Management Review* 32, no. 4 (2007); and D. M. Bergeron, A. J. Shipp, B. Rosen, and S. A. Furst, "Organizational Citizenship Behavior and Career Outcomes: The Cost of Being a Good Citizen," *Journal of Management* 39, no. 4 (2013), pp. 958–984.

Goal-Setting Theory

Gene Broadwater, coach of the Hamilton High School cross-country team, gave his squad these last words before they approached the starting line for the league championship race: "Each one of you is physically ready. Now, get out there and do your best. No one can ever ask more of you than that."

You've heard the sentiment a number of times yourself: "Just do your best. That's all anyone can ask." But what does "do your best" mean? Do we ever know whether we've achieved that vague goal? Would the cross-country runners have recorded faster times if Coach Broadwater had given each a specific goal? Research on **goal-setting theory** in fact reveals impressive effects of goal specificity, challenge, and feedback on performance.

goal-setting theory *A theory that says that specific and difficult goals, with feedback, lead to higher performance.*

In the late 1960s, Edwin Locke proposed that intentions to work toward a goal are a major source of work motivation.[37] That is, goals tell an employee what needs to be done and how much effort is needed.[38] Evidence strongly suggests that specific goals increase performance; that difficult goals, when accepted, result in higher performance than do easy goals; and that feedback leads to higher performance than does nonfeedback.[39]

Specific goals produce a higher level of output than the generalized goal "do your best." Why? Specificity itself seems to act as an internal stimulus. When a trucker commits to making 12 round-trip hauls between Toronto and Buffalo, New York, each week, this intention gives him a specific objective to attain. All things being equal, he will outperform a counterpart with no goals or the generalized goal "do your best."

If factors such as acceptance of goals are held constant, the more difficult the goal, the higher the level of performance. Of course, it's logical to assume easier goals are more likely to be accepted. But once a hard task is accepted, we can expect the employee to exert a high level of effort to try to achieve it.

Photo 7-2 Co-founders Anthony Thomson, left, and Vernon Hill, right, launched their first Metro Bank in London with a long-term goal of adding 200 new branches and capturing up to 10 percent of London's banking market. Metro challenges employees to reach these high goals by giving customers exceptionally friendly, convenient, and flexible service.

Source: REUTERS/Toby Melville.

Why are people motivated by difficult goals?[40] First, challenging goals get our attention and help us focus. Second, difficult goals energize us because we have to work harder to attain them. Do you study as hard for an easy exam as you do for a difficult one? Probably not. Third, when goals are difficult, people persist in trying to attain them. Finally, difficult goals lead us to discover strategies that help us perform the job or task more effectively. If we have to struggle to solve a difficult problem, we often think of a better way to go about it.

People do better when they get feedback on how well they are progressing toward their goals because it helps identify discrepancies between what they have done and what they want to do—that is, feedback guides behavior. But all feedback is not equally potent. Self-generated feedback—with which employees are able to monitor their own progress or receive feedback from the task process itself—is more powerful than externally generated feedback.[41] Recent research has also shown that people monitor their progress differently depending on how close they are to goal accomplishment. When they have just begun pursuing a goal, they derive motivation from believing that the goal is attainable, so they exaggerate their level of progress in order to stay motivated. However, when they are close to accomplishing their goal, they derive motivation from believing a discrepancy still exists between where they are currently and where they'd like to be, so they downplay their progress to date to signal a need for higher effort.[42]

If employees can participate in the setting of their own goals, will they try harder? The evidence is mixed. In some cases, participatively set goals yielded superior performance; in others, individuals performed best when assigned goals by their boss. But a major advantage of participation may be that it increases acceptance of the goal as a desirable one toward which to work.[43] Without participation, the individual pursuing the goal needs to clearly understand its purpose and importance.[44]

In addition to feedback, three other factors influence the goals–performance relationship: goal commitment, task characteristics, and national culture.

Goal-setting theory assumes an individual is committed to the goal and determined not to lower or abandon it. The individual (1) believes he or she can achieve the goal and (2) wants to achieve it.[45] Goal commitment is most likely to occur when goals are made public, when the individual has an internal locus of control, when the goals are self-set rather than assigned, and when goals are based at least partially on individual ability.[46] Goals themselves seem to affect performance more strongly when tasks are simple rather than complex, well learned rather than novel, independent rather than interdependent, and are on the high end of achievable goals.[47] On interdependent tasks, group goals are preferable. Paradoxically, goal abandonment following an initial failure is more likely for individuals who self-affirm their core values, possibly because they internalize the implications of failure.[48]

Finally, setting specific, difficult, individual goals may have different effects in different cultures. Most goal-setting research has been done in the United States and Canada, where individual achievement and performance are most highly valued. To date, research has not shown that group-based goals are more effective in collectivist than in individualist cultures. In collectivistic and high-power-distance cultures, achievable moderate goals can be more highly motivating than difficult ones.[49] Finally, assigned goals appear to generate greater goal commitment in high than in low power-distance cultures.[50] More research is needed to assess how goal constructs might differ across cultures.

Although goal-setting has positive outcomes, it's not unequivocally beneficial. For example, some goals may be *too* effective.[51] When learning something is important, goals related to performance undermine adaptation and creativity because people become too focused on outcomes and ignore changing conditions. In this case, a goal to learn and generate alternative solutions will be more effective than a goal to perform. In addition, some authors argue goals can lead employees to focus on a single standard and exclude all others. A goal to boost short-term stock prices may lead organizations to ignore long-term success and even to engage in unethical behavior such as "cooking the books" to meet those goals. Other studies show that employees low in conscientiousness and emotional stability experience greater emotional exhaustion when their leaders set goals.[52] Finally, individuals may fail to give up on an unattainable goal, even when it might be beneficial to do so. Despite differences of opinion, most researchers do agree that goals are powerful in shaping behavior. Managers should make sure goals are aligned with company objectives.

Research has found that people differ in the way they regulate their thoughts and behaviors during goal pursuit. Generally, people fall into one of two categories, though they could belong to both. Those with a **promotion focus** strive for advancement and accomplishment and approach conditions that move them closer toward desired goals. Those with a **prevention focus** strive to fulfill duties and obligations and avoid conditions that pull them away from desired goals. Although you would be right in noting that both strategies are in the service of goal accomplishment, the manner in which they get there is quite different. As an example, consider studying for an exam. You could engage in promotion-focused activities such as reading class materials and notes, or you could engage in prevention-focused activities such as refraining from things that would get in the way of studying, such as playing video games or going out with friends. Or, you could do both activities.

You may ask, "Which is the better strategy?" Well, the answer to that question depends on the outcome you are striving for. While a promotion (but not a prevention) focus is related to higher levels of task performance, citizenship behavior, and innovation, a prevention (but not a promotion) focus is related to safety performance. Ideally, it's probably best to be both promotion *and* prevention oriented.[53]

promotion focus   *A self-regulation strategy that involves striving for goals through advancement and accomplishment.*

prevention focus   *A self-regulation strategy that involves striving for goals by fulfilling duties and obligations.*

SELF-ASSESSMENT LIBRARY

What Are My Course Performance Goals?

In the Self-Assessment Library (available in MyManagementLab), take assessment I.C.5 (What Are My Course Performance Goals?).

Implementing Goal-Setting   How do managers make goal-setting theory operational? That's often left up to the individual. Some managers set aggressive performance targets—what General Electric called "stretch goals." Some CEOs, such as Procter & Gamble's Robert McDonald and Best Buy's Hubert Joly, are known for demanding performance goals. But many managers don't set goals. When asked whether their job had clearly defined goals, only a minority of employees in a survey said yes.[54]

A more systematic way to utilize goal-setting is with **management by objectives (MBO)**, which emphasizes participatively set goals that are tangible, verifiable, and measurable. As in Exhibit 7-4, the organization's overall objectives are translated into specific objectives for each level (divisional, departmental, individual). But because lower-unit managers jointly participate in setting their own goals, MBO works from the bottom up as well as from the top down. The result is a hierarchy that links objectives at one level to those at the next. And for the individual employee, MBO provides specific personal performance objectives.

Four ingredients are common to MBO programs: goal specificity, participation in decision making (including the setting of goals or objectives), an explicit time

management by objectives (MBO)   *A program that encompasses specific goals, participatively set, for an explicit time period, with feedback on goal progress.*

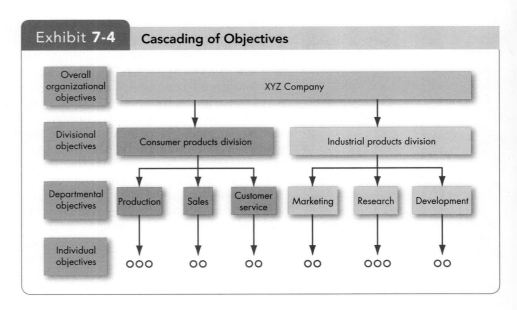

Exhibit 7-4 **Cascading of Objectives**

period, and performance feedback.[55] Many elements in MBO programs match propositions of goal-setting theory. For example, having an explicit time period to accomplish objectives matches goal-setting theory's emphasis on goal specificity. Similarly, we noted earlier that feedback about goal progress is a critical element of goal-setting theory. The only area of possible disagreement between MBO and goal-setting theory is participation: MBO strongly advocates it, whereas goal-setting theory demonstrates that managers' assigned goals are usually just as effective.

You'll find MBO programs in many business, health care, educational, government, and nonprofit organizations.[56] Their popularity does not mean they always work.[57] When MBO fails, the culprits tend to be unrealistic expectations, lack of commitment by top management, and inability or unwillingness to allocate rewards based on goal accomplishment.

Self-Efficacy Theory

self-efficacy theory *An individual's belief that he or she is capable of performing a task.*

Self-efficacy theory, also known as *social cognitive theory* or *social learning theory*, refers to an individual's belief that he or she is capable of performing a task.[58] The higher your self-efficacy, the more confidence you have in your ability to succeed. So, in difficult situations, people with low self-efficacy are more likely to lessen their effort or give up altogether, while those with high self-efficacy will try harder to master the challenge.[59] Self-efficacy can create a positive spiral in which those with high efficacy become more engaged in their tasks and then, in turn, increase performance, which increases efficacy further.[60] Changes in self-efficacy over time are related to changes in creative performance as well.[61] Individuals high in self-efficacy also seem to respond to negative feedback with increased effort and motivation, while those low in self-efficacy are likely to lessen their effort after negative feedback.[62] How can managers help their employees achieve high levels of self-efficacy? By bringing goal-setting theory and self-efficacy theory together.

Goal-setting theory and self-efficacy theory don't compete; they complement each other. As Exhibit 7-5 shows, employees whose managers set difficult goals for them will have a higher level of self-efficacy and set higher goals for their own performance. Why? Setting difficult goals for people communicates your confidence in them. Imagine you learn your boss sets a higher goal for you than for your coworkers. How would you interpret this? As long as you didn't feel you were being picked on, you would probably think, "Well, I guess my boss thinks I'm capable

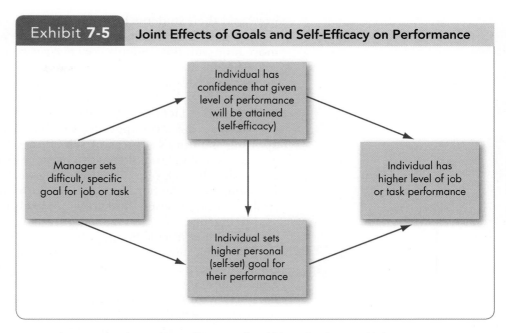

Exhibit 7-5   Joint Effects of Goals and Self-Efficacy on Performance

Individual has confidence that given level of performance will be attained (self-efficacy)

Manager sets difficult, specific goal for job or task

Individual has higher level of job or task performance

Individual sets higher personal (self-set) goal for their performance

Source: Based on E. A. Locke and G. P. Latham, "Building a Practically Useful Theory of Goal Setting and Task Motivation: A 35-Year Odyssey," *American Psychologist* (September 2002), pp. 705–717.

of performing better than others." This sets in motion a psychological process in which you're more confident in yourself (higher self-efficacy) and you set higher personal goals, performing better both inside and outside the workplace.

The researcher who developed self-efficacy theory, Albert Bandura, proposes four ways self-efficacy can be increased:[63]

1. Enactive mastery.
2. Vicarious modeling.
3. Verbal persuasion.
4. Arousal.

According to Bandura, the most important source of increasing self-efficacy is *enactive mastery*—that is, gaining relevant experience with the task or job. If you've been able to do the job successfully in the past, you're more confident you'll be able to do it in the future.

The second source is *vicarious modeling*—becoming more confident because you see someone else doing the task. If your friend slims down, it increases your confidence that you can lose weight, too. Vicarious modeling is most effective when you see yourself as similar to the person you are observing. Watching Tiger Woods play a difficult golf shot might not increase your confidence in being able to play the shot yourself, but if you watch a golfer with a handicap similar to yours, it's persuasive.

The third source is *verbal persuasion:* becoming more confident because someone convinces you that you have the skills necessary to be successful. Motivational speakers use this tactic.

Finally, Bandura argues that *arousal* increases self-efficacy. Arousal leads to an energized state, so the person gets "psyched up" and performs better. But if the task requires a steady, lower-key perspective (say, carefully editing a manuscript), arousal may in fact hurt performance.

The best way for a manager to use verbal persuasion is through the *Pygmalion effect* or the *Galatea effect.* The Pygmalion effect is a form of self-fulfilling prophecy in which believing something can make it true. In some studies, teachers were told their students had very high IQ scores when, in fact, they spanned a range from high to low. Consistent with the Pygmalion effect, the teachers spent more time with the students they *thought* were smart, gave them more challenging assignments, and expected more of them—all of which led to higher student self-efficacy and better grades.[64] This strategy also has been used in the workplace.[65] Also, sailors who were told convincingly that they would not get seasick were in fact much less likely to do so.[66]

What are the OB implications of self-efficacy theory? Well, it's a matter of applying Bandura's sources of self-efficacy to the work setting. Training programs often make use of enactive mastery by having people practice and build their skills. In fact, one reason training works is that it increases self-efficacy.[67] Individuals with higher levels of self-efficacy also appear to reap more benefits from training programs and are more likely to use their training on the job.[68]

Intelligence and personality are absent from Bandura's list, but they can increase self-efficacy.[69] People who are intelligent, conscientiousness, and emotionally stable are so much more likely to have high self-efficacy that some researchers argue self-efficacy is less important than prior research would suggest.[70] They believe it is partially a by-product in a smart person with a confident personality. Although Bandura strongly disagrees with this conclusion, more research is needed.

Reinforcement Theory

reinforcement theory   *A theory that says that behavior is a function of its consequences.*

Goal-setting is a cognitive approach, proposing that an individual's purposes direct his action. **Reinforcement theory**, in contrast, takes a behavioristic view, arguing that reinforcement conditions behavior. The two theories are clearly at odds philosophically. Reinforcement theorists see behavior as environmentally caused.

An Ethical Choice

Motivated by Big Brother

Technology is a great thing. The Internet provides us with instant access to an abundance of information, and smartphones allow us to stay easily connected with others through e-mail, texting, tweeting, and conversation. Yet that ease of connectivity has also left employees feeling like they can't leave work . . . which is becoming true.

Some companies are using technology to track their employees' activities, and some of this tracking is done in the name of science. Bank of America Corp. wanted to learn whether face-to-face interaction made a difference to the productivity of its call-center teams, so it asked around 100 workers to wear badges for a few weeks that tracked their whereabouts. Discovering that the most productive workers

interacted most frequently with others, the company scheduled work breaks in groups rather than individually.

Other companies track employees to ensure they are hard at work. Accurate Biometrics, for example, uses computer monitoring to oversee its telecommuters. Says Timothy Daniels, VP of operations, looking at websites his employees have visited "enables us to keep a watchful eye without being over-invasive." Gartner Inc., a technology-research company, predicts that by 2015, 60 percent of employers will use some form of computer security-monitoring to track their employees' work habits.

As a manager, if you have the ability to monitor your employees, how could you do so in an ethical way? First and foremost, employees should be

informed their activities will be tracked. Second, the purpose of tracking should be made clear to employees. Are they being monitored to learn something that might help them and the organization as a whole? Or are they being monitored to ensure they never slack off? Finally, it should be made clear which behaviors are inappropriate. Taking a legitimate work break is different from spending hours on a social networking site. These guidelines should increase the likelihood that monitoring programs are accepted and perceived to be fair.

Sources: S. Shellenbarger, "Working from Home Without Slacking Off," *The Wall Street Journal* (July 13–15, 2012), p. 29; and R. E. Silverman, "Tracking Sensors Invade the Workplace," *The Wall Street Journal* (March 7, 2003), www.wsj.com.

You need not be concerned, they would argue, with internal cognitive events; what controls behavior is reinforcers—any consequences that, when immediately following responses, increase the probability that the behavior will be repeated.

Reinforcement theory ignores the inner state of the individual and concentrates solely on what happens when he or she takes some action. Because it does not concern itself with what initiates behavior, it is not, strictly speaking, a theory of motivation. But it does provide a powerful means of analyzing what controls behavior, and this is why we typically consider it in discussions of motivation.[71]

Operant conditioning theory, probably the most relevant component of reinforcement theory for management, argues that people learn to behave to get something they want or to avoid something they don't want. Unlike reflexive or unlearned behavior, operant behavior is influenced by the reinforcement or lack of reinforcement brought about by its consequences. Therefore, reinforcement strengthens a behavior and increases the likelihood it will be repeated.[72]

B. F. Skinner, one of the most prominent advocates of operant conditioning, argued that creating pleasing consequences to follow specific forms of behavior would increase the frequency of that behavior. He demonstrated that people will most likely engage in desired behaviors if they are positively reinforced for doing so; that rewards are most effective if they immediately follow the desired response; and that behavior that is not rewarded, or is punished, is less likely to be repeated. We know a professor who places a mark by a student's name each time the student makes a contribution to class discussions. Operant conditioning would argue this practice is motivating because it conditions a student to expect a reward (earning class credit) each time she demonstrates a specific behavior (speaking up in class). The concept of operant conditioning was part of Skinner's broader concept of **behaviorism**, which argues that behavior follows stimuli in a relatively unthinking manner. Skinner's form of radical behaviorism rejects feelings, thoughts, and other states of mind as causes of behavior. In short, people learn to associate stimulus and response, but their conscious awareness of this association is irrelevant.[73]

behaviorism   *A theory that argues that behavior follows stimuli in a relatively unthinking manner.*

You can see illustrations of operant conditioning everywhere that reinforcements are contingent on some action on your part. Your instructor says if you want a high grade in the course, you must supply correct answers on the test. A commissioned salesperson wanting to earn a sizable income finds doing so is contingent on generating high sales in her territory. Of course, the linkage can also teach individuals to engage in behaviors that work against the best interests of the organization. Assume your boss says if you work overtime during the next 3-week busy season you'll be compensated for it at your next performance appraisal. However, when performance-appraisal time comes, you are given no positive reinforcement for your overtime work. The next time your boss asks you to work overtime, what will you do? You'll probably decline! Your behavior can be explained by operant conditioning: If a behavior fails to be positively reinforced, the probability it will be repeated declines.

Although reinforcers such as pay can motivate people, the process is much more complicated than stimulus–response. In its pure form, reinforcement theory ignores feelings, attitudes, expectations, and other cognitive variables known to affect behavior. In fact, some researchers look at the same experiments reinforcement theorists use to support their position and interpret the findings in a *cognitive* framework.[74]

Reinforcement is undoubtedly an important influence on behavior, but few scholars are prepared to argue it is the only one. The behaviors you engage in at work and the amount of effort you allocate to each task are affected by the consequences that follow. If you're consistently reprimanded for outproducing your colleagues, you'll likely reduce your productivity. But we might also explain your lower productivity in terms of goals, inequity, or expectancies.

Photo 7-3 Toyota Motor Corporation applies social learning theory in teaching employees skills they need to meet the company's high standards of quality and efficiency. At Toyota's global production centers, trainees learn manufacturing techniques under the tutelage of experienced production masters and then practice the skills.

Source: TORU YAMANAKA/AFP/GETTY IMAGES/Newscom.

Individuals can learn by being told or by observing what happens to other people, as well as through direct experiences. Much of what we have learned comes from watching models—parents, teachers, peers, film and television performers, bosses, and so forth. This view that we can learn through both observation and direct experience is called **social-learning theory**.[75]

Although social-learning theory is an extension of operant conditioning—that is, it assumes behavior is a function of consequences—it also acknowledges the effects of observational learning and perception. People respond to the way they perceive and define consequences, not to the objective consequences themselves.

Models are central to the social-learning viewpoint. Four processes determine their influence on an individual:

1. **Attentional processes.**   People learn from a model only when they recognize and pay attention to its critical features. We tend to be most influenced by models that are attractive, repeatedly available, important to us, or similar to us in our estimation.
2. **Retention processes.**   A model's influence depends on how well the individual remembers the model's action after the model is no longer readily available.
3. **Motor reproduction processes.**   After a person has seen a new behavior by observing the model, watching must be converted to doing. This process demonstrates that the individual can perform the modeled activities.
4. **Reinforcement processes.**   Individuals are motivated to exhibit the modeled behavior if positive incentives or rewards are provided. Positively reinforced behaviors are given more attention, learned better, and performed more often.

Equity Theory/Organizational Justice

Ainsley is a student at State University working toward a bachelor's degree in finance. In order to gain some work experience and increase her marketability, she has accepted a summer internship in the finance department at a pharmaceutical company. She is quite pleased at the pay: $15 an hour is

social-learning theory   *The view that we can learn through both observation and direct experience.*

6   Demonstrate how organizational justice is a refinement of equity theory.

more than other students in her cohort were receiving for their summer internships. At work she meets Josh, a recent graduate of State University working as a middle manager in the same finance department. Josh makes $30 an hour.

On the job, Ainsley could be described as a go-getter. She's engaged, satisfied, and always seems willing to help others. Josh is quite the opposite. He often seems disinterested in his job and even has thoughts about quitting. When pressed one day about why he is unhappy, Josh cites his pay as the main reason. Specifically, he tells Ainsley that, compared to managers at other pharmaceutical companies, he makes much less. "It isn't fair," he complains. "I work just as hard as they do, yet I don't make as much. Maybe I should go work for the competition."

How could someone making $30 an hour be less satisfied with his pay than someone making $15 an hour and be less motivated as a result? The answer lies in **equity theory** and, more broadly, in principles of organizational justice. According to equity theory, employees compare what they get from their job (their "outcomes," such as pay, promotions, recognition, or having the corner office) to what they put into it (their "inputs," such as effort, experience, and education). They take the ratio of their outcomes to their inputs and compare it to the ratio of others, usually someone similar like a co-worker or someone doing the same job. This is shown in Exhibit 7-6. If we believe our ratio to be equal to those with whom we compare ourselves, a state of equity exists and we perceive the situation as fair. J. Stacy Adams proposed that this negative state of tension provides the motivation to do something to correct it.[76]

Based on equity theory, employees who perceive inequity will make one of six choices:[77]

1. Change inputs (exert less effort if underpaid or more if overpaid).
2. Change outcomes (individuals paid on a piece-rate basis can increase their pay by producing a higher quantity of units of lower quality).
3. Distort perceptions of self ("I used to think I worked at a moderate pace, but now I realize I work a lot harder than everyone else.").
4. Distort perceptions of others ("Mike's job isn't as desirable as I thought.").
5. Choose a different referent ("I may not make as much as my brother-in-law, but I'm doing a lot better than my Dad did when he was my age.").
6. Leave the field (quit the job).

Some of these propositions have been supported, but others haven't.[78] First, inequities created by overpayment do not seem to significantly affect behavior in most work situations. So don't expect an employee who feels overpaid to

equity theory *A theory that says that individuals compare their job inputs and outcomes with those of others and then respond to eliminate any inequities.*

Exhibit 7-6	Equity Theory

Ratio Comparisons*	Perception
$\frac{O}{I_A} < \frac{O}{I_B}$	Inequity due to being underrewarded
$\frac{O}{I_A} = \frac{O}{I_B}$	Equity
$\frac{O}{I_A} > \frac{O}{I_B}$	Inequity due to being overrewarded

*Where $\frac{O}{I_A}$ represents the employee; and $\frac{O}{I_B}$ represents relevant others

give back part of her salary or put in more hours to make up for the inequity. Although individuals may sometimes perceive that they are overrewarded, they restore equity by rationalizing their situation ("I'm worth it because I work harder than everyone else"). Second, not everyone is equity-sensitive.[79] A few actually prefer outcome–input ratios lower than the referent comparisons. Predictions from equity theory are not likely to be very accurate about these "benevolent types."

Although equity theory's propositions have not all held up, the hypothesis served as an important precursor to the study of **organizational justice**, or more simply fairness, in the workplace.[80] Organizational justice is concerned more broadly with how employees feel authorities and decision-makers at work treat them. For the most part, employees evaluate how fairly they are treated along four dimensions, shown in Exhibit 7-7.

Distributive justice is concerned with the fairness of the outcomes, such as pay and recognition, that employees receive. Outcomes can be allocated in many ways. For example, we could distribute raises equally among employees, or we could base them on which employees need money the most. However, as we discussed about equity theory, employees tend to perceive their outcomes are fairest when they are distributed equitably.

Does the same logic apply to teams? At first glance, it would seem that distributing rewards equally among team members is best for boosting morale and teamwork—that way, no one is favored more than another. A recent study of National Hockey League teams suggests otherwise. Differentiating the pay of team members on the basis of their inputs (how well they performed in games) attracted better players to the team, made it more likely they would stay, and increased team performance.[81]

organizational justice *An overall perception of what is fair in the workplace, composed of distributive, procedural, informational, and interpersonal justice.*

distributive justice *Perceived fairness of the amount and allocation of rewards among individuals.*

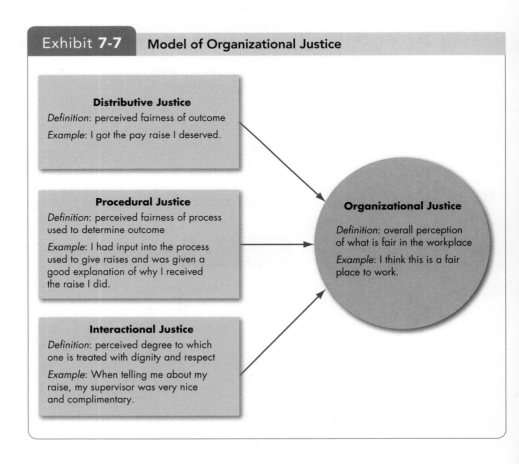

Exhibit **7-7**   **Model of Organizational Justice**

Distributive Justice

Definition: perceived fairness of outcome

Example: I got the pay raise I deserved.

Procedural Justice

Definition: perceived fairness of process used to determine outcome

Example: I had input into the process used to give raises and was given a good explanation of why I received the raise I did.

Interactional Justice

Definition: perceived degree to which one is treated with dignity and respect

Example: When telling me about my raise, my supervisor was very nice and complimentary.

Organizational Justice

Definition: overall perception of what is fair in the workplace

Example: I think this is a fair place to work.

The way we have described things so far, it would seem that distributive justice and equity are gauged in a rational, calculative way as individuals compare their outcome–input ratios to others. But the experience of justice, and especially injustice, is often not so cold and calculated. Instead, people base distributive judgments on a feeling or an emotional reaction to the way they think they are being treated relative to others, and their reactions are often "hot" and emotional as well.[82]

Although employees care a lot about *what* outcomes are distributed (distributive justice), they also care a lot about *how* outcomes are distributed. While distributive justice looks at *what* outcomes are allocated, **procedural justice** examines with *how* outcomes are allocated.[83] What makes procedures more or less fair? There are several factors. For one, employees perceive that procedures are fairer when they are given a say in the decision-making process. Having direct influence over how decisions or made, or at the very least being able to present your opinion to decision makers, creates a sense of control and makes us feel empowered (we discuss empowerment more in the next chapter). Employees also perceive that procedures are fairer when decision makers follow several "rules." These include making decisions in a consistent manner (across people and over time), avoiding bias (not favoring one group or person over another), using accurate information, considering the groups or people their decisions affect, acting ethically, and remaining open to appeals or correction.

procedural justice *The perceived fairness of the process used to determine the distribution of rewards.*

It turns out that procedural and distributive justice combine to influence people's perceptions of fairness. If outcomes are favorable and individuals get what they want, they care less about the process, so procedural justice doesn't matter as much when distributions are perceived to be fair. It's when outcomes are unfavorable that people pay close attention to the process. If the process is judged to be fair, then employees are more accepting of unfavorable outcomes.[84] Why is this the case? It's likely that employees believe that fair procedures, which often have long-lasting effects, will eventually result in a fair outcome, even if the immediate outcome is unfair. Think about it. If you are hoping for a raise and your manager informs you that you did not receive one, you'll probably want to know how raises were determined. If it turns out that your manager allocated

Photo 7-4 Procedural justice perceived by employees of The Container Store contributes to high job satisfaction and employee trust. As part of its "Putting Employees First" belief, the retailer involves employees in the decision-making process by empowering them to make decisions that directly affect how they work.

Source: Richard Sennott/ZUMAPRESS/Newscom.

raises based on merit, and you were simply outperformed by a co-worker, then you're more likely to accept your manager's decision than if raises were based on favoritism. Of course, if you get the raise in the first place, then you'll be less concerned with how the decision was made.

Beyond outcomes and procedures, research has shown that employees care about two other types of fairness that have to do with the way they are treated during interactions with others. The first type is **informational justice**, which reflects whether managers provide employees with explanations for key decisions and keep them informed of important organizational matters. The more detailed and candid managers are with employees, the more fairly treated those employees feel.

informational justice *The degree to which employees are provided truthful explanations for decisions.*

Though it may seem obvious that managers should be honest with their employees and not keep them in the dark about organizational matters, many managers are hesitant to share information. This is especially the case with bad news, which is uncomfortable for both the manager delivering it and the employee receiving it. For example, managers may fail to provide an adequate explanation for bad news such as a layoff or temporary pay cut out of a fear of being blamed, worries about making the situation worse, or concerns about triggering legal action.[85] In fact, research has linked the *absence* of explanations to increased litigation intentions by employees who have been laid off.[86] Explanations for bad news are beneficial when they take the form of post hoc excuses ("I know this is bad, and I wanted to give you the office, but it wasn't my decision") rather than justifications ("I decided to give the office to Sam, but having it isn't a big deal.").[87]

interpersonal justice *The degree to which employees are treated with dignity and respect.*

The second type of justice relevant to interactions between managers and employees is **interpersonal justice**, which reflects whether employees are treated with dignity and respect. Compared to the three other forms of justice we've discussed, interpersonal justice is unique in that it can occur in everyday interactions between managers and employees.[88] This quality allows manages to take advantage of (or miss out on) opportunities to make their employees feel fairly treated. Many managers may view treating employees politely and respectfully as too "soft," choosing more aggressive tactics out of a belief that doing so will be more motivating. Although displays of negative emotions such as anger may be motivating in some cases,[89] managers sometimes take this too far. Consider the recent firing of the Rutgers University men's basketball coach, Mike Rice, who was terminated after video surfaced of him verbally and even physically abusing players.[90]

After all this talk about types of justice, how much does justice really matter to employees? A great deal, as it turns out. When employees feel fairly treated, they respond in a number of positive ways. All four types of justice discussed in this section have been linked to higher levels of task performance and citizenship behaviors such as helping co-workers, as well as lower levels of counterproductive behaviors such as shirking job duties. Distributive and procedural justice are more strongly associated with task performance, while informational and interpersonal justice are more strongly associated with citizenship behavior. Even more physiological outcomes, such as how well employees sleep and the state of their health, have been linked to fair treatment.[91] Why does justice have these positive effects? First, fair treatment enhances commitment to the organization and makes employees feel it cares about their well-being. In addition, employees who feel fairly treated trust their supervisors more, which reduces uncertainty and fear of being exploited by the organization. Finally, fair treatment elicits positive emotions, which in turn prompts behaviors like citizenship.[92]

Studies suggest that managers are indeed motivated to foster employees' perceptions of justice because they wish to ensure compliance, maintain a positive identity, and establish fairness at work.[93] To enhance perceptions of justice, they should realize that employees are especially sensitive to unfairness in procedures when bad news has to be communicated (that is, when distributive justice is low). Thus, it's especially important to openly share information about how allocation decisions are made, follow consistent and unbiased procedures, and engage in similar practices to increase the perception of procedural justice. However, it may be that managers are constrained in how much they can affect distributive and procedural justice because of formal organizational policies or cost constraints. Interpersonal and informational justice are less likely to be governed by these mechanisms, because providing information and treating employees with dignity are practically "free." In such cases, managers wishing to promote fairness could focus their efforts more on informational and interpersonal justice.[94]

Despite all attempts to enhance fairness, perceived injustices are still likely to occur. Fairness is often subjective; what one person sees as unfair, another may see as perfectly appropriate. In general, people see allocations or procedures favoring themselves as fair.[95] So, when addressing perceived injustices, managers need to focus their actions on the source of the problem. In addition, if employees feel they have been treated unjustly, having opportunities to express their frustration has been shown to reduce their desire for retribution.[96]

In terms of cultural differences, meta-analytic evidence shows individuals in both individualistic and collectivistic cultures prefer an equitable distribution of rewards over an equal division (everyone gets paid the same regardless of performance).[97] Across nations, the same basic principles of procedural justice are respected, and workers around the world prefer rewards based on performance and skills over rewards based on seniority.[98] However, in collectivist cultures employees expect rewards to reflect their individual needs as well as their performance.[99] Other research suggests that inputs and outcomes are valued differently in various cultures.[100] Some cultures emphasize status over individual achievement as a basis for allocating resources. Materialistic cultures are more likely to see cash compensation and rewards as the most relevant outcomes of work, whereas relational cultures will see social rewards and status as important outcomes. International managers must consider the cultural preferences of each group of employees when determining what is "fair" in different contexts.

Expectancy Theory

7 Apply the key tenets of expectancy theory to motivating employees.

expectancy theory *A theory that says that the strength of a tendency to act in a certain way depends on the strength of an expectation that the act will be followed by a given outcome and on the attractiveness of that outcome to the individual.*

One of the most widely accepted explanations of motivation is Victor Vroom's **expectancy theory**.[101] Although it has its critics, most of the evidence supports the theory.[102]

Expectancy theory argues that the strength of our tendency to act a certain way depends on the strength of our expectation of a given outcome and its attractiveness. In more practical terms, employees will be motivated to exert a high level of effort when they believe it will lead to a good performance appraisal; that a good appraisal will lead to organizational rewards, such as salary increases and/or intrinsic rewards; and that the rewards will satisfy the employees' personal goals. The theory, therefore, focuses on three relationships (see Exhibit 7-8):

1. **Effort–performance relationship.** The probability perceived by the individual that exerting a given amount of effort will lead to performance.
2. **Performance–reward relationship.** The degree to which the individual believes performing at a particular level will lead to the attainment of a desired outcome.
3. **Rewards–personal goals relationship.** The degree to which organizational rewards satisfy an individual's personal goals or needs and the attractiveness of those potential rewards for the individual.[103]

Exhibit **7-8**	**Expectancy Theory**

Individual effort → ① → Individual performance → ② → Organizational rewards → ③ → Personal goals

① Effort–performance relationship
② Performance–reward relationship
③ Rewards–personal goals relationship

Expectancy theory helps explain why a lot of workers aren't motivated on their jobs and do only the minimum necessary to get by. Let's frame the theory's three relationships as questions employees need to answer in the affirmative if their motivation is to be maximized.

First, *if I give a maximum effort, will it be recognized in my performance appraisal?* For many employees, the answer is "no." Why? Their skill level may be deficient, which means no matter how hard they try, they're not likely to be high performers. The organization's performance appraisal system may be designed to assess nonperformance factors such as loyalty, initiative, or courage, which means more effort won't necessarily result in a higher evaluation. Another possibility is that employees, rightly or wrongly, perceive the boss doesn't like them. As a result, they expect a poor appraisal, regardless of effort. These examples suggest that people will only be motivated if they perceive a link between their effort and their performance.

Second, *if I get a good performance appraisal, will it lead to organizational rewards?* Many organizations reward things besides performance. When pay is based on factors such as having seniority, being cooperative, or "kissing up" to the boss, employees are likely to see the performance–reward relationship as weak and demotivating.

Photo 7-5 The performance–reward relationship is strong at Mary Kay Cosmetics, which offers a rewards and recognition program based on the achievement of personal goals set by each salesperson. The women shown here in China pose before pink sedans, one of many different rewards that motivate Mary Kay's independent sales force.

Finally, *if I'm rewarded, are the rewards attractive to me?* The employee works hard in the hope of getting a promotion but gets a pay raise instead. Or the employee wants a more interesting and challenging job but receives only a few words of praise. Unfortunately, many managers are limited in the rewards they can distribute, which makes it difficult to tailor rewards to individual employee needs. Some incorrectly assume all employees want the same thing, thus overlooking the motivational effects of differentiating rewards. In either case, employee motivation is submaximized.

As a vivid example of how expectancy theory can work, consider stock analysts. They make their living trying to forecast a stock's future price; the accuracy of their buy, sell, or hold recommendations is what keeps them in work or gets them fired. But it's not quite that simple. Analysts place few sell ratings on stocks, although in a steady market, by definition, as many stocks are falling as are rising. Expectancy theory provides an explanation: Analysts who place a sell rating on a company's stock have to balance the benefits they receive by being accurate against the risks they run by drawing that company's ire. What are these risks? They include public rebuke, professional blackballing, and exclusion from information. When analysts place a buy rating on a stock, they face no such trade-off because, obviously, companies love it when analysts recommend that investors buy their stock. So the incentive structure suggests the expected outcome of buy ratings is higher than the expected outcome of sell ratings, and that's why buy ratings vastly outnumber sell ratings.[104]

Does expectancy theory work? Some critics suggest it has only limited use and is more valid where individuals clearly perceive effort–performance and performance–reward linkages.[105] Because few individuals do, the theory tends to be idealistic. If organizations actually rewarded individuals for performance rather than seniority, effort, skill level, and job difficulty, expectancy theory might be much more valid. However, rather than invalidating it, this criticism can explain why a significant segment of the workforce exerts low effort on the job.

Integrating Contemporary Theories of Motivation

8 Compare contemporary theories of motivation.

Things might be simpler if, after presenting a half dozen theories, we could say only one was found valid. But many of the theories in this chapter are complementary. We now tie them together to help you understand their interrelationships.[106]

Exhibit 7-9 integrates much of what we know about motivation. Its basic foundation is the expectancy model shown in Exhibit 7-8. Let's walk through Exhibit 7-9. (We will look at job design closely in Chapter 8.)

We begin by explicitly recognizing that opportunities can either aid or hinder individual effort. The individual effort box on the left also has another arrow leading into it, from the person's goals. Consistent with goal-setting theory, the goals–effort loop is meant to remind us that goals direct behavior.

Expectancy theory predicts employees will exert a high level of effort if they perceive a strong relationship between effort and performance, performance and rewards, and rewards and satisfaction of personal goals. Each of these relationships is, in turn, influenced by other factors. For effort to lead to good performance, the individual must have the ability to perform and perceive the performance appraisal system as fair and objective. The performance–reward

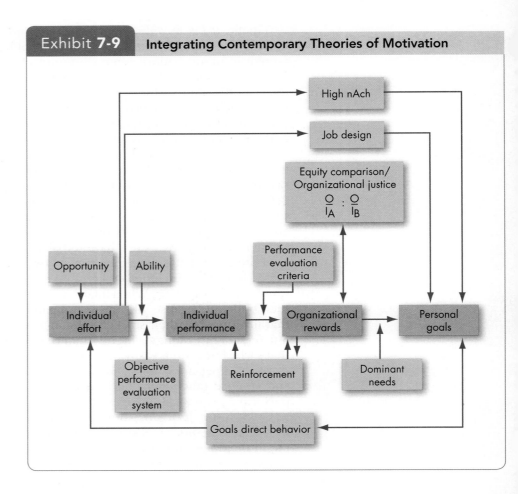

Exhibit 7-9 Integrating Contemporary Theories of Motivation

relationship will be strong if the individual perceives that performance (rather than seniority, personal favorites, or other criteria) is rewarded. If cognitive evaluation theory were fully valid in the actual workplace, we would predict here that basing rewards on performance should decrease the individual's intrinsic motivation. The final link in expectancy theory is the rewards–goals relationship. Motivation is high if the rewards for high performance satisfied the dominant needs consistent with individual goals.

A closer look at Exhibit 7-9 also reveals that the model considers achievement motivation, job design, reinforcement, and equity theories/organizational justice. A high achiever is not motivated by an organization's assessment of performance or organizational rewards, hence the jump from effort to personal goals for those with a high nAch. Remember, high achievers are internally driven as long as their jobs provide them with personal responsibility, feedback, and moderate risks. They are not concerned with the effort–performance, performance–rewards, or rewards–goal linkages.

Reinforcement theory enters the model by recognizing that the organization's rewards reinforce the individual's performance. If employees see a reward system as "paying off" for good performance, the rewards will reinforce and encourage good performance. Rewards also play the key part in organizational justice research. Individuals will judge the favorability of their outcomes (for example, their pay) relative to what others receive but also with respect to how they are treated: When people are disappointed in their rewards, they are likely to be sensitive to the perceived fairness of the procedures used and the consideration given to them by their supervisor.

Summary

The motivation theories in this chapter differ in their predictive strength. Maslow's hierarchy, McClelland's needs, and the two-factor theory focus on needs. None has found widespread support, although McClelland's is the strongest, particularly regarding the relationship between achievement and productivity. Self-determination theory and cognitive evaluation theory have merits to consider. Goal-setting theory can be helpful but does not cover absenteeism, turnover, or job satisfaction. Reinforcement theory can be helpful, but not regarding employee satisfaction or the decision to quit. Equity theory's strongest legacy is that it provided the spark for research on organizational justice, which has more support in the literature. Expectancy theory can be helpful, but assumes employees have few constraints on decision making, such as bias or incomplete information, and this limits its applicability.

Implications for Managers

- Make sure extrinsic rewards for employees are not viewed as coercive, but instead provide information about competence and relatedness.
- Consider goal-setting theory: Clear and difficult goals often lead to higher levels of employee productivity.
- Consider reinforcement theory regarding quality and quantity of work, persistence of effort, absenteeism, tardiness, and accident rates.
- Consult equity theory to help understand productivity, satisfaction, absence, and turnover variables.
- Expectancy theory offers a powerful explanation of performance variables such as employee productivity, absenteeism, and turnover.

Goals Get You to Where You Want to Be

POINT

Of course this is a true statement. Goal-setting theory is one of *the* best-supported theories in all the motivation literature. Study after study has consistently shown the benefits of goals. Want to excel on a test, lose a certain amount of weight, obtain a job with a particular income level, or improve your golf game? If you want to be a high performer, merely set a specific, difficult goal and let nature take its course. That goal will dominate your attention, cause you to focus, and make you try harder.

All too often, people are told by others to simply "do their best." Could anything be more vague? What does "do your best" actually mean? Maybe you feel that your "best" on one day is to muster a grade of 50 percent on an exam, while your "best" on another day is an 80. But if you were given a more difficult goal—say, to score a 95 on the exam—and you were committed to that goal, you would ultimately perform better.

Edwin Locke and Gary Latham, the researchers best known for goal-setting theory, put it best when they said: "The effects of goal setting are very reliable." In short, goal-setting theory is among the most valid and practical theories of motivation in organizational psychology.

COUNTERPOINT

Sure, a lot of research has shown the benefits of goal-setting, but those studies ignore the harm that's often done. For one, how often have you set a "stretch" goal, only to see yourself later fail? Goals create anxiety and worry about reaching them, and they often create unrealistic expectations as well. Imagine those who had set a goal to earn a promotion in a certain period of time (a specific, difficult goal), only to find themselves laid off once the recession hit. Or how about those who envisioned a retirement of leisure yet were forced to take on a part-time job or delay retirement altogether in order to continue to make ends meet. When too many things are out of our control, our difficult goals become impossible.

Or, consider this: Goals can lead to unethical behavior and poorer performance. How many reports have you heard over the years about teachers who "fudged" students' test scores in order to achieve educational standards? Another example: When Ken O'Brian, a professional quarterback for the New York Jets, was penalized for every interception he threw, he achieved his goal of fewer interceptions quite easily—by refusing to throw the ball even when he should have.

In addition to this anecdotal evidence, research has directly linked goal-setting to cheating. We should heed the warning of Professor Maurice E. Schweitzer—"Goal-setting is like a powerful medication"—before blindly accepting that specific, difficult goal.

Sources: E. A. Locke and G. P. Latham, "Building a Practically Useful Theory of Goal Setting and Task Motivation," *American Psychologist* 57 (2002), pp. 705–771; A. Tugend, "Expert's Advice to the Goal-Oriented: Don't Overdo It," *The New York Times* (October 6, 2012), p. B5; and C. Richards, "Letting Go of Long-Term Goals," *The New York Times* (August 4, 2012).

END-OF-CHAPTER REVIEW

MyManagementLab

Go to **mymanagementlab.com** to complete the problems marked with this icon. ⭐

QUESTIONS FOR REVIEW

7-1 What are the three key elements of motivation?

7-2 What are some early theories of motivation? How applicable are they today?

7-3 How do the predictions of self-determination theory apply to intrinsic and extrinsic rewards?

7-4 What are the implications of employee job engagement for management?

7-5 What are the key principles of goal-setting theory, self-efficacy theory, and reinforcement theory?

7-6 How is organizational justice a refinement of equity theory?

7-7 What are the key tenets of expectancy theory?

7-8 What are some contemporary theories of motivation, and how do they compare to one another?

EXPERIENTIAL EXERCISE Organizational Justice Task

Purpose
This exercise will highlight the four primary sources of organizational justice and help you understand what managers can do to ensure fairness in the workplace.

Time
Approximately 20 to 30 minutes.

Instructions
- Break into groups of three or four.

   7-9. Each person should recall an instance in which he or she was (a) treated especially fairly and (b) treated especially unfairly. Work-related instances are preferable, but nonwork examples are fine too.

7-10. Spend several minutes discussing whether the instance was more distributive, procedural, informational, or interpersonal in nature. What was the source of the fair/unfair treatment? How did you feel, and how did you respond? Was it easier to remember the fair or the unfair instance, and why do you think that is?

7-11. Each group should develop a set of recommendations for handling the unfair situations in a fairer manner. Select a leader for your group who will briefly summarize the unfair instances, along with the group's recommendations for handling them better. The discussion should reflect the four types of justice discussed in this chapter (distributive, procedural, informational, and interpersonal).

ETHICAL DILEMMA Grade Inflation

Oscar-nominated actor James Franco made headlines when he received a D in "Directing the Actor II," a graduate-level class at New York University. The subsequent firing of his professor, José Santana, which prompted a wrongful-termination lawsuit, raised questions about grade inflation. Grade inflation is of particular concern in graduate programs, where it is not uncommon for 75 percent of grades to be A's. Of course, along with grade inflation

we have seen tuition inflation, and educators have commented about a possible link between the two. As Professor Santana commented, "There's pressure to retain students."

Questions
   7-12. James Franco missed all but two of his classes in Professor Santana's course. Is that grounds for a D? What would constitute grounds for failure?

7-13. If around 75 percent of grades in graduate programs are A's, are grades now meaningless?

7-14. State funding of many schools has decreased dramatically over the years, increasing pressure on administrators to generate revenue through tuition increases and other means. How might this pressure create ethical tensions between the need to generate revenue, student retention, and grading?

Sources: Based on A. Ellin, "Failure Is Not an Option," *The New York Times* (April 15, 2012), pp. 13–14.

CASE INCIDENT 1 Equity and Executive Pay

Few topics in the business press grab headlines and ignite the public like the compensation packages received by top management, which continue to rise. For companies in the United States with more than $5 billion in revenue, the median CEO compensation was $14 million in 2012—a 2.8 percent increase over 2011.

How do compensation committees set executive compensation? In many cases, it comes down to equity theory and depends on the referent others to which the CEO is compared. To determine a "fair" level of pay for a given CEO, members of a compensation board find out how much CEOs with similar levels of experience in similar firms (similar inputs) are being paid and attempt to adjust compensation (outcomes) to be similar. So, CEOs in large tech firms are paid similarly to CEOs in other large tech firms, CEOs in small hospitals are paid similarly to CEOs in other small hospitals, and so forth. Proponents of this practice consider it to be "fair" because it achieves equity.

However, critics of high CEO pay want to change the perspective by comparing the CEO's pay to the pay of the company's lowest-ranking employees. For example, the average S&P 500 CEO is paid 263 times what the lowest-ranking employee makes—a ratio eight times higher than the same ratio from the 1950s. From this perspective, CEO pay is grossly inequitable and thus "unfair."

In response, many CEOs, such as Mark Zuckerberg of Facebook and Larry Page of Google, have taken $1 annual salaries, though they still earn substantial compensation by exercising their stock options. In addition, shareholders of some companies, such as Verizon, are playing a greater role in setting CEO compensation by reducing awards when the company underperforms.

Questions

7-15. How does the executive compensation issue relate to equity theory? Who do you think should be the comparative others in these equity judgments? How should we determine what is a "fair" level of pay for top executives?

7-16. Can you think of procedural justice implications related to the ways pay policies for top executives have been instituted? Do these pay-making decisions follow the procedural justice principles outlined in the chapter?

✪ **7-17.** Are there any positive motivational consequences of tying compensation pay closely to firm performance?

Sources: J. Bizjak, M. Lemmon, and T. Nguyen, "Are All CEOs Above Average? An Empirical Analysis of Compensation Peer Groups and Pay Design," *Journal of Financial Economics* 100, no. 3 (2011), pp. 538–555; R. Foroohar, "Stuffing Their Pockets: For CEOs, A Lucrative Recession" *Newsweek* (September 13, 2010), www.newsweek.com; A. Kleinman, "Mark Zuckerberg $1 Salary Puts Him in Elite Group of $1 CEOs," *The Huffington Post* (April 29, 2013), www.huffingtonpost.com; and G. Morgenson, "If Shareholders Say 'Enough Already,' the Board May Listen," *The New York Times* (April 6, 2013). www.newyorktimes.com.

CASE INCIDENT 2 Sleeping on the Job

Although the recession has been receding for several years now, many U.S. workers still feel pushed to the limit as they work long hours.

One consequence is that sleep has taken a back seat to other matters deemed more important. But rather than tread through the workday in a zombie-like, sleep-deprived state, some workers are turning to secret "power naps" in order to recharge. For example, Ronit Rogosziniski, a 45-year-old financial planner, wakes up at 5 a.m. each day, works, and at noon sneaks to her car for a quick snooze. She is not alone, as evidenced by the comments on Wall Street Oasis, a website frequently visited by investment bankers who blog about their travails. Their advice? When power-napping on a toilet, put the seat down and keep your pants up, "for maximum comfort."

Though the thought of an investment banker napping on a toilet in a power suit might be amusing, many believe lack of sleep is no laughing matter. Research examining the effects of sleep deprivation has found that tired workers experience higher levels of back pain, depression, and job dissatisfaction, along with lower levels of performance. Losing even an hour of sleep as a result of the shift to daylight savings time is enough to prompt higher levels of cyberloafing.

Some companies are paying attention to the costs associated with sleep deprivation and are encouraging napping at work. One survey of 600 companies conducted by the Society for Human Resource Management revealed that 6 percent had dedicated nap rooms in 2011. In addition, a poll of 1,508 workers conducted by the National Sleep Foundation found that 34 percent said they were allowed to nap at work.

Questions

7-18. Should organizations be concerned about their employees being sleep-deprived? What factors influencing sleep might be more or less under the control of an organization?

7-19. How might reinforcement theory play a role in the extent to which employees are sleep-deprived?

7-20. How might sleep deprivation influence aspects of expectancy theory? How might the incorporation of "nap rooms" for sleep-deprived employees influence aspects of equity theory?

✪ 7-21. If you were a manager who noticed your employees were sleep-deprived, what steps might you take to help them? What theories of motivation could you use to help them?

Sources: Based on C. Delo, "Why Companies are Cozying Up to Napping at Work," *CNN* (August 18, 2011), www.management.fortune.cnn.com; D. T. Wagner, C. M. Barnes, V. K. G. Lim, and D. L. Ferris, "Lost Sleep and Cyberloafing: Evidence from the Laboratory and a Daylight Saving Time Quasi-Experiment," *Journal of Applied Psychology* 97 (2012), pp. 1068–1076; and D. Wescott, "Do Not Disturb," *Bloomberg Businessweek* (April 23–29, 2012), p. 90.

MyManagementLab

Go to **mymanagementlab.com** for Auto-graded writing questions as well as the following Assisted-graded writing questions:

7-22. After reading the Ethical Dilemma, do you think grade inflation is a problem at colleges and universities? Do schools have an obligation to ensure that students succeed and get "good" grades? Why or why not?

7-23. In considering Case Incident 1, do you think the government has a legitimate role in controlling executive compensation? How might aspects of justice (distributive, procedural, and informational) inform this debate?

7-24. MyManagementLab Only—comprehensive writing assignment for this chapter.

Motivation: From Concepts to Applications

TELECOMMUTING? NO.
EXTRA MATERNITY LEAVE? YES

Yahoo! CEO Marissa Mayer has received her fair share of media attention since taking over the reins of the aging tech giant. But the move that received the most attention so far was her decision to ban telecommuting practices at Yahoo!, citing the need for face-to-face contact to boost productivity. Mayer's action bucks the recent trend of employees working more frequently from their homes—particularly among technology firms. For example, between 2005 and 2009, the Silicon Valley workforce—which includes employees at tech companies Google, Intel, Apple, and Oracle—grew by less than 10 percent, while telecommuting increased by nearly 130 percent.

Critics blasted Mayer's decision, claiming that the move was anti-feminist and would hurt employees trying to achieve a greater balance between work and family. They also pointed out that Mayer, who gave birth to her first child shortly after taking the reins at Yahoo!, returned to work only 2 weeks later. The fact that she had a nursery built right next to her office only added fuel to their fire.

Not all Mayer's moves have been at odds with ideals of work–family balance. Nine months after having her baby, Mayer announced that new mothers and fathers can take 8 weeks of paid leave, with mothers eligible for an additional 8 weeks. In addition, parents are provided with $500 to help with initial child care costs. The company said the decision was made "to support the happiness and well-being of Yahoos and their families." Mayer's former employer, Google, offers comparable benefits: 18 to 22 weeks of paid time for new mothers and 7 weeks for new fathers. Neither company comes close to Facebook, which offers mothers and fathers 4 paid months and $4,000 in "baby cash."

Although the media has focused on Yahoo!'s work–family policies, Mayer seems to be focused on turning the company around. Only time will tell whether her decision will yield higher employee productivity or, perhaps, higher turnover.

Sources: J. Kotkin, "Marissa Mayer's Misstep and the Unstoppable Rise of Telecommuting," *Forbes* (March 26, 2013); J. Pepitone, "Marissa Mayer Extends Yahoo's Maternity Leave," *CNNMoney.com* (April 30, 2013); and C. Tkaczyk, "Marissa Mayer Breaks Her Silence on Yahoo's Telecommuting Policy," *CNN Money* (April 19, 2013), http://tech.fortune.cnn.com/2013/04/19/marissa-mayer-telecommuting/.

LEARNING OBJECTIVES

After studying this chapter, you should be able to:

1 Describe the job characteristics model and the way it motivates by changing the work environment.

2 Compare the main ways jobs can be redesigned.

3 Explain how specific alternative work arrangements can motivate employees.

4 Describe how employee involvement measures can motivate employees.

5 Demonstrate how the different types of variable-pay programs can increase employee motivation.

6 Show how flexible benefits turn benefits into motivators.

7 Identify the motivational benefits of intrinsic rewards.

As we can see in the ongoing saga of Yahoo!, pay is not the only motivator for working individuals. Pay is a central means of motivation, but working conditions and benefits matter, too. The process of motivating employees is complex and, as the opening story indicates, people feel strongly about the implications of changes to their extrinsic or intrinsic benefits. The following self-assessment will provide information about how intrinsically motivating *your* job might be.

In Chapter 7, we focused on motivation theories. In this chapter, we start applying motivation concepts to practices because while it's important to understand the underlying concepts, it's even more important to see how, as a manager, you can use them.

What's My Job's Motivating Potential?

In the Self-Assessment Library (available in MyManagementLab), take assessment I.C.9 (What's My Job's Motivating Potential?) and answer the following questions. If you currently do not have a job, answer the questions for your most recent position.

1. How did you score relative to your classmates?
2. Did your score surprise you? Why or why not?
3. How might your results affect your career path?

Motivating by Job Design: The Job Characteristics Model

1   Describe the job characteristics model and the way it motivates by changing the work environment.

job design   *The way the elements in a job are organized.*

job characteristics model (JCM)   *A model that proposes that any job can be described in terms of five core job dimensions: skill variety, task identity, task significance, autonomy, and feedback.*

skill variety   *The degree to which a job requires a variety of different activities.*

task identity   *The degree to which a job requires completion of a whole and identifiable piece of work.*

task significance   *The degree to which a job has a substantial impact on the lives or work of other people.*

autonomy   *The degree to which a job provides substantial freedom and discretion to the individual in scheduling the work and in determining the procedures to be used in carrying it out.*

Increasingly, research on motivation focuses on approaches that link motivational concepts to changes in the way work is structured. Research in **job design** suggests the way the elements in a job are organized can increase or decrease effort and also suggests what those elements are. We'll first review the job characteristics model and then discuss some ways jobs can be redesigned. Finally, we'll explore alternative work arrangements.

The Job Characteristics Model

Developed by J. Richard Hackman and Greg Oldham, the **job characteristics model (JCM)** says we can describe any job in terms of five core job dimensions:[1]

1. **Skill variety** is the degree to which a job requires a variety of different activities so the worker can use specialized skills and talents. The work of a garage owner-operator who does electrical repairs, rebuilds engines, does bodywork, and interacts with customers scores high on skill variety. The job of a bodyshop worker who sprays paint 8 hours a day scores low on this dimension.

2. **Task identity** is the degree to which a job requires completion of a whole and identifiable piece of work. A cabinetmaker who designs a piece of furniture, selects the wood, builds the object, and finishes it to perfection has a job that scores high on task identity. A job scoring low on this dimension is operating a factory lathe solely to make table legs.

3. **Task significance** is the degree to which a job affects the lives or work of other people. The job of a nurse handling the diverse needs of patients in a hospital intensive care unit scores high on task significance; sweeping floors in a hospital scores low.

4. **Autonomy** is the degree to which a job provides the worker freedom, independence, and discretion in scheduling work and determining the procedures for carrying it out. A salesperson who schedules his or her own work each day and decides on the sales approach for each customer without supervision has a highly autonomous job. A salesperson who is given a set

feedback *The degree to which carrying out the work activities required by a job results in the individual obtaining direct and clear information about the effectiveness of his or her performance.*

of leads each day and is required to follow a standardized sales script with potential customers has a job low on autonomy.

5. **Feedback** is the degree to which carrying out work activities generates direct and clear information about your own performance. A job with high feedback is assembling iPads and testing them to see whether they operate properly. A factory worker who assembles iPads but then routes them to a quality-control inspector for testing and adjustments receives low feedback from his or her activities.

Exhibit 8-1 presents the job characteristics model (JCM). Note how the first three dimensions—skill variety, task identity, and task significance—combine to create meaningful work the incumbent will view as important, valuable, and worthwhile. Jobs with high autonomy give incumbents a feeling of personal responsibility for the results; if a job provides feedback, employees will know how effectively they are performing. From a motivational standpoint, the JCM proposes that individuals obtain internal rewards when they learn (knowledge of results) that they personally have performed well (experienced responsibility) on a task they care about (experienced meaningfulness).[2] The more these three psychological states are present, the greater will be employees' motivation, performance, and satisfaction, and the lower their absenteeism and likelihood of leaving. As Exhibit 8-1 also shows, individuals with a high growth need are more likely to experience the critical psychological states when their jobs are enriched—and respond to them more positively—than are their counterparts with a low growth need.

motivating potential score (MPS) *A predictive index that suggests the motivating potential in a job.*

We can combine the core dimensions into a single predictive index, called the **motivating potential score (MPS)**, and calculated as follows:

$$\text{MPS} = \frac{\text{Skill variety} + \text{Task identity} + \text{Task significance}}{3} \times \text{Autonomy} \times \text{Feedback}$$

To be high on motivating potential, jobs must be high on at least one of the three factors that lead to experienced meaningfulness and high on both autonomy

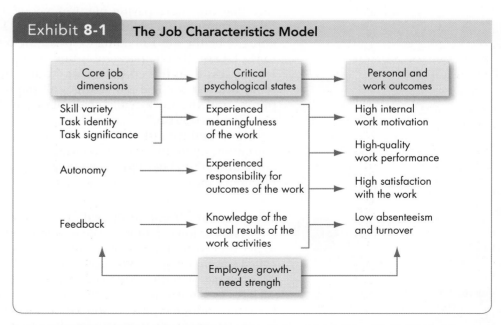

Exhibit 8-1   The Job Characteristics Model

Source: Adaptation of Job Characteristics Model, pp. 78–80 from J. Richard Hackman & Greg R. Oldham, *Work Redesign*, 1st Edition, © 1980. Adapted by permission of Pearson Education, Inc., Upper Saddle River, NJ.

and feedback. If jobs score high on motivating potential, the model predicts motivation, performance, and satisfaction will improve, while absence and turnover will be reduced.

Much evidence supports the JCM concept that the presence of a set of job characteristics—variety, identity, significance, autonomy, and feedback—does generate higher and more satisfying job performance.[3] But we can better calculate motivating potential by simply adding the characteristics rather than using the formula. Think about your job. Do you have the opportunity to work on different tasks, or is your day routine? Are you able to work independently, or do you constantly have a supervisor or co-worker looking over your shoulder? What do you think your answers to these questions say about your job's motivating potential? Revisit your answers to the self-assessment at the beginning of this chapter, then calculate your MPS from the job characteristics model. You might try computing your MPS score two ways: using the traditional MPS formula, and simply adding the dimensions. Then compare.

A few studies have tested the job characteristics model in different cultures, but the results aren't consistent. One study suggested that when employees were "other oriented" (concerned with the welfare of others at work), the relationship between intrinsic job characteristics and job satisfaction was weaker. The fact that the job characteristics model is relatively individualistic (it considers the relationship between the employee and his or her work) suggests job enrichment strategies may not have the same effects in collectivistic cultures as in individualistic cultures (such as the United States).[4] However, another study suggested the degree to which jobs had intrinsic job characteristics predicted job satisfaction and job involvement equally well for U.S., Japanese, and Hungarian employees.[5]

How Can Jobs Be Redesigned?

2   Compare the main ways jobs can be redesigned.

"Every day was the same thing," Frank said. "Stand on that assembly line. Wait for an instrument panel to be moved into place. Unlock the mechanism and drop the panel into the Jeep Liberty as it moved by on the line. Then I plugged in the harnessing wires. I repeated that for eight hours a day. I don't care that they were paying me twenty-four dollars an hour. I was going crazy. I did it for almost a year and a half. Finally, I just said to my wife that this isn't going to be the way I'm going to spend the rest of my life. My brain was turning to JELL-O on that Jeep assembly line. So I quit. Now I work in a print shop and I make less than fifteen dollars an hour. But let me tell you, the work I do is really interesting. The job changes all the time, I'm continually learning new things, and the work really challenges me! I look forward every morning to going to work again."

The repetitive tasks in Frank's job at the Jeep plant provided little variety, autonomy, or motivation. In contrast, his job in the print shop is challenging and stimulating. Let's look at some of the ways to put JCM into practice to make jobs more motivating.

Job Rotation   If employees suffer from over-routinization of their work, one alternative is **job rotation**, or the periodic shifting of an employee from one task to another with similar skill requirements at the same organizational level (also called *cross-training*). At Singapore Airlines, a ticket agent may take on the duties of a baggage handler. Extensive job rotation is among the reasons Singapore Airlines is rated one of the best airlines in the world.[6] Many manufacturing firms have adopted job rotation as a means of increasing flexibility and avoiding layoffs. Managers at these companies train workers on all their equipment so they can move around as needed in response to incoming orders. Although

job rotation   *The periodic shifting of an employee from one task to another.*

"Money Can't Buy Happiness"

In addition to this clichéd statement, you've probably heard the alternative: that money *does* buy happiness. Those who say how much money you have has no bearing on your happiness often refer to the Easterlin paradox, named after the economist Richard Easterlin who argued that once basic financial needs have been met, more money doesn't really do much to make a person happy. Other researchers point to data that agree with Easterlin's assertion. For example, when Robert Kenny surveyed 165 households earning $25 million or more, most said their money is not always helpful. They worried about how their children would be treated by others and whether they would be motivated to be independent.

Does that mean we should stop making money because it will make us miserable? Not so fast. Recent research surveying a much broader set of people, including people in various countries, indicates the exact opposite: The more money, the better. Using data collected by the Gallup organization,

economists Betsy Stevenson and Justin Wolfers of the University of Michigan found that people all over the world, from countries including the United States, Mexico, Britain, Brazil, France, Germany, Japan, India, Nigeria, Iran, and Russia, reported greater happiness as they grew richer. More interesting is the finding that the relationship between income and happiness doesn't change for the very rich. So going from richer to richest increases happiness about as much as moving from the poorest to less poor. The authors say, "The relationship between well-being and income . . . does not diminish as incomes rise. If there is a satiation point, we are yet to reach it."

The relationship between happiness and income also seems to be the same whether we look within a given country (you're happier if you're wealthier than your fellow citizens) or between countries (people from countries with higher per capita gross domestic product levels are happier than those from countries with lower levels).

Still, Stevenson and Wolfers caution against causal inferences. Income may contribute to happiness, but happiness may also contribute to higher income if those who are cheerful and pleasant get promoted more than those who are grumpy. Says Wolfers, "I suspect what's actually going on is that income is a marker for something else. It may be that what really makes us happy is leading fulfilling lives. It's not income per se, but it's having a broad set of choices, including the choice to have a healthy income."

Sources: R. Easterlin, "Does Economic Growth Improve the Human Lot? Some Empirical Evidence," in P. A. David and M. W. Reder (eds.), *Nations and Households in Economic Growth: Essays in Honor of Moses Abramovitz* (New York: Academic Press, 1974); D. Kurtzleben, "Finally: Proof That Money Buys Happiness (Sort Of)," *USNews.com* (April 29, 2013); A. Novotney, "Money Can't Buy Happiness," *Monitor on Psychology* (July/August 2012), pp. 24–26; B. Stevenson and J. Wolfers, "Subjective Well-Being and Income: Is There Any Evidence of Satiation?" NBER Working Paper 18992 (April 2013); and "Money Can Buy Happiness," *Economist.com* (May 2, 2013).

job rotation has often been conceptualized as an activity for assembly line and manufacturing employees, many organizations use job rotation for new managers to help them get a picture of the whole business as well.[7]

The strengths of job rotation are that it reduces boredom, increases motivation, and helps employees better understand how their work contributes to the organization. International evidence from Italy, Britain, and Turkey shows that job rotation is associated with higher levels of organizational performance in manufacturing settings.[8] However, job rotation has drawbacks. Training costs increase, and moving a worker into a new position reduces productivity just when efficiency at the prior job is creating organizational economies. Work that is done repeatedly may become habitual and "routine," which makes decision making more automatic and efficient. Job rotation creates disruptions when members of the work group have to adjust to new employees. And supervisors may have to spend more time answering questions and monitoring the work of recently rotated employees.

job enrichment *The vertical expansion of jobs, which increases the degree to which the worker controls the planning, execution, and evaluation of the work.*

Job Enrichment Job enrichment expands jobs by increasing the degree to which the worker controls the planning, execution, and evaluation of the work. An enriched job allows the worker to do a complete activity, increases

Exhibit 8-2   Guidelines for Enriching a Job

Suggested Action	Core Job Dimensions
Combine tasks	Skill variety
Form natural work units	Task identity
Establish client relationships	Task significance
Expand jobs vertically	Autonomy
Open feedback channels	Feedback

Source: J. R. Hackman and J. L. Suttle (eds.), *Improving Life at Work* (Glenview, IL: Scott Foresman, 1977), p. 138. Reprinted by permission of Richard Hackman and J. Lloyd Suttle.

the employee's freedom and independence, increases responsibility, and provides feedback so individuals can assess and correct their own performance.[9]

How does management enrich an employee's job? Exhibit 8-2 offers suggested guidelines based on the job characteristics model. *Combining tasks* puts fractionalized tasks back together to form a new and larger module of work. *Forming natural work units* makes an employee's tasks create an identifiable and meaningful whole. *Establishing client relationships* increases the direct relationships between workers and their clients (clients can be internal as well as outside the organization). *Expanding jobs vertically* gives employees responsibilities and control formerly reserved for management. *Opening feedback channels* lets employees know how well they are doing and whether their performance is improving, deteriorating, or remaining constant.

Another method for improving the meaningfulness of work is providing employees with mutual assistance programs.[10] Employees who can help each other directly through their work come to see themselves, and the organizations for which they work, in more positive, pro-social terms. This, in turn, can increase employee affective commitment.

The evidence on job enrichment shows it reduces absenteeism and turnover costs and increases satisfaction, but not all programs are equally effective.[11] A review of 83 organizational interventions designed to improve performance management showed that frequent, specific feedback related to solving problems was linked to consistently higher performance, but infrequent feedback that focused more on past problems than future solutions was much less effective.[12] Some recent evidence suggests job enrichment works best when it compensates for poor feedback and reward systems.[13] Work design may also not affect everyone in the same way. One recent study showed employees with a higher preference for challenging work experienced larger reductions in stress following job redesign than individuals who did not prefer challenging work.[14]

Relational Job Design

While redesigning jobs on the basis of job characteristics theory is likely to make work more intrinsically motivating to people, more contemporary research is focusing on how to make jobs more prosocially motivating to people. In other words, how can managers design work so employees are motivated to promote the well-being of the organization's beneficiaries? Beneficiaries of organizations might include customers, clients, patients, and users of products or services. This view of job design shifts the spotlight from the employee to those whose lives are affected by the job that employee performs.[15]

One way to make jobs more prosocially motivating is to better connect employees with the beneficiaries of their work, for example, by relating stories from customers who have found the company's products or services to be helpful. The medical device manufacturer Medtronic invites people to describe how Medtronic products have improved, or even saved, their lives and shares these stories with employees during annual meetings, providing a powerful reminder of the impact of their work. One study found that radiologists who saw photographs of patients whose scans they were examining made more accurate diagnoses of their medical problems. Why? Seeing the photos made it more personal, which elicited feelings of empathy in the radiologists.[16]

Even better, in some cases managers may be able to connect employees directly with beneficiaries. Researchers found that when university fundraisers briefly interacted with the undergraduates who would receive the scholarship money they raised, they persisted 42 percent longer, and raised nearly twice as much money, as those who didn't interact with potential recipients.[17] The positive impact of connecting employees was apparent even when they met with just a single scholarship recipient.

Why do these connections have such positive consequences? There are several reasons. Meeting beneficiaries firsthand allows employees to see that their actions affect a real, live person and that their jobs have tangible consequences. In addition, connections with beneficiaries make customers or clients more accessible in memory and more emotionally vivid, which leads employees to consider the effects of their actions more. Finally, connections allow employees to easily take the perspective of beneficiaries, which fosters higher levels of commitment.

You might be wondering whether connecting employees is already covered by the idea of task significance in job characteristics theory. However, some differences make beneficiary contact unique. For one, many jobs might be perceived to be high in significance, yet employees in those jobs never meet the individuals affected by their work. Second, beneficiary contact seems to have a distinct relationship with prosocial behaviors such as helping others. One study found that lifeguards who read stories about how their actions benefited swimmers were rated as more helpful by their bosses; this was not the case for lifeguards who read stories about the personal benefits of their work.[18] The upshot? There are many ways you can design jobs to be more motivating, and the choice should depend on the outcome or outcomes you'd like to achieve.

Alternative Work Arrangements

3 Explain how specific alternative work arrangements can motivate employees.

Another approach to motivation is to alter work arrangements with flextime, job sharing, or telecommuting. These are likely to be especially important for a diverse workforce of dual-earner couples, single parents, and employees caring for a sick or aging relative.

Flextime   Susan is the classic "morning person." She rises at 5:00 A.M. sharp each day, full of energy. However, as she puts it, "I'm usually ready for bed right after the 7:00 P.M. news."

Susan's work schedule as a claims processor at The Hartford Financial Services Group is flexible. Her office opens at 6:00 A.M. and closes at 7:00 P.M. It's up to her how she schedules her 8-hour day within this 13-hour period. Because Susan is a morning person and also has a 7-year-old son who gets out of school at

3:00 P.M. every day, she opts to work from 6:00 A.M. to 3:00 P.M. "My work hours are perfect. I'm at the job when I'm mentally most alert, and I can be home to take care of my son after he gets out of school."

flextime *Flexible work hours.*

Susan's schedule is an example of **flextime**, short for "flexible work time." Employees must work a specific number of hours per week but are free to vary their hours of work within certain limits. As in Exhibit 8-3, each day consists of a common core, usually 6 hours, with a flexibility band surrounding it. The core may be 9:00 A.M. to 3:00 P.M., with the office actually opening at 6:00 A.M. and closing at 6:00 P.M. All employees are required to be at their jobs during the common core period, but they may accumulate their other 2 hours before, after, or before *and* after that. Some flextime programs allow employees to accumulate extra hours and turn them into a free day off each month.

Flextime has become extremely popular. According to a recent survey, a majority (53 percent) of organizations now offer some form of flextime.[19] And this is not just a U.S. phenomenon. In Germany, for instance, 73 percent of businesses offer flextime, and such practices are becoming more widespread in Japan as well.[20] In fact, in Germany, Belgium, the Netherlands, and France, by law, employers are not allowed to refuse an employee's request for either a part-time or a flexible work schedule as long as that request is reasonable, such as to care for an infant child.[21]

Exhibit 8-3	Possible Flextime Staff Schedules

Schedule 1	
Percent Time:	100% = 40 hours per week
Core Hours:	9:00 A.M.–5:00 P.M., Monday through Friday (1 hour lunch)
Work Start Time:	Between 8:00 A.M. and 9:00 A.M.
Work End Time:	Between 5:00 P.M. and 6:00 P.M.

Schedule 2	
Percent Time:	100% = 40 hours per week
Work Hours:	8:00 A.M.–6:30 P.M., Monday through Thursday (1/2 hour lunch)
	Friday off
Work Start Time:	8:00 A.M.
Work End Time:	6:30 P.M.

Schedule 3	
Percent Time:	90% = 36 hours per week
Work Hours:	8:30 A.M.–5:00 P.M., Monday through Thursday (1/2 hour lunch)
	8:00 A.M.–Noon Friday (no lunch)
Work Start Time:	8:30 A.M. (Monday–Thursday); 8:00 A.M. (Friday)
Work End Time:	5:00 P.M. (Monday–Thursday); Noon (Friday)

Schedule 4	
Percent Time:	80% = 32 hours per week
Work Hours:	8:00 A.M.–6:00 P.M., Monday through Wednesday (1/2 hour lunch)
	8:00 A.M.–11:30 A.M. Thursday (no lunch)
	Friday off
Work Start Time:	Between 8:00 A.M. and 9:00 A.M.
Work End Time:	Between 5:00 P.M. and 6:00 P.M.

Photo 8-1 Jobs at FedEx involved in the physical transport of packages are not suitable for telecommuting. But in operating one of the world's largest telecommunications networks for recording and tracking shipments, FedEx provides many computer-based jobs for telecommuters who help the firm process more than 20 million transactions daily.

Source: Russell Gordon/DanitaDelimont.com "Danita Delimont Photography"/Newscom.

Claimed benefits include reduced absenteeism, increased productivity, reduced overtime expenses, reduced hostility toward management, reduced traffic congestion around work sites, elimination of tardiness, and increased autonomy and responsibility for employees—any of which may increase employee job satisfaction.[22] But what's flextime's actual record?

Most of the evidence stacks up favorably. Flextime tends to reduce absenteeism and frequently improves worker productivity,[23] probably for several reasons. Employees can schedule their work hours to align with personal demands, reducing tardiness and absences, and they can work when they are most productive. Flextime can also help employees balance work and family lives; it is a popular criterion for judging how "family friendly" a workplace is.

Flextime's major drawback is that it's not applicable to every job or every worker. It works well with clerical tasks for which an employee's interaction with people outside his or her department is limited. It is not a viable option for receptionists, sales personnel in retail stores, or people whose service jobs require them to be at their workstations at predetermined times. It also appears that people who have a stronger desire to separate their work and family lives are less prone to take advantage of opportunities for flextime.[24] Overall, employers need to consider the appropriateness of both the work and the workers before implementing flextime schedules.

Job Sharing   **Job sharing** allows two or more individuals to split a traditional 40-hour-a-week job. One might perform the job from 8:00 A.M. to noon and the other from 1:00 P.M. to 5:00 P.M., or the two could work full but alternate days. For example, top Ford engineers Julie Levine and Julie Rocco engaged in a job-sharing program that allowed both of them to spend time with their families while working on the time-intensive job of redesigning the Explorer crossover. Typically, one of the pair would work late afternoons and evenings while the other worked mornings. They both agreed that the program worked well, although making such a relationship work required a great deal of time and preparation.[25]

job sharing *An arrangement that allows two or more individuals to split a traditional 40-hour-a-week job.*

Only 12 percent of large organizations now offer job sharing, a decline from 18 percent in 2008.[26] Reasons it is not more widely adopted are likely the difficulty of finding compatible partners to share a job and the historically negative perceptions of individuals not completely committed to their jobs and employers.

Job sharing allows an organization to draw on the talents of more than one individual for a given job. It also opens the opportunity to acquire skilled workers—for instance, women with young children and retirees—who might not be available on a full-time basis. From the employee's perspective, job sharing increases flexibility and can increase motivation and satisfaction when a 40-hour-a-week job is just not practical. But the major drawback is finding compatible pairs of employees who can successfully coordinate the intricacies of one job.[27]

An employer's decision to use job sharing is often based on economics and national policy. Two part-time employees sharing a job can be less expensive than one full-time employee, but experts suggest this is not the case because training, coordination, and administrative costs can be high. In the United States, the national Affordable Care Act may create an incentive for companies to increase job sharing arrangements in order to avoid the fees employees must pay the government for full-time employees.[28] Many German and Japanese[29] firms have been using job sharing—but for a very different reason. Germany's Kurzarbeit program, which is now close to 100 years old, has kept employment levels from plummeting throughout the economic crisis by switching full-time workers to part-time job sharing work.[30]

telecommuting *Working from home at least two days a week on a computer that is linked to the employer's office.*

Telecommuting   It might be close to the ideal job for many people. No commuting, flexible hours, freedom to dress as you please, and few or no interruptions from colleagues. It's called **telecommuting**, and it refers to working at home at least 2 days a week on a computer linked to the employer's office.[31] (A closely related term—the *virtual office*—describes working from home on a relatively permanent basis.) As noted in the opening vignette, telecommuting has been a popular topic lately as a result of companies such as Yahoo! (and Best Buy) eliminating this form of flexible work.[32]

The U.S. Department of the Census estimated there was a 25 percent increase in self-employed home-based workers from 1999 to 2005 and a 20 percent increase in employed workers who work exclusively from home.[33] One recent

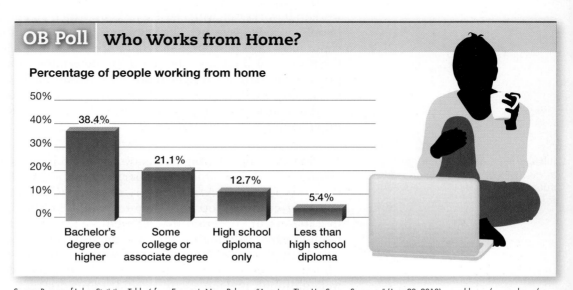

OB Poll   Who Works from Home?

Percentage of people working from home

- Bachelor's degree or higher: 38.4%
- Some college or associate degree: 21.1%
- High school diploma only: 12.7%
- Less than high school diploma: 5.4%

Source: Bureau of Labor Statistics, Table 6 from Economic News Release, "American Time Use Survey Summary" (June 20, 2013), www.bls.gov/news.release/atus.t06.htm.

survey of nearly 500 organizations found that 57 percent of organizations offered telecommuting, with 36 percent allowing employees to telecommute at least part of the time and 20 percent allowing employees to telecommute full-time, and these percentages have remained relatively stable since 2008.[34] Well-known organizations that actively encourage telecommuting include AT&T, IBM, American Express, Sun Microsystems, and a number of U.S. government agencies.[35]

What kinds of jobs lend themselves to telecommuting? There are three categories: routine information-handling tasks, mobile activities, and professional and other knowledge-related tasks.[36] Writers, attorneys, analysts, and employees who spend the majority of their time on computers or the telephone—including telemarketers, customer-service representatives, reservation agents, and product-support specialists—are natural candidates. As telecommuters, they can access information on their computers at home as easily as in the company's office.

There are several potential benefits of telecommuting. They include a larger labor pool from which to select, higher productivity, less turnover, improved morale, and reduced office-space costs. A positive relationship exists between telecommuting and supervisor performance ratings, but any relationship between telecommuting and potentially lower turnover intentions has not been substantiated in research to date.[37] Beyond the benefits to organizations and its employees, telecommuting has potential benefits to society. One study estimates that, in the United States, if people telecommuted half the time, carbon emissions would be reduced by approximately 51 metric tons per year. Environmental savings could also come about from lower office energy consumption, fewer traffic jams that emit greenhouse gasses, and fewer road repairs.[38]

However, there are also several downsides. The major one for management is less direct supervision of employees. In today's team-focused workplace, telecommuting may make it more difficult to coordinate teamwork and can reduce knowledge transfer in organizations.[39] From the employee's standpoint, telecommuting can offer a considerable increase in flexibility and job satisfaction—but not without costs.[40] For employees with a high social need, telecommuting can increase feelings of isolation and reduce job satisfaction. And all telecommuters are vulnerable to the "out of sight, out of mind" effect.[41] Employees who aren't at their desks, who miss meetings, and who don't share in day-to-day informal workplace interactions may be at a disadvantage when it comes to raises and promotions because they're perceived as not putting in the requisite "face-time."

The Social and Physical Context of Work

Robin and Chris both graduated from college a couple years ago with degrees in elementary education and became first-grade teachers in different school districts. Robin immediately confronted a number of obstacles: Several long-term employees were hostile to her hiring, there was tension between administrators and teachers, and students had little interest in learning. Chris had a colleague who was excited to work with a new graduate, students who were excited about academics, and a highly supportive principal. Not surprisingly, at the end of the first year, Chris had been a considerably more effective teacher than Robin.

The job characteristics model shows most employees are more motivated and satisfied when their intrinsic work tasks are engaging. However, having the most interesting workplace characteristics in the world may not always lead to satisfaction if you feel isolated from your co-workers, and having good social relationships can make even the most boring and onerous tasks more fulfilling. Research demonstrates that social aspects and work context are as important as other job design features.[42] Policies such as job rotation, worker empowerment, and employee participation have positive effects on productivity, at least partially because they encourage more communication and a positive social environment.

Some social characteristics that improve job performance include interdependence, social support, and interactions with other people outside of work. Social interactions are strongly related to positive moods and give employees opportunities to clarify their work role and how well they are performing. Social support gives employees greater opportunities to obtain assistance with their work. Constructive social relationships can bring about a positive feedback loop as employees assist one another in a "virtuous circle."

The work context is also likely to affect employee satisfaction. Hot, loud, and dangerous work is less satisfying than work conducted in climate-controlled, relatively quiet, and safe environments. This is probably why most people would rather work in a coffee shop than a metalworking foundry. Physical demands make people physically uncomfortable, which is likely to show up in lower levels of job satisfaction.

To assess why an employee is not performing to his or her best level, see whether the work environment is supportive. Does the employee have adequate tools, equipment, materials, and supplies? Does the employee have favorable working conditions, helpful co-workers, supportive work rules and procedures, sufficient information to make job-related decisions, and adequate time to do a good job? If not, performance will suffer.

Employee Involvement

employee involvement   *A participative process that uses the input of employees and is intended to increase employee commitment to an organization's success.*

Employee involvement is a participative process that uses employees' input to increase their commitment to the organization's success. The logic is that if we engage workers in decisions that affect them and increase their autonomy and control over their work lives, they will become more motivated, more committed to the organization, more productive, and more satisfied with their jobs. These benefits don't stop with individuals—when teams are given more control over their work, morale and performance increases.[43]

Employee involvement programs differ among countries.[44] A study of four countries, including the United States and India, confirmed the importance of modifying practices to reflect national culture.[45] While U.S. employees readily accepted employee involvement programs, managers in India who tried to empower their employees were rated low by those employees. These reactions are consistent with India's high power–distance culture, which accepts and expects differences in authority. Similarly, Chinese workers who were very accepting of traditional Chinese values showed few benefits from participative decision making, but workers who were less traditional were more satisfied and had higher performance ratings under participative management.[46] Another study conducted in China, however, showed that involvement increased employees' thoughts and feelings of job security, enhancing their well-being.[47]

Examples of Employee Involvement Programs

Let's look at two major forms of employee involvement—participative management and representative participation—in more detail.

Photo 8-2 At Wegmans Food Markets, subordinates share a significant degree of decision-making power with their immediate superiors. Wegmans believes that involving employees, like the store chef shown here, in making decisions that affect their work and please customers leads to higher job satisfaction and productivity.

Source: AP Photo/Jacquelyn Martin.

participative management *A process in which subordinates share a significant degree of decision-making power with their immediate superiors.*

representative participation *A system in which workers participate in organizational decision making through a small group of representative employees.*

4 Describe how employee involvement measures can motivate employees.

Participative Management   Common to all **participative management** programs is joint decision making, in which subordinates share a significant degree of decision-making power with their immediate superiors. Participative management has, at times, been promoted as a panacea for poor morale and low productivity. For participative management to be effective, followers must have trust and confidence in their leaders. Leaders should refrain from coercive techniques and instead stress the organizational consequences of decision making to their followers.[48]

Studies of the participation–performance relationship have yielded mixed findings.[49] Organizations that institute participative management do have higher stock returns, lower turnover rates, and higher estimated labor productivity, although these effects are typically not large.[50] A careful review of research at the individual level shows participation typically has only a modest influence on employee productivity, motivation, and job satisfaction. Of course, this doesn't mean participative management can't be beneficial under the right conditions. However, it is not a sure means for improving performance.

Representative Participation   Almost every country in western Europe requires companies to practice **representative participation**, called "the most widely legislated form of employee involvement around the world."[51] Its goal is to redistribute power within an organization, putting labor on a more equal footing with the interests of management and stockholders by letting workers be represented by a small group of employees who actually participate.

The two most common forms are works councils and board representatives.[52] Works councils are groups of nominated or elected employees who must be consulted when management makes decisions about employees. Board representatives are employees who sit on a company's board of directors and represent employees' interests.

The influence of representative participation on working employees seems to be minimal.[53] Works councils are dominated by management and have little impact on employees or the organization. While participation might increase the motivation and satisfaction of employee representatives, there is little evidence this trickles down to the employees they represent. Overall, "the greatest value of representative participation is symbolic. If one is interested in changing employee attitudes or in improving organizational performance, representative participation would be a poor choice."[54]

Linking Employee Involvement Programs and Motivation Theories

Employee involvement draws on a number of the motivation theories we discussed in Chapter 7. Theory Y is consistent with participative management and Theory X with the more traditional autocratic style of managing people. In terms of two-factor theory, employee involvement programs could provide intrinsic motivation by increasing opportunities for growth, responsibility, and involvement in the work itself. The opportunity to make and implement decisions—and then see them work out—can help satisfy an employee's needs for responsibility, achievement, recognition, growth, and enhanced self-esteem. Extensive employee involvement programs clearly have the potential to increase employee intrinsic motivation in work tasks. And giving employees control over key decisions, along with ensuring that their interests are represented, can enhance feelings of procedural justice.

Using Rewards to Motivate Employees

5 Demonstrate how the different types of variable-pay programs can increase employee motivation.

As we saw in Chapter 3, pay is not a primary factor driving job satisfaction. However, it does motivate people, and companies often underestimate its importance in keeping top talent. A 2006 study found that while 45 percent of employers thought pay was a key factor in losing top talent, 71 percent of top performers called it a top reason.[55]

Given that pay is so important, will the organization lead, match, or lag the market in pay? How will individual contributions be recognized? In this section, we consider (1) what to pay employees (decided by establishing a pay structure), (2) how to pay individual employees (decided through variable-pay plans and skill-based pay plans), (3) what benefits and choices to offer (such as flexible benefits), and (4) how to construct employee recognition programs.

What to Pay: Establishing a Pay Structure

There are many ways to pay employees. The process of initially setting pay levels entails balancing *internal equity*—the worth of the job to the organization (usually established through a technical process called job evaluation)—and *external equity*—the external competitiveness of an organization's pay relative to pay elsewhere in its industry (usually established through pay surveys). Obviously, the best pay system pays what the job is worth (internal equity) while also paying competitively relative to the labor market.

Some organizations prefer to pay above the market, while some may lag the market because they can't afford to pay market rates, or they are willing to bear the costs of paying below market (namely, higher turnover as people are lured to better-paying jobs). Some companies who have realized impressive gains in income and profit margins have done so partially by holding down employee wages, such as Comcast, Walt Disney, McDonald's, and AT&T.[56]

Pay more, and you may get better-qualified, more highly motivated employees who will stay with the organization longer. A study covering 126 large organizations found employees who believed they were receiving a competitive pay level had higher morale and were more productive, and customers were more satisfied as well.[57] But pay is often the highest single operating cost for an organization, which means paying too much can make the organization's products or services too expensive. It's a strategic decision an organization must make, with clear trade-offs.

In the case of Walmart, it appears that its strategic decision has not been working as of late. While annual growth in U.S. stores has slowed to around 1 percent, one of Walmart's larger competitors, Costco, has grown around 8 percent. The average worker at Costco made approximately $45,000 in 2011, compared to approximately $17,500 for the average worker at Walmart-owned Sam's Club. Costco's strategy is that they will get more if they pay more—higher wages are resulting in increased employee productivity and reduced turnover.

How to Pay: Rewarding Individual Employees Through Variable-Pay Programs

"Why should I put any extra effort into this job?" asked Anne Garcia, a fourth-grade elementary schoolteacher in Denver, Colorado. "I can excel or I can do the bare minimum. It makes no difference. I get paid the same. Why do anything above the minimum to get by?" Comments like Anne's have been voiced by schoolteachers for decades because pay increases were tied to seniority.

Recently, however, a number of states have revamped their compensation systems to motivate people like Anne by tying teacher pay levels to results in the classroom in various ways, and other states are considering such programs.[58]

A number of organizations are moving away from paying solely on credentials or length of service. Piece-rate plans, merit-based pay, bonuses, profit sharing, gainsharing, and employee stock ownership plans are all forms of a **variable-pay program**, which bases a portion of an employee's pay on some individual and/or organizational measure of performance. Earnings therefore fluctuate up and down.[59]

variable-pay program *A pay plan that bases a portion of an employee's pay on some individual and/or organizational measure of performance.*

Variable-pay plans have long been used to compensate salespeople and executives. Globally, around 80 percent of companies offer some form of variable-pay plan. In Latin America, more than 90 percent of companies offer some form of variable-pay plan. Latin American companies also have the highest percentage of total payroll allocated to variable pay, at nearly 18 percent. European and U.S. companies are relatively lower, at about 12 percent.[60] When it comes to executive compensation, Asian companies are outpacing Western companies in their use of variable pay.[61]

Recent research shows that 26 percent of U.S. companies have either increased or plan to increase the proportion of variable pay in employee pay programs, and another 40 percent have already recently increased the proportion of variable pay.[62] Unfortunately, not all employees see a strong connection between pay and performance. The results of pay-for-performance plans are mixed; context and the receptivity of the individual to the plans play a large role. A recent study of 415 companies in South Korea suggested that group-based pay-for-performance plans can have a strong positive effect on organizational performance.[63]

The fluctuation in variable pay is what makes these programs attractive to management. It turns part of an organization's fixed labor costs into a variable cost, thus reducing expenses when performance declines. When the U.S. economy encountered a recession in 2001 and again in 2008, companies with variable pay were able to reduce their labor costs much faster than others.[64] When pay is tied to performance, the employee's earnings also recognize contribution rather than being a form of entitlement. Over time, low performers' pay stagnates, while high performers enjoy pay increases commensurate with their contributions.

Let's examine the different types of variable-pay programs in more detail.

Photo 8-3 Following the widespread adoption of variable-pay plans in businesses and government agencies, many schools are moving toward rewarding teachers with bonuses for individual performance. The teacher shown here can earn a bonus based on her performance rather than only on her seniority or academic degrees.

Source: AP Photo/David J. Phillip.

piece-rate pay plan *A pay plan in which workers are paid a fixed sum for each unit of production completed.*

Piece-Rate Pay The **piece-rate pay plan** has long been popular as a means of compensating production workers with a fixed sum for each unit of production completed. A pure piece-rate plan provides no base salary and pays the employee only for what he or she produces. Ballpark workers selling peanuts and soda are frequently paid this way. If they sell 40 bags of peanuts at $1 each for their earnings, their take is $40. The harder they work and the more peanuts they sell, the more they earn. The limitation of these plans is that they're not feasible for many jobs. Surgeons earn significant salaries regardless of their patients' outcomes. Would it be better to pay them only if their patients fully recover? It seems unlikely that most would accept such a deal, and it might cause unanticipated consequences as well (such as surgeons avoiding patients with complicated or terminal conditions). So, although incentives are motivating and relevant for some jobs, it is unrealistic to think they can constitute the only piece of some employees' pay.

merit-based pay plan *A pay plan based on performance appraisal ratings.*

Merit-Based Pay A **merit-based pay plan** pays for individual performance based on performance appraisal ratings. A main advantage is that people thought to be high performers can get bigger raises. If designed correctly, merit-based plans let individuals perceive a strong relationship between their performance and their rewards.[65]

Most large organizations have merit pay plans, especially for salaried employees. Merit pay is slowly taking hold in the public sector. Most government employees are unionized, and the unions that represent them have usually demanded that pay raises be based solely on seniority. Claiming a new era of accountability, however, New Jersey Governor Chris Christie recently implemented merit pay for teachers. The Newark teachers union approved the plan, which included funding from Facebook CEO Mark Zuckerberg.[66] In another unusual move, New York City's public hospital system, instead of granting automatic annual raises, pays doctors based on how well they reduce costs, increase patient satisfaction, and improve the quality of care.[67]

A move away from merit pay, on the other hand, is coming from some organizations that don't feel it separates high and low performers enough. "There's a very strong belief and there's evidence and academic research that shows that variable pay does create focus among employees," said Ken Abosch, a compensation manager at human-resource consulting firm Aon Hewitt. Even those companies that have retained merit pay are rethinking the allocation.[68]

Although you might think a person's average level of performance is the key factor in merit pay decisions, recent research indicates that the projected level of future performance also plays a role. One study found that National Basketball Association players whose performance was on an upward trend were paid more than their average performance would have predicted. The upshot? Managers may unknowingly be basing merit pay decisions on how they *think* employees will perform, which may result in overly optimistic (or pessimistic) pay decisions.[69]

Despite their intuitive appeal, merit pay plans have several limitations. One is that they are typically based on an annual performance appraisal and thus are only as valid as the performance ratings. Another limitation is that the pay-raise pool fluctuates on economic or other conditions that have little to do with individual performance. One year, a colleague at a top university who performed very well in teaching and research was given a pay raise of $300. Why? Because the pay-raise pool was very small. Yet that is hardly pay-for-performance. Finally, unions typically resist merit pay plans. Relatively few teachers are covered by merit pay for this reason. Instead, seniority-based pay, where all employees get the same raises, predominates.

Photo 8-4 Chinese Internet firm Tencent Holdings rewards employees with attractive incentives that include cash bonuses for lower-ranking employees. The young men shown here were among 5,000 employees who received a special bonus tucked in red envelopes and personally handed out by Tencent's CEO and co-founder Pony Ma.

Source: Imaginechina via AP Images.

bonus *A pay plan that rewards employees for recent performance rather than historical performance.*

Bonuses An annual **bonus** is a significant component of total compensation for many jobs. Among *Fortune* 100 CEOs, the bonus (mean of $1.01 million) generally exceeds the base salary (mean of $863,000). But bonus plans increasingly include lower-ranking employees; many companies now routinely reward production employees with bonuses in the thousands of dollars when profits improve. The incentive effects of performance bonuses should be higher than those of merit pay because, rather than paying for performance years ago (that was rolled into base pay), bonuses reward recent performance. When times are bad, firms can cut bonuses to reduce compensation costs. Workers on Wall Street, for example, saw their average bonus drop by more than a third in 2012 as their firms faced greater scrutiny.[70]

This example also highlights the downside of bonuses: Employees' pay is more vulnerable to cuts. This is problematic when bonuses are a large percentage of total pay or when employees take bonuses for granted. "People have begun to live as if bonuses were not bonuses at all but part of their expected annual income," said Jay Lorsch, a Harvard Business School professor. KeySpan Corp., a 9,700-employee utility company in New York, tried to combine yearly bonuses with a smaller merit-pay raise. Elaine Weinstein, KeySpan's senior vice president of HR, credits the plan with changing the culture from "entitlement to meritocracy."[71]

Recent research has shown that the way bonuses and rewards are categorized also affects peoples' motivation. Dividing rewards and bonuses into multiple categories—even if those categories are meaningless—makes people work harder. Why? Because they are more likely to feel as if they "missed out" on a reward if they don't receive one from each category. Although admittedly a bit manipulative sounding, taking rewards and bonuses and splitting them into categories may increase motivation.[72]

skill-based pay *A pay plan that sets pay levels on the basis of how many skills employees have or how many jobs they can do.*

Skill-Based Pay Skill-based pay (also called *competency-based* or *knowledge-based pay*) is an alternative to job-based pay that bases pay levels on how many skills employees have or how many jobs they can do.[73] For employers, the lure of skill-based pay plans is increased flexibility of the workforce: Staffing is easier when employee skills are interchangeable. Skill-based pay also facilitates communication across the organization because people gain a better understanding of each other's jobs. One study found that across 214 different organizations, skill-based pay was related to higher levels of workforce flexibility, positive attitudes, membership behaviors, and productivity.[74] Another study found that over 5 years, a skill-based pay plan was associated with higher levels of individual skill change and skill maintenance.[75] These results suggest that skill-based pay plans are effective in achieving their stated goals.

What about the downsides? People can "top out"—that is, they can learn all the skills the program calls for them to learn. This can frustrate employees after they've been challenged by an environment of learning, growth, and continual pay raises. Plus, skill-based plans don't address the level of performance but only whether someone can perform the skill. Perhaps reflecting these weaknesses, one study of 97 U.S. companies using skill-based pay plans found that 39 percent had switched to a more traditional market-based pay plan 7 years later.[76]

profit-sharing plan *An organization-wide program that distributes compensation based on some established formula designed around a company's profitability.*

Profit-Sharing Plans   A **profit-sharing plan** distributes compensation based on some established formula designed around a company's profitability. Compensation can be direct cash outlays or, particularly for top managers, allocations of stock options. When you read about executives like Oracle's Larry Ellison, the top-earning U.S. CEO, earning $96.2 million, much of it ($90.7 million) comes from stock options previously granted based on company profit performance.[77] Or, take Facebook's Mark Zuckerberg, who despite accepting a $1 salary, made a whopping $2.3 billion in 2012 after cashing out 60,000 stock options.[78] Of course, the vast majority of profit-sharing plans are not so grand in scale. Jacob Luke, age 13, started his own lawn-mowing business after getting a mower from his uncle. Jacob employs his brother, Isaiah, and friend, Marcel Monroe, and pays them each 25 percent of the profits he makes on each yard. Profit-sharing plans at the organizational level appear to have positive impacts on employee attitudes; employees report a greater feeling of psychological ownership.[79]

gainsharing *A formula-based group incentive plan.*

Gainsharing   **Gainsharing**[80] is a formula-based group incentive plan that uses improvements in group productivity from one period to another to determine the total amount of money allocated. Its popularity seems narrowly focused among large manufacturing companies, although some health care organizations have experimented with it as a cost-saving mechanism. Gainsharing differs from profit sharing in tying rewards to productivity gains rather than profits, so employees can receive incentive awards even when the organization isn't profitable. Because the benefits accrue to groups of workers, high performers pressure weaker ones to work harder, improving performance for the group as a whole.[81]

employee stock ownership plan (ESOP) *A company-established benefits plan in which employees acquire stock, often at below-market prices, as part of their benefits.*

Employee Stock Ownership Plans   An **employee stock ownership plan (ESOP)** is a company-established benefit plan in which employees acquire stock, often at below-market prices, as part of their benefits. Companies as varied as Publix Supermarkets and W. L. Gore & Associates are now more than 50 percent employee-owned.[82] But most of the 10,000 or so ESOPs in the United States are in small, privately held companies.[83]

Research on ESOPs indicates they increase employee satisfaction and innovation.[84] But their impact on performance is less clear. ESOPs have the potential to increase employee job satisfaction and work motivation, but employees need to psychologically experience ownership.[85] That is, in addition to their financial stake in the company, they need to be kept regularly informed of the status of the business and have the opportunity to influence it in order to significantly improve the organization's performance.[86]

ESOP plans for top management can reduce unethical behavior. CEOs are more likely to manipulate firm earnings reports to make themselves look good in the short run when they don't have an ownership share, even though this manipulation will eventually lead to lower stock prices. However, when CEOs own a large amount of stock, they report earnings accurately because they don't want the negative consequences of declining stock prices.[87]

Evaluation of Variable Pay   Do variable-pay programs increase motivation and productivity? Studies generally support the idea that organizations with profit-sharing plans have higher levels of profitability than those without them.[88] Profit-sharing plans have also been linked to higher levels of employee affective commitment, especially in small organizations.[89] One study found that whereas piece-rate pay-for-performance plans stimulated higher levels of productivity, this positive affect was not observed for risk-averse employees. Thus, economist Ed Lazear seems generally right when he says, "Workers respond to prices just as economic theory predicts. Claims by sociologists and others that monetizing incentives may actually reduce output are unambiguously refuted by the data." But that doesn't mean everyone responds positively to variable-pay plans.[90]

You'd probably think individual pay systems such as merit pay or pay-for-performance work better in individualistic cultures such as the United States or that group-based rewards such as gainsharing or profit sharing work better

An Ethical Choice

Sweatshops and Worker Safety

The United States, as well as many other countries, has come a long way in terms of worker safety and compensation. The number of worker-related injuries has decreased substantially over generations, and many employees earn better wages. Unfortunately, the same cannot be said for other parts of the world.

To keep costs down, many companies and their managers turn to developing nations, where people are willing to work for low pay and no benefits. The poor, often unregulated working conditions of manual labor "sweatshops" are common, especially in the garment industry. However, three recent accidents in Bangladesh are raising ethical questions about using this type of labor. In November 2012, a fire at the Tazreen Fashion factory that made low-cost garments for U.S. stores, including Walmart, killed 112 workers. In April 2013, the collapse of Rana Plaza, home to a number of

garment factories, killed more than 1,100 workers. And in May 2013, a fire at the Tung Hai Sweater Company killed 8 workers. An investigation of the Rana Plaza incident revealed that the building had been constructed without permits, using poor materials. Although workers there reported seeing and hearing cracks in the structure of the building, they were ordered back to work. Because these individuals work in top-down management structures without participative management opportunities, and do not have unions to represent them, their concerns were not heeded.

Although pulling completely out of countries such as Bangladesh may only hurt individuals there who rely on this work to make a living, managers should take steps to raise safety standards. Some companies, such as PVH, owner of Tommy Hilfiger and Calvin Klein, as well as Tchibo, a German retailer, have signed the legally binding

"IndustriALL" proposal, which requires manufacturers to conduct building and fire-safety inspections regularly and to make their findings public. Many other companies have not signed, and it remains to be seen if this standard will effect real change for the workers, at least in terms of their safety. Some companies are attracted to countries with sweatshops precisely because they lack regulation and oversight and offer workers willing to work for less than $50 a month. Managers thus face a decision about whether to spend extra effort and money to ensure safe and equitable working conditions for all of their workers, either at home or abroad.

Sources: J. O'Donnell and C. Macleod, "Latest Bangladesh Fire Puts New Pressure on Retailers," *USA Today* (May 9, 2013), www.usatoday.com; and T. Hayden, "Tom Hayden: Sweatshops Attract Western Investors," *USA Today* (May 17, 2013), www.usatoday.com.

in collectivistic cultures. Unfortunately, there isn't much research on the issue. One recent study did suggest that employee beliefs about the fairness of a group incentive plan were more predictive of pay satisfaction in the United States than in Hong Kong. One interpretation is that U.S. employees are more critical in appraising a group pay plan, and therefore, it's more critical that the plan be communicated clearly and administered fairly.[91]

Flexible Benefits: Developing a Benefits Package

6   Show how flexible benefits turn benefits into motivators.

Todd E. is married and has three young children; his wife is at home full-time. His Citigroup colleague Allison M. is married too, but her husband has a high-paying job with the federal government, and they have no children. Todd is concerned about having a good medical plan and enough life insurance to support his family in case it's needed. In contrast, Allison's husband already has her medical needs covered on his plan, and life insurance is a low priority. Allison is more interested in extra vacation time and long-term financial benefits such as a tax-deferred savings plan.

A standardized benefits package would be unlikely to meet the needs of Todd and Allison well. Citigroup could, however, cover both sets of needs with flexible benefits.

flexible benefits *A benefits plan that allows each employee to put together a benefits package individually tailored to his or her own needs and situation.*

Consistent with expectancy theory's thesis that organizational rewards should be linked to each individual employee's goals, **flexible benefits** individualize rewards by allowing each employee to choose the compensation package that best satisfies his or her current needs and situation. These plans replace the "one-benefit-plan-fits-all" programs designed for a male with a wife and two children at home that dominated organizations for more than 50 years.[92] Fewer than 10 percent of employees now fit this image: About 25 percent are single, and one-third are part of two-income families with no children. Flexible benefits can accommodate differences in employee needs based on age, marital status, spouses' benefit status, and number and age of dependents.

The three most popular types of benefits plans are modular plans, core-plus options, and flexible spending accounts.[93] *Modular plans* are predesigned packages or modules of benefits, each of which meets the needs of a specific group of

Photo 8-5 Accounting firm Ernst & Young has a culture of flexibility that includes flexible benefit plans to meet specific individual needs of its diverse work force. Employees like Gregston Chu in EY's security operations can choose benefits that accommodate needs based on age, marital, and parental status, and age of dependents.

Source: AP Photo/The Honolulu Advertiser, Bruce Asato.

employees. A module designed for single employees with no dependents might include only essential benefits. Another, designed for single parents, might have additional life insurance, disability insurance, and expanded health coverage. *Core-plus plans* consist of a core of essential benefits and a menulike selection of others from which employees can select. Typically, each employee is given "benefit credits," which allow the purchase of additional benefits that uniquely meet his or her needs. *Flexible spending plans* allow employees to set aside pretax dollars up to the dollar amount offered in the plan to pay for particular benefits, such as health care and dental premiums. Flexible spending accounts can increase take-home pay because employees don't pay taxes on the dollars they spend from these accounts.

Today, almost all major corporations in the United States offer flexible benefits. And they're becoming the norm in other countries, too. A recent survey of 211 Canadian organizations found that 60 percent offer flexible benefits, up from 41 percent in 2005.[94] And a similar survey of firms in the United Kingdom found that nearly all major organizations were offering flexible benefits programs, with options ranging from private supplemental medical insurance to holiday trading, discounted bus travel, and child care vouchers.[95]

Intrinsic Rewards: Employee Recognition Programs

7 Identify the motivational benefits of intrinsic rewards.

Laura makes only $8.50 per hour working at her fast-food job in Pensacola, Florida, and the job isn't very challenging or interesting. Yet Laura talks enthusiastically about the job, her boss, and the company that employs her. "What I like is the fact that Guy [her supervisor] appreciates the effort I make. He compliments me regularly in front of the other people on my shift, and I've been chosen Employee of the Month twice in the past six months. Did you see my picture on that plaque on the wall?"

Organizations are increasingly recognizing what Laura knows: Important work rewards can be both intrinsic and extrinsic. Rewards are intrinsic in the form of employee recognition programs and extrinsic in the form of compensation systems. In this section, we deal with ways in which managers can reward and motivate employee performance.

Employee recognition programs range from a spontaneous and private thank-you to widely publicized formal programs in which specific types of behavior are encouraged and the procedures for attaining recognition are clearly identified. Some research suggests financial incentives may be more motivating in the short term, but in the long run it's nonfinancial incentives.[96]

A few years ago, 1,500 employees were surveyed in a variety of work settings to find out what they considered the most powerful workplace motivator. Their response? Recognition, recognition, and more recognition. As illustrated in Exhibit 8-4, Phoenix Inn, a West Coast chain of small hotels, encourages employees to smile by letting customers identify this desirable behavior and then recognizing winning employees with rewards and publicity.

An obvious advantage of recognition programs is that they are inexpensive because praise is free![97] As companies and government organizations face tighter budgets, nonfinancial incentives become more attractive. Everett Clinic in Washington State uses a combination of local and centralized initiatives to encourage managers to recognize employees.[98] Employees and managers give "Hero Grams" and "Caught in the Act" cards to colleagues for exceptional accomplishments at work. Part of the incentive is simply to receive recognition, but there are also drawings for prizes based on the number of cards a person receives. Managers are trained to use the programs frequently and effectively to reward good performance. Multinational corporations like Symantec Corporation have also increased their use of recognition programs. Centralized

Exhibit **8-4**

PHOENIX INN SUITES

I GOT CAUGHT SMILING!

WHO WAS THE PHOENIX INN SUITES EMPLOYEE THAT MADE YOUR STAY <u>EXCEPTIONAL?</u>

EMPLOYEE NAME_____

GUEST NAME _____

ROOM # _____

DATE OF STAY _____

PLEASE EITHER LEAVE THIS IN YOUR ROOM OR DROP OFF AT THE FRONT DESK

glOBalization!

Outcry Over Executive Pay Is Heard Everywhere

Executive compensation has always been a hot topic in the media, especially following the financial crisis on Wall Street in 2008. Public outrage has flared over annual salaries, stock options, and bonuses in the millions for CEOs. In fact, it is hard to go a day without hearing or reading about executive compensation in the United States. However, the United States is not alone.

In Great Britain, for example, the total average pay of CEOs increased by 33 percent in 2010, while companies' average market value grew by 24 percent. And a study by the London School of Economics found that a 10 percent increase in a company's market value was associated with a 0.2 percent increase in worker pay but a 3 percent increase in the chief executive's pay. Public anger over the disparity in compensation has led Prime Minister David Cameron to back calls by investors to have more control over executive pay packages. Large packages, he said, understandably "made people's blood boil."

In China, CEOs are paid much less. When the Industrial and Commercial Bank of China made a whopping $38.5 billion in net profits in 2012, its chairman, Jiang Jianqing, was paid $185,000. That's less than 1 percent of what Lloyd Blankfein, CEO of Goldman Sachs, received. Yet Mr. Jianqing's compensation made him the highest paid among his peers running China's other large banks.

Despite the fact the Chinese executives are among the lowest paid relative to CEOs in other developed countries, their pay levels are still controversial. Like the public in the United States and Britain, the Chinese public is angered over the large inequalities between CEOs and workers. However, many Chinese academics and analysts argue that CEOs in China are paid too *little*, making it difficult to create pay-for-performance systems that better match company profits with compensation.

Sources: S. Rabinovitch, "China's Bosses Criticised Over High Pay," *Financial Times .com* (2013); and J. Werdigier, "In Britain, Rising Outcry Over Executive Pay That Makes 'People's Blood Boil,'" *The New York Times* (January 23, 2012), p. B5.

programs across multiple offices in different countries can help ensure that all employees, regardless of where they work, can be recognized for their contribution to the work environment.[99] Another study found that recognition programs are common in Canadian and Australian firms as well.[100]

Despite the increased popularity of employee recognition programs, critics argue they are highly susceptible to political manipulation by management. When applied to jobs for which performance factors are relatively objective, such as sales, recognition programs are likely to be perceived by employees as fair. However, in most jobs, the criteria for good performance aren't self-evident, which allows managers to manipulate the system and recognize their favorites. Abuse can undermine the value of recognition programs and demoralize employees.

Summary

As we've seen in the chapter, the study of what motivates individuals is ultimately key to organizational performance. Employees whose differences are recognized, who feel valued, and who have the opportunity to work in jobs that are tailored to their strengths and interests will be motivated to perform at the highest levels. Employee participation also can increase employee productivity, commitment to work goals, motivation, and job satisfaction.

Implications for Managers

- *Recognize individual differences.*   Spend the time necessary to understand what's important to each employee. Design jobs to align with individual needs and maximize their motivation potential.
- *Use goals and feedback.*   You should give employees firm, specific goals, and they should get feedback on how well they are faring in pursuit of those goals.
- *Allow employees to participate in decisions that affect them.*   Employees can contribute to setting work goals, choosing their own benefits packages, and solving productivity and quality problems.
- *Link rewards to performance.*   Rewards should be contingent on performance, and employees must perceive the link between the two.
- *Check the system for equity.*   Employees should perceive that experience, skills, abilities, effort, and other obvious inputs explain differences in performance and hence in pay, job assignments, and other obvious rewards.

"Face-Time" Matters

Although allowing employees to work from home is gaining popularity, telecommuting is a practice that will only hurt them and their employers. Sure, employees say they're happier when their organization allows them the flexibility to work wherever they choose, but who wouldn't like to hang around at home in their pajamas pretending to work? I know plenty of colleagues who say, with a wink, that they're taking off to "work from home" the rest of the day. Who knows whether they are really contributing?

The bigger problem is the lack of face-to-face interaction between employees. Studies have shown that great ideas are born through interdependence, not independence. It's during those informal interactions around the water cooler or during coffee breaks that some of the most creative ideas arise. If you take that away, you stifle the organization's creative potential.

Trust is another problem. Ever trust someone you haven't met? I didn't think so. Again, face-to-face interactions allow people to establish trusting relationships more quickly, which fosters smoother social interactions and allows the company to perform better.

But enough about employers. Employees also would benefit by burning the midnight oil at the office. If you're out of sight, you're out of mind. Want that big raise or promotion? You're not going to get it if your supervisor doesn't even know who you are.

So think twice the next time you either want to leave the office early or not bother coming in at all, to "work from home."

Please. So-called face-time is overrated. If all managers do is reward employees who hang around the office the longest, they aren't being very good managers. Those who brag about the 80 hours they put in at the office (being sure to point out they were there on weekends) aren't necessarily the top performers. Being present is not the same thing as being efficient.

Besides, there are all sorts of benefits for employees and employers who take advantage of telecommuting practices. For one, it's seen as an attractive perk companies can offer. With so many dual-career earners, the flexibility to work from home on some days can go a long way toward achieving a better balance between work and family. That translates into better recruiting and better retention. In other words, you'll get and keep better employees if you offer the ability to work from home.

Plus, studies have shown that productivity is *higher*, not lower, when people work from home. This result is not limited to the United States. For example, one study found that Chinese call center employees who worked from home outproduced their "face-time" counterparts by 13 percent.

You say all these earth-shattering ideas would pour forth if people interacted. I say consider that one of the biggest workplace distractions is chatty co-workers. So, although I concede there are times when "face-time" is beneficial, the benefits of telecommuting far outweigh the drawbacks.

Sources: J. Surowiecki, "Face Time," *The New Yorker* (March 18, 2013), www.newyorker.com; and L. Taskin and F. Bridoux, "Telework: A Challenge to Knowledge Transfer in Organizations," *International Journal of Human Resource Management* 21, no. 13 (2010), pp. 2503–2520.

END-OF-CHAPTER REVIEW

MyManagementLab

Go to **mymanagementlab.com** to complete the problems marked with this icon. ⭐

QUESTIONS FOR REVIEW

8-1 What is the job characteristics model? How does it motivate employees?

8-2 What are the three major ways that jobs can be redesigned? In your view, in what situations would one of the methods be favored over the others?

8-3 What are the three alternative work arrangements of flextime, job sharing, and telecommuting? What are the advantages and disadvantages of each?

8-4 What are employee involvement programs? How might they increase employee motivation?

8-5 What is variable pay? What are the variable-pay programs that are used to motivate employees? What are their advantages and disadvantages?

8-6 How can flexible benefits motivate employees?

8-7 What are the motivational benefits of intrinsic rewards?

EXPERIENTIAL EXERCISE   Applying the Job Characteristics Model

Purpose
This exercise will help you understand how the job characteristics model relates to different occupations.

Time
Approximately 30 minutes.

Instructions
- Break into groups of three to five.

  8-8. As a group, consider each of the five job characteristics (skill variety, task identity, task significance, autonomy, and feedback). Then, write down jobs that have high levels of each characteristic (if you

can think of jobs that have high levels of multiple characteristics, note those as well). Do you think the jobs you identified are high or low paying? Why?

8-9. Next, write down jobs that have low levels of each characteristic (and if you can think of jobs that have low levels of multiple characteristics, note those as well.) Do you think the jobs you identified are high or low paying? Why?

8-10. For those jobs you identified as having low levels of job characteristics, come up with some strategies to increase them. Be specific in your recommendations. Class discussion will follow.

ETHICAL DILEMMA   Inmates for Hire

We've all heard about how companies are using overseas workers to reduce labor costs, but the real cost savings for some jobs may lie with prison workers. Federal Prison Industries (FPI, also called UNICOR) is a company that is owned by the government but employs prison inmates. Like some overseas sweatshop workers, prisoners are paid exceptionally low at 23 cents to $1.15 an hour, receive no benefits for their work, and do not work in a participative management environment. The motivation for them to work hard is instead completely intrinsic: to learn trade skills and the value of work while they are incarcerated, in hopes that they will be more employable upon their release.

Although the organization is unable to supply workers to the private sector, federal agencies are required to purchase goods produced by its workers whenever FPI's bids are competitive. Steven Eisen, chief financial officer of Tennier Industries, came face-to-face with FPI when his company lost a $45 million contract to manufacture clothing for the U.S. Defense Department. One hundred of Tennier's workers were laid off as a result. He argues it is wrong to give jobs to prison inmates at the expense of law-abiding citizens who may be struggling to find employment. "Our government screams, howls, and yells how the rest of the world is using prisoners or slave labor to manufacture items, and here we take the items right out of the mouths of people who need it," says Eisen.

Proponents of the program say it is beneficial to inmates, pointing to data from the Bureau of Prisons showing that inmates who work for FPI are 24 percent less likely to be incarcerated again and 14 percent more likely to be employed when released. Traci Billingsley, speaking for the Bureau of Prisons, states, "FPI supplies only a small fraction of the government's goods and services. FPI also helps support American jobs as it often partners with private American companies as a supplier."

Questions

8-11. Do you think it is fair for companies to have to compete against prison inmates for government work? Why or why not?

✪ **8-12.** Michigan Representative Bill Huizenga says, "If China did this—having their prisoners work at subpar wages in prisons—we would be screaming bloody murder." Do you agree or disagree with his statement? Is it ever okay to use prison labor? If so, when? If not, why not?

8-13. Do you think prisoner employees should have any benefits other workers have? Why or why not?

Sources: Based on D. Cardwell, "Competing with Prison Labor," *The New York Times* (March 15, 2012), pp. 1, 4.

CASE INCIDENT 1   Motivation for Leisure

"When I have time I don't have money. When I have money I don't have time," says Glenn Kelman, chief executive officer of Redfin. He's not alone. While many workers find themselves faced with 60-, 70-, or 80-hour weeks (and sometimes more); others who are unemployed can find themselves with too much time on their hands. Take Dennis Lee, a sales associate working in Chicago whose girlfriend is unemployed. She has time to spare, but he says her unemployment makes it "financially impossible for me to support the both of us, even if we just go on a small trip, like, to Wisconsin and get a small hotel and stay for a couple of days."

Yet some argue that individuals choose to be unemployed to take advantage of social safety nets and enjoy a more leisurely lifestyle. Casey Mulligan, a University of Chicago economist, says, "I estimate that half of the drop in the employment-population ratio came from an expansion of the social safety net."

Those who are employed and who may have the financial means to take a vacation often leave those vacation days on the table. The average U.S. worker gets 2.6 weeks of vacation a year, yet only 43 percent take that time. Although the reasons U.S. employees may not be motivated to take their vacation time vary from a sense of job insecurity to heavy employer workload demands, some companies now let employees trade vacation days for cash, essentially selling the vacation hours they do not intend to use. Other employers cap the amount of vacation time that can be accrued.

The challenge of taking leisure time does not seem to be a problem for many European countries. Take the French, who get 30 days of vacation and say they take all of them. In fact, if you work in the European Union and get sick on vacation, the European Court of Justice says you are entitled to take a make-up vacation.

Questions

8-14. Why do you think U.S. workers are given so little vacation time relative to norms in other countries?

✪ **8-15.** Why do you think U.S. workers often do not take all of their allotted vacation time, even when sometimes faced with losing the benefit when vacation days are capped? Are these personal choices, or are they driven more by society, or by organizational culture?

8-16. If many unemployed are spending around two hours/day looking for work as some research indicates, do you think that means they are enjoying a "leisurely" lifestyle? Why or why not? If unemployed, how would you spend your days?

Sources: P. Coy, "The Leisure Gap," *Bloomberg Businessweek,* (July 23–29, 2012), pp. 8–10; A. B. Krueger and A. I. Mueller, "Time Use, Emotional Well-Being, and Unemployment: Evidence from Longitudinal Data," *American Economic Review* (May 2012), pp. 594–599; and L. Kwoh, "More Firms Offer Option to Swap Cash for Time," *The Wall Street Journal* (September 26, 2012), p. B6.

CASE INCIDENT 2 Attaching the Carrot to the Stick

It seems like commonsense that people work harder when there are incentives at stake, but many scholars question this premise. Alfie Kohn has long suggested that workers are "punished by rewards" and urges that organizations avoid tying rewards to performance because of the negative consequences that can result. As an alternative to rewards, some experts recommend that managers foster a positive, upbeat work environment in hopes that enthusiasm will translate into motivation.

Although rewards *can* be motivating, they can reduce employees' intrinsic interest in the tasks they are doing. Along these lines, Mark Lepper of Stanford University found that children rewarded for drawing with felt-tip pens no longer wished to use the pens at all when rewards were removed, whereas children who were not rewarded for using the pens were eager to use them. And neuroimaging researchers at Cal Tech found that when incentives reached a certain threshold, the brain's reward center began to shut down and people became distracted. According to Vikram Chib, the lead researcher on the project, people begin to worry about losing the carrot when the stakes get too high, which leads to failure.

Rewards can also lead to misbehavior by workers. Psychologist Edward Deci notes, "Once you start making people's rewards dependent on outcomes rather than behaviors, the evidence is people will take the shortest route to those outcomes." Consider factory workers paid purely based on the number of units they produce. Because only quantity is rewarded, workers may neglect quality. Executives rewarded strictly on the basis of the quarterly stock price will tend to ignore the long-term profitability and survival of the firm; they might even engage in illegal or unethical behavior to increase their compensation.

Some rewards may also have legal implications. An increasing number of companies are providing financial rewards to employees who meet health goals or participate in wellness programs, but such efforts raise concerns about discrimination against those unable to reach the goals. Incentives might not motivate employees to take a more active role in managing their health in any case. As David Anderson, vice president and chief health officer at Stay-Well Health Management, says, "An incentive itself doesn't necessarily buy engagement. It buys compliance."

However, the majority of research cited in this and the previous chapter shows that individuals given rewards for behavior will be more likely to engage in the rewarded behaviors. It is also unlikely that individuals engaged in very boring, repetitive tasks will lose their intrinsic motivation if the task is rewarded because they never had any intrinsic motivation to begin with. The real issue for managers is finding an appropriate way to reward behaviors so desired behavior is increased while less-desired behavior is reduced.

Questions

8-17. Do you think that, as a manager, you should use incentives regularly? Why or why not?

8-18. Can you think of a time in your own life when the possibility of receiving an incentive *reduced* your motivation?

8-19. What employee behaviors do you think might be best encouraged by offering incentive rewards?

Sources: Based on V. S. Chib, B. DeMartino, S. Shimojo, and J. P. O'Doherty, "Neural Mechanisms Underlying Paradoxical Performance for Monetary Incentives Are Driven by Loss Aversion," *Neuron* 74 (2012), pp. 582–594; N. Fleming, "The Bonus Myth" *New Scientist* 210 (2011), pp. 40–43; D. Woodward, "Perking Up the Workplace," *Director* (February 2011), pp. 33–34; S. Ladika, "Are Wellness Incentives Bad for Your Company's Health?" *Workforce Management* (February 2013), p. 6; and G. G. Scott, "How to Create a Motivating Environment," *Nonprofit World* 28 (September/October 2010), p. 9.

MyManagementLab

Go to **mymanagementlab.com** for Auto-graded writing questions as well as the following Assisted-graded writing questions:

8-20. How would you design a bonus/reward program to avoid the problems mentioned in Case Incident 2?

8-21. Considering the case in the Ethical Dilemma, critics of FPI point to the loss of jobs for law-abiding citizens, while advocates point to the societal benefits. At what point do programs such as FPI do more harm than good, or more good than harm?

8-22. MyManagementLab Only—comprehensive writing assignment for this chapter.

9
Foundations of Group Behavior

Source: Bloomberg via Getty Images.

BULLS AND BEARS, BUT WHAT ABOUT WOMEN?

It is never easy to be part of an outgroup, but research indicates you may be able to bridge the gap by sharing information to build relationships. Ironically, women are traditionally good at this skill, but are sometimes in the outgroup simply because they're women. People in the outgroup find it difficult to succeed even when they can objectively prove worthiness. The statistics suggest this may be the case on Wall Street. Although women make up half the workforce in the financial industry, few make it to the top of the executive ranks. Granted, the situation has improved since the 1980s, where women were few and far between, yet many are still concerned about the slow progress toward gender equality, especially in upper management.

Sallie Krawcheck (in photo) believes that her roller-coaster career is due to subtle group discrimination against her as a woman. She led Sanford C. Bernstein & Company until joining Citigroup in 2002 and eventually became chief financial officer. That lasted until 2007, when she was moved downward to oversee the brokerage unit. Then came Bank of America in 2009, where she worked until she was laid off in 2011 as a result of company restructuring.

Of course, Krawcheck was not the only person, male or female, who struggled with job security throughout the recent financial crisis. Yet she argues that the turmoil on Wall Street has resulted in a huge setback for women trying to reach the upper echelons of their companies. Why? The main reasons, she says, is that male executives are forming tighter, homogeneous groups that exclude women. "Think about it. You're going through this horrible downturn. You're a CEO. You want people who you worked with for 10 years or 20 years who you can trust. These moves have led to more homogeneous leadership teams." In other words, if you're female, you don't fit in with the "old boys' network."

Irene Dorner, chief executive at HSBC, believes that exclusivity is a mistake. "I think you are insane commercially if you run any corporation and you turn down the opportunity for different views, innovation, and a different way of thinking," she says. While it is natural for people to form groups based on their obvious similarities, such as gender, research indicates that diverse groups perform better.

Sources: E. Bernstein, "To Charm and Make Friends Fast: Share, Don't Overshare," *The Wall Street Journal* (February 19, 2013), p. D1; A. R. Sorkin, "Women in a Man's World," *The New York Times* (April 3, 2013), pp. F1, F2; and S. Craig, "Lessons on Being a Success on Wall St., and Being a Casualty," *The New York Times* (April 3, 2013), p. F2.

LEARNING OBJECTIVES

After studying this chapter, you should be able to:

1 Define *group*, and distinguish the different types of groups.

2 Identify the five stages of group development.

3 Show how role requirements change in different situations.

4 Demonstrate how norms and status exert influence on an individual's behavior.

5 Show how group size affects group performance.

6 Contrast the benefits and disadvantages of cohesive groups.

7 Explain the implications of diversity for group effectiveness.

8 Contrast the strengths and weaknesses of group decision making.

9 Compare the effectiveness of interacting, brainstorming, and the nominal group technique.

Groups have their place—and their pitfalls. Before we discuss them, examine your own attitude toward working in groups. Take the following self-assessment and answer the accompanying questions.

The objectives of this chapter and Chapter 10 are to introduce you to basic group concepts, provide you with a foundation for understanding how groups work, and show you how to create effective teams. Let's begin by defining a *group* and explaining why people join groups.

SELF-ASSESSMENT LIBRARY

Do I Have a Negative Attitude Toward Working in Groups?

In the Self-Assessment Library (available in MyManagementLab), take assessment IV.E.1 (Do I Have a Negative Attitude Toward Working in Groups?), and answer the following questions.

1. Are you surprised by your results? If yes, why? If no, why not?
2. Do you think it is important to always have a positive attitude toward working in groups? Why or why not?

Defining and Classifying Groups

1 Define *group*, and distinguish the different types of groups.

group   *Two or more individuals, interacting and interdependent, who have come together to achieve particular objectives.*

formal group   *A designated work group defined by an organization's structure.*

informal group   *A group that is neither formally structured nor organizationally determined; such a group appears in response to the need for social contact.*

social identity theory   *Perspective that considers when and why individuals consider themselves members of groups.*

We define a **group** as two or more individuals, interacting and interdependent, who have come together to achieve particular objectives. Groups can be either formal or informal. By a **formal group**, we mean one defined by the organization's structure, with designated work assignments establishing tasks. In formal groups, the behaviors team members should engage in are stipulated by and directed toward organizational goals. The six members of an airline flight crew are a formal group. In contrast, an **informal group** is neither formally structured nor organizationally determined. Informal groups are natural formations in the work environment that appear in response to the need for social contact. Three employees from different departments who regularly have lunch or coffee together are an informal group. These types of interactions among individuals, though informal, deeply affect their behavior and performance.

Why Do People Form Groups?

Why do people form groups, and why do they feel so strongly about them? Consider the celebrations that follow a sports team's winning a national championship. Fans have staked their own self-image on the performance of someone else. The winner's supporters are elated, and sales of team-related shirts, jackets, and hats declaring support for the team skyrocket. Fans of the losing team feel dejected, even embarrassed. Our tendency to take personal pride or offense for the accomplishments of a group is the territory of **social identity theory**.

Social identity theory proposes that people have emotional reactions to the failure or success of their group because their self-esteem gets tied into the group's performance.[1] When your group does well, you bask in reflected glory, and your own self-esteem rises. When your group does poorly, you might feel bad about yourself, or you might even reject that part of your identity, like "fair weather fans." Social identities can even lead people to experience pleasure as a result of seeing another group suffer. We often see these feelings of *schadenfreude* as the joy fans experience when a hated team loses.[2]

People develop many identities through the course of their lives. You might define yourself in terms of the organization you work for, the city you live in,

Photo 9-1 Jeffrey Webster, director of human resources at a Nissan plant in Mississippi, serves as the director of a gospel choir at the facility. Choir members are a diverse group of employees who identify with each other as they all share a love of singing and performing for fellow workers, company executives, state officials, and community events.

Source: AP Photo/Rogelio V. Solis.

ingroup favoritism   *Perspective in which we see members of our ingroup as better than other people, and people not in our group as all the same.*

your profession, your religious background, your ethnicity, or your gender. A U.S. expatriate working in Rome might be very aware of being from the United States, for instance, but won't give this national identity a second thought when transferring from Tulsa to Tucson.[3]

Social identities help us understand who we are and where we fit in with other people, but they can have a negative side as well. Beyond feelings of *schadenfreude*, **ingroup favoritism** occurs when we see members of our ingroup as better than other people and people not in our group as all the same. This obviously paves the way for stereotyping.

When do people develop a social identity? Several characteristics make a social identity important to a person:

- **Similarity.**   Not surprisingly, people who have the same values or characteristics as other members of their organization have higher levels of group identification.[4] Demographic similarity can also lead to stronger identification for new hires, while those who are demographically different may have a hard time identifying with the group as a whole.[5]

- **Distinctiveness.**   People are more likely to notice identities that show how they are different from other groups. For example, veterinarians who work in veterinary medicine (where everyone is a veterinarian) identify with their organization, and veterinarians in nonveterinary medicine fields such as animal research or food inspection (where being a veterinarian is a more distinctive characteristic) identify with their profession.[6]

- **Status.**   Because people use identities to define themselves and increase self-esteem, it makes sense that they are most interested in linking themselves to high-status groups. People are likely to not identify with a low-status organization and will be more likely to quit in order to leave that identity behind.[7]

- **Uncertainty reduction.**   Membership in a group also helps some people understand who they are and how they fit into the world.[8] One study showed how the creation of a spin-off company produced questions about how employees should develop a unique identity that corresponded more closely to what the division was becoming.[9] Managers worked to define and communicate an idealized identity for the new organization when it became clear employees were confused.

Stages of Group Development

2 Identify the five stages of group development.

Groups generally pass through a predictable sequence in their evolution. Although not all groups follow this five-stage model, it is a useful framework for understanding group development. In this section, we describe the five-stage model and an alternative for temporary groups with deadlines.

The Five-Stage Model

five-stage group-development model *The five distinct stages groups go through: forming, storming, norming, performing, and adjourning.*

As shown in Exhibit 9-1, the **five-stage group-development model** characterizes groups as proceeding through the distinct stages of forming, storming, norming, performing, and adjourning.[10]

forming stage *The first stage in group development, characterized by much uncertainty.*

The first stage, **forming stage**, is characterized by a great deal of uncertainty about the group's purpose, structure, and leadership. Members "test the waters" to determine what types of behaviors are acceptable. This stage is complete when members have begun to think of themselves as part of a group.

storming stage *The second stage in group development, characterized by intragroup conflict.*

The **storming stage** is one of intragroup conflict. Members accept the existence of the group but resist the constraints it imposes on individuality. There is conflict over who will control the group. When this stage is complete, there will be a relatively clear hierarchy of leadership within the group.

norming stage *The third stage in group development, characterized by close relationships and cohesiveness.*

In the third stage, close relationships develop and the group demonstrates cohesiveness. There is now a strong sense of group identity and camaraderie. This **norming stage** is complete when the group structure solidifies and the group has assimilated a common set of expectations of what defines correct member behavior.

performing stage *The fourth stage in group development, during which the group is fully functional.*

The fourth stage is **performing**. The structure at this point is fully functional and accepted. Group energy has moved from getting to know and understand each other to performing the task at hand.

adjourning stage *The final stage in group development for temporary groups, characterized by concern with wrapping up activities rather than task performance.*

For permanent work groups, performing is the last stage in development. However, for temporary committees, teams, task forces, and similar groups that have a limited task to perform, the **adjourning stage** is for wrapping up activities and preparing to disband. Some group members are upbeat, basking in the group's accomplishments. Others may be depressed over the loss of camaraderie and friendships gained during the work group's life.

Many interpreters of the five-stage model have assumed a group becomes more effective as it progresses through the first four stages. Although this may be generally true, what makes a group effective is actually more complex.[11] First, groups proceed through the stages of group development at different rates. Those with a strong sense of purpose and strategy rapidly achieve high performance and improve over time, whereas those with less sense of purpose actually

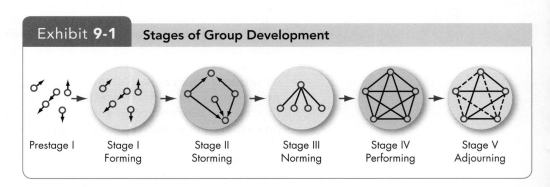

| Exhibit **9-1** | Stages of Group Development |

Prestage I   Stage I Forming   Stage II Storming   Stage III Norming   Stage IV Performing   Stage V Adjourning

Note: Society for Human Resources Management (SHRM) survey of 501 individuals and how drinking is viewed in their organization at a range of work-related activities.
Source: Based on S. M. Heathfield, "To Drink or Not to Drink: Does Alcohol Drinking Mix Safely with Work Events?" *About.com Guide* (2013). http://humanresources .about.com/od/networking/qt/drink_i3.htm.

see their performance worsen over time. Similarly, groups that begin with a positive social focus appear to achieve the "performing" stage more rapidly. Nor do groups always proceed clearly from one stage to the next. Storming and performing can occur simultaneously, and groups can even regress to previous stages.

An Alternative Model for Temporary Groups with Deadlines

punctuated-equilibrium model
A set of phases that temporary groups go through that involves transitions between inertia and activity.

Temporary groups with deadlines don't seem to follow the usual five-stage model. Studies indicate they have their own unique sequencing of actions (or inaction): (1) Their first meeting sets the group's direction, (2) the first phase of group activity is one of inertia, (3) a transition takes place exactly when the group has used up half its allotted time, (4) this transition initiates major changes, (5) a second phase of inertia follows the transition, and (6) the group's last meeting is characterized by markedly accelerated activity.[12] This pattern, called the **punctuated-equilibrium model**, is shown in Exhibit 9-2.

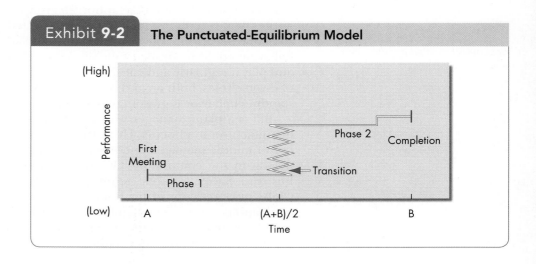

Exhibit 9-2   The Punctuated-Equilibrium Model

The first meeting sets the group's direction, and then a framework of behavioral patterns and assumptions through which the group will approach its project emerges, sometimes in the first few seconds of the group's existence. Once set, the group's direction is solidified and is unlikely to be reexamined throughout the first half of its life. This is a period of inertia—the group tends to stand still or become locked into a fixed course of action even if it gains new insights that challenge initial patterns and assumptions.

One of the most interesting discoveries in work team studies[13] was that groups experienced their transition precisely halfway between the first meeting and the official deadline—whether members spent an hour on their project or 6 months. The midpoint appears to work like an alarm clock, heightening members' awareness that their time is limited and they need to get moving. This transition ends phase 1 and is characterized by a concentrated burst of changes, dropping of old patterns, and adoption of new perspectives. The transition sets a revised direction for phase 2, a new equilibrium or period of inertia in which the group executes plans created during the transition period.

The group's last meeting is characterized by a final burst of activity to finish its work. In summary, the punctuated-equilibrium model characterizes groups as exhibiting long periods of inertia interspersed with brief revolutionary changes triggered primarily by members' awareness of time and deadlines. Keep in mind, however, that this model doesn't apply to all groups but is suited to the finite quality of temporary task groups working under a time deadline.[14]

Group Properties: Roles, Norms, Status, Size, Cohesiveness, and Diversity

3 Show how role requirements change in different situations.

Work groups are not unorganized mobs; they have properties that shape members' behavior and help explain and predict individual behavior within the group as well as the performance of the group itself. Some of these properties are roles, norms, status, size, cohesiveness, and diversity.

Group Property 1: Roles

Shakespeare said, "All the world's a stage, and all the men and women merely players." Using the same metaphor, all group members are actors, each playing a **role**. By this term, we mean a set of expected behavior patterns attributed to someone occupying a given position in a social unit. Our understanding of role behavior would be dramatically simplified if each of us could choose one role and play it regularly and consistently. Instead, we are required to play a number of diverse roles, both on and off our jobs. As we'll see, one of the tasks in understanding behavior is grasping the role a person is currently playing.

role *A set of expected behavior patterns attributed to someone occupying a given position in a social unit.*

Bill is a plant manager with EMM Industries, a large electrical equipment manufacturer in Phoenix. He fulfills a number of roles—EMM employee, member of middle management, electrical engineer, and primary company spokesperson in the community. Off the job, Bill finds himself in still more roles: husband, father, Catholic, tennis player, member of the Thunderbird Country Club, and president of his homeowners' association. Many of these roles are compatible; some create conflicts. How does Bill's religious commitment influence his managerial decisions regarding layoffs, expense account padding, and provision of accurate information to government agencies? A recent offer of promotion requires Bill to relocate, yet his family wants to stay in Phoenix. Can the role demands of his job be reconciled with the demands of his husband and father roles?

Like Bill we are all required to play a number of roles, and our behavior varies with each. Different groups impose different role requirements on individuals.

role perception *An individual's view of how he or she is supposed to act in a given situation.*

Role Perception   Our view of how we're supposed to act in a given situation is a **role perception**. We get role perceptions from stimuli all around us—for example, friends, books, films, television, as when we form an impression of the work of doctors from watching *Grey's Anatomy*. Of course, the primary reason apprenticeship programs exist in many trades and professions is to allow beginners to watch an expert so they can learn to act as they should.

role expectations *How others believe a person should act in a given situation.*

Role Expectations   **Role expectations** are the way others believe you should act in a given context. A U.S. federal judge is viewed as having propriety and dignity, while a football coach is seen as aggressive, dynamic, and inspiring to his players.

psychological contract *An unwritten agreement that sets out what management expects from an employee and vice versa.*

In the workplace, we look at role expectations through the perspective of the **psychological contract**: an unwritten agreement that exists between employees and employer. This agreement sets out mutual expectations: what management expects from workers and vice versa.[15] Management is expected to treat employees justly, provide acceptable working conditions, clearly communicate what is a fair day's work, and give feedback on how well an employee is doing. Employees are expected to respond by demonstrating a good attitude, following directions, and showing loyalty to the organization.

What happens if management is derelict in keeping its part of the bargain? We can expect negative effects on employee performance and satisfaction. One study among restaurant managers found that psychological contract violations were related to greater intentions to quit the job, while another study of a variety of different industries found they were associated with lower levels of productivity, higher levels of theft, and greater work withdrawal.[16] However, there is evidence that perceptions of psychological contracts vary across cultures. In France, where people are individualist and power is more asymmetric, contracts are perceived as self-interested yet favoring the more powerful party. In Canada,

Photo 9-2 Les Hatton, manager of a new Recreational Equipment Inc. store in Manhattan, pumps up employees before the store's grand opening. Part of the psychological contract between REI and its employees is the expectation that salespeople will display enthusiasm and generate excitement in welcoming and serving customers.

where people are individualist but power is more symmetric, contracts are perceived as self-interested yet focused on balanced reciprocity. In China, where people are collectivist and power is more asymmetric, contracts are perceived as going beyond the work context into employees' lives. And in Norway, where people are collectivist but power is more symmetric, contracts are perceived as more relational and based on trust.[17]

Role Conflict   When compliance with one role requirement may make it difficult to comply with another, the result is **role conflict**.[18] At the extreme, two or more role expectations are mutually contradictory.

role conflict   *A situation in which an individual is confronted by divergent role expectations.*

From the example on pp. 248–249, Bill had to deal with role conflicts, such as his attempt to reconcile the expectations placed on him as a husband and father with those placed on him as an executive with EMM Industries. Bill's wife and children want to remain in Phoenix, while EMM expects its employees to be responsive to the company's needs and requirements. Although it might be in Bill's financial and career interests to accept a relocation, the conflict comes down to choosing between family and career role expectations. Indeed, a great deal of research demonstrates that conflict between work and family roles is one of the most significant sources of stress for most employees.[19]

Most employees are simultaneously in occupations, work groups, divisions, and demographic groups, and these different identities can come into conflict when the expectations of one clash with the expectations of another.[20] During mergers and acquisitions, employees can be torn between their identities as members of their original organization and of the new parent company.[21] Organizations structured around multinational operations also have been shown to lead to dual identification, with employees distinguishing between the local division and the international organization.[22]

Zimbardo's Prison Experiment   One of the most illuminating role and identity experiments was done a number of years ago by Stanford University psychologist Philip Zimbardo and his associates.[23] They created a "prison" in the basement of the Stanford psychology building, hired at $15 a day two dozen emotionally stable, physically healthy, law-abiding students who scored "normal average" on extensive personality tests, randomly assigned them the role of either "guard" or "prisoner", and established some basic rules.

It took little time for the "prisoners" to accept the authority positions of the "guards" and for the mock guards to adjust to their new authority roles. Consistent with social identity theory, the guards came to see the prisoners as a negative outgroup, and their comments to researchers showed they had developed stereotypes about the "typical" prisoner personality type. After the guards crushed a rebellion attempt on the second day, the prisoners became increasingly passive. Whatever the guards "dished out," the prisoners took. The prisoners actually began to believe and act inferior and powerless, as the guards constantly reminded them. Every guard, at some time during the simulation, engaged in abusive, authoritative behavior. One said, "I was surprised at myself. . . . I made them call each other names and clean the toilets out with their bare hands. I practically considered the prisoners cattle, and I kept thinking: 'I have to watch out for them in case they try something.'" Surprisingly, during the entire experiment—even after days of abuse—not one prisoner said, "Stop this. I'm a student like you. This is just an experiment!"

The simulation actually proved *too successful* in demonstrating how quickly individuals learn new roles. The researchers had to end it after only 6 days because of the participants' pathological reactions. And remember, these were individuals chosen precisely for their normalcy and emotional stability.

What can we conclude from this prison simulation? Like the rest of us, the participants had learned stereotyped conceptions of guard and prisoner roles from the mass media and their own personal experiences in power and powerlessness relationships gained at home (parent–child), in school (teacher–student), and in other situations. This background allowed them easily and rapidly to assume roles very different from their inherent personalities and, with no prior personality pathology or training in the parts they were playing, execute extreme forms of behavior consistent with those roles.

A follow-up reality television show conducted by the BBC that used a lower-fidelity simulated prison setting provides some insights into these results.[24] The BBC results were dramatically different from those of the Stanford experiment. The "guards" were far more careful in their behavior and limited the aggressive treatment of "prisoners." They often described their concerns about how their actions might be perceived. In short, they did not fully take on their roles, possibly because they knew their behavior was being observed by millions of viewers. Philip Zimbardo has contended that the BBC study is not a replication of his study for several reasons, but he acknowledges the results demonstrate how both guards and prisoners act differently when closely monitored. These results suggest abuse of roles can be limited when people are made conscious of their behavior.

Myth or Science?

"U.S. Workers Are More Biased Than Asians"

This statement has some truth to it. But first let's review what we mean by "bias."

When people are placed into groups, they often exhibit an *ingroup bias*—they tend to favor members of their group regardless of whether they deserve it. Characteristics such as race, gender, and nationality are commonly investigated causes of ingroup bias. However, nearly any identity can activate ingroup bias, even when individuals are randomly assigned to groups and given a group identity. So, if you're placed arbitrarily in the "Slytherin" group, you automatically favor them over "Hufflepuff," "Gryffindor," and "Ravenclaw."

Ingroup bias happens because when group identity is salient to people—which it often is—they tend to simplify; they see themselves as more similar to other group members, and less similar to outgroup members, than is really the case.

Recent research suggests that Asians exhibit less ingroup bias than U.S. workers. One study asked Chinese students at Peking University and U.S. students at University of California–Berkeley to describe the degree to which a set of 16 favorable/unfavorable characteristics (intelligent/foolish, loyal/undependable) described the family member they were closest to. Chinese students described their closest family members significantly less favorably than did the U.S. students. In another study, when Chinese and U.S. subjects were asked to evaluate cultural stereotypes of their nationalities in general (intelligent, hardworking, leaderlike, and so on), the U.S. respondents were more likely to favor their group than were the Chinese.

Although Asians demonstrate less ingroup bias, they appear to stereotype more than U.S. workers. In other words, they tend to ascribe individual traits to entire groups of people and then infer traits on the basis of a person's perceived group membership ("information technology people are nerdy; Jerry works in information technology, therefore Jerry is nerdy"). Why do these differences exist? Regarding intergroup bias, it may be that Asians score higher on *dialecticism*—the tendency to be more comfortable with contradiction (yin and yang), change (nothing is permanent), and holism (everything has both good and bad). Regarding stereotyping, it may be that Asians, because they are more collectivist than U.S. workers, place a greater importance on social groups and thus arrange their perceptions more in terms of group memberships.

Sources: C. Ma-Kellams, J. Spencer-Rodgers, and K. Peng, "I Am Against Us? Unpacking Cultural Differences in Ingroup Favoritism Via Dialecticism," *Personality and Social Psychology Bulletin* 37, no. 1 (2011), pp. 15–27; A. E. Giannakakis and I. Fritsche, "Social Identities, Group Norms, and Threat: On the Malleability of Ingroup Bias," *Personality and Social Psychology Bulletin* 37, no. 1 (2011), pp. 82–93; T. E. DiDonato, J. Ullrich, and J. I. Krueger, " Social Perception as Induction and Inference: An Integrative Model of Intergroup Differentiation, Ingroup Favoritism, and Differential Accuracy," *Journal of Personality and Social Psychology* 100, no. 1 (2011), pp. 66–83; and J. Spencer-Rodgers, M. J. Williams, D. L. Hamilton, K. Peng, and L. Wang, "Culture and Group Perception: Dispositional and Stereotypic Inferences About Novel and National Groups," *Journal of Personality and Social Psychology* 93, no. 4 (2007), pp. 525–543.

Do I Trust Others?

In the Self-Assessment Library (available in MyManagementLab), take assessment II.B.3 (Do I Trust Others?). You can also check out assessment II.B.4 (Do Others See Me as Trusting?).

Group Property 2: Norms

4 Demonstrate how norms and status exert influence on an individual's behavior.

norms *Acceptable standards of behavior within a group that are shared by the group's members.*

Did you ever notice that golfers don't speak while their partners are putting on the green or that employees don't criticize their bosses in public? Why not? The answer is norms.

All groups have established **norms**—acceptable standards of behavior shared by their members that express what they ought and ought not to do under certain circumstances. When agreed to and accepted by the group, norms influence members' behavior with a minimum of external controls. Different groups, communities, and societies have different norms, but they all have them.[25]

Norms can cover virtually any aspect of group behavior.[26] Probably the most common is a *performance norm,* providing explicit cues about how hard members should work, what the level of output should be, how to get the job done, what level of tardiness is appropriate, and the like. These norms are extremely powerful and are capable of significantly modifying a performance prediction based solely on ability and level of personal motivation. Other norms include *appearance norms* (dress codes, unspoken rules about when to look busy), *social arrangement norms* (with whom to eat lunch, whether to form friendships on and off the job), and *resource allocation norms* (assignment of difficult jobs, distribution of resources like pay or equipment).

The Hawthorne Studies   Full-scale appreciation of the influence of norms on worker behavior did not occur until the early 1930s, following studies undertaken between 1924 and 1932 at the Western Electric Company's Hawthorne Works in Chicago.[27]

The Hawthorne researchers began by examining the relationship between the physical environment and productivity. As they increased the light level for the experimental group of workers, output rose for that unit and the control group. But to their surprise, as they dropped the light level in the experimental group, productivity continued to increase in both groups. In fact, productivity in the experimental group decreased only when the light intensity had been reduced to that of moonlight.

As a follow-up, the researchers began a second set of experiments at Western Electric. A small group of women assembling telephone relays was isolated from the main work group so their behavior could be more carefully observed. Observations covering a multiyear period found this small group's output increased steadily. The number of personal and out-sick absences was approximately one-third that recorded by women in the regular production department. It became evident this group's performance was significantly influenced by its status as "special." The members thought being in the experimental group was fun, that they were in an elite group, and that management showed concern about their interests by engaging in such experimentation. In essence, workers in both the illumination and assembly-test-room experiments were really reacting to the increased attention they received.

A third study, in the bank wiring observation room, was introduced to study the effect of a sophisticated wage incentive plan. The most important finding was that employees did not individually maximize their output. Rather, their output became controlled by a group norm that determined a proper day's work. Interviews determined the group was operating well below its capability and leveling output to protect itself. Members were afraid that if they significantly increased their output, the unit incentive rate would be cut, the expected daily

Photo 9-3 From studies of employees at the Western Electric Company's Hawthorne Works in Chicago, researchers gained valuable insights into how individual behavior is influenced by group norms. They also learned that money was less a factor in determining worker output than were group standards, sentiments, and security.

Source: Hawthorne Works Factory of Morton College.

output would be increased, layoffs might occur, or slower workers would be reprimanded. So the group established its idea of a fair output—neither too much nor too little. Members helped each other ensure their reports were nearly level.

The norms the group established included a number of "don'ts." *Don't* be a rate-buster, turning out too much work. *Don't* be a chiseler, turning out too little work. *Don't* squeal on any of your peers. How did the group enforce these norms? The methods included sarcasm, name-calling, ridicule, and even punches to the upper arm of any member who violated the group's norms. Members also ostracized individuals whose behavior was against the group's interest.

Conformity   As a member of a group, you desire acceptance by the group. Thus, you are susceptible to conforming to the group's norms. Considerable evidence suggests that groups can place strong pressures on individual members to change their attitudes and behaviors to conform to the group's standard.[28] There are numerous reasons for conformity, with recent research highlighting the importance of a desire to form accurate perceptions of reality based on group consensus, to develop meaningful social relationships with others, and to maintain a favorable self-concept.

conformity *The adjustment of one's behavior to align with the norms of the group.*

The impact that group pressures for **conformity** can have on an individual member's judgment was demonstrated in studies by Solomon Asch.[29] Asch made up groups of seven or eight people who were asked to compare two cards held by the experimenter. One card had one line, and the other had three lines of varying length, one of which was identical to the line on the one-line card, as Exhibit 9-3 shows. The difference in line length was quite obvious; in fact, under ordinary conditions, subjects made fewer than 1 percent errors in announcing aloud which of the three lines matched the single line. But what happens if members of the group begin giving incorrect answers? Will pressure to conform cause an unsuspecting subject (USS) to alter an answer? Asch arranged the group so only the USS was unaware the experiment was rigged. The seating was prearranged so the USS was one of the last to announce a decision.

Using Peer Pressure as an Influence Tactic

We've all experienced peer pressure, and it can be hard to behave differently from your friends and co-workers. As more work in organizations is performed in groups and teams, the possibilities and pitfalls of such pressure have become an increasingly important ethical issue for managers.

Peer pressure can be a positive force in some ways. In groups or departments where high effort and performance are the norms, peer pressure from co-workers, whether direct or indirect, can encourage high performance from those not meeting expectations. For example, vehicle accidents at a Ghanaian gold mine were lowered when good drivers, rather than managers or staff professionals, trained new drivers. A team with a norm toward behaving ethically could also use peer pressure directly to minimize negative

behavior. Thus, peer pressure can promote all sorts of good behaviors, from donating to charity to working for the Salvation Army.

However, as the chapter has shown, peer pressure can also be destructive. It can create a feeling of exclusion in those who do not go along with group norms and can be very stressful and hurtful for those who don't see eye-to-eye with the rest of the group. Peer pressure itself might become an unethical practice that unduly influences workers' behavior and thoughts. And while groups might pressure others into performing good behaviors, they can just as easily pressure them into performing bad behaviors.

Should you use group peer pressure? As a leader, you may need to. One recent survey found that only 6 percent of leaders reported being

able to successfully influence their employees. If you do use peer pressure to encourage individuals to work toward team goals and behave consistently with organizational values, it can enhance ethical performance. But your behavior should emphasize acceptance and rewarding of positive behavior, rather than rejection and exclusion, as a means of getting everyone to behave consistently in a group.

Sources: Based on: A. Verghese, "The Healing Power of Peer Pressure," *Newsweek* (March 14, 2011), www.newsweek.com; T. Rosenberg, *Join the Club: How Peer Pressure Can Transform the World* (New York: W. W. Norton & Company, 2011); J. Meer, "Brother, Can You Spare a Dime? Peer Pressure in Charitable Solicitation," *Journal of Public Economics* 95, no. 7–8 (2011), pp. 926–941; and L. Potter, "Lack Influence at Work? Why Most Leaders Struggle to Lead Positive Change," *The Wall Street Journal* (May 14, 2013), downloaded on May 28, 2013, from www.online.wsj.com.

The experiment began with several sets of matching exercises. All the subjects gave the right answers. On the third set, however, the first subject gave an obviously wrong answer—for example, saying "C" in Exhibit 9-3. The next subject gave the same wrong answer, and so did the others. Now the dilemma confronting the USS was this: publicly state a perception that differs from the announced position of the others in the group, or give an incorrect answer in order to agree with the others.

The results over many experiments and trials showed 75 percent of subjects gave at least one answer that conformed—that they knew was wrong but was consistent with the replies of other group members—and the average conformer gave wrong answers 37 percent of the time. What meaning can we draw from these results? They suggest group norms press us toward conformity. We desire to be one of the group and therefore avoid being visibly different.

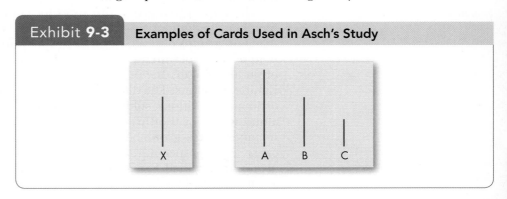

Exhibit 9-3   Examples of Cards Used in Asch's Study

This research was conducted more than 50 years ago. Has time altered the conclusions' validity? And should we consider them generalizable across cultures? Evidence indicates levels of conformity have steadily declined since Asch's studies in the early 1950s, and his findings *are* culture-bound.[30] Conformity to social norms is higher in collectivist cultures, but it is still a powerful force in groups in individualist countries.

Do individuals conform to the pressures of all groups to which they belong? Obviously not, because people belong to many groups, and their norms vary and sometimes are contradictory. People conform to the important groups to which they belong or hope to belong. These important groups are **reference groups**, in which a person is aware of other members, defines himself or herself as a member or would like to be a member, and feels group members are significant to him or her. The implication, then, is that all groups do not impose equal conformity pressures on their members.

Deviant Workplace Behavior   LeBron is frustrated by a co-worker who constantly spreads malicious and unsubstantiated rumors about him. Debra is tired of a member of her work team who, when confronted with a problem, takes out his frustration by yelling and screaming at her and other members. And Mi-Cha recently quit her job as a dental hygienist after being constantly sexually harassed by her employer.

What do these three episodes have in common? They represent employees exposed to acts of deviant workplace behavior.[31] **Deviant workplace behavior** (also called *antisocial behavior* or *workplace incivility*) is voluntary behavior that violates significant organizational norms and, in doing so, threatens the well-being of the organization or its members. Exhibit 9-4 provides a typology of deviant workplace behaviors, with examples of each.

Few organizations will admit to creating or condoning conditions that encourage and maintain deviant norms. Yet they exist. Employees report an increase in rudeness and disregard toward others by bosses and co-workers in recent years. And nearly half of employees who have suffered this incivility say it has led them to think about changing jobs; 12 percent actually quit because of it.[32] A study of nearly 1,500 respondents found that in addition to increasing turnover intentions, incivility at work increased reports of psychological stress and physical

reference groups   *Important groups to which individuals belong or hope to belong and with those whose norms individuals are likely to conform.*

deviant workplace behavior   *Voluntary behavior that violates significant organizational norms and, in so doing, threatens the well-being of the organization or its members. Also called antisocial behavior or workplace incivility.*

| Exhibit 9-4 | Typology of Deviant Workplace Behavior |

Category	Examples
Production	Leaving early Intentionally working slowly Wasting resources
Property	Sabotage Lying about hours worked Stealing from the organization
Political	Showing favoritism Gossiping and spreading rumors Blaming co-workers
Personal aggression	Sexual harassment Verbal abuse Stealing from co-workers

Sources: Based on S. L. Robinson and R. J. Bennett, "A Typology of Deviant Workplace Behaviors: A Multidimensional Scaling Study," *Academy of Management Journal* (April 1995), p. 565. Copyright 1995 by Academy of Management (NY); S. H. Appelbaum, G. D. Iaconi, and A. Matousek, "Positive and Negative Deviant Workplace Behaviors: Causes, Impacts, and Solutions," *Corporate Governance* 7, no. 5 (2007), pp. 586–598; and R. W. Griffin, and A. O'Leary-Kelly, *The Dark Side of Organizational Behavior* (New York: Wiley, 2004).

Photo 9-4 Winning a brown apron in a Starbucks Ambassador Cup competition is a symbol of high status that signifies achieving the highest level of coffee knowledge. Held throughout the world, the contests involve making coffee drinks, identifying coffees in blind taste tests, and testing contestants' knowledge about the coffee industry.

illness.[33] Recent research also suggests that lack of sleep, which hinders a person's ability to regulate emotions and behaviors, can lead to deviant behavior. As organizations have tried to do more with less, pushing their employees to work extra hours, they may indirectly be facilitating deviant behavior.[34]

Like norms in general, individual employees' antisocial actions are shaped by the group context within which they work. Evidence demonstrates deviant workplace behavior is likely to flourish where it's supported by group norms.[35] Workers who socialize either at or outside work with people who are frequently absent from work are more likely to be absent themselves.[36] What this means for managers is that when deviant workplace norms surface, employee cooperation, commitment, and motivation are likely to suffer.

What are the consequences of workplace deviance for teams? Some research suggests a chain reaction occurs in a group with high levels of dysfunctional behavior.[37] The process begins with negative behaviors like shirking, undermining co-workers, or being generally uncooperative. As a result of these behaviors, the team collectively starts to have negative moods. These negative moods then result in poor coordination of effort and lower levels of group performance, especially when there is a lot of nonverbal negative communication between members.

Group Property 3: Status

status *A socially defined position or rank given to groups or group members by others.*

Status—a socially defined position or rank given to groups or group members by others—permeates every society. Even the smallest group will develop roles, rights, and rituals to differentiate its members. Status is a significant motivator and has major behavioral consequences when individuals perceive a disparity between what they believe their status is and what others perceive it to be.

status characteristics theory *A theory that states that differences in status characteristics create status hierarchies within groups.*

What Determines Status?   According to **status characteristics theory**, status tends to derive from one of three sources:[38]

1. **The power a person wields over others.**   Because they likely control the group's resources, people who control the outcomes tend to be perceived as high status.
2. **A person's ability to contribute to a group's goals.**   People whose contributions are critical to the group's success tend to have high status. Some

thought NBA star Kobe Bryant had more say over player decisions than his coaches (though not as much as Bryant wanted!).

3. **An individual's personal characteristics.**   Someone whose personal characteristics are positively valued by the group (good looks, intelligence, money, or a friendly personality) typically has higher status than someone with fewer valued attributes.

Status and Norms   Status has some interesting effects on the power of norms and pressures to conform. High-status individuals are often given more freedom to deviate from norms than are other group members.[39] Physicians actively resist administrative decisions made by lower-ranking insurance company employees.[40] High-status people are also better able to resist conformity pressures than their lower-status peers. An individual who is highly valued by a group but doesn't need or care about the group's social rewards is particularly able to disregard conformity norms.[41] Research indicates that bringing high-status members into a group may improve performance, but only up to a point, perhaps because they may introduce counterproductive norms.[42]

Status and Group Interaction   High-status people tend to be more assertive group members.[43] They speak out more often, criticize more, state more commands, and interrupt others more often. But status differences actually inhibit diversity of ideas and creativity in groups because lower-status members tend to participate less actively in group discussions. When they possess expertise and insights that could aid the group, failure to fully utilize them reduces the group's overall performance.

Status Inequity   It is important for group members to believe the status hierarchy is equitable. Perceived inequity creates disequilibrium, which inspires various types of corrective behavior. Hierarchical groups can lead to resentment among those at the lower end of the status continuum. Large differences in status within groups are also associated with poorer individual performance, lower health, and higher intentions to leave the group.[44]

Groups generally agree within themselves on status criteria; hence, there is usually high concurrence in group rankings of individuals. Managers who occupy central positions in their social networks are typically seen as higher in status by their subordinates, and this position translates into greater influence over the group's functioning.[45] Groups generally form an informal status order based on ranking and who has access to needed resources.[46] Individuals can find themselves in conflicts when they move between groups whose status criteria are different, or when they join groups whose members have heterogeneous backgrounds. Business executives may use personal income or the growth rate of their companies as determinants of status. Government bureaucrats may use the size of their budgets, and blue-collar workers may use their years of seniority. Cultures also differ in their criteria for conferring status upon individuals. When groups are heterogeneous or when heterogeneous groups must be interdependent, status differences may initiate conflict as the group attempts to reconcile the differing hierarchies. As we'll see in Chapter 10, this can be a problem when management creates teams of employees from varied functions.

Status and Stigmatization   Although it's clear that your own status affects the way people perceive you, the status of people with whom you are affiliated can also affect others' views of you. Studies have shown that people who are stigmatized against can "infect" others with their stigma. This "stigma by association" effect can result in negative opinions and evaluations of the person affiliated with the stigmatized individual, even if the association is brief and purely coincidental.

For example, men interviewing for a job were viewed as less qualified when they were sitting next to an obese woman in a waiting room. Another study looking at the effects of being associated with an overweight person found that even when onlookers were told the target person and the overweight person were unrelated, the target person was still devalued.[47]

While affiliating with a stigmatized individual can damage a person's reputation, the opposite is true when it comes to affiliating with a high-status person. It's not the actual relationship that matters; all that's important for the target person to garner a more favorable reputation is for people to perceive a relationship with the high-status person exists.[48] Although this likely sounds (and is) highly unfair, it appears that George Washington was on to something when he encouraged people to, "Associate yourself with men of good quality if you esteem your own reputation for 'tis better to be alone than in bad company."

Group Property 4: Size

5 Show how group size affects group performance.

Does the size of a group affect the group's overall behavior? Yes, but the effect depends on what dependent variables we look at. Groups with a dozen or more members are good for gaining diverse input. If the goal is fact-finding, larger groups should be more effective. Smaller groups of about seven members are better at doing something productive with that input.

One of the most important findings about the size of a group concerns **social loafing**, the tendency for individuals to expend less effort when working collectively than alone.[49] It directly challenges the assumption that the productivity of the group as a whole should at least equal the sum of the productivity of the individuals in it.

social loafing *The tendency for individuals to expend less effort when working collectively than when working individually.*

Does team spirit spur individual effort and enhance a group's overall productivity? In the late 1920s, German psychologist Max Ringelmann compared the results of individual and group performance on a rope-pulling task.[50] He expected that three people pulling together should exert three times as much pull on a rope as one person, and eight people eight times as much. But one person pulling on a rope alone exerted an average of 63 kilograms of force. In groups of three, the per-person force dropped to 53 kilograms. And in groups of eight, it fell to only 31 kilograms per person.

Photo 9-5 Although social loafing is consistent with individualistic cultures, it is not consistent with collectivist societies such as China. The young employees shown here celebrating the opening of a new KFC restaurant in Shanghai are motivated by ingroup goals and perform better in a group than they do by working individually.

Replications of Ringelmann's research with similar tasks have generally supported his findings.[51] Total group performance increases with group size, but the addition of new members has diminishing returns on individual productivity. So more may be better in that total productivity of a group of four is greater than that of three, but the individual productivity of each member declines.

What causes social loafing? It may be a belief that others in the group are not carrying their fair share. If you see others as lazy or inept, you can reestablish equity by reducing your effort. But simply failing to contribute may not be enough to be labeled a "free rider." Instead, the group must believe the social loafer is acting in an exploitive manner (benefitting at the expense of other team members).[52] Another explanation for social loafing is the dispersion of responsibility. Because group results cannot be attributed to any single person, the relationship between an individual's input and the group's output is clouded. Individuals may then be tempted to become free riders and coast on the group's efforts. The implications for OB are significant. When managers use collective work situations to enhance morale and teamwork, they must also be able to identify individual efforts. Otherwise, they must weigh the potential losses in productivity from using groups against the possible gains in worker satisfaction.[53]

Social loafing appears to have a Western bias. It's consistent with individualist cultures, such as the United States and Canada, that are dominated by self-interest. It is *not* consistent with collectivist societies, in which individuals are motivated by in-group goals. In studies comparing U.S. employees with employees from the People's Republic of China and Israel (both collectivist societies), the Chinese and Israelis showed no propensity to engage in social loafing and actually performed better in a group than alone.

Recent research indicates that the stronger an individual's work ethic is, the less likely that person is to engage in social loafing.[54] There are also several ways to prevent social loafing: (1) set group goals, so the group has a common purpose to strive toward; (2) increase intergroup competition, which focuses on the shared outcome; (3) engage in peer evaluation, so each person evaluates each other person's contribution; (4) select members who have high motivation and prefer to work in groups; and (5) if possible, base group rewards in part on each member's unique contributions.[55] Although no magic bullet will prevent social loafing in all cases, these steps should help minimize its effect.

Group Property 5: Cohesiveness

6 Contrast the benefits and disadvantages of cohesive groups.

cohesiveness *The degree to which group members are attracted to each other and are motivated to stay in the group.*

Groups differ in their **cohesiveness**—the degree to which members are attracted to each other and motivated to stay in the group. Some work groups are cohesive because the members have spent a great deal of time together, the group's small size facilitates high interaction, or external threats have brought members close together.

Cohesiveness affects group productivity. Studies consistently show that the relationship between cohesiveness and productivity depends on the group's performance-related norms.[56] If norms for quality, output, and cooperation with outsiders are high, for instance, a cohesive group will be more productive than will a less cohesive group. But if cohesiveness is high and performance norms are low, productivity will be low. If cohesiveness is low and performance norms are high, productivity increases, but less than in the high-cohesiveness/high-norms situation. When cohesiveness and performance-related norms are both low, productivity tends to fall into the low-to-moderate range. These conclusions are summarized in Exhibit 9-5.

What can you do to encourage group cohesiveness? (1) Make the group smaller, (2) encourage agreement with group goals, (3) increase the time members spend together, (4) increase the group's status and the perceived difficulty of attaining membership, (5) stimulate competition with other groups, (6) give rewards to the group rather than to individual members, and (7) physically isolate the group.[57]

Making Global Virtual Teams Effective

Having a group whose members live and work in different countries once seemed impossible, but today virtual teams have become relatively common. In some cases, the group members never meet face-to-face, instead conducting all their work over e-mail, phone calls, and videoconferencing tools such as Skype.

Although global virtual teams present challenges, such as ensuring smooth coordination, establishing trust, and overcoming cultural differences in communication, they also present opportunities. Many companies utilize them to make sure the most qualified individuals are assigned to top projects.

Besides providing advanced technology to facilitate communication, organizations can do a number of things to make it more likely that global virtual teams succeed. These include ensuring sufficient time for preparation activities such as setting goals, formulating group strategy, and conducting ongoing analyses of the group's mission. This preparation, along with making tasks interdependent to create the need for collaborative interaction, ensures that everyone in the group has the same understanding of who knows what and who does what.

If you find yourself on a global virtual team, be aware that individuals from different cultures arrive at decisions differently. For example, while U.S. managers prefer to gather input from others and quickly implement a decision, managers from Sweden lean toward consensus building, which although lengthy can lead to greater commitment to the ultimate decision. And in France, debate and conflict are viewed as part of good decision making. Thus, both organizations and employees need to recognize that global virtual teams often require different strategies from traditional teams in order to be effective.

Sources: E. Meyer, "The Four Keys to Success with Virtual Teams," *Forbes* (August 19, 2010), downloaded on May 31, 2013, from www.forbes.com; and M. T. Maynard, J. E. Mathieu, T. L. Rapp, and L. L. Gibson, "Something(s) Old and Something(s) New: Modeling Drivers of Global Virtual Team Effectiveness," *Journal of Organizational Behavior* 33 (2012), pp. 342–365.

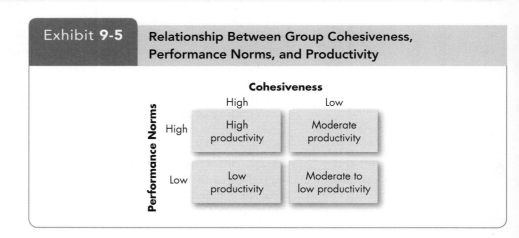

Exhibit 9-5 Relationship Between Group Cohesiveness, Performance Norms, and Productivity

Group Property 6: Diversity

7 Explain the implications of diversity for group effectiveness.

diversity *The extent to which members of a group are similar to, or different from, one another.*

The final property of groups we consider is **diversity** in the group's membership, or the degree to which members of the group are similar to, or different from, one another. A great deal of research is being done on how diversity influences group performance. Some research looks at cultural diversity and some at racial, gender, and other differences. Overall, studies identify both costs and benefits from group diversity.

Diversity appears to increase group conflict, especially in the early stages of a group's tenure, which often lowers group morale and raises dropout rates. One study compared groups that were culturally diverse (composed of people from different countries) and homogeneous (composed of people from the same country). On a wilderness survival exercise (not unlike the Experiential Exercise at the end of this chapter), the groups performed equally well, but the members from the diverse groups were less satisfied with their groups, were less cohesive, and had more conflict.[58] Another study examined the effect of differences in tenure on the performance of 67 engineering research and development groups.[59] When most people had roughly the same level of tenure, performance was high, but as tenure diversity increased, performance dropped off. There was an important qualifier: Higher levels of tenure diversity were not related to lower performance for groups when there were effective team-oriented human resources practices. Teams in which members' values or opinions differ tend to experience more conflict, but leaders who can get the group to focus on the task at hand and encourage group learning are able to reduce these conflicts and enhance discussion of group issues.[60] It seems diversity can be bad for performance even in creative teams, but appropriate organizational support and leadership might offset the problems.

Culturally and demographically diverse groups may perform better over time—if they can get over their initial conflicts. Why might this be so?

Surface-level diversity—in observable characteristics such as national origin, race, and gender—alerts people to possible deep-level diversity—in underlying attitudes, values, and opinions. One researcher argues, "The mere presence of diversity you can see, such as a person's race or gender, actually cues a team that there's likely to be differences of opinion."[61] Although those differences can lead to conflict, they also provide an opportunity to solve problems in unique ways.

One study of jury behavior found diverse juries more likely to deliberate longer, share more information, and make fewer factual errors when discussing evidence. Two studies of MBA student groups found surface-level diversity led to greater openness even without deep-level diversity. Here, surface-level diversity may subconsciously cue team members to be more open-minded in their views.[62]

The impact of diversity on groups is mixed. It is difficult to be in a diverse group in the short term. However, if members can weather their differences, over time diversity may help them be more open-minded and creative and to do better. But even positive effects are unlikely to be especially strong. As one review stated, "The business case (in terms of demonstrable financial results) for diversity remains hard to support based on the extant research."[63]

Faultlines   One possible side effect in diverse teams—especially those that are diverse in terms of surface level characteristics—is **faultlines**, or perceived divisions that split groups into two or more subgroups based on individual differences such as sex, race, age, work experience, and education.

faultlines *The perceived divisions that split groups into two or more subgroups based on individual differences such as sex, race, age, work experience, and education.*

For example, let's say group A is composed of three men and three women. The three men have approximately the same amount of work experience and backgrounds in marketing. The three women also have about the same amount of work experience and backgrounds in finance. Group B has three men and three women, but they all differ in terms of their experience and backgrounds. Two of the men are relatively experienced, while the other is new. One of the women has worked at the company for several years, while the other two are new. In addition, two of the men and one woman in group B have backgrounds in marketing, while the other men and the remaining two women have backgrounds in finance. It is thus likely that a faultline will result in subgroups of males and females in group A but not in group B.

Research on faultlines has shown that splits are generally detrimental to group functioning and performance. Subgroups may wind up competing with each other, which takes time away from core tasks and harms group performance. Groups that have subgroups learn more slowly, make more risky decisions, are less creative, and experience higher levels of conflict. Subgroups are less likely to trust each other. Finally, although the overall group's satisfaction is lower when faultlines are present, satisfaction with subgroups is generally high.[64]

Are faultlines ever a good thing? One study suggested that faultlines based on differences in skill, knowledge, and expertise could be beneficial when the groups were in organizational cultures that strongly emphasized results. Why?

A results-driven culture focuses people's attention on what's important to the company rather than on problems arising from subgroups.[65] Another study showed that problems stemming from strong faultlines based on gender and educational major were counteracted when their roles were cross-cut and the group as a whole was given a common goal to strive for. Together, these strategies force collaboration between members of subgroups and focus their efforts on accomplishing a goal that transcends the boundary imposed by the faultline.[66]

Overall, although research on faultlines suggests that diversity in groups is a potential double-edged sword, recent work indicates they can be strategically employed to improve performance.

Group Decision Making

8 Contrast the strengths and weaknesses of group decision making.

The belief—characterized by juries—that two heads are better than one has long been accepted as a basic component of the U.S. legal system and those of many other countries. Today, many decisions in organizations are made by groups, teams, or committees.

Groups versus the Individual

Decision-making groups may be widely used in organizations, but are group decisions preferable to those made by an individual alone? The answer depends on a number of factors. Let's begin by looking at the strengths and weaknesses of group decision making.[67]

Strengths of Group Decision Making   Groups generate *more complete information and knowledge.* By aggregating the resources of several individuals, groups bring more input as well as heterogeneity into the decision process. They offer *increased diversity of views.* This opens up the opportunity to consider more approaches and alternatives. Finally, groups lead to increased *acceptance of a solution.* Group members who participated in making a decision are more likely to enthusiastically support and encourage others to accept it.

Weaknesses of Group Decision Making   Group decisions are time consuming because groups typically take more time to reach a solution. There are *conformity pressures.* The desire by group members to be accepted and considered an asset to the group can squash any overt disagreement. Group discussion can be *dominated by one or a few members.* If they're low- and medium-ability members, the group's overall effectiveness will suffer. Finally, group decisions suffer from *ambiguous responsibility.* In an individual decision, it's clear who is accountable for the final outcome. In a group decision, the responsibility of any single member is diluted.

Effectiveness and Efficiency   Whether groups are more effective than individuals depends on how you define effectiveness. Group decisions are generally more *accurate* than the decisions of the average individual in a group, but less accurate than the judgments of the most accurate.[68] In terms of *speed,* individuals are superior. If *creativity* is important, groups tend to be more effective. And if effectiveness means the degree of *acceptance* the final solution achieves, the nod again goes to the group.[69]

But we cannot consider effectiveness without also assessing efficiency. With few exceptions, group decision making consumes more work hours than an individual tackling the same problem alone. The exceptions tend to be the instances in which, to achieve comparable quantities of diverse input, the single decision maker must spend a great deal of time reviewing files and talking to other people.

In deciding whether to use groups, then, managers must assess whether increases in effectiveness are more than enough to offset the reductions in efficiency.

Summary   In summary, groups are an excellent vehicle for performing many steps in the decision-making process and offer both breadth and depth of input for information gathering. If group members have diverse backgrounds, the alternatives generated should be more extensive and the analysis more critical. When the final solution is agreed on, there are more people in a group decision to support and implement it. These pluses, however, can be more than offset by the time consumed by group decisions, the internal conflicts they create, and the pressures they generate toward conformity. In some cases, therefore, we can expect individuals to make better decisions than groups.

Groupthink and Groupshift

Two by-products of group decision making have the potential to affect a group's ability to appraise alternatives objectively and arrive at high-quality solutions.

The first, called **groupthink**, relates to norms. It describes situations in which group pressures for conformity deter the group from critically appraising unusual, minority, or unpopular views. Groupthink is a disease that attacks many groups and can dramatically hinder their performance. The second phenomenon is **groupshift**, which describes the way group members tend to exaggerate the initial positions they hold when discussing a given set of alternatives and arriving at a solution. In some situations, caution dominates and there is a conservative shift, while in other situations groups tend toward a risky shift. Let's look at each phenomenon in detail.

Groupthink   Have you ever felt like speaking up in a meeting, a classroom, or an informal group but decided against it? One reason may have been shyness. Or you may have been a victim of groupthink, which occurs when the norm for consensus overrides the realistic appraisal of alternative courses and the full expression of deviant, minority, or unpopular views. The individual's mental efficiency, reality testing, and moral judgment deteriorate as a result of group pressures.[70]

We have all seen the symptoms of groupthink:

1. Group members rationalize any resistance to the assumptions they've made. No matter how strongly the evidence may contradict their basic assumptions, they behave so as to reinforce them.
2. Members apply direct pressures on those who momentarily express doubts about any of the group's shared views, or who question the validity of arguments supporting the alternative favored by the majority.
3. Members who have doubts or differing points of view seek to avoid deviating from what appears to be group consensus by keeping silent about misgivings and even minimizing to themselves the importance of their doubts.
4. There is an illusion of unanimity. If someone doesn't speak, it's assumed he or she is in full accord. Abstention becomes a "yes" vote.[71]

Groupthink appears closely aligned with the conclusions Solomon Asch drew in his experiments with a lone dissenter. Individuals who hold a position different from that of the dominant majority are under pressure to suppress, withhold, or modify their true feelings and beliefs. As members of a group, we find it more pleasant to be in agreement—to be a positive part of the group—than to be a disruptive force, even if disruption is necessary to improve the effectiveness of the group's decisions. Groups that are more focused on performance than on learning are especially likely to fall victim to groupthink and to suppress the opinions of those who do not agree with the majority.[72]

Does groupthink attack all groups? No. It seems to occur most often when there is a clear group identity, when members hold a positive image of their

groupthink   *A phenomenon in which the norm for consensus overrides the realistic appraisal of alternative courses of action.*

groupshift   *A change between a group's decision and an individual decision that a member within the group would make; the shift can be toward either conservatism or greater risk but it generally is toward a more extreme version of the group's original position.*

group that they want to protect, and when the group perceives a collective threat to this positive image.[73] So groupthink is not a dissenter-suppression mechanism as much as it's a means for a group to protect its positive image. One study showed that those influenced by groupthink were more confident about their course of action early on.[74] Groups that believe too strongly in the correctness of their course of action are more likely to suppress dissent and encourage conformity than are groups that are more skeptical about their course of action.

What can managers do to minimize groupthink?[75] First, they can monitor group size. People grow more intimidated and hesitant as group size increases, and although there is no magic number that will eliminate groupthink, individuals are likely to feel less personal responsibility when groups get larger than about 10 members. Managers should also encourage group leaders to play an impartial role. Leaders should actively seek input from all members and avoid expressing their own opinions, especially in the early stages of deliberation. In addition, managers should appoint one group member to play the role of devil's advocate, overtly challenging the majority position and offering divergent perspectives. Still another suggestion is to use exercises that stimulate active discussion of diverse alternatives without threatening the group or intensifying identity protection. Have group members delay discussion of possible gains so they can first talk about the dangers or risks inherent in a decision. Requiring members to initially focus on the negatives of an alternative makes the group less likely to stifle dissenting views and more likely to gain an objective evaluation.

Groupshift or Group Polarization   There are differences between group decisions and the individual decisions of group members.[76] What appears to happen in groups is that the discussion leads members toward a more extreme view of the position they already held. Conservatives become more cautious, and more aggressive types take on more risk. The group discussion tends to exaggerate the initial position of the group.

We can view group polarization as a special case of groupthink. The group's decision reflects the dominant decision-making norm that develops during discussion. Whether the shift in the group's decision is toward greater caution or more risk depends on the dominant pre-discussion norm.

The shift toward polarization has generated several explanations.[77] It's been argued, for instance, that discussion makes the members more comfortable with each other and, thus, more willing to express extreme versions of their original positions. Another argument is that the group diffuses responsibility. Group decisions free any single member from accountability for the group's final choice, so a more extreme position can be taken. It's also likely that people take on extreme positions because they want to demonstrate how different they are from the outgroup.[78] People on the fringes of political or social movements take on ever-more extreme positions just to prove they are really committed to the cause, whereas those who are more cautious tend to take moderate positions to demonstrate how reasonable they are.

So how should you use the findings on groupshift? Recognize that group decisions exaggerate the initial position of the individual members, that the shift has been shown more often to be toward greater risk, and that which way a group will shift is a function of the members' pre-discussion inclinations.

We now turn to the techniques by which groups make decisions. These reduce some of the dysfunctional aspects of group decision making.

Group Decision-Making Techniques

The most common form of group decision making takes place in **interacting groups**. Members meet face-to-face and rely on both verbal and nonverbal interaction to communicate. But as our discussion of groupthink demonstrated,

9   Compare the effectiveness of interacting, brainstorming, and the nominal group technique.

interacting groups *Typical groups in which members interact with each other face to face.*

brainstorming *An idea-generation process that specifically encourages any and all alternatives while withholding any criticism of those alternatives.*

nominal group technique *A group decision-making method in which individual members meet face to face to pool their judgments in a systematic but independent fashion.*

interacting groups often censor themselves and pressure individual members toward conformity of opinion. Brainstorming and the nominal group technique can reduce problems inherent in the traditional interacting group.

Brainstorming can overcome the pressures for conformity that dampen creativity[79] by encouraging any and all alternatives while withholding criticism. In a typical brainstorming session, a half-dozen to a dozen people sit around a table. The group leader states the problem in a clear manner so all participants understand. Members then freewheel as many alternatives as they can in a given length of time. To encourage members to "think the unusual," no criticism is allowed, even of the most bizarre suggestions, and all ideas are recorded for later discussion and analysis.

Brainstorming may indeed generate ideas—but not in a very efficient manner. Research consistently shows individuals working alone generate more ideas than a group in a brainstorming session. One reason for this is "production blocking." When people are generating ideas in a group, many are talking at once, which blocks the thought process and eventually impedes the sharing of ideas.[80] The following two techniques go further than brainstorming by helping groups arrive at a preferred solution.[81]

The **nominal group technique** restricts discussion or interpersonal communication during the decision-making process, hence the term *nominal*. Group members are all physically present, as in a traditional committee meeting, but they operate independently. Specifically, a problem is presented and then the group takes the following steps:

1. Before any discussion takes place, each member independently writes down ideas on the problem.
2. After this silent period, each member presents one idea to the group. No discussion takes place until all ideas have been presented and recorded.
3. The group discusses the ideas for clarity and evaluates them.
4. Each group member silently and independently rank-orders the ideas. The idea with the highest aggregate ranking determines the final decision.

The chief advantage of the nominal group technique is that it permits a group to meet formally but does not restrict independent thinking, as does an interacting group. Research generally shows nominal groups outperform brainstorming groups.[82]

Each of the group-decision techniques has its own set of strengths and weaknesses. The choice depends on what criteria you want to emphasize and the cost–benefit trade-off. As Exhibit 9-6 indicates, an interacting group is good for achieving commitment to a solution, brainstorming develops group cohesiveness, and the nominal group technique is an inexpensive means for generating a large number of ideas.

Exhibit 9-6   Evaluating Group Effectiveness

Effectiveness Criteria	Type of Group		
	Interacting	Brainstorming	Nominal
Number and quality of ideas	Low	Moderate	High
Social pressure	High	Low	Moderate
Money costs	Low	Low	Low
Speed	Moderate	Moderate	Moderate
Task orientation	Low	High	High
Potential for interpersonal conflict	High	Low	Moderate
Commitment to solution	High	Not applicable	Moderate
Development of group cohesiveness	High	High	Moderate

Summary

We can draw several implications from our discussion of groups. First, norms control behavior by establishing standards of right and wrong. The norms of a given group can help explain members' behaviors for managers. Second, status inequities create frustration and can adversely influence productivity and willingness to remain with an organization. Third, the impact of size on a group's performance depends on the type of task. Larger groups are associated with lower satisfaction. Fourth, cohesiveness may influence a group's level of productivity, depending on the group's performance-related norms. Fifth, diversity appears to have a mixed impact on group performance, with some studies suggesting that diversity can help performance and others suggesting it can hurt it. Sixth, role conflict is associated with job-induced tension and job dissatisfaction.[83] Lastly, people generally prefer to communicate with others at their own status level or a higher one, rather than with those below them.[84] The next chapter will explore several of these conclusions in greater depth.

Implications for Managers

- Consider that the degree of congruence between the employee's and the manager's perception of the employee's job influences the degree to which the manager will judge that employee effective. Therefore, be certain your employees fully understand their roles so you can accurately assess their performance.
- In group situations where the norms support high output, you can expect markedly higher individual performance than when the norms restrict output. Group norms that support antisocial behavior increase the likelihood that individuals will engage in deviant workplace activities.
- Pay attention to the organizational status levels of the employee groups you create. Because lower-status people tend to participate less in group discussions, groups with high status differences are likely to inhibit input from lower-status members and reduce their potential.
- When forming employee groups, use larger groups for fact-finding activities and smaller groups for action-taking tasks. When creating larger groups, you should also provide measures of individual performance.
- To increase employee satisfaction, work on making certain your employees perceive their job roles the same way you perceive their roles.

People Are More Creative when They Work Alone

POINT   **COUNTERPOINT**

I know groups are all the rage. Businesses are knocking down walls and cubicles to create more open, "collaborative" environments. "Self-managing teams" are replacing the traditional middle manager. Students in universities are constantly working on group projects, and even young children are finding themselves learning in small groups.

I also know *why* groups are all the rage. Work, they say, has become too complex for individuals to perform alone. Groups are better at brainstorming and coming up with creative solutions to complicated problems. Groups also produce higher levels of commitment and satisfaction—so long as group members develop feelings of cohesiveness and trust one another.

But for every group that comes up with a creative solution, I'll show you twice as many individuals who would come up with a better solution had they only been left alone. Consider creative geniuses like DaVinci, Newton, and Picasso. Or more recently, Steve Wozniak, the co-founder of Apple Computer. All were introverts who toiled by themselves. According to Wozniak, "I'm going to give you some advice that might be hard to take. That advice is: Work alone . . . not on a committee. Not on a team."

But enough anecdotal evidence. Research has also shown that groups can kill creativity. One study found that computer programmers at companies that give them privacy and freedom from interruptions outperformed their counterparts at companies that forced more openness and collaboration. Or consider Adrian Furnham, an organizational psychologist whose research led him to conclude that "business people must be insane to use brainstorming groups." People slack off in groups, and they're afraid to communicate any ideas that might make them sound dumb. These problems don't exist when people work alone.

So take Picasso's advice: "Without great solitude, no serious work is possible."

I'll grant your point that there are circumstances in which groups can hinder creative progress, but if the right conditions are put in place, groups are simply much better at coming up with novel solutions to problems than are individuals. Using strategies such as the nominal group technique, generating ideas electronically rather than face-to-face, and ensuring that individuals do not evaluate others' ideas until all have been generated are just a few ways you can set up groups for creative success.

The fact of the matter is that problems *are* too complex these days for individuals to effectively perform alone. Consider the Rovers launched by NASA to roam around Mars collecting data. An accomplishment like that is made possible only by a group, not a lone individual. Steve Wozniak's collaboration with Steve Jobs is what really made Apple sail as a company.

In addition, the most influential research is conducted by teams of academics, rather than individuals. Indeed, if you look at recent Nobel Prize winners in areas such as economics, physics, and chemistry, the majority have been won by academics who collaborated on the research.

So if you want creativity, two heads are in fact better than one.

Sources: S. Cain, "The Rise of the New Groupthink," *The New York Times* (January 15, 2012), pp. 1, 6; and C. Faure, "Beyond Brainstorming: Effects of Different Group Procedures on Selection of Ideas and Satisfaction with the Process," *Journal of Creative Behavior* 38 (2004), pp. 13–34.

END-OF-CHAPTER REVIEW

MyManagementLab

Go to **mymanagementlab.com** to complete the problems marked with this icon. ⭐

QUESTIONS FOR REVIEW

9-1 Define *group*. What are the different types of groups?

9-2 What are the five stages of group development?

9-3 Do role requirements change in different situations? If so, how?

9-4 How do group norms and status influence an individual's behavior?

9-5 How does group size affect group performance?

9-6 What are the advantages and limitations of cohesive groups?

9-7 What are the implications of diversity for group effectiveness?

9-8 What are the strengths and weaknesses of group (versus individual) decision making?

9-9 How effective are interacting, brainstorming, and the nominal group technique?

EXPERIENTIAL EXERCISE Surviving the Wild: Join a Group or Go It Alone?

You are a member of a hiking party. After reaching base camp on the first day, you decide to take a quick sunset hike by yourself. After a few exhilarating miles, you decide to return to camp. On your way back, you realize you are lost. You have shouted for help, to no avail. It is now dark. And getting cold.

Your Task

Without communicating with anyone else in your group, read the following scenarios and choose the best answer. Keep track of your answers on a sheet of paper. You have 10 minutes to answer the 10 questions.

9-10. The first thing you decide to do is to build a fire. However, you have no matches, so you use the bow-and-drill method. What is the bow-and-drill method?
   a. A dry, soft stick is rubbed between the hands against a board of supple green wood.
   b. A soft green stick is rubbed between the hands against a hardwood board.
   c. A straight stick of wood is quickly rubbed back and forth against a dead tree.
   d. Two sticks (one being the bow, the other the drill) are struck to create a spark.

9-11. It occurs to you that you can also use the fire as a distress signal. How do you form the international distress signal with fire?
   a. 2 fires
   b. 4 fires in a square
   c. 4 fires in a cross
   d. 3 fires in a line

9-12. You are very thirsty. You go to a nearby stream and collect some water in the small metal cup you have in your backpack. How long should you boil the water?
   a. 15 minutes
   b. A few seconds
   c. 1 minute
   d. It depends on the altitude.

9-13. You are very hungry, so you decide to eat what appear to be edible berries. When performing the universal edibility test, what should you do?
   a. Do not eat for 2 hours before the test.
   b. If the plant stings your lip, confirm the sting by holding it under your tongue for 15 minutes.
   c. If nothing bad has happened 2 hours after digestion, eat half a cup of the plant and wait again.
   d. Separate the plant into its basic components and eat each component, one at a time.

9-14. Next, you decide to build a shelter for the evening. In selecting a site, what do you *not* have to consider?
  a. It must contain material to make the type of shelter you need.
  b. It must be free of insects, reptiles, and poisonous plants.
  c. It must be large enough and level enough for you to lie down comfortably.
  d. It must be on a hill so you can signal rescuers and keep an eye on your surroundings.

9-15. In the shelter that you built, you notice a spider. You heard from a fellow hiker that black widow spiders populate the area. How do you identify a black widow spider?
  a. Its head and abdomen are black; its thorax is red.
  b. It is attracted to light.
  c. It runs away from light.
  d. It is dark with a red or orange marking on the female's abdomen.

9-16. After getting some sleep, you notice that the night sky has cleared, so you decide to try to find your way back to base camp. You believe you should travel north and can use the North Star for navigation. How do you locate the North Star?
  a. Hold your right hand up as far as you can and look between your index and middle fingers.
  b. Find Sirius and look 60 degrees above it and to the right.
  c. Look for the Big Dipper and follow the line created by its cup end.
  d. Follow the line of Orion's belt

9-17. You come across a fast-moving stream. What is the best way to cross it?
  a. Find a spot downstream from a sandbar, where the water will be calmer.
  b. Build a bridge.
  c. Find a rocky area, because the water will be shallow and you will have hand- and footholds.
  d. Find a level stretch where it breaks into a few channels.

9-18. After walking for about an hour, you feel several spiders in your clothes. You don't feel any pain, but you know some spider bites are painless. Which of these spider bites is painless?
  a. Black widow
  b. Brown recluse
  c. Wolf spider
  d. Harvestman (daddy longlegs)

9-19. You decide to eat some insects. Which insects should you avoid?
  a. Adults that sting or bite
  b. Caterpillars and insects that have a pungent odor
  c. Hairy or brightly colored ones
  d. All the above

Group Task

Break into groups of five or six people. Now imagine your whole group is lost. Write down your own answers first, and then compile your group's answers by reaching consensus as a group. Once the group comes to an agreement, write your decision on the same sheet of paper you used for your individual answers. You will have approximately 20 minutes for the group task.

Scoring Your Answers

Your instructor will provide you with the correct answers, which are based on expert judgments in these situations. Once you have received the answers, calculate (A) your individual score; (B) your group's score; (C) the average individual score in the group; and (D) the best individual score in the group. Write these down and consult with your group to ensure that these scores are accurate.

  A. Your individual score _____
  B. Your group's score _____
  C. Average individual score in group _____
  D. Best individual score in group _____

Discussion Questions

9-20. How did your group (B) perform relative to yourself (A)?

9-21. How did your group (B) perform relative to the average individual score in the group (C)?

9-22. How did your group (B) perform relative to the best individual score in the group (D)?

9-23. Compare your results with those of other groups. Did some groups do a better job of outperforming individuals than others?

9-24. What do these results tell you about the effectiveness of group decision making?

9-25. What can groups do to make group decision making more effective?

9-26. What circumstances might cause a group to perform worse than its best individual?

ETHICAL DILEMMA   Is Social Loafing Unethical?

As we discussed in this chapter, social loafing is one potential downside of working in groups. Regardless of the type of task—from games of Tug of War to working on group projects—research suggests that when working in a group, most individuals contribute less than if they were working on their own. Sometimes, these people are labeled shirkers, because they don't fulfill their responsibilities as group members. Other times, social loafing is overlooked, and the industrious employees do the work alone to meet the group's performance goals. Either way, social loafing is an ethical dilemma.

Whether in class projects or in jobs we've held, most of us have experienced social loafing, or shirking, in groups. And there may have even been times when we were guilty of social loafing ourselves. We discussed earlier in this chapter some ways of discouraging social loafing, such as limiting group size, holding individuals responsible for their contributions, setting group goals, and providing "hybrid" incentives that reward both individual and group performance. Although these strategies might help to reduce the occurrence of social loafing, in many cases, it seems that people just try to work around shirkers rather than motivate them to perform at higher levels.

Managers and employees must decide the ethics of social loafing acceptance. Managers must determine what level of social loafing for groups and for individual employees will be tolerated in terms of time wasted in nonproductive meetings, performance expectations, and counterproductive work behaviors. Employees must decide what limits to social loafing they will impose on themselves and what tolerance they have for social loafers in their work groups.

Questions

9-27. Do group members have an ethical responsibility to report shirkers to leadership? If you were working on a group project for a class and a group member was social loafing, would you communicate this information to the instructor? Why or why not?

9-28. Do you think social loafing is always shirking (failing to live up to your responsibilities)? Are there times when shirking is ethical or even justified?

9-29. Social loafing has been found to be higher in Western, more individualist, nations than in other countries. Do you think this means we should tolerate shirking on the part of U.S. students and workers to a greater degree than if it occurred with someone from Asia?

CASE INCIDENT 1   The Calamities of Consensus

When it is time for groups to reach a decision, many turn to consensus. Consensus, a situation of agreement, seems like a good idea. To achieve consensus, groups must cooperate and collaborate, which ultimately will produce higher levels of camaraderie and trust. In addition, if everyone agrees, then the prevailing wisdom is that everyone will be more committed to the decision.

However, there are times when the need for consensus can be detrimental to group functioning. Consider the recent "fiscal cliff" faced by the U.S. government toward the end of 2012. The White House and Congress needed to reach a deal that would reduce the swelling budget deficit. However, many Republicans and Democrats stuck to their party lines, refusing to compromise. Many viewed the end product that achieved consensus as a less than optimal solution. The public gave Congress an approval rating of only 13 percent, expressing frustration with the lack of compromise, but the group may not have been able to function well partly because of the need for consensus.

If consensus is reached, does that mean the decision is the right one? Consider the Supreme Court's recent ruling to uphold "Obamacare." In the days leading up to the decision,

the general consensus was that the law requiring U.S. citizens to purchase health care insurance would be deemed unconstitutional. Ultimately, that consensus proved to be wrong.

Critics of consensus-based methods argue that any decisions that are ultimately reached are inferior to decisions using other methods such as voting or having a team members provide input to their leader, who then makes the final decision. Critics also argue that because of pressures to conform, groupthink is much more likely, and decisions reached through consensus are simply those that are disliked the least by everyone.

Questions

9-30. Is consensus a good way for groups to make decisions? Why or why not?

9-31. Can you think of a time where a group of which you were part relied on consensus? How do you think the decision turned out?

9-32. Martin Luther King Jr. once proclaimed, "A genuine leader is not a seeker of consensus but a modeler of consensus." What do you think he meant by that statement? Do you agree with it? Why or why not?

Sources: D. Leonhardt, "When the Crowd Isn't Wise," The New York Times (July 8, 2012), p. SR BW 4; and K. Jensen, "Consensus Is Poison! Who's With Me?" Forbes (May 20, 2013), downloaded on May 30, 2013, from www.forbes.com.

CASE INCIDENT 2   **Investing in the Herd**

It is sometimes easy to forget that humans are not unlike other animals. Economist John Maynard Keynes recognized this when he commented, "Most, probably, of our decisions to do something positive, the full consequences of which will be drawn out over many days to come, can only be taken as the result of animal spirits—a spontaneous urge to action rather than inaction, and not as the outcome of a weighted average of quantitative benefits multiplied by quantitative probabilities."

Such "animal spirits" are particularly dangerous at the collective level. One animal's decision to charge over a cliff is a tragedy for the animal, but it may also lead the entire herd over the cliff.

You may be wondering how this is applicable to organizational behavior. As it turns out, "herd behavior," a term coined by Yale Economist Robert Shiller, is relevant to many aspects of organizational behavior. For example, consider the recent housing bubble and its subsequent and enduring collapse. As housing prices rose ever higher, people discounted risk. Homeowners and investors rushed to buy properties because everyone else was doing it. Banks rushed to provide loans with little due diligence because, well, everyone else was doing it. "Banks didn't want to get left behind. Everybody lowered their underwriting standards, no matter who they are," said Regions Bank executive Michael Menk. "As bankers that's who we are; we follow the herd."

Or, consider the initial public offering (IPO) of Facebook. Investors flocked to purchase its stock, responding to an incredible amount of hype. You can't blame them—after all, the company was initially valued at an astonishing $104 billion. Many predicted the stock would immediately soar after the IPO, allowing investors to quickly cash in. Initially, the hype seemed justified. Soon after trading began on May 18, 2012, Facebook's stock price jumped from the initial offering price of $38 to $43. One year later, shares were down more than 30 percent from that high. Although Facebook itself profited from the IPO, many investors feel the company's public stock offering was one of the worst in history.

A recent study in behavioral finance confirmed herd behavior in investment decisions and showed that analysts were especially likely to follow other analysts' behavior when they had private information that was less accurate or reliable. For better or for worse, people often rely heavily on the behavior of groups in formulating decisions about what they should do.

Questions

9-33. Some research suggests herd behavior increases as the size of the group increases. Why do you think this might be the case?

9-34. The examples of the housing bubble and Facebook's IPO show the potential downsides of herd behavior. Can you think of examples in which herd behavior might have upsides?

9-35. Shiller argues that herd behavior can go both ways: It explains the housing bubble, but it also explains the bust. As he notes, "Rational individuals become excessively pessimistic as they see others bidding down home prices to abnormally low levels." Do you agree with Shiller?

Sources: Based on R. J. Shiller, "How a Bubble Stayed Under the Radar," *The New York Times* (March 2, 2008), p. BU6; W. Hobson, "Reversal of Fortune," *Panama City News Herald* (March 22, 2009), www .newsherald.com; P. Leoni, "Pack Behavior," *Journal of Mathematical Psychology* 52, no. 6 (2008), pp. 348–351; J. Reiczigel, Z. Lang, L. Rózsa, and B. Tóthmérész, "Measures of Sociality: Two Different Views of Group Size," *Animal Behaviour* 75, no. 2 (2008), pp. 715–721; and S. Gustin, "Facebook's IPO One Year Later: Mobile Growth, Legal Headaches, and a Stalled Stock Price," *Time* (May 17, 2013), downloaded on May 28, 2013, from www.business.time.com.

MyManagementLab

Go to **mymanagementlab.com** for Auto-graded writing questions as well as the following Assisted-graded writing questions:

9-36. Considering Case Incident 1, what are some ways groups can improve the effectiveness of consensus methods to make decisions?

9-37. After reading Case Incident 2, what would you recommend organizations do to combat the problems resulting from herd behavior?

9-38. MyManagementLab Only—comprehensive writing assignment for this chapter.

10 Understanding Work Teams

SLAYING TEAMWORK

You might not think a band with albums titled *Reign in Blood* and *Seasons in the Abyss* and songs called "Angel of Death" and "Public Display of Dismemberment" could teach us anything about effective teamwork. However, effective teamwork is actually one of the reasons Slayer has been among the most successful bands in the "thrash metal" genre.

Formed in 1981 by guitarists Kerry King and Jeff Hanneman, drummer Dave Lombardo, and joined by lead singer Tom Araya, Slayer quickly drew attention for their controversial and angry lyrics, blistering pace, and shocking album covers. In addition to developing a loyal fan base, Slayer has earned critical praise, winning back-to-back Grammy awards in 2007 and 2008. Their 2006 album, *Christ's Illusion*, debuted at number 5 on the Billboard chart, their highest position ever.

Members' lives outside the band look very different from the macabre personae they convey onstage. Araya operates a farm with his wife and two kids, King is an advocate against drug use, and Dave Lombardo has recorded classical music in Italy. (In May 2013, the band lost Hanneman, who died of liver failure resulting after a spider bite caused necrotizing fasciitis.)

How did Slayer remain a fixture in the heavy metal scene for more than 30 years, even when the genre faded in popularity? For one, they knew their product and how to sell it. "We scare people," says Araya. Just as important, however, was their teamwork and camaraderie. King and Hanneman easily and often alternated playing lead and rhythm. As King explained, "There is nothing like 'I need more leads than you' or 'I have to have the same amount of leads as you'" to create problems. And when it came to decisions, members were encouraged to communicate openly with each other and voice their opinions. Then, like a small democracy, they voted. Hanneman explained that the process was effective because, even when the group went a different way than what he wanted, his opinion was at least heard.

Ultimately, the importance of effective teamwork for Slayer was summarized by Araya, who stated, "The four of us—we try to make sure we're all together. Cause if one person stumbles, it takes a while to catch up."

Sources: A. Barker, "Jeff Hanneman Dead: Slayer Guitarist was 49," *Variety* (May 2, 2013), http://variety.com/2013/music/people-news/jeff-hanneman-dead-slayer-guitarist-1200442635/; R. Blatt, "Business Lessons from Slayer: A Reflection in Honor of Jeff Hanneman," *Forbes* (May 12, 2013), downloaded on June 4, 2013, from www.forbes.com; and D. Lang, "Jeff Hanneman Dead: Slayer Guitarist Dies at Age 49," *The Huffington Post* (May 2, 2013), www.huffingtonpost.com/2013/05/02/jeff-hanneman-dead_n_3205149.html.

LEARNING OBJECTIVES

After studying this chapter, you should be able to:

1 Analyze the growing popularity of teams in organizations.

2 Contrast groups and teams.

3 Contrast the five types of teams.

4 Identify the characteristics of effective teams.

5 Show how organizations can create team players.

6 Decide when to use individuals instead of teams.

eams are increasingly the primary means for organizing work in contemporary business firms. In fact, there are few more damaging insults than "not a team player." Do you think you're a team player? Take the following self-assessment to find out.

How Good Am I at Building and Leading a Team?

In the Self-Assessment Library (available in MyManagementLab), take assessment II.B.6 (How Good Am I at Building and Leading a Team?), and answer the following questions.

1. Did you score as high as you thought you would? Why or why not?
2. Do you think you can improve your score? If so, how? If not, why not?
3. Do you think there is such a thing as team players? If yes, what are their behaviors?

Why Have Teams Become So Popular?

1 Analyze the growing popularity of teams in organizations.

Decades ago, when companies such as W. L. Gore, Volvo, and General Foods introduced teams into their production processes, it made news because no one else was doing it. Today, it's just the opposite. The organization that *doesn't* use teams has become newsworthy. Teams are everywhere.

How do we explain the current popularity of teams? As organizations have restructured themselves to compete more effectively and efficiently, they have turned to teams as a better way to use employee talents. Teams are more flexible and responsive to changing events than traditional departments or other forms of permanent groupings. They can quickly assemble, deploy, refocus, and disband. But don't overlook the motivational properties of teams. Consistent with our discussion in Chapter 7 of employee involvement as a motivator, teams facilitate employee participation in operating decisions. Thus, another explanation

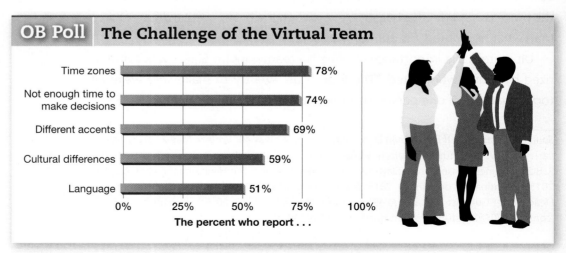

Note: Data is from a survey of 3,301 respondents from 102 countries.
Source: Based on RW3 CultureWizard, "The Challenges of Working in Virtual Teams: Virtual Teams Survey Report—2012," www.rw-3.com/2012Virtual TeamsSurveyReport.pdf, p. 4.

for their popularity is that they are an effective means for management to democratize organizations and increase employee motivation.

The fact that organizations have turned to teams doesn't necessarily mean they're always effective. Decision makers, as humans, can be swayed by fads and herd mentality. Are teams truly effective? What conditions affect their potential? How do members work together? These are some of the questions we'll answer in this chapter.

Differences Between Groups and Teams

2 Contrast groups and teams.

work group *A group that interacts primarily to share information and to make decisions to help each group member perform within his or her area of responsibility.*

work team *A group whose individual efforts result in performance that is greater than the sum of the individual inputs.*

Groups and teams are not the same thing. In this section, we define and clarify the difference between work groups and work teams.[1]

In Chapter 9, we defined a *group* as two or more individuals, interacting and interdependent, who have come together to achieve particular objectives. A **work group** is a group that interacts primarily to share information and make decisions to help each member perform within his or her area of responsibility.

Work groups have no need or opportunity to engage in collective work that requires joint effort. So their performance is merely the summation of each group member's individual contribution. There is no positive synergy that would create an overall level of performance greater than the sum of the inputs.

A **work team**, on the other hand, generates positive synergy through coordinated effort. The individual efforts result in a level of performance greater than the sum of those individual inputs. In both work groups and work teams, there are often behavioral expectations of members, collective normalization efforts, active group dynamics, and some level of decision making (even if just informally about the scope of membership). Both work groups and work teams may be called upon to generate ideas, pool resources, or coordinate logistics such as work schedules; for the work group, however, this effort will be limited to information gathering for decision makers outside the group (not team actionable).

Whereas we can think of a work team as a subset of a work group, the team is constructed to be purposeful (symbiotic) in its member interaction. The distinction between a work group and a work team should be kept even when the terms are mentioned interchangeably in differing contexts. Exhibit 10-1 highlights the differences between work groups and work teams.

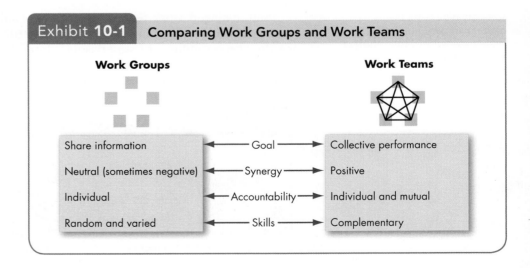

Exhibit 10-1 | **Comparing Work Groups and Work Teams**

Work Groups		Work Teams
Share information	← Goal →	Collective performance
Neutral (sometimes negative)	← Synergy →	Positive
Individual	← Accountability →	Individual and mutual
Random and varied	← Skills →	Complementary

These definitions help clarify why so many organizations have recently restructured work processes around teams. Management is looking for positive synergy that will allow the organizations to increase performance. The extensive use of teams creates the *potential* for an organization to generate greater outputs with no increase in inputs. Notice, however, that we said *potential*. There is nothing magical that ensures the achievement of positive synergy in the creation of teams. Merely calling a *group* a *team* doesn't automatically improve its performance. As we show later in this chapter, effective teams have certain common characteristics. If management hopes to gain increases in organizational performance through the use of teams, its teams must possess these.

Types of Teams

3 Contrast the five types of teams.

Teams can make products, provide services, negotiate deals, coordinate projects, offer advice, and make decisions.[2] In this section, first we describe four common types of teams in organizations: *problem-solving teams, self-managed work teams, cross-functional teams*, and *virtual teams* (see Exhibit 10-2). Then, we describe *multiteam systems*, which utilize a "team of teams" and are becoming increasingly widespread as work increases in complexity.

Problem-Solving Teams

In the past, teams were typically composed of 5 to 12 hourly employees from the same department who met for a few hours each week to discuss ways of improving quality, efficiency, and the work environment.[3] These **problem-solving teams** rarely have the authority to unilaterally implement any of their suggestions. Merrill Lynch created a problem-solving team to figure out ways to reduce the number of days it took to open a new cash management account.[4] By suggesting cutting the number of steps from 46 to 36, the team reduced the average number of days from 15 to 8.

problem-solving teams *Groups of 5 to 12 employees from the same department who meet for a few hours each week to discuss ways of improving quality, efficiency, and the work environment.*

Self-Managed Work Teams

Problem-solving teams only make recommendations. Some organizations have gone further and created teams that not only solve problems, but also implement solutions and take responsibility for outcomes.

self-managed work teams *Groups of 10 to 15 people who take on responsibilities of their former supervisors.*

    Self-managed work teams are groups of employees (typically 10 to 15 in number) who perform highly related or interdependent jobs and take on many of the responsibilities of supervisors.[5] Typically, these tasks are planning and scheduling work, assigning tasks to members, making operating decisions, taking action on problems, and working with suppliers and customers. Fully

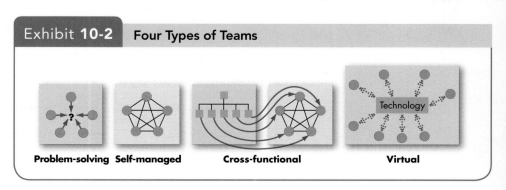

Exhibit **10-2**   Four Types of Teams

Problem-solving   Self-managed   Cross-functional   Virtual self-managed work teams even select their own members and evaluate each other's performance. Supervisory positions take on decreased importance and are sometimes even eliminated.

Research on the effectiveness of self-managed work teams has not been uniformly positive.[6] Self-managed teams do not typically manage conflicts well. When disputes arise, members stop cooperating and power struggles ensue, which leads to lower group performance.[7] However, when team members feel confident that they can speak up without being embarrassed, rejected, or punished by other team members—in other words, when they feel psychologically safe—conflict is actually beneficial and boosts performance.[8] In addition, one study of 45 self-managing teams of factory workers found that when team members perceived that economic rewards such as pay were dependent on input from their teammates, performance improved for both individuals and the team as a whole.[9]

Finally, although individuals on teams report higher levels of job satisfaction than other individuals, they also sometimes have higher absenteeism and turnover rates. One large-scale study of labor productivity in British establishments found that although using teams in general does improve labor productivity, no evidence supported the claim that self-managed teams performed better than traditional teams with less decision-making authority.[10] Thus, it appears that for self-managing teams to be advantageous, a number of situational factors must be in place.

Cross-Functional Teams

cross-functional teams Employees from about the same hierarchical level, but from different work areas, who come together to accomplish a task.

Starbucks created a team of individuals from production, global PR, global communications, and U.S. marketing to develop its Via brand of instant coffee. The team's suggestions resulted in a product that would be cost-effective to produce and distribute and that was marketed with a tightly integrated, multifaceted strategy.[11] This example illustrates the use of **cross-functional teams**, made up of employees from about the same hierarchical level but different work areas, who come together to accomplish a task.

Photo 10-1 Sprig Toys CEO Craig Storey (standing, left) and the firm's co-founders shown here promote cross-functional teamwork in creating eco-friendly toys made from recycled products. Teams include toy designers and specialists in patent development, market research, merchandising, branding, packaging, and marketing.

Source: AP Photo/The Coloradoan, V. Richard Haro.

Many organizations have used horizontal, boundary-spanning teams for decades. In the 1960s, IBM created a large task force of employees from across departments to develop its highly successful System 360. Today, cross-functional teams are so widely used it is hard to imagine a major organizational undertaking without one. All the major automobile manufacturers—Toyota, Honda, Nissan, BMW, GM, Ford, and Chrysler—currently use this form of team to coordinate complex projects. Cisco relies on specific cross-functional teams to identify and capitalize on new trends in several areas of the software market. Cisco's teams are the equivalent of social-networking groups that collaborate in real time to identify new business opportunities in the field and then implement them from the bottom up.[12]

Cross-functional teams are an effective means of allowing people from diverse areas within or even between organizations to exchange information, develop new ideas, solve problems, and coordinate complex projects. Of course, cross-functional teams are no picnic to manage. Their early stages of development are often long, as members learn to work with diversity and complexity. It takes time to build trust and teamwork, especially among people from varying backgrounds with different experiences and perspectives.

Virtual Teams

virtual teams *Teams that use computer technology to tie together physically dispersed members in order to achieve a common goal.*

The teams described in the preceding section do their work face-to-face. **Virtual teams** use computer technology to unite physically dispersed members and achieve a common goal.[13] They collaborate online—using communication links such as wide-area networks, videoconferencing, or e-mail—whether they're a room away or continents apart. Virtual teams are so pervasive, and technology has advanced so far, that it's probably a bit of a misnomer to call them "virtual." Nearly all teams today do at least some of their work remotely.

Despite becoming more widespread, virtual teams face special challenges. They may suffer because there is less social rapport and direct interaction among members, leaving some feeling isolated. One study showed that team leaders can reduce feelings of isolation, however, by communicating frequently and consistently with team members so none feel unfairly disfavored.[14] In addition, evidence from 94 studies entailing more than 5,000 groups found that virtual teams are better at sharing unique information (information held by individual members but not the entire group), but they tend to share less information overall.[15] As a result, low levels of virtuality in teams results in higher levels of information sharing, but high levels of virtuality hinder it. For virtual teams to be effective, management should ensure that (1) trust is established among members (one inflammatory remark in an e-mail can severely undermine team trust), (2) team progress is monitored closely (so the team doesn't lose sight of its goals and no team member "disappears"), and (3) the efforts and products of the team are publicized throughout the organization (so the team does not become invisible).[16]

Multiteam Systems

multiteam system *A collection of two or more interdependent teams that share a superordinate goal; a team of teams.*

The types of teams we've described so far are typically smaller, standalone teams, though their activities relate to the broader objectives of the organization. As tasks become more complex, teams are often made bigger. However, increases in team size are accompanied by higher coordination demands, creating a tipping point at which the addition of another member does more harm than good. To solve this problem, organizations are employing **multiteam systems**, collections of two or more interdependent teams that share a superordinate goal. In other words, multiteam systems are a "team of teams."[17]

To picture a multiteam system, imagine the coordination of response needed after a major car accident. There is the emergency medical services team, which responds first and transports the injured to the hospital. An emergency room team then takes over, providing medical care, followed by a recovery team.

Virtual Teams Leave a Smaller Carbon Footprint

Despite being in different countries, or even on different continents, many teams in geographically dispersed teams are able to communicate effectively without meeting face-to-face, thanks to technology such as videoconferencing, instant messaging, and e-mail. In fact, members of some of these virtual teams may never meet each other in person. Although the merits of face-to-face versus electronic communication have been debated, there may be a strong *ethical* argument for virtual teams. Keeping team members where they are, as opposed to having them travel every time they need to meet, may be a more environmentally responsible choice. A very large proportion of airline, rail, and car transport is for business purposes and contributes greatly to global carbon dioxide emissions.

When teams are able to meet virtually rather than face-to-face, they dramatically reduce their "carbon footprint."

In a globally connected world, what sorts of actions might you take to minimize your organization's environmental impact from business travel? Several tips might help to get you started thinking about ways that virtual teams can be harnessed for greater sustainability:

1. Encourage all team members to think about whether a face-to-face meeting is really necessary and to try to utilize alternative communication methods whenever possible.
2. Communicate as much information as possible through virtual means, including e-mail, telephone calls, and videoconferencing.
3. When traveling to team meetings, choose the most environmentally

responsible methods possible. Also, check the environmental profile of hotels before booking rooms.
4. If the environmental savings are not enough motivation to reduce travel, consider the financial savings. According to a recent survey, businesses spend about 8 to 12 percent of their entire budget on travel. Communicating electronically can therefore result in two benefits: (a) it's cheaper and (b) it's good for the environment.

Sources: P. Tilstone, "Cut Carbon . . . and Bills," *Director* (May 2009), p. 54; L. C. Latimer, "6 Strategies for Sustainable Business Travel," *Greenbiz* (February 11, 2011), www.greenbiz .com; and F. Gebhart, "Travel Takes a Big Bite Out of Corporate Expenses," *Travel Market Report* (May 30, 2013), downloaded on June 9, 2013, from www.travelmarketreport.com.

Although the emergency services team, the emergency room team, and the recovery team are technically independent, their activities are interdependent, and the success of one depends on the success of the others. Why? Because they all share the higher goal of saving lives.

Some factors that make smaller, more traditional teams effective do not necessarily apply to multiteam systems and can even hinder their performance. One study showed that multiteam systems performed better when they had "boundary spanners" whose job was to coordinate with members of the other subteams. This reduced the need for some team member communication. Restricting the lines of communication was helpful because it reduced coordination demands.[18] Research on smaller, standalone teams tends to find that opening up all lines of communication is better for coordination, but when it comes to multiteam systems, the same rules do not always apply.

Creating Effective Teams

4 Identify the characteristics of effective teams.

Many people have tried to identify factors related to team effectiveness.[19] To help, some studies have organized what was once a "veritable laundry list of characteristics"[20] into a relatively focused model.[21] Exhibit 10-3 summarizes what we currently know about what makes teams effective. As you'll see, it builds on many of the group concepts introduced in Chapter 9.

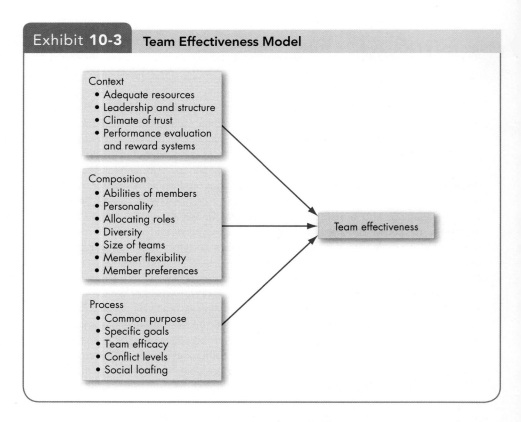

Exhibit 10-3   Team Effectiveness Model

Context
- Adequate resources
- Leadership and structure
- Climate of trust
- Performance evaluation and reward systems

Composition
- Abilities of members
- Personality
- Allocating roles
- Diversity
- Size of teams
- Member flexibility
- Member preferences

Process
- Common purpose
- Specific goals
- Team efficacy
- Conflict levels
- Social loafing

Team effectiveness

In considering the team effectiveness model, keep in mind two points. First, teams differ in form and structure. The model attempts to generalize across all varieties of teams, but avoids rigidly applying its predictions to all teams.[22] Use it as a guide. Second, the model assumes teamwork is preferable to individual work. Creating "effective" teams when individuals can do the job better is like perfectly solving the wrong problem.

We can organize the key components of effective teams into three general categories. First are the resources and other *contextual* influences that make teams effective. The second relates to the team's *composition*. Finally, *process* variables are events within the team that influence effectiveness. What does *team effectiveness* mean in this model? Typically, it has included objective measures of the team's productivity, managers' ratings of the team's performance, and aggregate measures of member satisfaction.

Context: What Factors Determine Whether Teams Are Successful

The four contextual factors most significantly related to team performance are adequate resources, effective leadership, a climate of trust, and a performance evaluation and reward system that reflects team contributions.

Adequate Resources   Teams are part of a larger organization system; every work team relies on resources outside the group to sustain it. A scarcity of resources directly reduces the ability of a team to perform its job effectively and achieve its goals. As one study concluded after looking at 13 factors related to group performance, "perhaps one of the most important characteristics of an effective work group is the support the group receives from the organization."[23] This support includes timely information, proper equipment, adequate staffing, encouragement, and administrative assistance.

Developing Team Members' Trust Across Cultures

The development of trust is critical in any work situation, but especially in multicultural teams, where differences in communication and interaction styles may lead to misunderstandings, eroding members' trust in one another.

Are there cultural differences in how much people trust others in general? Are there cultural differences in the factors people take into account when deciding how much to trust others? Researchers say "yes" to both questions—for the most part. Regarding the first question, some studies have shown that overall levels of trust differ across cultures. For example, Germans have been found to be less trusting of people from other countries, such as Mexicans and Czechs. Japanese have been found to be more trusting of U.S. counterparts than the other way around, but only in long-lasting relationships. Chinese and U.S. workers seem to trust each other equally.

For the second question, some evidence suggests people from different cultures do pay attention to different factors when deciding whether someone is trustworthy. Risk taking appears to be more critical to building trust for U.S. workers than for Japanese, perhaps reflecting that the United States is lower in uncertainty avoidance than Japan. Both Chinese and Mexicans appear to rely more than U.S. employees on emotional cues such as mutual understanding, openness, and social bonding, and less on cognitive cues such as reliability, professionalism, and economic cooperation.

When interacting with others from different cultures, whether in a formal team setting or not, it seems that what drives you to trust your colleagues may differ from what drives your colleagues to trust you, and recognizing these differences can help to facilitate higher levels of trust.

Sources: Based on D. L. Ferrin and N. Gillespie, "Trust Differences Across National-Societal Cultures: Much To Do, or Much Ado About Nothing," in M. N. K. Sanders, D. Skinner, G. Dietz, N. Gillespie, and Roy J. Lewicki (eds.), *Organizational Trust: A Cultural Perspective* (New York: Cambridge University Press, 2010), pp. 42–86; and J. Lauring and J. Selmer, "Openness to Diversity, Trust and Conflict in Multicultural Organizations," *Journal of Management & Organization* (November 2012), pp. 795–806.

Leadership and Structure   Teams can't function if they can't agree on who is to do what and ensure all members share the workload. Agreeing on the specifics of work and how they fit together to integrate individual skills requires leadership and structure, either from management or from the team members themselves. It's true in self-managed teams that team members absorb many of the duties typically assumed by managers. However, a manager's job then becomes managing *outside* (rather than inside) the team.

Leadership is especially important in multiteam systems. Here, leaders need to empower teams by delegating responsibility to them, and they play the role of facilitator, making sure the teams work together rather than against one another.[24] Teams that establish shared leadership by effectively delegating it are more effective than teams with a traditional single-leader structure.[25]

Climate of Trust   Members of effective teams trust each other. They also exhibit trust in their leaders.[26] Interpersonal trust among team members facilitates cooperation, reduces the need to monitor each others' behavior, and bonds members around the belief that others on the team won't take advantage of them. Team members are more likely to take risks and expose vulnerabilities when they believe they can trust others on their team. And, as we discuss in Chapter 12, trust is the foundation of leadership. It allows a team to accept and commit to its leader's goals and decisions. But it's not just the overall level of trust in a team that's important. How trust is dispersed among team members also matters. Trust levels that are asymmetric and imbalanced between team members can mitigate the performance advantages of a high overall level of trust.[27]

Performance Evaluation and Reward Systems   How do you get team members to be both individually and jointly accountable? Individual performance evaluations and incentives may interfere with the development of high-performance teams. So, in addition to evaluating and rewarding employees for their individual contributions, management should modify the traditional, individually oriented evaluation and reward system to reflect team performance and focus on hybrid systems that recognize individual members for their exceptional contributions and reward the entire group for positive outcomes.[28] Group-based appraisals, profit sharing, gainsharing, small-group incentives, and other system modifications can reinforce team effort and commitment.

Team Composition

The team composition category includes variables that relate to how teams should be staffed—the ability and personality of team members, allocation of roles, diversity, size of the team, and members' preference for teamwork.

Abilities of Members   Part of a team's performance depends on the knowledge, skills, and abilities of individual members.[29] It's true we occasionally read about an athletic team of mediocre players who, because of excellent coaching, determination, and precision teamwork, beat a far more talented group. But such cases make the news precisely because they are unusual. A team's performance is not merely the summation of its individual members' abilities. However, these abilities set limits on what members can do and how effectively they will perform on a team.

Research reveals some insights into team composition and performance. First, when the task entails considerable thought (solving a complex problem such as reengineering an assembly line), high-ability teams—composed of mostly intelligent members—do better than lower-ability teams, especially

Myth or Science?

"Team Members Who Are 'Hot' Should Make the Play"

Before we tell you whether this statement is true or false, we need to take a step back and address another question: "Can individuals go on 'hot' streaks?" In teams, and especially in sports, we often hear about players who are on a streak and have the "hot hand." Basketball player LeBron James scores five baskets in a row, golfer Rory McIlroy makes three birdies in a row for the European Ryder Cup team, and tennis player Serena Williams hits four aces in a row during a doubles match with her sister Venus. Most people (around 90 percent) believe LeBron, Rory, and Serena will continue to score well because they are on a hot streak, performing above their average.

Although people *believe* in the "hot hand," the score is tied on whether it actually exists. About half the relevant studies have shown that it does, while the remaining half show it does not. But perception is often reality, so perhaps the more important question is whether belief in the hot hand affects teams' strategies. One study of volleyball players showed that coaches and players allocate more balls to players who are believed to have the hot hand. Is this a good strategy? If the hot player's performance is typically lower than her teammates', then giving her more balls to hit will hurt the team because the better players aren't getting enough chances to hit. But if the player's

performance is typically higher than that of her teammates, giving her more balls to hit will likely help the team.

Considering all the research to date, however, the opening statement appears to be false.

_____

Sources: M. Raab, B. Gula, and G. Gigerenzer, "The Hot Hand Exists in Volleyball and Is Used for Allocation Decisions," *Journal of Experimental Psychology: Applied* 18, no. 1 (2012), pp. 81–94; T Gilovich, R. Vallone, and A. Tversky, "The Hot Hand in Basketball: On the Misperception of Random Sequences," *Cognitive Psychology* 17 (1985), pp. 295–314; and M. Bar-Eli, S. Avugos, and M. Raab, "Twenty Years of 'Hot Hand' Research: The Hot Hand Phenomenon: Review and Critique," *Psychology, Sport, and Exercise* 7 (2006), pp. 525–553.

Photo 10-2 Mike Weightman (second from left) led an 18-member, high-ability global team created by the International Atomic Energy Agency to study a nuclear power plant accident triggered by an earthquake in Japan. Team members from 12 countries provided experience and expertise in safety and a wide range of nuclear specialties.

Source: TEPCO/AFLO/Newscom.

when the workload is distributed evenly. That way, team performance does not depend on the weakest link. High-ability teams are also more adaptable to changing situations; they can more effectively apply existing knowledge to new problems.

Finally, the ability of the team's leader also matters. Smart team leaders help less-intelligent team members when they struggle with a task. A less intelligent leader can conversely neutralize the effect of a high-ability team.[30]

Personality of Members We demonstrated in Chapter 5 that personality significantly influences individual employee behavior. Some dimensions identified in the Big Five personality model are relevant to team effectiveness; a review of the literature identified three.[31] Specifically, teams that rate higher on mean levels of conscientiousness and openness to experience tend to perform better, and the minimum level of team member agreeableness also matters: teams did worse when they had one or more highly disagreeable members. Perhaps one bad apple *can* spoil the whole bunch!

Research has provided us with a good idea about why these personality traits are important to teams. Conscientious people are good at backing up other team members, and they're good at sensing when their support is truly needed. One study found that specific behavioral tendencies such as personal organization, cognitive structuring, achievement orientation, and endurance were all related to higher levels of team performance.[32] Open team members communicate better with one another and throw out more ideas, which makes teams composed of open people more creative and innovative.[33]

Suppose an organization needs to create 20 teams of 4 people each and has 40 highly conscientious people and 40 who score low on conscientiousness. Would the organization be better off (1) forming 10 teams of highly conscientious people and 10 teams of members low on conscientiousness, or (2) "seeding" each team with 2 people who scored high and 2 who scored low on conscientiousness? Perhaps surprisingly, evidence suggests option 1 is the best choice; performance across the teams will be higher if the organization forms 10 highly conscientious teams and 10 teams low in conscientiousness. The reason is that a team with varying conscientiousness levels will not work to the peak performance of the highly conscientious members. Instead, a group normalization dynamic (or simple resentment) will complicate interactions and force the highly conscientious members to lower their expectations, reducing the group's performance. In cases like this, it does appear to make sense to "put all of one's eggs [conscientious team members] into one basket [into teams with other conscientious members]."[34]

Allocation of Roles   Teams have different needs, and members should be selected to ensure all the various roles are filled. A study of 778 major league baseball teams over a 21-year period highlights the importance of assigning roles appropriately.[35] As you might expect, teams with more experienced and skilled members performed better. However, the experience and skill of those in core roles who handle more of the workflow of the team, and who are central to all work processes (in this case, pitchers and catchers), were especially vital. In other words, put your most able, experienced, and conscientious workers in the most central roles in a team.

We can identify nine potential team roles (see Exhibit 10-4). Successful work teams have selected people to play all these roles based on their skills and preferences.[36] (On many teams, individuals will play multiple roles.) To increase the likelihood team members will work well together, managers need to understand the individual strengths each person can bring to a team, select members with their strengths in mind, and allocate work assignments that fit with members' preferred styles.

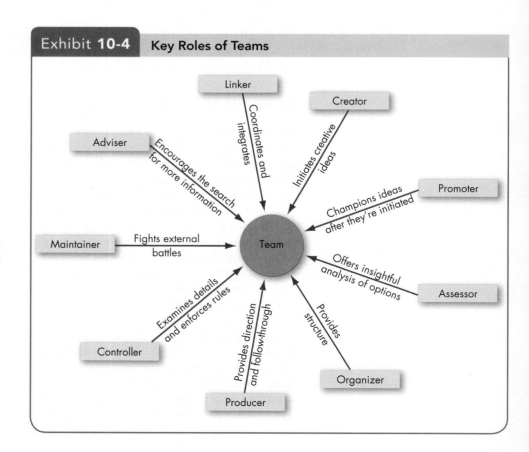

Exhibit **10-4**   **Key Roles of Teams**

Diversity of Members   In Chapter 9, we discussed research on the effect of diversity on groups. How does *team* diversity affect *team* performance? The degree to which members of a work unit (group, team, or department) share a common demographic attribute, such as age, sex, race, educational level, or length of service in the organization is the subject of **organizational demography**. Organizational demography suggests that attributes such as age or the date of joining should help us predict turnover. The logic goes like this: Turnover will be greater among those with dissimilar experiences because communication is more difficult and conflict is more likely. Increased conflict makes membership less attractive, so employees are more likely to quit. Similarly, the losers in a power struggle are more apt to leave voluntarily or be forced out.[37]

Many of us hold the optimistic view that diversity should be a good thing—diverse teams should benefit from differing perspectives. Two meta-analytic reviews of the research literature show, however, that demographic diversity is essentially unrelated to team performance overall, while a third review actually suggests that race and gender diversity are negatively related to team performance.[38] One qualifier is that gender and ethnic diversity have more negative effects in occupations dominated by white or male employees, but in more demographically balanced occupations, diversity is less of a problem. Diversity in function, education, and expertise are positively related to group performance, but these effects are quite small and depend on the situation.

Proper leadership can also improve the performance of diverse teams.[39] One study of 68 teams in China found that teams diverse in terms of knowledge, skills, and ways of approaching problems were more creative, but only when their leaders were transformational and inspiring.[40]

We have discussed research on team diversity in race or gender. But what about diversity created by national differences? Like the earlier research, evidence here indicates these elements of diversity interfere with team processes, at least in the short term.[41] Cultural diversity does seem to be an asset for tasks that call for a variety of viewpoints. But culturally heterogeneous teams have more difficulty learning to work with each other and solving problems. The good news is that these difficulties seem to dissipate with time. Although newly formed culturally diverse teams underperform newly formed culturally homogeneous teams, the differences disappear after about 3 months.[42]

Size of Teams   Most experts agree, keeping teams small is a key to improving group effectiveness.[43] Generally speaking, the most effective teams have five to nine members. Experts suggest using the smallest number of people who can do the task. Unfortunately, managers often err by making teams too large. It may require only four or five members to develop diversity of views and skills, while coordination problems can increase exponentially as team members are added. When teams have excess members, cohesiveness and mutual accountability decline, social loafing increases, and people communicate less. Members of large teams have trouble coordinating with one another, especially under time pressure. When a natural working unit is larger and you want a team effort, consider breaking the group into subteams if it's difficult to develop effective coordination processes.[44]

Member Preferences   Not every employee is a team player. Given the option, many employees will select themselves *out* of team participation. When people who prefer to work alone are required to team up, there is a direct threat to the team's morale and to individual member satisfaction.[45] This suggests that, when selecting team members, managers should consider individual preferences along with abilities, personalities, and skills. High-performing teams are likely to be composed of people who prefer working as part of a group.

organizational demography *The degree to which members of a work unit share a common demographic attribute, such as age, sex, race, educational level, or length of service in an organization, and the impact of this attribute on turnover.*

Photo 10-3 A Japanese nurse (left) served on a seven-member medical team formed by the International Committee of the Red Cross and deployed to the Philippines after a typhoon hit Mindanoa Island. The small team of health care workers had the capacity to respond quickly and effectively in providing patients with emergency medical care.

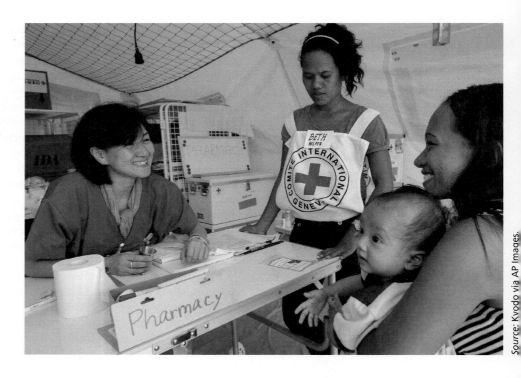

Source: Kyodo via AP Images.

Team Processes

The final category related to team effectiveness includes process variables such as member commitment to a common purpose, establishment of specific team goals, team efficacy, a managed level of conflict, and minimized social loafing. These will be especially important in larger teams and in teams that are highly interdependent.[46]

Why are processes important to team effectiveness? Let's return to the topic of social loafing. We found that $1+1+1$ doesn't necessarily add up to 3. When each member's contribution is not clearly visible, individuals tend to decrease their effort. Social loafing, in other words, illustrates a process loss from using teams. But teams should create outputs greater than the sum of their inputs, as when a diverse group develops creative alternatives. Exhibit 10-5 illustrates how group processes can have an impact on a group's actual effectiveness.[47] Teams are often used in research laboratories because they can draw on the diverse skills of various individuals to produce more meaningful research than researchers working independently—that is, they produce positive synergy, and their process gains exceed their process losses.

Common Plan and Purpose Effective teams begin by analyzing the team's mission, developing goals to achieve that mission, and creating strategies for achieving the goals. Teams that consistently perform better have established a clear sense of what needs to be done and how.[48]

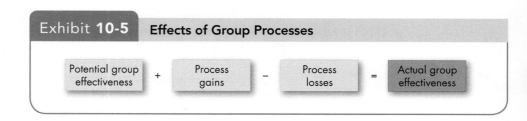

Exhibit 10-5 **Effects of Group Processes**

Potential group effectiveness + Process gains − Process losses = Actual group effectiveness

Members of successful teams put a tremendous amount of time and effort into discussing, shaping, and agreeing on a purpose that belongs to them both collectively and individually. This common purpose, when accepted by the team, becomes what GPS is to a ship captain: It provides direction and guidance under any and all conditions. Like a ship following the wrong course, teams that don't have good planning skills are doomed; perfectly executing the wrong plan is a lost cause.[49] Teams should agree on whether their goal is to learn about and master a task or simply to perform the task; evidence suggest that different perspectives on learning versus performance goals lead to lower levels of team performance overall.[50] It appears that these differences in goal orientation produce their effects by reducing discussion and sharing of information. In sum, having all employees on a team strive for the same *type* of goal is important.

Effective teams show **reflexivity**, meaning they reflect on and adjust their master plan when necessary. A team has to have a good plan, but it also has to be willing and able to adapt when conditions call for it.[51] Interestingly, some evidence does suggest that teams high in reflexivity are better able to adapt to conflicting plans and goals among team members.[52]

reflexivity *A team characteristic of reflecting on and adjusting the master plan when necessary.*

Specific Goals Successful teams translate their common purpose into specific, measurable, and realistic performance goals. Specific goals facilitate clear communication. They help teams maintain their focus on getting results.

Consistent with the research on individual goals, team goals should also be challenging. Difficult but achievable goals raise team performance on those criteria for which they're set. So, for instance, goals for quantity tend to raise quantity, goals for accuracy raise accuracy, and so on.[53]

Team Efficacy Effective teams have confidence in themselves; they believe they can succeed. We call this *team efficacy*.[54] Teams that have been successful raise their beliefs about future success, which, in turn, motivates them to work harder. In addition, teams that have a shared knowledge of who knows what within the team can strengthen the link between team members' self-efficacy and their individual creativity because members can more effectively solicit opinions and advice from their teammates.[55] What can management do to increase team efficacy? Two options are helping the team achieve small successes that build confidence and providing training to improve members' technical and interpersonal skills. The greater the abilities of team members, the more likely the team will develop confidence and the ability to deliver on that confidence.

Photo 10-4 Pit crew team members of NASCAR race car driver Danica Patrick work toward the common goal of winning the race. Each member has a specific job and a clear sense of what needs to be done to execute the crew's plan of working at top speed with no errors in checking the car, fixing parts, changing tires, and pumping gas.

Source: Brandon Wade/MCT/Newscom.

mental models *Team members' knowledge and beliefs about how the work gets done by the team.*

Mental Models   Effective teams share accurate **mental models**—organized mental representations of the key elements within a team's environment that team members share.[56] If team members have the wrong mental models, which is particularly likely in teams under acute stress, their performance suffers.[57] The similarity of team members' mental models matters, too. If team members have different ideas about how to do things, the team will fight over methods rather than focus on what needs to be done.[58] One review of 65 independent studies of team cognition found that teams with shared mental models engaged in more frequent interactions with one another, were more motivated, had more positive attitudes toward their work, and had higher levels of objectively rated performance.[59]

Conflict Levels   Conflict on a team isn't necessarily bad. As we discuss in Chapter 15, conflict has a complex relationship with team performance. *Relationship conflicts*—those based on interpersonal incompatibility, tension, and animosity toward others—are almost always dysfunctional. However, when teams are performing nonroutine activities, disagreements about task content—called *task conflicts*—stimulate discussion, promote critical assessment of problems and options, and can lead to better team decisions. A study conducted in China found that moderate levels of task conflict during the initial phases of team performance were positively related to team creativity, but both very low and very high levels of task conflict were negatively related to team performance.[60] In other words, both too much and too little disagreement about how a team should initially perform a creative task can inhibit performance.

The way conflicts are resolved can also make the difference between effective and ineffective teams. A study of ongoing comments made by 37 autonomous work groups showed that effective teams resolved conflicts by explicitly discussing the issues, whereas ineffective teams had conflicts focused more on personalities and the way things were said.[61]

Social Loafing   As we noted earlier, individuals can engage in social loafing and coast on the group's effort when their particular contributions can't be identified. Effective teams undermine this tendency by making members individually and jointly accountable for the team's purpose, goals, and approach.[62] Therefore, members should be clear on what they are individually responsible for and what they are jointly responsible for on the team.

SELF-ASSESSMENT LIBRARY

What Is My Team Efficacy?

In the Self-Assessment Library (available in MyManagementLab), take assessment IV.E.2 (What Is My Team Efficacy?).

Turning Individuals into Team Players

5   Show how organizations can create team players.

We've made a strong case for the value and growing popularity of teams. But many people are not inherently team players, and many organizations have historically nurtured individual accomplishments. Teams fit well in countries that score high on collectivism, but what if an organization wants to introduce teams into a work population of individuals born and raised in an individualistic society? A veteran employee of a large company, who had done well working in an individualistic company in an individualist country, described the experience of joining a team: "I'm learning my lesson. I just had my first negative performance appraisal in 20 years."[63]

So what can organizations do to enhance team effectiveness—to turn individual contributors into team members? Here are options for managers trying to turn individuals into team players.

Selecting: Hiring Team Players

Some people already possess the interpersonal skills to be effective team players. When hiring team members, be sure candidates can fulfill their team roles as well as technical requirements.[64]

When faced with job candidates who lack team skills, managers have three options. First, don't hire them. If you have to hire them, assign them to tasks or positions that don't require teamwork. If that is not feasible, the candidates can undergo training to make them into team players. In established organizations that decide to redesign jobs around teams, some employees will resist being team players and may be untrainable. Unfortunately, they typically become casualties of the team approach.

Creating teams often means resisting the urge to hire the best talent no matter what. The New York Knicks professional basketball team pays Carmelo Anthony nearly $20 million per year, and while he scores a lot of points for his team, statistics show he scores many of them by taking more shots than other highly paid players in the league, which means fewer shots for his teammates.[65] Personal traits also appear to make some people better candidates for working in diverse teams. Teams made up of members who like to work through difficult mental puzzles also seem more effective and able to capitalize on the multiple points of view that arise from diversity in age and education.[66]

Training: Creating Team Players

Training specialists conduct exercises that allow employees to experience the satisfaction teamwork can provide. Workshops help employees improve their problem-solving, communication, negotiation, conflict-management, and coaching skills. L'Oréal, for example, found that successful sales teams required much more than being staffed with high-ability salespeople: Management had to focus much of its efforts on team building. "What we didn't account for was that many members of our top team in sales had been promoted because they had excellent technical and executional skills," said L'Oréal's senior VP of sales, David Waldock. As a result of the focus on team training, Waldock says, "We are no longer a team just on paper, working independently. We have a real group dynamic now, and it's a good one."[67] Employees also learn the five-stage group development model described in Chapter 9. Developing an effective team doesn't happen overnight—it takes time.

Rewarding: Providing Incentives to Be a Good Team Player

An organization's reward system must be reworked to encourage cooperative efforts rather than competitive ones.[68] Hallmark Cards Inc. added to its basic individual-incentive system an annual bonus based on achievement of team goals. Whole Foods directs most of its performance-based rewards toward team performance. As a result, teams select new members carefully so they will contribute to team effectiveness (and, thus, team bonuses).[69] It is usually best to

Photo 10-5 New engineering employees of India's Tata Consultancy Services work in teams to construct paper boats during a team-building exercise at the firm's training center. Creating team players is essential to the success of TCS because employees must collaborate and work cohesively in providing IT consulting services and business solutions for global clients.

Source: Bloomberg via Getty Images.

set a cooperative tone as soon as possible in the life of a team. As we already noted, teams that switch from a competitive to a cooperative system do not immediately share information, and they still tend to make rushed, poor-quality decisions.[70] Apparently, the low trust typical of the competitive group will not be readily replaced by high trust with a quick change in reward systems. These problems are not seen in teams that have consistently cooperative systems.

Promotions, pay raises, and other forms of recognition should be given to individuals who work effectively as team members by training new colleagues, sharing information, helping resolve team conflicts, and mastering needed new skills. This doesn't mean individual contributions should be ignored; rather, they should be balanced with selfless contributions to the team.

Finally, don't forget the intrinsic rewards, such as camaraderie, that employees can receive from teamwork. It's exciting to be part of a successful team. The opportunity for personal development of self and teammates can be a very satisfying and rewarding experience.

Beware! Teams Aren't Always the Answer

6 Decide when to use individuals instead of teams.

Teamwork takes more time and often more resources than individual work. Teams have increased communication demands, conflicts to manage, and meetings to run. So, the benefits of using teams have to exceed the costs, and that's not always the case.[71] Before you rush to implement teams, carefully assess whether the work requires or will benefit from a collective effort.

How do you know whether the work of your group would be better done in teams? You can apply three tests.[72] First, can the work be done better by more than one person? A good indicator is the complexity of the work and the need for different perspectives. Simple tasks that don't require diverse input are probably better left to individuals. Second, does the work create a common purpose or set of goals for the people in the group that is more than the aggregate of individual goals? Many service departments of new-vehicle dealers have introduced teams that link customer-service people, mechanics, parts specialists, and sales representatives. Such teams can better manage collective responsibility for ensuring customer needs are properly met.

The final test is to determine whether the members of the group are interdependent. Using teams makes sense when there is interdependence among tasks—the success of the whole depends on the success of each one, *and* the success of each one depends on the success of the others. Soccer, for instance, is an obvious *team* sport. Success requires a great deal of coordination between interdependent players. Conversely, except possibly for relays, swim teams are not really teams. They're groups of individuals performing individually, whose total performance is merely the aggregate summation of their individual performances.

Summary

Few trends have influenced jobs as much as the massive movement to introduce teams into the workplace. The shift from working alone to working on teams requires employees to cooperate with others, share information, confront differences, and sublimate personal interests for the greater good of the team.

Implications for Managers

- Effective teams have common characteristics. They have adequate resources, effective leadership, a climate of trust, and a performance evaluation and reward system that reflects team contributions. These teams have individuals with technical expertise as well as problem-solving, decision-making, and interpersonal skills and the right traits, especially conscientiousness and openness.
- Effective teams also tend to be small—with fewer than 10 people, preferably of diverse backgrounds. They have members who fill role demands and who prefer to be part of a group. And the work that members do provides freedom and autonomy, the opportunity to use different skills and talents, the ability to complete a whole and identifiable task or product, and work that has a substantial impact on others.
- Effective teams have members who believe in the team's capabilities and are committed to a common plan and purpose, have an accurate shared mental model of what is to be accomplished, share specific team goals, maintain a manageable level of conflict, and show a minimal degree of social loafing.
- Because individualistic organizations and societies attract and reward individual accomplishments, it can be difficult to create team players in these environments. To make the conversion, try to select individuals who have the interpersonal skills to be effective team players, provide training to develop teamwork skills, and reward individuals for cooperative efforts.

To Get the Most Out of Teams, Empower Them

POINT

If you want high-performing teams with members who like each other and their jobs, I have a simple solution. Remove the leash tied to them by management and let them make their own decisions. In other word, empower them. This trend started a long time ago, when organizations realized that creating layers upon layers of bureaucracy thwarts innovation, slows progress to a trickle, and merely provides hoops for people to jump through in order to get anything done.

You can empower teams in two ways. One way is structurally, by transferring decision making from managers to team members and giving teams the official power to develop their own strategies. The other way is psychologically, by enhancing team members' beliefs that they have more authority, even though legitimate authority still rests with the organization's leaders. However, structural empowerment leads to heightened feelings of psychological empowerment, giving teams (and organizations) the best of both worlds.

Research suggests empowered teams benefit in a number of ways. Members are more motivated. They exhibit higher levels of commitment to the team and to the organization. And they perform much better too. Empowerment sends a signal to the team that it is trusted and doesn't have to be constantly micromanaged by upper leadership. And when teams get the freedom to make their own choices, they accept more responsibility for and take ownership of both the good and the bad.

Granted, that responsibility also means empowered teams must take the initiative to foster their ongoing learning and development, but teams entrusted with the authority to guide their own destiny do just that. So, do yourself (and your company) a favor and make sure that teams, rather than needless layers of middle managers, are the ones making the decisions that count.

COUNTERPOINT

Empowerment advocates cite the benefits yet neglect the harm that can be done when too much decision-making power is given to teams. They think that, to create effective teams, all you have to do as a leader is nothing because, by empowering teams, you've effectively stepped away as a leader and have lost your authority. Empowerment can do some good in certain circumstances, but it's certainly not a cure-all.

Yes, organizations have become flatter over the past several decades, paving the way for decision-making authority to seep into the lower levels of the organization. But consider that many teams are "empowered" simply because the management ranks have been so thinned that there is no one left to make the key calls. Empowerment is then just an excuse to ask teams to take on more responsibility without an accompanying increase in tangible benefits like pay.

In addition, the organization's leadership already has a good idea of what it would like its teams (and individual employees) to accomplish. If managers leave teams to their own devices, how likely is it that those teams will always choose what the manager wanted? Even if the manager offers suggestions about how the team might proceed, empowered teams can easily ignore that advice. Instead, they need direction on what goals to pursue and how to pursue them. That's what effective leadership is all about.

Consider what happens when decision-making authority is distributed among team members. The clarity of each team member's role becomes fuzzy, and members lack a leader to whom they can go for advice. And finally, when teams are self-managed, they become like silos, disconnected from the rest of the organization and its mission. Simply handing people authority is no guarantee they will use it effectively. So, leave the power to make decisions in the hands of those who have worked their way up the organization. After all, they got to be leaders for a reason.

Sources: S. I. Tannenbaum, J. Mathieu, E. Salas, and D. Cohen, "Teams Are Changing: Are Research and Practice Evolving Fast Enough," *Industrial and Organizational Psychology* 5 (2012), pp. 2–24; and R. Ashkenas, "How to Empower Your Team for Non-Negotiable Results," *Forbes* (April 24, 2013), downloaded on June 10, 2013, from www.forbes.com.

END-OF-CHAPTER REVIEW

MyManagementLab   Go to **mymanagementlab.com** to complete the problems marked with this icon. ⭐

QUESTIONS FOR REVIEW

10-1 How do you explain the growing popularity of teams in organizations?

10-2 What is the difference between a group and a team?

10-3 What are the five types of teams?

10-4 What conditions or context factors determine whether teams are effective?

10-5 How can organizations create team players?

10-6 When is work performed by individuals preferred over work performed by teams?

EXPERIENTIAL EXERCISE   Composing the "Perfect" Team

Break into teams of four to five. Assume you work for a company that redesigns existing products to improve them, from computer keyboards to bicycle helmets to toothbrushes. As a result, creativity is a key factor in whether your company succeeds in developing a product that is marketable.

You need to staff a new team of 5 individuals, and you have a pool of 20 to choose from. For each person, you have information about the following characteristics: intelligence, work experience, conscientiousness, agreeableness, neuroticism, openness to experience, and extraversion.

Your team is to answer the following questions:

10-7. If you could form your perfect team for this context, what would it look like? In other words, what characteristics would you choose for each of the five members—a lot of work experience or a little; high, moderate, or low conscientiousness; and so on? Why?

10-8. How, if at all, would your choices change if the task required teams to make quick decisions that were not necessarily the most creative? Why?

⭐**10-9.** Each member of your group should describe his or her ideal individual—one hypothetical person you'd most like to work with for this context (use the same criteria as in question 1). As a group, compare your responses. Does every person's ideal individual share the same characteristics, or are there differences? If you could, would you compose a team entirely of your ideal individuals? Why or why not?

ETHICAL DILEMMA   It's Easy to Be Unethical When Everyone Else Is

We often think of unethical behavior as individual behavior. However, in many cases, it's a team effort. Consider the doping scandal involving Tour de France cyclist Lance Armstrong and his teammates on the U.S. Postal Service Team. According to the U.S. Anti-Doping Agency, Armstrong, his coaches, and several of his teammates "ran the most sophisticated, professionalized and successful doping program the sport has ever seen." Five of eight riders on Armstrong's 1999 team admitted using performance-enhancing drugs, and Armstrong himself came clean in a widely publicized interview with Oprah Winfrey.

Teams in which unethical behavior occur are often high in status. Does unethical behavior occur only in elite teams like top management and sports? Or can it also occur in everyday work teams?

A study of 126 three-member teams of undergraduates suggests that unethical team behavior can occur beyond top management teams. In this study, teams were given a problem on which to work, with the following instructions:

> You are assigned a team project in one of your finance courses. Your team waits until the last minute to begin working. To save time, a friend suggests using an old project out of his fraternity files. Does your team go along with this plan?

How many of the teams decided to cheat? About 37 percent decided to use the old project.

Because this exercise was hypothetical, the authors also studied team cheating in another way—by allowing teams to self-grade a "decoy" assignment (an aspect of their assignment that did not in reality exist) that they thought counted as 2 percent of their course grade. How many teams cheated here? About one in four.

This study found that team cheating was greater when a team was composed of utilitarian members (those who think the ends justify the means). However, utilitarian attitudes were more likely to translate into team cheating when team members felt interpersonally "safe"—when they felt there was little risk within the team of being attacked or ridiculed for propositions or arguments they made.

The upshot? It appears that in the right circumstances, all types of teams are capable of behaving unethically. By holding individual team members accountable, and by providing a climate of "voice" where dissenting team members feel free to speak up, managers can discourage team unethical behavior.

Questions

10-10. Why do you think Lance Armstrong's teammates blew the whistle? What circumstances may have contributed to doping by Lance and his teammates?

10-11. Do you know for certain that you would have refused to agree to the unethical behavior in the experiment?

10-12. In this study, all team members were required to sign a response form indicating they agreed with the group decision, which was ultimately the decision to cheat. Do you think the results would change if consensus or a signature was not required?

Sources: M. J. Pearsall and A. P. J. Ellis, "Thick as Thieves: The Effects of Ethical Orientation and Psychological Safety on Unethical Team Behavior," *Journal of Applied Psychology* 96, no. 2 (2011), pp. 401–411; D. W. White and E. Lean, "The Impact of Perceived Leader Integrity on Subordinates in a Work Team Environment," *Journal of Business Ethics* 81, no. 4 (2008), pp. 765–778; and N. Karlinsky, "Lance Armstrong's Teammates Say He Doped," *ABC News* (October 10, 2012), downloaded on June 5, 2013, from www.abcnews.com.

CASE INCIDENT 1   Tongue-Tied in Teams

Thirty-one year old Robert Murphy has the best intentions to participate in team meetings, but when it's "game time," he chokes. An online marketing representative, Robert cannot be criticized for lack of preparation. After being invited to a business meeting with six of his co-workers and his supervisor, Robert began doing his research on the meeting's subject matter. He compiled notes, arranged them neatly, and walked into the meeting room. As soon as the meeting began, "I just sat there like a lump, fixated on the fact that I was quiet." The entire meeting passed without Robert contributing a word.

Robert is certainly not the first person, nor is he the last, to fail to speak up during meetings. While some employees may actually lack ability, the highly intelligent also freeze. One study found that if we believe our peers are smarter, we experience anxiety that temporarily blocks our ability to think effectively. In other words, worrying about what the group thinks of you makes you dumber. The study also found the effect was worse for women, perhaps because they are more socially attuned.

In other cases, failing to speak up may be attributed to personality. While the extraverted tend to be assertive and assured in group settings, the more introverted prefer to collect their thoughts before speaking—if they speak at all. But again, even those who are extraverted can remain quiet, especially when they feel they cannot contribute.

What to do? Michael Woodward, an organizational psychologist, suggests pairing up with someone more assertive who can pull you into the conversation. Preparation is key, even if it means talking to the person facilitating the meeting beforehand to discuss your thoughts. And finally, the realization that others may be feeling the same anxiety can also help spark the confidence to speak up.

Questions

10-13. Recall a time when you failed to speak up during a group meeting. What were the reasons for your silence? Are they similar to or different from the reasons discussed here?

10-14. Beyond the tips provided in this Case Incident, can you think of other strategies that can help the tongue-tied?

10-15. Imagine you are leading a team meeting and you notice that a couple of team members are not contributing. What specific steps might you take to try to increase their contributions?

Sources: E. Bernstein, "Speaking Up Is Hard to Do: Researchers Explain Why," *The Wall Street Journal* (February 7, 2012), p. D1; and H. Leroy et al., "Behavioral Integrity for Safety, Priority of Safety, Psychological Safety, and Patient Safety: A Team-Level Study," *Journal of Applied Psychology* (November 2012), pp. 1273–1281.

CASE INCIDENT 2 Multicultural Multinational Teams

As work has become more global, companies are realizing the benefits of composing teams of employees who not only have different cultural backgrounds, but who live in different countries. These multicultural, multinational teams are extremely diverse, allowing companies to leverage widely different points of view about business problems.

One company known for using multicultural, multinational teams is IBM. Although at one time IBM was famous for its written and unwritten rules—such as its no-layoff policy, focus on individual promotions and achievement, expectation of lifetime service at the company, and requirement of suits and white shirts at work—times have changed.

IBM has clients in 170 countries and now does two-thirds of its business outside the United States. As a result, it has overturned virtually all aspects of its old culture. One relatively new focus is on teamwork. To foster appreciation of a variety of cultures and open up emerging markets, IBM sends hundreds of its employees to month-long volunteer project teams in regions of the world where most big companies don't do business. Al Chakra, a software development manager located in Raleigh, North Carolina, was sent to join GreenForest, a furniture manufacturing team in Timisoara, Romania. With Chakra were IBM employees from five other countries. Together, the team helped GreenForest become more computer-savvy to increase its business. In return for the IBM team's assistance, GreenForest was charged nothing. IBM firmly believes these multicultural, multinational teams are good investments, because they help lay the groundwork for uncovering business in emerging economies. IBM is not the only company to use multicultural, multinational teams. Intel Corp., for example, has teams of employees located in the United States, Israel, and Ireland.

To manage these types of teams effectively, leaders must possess certain characteristics. These include obvious factors like openness to cultural diversity and cultural intelligence. And according to a survey conducted by Miriam Erez, a faculty member at the Technion-Israel Institute of Technology, it is better for leaders to have a global rather than a cross-cultural perspective. What's the difference? A global perspective means integrating culturally different and geographically different individuals into a single, unified team. Leaders with a global perspective develop a global identity in addition to their local or national identity, while leaders with a cross-cultural perspective do not perceive themselves as belonging to more than one culture.

Questions

10-16. If you calculate the person-hours devoted to IBM's team projects, they amount to more than 180,000 hours of management time each year. Do you think this is a wise investment of IBM's human resources? Why or why not?

10-17. Would you like to work on a multicultural, multinational project team? Why or why not?

10-18. Multicultural project teams often face problems with communication, expectations, and values. How do you think some of these challenges can be overcome?

Sources: Based on C. Hymowitz, "IBM Combines Volunteer Service, Teamwork to Cultivate Emerging Markets," *The Wall Street Journal* (August 4, 2008), p. B6; S. Gupta, "Mine the Potential of Multicultural Teams," *HR Magazine* (October 2008), pp. 79–84; H. Aguinis and K. Kraiger, "Benefits of Training and Development for Individuals and Teams, Organizations, and Society," *Annual Review of Psychology* 60, no. 1 (2009), pp. 451–474; and K. Gurchiek, "Global Training Sought for Leaders of Multicultural Teams," *Society for Human Resource Management* (September 15, 2011), downloaded on June 5, 2013, from www.shrm.org.

MyManagementLab

Go to **mymanagmentlab.com** for Auto-graded writing questions as well as the following Assisted-graded writing questions:

10-19. List the characteristics of an optimally successful team.
10-20. In reference to Case Incident 2 , how could you foster a "global perspective" in a multicultural, multinational team, rather than just a "cross-cultural perspective?" Is this an important distinction to make?
10-21. MyManagementLab Only—comprehensive writing assignment for this chapter.

Communication

MyManagementLab®

⭐ **Improve Your Grade!**

When you see this icon, visit **www.mymanagementlab.com** for activities that are applied, personalized, and offer immediate feedback.

COMMUNICATION INCOMPATIBILITY

Ashley was greeting her client when her cell phone buzzed the first time. Turning to sit down, she instinctively reached into her pocket to check: just a Facebook notification from business partner Chris. Ashley smiled at her client and opened the folder on the table between them.

"Bzzt," went her phone again. Ashley glanced: a tweet from Chris. Before she could click open her pen, her phone gave an insistent "Bzzt Bzzt." She glanced down. It was Chris again, now texting, who knew she was closing an important sale this afternoon. With a murmured apology to the client, whose smile had melted into a frown, Ashley ducked into the hallway. Her first call went to Chris's answering service, but her second call was answered before it rang. "Why didn't you *write* me back?" Chris whispered furiously. "Don't call. I told you I was in a meeting!"

Facebook, Twitter, Skype, e-mail, texts, phone calls, messages, live interaction—there have never been more ways to communicate. But few of us want to be available every minute. When people don't want to interact through the same medium, they suffer the frustration of communication incompatibility.

The communication incompatibility between Ashley and Chris may be minor, but the communication incompatibility between Ashley and her client may have serious business consequences. Because Ashley and Chris have an ongoing relationship, they may later decide to turn off their phones in meetings, but Ashley may have to repair her client's perception that she wasn't engaged in their meeting. Or it may be the other way around: The client might have liked to see Ashley's responsiveness to a perceived business emergency, while Ashley might think Chris doesn't respect her enough to recognize boundaries, and Chris might feel Ashley is unresponsive in their team effort.

Expert observers of communication incompatibility suggest the root of the phenomenon is lack of empathy. "People don't think to themselves, 'How does this other person want to be communicated with?' They just do what's easiest for them," observes communications writer Richard Laermer. When we cannot see the other person's perspective, we tend to make judgments about their motives for not communicating in the styles we prefer. For some people, "The idea that I have to monitor my Twitter account, email, Facebook, cellphone and land line in order to keep in touch—and to keep straight how other people prefer to talk—is too much," according to psychologist Sherry Turkle. Yet few people share their preferred communication method and style, leaving others to guess . . . and infer. The organizational consequences from communications breakdowns—lost clients, missed opportunities, misperceived levels of engagement—can be disastrous for employees and organizations.

Experts contend that many communication breakdowns occur when we decide what another person's unresponsiveness means. For instance, when

LEARNING OBJECTIVES

After studying this chapter, you should be able to:

1 Identify the main functions of communication.

2 Describe the communication process and formal and informal communication.

3 Contrast downward, upward, and lateral communication.

4 Compare and contrast formal small-group networks and the grapevine.

5 Contrast oral, written, and nonverbal communication.

6 Show how channel richness underlies the choice of communication channel.

7 Differentiate between automatic and controlled processing of persuasive messages.

8 Identify common barriers to effective communication.

9 Show how to overcome the potential problems in cross-cultural communication.

consultant Lisa Richens began to work from home, she ignored the "howdy" phone calls her husband Deron made during breaks at his office. She said, "I felt that when he had a minute he expected me to have a minute." When Deron kept calling, she answered the phone only to say, "Text me." Deron believed, "You can get everything knocked out in one quick conversation," but Lisa felt the phone calls were intrusive. The same thing happens when we don't respond to an e-mail; whether it is because we don't have time yet or because we don't use that account anymore, the sender may feel offended. The way we view others' responses depends on our own preferred style. "There are too many ways to converse, each of us has a favorite method . . . and no one wants to compromise," observed *Wall Street Journal* journalist Elizabeth Bernstein.

To resolve communications incompatibility, Turkle and other experts recommend having "necessary and difficult" conversations to say, "'Technology has created a situation where we are treating each other as though we were stalkers, but I don't want to think of you that way.'" Or you can try setting ground rules, but this might be easier said than done. When Laermer called his contacts to explain his preference for e-mail "because it allows for more depth than text, and it has a subject line," they texted him back. He ignored the texts; they called to complain. "They thought I was being a jerk about not texting," he said. "If they insist on only texting, they're not my kind of person anyway." These end-game strategies highlight the emotional escalation many people feel when there is communications incompatibility.

Sources: A. K. C. Au, and D. K.-S. Chang, "Organizational Media Choice in Performance Feedback: A Multifaceted," *Journal of Applied Social Psychology* (February 2013), pp. 397–407; E. Bernstein, "The Miscommunicators," *The Wall Street Journal* (July 3, 2012), pp. D1, D3; and N. Park, J. E. Chung, and L. Seungyoon, "Explaining the Use of Text-Based Communication Media: An Examination of Three Theories of Media Use," *Cyberpsychology Behavior and Social Networking* (July 2012), pp. 357–363.

T he story of Ashley and Chris illustrates one of the many challenges of communicating in organizations. In this chapter, we'll analyze the power of communication and ways in which we can make it more effective. One of the topics we'll discuss is gossip. Consider the following self-assessment, and see how you score on your attitudes toward gossip at work.

No individual, group, or organization can exist without sharing meaning among its members. It is only thus that we can convey information and ideas. Communicating is more than merely imparting meaning; that meaning must also be understood. If one group member speaks only German and the others do not know the language, the German speaker will not be fully understood. Therefore, **communication** must include both the *transfer* and *the understanding of meaning*. In perfect communication, if it existed, a thought would be transmitted so the receiver understood the same mental picture the sender intended. Though it sounds elementary, perfect communication is never achieved in practice, for reasons we shall see later in this chapter.

First let's review the functions communication performs and describe the communication process.

Am I a Gossip?

In the Self-Assessment Library (available in MyManagementLab), take assessment IV.E.3 (Am I a Gossip?) and answer the following questions.

1. How did you score relative to your classmates?
2. Do you think gossiping is morally wrong? Why or why not?

Functions of Communication

1 Identify the main functions of communication.

communication *The transfer and understanding of meaning.*

Communication serves four major functions within a group or organization: control, motivation, emotional expression, and information.[1]

Communication acts to *control* member behavior in several ways. Organizations have authority hierarchies and formal guidelines employees are required to follow. When employees communicate a job-related grievance, follow their job description, or comply with company policies, communication performs a control function. Informal communication controls behavior too. When work groups tease or harass a member who produces too much (and makes the rest of the group look bad), they are informally communicating, and controlling, the member's behavior.

Communication fosters *motivation* by clarifying to employees what they must do, how well they are doing it, and how they can improve their performance. We saw this operating in our review of goal-setting theory in Chapter 7. Formation of goals, feedback on progress, and reward for desired behavior all stimulate motivation and require communication.

Photo 11-1 Rene Brookbank, marketing consultant and director of client relations at Cummins & White law firm, jokes with her co-workers during a fashion event for employees. Communication interactions like this that take place in organizations perform the function of fulfilling social needs and providing for the emotional expression of feelings.

Source: H. Lorren Au Jr/ZUMAPRESS/Newscom.

The work group is a primary source of social interaction for many employees. Communication within the group is a fundamental mechanism by which members show satisfaction and frustration. Communication, therefore, provides for the *emotional expression* of feelings and fulfillment of social needs.

The final function of communication is to facilitate decision making. Communication provides the *information* individuals and groups need to make decisions by transmitting the data needed to identify and evaluate choices.

Almost every communication interaction that takes place in a group or organization performs one or more of these functions, and none of the four is more important than the others. To perform effectively, groups need to maintain some control over members, stimulate members to perform, allow emotional expression, and make decision choices.

glOBalization!

Multinational Firms Adopt English as Global Language Strategy

As companies "go global" from wherever they are headquartered, they are forced to address language barriers with their overseas employees and customers. Global organizations are increasingly choosing English as their common communication language, even though more people speak Chinese worldwide than any other language. Adopters of English include Airbus (headquartered in France), Daimler-Chrysler (United States), Fast Retailing (Japan), Nokia (Finland), Samsung (Seoul), and SAP (Germany).

A worldwide study indicated that 25 percent of jobs require employees to interact with people in other countries, including jobs for more than half the workers in India, Singapore, and Saudi Arabia. Of these jobs, two-thirds require English. "English has emerged as the default language for business around the world," concluded Darrell Bricker, CEO of Ipsos Public Affairs.

One reason English is the dominant language of business and of the Internet is that it is the native language in more than 60 nations, and increasingly the official secondary language elsewhere. While employees in native English-speaking countries are at a distinct advantage, so are employees in countries where English proficiency is high, such as Singapore, Malaysia, Scandinavia, and the Netherlands. Employees in other nations where English proficiency is lower—such as Panama, Saudi Arabia, Thailand, and Libya—are conversely disadvantaged.

Establishing English is not just a matter of teaching employees the language. Change brings shock and threatens the cultural identity of some people, while others may not be able to master a new language quickly. As a result, team dynamics and performance can suffer, compliance may be unreliable, cohesiveness may faction, employees may stop sharing needed information, and people may terminate their employment.

Careful implementation plans facilitate "Englishnization," says CEO Hiroshi Mikitani of Japan's Rakuten. OB research suggests that managers should offer employees opportunities to gain experience (such as in overseas job rotations and language immersion training specific to the industry), model positive attitudes, identify and encourage talent, market the initiative through success stories on blogs, and encourage corporate social networking with cross-national interactions.

Once organizations pass the implementation phase, research indicates that a global corporate language policy helps create a positive diversity climate; an English standard may actually lead employees to learn about other cultures. And that's good for business. As *Language Magazine* editor Daniel Ward observed, embracing cultures "will not only improve their business relationships, it will make them more fulfilling by enabling them to better understand and appreciate other cultures."

Sources: D. Clarke, "English—The Language of Global Business?" *Forbes* (October 26, 2012), www.forbes.com/sites/dorieclark/2012/10/26/english-the-language-of-global-business/; J. Lauring and J. Selmer, "International Language Management and Diversity Climate in Multicultural Organizations," *International Business Review* (April 2012), pp. 156–166; L. Louhiala-Salminen and A. Kankaaranta, "Language as an Issue in International Internal Communication: English or Local Language? If English, what English?" *Public Relations Review* (June 2012), pp. 262–269; C. Michaud, "English the Preferred Language for Business: Poll," *Reuters* (May 16, 2012), www.reuters.com/article/2012/05/16/us-language-idUSBRE84F0OK20120516; and T. Neeley, "Global Business Speaks English: Why You Need a Language Strategy Now," *Harvard Business Review* (May 2012), pp. 117–124.

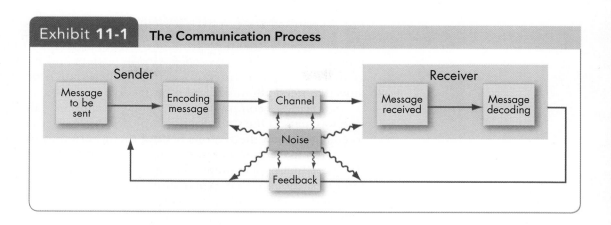

Exhibit **11-1**   The Communication Process

The Communication Process

2 Describe the communication process and formal and informal communication.

communication process *The steps between a source and a receiver that result in the transfer and understanding of meaning.*

formal channels *Communication channels established by an organization to transmit messages related to the professional activities of members.*

informal channels *Communication channels that are created spontaneously and that emerge as responses to individual choices.*

Before communication can take place it needs a purpose, a message to be conveyed between a sender and a receiver. The sender encodes the message (converts it to a symbolic form) and passes it through a medium (channel) to the receiver, who decodes it. The result is transfer of meaning from one person to another.[2]

Exhibit 11-1 depicts this **communication process**. The key parts of this model are (1) the sender, (2) encoding, (3) the message, (4) the channel, (5) decoding, (6) the receiver, (7) noise, and (8) feedback.

The *sender* initiates a message by encoding a thought. The *message* is the actual physical product of the sender's *encoding*. When we speak, the speech is the message. When we write, the writing is the message. When we gesture, the movements of our arms and the expressions on our faces are the message. The *channel* is the medium through which the message travels. The sender selects it, determining whether to use a formal or informal channel. **Formal channels** are established by the organization and transmit messages related to the professional activities of members. They traditionally follow the authority chain within the organization. Other forms of messages, such as personal or social, follow **informal channels**, which are spontaneous and emerge as a response to individual choices.[3] The *receiver* is the person(s) to whom the message is directed, who must first translate the symbols into understandable form. This step is the *decoding* of the message. *Noise* represents communication barriers that distort the clarity of the message, such as perceptual problems, information overload, semantic difficulties, or cultural differences. The final link in the communication process is a feedback loop. *Feedback* is the check on how successful we have been in transferring our messages as originally intended. It determines whether understanding has been achieved.

Direction of Communication

3 Contrast downward, upward, and lateral communication.

Communication can flow vertically or laterally. We subdivide the vertical dimension into downward and upward directions.[4]

Downward Communication

Communication that flows from one level of a group or organization to a lower level is *downward communication*. Group leaders and managers use it to assign goals, provide job instructions, explain policies and procedures, point out problems that need attention, and offer feedback.

In downward communication, managers must explain the reasons *why* a decision was made. One study found employees were twice as likely to be committed to changes when the reasons behind them were fully explained. Although this may seem like common sense, many managers feel they are too busy to explain things or that explanations will "open up a big can of worms." Evidence clearly indicates, though, that explanations increase employee commitment and support of decisions.[5] Although managers might think that sending a message one time is enough to get through to lower-level employees, most research suggests managerial communications must be repeated several times and through a variety of different media to be truly effective.[6]

Another problem in downward communication is its one-way nature; generally, managers inform employees but rarely solicit their advice or opinions. Research affirms that employees will not provide input, even when conditions are favorable, if doing so seems against their best interests.[7] A study revealed that nearly two-thirds of employees say their boss rarely or never asks their advice. The study noted, "Organizations are always striving for higher employee engagement, but evidence indicates they unnecessarily create fundamental mistakes. People need to be respected and listened to." Companies like cell phone maker Nokia actively listen to employee's suggestions, a practice the company thinks is especially important to innovation.[8]

The best communicators explain the reasons behind their downward communications but also solicit communication from the employees they supervise. That leads us to the next direction: upward communication.

Upward Communication

Upward communication flows to a higher level in the group or organization. It's used to provide feedback to higher-ups, inform them of progress toward goals, and relay current problems. Upward communication keeps managers aware of how employees feel about their jobs, co-workers, and the organization in general. Managers also rely on upward communication for ideas on how conditions can be improved.

Given that most managers' job responsibilities have expanded, upward communication is increasingly difficult because managers are overwhelmed and easily distracted. To engage in effective upward communication, try to communicate in headlines not paragraphs, support your headlines with actionable items, and prepare an agenda to make sure you use your boss's attention well.[9]

Lateral Communication

When communication takes place among members of the same work group, members of work groups at the same level, managers at the same level, or any other horizontally equivalent workers, we describe it as *lateral communication*.

Lateral communication saves time and facilitates coordination. Some lateral relationships are formally sanctioned. More often, they are informally created to short-circuit the vertical hierarchy and expedite action. So from management's viewpoint, lateral communications can be good or bad. Because strictly adhering to the formal vertical structure for all communications can be inefficient, lateral communication occurring with management's knowledge and

Photo 11-2 Burger King improved the lateral communication among its executives by eliminating their closed-door offices and organizing their desks in an open-space setting. Shown here, from left, are executives Jonathan Fitzpatrick, Jose Tomas, and Daniel Schwartz communicating in their new work area at company headquarters in Miami.

Source: C.W. Griffin/MCT/Newscom.

support can be beneficial. But it can create dysfunctional conflicts when the formal vertical channels are breached, when members go above or around their superiors to get things done, or when bosses find actions have been taken or decisions made without their knowledge.

Organizational Communication

4 Compare and contrast formal small-group networks and the grapevine.

Formal Small-Group Networks

Formal organizational networks can be complicated, including hundreds of people and a half-dozen or more hierarchical levels. To simplify, we've condensed these networks into three common small groups of five people each (see Exhibit 11-2): chain, wheel, and all channel.

Exhibit **11-2**	Three Common Small-Group Networks

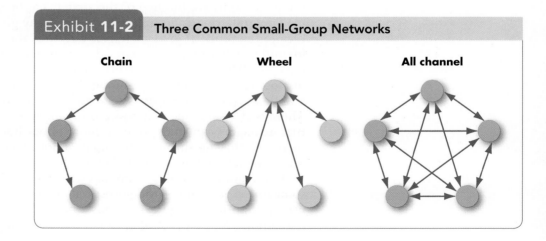

Chain   Wheel   All channel

	Networks		
Criteria	Chain	Wheel	All Channel
Speed	Moderate	Fast	Fast
Accuracy	High	High	Moderate
Emergence of a leader	Moderate	High	None
Member satisfaction	Moderate	Low	High

Exhibit 11-3   Small-Group Networks and Effective Criteria

The *chain* rigidly follows the formal chain of command; this network approximates the communication channels you might find in a rigid three-level organization. The *wheel* relies on a central figure to act as the conduit for all group communication; it simulates the communication network you would find on a team with a strong leader. The *all-channel* network permits group members to actively communicate with each other; it's most often characterized in practice by self-managed teams, in which group members are free to contribute and no one person takes on a leadership role.

As Exhibit 11-3 demonstrates, the effectiveness of each network depends on the dependent variable that concerns you. The structure of the wheel facilitates the emergence of a leader, the all-channel network is best if you desire high member satisfaction, and the chain is best if accuracy is most important. Exhibit 11-3 leads us to the conclusion that no single network will be best for all occasions.

The Grapevine

grapevine *An organization's informal communication network.*

The informal communication network in a group or organization is called the **grapevine**.[10] Although rumors and gossip transmitted through the grapevine may be informal, it's still an important source of information for employees and candidates. Grapevine or word-of-mouth information from peers about a company has important effects on whether job applicants join an organization.[11]

Rumors emerge as a response to situations that are *important* to us, when there is *ambiguity,* and under conditions that arouse *anxiety.*[12] The fact that work situations frequently contain these three elements explains why rumors flourish in organizations. The secrecy and competition that typically prevail—around the appointment of new bosses, the relocation of offices, downsizing decisions, or the realignment of work assignments—encourage and sustain rumors on the grapevine. A rumor will persist until either the wants and expectations creating the uncertainty are fulfilled or the anxiety has been reduced.

The grapevine is an important part of any group or organization communication network. It gives managers a feel for the morale of their organization, identifies issues employees consider important, and helps tap into employee anxieties. The grapevine also serves employees' needs: small talk creates a sense of closeness and friendship among those who share information, although research suggests it often does so at the expense of those in the "out" group.[13] There is also evidence that gossip is driven largely by employee social networks that managers can study to learn more about how positive and negative information is flowing through the organization.[14] Thus, while the grapevine may not be sanctioned or controlled by the organization, it can be understood.

Can managers entirely eliminate rumors? No. Research indicates that even some forms of gossip provide prosocial motivation.[15] What they should do, however, is minimize the negative consequences of rumors by limiting their range and impact. Exhibit 11-4 offers a few practical suggestions.

Exhibit 11-4	Suggestions for Reducing the Negative Consequences of Rumors

1. **Provide** information—in the long run, the best defense against rumors is a good offense (in other words, rumors tend to thrive in the absence of formal communication).
2. **Explain** actions and decisions that may appear inconsistent, unfair, or secretive.
3. **Refrain** from shooting the messenger—rumors are a natural fact of organizational life, so respond to them calmly, rationally, and respectfully.
4. **Maintain** open communication channels—constantly encourage employees to come to you with concerns, suggestions, and ideas.

Source: Based on L. Hirschhorn, "Managing Rumors," in L. Hirschhorn (ed.), *Cutting Back* (San Francisco: Jossey-Bass, 1983), pp. 54–56.

Modes of Communication

5 Contrast oral, written, and nonverbal communication.

How do group members transfer meaning among each other? They rely on oral, written, and nonverbal communication.

Oral Communication

A primary means of conveying messages is oral communication. Speeches, formal one-on-one and group discussions, and the informal rumor mill or grapevine are popular forms of oral communication.

The advantages of oral communication are speed and feedback. We can convey a verbal message and receive a response in minimal time. If the receiver is unsure of the message, rapid feedback allows the sender to quickly detect and correct it. As one professional put it, "Face-to-face communication on a consistent basis is still the best way to get information to and from employees."[16]

One major disadvantage of oral communication surfaces whenever a message has to pass through a number of people: the more people, the greater the potential distortion. If you've ever played the game "Telephone," you know the problem. Each person interprets the message in his or her own way. The message's content, when it reaches its destination, is often very different from the original. In an organization, where decisions and other communiqués are verbally passed up and down the authority hierarchy, opportunities arise for messages to become distorted.

Meetings Meetings can be formal or informal, include two or more people, and take place in almost any venue. Framing even our casual business interactions with others as meetings helps us stay focused on progress. Every meeting is an opportunity to "get stuff done," as CEO Kris Duggan of Badgeville said, and to "sparkle." He noted, "You may be an expert in your field, but if you don't communicate well, or if you don't get people excited, or you're not passionate or enthusiastic, that's going to be a hindrance."[17] Good interpersonal communication is important for making meetings effective. Some experts recommend using humor as an ice breaker; public relations firm Peppercomm even offers stand-up comedy workshops to help businesses teach people how to use humor.[18]

Videoconferencing *Videoconferencing* permits employees and clients to conduct real-time meetings with people at different locations. Live audio and video images let us see, hear, and talk with each other without being physically in the same location.

Peter Quirk, a program manager with EMC Corporation, uses videoconferencing to hold monthly meetings of employees at various locations to save travel expenses and time. However, Quirk notes it's important to stimulate questions and involve all participants in order to avoid having someone who is linked in but disengaged. Sun Microsystem's Karen Rhode agrees special efforts must be made to engage remote participants, suggesting, "You can poll people, people can ask questions, you can do an engaging presentation."[19]

Telephone   The telephone has been around so long that we can overlook its efficiency as a mode of communication. Telephone communication offers many of the benefits of meetings, and the ringing of the phone can prompt immediate response. Phone calls can be formal meetings or informal chats, either scheduled or spontaneous. Communication by telephone is fast, effective, and less ambiguous than e-mail. However, telephone messages can be easily overlooked.

Written Communication

Written communication includes letters, e-mail, instant messaging, organizational periodicals, and any other method that conveys written words or symbols. We will discuss written business communication via letters, PowerPoint, e-mail, instant messaging, text messaging, social media, and blogs later in this section.

Myth or Science?

"Today, Writing Skills Are More Important than Speaking Skills"

Never before have the writing skills of managers and employees been more on display. Whether we are tapping a keyboard or a screen, our communication with others is often unedited. (Thank goodness for spellcheck.) With all the written communication methods we currently employ, it would be easy to think upper management values writing skills over speaking skills. However, evidence suggests this is not the case.

As we discussed in Chapter 1, soft skills matter most to employers, regardless of industry. According to Nick Schultz of the American Enterprise Institute, "Considerable evidence suggests that many employers would be happy just to find applicants who have the sort of 'soft' skills that used to be almost taken for granted." Though soft skills refer to all interpersonal skills evident through speaking and writing, they are most on display in one-on-one discussions, interviews, meetings, and presentations. The ability to speak well, particularly English, has become a job prerequisite for many multinational corporations.

The good news is that speaking ability—knowledge of when to speak, how to speak, how to sound, what to say—can be improved through training. According to leadership coach and author Kristi Hedges, most people can train on their own and do not need formal presentation classes. Speaking well hinges on clarity and sincerity of expression, so you can make significant improvements by researching speaking techniques, watching videos of practice sessions, and practicing new techniques in meetings. If learning to speak a foreign language fluently is a problem, full immersion through overseas assignments to native-speaking territories can be helpful if it is an option, as well as listening to and mimicking television and radio broadcasts in the other language. While it is a mistake to believe writing skills have become more important than speaking skills, we can all make significant improvements in our verbal communications relatively quickly.

Sources: R. J. Aldrick and J. Kasuku, "Escaping from American Intelligence: Culture, Ethnocentrism and the Anglosphere," *International Affairs* (September 2012), pp. 1009–1028; K. Hedges, "Confessions of a Former Public Speaking Trainer: Don't Waste Your Money," *Forbes* (April 19, 2012), www.forbes.com/sites/work-in-progress/2012/04/19/public-speaking-trainer-confesses-dont-waste-your-money-on-this/; and N. Schultz, "Hard Unemployment Truths About 'Soft' Skills," *The Wall Street Journal* (September 20, 2012), p. A15.

Letters   With all the technology available, why would anyone write, print, and send a letter? Of all the forms of written communication, letter writing is the oldest—and the most enduring. We have scrolls of writing from thousands of years ago, yet we still put ink on paper when we want to create a lasting record. The same cannot be said of electronic writing; sometimes these communications are difficult to find later, and documents may not open when computer programs change.

PowerPoint   PowerPoint and other slide formats like Prezi can be an excellent mode of communication because slide-generating software combines words with visual elements to engage the reader and help explain complex ideas. PowerPoint is often used in conjunction with oral presentations, but its appeal is so intuitive that it can serve as a primary mode of communication. It is not without its detractors, however, who argue that it is too impersonal, disengaging, and frequently misused.

E-Mail   The growth of e-mail since its inception nearly 50 years ago has been spectacular, and its use is so pervasive it's hard to imagine life without it. Recent research found there are more than 3.1 billion active e-mail accounts worldwide, and corporate employees average 105 e-mails each day.[20] Exhibit 11-5 shows the time managers and professionals spend daily on various tasks. Many managers report that they spend too much time on e-mail.

E-mail messages can be quickly written, edited, and stored. They can be distributed to one person or thousands with the same click of a key, though some companies (such as data company Nielson) have banned the "reply to all"

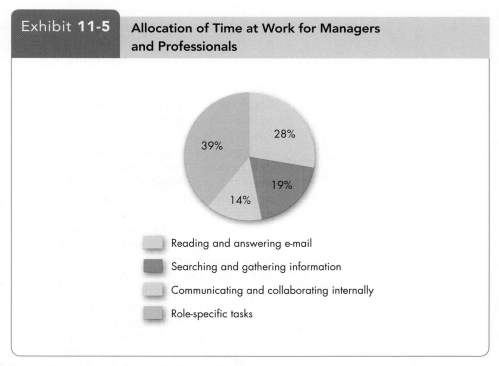

| Exhibit **11-5** | Allocation of Time at Work for Managers and Professionals |

- Reading and answering e-mail
- Searching and gathering information
- Communicating and collaborating internally
- Role-specific tasks

Source: Based on M. Chui et al., "The Social Economy: Unlocking Value and Productivity through Social Technologies," McKinsey & Company (July 2012), http://www.mckinsey.com/insights/high_tech_telecoms_internet/the_social_economy.

feature.[21] The cost of sending formal e-mail messages to employees is a fraction of the cost of printing, duplicating, and distributing a comparable letter or brochure.[22] E-mail is not without cost, however. In fact, according to e-mail software company Messagemind, corporations lose $650 billion each year from time spent in processing unnecessary e-mail communication.[23] A recent study also indicated that people focus longer on tasks and are less stressed when they are cut off from checking e-mail.[24]

Instant Messaging   Like e-mail, instant messaging (IM) is usually done via computer. It is a synchronous technology, meaning you need to be there to receive the message. In this way, IM operates like a telephone without an answering machine: If you are present when the IM comes in, you can respond in real time to engage in online typed dialogue. If you miss the incoming IM, you may be alerted when you next log on that a person tried to reach you. However, unlike the case with e-mail, you are not then usually expected to reply.

Text Messaging   Text messaging (TM) is similar to instant messaging in that both are synchronous technologies, but text messaging is usually done via cell phone and often as a real-time alternative to phone calls. The guidelines for the business use of texting are still evolving.

Social Media   Nowhere has communication been more transformed than in the rise of social networks like Facebook and LinkedIn, and business is taking advantage of the opportunities these social media present. Many organizations have developed their own in-house social networking applications, known as *enterprise social software*, and most have their own Facebook page and Twitter feeds.[25] According to research advisory firm Gartner Inc., companies that use social media as more than a marketing tool may lead their industries in growth by 2015.[26]

Rather than being one huge site, Facebook, with more than 1.11 billion active users per month,[27] is composed of separate networks based on schools, companies, or regions. According to Facebook's 2013 first quarter earnings report, the lowest numbers of monthly active users are in the United States and Canada; Europe has a larger number of users, and Asia has an even larger number.[28] Users can send public messages to other users either by posting on their walls or through messages or chats. Privacy remains a high concern for many Facebook users.

Unlike many social media venues, LinkedIn was created as an online business network. User profiles on the site are like virtual résumés. Communication is sometimes limited to endorsements of others' skills and establishment of business connections, though direct private communication is available and users can form and belong to groups.

Twitter is a hybrid social networking service for users to post "micro-blog" entries of 140 characters to their subscribers about any topic, including work. While only 4 percent of CEOs are on Twitter, some have many followers, such as Richard Branson of Virgin Group, who has 2.5 million. As Harvard professor and former Medtronic CEO Bill George noted, "Can you think of a more cost-effective way of getting to your customers and employees?"[29] Having many followers can be an advantage to a firm or a manager, and a huge liability when posts (tweets) are badly written or negative.

If your job includes using a Twitter account, you probably can't take the account with you if you leave the company. Editor and video blogger Noah Kravitz tried to take his 17,000 followers with him when he left PhoneDog, a company that offers mobile phone news and reviews, but the firm sued him for taking its customers. Generally, says cyberlaw attorney Eric Menhart, "If working for an employer creates value under an employment agreement, that value is effectively owned by the employer." Kravitz's attorney says, "No one has actually had a case exactly like this before," but there are sure to be others as Twitter's business usage grows.[30]

Blogs   A *blog* (short for web log) is a website about a single person or company. Experts estimate that more than 156 million blogs now exist, many maintained by U.S. employees. And, of course, many organizations and organizational leaders have blogs that speak for the organization.

Others   Flickr, Pinterest, Google+, YouTube, Wikis, Jive, Socialtext, and Social Cast are just a few of the many public and industry-specific social platforms, with new ones launching daily. Some are designed for only one type of posting: YouTube accepts only videos, for instance, and Flickr only videos and images. Other sites have a particular culture, such as Pinterest's informal posts sharing recipes or decorating tips. There is likely to soon be a social media site tailored to every type of communication.

Nonverbal Communication

Every time we deliver a verbal message, we also impart a nonverbal message.[31] Sometimes the nonverbal component may stand alone. No discussion of communication would thus be complete without consideration of *nonverbal communication*—which includes body movements, the intonations or emphasis we give to words, facial expressions, and the physical distance between the sender and receiver.

We could argue that every *body movement* has meaning, and no movement is accidental (though some are unconscious). We act out our state of being with nonverbal body language. We can smile to project trustworthiness, uncross our arms to appear approachable, and stand to signal authority.[32]

Body language can convey status, level of engagement, and emotional state.[33] Body language adds to, and often complicates, verbal communication. A body position or movement can communicate something of the emotion behind a message, but when it is linked with spoken language, it gives fuller meaning to a sender's message. Studies indicate that people read much more about another's attitude and emotions from their nonverbal cues than their words. If the nonverbal cues conflict with the speaker's verbal message, the nonverbal cues are sometimes more likely to be believed by the listener.[34]

If you read the minutes of a meeting, you wouldn't grasp the impact of what was said the same way as if you had been there or could see the meeting on video. Why? There is no record of nonverbal communication. The emphasis given to words or phrases is missing. Exhibit 11-6 illustrates how *intonations* can change the meaning of a message. *Facial expressions* also convey meaning. Facial expressions, along with intonations, can show arrogance, aggressiveness, fear, shyness, and other characteristics.

Physical distance also has meaning. What is considered proper spacing between people largely depends on cultural norms. A businesslike distance in some European countries feels intimate in many parts of North America. If someone stands closer to you than is considered appropriate, it may indicate aggressiveness or sexual interest; if farther away, it may signal disinterest or displeasure with what is being said.

Exhibit 11-6   Intonations: It's the Way You Say It!

Change your tone and you change your meaning:

Placement of the Emphasis	What It Means
Why don't I take **you** to dinner tonight?	I was going to take someone else.
Why don't **I** take you to dinner tonight?	Instead of the guy you were going with.
Why **don't** I take you to dinner tonight?	I'm trying to find a reason why I **shouldn't** take you.
Why don't I take you to dinner tonight?	Do you have a problem with me?
Why don't I **take** you to dinner tonight?	Instead of going on your own.
Why don't I take you to **dinner** tonight?	Instead of lunch tomorrow.
Why don't I take you to dinner **tonight**?	Not tomorrow night.

Source: Based on M. Kiely, "When 'No' Means 'Yes,'" *Marketing* (October 1993), pp. 7–9. Reproduced in A. Huczynski and D. Buchanan, *Organizational Behavior*, 4th ed. (Essex, UK: Pearson Education, 2001), p. 194.

Choice of Communication Channel

6 Show how channel richness underlies the choice of communication channel.

Why do people choose one channel of communication over another? A model of media richness helps explain channel selection among managers.[35]

Channel Richness

Channels differ in their capacity to convey information. Some are *rich* in that they can (1) handle multiple cues simultaneously, (2) facilitate rapid feedback, and (3) be very personal. Others are *lean* in that they score low on these factors. As Exhibit 11-7 illustrates, face-to-face conversation scores highest in

Exhibit 11-7   Information Richness and Communication Channels

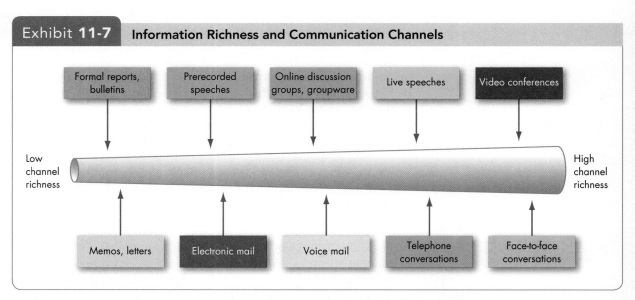

Sources: Based on R. H. Lengel and R. L. Daft, "The Selection of Communication Media as an Executive Skill," *Academy of Management Executive* (August 1988), pp. 225–232; and R. L. Daft and R. H. Lengel, "Organizational Information Requirements, Media Richness, and Structural Design," *Managerial Science* (May 1996), pp. 554–572. Reproduced from R. L. Daft and R. A. Noe, *Organizational Behavior* (Fort Worth, TX: Harcourt, 2001), p. 311.

channel richness *The amount of information that can be transmitted during a communication episode.*

channel richness because it transmits the most information per communication episode—multiple information cues (words, postures, facial expressions, gestures, intonations), immediate feedback (both verbal and nonverbal), and the personal touch of being present. Impersonal written media such as formal reports and bulletins rate lowest in richness.

Choosing Communication Methods

The choice of channel depends on whether the message is routine. Routine messages tend to be straightforward and have minimal ambiguity; channels low in richness can carry them efficiently. Nonroutine communications are likely to be complicated and have the potential for misunderstanding. Managers can communicate them effectively only by selecting rich channels.

Often, a variety of modes of communication work best to convey important ideas. When tough times hit Manpower Business Solutions during the recent economic recession, the company elected to communicate with employees daily in a variety of media to ensure that everyone remained informed.[36] Employees were given updates about the company's plans for dealing with economic problems, including advance warning before layoffs. The company believes its strategy of using rich communication channels for nonroutine information has paid off by reducing employee anxiety and increasing engagement with the organization.

Channel richness is a helpful framework for choosing your mode of communication. It is not always easy to know when to choose oral rather than written communication, for instance. Experts say oral communication or "face time" with co-workers, clients, and upper management is key to success. However, if you seek out the CEO just to say hello, you may be remembered as an annoyance rather than a star, and signing up for every meeting on the calendar to increase your face time is counterproductive to getting the work of the organization done. Your communication choice is worth a moment's thought: Is the message you need to communicate better suited to a discussion, or a diagram?

Whenever you need to gauge the receiver's receptivity, *oral communication* is usually the better choice. The marketing plan for a new product, for instance, may need to be worked out with clients in person, so you can see their reactions to each idea you are proposing. Also consider the receiver's preferred mode of communication; some individuals focus on content better over the phone than in meetings. The pace of your work environment matters too. If your manager requests a meeting with you, you may not want to ask for an exchange of e-mails instead. A fast-paced workplace may thrive on pop-by meetings, while a deadline-heavy team project may progress faster with scheduled Skype video-conferences. Sometimes we cannot choose between a face-to-face meeting and a telephone meeting because of distance. Other times, there is an option.

Much of what we communicate face-to-face is in the delivery, so also consider your speaking skills when choosing your communication method. Research indicates that the sound of your voice is twice as important as what you are saying. A good speaking voice—clear, moderated—can be a help to your career, while loud, questioning, irritating, immature, falsetto, breathy, or monotone voice tones can hinder you. If your voice is problematic, work teams can help you raise your awareness so you can make changes, or you may benefit from the help of a voice coach.[37]

Written communication is generally the most reliable mode for complex and lengthy communications, and it can be the most efficient method for short messages as well, as when a two-sentence text can take the place of a 10-minute phone call. But keep in mind that written communication can be limited in its emotional expression.

Photo 11-3 To enhance her personal face-to-face office visits with patients, pediatric physician Dr. Natasha Burgert uses written messages in communicating with them through e-mail and texting and on her blog. These written communications enable her to share reliable and timely medical information with patients' families, so they can provide better care for their children.

Choose written communication when you want the information to be tangible and verifiable. Both you and the receiver(s) will have a record of the message. People are usually forced to think more thoroughly about what they want to convey in a written message than in a spoken one, so your written communications can also be well thought out, logical, and clear. But be aware that, as with oral communication, your delivery is just as important as the content. Managers report that grammar mistakes and lack of business formality is unprofessional . . . and unacceptable. "People get passionate about grammar," corporate writing instructor and author Jack Appleman noted, and a recent study found that 45 percent of employers were adding training programs to teach grammar and communication skills. Other experts argue that the use of social media jargon and abbreviations are good for business. James Grimes, marketing vice president of software firm RescueTime, advocates his employees stay culturally relevant. He says, "Those who can be sincere, and still text and Twitter . . . those are the ones who are going to succeed." Of course, his advice might be best suited to his computer-based industry. For your professional success, know your audience when possible, and use good grammar.

Letters are used in business primarily for networking purposes and when signatures need to be authentic. A handwritten thank-you note is never a wrong choice for an applicant to send after an employment interview, for instance, and handwritten envelopes often are put right on the receiver's desk unopened by administrative staff. Although electronic written communication provides authentication by indicating the sender and date/time sent, a handwritten signature is still preferred and sometimes required for letters and contracts.

Here are some issues to consider when choosing *e-mail*:

- **Risk of misinterpreting the message.** One research team at New York University found we can accurately decode an e-mail's intent and tone only 50 percent of the time, yet most of us vastly overestimate our ability to send and interpret clear messages. If you're sending an important message, make sure you reread it for clarity first.[38] Watch also for tone, even in your subject line. Subject lines should be direct, straightforward, and without sexual references. Recent research indicated that short subject lines—fewer than 50 characters—get more clicks.[39]

- **Fallout from negative messages.** When Radio Shack decided to lay off 400 employees, it drew an avalanche of scorn inside and outside the company by doing it via e-mail. Employees need to be careful when communicating negative messages via e-mail, too. Inappropriate or negative content could jeopardize your current job or eliminate you from consideration for a new position.

- **Time-consuming nature.** Sorting and reading e-mails takes a long time. Writing e-mails can take even longer, whether you are typing with ten fingers on a keyboard or two thumbs on a smartphone. Most of us have trouble keeping up with our e-mail, especially as we advance in our careers. Experts suggest the following strategies:
  - Don't check e-mail in the morning.
  - Check e-mail in batches, not throughout the day.
  - Unsubscribe to the extra clutter of e-newsletters and product endorsements.

- **Limited expression of emotions.** Some researchers say the lack of visual and vocal cues means emotionally positive messages, like those including praise, will be seen as more emotionally neutral than the sender intended.[40] E-mail tends to have a disinhibiting effect on people; without the recipient's facial expression to temper their emotional expression, senders write things they'd never be comfortable saying in person. When others send flaming messages, remain calm and try not to respond in kind. Try to see the message from the other party's point of view.[41]

- **Privacy concerns.** There are many privacy issues with e-mail.[42] First, your e-mails may be monitored. The growing field of digital forensics focuses on investigating e-mails from all company devices (computers, smartphones, etc.) sent by employees, particularly on e-mails sent to an organization's competitors.[43] Many employers sift through e-mails, using software to catch not only obvious key words ("insider trading"), but also vague ("that thing we talked about") or guilt-ridden ("regret") phrases. You can't always trust the recipient of your e-mail to keep it confidential, either. For these reasons, you shouldn't write anything you wouldn't want made public. Also, exercise caution in forwarding e-mail from your company's e-mail account to a personal or "public" e-mail. These accounts often aren't as secure as corporate accounts, so when you forward a company e-mail to them, you may violate your organization's policy or unintentionally disclose confidential data.

- **Professionalism.** It is important to not let the informality of text messaging spill over into business e-mails. Many prefer to keep business communication relatively formal. A survey of employers revealed that 58 percent rate grammar, spelling, and punctuation as "very important" in e-mails. Avoid jargon and slang, use formal titles, use formal e-mail addresses for yourself, and make your message concise and well written.

In general, respond to *instant messages* only when they are professional, and initiate them only when you know they will be welcome. Remember that the information conveyed in an IM is more public than you might want (you can't be sure who is reading it), and that your conversation will not be stored for later reference.

There are significant gains and challenges from the introduction of *text messaging* in business settings. Texts are cheap to send and receive, and the willingness to be available for quick communications from clients and managers is conducive to good business. However, some users—and managers—view text messaging as intrusive and distracting. The rules of business etiquette are not yet established, resulting in offenses ranging from texts at unreasonable hours to serial texting in bursts of short messages that keep receivers' phones buzzing annoyingly. Such a continual presence can also make it hard for employees to concentrate and stay focused. A survey of managers revealed that in 86 percent of meetings, at least some participants checked their incoming texts, and another survey revealed 20 percent of managers report having been scolded for using wireless devices during meetings. Because instant messages can be intercepted easily, many organizations are concerned about the security of texting. For these reasons, it is best to severely limit personal text messages during office hours and be cautious in using texting for business purposes. You should discuss using texting for business with people before you text them for the first time, set up general availability ground rules, and take your cues about when to text from the other person. The level of informality and abbreviations we use in personal text messages is usually not advisable at work.[44] For longer messages, it is better to use e-mail; even though the receiver still might scroll through the message on a smartphone, the option of viewing—and saving—your message on a computer is preferable.

On the corporate level, the returns on using *social media* are mixed. Some of the most spectacular gains are in the sales arena, both business-to-public and business-to-business. For instance, one sales representative for virtual-meetings company PGi landed his fastest sale ever by instantly connecting with a potential client after TweetDeck alerted him that a CEO was tweeting his frustration about web conferencing.[45] Companies are also developing their own internal social networking platforms to encourage employees to collaborate and to improve training, reporting a recent 300 percent annual increase in corporate network activity. However, the return on using social media in human resources is undetermined, especially for recruiting purposes. UPS has been tracking social media ROI, measuring click-through rates on the company website against the $7,500 cost for each Twitter and Facebook career page as well as social media personnel labor costs. "In social media," UPS's director of talent acquisition Matt Lavery said, "The investment is more about the time and effort of your recruiting staff than it is about other dollars."[46]

The choice to use a social media outlet for business use remains controversial. As a manager, you should "think about business issues first, and then talk about technology second," advises Oracle director Steve Boese.[47] The same is true for employees. Does the social media outlet support the organization's and

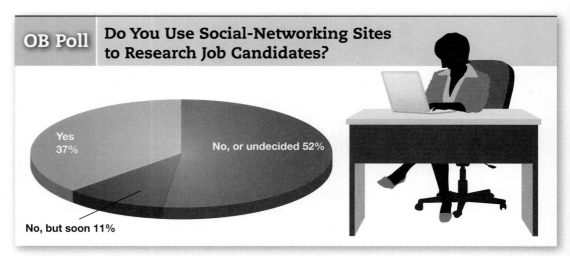

Note: CareerBuilder survey of over 2,000 hiring professionals.

Source: Based on CareerBuilder at http://www.careerbuilder.com/JobPoster/Resources/page.aspx?pagever=2012SocialMedia&template=none.

your efforts? Collaborative and learning opportunities gained through your participation in corporate social networking can be a big benefit to your career and the organization. For the organization, there are potential gains from encouraging employees to tout company products on their Facebook pages to thousands of friends, but there are liability and compensation issues to consider.

Some companies have policies governing the use of social media, but many don't. It is difficult for management to control the content employees post; even well-intentioned employees post comments that could be construed as harmful to their company's reputation or that reveal confidential or sensitive information. Software that mines social media sites can check up on a job applicant, and the growing field of digital forensics helps investigate potential problems with current employees, but cybersleuthing can be time-consuming and expensive.[48] And acting upon violations of an organization's social media policy is tricky. Thus, if you want to use social media for business purposes as a manager, make certain you are connected with all levels of management engaged in the effort. And if you would like to mention your business in your personal social media, communicate with your organization about what you would like to do, and what you think the potential return for the company may be. Use discretion about which personal social media platforms are acceptable for business communication. Finally, make sure you know your company's social media policies about corporate confidentiality and your company's view on your privacy.[49]

As an individual, you may choose to post a *blog* to your own blog page, or you may choose to comment on another person's blog. Both options are more public than you may think, and your words are easily reachable by your name via search engines like Google. If someone in the company happens to read a critical or negative blog entry or post, there is nothing to keep him or her from sharing that information with others. You could be dismissed as a result. Beware also of posting personal blog entries from work because your Internet connections may be monitored.

It's important to be alert to *nonverbal* aspects of communication and look for nonverbal cues as well as the literal meaning of a sender's words. You should particularly be aware of contradictions between the messages. Someone who frequently glances at her wristwatch is giving the message that she would prefer to terminate the conversation no matter what she actually says, for instance. We misinform others when we express one message verbally, such as trust, but nonverbally communicate a contradictory message that reads, "I don't have confidence in you."

Information Security

Security is a huge concern for nearly all organizations with private or proprietary information about clients, customers, and employees. Organizations worry about the security of the electronic information they seek to protect, such as hospital patient data, the physical information they still keep in file cabinets, and the security of the information they entrust their employees with knowing, such as Apple's need-to-know-only information sharing. The recent adoption of cloud-based electronic data storage has brought a new level of worry; 51 percent of managers in a recent survey were considering cloud-based human resources software. Fears about cloud computing seem unwarranted, so its business use will likely increase.[50] As we've discussed, most companies actively monitor employee Internet use and e-mail records, and some even use video surveillance and record phone conversations. Necessary though they may be, such practices can seem invasive to employees. An organization can relieve employee concerns by engaging them in the creation of information-security policies and giving them some control over how their personal information is used.[51]

Using Employees in Organizational Social Media Strategy

Social media are good for business communication, but their use is an ethical minefield for employers and employees. In a recent study of 24 industries in 115 countries, 63 percent of managers believed social media will be important to their businesses in 3 years. Although most companies are still in the early adoption stage, research suggests that social media use is an indicator of profitability firm equity value. Companies at the forefront include McDonald's, IBM, Salesforce, SAP, and Yammer. Social media can turn oblivious customers into fans through increased, personalized communication, and quick and appropriate response to customers' communication can turn those fans— and employees—into spokespeople for the brand. The key is forming emotional bonds or capitalizing on current relationships to spread the good word about the company to potential clients. With more than 1 billion Facebook users, 100 million active users on Twitter, and 65 million Google+ users, companies want to optimize their social media contacts.

Social media sites open a host of ethical concerns. Employees with a huge online presence who use it for both personal and company promotion (known as co-branded employees) become a liability if they leak corporate information, present a bad image, or leave the company. There are also ethical concerns about employees' privacy and right to free speech: If an employee who monitors the company Twitter feed and wins a customer over later tweets from her personal account, "Score for us: another happy customer," that may present no concern. But she would hurt the company if she tweeted instead, "Epic fail: we blew it again."

Other ethical concerns with few tested guidelines include ensuring employees make proper use of company time, compensating them for time they spend promoting the company through their personal social media connection, clarifying who should own the personal devices used for company promotion, setting limits on company expectations of employees' promotion, dealing with permissions/attributions, and clearing any legal hurdles.

Experts advise organizations to draft social media policies that reflect their company ethics rather than seek to "cover all the bases" of their potential liability. While an organization could require job applicants to share their online passwords, for instance, this may violate trust and personal privacy rules. Policies that define ethical expectations for employee online behavior, discuss monitoring, define consequences for nonconformance, and explain the logic of the guidelines will be the most effective. Even still, the National Labor Relations Board (NLRB) finds many corporate policies aimed at the ethics of social media usage violate the National Labor Relations Act. A good social media policy can affirm the ethical expectations of the corporation and improve organizational culture.

Sources: S. F. Gale, "Policies Must Score a Mutual Like," *Workforce Management* (August 2012), p. 18; B. Giamanco and K. Gregoire, "Tweet Me, Friend Me, Make Me Buy," *Harvard Business Review* (July–August 2012), pp. 88–93; D. Kiron, D. Palmer, A. N Phillips, and N. Kruschwitz, "What Managers Really Think About Social Business," *MIT Sloan Management Review* (Summer 2012), pp. 51–60; X. Luo, J. Zhang, and W. Duan, "Social Media and Firm Equity Value," *Information Systems Research* (March 2013), pp. 146–163; C. M. Sashi, "Customer Engagement, Buyer-Seller Relationships, and Social Media," *Management Decision,* 50 (2012), pp. 253–272; and A. Smith, "NLRB Finds Social Media Policies Unlawful," *HR Magazine* (August 2012), p. 18.

Persuasive Communication

7 Differentiate between automatic and controlled processing of persuasive messages.

We've discussed a number of methods for communication up to this point. Now we turn our attention to one of the functions of communication and the features that might make messages more or less persuasive to an audience.

Automatic and Controlled Processing

To understand the process of communication, it is useful to consider two different ways that we process information.[52] Think about the last time you bought a can of soda. Did you carefully research brands, or did you reach for the can that

automatic processing *A relatively superficial consideration of evidence and information making use of heuristics.*

had the most appealing advertising images? If we're honest, we'll admit glitzy ads and catchy slogans do indeed have an influence on our choices as consumers. We often rely on **automatic processing**, a relatively superficial consideration of evidence and information making use of heuristics like those we discussed in Chapter 6. Automatic processing takes little time and low effort, so it makes sense to use it for processing persuasive messages related to topics you don't care much about. The disadvantage is that it lets us be easily fooled by a variety of tricks, like a cute jingle or glamorous photo.

Now consider the last time you chose a place to live. You probably did some independent research among experts who know something about the area, gathered information about prices from a variety of sources, and considered the costs and benefits of renting versus buying. Here, you're relying on more effortful **controlled processing**, a detailed consideration of evidence and information relying on facts, figures, and logic. Controlled processing requires effort and energy, but it's harder to fool someone who has taken the time and effort to engage in it. So what makes someone engage in either shallow or deep processing? There are a few rules of thumb for determining what types of processing an audience will use.

controlled processing *A detailed consideration of evidence and information relying on facts, figures, and logic.*

Interest Level

One of the best predictors of whether people will use an automatic or controlled process for reacting to a persuasive message is their level of interest in it.[53] Interest levels reflect the impact a decision is going to have on your life. When people are very interested in the outcome of a decision, they're more likely to process information carefully. That's probably why people look for so much more information when deciding about something important (like where to live) than something relatively unimportant (like which soda to drink).

Prior Knowledge

People who are very well informed about a subject area are more likely to use controlled processing strategies. They have already thought through various arguments for or against a specific course of action, and therefore they won't readily change their position unless very good, thoughtful reasons are provided. On the other hand, people who are poorly informed about a topic can change their minds more readily, even in the face of fairly superficial arguments presented without a great deal of evidence. In other words, a better-informed audience is likely to be much harder to persuade.

Personality

Do you always read at least five reviews of a movie before deciding whether to see it? Perhaps you even research recent films by the same stars and director. If so, you are probably high in *need for cognition,* a personality trait of individuals who are most likely to be persuaded by evidence and facts.[54] Those who are lower in need for cognition are more likely to use automatic processing strategies, relying on intuition and emotion to guide their evaluation of persuasive messages.

Message Characteristics

Another factor that influences whether people use an automatic or controlled processing strategy is the characteristics of the message itself. Messages provided through relatively lean communication channels, with little opportunity for users to interact with the content of the message, encourage automatic processing. Conversely, messages provided through richer communication channels tend to encourage more deliberative processing.

Photo 11-4 Managers of Germany's construction firm Hochtief relied on controlled processing during a meeting when they presented rational arguments against a takeover bid by another firm. Fearing that a takeover would put their jobs at risk, Hochtief employees had a high level of interest in the takeover attempt and learning about managers' plans to prevent it.

Source: Bernd Thissen/dpa/picture-alliance/Newscom

The most important implication is to match your persuasive message to the type of processing your audience is likely to use. When the audience is not interested in a persuasive message topic, when they are poorly informed, when they are low in need for cognition, and when information is transmitted through relatively lean channels, they'll be more likely to use automatic processing. In these cases, use messages that are more emotionally laden and associate positive images with your preferred outcome. On the other hand, when the audience is interested in a topic, when they are high in need for cognition, or when the information is transmitted through rich channels, then it is a better idea to focus on rational arguments and evidence to make your case.

Barriers to Effective Communication

8 Identify common barriers to effective communication.

A number of barriers can slow or distort effective communication. In this section, we highlight the most important.

Filtering

filtering *A sender's manipulation of information so that it will be seen more favorably by the receiver.*

Filtering refers to a sender's purposely manipulating information so the receiver will see it more favorably. A manager who tells his boss what he feels the boss wants to hear is filtering information.

The more vertical levels in the organization's hierarchy, the more opportunities there are for filtering. But some filtering will occur wherever there are status differences. Factors such as fear of conveying bad news and the desire to please the boss often lead employees to tell their superiors what they think they want to hear, thus distorting upward communications.

Selective Perception

We have mentioned selective perception before in this book. It appears again here because selective perception is important because the receivers in the communication process selectively see and hear based on their needs, motivations, experience, background, and other personal characteristics. Receivers also project their interests and expectations into communications as they decode them. An employment interviewer who expects a female job applicant to put her family ahead of her career is likely to see that in all female applicants, regardless of whether they actually feel that way. As we said in Chapter 6, we don't see reality; we interpret what we see and call it reality.

Information Overload

information overload *A condition in which information inflow exceeds an individual's processing capacity.*

Individuals have a finite capacity for processing data. When the information we have to work with exceeds our processing capacity, the result is information overload. We've seen that dealing with it has become a huge challenge for individuals and for organizations. It's a challenge you can manage—to some degree—by following the steps outlined earlier in this chapter.

What happens when individuals have more information than they can sort and use? They tend to select, ignore, pass over, or forget. Or they may put off further processing until the overload situation ends. In any case, lost information and less effective communication results, making it all the more important to deal well with overload.

We have already reviewed some ways of reducing the time sunk into e-mails. More generally, as an Intel study shows, it may make sense to connect to technology less frequently, to, in the words of one article, "avoid letting the drumbeat of digital missives constantly shake up and reorder to-do lists." Lynaia Lutes, an account supervisor for a small Texas company, was able to think much more strategically by taking a break from digital information each day. In the past, she said, "I basically completed an assignment" but didn't approach it strategically. By creating such breaks for yourself, you may be better able to prioritize, think about the big picture, and thereby be more effective.[55]

As information technology and immediate communication have become a more prevalent component of modern organizational life, more employees find they are never able to get offline. Some business travelers were disappointed when airlines began offering wireless Internet connections in flight because they could no longer use their travel time as a rare opportunity to relax without a constant barrage of organizational communications. The negative impacts of these communication devices can spill over into employees' personal lives as well. Both workers and their spouses relate the use of electronic communication technologies outside work to higher levels of work–life conflict.[56] Employees must balance the need for constant communication with their own personal need for breaks from work, or they risk burnout from being on call 24 hours a day.

Emotions

You may interpret the same message differently when you're angry or distraught than when you're happy. For example, individuals in positive moods are more confident about their opinions after reading a persuasive message, so well-designed arguments have stronger impacts on their opinions.[57] People in negative moods are more likely to scrutinize messages in greater detail, whereas those in positive moods tend to accept communications at face value.[58] Extreme emotions such as jubilation or depression are most likely to hinder effective communication. In such instances, we are most prone to disregard our rational and objective thinking processes and substitute emotional judgments.

Photo 11-5 Communication barriers exist between these call-center employees in Manila, Philippines, and their U.S. and Canadian customers, even though they communicate in the common language of English. Training in pronunciation, intonation, vocabulary, and grammar helps employees to get messages across effectively to their customers.

Source: Dondi Tawatao/Getty Images

Language

Even when we're communicating in the same language, words mean different things to different people. Age and context are two of the biggest factors that influence such differences.

When business consultant Michael Schiller asked his 15-year-old daughter where she was going with friends, he said, "You need to recognize your ARAs and measure against them." Schiller said that in response, his daughter "looked at him like he was from outer space." (For the record, ARA stands for accountability, responsibility, and authority.) Those new to corporate lingo may find acronyms such as ARA, words such as *deliverables* (verifiable outcomes of a project), and phrases such as *get the low-hanging fruit* (deal with the easiest parts first) bewildering, in the same way parents may be mystified by teen slang.[59]

Our use of language is far from uniform. If we knew how each of us modifies the language, we could minimize communication difficulties, but we usually don't know. Senders tend to incorrectly assume the words and terms they use mean the same to the receiver as to them.

Silence

It's easy to ignore silence or lack of communication because it is defined by the absence of information. However, research suggests using silence and withholding communication are common and problematic.[60] One survey found that more than 85 percent of managers reported remaining silent about at least one issue of significant concern.[61] Employee silence means managers lack information about ongoing operational problems. And silence regarding discrimination, harassment, corruption, and misconduct means top management cannot take action to eliminate this behavior. Finally, employees who are silent about important issues may also experience psychological stress.

Silence is less likely where minority opinions are treated with respect, work-group identification is high, and high procedural justice prevails.[62] Practically, this means managers must make sure they behave in a supportive manner when employees voice divergent opinions or concerns, and they must take these under advisement. One act of ignoring or belittling an employee for expressing concerns may well lead the employee to withhold important future communication.

Communication Apprehension

communication apprehension
Undue tension and anxiety about oral communication, written communication, or both.

An estimated 5 to 20 percent of the population suffers debilitating **communication apprehension**, or social anxiety.[63] These people experience undue tension and anxiety in oral communication, written communication, or both.[64] They may find it extremely difficult to talk with others face-to-face or may become extremely anxious when they have to use the phone, relying on memos or e-mails when a phone call would be faster and more appropriate.

Oral-communication apprehensives avoid situations, such as teaching, for which oral communication is a dominant requirement.[65] But almost all jobs require *some* oral communication. Of greater concern is evidence that high oral-communication apprehensives distort the communication demands of their jobs in order to minimize the need for communication. Be aware that some people severely limit their oral communication and rationalize their actions by telling themselves communicating isn't necessary for them to do their job effectively.

Lying

The final barrier to effective communication is outright misrepresentation of information, or lying. People differ in their definition of a lie. For example, is deliberately withholding information about a mistake a lie, or do you have to actively deny your role in the mistake to pass the threshold? While the definition of a lie befuddles ethicists and social scientists, there is no denying the prevalence of lying. In one diary study, the average person reported telling one to two lies per day, with some individuals telling considerably more.[66] Compounded across a large organization, this is an enormous amount of deception happening every single day. Evidence shows that people are more comfortable lying over the phone than face-to-face and more comfortable lying in e-mails than when they have to write with pen and paper.[67]

Can you detect liars? The literature suggests most people are not very good at detecting deception in others.[68] The problem is there are no nonverbal or verbal cues unique to lying—averting your gaze, pausing, and shifting your posture can also be signals of nervousness, shyness, or doubt. Most people who lie take steps to guard against being detected, so they might look a person in the eye when lying because they know that direct eye contact is (incorrectly) assumed to be a sign of truthfulness. Finally, many lies are embedded in truths; liars usually give a somewhat true account with just enough details changed to avoid detection.

In sum, the frequency of lying and the difficulty in detecting liars makes this an especially strong barrier to effective communication.

Global Implications

9 Show how to overcome the potential problems in cross-cultural communication.

Effective communication is difficult under the best of conditions. Cross-cultural factors clearly create the potential for increased communication problems. A gesture that is well understood and acceptable in one culture can be meaningless or lewd in another. Only 18 percent of companies have documented strategies for communicating with employees across cultures, and only 31 percent require that corporate messages be customized for consumption in other cultures. Procter & Gamble seems to be an exception; more than half the company's employees don't speak English as their first language, so the company focuses on simple messages to make sure everyone knows what's important.[69]

Cultural Barriers

Researchers have identified a number of problems related to language difficulties in cross-cultural communications.[70]

First are *barriers caused by semantics*. Words mean different things to different people, particularly people from different national cultures. Some words don't translate between cultures. The Finnish word *sisu* means something akin to "guts" or "dogged persistence" but is essentially untranslatable into English. The new capitalists in Russia may have difficulty communicating with British or Canadian counterparts because English terms such as *efficiency, free market,* and *regulation* have no direct Russian equivalents.

Second are *barriers caused by word connotations*. Words imply different things in different languages. Negotiations between U.S. and Japanese executives can be difficult because the Japanese word *hai* translates as "yes," but its connotation is "Yes, I'm listening" rather than "Yes, I agree."

Third are *barriers caused by tone differences*. In some cultures, language is formal; in others, it's informal. In some cultures, the tone changes depending on the context: People speak differently at home, in social situations, and at work. Using a personal, informal style when a more formal style is expected can be inappropriate.

Fourth are *differences in tolerance for conflict and methods for resolving conflicts*. Individuals from individualist cultures tend to be more comfortable with direct conflicts and will make the source of their disagreements overt. Collectivists are more likely to acknowledge conflict only implicitly and avoid emotionally charged disputes. They may attribute conflicts to the situation more than to the individuals and therefore may not require explicit apologies to repair relationships, whereas individualists prefer explicit statements accepting responsibility for conflicts and public apologies to restore relationships.

Cultural Context

Cultures tend to differ in the degree to which context influences the meaning individuals take from communication.[71] In **high-context cultures** such as China, Korea, Japan, and Vietnam, people rely heavily on nonverbal and subtle situational cues in communicating with others, and a person's official status, place in society, and reputation carry considerable weight. What is *not* said may be more significant than what *is* said. In contrast, people from Europe and North America reflect their **low-context cultures**. They rely essentially on spoken and written words to convey meaning; body language and formal titles are secondary (see Exhibit 11-8).

These contextual differences actually mean quite a lot in terms of communication. Communication in high-context cultures implies considerably more trust by both parties. What may appear to be casual and insignificant conversation in fact reflects the desire to build a relationship and create trust. Oral agreements imply strong commitments in high-context cultures. And who you are—your age, seniority, rank in the organization—is highly valued and heavily influences your credibility. But in low-context cultures, enforceable contracts tend to be in writing, precisely worded, and highly legalistic. Similarly, low-context cultures value directness. Managers are expected to be explicit and precise in conveying intended meaning. It's quite different in high-context cultures, in which managers tend to "make suggestions" rather than give orders.

high-context cultures *Cultures that rely heavily on nonverbal and subtle situational cues in communication.*

low-context cultures *Cultures that rely heavily on words to convey meaning in communication.*

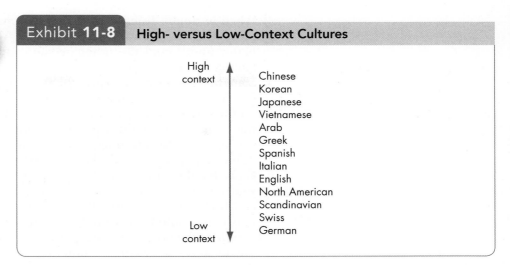

Exhibit 11-8   **High- versus Low-Context Cultures**

High context ↑ Chinese
Korean
Japanese
Vietnamese
Arab
Greek
Spanish
Italian
English
North American
Scandinavian
Swiss
Low context ↓ German

A Cultural Guide

There is much to be gained from business intercultural communications. It is safe to assume every single one of us has a different viewpoint that is culturally shaped. Because we do have differences, we have an opportunity to reach the most creative solutions possible with the help of others if we communicate effectively.

According to Fred Casmir, a leading expert in intercultural communication research, we often do not communicate well with people outside of our culture because we tend to generalize from only knowing their cultural origin. This can be insensitive and potentially disastrous, especially when we make assumptions based on observable characteristics. Many of us have a richly varied ethnic background and would be offended if someone addressed us according to what culture our physical features might favor, for instance. Also, attempts to be culturally sensitive to another person are often based on stereotypes propagated by media. These stereotypes usually do not have a correct or current relevance.

Casmir noted that because there are far too many cultures for anyone to understand completely, and individuals interpret their own cultures differently, intercultural communication should be based on sensitivity and pursuit of common goals. He found the ideal condition is an ad hoc "third culture" a group can form when they seek to incorporate aspects of each member's cultural communication preferences. The norms this subculture establishes through appreciating individual differences create a common ground for effective communication. Intercultural groups that communicate effectively can be highly productive and innovative.

When communicating with people from a different culture, what can you do to reduce misinterpretations? Casmir and other experts offer the following suggestions:

1. **Know yourself.**   Recognizing your own cultural identity and biases is critical to then understanding the unique viewpoint of other people.
2. **Foster a climate of mutual respect, fairness, and democracy.**   Clearly establish an environment of equality and mutual concern. This will be your "third culture" context for effective intercultural communication that transcends each person's cultural norms.
3. **Learn the cultural context of each person.**   You may find more similarities or differences to your own frame of reference than you might expect. Be careful not to categorize them by culture of origin, however.

4. **When in doubt, listen.**   If you speak your opinions too early, you may be more likely to offend the other person. You will also want to listen first to better understand the other person's intercultural language fluency and familiarity with your culture.

5. **State facts, not your interpretation.**   Interpreting or evaluating what someone has said or done draws more on your own culture and background than on the observed situation. If you state only facts, you will have the opportunity to benefit from the other person's interpretation. Delay judgment until you've had sufficient time to observe and interpret the situation from the differing perspectives of all concerned.

6. **Consider the other person's viewpoint.**   Before sending a message, put yourself in the recipient's shoes. What are his or her values, experiences, and frames of reference? What do you know about his or her education, upbringing, and background that can give you added insight? Try to see the people in the group as they really are first, and take a collaborative problem-solving approach whenever potential conflicts arise.

7. **Proactively maintain the identity of the group.**   Like any culture, the establishment of a common-ground "third culture" for effective intercultural communication takes time and nurturing. Remind members of the group of your common goals, mutual respect, and need to adapt to individual communication preferences.[72]

SELF-ASSESSMENT LIBRARY

How Good Are My Listening Skills?

In the Self-Assessment Library (available in MyManagementLab), take assessment II.A.2 (How Good Are My Listening Skills?).

Summary

You've probably discovered the link between communication and employee satisfaction in this chapter: the less uncertainty, the greater the satisfaction. Distortions, ambiguities, and incongruities between verbal and nonverbal messages all increase uncertainty and reduce satisfaction.

Implications for Managers

- Remember that your communication mode will partly determine your communication effectiveness.
- Obtain feedback from your employees to make certain your messages—however they are communicated—are understood.
- Remember that written communication creates more misunderstandings than oral communication; communicate with employees through in-person meetings when possible.
- Make sure you use communication strategies appropriate to your audience and the type of message you're sending.
- Keep in mind communication barriers such as gender and culture.

Social Media Presence

POINT   **COUNTERPOINT**

Everyone uses social media. Well, almost everyone: A recent Pew Research Study found that the highest percentage of adults who use social networking sites was in Israel at 53 percent, followed by 50 percent in the United States, 43 percent in Russia and Britain, and 42 percent in Spain.

Business is social, and using employees' social contacts to increase business has always been a facet of marketing. Organizations that don't follow their employees' social media presence are missing an opportunity to expand their business and strengthen their workforce. Employees are key representatives of their companies to the outside world. With social media, the potential scope of that influence is hugely increased, and the company can monitor and identify employees with the best endorsement potential. The Honda employee who once told 30 friends that Honda is best can now tell 300 Facebook friends and 500 Twitter followers about the latest model. Employees savvy about social media can have a substantial positive effect on the bottom line.

Monitoring employees' social media presence can also strengthen the workforce by identifying the best talent. Managers can look for potential online celebrities—frequent bloggers and Twitter users with many followers—to approach for co-branding partnerships. Scrutiny can also help employers spot problems. For example, consider the employee who is fired one day and turns violent. A manager who had been monitoring the employee's social media posts may have been able to detect warning signs. A human resources department monitoring employees' social media activity may be able to identify a substance abuse problem and provide help for the employee through the company's intervention policies.

A job candidate's social media presence provides one more input to hiring and retention decisions that many companies already take advantage of. In reality, there is no difference between the employee and the person—they are one and the same, on or off working hours.

Employers that monitor social media can also identify employees who use their platforms to send out bad press or who leak proprietary information. For this reason, managers may someday be *required* to monitor employees' social media postings and to act upon infringements of company policies. Many do so already.

Managers should therefore develop enforceable social media policies and create a corporate infrastructure to regularly research and monitor social media activity. The potential increase in business and limit on liability is ample return for dedicating staff and work hours to building a successful monitoring program.

There is little to be gained and much to be lost when organizations follow candidates' and employees' presence on social media. Managers may be able to learn more about individuals through their online activity, and organizations may be able to catch some good press from employee postings, but the risk of liability for this intrusion on privacy is inescapable. Managers are ill-equipped to monitor, interpret, and act upon employees' social media postings, and few have any experience with relating the medium to business use.

Managers may also easily misinterpret information they find. Few companies have training programs for the proper use of social media; only 40 percent have social media policies of any kind. Those that do are skating on thin ice because monitoring policies can conflict with privacy regulations.

An employee's online image doesn't reveal much that is relevant to the job, certainly not enough to warrant the time and money a business would spend on monitoring. Most users view social media as a private, recreational venue, and their membership on Facebook and other sites should be regarded with the same respect as would membership in a club. In this light, monitoring employees' social media accounts is an unethical violation of their right to privacy.

Equal Employment Opportunity laws require companies to hire without respect to race, age, religion, national origin, or disability. But managers who check into candidates' social media postings often find out more than the candidate wanted to share, and then there is no way to keep that information from affecting the hiring decision. Searching through social media can, therefore, expose a company to a costly discrimination claim.

Using employees' personal social media presence as a marketing tool through company-supportive postings is unethical from many standpoints. First, it is unethical to expect employees to expand the company's client base through their personal contacts. Second, it is unreasonable to expect them to endorse the company after working hours. And the practice of asking employees for their social media passwords is an obvious intrusion into their personal lives.

In sum, people have a right to a professional and a private image. Unless the employee is offering to "friend" the company in a social media partnership, there is no question that employers should stay out of their personal business.

Sources: S. F. Gale, "Policies Must Score a Mutual Like," *Workforce Management* (August 2012); R. Huggins and S. Ward, "Countries with the Highest Percentage of Adults Who Use Social Networking Sites," *USA Today* (February 8, 2012), p. 1A; A. L. Kavanaugh et al., "Social Media Use by Government: From the Routine to the Critical," *Government Information Quarterly* (October 2012), pp. 480–491; and S. Johnson, "Those Facebook Posts Could Cost You a Job," *San Jose Mercury News* (January 16, 2012), www.mercurynews.com/business/ci_19754451.

END-OF-CHAPTER REVIEW

MyManagementLab

Go to **mymanagementlab.com** to complete the problems marked with this icon. ★

QUESTIONS FOR REVIEW

11-1 What are the primary functions of the communication process in organizations?

11-2 What are the key parts of the communication process, and how do you distinguish formal and informal communication?

11-3 What are the differences among downward, upward, and lateral communication?

11-4 What are the differences between formal small-group networks and the grapevine?

11-5 What are the methods of oral communication, written communication, and nonverbal communication?

11-6 How does channel richness underlie the choice of communication channel?

11-7 What is the difference between automatic and controlled processing of persuasive messages?

11-8 What are some common barriers to effective communication?

11-9 What unique problems underlie cross-cultural communication?

EXPERIENTIAL EXERCISE An Absence of Nonverbal Communication

This exercise will help you to see the value of nonverbal communication to interpersonal relations.

- The class is to split up into pairs (party A and party B).
  11-10. Party A is to select a topic from the following list:
  a. Managing in the Middle East is significantly different from managing in North America.
  b. Employee turnover in an organization can be functional.
  c. Some conflict in an organization is good.
  d. Whistle-blowers do more harm than good for an organization.
  e. An employer has a responsibility to provide every employee with an interesting and challenging job.
  f. Everyone should register to vote.
  g. Organizations should require all employees to undergo regular drug tests.
  h. Individuals who have majored in business or economics make better employees than those who have majored in history or English.
  i. The place where you get your college degree is more important in determining your career success than what you learn while you're there.

  j. It's unethical for a manager to purposely distort communications to get a favorable outcome.

  11-11. Party B is to choose a position on this topic (for example, arguing *against* the view "Some conflict in an organization is good"). Party A now must automatically take the opposite position.

- The two parties have 10 minutes in which to debate their topic. The catch is that the individuals can only communicate verbally. They may *not* use gestures, facial movements, body movements, or any other nonverbal communication. It may help for each party to sit on their hands to remind them of their restrictions and to maintain an expressionless look.

  11-12. After the debate is over, form groups of six to eight and spend 15 minutes discussing the following:
  a. How effective was communication during these debates?
  b. What barriers to communication existed?
  c. What purposes does nonverbal communication serve?
  d. Relate the lessons learned in this exercise to problems that might occur when communicating on the telephone or through e-mail.

ETHICAL DILEMMA   Pitfalls of E-Mail

While e-mail may be a very useful—even indispensable—form of communication in organizations, it certainly has its limits and dangers. Indeed, e-mail can get you into trouble with more people, more quickly, than almost any other form of communication.

Ask Bill Cochran. Cochran, 44, is a manager at Richmond Group, a Dallas-based advertising agency. As Richmond was gearing up to produce a Superbowl ad for one its clients—Bridgestone—Cochran's boss sent an e-mail to 200 people describing the internal competition to determine which ad idea would be presented. Cochran chose the occasion to give a pep talk to his team. Using "locker room talk," he composed an e-mail criticizing the other Richmond teams, naming employees he thought would provide them real competition—and those who wouldn't.

What Cochran did next—hit the Send key—seemed so innocuous. But it was a keystroke he would soon wish he could undo. Shortly after he sent the e-mail, a co-worker,

Wendy Mayes, wrote to him: "Oh God. . . Bill. You just hit REPLY ALL!"

Questions

11-13. After realizing what he had done, how should Cochran have responded to this situation?

11-14. After the incident, Mayes says of Cochran: "His name soon became synonymous with 'idiotic behavior' such as 'don't pull a Cochran.'" Is it unethical to participate in such ribbing?

⭐ **11-15.** Kaspar Rorsted, CEO of Henkil, a consumer and industrial products company based in Germany, vsays that copying others on e-mails is overused. "It's a waste of time," he said. "If they want to write me, they can write me. People often copy me to cover their back." Do you agree? How can you decide when copying others is necessary versus "a waste of time"?

Sources: E. Bernstein, "Reply All: The Button Everyone Loves to Hate," *The Wall Street Journal* (March 8, 2011), pp. D1, D4; A. Bryant, "No Need to Hit The 'Send' Key. Just Talk to Me," *The New York Times* (August 29, 2010), p. 2; and R. E. Silverman, "Ban 'Reply to All,'" *The Wall Street Journal* (January 2, 2013), pp. B1, B4.

CASE INCIDENT 1   Using Social Media to Your Advantage

As you know, social media have transformed the way we interact. The transparent, rapid-fire communication they make possible means people can spread information about companies more rapidly than ever.

Do organizations understand yet how to use social media effectively? Perhaps not. Recent findings indicated that only three out of ten CEOs in the *Fortune* 500 have any presence on national social media sites. Many executives are wary of these new technologies because they cannot always control the outcomes of their communications. However, whether they are directly involved with social media or not, companies should recognize that these messages are out there, so it behooves them to make their voices heard. Some experts say social media tools improve productivity because they keep employees connected to their companies during nonoffice hours. And social media can be an important way to learn about emerging trends. André Schneider, chief operating officer of the World Economic Forum, uses feedback from LinkedIn discussion groups and Facebook friends to discover emerging trends and issues worldwide. Padmasree Warrior, chief technology officer of Cisco, has used social media to refine her presentations before a "test" audience.

The first step in developing a social media strategy is establishing a brand for your communications—define what you want your social media presence to express. Experts recommend that companies begin their social media strategy by leveraging their internal corporate networks to test their strategy in a medium that's easier to control. Most companies already have the technology to use social media through their corporate websites. Begin by using these platforms for communicating with employees and facilitating social networks for general information sharing. As social networking expert Soumitra Dutta from Insead notes, "My advice is to build your audience slowly and be selective about your contacts."

Despite the potential advantages, companies also need to be aware of significant drawbacks to social media. First, it's very difficult to control social media communications. Microsoft found this out when the professional blogger it hired spent more time promoting himself than getting positive information out about the company. Second, important intellectual capital might leak out. Companies need to establish very clear policies and procedures to ensure that sensitive information about ongoing corporate strategies is not disseminated via social media. Finally, managers should maintain motivation and interest beyond their initial forays into social media. A site that's rarely updated can send a very negative message about the organization's level of engagement with the world.

Questions

11-16. Do you think organizations need to have a social media presence today? Are the drawbacks sufficient to make you think it's better for them to avoid certain media?

⭐ **11-17.** What features would you look for in a social media outlet? What types of information would you avoid making part of your social media strategy?

11-18. What do you think is the future direction of social media? How might emerging technologies change them?

Sources: B. Acohido, "Social-Media Tools Boost Productivity," *USA Today* (August 13, 2012), p. 1B; S. Dutta, "What's Your Personal Social Media Strategy," *Harvard Business Review* (November 2010), pp. 127–130; and G. Connors, "10 Social Media Commandments for Employers," *Workforce Management Online* (February 2010), www.workforce.com; and L. Kwoh and M. Korn, "140 Characters of Risk: CEOs on Twitter," The *Wall Street Journal* (September 26, 2012), pp. B1, B8.

CASE INCIDENT 2 PowerPoint Purgatory

We've all been there, done that: 10 minutes, 20 PowerPoint slides. Whether you've been the harried presenter racing through the slides or the hapless listener choosing between reading the slides or listening to the talk, it's miserable. Three hundred fifty PowerPoint presentations are given per second worldwide, and the program commands 95 percent of the presentation software market. Why do we do this to ourselves?

The short answer seems to be because we know how, or at least we think we do. Joel Ingersoll of Lorton Data, a Minneapolis database company, said, "You say to yourself, 'I'll start vomiting information I found on my hard drive until I hit, oh, about 20 slides, and then I'll wing the talking-to-people part.'" Bombarding audiences with stark phrases is only one possible pitfall, says Rick Altman, author of *Why Most PowerPoint Presentations Suck*. Another is to overdesign your presentation. Most of us spend 36 percent of our prep time on design, according to a recent study, yet we fail to remember that "less is more." The poor choices that sometimes result (such as using cartoonish typefaces for a serious presentation) can undermine your intended message. Altman cautions against using layer after layer of bullet points to write out what you should say instead, and he recommends making sparing use of holograms, 3D, and live Twitter feeds that only detract from your message.

Successful talks are about a story and an interaction. "Even if you're a middle manager delivering financials to your department in slides, you're telling a story. A manager is constantly trying to persuade," said Nancy Duarte, owner of a presentation design company. Equally important is the audience. "Everyone is sick of the one-way diatribe," Duarte observed, and Altman recommends engaging people "as if they're in preschool waiting to get picked up by their parents." According to Keith Yamashita, founder of SYPartners communications, this may mean ditching PowerPoint altogether. "There are endless techniques that are more appropriate than PowerPoint," he contends. Like what?

Experts suggest fewer visual aids and more live interaction with the audience. High tech does not guarantee better storytelling. "Pin up butcher paper on the walls, draw a map of your thinking, and hand that out," Yamashita says, or use a white board. The results can amaze you. When sales engineer Jason Jones had trouble launching his 2-hour slide presentation to a dozen clients, buddy Dave Eagle stepped in. "All right, I got two presentations for y'all," Eagle told the dozen clients, one where the presentation was "on the wall" with slides, and the other just spoken. The clients chose the latter, and they won the account.

Questions

11-19. What are some of the ways people misuse PowerPoint? What are the potential consequences?

11-20. Have you used PowerPoint in your school projects or at work? In what presentations did you find PowerPoint most effective in communicating your message? In what presentations did PowerPoint hinder your successful communication?

11-21. List the pros and cons you see for managers avoiding PowerPoint as a mode of communication.

Sources: A. A. Buchko, K. J. Buchko, and J. M Meyer, "Is There Power in PowerPoint? A Field Test of the Efficacy of PowerPoint on Memory and Recall of Religious Sermons," *Computers in Human Behavior* (March 2012), pp. 688–695; "Full Text of Iran's Proposals to Six World Powers in Moscow," FARS News Agency (Tehran), http://english.farsnews.com/newstext.php?nn=9103085486; and B. Parks, "Death to PowerPoint," *Bloomberg Businessweek* (September 3–9, 2012), pp. 83–85.

MyManagementLab

Go to **mymanagementlab.com** for Auto-graded writing questions as well as the following Assisted-graded writing questions:

11-22. Based on Case Incident 1 and your chapter reading of this text's material, which social media sources do you think are most useful for sending an organization's communications to external stakeholders, like stockholders or customers? Are different social media more appropriate for communicating with employees?

11-23. In consideration of Case Incident 2 and the chapter material in this text, what are the positive aspects of PowerPoint as a communication method? A recent study found no difference in memory recall of listeners after presentations with (a) PowerPoint words only, (b) visual-only slides, (c) words and visual aids, and (d) no slides. How does this change your view of the usefulness of PowerPoint as a communication tool?

11-24. MyManagementLab Only—comprehensive writing assignment for this chapter.

12

Leadership

THE RIGHT STUFF: JEFF BEZOS OF AMAZON

For Amazon founder and CEO Jeff Bezos, the sky's the limit—literally. Bezos' private space firm Blue Origin recently burst into space—45,000 feet above Texas at 1.2 Mach speed—when its unmanned rocket made a break for the stratosphere . . . and exploded into flames. If Bezos was discouraged about the expensive loss, he recovered quickly. In a blog post typical of the leadership approach that makes him *Forbes'* number-one CEO in America, he wrote: "Not the outcome any of us wanted, but we're signed up for this to be hard, and the Blue Origin team is doing an outstanding job. We're already working on our next development vehicle."

Onward and upward seems to be Bezos' credo. Amazon's stock has recently rocketed up almost 400 percent in five years, and his $19 billion personal net worth has made him one of the 30 richest men in the world. Like Blue Origin's flight path, the dot-com crash-and-burn era threatened the transformation of Amazon from online bookseller to retailing giant. While Amazon's financial performance flat-lined from mid-2003 to 2007, Bezos stayed true to his mission of service. He let customers dictate the specifications for Amazon products, sold them access to Amazon's own software architecture, and launched Amazon Web Services to offer businesses cloud-based computer services. Investors noticed, and Amazon took off. A visionary leader, Bezos philosophically takes the long view on all his projects. "We are willing to be misunderstood for long periods of time," he says.

Bezos' unwavering dedication to driving the business by what the customer wants is legendary. It starts with the empty chair he pulls up to the conference table during meetings for "the most important person in the room"—the customer. Employees and managers abide by his "culture of metrics" that tracks company performance against 500 goals to provide data-driven customer service. Bezos requires managers to attend yearly call-center training to better understand the company's 164 million customers, which he also attends. And he reads his customer e-mails. "We're not satisfied until [customer satisfaction] is 100 percent," he says.

As the leader of 56,000 employees, Bezos focuses on hiring good people. "I'd rather interview 50 people and not hire anyone than hire the wrong person," he says. He empowers employees to solve the challenges customers face, which resulted in the worldwide success of the Kindle e-reader, for instance. Bezos respects the metrics employees present, saying, "The great thing about fact-based decisions is that they overrule the hierarchy. The most junior person in the company can win an argument with the most senior person with regard to a fact-based decision. For intuitive decisions . . . you have to rely on experienced executives who've honed their instincts." And he works alongside his employees, earning a modest salary of $82,000 while

LEARNING OBJECTIVES

After studying this chapter, you should be able to:

1 Contrast leadership and management.

2 Summarize the conclusions of trait theories of leadership.

3 Identify the central tenets and main limitations of behavioral theories.

4 Assess contingency theories of leadership by their level of support.

5 Contrast *charismatic* and *transformational leadership*.

6 Define *authentic leadership*.

7 Demonstrate the role mentoring plays in our understanding of leadership.

8 Address challenges to the effectiveness of leadership.

hoping for that big stock payoff (a strategy that has paid off), practicing frugality, constantly critiquing, being self-reliant, and laughing a lot. He expects of others what he expects of himself.

In these ways, Bezos may be the ultimate servant leader. As we discuss in this chapter, servant leaders look beyond their own self-interests. They have ethical standards they impose on themselves as well as others, and they are not narcissistic: They feel rewarded by creating benefit, not just by receiving personal rewards. Research suggests that company founders are often servant leaders, and that CEO servant leadership predicts corporate financial performance.

Generally, exceptional leaders manage to be exceptional at one role—a visionary like Chipotle CEO Steve Ells, or a servant leader like Japan Airlines CEO Haruka Nishimatsu, for instance. Jeff Bezos appears to have mastered both.

Sources: G. Anders, "Jeff Bezos Gets It," *Forbes* (April 23, 2012), pp. 76–86; J. Greathouse, "5 Time-Tested Success Tips from Amazon Founder Jeff Bezos," *Forbes* (April 30, 2013), www.forbes.com/sites/johngreathouse/2013/04/30/5-time-tested-success-tips-from-amazon-founder-jeff-bezos/2/; C. O'Connor, "Jeff Bezos' Spacecraft Blows Up In Secret Test Flight; Locals Describe 'Challenger-Like' Explosion," *Forbes* (September 2, 2011), www.forbes.com/sites/clareoconnor/2011/09/02/jeff-bezos-spacecraft-blows-up-in-secret-test-flight-locals-describe-challenger-like-explosion/2/; and S. J. Peterson, B. M. Galvin, and D. Lane, "CEO Servant Leadership: Exploring Executive Characteristics and Firm Performance," *Personnel Psychology* 65 (2012), pp. 565–596.

Before we define leadership and discuss what makes an effective leader exceptional, take the assessment to find out your own leadership style.

SELF-ASSESSMENT LIBRARY

What's My Leadership Style?

In the Self-Assessment Library (available in MyManagementLab) take assessment II.B.1 (What's My Leadership Style?) and answer the following questions.

1. How did you score on the two scales?
2. Do you think your leadership style will change over time? Why or why not?

What Is Leadership?

1 Contrast leadership and management.

leadership *The ability to influence a group toward the achievement of a vision or set of goals.*

We define **leadership** as the ability to influence a group toward the achievement of a vision or set of goals. The source of this influence may be formal, such as that provided by managerial rank in an organization. But not all leaders are managers, nor are all managers leaders. Just because an organization provides its managers with certain formal rights is no assurance they will lead effectively. Nonsanctioned leadership—the ability to influence that arises outside the formal structure of the organization—is often as important or more important than formal influence. Leaders can emerge from within a group as well as by formal appointment.

Organizations need strong leadership *and* strong management for optimal effectiveness. We need leaders to challenge the status quo, create visions of the

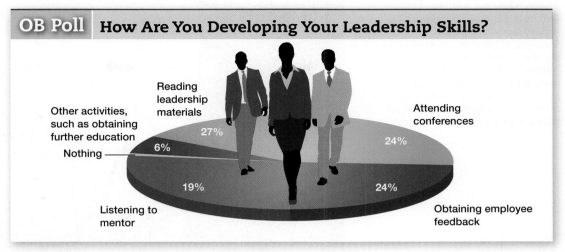

OB Poll | **How Are You Developing Your Leadership Skills?**

Other activities, such as obtaining further education

Reading leadership materials — 27%

Nothing

6%

19%

Listening to mentor

24% — Attending conferences

24%

Obtaining employee feedback

Note: Survey of 700 respondents.
Source: Based on J. Brox, "The Results Are In: How Do You Ensure You're Constantly Developing as a Leader?" (May 14, 2013), http://www.refreshleadership.com/index.php/2013/05/results-ensure-youre-constantly-developing-leader/#more-4732."

future, and inspire organizational members to achieve the visions. We also need managers to formulate detailed plans, create efficient organizational structures, and oversee day-to-day operations.

Trait Theories

2 Summarize the conclusions of trait theories of leadership.

trait theories of leadership *Theories that consider personal qualities and characteristics that differentiate leaders from nonleaders.*

Throughout history, strong leaders have been described by their traits. **Trait theories of leadership** focus on personal qualities and characteristics. The search for personality, social, physical, or intellectual attributes that differentiate leaders from nonleaders goes back to the earliest stages of leadership research.

Early efforts to isolate leadership traits resulted in a number of dead ends. A research review in the late 1960s identified nearly 80 leadership traits, but only 5 were common to 4 or more of the investigations.[1] By the 1990s, we could say most leaders "are not like other people," but the particular traits that characterized them varied a great deal from review to review.[2] Identifying leadership traits remained a challenge.

A breakthrough came when researchers began organizing traits around the Big Five personality framework (see Chapter 5).[3] Most of the dozens of traits in various leadership reviews fit under one of the Big Five (ambition and energy are part of extraversion, for instance), giving strong support to certain traits as predictors of leadership.

A comprehensive review of the leadership literature organized around the Big Five has found extraversion to be the most predictive trait of effective leadership,[4] but it is more strongly related to the way leaders emerge than to their effectiveness. Sociable and dominant people are more likely to assert themselves in group situations, but leaders need to make sure they're not too assertive. One study found leaders who scored very high on assertiveness were less effective than those who were moderately high.[5]

Unlike agreeableness and emotional stability, conscientiousness and openness to experience also showed strong relationships to leadership, though not

Photo 12-1 Indra Nooyi, CEO and board chairman of PepsiCo, is described as fun-loving, sociable, agreeable, conscientious, emotionally stable, and open to experiences. Recognized as one of the most powerful women in business, Nooyi's personal qualities and traits have contributed to her job performance and career success.

quite as strong as extraversion. Overall, the trait approach does have something to offer. Leaders who like being around people and are able to assert themselves (extraverted), who are disciplined and able to keep commitments they make (conscientious), and who are creative and flexible (open) do have an apparent advantage when it comes to leadership, suggesting good leaders do have key traits in common. One reason is that conscientiousness and extraversion are positively related to leaders' self-efficacy, which explained most of the variance in subordinates' ratings of leader performance.[6] People are more likely to follow someone who is confident she's going in the right direction.

Another trait that may indicate effective leadership is emotional intelligence (EI), discussed in Chapter 4. Advocates of EI argue that without it, a person can have outstanding training, a highly analytical mind, a compelling vision, and an endless supply of terrific ideas but still not make a great leader. This may be especially true as individuals move up in an organization.[7] A core component of EI is empathy. Empathetic leaders can sense others' needs, listen to what followers say (and don't say), and read the reactions of others. A leader who effectively displays and manages emotions will find it easier to influence the feelings of followers by expressing genuine sympathy and enthusiasm for good performance, and by showing irritation when employees fail to perform.[8]

The link between EI and leadership effectiveness may be worth investigating in greater detail.[9] Recent research has demonstrated that people high in EI are more likely to emerge as leaders, even after taking cognitive ability and personality into account.[10]

Based on the latest findings, we offer two conclusions. First, contrary to what we believed 20 years ago and thanks to the Big Five, we can say that traits can predict leadership. Second, traits do a better job predicting the emergence of leaders and the appearance of leadership than distinguishing between *effective* and *ineffective* leaders.[11] The fact that an individual exhibits the right traits and that others consider him or her a leader does not necessarily mean the leader is successful at getting the group to achieve its goals.

Behavioral Theories

3 Identify the central tenets and main limitations of behavioral theories.

behavioral theories of leadership *Theories proposing that specific behaviors differentiate leaders from nonleaders.*

initiating structure *The extent to which a leader is likely to define and structure his or her role and those of subordinates in the search for goal attainment.*

consideration *The extent to which a leader is likely to have job relationships characterized by mutual trust, respect for subordinates' ideas, and regard for their feelings.*

The failures of early trait studies led researchers in the late 1940s through the 1960s to wonder whether there was something unique in the way effective leaders *behave*. Trait research provides a basis for *selecting* the right people for leadership. In contrast, **behavioral theories of leadership** implied we could *train* people to be leaders.

The most comprehensive theories resulted from the Ohio State Studies in the late 1940s,[12] which sought to identify independent dimensions of leader behavior. Beginning with more than a thousand dimensions, the studies narrowed the list to two that substantially accounted for most of the leadership behavior described by employees: *initiating structure* and *consideration*.

Initiating structure is the extent to which a leader is likely to define and structure his or her role and those of employees in the search for goal attainment. It includes behavior that attempts to organize work, work relationships, and goals. A leader high in initiating structure is someone who "assigns group members to particular tasks," "expects workers to maintain definite standards of performance," and "emphasizes the meeting of deadlines."

Consideration is the extent to which a person's job relationships are characterized by mutual trust, respect for employees' ideas, and regard for their feelings. A leader high in consideration helps employees with personal problems, is friendly and approachable, treats all employees as equals, and expresses appreciation and support. In a recent survey, when asked to indicate what most motivated them at work, 66 percent of employees mentioned appreciation.[13]

Leadership studies at the University of Michigan's Survey Research Center had similar objectives to the Ohio State Studies: to locate behavioral characteristics of leaders that appeared related to performance effectiveness. The

Photo 12-2 Morgan Smith (left) is an employee-oriented leader who takes a personal interest in the needs of his employees. As former owner and managing partner of Boneheads Restaurant in Lake Forest, California, Smith is described as a generous, kind, and cheerful manager who shows respect for employees and helps them to reach their full potential.

Source: Jebb Harris/ZUMAPRESS/Newscom.

employee-oriented leader *A leader who emphasizes interpersonal relations, takes a personal interest in the needs of employees, and accepts individual differences among members.*

production-oriented leader *A leader who emphasizes technical or task aspects of the job.*

Michigan group also identified two behavioral types: the **employee-oriented leader** emphasized interpersonal relationships by taking a personal interest in employees' needs and accepting individual differences among them, and the **production-oriented leader** emphasized technical or task aspects of jobs, focusing on accomplishing the group's tasks. These dimensions are closely related to the Ohio State dimensions. Employee-oriented leadership is similar to consideration, and production-oriented leadership is similar to initiating structure. In fact, most researchers use the terms synonymously.[14]

At one time, the results of behavioral theories tests were thought to be disappointing. However, a review of 160 studies found the followers of leaders high in consideration were more satisfied with their jobs, were more motivated, and had more respect for their leaders. Initiating structure was more strongly related to higher levels of group and organization productivity and more positive performance evaluations.

Research from the GLOBE study suggests there are international differences in the preference for initiating structure and consideration.[15] Based on the values of Brazilian employees, for instance, a U.S. manager leading a team in Brazil would need to be team oriented, participative, and humane. Leaders high in consideration would succeed best in this culture. As one Brazilian manager said in the study, "We do not prefer leaders who take self-governing decisions and

glOBalization!

Leaders Broaden Their Span of Control in Multinational Organizations

In the past 20 years, senior corporate leaders have increased their average number of direct reports from 5 to 10 as their organizations have spread into new multinational territories. You may think this is yet another example of organization bloat. In reality, it has more to do with the desire of today's CEOs to directly engage with all areas of their business interests, bringing in representatives from new overseas ventures and even eliminating a significant middle layer of hierarchy (the role of the deputy, or COO, is on the decline among *Fortune* 500 companies). In fact, 80 percent of the new managers reporting to CEOs are functional leaders, who have been increasingly taking on general manager roles.

While the jump from 5 to 10 may not seem big in terms of headcount, the fact that these new direct reports represent diverse corporate interests poses a challenge for leadership. Research suggests the number of direct reports should be fewer than five if significant cross-organizational collaboration is needed, as in most multinational organizations. Experts also advise limiting the CEO's span of control when organizations are in transition, as globally expanding businesses are by definition.

The type of leadership the organization's particular CEO embodies should also suggest the optimal span of control, as should the national cultures of top overseas managers. A study from 23 countries showed that, in agreement with leader–member exchange (LMX) theory discussed in this chapter, individuals whose leaders treat them as favorites trust their leaders more in individualistic than in collectivistic cultures. This suggests that a CEO may be effective with a higher number of direct reports when they are from the organization's Asian business interests, for example, because the collectivist culture's respect for authority does not depend on personalized LMX attention. A CEO managing Western-culture direct reports might be better advised to keep the number to five or fewer in order to leverage the positive outcomes of high LMX.

Leadership issues are always at the forefront as companies expand. Companies have stretched and flattened their organizational structures to meet their global aspirations, but few leaders have directly addressed the high need for mental proximity—the ability to connect closely with their key employees, who are, after all, influential leaders themselves.

Sources: B. Groysberg and M. Slind, "Leadership Is a Conversation," *Harvard Business Review* (June 2012), pp. 76–84; G. L. Neilson and J. Wulf, "How Many Direct Reports?" *Harvard Business Review* (April 2012), pp. 112–119; and T. Rockstuhl, J. H. Dulebohn, S. Ang, and L. M. Shore, "Leader-Member Exchange (LMX) and Culture: A Meta-Analysis of Correlates of LMX across 23 Countries," *Journal of Applied Psychology* 97 (2012), pp. 1097–1130.

act alone without engaging the group. That's part of who we are." Compared to U.S. employees, the French have a more bureaucratic view of leaders and are less likely to expect them to be humane and considerate. A leader high in initiating structure (relatively task-oriented) will do best and can make decisions in a relatively autocratic manner. A manager who scores high on consideration (people oriented) may find that style backfires in France. According to the study, Chinese culture emphasizes being polite, considerate, and unselfish, but it has a high performance orientation. Thus, consideration and initiating structure may both be important.

Summary of Trait Theories and Behavioral Theories

Leaders who have certain traits and who display consideration and structuring behaviors do appear to be more effective. Perhaps you're wondering whether conscientious leaders (trait) are more likely to be structuring (behavior) and extraverted leaders (trait) to be considerate (behavior). Unfortunately, we are not sure there is a connection. Future research is needed to integrate these approaches.

Some leaders may have the right traits or display the right behaviors and still fail. As important as traits and behaviors are in identifying effective or ineffective leaders, they do not guarantee success. Context matters, too, which has given rise to the contingency theories we discuss next.

Contingency Theories

4 Assess contingency theories of leadership by their level of support.

Some tough-minded leaders seem to gain a lot of admirers when they take over struggling companies and lead them out of the doldrums. However, predicting leadership success is more complex than isolating a few traits or behaviors. What works in very bad times and in very good times doesn't seem to translate into long-term success. When researchers looked at situational influences, it appeared that under condition *a*, leadership style *x* would be appropriate, whereas style *y* was more suitable for condition *b*, and style *z* for condition *c*. But what *were* conditions *a*, *b*, and *c*? We next consider four approaches to isolating situational variables: the Fiedler model, situational theory, path–goal theory, and the leader-participation model.

The Fiedler Model

Fred Fiedler developed the first comprehensive contingency model for leadership.[16] The **Fiedler contingency model** proposes that effective group performance depends on the proper match between the leader's style and the degree to which the situation gives the leader control.

Fiedler contingency model *The theory that effective groups depend on a proper match between a leader's style of interacting with subordinates and the degree to which the situation gives control and influence to the leader.*

least preferred co-worker (LPC) questionnaire *An instrument that purports to measure whether a person is task or relationship oriented.*

Identifying Leadership Style Fiedler believes a key factor in leadership success is the individual's basic leadership style. He created the **least preferred co-worker (LPC) questionnaire** to identify that style by measuring whether a person is task or relationship oriented. The LPC questionnaire asks respondents to think of all the co-workers they have ever had and describe the one they *least enjoyed* working with by rating that person on a scale of 1 to 8 for each of 16 sets of contrasting adjectives (such as pleasant–unpleasant, efficient–inefficient, open–guarded, supportive–hostile). If you describe the person you are least able to work with in favorable terms (a high LPC score), Fiedler would label you *relationship oriented*. If you see your least-preferred coworker in unfavorable terms (a low LPC score), you are primarily interested in productivity and are *task oriented*. About 16 percent of respondents score in the middle range[17] and thus fall outside the theory's predictions. Our discussion relates to the 84 percent who score in the high or low range of the LPC questionnaire.

Fiedler assumes an individual's leadership style is fixed; if a situation requires a task-oriented leader and the person in the leadership position is relationship oriented, either the situation has to be modified or the leader has to be replaced to achieve optimal effectiveness.

SELF-ASSESSMENT LIBRARY

What's My LPC Score?

In the Self-Assessment Library (available in MyManagementLab), take assessment IV.E.5 (What's My LPC Score?).

leader–member relations
The degree of confidence, trust, and respect subordinates have in their leader.

task structure *The degree to which job assignments are procedurized.*

position power *Influence derived from one's formal structural position in the organization; includes power to hire, fire, discipline, promote, and give salary increases.*

Defining the Situation   After assessing an individual's basic leadership style through the LPC questionnaire, we match the leader with the situation. Fiedler identified three contingency or situational dimensions:

1. **Leader–member relations** is the degree of confidence, trust, and respect members have in their leader.
2. **Task structure** is the degree to which the job assignments are procedurized (that is, structured or unstructured).
3. **Position power** is the degree of influence a leader has over power variables such as hiring, firing, discipline, promotions, and salary increases.

We evaluate the situation in terms of these three variables. Fiedler states that the better the leader–member relations, the more highly structured the job, and the stronger the position power, the more control the leader has. A very favorable situation (in which the leader has a great deal of control) might include a payroll manager who is well respected and whose employees have confidence in him (good leader–member relations), activities that are clear and specific—such as wage computation, check writing, and report filing (high task structure), and provision of considerable freedom to reward and punish employees (strong position power). An unfavorable situation might be that of the disliked chairperson of a volunteer United Way fundraising team. In this job, the leader has very little control.

Matching Leaders and Situations   Combining the three contingency dimensions yields eight possible situations in which leaders can find themselves (Exhibit 12-1). The Fiedler model proposes matching an individual's LPC score and these eight situations to achieve maximum leadership effectiveness.[18] Fiedler concluded that task-oriented leaders perform better in situations very favorable to them and very unfavorable. So, when faced with a category I, II, III, VII, or VIII situation, task-oriented leaders perform better. Relationship-oriented leaders, however, perform better in moderately favorable situations—categories IV, V, and VI. Fiedler later condensed these eight situations down to three.[19] Task-oriented leaders perform best in situations of high and low control, while relationship-oriented leaders perform best in moderate control situations.

How would you apply Fiedler's findings? You would match leaders—in terms of their LPC scores—with the type of situation—in terms of leader–member

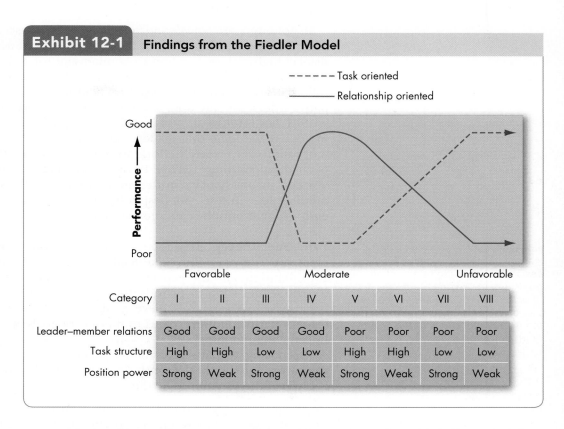

Exhibit 12-1   Findings from the Fiedler Model

Category	I	II	III	IV	V	VI	VII	VIII
Leader–member relations	Good	Good	Good	Good	Poor	Poor	Poor	Poor
Task structure	High	High	Low	Low	High	High	Low	Low
Position power	Strong	Weak	Strong	Weak	Strong	Weak	Strong	Weak

relationships, task structure, and position power—for which they were best suited. But remember that Fiedler views an individual's leadership style as fixed. Therefore, there are only two ways to improve leader effectiveness.

First, you can change the leader to fit the situation—as a baseball manager puts a right- or left-handed pitcher into the game depending on the hitter. If a group situation rates highly unfavorable but is currently led by a relationship-oriented manager, for example, the group's performance could be improved under a manager who is task-oriented. The second alternative is to change the situation to fit the leader by restructuring tasks or increasing or decreasing the leader's power to control factors such as salary increases, promotions, and disciplinary actions.

Evaluation   Studies testing the overall validity of the Fiedler model find considerable evidence to support substantial parts of it.[20] If we use three categories rather than the original eight, ample evidence supports Fiedler's conclusions.[21] But the logic underlying the LPC questionnaire is not well understood, and respondents' scores are not stable.[22] The contingency variables are also complex and difficult for practitioners to assess.[23]

Other Contingency Theories

Although LPC theory is the most researched contingency theory, three others deserve mention.

situational leadership theory (SLT) *A contingency theory that focuses on followers' readiness.*

Situational Leadership Theory   Situational leadership theory (SLT) focuses on the followers. It says successful leadership depends on selecting the right leadership style contingent on the followers' *readiness,* the extent to which they are willing and able to accomplish a specific task. A leader should choose one of four behaviors depending on follower readiness.

If followers are *unable* and *unwilling* to do a task, the leader needs to give clear and specific directions; if they are *unable* and *willing*, the leader needs to display high task orientation to compensate for followers' lack of ability, and high relationship orientation to get them to "buy into" the leader's desires. If followers are *able* and *unwilling*, the leader needs to use a supportive and participative style; if they are both *able* and *willing*, the leader doesn't need to do much.

SLT has intuitive appeal. It acknowledges the importance of followers and builds on the logic that leaders can compensate for their limited ability and motivation. Yet research efforts to test and support the theory have generally been disappointing.[24] Why? Possible explanations include internal ambiguities and inconsistencies in the model itself as well as problems with research methodology in tests. So, despite its intuitive appeal and wide popularity, any endorsement must be cautious for now.

path–goal theory *A theory that states that it is the leader's job to assist followers in attaining their goals and to provide the necessary direction and/or support to ensure that their goals are compatible with the overall objectives of the group or organization.*

Path–Goal Theory   Developed by Robert House, **path–goal theory** extracts elements from the Ohio State leadership research on initiating structure and consideration, and the expectancy theory of motivation.[25] The theory suggests it's the leader's job to provide followers with information, support, or other resources necessary to achieve goals. (The term *path–goal* implies effective leaders clarify followers' paths to their work goals and make the journey easier by reducing roadblocks.)

According to path–goal theory, whether a leader should be directive or supportive, or should demonstrate some other behavior, depends on complex analysis of the situation. The theory predicts:

- Directive leadership yields greater satisfaction when tasks are ambiguous or stressful than when they are highly structured and well laid out.
- Supportive leadership results in high performance and satisfaction when employees are performing structured tasks.
- Directive leadership is likely to be perceived as redundant among employees with high ability or considerable experience.

Photo 12-3 CEO Alan Mulally led a successful turnaround effort at Ford Motor Company by applying the path–goal theory. He directed managers and employees toward the goal of making Ford globally competitive and profitable and developed the Way Forward plan that focused on everyone in the company operating as one team around the world.

In a study of 162 workers in a document-processing organization, researchers found workers' conscientiousness was related to higher levels of performance only when supervisors set goals and defined roles, responsibilities, and priorities.[26] Other research has found that goal-focused leadership can lead to higher levels of emotional exhaustion for subordinates who are low in conscientiousness and emotional stability.[27] These studies demonstrate that leaders who set goals enable conscientious followers to achieve higher performance but may cause stress for workers who are low in conscientiousness.

Leader-Participation Model   The final contingency theory we cover argues that *the way* the leader makes decisions is as important as *what* she or he decides. Victor Vroom and Phillip Yetton's **leader-participation model** relates leadership behavior and participation in decision making.[28] Like path–goal theory, it says leader behavior must adjust to reflect the task structure. The model is normative—it provides a decision tree of seven contingencies and five leadership styles for determining the form and amount of participation in decision making.

As one leadership scholar noted, "Leaders do not exist in a vacuum"; leadership is a symbiotic relationship between leaders and followers.[29] But the theories we've covered to this point assume leaders use a fairly homogeneous style with everyone in their work unit. Think about your experiences in groups. Did leaders often act very differently toward different people? Our next theory considers *differences* in the relationships leaders form with diverse followers.

leader-participation model   *A leadership theory that provides a set of rules to determine the form and amount of participative decision making in different situations.*

Leader–Member Exchange (LMX) Theory

leader–member exchange (LMX) theory   *A theory that supports leaders' creation of ingroups and outgroups; subordinates with ingroup status will have higher performance ratings, less turnover, and greater job satisfaction.*

Think of a leader you know. Does this leader have favorites who make up his or her ingroup? If you answered "yes," you're acknowledging the foundation of leader–member exchange theory.[30] **Leader–member exchange (LMX) theory** argues that, because of time pressures, leaders establish a special relationship with a small group of their followers. These individuals make up the ingroup—they are trusted, get a disproportionate amount of the leader's attention, and are more likely to receive special privileges. Other followers fall into the outgroup.

LMX theory proposes that early in the history of the interaction between a leader and a given follower, the leader implicitly categorizes the follower as an "in" or an "out"; that relationship is relatively stable over time. Leaders induce LMX by rewarding employees with whom they want a closer linkage and punishing those with whom they do not.[31] For the LMX relationship to remain intact, the leader and the follower must invest in the relationship.

Just how the leader chooses who falls into each category is unclear, but there is evidence ingroup members have demographic, attitude, and personality characteristics similar to those of their leader or a higher level of competence than outgroup members[32] (see Exhibit 12-2). Leaders and followers of the same gender tend to have closer (higher LMX) relationships than those of different genders.[33] Even though the leader does the choosing, the follower's characteristics drive the categorizing decision.

Research to test LMX theory has been generally supportive, with substantive evidence that leaders do differentiate among followers; these disparities are far from random; and followers with ingroup status will have higher performance ratings, engage in more helping or "citizenship" behaviors at work, and report

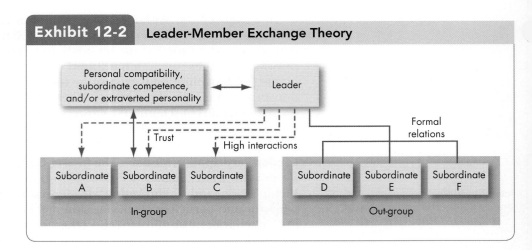

Exhibit 12-2   Leader-Member Exchange Theory

greater satisfaction with their superior.[34] One study conducted in Portugal and the United States found that leader–member exchange was associated strongly with followers' commitment to the organization when leaders were seen as embodying the values and identity of the organization.[35] These findings for ingroup members shouldn't be surprising, given our knowledge of self-fulfilling prophecy (see Chapter 6). Leaders invest resources with those they expect to perform best. Believing ingroup members are the most competent, leaders treat them as such and unwittingly fulfill their prophecy.

Leader–follower relationships may be stronger when followers have a more active role in shaping their own job performance. A study in Turkey demonstrated that when leaders differentiated strongly among their followers in terms of their relationships (some followers had very positive leader–member exchange, others very poor), employees responded with more negative work attitudes and higher levels of withdrawal behavior.[36] Research on 287 software developers and 164 supervisors showed leader–member relationships have a stronger impact on employee performance and attitudes when employees have higher levels of autonomy and a more internal locus of control.[37]

Charismatic Leadership and Transformational Leadership

5 Contrast *charismatic* and *transformational leadership*.

In this section, we present two contemporary leadership theories—charismatic leadership and transformational leadership—with a common theme: They view leaders as individuals who inspire followers through words, ideas, and behaviors.

Charismatic Leadership

Martin Luther King Jr., Ronald Reagan, Mary Kay Ash (founder of Mary Kay Cosmetics), and Steve Jobs (co-founder of Apple Computer) are frequently cited as charismatic leaders. What do they have in common?

What Is Charismatic Leadership? Sociologist Max Weber defined *charisma* (from the Greek for "gift") more than a century ago as "a certain quality of an individual personality, by virtue of which he or she is set apart from

Exhibit 12-3	Key Characteristics of a Charismatic Leader

1. *Vision and articulation.* Has a vision—expressed as an idealized goal—that proposes a future better than the status quo; and is able to clarify the importance of the vision in terms that are understandable to others.
2. *Personal risk.* Willing to take on high personal risk, incur high costs, and engage in self-sacrifice to achieve the vision.
3. *Sensitivity to follower needs.* Perceptive of others' abilities and responsive to their needs and feelings.
4. *Unconventional behavior.* Engages in behaviors that are perceived as novel and counter to norms.

Source: Based on J. A. Conger and R. N. Kanungo, *Charismatic Leadership in Organizations* (Thousand Oaks, CA: Sage, 1998), p. 94.

charismatic leadership theory
A leadership theory that states that followers make attributions of heroic or extraordinary leadership abilities when they observe certain behaviors.

ordinary people and treated as endowed with supernatural, superhuman, or at least specifically exceptional powers or qualities. These are not accessible to the ordinary person and are regarded as of divine origin or as exemplary, and on the basis of them the individual concerned is treated as a leader."[38] Weber argued that charismatic leadership was one of several ideal types of authority.

The first researcher to consider charismatic leadership in terms of OB was Robert House. According to House's **charismatic leadership theory**, followers attribute heroic or extraordinary leadership abilities when they observe certain behaviors, and tend to give these leaders power.[39] A number of studies have attempted to identify the characteristics of charismatic leaders: They have a vision, are willing to take personal risks to achieve that vision, are sensitive to follower needs, and exhibit extraordinary behaviors[40] (see Exhibit 12-3).

Are Charismatic Leaders Born or Made?   Are charismatic leaders born with their qualities? Or can people actually learn to be charismatic leaders? Yes, and yes.

Individuals *are* born with traits that make them charismatic. In fact, studies of identical twins have found they score similarly on charismatic leadership measures, even if they were raised in different households and never met. Personality is also related to charismatic leadership; charismatic leaders are likely to be extraverted, self-confident, and achievement oriented.[41] Consider Presidents Barack Obama and Ronald Reagan: Like them or not, they are often compared because both possess the qualities of charismatic leaders.

To develop an aura of charisma by maintaining an optimistic view, use passion as a catalyst for generating enthusiasm, and communicate with the whole body, not just with words. Use an animated voice, reinforce your message with eye contact and enthusiastic expressions, and use gestures for emphasis. Draw others in by creating a bond that inspires them to follow. Bring out the potential in followers by tapping into their emotions. Recent research indicates that your presence matters as well in creating a charismatic impression. If you stay active and central in your leadership roles, you will naturally communicate your vision for achieving goals to your followers, which increases the likelihood that you will be seen as charismatic.[42]

vision   *A long-term strategy for attaining a goal or goals.*

How Charismatic Leaders Influence Followers   How do charismatic leaders actually influence followers? By articulating an appealing **vision**, a long-term strategy for attaining a goal by linking the present with a better future for the organization. Desirable visions fit the times and circumstances and reflect the uniqueness of the organization.

vision statement *A formal articulation of an organization's vision or mission.*

A vision needs an accompanying **vision statement**, a formal articulation of an organization's vision or mission. Charismatic leaders may use vision statements to imprint on followers an overarching goal and purpose. They build followers' self-esteem and confidence with high performance expectations and the belief that followers can attain them. Next, through words and actions the leader conveys a new set of values and sets an example for followers to imitate. One study of Israeli bank employees showed charismatic leaders were more effective because their employees personally identified with them. Charismatic leaders also set a tone of cooperation and mutual support. A study of 115 government employees found they had a stronger sense of personal belonging at work when they had charismatic leaders, increasing their willingness to engage in helping and compliance-oriented behavior.[43]

Finally, the charismatic leader engages in emotion-inducing and often unconventional behavior to demonstrate courage and conviction about the vision. Followers "catch" the emotions their leader is conveying.[44]

Does Effective Charismatic Leadership Depend on the Situation? People working for charismatic leaders are motivated to exert extra effort and, because they like and respect their leaders, express greater satisfaction. Organizations with charismatic CEOs are more profitable, and charismatic college professors enjoy higher course evaluations.[45] Even in laboratory studies, when people are psychologically aroused, they are more likely to respond to charismatic leaders.[46] This may explain why, when charismatic leaders surface, it's likely to be in politics or religion, or during wartime, or when a business is in its infancy or facing a life-threatening crisis. Franklin D. Roosevelt offered a vision to get the United States out of the Great Depression in the 1930s. In 1997, when Apple Computer was floundering and lacking direction, the board persuaded charismatic co-founder Steve Jobs to return as interim CEO and restore the company to its innovative roots.

Another situational factor limiting charisma is the level in the organization. Top executives create vision; it's more difficult to utilize a person's charismatic leadership qualities in lower-level management jobs or to align his or her vision with the larger goals of the organization.

Finally, people are especially receptive to charismatic leadership when they sense a crisis, when they are under stress, or when they fear for their lives. Charismatic leaders are able to reduce stress for their employees, perhaps because they help make work seem more meaningful and interesting.[47] Some peoples' personalities are especially susceptible to charismatic leadership.[48] Consider self-esteem. An individual who lacks self-esteem and questions his or her self-worth is more likely to absorb a leader's direction rather than establish his or her own way of leading or thinking.

The Dark Side of Charismatic Leadership Charismatic business leaders like GE's Jack Welch, Apple's Steve Jobs, Southwest Airlines' Herb Kelleher, and Microsoft's Steven Ballmer became celebrities on the order of Kate Middleton and Brad Pitt. Every company wanted a charismatic CEO, and to attract them, boards of directors gave them unprecedented autonomy and resources—the use of private jets and multimillion-dollar penthouses, interest-free loans to buy beach homes and artwork, security staffs, and similar benefits befitting royalty. One study showed charismatic CEOs were able to leverage higher salaries even when their performance was mediocre.[49]

Unfortunately, charismatic leaders who are larger than life don't necessarily act in the best interests of their organizations.[50] Many have allowed their personal goals to override the goals of the organization. The results at companies such as Enron, Tyco, WorldCom, and HealthSouth were leaders who recklessly used organizational resources for their personal benefit and executives who violated laws and ethical boundaries to inflate stock prices and allow leaders to cash in millions of dollars in stock options. Research has shown that individuals who are narcissistic are also higher in some behaviors associated with charismatic leadership.[51]

It's not that charismatic leadership isn't effective; overall, it is. But a charismatic leader isn't always the answer. Success depends, to some extent, on the situation and on the leader's vision. Some charismatic leaders—Hitler, for example—are all too successful at convincing their followers to pursue a vision that can be disastrous.

SELF-ASSESSMENT LIBRARY

How Charismatic Am I?

In the Self-Assessment Library (available in MyManagementLab), take assessment II.B.2 (How Charismatic Am I?).

transactional leaders *Leaders who guide or motivate their followers in the direction of established goals by clarifying role and task requirements.*

transformational leaders *Leaders who inspire followers to transcend their own self-interests and who are capable of having a profound and extraordinary effect on followers.*

Transformational Leadership

A stream of research has focused on differentiating transformational from transactional leaders.[52] The Ohio State studies, Fiedler's model, and path–goal theory describe **transactional leaders**, who guide their followers toward established goals by clarifying role and task requirements. **Transformational leaders** inspire followers to transcend their self-interests for the good of the organization. Transformational leaders can have an extraordinary effect on their followers. Richard Branson of the Virgin Group is a good example of a transformational leader. He

Myth or Science?

"Top Leaders Feel the Most Stress"

Leaders of corporations fight pressures from their boards, customers, managers, and employees. Wouldn't it stand to reason they are the most stressed people in their organizations? Apparently not. According to studies from Harvard University, the University of California–San Diego, and Stanford University, leadership brings a blissful relief from the stress felt by individuals who are not in managerial roles. Not only did leaders report less anxiety than nonleaders, but their cortisol (stress hormone) levels were also lower, indicating they biologically are less likely to register stress. Another study found that individuals in higher-status occupational groups registered

less perceived stress and lower blood pressure readings than those in lower status occupations.

If you're thinking this is one more reason "it's better at the top," you may be right, if only partially. It is true that leaders appear to show fewer signs of stress by virtue of being leaders, regardless of higher income or longer job tenure. However, researchers found no "magic level" in an organization at which employees feel a reduction in stress levels.

One study found that stress reduction correlates with feelings of control. Leaders with more subordinates and greater power felt less stress than other individuals who knew they had

less control over outcomes. Top leaders who control the resources of their corporations and have plenty of employees to carry out their directives therefore can fight stressors before they affect them.

Sources: M. Korn, "Top-Level Leaders Have Less Stress Than Others," *The Wall Street Journal* (October 3, 2012), p. B6; G. D. Sherman et al. "Leadership Is Associated with Lower Levels of Stress," *Proceedings of the National Academy of Sciences of the United States of America* (October 30, 2012), pp. 17903–17907; and E. Wiernik et al., "Occupational Status Moderates the Association between Current Perceived Stress and High Blood Pressure: Evidence from the IPC Cohort Study," *Hypertension* (March 2013), pp. 571–577.

| Exhibit 12-4 | Characteristics of Transactional and Transformational Leaders |

Transactional Leader

Contingent Reward: Contracts exchange of rewards for effort, promises rewards for good performance, recognizes accomplishments.

Management by Exception (active): Watches and searches for deviations from rules and standards, takes correct action.

Management by Exception (passive): Intervenes only if standards are not met.

Laissez-Faire: Abdicates responsibilities, avoids making decisions.

Transformational Leader

Idealized Influence: Provides vision and sense of mission, instills pride, gains respect and trust.

Inspirational Motivation: Communicates high expectations, uses symbols to focus efforts, expresses important purposes in simple ways.

Intellectual Stimulation: Promotes intelligence, rationality, and careful problem solving.

Individualized Consideration: Gives personal attention, treats each employee individually, coaches, advises.

Sources: Based on A. H. Eagly, M. C. Johannesen-Schmidt, and M. L. Van Engen, "Transformational, Transactional, and Laissez-faire Leadership Styles: A Meta-Analysis Comparing Women and Men," *Psychological Bulletin* 129, no. 4 (2003), pp. 569–591; and T. A. Judge and J. E. Bono, "Five Factor Model of Personality and Transformational Leadership," *Journal of Applied Psychology* 85, no. 5 (2000), pp. 751–765.

pays attention to the concerns and needs of individual followers, changes followers' awareness of issues by helping them look at old problems in new ways, and excites and inspires followers to put forth extra effort to achieve group goals. Recent research suggests that transformational leaders are most effective when their followers are able to see the positive impact of their work through direct interaction with customers or other beneficiaries.[53] Exhibit 12-4 briefly identifies and defines characteristics that differentiate these two types of leaders.

Transactional and transformational leadership complement each other; they aren't opposing approaches to getting things done.[54] Transformational leadership *builds on* transactional leadership and produces levels of follower effort and performance beyond what transactional leadership alone can do. But the reverse isn't true. So if you are a good transactional leader but do not have transformational qualities, you'll likely only be a mediocre leader. The best leaders are transactional *and* transformational.

Full Range of Leadership Model   Exhibit 12-5 shows the full range of leadership model. Laissez-faire is the most passive and therefore least effective of leader behaviors.[55] Management by exception—active or passive—is slightly better, but it's still considered ineffective. Management-by-exception leaders tend to be available only when there is a problem, which is often too late. Contingent reward leadership can be an effective style of leadership but will not get employees to go above and beyond the call of duty.

Only with the four remaining styles—all aspects of transformational leadership—are leaders able to motivate followers to perform above expectations and transcend their self-interest for the sake of the organization. Individualized consideration, intellectual stimulation, inspirational motivation, and idealized influence (known as the "four I's") all result in extra effort from workers, higher productivity, higher morale and satisfaction, higher organizational

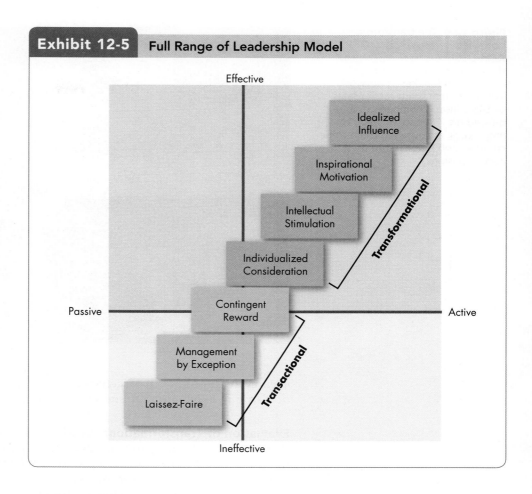

Exhibit 12-5   Full Range of Leadership Model

effectiveness, lower turnover, lower absenteeism, and greater organizational adaptability. Based on this model, leaders are generally most effective when they regularly use the four I's.

How Transformational Leadership Works   Transformational leaders are more effective because they are creative, but also because they encourage those who follow them to be creative, too.[56] Companies with transformational leaders have greater decentralization of responsibility, managers have more propensity to take risks, and compensation plans are geared toward long-term results—all of which facilitate corporate entrepreneurship.[57] One study of information technology workers in China found empowering leadership behavior led to feelings of positive personal control among workers, which increased their creativity at work.[58] Another recent study indicated that abusive supervisors negatively affect creativity, not for just their direct reports but for whole teams.[59]

Companies with transformational leaders show greater agreement among top managers about the organization's goals, which yields superior organizational performance.[60] The Israeli military has seen similar results, showing that transformational leaders improve performance by building consensus among group members.[61] Transformational leaders are able to increase follower self-efficacy, giving the group a "can do" spirit.[62] Followers are more likely to pursue ambitious goals, agree on the strategic goals of the organization, and believe the goals they are pursuing are personally important.[63]

Just as vision helps explain how charismatic leadership works, it also explains part of the effect of transformational leadership. One study found vision was

Source: Imaginechina via AP Images.

Photo 12-4 The transformational leadership of Cisco CEO John Chambers has helped grow the company into the top global designer and maker of networking equipment, with record sales of $46 billion. Chambers communicated his visionary strategy to employees, encouraged them to be creative, and empowered them to make decisions.

even more important than a charismatic (effusive, dynamic, lively) communication style in explaining the success of entrepreneurial firms.[64]

Evaluation of Transformational Leadership   Transformational leadership has been supported at diverse job levels and occupations (school principals, teachers, marine commanders, ministers, presidents of MBA associations, military cadets, union shop stewards, sales reps). One study of R&D firms found teams whose project leaders scored high on transformational leadership produced better-quality products as judged one year later and higher profits five years later.[65] Another study looking at employee creativity and transformational leadership found employees with transformational leaders had more confidence in their ability to be creative at work and higher levels of creative performance.[66] A review of 117 studies testing transformational leadership found it was related to higher levels of individual follower performance, team performance, and organizational performance.[67]

Transformational leadership isn't equally effective in all situations. It has a greater impact on the bottom line in smaller, privately held firms than in more complex organizations.[68] Transformational leadership may be more effective when leaders can directly interact with the workforce to make decisions than when they report to an external board of directors or deal with a complex bureaucratic structure. One study showed transformational leaders were more effective in improving group potency in teams higher in power distance and collectivism.[69] Other research using a sample of employees both in China and the United States found that transformational leadership had a more positive relationship with perceived procedural justice among individuals who were lower in power-distance orientation, which in turn related to a stronger transformational leadership-citizenship behavior relationship among those higher in power distance.[70] Transformational leaders also obtain higher levels of trust, which reduces stress for followers.[71] In short, transformational leadership works through a number of different processes.

One study examined how different types of transformational leadership can be effective depending on whether work is evaluated at the team or the individual level.[72] Individual-focused transformational leadership is behavior that empowers individual followers to develop, enhance their abilities, and increase self-efficacy. Team-focused transformational leadership emphasizes group goals, shared values and beliefs, and unified efforts. Evidence from a sample of 203 team members and 60 leaders in a business unit found individual transformational leadership associated with higher individual-level performance, whereas team-focused transformational leadership drew higher group-level performance.

Transformational leadership theory is not perfect. Contingent reward leadership may not characterize transactional leaders only. And contrary to the full range of leadership model, the four I's of transformational leadership are not always superior in effectiveness to transactional leadership; contingent reward leadership sometimes works as well as transformational leadership.

In summary, transformational leadership is more strongly correlated than transactional leadership with lower turnover rates, higher productivity, lower employee stress and burnout, and higher employee satisfaction.[73] Like charisma, it can be learned. One study of Canadian bank managers found branches managed by those who underwent transformational leadership training performed significantly better than branches whose managers did not receive training.

The GLOBE study—of 18,000 leaders from 825 organizations in 62 countries—links a number of elements of transformational leadership with effective leadership, regardless of country.[74] This conclusion is very important because it disputes the contingency view that leadership style needs to adapt to cultural differences.

What elements of transformational leadership appear universal? Vision, foresight, providing encouragement, trustworthiness, dynamism, positiveness, and proactiveness top the list. The GLOBE team concluded that "effective business leaders in any country are expected by their subordinates to provide a powerful and proactive vision to guide the company into the future, strong motivational skills to stimulate all employees to fulfill the vision, and excellent planning skills to assist in implementing the vision."[75] A vision is important in any culture, but the way it is formed and communicated may need to be adapted.

Authentic Leadership: Ethics and Trust

6 Define *authentic leadership.*

Although theories have increased our understanding of effective leadership, they do not explicitly deal with the role of ethics and trust, which some argue is essential to complete the picture. Here, we consider these two concepts under the rubric of authentic leadership.[76]

What Is Authentic Leadership?

SAP's Co-CEO Bill McDermott's motto is "Stay Hungry, Stay Humble," and he appears to practice what he preaches. Campbell Soup's CEO Denise Morrison decided to lower sodium in the company's soup products simply because it was the right thing to do. McDermott and Morrison appear to be good exemplars of authentic leadership.[77]

authentic leaders *Leaders who know who they are, know what they believe in and value, and act on those values and beliefs openly and candidly. Their followers would consider them to be ethical people.*

Authentic leaders know who they are, know what they believe in and value, and act on those values and beliefs openly and candidly. Their followers consider them ethical people. The primary quality produced by authentic leadership is trust. Authentic leaders share information, encourage open communication, and stick to their ideals. The result: People come to have faith in them.

Photo 12-5 Entrepreneur Grace Liu is an authentic leader. Shown here with her employees, Liu is co-founder and managing director of Asianera, a maker of hand-painted bone china. She built her successful business of high-quality porcelain and innovative design based on her strong personal core values of respecting the individual and operating with integrity.

Source: Ton Koene/71JMApress/Newscom.

There has been limited research on authentic leadership to date. However, recent research indicates that authentic leadership, especially when shared among top management team members, created a positive energizing effect (see affective events theory, discussed in Chapter 4) that heightened firm performance.[78] Authentic leadership is a promising way to think about ethics and trust in leadership because it focuses on the moral aspects of being a leader. Transformational or charismatic leaders can have a vision and communicate it persuasively, but sometimes the vision is wrong (as in the case of Hitler), or the leader is more concerned with his or her own needs or pleasures, as were Dennis Kozlowski (ex-CEO of Tyco), Jeff Skilling (ex-CEO of Enron), and Raj Rajaratnam (founder of the Galleon Group).[79]

SELF-ASSESSMENT LIBRARY

Am I an Ethical Leader?

In the Self-Assessment Library (available in MyManagementLab), take assessment IV.E.4 (Am I an Ethical Leader?).

Ethical Leadership

Researchers have begun to study the ethical implications in leadership.[80] Why now? One reason may be the growing interest in ethics throughout the field of management. Another may be the discovery that many past leaders—such as Martin Luther King Jr., John F. Kennedy, and Thomas Jefferson—suffered ethical shortcomings. Another reason may be the growing realization that although every member of an organization is responsible for ethical behavior, many initiatives aimed at increasing organizational ethical behavior are focused on the leaders. The role of the leader in creating the ethical expectations for all members is crucial.[81] A recent study of 2,572 U.S. Army soldiers underscored that ethical top leadership influences not only direct followers, but across all organizational levels, because these top leaders create an ethical culture and expect lower-level leaders to behave along ethical guidelines.[82]

Ethics and leadership intersect at a number of junctures. Transformational leadership has ethical implications since these leaders change the way followers think. Charisma, too, has an ethical component. Unethical leaders use their charisma to enhance power over followers, directed toward self-serving ends. Leaders who treat their followers with fairness, especially by providing honest, frequent, and accurate information, are seen as more effective.[83] Related to this is the concept of humbleness, another characteristic ethical leaders often exhibit as part of being authentic. Research indicates that leaders who model humility help followers to understand the growth process for their own development.[84] Leaders rated as highly ethical tend to have followers who engage in more organizational citizenship behaviors and who are more willing to bring problems to the leaders' attention.[85] Recent research also found that ethical leadership reduced interpersonal conflicts.[86]

Because top executives set the moral tone for an organization, they need to set high ethical standards, demonstrate them through their own behavior, and encourage and reward integrity in others while avoiding abuses of power such as giving themselves large raises and bonuses while laying off employees. A recent research review found that role modeling by top leaders positively influenced managers throughout their organizations to behave ethically and fostered a climate that reinforced group-level ethical conduct. The findings suggest that organizations should invest in ethical leadership training programs, especially in industries with few ethical regulations. The researchers furthermore advised that ethical leadership training programs to teach cultural values should be mandated for leaders who take foreign assignments or manage multicultural work teams.[87]

For ethical leadership to be effective, it is not enough for the leader to simply possess high moral character. After all, there is no universal standard for ethical behavior, and ethical norms vary by culture, by industry, and even sometimes within an organization. Leaders must be willing to express their ethical beliefs and persuade others to follow their standards. Followers must believe in both the leader and the overlying principles, even if they don't personally agree with every minor stance.

To convey their beliefs, leaders should learn to express their moral convictions in statements that reflect values shared with their organization's members. Leaders can build on this foundation of trust to show their character, enhance a sense of unity, and create buy-in from followers. The leader's message should announce high goals and confidence that they can be reached.

Ethical leaders' statements are often positive messages, such as Winston Churchill's opening for his World War II victory speech: "This is your hour. This is not a victory of a party of or any class. It's a victory of the great British nation as a whole." An example of an ethical leader's negative message is this speech by Gandhi: "Even if all the United Nations opposes me, even if the whole of India forsakes me, I will say, 'You are wrong. India will wrench with nonviolence her liberty from unwilling hands.'" Positive and negative ethical leader statements can be equally effective when they deliver clear, moral, inclusive, goal-setting statements with persuasiveness. In fact, they can set trends in motion to make the seemingly far-fetched become real.[88]

Leadership is not value-free. In assessing its effectiveness, we need to address the *means* a leader uses to achieve goals as well as the content of those goals. Scholars have tried to integrate ethical and charismatic leadership by advancing the idea of **socialized charismatic leadership**—leadership that conveys other-centered (not self-centered) values by leaders who model ethical conduct.[89] Socialized charismatic leaders are able to bring employee values in line with their own values through their words and actions.[90]

socialized charismatic leadership *A leadership concept that states that leaders convey values that are other centered versus self centered and who role-model ethical conduct.*

Holding Leaders Ethically Accountable

No one thinks leaders shouldn't be accountable. Leaders must balance many and conflicting stakeholder demands. The first, largely unspoken, demand is for strong financial performance; leaders are probably terminated more often for missing this goal than for all other factors combined. When one balances the often-extreme pressure for financial performance with the desire most leaders have to act ethically toward their employees, there is unfortunately little leadership accountability to ensure ethical leadership is happening. Given that pressure, ethical leadership may be under-rewarded and depend solely on the leader's innate decency.

Ethical leadership is a relatively new area of research attention. Demonstrating fairness and social responsibility and abiding by the law even run counter to many old-school models of leadership. Consider, for example, legendary management guru Peter Drucker's advice (1967): "It is the duty of the executive to remove ruthlessly anyone—and especially any manager—who consistently fails to perform with high distinction. To let such a man stay on corrupts the others." Modern ethical leadership guidelines say this cut-throat mindset fails to consider the moral implications of treating people as objects at an organization's disposal.

While few organizations still require "performance at all costs," financiers, shareholders, and boards have the reward power to teach leaders which outcomes to value. Ethical leadership resounds positively throughout all organizational levels, resulting in responsible and potentially highly profitable outcomes, but the ultimate ethical test will come when shareholders—and leaders—show signs of balancing these accountabilities themselves.

Sources: T. E. Ricks, "What Ever Happened to Accountability?" *Harvard Business Review* (October 2012), pp. 93–100; J. M. Schaubroeck et al., "Embedding Ethical Leadership Within and Across Organizational Levels," *Academy of Management Journal* 55 (2012), pp. 1053–1078; and J. Stouten, M. van Dijke, and D. De Cremer, "Ethical Leadership," *Journal of Personnel Psychology* 11 (2012), pp. 1–6.

Servant Leadership

servant leadership *A leadership style marked by going beyond the leader's own self-interest and instead focusing on opportunities to help followers grow and develop.*

Scholars have recently considered ethical leadership from a new angle by examining **servant leadership**.[91] Servant leaders go beyond their self-interest and focus on opportunities to help followers grow and develop. They don't use power to achieve ends; they emphasize persuasion. Characteristic behaviors include listening, empathizing, persuading, accepting stewardship, and actively developing followers' potential. A recent study of 126 CEOs found that servant leadership is negatively correlated with the trait of narcissism.[92] Because servant leadership focuses on serving the needs of others, research has focused on its outcomes for the well-being of followers.

What are the effects of servant leadership? One study of 123 supervisors found it resulted in higher levels of commitment to the supervisor, self-efficacy, and perceptions of justice, which all were related to organizational citizenship behavior.[93] This relationship between servant leadership and follower OCB appears to be stronger when followers are focused on being dutiful and responsible.[94] Second, servant leadership increases team potency (a belief that one's team has above-average skills and abilities), which in turn leads to higher levels of group performance.[95] Third, a study with a nationally representative sample found higher levels of citizenship associated with a focus on growth and advancement, which in turn was associated with higher levels of creative performance.[96]

Servant leadership may be more prevalent and more effective in certain cultures.[97] When asked to draw images of leaders, for example, U.S. subjects tend to draw them in front of the group, giving orders to followers. Singaporeans tend to draw leaders at the back of the group, acting more to gather a group's opinions together and then unify them from the rear. This suggests the East

Asian prototype is more like a servant leader, which might mean servant leadership is more effective in these cultures.

Trust and Leadership

trust *A positive expectation that another will not act opportunistically.*

Trust is a psychological state that exists when you agree to make yourself vulnerable to another because you have positive expectations about how things are going to turn out.[98] Although you aren't completely in control of the situation, you are willing to take a chance that the other person will come through for you. Trust is a primary attribute associated with leadership; breaking it can have serious adverse effects on a group's performance.[99]

Followers who trust a leader are confident their rights and interests will not be abused.[100] Transformational leaders create support for their ideas in part by arguing that their direction will be in everyone's best interests. People are unlikely to look up to or follow someone they perceive as dishonest or likely to take advantage of them. Thus, as you might expect, transformational leaders do generate higher levels of trust from their followers, which in turn is related to higher levels of team confidence and, ultimately, higher levels of team performance.[101]

In a simple contractual exchange of goods and services, your employer is legally bound to pay you for fulfilling your job description. But today's rapid reorganizations, diffusion of responsibility, and collaborative team-based work style mean employment relationships are not stable long-term contracts with explicit terms. Rather, they are more fundamentally based on trusting relationships than ever before. You have to trust that if you show your supervisor a creative project you've been working on, he or she won't steal the credit behind your back. You have to trust that the extra work you've been doing will be recognized in your performance appraisal. In contemporary organizations, where work is less closely documented and specified, voluntary employee contribution based on trust is absolutely necessary. Only a trusted leader will be able to encourage employees to reach beyond themselves to a transformational goal.

How Is Trust Developed?

Trust isn't just about the leader; the characteristics of followers also influence its development. What key characteristics lead us to believe a leader is trustworthy? Evidence has identified three: integrity, benevolence, and ability (see Exhibit 12-6).[102]

Integrity refers to honesty and truthfulness. When 570 white-collar employees were given a list of 28 attributes related to leadership, they rated honesty the

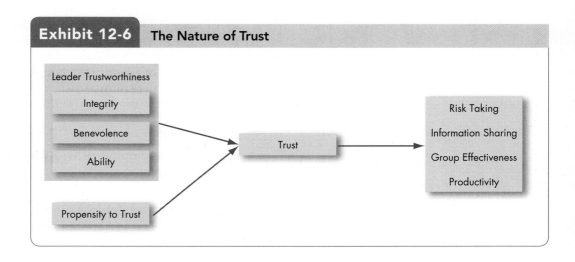

Exhibit 12-6   The Nature of Trust

Leader Trustworthiness
- Integrity
- Benevolence
- Ability

Propensity to Trust

→ Trust →

- Risk Taking
- Information Sharing
- Group Effectiveness
- Productivity

most important by far.[103] Integrity also means having consistency between what you do and say.

Benevolence means the trusted person has your interests at heart, even if yours aren't necessarily in line with theirs. Caring and supportive behavior is part of the emotional bond between leaders and followers.

Ability encompasses an individual's technical and interpersonal knowledge and skills. Even a highly principled person with the best intentions in the world won't be trusted to accomplish a positive outcome for you if you don't have faith in his or her ability to get the job done. Does the person know what he or she is talking about? You're unlikely to listen to or depend on someone whose abilities you don't believe in.

Trust as a Process

Trust propensity refers to how likely a particular employee is to trust a leader. Some people are simply more likely to believe others can be trusted.[104] Those who carefully document every promise or conversation with their supervisors aren't very high in trust propensity, and they probably aren't going to take a leader's word for anything. Those who think most people are basically honest and forthright will be much more likely to seek out evidence that their leaders have behaved in a trustworthy manner. Trust propensity is closely linked to the personality trait of agreeableness, and people with lower self-esteem are less likely to trust others.[105]

Time is the final component for building trust. We come to trust people based on observing their behavior over a period of time.[106] Leaders need to demonstrate they have integrity, benevolence, and ability in situations where trust is important—say, where they could behave opportunistically or let employees down. Trust can be won in the ability domain by demonstrating competence. Recent research with 100 companies around the world suggests that leaders can build trust by shifting their communication style from top-down commands to ongoing organizational dialogue. When leaders regularly create interpersonal conversations with their employees that are intimate, interactive, and inclusive and that intentionally follow an agenda, followers demonstrate trust with high levels of engagement.[107]

Leaders who break the psychological contract with workers, demonstrating they aren't trustworthy, will find employees are less satisfied and less committed, have a higher intent toward turnover, engage in less citizenship behavior, and have lower levels of task performance.[108] Leaders who betray trust are especially likely to be evaluated negatively by followers if there is already a low level of leader–member exchange.[109] Once it is violated, trust can be regained, but only in certain situations and depending on the type of violation.[110] If the cause is lack of ability, it's usually best to apologize and recognize you should have done better. When lack of integrity is the problem, apologies don't do much good. Regardless of the violation, saying nothing or refusing to confirm or deny guilt is never an effective strategy for regaining trust. Trust can be restored when we observe a consistent pattern of trustworthy behavior by the transgressor. However, if the transgressor used deception, trust never fully returns, not even after apologies, promises, or a consistent pattern of trustworthy actions.[111]

What Are the Consequences of Trust?

Trust between supervisors and employees has a number of advantages. Here are just a few that research has shown:

- **Trust encourages taking risks.** Whenever employees decide to deviate from the usual way of doing things, or to take their supervisors' word on a new direction, they are taking a risk. In both cases, a trusting relationship can facilitate that leap.

- **Trust facilitates information sharing.** One big reason employees fail to express concerns at work is that they don't feel psychologically safe revealing their views. When managers demonstrate they will give employees' ideas a fair hearing and actively make changes, employees are more willing to speak out.[112]
- **Trusting groups are more effective.** When a leader sets a trusting tone in a group, members are more willing to help each other and exert extra effort, which increases trust. Members of mistrusting groups tend to be suspicious of each other, constantly guard against exploitation, and restrict communication with others in the group. These actions tend to undermine and eventually destroy the group.
- **Trust enhances productivity.** The bottom-line interest of companies appears to be positively influenced by trust. Employees who trust their supervisors tend to receive higher performance ratings.[113] People respond to mistrust by concealing information and secretly pursuing their own interests.

Leading for the Future: Mentoring

7 Demonstrate the role mentoring plays in our understanding of leadership.

Leaders often take responsibility for developing future leaders. Let's consider what makes mentoring valuable as well as its potential pitfalls.

Mentoring

mentor *A senior employee who sponsors and supports a less-experienced employee, called a protégé.*

A **mentor** is a senior employee who sponsors and supports a less-experienced employee, a protégé. Successful mentors are good teachers. They present ideas clearly, listen well, and empathize with protégés' problems. Mentoring relationships serve career functions and psychosocial functions (see Exhibit 12-7).[114]

Traditional informal mentoring relationships develop when leaders identify a less experienced, lower-level employee who appears to have potential for future development.[115] The protégé is often tested with a particularly challenging assignment. If he or she performs acceptably, the mentor will develop the

---

Exhibit 12-7   **Career and Psychological Functions of the Mentoring Relationship**

Career Functions	Psychosocial Functions
• Lobbying to get the protégé challenging and visible assignments	• Counseling the protégé to bolster his or her self-confidence
• Coaching the protégé to help develop his or her skills and achieve work objectives	• Sharing personal experiences with the protégé
• Providing exposure to influential individuals within the organization	• Providing friendship and acceptance
• Protecting the protégé from possible risks to his or her reputation	• Acting as a role model
• Sponsoring the protégé by nominating him or her for potential advances or promotions	
• Acting as a sounding board for ideas the protégé might be hesitant to share with a direct supervisor	

relationship, informally showing the protégé how the organization *really* works outside its formal structures and procedures.

Why would a leader want to be a mentor?[116] Many feel they have something to share with the younger generation and want to provide a legacy. Mentoring provides unfiltered access to the attitudes of employees, and protégés can be an excellent source of early warning signals that identify potential organizational problems.

Are all employees in an organization likely to participate in a mentoring relationship? Unfortunately, no.[117] However, research continues to indicate that employers should establish mentoring programs because they benefit both mentors and protégés. A recent study in Korea found that mentors achieved higher levels of transformational leadership abilities as a result of the process, while organizational commitment and well-being increased for both mentors and protégés.[118]

Although begun with the best intentions, these formal relationships are not as effective as informal ones.[119] Poor planning and design may often be the reason. Mentor commitment is critical to program effectiveness; mentors must see the relationship as beneficial to themselves and the protégé. The protégé must feel he or she has input into the relationship; someone who feels it's foisted on him or her will just go through the motions.[120] Formal mentoring programs are also most likely to succeed if they appropriately match the work style, needs, and skills of protégé and mentor.[121]

You might assume mentoring is valuable for objective outcomes like compensation and job performance, but research suggests the gains are primarily psychological. Research indicates that while mentoring can have an impact on career success, it is not as much of a contributing factor as ability and personality. It may *feel* nice to have a mentor, but it doesn't appear that having a good mentor, or any mentor, is critical to your career. Mentors may be effective not because of the functions they provide, but because of the resources they can obtain; a mentor connected to a powerful network can build relationships that will help the protégé advance. Network ties, whether built through a mentor or not, are a significant predictor of career success.[122] If a mentor is not well connected or not a very strong performer, the best mentoring advice in the world will not be very beneficial.

Challenges to the Leadership Construct

8 Address challenges to the effectiveness of leadership.

"In the 1500s, people ascribed all events they didn't understand to God. Why did the crops fail? God. Why did someone die? God. Now our all-purpose explanation is leadership."[123] But much of an organization's success or failure is due to factors outside the influence of leadership. Sometimes it's a matter of being in the right or wrong place at a given time. In this section, we present two perspectives and one technological change that challenge accepted beliefs about the value of leadership.

attribution theory of leadership
A leadership theory that says that leadership is merely an attribution that people make about other individuals.

Leadership as an Attribution

As you may remember from Chapter 6, attribution theory examines how people try to make sense of cause-and-effect relationships. The **attribution theory of leadership** says leadership is merely an attribution people make about other individuals.[124] We attribute to leaders intelligence, outgoing personality, strong verbal skills, aggressiveness, understanding, and industriousness.[125] At the organizational level, we tend, rightly or wrongly, to see leaders as responsible for both extremely negative and extremely positive performance.[126]

One study of 128 major U.S. corporations found that whereas perceptions of CEO charisma did not lead to objectively better company performance, company performance did lead to perceptions of charisma.[127] Employee perceptions of leaders' behaviors are significant predictors of whether they blame the leader for failure, regardless of how the leader assesses him- or herself.[128] A study of more than 3,000 employees from western Europe, the United States, and the Middle East found people who tended to "romanticize" leadership in general were more likely to believe their own leaders were transformational.[129]

When Merrill Lynch began to lose billions in 2008 as a result of its investments in mortgage securities, it wasn't long before CEO Stan O'Neal lost his job. O'Neal appeared before the House Oversight and Government Reform Committee of the U.S. Congress for what one committee member termed "a public flogging." Some called him a "criminal" and others suggested Merrill's losses during his tenure represented "attempted destruction."[130]

Whether O'Neal was responsible for the losses at Merrill or deserved his nine-figure severance package is difficult to answer. However, we can argue that he probably changed very little between 2004 when *Fortune* described him as a "turnaround genius" and 2009 when he was fired. What changed was the performance of the organization he led. It's not necessarily wrong to terminate a CEO for flagging financial performance. However, O'Neal's story illustrates the power of the attribution approach to leadership: hero and genius when things are going well, villain when they aren't.

We make demographic assumptions about leaders. Respondents in a study assumed a leader described with no identifying racial information was white at a rate beyond the base rate of white employees in a company. In scenarios where identical leadership situations are described but the leaders' race is manipulated, white leaders are rated as more effective than leaders of other racial groups.[131] One large-scale summary study (a meta-analysis) found that many individuals hold stereotypes of men as having more leader characteristics than women, although as you might expect, this tendency to equate leadership with masculinity has decreased over time.[132] Other data suggest women's perceived success as transformational leaders may be based on demographic characteristics. Teams prefer male leaders when aggressively competing against other teams, but they prefer female leaders when the competition is within teams and calls for improving positive relationships within the group.[133]

Attribution theory suggests what's important is projecting the *appearance* of being a leader rather than focusing on *actual accomplishments*. Leader-wannabes who can shape the perception that they're smart, personable, verbally adept, aggressive, hardworking, and consistent in their style can increase the probability their bosses, colleagues, and employees will view them as effective leaders.

Substitutes for and Neutralizers of Leadership

One theory of leadership suggests that in many situations leaders' actions are irrelevant.[134] Experience and training are among the **substitutes** that can replace the need for a leader's support or ability to create structure. Recently, companies such as videogame producer Valve Corporation, Gore-Tex maker W. L. Gore, and collaboration-software firm GitHub have experimented with eliminating leaders and management. Governance in the "bossless" work environment is achieved through accountability to co-workers, who determine team composition and even sometimes pay.[135] Organizational characteristics such as

substitutes *Attributes, such as experience and training, that can replace the need for a leader's support or ability to create structure.*

Exhibit 12-8 Substitutes for and Neutralizers of Leadership

Defining Characteristics	Relationship-Oriented Leadership	Task-Oriented Leadership
Individual		
Experience/training	No effect on	Substitutes for
Professionalism	Substitutes for	Substitutes for
Indifference to rewards	Neutralizes	Neutralizes
Job		
Highly structured task	No effect on	Substitutes for
Provides its own feedback	No effect on	Substitutes for
Intrinsically satisfying	Substitutes for	No effect on
Organization		
Explicit formalized goals	No effect on	Substitutes for
Rigid rules and procedures	No effect on	Substitutes for
Cohesive work groups	Substitutes for	Substitutes for

Source: Based on S. Kerr and J. M. Jermier, "Substitutes for Leadership: Their Meaning and Measurement," *Organizational Behavior and Human Performance* (December 1978), p. 378.

neutralizers *Attributes that make it impossible for leader behavior to make any difference to follower outcomes.*

explicit formalized goals, rigid rules and procedures, and cohesive work groups can replace formal leadership, while indifference to organizational rewards can neutralize its effects. **Neutralizers** make it impossible for leader behavior to make any difference to follower outcomes (see Exhibit 12-8).

It's simplistic to think employees are guided to goal accomplishments solely by the actions of their leaders. We've introduced a number of variables—such as attitudes, personality, ability, and group norms—that affect employee performance and satisfaction. Leadership is simply another independent variable in our overall OB model.

Sometimes the difference between substitutes and neutralizers is fuzzy. If I'm working on a task that's intrinsically enjoyable, theory predicts leadership will be less important because the task provides motivation. But does that mean intrinsically enjoyable tasks neutralize leadership effects, or substitute for them, or both? Another problem is that while substitutes for leadership (such as employee characteristics, the nature of the task, etc.) matter to performance, that doesn't necessarily mean leadership doesn't.[136]

Online Leadership

How do you lead people who are physically separated from you and with whom you communicate electronically? This question needs attention from OB researchers.[137] Today's managers and employees are increasingly linked by networks rather than geographic proximity.

We propose that online leaders have to think carefully about what actions they want their digital messages to initiate. They confront unique challenges, the greatest of which appears to be developing and maintaining trust. **Identification-based trust**, based on a mutual understanding of each other's intentions and appreciation of the other's wants and desires, is particularly difficult to achieve without face-to-face interaction.[138] Online negotiations can also be hindered because parties express lower levels of trust.[139]

identification-based trust *Trust based on a mutual understanding of each other's intentions and appreciation of each other's wants and desires.*

We believe good leadership skills will soon include the ability to communicate support, trust, and inspiration through electronic communication and to accurately read emotions in others' messages. In electronic communication, writing skills are likely to become an extension of interpersonal skills.

Finding and Creating Effective Leaders

How can organizations find or create effective leaders? Let's try to answer that question.

Selecting Leaders

The process organizations go through to fill management positions is an exercise in the identification of effective leaders. You might begin by reviewing the knowledge, skills, and abilities needed to do the job effectively. Personality tests can identify traits associated with leadership—extraversion, conscientiousness, and openness to experience. High self-monitors are better at reading situations and adjusting their behavior accordingly. Candidates with high emotional intelligence should have an advantage, especially in situations requiring transformational leadership.[140] Experience is a poor predictor of leader effectiveness, but situation-specific experience is relevant.

Because nothing lasts forever, the most important event an organization needs to plan for is a change in leadership. JCPenney recently hired a CEO with no department store experience who promptly changed its overall strategy, a maneuver so disastrous that Penney's stock fell 69 percent in the roughly one year he lasted (at which time Penney rehired the old CEO it had forced out). Organizations seem to spend no time on leadership succession and are surprised when their picks turn out poorly. HP is on its fourth CEO in 7 years, including one who lasted a matter of months, causing observers to wonder whether HP's and JCPenney's boards of directors had done their homework in leadership succession.

Training Leaders

Organizations spend billions of dollars on leadership training and development.[141] These take many forms, including $50,000 executive leadership programs offered by universities such as Harvard to sailing experiences offered by the Outward Bound program. Business schools are placing renewed emphasis on leadership development. Some companies place a lot of emphasis on leadership development. Goldman Sachs is well known for developing leaders; at one point, *BusinessWeek* called it the "Leadership Factory."[142]

How can managers get the most from their leadership-training budgets? First, leadership training is likely to be more successful with high self-monitors. Such individuals have the flexibility to change their behavior. Second, organizations can teach implementation skills. Third, we can teach skills such as trust building and mentoring. Leaders can be taught situational-analysis skills. They can learn how to evaluate situations, modify them to better fit their style, and assess which leader behaviors might be most effective in given situations. BHP Billiton, Best Buy, Nokia, and Adobe have hired coaches to help top executives one on one to improve their interpersonal skills and act less autocratically.[143]

Fourth, behavioral training through modeling exercises can increase an individual's ability to exhibit charismatic leadership qualities. Recent research also indicates that leaders should engage in regularly reviewing their leadership after key organizational events as part of their development. These after-event reviews are especially effective for leaders who are high in conscientiousness and openness to experience, and who are emotionally stable (low in neuroticism).[144]

Finally, leaders can be trained in transformational leadership skills that have bottom-line results, whether in the financial performance of Canadian banks or the effectiveness of soldiers in the Israeli Defense Forces.[145]

Summary

Leadership plays a central part in understanding group behavior because it's the leader who usually directs us toward our goals. Knowing what makes a good leader should thus be valuable in improving group performance. The early search for a set of universal leadership traits failed. However, recent efforts using the Big Five personality framework show strong and consistent relationships between leadership and extraversion, conscientiousness, and openness to experience. The behavioral approach's major contribution was narrowing leadership into task-oriented (initiating structure) and people-oriented (consideration) styles. By considering the situation in which the leader operates, contingency theories promised to improve on the behavioral approach, but only LPC theory has fared well in leadership research. Research on charismatic and transformational leadership has made major contributions to our understanding of leadership effectiveness.

Implications for Managers

- For management positions, hire candidates who exhibit transformational leadership qualities and who have demonstrated vision and charisma.
- Tests and interviews can help you identify people with leadership qualities.
- Hire candidates whom you believe are ethical and trustworthy for management roles and train current managers in your organization's ethical standards in order to increase leadership effectiveness.
- Seek to develop trusting relationships with followers because, as organizations have become less stable and predictable, strong bonds of trust are replacing bureaucratic rules in defining expectations and relationships.
- Consider investing in leadership training such as formal courses, workshops, rotating job responsibilities, coaching, and mentoring.

Heroes Are Made, Not Born

POINT

We often ascribe heroic qualities to our leaders. They are courageous in the face of great risk. They persevere when few would. They take action when most sit by. Heroes are exceptional people who display exceptional behavior.

But some social psychologists question this conventional wisdom. They note that heroism can be found in many spheres of life, including in the behavior of whistleblowers, explorers, religious leaders, scientists, Good Samaritans, and those who beat the odds. At some time in our lives, we all show heroism when the situation allows us to. If we want to see more heroic behavior, we need to create more situations that produce it.

Stanford psychologist Phil Zimbardo goes even further to argue that our romantic view that heroes are born is misplaced:

> The banality of evil is matched by the banality of heroism. Neither is the consequence of dispositional tendencies . . . Both emerge in particular situations at particular times, when situational forces play a compelling role in moving individuals across the line from inaction to action.

People exhibit brave behavior every day. The workers who risked their lives to contain Japan's earthquake-ravaged nuclear reactors in 2011 are a great example. Thus, we err when we think leaders are uniquely positioned to behave heroically. We all can be heroes in the right situation.

COUNTERPOINT

Of course heroes are not like everyone else. That's what makes them heroes.

A generation of evidence from behavioral genetics reveals that "everything is genetic," meaning we have yet to discover an important human behavior that does not have genetic origins. Though we're not aware of any such study with respect to heroism, it would be surprising if courageous behavior were not at least partly genetic.

It's foolish to think courageous people aren't exceptional because of who they are. Just as we know there is an entrepreneurial personality and a leader personality, there is a heroic personality. Research suggests, for example, that people who score high on conscientiousness are more likely to engage in courageous behavior.

Not all leaders are heroes, but many have exhibited courageous behavior. CEO Richard Branson may or may not be a hero, but when he launches his latest attempt to set the world record for an around-the-world balloon flight or sloop sailing, he exhibits the same courageous behavior when he is leading conglomerate Virgin Group. Virgin Group now includes more than 400 companies, including Virgin Galactic, a space tourism company, and Virgin Fuels, whose goal is to revolutionize the industry by providing sustainable fuels for automobiles and aircraft. Same leader, same heroic behavior—in work and in life.

Are we really to believe that Richard Branson and other courageous leaders are just like everyone else?

Sources: Z. E. Franco, K. Blau, and P. G. Zimbardo, "Heroism: A Conceptual Analysis and Differentiation Between Heroic Action and Altruism," Review of General Psychology 15, no. 2 (2011), pp. 99–113; O. Dorell, "At Nuke Plant, Heroes Emerge," USA Today (March 25, 2011), pp. 1A, 2A; G. R. Goethals and S. C. Allison, "Making Heroes: The Construction of Courage, Competence, and Virtue," Advances in Experimental Psychology 46 (2012), pp. 183–235; L. J. Walker, J. A. Frimer, and W. L. Dunlop, "Varieties of Moral Personality: Beyond the Banality of Heroism," Journal of Personality 78, no. 3 (2010), pp. 907–942; and J. Lehrer, "Are Heroes Born, or Can They Be Made?" The Wall Street Journal (December 11, 2010), p. C12.

END-OF-CHAPTER REVIEW

MyManagementLab   Go to mymanagementlab.com to complete the problems marked with this icon. ⭐

QUESTIONS FOR REVIEW

12-1 Are leadership and management different from oneanother? If so, how?

12-2 What is the difference between trait and behavioral theories? Are the theories valid?

12-3 What are the main limitations of behavioral theories of leadership?

12-4 What is Fiedler's contingency model? Has it been supported in research?

12-5 How do charismatic and transformational leadership compare and contrast? Are they valid?

12-6 What is authentic leadership? Why do ethics and trust matter to leadership?

12-7 How is mentoring valuable to leadership? What are the keys to effective mentoring?

12-8 How can organizations select and develop effective leaders?

EXPERIENTIAL EXERCISE What Is Leadership?

- Break the class into six groups: GROUP A: Government Leaders (president, senator, governor, representative, assemblyperson); GROUP B: Business Leaders (CEO, president, leader in business); GROUP C: School Leaders (class president, informal leader); GROUP D: Sports Leaders (team captain, informal team leader, coach); GROUPS E and F: Effective Managers (manager who demonstrates competence/effectiveness in position).

12-9. Each group is to identify its defining characteristics, not simply by brainstorming, but by deciding upon

descriptors that most of the group agrees are defining characteristics.

12-10. Reconvene the class. Draw six columns for each group and list the characteristics for each group. What similarities do you see between the lists? From the results of this exercise, does it appear that what it takes to be a good leader is different from what it takes to be a good manager? Does this mean leadership and management are different?

ETHICAL DILEMMA Undercover Leaders

The television show *Undercover Boss* features a leader working undercover in his or her own company to find out how the organization really works. Here, we consider the ethical leadership lessons it might offer.

Executives from DirecTV, Hooters, 7-Eleven, NASCAR, Chiquita, and Choice Hotels have been featured on the show. Typically, the executive works undercover for a week. Then the employees with whom and under whom the leader has worked are summoned to company headquarters and rewarded, or punished, for their actions.

In one episode, Waste Management's president Larry O'Donnell, sporting gray stubble and work clothes,

works the back of a trash truck. Later, he sorts recyclables from a fast-moving conveyer belt. Under the barking orders of a supervisor, he even cleans a long line of portable toilets.

Some criticize the show for its faux realism. The CEOs know they are on camera, so every word and facial expression is for the cameras. Many employees know they are on camera, too. One critic commented, "Because the series' very existence requires cooperation from the executives that it purports to make suffer for their sins, it has to raise them higher, in the end, than it found them at the start."

Realistic or not, the series continues to be popular. And the effects on the bosses featured in the episodes—and their employees—are profound. After CEO Mitchell Modell of the sporting goods chain Modell's spent days struggling to keep up with his lowest-paid employees in the warehouse and the office, he reported, "I tell everybody if you're fortunate enough to be on 'Undercover Boss' to do it in a heartbeat," he said. "If you're not fortunate enough, then go work on the front lines. It's an eye-opening experience." As a result of the insight he gained, Modell overhauled the company's approach to customer service and learned new ways to increase profitability and organization performance. He said, "As CEO, one of the things you always wonder about is what your associates (employees) are really thinking and what their days are like. It was a great education."

The idea has moved beyond television too. Recently, the Australian government created a program that places CEOs undercover in their own workplaces. One participating CEO, Phil Smith of clothing retailer Fletcher Jones, said tearfully, "I learnt a lot from this that I wouldn't have found out any other way."

Questions

✪ 12-11. Do you think it is ethical for a leader to go undercover in his or her organization? Why or why not?

12-12. Do you think leaders who work undercover are really changed as a result of their experiences?

12-13. Would you support a government program that gave companies incentives to send leaders undercover?

Sources: K. Jones, "CEOs Go Undercover Over Workplace Safety," *SafetyAtWorkBlog* (February 5, 2011), downloaded June 10, 2011, from http://safetyatworkblog.wordpress.com/; D. Kaplan, "'Undercover Boss' a Life-Changing Experience for Sporting Goods Mogul Mitchell Modell" (March 1, 2013), www.nydailynews.com/entertainment/tv-movies/undercover-boss-life-changer-modell-ceo-article-1.1276376; K. Kern, "The Fakery of CEOs Undercover," *Bloomberg Businessweek* (February 15, 2010), pp. 78–79.

CASE INCIDENT 1 Leadership Mettle Forged in Battle

In 2008, facing a serious shortage of leadership-ready employees at the store management level, Walmart decided to recruit from the U.S. military. The company sent recruiters to military job fairs and hired 150 junior military officers, pairing them with store mentors to learn on the job. The result: Walmart claims that it's been able to bring in world-class leaders who were ready to take over once they had learned the retail business that Walmart could easily teach them. Other organizations that have heavily recruited from the military in recent years include GE, Home Depot, Lowe's, State Farm Insurance, Merck, and Bank of America.

It's not really surprising to see companies turn to the military for leadership potential. A long tradition of books and seminars advises leaders to think like military leaders ranging from Sun Tzu to Norman Schwarzkopf. And military veterans do have a variety of valuable skills learned through experience. General David Petraeus notes, "Tell me anywhere in the business world where a 22- or 23-year-old is responsible for 35 or 40 other individuals on missions that involve life and death . . . They're under enormous scrutiny, on top of everything else. These are pretty formative experiences. It's a bit of a crucible-like experience that they go through." Military leaders are also used to having to make due in less than optimal conditions, negotiate across cultures, be highly accountable, and operate under extreme stress.

However, they do have to relearn some lessons from the service. Some may not be used to leading someone like an eccentric computer programmer who works strange hours, dresses like a slob, but brings more to the company's bottom line than a conventional employee. Indeed, in some companies like Google, there is nothing like the chain of command military leaders are used to. Still, most forecasts suggest there will be an ample supply of battle-tested military leaders ready to report for corporate duty in the near future, and many companies are eager to have them.

Questions

12-14. Do you think leaders in military contexts exhibit the same qualities as organizational leaders? Why or why not?

✪ 12-15. In what ways not mentioned in the case would military leadership lessons *not* apply in the private sector? What might military leaders have to relearn to work in business?

12-16. Are specific types of work or situations more likely to benefit from the presence of "battle-tested" leaders? List a few examples.

Sources: B. O'Keefe, J. Birger, and D. Burke, "Battle Tested," *Fortune* (March 22, 2010), p. 108–118; B. Whitmore, "Hiring Military Veterans Is Good Business," *Huntington WV Herald-Dispatch* (November 6, 2010), www.herald-dispatch.com; B. Wansink, C. R. Payne, and K. van Ittersum, "Profiling the Heroic Leader: Empirical Lessons from Combat-Decorated Veterans of World War II," *Leadership Quarterly* 19, no. 5 (2008), pp. 547–555; and T. E. Ricks, "What Ever Happened to Accountability?" *Harvard Business Review* (October 2012), pp. 93–100.

CASE INCIDENT 2 Leadership by Algorithm

Is there one right way to lead? Research suggests not, the methods explored in this chapter suggest not, and commonsense suggests a "one size fits all" approach could be disastrous because organizations exist for diverse purposes and develop unique cultures. Leadership development programs generally teach a best-practices model, but experts suggest that individuals trained in leadership techniques that are contrary to their own natures risk losing the authenticity crucial to effective leadership. The real path to leadership may lie in algorithms.

If you've ever taken a strengths-based assessment such as the Harrison Assessment or Gallup's Clifton StrengthsFinder, you know that surveys aimed at discovering your personality, skills, and preferences result in a personal profile. This tool is helpful in leadership development, but algorithms can take your leadership development to the next level of personalization and application. They can take the results from each survey you complete, for instance, and use them to create a leadership program that matches your needs and abilities.

As the founder of TMBC and author of *StandOut*, Marcus Buckingham is an expert on the creating leadership programs. He recommends the following steps:

Step 1. Find or develop the assessment tools. These might include a personality component, such as a Big Five inventory test, and will include other tests companies can resource or create according to what leadership characteristics they are seeking to monitor.

Step 2. Identify the top leaders in the organization and administer the test to them. Similarities in their profiles may not emerge across the broad spectrum of all top leaders. This step is not to determine what all the leaders have in common, but to group the top leaders into categories by their similar profiles.

Step 3. Interview the leaders within each profile category to learn about the techniques they use that work. Often these will be unique, unscripted, and revealingly correlated to the strengths in their assessment profile. Compile the techniques within each profile category.

Step 4. The results of top leader profile categories and their techniques can be used to create an algorithm, or tailored method, for developing leaders. Administer the assessment tests to developing leaders and determine their profile categories. The techniques from successful leaders can now be shared with the developing leaders who are most like them because they share the same profile category.

These steps provide a means for successful leaders to pass along to developing leaders techniques that are likely to feel authentic to the developing leaders and that encourage creativity. The techniques can be delivered in an ongoing process as short, personalized, interactive, and readily applicable tips and advice, for results no two-week leadership development course could achieve.

Questions

12-17. If you have participated in leadership development programs, how effective did you find them in (a) teaching you techniques and (b) giving you practical strategies you could use? What could they do better?

12-18. What are some potential negatives of using Buckingham's approach to leadership development?

12-19. Would you suggest applying Buckingham's steps to your organization? Why or why not?

Sources: M. Buckingham, "Leadership Development in the Age of the Algorithm," *Harvard Business Review* (June 2012), pp. 86–94; M. D. Watkins, "How Managers Become Leaders," *Harvard Business Review* (June 2012), pp. 64–72; and J. M. Podolny, "A Conversation with James G. March on Learning About Leadership," *Academy of Management Learning & Education* 10 (2011), pp. 502–506.

MyManagementLab

Go to **mymanagementlab.com** for Auto-graded writing questions as well as the following Assisted-graded writing questions:

12-20. Considering the chapter and Case Incident 2, why would a personalized leadership development program be preferable to a best-practices teaching program?

12-21. What are your suggestions for creating ethical leadership in organizations?

12-22. MyManagementLab Only—comprehensive writing assignment for this chapter.

13

Power and Politics

FROM POWER TO PRISON

Rajat Gupta is one of the "1-percenters" in every way. He led one of the world's most trusted and prestigious consulting firms, McKinsey & Company. As a philanthropist, he raised tens of millions of dollars for health care, education, and AIDS. He served on the boards of directors of some of the world's most respected companies, including Goldman Sachs, Procter & Gamble, and American Airlines. He attended numerous meetings and state dinners in the White House and was on a first-name basis with three presidents (Clinton, Bush, and Obama).

Now Gupta is a convicted felon awaiting, on appeal, his sentence to federal prison. His positions, memberships, and networks have dissolved.

From Bernie Madoff to Ken Lay, there have been many stunning falls from grace in recent times. If power is measured from multiple angles—wealth, reputation, status, influence, networks—it is hard to imagine a steeper fall than Gupta's.

Gupta not only had power, he appeared to be humbled by it. People described him as "modest" and "egoless." His colleagues at McKinsey admired him for the value he placed on family. He described himself as a "servant leader." *Bloomberg Businessweek* noted that he was "that rare businessman whose integrity was beyond reproach."

Life began to unravel for Gupta in 2011. When the FBI and SEC were investigating Galleon Group founder and CEO Raj Rajaratnam (convicted in 2011 on 14 charges of fraud and insider trading), they uncovered a "flurry" of phone conversations between Rajaratnam and Gupta. In wiretapped calls, Gupta alerted Rajaratnam to an upcoming $5 billion investment in Goldman by Berkshire Hathaway. On another occasion, 23 seconds after hanging up on a Goldman conference call, Gupta called Rajaratnam with news that Goldman would report a quarterly loss. All the while, Gupta was investing in and profiting from Galleon's profits on these and other trades. Rajaratnam also "loaned" Gupta millions so he could increase his investments in Galleon.

Did power corrupt Gupta's values? Or was he always the opposite of who he pretended to be? It appears more of the former than the latter. When Gupta became managing partner at McKinsey, he turned down more lucrative offers because once in the position, according to his wife, "he enjoyed the stature that came with his job." Over time, as he increasingly rubbed elbows with the world's wealthiest most powerful people, he wanted more. Giving a talk at Columbia before being charged, Gupta admitted that wealth and power only made him want more. "However much you say that you will not fall into the trap of it, you do fall into the trap of it," he said.

_____

Sources: A. Raghavan, "Rajat Gupta's Lust for Zeros," *The New York Times* (May 17, 2013), downloaded May 23, 2013, from www.nytimes.com/; S. Deb, *Fallen Angel: The Making and Unmaking of Rajat Gupta*, (Calcutta, India: Rupa & Co, 2013); and K. Scannell, "Lawyers for Rajat Gupta Argue for New Trial," *Financial Times* (May 21, 2013), downloaded May 24, 2013, from www.ft.com/.

n both research and practice, *power* and *politics* have been described as the last dirty words. It is easier for most of us to talk about sex or money than about power or political behavior. As the Rajat Gupta case shows, power is seductive. People who have power deny it, people who want it try not to look like they're seeking it, and those who are good at getting it are secretive about how they do so.[1] To see whether you think your work environment is political, take the accompanying self-assessment.

A major theme of this chapter is that power and political behavior are natural processes in any group or organization. Given that, you need to know how power is acquired and exercised if you are to fully understand organizational behavior. Although you may have heard that "Power corrupts, and absolute power corrupts absolutely," power is not always bad. As one author noted, most medicines can kill if taken in the wrong amount, and thousands die each year in automobile accidents, but we don't abandon chemicals or cars because of the dangers associated with them. Rather, we consider danger an incentive to get training and information that will help us to use these forces productively.[2] The same applies to power. It's a reality of organizational life, and it's not going to go away. By learning how power works in organizations, you'll be better able to use your knowledge to become a more effective manager.

SELF-ASSESSMENT LIBRARY

Is My Workplace Political?

In the Self-Assessment Library (available in MyManagementLab), take assessment IV.F.1 (Is My Workplace Political?). If you don't currently have a job, answer for your most recent job. Then answer the following questions.

1. How does your score relate to those of your classmates? Do you think your score is accurate? Why or why not?
2. Do you think a political workplace is a bad thing? If yes, why? If no, why not?
3. What factors cause your workplace to be political?

A Definition of Power

1 Define *power* and contrast leadership and power.

power *A capacity that A has to influence the behavior of B so that B acts in accordance with A's wishes.*

dependence *B's relationship to A when A possesses something that B requires.*

Power refers to a capacity that *A* has to influence the behavior of *B* so *B* acts in accordance with *A*'s wishes.[3]

Someone can thus have power but not use it; it is a capacity or potential. Probably the most important aspect of power is that it is a function of **dependence**. The greater *B*'s dependence on *A*, the greater *A*'s power in the relationship. Dependence, in turn, is based on alternatives that *B* perceives and the importance *B* places on the alternative(s) *A* controls. A person can have power over you only if he or she controls something you desire. If you want a college degree and have to pass a certain course to get it, and your current instructor is the only faculty member in the college who teaches that course, he or she has power over you. Your alternatives are highly limited, and you place a high degree of importance on obtaining a passing grade. Similarly, if you're attending college on funds totally provided by your parents, you probably recognize the power they hold over you. You're dependent on them for financial support. But once you're out of school, have a job, and are making a good income, your parents' power is reduced significantly. Who among us, though, has not known or heard of a rich relative who is able to control a large number of family members merely through the implicit or explicit threat of "writing them out of the will"?

In a disturbing example of the power of dependence, Wall Street portfolio manager Ping Jiang allegedly was able to coerce analyst Andrew Tong into taking female hormones and wearing lipstick and makeup. Why such power? Jiang controlled Tong's access to day trading. That's how much power dependency can bring.[4]

Contrasting Leadership and Power

A careful comparison of our description of power with our description of leadership in Chapter 12 reveals the concepts are closely intertwined. Leaders use power as a means of attaining group goals.

How are the two terms different? Power does not require goal compatibility, merely dependence. Leadership, on the other hand, requires some congruence between the goals of the leader and those being led. A second difference relates to the direction of influence. Leadership focuses on the downward influence on followers. It minimizes the importance of lateral and upward influence patterns. Power does not. In still another difference, leadership research, for the most part, emphasizes style. It seeks answers to questions such as these: How supportive should a leader be? How much decision making should be shared with followers? In contrast, the research on power focuses on tactics for gaining compliance. It goes beyond the individual as the exerciser of power because groups as well as individuals can use power to control other individuals or groups.

Bases of Power

2   Contrast the five bases of power.

Where does power come from? What gives an individual or a group influence over others? We answer by dividing the bases or sources of power into two general groupings—formal and personal—and then breaking each of these down into more specific categories.[5]

Formal Power

Formal power is based on an individual's position in an organization. It can come from the ability to coerce or reward, or from formal authority.

coercive power   *A power base that is dependent on fear of the negative results from failing to comply.*

Coercive Power   The **coercive power** base depends on fear of the negative results from failing to comply. It rests on the application, or the threat of application, of physical sanctions such as the infliction of pain, frustration through restriction of movement, or the controlling by force of basic physiological or safety needs.

At the organizational level, *A* has coercive power over *B* if *A* can dismiss, suspend, or demote *B*, assuming *B* values his or her job. If *A* can assign *B* work activities *B* finds unpleasant, or treat *B* in a manner *B* finds embarrassing, *A* possesses coercive power over *B*. Coercive power can also come from withholding key information. People in an organization who have data or knowledge others need can make others dependent on them.

reward power *Compliance achieved based on the ability to distribute rewards that others view as valuable.*

Reward Power The opposite of coercive power is **reward power**, with which people comply because it produces positive benefits; someone who can distribute rewards others view as valuable will have power over them. These rewards can be either financial—such as controlling pay rates, raises, and bonuses—or nonfinancial, including recognition, promotions, interesting work assignments, friendly colleagues, and preferred work shifts or sales territories.[6]

legitimate power *The power a person receives as a result of his or her position in the formal hierarchy of an organization.*

Legitimate Power In formal groups and organizations, probably the most common access to one or more of the power bases is through **legitimate power**. It represents the formal authority to control and use organizational resources based on structural position in the organization.

Legitimate power is broader than the power to coerce and reward. Specifically, it includes members' acceptance of the authority of a position. We associate power so closely with the concept of hierarchy that just drawing longer lines in an organization chart leads people to infer the leaders are especially powerful, and when a powerful executive is described, people tend to put the person at a higher position when drawing an organization chart.[7] When school principals, bank presidents, or army captains speak (assuming their directives are viewed as within the authority of their positions), teachers, tellers, and first lieutenants listen and usually comply.

Personal Power

Many of the most competent and productive chip designers at Intel have power, but they aren't managers and have no formal power. What they have is *personal power*, which comes from an individual's unique characteristics. There are two bases of personal power: expertise and the respect and admiration of others.

expert power *Influence based on special skills or knowledge.*

Expert Power **Expert power** is influence wielded as a result of expertise, special skill, or knowledge. As jobs become more specialized, we become increasingly dependent on experts to achieve goals. It is generally acknowledged that physicians have expertise and hence expert power: Most of us follow our doctor's advice. Computer specialists, tax accountants, economists, industrial psychologists, and other specialists wield power as a result of their expertise.

referent power *Influence based on identification with a person who has desirable resources or personal traits.*

Referent Power **Referent power** is based on identification with a person who has desirable resources or personal traits. If I like, respect, and admire you, you can exercise power over me because I want to please you.

Referent power develops out of admiration of another and a desire to be like that person. It helps explain, for instance, why celebrities are paid millions of dollars to endorse products in commercials. Marketing research shows people such as LeBron James and Tom Brady have the power to influence your choice of athletic shoes and credit cards. With a little practice, you and I could probably deliver as smooth a sales pitch as these celebrities, but the buying public doesn't identify with you and me. Some people who are not in formal leadership positions nonetheless have referent power and exert influence over others because of their charismatic dynamism, likability, and emotional effects on us.

Photo 13-1 Internet entrepreneur Mark Zuckerberg, co-founder and CEO of Facebook, has expert power. Shown here talking with employees, Zuckerberg earned the title "software guy" during college because of his expertise in computer programming. Facebook depends on Zuckerberg's programming expertise to achieve company goals.

Source: AP Photo/Tony Avelar.

Which Bases of Power Are Most Effective?

Of the three bases of formal power (coercive, reward, legitimate) and two bases of personal power (expert, referent), which is most important to have? Research suggests pretty clearly that the personal sources of power are most effective. Both expert and referent power are positively related to employees' satisfaction with supervision, their organizational commitment, and their performance, whereas reward and legitimate power seem to be unrelated to these outcomes. One source of formal power—coercive power—actually can backfire in that it is negatively related to employee satisfaction and commitment.[8]

Consider Steve Stoute's company, Translation, which matches pop-star spokespersons with corporations that want to promote their brands. Stoute has paired Gwen Stefani with HP, Justin Timberlake with McDonald's, Beyoncé Knowles with Tommy Hilfiger, and Jay-Z with Reebok. Stoute's business seems to be all about referent power. His firm's work aims to use the credibility of these artists and performers to reach youth culture.[9] In other words, people buy products associated with cool figures because they wish to identify with and emulate them.

Dependence: The Key to Power

3 Explain the role of dependence in power relationships.

The most important aspect of power is that it is a function of dependence. In this section, we show how understanding dependence helps us understand power itself.

The General Dependence Postulate

Let's begin with a general postulate: *The greater* B*'s dependence on* A, *the more power* A *has over* B. When you possess anything others require that you alone control, you make them dependent on you, and therefore you gain power over them.[10]

If something is plentiful, possessing it will not increase your power. But as the old saying goes, "In the land of the blind, the one-eyed man is king!" Conversely, the more you can expand your own options, the less power you place in the hands of others. This explains why most organizations develop multiple suppliers rather than give their business to only one. It also explains why so many aspire to financial independence. Independence reduces the power others can wield to limit our access to opportunities and resources.

What Creates Dependence?

Dependence increases when the resource you control is important, scarce, and nonsubstitutable.[11]

Importance   If nobody wants what you have, it's not going to create dependence. Because organizations, actively seek to avoid uncertainty,[12] we should expect that individuals or groups that can absorb uncertainty will be perceived as controlling an important resource. For instance, a study of industrial organizations found their marketing departments were consistently rated the most powerful.[13] The researcher concluded that the most critical uncertainty facing these firms was selling their products, suggesting that engineers, as a group, would be more powerful at technology company Matsushita than at consumer products giant Procter & Gamble. These inferences appear to be generally valid. Matsushita, which is heavily technologically oriented, depends on its engineers to maintain its products' technical advantages and quality, and so they are a powerful group. At Procter & Gamble, marketing is the name of the game, and marketers are the most powerful occupational group.

Scarcity   Ferruccio Lamborghini, who created the exotic supercars that still carry his name, understood the importance of scarcity and used it to his advantage during World War II. Lamborghini was in Rhodes with the Italian army. His

Photo 13-2 Mary Pochobradsky (center) is in a position of power at Procter & Gamble. She is the North American marketing director for P&G's fabric enhancing products like Downy, a brand that generates $1 billion in annual sales. P&G marketers are powerful occupational groups because they control the important resource of selling products.

superiors were impressed with his mechanical skills because he demonstrated an almost uncanny ability to repair tanks and cars no one else could fix. After the war, he admitted his ability was largely due to his having been the first person on the island to receive the repair manuals, which he memorized and then destroyed so as to become indispensable.[14]

We see the scarcity–dependence relationship in the power of occupational categories. Where the supply of labor is low relative to demand, workers can negotiate compensation and benefits packages far more attractive than can those in occupations with an abundance of candidates. College administrators have no problem today finding English instructors. The market for network systems analysts, in contrast, is comparatively tight, with demand high and supply limited. The bargaining power of computer-engineering faculty allows them to negotiate higher salaries, lighter teaching loads, and other benefits.

Nonsubstitutability   The fewer viable substitutes for a resource, the more power control that resource provides. At universities with strong pressures on the faculty to publish, the more recognition the faculty member receives through publication, the more mobile he or she is, because other universities want faculty who are highly published and visible. Although tenure can alter this relationship by restricting the department head's alternatives, faculty members with few or no publications have the least mobility and are subject to the greatest influence from their superiors.

Power Tactics

4 Identify nine power or influence tactics and their contingencies.

power tactics   *Ways in which individuals translate power bases into specific actions.*

What **power tactics** do people use to translate power bases into specific action? What options do they have for influencing their bosses, co-workers, or employees? In this section, we review popular tactical options and the conditions that may make one more effective than another.

Research has identified nine distinct influence tactics:[15]

- **Legitimacy.** Relying on your authority position or saying a request accords with organizational policies or rules.
- **Rational persuasion.** Presenting logical arguments and factual evidence to demonstrate a request is reasonable.
- **Inspirational appeals.** Developing emotional commitment by appealing to a target's values, needs, hopes, and aspirations.
- **Consultation.** Increasing the target's support by involving him or her in deciding how you will accomplish your plan.
- **Exchange.** Rewarding the target with benefits or favors in exchange for following a request.
- **Personal appeals.** Asking for compliance based on friendship or loyalty.
- **Ingratiation.** Using flattery, praise, or friendly behavior prior to making a request.
- **Pressure.** Using warnings, repeated demands, and threats.
- **Coalitions.** Enlisting the aid or support of others to persuade the target to agree.

Some tactics are more effective than others. Rational persuasion, inspirational appeals, and consultation tend to be the most effective, especially when the audience is highly interested in the outcomes of a decision process. Pressure tends to backfire and is typically the least effective of the nine tactics.[16] You can also increase your chance of success by using two or more tactics together or sequentially, as long as your choices are compatible.[17] Using both ingratiation and legitimacy can lessen negative reactions to your appearing to dictate outcomes, but only when the audience does not really care about the outcome of a decision process or the policy is routine.[18]

Let's consider the most effective way of getting a raise. You can start with rational persuasion: Figure out how your pay compares to that of peers, or land a competing job offer, or show objective results that testify to your performance. Kitty Dunning, a vice president at Don Jagoda Associates, landed a 16 percent raise when she e-mailed her boss numbers showing she had increased sales.[19] You can also make good use of salary calculators such as Salary.com to compare your pay with comparable others.

But the effectiveness of some influence tactics depends on the direction of influence.[20] As Exhibit 13-1 shows, rational persuasion is the only tactic effective across organizational levels. Inspirational appeals work best as a downward-influencing tactic with subordinates. When pressure works, it's generally downward only. Personal appeals and coalitions are most effective as lateral influence. Other factors that affect the effectiveness of influence include the sequencing of tactics, a person's skill in using the tactic, and the organizational culture.

You're more likely to be effective if you begin with "softer" tactics that rely on personal power, such as personal and inspirational appeals, rational persuasion, and consultation. If these fail, you can move to "harder" tactics, such as exchange, coalitions, and pressure, which emphasize formal power and incur greater costs and risks.[21] Interestingly, a single soft tactic is more effective than a single hard tactic, and combining two soft tactics or a soft tactic and rational persuasion is more effective than any single tactic or combination of hard tactics.[22] The effectiveness of tactics depends on the audience.[23] People especially likely to comply with soft power tactics tend to be more reflective and intrinsically motivated; they have high self-esteem and greater desire for control. Those likely to comply with hard power tactics are more action-oriented and extrinsically motivated and are more focused on getting along with others than on getting their own way.

People in different countries prefer different power tactics.[24] Those from individualistic countries tend to see power in personalized terms and as a legitimate means of advancing their personal ends, whereas those in collectivistic countries see power in social terms and as a legitimate means of helping others.[25] A study comparing managers in the United States and China found that U.S. managers prefer rational appeal, whereas Chinese managers preferred coalition tactics.[26] These differences tend to be consistent with the values in

Exhibit 13-1	Preferred Power Tactics by Influence Direction	
Upward Influence	**Downward Influence**	**Lateral Influence**
Rational persuasion	Rational persuasion	Rational persuasion
	Inspirational appeals	Consultation
	Pressure	Ingratiation
	Consultation	Exchange
	Ingratiation	Legitimacy
	Exchange	Personal appeals
	Legitimacy	Coalitions

these two countries. Reason is consistent with the U.S. preference for direct confrontation and rational persuasion to influence others and resolve differences, while coalition tactics align with the Chinese preference for meeting difficult or controversial requests with indirect approaches. Research also has shown that individuals in Western, individualistic cultures tend to engage in more self-enhancement behaviors (such as self-promotion) than individuals in more collectivistic Eastern cultures.[27]

political skill *The ability to influence others in such a way as to enhance one's objectives.*

People differ in their **political skill**, or their ability to influence others to enhance their own objectives. The politically skilled are more effective users of all the influence tactics. Political skill also appears more effective when the stakes are high—such as when the individual is accountable for important organizational outcomes. Finally, the politically skilled are able to exert their influence without others detecting it, a key element in being effective (it's damaging to be labeled political).[28] However, these individuals also appear most able to use their political skills in environments marked by low levels of procedural and distributive justice. When an organization is run with open and fairly applied rules, free of favoritism or biases, political skill is actually negatively related to job performance ratings.[29]

Finally, we know cultures within organizations differ markedly—some are warm, relaxed, and supportive; others are formal and conservative. Some encourage participation and consultation, some encourage reason, and still others rely on pressure. People who fit the culture of the organization tend to obtain more influence.[30] Specifically, extraverts tend to be more influential in team-oriented organizations, and highly conscientious people are more influential in organizations that value working alone on technical tasks. People who fit the culture are influential because they can perform especially well in the domains deemed most important for success. In other words, they are influential because they are competent. Thus, the organization itself will influence which subset of power tactics is viewed as acceptable for use.

How Power Affects People

To this point, we've discussed what power is and how it is acquired. But we've not yet answered one important question: Does power corrupt?

There is certainly evidence that there are corrupting aspects of power. Evidence suggests that power leads people to place their own interests ahead of others. Why does this happen? Interestingly, research suggests that power not only leads people to focus on their self-interests because they can, it also liberates people to focus inward, and thus come to place greater weight on their goals and interests. Power also appears to lead individuals to "objectify" others (to see them as tools to obtain their instrumental goals), to value relations with people with less power, and to see relationships as more peripheral.[31]

That's not all. Powerful people react—especially negatively—to any threats to their competence. They're more willing to denigrate others. People given power are more likely to make self-interested decisions when faced with a moral hazard (such as when hedge fund managers take more risks with other people's money because they're rewarded for gains but less often punished for losses). Power also leads to overconfident decision making.[32]

Frank Lloyd Wright, perhaps America's greatest architect, is a good example of power's corrupting effects. Early in his career, Wright worked for and was mentored by a renowned architect, Louis Sullivan (sometimes known as "the father of the skyscraper"). Before he achieved greatness, Wright was copious in his praise for Sullivan. Later in his career, that praise faded, and Wright even took credit for one of Sullivan's noted designs. Wright was never a benevolent man, but as his power accumulated, so did his potential to behave in a "monstrous" way toward others.[33]

So, yes, power does appear to have some important disturbing effects on us. But that is hardly the whole story—it's more complicated than that. Power doesn't affect everyone in the same way, and there are even positive effects of power. Let's consider each of these in turn.

First, the toxic effects of power depend on one's personality. Research suggests that if we have an anxious personality, power does not corrupt us because we are less likely to think that using power benefits us.[34] Second, the corrosive effect of power can be contained by organizational systems. One study found, for example, that while power made people behave in a self-serving manner, when accountability of this behavior was initiated, the self-serving behavior stopped. Third, forgive the pun, but we have the power to blunt the negative effects of power. One study showed that simply expressing gratitude toward powerful others made them less likely to aggress against us. Finally, remember the aphorism that those with little power grab and abuse what little they have? There appears to be some truth to this in that the people most likely to abuse power are those who are low in status and gain power. Why is this the case? It appears that having low status is threatening, and this fear is used in negative ways if power is given.[35]

As you can see, there are factors that can ameliorate the negative effects of power. But there also appear to be general positive effects. Power energizes and leads to approach motivation (that is, more motivated to achieve goals). It also can enhance people's motivation to help others, at least for certain people. One study found, for example, that values toward helping others only translated into actual work behavior when people felt a sense of power.[36]

This study points to an important insight about power. It is not so much that power corrupts as it *reveals*. Supporting this line of reasoning, another study revealed that power led to self-interested behavior only for those with weak moral identities (that is, the degree to which morals are core to one's identity). For those with strong moral identities, power actually enhanced their moral awareness.[37]

Sexual Harassment: Unequal Power in the Workplace

5   Show the connection between sexual harassment and the abuse of power.

Sexual harassment is wrong. It can also be costly to employers. Just ask executives at Walmart, the World Bank, and the United Nations.[38] Mitsubishi paid $34 million to settle a sexual harassment case. And a former UPS manager won an $80 million suit against UPS on her claims it fostered a hostile work environment when it failed to listen to her complaints of sexual harassment. Of course, it's not only big organizations that run into trouble: A jury awarded Janet Bianco, a nurse at New York's Flushing Hospital, $15 million for harassment she suffered from Dr. Matthew Miller. After the verdict, Bianco said, "I think that people take it lightly when you say sexual harassment. They don't understand how it affects your life, not only in your job, but in your home, with your friends."[39]

In addition to the legal dangers to sexual harassment, obviously it can have a negative impact on the work environment, too. Sexual harassment negatively affects job attitudes and leads those who feel harassed to withdraw from the

Photo 13-3 A federal jury awarded this woman a $95 million judgment in a sexual harassment lawsuit against her employer for harassment from her supervisor that included unwanted physical contact. The jury found the supervisor guilty of assault and battery and the company liable for negligent supervision and sexual harassment.

Source: BILL GREENBLATT/UPI/Newscom.

sexual harassment   *Any unwanted activity of a sexual nature that affects an individual's employment and creates a hostile work environment.*

organization. In fact, perceptions of sexual harassment are more likely to lead to withdrawal than workplace bullying leads to withdrawal.[40] It even appears that sexual harassment has health consequences. Women exposed to sexual harassment reported psychological distress 2 years after the harassment occurred.[41]

Sexual harassment is defined as any unwanted activity of a sexual nature that affects an individual's employment and creates a hostile work environment. The U.S. Supreme Court helped to clarify this definition by adding a key test for determining whether sexual harassment has occurred—when comments or behavior in a work environment "would reasonably be perceived, and [are] perceived, as hostile or abusive."[42] But disagreement continues about what *specifically* constitutes sexual harassment. Organizations have generally made progress toward limiting overt forms of sexual harassment. This includes unwanted physical touching, recurring requests for dates when it is made clear the person isn't interested, and coercive threats that a person will lose his or her job for refusing a sexual proposition. Problems are likely to surface around more subtle forms of sexual harassment—unwanted looks or comments, off-color jokes, sexual artifacts like pinups posted in the workplace, or misinterpretations of where the line between being friendly ends and harassment begins.

Surveys indicate that between 25 and 40 percent of individuals report being sexually harassed.[43] Data from the Equal Employment Opportunity Commission (EEOC) suggests that sexual harassment is decreasing: Sexual harassment claims now make up 10 percent of all discrimination claims, compared with 20 percent in the mid-1990s. However, claims from men have increased from 11 percent of claims in 1997 to 17 percent today.[44] Even if claims have dropped to some degree, sexual harassment remains prevalent, particularly for women in certain types of positions. The Department of Veterans Affairs found that almost half of women in the military reported being victims of sexual harassment, with one in four reporting being sexually assaulted.[45]

One problem with reporting is that sexual harassment is, to some degree, in the eye of the beholder. Witnesses offering sexual harassment testimony also find that victims who took either an aggressive or a passive tone in making their complaints were seen as less plausible than victims who took a more neutral tone. This research suggests that people may not be able to be entirely objective when listening to sexual harassment complaints, taking the tone of the victim into account when making judgments rather than simply relying on the facts of the case at hand.[46] The best approach is to be careful—refrain from any behavior that may be taken as harassing, even if that was not the intent. Realize that what you see as an innocent joke or hug may be seen as harassment by the other party.

Most studies confirm that the concept of power is central to understanding sexual harassment.[47] This seems true whether the harassment comes from a supervisor, a co-worker, or an employee. And sexual harassment is more likely to occur when there are large power differentials. The supervisor–employee dyad best characterizes an unequal power relationship, where formal power gives the supervisor the capacity to reward and coerce. Because employees want favorable performance reviews, salary increases, and the like, supervisors control resources most employees consider important and scarce. Thus, sexual harassment by the boss typically creates the greatest difficulty for those being harassed. If there are no witnesses, it is the victim's word against the harasser's. Has this boss harassed others, and, if so, will they come forward or fear retaliation? Male respondents in one study in Switzerland who were high in hostile sexism reported higher intentions to sexually harass in organizations that had low levels of justice, suggesting that failure to have consistent policies and procedures for all employees might actually increase levels of sexual harassment.[48]

Women in positions of power in an organization can be subjected to sexual harassment from males who occupy less powerful positions, although this situation doesn't get nearly as much attention as harassment by a supervisor. The employee devalues the woman in power by highlighting traditional gender

glOBalization!

Power, Gender, and Sexual Harassment in France

For centuries, France has been known as a place of cultural refinement and progressive thought. France's égalité, however, does not appear to be universal. Among advanced democracies, France scores relatively low on the gender equality index (57th)—a measure of whether roles for men and women in society are free and on an equal footing. In wage equality, France ranks even worse—129th.

Recently, when French Housing Minister Cécile Duflot, wearing a floral dress, spoke to the National Assembly about an architecture project, male legislators hooted and made catcalls as she tried to speak. "We were just admiring her," said legislator Patrick Balkany. Then there is the case of Dominique Strauss-Kahn, former head of the International Monetary Fund. Strauss-Kahn, a socialist and at one time a "lock" to be the current Prime Minister, had been accused of repeated sexual harassment and several sexual assaults, to little effect. Even current Prime Minister François Hollande commented that while he would like to increase the percentage of women in his government, that didn't "mean that they will have the same responsibilities."

Last year in France, penalties for sexual harassment were levied in only 80 cases—quite low for a country of 65 million people (in comparison, the figure is roughly 10,000 U.S. employers if settlements with employer penalties are included). France recently passed a more comprehensive law against sexual harassment in the workplace, but some question whether it will be effective, pointing to the many loopholes and gray areas in the law. As one observer noted, "Sexual harassment laws are on the books. But they are rarely enforced or prosecuted."

Sources: R. Marquand, "France's 'Boys Will Be Boys' Mentality Challenges Gender Equality," *Christian Science Monitor* (January 8, 2013), downloaded May 20, 2013, from www.csmonitor.com/; M. de la Baume, "France Is Expected to Pass a New Harassment Law," *The New York Times* (July 28, 2012), p. A8; and H. Fouquet and T. Patel, " 'Macho' France Dismays Women Seeking Égalité in Election," *Bloomberg Businessweek* (March 8, 2012), downloaded May 22, 2013, from www.businessweek.com/.

stereotypes that reflect negatively on her (such as helplessness, passivity, or lack of career commitment), usually in an attempt to gain power over her or minimize power differentials. Increasingly, too, there are cases of women in positions of power harassing male employees.

Sexual harassment can wreak havoc on an organization, not to mention on the victims themselves, but it can be avoided. The manager's role is critical. Here are some ways managers can protect themselves and their employees from sexual harassment:

1. Make sure an active policy defines what constitutes sexual harassment, informs employees they can be fired for sexually harassing another employee, and establishes procedures for making complaints.
2. Reassure employees they will not encounter retaliation if they file a complaint.
3. Investigate every complaint, and inform the legal and human resource departments.
4. Make sure offenders are disciplined or terminated.
5. Set up in-house seminars to raise employee awareness of sexual harassment issues.

The bottom line is that managers have a responsibility to protect their employees from a hostile work environment, but they also need to protect themselves. Managers may be unaware that one of their employees is being sexually harassed.

An Ethical Choice

Should All Sexual Behavior Be Prohibited at Work?

The difficulty in monitoring and defining sexual harassment at work has led some organizations to go beyond discouraging overt sexually harassing behaviors. Companies ranging from Walmart to Staples to Xerox have disciplined employees for workplace romances and upheld policies that ban hierarchical romantic relationships, such as between a supervisor and subordinate. The idea is that such relationships are so fraught with potential for abuse of power that they cannot possibly be consensual for extended periods of time. Surveys by the Society of Human Resource Management suggest that concerns about both potential sexual harassment and lowered productivity have motivated prohibitions on workplace romances. However, ethicists and legal scholars have thrown some "no romance" policies into question on the grounds they are patronizing or invade employee privacy.

What does organizational behavior research have to say about *consensual* sexual behavior at work? One study of more than 1,000 respondents found 40 percent were exposed to sexual behavior in some form in the past year. Counter to the idea that all sexual behavior at work is negative, some female and many male respondents reported enjoying the experience. However, exposure to sexual behavior at work was negatively related to performance and psychological well-being. People may report enjoying it, but it might be hurting their productivity and well-being anyway.

When thinking about a sexual harassment policy for your own organization that might prohibit all workplace romances, consider the following questions:

1. Are there potential problems in monitoring and enforcing such a comprehensive policy on all employees?

2. Does the organization have the right to actively determine what types of behaviors consenting employees engage in outside the work environment?

3. Can the policy be written in a less restrictive manner, such as by prohibiting employees who work together closely from having workplace romances? In this way, the organization might be able to transfer employees who are in a relationship so they don't work directly with one another, and thus they can be retained in the organization and their personal privacy respected.

Sources: Based on J. L. Berdahl and K. Aquino, "Sexual Behavior at Work: Fun or Folly?" *Journal of Applied Psychology* 94, no. 1 (2009), pp. 34–47; and C. Boyd, "The Debate over the Prohibition of Romance in the Workplace," *Journal of Business Ethics* 97, no. 2 (2010), pp. 325–338.

But being unaware does not protect them or their organization. If investigators believe a manager could have known about the harassment, both the manager and the company can be held liable.

Politics: Power in Action

When people get together in groups, power will be exerted. People want to carve out a niche from which to exert influence, earn rewards, and advance their careers. When employees in organizations convert their power into action, we describe them as being engaged in politics. Those with good political skills have the ability to use their bases of power effectively.[49]

Definition of Organizational Politics

political behavior *Activities that are not required as part of a person's formal role in the organization but that influence, or attempt to influence, the distribution of advantages and disadvantages within the organization.*

There is no shortage of definitions of *organizational politics.* Essentially, this type of politics focuses on the use of power to affect decision making in an organization, or on self-serving and organizationally unsanctioned behaviors.[50] For our purposes, **political behavior** in organizations consists of activities that are not required as part of an individual's formal role but that influence, or attempt to influence, the distribution of advantages and disadvantages within the organization.[51]

This definition encompasses what most people mean when they talk about organizational politics. Political behavior is outside specified job requirements. It requires some attempt to use power bases. It includes efforts to influence the goals, criteria, or processes used for decision making. Our definition is broad enough to include varied political behaviors such as withholding key information from decision makers, joining a coalition, whistleblowing, spreading rumors, leaking confidential information to the media, exchanging favors with others in the organization for mutual benefit, and lobbying on behalf of or against a particular individual or decision alternative.

OB Poll | **Importance of Organizational Politics**

How do employees get ahead in your organization?

- Creativity 4%
- Initiative 18%
- Hard work 27%
- Politics 51%

Source: D. Crampton, "Is How Americans Feel about Their Jobs Changing?" (September 28, 2012), http://corevalues.com/employee-motivation/is-how-americans-feel-about-their-jobs-changing.

Photo 13-4 Whistleblower Michael Woodford was fired from his position as CEO of Japan's camera-maker Olympus after informing company officials about accounting irregularities. Although not part of his role as CEO, Woodford engaged in the political behavior of whistleblowing that uncovered a 13-year accounting fraud by some Olympus executives.

Source: REUTERS/Luke MacGregor.

The Reality of Politics

Interviews with experienced managers show that most believe political behavior is a major part of organizational life.[52] Many managers report some use of political behavior is both ethical and necessary, as long as it doesn't directly harm anyone else. They describe politics as a necessary evil and believe someone who *never* uses political behavior will have a hard time getting things done. Most also indicate they had never been trained to use political behavior effectively. But why, you may wonder, must politics exist? Isn't it possible for an organization to be politics free? It's *possible*—but unlikely.

Organizations are made up of individuals and groups with different values, goals, and interests.[53] This sets up the potential for conflict over the allocation of limited resources, such as departmental budgets, space, project responsibilities, and salary adjustments.[54] If resources were abundant, then all constituencies within the organization could satisfy their goals. But because they are limited, not everyone's interests can be satisfied. Furthermore, gains by one individual or group are often *perceived* as coming at the expense of others within the organization (whether they are or not). These forces create real competition among members for the organization's limited resources.

Maybe the most important factor leading to politics within organizations is the realization that most of the "facts" used to allocate the limited resources are open to interpretation. What, for instance, is *good* performance? What's an *adequate* improvement? What constitutes an *unsatisfactory* job? One person's "selfless effort to benefit the organization" is seen by another as a "blatant attempt to further one's interest."[55] The manager of any major league baseball team knows a .400 hitter is a high performer and a .125 hitter is a poor performer. You don't need to be a baseball genius to know you should play your .400 hitter and send the .125 hitter back to the minors. But what if you have to choose between players who hit .280 and .290? Then less objective factors come into play: fielding expertise, attitude, potential, ability to perform in a clutch, loyalty to the team, and so on. More managerial decisions resemble the choice

Exhibit 13-2	Politics Is in the Eye of the Beholder

A behavior one person labels as "organizational politics" is very likely to seem like "effective management" to another. The fact is not that effective management is necessarily political, although in some cases it might be. Rather, a person's reference point determines what he or she classifies as organizational politics. For example, one experimental study showed that power-oriented behavior performed by a permanent, tenured employee is seen as more legitimate and less harsh than the same behavior performed by a temporary employee. Take a look at the following labels used to describe the same phenomenon. These suggest that politics, like beauty, is in the eye of the beholder.

"Political" Label		"Effective Management" Label
1. Blaming others	vs.	Fixing responsibility
2. "Kissing up"	vs.	Developing working relationships
3. Apple polishing	vs.	Demonstrating loyalty
4. Passing the buck	vs.	Delegating authority
5. Covering your rear	vs.	Documenting decisions
6. Creating conflict	vs.	Encouraging change and innovation
7. Forming coalitions	vs.	Facilitating teamwork
8. Whistle-blowing	vs.	Improving efficiency
9. Scheming	vs.	Planning ahead
10. Overachieving	vs.	Competent and capable
11. Ambitious	vs.	Career minded
12. Opportunistic	vs.	Astute
13. Cunning	vs.	Practical minded
14. Arrogant	vs.	Confident
15. Perfectionist	vs.	Attentive to detail

Source: Based on T. C. Krell, M. E. Mendenhall, and J. Sendry, "Doing Research in the Conceptual Morass of Organizational Politics," paper presented at the Western Academy of Management Conference, Hollywood, CA, April 1987.

between a .280 and a .290 hitter than between a .125 hitter and a .400 hitter. It is in this large and ambiguous middle ground of organizational life—where the facts *don't* speak for themselves—that politics flourish (see Exhibit 13-2).

Finally, because most decisions have to be made in a climate of ambiguity—where facts are rarely fully objective and thus are open to interpretation—people within organizations will use whatever influence they can to taint the facts to support their goals and interests. That, of course, creates the activities we call *politicking*.

Therefore, to answer the question whether it is possible for an organization to be politics-free, we can say "yes"—if all members of that organization hold the same goals and interests, if organizational resources are not scarce, and if performance outcomes are completely clear and objective. But that doesn't describe the organizational world in which most of us live.

Causes and Consequences of Political Behavior

6 Identify the causes and consequences of political behavior.

Factors Contributing to Political Behavior

Not all groups or organizations are equally political. In some organizations, for instance, politicking is overt and rampant, while in others politics plays a small role in influencing outcomes. Why this variation? Recent research and observation have identified a number of factors that appear to encourage political

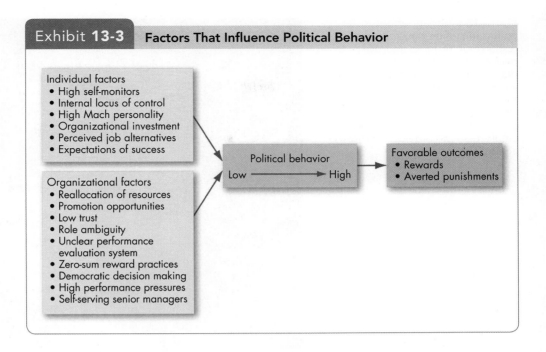

Exhibit 13-3 Factors That Influence Political Behavior

Individual factors
- High self-monitors
- Internal locus of control
- High Mach personality
- Organizational investment
- Perceived job alternatives
- Expectations of success

Organizational factors
- Reallocation of resources
- Promotion opportunities
- Low trust
- Role ambiguity
- Unclear performance evaluation system
- Zero-sum reward practices
- Democratic decision making
- High performance pressures
- Self-serving senior managers

Political behavior
Low ——→ High

Favorable outcomes
- Rewards
- Averted punishments

behavior. Some are individual characteristics, derived from the unique qualities of the people the organization employs; others are a result of the organization's culture or internal environment. Exhibit 13-3 illustrates how both individual and organizational factors can increase political behavior and provide favorable outcomes (increased rewards and averted punishments) for both individuals and groups in the organization.

Individual Factors   At the individual level, researchers have identified certain personality traits, needs, and other factors likely to be related to political behavior. In terms of traits, we find that employees who are high self-monitors, possess an internal locus of control, and have a high need for power are more likely to engage in political behavior.[56] The high self-monitor is more sensitive to social cues, exhibits higher levels of social conformity, and is more likely to be skilled in political behavior than the low self-monitor. Because they believe they can control their environment, individuals with an internal locus of control are more prone to take a proactive stance and attempt to manipulate situations in their favor. Not surprisingly, the Machiavellian personality—characterized by the will to manipulate and the desire for power—is comfortable using politics as a means to further his or her self-interest.

In addition, an individual's investment in the organization, perceived alternatives, and expectations of success influence the degree to which he or she will pursue illegitimate means of political action.[57] The more a person expects increased future benefits from the organization, the more that person has to lose if forced out and the less likely he or she is to use illegitimate means. The more alternative job opportunities an individual has—due to a favorable job market or the possession of scarce skills or knowledge, a prominent reputation, or influential contacts outside the organization—the more likely that individual is to risk illegitimate political actions. Finally, an individual with low expectations of success from illegitimate means is unlikely to use them. High expectations from such measures are most likely to be the province of both experienced and powerful individuals with polished political skills and inexperienced and naïve employees who misjudge their chances.

Photo 13-5 Organizations foster politicking when they reduce resources in order to improve performance. After announcing plans to downsize its global workforce of 100,000 employees to increase its competitiveness, French pharmaceutical firm Sanofi stimulated political activity among employees who organized protests against the job cuts.

Source: REUTERS/Robert Pratta

Organizational Factors   Although we acknowledge the role individual differences can play, the evidence more strongly suggests that certain situations and cultures promote politics. Specifically, when an organization's resources are declining, when the existing pattern of resources is changing, and when there is opportunity for promotions, politicking is more likely to surface.[58] When organizations downsize to improve efficiency, resources must be reduced, and people may engage in political actions to safeguard what they have. But *any* changes, especially those that imply significant reallocation of resources within the organization, are likely to stimulate conflict and increase politicking. The opportunity for promotions or advancement has consistently been found to encourage competition for a limited resource as people try to positively influence the decision outcome.

Cultures characterized by low trust, role ambiguity, unclear performance evaluation systems, zero-sum reward allocation practices, democratic decision making, high pressures for performance, and self-serving senior managers will also create breeding grounds for politicking.[59] The less trust within the organization, the higher the level of political behavior and the more likely it will be of the illegitimate kind. So, high trust should suppress political behavior in general and inhibit illegitimate actions in particular.

Role ambiguity means the prescribed employee behaviors are not clear. There are, therefore, fewer limits to the scope and functions of the employee's political actions. Because political activities are defined as those not required as part of the employee's formal role, the greater the role ambiguity, the more employees can engage in unnoticed political activity.

Performance evaluation is far from a perfect science. The more organizations use subjective criteria in the appraisal, emphasize a single outcome measure, or allow significant time to pass between the time of an action and its appraisal, the greater the likelihood that an employee can get away with politicking. Subjective

"Powerful Leaders Keep Their (Fr)Enemies Close"

This statement appears to be true. We all have heard the term "frenemies" to describe friends who are also rivals or people who act like friends but secretly dislike each other. Some observers have argued that frenemies are increasing at work due to the "abundance of very close, intertwined relationships that bridge people's professional and personal lives."

Keeping enemies close may be one reason Barack Obama appointed Hillary Clinton secretary of state after their bitter battle for the presidency. Or, in the business world, why one entrepreneur decided not to sue a former college classmate who, after working for her startup as a consultant, took that knowledge and started his own, competing company with the first company.

Is it really wise to keep your enemies close? And, if so, why?

New research suggests answers to these questions. This research conducted three experimental studies where individuals chose to work in the same room with the rival, even when instructed that they would probably perform better apart; to sit closer to rivals when working together; and to express an explicit preference to be closer to the rival. The researchers further found that the primary reason for the "being closer" effect was the desire to monitor the behavior and performance of the rival.

The researchers also found that the "keeping enemies closer" effect was strong under certain conditions—when the individual was socially dominant, when the individual felt more competition from the team member, and when rewards and ability to serve as leader were dependent on their performance.

These results suggest that the concept of frenemies is very real and that we choose to keep our rivals close so we can keep an eye on the competition they provide.

Sources: M. Thompson, "How to Work with Your Startup Frenemies," *VentureBeat* (December 22, 2012), downloaded May 9, 2013, from http://venturebeat.com/; and N. L. Mead and J. K. Maner, "On Keeping Your Enemies Close: Powerful Leaders Seek Proximity to Ingroup Power Threats," *Journal of Personality and Social Psychology* 102 (2012), pp. 576–591.

performance criteria create ambiguity. The use of a single outcome measure encourages individuals to do whatever is necessary to "look good" on that measure, but that often occurs at the cost of good performance on other important parts of the job that are not being appraised. The longer the time between an action and its appraisal, the more unlikely it is that the employee will be held accountable for political behaviors.

The more an organization's culture emphasizes the zero-sum or win–lose approach to reward allocations, the more employees will be motivated to engage in politicking. The zero-sum approach treats the reward "pie" as fixed, so any gain one person or group achieves has to come at the expense of another person or group. If $15,000 in annual raises is to be distributed among five employees, any employee who gets more than $3,000 takes money away from one or more of the others. Such a practice encourages making others look bad and increasing the visibility of what you do.

Finally, when employees see the people on top engaging in political behavior, especially doing so successfully and being rewarded for it, a climate is created that supports politicking. Politicking by top management in a sense gives those lower in the organization permission to play politics by implying that such behavior is acceptable.

How Do People Respond to Organizational Politics?

Trish loves her job as a writer on a weekly television comedy series but hates the internal politics. "A couple of the writers here spend more time kissing up to the executive producer than doing any work. And our head writer clearly has his favorites. While they pay me a lot and I get to really use my creativity,

I'm sick of having to be on alert for backstabbers and constantly having to self-promote my contributions. I'm tired of doing most of the work and getting little of the credit." Are Trish's comments typical of people who work in highly politicized workplaces? We all know friends or relatives who regularly complain about the politics at their job. But how do people in general react to organizational politics? Let's look at the evidence.

In our earlier discussion in this chapter of factors that contribute to political behavior, we focused on the favorable outcomes. But for most people—who have modest political skills or are unwilling to play the politics game—outcomes tend to be predominantly negative. Exhibit 13-4 summarizes the extensive research (mostly conducted in the United States) on the relationship between organizational politics and individual outcomes.[60] Very strong evidence indicates, for instance, that perceptions of organizational politics are negatively related to job satisfaction.[61] The perception of politics also tends to increase job anxiety and stress, possibly because people believe they may be losing ground to others who are active politickers or, conversely, because they feel additional pressures from entering into and competing in the political arena.[62] Politics may lead to self-reported declines in employee performance, perhaps because employees perceive political environments to be unfair, which demotivates them.[63] Not surprisingly, when politicking becomes too much to handle, it can lead employees to quit.[64]

When employees of two agencies in a study in Nigeria viewed their work environments as political, they reported higher levels of job distress and were less likely to help their co-workers. Thus, although developing countries such as Nigeria are perhaps more ambiguous and more political environments in which to work, the negative consequences of politics appear to be the same as in the United States.[65]

Researchers have also noted several interesting qualifiers. First, the politics–performance relationship appears to be moderated by an individual's understanding of the "hows" and "whys" of organizational politics. "An individual who has a clear understanding of who is responsible for making decisions and why they were selected to be the decision makers would have a better understanding

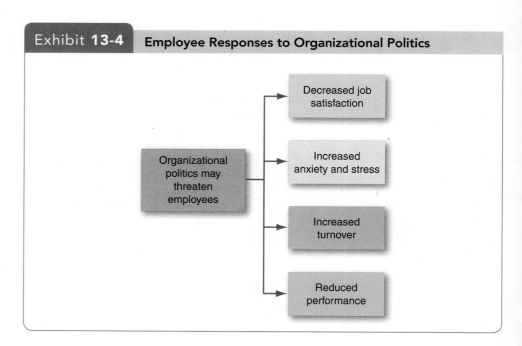

Exhibit 13-4   Employee Responses to Organizational Politics

Organizational politics may threaten employees

- Decreased job satisfaction
- Increased anxiety and stress
- Increased turnover
- Reduced performance

of how and why things happen the way they do than someone who does not understand the decision-making process in the organization."[66] When both politics and understanding are high, performance is likely to increase because the individual will see political actions as an opportunity. This is consistent with what you might expect among individuals with well-honed political skills. But when understanding is low, individuals are more likely to see politics as a threat, which can have a negative effect on job performance.[67]

Second, political behavior at work moderates the effects of ethical leadership.[68] One study found that male employees were more responsive to ethical leadership and showed the most citizenship behavior when levels of both politics and ethical leadership were high. Women, on the other hand, appear most likely to engage in citizenship behavior when the environment is consistently ethical and *apolitical*.

Third, when employees see politics as a threat, they often respond with **defensive behaviors**—reactive and protective behaviors to avoid action, blame, or change.[69] (Exhibit 13-5 provides some examples of these behaviors.) And defensive behaviors are often associated with negative feelings toward the job and work environment.[70] In the short run, employees may find that defensiveness protects their self-interest, but in the long run it wears them down. People who consistently rely on defensiveness find that, eventually, it is the only way they know how to behave. At that point, they lose the trust and support of their peers, bosses, employees, and clients.

defensive behaviors *Reactive and protective behaviors to avoid action, blame, or change.*

Exhibit 13-5   Defensive Behaviors

Avoiding Action

Overconforming. Strictly interpreting your responsibility by saying things like "The rules clearly state . . . " or "This is the way we've always done it."

Buck passing. Transferring responsibility for the execution of a task or decision to someone else.

Playing dumb. Avoiding an unwanted task by falsely pleading ignorance or inability.

Stretching. Prolonging a task so that one person appears to be occupied—for example, turning a two-week task into a 4-month job.

Stalling. Appearing to be more or less supportive publicly while doing little or nothing privately.

Avoiding Blame

Buffing. This is a nice way to refer to "covering your rear." It describes the practice of rigorously documenting activity to project an image of competence and thoroughness.

Playing safe. Evading situations that may reflect unfavorably. It includes taking on only projects with a high probability of success, having risky decisions approved by superiors, qualifying expressions of judgment, and taking neutral positions in conflicts.

Justifying. Developing explanations that lessen one's responsibility for a negative outcome and/or apologizing to demonstrate remorse, or both.

Scapegoating. Placing the blame for a negative outcome on external factors that are not entirely blameworthy.

Misrepresenting. Manipulation of information by distortion, embellishment, deception, selective presentation, or obfuscation.

Avoiding Change

Prevention. Trying to prevent a threatening change from occurring.

Self-protection. Acting in ways to protect one's self-interest during change by guarding information or other resources.

SELF-ASSESSMENT LIBRARY

7 Apply impression management techniques.

impression management (IM)
The process by which individuals attempt to control the impression others form of them.

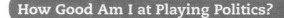

How Good Am I at Playing Politics?

In the Self-Assessment Library (available in MyManagementLab), take assessment II.C.3 (How Good Am I at Playing Politics?).

Impression Management

We know people have an ongoing interest in how others perceive and evaluate them. For example, North Americans spend billions of dollars on diets, health club memberships, cosmetics, and plastic surgery—all intended to make them more attractive to others. Being perceived positively by others should have benefits for people in organizations. It might, for instance, help them initially to get the jobs they want in an organization and, once hired, to get favorable evaluations, superior salary increases, and more rapid promotions. In a political context, it might help sway the distribution of advantages in their favor. The process by which individuals attempt to control the impression others form of them is called **impression management (IM)**.[71]

Who might we predict will engage in IM? No surprise here. It's our old friend, the high self-monitor.[72] Low self-monitors tend to present images of themselves that are consistent with their personalities, regardless of the beneficial or detrimental effects for them. In contrast, high self-monitors are good at reading situations and molding their appearances and behavior to fit each situation. If you want to control the impression others form of you, what IM techniques can you use? Exhibit 13-6 summarizes some of the most popular and provides an example of each.

Keep in mind that when people engage in IM, they are sending a false message that might be true under other circumstances.[73] Excuses, for instance, may be offered with sincerity. Referring to the example in Exhibit 13-6, you can *actually* believe that ads contribute little to sales in your region. But misrepresentation can have a high cost. If you "cry wolf" once too often, no one is likely to believe you when the wolf really comes. So the impression manager must be cautious not to be perceived as insincere or manipulative.[74] Consider the effect of implausible name-dropping as an example of this principle. Participants in a study in Switzerland disliked an experimental confederate who claimed to be a personal friend of the well-liked Swiss tennis star Roger Federer, but they generally liked confederates who just said they were fans.[75] Another study found that when managers attributed an employee's citizenship behaviors to impression management, they actually felt angry (probably because they felt manipulated) and gave subordinates lower performance ratings. When managers attributed the same behaviors to prosocial values and concern about the organization, they felt happy and gave higher performance ratings.[76] In sum, people don't like to feel others are manipulating them through impression management, so such tactics should be employed with caution.

Most of the studies undertaken to test the effectiveness of IM techniques have related it to two criteria: interview success and performance evaluations. Let's consider each of these.

The evidence indicates most job applicants use IM techniques in interviews and that it works.[77] In one study, for instance, interviewers felt applicants for a position as a customer service representative who used IM techniques performed better in the interview, and they seemed somewhat more inclined to hire these people.[78] Moreover, when the researchers considered applicants' credentials, they concluded it was the IM techniques alone that influenced the interviewers—that is, it didn't seem to matter whether applicants were well or poorly qualified. If they used IM techniques, they did better in the interview.

| Exhibit 13-6 | Impression Management (IM) Techniques |

Conformity

Agreeing with someone else's opinion to gain his or her approval is a *form of ingratiation.*

Example: A manager tells his boss, "You're absolutely right on your reorganization plan for the western regional office. I couldn't agree with you more."

Favors

Doing something nice for someone to gain that person's approval is a *form of ingratiation.*

Example: A salesperson says to a prospective client, "I've got two tickets to the theater tonight that I can't use. Take them. Consider it a thank-you for taking the time to talk with me."

Excuses

Explanations of a predicament-creating event aimed at minimizing the apparent severity of the predicament is a *defensive IM technique.*

Example: A sales manager says to her boss, "We failed to get the ad in the paper on time, but no one responds to those ads anyway."

Apologies

Admitting responsibility for an undesirable event and simultaneously seeking to get a pardon for the action is a *defensive IM technique.*

Example: An employee says to his boss, "I'm sorry I made a mistake on the report. Please forgive me."

Self-Promotion

Highlighting one's best qualities, downplaying one's deficits, and calling attention to one's achievements is a *self-focused IM technique.*

Example: A salesperson tells his boss, "Matt worked unsuccessfully for three years to try to get that account. I sewed it up in six weeks. I'm the best closer this company has."

Enhancement

Claiming that something you did is more valuable than most other members of the organizations would think is a *self-focused IM technique.*

Example: A journalist tells his editor, "My work on this celebrity divorce story was really a major boost to our sales" (even though the story only made it to page 3 in the entertainment section).

Flattery

Complimenting others about their virtues in an effort to make oneself appear perceptive and likeable is an *assertive IM technique.*

Example: A new sales trainee says to her peer, "You handled that client's complaint so tactfully! I could never have handled that as well as you did."

Exemplification

Doing more than you need to in an effort to show how dedicated and hard working you are is an *assertive IM technique.*

Example: An employee sends e-mails from his work computer when he works late so that his supervisor will know how long he's been working.

Sources: Based on B. R. Schlenker, *Impression Management* (Monterey, CA: Brooks/Cole, 1980); M. C. Bolino, K. M. Kacmar, W. H. Turnley, and J. B. Gilstrap, "A Multi-Level Review of Impression Management Motives and Behaviors," *Journal of Management* 34, no. 6 (2008), pp. 1080–1109; and R. B. Cialdini, "Indirect Tactics of Image Management Beyond Basking," in R. A. Giacalone and P. Rosenfeld (eds.), *Impression Management in the Organization* (Hillsdale, NJ: Lawrence Erlbaum, 1989), pp. 45–71.

Some IM techniques work better in interviews than others. Researchers have compared applicants whose IM techniques focused on promoting their accomplishments (called *self-promotion*) to those who focused on complimenting the interviewer and finding areas of agreement (referred to as *ingratiation*).

In general, applicants appear to use self-promotion more than ingratiation.[79] What's more, self-promotion tactics may be more important to interviewing success. Applicants who work to create an appearance of competence by enhancing their accomplishments, taking credit for successes, and explaining away failures do better in interviews. These effects reach beyond the interview: Applicants who use more self-promotion tactics also seem to get more follow-up job-site visits, even after adjusting for grade-point average, gender, and job type. Ingratiation also works well in interviews; applicants who compliment the interviewer, agree with his or her opinions, and emphasize areas of fit do better than those who don't.[80]

In terms of performance ratings, the picture is quite different. Ingratiation is positively related to performance ratings, meaning those who ingratiate with their supervisors get higher performance evaluations. However, self-promotion appears to backfire: Those who self-promote actually seem to receive *lower* performance evaluations.[81] There is an important qualifier to this general result. It appears that individuals high in political skill are able to translate IM into higher performance appraisals, whereas those lower in political skill are more likely to be hurt by their IM attempts.[82] Another study of 760 boards of directors found that individuals who ingratiate themselves to current board members (express agreement with the director, point out shared attitudes and opinions, compliment the director) increase their chances of landing on a board.[83]

What explains these results? If you think about them, they make sense. Ingratiating always works because everyone—both interviewers and supervisors—likes to be treated nicely. However, self-promotion may work only in interviews and backfire on the job because, whereas the interviewer has little idea whether you're blowing smoke about your accomplishments, the supervisor knows because it's his or her job to observe you. Thus, if you're going to self-promote, remember that what works in an interview won't always work once you're on the job.

Are our conclusions about responses to politics globally valid? Should we expect employees in Israel, for instance, to respond the same way to workplace politics that employees in the United States do? Almost all our conclusions on employee reactions to organizational politics are based on studies conducted in North America. The few studies that have included other countries suggest some minor modifications.[84] One study of managers in U.S. culture and three Chinese cultures (People's Republic of China, Hong Kong, and Taiwan) found U.S. managers evaluated "gentle persuasion" tactics such as consultation and inspirational appeal as more effective than did their Chinese counterparts.[85] Other research suggests that effective U.S. leaders achieve influence by focusing on personal goals of group members and the tasks at hand (an analytical approach), whereas influential East Asian leaders focus on relationships among group members and meeting the demands of the people around them (a holistic approach).[86]

As another example, Israelis and the British seem to generally respond as do North Americans—that is, their perception of organizational politics relates to decreased job satisfaction and increased turnover.[87] But in countries that are more politically unstable, such as Israel, employees seem to demonstrate greater tolerance of intense political processes in the workplace, perhaps because they are used to power struggles and have more experience in coping with them.[88] This suggests that people from politically turbulent countries in the Middle East or Latin America might be more accepting of organizational politics, and even more willing to use aggressive political tactics in the workplace, than people from countries such as Great Britain or Switzerland.

The Ethics of Behaving Politically

8 Determine whether a political action is ethical.

Although there are no clear-cut ways to differentiate ethical from unethical politicking, there are some questions you should consider. For example, what is the utility of engaging in politicking? Sometimes we do it for little good reason. Major league baseball player Al Martin claimed he played football at USC when in fact he never did. As a baseball player, he had little to gain by pretending to have played football. Outright lies like this may be a rather extreme example of impression management, but many of us have at least distorted information to make a favorable impression. One thing to keep in mind is whether it's really worth the risk. Another question to ask is this: How does the utility of engaging in the political behavior balance out any harm (or potential harm) it will do to others? Complimenting a supervisor on his or her appearance in order to curry favor is probably much less harmful than grabbing credit for a project that others deserve.

Finally, does the political activity conform to standards of equity and justice? Sometimes it is difficult to weigh the costs and benefits of a political action, but its ethicality is clear. The department head who inflates the performance evaluation of a favored employee and deflates the evaluation of a disfavored employee—and then uses these evaluations to justify giving the former a big raise and nothing to the latter—has treated the disfavored employee unfairly.

Unfortunately, powerful people can become very good at explaining self-serving behaviors in terms of the organization's best interests. They can persuasively argue that unfair actions are really fair and just. Our point is that immoral people can justify almost any behavior. Those who are powerful, articulate, and persuasive are most vulnerable to ethical lapses because they are likely to be able to get away with unethical practices successfully. When faced with an ethical dilemma regarding organizational politics, try to consider whether playing politics is worth the risk and whether others might be harmed in the process. If you have a strong power base, recognize the ability of power to corrupt. Remember that it's a lot easier for the powerless to act ethically, if for no other reason than they typically have very little political discretion to exploit.

Mapping Your Political Career

As we have seen, politics are not just for politicians. You can use the concepts presented in this chapter is some very tangible ways we have outlined. However, there is another application: You.

One of the most useful ways to think about power and politics is in terms of your own career. Think about your career in your organization of choice. What are your ambitions? Who has the power to help you get there? What is your relationship with these people? The best way to answer these questions is with a political map, which can help you sketch out your relationships with the people upon whom your career depends. Exhibit 13-7 contains such a political map.[89] Let's walk through it.

Assume that your future promotion depends on five people, including Jamie, your immediate supervisor. As you can see in the exhibit, you have a

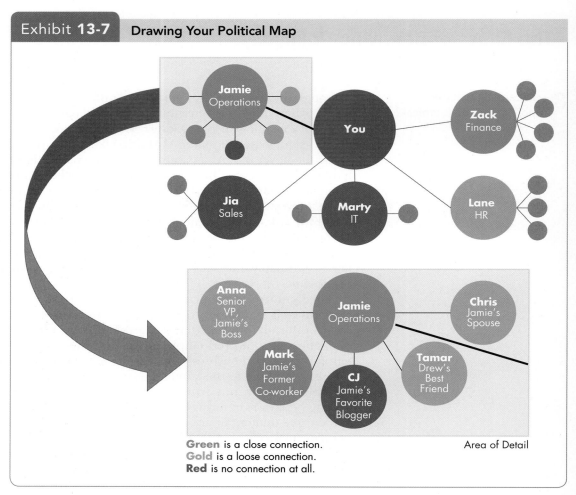

Exhibit 13-7   **Drawing Your Political Map**

Green is a close connection.
Gold is a loose connection.
Red is no connection at all.

Area of Detail

Source: Based on Clark, "A Campaign Strategy for Your Career," *Harvard Business Review* (November 2012), pp. 131–134.

close relationship with Jamie (you would be in real trouble otherwise). You also have a close relationship with Zack in finance. However, for the others, you either have a loose relationship (Lane), or none at all (Jia, Marty). One obvious implication of this map is to formulate a plan for more influence over, and a closer relationship with, these people. How might you do that?

The map also provides for a useful way to think about that. Assume that the five individuals have their own networks. In this case, though, assume these aren't so much power networks as in your case, but influence networks representing your knowledge of the people who influence them.

One of the best ways to influence people is indirectly. What if you played in a tennis league with Mark, Jamie's former co-worker who you know remains friends with Jamie? To influence Mark, in many cases, may also be to influence Marty. Why not post an entry on CJ's blog? This same analysis can then be completed with the other four decision-makers.

Of course, this map doesn't show you everything you need to know—no map does. For example, rarely would all five people have the same amount of power. Moreover, maps are harder to construct in the era of large social networks. Try to keep this basic, to the people who *really* matter to your career.

All of this may seem a bit Machiavellian to you. However, remember, only one person gets the promotion, and your competition may have a map of his or her own. As we noted in the early part of the chapter, power and politics are a part of organizational life. To decide not to play is deciding not to be effective. Better to be explicit about it with a political map than to proceed as if power and politics didn't matter.

Summary

An effective manager accepts the political nature of organizations. Some people are significantly more politically astute than others, meaning that they are aware of the underlying politics and can manage impressions. Those who are good at playing politics can be expected to get higher performance evaluations and, hence, larger salary increases and more promotions than the politically naïve or inept. The politically astute are also likely to exhibit higher job satisfaction and be better able to neutralize job stressors.

Few employees relish being powerless in their job and organization. People respond differently to the various power bases. Expert and referent power are derived from an individual's personal qualities. In contrast, coercion, reward, and legitimate power are essentially organizationally derived. Competence especially appears to offer wide appeal, and its use as a power base results in high performance by group members.

Implications for Managers

If you want to get things done in a group or an organization, it helps to have power. Here are several suggestions for how to deal with power in your own work life:

- As a manager who wants to maximize your power, you will want to increase others' dependence on you. You can, for instance, increase your power in relation to your boss by developing knowledge or a skill she needs and for which she perceives no ready substitute.
- You will not be alone in attempting to build your power bases. Others, particularly employees and peers, will be seeking to increase your dependence on them, while you are trying to minimize it and increase their dependence on you. The result is a continual battle.
- Try to avoid putting others in a position where they feel they have no power.
- By assessing behavior in a political framework, you can better predict the actions of others and use that information to formulate political strategies that will gain advantages for you and your work unit.
- Consider that employees who have poor political skills or are unwilling to play the politics game generally relate perceived organizational politics to lower job satisfaction and self-reported performance, increased anxiety, and higher turnover. Therefore, if you are adept at organizational politics, help your employees understand the importance of becoming politically savvy.

Everyone Wants Power

POINT   **COUNTERPOINT**

Not everything we secretly want we admit to wanting. Money is one example. One psychologist found that few people would admit to wanting money, but they thought everyone else wanted it. They were half right—everyone wants money. And everyone wants power.

Harvard psychologist David McClelland was justifiably famous for his study of underlying motives. McClelland would measure people's motivation for power from his analysis of how people described pictures (called the Thematic Apperception Test, or TAT). Why didn't he simply ask people how much they wanted power? Because he believed that many more people really wanted power than would admit, or even consciously realize. And that is exactly what he found.

Why do we want power? Because it is good for us. It gives us more control over our own lives. It gives us more freedom to do as we wish. There are few things worse in life than feeling helpless, and few better than feeling in charge of your destiny.

Take Steve Cohen, founder of SAC Capital Advisors and the most powerful man on Wall Street. He buys Picassos, he lives in a mansion, he has white-gloved butlers, he travels the world first class. People will do almost anything to please him—or to even get near him. One writer notes, "Inside his offices, vast fortunes are won and lost. Careers are made and unmade. Type-A egos are inflated and crushed, sometimes in the space of hours." All of this is bad for Steve Cohen how?

Research shows that people with power and status command more respect from others, have higher self-esteem (no surprise there), and enjoy better health than those of less stature.

Usually, people who tell you power doesn't matter are those who have no hope of getting it. Being jealous, like wanting power, is one of those people just won't admit to.

Of course it is true that some people desire power—and often behave ruthlessly to get it. For most of us, however, power is not high on our list of priorities, and for some people, power is actually undesirable.

Research shows that most individuals feel uncomfortable when placed in powerful positions. One study asked individuals, before they began work in a four-person team, to "rank, from 1 [highest] to 4 [lowest], in terms of status and influence within the group, would you like to achieve." You know what? Only about one-third (34 percent) of participants chose the highest rank. In a second study, researchers studied employees participating in Amazon's Mechanical Turk online service. They found, when employees were asked about their reasons for belonging to the three groups (which would be a workplace, a volunteer group, a congregation, etc.) that were most important in their life, that the main reason people want power is to earn respect. If they can get respect without gaining power, that is what most preferred. In a third study, the authors found that individuals preferred power only when they had high ability—in other words, where their influence helped their groups.

This interesting research suggests that we often confuse the desire for power with other things—like the desire to be respected and to help our groups and organizations succeed. In these cases, power is something most of us seek for more benevolent ends—and only in cases when we think the power does good.

Another study found that the majority of people want respect from their peers, not power. Cameron Anderson, the author of this research, sums it up nicely: "You don't have to be rich to be happy, but instead be a valuable contributing member to your groups," he comments. "What makes a person high in status in a group is being engaged, generous with others, and making self sacrifices for the greater good."

Oh, and about Stevie Cohen . . . you realize that he is being investigated by the SEC? The SEC investigator: Preet Bharara, the same one who got Rajat Gupta.

Sources: B. Burrough and B. McLean, "The Hunt for Steve Cohen," *Vanity Fair* (June 2013), downloaded May 13, 2013, from www.vanityfair.com/; C. Anderson, R. Willer, G. J. Kilduff, and C. E. Brown, "The Origins of Deference: When Do People Prefer Lower Status?" *Journal of Personality and Social Psychology* 102 (2012), pp. 1077–1088; C. Anderson, M. W Kraus, A. D. Galinsky, and D. Keltner, "The Local-Ladder Effect: Social Status and Subjective Well-Being," *Psychological Science* 23(7), (2012), pp. 764–771; and S. Kennelly, "Happiness Is About Respect, Not Riches," *Greater Good* (July 13, 2012), downloaded May 4, 2013, from http://greatergood.berkeley.edu/.

END-OF-CHAPTER REVIEW

MyManagementLab

Go to **mymanagementlab.com** to complete the problems marked with this icon. ★

QUESTIONS FOR REVIEW

13-1 What is power? How is leadership different from power?

13-2 What are the similarities and differences among the five bases of power?

13-3 What is the role of dependence in power relationships?

13-4 What are the nine most often identified power or influence tactics and their contingencies?

13-5 What is the connection between sexual harassment and the abuse of power?

13-6 What are the causes and consequences of political behavior?

13-7 What are some examples of impression management techniques?

13-8 What standards can you use to determine whether a political action is ethical?

EXPERIENTIAL EXERCISE Power Dynamics in Teams

General Context

Power dynamics often exist in organizations at the team level, such that one work team or unit has much more power than another. In fact, power differences can be as big between teams as within them. This exercise will simulate those dynamics, within the limitations of a classroom context.

Generate Revenue Pool

Each student is to turn in a dollar bill (or similar value of currency) to the instructor. This pool comprises the revenue of the organization, and $1 is equal to $1 million. (For purposes of distribution after the assignment, however, dollars revert back to their original value.)

Form Teams and Understand Different Rules for Different Teams

Students are assigned to one of three teams. Each team operates under different rules, as follows:

Top team. Members of the top team are free to enter the space of either of the other teams. They are also free to communicate whatever they want, whenever they want. *Members of the top team have the authority to make any change in the rules they want, at any time, with or without notice.*

Middle team. Members of the middle team may enter the space of the bottom team when they want. They must, however, request permission from the top team to enter the top team's space (the top team can refuse).

Bottom team. Members of the bottom team may not disturb the top team in any way unless specifically invited to. They do have the right to knock on the door of the middle team and request permission to communicate (which can also be refused).

Instructions

Recall that the pool of money represents the revenue of the organization. The teams' assignment is to distribute this revenue in the most effective way possible.

Before beginning, divide the money into thirds and physically give two-thirds of it to the top team, one-third to the middle team, and none to the bottom team.

Perform the Assignment

Teams go to their assigned spaces with 30 minutes to complete their assignment. The particulars of the assignment differ by team, in the following manner:

Top team. The top team is responsible for the overall effectiveness of the organization. In particular, this team is responsible for learning from the exercise and deciding how to use its money.

Middle team. The middle team's assignment is to assist the top team in providing for the overall welfare of the organization and deciding how to use its money.

Bottom team. The bottom team's assignment is to identify the organization's resources and decide how best to provide for learning and the overall effectiveness of the organization.

Debriefing

Each of the three teams chooses two representatives to go to the front of the class and discuss the following:

13.9. Summarize what occurred within and among the three teams.

13.10. Is it different being in the top team than in the middle team? If so, what are the differences your team perceived?

13.11. What lessons about power does this exercise teach us?

13.12. In your team's opinion, does this exercise reflect, in part, the reality of resource allocation decisions in organizations? Why or why not?

Sources: Based loosely on L. Bolman and T. E. Deal, *Exchange* 3, no. 4 (1979), pp. 38–42.

ETHICAL DILEMMA   How Much Should You Defer to Those in Power?

Though it is not always easy to admit to ourselves, often we adapt our behavior to suit those in power. To some degree, it is important for organizational success that we do so. After all, people are in positions of authority for a reason, and if no one paid attention to the rules put in place by these people, chaos would rule.

At other times, however, and more often that we acknowledge, powerful individuals in organizations push our actions into ethical gray areas, or worse.

In Stanley Milgram's famous experiments, most individuals delivered what they thought were severe shocks only because an authority figure directed them to do so.

More recently, managers of restaurants and stores (including McDonald's, Applebee's, Taco Bell, Winn Dixie, and others) were persuaded to strip search customers or employees when an individual impersonating a police officer phoned in and instructed them to do so.

These powerful examples aside, there are more prosaic ways power persuades us. For example, many stock analysts report pressure from their bosses to promote funds from which the organization profits most (which, in such situations, is not disclosed to their clients).

Few of us are going to deliver electric shocks or perform strip searches. But these examples, as well as the scandals at Abu Ghraib and Penn State, do highlight the disturbing tendency for many of us to conform to the wishes of those in power.

Questions

⭐ **13-13.** Do you think people tailor their behavior to suit those in power more than they admit? Do you?

13-14. One writer commented that these acts of bending behavior to suit those in power remind "anyone who is under pressure to carry out orders from 'above' to constantly question the validity and prudence of what they're being asked to do." Why don't we do this more often?

13-15. Why do some individuals resist the effects of power more strongly than others?

Sources: J. Sancton, "Milgram at McDonald's," *Bloomberg Businessweek* (September 2, 2012), pp. 74–75; and A. Wolfson, "Compliance' Re-Creates McDonald's Strip-Search Ordeal," *USA Today* (September 1, 2012), downloaded on May 21, 2013, from http://usatoday.com/.

CASE INCIDENT 1   Delegate Power, or Keep It Close?

Samantha Parks is the owner and CEO of Sparks, a small New York agency that develops advertising, promotions, and marketing materials for high-fashion firms. Parks has tended to keep a tight rein on her business, overseeing most projects from start to finish. However, as the firm has grown, she has found it necessary to delegate more and more decisions to her associates. She's recently been approached by a hairstyling chain that wants a comprehensive redefinition of its entire marketing and promotions look. Should Samantha try to manage this project in her traditional way, or should she delegate major parts to her employees?

Most managers confront this question at some point in their careers. Some experts propose that top executives need to stay very close to the creative core of their business, which means that even if their primary responsibility is to manage, CEOs should never cede too much control to committees of creative individuals or they can lose sight of the firm's overall future direction. Moreover, executives who do fall out of touch with the creative process risk being passed over by a new generation of "plugged in" employees who better understand how the business really works.

Others offer the opposite advice, saying it's not a good idea for a CEO to "sweat the small stuff" like managing individual client accounts or projects. These experts advise executives to identify everything they can "outsource" to other employees and to delegate as much as possible. By eliminating trivial tasks, executives will be better able to focus their attention on the most important decision making and control aspects of their jobs, which will help the business and also ensure that the top executive maintains control over the functions that really matter.

These pieces of advice are not necessarily in conflict with one another. The real challenge is to identify what you can delegate effectively without ceding too much power and control away from the person with the unifying vision. That is certainly easier said than done, though.

Questions

13-16. If you were Samantha Parks, how would you prioritize which projects or parts of projects to delegate?

13-17. In explaining what makes her decisions hard, Parks said, "I hire good people, creative people, to run these projects, and I worry that they will see my oversight and authority as interfering with their creative process." How can she deal with these concerns without giving up too much control?

13-18. Should executives try to control projects to maintain their position of authority? Do they have a right to control projects and keep in the loop on important decisions just so they can remain in charge?

Sources: Based on M. L. Tushman, W. K. Smith, and A. Binns, "The Ambidextrous CEO," *Harvard Business Review* (June 2011), pp. 74–79; and S. Bogan, "Find Your Focus," *Financial Planning* (February 2011), p. 72.

CASE INCIDENT 2   Barry's Peer Becomes His Boss

As Barry looked out the window of his office in Toronto, the gloomy October skies obscured his usual view of CN Tower. "That figures," Barry thought to himself—his mood was just as gloomy.

Five months ago, last May, Barry's company, CTM, a relatively small but growing technology company, reorganized itself. Although such reorganizations often imperil careers, Barry felt the change only improved his position. Barry's co-worker, Raphael, was promoted to a different department, which made sense because Raphael had been with the company for a few more years and had worked with the CEO on a successful project. Because Raphael was promoted and their past work roles were so similar, Barry thought his own promotion was soon to come.

However, 6 weeks ago, Barry's boss left. Raphael was transferred back to the same department and became Barry's boss. Although Barry felt a bit overlooked, he knew he was still relatively junior in the company and felt that his good past relationship with Raphael would bode well for his future prospects.

The past 6 weeks, however, had brought nothing but disappointment. Although Raphael often told Barry he was doing a great job, drawing from several observations, Barry felt that opinion was not being shared with the higher-ups. Worse, a couple of Barry's friends in the company showed Barry several e-mails where Raphael had taken credit for Barry's work.

"Raphael is not the person I thought he was," thought Barry.

What was his future in the company if no one saw the outcomes of his hard work? How would it affect his career to work for someone who apparently was willing to do anything to get ahead, even at others' expense? He thought about looking for work, but that prospect only darkened his mood further. He liked the company. He felt he did good work there.

As Barry looked again out his window, a light rain began to fall. The CN Tower was no more visible than before. He just didn't know what to do.

Questions

13-19. Should Barry complain about his treatment? To whom? If he did complain, what power tactics should Barry use?

13-20. Studies have shown that those prone to complaining or "whining" tend to have less power in an organization. Do you think whining leads to diminished power and influence, or the other way around? How can Barry avoid appearing to be a whiner?

13-21. Do you think Barry should look for another job? Why or why not?

Sources: Based on M. G. McIntyre, "Disgruntlement Won't Advance Your Career," *Pittsburgh Post-Gazette* (September 23, 2012), downloaded May 14, 2013, from www.post-gazette.com/; and S. Shellenbarger, "What to Do with a Workplace Whiner," *The Wall Street Journal* (September 12, 2012), pp. D1, D3.

MyManagementLab

Go to **mymanagementlab.com** for Auto-graded writing questions as well as the following Assisted-graded writing questions:

13-22. In consideration of your reading of the chapter and Case Incident 1, what do you think are some tasks in an organization that a top executive should never delegate to others?

13-23. After reading the chapter and Case Incident 2, what impression management techniques would you say Raphael is using?

13-24. MyManagementLab Only—comprehensive writing assignment for this chapter.

14

Conflict and Negotiation

JAMIE DIMON AND THE LONDON WHALE

In the aftermath of the financial crisis of 2007–2009, JPMorgan Chase emerged as the largest U.S. bank—with a stronger competitive position than ever. Its stock price is nearly 20 percent higher than when the meltdown began. In the past 10 years, it has never reported a quarterly loss and has paid a dividend to its shareholders every quarter, even during the dark days in 2008 and 2009.

Yet JPMorgan Chase and its chief executive, Jamie Dimon, also committed one of the largest blunders in banking history—a $6.2 billion loss tied to the investments of a single, small-scale trader in the bank's tower at Canary Wharf in east London. The trader, Bruno Iksil, tried covering his losses in derivatives trading and misleading his superiors about the extent of the damage. As his trades became larger and lost more, clients began to refer to Iksil as the "Whale."

Of course, figuring large in explanations for the London Whale losses are problems in financial decision making. Derivatives—investments meant to hedge against risk—are risky. Some people, however, have pointed to the conflict-averse culture at JPMorgan Chase as the main culprit in Iksil's huge losses.

Like any investment bank, JPMorgan Chase doesn't like to lose money. After seeing colleagues rebuked for reporting losses, many managers began to think the best way to avoid similar conflicts was to hide problems. In testimony before Carl Levin, the head of the U.S. Senate banking committee, a senior regulator named Scott Waterhouse reported an episode in which Dimon berated Douglas Braunstein, Chase's chief financial officer, for delivering negative reports. Here is an excerpt of the testimony:

> *Levin:* So apparently he [Dimon] had decided to stop the reports?
> *Waterhouse:* I took it that way, yes, sir.
> *Levin:* Did he raise his voice?
> *Waterhouse:* He did.

This may not seem like a big admission, but it revealed the tip of the iceberg of the contentious culture JPMorgan Chase didn't want anyone to talk about. As a result, no one wanted to be the bearer of bad news. This interacted with two other credos in JPMorgan Chase's culture: "Always have a follow-up list" and "Get stuff done." But what happens when there are problems to report? What if those problems are not amenable to instant checklists—what if resolving them requires some discussion, debate, and perhaps even disagreement?

Dimon is, by most reports and by the results, an excellent CEO. In discussing the London Whale, he says he himself didn't encourage enough divergent thinking to work its way up the organization chart. In other words, he

LEARNING OBJECTIVES

After studying this chapter, you should be able to:

1 Differentiate between the traditional and interactionist views of conflict.

2 Describe the three types of conflict and the two loci of conflict.

3 Outline the conflict process.

4 Contrast distributive and integrative bargaining.

5 Apply the five steps of the negotiation process.

6 Show how individual differences influence negotiations.

7 Assess the roles and functions of third-party negotiations.

created a culture that didn't tolerate opposing ideas and the communication of negative information. He told a *Forbes* reporter of several lessons he had learned: "Fighting complacency, asking hard questions instead of shying away from conflict, and matching controls and risk limits to the activities they govern."

In the end, Iksil, his boss, and his boss's boss were fired. In 2013, Dimon survived a vote by shareholders to replace him as chairman, and he and JPMorgan Chase live to fight another day. "I intend to be here for many more years," Dimon says. But the London Whale saga does show what can happen when a culture becomes so conflict-averse that any information that might provoke a clash is squelched.

———————

Sources: S. Schaefer, " Jamie Dimon: What I Learned from The London Whale," *Forbes* (April 10, 2013), downloaded May 28, 2013, from www.forbes.com/; J. Cassidy, "Will the London Whale Swallow Jamie Dimon?" *The New Yorker* (March 16, 2013), downloaded May 28, 2013, from www.newyorker .com/; and W. D. Cohan and B. McLean, "Jamie Dimon on the Line," *Vanity Fair* (November 2012), downloaded May 24, 2013, from www.vanityfair.com/.

As we see in the JP Morgan Chase example, the presence and absence of conflict and negotiation are often complex—and controversial—interpersonal processes. While we generally see conflict as a negative topic and negotiation as a positive one, what we deem positive or negative often depends on our perspective. Let's gauge how you handle conflict with the following self-assessment.

SELF-ASSESSMENT LIBRARY

What's My Preferred Conflict-Handling Style?

In the Self-Assessment Library (available in MyManagementLab), take assessment II.C.5 (What's My Preferred Conflict-Handling Style?), and answer the following questions.

1. Judging from your highest score, what's your primary conflict-handling style?
2. Do you think your style varies, depending on the situation?
3. Would you like to change any aspects of your conflict-handling style?

A Definition of Conflict

1 Differentiate between the traditional and interactionist views of conflict.

There has been no shortage of definitions of *conflict*,[1] but common to most is the idea that conflict is a perception. If no one is aware of a conflict, then it is generally agreed no conflict exists. Also needed to begin the conflict process are opposition or incompatibility and interaction.

We define **conflict** broadly as a process that begins when one party perceives another party has or is about to negatively affect something the first party cares about.[2] Conflict describes the point in ongoing activity when interaction

conflict *A process that begins when one party perceives that another party has negatively affected, or is about to negatively affect, something that the first party cares about.*

becomes interparty disagreement. There is a wide range of conflicts people experience in organizations: incompatibility of goals, differences over interpretations of facts, disagreements based on behavioral expectations, and the like. Our definition covers the full range of conflict levels from overt and violent acts to subtle forms of disagreement.

There has been disagreement over the role of conflict in groups and organizations. One school of thought argues that conflict must be avoided—that it indicates a malfunctioning within the group. We call this the *traditional* view. Another perspective proposes not only that conflict can be a positive force in a group but that some conflict is absolutely necessary for a group to perform effectively. We label this the *interactionist* view. Let's take a closer look at each.

The Traditional View of Conflict

traditional view of conflict *The belief that all conflict is harmful and must be avoided.*

The **traditional view of conflict** was consistent with attitudes about group behavior that prevailed in the 1930s and 1940s. Conflict was seen as a dysfunctional outcome resulting from poor communication, a lack of openness and trust between people, and the failure of managers to be responsive to the needs and aspirations of their employees. Conflict was discussed with the terms *violence*, *destruction*, and *irrationality*.

While the idea that all conflict is bad and should be avoided certainly offers a simple approach to looking at the behavior of people who create disagreements, researchers realized that some level of conflict was inevitable. We need merely study the causes of conflict and correct those malfunctions to improve group and organizational performance.

The Interactionist View of Conflict

interactionist view of conflict *The belief that conflict is not only a positive force in a group but also an absolute necessity for a group to perform effectively.*

The **interactionist view of conflict** encourages conflict on the grounds that a harmonious, peaceful, tranquil, and cooperative group is prone to becoming static, apathetic, and unresponsive to needs for change and innovation.[3] The major contribution of this view is recognizing that a minimal level of conflict can help keep a group viable, self-critical, and creative.

Photo 14-1 Under the leadership of George Zimmer, the founder of Men's Warehouse and its advertising spokesman, the retailer grew to a multi-million-dollar firm with 1,143 stores. But dysfunctional conflict between Zimmer and MW's board of directors resulted in the board removing Zimmer from his leadership role of executive chairman.

Source: Bloomberg via Getty Images.

functional conflict *Conflict that supports the goals of the group and improves its performance.*

dysfunctional conflict *Conflict that hinders group performance.*

The interactionist view does not propose that all conflicts are good. Rather, **functional conflict** supports the goals of the group, improves its performance, and is thus a constructive form of conflict. Conflict that hinders group performance is destructive or **dysfunctional conflict**. What differentiates functional from dysfunctional conflict? To a large degree, this depends on the *type* of conflict and the *locus* of conflict.

Next we review each of these in turn.

Types and Loci of Conflict

2 Describe the three types of conflict and the two loci of conflict.

task conflict *Conflict over content and goals of the work.*

relationship conflict *Conflict based on interpersonal relationships.*

process conflict *Conflict over how work gets done.*

Types of Conflict

One means of understanding conflict is to identify the *type* of disagreement, or what the conflict is about. Is it a disagreement about goals? Is it about people who just rub one another the wrong way? Or is it about the best way to get things done? Although each conflict is unique, researchers have classified conflicts into three categories: task, relationship, or process.

Task conflict relates to the content and goals of the work. **Relationship conflict** focuses on interpersonal relationships. **Process conflict** is about how the work gets done. Studies demonstrate that relationship conflicts, at least in work settings, are almost always dysfunctional.[4] Why? It appears that the friction and interpersonal hostilities inherent in relationship conflicts increase personality clashes and decrease mutual understanding, which hinders the completion of organizational tasks. Of the three types, relationship conflicts also appear to be the most psychologically exhausting to individuals.[5] Because they tend to revolve around personalities, you can see how relationship conflicts can become destructive. After all, we can't expect to change our co-workers' personalities, and we would generally take offense at criticisms directed at who we *are* as opposed to how we behave.

While scholars agree that relationship conflict is dysfunctional, there is considerably less agreement as to whether task and process conflicts are functional. Early research suggested that task conflict within groups was associated with higher group performance, but a recent review of 116 studies found that task conflict was essentially unrelated to group performance. However, there were factors that could create a relationship between conflict and performance.[6]

One such factor was whether the conflict included top management or occurred lower in the organization. Task conflict among top management teams was positively associated with their performance, whereas conflict lower in the organization was negatively associated with group performance. This review also found that it mattered whether other types of conflict were occurring at the same time. If task and relationship conflict occurred together, task conflict was more likely negative, whereas if task conflict occurred by itself, it more likely was positive. Finally, some scholars have argued that the strength of conflict is important—if task conflict is very low, people aren't really engaged or addressing the important issues. If task conflict is too high, however, infighting will quickly degenerate into personality conflict. According to this view, moderate levels of task conflict are optimal. Supporting this argument, one study in China found that moderate levels of task conflict in the early development stage increased creativity in groups, but high levels decreased team performance.[7]

Finally, the personalities of the teams appear to matter. A recent study demonstrated that teams made up of individuals who are, on average, high in openness and emotional stability are better able to turn task conflict into increased group performance.[8] The reason may be that open and emotionally stable teams can put task conflict in perspective and focus on how the variance in ideas can help solve the problem, rather than letting it degenerate into relationship conflicts.

What about process conflict? Researchers found that process conflicts revolve around delegation and roles. Conflicts over delegation often revolve around shirking, and conflicts over roles can leave some group members feeling marginalized. Thus, process conflicts often become highly personalized and quickly devolve into relationship conflicts. It's also true, of course, that arguing about how to do something takes time away from actually doing it. We've all been part of groups in which the arguments and debates about roles and responsibilities seem to go nowhere.

Loci of Conflict

dyadic conflict *Conflict that occurs between two people.*

intragroup conflict *Conflict that occurs within a group or team.*

intergroup conflict *Conflict between different groups or teams.*

Another way to understand conflict is to consider its *locus,* or where the conflict occurs. Here, too, there are three basic types. **Dyadic conflict** is conflict between two people. **Intragroup conflict** occurs *within* a group or team. **Intergroup conflict** is conflict *between* groups or teams.

Nearly all the literature on task, relationship, and process conflict considers intragroup conflict (within the group). That makes sense given that groups and teams often exist only to perform a particular task. However, it doesn't necessarily tell us about the other loci of conflict. For example, research has found that for intragroup task conflict to influence performance within the team, it is important that the teams have a supportive climate in which mistakes aren't penalized and every team member "[has] the other's back."[9] But is this concept useful for understanding the effects of intergroup conflict for the organization? Think about, say, NFL football. For a team to adapt and improve, perhaps a certain amount of task conflict is good for team performance, especially when the team members support one another. But would we care whether members from one team supported members from another team? Probably not. In fact, if groups are competing with one another so that only one team can "win," interteam conflict seems almost inevitable. When is that helpful, and when is it a concern?

One study that did focus on intergroup conflict found an interplay between an individual's position within a group and the way that individual managed conflict between groups. Group members who were relatively peripheral in their own groups were better at resolving conflicts between their group and another one. But this happened only when those peripheral members were still accountable to their group.[10] Thus, being at the core of your work group does not necessarily make you the best person to manage conflict with other groups.

Another intriguing question about loci is whether conflicts interact or buffer one another. Assume, for example, that Dana and Scott are on the same team. What happens if they don't get along interpersonally (dyadic conflict) *and* their team also has high personality conflict? What happens to their team if two other team members, Shawna and Justin, do get along well? It's also possible to ask this question at the intragroup and intergroup level. Intense intergroup conflict can be quite stressful to group members and might well affect the way they interact. One study found, for example, that high levels of conflict between teams caused individuals to focus on complying with norms within their teams.[11]

Thus, understanding functional and dysfunctional conflict requires not only that we identify the type of conflict; we also need to know where it occurs. It's possible that while the concepts of task, relationship, and process conflict are useful in understanding intragroup or even dyadic conflict, they are less useful in explaining the effects of intergroup conflict.

In sum, the traditional view that all conflict should be eliminated is short-sighted. The interactionist view that conflict can stimulate active discussion without spilling over into negative, disruptive emotions is incomplete. Thinking about conflict in terms of type and locus helps us realize that it is probably inevitable in most organizations, and when it does occur, we can attempt to make it as productive as possible.

The Conflict Process

3   Outline the conflict process.

conflict process   *A process that has five stages: potential opposition or incompatibility, cognition and personalization, intentions, behavior, and outcomes.*

The **conflict process** has five stages: potential opposition or incompatibility, cognition and personalization, intentions, behavior, and outcomes (see Exhibit 14-1).

Stage I: Potential Opposition or Incompatibility

The first stage of conflict is the appearance of conditions—causes or sources—that create opportunities for it to arise. These conditions *need not* lead directly to conflict, but one of them is necessary if it is to surface. We group the conditions into three general categories: communication, structure, and personal variables.

Communication   Susan had worked in supply chain management at Bristol-Myers Squibb for three years. She enjoyed her work largely because her manager, Harry, was a great boss. Then Harry was promoted and Chuck took his place. Six months later, Susan says her job is frustrating. "Harry and I were on the same wavelength. It's not that way with Chuck. He tells me something, and I do it. Then he tells me I did it wrong. I think he means one thing but says something else. It's been like this since the day he arrived. I don't think a day goes by when he isn't yelling at me for something. You know, there are some people you just find it easy to communicate with. Well, Chuck isn't one of those!"

Susan's comments illustrate that communication can be a source of conflict.[12] Her experience represents the opposing forces that arise from semantic

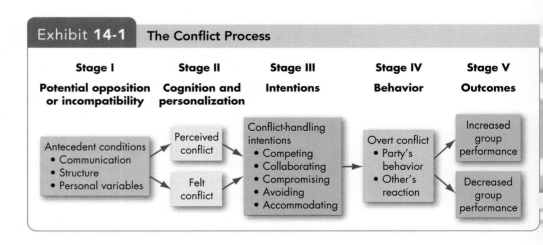

Exhibit **14-1**   The Conflict Process

Stage I	Stage II	Stage III	Stage IV	Stage V
Potential opposition or incompatibility	Cognition and personalization	Intentions	Behavior	Outcomes

Antecedent conditions
• Communication
• Structure
• Personal variables

Perceived conflict

Felt conflict

Conflict-handling intentions
• Competing
• Collaborating
• Compromising
• Avoiding
• Accommodating

Overt conflict
• Party's behavior
• Other's reaction

Increased group performance

Decreased group performance

difficulties, misunderstandings, and "noise" in the communication channel (Chapter 11). These factors, along with jargon and insufficient information, can be barriers to communication and potential antecedent conditions to conflict. The potential for conflict has also been found to increase with too little or *too much* communication. Communication is functional up to a point, after which it is possible to overcommunicate, increasing the potential for conflict.

Structure   Charlotte is a salesperson and Mercedes is the company credit manager at Portland Furniture Mart, a large discount furniture retailer. The women have known each other for years and have much in common: They live two blocks apart, and their oldest daughters attend the same middle school and are best friends. If Charlotte and Mercedes had different jobs, they might be friends, but at work they constantly disagree. Charlotte's job is to sell furniture, and she does it well. Most of her sales are made on credit. Because Mercedes' job is to minimize credit losses, she regularly has to turn down the credit applications of Charlotte's customers. It's nothing personal between the women; the requirements of their jobs just bring them into conflict.

The conflicts between Charlotte and Mercedes are structural in nature. The term *structure* in this context includes variables such as size of group, degree of specialization in tasks assigned to group members, jurisdictional clarity, member–goal compatibility, leadership styles, reward systems, and degree of dependence between groups.

Size and specialization can stimulate conflict. The larger the group and the more specialized its activities, the greater the likelihood of conflict. Tenure and conflict are inversely related; potential for conflict is greatest when group members are younger and when turnover is high.

The greater the ambiguity about where responsibility for actions lies, the greater the potential for conflict. Jurisdictional ambiguities increase intergroup fighting for control of resources and territory. Diversity of goals among groups is also a major source of conflict. When groups within an organization seek diverse ends, some of which—like sales and credit at Portland Furniture Mart—are inherently at odds, opportunities for conflict increase. Reward systems, too, create conflict when one member's gain comes at another's expense. Finally, if a group is dependent on another group (in contrast to the two being mutually independent), or if interdependence allows one group to gain at another's expense, opposing forces are stimulated.

Personal Variables   Have you ever met someone you immediately disliked? Perhaps you disagreed with most of his opinions. Even insignificant characteristics—the sound of his voice, his facial expressions, his word choice—may have annoyed you. Sometimes our impressions are negative. When you have to work with people you don't like, the potential for conflict arises.

Our last category of potential sources of conflict is personal variables, which include personality, emotions, and values. People high in the personality traits of disagreeableness, neuroticism, or self-monitoring are prone to tangle with other people more often—and to react poorly when conflicts occur.[13] Emotions can also cause conflict even when they are not directed at others. An employee who shows up to work irate from her hectic morning commute may carry that anger into her workday and result in a tension-filled meeting.[14] People are furthermore more likely to cause conflict when their values are opposed.

Stage II: Cognition and Personalization

If the conditions cited in Stage I negatively affect something one party cares about, then the potential for opposition or incompatibility becomes actualized in the second stage.

perceived conflict *Awareness by one or more parties of the existence of conditions that create opportunities for conflict to arise.*

felt conflict *Emotional involvement in a conflict that creates anxiety, tenseness, frustration, or hostility.*

As we noted in our definition of conflict, one or more of the parties must be aware that antecedent conditions exist. However, because a disagreement is a **perceived conflict** does not mean it is personalized. In other words, "*A* may be aware that *B* and *A* are in serious disagreement . . . but it may not make *A* tense or anxious, and it may have no effect whatsoever on *A*'s affection toward *B*."[15] It is at the **felt conflict** level, when individuals become emotionally involved, that they experience anxiety, tension, frustration, or hostility.

Keep in mind two points. First, Stage II is important because it's where conflict issues tend to be defined, where the parties decide what the conflict is about.[16] If our salary disagreement is a zero-sum situation (the increase in pay you want means there will be that much less for me), I am going to be far less willing to compromise than if I frame the conflict as a potential win–win situation (the dollars in the salary pool might be increased so both of us could get the added pay we want). The definition of conflict is important because it delineates the set of possible settlements.

Our second point is that emotions play a major role in shaping perceptions.[17] Negative emotions allow us to oversimplify issues, lose trust, and put negative interpretations on the other party's behavior.[18] In contrast, positive feelings increase our tendency to see potential relationships among elements of a problem, take a broader view of the situation, and develop innovative solutions.[19]

Stage III: Intentions

intentions *Decisions to act in a given way.*

Intentions intervene between people's perceptions and emotions and their overt behavior. They are decisions to act in a given way.[20]

Intentions are a distinct stage because we have to infer the other's intent to know how to respond to his or her behavior. Many conflicts escalate simply because one party attributes the wrong intentions to the other. There is slippage between intentions and behavior, so behavior does not always accurately reflect a person's intentions.

Exhibit 14-2 represents one author's effort to identify the primary conflict-handling intentions. Using two dimensions—*cooperativeness* (the degree to which one party attempts to satisfy the other party's concerns) and *assertiveness* (the degree to which one party attempts to satisfy his or her own concerns)— we can identify five conflict-handling intentions: *competing* (assertive and

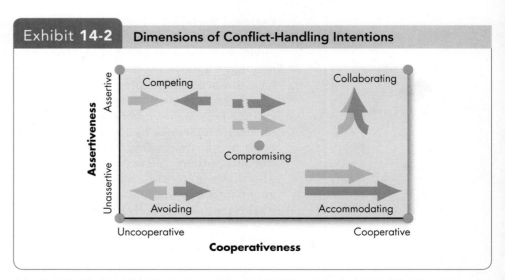

Exhibit 14-2   **Dimensions of Conflict-Handling Intentions**

Source: Figure from "Conflict and Negotiation Processes in Organizations" by K. Thomas in *Handbook of Industrial and Organizational Psychology*, 2/e, Vol. 3, ed. by M. D. Dunnette and L. M. Hough, p. 668 (Palo Alto, CA: Consulting Psychologists Press, 1992).

uncooperative), *collaborating* (assertive and cooperative), *avoiding* (unassertive and uncooperative), *accommodating* (unassertive and cooperative), and *compromising* (midrange on both assertiveness and cooperativeness).[21]

Competing   When one person seeks to satisfy his or her own interests regardless of the impact on the other parties to the conflict, that person is **competing**. You compete when you place a bet that only one person can win, for example.

competing   *A desire to satisfy one's interests, regardless of the impact on the other party to the conflict.*

Collaborating   When parties in conflict each desire to fully satisfy the concerns of all parties, there is cooperation and a search for a mutually beneficial outcome. In **collaborating**, parties intend to solve a problem by clarifying differences rather than by accommodating various points of view. If you attempt to find a win–win solution that allows both parties' goals to be completely achieved, that's collaborating.

collaborating   *A situation in which the parties to a conflict each desire to satisfy fully the concerns of all parties.*

Avoiding   A person may recognize a conflict exists and want to withdraw from or suppress it. Examples of **avoiding** include trying to ignore a conflict and avoiding others with whom you disagree.

avoiding   *The desire to withdraw from or suppress a conflict.*

Accommodating   A party who seeks to appease an opponent may be willing to place the opponent's interests above his or her own, sacrificing to maintain the relationship. We refer to this intention as **accommodating**. Supporting someone else's opinion despite your reservations about it, for example, is accommodating.

accommodating   *The willingness of one party in a conflict to place the opponent's interests above his or her own.*

Compromising   In **compromising**, there is no winner or loser. Rather, there is a willingness to ration the object of the conflict and accept a solution with incomplete satisfaction of both parties' concerns. The distinguishing characteristic of compromising, therefore, is that each party intends to give up something.

compromising   *A situation in which each party to a conflict is willing to give up something.*

Intentions are not always fixed. During the course of a conflict, they might change if the parties are able to see the other's point of view or respond emotionally to the other's behavior. People generally have preferences among the five conflict-handling intentions. We can predict a person's intentions rather well from a combination of intellectual and personality characteristics.

Stage IV: Behavior

When most people think of conflict, they tend to focus on Stage IV because this is where conflicts become visible. The behavior stage includes statements, actions, and reactions made by conflicting parties, usually as overt attempts to implement their own intentions. As a result of miscalculations or unskilled enactments, overt behaviors sometimes deviate from original intentions.[22]

Stage IV is a dynamic process of interaction. For example, you make a demand on me, I respond by arguing, you threaten me, I threaten you back, and so on. Exhibit 14-3 provides a way of visualizing conflict behavior. All conflicts exist somewhere along this continuum. At the lower part are conflicts characterized by subtle, indirect, and highly controlled forms of tension, such as a student questioning in class a point the instructor has just made. Conflict intensities escalate as they move upward along the continuum until they become highly destructive. Strikes, riots, and wars clearly fall in this upper range. Conflicts that reach the upper ranges of the continuum are almost always dysfunctional. Functional conflicts are typically confined to the lower range of the continuum.

If a conflict is dysfunctional, what can the parties do to de-escalate it? Or, conversely, what options exist if conflict is too low and needs to be increased? This brings us to techniques of **conflict management**. Exhibit 14-4 lists the major resolution

conflict management   *The use of resolution and stimulation techniques to achieve the desired level of conflict.*

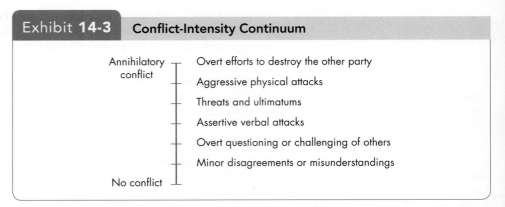

Exhibit **14-3**   Conflict-Intensity Continuum

Sources: Based on S. P. Robbins, *Managing Organizational Conflict: A Nontraditional Approach* (Upper Saddle River, NJ: Prentice Hall, 1974), pp. 93–97; and F. Glasi, "The Process of Conflict Escalation and the Roles of Third Parties," in G. B. J. Bomers and R. Peterson (eds.), *Conflict Management and Industrial Relations* (Boston: Kluwer-Nijhoff, 1982), pp. 119–140.

and stimulation techniques that allow managers to control conflict levels. We have already described several as conflict-handling intentions. Under ideal conditions, a person's intentions should translate into comparable behaviors.

Stage V: Outcomes

The action–reaction interplay between conflicting parties creates consequences. As our model demonstrates (see Exhibit 14-1), these outcomes may be functional, if the conflict improves the group's performance, or dysfunctional, if it hinders performance.

Exhibit **14-4**   Conflict Management Techniques

Conflict-Resolution Techniques

Problem solving	Face-to-face meeting of the conflicting parties for the purpose of identifying the problem and resolving it through open discussion.
Superordinate goals	Creating a shared goal that cannot be attained without the cooperation of each of the conflicting parties.
Expansion of resources	When a conflict is caused by the scarcity of a resource (for example, money, promotion, opportunities, office space), expansion of the resource can create a win-win solution.
Avoidance	Withdrawal from or suppression of the conflict.
Smoothing	Playing down differences while emphasizing common interests between the conflicting parties.
Compromise	Each party to the conflict gives up something of value.
Authoritative command	Management uses its formal authority to resolve the conflict and then communicates its desires to the parties involved.
Altering the human variable	Using behavioral change techniques such as human relations training to alter attitudes and behaviors that cause conflict.
Altering the structural variables	Changing the formal organization structure and the interaction patterns of conflicting parties through job redesign, transfers, creation of coordinating positions, and the like.

Conflict-Stimulation Techniques

Communication	Using ambiguous or threatening messages to increase conflict levels.
Bringing in outsiders	Adding employees to a group whose backgrounds, values, attitudes, or managerial styles differ from those of present members.
Restructuring the organization	Realigning work groups, altering rules and regulations, increasing interdependence, and making similar structural changes to disrupt the status quo.
Appointing a devil's advocate	Designating a critic to purposely argue against the majority positions held by the group.

Source: Based on S. P. Robbins, *Managing Organizational Conflict: A Nontraditional Approach* (Upper Saddle River, NJ: Prentice Hall, 1974), pp. 59–89.

Functional Outcomes How might conflict act as a force to increase group performance? It is hard to visualize a situation in which open or violent aggression could be functional. But it's possible to see how low or moderate levels of conflict could improve group effectiveness. Note that all our examples focus on task and process conflicts and exclude the relationship variety.

Conflict is constructive when it improves the quality of decisions, stimulates creativity and innovation, encourages interest and curiosity among group members, provides the medium for problems to be aired and tensions released, and fosters self-evaluation and change. Conflict is an antidote for groupthink. It doesn't allow the group to passively rubber-stamp decisions that may be based on weak assumptions, inadequate consideration of relevant alternatives, or other debilities. Conflict challenges the status quo and furthers the creation of new ideas, promotes reassessment of group goals and activities, and increases the probability that the group will respond to change. An open discussion focused on higher-order goals can make functional outcomes more likely. Groups that are extremely polarized do not manage their underlying disagreements effectively and tend to accept suboptimal solutions, or they avoid making decisions altogether rather than working out the conflict.[23] Research studies in diverse settings confirm the functionality of active discussion. Team members with greater differences in work styles and experience also tend to share more information with one another.[24]

These observations lead us to predict benefits to organizations from the increasing cultural diversity of the workforce. And that's what the evidence indicates, under most conditions. Heterogeneity among group and organization members can increase creativity, improve the quality of decisions, and facilitate change by enhancing member flexibility.[25] Researchers compared decision-making groups composed of all-Caucasian individuals with groups that also contained members from Asian, Hispanic, and Black ethnic groups. The ethnically diverse groups produced more effective and more feasible ideas, and the unique ideas they generated tended to be higher quality than the unique ideas produced by the all-Caucasian group.

Photo 14-2 IBM benefits from the diversity of employees like Greg Labows (left) and Tsegga Medhin, who engage in functional conflict that improves the company's performance. At IBM, diversity drives innovation. For innovation to flourish, IBM relies on the creative tension from different ideas, experiences, perspectives, skills, interests, and thinking.

Source: Chris Seward/MCT/Newscom.

Dysfunctional Outcomes   The destructive consequences of conflict on the performance of a group or an organization are generally well known: Uncontrolled opposition breeds discontent, which acts to dissolve common ties and eventually leads to the destruction of the group. And, of course, a substantial body of literature documents how dysfunctional conflicts can reduce group effectiveness.[26] Among the undesirable consequences are poor communication, reductions in group cohesiveness, and subordination of group goals to the primacy of infighting among members. All forms of conflict—even the functional varieties—appear to reduce group member satisfaction and trust.[27] When active discussions turn into open conflicts between members, information sharing between members decreases significantly.[28] At the extreme, conflict can bring group functioning to a halt and threaten the group's survival.

We noted that diversity can usually improve group performance and decision making. However, if differences of opinion open up along demographic fault lines, harmful conflicts result and information sharing decreases.[29] For example, if differences of opinion in a gender-diverse team line up so that men all hold one opinion and women hold another, group members tend to stop listening to one another. They fall into ingroup favoritism and won't take the other side's point of view into consideration. Managers in this situation need to pay special attention to these fault lines and emphasize the shared goals of the team.

Managing Functional Conflict   If managers recognize that in some situations conflict can be beneficial, what can they do to manage conflict effectively in their organizations? Let's look at some approaches organizations are using to encourage their people to challenge the system and develop fresh ideas.

One of the keys to minimizing counterproductive conflicts is recognizing when there really is a disagreement. Many apparent conflicts are due to people using different language to discuss the same general course of action. For example, someone in marketing might focus on "distribution problems," while someone from operations will talk about "supply chain management" to describe essentially the same issue. Successful conflict management recognizes these different approaches and attempts to resolve them by encouraging open, frank discussion focused on interests rather than issues (we'll have more to say about this when we contrast distributive and integrative bargaining styles). Another approach is to have opposing groups pick parts of the solution that are most important to them and then focus on how each side can get its top needs satisfied. Neither side may get exactly what it wants, but each side will get the most important parts of its agenda.[30]

Groups that resolve conflicts successfully discuss differences of opinion openly and are prepared to manage conflict when it arises.[31] The most disruptive conflicts are those that are never addressed directly. An open discussion makes it much easier to develop a shared perception of the problems at hand; it also allows groups to work toward a mutually acceptable solution. Managers need to emphasize shared interests in resolving conflicts, so groups that disagree with one another don't become too entrenched in their points of view and start to take the conflicts personally. Groups with cooperative conflict styles and a strong underlying identification to the overall group goals are more effective than groups with a competitive style.[32]

Differences across countries in conflict resolution strategies may be based on collectivistic tendencies and motives.[33] Collectivist cultures see people as deeply embedded in social situations, whereas individualist cultures see them as autonomous. As a result, collectivists are more likely to seek to preserve relationships and promote the good of the group as a whole. They will avoid direct expression of conflicts, preferring indirect methods for resolving differences of opinion. Collectivists may also be more interested in demonstrations of concern and working through third parties to resolve disputes, whereas individualists will be more likely to confront differences of opinion directly and openly.

Some research does support this theory. Compared to collectivist Japanese negotiators, their more individualist U.S. counterparts are more likely to see offers from their counterparts as unfair and to reject them. Another study revealed that whereas U.S. managers were more likely to use competing tactics in the face of conflicts, compromising and avoiding are the most preferred methods of conflict management in China.[34] Interview data, however, suggests that top management teams in Chinese high-technology firms prefer collaboration even more than compromising and avoiding.[35]

Having considered conflict—its nature, causes, and consequences—we now turn to negotiation, which often resolves conflict.

Negotiation

4 Contrast distributive and integrative bargaining.

Negotiation permeates the interactions of almost everyone in groups and organizations. There's the obvious: Labor bargains with management. There's the not-so-obvious: Managers negotiate with employees, peers, and bosses; salespeople negotiate with customers; purchasing agents negotiate with suppliers. And there's the subtle: An employee agrees to cover for a colleague for a few minutes in exchange for future benefit. In today's loosely structured organizations, in which members work with colleagues over whom they have no direct authority and with whom they may not even share a common boss, negotiation skills are critical.

negotiation *A process in which two or more parties exchange goods or services and attempt to agree on the exchange rate for them.*

We can define **negotiation** as a process that occurs when two or more parties decide how to allocate scarce resources.[36] Although we commonly think of the outcomes of negotiation in one-shot economic terms, like negotiating over the price of a car, every negotiation in organizations also affects the relationship between negotiators and the way negotiators feel about themselves.[37] Depending on how much the parties are going to interact with one another, sometimes maintaining the social relationship and behaving ethically will be just as important as achieving an immediate outcome of bargaining. Note that we use the terms *negotiation* and *bargaining* interchangeably. In this section, we contrast two bargaining strategies, provide a model of the negotiation process, ascertain the role of individual differences in negotiation effectiveness, and take a brief look at third-party negotiations.

Bargaining Strategies

There are two general approaches to negotiation—*distributive bargaining* and *integrative bargaining*.[38] As Exhibit 14-5 shows, they differ in their goal and motivation, focus, interests, information sharing, and duration of relationship. Let's define each and illustrate the differences.

distributive bargaining *Negotiation that seeks to divide up a fixed amount of resources; a win–lose situation.*

Distributive Bargaining   You see a used car advertised for sale online that looks great. You go see the car. It's perfect, and you want it. The owner tells you the asking price. You don't want to pay that much. The two of you negotiate. The negotiating strategy you're engaging in is called **distributive bargaining**. Its identifying feature is that it operates under zero-sum conditions—that is, any gain I make is at your expense, and vice versa. Every dollar you can get the seller to cut from the car's price is a dollar you save, and every dollar the seller

Exhibit 14-5   Distributive Versus Integrative Bargaining

Bargaining Characteristic	Distributive Bargaining	Integrative Bargaining
Goal	Get as much of the pie as possible	Expand the pie so that both parties are satisfied
Motivation	Win–lose	Win–win
Focus	Positions ("I can't go beyond this point on this issue.")	Interests ("Can you explain why this issue is so important to you?")
Interests	Opposed	Congruent
Information sharing	Low (Sharing information will only allow other party to take advantage)	High (Sharing information will allow each party to find ways to satisfy interests of each party)
Duration of relationship	Short term	Long term

fixed pie *The belief that there is only a set amount of goods or services to be divvied up between the parties.*

can get from you comes at your expense. The essence of distributive bargaining is negotiating over who gets what share of a fixed pie. By **fixed pie**, we mean a set amount of goods or services to be divvied up. When the pie is fixed, or the parties believe it is, they tend to bargain distributively.

The most widely cited example of distributive bargaining may be labor–management negotiations over wages. Typically, labor's representatives come to the bargaining table determined to get as much money as possible from management. Because every cent labor negotiates increases management's costs, each party bargains aggressively and treats the other as an opponent to defeat.

The essence of distributive bargaining is depicted in Exhibit 14-6. Parties *A* and *B* represent two negotiators. Each has a *target point* that defines what he or she would like to achieve. Each also has a *resistance point,* which marks the lowest acceptable outcome—the point below which the party would break off negotiations rather than accept a less favorable settlement. The area between these two points makes up each party's aspiration range. As long as there is some overlap between *A*'s and *B*'s aspiration ranges, there exists a settlement range in which each one's aspirations can be met.

When you are engaged in distributive bargaining, one of the best things you can do is make the first offer, and make it an aggressive one. Making the first offer shows power; individuals in power are much more likely to make initial offers, speak first at meetings, and thereby gain the advantage. Another reason this is a good strategy is the anchoring bias, mentioned in Chapter 6. People tend to fixate on initial information. Once that anchoring point is set, they fail

Exhibit 14-6   Staking Out the Bargaining Zone

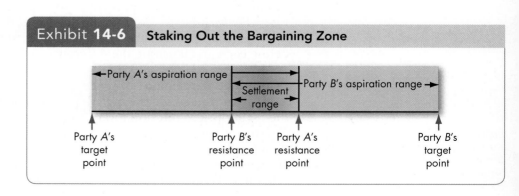

to adequately adjust it based on subsequent information. A savvy negotiator sets an anchor with the initial offer, and scores of negotiation studies show that such anchors greatly favor the person who sets them.[39]

Say you have a job offer, and your prospective employer asks you what sort of starting salary you'd want. You've just been given a gift—you have a chance to set the anchor, meaning you should ask for the highest salary you think the employer could reasonably offer. Asking for a million dollars is only going to make most of us look ridiculous, which is why we suggest being on the high end of what you think is *reasonable*. Too often, we err on the side of caution, afraid of scaring off the employer and thus settling for far too little. It *is* possible to scare off an employer, and it's true employers don't like candidates to be assertive in salary negotiations, but liking isn't the same as doing what it takes to hire or retain someone.[40] What happens much more often is that we ask for less than we could have obtained.

Another distributive bargaining tactic is revealing a deadline. Erin is a human resources manager. She is negotiating salary with Ron, who is a highly sought-after new hire. Because Ron knows the company needs him, he plays hardball and asks for an extraordinary salary and benefit package. Erin tells Ron the company can't meet his requirements. Ron tells Erin he is going to have to think things over. Worried the company is going to lose Ron to a competitor, Erin tells Ron she is under time pressure and needs to reach an agreement with him immediately, or she will have to offer the job to another candidate. Would you consider Erin to be a savvy negotiator? Well, she is. Negotiators who reveal deadlines speed concessions from their negotiating counterparts, making them reconsider their position. Even though negotiators don't *think* this tactic works, in reality, negotiators who reveal deadlines do better.[41]

Integrative Bargaining   Jake is a 5-year-old Chicago luxury boutique owned by Jim Wetzel and Lance Lawson. In the early days of the business, Wetzel and Lawson moved millions of dollars of merchandise from many up-and-coming designers. They developed such a good rapport that many designers would send allotments to Jake without requiring advance payment. When the economy soured in 2008, Jake had trouble selling inventory, and designers were not being paid for what they had shipped to the store. Despite the fact that many designers were willing to work with the store on a delayed payment plan, Wetzel and Lawson stopped returning their calls. Lamented one designer, Doo-Ri Chung, "You kind of feel this familiarity with people who supported you for so long. When they have cash-flow issues, you want to make sure you are there for them as well."[42] Ms. Chung's attitude shows the promise of **integrative bargaining**. In contrast to distributive bargaining, integrative bargaining assumes that one or more of the possible settlements can create a win–win solution. Of course, as the Jake example shows and we'll highlight later, both parties must be engaged for integrative bargaining to work.

In terms of intraorganizational behavior, integrative bargaining is preferable to distributive bargaining because the former builds long-term relationships. Integrative bargaining bonds negotiators and allows them to leave the bargaining table feeling they have achieved a victory. Distributive bargaining, however, leaves one party a loser. It tends to build animosity and deepen divisions when people have to work together on an ongoing basis. Research shows that over repeated bargaining episodes, a losing party who feels positive about the negotiation outcome is much more likely to bargain cooperatively in subsequent negotiations. This points to an important advantage of integrative negotiations: Even when you win, you want your opponent to feel good about the negotiation.[43]

Why, then, don't we see more integrative bargaining in organizations? The answer lies in the conditions necessary for it to succeed. These include opposing

integrative bargaining   *Negotiation that seeks one or more settlements that can create a win–win solution.*

Photo 14-3 Officials of United Auto Workers (left) and Ford Motor Company are committed to integrative bargaining in negotiating contracts. Both UAW and Ford share information that addresses difficult business challenges and work toward providing mutually acceptable solutions for win–win settlements that boost the company's competitiveness.

parties who are open with information and candid about concerns, are sensitive to the other's needs and trust, and maintain flexibility.[44] Because these conditions seldom exist in organizations, negotiations often take a win-at-any-cost dynamic.

Individuals who bargain in teams reach more integrative agreements than those who bargain individually because more ideas are generated when more people are at the bargaining table.[45] Another way to achieve higher joint-gain settlements is to put more issues on the table. The more negotiable issues introduced into a negotiation, the more opportunity for "logrolling," where issues are traded off according to individual different preferences. This creates better outcomes for each side than if they negotiated each issue individually.[46] Focus also on the underlying interests of both sides rather than on issues. In other words, it is better to concentrate on *why* an employee wants a raise rather than to focus just on the raise amount—some unseen potential for integrative outcomes may arise if both sides concentrate on what they really want rather than on specific items they're bargaining over. Typically, it's easier to concentrate on underlying interests when parties stay focused on broad, overall goals rather than on immediate outcomes of a specific decision.[47] Negotiations when both parties are focused on learning and understanding the other side tend to yield higher joint outcomes than those in which parties are more interested in their individual bottom-line outcomes.[48]

Compromise may be your worst enemy in negotiating a win–win agreement. Compromising reduces the pressure to bargain integratively. After all, if you or your opponent caves in easily, no one needs to be creative to reach a settlement. People then settle for less than they could have obtained if they had been forced to consider the other party's interests, trade off issues, and be creative.[49] Consider a classic example in which two sisters are arguing over who gets an orange. Unknown to them, one sister wants the orange to drink the juice, whereas the

"Teams Negotiate Better than Individuals in Collectivistic Cultures"

According to a recent study, this statement appears to be false.

In general, the literature has suggested that teams negotiate more effectively than individuals negotiating alone. Some evidence indicates that team negotiations create more ambitious goals, and that teams communicate more with each other than individual negotiators do.

Commonsense suggests that if this is indeed the case, it is especially true in collectivistic cultures, where individuals are more likely to think of collective goals and be more comfortable working in teams. A recent study of the negotiation of teams in the United States and in Taiwan, however,

suggests that this commonsense is wrong. The researchers conducted two studies comparing two-person teams with individual negotiators. They defined negotiating effectiveness as the degree to which the negotiation produced an optimal outcome for both sides. U.S. teams did better than solo individuals in both studies. In Taiwan, solo individuals did better than teams.

Why did this happen? The researchers determined that in Taiwan norms respecting harmony already exist, and negotiating in teams only amplifies that tendency. This poses a problem because when norms for cooperation are exceptionally high, teams "satisfice" to avoid conflict. In contrast, because

the United States is individualistic, solo teams may only amplify their tendencies to focus solely on their own interests, which makes reaching integrative solutions harder.

Overall, these findings suggest that negotiating individually works best in collectivistic cultures, and negotiating in teams works best in individualistic cultures.

Sources: Based on M. J. Gelfand et al., "Toward a Culture-by-Context Perspective on Negotiation: Negotiating Teams in the United States and Taiwan," *Journal of Applied Psychology* 98 (2013), pp. 504–513; and A. Graf, S. T. Koeszegi, and E.-M. Pesendorfer, "Electronic Negotiations in Intercultural Interfirm Relationships," *Journal of Managerial Psychology* 25 (2010), pp. 495–512.

other wants the orange peel to bake a cake. If one sister capitulates and gives the other sister the orange, they will not be forced to explore their reasons for wanting the orange, and thus they will never find the win–win solution: They could *each* have the orange because they want different parts.

The Negotiation Process

5 Apply the five steps of the negotiation process.

Exhibit 14-7 provides a simplified model of the negotiation process. It views negotiation as made up of five steps: (1) preparation and planning, (2) definition of ground rules, (3) clarification and justification, (4) bargaining and problem solving, and (5) closure and implementation.[50]

Preparation and Planning   Before you start negotiating, do your homework. What's the nature of the conflict? What's the history leading up to this negotiation? Who's involved and what are their perceptions of the conflict? What do you want from the negotiation? What are *your* goals? If you're a supply manager at Dell Computer, for instance, and your goal is to get a significant cost reduction from your supplier of keyboards, make sure this goal stays paramount in discussions and doesn't get overshadowed by other issues. It helps to put your goals in writing and develop a range of outcomes—from "most hopeful" to "minimally acceptable"—to keep your attention focused.

You should assess what you think are the other party's goals. What are they likely to ask? How entrenched is their position likely to be? What intangible or hidden interests may be important to them? On what might they be willing to settle? When you can anticipate your opponent's position, you are better equipped to counter arguments with facts and figures that support your position.

Relationships change as a result of negotiation, so take that into consideration. If you could "win" a negotiation but push the other side into resentment

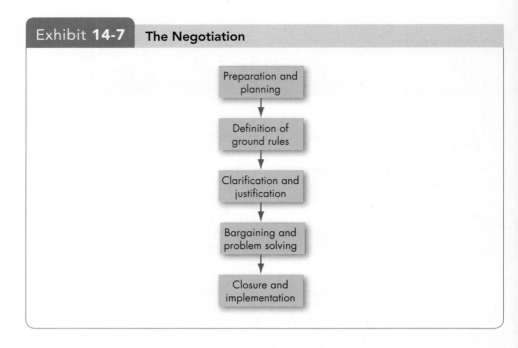

Exhibit 14-7   The Negotiation

- Preparation and planning
- Definition of ground rules
- Clarification and justification
- Bargaining and problem solving
- Closure and implementation

or animosity, it might be wiser to pursue a more compromising style. If preserving the relationship will make you seem easily exploited, you may consider a more aggressive style. As an example of how the tone of a relationship set in negotiations matters, people who feel good about the *process* of a job offer negotiation are more satisfied with their jobs and less likely to turn over a year later regardless of their actual *outcomes* from these negotiations.[51]

Once you've gathered your information, develop a strategy. For example, expert chess players know how they will respond to any given situation. You should determine your and the other side's **b**est **a**lternative **t**o a **n**egotiated **a**greement, or **BATNA**.[52] Your BATNA determines the lowest value acceptable to you for a negotiated agreement. Any offer you receive that is higher than your BATNA is better than an impasse. Conversely, you shouldn't expect success in your negotiation effort unless you're able to make the other side an offer it finds more attractive than its BATNA. If you go into your negotiation having a good idea of what the other party's BATNA is, you might be able to elicit a change even if you're not able to meet it. Think carefully about what the other side is willing to give up. People who underestimate their opponent's willingness to give on key issues before the negotiation even starts end up with lower outcomes from a negotiation.[53]

Definition of Ground Rules   Once you've done your planning and developed a strategy, you're ready to begin defining with the other party the ground rules and procedures of the negotiation itself. Who will do the negotiating? Where will it take place? What time constraints, if any, will apply? To what issues will negotiation be limited? Will you follow a specific procedure if an impasse is reached? During this phase, the parties will also exchange their initial proposals or demands.

Clarification and Justification   When you have exchanged initial positions, you and the other party will explain, amplify, clarify, bolster, and justify your original demands. This step needn't be confrontational. Rather, it's an opportunity for educating each other on the issues, why they are important, and how you arrived

BATNA   *The best alternative to a negotiated agreement; the least the individual should accept.*

at your initial demands. Provide the other party with any documentation that supports your position.

Bargaining and Problem Solving   The essence of the negotiation process is the actual give-and-take in trying to hash out an agreement. This is where both parties need to make concessions.

Closure and Implementation   The final step in the negotiation process is formalizing your agreement and developing procedures necessary for implementing and monitoring it. For major negotiations—from labor–management negotiations to bargaining over lease terms—this requires hammering out the specifics in a formal contract. For other cases, closure of the negotiation process is nothing more formal than a handshake.

Individual Differences in Negotiation Effectiveness

6 Show how individual differences influence negotiations.

Are some people better negotiators than others? The answer is complex. Four factors influence how effectively individuals negotiate: personality, mood/emotions, culture, and gender.

Personality Traits in Negotiation   Can you predict an opponent's negotiating tactics if you know something about his or her personality? Because personality and negotiation outcomes are related but only weakly, the answer is, at best, "sort of." Most research has focused on the Big Five trait of agreeableness, for obvious reasons—agreeable individuals are cooperative, compliant, kind, and conflict-averse. We might think such characteristics make agreeable individuals easy prey in negotiations, especially distributive ones. The evidence suggests, however, that overall agreeableness is weakly related to negotiation outcomes. Why is this the case?

glOBalization!

Trust Is an Issue

Research has shown that one of the greatest barriers in negotiating across cultures is trust. People in one culture are generally less trusting of those in another, including when negotiating.

One study of Indian and U.S. negotiators found, for example, that respondents reported having less trust in their cross-culture negotiation counterparts. These lower levels of trust were associated with lower discovery of common interests between parties, which occurred because cross-culture negotiators were less willing to disclose and solicit information.

Another study found that both U.S. and Chinese negotiators tended to have an ingroup bias, which led them to favor negotiating partners from their own cultures. For Chinese negotiators, this was particularly true when accountability requirements were high.

So what can we do to establish trust and reduce ingroup cultural favoritism? The first and foremost step is to recognize that it is critical to *build* trust: Try to get to know your counterpart, begin with small wins, and continue to communicate your interests and check your understanding of your counterpart's interests. The challenges

of cross-cultural negotiation mean that the tactics we've described in this chapter are even more important to successful negotiations.

Sources: Based on B. Gunia, J. Brett, and A. Nandkeolyar, "In Global Negotiations, It's All About Trust," *Harvard Business Review* (December 2012), p. 26; W. Liu, R. Friedman, and Y. Hong, "Culture and Accountability in Negotiation: Recognizing the Importance of In-Group Relations," *Organizational Behavior and Human Decision Processes* 117 (2012), pp. 221–234; and B. C. Gunia, J. M. Brett, A. K. Nandkeolyar, and D. Kamdar, "Paying a Price: Culture, Trust, and Negotiation Consequences," *Journal of Applied Psychology* 96, no. 4 (2010), pp. 774–789.

It appears that the degree to which agreeableness, and personality more generally, affects negotiation outcomes depends on the situation. The importance of being extraverted in negotiations, for example, will very much depend on how the other party reacts to someone who is assertive and enthusiastic. One complicating factor for agreeableness is that it has two facets: The tendency to be cooperative and compliant is one, but so is the tendency to be warm and empathetic.[54] It may be that while the former is a hindrance to negotiating favorable outcomes, the latter helps. Empathy, after all, is the ability to take the perspective of another person and to gain insight/understanding of them. We know so-called perspective-taking benefits integrative negotiations, so perhaps the null effect for agreeableness is due to the two tendencies pulling against one another. If this is the case, then the best negotiator is a competitive but empathetic one, and the worst is a gentle but empathetic one.

A recent study suggested that the type of negotiations matter as well. In this study, agreeable individuals reacted more positively and felt less stress (measured by their cortisol levels) in integrative negotiations than in distributive ones. Low levels of stress, in turn, made for more effective negotiation outcomes.[55] Similarly, in "hard-edged" distributive negotiations, where giving away information leads to a disadvantage, extraverted negotiators do less well because they tend to share more information than they should.[56]

Research suggests intelligence predicts negotiation effectiveness, but, as with personality, the effects aren't especially strong.[57] In a sense, these weak links mean you're not severely disadvantaged, even if you're an agreeable extravert, when it's time to negotiate. We all can learn to be better negotiators.[58]

Using Empathy to Negotiate More Ethically

You may have noticed that much of our advice for negotiating effectively depends on understanding the perspective and goals of the person with whom you are negotiating. Preparing checklists of your negotiation partner's interests, likely tactics, and BATNA have all been shown to improve negotiation outcomes. Can these steps make you a more ethical negotiator as well? Studies suggest that they might.

Researchers asked respondents to indicate how much they tended to think about other people's feelings and emotions and to describe the types of tactics they engaged in during a negotiation exercise. More empathetic individuals consistently engaged in fewer unethical negotiation behaviors like making false promises and manipulating information, and emotions. To put this in terms familiar to you from personality research, it appears that individuals who are higher in agreeableness will be more ethical negotiators.

When considering how to improve your ethical negotiation behavior, follow these guidelines:

1. Try to understand your negotiation partner's perspective, not just by understanding cognitively what the other person wants, but by empathizing with the emotional reaction he or she will have to the possible outcomes.
2. Be aware of your own emotions, because many moral reactions are fundamentally emotional. One study found that engaging in unethical negotiation strategies increased feelings of guilt, so by extension, feeling guilty in a negotiation may mean you are engaging in behavior you'll regret later.
3. Beware of empathizing so much that you work against your own interests. Just because you try to understand the motives and emotional reactions of the other side does not mean you have to assume the other person is going to be honest and fair in return. So be on guard.

Sources: Based on T. R. Cohen, "Moral Emotions and Unethical Bargaining: The Differential Effects of Empathy and Perspective Taking in Deterring Deceitful Negotiation," Journal of Business Ethics 94, no. 4 (2010), pp. 569–579; and R. Volkema, D. Fleck, and A. Hofmeister, "Predicting Competitive-Unethical Negotiating Behavior and Its Consequences," Negotiation Journal 26, no. 3 (2010), pp. 263–286.

Moods/Emotions in Negotiation   Do moods and emotions influence negotiation? They do, but the way they work depends on the emotion as well as the context. A negotiator who shows anger generally induces concessions, for instance, because the other negotiator believes no further concessions from the angry party are possible. One factor that governs this outcome, however, is power— you should show anger in negotiations only if you have at least as much power as your counterpart. If you have less, showing anger actually seems to provoke "hardball" reactions from the other side.[59] Another factor is how genuine your anger is—"faked" anger, or anger produced from so-called surface acting (see Chapter 4), is not effective, but showing anger that is genuine (so-called deep acting) does.[60] It also appears that having a history of showing anger, rather than sowing the seeds of revenge, actually induces more concessions because the other party perceives the negotiator as "tough."[61] Finally, culture seems to matter. For instance, one study found that when East Asian participants showed anger, it induced more concessions the negotiator expressing anger was from the United States or Europe, perhaps because of the stereotype of East Asians as refusing to show anger.[62]

Another relevant emotion is disappointment. Generally, a negotiator who perceives disappointment from his or her counterpart concedes more because disappointment makes many negotiators feel guilty. In one study, Dutch students were given 100 chips to bargain over. Negotiators who expressed disappointment were offered 14 more chips than those who didn't. In a second study, showing disappointment yielded an average concession of 12 chips. Unlike a show of anger, the relative power of the negotiators made no difference in either study.[63]

Anxiety also appears to have an impact on negotiation. For example, one study found that individuals who experienced more anxiety about a negotiation used more deceptions in dealing with others.[64] Another study found that anxious negotiators expect lower outcomes, respond to offers more quickly, and exit the bargaining process more quickly, leading them to obtain worse outcomes.[65]

As you can see, emotions—especially negative ones—matter to negotiation. Even emotional unpredictability affects outcomes; researchers have found that negotiators who express positive and negative emotions in an unpredictable way extract more concessions because it makes the other party feel less in control.[66] As one negotiator put it, "Out of the blue, you may have to react to something you have been working on in one way, and then something entirely new is introduced, and you have to veer off and refocus."[67]

Culture in Negotiations   Do people from different cultures negotiate differently? The simple answer is the obvious one: Yes, they do. However, there are many nuances in the way this works. It isn't as simple as "U.S. negotiators are the best"; indeed, success in negotiations depends on the context.

So what can we say about culture and negotiations? First, it appears that people generally negotiate more effectively within cultures than between them. For example, a Colombian is apt to do better negotiating with a Colombian than with a Sri Lankan. Second, it appears that in cross-cultural negotiations, it is especially important that the negotiators be high in openness. This suggests choosing cross-cultural negotiators who are high on openness to experience, but also avoiding factors—such as time pressures—that tend to inhibit learning to understand the other party.[68]

Finally, because emotions are culturally sensitive, negotiators need to be especially aware of the emotional dynamics in cross-cultural negotiation. One study, for example, explicitly compared how U.S. and Chinese negotiators react to an angry counterpart. Chinese negotiators increased their use of distributive negotiating tactics, whereas U.S. negotiators decreased their use of these tactics.

Photo 14-4 In general, people negotiate more effectively within cultures than between them. Politeness and positivity characterize the typical conflict-avoidant negotiations in Japan such as those of labor union leader Hidekazu Kitagawa (right), shown here presenting wage and benefits demands to Ikuo Mori, president of Fuji Heavy Industries, maker of Subaru vehicles.

That is, Chinese negotiators began to drive a harder bargain once they saw that their negotiation partner was becoming angry, whereas U.S. negotiators actually capitulated somewhat in the face of angry demands. Why the difference? It may be that individuals from East Asian cultures feel that using anger to get their way in a negotiation is not a legitimate tactic, so they respond by refusing to cooperate when their opponents become upset.[69]

Gender Differences in Negotiations   There are many areas of organizational behavior in which men and women are not that different. Negotiation is not one of them. It now seems fairly clear that men and women negotiate differently, and these differences affect outcomes.

A popular stereotype is that women are more cooperative and pleasant in negotiations than are men. Though this is controversial, there is some merit to it. Men tend to place a higher value on status, power, and recognition, whereas women tend to place a higher value on compassion and altruism. Moreover, women do tend to value relationship outcomes more than men, and men tend to value economic outcomes more than women.[70]

Source: A. Gouveia, "Why Americans are Too Scared to Negotiate Salary," *San Francisco Chronicle* (April 3, 2013), downloaded May 30, 2013 from http://www.sfgate.com/jobs/.

These differences affect both negotiation behavior and negotiation outcomes. Compared to men, women tend to behave in a less assertive, less self-interested, and more accommodating manner. As one recent review concluded, women "are more reluctant to initiate negotiations, and when they do initiate negotiations, they ask for less, are more willing to accept [the] offer, and make more generous offers to their negotiation partners than men do."[71] A study of MBA students at Carnegie-Mellon University found that male MBA students took the step of negotiating their first offer 57 percent of the time, compared to 4 percent for female MBA students. The net result? A $4,000 difference in starting salaries.[72]

However, the disparity goes even further than that. Because of the way women approach negotiation, other negotiators seek to exploit female negotiators by, for example, making lower salary offers. As a result, "female negotiators obtain poorer individual outcomes than male negotiators do, and two women negotiating together build less total value than do two male negotiators."[73]

This is not a "fix the woman" problem for two reasons. First, as is the case with any stereotype that has some validity, we always find individual variation. There are average differences between men and women in negotiation, but this hardly means that every man's behavior is more assertive than every woman's in negotiation. Second, there is some evidence that men hold a gender double standard—when women behave stereotypically, men are more likely to take advantage of the cooperative behavior, but when women behave assertively, their assertive behavior is viewed more negatively than if the same behavior were demonstrated by men.

So what can be done to change this troublesome state of affairs? First, organizational culture plays a role here. If an organization, even unwittingly, encourages a predominantly competitive model for negotiators, this will tend to increase gender-stereotypic behaviors (men negotiating competitively, women negotiating cooperatively), and it will also increase backlash when women go against stereotype. Men and women need to know that it is acceptable for each to show a full range of negotiating behaviors. Thus, a female negotiator who behaves competitively and a male negotiator who behaves cooperatively need to know that they are not violating expectations.

Second, at an individual level, women cannot directly control male stereotypes of women. Fortunately, such stereotypes are fading. However, women *can* control their own negotiating behavior. Does this mean they should always behave aggressively and in a self-interested manner in negotiations? If economic outcomes are valued, then the answer, in general, is yes. And, of course, the shoe can be put on the other foot—if men value social outcomes, they should consider behaving in a more cooperative manner.

Sometimes the change can be fairly simple. Take the example of freelance writer Alina Tugend. She decided that, when given an offer for her work, she would simply say, "I expected more." Although Tugend initially found this strategy difficult, it became easier when she found that it earned her a few hundred extra dollars per story. Also, do your homework. When web designer Kate Gilbert wondered whether her $30/hour fee was too low, she started asking around. She found she was asking too little—way too little. She now starts her rate at $80/hour.[74]

Research is less clear as to whether women can improve their outcomes even further by showing some gender-stereotypic behaviors. An article by Laura Kray and colleagues suggested that female negotiators who were instructed to behave with "feminine charm" (be animated in body movements, make frequent eye contact with their partner, smile, laugh, be playful, and frequently compliment their partner) did better in negotiations than women not so instructed. These behaviors didn't work for men regardless of the gender of their negotiating partner.[75]

Other researchers disagree and argue that what can best benefit women is to break down gender stereotypes on the part of individuals who hold them.[76] It's possible this is a short-term/long-term situation: In the short term, women can gain an advantage in negotiation by being both assertive and flirtatious, but in the long term, their interests are best served by eliminating these sorts of sex role stereotypes.

SELF-ASSESSMENT LIBRARY

What's My Negotiating Style?

In the Self-Assessment Library (available in MyManagementLab), take assessment II.C.6 (What's My Negotiating Style?).

Evidence suggests women's own attitudes and behaviors hurt them in negotiations. Managerial women demonstrate less confidence than men in anticipation of negotiating and are less satisfied with their performance afterward, even when their performance and the outcomes they achieve are similar to those for men.[77] Women are also less likely than men to see an ambiguous situation as an opportunity for negotiation. Women may unduly penalize themselves by failing to engage in negotiations that would be in their best interests. Some research suggests that women are less aggressive in negotiations because they are worried about backlash from others. There is an interesting qualifier to this result: Women are more likely to engage in assertive negotiation when they are bargaining on behalf of someone else than when they are bargaining on their own behalf.[78]

Third-Party Negotiations

7 Assess the roles and functions of third-party negotiations.

To this point, we've discussed bargaining in terms of direct negotiations. Occasionally, however, individuals or group representatives reach a stalemate and are unable to resolve their differences through direct negotiations. In such cases, they may turn to a third party to help them find a solution. There are three basic third-party roles: mediator, arbitrator, and conciliator.

mediator *A neutral third party who facilitates a negotiated solution by using reasoning, persuasion, and suggestions for alternatives.*

A **mediator** is a neutral third party who facilitates a negotiated solution by using reasoning and persuasion, suggesting alternatives, and the like. Mediators are widely used in labor–management negotiations and in civil court disputes. Their overall effectiveness is fairly impressive. The settlement rate is approximately 60 percent, with negotiator satisfaction at about 75 percent. But the situation is the key to whether mediation will succeed; the conflicting parties must be motivated to bargain and resolve their conflict. In addition, conflict intensity can't be too high; mediation is most effective under moderate levels of conflict. Finally, perceptions of the mediator are important; to be effective, the mediator must be perceived as neutral and noncoercive.

arbitrator *A third party to a negotiation who has the authority to dictate an agreement.*

An **arbitrator** is a third party with the authority to dictate an agreement. Arbitration can be voluntary (requested by the parties) or compulsory (forced on the parties by law or contract). The big plus of arbitration over mediation is that it always results in a settlement. Whether there is a negative side depends on how heavy-handed the arbitrator appears. If one party is left feeling overwhelmingly defeated, that party is certain to be dissatisfied and the conflict may resurface at a later time.

conciliator *A trusted third party who provides an informal communication link between the negotiator and the opponent.*

A **conciliator** is a trusted third party who provides an informal communication link between the negotiator and the opponent. This role was made famous by Robert Duval in the first *Godfather* film. As Don Corleone's adopted son and a lawyer by training, Duval acted as an intermediary between the Corleones and the other Mafioso families. Comparing conciliation to mediation in terms of effectiveness has proven difficult because the two overlap a great deal. In practice, conciliators typically act as more than mere communication conduits. They also engage in fact-finding, interpret messages, and persuade disputants to develop agreements.

Summary

While many people assume conflict lowers group and organizational performance, this assumption is frequently incorrect. Conflict can be either constructive or destructive to the functioning of a group or unit. As shown in Exhibit 14-8,

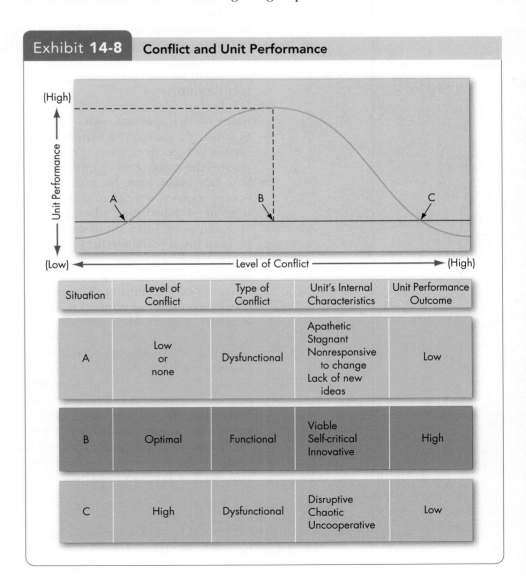

Exhibit 14-8   Conflict and Unit Performance

Situation	Level of Conflict	Type of Conflict	Unit's Internal Characteristics	Unit Performance Outcome
A	Low or none	Dysfunctional	Apathetic Stagnant Nonresponsive to change Lack of new ideas	Low
B	Optimal	Functional	Viable Self-critical Innovative	High
C	High	Dysfunctional	Disruptive Chaotic Uncooperative	Low

levels of conflict can be either too high or too low to be constructive. Either extreme hinders performance. An optimal level is one that prevents stagnation, stimulates creativity, allows tensions to be released, and initiates the seeds of change without being disruptive or preventing coordination of activities.

Implications for Managers

- As Exhibit 14-8 suggests, choose an authoritarian management style in emergencies, when unpopular actions need to be implemented (such as cost cutting, enforcement of unpopular rules, discipline), and when the issue is vital to the organization's welfare. Be certain to communicate your logic when possible to make certain employees remain engaged and productive.
- Seek integrative solutions when your objective is to learn, when you want to merge insights from people with different perspectives, when you need to gain commitment by incorporating concerns into a consensus, and when you need to work through feelings that have interfered with a relationship.
- It is best to avoid an issue when it is trivial or symptomatic of other issues, when more important issues are pressing, when you perceive no chance of satisfying everyone's concerns, when people need to cool down and regain perspective, when gathering information, and when others can resolve the conflict more effectively.
- You can build trust by accommodating others when you find you're wrong, when you need to demonstrate reasonableness, when other positions need to be heard, when issues are more important to others than to yourself, when you want to satisfy others and maintain cooperation, when you can build social credits for later issues, to minimize loss when you are outmatched and losing, and when employees should learn from their own mistakes.
- Consider compromising when goals are important but not worth potential disruption, when opponents with equal power are committed to mutually exclusive goals, and when you need temporary settlements to complex issues.
- Distributive bargaining can resolve disputes, but it often reduces the satisfaction of one or more negotiators because it is confrontational and focused on the short term. Integrative bargaining, in contrast, tends to provide outcomes that satisfy all parties and build lasting relationships.
- Make sure you set aggressive negotiating goals and try to find creative ways to achieve the objectives of both parties, especially when you value the long-term relationship with the other party. That doesn't mean sacrificing your self-interest; rather, it means trying to find creative solutions that give both parties what they really want.

Pro Sports Strikes Are Caused by Greedy Owners

POINT

I'm as sick as anyone of the constant strikes, lockouts, and back-and-forth negotiations between sports teams and the players' unions. Of the major pro sports leagues, Major League Baseball (MLB) is the only one not to have had a strike or lockout since 2010—and it has already had eight in its history. You've got to wonder why this keeps happening. Here's why: Owners' greed knows no limit.

In nearly every recent strike or lockout, the main issue was money and how to divide it.

When the National Hockey League (NHL) locked out the players during the 2012–2013 season, the owners were the in-stigators. They wanted to reduce the players' share of hockey revenues. They wanted to eliminate salary arbitration. They wanted to introduce term limits to contracts. They wanted to change free-agency rules and eliminate signing bonuses. On a philosophical level, some of these proposals are interesting because they reveal that owners want to restrict competition when it suits them and increase it when it benefits them.

This summer, while the owners were whining about the un-fairness of long-term contracts, the Minnesota Wild's owner Craig Leipold, a noted negotiations hawk, signed Zach Parise and Ryan Suter to identical 13-year, $98 million contracts. Contracts like these suggest that owners want the players' union to save them from themselves.

Perhaps some of this would make sense if the owners were losing money hand over fist, but that is hardly the case. The NHL is now a $3.3 billion business, and it continues to grow. The own-ers aren't hurting, either. Most are millionaires many times over. Los Angeles Kings owner Philip Anschutz is reported to have a net worth of $7 billion.

Forbes reports the average NFL team is now worth more than $1.1 billion and made $41 million last year. Even low-revenue and poorly run teams make money. Take the Jackson-ville Jaguars. Wayne Weaver paid $208 million for the team in 1993. It has never made it to the Super Bowl and is almost al-ways an also-ran in its division. Did the team's ineffectiveness really cost Weaver? He sold the club for $770 million in 2012.

In essence, what we have are rich owners trying to negoti-ate rules that keep them from competing with one another for players. It's a bald-faced and hypocritical attempt to use their own kind of union to negotiate favorable agreements, all the while criticizing the players' unions.

COUNTERPOINT

Major league owners are an easy target. But they have the most to lose from work stoppages. It's the players and their unions who push the envelope.

It's true that most major league players are well rewarded for their exceptional talents and the risks they take. It's also true that owners who are able to invest in teams are wealthy—investors usually are. But the fault for disputes lies with spoiled players—and the union leaders who burnish their credentials and garner the limelight by fanning the flames of discontent.

On this latter point, give all the credit in the world to the union negotiators (paid millions themselves), who do nothing if not hawk publicity and use hardball negotiating tactics. Take the NHL players' union boss Donald Fehr. For a recent "negotiation" set to begin at 10 A.M., he arrived at 11:15. At exactly 12:00, he announced he had a lunch meeting uptown and left.

As for the players, pro athletes are entitled almost by defini-tion. For example, one recently retired NFL player and union rep-resentative, Chester Pitts, was commenting about how he had to settle for an $85,000 Mercedes instead of a $250,000 car. Well, we all have to make sacrifices. One rookie, Jets' quarterback Geno Smith, fired his agent after signing "only" a four-year con-tract for roughly $4.99 million. Smith called the contract "hard to stomach." I see a future in the player's union for this guy.

Do we really need labor unions for workers whose average salaries are $1,900,000 (NFL), $2,400,000 (NHL), $3,310,000 (MLB), and $5,150,000 (NBA)? NHL clubs spent 76 percent of their gross revenues on players' salaries and collectively lost $273 million the year before the most recent lockout. It's not much better in the NBA, where many teams lose money. Take the Dallas Mavericks, who have rarely made money once since 2002, despite playing in the fourth-most populous metro area and winning the NBA title in 2012.

It's easy to argue that major league sports have an unusual number of labor disputes, but that's not necessarily accurate. Did you hear about the 2013 Turkish Airlines Strike or the world-wide strikes in the fast-food industry in 2013? Sports strikes in-terest us, but we shouldn't fall into the trap of blaming these on the owners.

Sources: J. Feinstein, "In the NHL Lockout, the Owners Have It All Wrong," *Washington Post* (December 25, 2012), down-loaded May 29, 2013, from http://articles.washingtonpost.com/; R. Cimini, "Geno Smith's Maturity Questioned," *ESPN* (May 3, 2013), downloaded May 3, 2013, from http://espn.go.com/; K. Campbell, "Thanks to Donald Fehr, NHL Negotiating against Itself . . . and Losing," *The Hockey News* (December 29, 2012), downloaded May 29, 2013, from http://sports.yahoo.com/; and M. Ozanian, "Dallas Cowboys Lead NFL with $2.1 Billion Valuation," *Forbes* (September 5, 2012), downloaded May 20, 2013, from www.forbes.com/.

END-OF-CHAPTER REVIEW

MyManagementLab

Go to mymanagementlab.com to complete the problems marked with this icon ⭐.

QUESTIONS FOR REVIEW

14-1 What are the differences between the traditional and interactionist views of conflict?

14-2 What are the three types of conflict and the two loci of conflict?

14-3 What are the steps of the conflict process?

14-4 What are the differences between distributive and integrative bargaining?

14-5 What are the five steps in the negotiation process?

14-6 How do individual differences influence negotiations?

14-7 What are the roles and functions of third-party negotiations?

EXPERIENTIAL EXERCISE A Negotiation Role-Play

This role-play is designed to help you develop your negotiating skills. The class is to break into pairs. One person will play the role of Alex, the department supervisor. The other person will play C. J., Alex's boss. Both participants should read "The Situation," "The Negotiation," and then their role only.

The Situation

Alex and C. J. work for Nike in Beaverton, Oregon. Alex supervises a research laboratory. C. J. is the manager of research and development. Alex and C. J. are former college runners who have worked for Nike for more than 6 years. C. J. has been Alex's boss for 2 years. One of Alex's employees has greatly impressed Alex. This employee is Lisa Roland. Lisa was hired 11 months ago. She is 24 years old and holds a master's degree in mechanical engineering. Her entry-level salary was $57,500 per year. Alex told her that, in accordance with corporation policy, she would receive an initial performance evaluation at 6 months and a comprehensive review after 1 year. Based on her performance record, Lisa was told she could expect a salary adjustment at the time of the 1-year evaluation.

Alex's evaluation of Lisa after 6 months was very positive. Alex commented on the long hours Lisa was putting in, her cooperative spirit, the fact that others in the lab enjoyed working with her, and that she was making an immediate positive impact on the project assigned to her. Now that Lisa's first anniversary is coming up, Alex has again reviewed Lisa's performance. Alex thinks Lisa may be the best new person the R&D group has ever hired. After only a year, Alex has ranked Lisa as the number-3 performer in a department of 11.

Salaries in the department vary greatly. Alex, for instance, has a base salary of $86,000, plus eligibility for a bonus that might add another $7,000 to $12,000 a year. The salary range of the 11 department members is $48,400 to $76,350. The individual with the lowest salary is a recent hire with a bachelor's degree in physics. The two people whom Alex has rated above Lisa earn base salaries of $69,200 and $76,350. They're both 27 years old and have been at Nike for 3 and 4 years, respectively. The median salary in Alex's department is $64,960.

Alex's Role

You want to give Lisa a big raise. Although she's young, she has proven to be an excellent addition to the department. You don't want to lose her. More importantly, she knows in general what other people in the department are earning, and she thinks she's underpaid. The company typically gives 1-year raises of 5 percent, although 10 percent is not unusual, and 20 to 30 percent increases have been approved on occasion. You'd like to get Lisa as large an increase as C. J. will approve.

C. J.'s Role

All your supervisors typically try to squeeze you for as much money as they can for their people. You understand this because you did the same thing when you were a supervisor, but your boss wants to keep a lid on costs. He wants you to keep raises for recent hires generally in the 5 to 8 percent range. In fact, he's sent a memo to all managers and supervisors saying this. He also said that managers will be evaluated on their ability to maintain budgetary control. However, your boss is also concerned with equity and paying people what they're worth. You feel assured that he will support any salary recommendation you make, as long as it can be justified. Your goal, consistent with cost reduction, is to keep salary increases as low as possible.

The Negotiation

Alex has a meeting scheduled with C. J. to discuss Lisa's performance review and salary adjustment. Take a couple of minutes to think through the facts in this exercise and to prepare a strategy. Then take up to 15 minutes to conduct your negotiation. When your negotiation is complete, the class will compare the various strategies used and pair outcomes.

ETHICAL DILEMMA The Lowball Applicant

Consider this first-person account:

I am a human resource manager, so I interview people every day. Sometimes the managers in my company ask me to pre-screen candidates, which I do after discussing the job at length with the manager. I usually start the candidate screening with a few personality–job fit tests; then conduct an interview, following a list of job-specific questions the manager has given me; and finally discuss the job requirements, our company, and the pay/benefits. By that time in the process, the candidate usually has a good idea of the job and is eager to suggest a high level of pay at the top of the advertised bracket or, often, above the pay bracket. However, this isn't always the case. One time in particular, an excellent candidate with outstanding qualifications surprised me by saying that since she wanted flextime, she would accept a rate below the pay bracket. Confused, I asked her if she wanted a reduction in hours below full-time. She said no, she expected to work full-time and only wanted to come in a little late and would leave a little late to make up the time. I guess she figured this was a concession worth slashing her salary for, but our company has flextime. In fact, she could have asked for 5 fewer hours per week, still been considered full-time by our company policies, and negotiated for above the advertised pay grade.

I knew the manager would be highly interested in this candidate and that he could probably get her to work the longer full-time hours at a lower rate of pay. That outcome might be best for the company, or it might not. She obviously didn't fully understand the company policies in her favor, and she was unsophisticated about her worth in the marketplace. What should I have done?

Questions

14-8. If the human resource manager coached the applicant to request a higher salary, did the coaching work against the interests of the organization? What was the responsibility of the human resource manager to put the organization's financial interests first?

14-9. What do you see as the potential downside of the human resource manager abstaining from discussing the pay issue further with the candidate?

14-10. If the candidate were hired at the reduced rate she proposed, how might the situation play out over the next year when she gets to know the organization and pay standards better?

CASE INCIDENT 1 Choosing Your Battles

While much of this chapter has discussed methods for achieving harmonious relationships and getting out of conflicts, it's also important to remember there are situations in which too little conflict can be a problem. As we noted, in creative problem-solving teams, some level of task conflict early in the process of formulating a solution can be an important stimulus to innovation.

However, the conditions must be right for productive conflict. In particular, individuals must feel psychologically safe in bringing up issues for discussion. If people fear that what they say is going to be held against them, they may be reluctant to speak up or rock the boat. Experts suggest that effective conflicts have three key characteristics: They should (1) speak to what is possible, (2) be compelling, and (3) involve uncertainty.

So how should a manager "pick a fight?" First, ensure that the stakes are sufficient to actually warrant a disruption. Second, focus on the future, and on how to resolve the conflict rather than on whom to blame. Third, tie the conflict to fundamental values. Rather than concentrating on winning or losing, encourage both parties to see how successfully exploring and resolving the conflict will lead to optimal outcomes for all. If managed successfully, some degree of open disagreement can be an important way for companies to manage simmering and potentially destructive conflicts.

Do these principles work in real organizations? The answer is yes. Dropping its old ways of handling scheduling and logistics created a great deal of conflict at Burlington Northern Santa Fe railroad, but applying these principles to managing the conflict helped the railroad adopt a more sophisticated system and recover its competitive position in the transportation industry. Doug Conant, CEO of Campbell Soup, increased functional conflicts in his organization by emphasizing a higher purpose to the organization's efforts rather than focusing on whose side was winning a conflict. Thus, a dysfunctional conflict environment changed dramatically, and the organization was able to move from one of the world's worst-performing food companies to one that was recognized as a top performer by both the Dow Jones Sustainability Index and *Fortune* 500 data on employee morale.

Questions

14-11. How would you ensure sufficient discussion of contentious issues in a work group? How can managers bring unspoken conflicts into the open without making them worse?

14-12. How can negotiators utilize conflict management strategies to their advantage so that differences in interests lead not to dysfunctional conflicts but rather to positive integrative solutions?

14-13. Can you think of situations in your own life in which silence has worsened a conflict between parties? What might have been done differently to ensure that open communication facilitated collaboration instead?

Sources: Based on S. A. Joni and D. Beyer, "How to Pick a Good Fight," *Harvard Business Review* (December 2009), pp. 48–57; and B. H. Bradley, B. E. Postlewaite, A. C. Klotz, M. R. Hamdani, and K. G. Brown, "Reaping the Benefits of Task Conflict in Teams: The Critical Role of Team Psychological Safety Climate," *Journal of Applied Psychology,* Advance publication (July 4, 2011), doi: 10.1037/a0024200.

CASE INCIDENT 2   Twinkies, Rubber Rooms, and Collective Bargaining

U.S. labor unions have seen a dramatic decline in membership in the private sector, where only 6.5 percent of the employees are unionized. The situation is very different in the public sector, however, where 40 percent of government employees are unionized. These numbers are the result of very different trends—in the 1950s, the situation was approximately reversed, with roughly 35 percent of private-sector workers and 12 percent of public-sector employees belonging to unions.

Research suggests two core reasons public-sector unions have grown. First, changes in state and national labor laws have made it easier for public-sector unions to organize. Some also argue that enforcement agencies have tolerated anti-union actions in the private sector. Second, the location of private-sector jobs has changed; high-paying union jobs in the manufacturing sector, the steel industry, and other former bastions of private-sector unionization have mostly gone overseas or to the South, where it's harder to organize workers. On the other hand, it's difficult to move government jobs away from the communities they serve. A Philadelphia school, for example, couldn't just decide it was going to relocate its teachers to Atlanta. Also, public-sector labor forces tend to be more static than in the private sector. More plants than post offices have closed.

Are these trends problems? Though this is partly a political question, let's look at it objectively in terms of pluses and minuses.

On the positive side, by negotiating as a collective, unionized workers are able to earn, on average, roughly 15 percent more than their nonunion counterparts. Unions also can protect the rights of workers against capricious actions by employers. Consider the following example:

> Lydia criticized the work of five of her co-workers. They were not amused and posted angry messages on a Facebook page. Lydia complained to her supervisor that the postings violated the employer's "zero tolerance" policy against "bullying and harassment." The employer investigated and, agreeing that its policy had been violated, fired the five. The National Labor Relations Board, however, ruled this an unfair labor practice and ordered reinstatements.

Most of us would probably prefer not to be fired for Facebook posts. This is a protection unions can provide.

On the negative side, public-sector unions at times have been able to negotiate employment arrangements that are hard to sustain. For more than 25 years, the union that represents California's prison guards—the California Correctional Peace Officers Association (CCPOA)—lobbied the state to increase the number of prisons and to increase sentences (such as via the "three strikes" law). The lobbying worked; prisons were built, the prison population exploded, and thousands of new guards were hired. The average CCPOA member now makes more than $100,000 per year and can retire at age 50 with 90 percent of salary as pension. California now spends more money on prisons than on education.

Further, it is often extremely difficult to fire a member of a public-sector union, even if performance is exceptionally poor. Aryeh Eller, 46, a former music teacher at Hillcrest High School in Queens, was pulled from the classroom for repeated sexual harassment of female students, a charge to which he has admitted. While in the "rubber room," where union members unfit to work are paid their full wage to just sit, Eller has seen his salary increase to $85,000 due to automatic seniority increases under the teachers' union contract. Such protections exist for teachers in nearly every state, protecting even those arrested for having sex with minors and giving minors drugs. Teachers are not alone. There are rubber rooms for many types of union jobs.

Reasonable people can disagree about the pros and cons of unions and whether they help or hinder an organization's ability to be successful. There isn't any dispute, however, that they often figure prominently in the study of workplace conflict and negotiation strategies.

Questions

14-14. Labor–management negotiations might be characterized as more distributive than integrative. Do you agree? Why do you think this is the case? What, if anything, would you do about it?

14-15. If unions have negotiated unreasonable agreements, what responsibility does management or the administration bear for agreeing to these terms? Why do you think they do agree?

✪ 14-16. If you were advising union and management representatives about how to negotiate an agreement, drawing from the concepts in this chapter, what would you tell them?

Sources: "Aryeh Eller, New York Teacher Removed from Classroom for Sexual Harassment, Paid Nearly $1 Million to Do Nothing," *Huffington Post* (January 28, 2013), downloaded May 20, 2013, from www.huffingtonpost.com; "Hispanics United of Buffalo, Inc. and Carlos Ortiz," Case 03–CA–027872, *National Labor Relations Board* (December 14, 2012), downloaded May 13, 2013, from www.nlrb.gov/cases-decisions/board-decisions; and J. Weissmann, "Who's to Blame for the Hostess Bankruptcy: Wall Street, Unions, or Carbs? *The Atlantic* (November 16, 2012), downloaded on May 29, 2013, from www.theatlantic.com/.

MyManagementLab

Go to **mymanagementlab.com** for Auto-graded writing questions as well as the following Assisted-graded writing questions:

14-17. From your reading of Case Incident 1 and the text, what do you think are the optimal conditions for negotiating?

14-18. In regard to Case Incident 2, failure to reach agreement can be costly—for both union members and the organization. In 2012, when negotiations between Hostess and its bakers' union fell apart, the maker of Twinkies was dissolved and its 18,500 workers were without jobs. Why do such apparent lose–lose negotiation outcomes happen?

14-19. MyManagementLab Only—comprehensive writing assignment for this chapter.

15 Foundations of Organization Structure

Source: Washington Post/Getty Images.

HEARD BUT NOT SEEN— THE VIRTUAL ASSISTANT

In this age where the debate is all about working in your home, office, cubicle, shared space, or the nearest coffeehouse, one underlying concern is how much face time we need with the people in our organizations. How about none? According to some employers, even the dynamic, complex, often personal role of the office assistant can be effectively accomplished by someone in another country whom you will probably never meet in person. Many of those employers report that such assistants are efficient, valuable, and multi-talented. From finding a perfect office party venue to designing a website, virtual assistants can handle just about anything someone in—or around the corner from—the office can.

"We've been very surprised at the breadth of capabilities" of virtual assistants, said Adam Neary, Profitability.com's founder and chief executive officer (CEO). "In fact, we've started using oDesk [a virtual assistant website] for all sorts of highly technical and specialized skills." Marc Plotkin, a software entrepreneur with 25 employees, agrees. Rather than find a local employee to handle his overloaded e-mail inbox, he used the Zirtual site to hire a former English teacher states away. Ben and Lydia Choi hired a virtual assistant to take over "an endless list of to-dos that neither of us wanted to tackle" for their house move while they maintained their executive jobs. Christine Durst, co-founder of RatRaceRebellion.com, noted that virtual assistants also handle paralegal work and architectural or engineering support.

Part temporary employee, part apprentice, the virtual office assistant can be a cost-effective hire. While fees paid to the matchmaking company range from $6/hour to $90/hour based on skills employed, employers can also pay monthly for a specified number of hours. The virtual assistant is not offered benefits, office space, or other compensation, but the employer's biggest savings may be in upfront costs. Employers are encouraged to hire more than one assistant initially and offer each the same task; because the assistants are paid by the hour, the employer can simply terminate the arrangement with lower-performing candidates.

But don't think the virtual worker doesn't need managing. The good ones need feedback, acknowledgment, and extrinsic rewards—just the way in-house employees do. According to Sue Shellenbarger of *The Wall Street Journal*, "Virtual assistants are like any employee, they like to have a chance to grow, and they really have a high regard for mutual respect."

While postings by candidates on clearinghouse websites have grown exponentially, with a one-year increase of 44 percent (to 50,000 assistants) on Elance alone, so has the number of employers seeking virtual assistants.

LEARNING OBJECTIVES

After studying this chapter, you should be able to:

1 Identify the six elements of an organization's structure.

2 Identify the characteristics of a bureaucracy.

3 Describe a matrix organization.

4 Identify the characteristics of a virtual organization.

5 Show why managers want to create boundaryless organizations.

6 Demonstrate how organizational structures differ, and contrast mechanistic and organic structural models.

7 Analyze the behavioral implications of different organizational designs.

Virtual office assistants are undoubtedly here to stay. Will your next co-worker report from India, the Philippines, China, Poland, India, Manila, Hong Kong, or around the corner?

———————

Sources: A. Baxter, "You Could Need a Virtual Hand," *Geelong Advertiser.com.au* (March 13, 2013), www.geelongadvertiser.com.au/article/2013/03/13/361054_business.html; S. Shellenbarger, "Get Me a Hair Appointment and Empty My Inbox," *The Wall Street Journal* (February 20, 2013), p. D1; and "Want More Hours in a Day? Hire a Virtual Assistant" (February 19, 2013), http://live.wsj.com/video/the-pros-and-cons-of-virtual-assistants/DF528DB3-79AC-4066-994B-76C6A6509F7B.html? KEYWORDS=virtual+assistant.

S tructural decisions like the incorporation of remote employees are arguably the most fundamental ones a leader has to make toward sustaining organizational growth.[1] Before we delve into the elements of an organization's structure and how they can affect behavior, consider how you might react to one type of organizational structure—the bureaucratic structure—by taking the following self-assessment.

SELF-ASSESSMENT LIBRARY

Do I Like Bureaucracy?

In the Self-Assessment Library (available in MyManagementLab), take assessment IV.F.2 (Do I Like Bureaucracy?) and answer the following questions.

1. Judging from the results, how willing are you to work in a bureaucratic organization?
2. Do you think scores on this measure matter? Why or why not?
3. Do you think people who score very low (or even very high) on this measure should try to adjust their preferences based on where they are working?

What Is Organizational Structure?

1 Identify the six elements of an organization's structure.

organizational structure *The way in which job tasks are formally divided, grouped, and coordinated.*

An **organizational structure** defines how job tasks are formally divided, grouped, and coordinated. Managers need to address six key elements when they design their organization's structure: work specialization, departmentalization, chain of command, span of control, centralization and decentralization, and formalization.[2] Exhibit 15-1 presents each of these elements as answers to an important structural question, and the following sections describe them.

Work Specialization

Early in the twentieth century, Henry Ford became rich by building automobiles on an assembly line. Every Ford worker was assigned a specific, repetitive task such as putting on the right front wheel or installing the right front door. By dividing jobs into small standardized tasks that could be performed over and over, Ford was able to produce a car every 10 seconds, using employees who had relatively limited skills.

Exhibit 15-1	Key Design Questions and Answers for Designing the Proper Organizational Structure

The Key Question	The Answer Is Provided by
1. To what degree are activities subdivided into separate jobs?	Work specialization
2. On what basis will jobs be grouped together?	Departmentalization
3. To whom do individuals and groups report?	Chain of command
4. How many individuals can a manager efficiently and effectively direct?	Span of control
5. Where does decision-making authority lie?	Centralization and decentralization
6. To what degree will there be rules and regulations to direct employees and managers?	Formalization

work specialization *The degree to which tasks in an organization are subdivided into separate jobs.*

Ford demonstrated that work can be performed more efficiently if employees are allowed to specialize. Today, we use the term **work specialization**, or *division of labor,* to describe the degree to which activities in the organization are divided into separate jobs. The essence of work specialization is to divide a job into a number of steps, each completed by a separate individual. In essence, individuals specialize in doing part of an activity rather than the entirety.

By the late 1940s, most manufacturing jobs in industrialized countries featured high work specialization. Because not all employees in an organization have the same skills, management saw specialization as a means of making the most efficient use of its employees' skills and even successfully improving them through repetition. Less time is spent in changing tasks, putting away tools and equipment from a prior step, and getting ready for another. Equally important, it's easier and less costly to find and train workers to do specific and repetitive tasks, especially in highly sophisticated and complex operations. Could Cessna produce one Citation jet a year if one person had to build the entire plane alone? Not likely! Finally, work specialization increases efficiency and productivity by encouraging the creation of special inventions and machinery.

Thus, for much of the first half of the twentieth century, managers viewed work specialization as an unending source of increased productivity. And they were probably right. When specialization was not widely practiced, its introduction almost always generated higher productivity. By the 1960s, it increasingly seemed a good thing could be carried too far. Human diseconomies from specialization began to surface in the form of boredom, fatigue, stress, low productivity, poor quality, increased absenteeism, and high turnover, which more than offset the economic advantages (see Exhibit 15-2). Managers could increase productivity now by enlarging, rather than narrowing, the scope of job activities. Giving employees a variety of activities to do, allowing them to do a whole and complete job, and putting them into teams with interchangeable skills often achieved significantly higher output, with increased employee satisfaction.

Most managers today recognize the economies specialization provides in certain jobs and the problems when it's carried too far. High work specialization helps McDonald's make and sell hamburgers and fries efficiently and aids medical specialists in most health maintenance organizations. Amazon's Mechanical Turk program, TopCoder, and others like it have facilitated a new

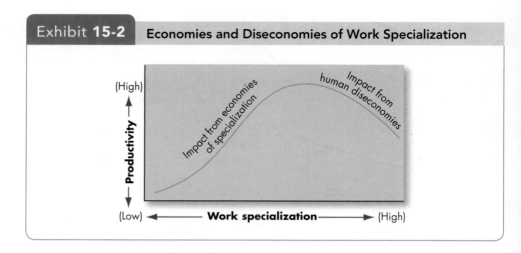

Exhibit 15-2 Economies and Diseconomies of Work Specialization

trend in microspecialization in which extremely small pieces of programming, data processing, or evaluation tasks are delegated to a global network of individuals by a program manager who then assembles the results.[3] For example, a manager who has a complex but routine computer program to write might send a request for specific subcomponents of the code to be written and tested by dozens of subcontracted individuals in the network (which spans the entire globe), enabling the project to be completed far more quickly than if a single programmer were writing the parts. This emerging trend suggests there still may be advantages to be had in specialization, particularly for offices where job sharing and part time work are prevalent.[4]

Wherever job roles can be broken down into specific tasks or projects, specialization is possible. This opens the potential for employers to use online platforms to assign multiple workers to tasks from a broader functional role like marketing.[5] Thus, whereas specialization of yesteryear focused on breaking manufacturing tasks into specific duties within the same plant, today's specialization breaks complex tasks into specific elements by technology, by expertise, and often globally. Yet the core principle is the same.

Departmentalization

Once jobs have been divided through work specialization, they must be grouped so common tasks can be coordinated. The basis by which jobs are grouped is called **departmentalization**.

One of the most popular ways to group activities is by *functions* performed. A manufacturing manager might organize a plant into engineering, accounting, manufacturing, personnel, and supply specialists departments. A hospital might have departments devoted to research, surgery, intensive care, accounting, and so forth. A professional football franchise might have departments entitled player personnel, ticket sales, and travel and accommodations. The major advantage of this type of functional departmentalization is efficiencies gained from putting like specialists together.

We can also departmentalize jobs by the type of *product* or *service* the organization produces. Procter & Gamble places each major product—such as Tide, Pampers, Charmin, and Pringles—under an executive who has complete global responsibility for it. The major advantage here is increased accountability for performance because all activities related to a specific product or service are under the direction of a single manager.

When a firm is departmentalized on the basis of *geography*, or territory, the sales function, for instance, may have western, southern, midwestern, and

departmentalization *The basis by which jobs in an organization are grouped together.*

Photo 15-1 Departmentalization by four customer segments—consumers, software developers, small businesses, and large corporations—helps Microsoft better understand and respond to each group's needs. Products and services Microsoft designs for consumers include Bing, Windows, Xbox, Surface, and Skype.

eastern regions, each, in effect, a department organized around geography. This form is valuable when an organization's customers are scattered over a large geographic area and have similar needs based on their location. Toyota recently changed its management structure into geographic regions "so that they may develop and deliver ever better products," said CEO Akio Toyoda.[6]

Process departmentalization works for processing customers as well as products. If you've ever been to a state motor vehicle office to get a driver's license, you probably went through several departments before receiving your license. In one typical state, applicants go through three steps, each handled by a separate department: (1) validation by the motor vehicles division, (2) processing by the licensing department, and (3) payment collection by the treasury department.

A final category of departmentalization uses the particular type of *customer* the organization seeks to reach. Microsoft, for example, is organized around four customer markets: consumers, large corporations, software developers, and small businesses. Customers in each department have a common set of problems and needs best met by having specialists for each.

Chain of Command

While the chain of command was once a basic cornerstone in the design of organizations, it has far less importance today.[7] But contemporary managers should still consider its implications, particularly for industries that deal with potential life-or-death situations. The **chain of command** is an unbroken line of authority that extends from the top of the organization to the lowest echelon and clarifies who reports to whom.

chain of command *The unbroken line of authority that extends from the top of the organization to the lowest echelon and clarifies who reports to whom.*

authority *The rights inherent in a managerial position to give orders and to expect the orders to be obeyed.*

unity of command *The idea that a subordinate should have only one superior to whom he or she is directly responsible.*

We can't discuss the chain of command without also discussing *authority* and *unity of command*. **Authority** refers to the rights inherent in a managerial position to give orders and expect them to be obeyed. To facilitate coordination, each managerial position is given a place in the chain of command, and each manager is given a degree of authority in order to meet his or her responsibilities. The principle of **unity of command** helps preserve the concept of an unbroken line of authority. It says a person should have one and only one superior to whom he or she is directly responsible. If the unity of command is broken, an employee might have to cope with conflicting demands or priorities from several superiors, as is often the case in organization charts' dotted-line reporting relationships.

Times change, and so do the basic tenets of organizational design. A low-level employee today can access information in seconds that was available only to top managers a generation ago. Operating employees are empowered to make decisions previously reserved for management. Add the popularity of self-managed and cross-functional teams as well as the creation of new structural designs that include multiple bosses, and you can see why authority and unity of command may appear to hold less relevance. Many organizations still find they can be most productive by enforcing the chain of command. Indeed, one survey of more than 1,000 managers found that 59 percent of them agreed with the statement, "There is an imaginary line in my company's organizational chart. Strategy is created by people above this line, while strategy is executed by people below the line."[8] However, this same survey found that lower-level employees' buy-in to the organization's strategy was inhibited by their reliance on the hierarchy for decision making.

Span of Control

span of control *The number of subordinates a manager can efficiently and effectively direct.*

How many employees can a manager efficiently and effectively direct? This question of **span of control** is important because it largely determines the number of levels and managers an organization has. All things being equal, the wider or larger the span, the more efficient the organization.

Assume two organizations each have about 4,100 operative-level employees. One has a uniform span of four and the other a span of eight. As Exhibit 15-3 illustrates, the wider span will have two fewer levels and approximately 800 fewer

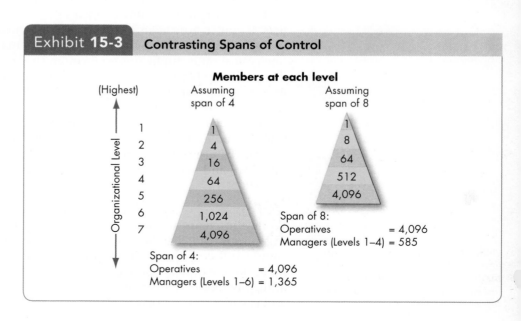

| Exhibit **15-3** | Contrasting Spans of Control |

Members at each level

Assuming span of 4:

Organizational Level	Members
1	1
2	4
3	16
4	64
5	256
6	1,024
7	4,096

Span of 4:
Operatives = 4,096
Managers (Levels 1–6) = 1,365

Assuming span of 8:

Organizational Level	Members
1	1
2	8
3	64
4	512
5	4,096

Span of 8:
Operatives = 4,096
Managers (Levels 1–4) = 585

managers. If the average manager makes $50,000 a year, the wider span will save $40 million a year in management salaries! Obviously, wider spans are more efficient in terms of cost. However, at some point when supervisors no longer have time to provide the necessary leadership and support, they reduce effectiveness and employee performance suffers.

Narrow or small spans have their advocates. By keeping the span of control to five or six employees, a manager can maintain close control.[9] But narrow spans have three major drawbacks. First, they're expensive because they add levels of management. Second, they make vertical communication in the organization more complex. The added levels of hierarchy slow down decision making and tend to isolate upper management. Third, narrow spans encourage overly tight supervision and discourage employee autonomy.

The trend in recent years has been toward wider spans of control. They're consistent with firms' efforts to reduce costs, cut overhead, speed decision making, increase flexibility, get closer to customers, and empower employees. However, to ensure performance doesn't suffer because of these wider spans, organizations have been investing heavily in employee training. Managers recognize they can handle a wider span best when employees know their jobs inside and out or can turn to co-workers when they have questions.

Centralization and Decentralization

centralization *The degree to which decision making is concentrated at a single point in an organization.*

Centralization refers to the degree to which decision making is concentrated at a single point in the organization. In *centralized* organizations, top managers make all the decisions, and lower-level managers merely carry out their directives. In organizations at the other extreme, *decentralized* decision making is pushed down to the managers closest to the action or even to work groups

The concept of centralization includes only formal authority—that is, the rights inherent in a position. An organization characterized by centralization is inherently different structurally from one that's decentralized. A decentralized organization can act more quickly to solve problems, more people provide input into decisions, and employees are less likely to feel alienated from those who make decisions that affect their work lives. Recent research indicates the effects of centralization and decentralization can be predicted: Centralized organizations are better for avoiding commission errors (bad choices), while decentralized organizations are better for avoiding omission errors (lost opportunities).[10]

Management efforts to make organizations more flexible and responsive have produced a recent trend toward decentralized decision making by lower-level managers, who are closer to the action and typically have more detailed knowledge about problems than top managers. Sears and JCPenney have given their store managers considerably more discretion in choosing what merchandise to stock. This allows those stores to compete more effectively against local merchants. Similarly, when Procter & Gamble empowered small groups of employees to make many decisions about new-product development independent of the usual hierarchy, it was able to rapidly increase the proportion of new products ready for market.[11] Research investigating a large number of Finnish organizations demonstrated that companies with decentralized research and development offices in multiple locations were better at producing innovation than companies that centralized all research and development in a single office.[12]

Decentralization is often necessary for companies with offshore sites because localized decision making is needed to respond to each region's profit opportunities, client base, and specific laws, while centralized oversight is needed to hold regional managers accountable. Failure to successfully balance these priorities can harm not only the company, but also its relationships with foreign governments, as in the groundbreaking 2013 case brought by Argentina's government against Britain's HSBC Holdings bank for wrongdoing at its Argentina subsidiary. If the charges in the case prove correct, the local branch aided tax evasion and money laundering through phantom accounts at the local subsidiary.[13] Perhaps this is a situation in which tighter corporate oversight could have made this impossible.

How Willing Am I to Delegate?

In the Self-Assessment Library (available in MyManagementLab), take assessment III.A.2 (How Willing Am I to Delegate?).

Formalization

formalization *The degree to which jobs within an organization are standardized.*

Formalization refers to the degree to which jobs within the organization are standardized. If a job is highly formalized, the incumbent has a minimal amount of discretion over what to do and when and how to do it. Employees can be expected always to handle the same input in exactly the same way, resulting in a consistent and uniform output. There are explicit job descriptions, lots of organizational rules, and clearly defined procedures covering work processes in organizations in which there is high formalization. Where formalization is low, job behaviors are relatively unprogrammed, and employees have a great deal of freedom to exercise discretion in their work. Formalization not only eliminates the possibility of employees engaging in alternative behaviors, but even removes the need for employees to consider alternatives.

The degree of formalization can vary widely between and within organizations. Publishing representatives who call on college professors to inform them of their company's new publications have a great deal of freedom in their jobs. They have only a general sales pitch, which they tailor as needed, and rules and procedures governing their behavior may be little more than the requirement to submit a weekly sales report and suggestions on what to emphasize about forthcoming titles. At the other extreme, clerical and editorial employees in the same publishing houses may need to be at their desks by 8:00 a.m. and follow a set of precise procedures dictated by management. Recent research from 94 high-technology Chinese firms showed that formalization is a detriment to team flexibility in decentralized organization structures, suggesting that formalization does not work as well where duties are inherently interactive, or where there is a need to be flexible and innovative.[14]

Common Organizational Designs

2 Identify the characteristics of a bureaucracy.

simple structure *An organization structure characterized by a low degree of departmentalization, wide spans of control, authority centralized in a single person, and little formalization.*

We now turn to three of the more common organizational designs: the *simple structure*, the *bureaucracy*, and the *matrix structure*.

The Simple Structure

What do a small retail store, an electronics firm run by a hard-driving entrepreneur, and an airline's "war room" in the midst of a pilot's strike have in common? They probably all use the **simple structure**.

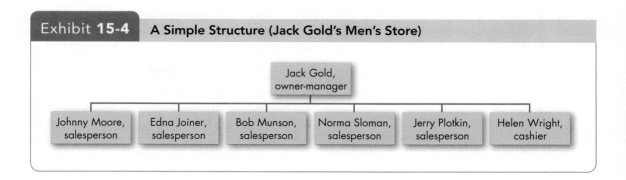

Exhibit 15-4   A Simple Structure (Jack Gold's Men's Store)

We can think of the simple structure in terms of what it is *not* rather than what it is. The simple structure is not elaborate.[15] It has a low degree of departmentalization, wide spans of control, authority centralized in a single person, and little formalization. It is a "flat" organization; it usually has only two or three vertical levels, a loose body of employees, and one individual in whom the decision-making authority is centralized.

Most companies start as a simple structure, and many innovative technology-based firms with short expected lifespans like cell phone app development firms remain compact by design.[16] The simple structure is most widely adopted in small businesses in which the manager and owner are one and the same. Exhibit 15-4 is an organization chart for a retail men's store owned and managed by Jack Gold. Jack employs five full-time salespeople, a cashier, and extra workers for weekends and holidays, but he "runs the show." Though he is typical, large companies in times of crisis often simplify their structures as a means of focusing their resources. When Anne Mulcahy took over as CEO at Xerox, its product mix and management structure were overly complex. She simplified both, cutting corporate overhead by 26 percent. "It's a case of placing your bets in a few areas," she said.[17]

The strength of the simple structure lies in its simplicity. It's fast, flexible, inexpensive to operate, and accountability is clear. One major weakness is that it becomes increasingly inadequate as an organization grows because its low formalization and high centralization tend to create information overload at the top. As size increases, decision making typically becomes slower and can eventually come to a standstill as the single executive tries to continue making all the decisions. This proves the undoing of many small businesses. If the structure isn't changed and made more elaborate, the firm often loses momentum and can eventually fail. The simple structure's other weakness is that it's risky—everything depends on one person. One illness can literally destroy the organization's information and decision-making center.

The Bureaucracy

Standardization! That's the key concept that underlies all bureaucracies. Consider the bank where you keep your checking account; the department store where you buy clothes; or the government offices that collect your taxes, enforce health regulations, or provide local fire protection. They all rely on standardized work processes for coordination and control.

The **bureaucracy** is characterized by highly routine operating tasks achieved through specialization, strictly formalized rules and regulations, tasks grouped into functional departments, centralized authority, narrow spans of control, and decision making that follows the chain of command. *Bureaucracy* is a dirty word in many people's minds. However, it does have advantages. Its primary strength is its ability to perform standardized activities in a highly efficient manner. Putting

bureaucracy *An organization structure with highly routine operating tasks achieved through specialization, very formalized rules and regulations, tasks that are grouped into functional departments, centralized authority, narrow spans of control, and decision making that follows the chain of command.*

like specialties together in functional departments results in economies of scale, minimum duplication of people and equipment, and employees who can speak "the same language" among their peers. Bureaucracies can get by with less talented—and hence less costly—middle- and lower-level managers because rules and regulations substitute for managerial discretion. Standardized operations and high formalization allow decision making to be centralized. There is little need for innovative and experienced decision makers below the level of senior executives.

Listen in on a dialogue among four executives in one company: "You know, nothing happens in this place until we *produce* something," said the production executive. "Wrong," commented the research and development manager. "Nothing happens until we *design* something!" "What are you talking about?" asked the marketing executive. "Nothing happens here until we *sell* something!" The exasperated accounting manager responded, "It doesn't matter what you produce, design, or sell. No one knows what happens until we *tally up the results!*" This conversation highlights that bureaucratic specialization can create conflicts in which functional-unit goals override the overall goals of the organization.

The other major weakness of a bureaucracy is something we've all witnessed: obsessive concern with following the rules. When cases don't precisely fit the rules, there is no room for modification. The bureaucracy is efficient only as long as employees confront familiar problems with programmed decision rules.

The Matrix Structure

3 Describe a matrix organization.

matrix structure *An organization structure that creates dual lines of authority and combines functional and product departmentalization.*

You'll find the **matrix structure** in advertising agencies, aerospace firms, research and development laboratories, construction companies, hospitals, government agencies, universities, management consulting firms, and entertainment companies.[18] It combines two forms of departmentalization: functional and product. Companies that use matrix-like structures include ABB, Boeing, BMW, IBM, and P&G.

The strength of functional departmentalization is putting like specialists together, which minimizes the number necessary while allowing the pooling

Photo 15-2 Hospitals benefit from standardized work processes and procedures common to a bureaucratic structure because they help employees perform their jobs efficiently. The nursing staff in the maternity ward of a New Zealand hospital shown here adhere to formal rules and regulations in providing care to moms and newborns.

Exhibit 15-5	Matrix Structure for a College of Business Administration

Programs / Academic Departments	Undergraduate	Master's	Ph.D.	Research	Executive Development	Community Service
Accounting						
Finance						
Decision and Information Systems						
Management						
Marketing						

and sharing of specialized resources across products. Its major disadvantage is the difficulty of coordinating the tasks of diverse functional specialists on time and within budget. Product departmentalization has exactly the opposite benefits and disadvantages. It facilitates coordination among specialties to achieve on-time completion and meet budget targets. It provides clear responsibility for all activities related to a product, but with duplication of activities and costs. The matrix attempts to gain the strengths of each while avoiding their weaknesses.

The most obvious structural characteristic of the matrix is that it breaks the unity-of-command concept. Employees in the matrix have two bosses: their functional department managers and their product managers.

Exhibit 15-5 shows the matrix form in a college of business administration. The academic departments of accounting, decision and information systems, marketing, and so forth are functional units. Overlaid on them are specific programs (that is, products). Thus, members in a matrix structure have a dual chain of command: to their functional department and to their product groups. A professor of accounting teaching an undergraduate course may report to the director of undergraduate programs as well as to the chairperson of the accounting department.

The strength of the matrix is its ability to facilitate coordination when the organization has a number of complex and interdependent activities. Direct and frequent contacts between different specialties in the matrix can let information permeate the organization and more quickly reach the people who need it. The matrix reduces "bureaupathologies"—the dual lines of authority reduce people's tendency to become so busy protecting their little worlds that the organization's goals become secondary.[19] A matrix also achieves economies of scale and facilitates the allocation of specialists by providing both the best resources and an effective way of ensuring their efficient deployment.

The major disadvantages of the matrix lie in the confusion it creates, its tendency to foster power struggles, and the stress it places on individuals.[20] Without the unity-of-command concept, ambiguity about who reports to who is significantly increased and often leads to conflict. It's not unusual for product managers to fight over getting the best specialists assigned to their products. Bureaucracy reduces the potential for power grabs by defining the rules of the game.

When those rules are "up for grabs" in a matrix, power struggles between functional and product managers result. For individuals who desire security and absence from ambiguity, this work climate can be stressful. Reporting to more than one boss introduces role conflict, and unclear expectations introduce role ambiguity. The comfort of bureaucracy's predictability is replaced by insecurity and stress.

New Design Options

Senior managers in a number of organizations have been developing new structural options with fewer layers of hierarchy and more emphasis on opening the boundaries of the organization.[21] In this section, we describe two such designs: the *virtual organization* and the *boundaryless organization*. We'll also discuss how efforts to reduce bureaucracy and increase strategic focus have made downsizing routine.

The Virtual Organization

4   Identify the characteristics of a virtual organization.

virtual organization   *A small, core organization that outsources major business functions.*

Why own when you can rent? That question captures the essence of the **virtual organization** (also sometimes called the *network,* or *modular,* organization), typically a small, core organization that outsources its major business functions.[22] In structural terms, the virtual organization is highly centralized, with little or no departmentalization.

The prototype of the virtual structure is today's movie-making organization. In Hollywood's golden era, movies were made by huge, vertically integrated corporations. Studios such as MGM, Warner Brothers, and 20th Century Fox owned large movie lots and employed thousands of full-time specialists—set designers, camera people, film editors, directors, and even actors. Today, most movies are made by a collection of individuals and small companies who come together and make films project by project.[23] This structural form allows each project to be staffed with the talent best suited to its demands, rather than just with the people employed by the studio. It minimizes bureaucratic overhead because there is no lasting organization to maintain. And it lessens long-term risks and their costs because there *is* no long term—a team is assembled for a finite period and then disbanded.

Philip Rosedale runs a virtual company called LoveMachine that lets employees send brief electronic messages to one another to acknowledge a job well done; the messages can be then used to facilitate company bonuses. The company has no full-time software development staff—instead, LoveMachine outsources assignments to freelancers who submit bids for projects like debugging software or designing new features. Programmers work from around the world, including Russia, India, Australia, and the United States.[24] Similarly, Newman's Own, the food products company founded by Paul Newman, sells hundreds of millions of dollars in food every year yet employs only 28 people. This is possible because it outsources almost everything: manufacturing, procurement, shipping, and quality control.

Exhibit 15-6 shows a virtual organization in which management outsources all the primary functions of the business. The core of the organization is a small group of executives whose job is to oversee directly any activities done in-house and to coordinate relationships with the other organizations that

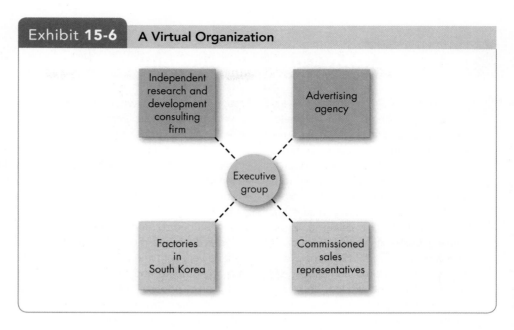

Exhibit 15-6   A Virtual Organization

manufacture, distribute, and perform other crucial functions for the virtual organization. The dotted lines represent the relationships typically maintained under contracts. In essence, managers in virtual structures spend most of their time coordinating and controlling external relations, typically by way of computer network links.

The major advantage of the virtual organization is its flexibility, which allows individuals with an innovative idea and little money to successfully compete against larger, more established organizations. Virtual organizations also save a great deal of money by eliminating permanent offices and hierarchical roles.[25]

Virtual organizations' drawbacks have become increasingly clear as their popularity has grown.[26] They are in a state of perpetual flux and reorganization, which means roles, goals, and responsibilities are unclear, setting the stage for political behavior. Cultural alignment and shared goals can be lost because of the low degree of interaction among members. Team members who are geographically dispersed and communicate infrequently find it difficult to share information and knowledge, which can limit innovation and slow response time. Sometimes, as with Lululemon's shipments of unintentionally see-through yoga pants, the consequences of having geographically remote managers can be embarrassing and even financially harmful to the company.[27] Ironically, some virtual organizations are less adaptable and innovative than those with well-established communication and collaboration networks. A leadership presence that reinforces the organization's purpose and facilitates communication is thus especially valuable.

The Boundaryless Organization

5 Show why managers want to create boundaryless organizations.

boundaryless organization *An organization that seeks to eliminate the chain of command, have limitless spans of control, and replace departments with empowered teams.*

General Electric's former chairman, Jack Welch, coined the term **boundaryless organization** to describe what he wanted GE to become: a "family grocery store."[28] That is, in spite of GE's monstrous size (2012 revenues were $144.8 billion),[29] Welch wanted to eliminate *vertical* and *horizontal* boundaries within it and break down *external* barriers between the company and its customers and suppliers. The boundaryless organization seeks to eliminate the chain of command, have limitless spans of control, and replace departments with empowered teams. Although GE has not yet achieved this boundaryless state—and probably never will—it has made significant progress toward that end. So have

The World Is My Corporate Headquarters

"Going global" has meant many things in the evolution of worldwide business: sourcing materials from abroad, selling products overseas, and sending employees worldwide among them. In all earlier models, the common theme was that the corporate office is *here*, and global means *out there*. This thinking is changing. Enter the rise of office-less companies such as Automattic Inc., with 123 employees working in 26 countries, and Kalypso LP, with 150 employees around the globe. Neither company has a corporate headquarters or, truly, an office of any sort. The implications of this new understanding of what it means to be a global business are logistical, structural, and human.

On the logistics end of getting work done, office-less companies utilize every technology available, from Skype to blogs. Sensitive information is limited to phone discussions, though the difficulty of scheduling virtual meetings can be tricky across a number of time zones. When needed and at least annually, employees fly to designated intermediate spots for face-to-face time. Employees live where they want or where a strategic company presence for clients is desired.

The office-less company isn't a good fit for every industry. The complete decentralization of the organization's physical structure dictates a nonhierarchical organization chart. High employee autonomy and empowerment to make decisions means supervision must be very light in order for the company to compete and take advantage of business opportunities specific to one employee's region, which the rest of the company cannot see.

With hiring possibilities worldwide, the company must also be clear about who can recruit new candidates and how to fit them into the organizational structure. Though the office-less company sounds like a good opportunity to maximize the worldwide talent pool, it presents challenges on a human level. According to Bill Poston, founding-partner of Kalypso, the office-less company doesn't work for people "who are uncomfortable with ambiguity." With the technology available, workers aren't isolated, but the necessary lack of hierarchy means some workers may feel underappreciated. Strong hiring and orientation methods may counteract these challenges, however, and Automattic even has job candidates work on projects before being hired to determine whether they will work well in its office-less environment. Research supports the idea that testing candidates for their natural fit is preferable to subjecting employees to surveillance technology, whether keystroke counts or body sensors.

The office-less company is still a rarity in the world, but its popularity is growing. It's very possible that truly global corporations of the future will need to consider a decentralization strategy that includes either many headquarters—or no headquarters at all.

Sources: T. Johns and L. Gratton, "The Third Wave of Virtual Work," *Harvard Business Review* (January–February 2013), pp. 66–73; R. E. Silverman, "Step Into the Office-Less Company," *The Wall Street Journal* (September 15, 2012), p. B6; and R. E. Silverman, "Tracking Sensors Invade the Workplace," *The Wall Street Journal* (March 7, 2013), p. B1.

other companies, such as Hewlett-Packard, AT&T, Motorola, and 3M. Let's see what a boundaryless organization looks like and what some firms are doing to make it a reality.

By removing vertical boundaries, management flattens the hierarchy and minimizes status and rank. Cross-hierarchical teams (which include top executives, middle managers, supervisors, and operative employees), participative decision-making practices, and the use of 360-degree performance appraisals (in which peers and others above and below the employee evaluate performance) are examples of what GE is doing to break down vertical boundaries. At Oticon A/S, a $160 million-per-year Danish hearing aid manufacturer, all traces of hierarchy have disappeared. Everyone works at uniform mobile workstations, and project teams, not functions or departments, coordinate work.

Functional departments create horizontal boundaries that stifle interaction among functions, product lines, and units. The way to reduce them is to replace functional departments with cross-functional teams and organize activities around processes. Xerox now develops new products through multidisciplinary

Photo 15-3 BMW Group operates as a boundaryless organization in designing, developing, and producing its BMW, Rolls-Royce, and Mini cars. The automaker's plant shown here in Jakarta, Indonesia, is part of BMW's flexible global production network that responds quickly to fluctuations in customer demands and market requirements.

Source: Bloomberg via Getty Images.

teams that work on a single process instead of on narrow functional tasks. Some AT&T units prepare annual budgets based not on functions or departments but on processes, such as the maintenance of a worldwide telecommunications network. Another way to lower horizontal barriers is to rotate people through different functional areas using lateral transfers. This approach turns specialists into generalists.

When fully operational, the boundaryless organization also breaks down geographic barriers. Today, most large U.S. companies see themselves as global corporations; many, like Coca-Cola and McDonald's, do as much business overseas as in the United States, and some struggle to incorporate geographic regions into their structure. In other cases, the boundaryless organization approach is need-based. Such is the case with Chinese companies, which have made 93 acquisitions in the oil and gas industry since 2008 to meet forecasted demand their resources in China cannot meet.[30] The boundaryless organization provides one solution because it considers geography more of a tactical, logistical issue than a structural one. In short, the goal is to break down cultural barriers.

One way to do so is through strategic alliances.[31] Firms such as NEC Corporation, Boeing, and Apple each have strategic alliances or joint partnerships with dozens of companies. These alliances blur the distinction between one organization and another as employees work on joint projects. Research from 119 international joint ventures (IJVs) in China indicates that these partnerships allow firms to learn from each other and obtain higher new product performance especially where a strong learning culture exists.[32] And some companies allow customers to perform functions previously done by management. Some AT&T units receive bonuses based on customer evaluations of the teams that serve them. Finally, telecommuting is blurring organizational boundaries. The security analyst with Merrill Lynch who does her job from her ranch in Montana or the software designer in Boulder, Colorado, who works for a San Francisco firm are just two of the millions of workers operating outside the physical boundaries of their employers' premises.

OB Poll The Incredible Shrinking Office

Office space per worker (sq ft)

2000	2010	2012	(2017)
270	225	176	151

Source: Based on February 28, 2012 press release "Office Space per Worker Will Drop to 100 Square Feet or Below." http://www.corenetglobal.org/files/home/info_center/global_press_releases/pdf/pr120227_officespace.pdf.

The Leaner Organization: Downsizing

The goal of the new organizational forms we've described is to improve agility by creating a lean, focused, and flexible organization. *Downsizing* is a systematic effort to make an organization leaner by closing locations, reducing staff, or selling off business units that don't add value.

The radical shrinking of Motorola Mobility in 2012 and 2013 is a case of downsizing to survive after its merger with Google. In response to declining demand for its smartphones, Motorola cut the workforce by 20 percent in August 2012. When the company posted a $350 million fourth-quarter loss in 2012, with a 40 percent revenue decline, it cut the workforce again, by 10 percent.

Photo 15-4 Naveen Selvadurai is the co-founder of Foursquare, a social networking service that transfers its inputs into outputs by using location-based mobile platform technology. Nonroutineness characterizes the work of employees at Foursquare, an organic organization that adapts quickly and flexibly to rapid changes in its environment.

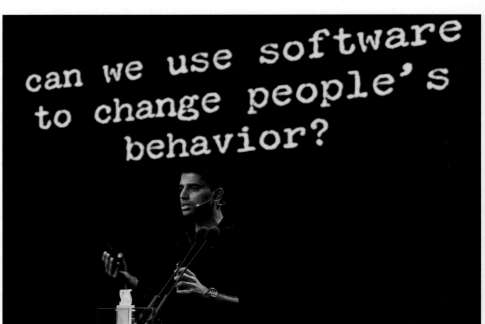

Google calls this "rightsizing" and hopes a new Motorola phone will save the company from further layoffs.[33]

Other firms downsize to direct all their efforts toward their core competencies. American Express claims to have been doing this in a series of layoffs over more than a decade: 7,700 jobs in 2001; 6,500 jobs in 2002; 7,000 jobs (10 percent of its workforce) in 2008; 4,000 jobs in 2009. The 2013 cut of 5,400 jobs (8.5 percent of the remaining workforce) represents "its biggest retrenchment in a decade." Each layoff has been accompanied by a restructuring to reflect changing customer preferences, away from personal customer service and toward online customer service. According to CEO Ken Chennault, these "restructuring initiatives" are "designed to make American Express more nimble, more efficient and more effective in using our resources to drive growth . . . and to maintain marketing and promotion investments."[34]

Some companies focus on lean management techniques to reduce bureaucracy and speed decision making. Starbucks adopted lean initiatives in 2009, which encompassed all levels of management and also focused on faster barista techniques and manufacturing processes. Customers have generally applauded the shortened wait times and product consistency at this well-run corporation. Starbucks continues to reap returns from its lean initiatives, posting notable revenue gains each quarter.[35]

Despite the advantages of being a lean organization, the impact of downsizing on organizational performance has been a source of controversy.[36] Reducing the size of the workforce has an immediately positive outcome in the form of lower wage costs. Companies downsizing to improve strategic focus often see positive effects on stock prices after the announcement. A recent example of this is with Russia's Gorky Automobile Factory (GAZ), which realized a profit for the first time in many years after President Bo Andersson fired 50,000 workers, half the workforce.[37] On the other hand, among companies that only cut employees but don't restructure, profits and stock prices usually decline. Part of the problem is the effect of downsizing on employee attitudes. Those who remain often feel worried about future layoffs and may be less committed to the organization.[38] Stress reactions can lead to increased sickness absences, lower concentration on the job, and lower creativity. In companies that don't invest much in their employees, downsizing can also lead to more voluntary turnover, so vital human capital is lost. The result is a company that is more anemic than lean.

Companies can reduce negative impacts by preparing in advance, thus alleviating some employee stress and strengthening support for the new direction.[39] Here are some effective strategies for downsizing. Most are closely linked to the principles for organizational justice we've discussed previously:

- **Investment.**   Companies that downsize to focus on core competencies are more effective when they invest in high-involvement work practices afterward.
- **Communication.**   When employers make efforts to discuss downsizing with employees early, employees are less worried about the outcomes and feel the company is taking their perspective into account.
- **Participation.**   Employees worry less if they can participate in the process in some way. Voluntary early-retirement programs or severance packages can help achieve leanness without layoffs.
- **Assistance.**   Severance, extended health care benefits, and job search assistance demonstrate a company cares about its employees and honors their contributions.

In short, companies that make themselves lean can be more agile, efficient, and productive—but only if they make cuts carefully and help employees through the process.

Ethical Concerns of Deskless Workplaces

Once upon a time, students fresh from business schools couldn't wait for that first cubicle to call home, mid-level managers aspired to an office of their own, and executives coveted the corner office on the top floor. These days, the walls are coming down. At online retailer Zappos, not even the CEO wants an office, and all 1,300 employees are welcome throughout the open spaces. Other firms like Google have followed the trend, giving rise to new workplace designs of public rooms with lounge areas and large, multiperson tables.

According to Edward Danyo, manager of workplace strategy at pharmaceuticals firm GlaxoSmithKline, shared environments create great work gains, including what he estimates is a 45 percent increase in the speed of decision making. But there are ethical concerns for the dismantling of the physical and mental organizational structure. Here are some questions for you to consider for managing employees in one of these workplaces of the future:

- Where will confidential discussions take place? As a manager, you need to be able to address issues with your employees privately, and your employees likewise need to feel welcome to meet with you and human resource professionals privately. In some contemporary workplace designs, ad hoc conference rooms address the need for separate gatherings. This may not be optimal if the walls are made of glass, if your employees will feel stigmatized when called into

a meeting room with you or a human resources professional, or if your employees become reluctant to approach human resources staff with issues. As a manager, you will need to be sensitive to employees' concerns.

- How can differences in personality traits be overcome? Just like in a middle-school cafeteria, employees high in extraversion will be more comfortable building collaborative relationships without assigned workspaces, while highly introverted individuals may be uncomfortable without an established office structure where they can get to know others over time. Your input on team building will be even more important to keep your projects moving forward.

- How can personal privacy be maintained? Zappos gives employees personal lockers, asks employees to angle laptop screens away from neighbors, and tries to make open spaces more private by encouraging ear buds to create a sound barrier between working employees. It may be best to think of the deskless office as being as public as, for instance, a library. You will need to communicate the company's expectations and protocol for reporting violations to your employees and respond to their concerns.

- How can you assure your clients of confidentiality? Even walled, soundproof rooms for virtual or live meetings may not provide the desired level of security for clients who

need to know their business will stay on a need-to-know basis. As a manager, you will need to help create an environment in which clients can trust that their interactions with your employees will be secure.

- Where will electronic and paper files be stored, and how will access to them be limited? Cloud-based storage is common, and paper files are at the lowest levels ever in organizations, but security issues for each need to be considered in organizational design, and access needs to be assigned from the organizational chart. You will be responsible for knowing which of your employees has access to files in the cloud and physically.

- How will expectations and accountabilities be enforced? In an environment without offices and sometimes without job titles, there is an even greater need for clearly assigned goals, roles, and expectations. Open, collaborative structures may foster the diffusion of responsibility we discussed as problems of groups and teams in Chapters 9 and 10.

Sources: S. Henn, "'Serendipitous Interaction' Key to Tech Firms's Workplace Design," *NPR* (March 13, 2013), www.npr.org/blogs/alltechconsidered/2013/03/13/174195695/serendipitous-interaction-key-to-tech-firms-workplace-design; H. El Nasser, "What Office? Laptops are Workspace," *USA Today* (June 6, 2012), pp. 1B–2B; R. W. Huppke, "Thinking Outside the Cubicle," *Chicago Tribune* (October 29, 2012), pp. 2-1, 2-3; "Inside the New Deskless Office," *Forbes* (July 16, 2012), p. 34; and E. Maltby, "My Space Is Our Space," *The Wall Street Journal* (May 21, 2012), p. R9.

Why Do Structures Differ?

6 Demonstrate how organizational structures differ, and contrast mechanistic and organic structural models.

mechanistic model   *A structure characterized by extensive departmentalization, high formalization, a limited information network, and centralization.*

organic model   *A structure that is flat, uses cross-hierarchical and cross-functional teams, has low formalization, possesses a comprehensive information network, and relies on participative decision making.*

We've described organizational designs ranging from the highly structured bureaucracy to the amorphous boundaryless organization. The other designs we discussed exist somewhere in between.

Exhibit 15-7 recaps our discussions by presenting two extreme models of organizational design. One we'll call the **mechanistic model**. It's generally synonymous with the bureaucracy in that it has highly standardized processes for work, high formalization, and more managerial hierarchy. The other extreme, the **organic model**, looks a lot like the boundaryless organization. It's flat, has fewer formal procedures for making decisions, has multiple decision makers, and favors flexible practices.[40]

With these two models in mind, let's ask a few questions: Why are some organizations structured along more mechanistic lines whereas others follow organic characteristics? What forces influence the choice of design? In this section, we present the major causes or determinants of an organization's structure.[41]

Organizational Strategy

Because structure is a means to achieve objectives, and objectives derive from the organization's overall strategy, it's only logical that structure should follow strategy. If management significantly changes the organization's strategy, the structure must change to accommodate.[42] Most current strategy frameworks focus on three strategy dimensions—innovation, cost minimization, and imitation—and the structural design that works best with each.[43]

innovation strategy   *A strategy that emphasizes the introduction of major new products and services.*

To what degree does an organization introduce major new products or services? An **innovation strategy** strives to achieve meaningful and unique innovations. Obviously, not all firms pursue innovation. Apple and 3M do, but

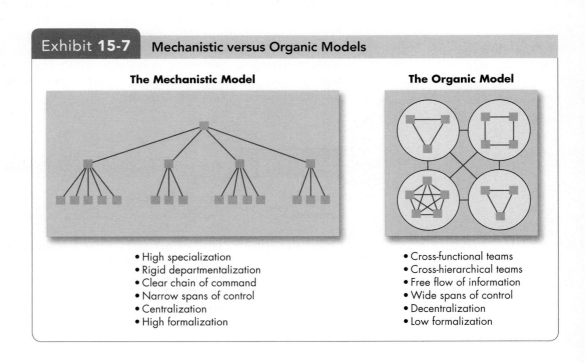

Exhibit **15-7**   Mechanistic versus Organic Models

The Mechanistic Model

- High specialization
- Rigid departmentalization
- Clear chain of command
- Narrow spans of control
- Centralization
- High formalization

The Organic Model

- Cross-functional teams
- Cross-hierarchical teams
- Free flow of information
- Wide spans of control
- Decentralization
- Low formalization

cost-minimization strategy *A strategy that emphasizes tight cost controls, avoidance of unnecessary innovation or marketing expenses, and price cutting.*

imitation strategy *A strategy that seeks to move into new products or new markets only after their viability has already been proven.*

conservative retailer Marks & Spencer doesn't. Innovative firms will use competitive pay and benefits to attract top candidates and motivate employees to take risks. Some degree of mechanistic structure can actually benefit innovation. Well-developed communication channels, policies for enhancing long-term commitment, and clear channels of authority all may make it easier for rapid changes to occur smoothly.

An organization pursuing a **cost-minimization strategy** tightly controls costs, refrains from incurring unnecessary expenses, and cuts prices in selling a basic product. This describes the strategy pursued by Walmart and the makers of generic or store-label grocery products. Cost-minimizing organizations pursue fewer policies meant to develop commitment among their workforce.

Organizations following an **imitation strategy** try to both minimize risk and maximize opportunity for profit, moving new products or entering new markets only after innovators have proven their viability. Mass-market fashion manufacturers that copy designer styles follow this strategy, as do firms such as Hewlett-Packard and Caterpillar. They follow smaller and more innovative competitors with superior products, but only after competitors have demonstrated the market is there. Italy's Moleskine SpA, a small maker of fashionable notebooks, is another example of imitation strategy, but in the reverse; looking to open more retail shops around the world, it is employing the expansion strategies of larger, successful fashion companies Salvatore Ferragamo SpA and Brunello Cucinelli.[44]

Exhibit 15-8 describes the structural option that best matches each strategy. Innovators need the flexibility of the organic structure, whereas cost minimizers seek the efficiency and stability of the mechanistic structure. Imitators combine the two structures. They use a mechanistic structure to maintain tight controls and low costs in their current activities but create organic subunits in which to pursue new undertakings.

Organization Size

An organization's size significantly affects its structure. Organizations that employ 2,000 or more people tend to have more specialization, more departmentalization, more vertical levels, and more rules and regulations than do small organizations. However, size becomes less important as an organization expands. Why? At around 2,000 employees, an organization is already fairly mechanistic; 500 more employees won't have much impact. But adding 500 employees to an organization of only 300 is likely to significantly shift it toward a more mechanistic structure.

Exhibit 15-8	The Strategy–Structure Relationship
Strategy	**Structural Option**
Innovation	**Organic:** A loose structure; low specialization, low formalization, decentralized
Cost minimization	**Mechanistic:** Tight control; extensive work specialization, high formalization, high centralization
Imitation	**Mechanistic and organic:** Mix of loose with tight properties; tight controls over current activities and looser controls for new undertakings

Photo 15-5 It's a common practice in China for managers in service businesses to gather employees before their workday and give them a pep talk and training. The barbershop employees shown here in Foshan accept the daily ritual because power distance is high in China, making workers tolerant of mechanistic structures.

Source: ChinaFotoPress/ZUMA Press/Newscom.

technology *The way in which an organization transfers its inputs into outputs.*

Technology

Technology describes the way an organization transfers inputs into outputs. Every organization has at least one technology for converting financial, human, and physical resources into products or services. Ford Motor Company uses an assembly-line process to make its products. Colleges may use a number of instructional technologies—the ever-popular lecture method, case analysis, the experiential exercise, programmed learning, and online instruction and distance learning. Regardless, organizational structures adapt to their technology.

Numerous studies have examined the technology–structure relationship.[45] What differentiates technologies is their *degree of routineness*. Routine activities are characterized by automated and standardized operations. Examples are injection-mold production of plastic knobs, automated transaction processing of sales transactions, and the printing and binding of this book. Nonroutine activities are customized and require frequent revision and updating. They include furniture restoring, custom shoemaking, genetic research, and the writing and editing of this book. In general, organizations engaged in nonroutine activities tend to prefer organic structures, while those performing routine activities prefer mechanistic structures.

Environment

environment *Institutions or forces outside an organization that potentially affect the organization's performance.*

An organization's **environment** includes outside institutions or forces that can affect its performance, such as suppliers, customers, competitors, government regulatory agencies, and public pressure groups. Dynamic environments create significantly more uncertainty for managers than do static ones. To minimize uncertainty in key market arenas, managers may broaden their structure to sense and respond to threats. For example, most companies, including Pepsi and Southwest Airlines, have added social networking departments to counter negative information posted on blogs. Or companies may form strategic alliances, such as when Microsoft and Yahoo! joined forces to better compete with Google in the online search provider arena.

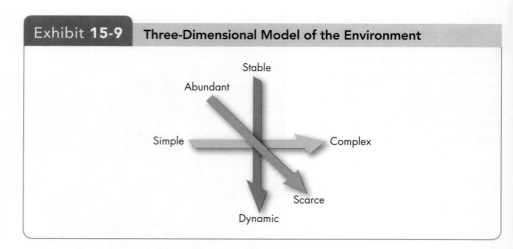

Exhibit **15-9**   Three-Dimensional Model of the Environment

Any organization's environment has three dimensions: capacity, volatility, and complexity.[46] *Capacity* refers to the degree to which the environment can support growth. Rich and growing environments generate excess resources, which can buffer the organization in times of relative scarcity.

Volatility describes the degree of instability in the environment. A dynamic environment with a high degree of unpredictable change makes it difficult for management to make accurate predictions. Because information technology changes at such a rapid place, for instance, more organizations' environments are becoming volatile.

Finally, *complexity* is the degree of heterogeneity and concentration among environmental elements. Simple environments—like the tobacco industry where the methods of production, competitive and regulatory pressures, and the like haven't changed in quite some time—are homogeneous and concentrated. Environments characterized by heterogeneity and dispersion—like the broadband industry—are complex and diverse, with numerous competitors.

Exhibit 15-9 summarizes our definition of the environment along its three dimensions. The arrows indicate movement toward higher uncertainty. Thus, organizations that operate in environments characterized as scarce, dynamic, and complex face the greatest degree of uncertainty because they have high unpredictability, little room for error, and a diverse set of elements in the environment to monitor constantly.

Given this three-dimensional definition of *environment*, we can offer some general conclusions about environmental uncertainty and structural arrangements. The more scarce, dynamic, and complex the environment, the more organic a structure should be. The more abundant, stable, and simple the environment, the more the mechanistic structure will be preferred.

Organizational Designs and Employee Behavior

7 Analyze the behavioral implications of different organizational designs.

We opened this chapter by implying that an organization's structure can have significant effects on its members. What might those effects be?

A review of the evidence leads to a pretty clear conclusion: You can't generalize! Not everyone prefers the freedom and flexibility of organic structures. Different factors stand out in different structures as well. In highly formalized,

"Employees Can Work Just as Well from Home"

This statement is true, but not unequivocally. Employees who work from home even part of the time report they are happier, and as we saw in Chapter 3, happier employees are likely to be more productive than their dissatisfied counterparts. From an organization's perspective, companies are realizing gains of 5 to 7 extra work hours a week for each employee working from home. There are also cost savings, from reduced overhead for office space and utilities to elimination of unproductive social time. Employers of a home-based workforce can establish work teams and organizational reporting relationships with little attention to office politics, opening the potential to more objectively assign roles and responsibilities. These may be some of the reasons organizations have increasingly endorsed the concept of telecommuting, to the point where 3.1 million U.S. employees are now company-employed to work from home.

Although we can all think of jobs that may never be conducive to working from home (such as many in the service industry), not all positions that *could* be based from home *should* be. Research indicates the success of a work-from-home position depends on the job's structure even more than on its tasks. The amount of interdependence needed between employees within a team or in a reporting relationship sometimes requires *epistemic interdependence*, which is each employee's ability to predict what other employees will do. Organization consultants pay attention to how employee roles relate in the *architecture* of the organization chart, realizing that intentional relationship building is key. Thus, while an employee may complete the tasks of a job well by working alone from home, the benefits of teamwork can be lost. We don't yet fully understand the impact of working at a physical distance without

sharing time or space with others, but it is perhaps the reason that Yahoo!, Best Buy, and other corporations are reining their employees back into the office.

The success of a work-from-home program depends on the individual, the job, and the culture of the organization. Work from home can be satisfying for employees and efficient for organizations, but we are learning that there are limits.

Sources: M. Mercer, "Shirk Work? Working at Home Can Mean Longer Hours," *TriCities.com* (March 4, 2013), www.tricities.com/news/opinion_columns/article_d04355b8-83cb-11e2-bc31-0019bb30f31a.html; P. Puranam, M. Raveendran, and T. Knudsen, "Organization Design: The Epistemic Interdependence Perspective," *Academy of Management Review* 37, no. 3 (2012), pp. 419–440; N. Shah, "More Americans Working Remotely," *The Wall Street Journal* (March 6, 2013), p. A3; and R. E. Silverman and Q. Fottrell, "The Home Office in the Spotlight," *The Wall Street Journal* (February 27, 2013), p. B6.

heavily structured, mechanistic organizations, the level of fairness in formal policies and procedures is a very important predictor of satisfaction. In more personal, individually adaptive organic organizations, employees value interpersonal justice more.[47] Some people are most productive and satisfied when work tasks are standardized and ambiguity minimized—that is, in mechanistic structures. So, any discussion of the effect of organizational design on employee behavior has to address individual differences. To do so, let's consider employee preferences for work specialization, span of control, and centralization.[48]

The evidence generally indicates that *work specialization* contributes to higher employee productivity—but at the price of reduced job satisfaction. However, work specialization is not an unending source of higher productivity. Problems start to surface, and productivity begins to suffer, when the human diseconomies of doing repetitive and narrow tasks overtake the economies of specialization. As the workforce has become more highly educated and desirous of jobs that are intrinsically rewarding, we seem to reach the point at which productivity begins to decline as a function of specialization more quickly than in the past. While decreased productivity often prompts companies to add oversight and inspection roles, the better answer may be to reorganize work functions and accountability.[49]

There is still a segment of the workforce that prefers the routine and repetitiveness of highly specialized jobs. Some individuals want work that makes minimal intellectual demands and provides the security of routine; for them, high work specialization is a source of job satisfaction. The question, of course, is whether they represent 2 percent of the workforce or 52 percent. Given that some self-selection operates in the choice of careers, we might conclude that negative behavioral outcomes from high specialization are most likely to surface in professional jobs occupied by individuals with high needs for personal growth and diversity.

It is probably safe to say no evidence supports a relationship between *span of control* and employee satisfaction or performance. Although it is intuitively attractive to argue that large spans might lead to higher employee performance because they provide more distant supervision and more opportunity for personal initiative, the research fails to support this notion. Some people like to be left alone; others prefer the security of a boss who is quickly available at all times. Consistent with several of the contingency theories of leadership discussed in Chapter 12, we would expect factors such as employees' experiences and abilities and the degree of structure in their tasks to explain when wide or narrow spans of control are likely to contribute to their performance and job satisfaction. However, some evidence indicates that a *manager's* job satisfaction increases as the number of employees supervised increases.

We find fairly strong evidence linking *centralization* and job satisfaction. In general, less centralized organizations have a greater amount of autonomy. And autonomy appears positively related to job satisfaction. But, again, while one employee may value freedom, another may find autonomous environments frustratingly ambiguous.

Our conclusion: To maximize employee performance and satisfaction, managers must take individual differences, such as experience, personality, and the work task, into account. Culture should factor in, too.

We can draw one obvious insight: other things equal, people don't select employers randomly. They are attracted to, are selected by, and stay with organizations that suit their personal characteristics.[50] Job candidates who prefer predictability are likely to seek out and take employment in mechanistic structures, and those who want autonomy are more likely to end up in an organic structure. Thus, the effect of structure on employee behavior is undoubtedly reduced when the selection process facilitates proper matching of individual characteristics with organizational characteristics. Furthermore, companies should strive to establish, promote, and maintain the unique identity of their structures since skilled employees may quit as a result of dramatic changes.[51]

Research suggests national culture influences the preference for structure.[52] Organizations that operate with people from high power-distance cultures, such as Greece, France, and most of Latin America, find their employees are much more accepting of mechanistic structures than are employees from low power-distance countries. So consider cultural differences along with individual differences when predicting how structure will affect employee performance and satisfaction.

Finally, the changing landscape of organizational structure designs has implications for the individual progressing on a career path. Recent research interviews with managers in Japan, the United Kingdom, and the United States indicate that employees who have weathered downsizing and resulting hybrid organizational structures consider their future career prospects diminished. While this may or may not be true, it shows that organizational structure does affect the employee and thus must be carefully designed.[53]

Summary

The theme of this chapter is that an organization's internal structure contributes to explaining and predicting behavior. That is, in addition to individual and group factors, the structural relationships in which people work has a bearing on employee attitudes and behavior. What's the basis for this argument? To the degree that an organization's structure reduces ambiguity for employees and clarifies concerns such as "What am I supposed to do?" "How am I supposed to do it?" "To whom do I report?" and "To whom do I go if I have a problem?" it shapes their attitudes and facilitates and motivates them to higher levels of performance. Exhibit 15-10 summarizes what we've discussed.

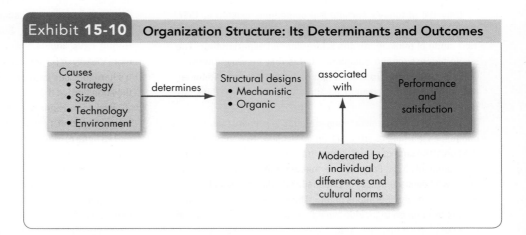

Exhibit 15-10   Organization Structure: Its Determinants and Outcomes

Implications for Managers

- Specialization can make operations more efficient, but remember that excessive specialization can create dissatisfaction and reduced motivation.
- Avoid designing rigid hierarchies that overly limit employees' empowerment and autonomy.
- Balance the advantages of virtual and boundaryless organizations against the potential pitfalls before adding flexible workplace options.
- Downsize your organization to realize major cost savings, and focus the company around core competencies—but only if necessary because downsizing can have a significant negative impact on employee affect.
- Consider the scarcity, dynamism, and complexity of the environment, and balance the organic and mechanistic elements when designing an organizational structure.

The End of Management

POINT | **COUNTERPOINT**

Management—at least as we know it—is dying. Formal organizational structures are giving way to flatter, less bureaucratic, less formal structures. And that's a good thing.

Today, leaders are celebrated for triumphing *over* structure rather than for working well within it. Innovative companies like Apple, Google, Facebook, Twitter, and Groupon were born and now thrive thanks not to a multilayered bureaucracy, but to an innovative idea that was creatively executed by a flexible group of people freely collaborating. Management in those companies exists to facilitate, rather than control.

Only 100 of today's *Fortune* 500 companies existed in 1957. Yet management theory and practice continue to adhere to a 1957 mode of thinking. As one future-minded expert noted, "The single biggest reason companies fail is that they overinvest in what is, as opposed to what might be." How does a traditional, formal, bureaucratic structure foster "what might be" thinking? It doesn't.

The new wave of eliminating job titles is a prime indicator of companies learning to structure for innovation. This trend is a reflection of the changes in job scope that have come with increased technological savvy. For instance, the fact that most managers do their own keyboarding has dramatically changed the job of the office secretary of generations before. The scope of what managers do has broadened to include typing, taking notes, and managing their own files/schedules, while the scope of what secretaries (or administrative assistants) do has broadened to include making social media posts and assuming technical duties. The most innovative firms have questioned whether they need job titles at all, instead emphasizing collaboration throughout the organization.

The best companies have eliminated offices altogether and encourage employees to mingle and form teams according to their project interests. This suits younger workers who never did want offices, who aspire to work *with* the top players rather than *report to* them, and who value flexible hours and work from home options. Job titles are gone, roles are ambiguous, and reporting relationships morph by project.

"There's a struggle right now between the old and the new," notes Adam Leitman Bailey, a New York real estate lawyer. "We don't what know works. In the end, it's what's going to be best for the talent we hire." The talent is ready for the elimination of management as we know it. The successful corporation of the future will have a flatter organizational structure and accountability based on performance.

There is no "right size fits all" approach to organizational structure. How flat, informal, and collaborative an organization should be depends on many factors, but no matter what, management structure is needed. Let's consider two cases.

People lauded how loosely and informally Warren Buffett structured his investment firm, Berkshire Hathaway. Buffett spends most of his day reading and talking informally "with highly gifted people whom he trusts and who trust him." This sounded wonderful until it was discovered Buffett's CFO and heir apparent David Sokol was on the take. Sokol made $3 million when he successfully lobbied for Berkshire Hathaway to acquire a firm in which he had secretly acquired a significant stake. His insider maneuvers discovered, Sokol was forced to resign. Wouldn't Buffett have known Sokol was compromised if he supervised more closely or had structures in place to check such "freedom"? It's hard to argue with Berkshire Hathaway's past successes, but they don't prove the company is ideally structured.

Berkshire Hathaway is a cautionary example of the perils of a structure that's *too* flat and informal. For the benefits of a formal structure, look no further than Honeywell International. CEO David Cote seems relaxed and fun-loving (witness his Harley-Davidson rides through upscale suburban streets, office attire of leather bomber jacket and jeans, and hip background music at corporate headquarters), but his hard-hitting work ethic is legendary. As the leader of a global technology and manufacturing conglomerate, Cote keeps a tight rein on the four industry divisions and 132,000 employees.

Cote's control focus doesn't end at the executive suite, thanks to a formal organizational structure with job titles, security clearances, role descriptions . . . the works, at all levels on the organization chart. At the factories, job titles are painted literally on the *floor* to indicate who needs to be present—and standing—at organizational meetings monitored with a clock hand that turns red when 15 minutes is up. Is Cote a control freak? Maybe, but you can't argue with success: Not only did he successfully merge three disparate company cultures and more than 250 factories, but the new Honeywell has climbed up the *Fortune* 500 ranks and pulls in $37.1 billion in annual sales. The company's profits have increased faster than sales, in part due to Cote's insistence on freezing raises and hiring only two to three employees for every four to five who exit.

The examples of Berkshire Hathaway and Honeywell illustrate the strong need for management structure in an ever-changing, diverse, worldwide marketplace.

Sources: A. Bryant, "Structure? The Flatter the Better," *The New York Times* (January 17, 2010), p. BU2; "Honeywell International: From Bitter to Sweet," *The Economist* (April 14, 2012), www.economist.com/node/21552631; A. Efrati and S. Morrison, "Chief Seeks More Agile Google," *The Wall Street Journal* (January 22, 2011), pp. B1, B4; H. El Nasser, "What Office? Laptops Are Workspace," *USA Today* (June 6, 2012); *Fortune* 500 rankings, http://money.cnn.com/magazines/fortune/fortune500/2012/full_list/; "Honeywell | Company Structure Information from ICIS," *ICIS.com,* www.icis.com/v2/companies/9145292/honeywell/structure.html; K. Linebaugh, "Honeywell's Hiring Is Bleak," *The Wall Street Journal* (March 6, 2013), p. B3; A. Murray, "The End of Management," *The Wall Street Journal* (August 21, 2010), p. W3; A. R. Sorkin, "Delegator in Chief," *The New York Times* (April 24, 2011), p. B4; and S. Tully, "How Dave Cote Got Honeywell's Groove Back," *CNN Money* (May 14, 2012), http://management.fortune.cnn.com/2012/05/14/500-honeywell-cote/.

END-OF-CHAPTER REVIEW

MyManagementLab

Go to **mymanagementlab.com** to complete the problems marked with this icon. ⭐

QUESTIONS FOR REVIEW

15-1 What are the six key elements that define an organization's structure?

15-2 What is a bureaucracy, and how does it differ from a simple structure?

15-3 What is a matrix organization?

15-4 What are the characteristics of a virtual organization?

15-5 How can managers create a boundaryless organization?

15-6 Why do organizational structures differ, and what is the difference between a mechanistic structure and an organic structure?

15-7 What are the behavioral implications of different organizational designs?

EXPERIENTIAL EXERCISE **Dismantling a Bureaucracy**

Pre-work

In order to understand how to improve an organizational structure, it is important to start with a clear understanding of how an organization is currently structured. For this exercise, you will perform research on the college or university you are attending or another organization that your professor identifies. Using the organization's website, find out about different administrative units, paying special attention to noncore functions like finance, information technology, and human resources. While doing this research, assemble a list of five features that resemble a bureaucracy and five features that you think might be successfully managed by an external partner.

Create Groups

Your instructor will form you into groups of at least four individuals at the start of class.

Assess Bureaucracy

Your initial task will be to share your assessments of the features of the organization that seem bureaucratic in nature. What are the common functions that tend to be run in a bureaucratic manner? Try to identify standardized work practices that enhance coordination and control. In particular, think of systems of rules, regulations, departments, and offices that have highly specific and specialized roles. Collectively, your team should allocate about 15 minutes to accomplish this task.

Dismantle Bureaucracy

To dismantle a bureaucracy, it is important to consider both the advantages and disadvantages of the current system. Thus, the goal of the second part of the exercise is to employ techniques related to boundaryless and virtual organizations to reduce bureaucracy in a debate format, with one person arguing for why changes can be good, while the other person argues for why changes might be disruptive.

The team will start by dividing into two subgroups and will work in these groups independently for about 10 minutes. One member will have the responsibility to identify alternative mechanisms that might be able to replace the current bureaucratic structure while still keeping all the same functions "in-house" by creating a boundaryless organization. How can the organizations get the same results but with a different set of control systems? Another member will identify reasons it might be difficult to transition from a bureaucracy to the system you advocated. What are the potential sources of resistance to change? These two members should work together to arrive at a consensus for how bureaucracy might be minimized without damaging organizational productivity and efficiency.

At the same time, the second group of two individuals will work on a different task. One member will consider how each organization can take on elements of a virtual organization as a way to become less bureaucratic. Identify elements of the organization that might be downsized or outsourced. Another member will identify why "going virtual" might be a bad idea, looking to potential loss of control and poor information exchange as possible obstacles. These two members will arrive at a consensus for how the organization can be made as lean as possible without damaging organizational productivity and efficiency.

Finally, all four members of the team will come together to arrive at a consensus for how to limit bureaucracy by either (1) using new systems that are consistent with a boundaryless organization or (2) using elements of a lean, virtual organization to strip off unnecessary bureaucratic layers. This final combination process should take about 10 minutes.

Debriefing

After each group has come to a consensus for how to limit bureaucracy, the instructor will lead an all-class discussion in which each group will describe its eventual approach to minimizing bureaucracy in its organization. Your instructor will provide additional insight into why it may be difficult to change a bureaucracy, as well as suggesting areas where bureaucracy can be effectively limited through either boundarylessness or virtuality.

ETHICAL DILEMMA Directing the Directors

One critical structural element of most corporations is the board of directors. In principle, chief executives report to the directors. In practice, however, boards do not always function as you might expect. Boards were implicated in many corporate scandals of the past decade—either because they actively condoned unethical behavior or because they turned a blind eye to it. Critics also blamed lax board oversight for the financial meltdown and ensuing recession. Business media have called boards "absolutely useless" and "a sham."

One of the keys to reforming board behavior is ensuring that boards function independently of the CEO. The Securities and Exchange Commission (SEC) and the New York Stock Exchange (NYSE) have set guidelines for the independence of directors—who should not be otherwise affiliated with, employed by, or connected to the organization they direct. The more independent the structure and composition of the board, the better the corporation will be governed, and the more effective both will be.

One example of potential conflict of interest can be found among board members of the Federal Reserve. Jamie Dimon, CEO of JPMorgan Chase, sits on the board of directors for the New York Federal Reserve, as do some other financial institution executives. Their appointments represent a huge potential conflict of interest—banks are motivated purely to produce their own best profits, while the Federal Reserve is charged with overseeing the good of all. Though the conflict is obvious, ironically this structure was set up by Congress when it created the Federal Reserve regulatory system in 1913.

Dimon may be able to remain impartial, but the facts in the case remain: (1) JPMorgan Chase recently reported multi-billion-dollar losses from financial gambles; (2) JPMorgan Chase received $390 billion in emergency funds, $29 billion to acquire Bear Stearns, and an 18-month exemption from risk-based leverage and capital requirements—among other helps—from the Federal Reserve. Senator Bernie Sanders, referencing his investigation, stated, "This report reveals the inherent conflicts of interest that exist at the Federal Reserve. At a time when small businesses could not get affordable loans to create jobs, the Fed was providing trillions in secret loans to some of the largest banks and corporations in America that were well represented on the boards of the Federal Reserve Banks. These conflicts must end."

Examples like this one seem to be egregious violations of independence in board structures. Yet, evidence on the link between board independence and firm performance is surprisingly weak. One recent review concluded, "There is no evidence of systematic relationships between board composition and corporate financial performance."

Another structural issue is how the roles of the CEO and chairperson are filled—for instance, whether these positions are held by different people. Most argue that for the board to function independently, the roles must be separate, and *Bloomberg Businessweek* estimates that 37 percent of the 500 largest U.S. corporations do split them. Yet here, too, the evidence is weak: It doesn't appear that corporations with separate CEOs and chairs perform any better than those where the CEO and chairperson are one and the same.

Questions

15-8. Do you think Jamie Dimon was wrong or justified in seeking help for JP Morgan Chase? Why?

15-9. Why do you think board structure doesn't appear to matter to corporate performance?

⭐ **15-10.** Do you think the roles of CEO and chairperson of the board of directors should always be separate? Why or why not?

Sources: A. Censky, "Why Is Jamie Dimon on a Federal Reserve Board?" *CNN Money* (May 21, 2012), http://money.cnn.com/2012/05/21/news/economy/jamie-dimon-new-york-fed/index.htm; D. R. Dalton and C. M. Dalton, "Integration of Micro and Macro Studies in Governance Research: CEO Duality, Board Composition, and Financial Performance," *Journal of Management* 37, no. 2 (2011), pp. 404–411; T. J. Neff and R. Charan, "Separating the CEO and Chairman Roles," *Bloomberg Businessweek* (January 15, 2010), www.businessweek.com/; Press release, "Fed Board Member Conflicts Detailed by GAO: Banks and Businesses Took $4 Trillion in Bailouts," The Office of Senator Bernie Sanders (June 12, 2012), www.commondreams.org/newswire/2012/06/12-2; and G. Zornick, "Senator Reveals Specifics on the Fed's Conflicts of Interest," *The Nation* (June 12, 2012), www.thenation.com/blog/168351/senator-reveals-specifics-feds-conflicts-interest#.

CASE INCIDENT 1 Creative Deviance: Bucking the Hierarchy?

One of the major functions of an organizational hierarchy is to increase standardization and control for top managers. Using the chain of command, managers can direct the activities of subordinates toward a common purpose. If the right person with a creative vision is in charge of a hierarchy, the results can be phenomenal. Until Steve Jobs's passing in October 2011, Apple had used a strongly top-down creative process in which most major decisions and innovations flowed directly through Jobs and then were delegated to sub-teams as specific assignments to complete.

Then there is creative deviance, in which individuals create extremely successful products despite being told by senior management to stop working on them. The electrostatic displays used in more than half of Hewlett-Packard's instruments, the tape slitter that was one of the most important process innovations in 3M's history, and Nichia's development of multi-billion-dollar LED bright lighting technology were all officially rejected by the management hierarchy. In all these cases, an approach like Apple's would have shut down some of the most successful products these companies ever produced. Doing "business as usual" can become such an imperative in a hierarchical organization that new ideas are seen as threats rather than opportunities for development.

It's not immediately apparent why top-down decision making works so well for one highly creative company like Apple, while hierarchy nearly ruined innovations at several other organizations. It may be that Apple's structure is actually quite simple, with relatively few layers and a great deal of responsibility placed on each individual for his or her own outcomes. Or it may be that Apple simply had a very unique leader who was able to rise above the conventional strictures of a CEO to create a culture of constant innovation.

Questions

⭐ **15-11.** Do you think it's possible for an organization to deliberately create an "anti-hierarchy" to encourage employees to engage in more acts of creative deviance? What steps might a company take to encourage creative deviance?

15-12. What are the dangers of an approach that encourages creative deviance?

15-13. Why do you think a company like Apple is able to be creative with a strongly hierarchical structure, whereas other companies find hierarchy limiting?

15-14. Do you think Apple's success has been entirely dependent upon Steve Jobs's role as head of the hierarchy? What are the potential liabilities of a company that is so strongly connected to the decision-making of a single individual?

Sources: C. Mainemelis, "Stealing Fire: Creative Deviance in the Evolution of New Ideas," *Academy of Management Review* 35, no. 4 (2010), pp. 558–578; and A. Lashinsky, "Inside Apple," *Fortune* (May 23, 2011), pp. 125–134.

CASE INCIDENT 2   Boeing Dreamliner: Engineering Nightmare or Organizational Disaster?

As a flight of imagination, Boeing's 787 Dreamliner was an excellent idea: made of composite materials, the plane would be lightweight enough to significantly reduce fuel costs while maintaining a passenger load up to 290 seats. Airline carriers chose options from a long list of unprecedented luxuries to entice the flying public and placed their orders well ahead of the expected completion dates. And then the problems started.

An airplane like the 787 has a design about as complex as that of a nuclear power plant, and Boeing's equally complex offshore organizational structure didn't help the execution. Boeing outsources 67 percent of its manufacturing and many of its engineering functions. While the official assembly site is in Everett, Washington, parts were manufactured at 100 supplier sites in countries across the globe, and some of those suppliers subcontracted piecework to other firms. Because the outsourcing plan allowed vendors to develop their own blueprints, language barriers became a problem back in Washington as workers struggled to understand multilingual assembly instructions. When components didn't fit together properly, the fixes needed along the supply chain and with engineering were almost impossible to implement. The first aircraft left the runway on a test flight in 2009, but Boeing had to buy one of the suppliers a year later (cost: $1 billion) to help make the planes. The first customer delivery was still years away.

If Boeing and industry watchers thought its troubles were over when the first order was delivered to All Nippon Airways (ANA) in 2011, three years behind schedule and after at least seven manufacturing delays, they were wrong. Besides the continuing woes of remaining behind schedule (848 planes have been ordered but only 6 percent have been delivered), Boeing's Dreamliner has suffered numerous mechanical problems. After the plane's technologically advanced lithium-ion batteries started a fire on one aircraft and forced another into an emergency landing in January 2013, ANA and Japan Airlines grounded their fleets. The FAA followed suit, grounding all 787s in the United States. The remaining 50 flying Dreamliners worldwide were then confined to the tarmac until a solution could be found.

While Boeing's CEO Jim McNerney says he is "confident we'll identify the root cause," it's difficult to know what he thinks will fix the Dreamliner's operational problems, chief among them the battery crisis. On the one hand, McNerney is a proponent of Six Sigma and other statistics analytics tools used to streamline production to exacting standards, so it is conceivable that he will try to apply standardization throughout the complex supply chain. He may also decide, along with his engineering team, that the long list of features complicates orders too much and therefore simplify the manufacturing process by eliminating options.

On the other hand, McNerney may approach this as an organizational structure problem, both at corporate headquarters and abroad. While he has been meeting daily with his top executives, there have been so many management changes during the 787's history that it would be difficult for him to identify responsibility for errors in order to make changes in the team or the organizational structure. For the work done abroad, McNerney might be looking to restructure reporting relationships in favor of smaller spans of control to heighten management accountability and tie suppliers to the organizational structure of corporate Boeing. Or he might be considering "reshoring" to bring manufacturing physically close to the final assembly site and under Boeing's control while centralizing the organization structure. If he doesn't do this for all components, he may continue to allow local suppliers to manufacture for Boeing, or he may follow current thinking that key components (generally, the most complex parts) should not be outsourced.

No matter what Boeing and McNerney decide, it is clear that the company must produce reliable aircraft consistently before worldwide government agencies will allow the planes to fly, which may be long before the public will consider trusting the safety of the Dreamliner.

Questions

15-15. Do you think this is a case of the difficulty of launching new technology (there are "bugs" in any system), or one of an unsuccessful launch?

15-16. What type of executive management structure do you think would be most conducive to getting the Dreamliner past the battery problem and back in flight? Is this a different structure than you would suggest for fixing the ongoing manufacturing problems? Sketch out the potential design.

15-17. What organizational structure would you suggest to effectively tie in Boeing's managers and suppliers abroad? Sketch your ideas. (Goals for managers might include facilitating teams, coordinating efforts, maintaining organizational transparency, and creating conversations.)

15-18. What do you think McNerney should do as an overall scheme?

Sources: S. Denning, "The Boeing Debacle: Seven Lessons Every CEO Must Learn," *Forbes* (January 17, 2013), www.forbes.com/sites/stevedenning/2013/01/17/the-boeing-debacle-seven-lessons-every-ceo-must-learn/; E. Frauenheim, "Homeward Bound," *Workforce Management* (February, 2013), pp. 26–31; C. Hymowitz, "Boeing CEO's Task: Get the Dreamliner Airborne Again," *Bloomberg Businessweek* (January 24, 2013), www.businessweek.com/articles/2013-01-24/boeing-ceos-task-get-the-dreamliner-airborne-again/; D. Nosowitz, "Why Is Boeing's 787 Dreamliner Such a Piece of Crap?" *Popsci* (January 17, 2013), www.popsci.com/technology/article/2013-01/why-boeings-787-dreamliner-such-piece-crap; J. Ostrower and A. Pasztor, "Boeing Plays Down 787 Woes; Net Falls 30%," *The Wall Street Journal* (January 31, 2013), p. B3; and D. Terdiman, "Boeing's Dreamliner Struggles Despite Tech Superiority," *C/Net* (February 24, 2012), http://news.cnet.com/8301-13772_3-57385001-52/boeings-dreamliner-struggles-despite-tech-superiority/.

MyManagementLab

Go to **mymanagementlab.com** for Auto-graded writing questions as well as the following Assisted-graded writing questions:

15-19. Which organizational designs do you think are best suited to incorporate employees who work from home? Why?

15-20. Based on what you've discovered about your personality traits on the Big Five Model through your organizational behavior studies in Chapter 5, in which organizational structures might you work best?

15-21. MyManagementLab Only—comprehensive writing assignment for this chapter.

16 Organizational Culture

MyManagementLab®
⭐ **Improve Your Grade!**

When you see this icon, visit **www.mymanagementlab.com** for activities that are applied, personalized, and offer immediate feedback.

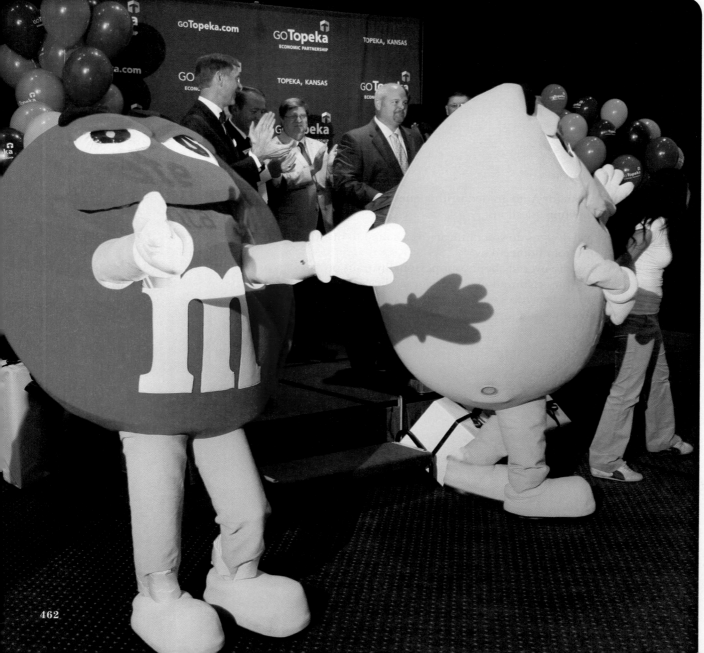

A CULTURE OUT OF THIS WORLD: MARS INC.

At first glance, it doesn't seem Mars Inc. would offer a positive organizational culture. Employers, managers, and even the president punch time clocks, and being late will cost you 10 percent of your daily pay. There are no stock options or pensions. There is no free lunch or comfy play area. There are few windows and the doors to the buildings are kept locked. Associates are called Martians.

Yet Mars, the $33 billion multinational candy and pet food producer behind iconic brands M&M, Uncle Ben's, and Pedigree pet food, is one of *Fortune*'s 100 Best Companies to Work For. Mars employees are loyal and longstanding. One family member or another of one 78-year-old associate has worked for Mars over the past six decades, and third-generation employees are not uncommon. Turnover in the United States, where a third of the company's 72,000 employees work, is only 5 percent.

Employees credit the organizational culture. One associate wrote upon his retirement after 33 years in the Hackettstown, New Jersey, facility, "What a wonderful company to have worked for . . . associates became like family . . . made hundreds of friends there." Nearly everyone posting on Glassdoor, a website for employees to post reviews of their organizations, lists the "open" organizational culture as the highlight of their Mars experience.

Five principles are posted throughout the company's 400 facilities in 73 countries and shape the Mars organizational culture: quality, responsibility, mutuality, efficiency, and freedom. The principles get results. For example, the principle of quality has resulted in a quality rejection rate for M&M's of only 2 percent at the New Jersey site. The principle of responsibility is practiced internally as fairness for employees, resulting in nonunionized worksites and 38 percent female management, and externally as paid time off for volunteering and in a significant corporate commitment to develop food crops for Africa.

The principle of mutuality means teamwork. In addition to mentorships and reverse internships (in which younger associates teach older associates social media strategy), the "open office environment spurs collaboration and approachability," one Mars Security Analyst in Chicago observed. The principle of efficiency is a good counterbalance to the quirky atmosphere and explains the lack of luxury in the third-largest private company in the United States. President Paul S. Michaels says, "Does it add value for the consumer [for] Snickers bars to pay for marble floors and Picassos?"

Freedom is the underlying principle that frames the Mars organizational culture—and the company's success. Associates are encouraged to innovate, experiment, and seek help in a nonhierarchical environment. They find senior management "approachable" and "available." One associate in England cites "a lot of freedom and responsibility the minute you walk through the door."

LEARNING OBJECTIVES

After studying this chapter, you should be able to:

1 Describe the common characteristics of organizational culture.

2 Compare the functional and dysfunctional effects of organizational culture on people and the organization.

3 Identify the factors that create and sustain an organization's culture.

4 Show how culture is transmitted to employees.

5 Demonstrate how an ethical culture can be created.

6 Describe a positive organizational culture.

7 Identify characteristics of a spiritual culture.

8 Show how national culture can affect the way organizational culture is transported to another country.

Martian culture is a unique blend of secrecy and transparency. To the outside world, it offers locked doors, loyal employees who won't divulge its secrets, and family owners who won't give interviews. But within, the culture is fully transparent. Company sales, earnings, cash flow, and site-efficiency data stream continuously across open-area screens, for instance, and bonuses are awarded on a team level. While no one would expect the organizational culture of people who call themselves Martians to be ordinary, the Mars experience seems exceptional. "This is a company you're not embarrassed to tell people you work for," Michaels said, and employees agree.

Sources: A. Gajdosik, "Mars, Inc. and Partners Offer Genome Data to the Public," *Candy Industry* (May 1, 2013), www.candyindustry.com/articles/85670-mars-inc-and-partners-offer-genome-data-to-the-public; D. A. Kaplan, "Inside Mars," *Fortune* (February 4, 2013), pp. 72–82; Mars Inc. Press Release, "Mars, Incorporated and Partners Confirm That Genome Data of Africa's 'Orphan Crops' to Be Made Public," *The Wall Street Journal* (April 29, 2013), www.marketwatch.com/story/mars-incorporated-and-partners-confirm-that-genome-data-of-africas-orphan-crops-to-be-made-public-2013-04-29; and reviews for Mars Inc., Mars Chocolate North America, and Mars Petcare on Glassdoor, www.glassdoor.com, accessed June 5, 2013.

A strong organizational culture provides stability to an organization. But as Mars Inc. illustrates, many minute components make up organizational culture. For some organizations, culture can be a major barrier to change. In this chapter, we show that every organization has a culture that, depending on its strength, can have a significant influence on the attitudes and behaviors of organization members. First let's figure out what kind of organizational culture you prefer. Take the self-assessment to find out.

SELF-ASSESSMENT LIBRARY

What's the Right Organizational Culture for Me?

In the Self-Assessment Library (available in MyManagementLab), take assessment III.B.1 (What's the Right Organizational Culture for Me?), and answer the following questions.

1. Judging from your results, do you fit better in a more formal and structured culture or in a more informal and unstructured culture?
2. Did your results surprise you? Why do you think you scored as you did?
3. How might your results affect your career path?

What Is Organizational Culture?

1 Describe the common characteristics of organizational culture.

An executive once was asked what he thought *organizational culture* meant. He gave essentially the same answer U.S. Supreme Court Justice Potter Stewart gave in defining pornography: "I can't define it, but I know it when I see it." In this section, we propose one definition and review several related ideas to better understand the phenomenon of organizational culture.

A Definition of Organizational Culture

Organizational culture refers to a system of shared meaning held by members that distinguishes the organization from other organizations.[1] Seven primary characteristics seem to capture the essence of an organization's culture:[2]

1. **Innovation and risk taking.**   The degree to which employees are encouraged to be innovative and take risks.
2. **Attention to detail.**   The degree to which employees are expected to exhibit precision, analysis, and attention to detail.
3. **Outcome orientation.**   The degree to which management focuses on results or outcomes rather than on the techniques and processes used to achieve them.
4. **People orientation.**   The degree to which management decisions take into consideration the effect of outcomes on people within the organization.
5. **Team orientation.**   The degree to which work activities are organized around teams rather than individuals.
6. **Aggressiveness.**   The degree to which people are aggressive and competitive rather than easygoing.
7. **Stability.**   The degree to which organizational activities emphasize maintaining the status quo in contrast to growth.

Each of these characteristics exists on a continuum from low to high. Appraising the organization on them, then, gives a composite picture of its culture and a basis for the shared understanding members have about the organization, how things are done in it, and the way they are supposed to behave. Let's identify where Mars Inc. may fall on each of these characteristics from the chapter opener. The Mars culture is likely to be high in innovation and risk-taking, high in attention to detail, and high in team orientation. The company's outcome orientation may be moderate because it is already a top industry performer, but it is consensus driven and promotes work–life balance. Its people orientation seems to be high, judging by the open culture, and, as Victoria Mars (great-granddaughter of founder Frank Mars) tells associates, "You are valued for you." The aggressiveness of Mars' culture may be moderate to low because there are few employee complaints of competitiveness, though we've noted it is also secretive, so perhaps employees don't discuss this element. Finally, it appears stable in terms of sustainability and seems moderately committed to growth. Exhibit 16-1 contrasts how companies may be very different along these dimensions.

Some research has conceptualized culture into four different types based on competing values:[3] the collaborative and cohesive *clan,* the innovative and adaptable *adhocracy,* the controlled and consistent *hierarchy,* and the competitive and customer focused *market.* A review of 94 studies found that job attitudes were especially positive in clan-based cultures, innovation was especially strong in market cultures, and financial performance was especially good in market cultures.[4] Although the competing values framework received some support, the review authors noted that further theoretical work is needed to ensure it is consistent with the actual cultural values found in organizations.

Culture Is a Descriptive Term

Organizational culture shows how employees perceive the characteristics of an organization's culture, not whether they like them—that is, it's a descriptive term. Research on organizational culture has sought to measure how employees see their organization: Does it encourage teamwork? Does it reward innovation? Does it stifle initiative? In contrast, job satisfaction seeks to measure how employees feel about the organization's expectations, reward practices, and the like. Although the two terms have overlapping characteristics, keep in mind that *organizational culture* is descriptive, whereas *job satisfaction* is evaluative.

Exhibit **16-1**	Contrasting Organizational Cultures

Organization A

This organization is a manufacturing firm. Managers are expected to fully document all decisions, and "good managers" are those who can provide detailed data to support their recommendations. Creative decisions that incur significant change or risk are not encouraged. Because managers of failed projects are openly criticized and penalized, managers try not to implement ideas that deviate much from the status quo. One lower-level manager quoted an often-used phrase in the company: "If it ain't broke, don't fix it."

There are extensive rules and regulations in this firm that employees are required to follow. Managers supervise employees closely to ensure there are no deviations. Management is concerned with high productivity, regardless of the impact on employee morale or turnover.

Work activities are designed around individuals. There are distinct departments and lines of authority, and employees are expected to minimize formal contact with other employees outside their functional area or line of command. Performance evaluations and rewards emphasize individual effort, although seniority tends to be the primary factor in the determination of pay raises and promotions.

Organization B

This organization is also a manufacturing firm. Here, however, management encourages and rewards risk taking and change. Decisions based on intuition are valued as much as those that are well rationalized. Management prides itself on its history of experimenting with new technologies and its success in regularly introducing innovative products. Managers or employees who have a good idea are encouraged to "run with it." And failures are treated as "learning experiences." The company prides itself on being market driven and rapidly responsive to the changing needs of its customers.

There are few rules and regulations for employees to follow, and supervision is loose because management believes that its employees are hardworking and trustworthy. Management is concerned with high productivity but believes that this comes through treating its people right. The company is proud of its reputation as being a good place to work.

Job activities are designed around work teams, and team members are encouraged to interact with people across functions and authority levels. Employees talk positively about the competition between teams. Individuals and teams have goals, and bonuses are based on achievement of these outcomes. Employees are given considerable autonomy in choosing the means by which the goals are attained.

Do Organizations Have Uniform Cultures?

Organizational culture represents a perception the organization's members hold in common. We should therefore expect individuals with different backgrounds or at different levels in the organization to describe its culture in similar terms.[5]

That doesn't mean, however, that there are no subcultures. Most large organizations have a dominant culture and numerous subcultures.[6] A **dominant culture** expresses the **core values** a majority of members share and that give the organization its distinct personality.[7] **Subcultures** tend to develop in large organizations to reflect common problems or experiences members face in the same department or location. The purchasing department can have a subculture that includes the core values of the dominant culture plus additional values unique to members of that department.

If organizations were composed only of numerous subcultures, organizational culture as an independent variable would be significantly less powerful. It is the "shared meaning" aspect of culture that makes it such a potent device for guiding and shaping behavior. That's what allows us to say, for example, that the Zappos culture values customer care and dedication over speed and efficiency, and to use that information to better understand the behavior of Zappos executives and employees.[8] But subcultures can influence members' behavior too.

dominant culture   *A culture that expresses the core values that are shared by a majority of the organization's members.*

core values   *The primary or dominant values that are accepted throughout the organization.*

subcultures   *Minicultures within an organization, typically defined by department designations and geographical separation.*

"An Organization's Culture Is Forever"

This is actually not true. Although research indicates organizational culture is difficult to change and that change can take a long time, it can be done. Sometimes it is essential to survival. For years, Wisconsin's Wellspring system provided a low-level nursing home environment in which inpatients had little input about their care and the organizational culture allowed lax standards to prevail. Then the network of 11 nursing homes launched a culture change initiative. Management focused on caregiver collaboration, education, accountability, and empowerment. The results were excellent. Wellspring realized fewer state standards infractions and higher retention rates at the facilities, but the results for the patients were even greater: fewer bedfast residents, less use of restraints and psychoactive medication, less incontinence, and fewer tube feedings than in other nursing homes.

The Wellspring program illustrates the significant effect positive organizational culture change can achieve. CEO Bob Flexon of Dynegy Inc., a Houston-based electric utility giant emerging from bankruptcy, is trying to save his company by changing the organizational culture. First, he ditched the cushy CEO office suite, $15,000 marble desk, and Oriental rugs for a small cubicle on a warehouse-style floor shared with all 235 headquarters employees. Next, he visited company facilities, trained "culture champions," and reinstated annual performance reviews as part of the plan to increase collaboration. He created a plaque as a reminder to "Be Here Now" instead of multitasking and banned smartphones from meetings. Flexon said, "The idea was to instill a winning spirit," and he counts on his visibility as CEO to broadcast the culture change down to

the lowest levels of the widespread organization.

Positive results have included a reduction in turnover from 8 percent in 2011 to 5.8 percent in 2012. Flexon said, "People are cautiously beginning to believe that we can win again." The company continues to report massive earnings losses, but Flexon is optimistic about Dynegy's rebound. He says, "Our ongoing focus on culture is what will make the difference."

Sources: J. Bellot, "Nursing Home Culture Change What Does It Mean to Nurses?" Research in Gerontological Nursing (October 2012), pp. 264–273; J. S. Lublin, "This CEO Used to Have an Office," The Wall Street Journal (March 13, 2013), pp. B1, B8; and J. Molineux, "Enabling Organizational Cultural Change Using Systemic Strategic Human Resource Management—A Longitudinal Case Study," International Journal of Human Resource Management (April 1, 2013), pp. 1588–1612.

Strong versus Weak Cultures

It's possible to differentiate between strong and weak cultures.[9] If most employees (responding to management surveys) have the same opinions about the organization's mission and values, the culture is strong; if opinions vary widely, the culture is weak.

strong culture *A culture in which the core values are intensely held and widely shared.*

In a **strong culture**, the organization's core values are both intensely held and widely shared.[10] The more members who accept the core values and the greater their commitment, the stronger the culture and the greater its influence on member behavior. This is because the high degree of shared values and intensity create a climate of high behavioral control. Nordstrom employees know in no uncertain terms what is expected of them, for example, and these expectations go a long way in shaping their behavior. In contrast, Nordstrom competitor Macy's, which has struggled through an identity crisis, is working to remake its culture.

A strong culture should reduce employee turnover because it demonstrates high agreement about what the organization represents. Such unanimity of purpose builds cohesiveness, loyalty, and organizational commitment. These qualities, in turn, lessen employees' propensity to leave.[11] One study found that the more employees agreed on customer orientation in a service organization, the higher the profitability of the business unit.[12] Another study found that when team managers and team members disagreed about perceptions of organizational support, there were more negative moods among team members, and the performance of teams was lower.[13] These negative effects are especially strong when managers believe the organization provides more support than employees think it does.

Culture versus Formalization

We've seen that high formalization creates predictability, orderliness, and consistency. A strong culture achieves the same end without the need for written documentation.[14] Therefore, we should view formalization and culture as two different roads to a common destination. The stronger an organization's culture, the less management need be concerned with developing formal rules and regulations to guide employee behavior. Those guides will be internalized in employees when they accept the organization's culture.

What Do Cultures Do?

2 Compare the functional and dysfunctional effects of organizational culture on people and the organization.

Let's review the role culture performs and whether it can ever be a liability for an organization.

The Functions of Culture

First, culture has a boundary-defining role: It creates distinctions between one organization and others. Second, it conveys a sense of identity for organization members. Third, culture facilitates commitment to something larger than individual self-interest. Fourth, it enhances the stability of the social system. Culture is the social glue that helps hold the organization together by providing standards for what employees should say and do. Finally, it is a sense-making and control mechanism that guides and shapes employees' attitudes and behavior. This last function is of particular interest to us.[15] Culture defines the rules of the game.

Today's trend toward decentralized organizations makes culture more important than ever, but ironically it also makes establishing a strong culture more difficult. When formal authority and control systems are reduced, culture's *shared meaning* can point everyone in the same direction. However, employees organized in teams may show greater allegiance to their team and its values than to the organization as a whole. In virtual organizations, the lack of frequent face-to-face contact makes establishing a common set of norms very difficult. Strong leadership that communicates frequently about common goals and priorities is especially important in innovative organizations.[16]

Individual–organization "fit"—that is, whether the applicant's or employee's attitudes and behavior are compatible with the culture—strongly influences who gets a job offer, a favorable performance review, or a promotion. It's no coincidence that Disney theme park employees appear almost universally attractive, clean, and wholesome with bright smiles. The company selects employees who will maintain that image. On the job, a strong culture supported by formal rules and regulations ensures employees will act in a relatively uniform and predictable way.

Culture Creates Climate

If you've worked with someone whose positive attitude inspired you to do your best, or with a lackluster team that drained your motivation, you've experienced the effects of climate. **Organizational climate** refers to the shared perceptions organizational members have about their organization and work environment.[17] This aspect of culture is like team spirit at the organizational

organizational climate *The shared perceptions organizational members have about their organization and work environment.*

Photo 16-1 Employees of French videogame publisher Ubisoft are shown working on the *Just Dance 3* game at the firm's creative studio near Paris. Imaginative employees who work in teams on challenging projects at Ubisoft's 26 creative studios around the world share the positive climate of creative collaboration that reflects the diversity of team members.

Source: REUTERS/Charles Platiau.

level. When everyone has the same general feelings about what's important or how well things are working, the effect of these attitudes will be more than the sum of the individual parts. One meta-analysis found that across dozens of different samples, psychological climate was strongly related to individuals' level of job satisfaction, involvement, commitment, and motivation.[18] A positive overall workplace climate has been linked to higher customer satisfaction and financial performance as well.[19]

Dozens of dimensions of climate have been studied, including innovation, creativity, communication, warmth and support, involvement, safety, justice, diversity, and customer service.[20] A person who encounters a positive climate for performance will think about doing a good job more often and will believe others support his or her success. Someone who encounters a positive climate for diversity will feel more comfortable collaborating with co-workers regardless of their demographic background. Climates can interact with one another to produce behavior. For example, a positive climate for worker empowerment can lead to higher levels of performance in organizations that also have a climate for personal accountability.[21] Climate also influences the habits people adopt. If the climate for safety is positive, everyone wears safety gear and follows safety procedures even if individually they wouldn't normally think very often about being safe—indeed, many studies have shown that a positive safety climate decreases the number of documented injuries on the job.[22]

The Ethical Dimension of Culture

Organizational cultures are not neutral in their ethical orientation, even when they are not openly pursuing ethical goals. Over time, the **ethical work climate (EWC)**, or the shared concept of right and wrong behavior in that workplace, develops as part of the organizational climate. The ethical climate reflects the true values of the organization and shapes the ethical decision-making of its members.

Researchers have developed ethical climate theory (ECT) and the ethical climate index (ECI) to categorize and measure the ethical dimensions of organizational cultures.[23] Of the nine identified climate categories, five are found to be most prevalent in organizations: *instrumental, caring, independence, law and*

ethical work climate (EWC) *The shared concept of right and wrong behavior in the workplace that reflects the true values of the organization and shapes the ethical decision-making of its members.*

code, and *rules.* Each explains the general mindset, expectations, and values of the managers and employees in relationship to their organization. For instance, in an *instrumental* ethical climate, managers may frame their decision making around the assumption that employees (and companies) are motivated by self-interest (egoistic). In a *caring* climate, conversely, managers may operate under the expectation that their decisions will positively affect the greatest number of stakeholders (employees, customers, suppliers) possible.

Ethical climates of *independence* rely on each individual's personal moral ideas to dictate his or her workplace behavior. *Law and code* climates require managers and employees to use an external standardized moral compass such as a professional code of conduct for norms, while *rules* climates tend to operate by internal standardized expectations from, perhaps, an organizational policy manual. Organizations often progress through different categories as they move through their business life cycle.

An organization's ethical climate powerfully influences the way its individual members feel they should behave, so much so that researchers have been able to predict organizational outcomes from the climate categories.[24] Instrumental climates are negatively associated with employee job satisfaction and organizational commitment, even though those climates appeal to self-interest (of the employee and the company). They are positively associated with turnover intentions, workplace bullying, and deviant behavior. Caring and rules climates have a positive association with job satisfaction. Caring, independence, rules, and law and code climates also reduce employee turnover intentions, workplace bullying, and dysfunctional behavior.

Studies of ethical climates and workplace outcomes suggest that some climate categories are likely to be found in certain organizations. Industries with exacting standards such as engineering, accounting, and law tend to have a rules or a law and code climate. Industries that thrive on competitiveness such as financial trading often have an instrumental ethical climate. Industries with missions of benevolence are likely to have a caring climate, even if they are for-profit as in an environmental protection firm.

Research is exploring why organizations tend to fall into certain climate categories by industry, especially successful organizations. We cannot conclude that instrumental climates are always bad or that caring climates are always good. Instrumental cultures may foster the individual success their companies need to thrive, for example, and they may help underperformers to recognize their self-interest is better served elsewhere. Managers in caring cultures may be thwarted from making the best decisions when only choices that serve the greatest number of employees are acceptable.[25] The ECI is one new way researchers are seeking to understand the context of ethical drivers in organizations. By measuring the collective levels of moral sensitivity, judgment, motivation, and character of our organizations, we may be able to judge the strength of the influence our ethical climates have on us.[26]

Although ECT was first introduced more than 25 years ago, researchers have recently been studying ethics in organizations more closely to determine not only how ethical climates behave (through ECI, for instance, introduced in 2010) but also how they might be fostered, even changed.[27] Eventually, we will be able to provide leaders with clear blueprints for designing effective ethical climates to improve the lives of an organization's members.

Culture and Innovation

The most innovative companies are often characterized by their open, unconventional, collaborative, vision-driven, accelerating cultures.[28] Startup firms often have innovative cultures by definition because they are usually small, agile, and focused on solving problems in order to survive and grow. Consider digital music leader Echo Nest. This startup has always been unconventional, flexible, and open, hosting music app "hack" days and permitting outsiders to use its unique technology for noncommercial experimentation.[29]

At the other end of the startup spectrum, consider 30-year-old Intuit, one of the World's 100 Most Innovative Companies according to *Forbes*. Intuit employees attend workshops to teach them how to think creatively . . . and unconventionally. Sessions have led to managers talking through puppets and holding bake sales to sell prototype apps with their cupcakes. The culture stresses open accountability. "I saw one senior guy whose idea they'd been working on for nine months get dis[ap]proved in a day because someone had a better way. He got up in front of everyone and said, 'This is my bad. I should have checked my hypothesis earlier,'" said an admiring Eric Ries, author of *The Lean Startup*. A consultant for entrepreneurs, Ries considers the older software company equally innovative because of its culture.

Alexion Pharmaceuticals is also one of *Forbes'* Most Innovative and, like Intuit, it has been in operation long past the usual innovation life-cycle stage. Unlike Intuit, though, the maker of life-saving medicines is not known for management shenanigans. The key to its continuing innovation is a culture of caring, which drives it to develop medicines that save victims of rare diseases, even when the patients affected are few, the cost of development is prohibitively high, and the probability of success is low.[30]

Culture as an Asset

As we have discussed, organizational culture can provide a positive ethical environment and foster innovation. Culture can also significantly contribute to an organization's bottom line in many ways.

ChildNet is a nonprofit child welfare agency in Florida whose organizational culture was described as "grim" from the time one of its foster children

Photo 16-2 Founded in 1969, Samsung Electronics of South Korea is past the usual innovation life-cycle stage yet continues to foster a climate of creativity and idea generation. Samsung seeks to emulate a startup culture through its Creative Labs, where employees like engineer Ki Yuhoon shown here take up to a year off from their regular jobs to work on innovative projects.

disappeared in 2000, through 2007 when the CEO was fired amid FBI allegations of fraud and forgery. "We didn't know if we would have jobs or who would take over. It was a very grim situation," employee Maggie Tilelli said. However, after intense turnaround efforts aimed at changing the organizational culture, Child-Net became Florida's top-ranked agency within four years and *Workforce Management*'s Optima award winner for General Excellence in 2012. President and CEO Emilio Benitez, who took charge in 2008, effected the transformation by changing the executive staff, employing new technology to support caseworkers in the field and managers at headquarters, acknowledging the stress employees and managers felt by establishing an employee recognition program, and creating cross-departmental roundtables (work groups) for creative problem-solving. The roundtables have been able to find solutions to difficult client cases, resulting in better placement of foster children into permanent homes. "From a business perspective, [the new problem-solving approach] was a tremendous cost savings," Benitez said. "But at the end of the day, it's about the families we serve."[31]

While ChildNet demonstrates how an organizational culture can positively affect the bottom line, Dish Network illustrates the elusiveness of matching a particular culture to an industry or organization. By every measure, Dish Network is a business success story—it is the second-largest U.S. satellite TV provider, and it has made founder Charlie Ergen one of the richest men in the world. Yet Dish was recently ranked as the worst U.S. company to work for, and employees say the fault is the micromanaging culture Ergen created and enforces. Employees describe arduous mandatory overtime, fingerprint scanners to record work hours to the minute, public berating (most notably from Ergen), management condescension and distrust, quarterly "bloodbath" layoffs, and no working from home. One employee advised another, "You're part of a poisonous environment . . . go find a job where you can use your talents for good rather than evil." Many employees do just that, but Dish thrives anyway, regularly exceeding its quarterly earnings estimates. However, its growth in subscribers has leveled out in the past several years, and even Ergen acknowledges, "We're a one-trick pony" with satellite TV as the only product.[32]

At ChildNet, positive changes to the organization's performance have been clearly attributed to the transformation of its organizational culture. Dish, on the other hand, may have succeeded *despite* its culture. Ergen is a clever entrepreneur, but the company has only 12 percent of the total U.S. television provider market.[33] We can only wonder how much more successful it could be if it reformed its toxic culture. There are many more cases of business success stories due to excellent organizational cultures than there are of success stories despite bad cultures, and almost no success stories because of bad ones.

Culture as a Liability

Culture can enhance organizational commitment and increase the consistency of employee behavior, clearly benefits to an organization. Culture is valuable to employees too, because it spells out how things are done and what's important. But we shouldn't ignore the potentially dysfunctional aspects of culture, especially a strong one, on an organization's effectiveness. Hewlett-Packard, once known as a premier computer manufacturer, has been rapidly losing market share and profits as the dysfunction of its top management team has trickled down, leaving employees disengaged, uncreative, unappreciated, and polarized.[34]

institutionalization *A condition that occurs when an organization takes on a life of its own, apart from any of its members, and acquires immortality.*

Institutionalization   When an organization undergoes **institutionalization** and becomes *institutionalized*—that is, it is valued for itself and not for the goods or services it produces—it takes on a life of its own, apart from its founders or members.[35] Institutionalized organizations often don't go out of business even if the original goals are no longer relevant. Acceptable modes of behavior become largely self-evident to members, and although this isn't entirely negative, it does mean behaviors and habits that should be questioned and analyzed become taken for granted, which can stifle innovation and make maintaining the organization's culture an end in itself.

Barriers to Change   Culture is a liability when the shared values don't agree with those that further the organization's effectiveness. This is most likely when an organization's environment is undergoing rapid change, and its entrenched culture may no longer be appropriate.[36] Consistency of behavior, an asset in a stable environment, may then burden the organization and make it difficult to respond to changes.

Barriers to Diversity   Hiring new employees who differ from the majority in race, age, gender, disability, or other characteristics creates a paradox:[37] Management wants to demonstrate support for the differences these employees bring to the workplace, but newcomers who wish to fit in must accept the organization's core cultural values. Because diverse behaviors and unique strengths are likely to diminish as people attempt to assimilate, strong cultures can become liabilities when they effectively eliminate these advantages. A strong culture that condones prejudice, supports bias, or becomes insensitive to people who are different can undermine formal corporate diversity policies.

Barriers to Acquisitions and Mergers   Historically, when management looked at acquisition or merger decisions, the key factors were financial advantage and product synergy. In recent years, cultural compatibility has become the primary concern.[38] All things being equal, whether the acquisition actually works seems to have much to do with how well the two organizations' cultures match up.

A survey by consulting firm A. T. Kearney revealed that 58 percent of mergers failed to reach their financial goals.[39] As one expert commented, "Mergers have an unusually high failure rate, and it's always because of people issues"—in other words, because of conflicting organizational cultures. The $183 billion merger between America Online (AOL) and Time Warner in 2001 was the largest in U.S. corporate history. It was also a disaster. Only 2 years later, the stock had fallen an astounding 90 percent, and the new company reported what was then the largest financial loss in U.S. history. Culture clash is commonly argued to be one of the causes of AOL Time Warner's problems.

Creating and Sustaining Culture

3 Identify the factors that create and sustain an organization's culture.

An organization's culture doesn't pop out of thin air, and once established it rarely fades away. What influences the creation of a culture? What reinforces and sustains it once in place?

How a Culture Begins

An organization's current customs, traditions, and general way of doing things are largely due to what it has done before and how successful it was in doing it. This leads us to the ultimate source of an organization's culture: the founders.[40]

Free of previous customs or ideologies, founders have a vision of what the organization should be, and the firm's small size makes it easy to impose that vision on all members.

Culture creation occurs in three ways.[41] First, founders hire and keep only employees who think and feel the same way they do. Second, they indoctrinate and socialize employees to their way of thinking and feeling. And finally, the founders' own behavior encourages employees to identify with them and internalize their beliefs, values, and assumptions. When the organization succeeds, the founders' personality becomes embedded in the culture.

The fierce, competitive style and disciplined, authoritarian nature of Hyundai, the giant Korean conglomerate, exhibits the same characteristics often used to describe founder Chung Ju-Yung. Other founders with immeasurable impact on their organization's culture include Bill Gates at Microsoft, Ingvar Kamprad at IKEA, Herb Kelleher at Southwest Airlines, Fred Smith at FedEx, and Richard Branson at the Virgin Group.

Keeping a Culture Alive

Once a culture is in place, practices within the organization maintain it by giving employees a set of similar experiences.[42] The selection process, performance evaluation criteria, training and development activities, and promotion procedures (all discussed in Chapter 17) ensure those hired fit in with the culture, reward those who support it, and penalize (or even expel) those who challenge it. Three forces play a particularly important part in sustaining a culture: selection practices, the actions of top management, and socialization methods. Let's look at each.

Selection   The explicit goal of the selection process is to identify and hire individuals with the knowledge, skills, and abilities to perform successfully. The final decision, because it's significantly influenced by the decision maker's judgment of how well the candidates will fit into the organization, identifies people whose values are essentially consistent with at least a good portion of the organization's.[43] Selection also provides information to applicants. Those who perceive a conflict between their values and those of the organization can remove themselves from the applicant pool. Selection thus becomes a two-way street, allowing employer or applicant to avoid a mismatch and sustaining an organization's culture by selecting out those who might attack or undermine its core values.

W. L. Gore & Associates, the maker of Gore-Tex fabric used in outerwear, prides itself on its democratic culture and teamwork. There are no job titles at Gore, nor bosses or chains of command. All work is done in teams. In Gore's selection process, teams of employees put job applicants through extensive interviews to ensure they can deal with the level of uncertainty, flexibility, and teamwork that's normal in Gore plants. Not surprisingly, W. L. Gore appears regularly on *Fortune*'s list of 100 Best Companies to Work For (number 21 in 2013).[44]

Top Management   The actions of top management also have a major impact on the organization's culture.[45] Through words and behavior, senior executives establish norms that filter through the organization about, for instance, whether risk taking is desirable, how much freedom managers give employees, what is appropriate dress, and what actions earn pay raises, promotions, and other rewards.

The culture of supermarket chain Wegmans—which believes driven, happy, and loyal employees are more eager to help one another and provide exemplary customer service—is a direct result of the beliefs of the Wegman family. The chain began in 1930 when brothers John and Walter Wegman opened their first grocery store in Rochester, New York. Their focus on fine foods quickly separated Wegmans from other grocers—a focus maintained by the company's employees, many of whom are hired based on their interest in food. In 1950, Walter's son Robert became president and added generous employee benefits such as profit sharing and fully paid medical coverage. Now Robert's son Danny is president, and he has continued the Wegmans tradition of taking care of employees. To date, Wegmans has paid more than $90 million in scholarships for more than 28,400 employees. Pay is well above market average, making annual turnover for full-time employees a mere 3.6 percent (the industry average is 24 percent). Wegmans regularly appears on *Fortune*'s list as well (number 5 in 2013).[46]

Socialization   No matter how good a job the organization does in recruiting and selection, new employees need help adapting to the prevailing culture. That help is **socialization**.[47] For example, all Marines must go through boot camp, where they prove their commitment and learn the "Marine way." The consulting firm Booz Allen Hamilton begins its process of bringing new employees onboard even before they start their first day of work. New recruits go to an internal web portal to learn about the company and engage in some activities that help them understand the culture of the organization. After they start work, they continue to learn about the organization through an ongoing social networking application that links new workers with more established members of the firm and helps ensure that culture is transmitted over time.[48] Clear Channel Communications, Facebook, Google, and other companies are adopting fresh onboarding (new hire) procedures, including assigning "peer coaches," holding socializing events, personalizing orientation programs, and giving out immediate work assignments. "When we can stress the personal identity of people, and let them bring more of themselves at work, they are more satisfied with their job and have better results," researcher Francesca Gino of Harvard said.[49]

We can think of socialization as a process with three stages: prearrival, encounter, and metamorphosis.[50] This process, shown in Exhibit 16-2, has an impact on the new employee's work productivity, commitment to the organization's objectives, and eventual decision to stay with the organization.

The **prearrival stage** recognizes that each individual arrives with a set of values, attitudes, and expectations about both the work and the organization. One major purpose of a business school, for example, is to socialize business students to the attitudes and behaviors business firms want. Newcomers to high-profile organizations with a strong market position will make their own assumptions about what it must be like to work there.[51] Most new recruits will expect Nike to be dynamic and exciting, a prestigious law firm to be high in pressure and

socialization   *A process that adapts employees to the organization's culture.*

prearrival stage   *The period of learning in the socialization process that occurs before a new employee joins the organization.*

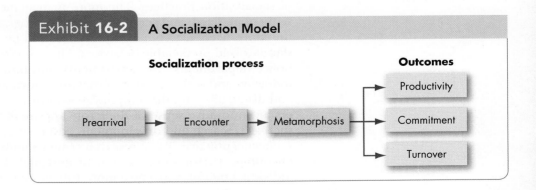

Exhibit **16-2**   A Socialization Model

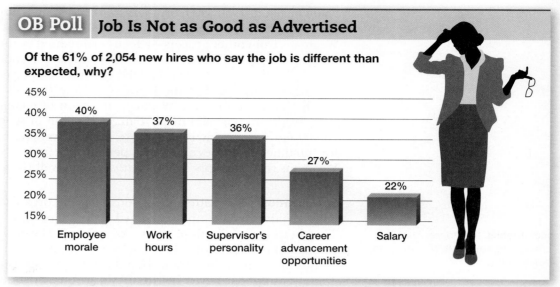

OB Poll | **Job Is Not as Good as Advertised**

Of the 61% of 2,054 new hires who say the job is different than expected, why?

Category	Percentage
Employee morale	40%
Work hours	37%
Supervisor's personality	36%
Career advancement opportunities	27%
Salary	22%

Source: S. Bates, "Majority of New Hires Say Job Is Not What They Expected," *Society for Human Resource Management* (May 28, 2012), http://www .shrm.org/hrdisciplines/employeerelations/articles/pages/newhiresfeelmisled.aspx.

rewards, and the Marine Corps to require both discipline and courage. No matter how well managers think they can socialize newcomers, however, the most important predictor of future behavior is past behavior. What people know before they join the organization, and how proactive their personality is, are critical predictors of how well they adjust to a new culture.[52]

One way to capitalize on prehire characteristics in socialization is to use the selection process to inform prospective employees about the organization as a whole. We've also seen how the selection process ensures the inclusion of the "right type"—those who will fit in.

encounter stage *The stage in the socialization process in which a new employee sees what the organization is really like and confronts the possibility that expectations and reality may diverge.*

On entry into the organization, the new member enters the **encounter stage** and confronts the possibility that expectations—about the job, co-workers, the boss, and the organization in general—may differ from reality. If expectations were fairly accurate, the encounter stage merely cements earlier perceptions. However, this is often not the case. At the extreme, a new member may become disillusioned enough to resign. Proper recruiting and selection should significantly reduce that outcome, along with encouraging friendship ties in the organization—newcomers are more committed when friends and co-workers help them "learn the ropes."[53]

metamorphosis stage *The stage in the socialization process in which a new employee changes and adjusts to the job, work group, and organization.*

Finally, to work out any problems discovered during the encounter stage, the new member changes or goes through the **metamorphosis stage**. The options presented in Exhibit 16-3 are alternatives designed to bring about the desired metamorphosis. Most research suggests there are two major "bundles" of socialization practices. The more management relies on formal, collective, sequential, fixed, and serial socialization programs and emphasizes divestiture, the more likely newcomers' differences will be stripped away and replaced by standardized predictable behaviors. These *institutional* practices are common in police departments, fire departments, and other organizations that value rule following and order. Programs that are informal, individual, random, variable, and disjunctive and that emphasize investiture are more likely to give newcomers an innovative sense of their role and methods of working. Creative fields, such as research and development, advertising, and filmmaking, rely on these *individual* practices. Most research suggests high levels of institutional practices encourage person–organization fit and high levels of commitment, whereas individual practices produce more role innovation.[54]

| Exhibit 16-3 | Entry Socialization Options |

Formal vs. Informal The more a new employee is segregated from the ongoing work setting and differentiated in some way to make explicit his or her newcomer's role, the more socialization is formal. Specific orientation and training programs are examples. Informal socialization puts the new employee directly into the job, with little or no special attention.

Individual vs. Collective New members can be socialized individually. This describes how it's done in many professional offices. They can also be grouped together and processed through an identical set of experiences, as in military boot camp.

Fixed vs. Variable This refers to the time schedule in which newcomers make the transition from outsider to insider. A fixed schedule establishes standardized stages of transition. This characterizes rotational training programs. It also includes probationary periods, such as the 8- to 10-year "associate" status used by accounting and law firms before deciding on whether or not a candidate is made a partner. Variable schedules give no advance notice of their transition timetable. Variable schedules describe the typical promotion system, in which one is not advanced to the next stage until one is "ready."

Serial vs. Random Serial socialization is characterized by the use of role models who train and encourage the newcomer. Apprenticeship and mentoring programs are examples. In random socialization, role models are deliberately withheld. New employees are left on their own to figure things out.

Investiture vs. Divestiture Investiture socialization assumes that the newcomer's qualities and qualifications are the necessary ingredients for job success, so these qualities and qualifications are confirmed and supported. Divestiture socialization tries to strip away certain characteristics of the recruit. Fraternity and sorority "pledges" go through divestiture socialization to shape them into the proper role.

The three-part entry socialization process is complete when new members have internalized and accepted the norms of the organization and their work group, are confident in their competence, and feel trusted and valued by their peers. They understand the system—not only their own tasks but the rules, procedures, and informally accepted practices as well. Finally, they know what is expected of them and what criteria will be used to measure and evaluate their work. As Exhibit 16-2 showed, successful metamorphosis should have a positive impact on new employees' productivity and their commitment to the organization and reduce their propensity to leave the organization.

Researchers have begun to examine how employee attitudes change during socialization by measuring at several points over the first few months. One study has documented patterns of "honeymoons" and "hangovers" for new workers, showing that the period of initial adjustment is often marked by decreases in job satisfaction as their idealized hopes come into contact with the reality of organizational life.[55] Other research suggests that role conflict and role overload for newcomers rise over time and that workers with the largest increases in these role problems experience the largest decreases in commitment and satisfaction.[56] It may be that the initial adjustment period for newcomers presents increasing demands and difficulties, at least in the short term.

Summary: How Cultures Form

Exhibit 16-4 summarizes how an organization's culture is established and sustained. The original culture derives from the founder's philosophy and strongly influences hiring criteria as the firm grows. Top managers' actions set the general climate, including what is acceptable behavior and what is not. The way employees are socialized will depend both on the degree of success achieved in matching new employees' values to those of the organization in the selection process and on top management's preference for socialization methods.

Exhibit 16-4   How Organization Cultures Form

Philosophy of organization's founders → Selection criteria → Top management / Socialization → Organization culture

How Employees Learn Culture

4 Show how culture is transmitted to employees.

Culture is transmitted to employees in a number of forms, the most potent being stories, rituals, material symbols, and language.

Stories

When Henry Ford II was chairman of Ford Motor Company, you would have been hard pressed to find a manager who hadn't heard how he reminded his executives, when they got too arrogant, "It's my name that's on the building." The message was clear: Henry Ford II ran the company.

A number of senior Nike executives spend much of their time serving as corporate storytellers.[57] When they tell how co-founder (and Oregon track coach) Bill Bowerman went to his workshop and poured rubber into a waffle iron to create a better running shoe, they're talking about Nike's spirit of innovation. When new hires hear tales of Oregon running star Steve Prefontaine's battles to make running a professional sport and attain better performance equipment, they learn of Nike's commitment to helping athletes.

Stories such as these circulate through many organizations, anchoring the present in the past and legitimating current practices. They typically include narratives about the organization's founders, rule breaking, rags-to-riches successes, reductions in the workforce, relocation of employees, reactions to past mistakes, and organizational coping.[58] Employees also create their own narratives about how they came to either fit or not fit with the organization during the process of socialization, including first days on the job, early interactions with others, and first impressions of organizational life.[59]

Rituals

rituals *Repetitive sequences of activities that express and reinforce the key values of the organization, which goals are most important, which people are important, and which are expendable.*

Rituals are repetitive sequences of activities that express and reinforce the key values of the organization—what goals are most important and which people are important and which are expendable.[60] One of the best known rituals is Walmart's company chant. Begun by the company's founder, the late Sam Walton, as a way to motivate his workforce, "Gimme a W, gimme an A, gimme an L, gimme a squiggle, give me an M, A, R, T!" became a ritual to bond workers together and reinforce Walton's belief that employees made the company successful. Other companies have nontraditional rituals to help support the values of their cultures. Kimpton Hotels & Restaurants, one of *Fortune*'s 100 Best Companies to Work For, maintains its customer-oriented culture with traditions like a Housekeeping Olympics that includes blindfolded bedmaking and vacuum races, for instance.[61] At marketing firm United Entertainment Group, employees work unusual hours a few times a year, arriving in the late afternoon and working until early morning. CEO Jarrod Moss does this to spark creativity. He says, "You mess with somebody's internal clock, and some interesting ideas come out."[62]

Symbols

material symbols *What conveys to employees who is important, the degree of egalitarianism top management desires, and the kinds of behavior that are appropriate.*

The layout of corporate headquarters, the types of automobiles top executives are given, and the presence or absence of corporate aircraft are a few examples of **material symbols**. Others include the size of offices, the elegance of furnishings, perks, and attire.[63] These convey to employees who is important, the degree of egalitarianism top management desires, and the kinds of behavior that are appropriate, such as risk-taking, conservative, authoritarian, participative, individualistic, or social.

Dynegy's headquarters doesn't look like your typical head-office operation. There are few individual offices, even for senior executives. The space is essentially made up of cubicles, common areas, and meeting rooms. This informality conveys to employees that Dynegy values openness, equality, creativity, and flexibility. Some corporations provide their top executives with chauffeur-driven limousines and a corporate jet. Other CEOs drive the company car themselves and travel in the economy section. At some firms, like Chicago shirtmaker Threadless, an "anything goes" atmosphere helps emphasize creativity. Meetings are held in an Airstream camper parked inside the company's converted FedEx warehouse, while employees in shorts and flip-flops work in bullpens featuring disco balls and garish decorations chosen by each team.[64]

Some cultures are known for the perks in their environments, such as Google's bocce courts, Factset Research's onsite Pie/Cheese/Cupcake trucks, software designer Autodesk's bring-your-dog office, SAS's free health care clinic, Microsoft's organic spa, and adventure-gear REI's free equipment rentals. Other companies communicate the values of their cultures through the gift of time to think creatively, either with leaders or offsite. Financial products developer Think Finance and other companies set up rotating focus groups and

Photo 16-3 At Sermo, an online community for physicians, a casual work environment and open office plan convey that the company values openness, creativity, and flexibility. Allowing employees to bring their pets to work, Daniel Palestrant (left), Sermo's founder and CEO, created a culture where employees are comfortable and able to have fun.

A Culture of Compassion

In the world of banking, success and ethical culture don't necessarily go hand in hand. Leaders who desire ethical cultures in their organizations must choose to build ethics into the company's definition of success in ways that translate into ethical actions for managers and employees. Contrast two financial success stories, Goldman Sachs and Wells Fargo. Both megabanks are among the *Fortune* 100 (the largest U.S. companies ranked by revenue). They are also two of *Fortune*'s World's Most Admired Companies, a list that ranks the largest companies in revenue by nine criteria including social responsibility. Yet their organizational cultures appear to be vastly different. Goldman Sachs seems to struggle to achieve an ethical culture for its employees and clients, while Wells Fargo seems to emanate a culture of compassion. Consider some recent headlines:

- Mefit "Mike" Mecevic was a loyal janitor for Goldman Sachs when Superstorm Sandy hit New York in October 2012. Mecevic and his coworkers rode out the storm in the company's Manhattan skyscraper and worked nonstop for days to keep floodwaters back. Then a Goldman Sachs manager threw him out without explanation. Mecevic said to him, " 'I live in Staten Island, there's a state of emergency, there are no cars, no trains, no lights. The water is up to our necks.' I was begging for my life. But he said 'Leave the building.' " Mecevic implored two other managers to help him, to no avail. He left but was later fired anyway. "I worked day and night," Mecevic said. "They destroyed my life for nothing. Nothing."
- A Wells Fargo branch in Atlanta was the scene of a March 2013 "Harlem Shake" video in which two actors

and numerous bank employees danced provocatively through roles of teller, customer, and masked robber. The video was shot after the bank closed and apparently with the approval of local management. In the background appears the Wells Fargo logo and this quote from founder Henry Wells: "We have one very powerful business rule. It is concentrated in one word: courtesy." Despite the fact that Wells Fargo disapproved of the nonprofessional video, it did not release the names of the managers or employees or reveal whether any action was taken against them. The bank said only, "This was something that our team members [the Wells Fargo term for 'employees'] participated in on their own time. It was not approved by the company and Wells Fargo did not produce the video."

- When Goldman Sachs executive director Greg Smith left the company in March 2012, he e-mailed his resignation to his boss and, 15 minutes later, to the Op-Ed page of *The New York Times*. "I look around today and see virtually no trace of the culture that made me love working for this firm for many years," he wrote. "It makes me ill how callously people talk about ripping their clients off. I have seen five different managing directors refer to their own clients as 'muppets' [British slang for 'idiots']." Smith received messages of support from clients, while top bank leaders denounced his claims. Smith will not likely be hired on Wall Street again, partly because Goldman Sachs launched an investigation and discredited him for over a year through numerous leaks and accusations shared with the media.
- The financial crisis in the housing market has dragged on longer than

forecasted, yet Wells Fargo has remained committed to keeping people in their foreclosed homes instead of carrying out repossessions that could boost company profitability. The bank is also committed to respecting its clients, even when those clients are in trouble. For the past few years, it has held "Home Preservation Workshops" where indebted homeowners can meet with "home retention" team members in confidential booths set up in large halls across the United States. Clients bring paperwork specific to their cases, and team members negotiate binding agreements. One client said, "It is a great feeling to not worry" about losing her home.

Organizational culture is where leaders' ethical choices demonstrate their expectations for others' decisions throughout the company. Both Goldman and Wells Fargo enjoy stellar reputations. But these examples suggest that the two companies make very different ethical choices with respect to their cultures.

Sources: B. Ross, A. Ng, and C. Siemaszko, "Ex-Goldman Sachs Janitor Sues for Being Forced into Post-Hurricane Sandy Destruction," *New York Daily News* (June 7, 2013), www.nydailynews.com/new-york/janitor-sues-tossed-aftermath-hurricane-sandy-article-1.1366334; M. Schifrin and H. Touryalai, "The Bank That Works," *Forbes* (February 13, 2012), pp. 66–74; C. Seward, "Wells Fargo Shakes Finger at 'Harlem Shake' YouTube Video," *The Atlanta Journal-Constitution* (March 27, 2013), http://blogs.ajc.com/business-beat/2013/03/27/wells-fargo-team-in-harlem-shake-youtube-video/; K. Roose, "Goldman Sachs Just Can't Quit Greg Smith," *New York Magazine* (March 14, 2013), http://nymag.com/daily/intelligencer/2013/03/goldman-sachs-just-cant-quit-greg-smith.html; and G. Smith, "Why I Am Leaving Goldman Sachs," *The New York Times* (March 14, 2012), www.nytimes.com/2012/03/14/opinion/why-i-am-leaving-goldman-sachs.html?_r=0.

town halls, where employees meet with top management to enhance an idea-sharing culture. CEO Ken Rees says, "At the end, I always ask, 'Tell me one thing you really like about the company and one thing that frustrates you about the company.' [It] is eye-opening." Biotech leader Genentech and many other top companies provide paid sabbaticals. Genentech offers every employee 6 weeks' paid leave for every 6 years of service to support a culture of equitability and innovative thinking.[65]

Language

Many organizations and subunits within them use language to help members identify with the culture, attest to their acceptance of it, and help preserve it. Unique terms describe equipment, officers, key individuals, suppliers, customers, or products that relate to the business. New employees may at first be overwhelmed by acronyms and jargon, that, once assimilated, act as a common denominator to unite members of a given culture or subculture.

Creating an Ethical Organizational Culture

5 Demonstrate how an ethical culture can be created.

The organizational culture most likely to shape high ethical standards among its members is high in risk tolerance, low to moderate in aggressiveness, and focused on means as well as outcomes.[66] This type of culture takes a long-term perspective and balances the rights of multiple stakeholders, including employees, stockholders, and the community. Managers are supported for taking risks and innovating, discouraged from engaging in unbridled competition, and guided to heed not just to *what* goals are achieved but also *how*.

If the culture is strong and supports high ethical standards, it should have a very powerful and positive influence on employee behavior. Marcus Baynes, an analyst/computer scientist with the U.S. National Security Agency, credits the organization's commitment to work–life balance and diversity for its ability to sustain a positive, ethical culture in a high-stakes, high-stress environment. "The work is demanding and important, but we have a lot of fun doing it," he said.[67]

Examples of organizations that have failed to establish proper codes of ethical conduct can be found in the media nearly every day. Some actively deceive customers or clients. Others produce products that harm consumers or the environment, or they harass or discriminate against certain groups of employees. Others are more subtle and cover up or fail to report wrongdoing. The negative consequences of a systematic culture of unethical behavior can be severe and include customer boycotts, fines, lawsuits, and government regulation of an organization's practices.

What can managers do to create a more ethical culture? They can adhere to the following principles:[68]

- **Be a visible role model.**   Employees will look to the actions of top management as a benchmark for appropriate behavior. Send a positive message.
- **Communicate ethical expectations.**   Minimize ethical ambiguities by sharing an organizational code of ethics that states the organization's primary values and ethical rules employees must follow.
- **Provide ethical training.**   Set up seminars, workshops, and training programs to reinforce the organization's standards of conduct, clarify what practices are permissible, and address potential ethical dilemmas.

- **Visibly reward ethical acts and punish unethical ones.**   Appraise managers on how their decisions measure up against the organization's code of ethics. Review the means as well as the ends. Visibly reward those who act ethically and conspicuously punish those who don't.
- **Provide protective mechanisms.**   Provide formal mechanisms so employees can discuss ethical dilemmas and report unethical behavior without fear of reprimand. These might include ethical counselors, ombudspeople, or ethical officers.

The work of setting a positive ethical climate has to start at the top of the organization.[69] A study of 195 managers demonstrated that when top management emphasizes strong ethical values, supervisors are more likely to practice ethical leadership. Positive ethical attitudes transfer down to line employees, who show lower levels of deviant behavior and higher levels of cooperation and assistance. A study involving auditors found perceived pressure from organizational leaders to behave unethically was associated with increased intentions to engage in unethical practices.[70] Clearly the wrong type of organizational culture can negatively influence employee ethical behavior. Finally, employees whose ethical values are similar to those of their department are more likely to be promoted, so we can think of ethical culture as flowing from the bottom up as well.[71]

Creating a Positive Organizational Culture

6 Describe a positive organizational culture.

positive organizational culture
A culture that emphasizes building on employee strengths, rewards more than punishes, and emphasizes individual vitality and growth.

At first blush, creating a positive culture may sound hopelessly naïve or like a Dilbert-style conspiracy. The one thing that makes us believe this trend is here to stay, however, are signs that management practice and OB research are converging.

A **positive organizational culture** emphasizes building on employee strengths, rewards more than it punishes, and emphasizes individual vitality and growth.[72] Let's consider each of these areas.

Building on Employee Strengths   Although a positive organizational culture does not ignore problems, it does emphasize showing workers how they can capitalize on their strengths. As management guru Peter Drucker said, "Most Americans do not know what their strengths are. When you ask them, they look at you with a blank stare, or they respond in terms of subject knowledge, which is the wrong answer." Wouldn't it be better to be in an organizational culture that helped you discover your strengths and learn how to make the most of them?

Larry Hammond, CEO of Auglaize Provico, an agribusiness based in Ohio, used this approach when you'd least expect it: during his firm's darkest days. In the midst of the firm's worst financial struggles, when it had to lay off one-quarter of its workforce, Hammond decided to try a different approach. Rather than dwell on what was wrong, he took advantage of what was right. "If you really want to [excel], you have to know yourself—you have to know what you're good at, and you have to know what you're not so good at," says Hammond. With the help of Gallup consultant Barry Conchie, Hammond focused on discovering and using employee strengths and helped the company turn itself around. "You ask Larry [Hammond] what the difference is, and he'll say that it's individuals using their natural talents," says Conchie.[73]

Photo 16-4 Market Technologies is a family-owned trading software developer that has a positive culture. The firm rewards employees in many small ways in appreciation for their contributions to its success, from fun dress-up events like tacky tourist day shown here to birthday and achievement celebrations and frequent family outings.

Source: St Petersburg Times/ZUMAPRESS/Newscom.

Rewarding More Than Punishing   Although most organizations are sufficiently focused on extrinsic rewards such as pay and promotions, they often forget about the power of smaller (and cheaper) rewards such as praise. Part of creating a positive organizational culture is "catching employees doing something right." Many managers withhold praise because they're afraid employees will coast or because they think praise is not valued. Employees generally don't ask for praise, and managers usually don't realize the costs of failing to give it.

Consider El´zbieta Górska-Kolodziejczyk, a plant manager for International Paper's facility in Kwidzyn, Poland. Employees worked in a bleak windowless basement. Staffing became roughly one-third its prior level, while production tripled. These challenges had done in the previous three managers. So when Górska-Kolodziejczyk took over, although she had many ideas about transforming the organization, at the top were recognition and praise. She initially found it difficult to give praise to those who weren't used to it, especially men. "They were like cement at the beginning," she said. "Like cement." Over time, however, she found they valued and even reciprocated praise. One day a department supervisor pulled her over to tell her she was doing a good job. "This I do remember, yes," she said.[74]

Emphasizing Vitality and Growth   No organization will get the best from employees who see themselves as mere cogs in the machine. A positive culture recognizes the difference between a job and a career. It supports not only what the employee contributes to organizational effectiveness but also how the organization can make the employee more effective—personally and professionally. Top companies recognize the value of helping people grow. Safelite AutoGlass, *Workforce Management*'s 2012 Optima award winner for Competitive Advantage, attributes its success in part to its PeopleFirst Plan talent development initiative. "The only way we can stand out is if we have the best people," says Senior Vice President Steve Miggo.[75]

Although it may take more creativity to encourage employee growth in some types of industries, consider the food industry. At Masterfoods in Belgium,

Philippe Lescornez led a team of employees including Didier Brynaert, who worked in Luxembourg, nearly 150 miles away. Brynaert was considered a good sales promoter who was meeting expectations when Lescornez decided Brynaert's job could be made more important if he were seen less as just another sales promoter and more as an expert on the unique features of the Luxembourg market. So Lescornez asked Brynaert for information he could share with the home office. He hoped that by raising Brynaert's profile in Brussels, he could create in him a greater sense of ownership for his remote sales territory. "I started to communicate much more what he did to other people [within the company], because there's quite some distance between the Brussels office and the section he's working in. So I started to communicate, communicate, communicate. The more I communicated, the more he started to provide material," said Lescornez. As a result, "Now he's recognized as the specialist for Luxembourg—the guy who is able to build a strong relationship with the Luxembourg clients," says Lescornez. What's good for Brynaert was, of course, also good for Lescornez, who got credit for helping Brynaert grow and develop.[76]

Limits of Positive Culture   Is a positive culture a cure-all? Though many companies have embraced aspects of a positive organizational culture, it is a new enough idea for us to be uncertain about how and when it works best.

Not all national cultures value being positive as much as U.S. culture does, and, even within U.S. culture, there surely are limits to how far U.S. companies should go. The limits may need to be dictated by the industry. For example, Admiral, a British insurance company, has established a Ministry of Fun in its call centers to organize poem writing, foosball, conker (a British game involving chestnuts), and fancy-dress days, while other companies in the insurance industry have maintained more serious cultures. When does the pursuit of a positive culture start to seem coercive or even Orwellian? As one critic notes, "Promoting a social orthodoxy of positiveness focuses on a particular constellation of desirable states and traits but, in so doing, can stigmatize those who fail to fit the template."[77] There may be benefits to establishing a positive culture, but an organization also needs to be objective and not pursue it past the point of effectiveness.

Spirituality and Organizational Culture

7 Identify characteristics of a spiritual culture.

What do Southwest Airlines, Hewlett-Packard, Ford, The Men's Wearhouse, Tyson Foods, Wetherill Associates, and Tom's of Maine have in common? They're among a growing number of organizations that have embraced workplace spirituality.

What Is Spirituality?

workplace spirituality   *The recognition that people have an inner life that nourishes and is nourished by meaningful work that takes place in the context of community.*

Workplace spirituality is *not* about organized religious practices. It's not about God or theology. **Workplace spirituality** recognizes that people have an inner life that nourishes and is nourished by meaningful work in the context of community.[78] Organizations that promote a spiritual culture recognize that people seek to find meaning and purpose in their work and desire to connect with other human beings as part of a community. Many of the topics we have discussed—ranging from job design (designing work that is meaningful to employees) to transformational leadership (leadership practices that emphasize a higher-order purpose and self-transcendent goals) are well matched to the concept of organizational spirituality. When a company emphasizes its commitment to paying Third World suppliers a fair (above-market) price for their coffee to facilitate community development—as did Starbucks—or encourages employees to share prayers or inspirational messages through e-mail—as did Interstate Batteries—it is encouraging a more spiritual culture.[79]

Why Spirituality Now?

As we noted in our discussion of emotions in Chapter 4, the myth of rationality assumed the well-run organization eliminated feelings. Concern about an employee's inner life had no role in the perfectly rational model. But just as we've now come to realize that the study of emotions improves our understanding of organizational behavior, an awareness of spirituality can help us better understand employee behavior in the twenty-first century.

Of course, employees have always had an inner life. So why has the search for meaning and purposefulness in work surfaced now? We summarize the reasons in Exhibit 16-5.

Characteristics of a Spiritual Organization

The concept of workplace spirituality draws on our previous discussions of values, ethics, motivation, and leadership. What differentiates spiritual organizations from their nonspiritual counterparts? Although research remains preliminary, several cultural characteristics tend to be evident in spiritual organizations:[80]

- **Benevolence.** Spiritual organizations value showing kindness toward others and promoting the happiness of employees and other organizational stakeholders.
- **Strong sense of purpose.** Spiritual organizations build their cultures around a meaningful purpose. Although profits may be important, they're not the primary value of the organization.
- **Trust and respect.** Spiritual organizations are characterized by mutual trust, honesty, and openness. Employees are treated with esteem and value, consistent with the dignity of each individual.
- **Open-mindedness.** Spiritual organizations value flexible thinking and creativity among employees.

Exhibit 16-5   Reasons for the Growing Interest in Spirituality

- Spirituality can counterbalance the pressures and stress of a turbulent pace of life. Contemporary lifestyles—single-parent families, geographic mobility, the temporary nature of jobs, new technologies that create distance between people—underscore the lack of community many people feel and increase the need for involvement and connection.

- Formalized religion hasn't worked for many people, and they continue to look for anchors to replace lack of faith and to fill a growing feeling of emptiness.

- Job demands have made the workplace dominant in many people's lives, yet they continue to question the meaning of work.

- People want to integrate personal life values with their professional lives.

- An increasing number of people are finding that the pursuit of more material acquisitions leaves them unfulfilled.

Photo 16-5 Target employee Steve Baxter is a volunteer for Project Homeless Connect, a community program that provides housing and other services for people in need. Target employees value benevolence and show kindness to fellow workers and to people in their communities by giving their time and talents to helping others.

Source: Flores Elizabeth/ZUMA Press/Newscom

SELF-ASSESSMENT LIBRARY

How Spiritual Am I?

In the Self-Assessment Library (available in MyManagementLab), take assessment IV.A.4 (How Spiritual Am I?). Note: People's scores on this measure vary from time to time, so take that into account when interpreting the results.

Achieving a Spiritual Organization

Many organizations have grown interested in spirituality but have had difficulty putting its principles into practice. Several types of practices can facilitate a spiritual workplace,[81] including those that support work–life balance. Leaders can demonstrate values, attitudes, and behaviors that trigger intrinsic motivation and a sense of calling through work. Encouraging employees to consider how their work provides a sense of purpose through community building also can help achieve a spiritual workplace; often this is done through group counseling and organizational development, a topic we take up in Chapter 18. A growing number of companies, including Taco Bell and Sturdisteel, offer employees the counseling services of corporate chaplains. Many chaplains are employed by agencies, such as Marketplace Chaplains USA, while some corporations such as R.J. Reynolds Tobacco and Tyson Foods employ chaplains directly. The workplace presence of corporate chaplains, who are usually ordained Christian ministers, is obviously controversial, although their role is not to increase spirituality, but to help human resources serve the employees who already have Christian beliefs.[82]

Criticisms of Spirituality

Critics of the spirituality movement in organizations have focused on three issues. First is the question of scientific foundation. What really is workplace spirituality? Is it just a new management buzzword? Second, are spiritual organizations legitimate? Specifically, do organizations have the right to impose spiritual values on their employees? Third is the question of economics: Are spirituality and profits compatible?

First, as you might imagine, there is comparatively little research on workplace spirituality. We don't know whether the concept will have staying power. Do the cultural characteristics we just identified really separate spiritual organizations? Spirituality has been defined so broadly in some sources that practices from job rotation to corporate retreats at meditation centers have been identified as spiritual. Questions need to be answered before the concept gains full credibility.

On the second point, an emphasis on spirituality can clearly make some employees uneasy. Critics have argued that secular institutions, especially business firms, have no business imposing spiritual values on employees.[83] This criticism is undoubtedly valid when spirituality is defined as bringing religion and God into the workplace. However, it seems less stinging when the goal is limited to helping employees find meaning and purpose in their work lives. If the concerns listed in Exhibit 16-5 truly characterize a large segment of the workforce, then perhaps organizations can do so.

Finally, whether spirituality and profits are compatible objectives is certainly relevant for managers and investors in business. The evidence, although limited,

glOBalization!

Creating a Multinational Organizational Culture

In the twenty-first century, globalization is good. But is it good for organizational culture? Research suggests that globalization can threaten even strong, positive organizational cultures because they are often based on the values of the company's original country.

Implementing a multinational organizational culture can create strife between employees of traditionally competing countries. When Swedish, Norwegian, Finnish, and Danish banks combined to form Nordea financial services, researchers found the stereotypes some employees held created a combative atmosphere. Many of these stereotypes were based on the countries' historical relationships: Finland had originally been a colony of Sweden, and Norway had been a part of Denmark and then of Sweden. The fact that none of the employees had yet been born when their countries were colonies didn't matter; the stereotypes of Swedes as "domineering swindlers," Norwegians as "nationalistic underdogs," Finnish as "sensitive little siblings," and Danes

as "politicking negotiators" fractured the organizational culture. Complex alliances within Nordea formed along nationalistic lines to combat the efforts of other alliances. The dysfunctional organizational culture threatened the company's survival.

The case of Nordea illustrates the need for creating a strong, ethical, unique organizational culture for successful globalization. Nordea employed intentional "Nordic" storytelling for employees to identify with positive aspects of their shared geographical region through press releases, corporate correspondence, equal country representation in top management, and championing of shared values. The storytelling was successful in defining a positive organizational culture, but the Nordic emphasis limited the company when it wanted to expand into Europe. Nordea then redefined its culture as "globalist" in orientation, again employing storytelling as the communication method. Unfortunately, not only is organizational culture change difficult, but the company name Nordea, a blend of "Nordic" and

"idea," brands it as uniquely regional. Nordea continues to struggle with culture issues.

Because culture strongly affects performance, organizations need to construct and clearly communicate a multinational culture that focuses on corporate values. These values should be unique and separate from identifiable country norms, emphasize respect and tolerance for cultural differences, and address the issue of cultural identity. Globalization can be an opportunity to positively change organizational culture.

Sources: P. Monin, N. Noorderhavin, E. Vaara, and D. Kroon, "Giving Sense to and Making Sense of Justice in Postmerger Integration," *Academy of Management Journal* (February 2013), pp. 256–284; A. Simha and J. B. Cullen, "Ethical Climates and Their Effects on Organizational Outcomes: Implications from the Past and Prophecies for the Future," *Academy of Management Perspectives* (November 2011), pp. 20–34; and E. Vaara and J. Tienari, "On the Narrative Construction of Multinational Corporations: An Antenarrative Analysis of Legitimation and Resistance in a Cross-Border Merger," *Organization Science* (March–April 2011), pp. 370–390.

indicates they are. In one study, organizations that provided their employees with opportunities for spiritual development have outperformed those that didn't.[84] Other studies reported that spirituality in organizations was positively related to creativity, employee satisfaction, job involvement, and organizational commitment.[85]

Global Implications

8 Show how national culture can affect the way organizational culture is transported to another country.

We considered global cultural values (collectivism–individualism, power distance, and so on) in Chapter 5. Here our focus is a bit narrower: How is organizational culture affected by a global context? Organizational culture is so powerful it often transcends national boundaries. But that doesn't mean organizations should, or could, ignore local culture.

Organizational cultures often reflect national culture. The culture at AirAsia, a Malaysian-based airline, emphasizes openness and friendships. The carrier has lots of parties, participative management, and no private offices, reflecting Malaysia's relatively collectivistic culture. The culture of many U.S. airlines do not reflect the same degree of informality. If U.S. airlines were to merge with AirAsia, they would need to take these cultural differences into account. Organizational culture differences are not always due to international cultures differences, however. One of the chief challenges of the merger between US Airways and American airlines is the integration of US Airway's "open-collar" culture with American's "button-down" culture.[86]

One of the primary things U.S. managers can do is to be culturally sensitive. The United States is a dominant force in business and in culture—and with that influence comes a reputation. "We are broadly seen throughout the world as arrogant people, totally self-absorbed and loud," says one U.S. executive. Some ways in which U.S. managers can be culturally sensitive include talking in a low tone of voice, speaking slowly, listening more, and avoiding discussions of religion and politics.

The management of ethical behavior is one area where national culture can rub up against corporate culture.[87] U.S. managers endorse the supremacy of anonymous market forces and implicitly or explicitly view profit maximization as a moral obligation for business organizations. This worldview sees bribery, nepotism, and favoring personal contacts as highly unethical. Any action that deviates from profit maximization may indicate that inappropriate or corrupt behavior may be occurring. In contrast, managers in developing economies are more likely to see ethical decisions as embedded in a social environment. That means doing special favors for family and friends is not only appropriate but possibly even an ethical responsibility. Managers in many nations also view capitalism skeptically and believe the interests of workers should be put on a par with the interests of shareholders.

U.S. employees are not the only ones who need to be culturally sensitive. Three times a week, employees at the Canadian unit of Japanese videogame maker Koei begin the day by standing next to their desks, facing their boss, and saying "Good morning" in unison. Employees then deliver short speeches on topics that range from corporate principles to 3D game engines. Koei also has employees punch a time clock and asks women to serve tea to top executive guests. Although these practices are consistent with Koei's culture, they do not fit Canadian culture very well. "It's kind of like school," says one Canadian employee.[88]

Another area of sensitivity relates to differing standards of wellness practices that contribute to the organizational culture. As national organizations seek to employ workers in overseas operations, management must decide whether to standardize the wellness plans and work–life balance initiatives offered in the home country or to tailor the plans for the norms of the satellite offices. At this point, there is no clear consensus on the best course of action, but the first step is for companies to be sensitive to differing standards. For instance, when U.S. company Rothenberg International introduced its alcohol abuse remediation plan to Russian employees as part of its employee assistance program (EAP), it didn't foresee that Russians resist the concept of "assistance" and prefer "support" instead. Rothenberg was able to adjust, but sometimes local laws intercede (as a help or a hindrance) when employers roll out homeland plans. Brazil has a government anti-HIV plan that employers can use, for instance, and the U.K.'s National Health Service pays for smoking cessation programs, while in Germany private insurance must pay for wellness plans.[89]

Employers are recognizing that workplace wellness plans and work–life balance initiatives contribute positively to the organizational culture and thus to the bottom line in improved productivity, reduced absenteeism, and lowered disability costs. The quality of care available around the world has also improved. With sensitivity, multinational companies can create unique organizational cultures to support their employees and, through them, their objectives.

Summary

Exhibit 16-6 depicts organizational culture as an intervening variable. Employees form an overall subjective perception of the organization based on factors such as degree of risk tolerance, team emphasis, and support of individuals. This overall perception becomes, in effect, the organization's culture or personality and affects employee performance and satisfaction, with stronger cultures having greater impact.

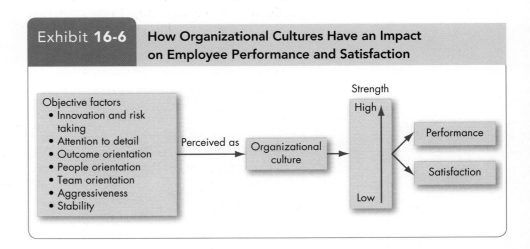

Exhibit 16-6   How Organizational Cultures Have an Impact on Employee Performance and Satisfaction

Implications for Managers

- Realize that an organization's culture is relatively fixed in the short term. To effect change, involve top management and strategize a long-term plan.
- Hire individuals whose values align with those of the organization; these employees will tend to remain committed and satisfied. Not surprisingly, "misfits" have considerably higher turnover rates.
- Understand that employees' performance and socialization depend to a considerable degree on their knowing what to do and not do. Train your employees well and keep them informed of changes to their job roles.
- As a manager, you can shape the culture of your work environment, sometimes as much as it shapes you. All managers can especially do their part to create an ethical culture and to consider spirituality and its role in creating a positive organizational culture.
- Be aware that your company's organizational culture may not be "transportable" to other countries. Understand the cultural relevance of your organization's norms before introducing new plans or initiatives overseas.

Organizations Should Strive to Create a Positive Organizational Culture

POINT

Organizations should do everything they can to establish a positive culture, because it works. Scores of recent studies have shown that individuals who are in positive states of mind at work and in life lead happier, more productive, and more fulfilling lives. Given the accumulating evidence, researchers are now studying ways to make that happen.

In a recent *Harvard Business Review* article, Wharton faculty member Adam Grant discusses an interesting concept: *outsourcing inspiration*. What does he mean by that? Grant writes: "A growing body of research shows that end users—customers, clients, patients, and others who benefit from a company's products and services—are surprisingly effective in motivating people to work harder, smarter, and more productively."

Some tangible examples of how this can work:

- Northwestern University's "buddy program" introduces Alzheimer's patients to scientists working to develop treatments for the disease.
- At a Merrill Lynch branch, weekly team meetings begin with stories about how the team has made a difference in customers' lives.
- "All Medtronic employees have a 'defining moment' in which they come face-to-face with a patient whose story deeply touches them," writes former CEO Bill George.

Of course, there are other ways of creating a positive organizational culture, including building on strengths and rewarding more than punishing.

Creating a positive organizational culture is not magic, but it tends to have extremely positive benefits for organizations that embrace it. *Outsourcing inspiration* is a great way for employees to feel appreciated, to experience empathy, and to see the impact of their work—all motivating outcomes that will lead organizations to be more effective and individuals more fulfilled in their work.

COUNTERPOINT

There are many unanswered questions about the merits of using positive organizational scholarship to build positive organizational cultures. Let's focus on three.

What is a positive culture? The employment relationship can be amicable and even mutually beneficial. However, glossing over natural differences in interests with the frosting of positive culture is intellectually dishonest and potentially harmful. From time to time, any organization needs to undertake unpopular actions. Can anyone terminate an employee positively (and honestly), or explain to someone why others received a raise? There's a danger in trying to sugarcoat. Positive relationships will develop—or not—on their own. We'd be better off preaching that people, and organizational cultures, should be honest and fair, rather than unabashedly positive.

Is practice ahead of science? Before we start beseeching organizations to build positive cultures, we should make sure these interventions work as we think they do. Many have unintended consequences, and we simply don't have enough research to support the claims put forth. As one reviewer noted, "Everyone wants to believe they could have greater control over their lives by simply changing the way they think. Research that supports this idea gets promoted loudly and widely." But it's not based on a mountain of evidence.

Is building a positive culture manipulative? Psychologist Lisa Aspinwall writes of "saccharine terrorism," where employees are coerced into positive mindsets by Happiness Coaches. You may think this an exaggeration, but companies like UBS, American Express, KPMG, FedEx, Adobe, and IBM use Happiness Coaches to do exactly that. As one critic noted, "Encouraging people to maintain a happy outlook in the face of less-than-ideal conditions is a good way of keeping citizens under control in spite of severe societal problems, or keeping employees productive while keeping pay and benefits low."

Sources: B. Azar, "Positive Psychology Advances, with Growing Pains," *Monitor on Psychology* (April 2011), pp. 32–36; A. Grant, "How Customers Can Rally Your Troops," *Harvard Business Review* (June 2011), downloaded on July 12, 2011, from http://hbr.org/; and J. McCarthy, "5 Big Problems with Positive Thinking (And Why You Should Do It Anyway)," *Positive Psychology* (October 2010), downloaded on July 10, 2011, from http://psychologyofwellbeing.com/.

END-OF-CHAPTER REVIEW

MyManagementLab

Go to mymanagementlab.com to complete the problems marked with this icon. ⭐

QUESTIONS FOR REVIEW

16-1 What is organizational culture, and what are its common characteristics?

16-2 What are the functional and dysfunctional effects of organizational culture?

16-3 What factors create and sustain an organization's culture?

16-4 How is culture transmitted to employees?

16-5 How can an ethical culture be created?

16-6 What is a positive organizational culture?

16-7 What are the characteristics of a spiritual culture?

16-8 How does national culture affect what happens when an organizational culture is transported to another country?

EXPERIENTIAL EXERCISE Rate Your Classroom Culture

Listed here are 14 statements. Using the 5-item scale (from strongly agree to strongly disagree), respond to each statement by circling the number that best represents your opinion.

	Strongly Agree	Agree	Neutral	Disagree	Strongly Disagree
16-9. I feel comfortable challenging statements made by my instructor.	1	2	3	4	5
16-10. My instructor heavily penalizes assignments that are not turned in on time.	1	2	3	4	5
16-11. My instructor believes that "It's final results that count."	1	2	3	4	5
16-12. My instructor is sensitive to my personal needs and problems.	1	2	3	4	5
16-13. A large portion of my grade depends on how well I work with others in the class.	1	2	3	4	5
16-14. I often feel nervous and tense when I come to class.	1	2	3	4	5
16-15. My instructor seems to prefer stability over change.	1	2	3	4	5
16-16. My instructor encourages me to develop new and different ideas.	1	2	3	4	5
16-17. My instructor has little tolerance for sloppy thinking.	1	2	3	4	5
16-18. My instructor is more concerned with how I came to a conclusion than with the conclusion itself.	1	2	3	4	5

	Strongly Agree	Agree	Neutral	Disagree	Strongly Disagree
16-19. My instructor treats all students alike.	1	2	3	4	5
16-20. My instructor frowns on class members helping each other with assignments.	1	2	3	4	5
16-21. Aggressive and competitive people have a distinct advantage in this class.	1	2	3	4	5
16-22. My instructor encourages me to see the world differently.	1	2	3	4	5

Calculate your total score by adding up the numbers you circled. Your score will fall between 14 and 70.

A high score (49 or above) describes an open, risk-taking, supportive, humanistic, team-oriented, easygoing, growth-oriented culture. A low score (35 or below) describes a closed, structured, task-oriented, individualistic, tense, and stability-oriented culture. Note that differences count, so a score of 60 is a more open culture than one

that scores 50. Also, realize that one culture isn't preferable over another. The "right" culture depends on you and your preferences for a learning environment.

Form teams of five to seven members each. Compare your scores. How closely do they align? Discuss and resolve any discrepancies. Based on your team's analysis, what type of student do you think would perform best in this class?

ETHICAL DILEMMA A Bankrupt Culture

Like many newspapers, the *Chicago Tribune* is in trouble. The paper was bought by real estate mogul Sam Zell in 2007, who promptly filed for bankruptcy. That didn't surprise experts. What Zell did next did.

Zell hired Randy Michaels as the Tribune Company's CEO. Soon after Michaels arrived, he launched an attack on the Tribune's culture. In an informal meeting with a group of fellow Tribune executives, Michaels said, "Watch this" and offered the waitress $100 to show her breasts. The group was dumbfounded.

But Michaels hardly stopped there.

Michaels was fond of a culture that included "sexual innuendo, poisonous workplace banter, and profane invective." One press release announced the hiring of Kim Johnson, who, it was said, was "a former waitress at 'Knockers—The Place for Hot Racks and Cold Brews.'" Another executive reporting to Michaels sent links to raunchy websites in e-mail messages. Michaels was heard loudly discussing with other executives he had brought with him the "sexual suitability of various employees."

When some complained about the change in the culture, Michaels rewrote the employee handbook. "Working at Tribune means accepting that you might hear a word that

you, personally, might not use," the new manual stated. "You might experience an attitude you don't share. You might hear a joke that you don't consider funny. That is because a loose, fun, nonlinear atmosphere is important to the creative process." It then concluded, "This should be understood, should not be a surprise, and not considered harassment."

Eventually Michaels was forced out, but the damage had been done. The Tribune was in bankruptcy through 2012, and the company may sell off its newspapers. More than 5,000 employees have lost their jobs. In retrospect, Zell has called his purchase "the deal from hell." It appears he appointed a CEO to match the deal.

Questions

16-23. What does this story tell you about the effect of top management on organizational culture?

16-24. Denise Brown, a former member of the Tribune's management, said, "If you spoke up, you were portrayed as a sissy." How would you have reacted if you witnessed some of these behaviors?

✪**16-25.** How can you determine when a line has been crossed between a fun and informal culture, and one that is offensive and inappropriate?

Sources: D. Carr, "At Debt-Ridden Tribune, a Culture Run Amok," *The New York Times* (October 6, 2010), pp. A1, A22; E. Lee, "Tribune CEO Says Protest Over Koch Newspaper Sale Is Premature," *Bloomberg* (May 16, 2013), www.bloomberg.com/news/2013-05-15/tribune-ceo-says-furor-over-possible-newspaper-sale-is-premature.html; M. Oneal and P. Rosenthal, "Tribune Co. CEO Randy Michaels Resigns Amid Accusations of Crass Behavior," *Chicago Tribune* (October 22, 2010), downloaded July 12, 2011, from http://articles.chicagotribune.com/; and P. Whoriskey, "Former Tribune, Times Mirror Executives, Editors Sue Shareholders," *Washington Post* (June 2, 2011), downloaded on July 11, 2011, from www.washingtonpost.com/.

CASE INCIDENT 1   Mergers Don't Always Lead to Culture Clashes

A lot of mergers lead to culture clashes and, ultimately, failure. So in 2005 when banking giant Bank of America (BOA) announced its $35 billion acquisition of credit card giant MBNA, many thought that in a few years this merger would join the heap of those done in by cultural differences.

MBNA's culture was characterized by a free-wheeling, entrepreneurial spirit that was also quite secretive. MBNA employees also were accustomed to the high life. Their corporate headquarters in Wilmington, Delaware, could be described as lavish, and employees throughout the company enjoyed high salaries and generous perks—from the private golf course at its headquarters to its fleet of corporate jets and private yachts.

Bank of America, in contrast, grew by thrift. It was a low-cost, no-nonsense operation. Unlike MBNA, it believed that size and smarts were more important than speed. It was an acquisition machine that some likened to *Star Trek*'s relentless Borg collective.

In short, the cultures in the two companies were very, very different.

Although these cultural differences seemed a recipe for disaster, it appears, judging from the reactions of BOA and MBNA employees, that the merger has worked. How can this be?

BOA had the foresight to know which MBNA practices to attempt to change and which to keep in place. Especially critical was BOA's appreciation and respect for MBNA's culture. "On Day 1, I was directed that this was not like the ones you are used to," said Clifford Skelton, who had helped manage BOA's acquisition of FleetBoston Financial before moving on to MBNA.

To try to manage the cultural transition, executives of both companies began by comparing thousands of practices covering everything from hiring to call-center operations. In many cases, BOA chose to keep MBNA's cultural practices in place. In other cases, BOA did impose its will on MBNA. For example, because MBNA's pay rates were well above market, many MBNA managers were forced to swallow a steep pay cut. Some MBNA employees left, but most remained.

In other cases, the cultures co-adapted. For example, MBNA's dress code was much more formal than BOA's business-casual approach. In the end, a hybrid code was adopted, where business suits were expected in the credit-card division's corporate offices and in front of clients, but business causal was the norm otherwise.

While most believe the merger has been successful, there are tensions. Some BOA managers see MBNA managers as arrogant and autocratic. Some MBNA managers see their BOA counterparts as bureaucratic.

Of course, BOA made another, more recent and much larger acquisition: Merrill Lynch. After a rough start, most evidence suggests this mega-merger saved Merrill from bankruptcy and appears to be working well, including January–March 2013 earnings gains that put it among the top three investment banks, according to a recent study. BOA may have found the secret to successful mega-mergers.

Questions

16-26. Why do you think Bank of America's and MBNA's cultures appeared to mesh rather than clash?

16-27. Do you think culture is important to the success of a merger/acquisition? Why or why not?

⭐**16-28.** How much of the smooth transition, if any, do you think comes from both companies glossing over real differences in an effort to make the merger work?

Sources: Based on E. Dash, "A Clash of Cultures, Averted," *The New York Times* (February 20, 2007), pp. B1, B3; L. Moyer, "Bank of America Lewis Must Wait on His Fate," *Forbes* (April 29, 2009), www.forbes .com; K. MacFadyen, "From the People Who Brought You BofA," *Mergers and Acquisitions* (October, 2009), pp. 38–40; and S. Slater, "JPMorgan Stays Top of Investment Banking in First Quarter: Study," *Reuters* (June 12, 2013), www.reuters.com/article/2013/06/12/us-investmentbanks-rankings-idUSBRE95B09P2 0130612?feedType=RSS&feedName=businessNews.

CASE INCIDENT 2   Did Toyota's Culture Cause Its Problems?

You may be familiar with the problems that have recently plagued Toyota. However, you may not know the whole story. First, the facts. In 2010, Toyota issued a series of recalls for various models. The most serious was for a defect called "unintended acceleration," which occurs when a car accelerates with no apparent input from the driver. Investigations revealed that unintended acceleration in Toyota cars has been the cause of 37 deaths since 2000. When the problems first surfaced, however, Toyota denied it was the cause. Eventually, Toyota apologized and recalled more than 9 million cars.

To many, the root cause of Toyota's problems was its insular, arrogant culture. *Fortune* argued: "Like GM before it, Toyota has gotten smug. It believes the Toyota Way is the only way." *Time* reported "a Toyota management team that had fallen in love with itself and become too insular to properly handle something like the current crisis." Transportation Secretary Ray LaHood described Toyota's culture as "safety-deaf."

But is this the reality? Increasingly, evidence suggests that Toyota's culture—or even the cars it produces—is not the source of the problem.

A 2011 report released by the U.S. National Highway Traffic Safety Administration (NHTSA) concluded that unintended acceleration was not caused by problems in the electronic circuitry. *The Wall Street Journal* wrote that "safety regulators, human-error experts and auto makers say driver error is the primary cause of sudden acceleration." *Forbes* and *The Atlantic* commented that most of the incidents of sudden acceleration in Toyota cars occurred with elderly drivers, and elderly drivers are known to be more prone to confusing pedals. Many other independent investigations, including ones conducted by automobile experts at *Popular Mechanics* and *Car and Driver*, reached the same conclusion: The main cause of unintended acceleration was drivers mistaking the gas pedal for the brake pedal.

In June 2013, another round of recalls rocked Toyota and again involved the braking systems, this time affecting 242,000 Prius hybrid models. Automotive analyst Neil King cautions against inferring that Toyota is a troubled company, however. "Recalls seem to be so commonplace these days, I don't see it having any major impact . . . they are not the only ones affected. There was a period when it seemed to be only Toyota."

Does Toyota have an insular and inbred corporate culture? Probably. But it's been that way for a long time, and it's far from clear that its organizational culture is responsible for failures in the increasingly complex technological systems in today's cars.

Questions

16-29. If Toyota is not the cause of unintended acceleration, why was it blamed for it?

16-30. Is it possible to have a strong—even arrogant— culture and still produce safe and high-quality vehicles?

16-31. If you were the CEO of Toyota when the story was first publicized, how would you have reacted?

Sources: J. Moulds, "Toyota Recalls 242,000 Prius Cars," *The Guardian* (June 5, 2013), www.guardian .co.uk/business/2013/jun/05/toyota-recalls-prius-cars-uk-brake-fault; A. Taylor, "How Toyota Lost Its Way," *Fortune* (July 26, 2010), pp. 108–117; P. Allen, "Anatomy of Toyota's Problem Pedal: Mechanic's Diary," *Popular Mechanics* (March 3, 2010), downloaded July 11, 2011, from www.popularmechanics .com/; B. Saporito, "Behind the Troubles at Toyota," *Time* (February 11, 2010), downloaded July 11, 2011, from www.time.com/; and B. Simon, "LaHood Voices Concerns Over Toyota Culture," *Financial Times* (February 24, 2010), downloaded July 11, 2011, from www.ft.com/.

MyManagementLab

Go to **mymanagementlab.com** for Auto-graded writing questions as well as the following Assisted-graded writing questions:

16-32. From your reading of Case Incident 1, in what ways were the cultures of Bank of America and MBNA incompatible?

16-33. In regard to Case Incident 2, how did the culture at Toyota possibly perpetuate the problem?

16-34. MyManagementLab Only—comprehensive writing assignment for this chapter.

17 Human Resource Policies and Practices

LASZLO BOCK IS A REAL PEOPLE PERSON

At Google, where most things are run unconventionally, the top position in Human Resources is Senior Vice President of People Operations. Laszlo Bock has held the title since the role was created in 2006 and is responsible for Google's HR strategy, including aggressive hiring policies that have increased headcount tenfold to more than 37,000.

A Romanian immigrant with a Yale MBA and a solid business background, Bock is a new type of HR professional, embodying a global viewpoint. Jason Hanold, director of global executive-search firm Russell Reynolds Associates, said many new HR executives "are just as likely to have MBAs as they are to have degrees in industrial relations, who have broader business acumen than we've traditionally seen and are making an impact earlier than normal." Google CEO Eric Schmidt says, "Innovation and data are at the core of who we are at Google, and Laszlo applies those same principles to HR. He drives cutting-edge people programs and uses rigorous analytics to guide decision-making."

To develop the people programs that shape Google's approach to human resources, Bock devised the Three Thirds, a cross-functional management team model to foster critical thinking and a statistical, research approach to decision making. It is one-third traditional HR, one-third strategy/consulting, and one-third analysis. The Three Thirds "is not only meant to transform the perception of HR, but to transform the capability of the HR function as well," Bock says. "The idea is that you are able to operate your HR function in a fundamentally different way. You can prove what you're doing, and you can understand your clients' businesses and your CEO's business in a way that's far deeper than you could if you had just grown up in a single function."

In the early days, says Bock, "There was a lot of pressure to grow as quickly as we could. One challenge was making sure that quality of hiring didn't slip." Another was to build Google's unique open culture and transmit it worldwide. Bock says, "We try to have as many channels for expression as we can, recognizing that different people, and different ideas, will percolate up in different ways."

The eternal challenge of keeping employees happy is met in part through employee recognition, companywide visibility, and career development. Google relies on internal surveys as a management tool. "We regularly survey employees about their managers, and then use that information to publicly recognize the best managers and enlist them as teachers and role models for the next year. The worst managers receive intense coaching and support, which helps 75 percent of them get better within a quarter," Bock said.

Bock feels that Google's HR model might yield successful results for other companies. His long-term friend, director of Advantage Testing Gus

LEARNING OBJECTIVES

After studying this chapter, you should be able to:

1 Identify the most useful initial selection methods.

2 Identify the most useful substantive selection methods.

3 Define *contingent selection*.

4 Compare the four main types of training.

5 Contrast formal and informal training methods.

6 Contrast on-the-job and off-the-job training.

7 List the methods of performance evaluation.

8 Show how managers can improve performance evaluations.

9 Describe the leadership role of HR in organizations.

Mattammal, says Bock hopes that "Google is the place to go and learn HR, where you can then go to other organizations and take what you learned there. He's got a great environment there in terms of trying new initiatives, and the company is committed to thinking about things differently." Bock cautions that much of what they do is "Google-specific," but says he thinks Google has "hit upon some fundamental truths . . . one is that, if you give people freedom, they will amaze you. They'll do remarkable things, and all you need to do is give them a little infrastructure and a lot of room to change the world. And I think that holds in any industry."

Sources: L. He, "Google's Secrets of Innovation: Empowering Its Employees," *Forbes* (March 29, 2013), www.forbes.com/sites/laurahe/2013/03/29/googles-secrets-of-innovation-empowering-its-employees/; C. Newton, "Google Revenue Hits $14.42B in Fourth Quarter, Up 36 Percent," *C/NET* (January 22, 2013), http://news.cnet.com/8301-1023_3-57565236-93/google-revenue-hits-$14.42b-in-fourth-quarter-up-36-percent/; and M. O'Brien, "Building a New Breed," *Human Resources Executive Online* (October 2, 2010), www.hreonline.com/HRE/view/story.jhtml?id=533322196.

The message of this chapter is that human resource (HR) policies and practices—such as employee recruitment, selection, training, and performance management—influence an organization's effectiveness.[1] Studies show that managers—even HR managers—often don't know which HR practices work and which don't, but innovators like Laszlo Bock are serving key leadership functions in their organizations. To see how much you know (before learning the right answers in this chapter), take the self-assessment.

SELF-ASSESSMENT LIBRARY

How Much Do I Know About Human Resource Management (HRM)?

In the Self-Assessment Library (available in MyManagementLab), take assessment IV.G.2 (How Much Do I Know About HRM?), and answer the following questions:

1. How did you score compared to your classmates'? Did the results surprise you?
2. How much of effective HRM is common sense?
3. Do you think your score will improve after you read this chapter?

Recruitment Practices

We are all familiar with the continued high unemployment rate brought on by the Great Recession. In many industries, numerous candidates apply for each open job position. Yet there is a skills shortage in some industries, particularly in the technology and manufacturing sectors, which requires human resource departments to launch recruiting efforts.[2] Companies are increasingly turning away from outside recruiting agencies and relying on their own executives and human resource professionals for talent searches.[3] They are also using a variety of online tools including job boards and social media to bring in applications. This method has yielded an exponential number of applications, especially because the means to identify the best online recruitment sources are still developing.[4] Some organizations are pioneering unique methods such as online programming contests that masquerade as games to identify individuals with top skill sets who may be convinced to apply for positions. This method has been successful for recruiting applicants from all over the globe.[5]

Selection Practices

One of the most important HR functions is hiring the right people. How do you figure out who the right people are? Identifying the right people is the objective of the selection process, which matches individual characteristics (ability, experience, and so on) with the requirements of the job.[6] When management fails to get a proper match, employee performance and satisfaction both suffer. With more applications coming in the door than ever, it is paramount to ensure that your organization has an effective method for selecting the most qualified applicants. Unfortunately, technology has not been developed yet that can reliably sort through applications to identify the unique combinations of traits and experience that yield top performers. Even technology to inform applicants of their status in the hiring process is only in the early stages of development.[7]

How the Selection Process Works

Exhibit 17-1 shows how the selection process works in most organizations. Having decided to apply for a job, applicants go through several stages—three are shown in the exhibit—during which they can be rejected at any time. In practice, some organizations forgo some of these steps in the interests of time. (A meat-packing plant may hire anyone who walks in the door, but there is not a long line of people who want to "thread" a pig's intestines for a living.) But most organizations follow a process that looks something like this exhibit. Let's go into a bit more detail about each stage.

Initial Selection

1 Identify the most useful initial selection methods.

Initial selection devices are the first information applicants submit and are used for preliminary rough cuts to decide whether the applicant meets the basic qualifications for a job. Application forms and résumés (including letters of recommendation) are initial selection devices. We list background checks as either an initial selection device or a contingent selection device, depending on how the organization handles them. Some organizations prefer to look into an applicant's background right away. Others wait until the applicant is about to be hired, contingent on everything else checking out. Still others seem barely to check anything, instead hiring friends and family. This practice is controversial, partly because it hurts workplace diversity, which has been shown to increase organizational performance.[8] And some companies deliberately set out to hire applicants who wouldn't pass background checks, like those with

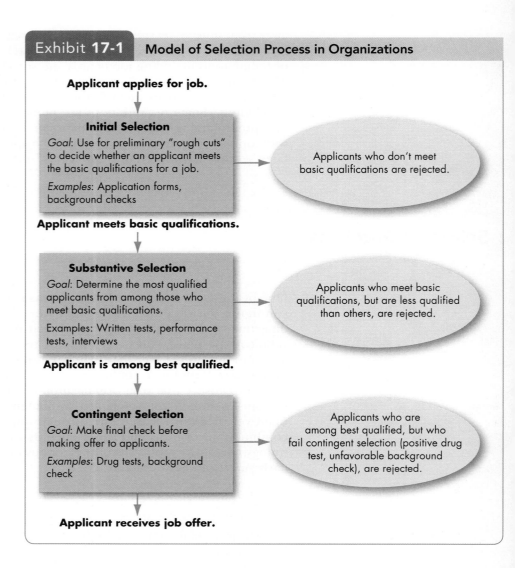

Exhibit 17-1 | Model of Selection Process in Organizations

Applicant applies for job.

Initial Selection

Goal: Use for preliminary "rough cuts" to decide whether an applicant meets the basic qualifications for a job.

Examples: Application forms, background checks

→ Applicants who don't meet basic qualifications are rejected.

Applicant meets basic qualifications.

Substantive Selection

Goal: Determine the most qualified applicants from among those who meet basic qualifications.

Examples: Written tests, performance tests, interviews

→ Applicants who meet basic qualifications, but are less qualified than others, are rejected.

Applicant is among best qualified.

Contingent Selection

Goal: Make final check before making offer to applicants.

Examples: Drug tests, background check

→ Applicants who are among best qualified, but who fail contingent selection (positive drug test, unfavorable background check), are rejected.

Applicant receives job offer.

criminal backgrounds. These organizations value "second chances" in their cultures and report that many of these workers become valuable contributors to their organizations and society. Such hires are not without risk, however, and so must be carefully managed.[9]

Application Forms   You've no doubt submitted your fair share of applications. By itself, the information submitted on an application form is not a very useful predictor of performance. However, it can be a good initial screen. For example, there's no sense spending time interviewing an applicant for a registered nurse position if he or she doesn't have the proper credentials (education, certification, experience). Many organizations encourage applicants to apply online. It takes only a few minutes, and the form can be forwarded to the people responsible for making the hiring decision. Most major corporations have a career page on their websites where prospective employees can search for available positions by location or job type and then apply online. These days, you are more likely to e-mail or upload your résumé than send anything by mail, and applicants are beginning to favor creating video résumés. Recent research in The Netherlands suggested that applicants from minority ethnic groups (Turkish and Moroccan) preferred the personal nature of the video résumé.[10]

Perceptions of Fairness in Selection Methods

Human resource professionals have a dozen or more tools at their disposal in the applicant selection process. These include interviews, résumés/applications, cognitive ability tests, personality measurements, graphology, honesty tests, and work samples. Assessments can be made in person, by telephone, or online, and HR managers can rate them analytically or subjectively.

But using the tools indiscriminately can cost the goodwill of candidates. Recent studies worldwide indicate that job candidates' judgment of the fairness of selection methods heavily influences the likelihood of their accepting a job and recommending the company to others. Those who do not think the selection methods are fair are also more likely to sue the company.

Perceptions of fairness differ by selection method and culture, but candidates worldwide perceive interviews most favorably, and graphology (handwriting analysis) and honesty tests unfavorably. Research indicates

that U.S., European, and Asian candidates consider work sample tests to be very fair, while those in India rate them unfavorably. U.S. and Asian candidates seem more consistently favorable in their fairness perceptions of cognitive ability tests and personality assessments than Indian candidates.

Researchers attribute the fairness perception differences to varying cultural contexts. For instance, Indian applicants favor methods that showcase personal characteristics (personal references, personality tests) over work-related assessments, perhaps because their culture does not emphasize personal privacy as strongly as more individualistic cultures. U.S. candidates rate the use of personal contacts favorably, while Asians prefer written tests, perhaps because Asian hiring practices were not historically objective. This reason may also apply to the finding that U.S. applicants favorably rate methods relying on subjective human interaction, while Asians rate practices using no direct interaction such as online

testing as more fair. Finally, when the method solicits personal information, applicants in low power distance countries are more likely to question its fairness than applicants in high power distance cultures where questioning authority is less acceptable.

Research supports the use of a variety of assessments chosen for their applicability to the job. A big-picture approach to global recruitment should also include consideration of the candidates' confidence in the organization's fairness practices.

Sources: G. W. Guimetti and E. F. Sinar, "Don't You Know Me Well Enough Yet? Comparing Reactions of Internal and External Candidates to Employment Testing," *International Journal of Selection and Assessment* (June 2012), pp. 139–147; T. G. Hoang, D. M. Truxillo, B. Erdogan, and T. N. Bauer, "Cross-cultural Examination of Applicant Reactions to Selection Methods: United States and Vietnam," *International Journal of Selection and Assessment* (June 2012), pp. 209–219; and J. Snyder and C. Shahani-Denning, "Fairness Reactions to Personnel Selection Methods: A Look at Professionals in Mumbai, India," *International Journal of Selection and Assessment* (September 2012), pp. 297–307.

Increasingly, employers are asking for photos with applicant submissions, and some are then scanning the photo with facial-recognition software to match the face to the applicant's home address, Social Security number, criminal record, and affiliations. While this seems like a good business practice, experts recommend against it unless the business operates in a high-security environment because applicants can claim discrimination based on their facial characteristics.[11]

Managers must be careful about the questions they ask on applications. It's pretty obvious that questions about race, gender, and nationality are disallowed. However, other questions also put companies in legal jeopardy. For example, it generally is not permissible to ask about prior arrest records or even convictions unless the answer is job related.

Be careful about what you put on your online applications. Many human resource departments, faced with an overwhelming number of electronic submissions, are using software to prescreen candidates based on keyword matches between applications and the qualifications needed for the job. Their software often seeks to screen out unacceptable candidates rather than select potentially good ones. While you will want to incorporate all the keywords that accurately describe your experience, including paid and volunteer work,[12] do use whatever prompts you are given to outline the personal characteristics that qualify you.[13]

Background Checks More than 80 percent of employers conduct both employment and personal reference checks on applicants at some point in the hiring process. The reason is obvious: They want to know how an applicant did in past jobs and whether former employers would recommend hiring the person. The problem is that rarely do former employers provide useful information. In fact, nearly two-thirds refuse to provide detailed references because they are afraid of being sued for saying something bad about a former employee. Although this concern is often unfounded (employers are safe as long as they stick to documented facts, and several states have passed laws protecting truthful information provided in reference checks), in our litigious society, most employers play it safe. The result is a paradox: Most employers want reference information, but few will give it out. Employers do call personal references for a more candid idea of the applicant; recent research also found that 30 percent of hiring managers regularly discovered references that were false or misleading.[14] Others have turned to reference-checking software that sends 10-minute surveys to references. Research indicates this new technology may result in better (more objective) information.[15]

Letters of recommendation are another form of background check. These also aren't as useful as they may seem. Applicants select references who will write good things about them, so almost all letters of recommendation are positive. In the end, readers either ignore them or read "between the lines" to try to find hidden meaning.

Many employers look for candidates online through a general Internet search or through a targeted search on social networking sites. The legality of this practice has come into question, but there is no doubt that many employers include an electronic search to see whether candidates have any history that might make them a dubious choice for employment. For some potential employees, an embarrassing or incriminating photo circulated through Facebook may make it hard to get a job. On the other hand, a recent study found that independent raters viewing candidate Facebook profiles were able to accurately determine candidate conscientiousness, agreeability, and intelligence that later translated into job performance scores as rated by supervisors.[16]

Some employers check credit histories. A bank hiring tellers, for example, would probably want to know about their credit history, but credit checks are increasingly being used for nonbanking jobs. There is some evidence in favor of this practice. Task performance, organizational citizenship behavior (OCB), and conscientiousness (which is a predictor of job performance) were found to be positively related to credit scores.[17] However, research also found that minority status was adversely related to credit scores, while age and educational attainment were positively related.[18] Because of these discrimination concerns and the invasive nature of credit checks, employers need to be sure there is a need for them.

Finally, some employers conduct criminal background checks. Currently, 65 million U.S. adults (one in four) have criminal records, and for many it is difficult or impossible to find work.[19] The Equal Employment Opportunity Commission (EEOC) states that candidates cannot be denied employment based only on the findings of background checks, and experts point out that they are often inaccurate anyway. Also, because job candidates are seldom told why they are turned down, individuals can be hurt without the opportunity for correction.[20] To further complicate matters, a criminal history can legally be used for rejection only if the violation relates to the job (an embezzler could be disqualified for jobs in finance, but not in, say, the medical field).[21] A civil rights movement currently seeks to ban employers from even asking applicants whether they have criminal convictions. Although it would seem best that employers refrain from conducting criminal background checks, *not* checking can carry a legal cost. Manor Park Nursing Home in Texas, for instance, failed to do a criminal background check of an employee who later sexually assaulted a resident of the home. The jury awarded the plaintiff $1.1 million, concluding the nursing home was negligent for failing to conduct a background check.[22]

Substantive Selection

2 Identify the most useful substantive selection methods.

If an applicant passes the initial screens, next are substantive selection methods. These are the heart of the selection process and include written tests, performance tests, and interviews.

Written Tests   Long popular as selection devices, written tests—called "paper-and-pencil" tests, though most are now available online—declined in use between the late 1960s and mid-1980s, especially in the United States. They were frequently characterized as discriminatory, and many organizations had not validated them as job related. The past 20+ years, however, have seen a resurgence, and today more than 60 percent of all U.S. organizations and most of the *Fortune* 1,000 use some type of employment test.[23] Managers recognize that valid tests can help predict who will be successful on the job.[24] Applicants, however, tend to view written tests as less valid and fair than interviews or performance tests.[25] Typical written tests include (1) intelligence or cognitive ability tests, (2) personality tests, (3) integrity tests, and (4) interest inventories.

Tests of intellectual ability, spatial and mechanical ability, perceptual accuracy, and motor ability have long proven valid predictors for many skilled, semiskilled, and unskilled operative jobs organizations.[26] Intelligence tests have proven to be particularly good predictors for jobs that include cognitively complex tasks (like learning the ever-more-complex playbooks in the NFL).[27] Many experts say intelligence tests are the *single best* selection measure across jobs and that they are at least as valid in the European Union (EU) as in the United States.[28] Some innovative employers are pioneering the use of tests designed to assess how a person thinks. Google, for instance, may ask candidates, "A man pushed his car to a hotel and lost his fortune. What happened?" Whether you answer, "The man was playing Monopoly" or not, the important choice is to give a thoughtful response.[29]

Photo 17-1 At this Sarku, Japan, fast-food restaurant, employees who apply for management positions must take written tests as part of the company's substantive selection process. Written tests for intelligence, integrity, personality, and interests are popular selection devices that help predict which applicants will be successful on the job.

Source: The Washington Post/Getty Images.

Personality tests are inexpensive and simple to administer, and their use has grown. The traits that best predict job performance are conscientiousness and positive self-concept.[30] This makes sense in that conscientious people tend to be motivated and dependable, and positive people are "can-do" oriented and persistent. However, concerns about applicants faking responses remain, partly because it's fairly easy to claim to be hard-working, motivated, and dependable when asked in a job application setting and partly because applicants aren't always aware they are faking.[31] A recent study of Croatian university students suggested that individuals can be partially successful in faking a desirable profile.[32] Another study in China indicated that the use of warning messages for potential faking behavior may help curb the behavior, but practical application for selection processes would be controversial.[33] Two reviews of studies comparing self-reported personality to observer-rated personality found that observer ratings are better predictors of job performance and other behaviors.[34] Thus, employers might want to consider asking employment references about an applicant's personality as part of the screening process.

As ethical problems have increased, integrity tests have gained popularity. These paper-and-pencil tests measure factors such as dependability, carefulness, responsibility, and honesty; they have proven to be powerful predictors of supervisory ratings of job performance and of theft, discipline problems, and excessive absenteeism.[35] However, recent research indicates the many available tests do not all predict job performance outcomes equally well. Managers must be careful to choose one that measures criteria matched to the job responsibilities.[36]

Performance-Simulation Tests   What better way to find out whether applicants can do a job successfully than by having them do it? That's precisely the logic of performance-simulation tests.

Although they are more complicated to develop and administer than written tests, performance-simulation tests have higher *face validity* (which measures whether applicants perceive the measures to be accurate), and their popularity has increased. The three best-known are work samples, assessment centers, and situational judgment tests.

Work sample tests are hands-on simulations of part or all of the work that applicants for routine jobs must perform. Each work sample element is matched with a job-performance element to measure applicants' knowledge, skills, and abilities with more validity than written aptitude and personality tests.[37] Work samples are widely used in the hiring of skilled workers, such as welders, machinists, carpenters, and electricians. Work sample tests are increasingly used for all levels of employment.

A more elaborate set of performance-simulation tests, specifically designed to evaluate a candidate's managerial potential, is administered in **assessment centers**. Line executives, supervisors, and/or trained psychologists evaluate candidates as they go through one to several days of exercises that simulate real problems they would confront on the job.[38] A candidate might be required to play the role of a manager who must decide how to respond to ten memos in an in-basket within a 2-hour period.

To reduce the costs of job simulations, many organizations have started to use *situational judgment tests* which ask applicants how they would perform in a variety of job situations and then compare their answers to those of high-performing employees.[39] Coaching can improve scores on these tests, however, raising questions about whether scores reflect true judgment or merely test preparation.[40] One study comparing situational judgment tests to assessment centers found the assessment center was a better predictor of job performance, although the

work sample tests *Hands-on simulations of part or all of the work that applicants for routine jobs must perform.*

assessment centers *A set of performance-simulation tests designed to evaluate a candidate's managerial potential.*

difference was not large.[41] Ultimately, the lower cost of the situational judgment test may make it a better choice for some organizations than a more elaborate work sample or assessment center.

Employers are increasingly using work sample methods that go beyond assessment testing into the realm of actual work performed and evaluated. These are sometimes known as realistic job previews or job tryouts, and they are given as a way to assess talent versus experience. Experts are finding they also decrease turnover because both employers and new hires know what they are getting into ahead of time.[42] When George McAfee applied for a vice president position in the tech industry, he was required to give presentations, conduct research, and hold talks with executives about their ongoing business concerns for over a week, all unpaid. He felt the employer was taking advantage of his free labor, but he said, "You just have to accept that and not be offended."[43] Human resources managers may risk losing qualified candidates who object to extensive testing and withdraw from the process. Those who identify with an organization's mission, people, or products will be less likely to withdraw, suggesting that HR managers should seek to engage candidates with the organization early in the selection process.[44]

Interviews   Of all the selection devices organizations around the globe use to differentiate candidates, the interview remains the most common.[45] It also tends to have a disproportionate amount of influence. Over-reliance on interviews is problematic because extensive evidence shows that impression management techniques like self-promotion have a strong effect on interviewer preferences even when unrelated to the job.[46] Conversely, the candidate who performs poorly in the employment interview is likely to be cut from the applicant pool regardless of experience, test scores, or letters of recommendation. And unfortunately, candidates can be rated lower for something as trivial as a blemish on their faces, a recent study found.[47]

These findings are relevant because of the interview's typical nature.[48] The popular unstructured interview—short, casual, and made up of random questions— is simply not a very effective selection device.[49] The data it gathers are typically biased and often only modestly related to future job performance. Still, managers are reluctant to use *structured interviews* in place of their favorite questions, such as "If you could be any animal, what would you be, and why?"[50] Harry West, CEO of innovation design firm Continuum, asks all candidates the same basic questions: "What is it you want to do? What is it that you're good at? What is it that you're not good at? Tell me about what you've done." This is an excellent start in that the questions are objective in nature, prompt open-ended responses, and are standardized for all candidates.[51]

Without structure, interviewers tend to favor applicants who share their attitudes, give undue weight to negative information, and allow the order in which applicants are interviewed to influence their evaluations.[52] To reduce such bias and improve the validity of interviews, managers should adopt a standardized set of questions, a uniform method of recording information, and standardized ratings of applicants' qualifications. Training interviewers to focus on specific dimensions of job performance, practicing evaluation procedures of candidates, and giving interviewers feedback on how well they focused on job-relevant characteristics significantly improves the accuracy of their ratings.[53] Interview effectiveness also improves when employers use *behavioral structured interviews*, probably because these assessments are less influenced by interviewer biases.[54] These interviews require applicants to describe how they handled specific problems and situations in previous jobs, based on the assumption that past behavior offers the best predictor of future behavior. Panel interviews also minimize the influence of individual biases and have higher validity.

OB Poll | Interview Derailment

When the interviewer goes off on a tangent, what do you do?

Gently redirect: 53%
Listen: 37%
Speak up: 10%

Note: Based on a survey of 150 job candidates.
Source: Based on J. Yang and P. Trap, *USA Today* (November 13, 2012), p. 1B.

In practice, most organizations use interviews as more than a prediction-of-performance device.[55] Companies as diverse as Southwest Airlines, Disney, Bank of America, Microsoft, Procter & Gamble, and Harrah's Entertainment use interviews to assess applicant—organization fit. So, in addition to evaluating specific, job-related skills, effective managers look at personality characteristics and personal values to find individuals who fit the organization's culture and image.

Contingent Selection

3 Define *contingent selection*.

If applicants pass the substantive selection methods, they are ready to be hired, contingent on final checks. One common contingent method is a drug test. Publix grocery stores make a tentative offer to applicants contingent on their passing such a test and checking out as drug-free.

Drug testing is controversial. Many applicants think testing without reasonable suspicion is invasive or unfair and say they should be tested on job-performance factors, not lifestyle choices that may not be relevant. Employers might counter that drug use and abuse are extremely costly, not just in financial terms but also in terms of people's safety. They have the law on their side. The U.S. Supreme Court has concluded that drug tests are "minimally invasive" selection procedures that as a rule do not violate individuals' rights.

Under the Americans with Disabilities Act, firms may not require employees to pass a medical exam before a job offer is made. However, they can conduct medical exams *after* making a contingent offer—to determine whether an applicant is physically or mentally able to do the job. Employers also sometimes use medical exams to find out whether and how they can accommodate employees with disabilities. For jobs requiring exposure to heavy physical or psychological demands, such as air traffic controllers or firefighters, medical exams are obviously an important indicator of the ability to perform.

International Variations in Selection Processes

Selection practices tend to be different in various business cultures. The use of educational qualifications in screening candidates seems to be a universal practice, but aside from this, different countries emphasize different selection techniques. Structured interviews are popular in some countries and nonexistent in others. Research shows that across The Netherlands, the United States,

Source: Bloomberg via Getty Images.

Photo 17-2 Arcadio Cruz (left) interviews a job applicant for a position at an Orchard Hardware Supply in Los Angeles. While selection practices differ among countries, the structured job interview is a popular selection method preferred by most applicants in the United States as well as in the Netherlands, France, Spain, Portugal, and Singapore.

France, Spain, Portugal, and Singapore, most applicants prefer interviews and work sample tests and dislike the use of personal contacts and integrity tests.[56] There was little variation in preferences across these countries.

Training and Development Programs

4 Compare the four main types of training.

Competent employees don't remain competent forever. Skills deteriorate and can become obsolete, and new skills need to be learned. That's why U.S. corporations with a hundred or more employees spent more than $125 billion on formal training in a recent year.[57]

Types of Training

Training can include everything from teaching employees basic reading skills to conducting advanced courses in executive leadership. Here we discuss four general skill categories—basic literacy, technical skills, interpersonal skills, and problem-solving skills—and civility and ethics training.

Basic Skills   One survey of more than 400 human resources professionals found that 40 percent of employers believe high school graduates lack basic skills in reading comprehension, writing, and math.[58] As work has become more sophisticated, the need for these basic skills has grown significantly, leading to a gap between employer demands for skills and the available skills in the workforce.[59] The challenge isn't unique to the United States. It's a worldwide problem from the most developed countries to the least.[60] For many undeveloped countries, widespread illiteracy means there is almost no hope of competing in a global economy.

Organizations increasingly have to teach employees basic reading and math skills. A literacy audit showed that employees at gun manufacturer Smith & Wesson needed at least an eighth-grade reading level to do typical workplace tasks.[61] Yet 30 percent of the company's 676 workers with no degree scored below eighth-grade levels in either reading or math. After the first round of basic-skills classes, company-paid and on company time, 70 percent of attendees brought their skills up to the target level, allowing them to do a better job. They displayed increased abilities to use fractions and decimals, better overall communication, greater ease in writing and reading charts, graphs, and bulletin boards—and a significant increase in confidence.

Technical Skills   Most training is directed at upgrading and improving an employee's technical skills, which is increasingly important for two reasons: new technology and new structural designs in the organization.

Indian companies have faced a dramatic increase in demand for skilled workers in areas like engineering for emerging technologies, but many recent engineering graduates lack up-to-date knowledge required to perform these technical tasks.[62] Companies like Tata and Wipro provide new hires with up to 3 months of training to ensure they have the knowledge to perform the technical work demanded. In addition, these organizations are attempting to form partnerships with engineering schools to ensure their curricula meet the needs of contemporary employers.

As organizations flatten their structures, expand their use of teams, and break down traditional departmental barriers, employees need mastery of a wider variety of tasks and increased knowledge of how their organization operates. The restructuring of jobs around empowered teams at Miller Brewing led management to introduce a comprehensive business literacy program to help employees better understand competition, the state of the beer industry, where the company's revenues come from, how costs are calculated, and where employees fit into the company's value chain.[63]

Problem-Solving Skills   Problem-solving training for managers and other employees can include activities to sharpen their logic, reasoning, and problem-defining skills as well as their abilities to assess causation, develop and analyze alternatives, and select solutions. Problem-solving training has become a part of almost every organizational effort to introduce self-managed teams or implement quality-management programs.

Interpersonal Skills   Most employees belong to a work unit, and their work performance depends on their ability to effectively interact with their co-workers and bosses. Some employees have excellent interpersonal abilities, but others require training to improve listening, communicating, and team-building skills. Although professionals are greatly interested in interpersonal skills training, most evidence suggests that skills learned in such training do not readily transfer back to the workplace.[64]

Civility Training   As human resource managers have become increasingly aware of the effects of social behavior in the workplace, they have paid more attention to the problems of incivility, bullying, and abusive supervision in organizations. Examples of incivility include being ignored, being excluded from social situations, having your reputation undermined in front of others, and experiencing other actions meant to demean or disparage. Researchers have shown that these forms of negative behavior can decrease satisfaction, reduce job performance, increase perceptions of unfair treatment, increase depression, and lead to psychological withdrawal from the workplace.[65]

Photo 17-3 After receiving many complaints from patients about rude and insulting behavior from its nursing staff, hospital officials at a clinic in southern China hired flight attendants to provide civility training for the nursing staff. During a training intervention, nurses learned how to greet patients politely and care for them with grace, kindness, and patience.

Source: Europics/Newscom.

Is there anything managers can do to minimize incivility, bullying, and abusive supervision? One possibility is training specifically targeted to building civility by having directed conversations about it and supporting the reduction of incivility on an ongoing process. Following a training intervention based on these principles, co-worker civility, respect, job satisfaction, and management trust increased, while supervisor incivility, cynicism, and absences decreased.[66] Thus, the evidence suggests that deliberate interventions to improve the workplace climate for positive behavior can indeed minimize the problems of incivility.

Ethics Training   A large percentage of employees working in the 1,000 largest U.S. corporations receive ethics training[67] either during new-employee orientation, as part of ongoing developmental programs, or as periodic reinforcement of ethical principles.[68] But the jury is still out on whether you can actually teach ethics.[69]

Critics argue that ethics are based on values, and value systems are learned by example at an early age. By the time employees are hired, their ethical values are fixed. Some research does suggest ethics training does not have a significant long-term effect on participants' values and even that exposure to business and law school programs *decreases* students' level of prosocial ethical values.[70]

Supporters of ethics training say values *can* be learned and changed after early childhood. And even if they couldn't, ethics training helps employees recognize ethical dilemmas and become more aware of the ethical issues underlying their actions. It also reaffirms an organization's expectations that members will act ethically. Individuals who have greater exposure to organizational ethics codes and ethics training do tend to be more satisfied and perceive their organizations as more socially responsible, so ethics training does have some positive effects.[71]

Training Methods

5   Contrast formal and informal training methods.

Historically, *training* meant "formal training," planned in advance and having a structured format. However, most workplace learning takes place in *informal training*—unstructured, unplanned, and easily adapted to situations and individuals. In reality, most informal training is nothing other than employees helping each other out, sharing information, and solving work-related problems together. Thus, many managers are now supportive of what used to be considered "idle chatter."

On-the-job training methods include job rotation, apprenticeships, understudy assignments, and formal mentoring programs. U.S. companies have been increasingly using longer-term job rotations to train managers for higher positions and foster collaboration.[72] But because on-the-job training methods often disrupt the workplace, organizations also invest in *off-the-job training*. The $125 billion figure we cited earlier for training was largely spent on the formal off-the-job variety, the most popular method being live classroom lectures. But it also encompasses public seminars, self-study programs, Internet courses, webinars, podcasts, and group activities that use role-plays and case studies. Larger organizations are increasingly building "Corporate Universities" to house formal training programs. The formal instruction given in the corporate university classes are often supplemented with informal online training.[73]

The fastest-growing training medium is probably computer-based training, or e-training.[74] E-learning systems emphasize learner control over the pace and content of instruction, allow e-learners to interact through online communities, and incorporate other techniques such as simulations and group discussions. Computer-based training that lets learners actively participate in exercises and quizzes can be more effective than traditional classroom instruction.[75] Recent research has also highlighted the ways in which computer-based training can be improved by providing learners with regular prompts to set goals for learning, use effective study strategies, and measure progress toward their learning goals.[76] Organizations are even exploring delivering e-training through micro-lessons, on-the-spot tips, and learning games sent to mobile devices.[77]

On the positive side, e-training increases flexibility because organizations can deliver materials anywhere, any time. It seems fast and efficient. On the other hand, it's expensive to design self-paced online materials, employees miss the social interaction of a classroom, online learners are more susceptible to distractions, and "clicking through" training without engaging in practice activities provides no assurance that employees have actually learned.[78]

6 Contrast on-the-job and off-the-job training.

Photo 17-4 Cold Stone Creamery employee Dan Lewis plays an Internet game as part of the company's computerized training program. The ice-cream parlor chain developed a propriety game named *Stone City* to help frontline employees learn about customer service and how ice-cream portions and inventory wastage affect the firm's profitability.

Evaluating Effectiveness

The *effectiveness* of a training program can refer to the level of student satisfaction, the amount students learn, the extent to which they transfer the material from training to their jobs, or the financial return on investments in training.[79] These results are not always related. Some people who have a positive experience in an upbeat, fun class learn very little; some who learn a great deal have difficulty figuring out how to use their knowledge at work; and changes in employee behavior are often not large enough to justify the expense of training. This means rigorous measurement of multiple training outcomes should be a part of every training effort.

The success of training also depends on the individual. If individuals are unmotivated, they will learn very little. What creates training motivation? Personality is important: Those with an internal locus of control, high conscientiousness, high cognitive ability, and high self-efficacy learn more. The climate also is important: When trainees believe there are opportunities and resources to let them apply their newly learned skills, they are more motivated and do better in training programs.[80] Finally, after-training support from supervisors and co-workers has a strong influence on whether employees transfer their learning into new behavior.[81] For a training program to be effective, it must not just teach the skills, but also change the work environment to support the trainees.

Performance Evaluation

7 List the methods of performance evaluation.

Would you study differently or exert a different level of effort for a college course graded on a pass–fail basis than for one that awarded letter grades A to F? Students typically tell us they study harder when letter grades are at stake. When they take a course on a pass–fail basis, they tend to do just enough to ensure a passing grade.

What applies in the college context also applies to employees at work. In this section, we show how the choice of a performance evaluation system and the way it's administered can be an important force influencing employee behavior.

What Is Performance?

In the past, most organizations assessed only how well employees performed the tasks listed on a job description, but today's less hierarchical and more service-oriented organizations require more. Researchers now recognize three major types of behavior that constitute performance at work:

task performance *The combination of effectiveness and efficiency at doing your core job tasks.*

citizenship *Actions that contribute to the psychological environment of the organization, such as helping others when not required.*

counterproductivity *Actions that actively damage the organization, including stealing, behaving aggressively toward co-workers, or being late or absent.*

1. **Task performance.** Performing the duties and responsibilities that contribute to the production of a good or service or to administrative tasks. This includes most of the tasks in a conventional job description.
2. **Citizenship.** Actions that contribute to the psychological environment of the organization, such as helping others when not required, supporting organizational objectives, treating co-workers with respect, making constructive suggestions, and saying positive things about the workplace.
3. **Counterproductivity.** Actions that actively damage the organization. These behaviors include stealing, damaging company property, behaving aggressively toward co-workers, and taking avoidable absences.

Most managers believe good performance means doing well on the first two dimensions and avoiding the third.[82] A person who does core job tasks very well but is rude and aggressive toward co-workers is not going to be considered a good employee in most organizations, and even the most pleasant and upbeat worker who can't do the main job tasks well is not going to be a good employee.

Purposes of Performance Evaluation

Performance evaluation serves a number of purposes.[83] One is to help management make general *human resource decisions* about promotions, transfers, and terminations. Evaluations also *identify training and development needs.* They *pinpoint employee skills and competencies* for which remedial programs can be developed. Finally, they *provide feedback to employees* on how the organization views their performance and are often the *basis for reward allocations,* including merit pay increases.

Because our interest is in organizational behavior, here we emphasize performance evaluation as a mechanism for providing feedback and determining reward allocations.

What Do We Evaluate?

The criteria management chooses to evaluate will have a major influence on what employees do. The three most popular sets of criteria are individual task outcomes, behaviors, and traits.

Individual Task Outcomes   If ends count rather than means, management should evaluate an employee's task on outcomes such as quantity produced, scrap generated, and cost per unit of production for a plant manager or on overall sales volume in the territory, dollar increase in sales, and number of new accounts established for a salesperson.

Behaviors   It is difficult to attribute specific outcomes to the actions of employees in advisory or support positions or employees whose work assignments are part of a group effort. We may readily evaluate the group's performance, but if it is hard to identify the contribution of each group member, management will often evaluate the employee's behavior. A plant manager might be evaluated on promptness in submitting monthly reports or leadership style, and a salesperson on average number of contact calls made per day or sick days used per year.

Measured behaviors needn't be limited to those directly related to individual productivity. As we pointed out in discussing organizational citizenship behavior (see Chapters 1 and 3), helping others, making suggestions for improvements, and volunteering for extra duties make work groups and organizations more effective and often are incorporated into evaluations of employee performance.

Traits   The weakest criteria, because they're furthest removed from actual job performance, are individual traits.[84] Having a good attitude, showing confidence, being dependable, looking busy, or possessing a wealth of experience may or may not be highly correlated with positive task outcomes, but it's naïve to ignore the reality that organizations still use such traits to assess job performance.

Who Should Do the Evaluating?

Who should evaluate an employee's performance? By tradition, the task has fallen to managers because they are held responsible for their employees' performance. But others may do the job better.

With many of today's organizations using self-managed teams, telecommuting, and other organizing devices that distance bosses from employees, the immediate superior may not be the most reliable judge of an employee's

Photo 17-5 Behaviors such as helping others and building trusting relationships with residents and their family members are important elements in evaluating the performance of caregivers at this nursing home in Yokohama, Japan. These subjective factors add to the home's effectiveness and reputation as a place where residents are treated with love and respect.

Source: Kyodo/ASSOCIATED PRESS.

performance. Peers and even subordinates are being asked to take part in the process, and employees are participating in their own evaluations. One survey found about half of executives and 53 percent of employees now have input into their performance evaluations.[85] As you might expect, self-evaluations often suffer from overinflated assessment and self-serving bias, and they seldom agree with superiors' ratings.[86] They are probably better suited to developmental than evaluative purposes and should be combined with other sources of information to reduce rating errors.

In most situations, it is highly advisable to use multiple sources of ratings. Any individual performance rating may say as much about the rater as about the person being evaluated. By averaging across raters, we can obtain a more reliable, unbiased, and accurate performance evaluation.

Another popular approach to performance evaluation is 360-degree evaluations.[87] These provide performance feedback from the employee's full circle of daily contacts, from mailroom workers to customers to bosses to peers (see Exhibit 17-2). The number of appraisals can be as few as 3 or 4 or as many as 25; most organizations collect 5 to 10 per employee.

What's the appeal of the 360-degree appraisal? By relying on feedback from co-workers, customers, and subordinates, organizations are hoping to give everyone a sense of participation in the review process and gain more accurate readings on employee performance.

Evidence on the effectiveness of the 360-degree evaluation is mixed.[88] It provides employees with a wider perspective on their performance, but many organizations don't spend the time to train evaluators in giving constructive criticism. Some 360-degree evaluations allow employees to choose the peers and subordinates who evaluate them, which can artificially inflate feedback. It's also difficult to reconcile disagreements between rater groups. There is clear evidence that

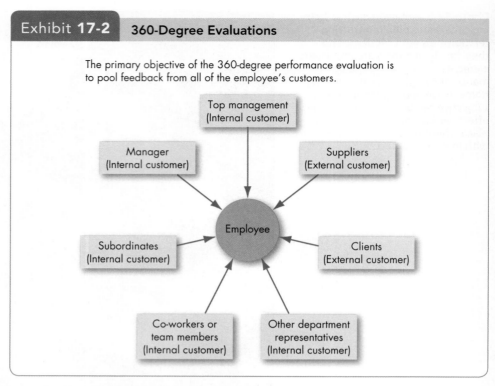

Exhibit 17-2 | **360-Degree Evaluations**

The primary objective of the 360-degree performance evaluation is to pool feedback from all of the employee's customers.

Top management
(Internal customer)

Manager
(Internal customer)

Suppliers
(External customer)

Employee

Subordinates
(Internal customer)

Clients
(External customer)

Co-workers or
team members
(Internal customer)

Other department
representatives
(Internal customer)

Source: Adapted from *Personnel Journal* (November 1994), p. 100.

peers tend to give much more lenient ratings than supervisors or subordinates, and peers also tend to make more errors in appraising performance.

Methods of Performance Evaluation

We've discussed *what* we evaluate and *who* should do the evaluating. Now we ask: *How* do we evaluate an employee's performance? What are the specific techniques for evaluation?

Written Essays   Probably the simplest method is to write a narrative describing an employee's strengths, weaknesses, past performance, potential, and suggestions for improvement. The written essay requires no complex forms or extensive training to complete. But, with this method, a useful appraisal may be determined as much by the evaluator's writing skill as by the employee's actual level of performance. It's also difficult to compare essays for different employees (or for the same employees written by different managers) because there is no standardized scoring key.

critical incidents   *A way of evaluating the behaviors that are key in making the difference between executing a job effectively and executing it ineffectively.*

Critical Incidents   **Critical incidents** focus the evaluator's attention on the difference between executing a job effectively and executing it ineffectively. The appraiser describes what the employee did that was especially effective or ineffective in a situation, citing only specific behaviors. A list of such critical incidents provides a rich set of examples to show the employee desirable behaviors and those that call for improvement.

graphic rating scales   *An evaluation method in which the evaluator rates performance factors on an incremental scale.*

Graphic Rating Scales   One of the oldest and most popular methods of evaluation is **graphic rating scales**. The evaluator goes through a set of performance factors—such as quantity and quality of work, depth of knowledge, cooperation, attendance, and initiative—and rates each on incremental scales. The scales may specify, say, five points, so *job knowledge* might be rated 1 ("is poorly informed about work duties") to 5 ("has complete mastery of all phases of the job"). Although they don't provide the depth of information that essays or critical incidents do, graphic rating scales are less time consuming to develop and administer and allow for quantitative analysis and comparison.

behaviorally anchored rating scales (BARS) *Scales that combine major elements from the critical incident and graphic rating scale approaches. The appraiser rates the employees based on items along a continuum, but the points are examples of actual behavior on the given job rather than general descriptions or traits.*

forced comparison *Method of performance evaluation where an employee's performance is made in explicit comparison to others (e.g., an employee may rank third out of ten employees in her work unit).*

group order ranking *An evaluation method that places employees into a particular classification, such as quartiles.*

individual ranking *An evaluation method that rank-orders employees from best to worst.*

Behaviorally Anchored Rating Scales   Behaviorally anchored rating scales (BARS) combine major elements from the critical incident and graphic rating scale approaches. The appraiser rates employees on items along a continuum, but the items are examples of actual behavior on the job rather than general descriptions or traits. To develop the BARS, participants first contribute specific illustrations of effective and ineffective behavior, which are translated into a set of performance dimensions with varying levels of quality.

Forced Comparisons   Forced comparisons evaluate one individual's performance against the performance of another or others. It is a relative rather than an absolute measuring device. The two most popular comparisons are group order ranking and individual ranking.

Group order ranking requires the evaluator to place employees into a particular classification, such as top one-fifth or second one-fifth. If a rater has 20 employees, only 4 can be in the top fifth and, of course, 4 must also be relegated to the bottom fifth. This method is often used in recommending students to graduate schools.

The **individual ranking** approach rank-orders employees from best to worst. If the manager is required to appraise 30 employees, the difference between the 1st and 2nd employee is assumed to be the same as that between the 21st and 22nd. Some employees may be closely grouped, but no ties are permitted. The result is a clear ordering from the highest performer to the lowest.

One parallel to forced ranking is forced distribution of college grades. Why would universities do this? As shown in Exhibit 17-3, average GPAs have gotten much higher over time.[89] Although it is not exactly clear why this increase has occurred over time, many attribute the rise in high letter grades to the popularity of student evaluations as a means of assessing professor performance. Generous grades might produce higher student evaluations. It's also the case that giving higher grades can help students become more competitive candidates for graduate school and jobs.

In response to grade inflation, some colleges have instituted forced grade distributions, whereby professors must give a certain percentage of A's, B's, and C's. This is exactly what Princeton recently did; each department can now give A's to no more than 35 percent of its students.

Suggestions for Improving Performance Evaluations

8   Show how managers can improve performance evaluations.

The performance evaluation process is a potential minefield. Evaluators can unconsciously inflate evaluations (positive leniency), understate performance (negative leniency), or allow the assessment of one characteristic to unduly influence the assessment of others (the halo error). Some appraisers bias their evaluations by unconsciously favoring people who have qualities and traits similar to their own (the similarity error). And some evaluators see the evaluation process as a political opportunity to overtly reward or punish employees they like or dislike. A review of the literature and several studies on performance appraisals demonstrates that many managers deliberately distort performance ratings in order to maintain a positive relationship with their subordinates or

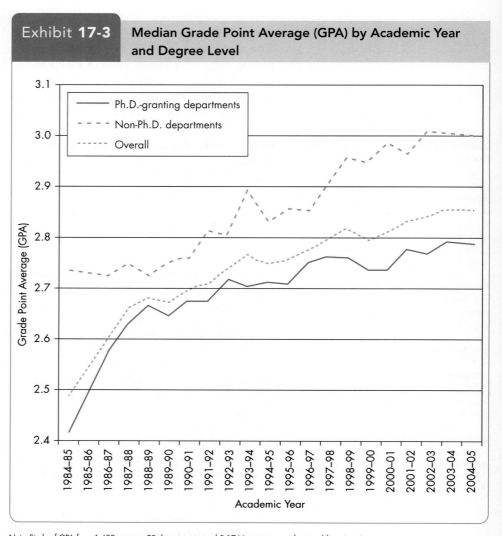

Exhibit **17-3** | Median Grade Point Average (GPA) by Academic Year and Degree Level

Note: Study of GPA from 1,683 courses, 28 departments, and 3,176 instructors at a large public university.
Source: R. Todd Jewell, M. A. McPherson, and M. A. Tieslau, "Whose Fault Is It? Assigning Blame for Grade Inflation in Higher Education," *Applied Economics* 45 (2013), pp. 1185–1200.

to achieve a positive image of themselves by showing that all their employees are performing well.[90] Although no protections *guarantee* accurate performance evaluations, the following suggestions can make the process more objective and fair.

Use Multiple Evaluators   As the number of evaluators increases, the probability of attaining more accurate information increases, as does the likelihood that the employee will accept the feedback as valid.[91] We often see multiple evaluators in competitions in such sports as diving and gymnastics. A set of evaluators judges a performance, the highest and lowest scores are dropped, and the final evaluation is made up of those remaining. The logic of multiple evaluators applies to organizations as well. If an employee has had ten supervisors, nine having rated her excellent and one poor, we can safely discount the one poor evaluation. By moving employees around within the organization to gain a number of evaluations, or by using multiple assessors (as in 360-degree appraisals), we increase the probability of achieving more valid and reliable evaluations.

Evaluate Selectively   To increase agreement among evaluations, appraisers should evaluate only where they have some expertise.[92] Appraisers should thus be as close as possible, in organizational level, to the individual being evaluated. The more levels that separate the evaluator from the employee, the less opportunity the evaluator has to observe the individual's behavior and, therefore, the greater the possibility for inaccuracies.

Train Evaluators   If you can't *find* good evaluators, *make* them. Training can produce more accurate raters.[93] Most rater training courses emphasize changing the raters' frame of reference by teaching them what to look for, so everyone in the organization defines *good performance* in the same way. Another effective training technique is to encourage raters to describe the employee's behavior in as much detail as possible. Providing more detail encourages raters to remember more about the employee's performance, rather than just acting on their feelings about the employee at the moment.

Provide Employees with Due Process   The concept of *due process* can be applied to appraisals to increase the perception that employees are being treated fairly.[94] Three features characterize due process systems: (1) Individuals are provided with adequate notice of what is expected of them, (2) all evidence relevant to a proposed violation is aired in a fair hearing so the individuals affected can respond, and (3) the final decision is based on the evidence and free of bias.

One technique organizations might consider to enhance due process is posting appraisals online so employees can see their own performance scores exactly as the supervisor enters them. One company that did so found employees believed rater accountability and employee participation were higher when appraisal information was available online prior to appraisal interviews.[95] It might be that raters were more sensitive to providing accurate ratings when they knew employees would be able to see their own information directly.

Providing Performance Feedback

Few activities are more unpleasant for many managers than providing performance feedback to employees. In fact, unless pressured by organizational policies and controls, managers are likely to ignore this responsibility.

Why? First, even though almost every employee could stand to improve in some areas, managers fear confrontation when presenting negative feedback. Second, many employees do tend to become defensive when their weaknesses are pointed out. Instead of accepting the feedback as constructive and a basis for improving performance, some criticize the manager or redirect blame to someone else. Finally, employees tend to have an inflated assessment of their own performance. Statistically speaking, half of all employees must be below-average performers. But the average employee's estimate of his or her own performance level generally falls much higher. So even when managers are providing good news, employees are likely to perceive it as not good enough.

The solution to the problem is not to ignore it but to train managers to conduct constructive feedback sessions. An effective review—in which the employee perceives the appraisal as fair, the manager as sincere, and the climate as constructive—can leave the employee feeling upbeat, informed about areas needing improvement, and determined to correct them.[96] It probably won't surprise you that employees in a bad mood are much less likely to take advice than employees in a good mood.[97] Appraisals should also be as specific as possible. People are most likely to overrate their own performance when asked about overall job performance, but they can be more objective when feedback is about a specific area.[98] It's also hard to figure out how to improve your performance globally—it's much easier to improve in specific areas. In addition, the performance review should be a counseling activity more than a judgment process, best accomplished by allowing it to evolve from the employee's own self-evaluation.

International Variations in Performance Appraisal

Let's examine performance evaluation globally in the context of cultural dimensions: individualism/collectivism, a person's relationship to the environment, time orientation, and focus of responsibility.

Individual-oriented cultures such as the United States emphasize formal performance evaluation systems more than informal systems. They advocate written evaluations performed at regular intervals, the results of which managers share with employees and use in the determination of rewards. On the other hand, the collectivist cultures that dominate Asia and much of Latin America are characterized by more informal systems—downplaying formal feedback and disconnecting reward allocations from performance ratings. Some of these differences may be narrowing, however. In Korea, Singapore, and Japan, the use of performance evaluation has increased dramatically in the past decade, though not always smoothly or without controversy. One survey of Korean employees revealed that a majority questioned the validity of their performance evaluation results.[99]

One recent study focused on the banking industry found significant differences across countries in performance appraisal practices.[100] Formal performance appraisals were used more frequently in countries that were high in assertiveness, high in uncertainty avoidance, and low in in-group collectivism. In other words, assertive countries that see performance as an individual responsibility, and that desire certainty about where people stand, were more likely to use formal performance appraisals. On the other hand, in high uncertainty avoidance cultures performance appraisals were also used more frequently for communication and development purposes (as opposed to being used for rewards and promotion). Another study found that individuals who were high in power distance and high in collectivism tend to give more lenient performance appraisals.[101]

SELF-ASSESSMENT LIBRARY

How Good Am I at Giving Performance Feedback?

In the Self-Assessment Library (available in MyManagementLab), take assessment III.A.3 (How Good Am I at Giving Performance Feedback?).

The Leadership Role of HR

9 Describe the leadership role of HR in organizations.

We have discussed the important functions HR departments serve in selection practices, training and development, and the performance evaluation process. Arguably, these are a business's most important tasks in managing its most valuable asset—its people. However, HR also plays a key leadership role in nearly all facets of the workplace environment, from designing and administering benefit programs to conducting attitude surveys to drafting and enforcing employment policies. HR is on the front lines in managing adversarial employment conditions such as work–life conflicts, mediations, terminations, and layoffs. HR is on the scene when an employee joins and leaves, and all along the way. HR departments uniquely represent both the employee's and the company's perspective as needed.

Companies have only recently begun to recognize the potential for HR to influence employee performance. Researchers have been examining the effects of a high-performance work system (HPWS), a group of "mutually reinforcing, overlapping, and synergistic individual human resource practices" that organizations have been developing. A recent study of 163 Spanish companies suggests that an HPWS can especially increase performance when the organization has a learning culture.[102] Another study found that employees' perceptions of an HPWS aimed at promoting their ability, motivation, and opportunity resulted in lowered absenteeism, increased intentions to stay, and increased organizational citizenship behavior.[103] Because employers and employees alike benefit from strong human resource practices, let's consider some of the leadership functions of human resources.

Designing and Administering Benefit Programs

As we've seen throughout this book, employers are more willing than ever to consider an infinite range of benefits to offer employees in efforts to recruit and retain the best talent. For every issue facing workers—health, child care, aging parents, education, workplace conditions, and others—there exists a potential benefit organizations may consider to meet the need. The responsibility for designing and administering an organization's benefit program falls to the HR department, with input from executive management.

Ideally, a benefit program should be uniquely suited to the organizational culture, reflect the values of the organization, demonstrate economic feasibility, and be sustainable in the long term. Such benefits will likely improve employees' psychological well-being and therefore increase organizational performance.[104]

Consider employees who are mothers of infant children. Benefit options HR might consider could range from support to intolerance. Should the company give paid time off for working mothers to breast-feed their babies? Should it provide a break room for mothers to breast-feed their babies at work? Should it allow mothers to pump milk at work to give to babies at home? What about mothers who are bottle-feeding? Federal laws do not require companies to provide any accommodation for breast-feeding mothers beyond an undefined "reasonable break time," and a recent case in Texas ruled against a woman who was fired for asking to use the back room to pump milk for her child.[105] An HR manager in a company that produced lactation pumps, supported La Leche League International, and employed women of child-bearing age may want to offer some benefit because the support would agree with the company's principles. An HR manager in a company unrelated to the issue may explore providing some benefit upon employee requests. Each manager may then perform an analysis of the costs associated with providing different levels of benefits, along with the positive organizational outcomes for each, to determine which benefit would be sustainable for the company long term. Of course, this is just one example of possible benefits to consider, and this benefit applies only to a segmented group of workers. Other benefits may affect a larger population of your workforce, such as health care options and vacation benefits.

Drafting and Enforcing Employment Policies

Along with benefits come responsibilities, and employees need to know what the organization expects from them. Employment policies that are informed by current laws but go beyond minimum requirements will help define a positive

HIV/AIDS and the Multinational Organization

It wasn't long ago that an AIDS diagnosis was a death sentence, and the ethical choices for HR departments revolved around palliative care and death benefits. Thankfully, those days are gone, at least for most. Now the ethical choice is about the standards of care and support organizations want to provide, for which employees worldwide, and for how long. "There has been an uptick with those employed that have HIV/AIDS" as the disease has become more chronic than fatal, said Randy Vogenberg of the Institute for Integrated Healthcare. However, whether someone can continue working still depends upon drug therapy, workplace accommodations, and employee education. In most countries, standards are not specifically mandated, leaving employers to choose the level of support to offer. "It's not a question of whether a business is going to be confronted with this," labor law attorney Peter Petesch says. "It's a question of how soon."

By current estimates, more than 1.18 million people in the United States and 34 million people globally live with HIV. Two-thirds of HIV infections are in sub-Saharan Africa, and more than 95 percent of infected individuals live in developing countries. Worldwide, there is little consistency in the approach to the problem. Few U.S. companies have specific HIV/AIDS policies, for example, and although benefit plans cover the illness, employees' out-of-pocket costs for the expensive drug therapy can range significantly. HIV/AIDS treatment is available in Europe through the national health care system. Some larger African companies run clinics where national health care or insurance is insufficient, but not all companies offer insurance. In India and China, insurers do not cover HIV/AIDS, so companies need to consider separate employee reimbursement to match their intentions for coverage.

When it comes to HIV/AIDS, an ounce of prevention is worth a pound of cure, or more literally, dramatic corporate savings. Recent research found that the investment companies spent on preventing the disease from spreading and on treating infected employees saved money and lives. HR initiatives like providing peer educators to teach employees about prevention and accommodation, free counseling services, free voluntary testing, and well-being monitoring have been effective worldwide.

"Nobody needs to die of this disease anymore," said Jenni Gillies, head of business development for beer brewer SABMiller, which has 70,000 employees in 75 countries and is committed to helping to eradicate HIV/AIDS through employee education and support. But there are costs and responsibilities associated with each decision about the level of care to support or supply, and how far companies should meet this need over other employee needs will be a constant question. Some organizations may conclude that governments and other systems are responsible for the care of citizens. It's a tough call. Meanwhile, individual managers can assist in preventing discrimination and encouraging education.

Sources: J. Mooney, "People with HIV and AIDS: Living and Working Longer," *HR Magazine* (June 2012), pp. 41–44; SABMiller corporate website, "Inside View" page, www.insideview.com/directory/sabmiller-plc, accessed June 18, 2013; and World Health Organization, "HIV/AIDS" fact page, www.who.int/immunization/topics/hiv/en/index1.html, accessed June 18, 2013.

organizational culture. Policies differ from benefits in that they provide the guidelines for behavior, not just the working conditions. In our example of working mothers with infant children, a company might provide a benefit of a special break room for mothers of young children, but a policy is needed to outline the expectation for conduct. May mothers elect to feed their babies in other places in the facility, or only in the break room? What timing is acceptable? Where can collected breast milk be stored? Establishing policies to address potential questions can help minimize confusion and awkwardness for all employees.

The lactation case is an example of a potential benefit and policy combination that will ensure employees recognize the benefit as an employer's aid to their well-being while understanding how and where to use it. However, any policy must have enforcement to be effective. Human resource managers are responsible for setting the organizational consequences of infractions and often for enforcing policies as well.

Sometimes, human resource managers will need to take action even when the employee's direct manager may not agree, especially if compliance with the law is at issue. For example, many companies in the entertainment, nonprofit, publishing, and marketing industries use unpaid post-college interns, who are supposed to receive on-the-job experience as compensation. The Labor Department stipulates that interns who are unpaid must be provided a vocational education experience and that their work cannot profit the employer. Interns report getting stuck doing menial tasks an employer would need to pay someone else to do. If these companies want to continue using unpaid interns, human resource managers need to set policies that clarify the assignments supervisors can give and then ensure the policies are followed. Otherwise, their organizations will face lawsuits like the one from Eric Glatt, an intern on the movie *Black Swan*, who is suing for minimum wage violations.[106] A judge in the U.S. District Court recently ruled that he was improperly catalogued as an intern.[107]

Managing Work–Life Conflicts

We introduced work–life balance in Chapter 1 and discussed the blurring lines between work life and personal life. Here, we specifically focus on what organizations can do to help employees reduce conflicts.

Work–life conflicts grabbed management's attention in the 1980s, largely as a result of the increased entry into the workforce of women with dependent children. In response, most major organizations took actions to make their

Myth or Science?

"Work–Family Policies Make Good Business Sense"

Surprisingly, this statement appears to be mostly false. At first glance, it would seem natural that work–family policies including flextime, child care assistance, and help with elder care would increase employee engagement, productivity, and commitment. After all, more workers are shouldering increased responsibilities at home than ever before. In more than half of U.S. married couples, both partners are working. Almost half of U.S. children live with one (most likely working) parent, and nearly half the workforce has elder care responsibilities. Employees say they want to work from home so dearly that 62 percent in a recent survey would be willing to give up social media, chocolate, vacation days, even salary increases for the benefit. Yet there seems to be a difference between policies employees say they want and those that yield positive outcomes.

Research findings are inconsistent about the benefits of work–family policies. Some studies have indicated they improve employee recruitment and retention, and others have suggested they may inspire higher commitment. Other studies, however, have found no relationship between work–family policies and employee job satisfaction or intention to stay. The utopia employees envision in their work-from-home scenario is different from the reality of juggling work and home demands simultaneously, in which tensions are increased and the personal resources of time, energy, and mood are depleted. Furthermore, the results of work-life policies on business outcomes such as productivity have been mixed and controversial.

When it comes to work–family policies, then, human resource professionals must balance providing the benefits employees value against the organizational costs of unclear business outcomes. The good news from a business perspective is that many employees will not use many work–family benefits. Yet, according to a recent meta-analysis, employees in organizations with multiple work–family policies were more likely to have positive attitudes, whether or not they exercised their options. The real benefit therefore seems to come with a workplace climate of work–family support, not particular policies that may or may not apply to an individual's unique situation. Research suggests human resource professionals adopt work–life measures that include trial periods and are varied, inexpensive to execute, and in line with employee values.

Sources: M. M. Butts, W. J. Casper, and T. S. Yang, "How Important Are Work-Family Support Policies? A Meta-analytic Investigation of Their Effects on Employee Outcomes," *Journal of Applied Psychology* 98 (2013), pp. 1–25; SHRM Online staff, "People Really Love Telecommuting," *HR Magazine* (April 2012), p. 20; and L. L. ten Brummelhuis, "A Resource Perspective on the Work-Home Interface," *American Psychologist* (October 2012), pp. 545–556.

workplaces more family-friendly.[108] They introduced onsite child care, summer day camps, flextime, job sharing, leaves for school functions, telecommuting, and part-time employment. But organizations quickly realized work–life conflicts were not limited to female employees with children. Male workers and women without children were also facing this problem. Heavy workloads and increased travel demands, for instance, made it increasingly hard for many employees to meet both work and personal responsibilities. A Boston College survey of nearly 1,000 fathers who have professional careers showed that the participants put more importance on job security and flexible, family-friendly working schedules than on high income and advancement opportunities.[109]

Organizations are modifying their workplaces with scheduling options and benefits to accommodate the varied needs of a diverse workforce. Employees at NestléPurina can bring their dogs into the office; SAS Institute has onsite child care, a health care center, and a fitness center; and other firms offer perks ranging from onsite laundry to food services to free child care.[110] Exhibit 17-4 lists some initiatives to help employees reduce work–life conflicts.

Time pressures aren't the primary problem underlying work–life conflicts.[111] The psychological incursion of work into the family domain—and vice versa—when people are worrying about personal problems at work and thinking about work problems at home creates conflict. This suggests organizations should spend less effort helping employees with time-management issues and more in helping them clearly segment their lives. Keeping workloads reasonable, reducing work-related travel, and offering onsite quality child care are examples of practices that can help in this endeavor. Employees can also reduce interference between work and home by increasing the amount of planning they do.[112]

Not surprisingly, people differ in their preference for scheduling options and benefits.[113] Some prefer organizational initiatives that better segment work from their personal lives, as flextime, job sharing, and part-time hours do by allowing employees to schedule work hours less likely to conflict with personal responsibilities. Other organizations prefer initiatives to integrate work and personal life, such as onsite child care, gym facilities, and company-sponsored family picnics. On average, most people prefer an organization that provides support for work–life balance. A study found that potential employees, particularly women, are more attracted to organizations that have a reputation for supporting employee work–life balance.[114]

Mediations, Terminations, and Layoffs

Human resource departments often take center stage when unpleasant events such as disputes, substandard performance, and downsizing occur. Employees need to be able to trust their human resource professionals to maintain appropriate confidentiality and a balanced perspective. Managers need to be able to trust HR, too, to know the laws and represent the company's perspective. The human resource professional should be well trained in mediation techniques and rely upon company policies to seek positive resolution. Sometimes, human resource managers are integral to the termination process, when employees are not able to resolve issues with management. Termination processes are subject to union labor contracts and laws, which can confound the situation. In Spain, for instance, labor laws have traditionally protected older workers with near-guaranteed employment.[115]

For departing employees, the HR department is often the last stop on their way out the door. Human resource managers are thus in charge of leaving a favorable impression with the employee and collecting helpful input from the exit interview. This is never more true than when organizations terminate employees in layoffs. Employees who think the layoff process was handled fairly are more

Exhibit 17-4	Work–Life Initiatives	
Time based strategies	• Flextime • Job sharing • Leave for new parents • Telecommuting • Paid time off	At Abbott, 97% of employees held jobs that permitted them to flex their schedules; at Lego 90% of employees do. Cisco provides job-sharing and videoconferencing facilities to minimize needs for travel away from family. Deloitte offers employees 4 unpaid weeks sabbatical, or 3 to 6 partially paid months off to volunteer. Deutsche Bank offers parents 20 days of free backup care per child per year, which they can redeem at local child care centers. Colgate offers employees extensive telecommuting options.
Information based strategies	• Work–life support • Relocation assistance • Elder care resources • Counseling services	Blue Cross Blue Shield of North Carolina provides ParentLife classes and seminars. Capital One provides a networking and counseling group for parents of children with autism. Genentech offers a CareerLab, which provides career counseling, skills workshops, and networking sessions. Hallmark offers employees monthly meetings to talk about career management for women. Johnson and Johnson offers work–life Webinars covering topics like single parenting, fatherhood, and elder care.
Money-based strategies	• Insurance subsidies • Flexible benefits • Adoption assistance • Discounts for child care tuition • Direct financial assistance • Domestic partner benefits • Scholarships, tuition reimbursement	Accenture offers a $5,000 adoption assistance benefit. Carlson offers employees scholarships of up to $20,000 to attend the University of Minnesota's Carlson School of Management. Citi employees can save up to $5,000 per year in pretax dependent care accounts, with a match of up to 30% from the company. Colgate-Palmolive provides up to $10,000 per year in annual tuition aid for job-related courses. IBM provides medical testing and therapy for children with special needs, up to a lifetime maximum of $50,000. Prudential employees can receive up to 15% off child care discounts.
Direct services	• Onsite child care • Fitness center • Summer child care • Onsite conveniences • Concierge services • Free or discounted company products	Allstate and SAS provide onsite child care center at company headquarters. Companies like AOL and Verizon have onsite fitness centers and discounts at gyms nationwide. Bristol-Myers Squibb offers full-time, part-time, and backup care for kids up to age 5, and summer camps for older children. Discovery Communications provides low-cost concierge services to help with to-do lists. Turner Broadcasting has a wellness center at headquarters that provides free exams, vaccinations, allergy shots, and health coaching. REI employees can participate in a program that offers large discounts on company products.
Culture-change strategies	• Establishing work–life balanced culture; training managers to help employees deal with work–life conflicts • Tie manager pay to employee satisfaction • Focus on employees' actual performance, not "face time"	At American Express, 80% of managers received training on how to supervise employees with flexible work arrangements. Bank of America's My Work program allows mothers to log in from home or a satellite office. General Mills has a flexibility manager to enhance work–life balance. Pearson developed a Flexible Work Options. Accountability Guide that trains managers in the use of flextime for their employees.

Sources: "2012 100 Best Companies" Working Mother, www.workingmother.com, accessed June 18, 2013; "100 Best Companies to Work For," CNNMoney, www.money.cnn.com, accessed June 18, 2013; and J. Smith, "25 Big Companies with the Best Work-Life Balance," Forbes (June 2, 2013), www.forbes.com/sites/jacquelynsmith/2013/06/03/the-best-big-companies-for-work-life-balance/.

apt to recommend the company to others and to return to work if asked.[116] Employees who survive a layoff and stay employed with the company also evaluate the fairness of the downsizing process, according to another study, particularly in individualistic countries. Organizations that are able to demonstrate fairness are, therefore, more likely to make hoped-for financial gains from downsizing.[117]

In sum, the role of HR is increasing for organizations worldwide, and top management is realizing human resource leadership is needed to create the cultures and positive business outcomes top corporations need to stay competitive.

Summary

An organization's human resource policies and practices create important forces that shape employee behavior and attitudes. In this chapter, we specifically discussed the influence of selection practices, training and development programs, and performance evaluation systems.

Implications for Managers

- An organization's selection practices can identify competent candidates and accurately match them to the job and the organization. Consider assessment methods that are most likely to evaluate the skills directly needed for jobs you are looking to fill.
- Use training programs for your employees to achieve direct improvement in the skills necessary to successfully complete the job. Employees who are motivated will use those skills for their greater productivity.
- Training programs increase an employee's self-efficacy—that is, a person's expectation that he or she can successfully execute the behaviors required to produce an outcome (see Chapter 7). Employees with high self-efficacy have strong expectations about their abilities to perform in new situations and are willing to exert the effort to get tasks done.
- Use performance evaluations to assess an individual's performance accurately and as a basis for allocating rewards. Make sure the performance evaluations are as fair as possible. As demonstrated in Chapter 7 in our discussion of equity theory, evaluations perceived as unfair can result in reduced effort, increases in absenteeism, or a search for another job.
- Give your employees the opportunity to participate in their evaluations so they understand the performance criteria and engage with the improvement process.

Social Media Is a Great Source of New Hires

POINT

Social media sites such as Facebook, LinkedIn, and Twitter, and job boards like Monster.com, are indispensable in today's marketplace for top talent.

It's true that an online presence with social media sites is a good way to sniff out fraud. Studies reveal that 45 percent of today's résumés contain at least one piece of false information. Mining social media sites is great at gaining a fuller—and more accurate—picture of a candidate.

One survey found that, today, 63 percent of employers use social media sites in recruitment and hiring decisions. Another revealed that 80 percent of employers plan to increase their presence on Facebook and LinkedIn in the future.

Not only can social media sites help you make more informed selection decisions, they can be a great help in recruiting more and better candidates to apply in the first place. Dawn Mitchell, a recruiter for business software company Red Hat, says it's about "living where the candidates are." She says that nearly all her recent hires have come from social media contacts. Tom Gimbel, CEO of LaSalle Network, a $35 million staffing and recruiting firm, recommends that employers advertise positions on social media sites.

Increasingly, recruiting firms that link applicants to companies are finding social media critical for their business, too. "Social media is the heart of everything we do," said Bill Peppler of Kavaliro Staffing Services. "We make numerous job placements that we never would have been able to do without Facebook," he said.

Accenture—the New York–based consulting firm—has mastered the art of using social media in hiring. John Campagnino, Accenture's global director of recruitment, says it has become "a centerpiece of our talent acquisition strategy." Campagnino says that Accenture interacts with potential hires on Facebook, LinkedIn, and Twitter; posts jobs on these sites daily; and creates "talent communities" by joining professional groups.

Hiring without heavy reliance on social media is backward-looking—and a missed opportunity.

COUNTERPOINT

Many employers are scaling back their presence on online job boards like Monster.com and social media sites like Facebook and LinkedIn because there is just too much chaff for the wheat. For example, McLean, Virginia–based Science Applications International Corporate (SAIC) reduced the number of job boards it uses from 15 to 6. SAIC found that it simply wasn't getting to enough of the right candidates early enough to staff its engineering and analyst positions. "We need to reach candidates earlier, before they're being pursued by competitors," the company said.

Paris-owned food services company Sodexo has slashed its online presence in half. Why? Because while recruiting via social media increased the number of applications, nearly all the increase was in unqualified applicants. "Recruiters had to put in all this extra time to read applications but we didn't get benefit from it," said Arie Ball, the company's talent acquisition vice president.

PNC also is scaling back due to the low signal-to-noise ratio. "We used to post everything," said the online banking company. "But you have to think strategically."

There is also the nontrivial issue of mistaken identity. A lot of mistaken hiring decisions have been made because a company accessed the wrong Facebook or LinkedIn profile. Applicants can post false information on social media sites, too.

Perhaps the biggest issue of all is objectivity. Says one employment expert, "Once an HR recruiter or administrator has been exposed to an applicant's social networking profile, it's difficult to remain objective and consider only the information that is relevant to the job."

Another recruiting manager voiced his skepticism regarding social media: "I'd love to drink the Kool-Aid if it did anything for me."

Sources: T. Gimbel, "How to Hire the Right 2013 College Grad," *Fox Business* (June 14, 2013), www.foxbusiness.com/business-leaders/2013/06/14/how-to-successfully-hire-2013-college-grad/; J. Light, "Recruiters Rethink Online Playbook," *The Wall Street Journal* (January 18, 2011), p. B7; R. Pyrillis, "The Bait Debate," *Workforce Management* (February 2011), pp. 16–22; and J. Bos, "Five Trends in Employee Screening: Is Your Company Prepared?" *Workforce Management* (March 2010), pp. 28–30.

END-OF-CHAPTER REVIEW

QUESTIONS FOR REVIEW

17-1 What are the most useful methods of initial selection?

17-2 What are the most useful methods of substantive selection?

17-3 What is *contingent selection*?

17-4 What are the similarities and differences among the four main types of training?

17-5 What are the similarities and differences between formal and informal training methods?

17-6 What are the similarities and differences between on-the-job and off-the-job training?

17-7 What are the methods of performance evaluation?

17-8 How can managers improve performance evaluations?

17-9 What are the various roles of HR in organizations?

EXPERIENTIAL EXERCISE Evaluating Performance and Providing Feedback

Objective

To experience the assessment of performance and observe the provision of performance feedback.

Time

Approximately 30 minutes.

Procedure

Select a class leader—either a volunteer or someone chosen by your instructor. The class leader will preside over the class discussion and perform the role of manager in the evaluation review.

Your instructor will leave the room. The class leader is then to spend up to 15 minutes helping the class to evaluate your instructor. Your instructor understands that this is only a class exercise and is prepared to accept criticism (and, of course, any praise you may want to convey). Your instructor also recognizes that the leader's evaluation is actually a composite of many students' input. So, be open

and honest in your evaluation and have confidence that your instructor will not be vindictive.

Research has identified seven performance dimensions to the college instructor's job: (1) instructor knowledge, (2) testing procedures, (3) student–teacher relations, (4) organizational skills, (5) communication skills, (6) subject relevance, and (7) utility of assignments. The discussion of your instructor's performance should focus on these seven dimensions. The leader may want to take notes for personal use but will not be required to give your instructor any written documentation.

When the 15-minute class discussion is complete, the leader will invite the instructor back into the room. The performance review will begin as soon as the instructor walks through the door, with the class leader becoming the manager and the instructor playing himself or herself.

When completed, class discussion will focus on performance evaluation criteria and how well your class leader did in providing performance feedback.

ETHICAL DILEMMA Credit Checking

Is it unethical—or illegal—for a hiring organization to check an applicant's credit history? The Equal Employment Opportunity Commission (EEOC) seems to think

so. It is suing Kaplan Higher Education Corporation for its use of credit checks, alleging that relying on poor credit histories to reject applicants has adverse impact on minority applicants, with no legitimate purpose justifying its use. Justine Lisser, an EEOC spokesperson, said, "Credit histories were not compiled to show responsibility. They were compiled to show whether or not someone was paying the bills, which is not always the same thing."

In its defense, Kaplan maintained that it typically conducted credit checks: "The checks are job-related and necessary for our organization to ensure that staffing handling financial matters, including financial aid, are properly screened." However, research indicates that credit scores are not correlated with workplace deviance.

A 2011 survey of employers revealed that 21 percent conducted credit checks on all applicants. That was up from 15 percent the year before. Two-thirds conduct credit checks on some applicants, up from 61 percent in 2010.

Joey Price, with BL Seamon, thought she had found the perfect candidate for a conference planner position. The candidate was fresh out of college but had experience

planning conferences and a good academic record. But when Price found out she had multiple car repossessions, extremely high credit card bills, and collection agencies after her, she rejected the candidate. "A credit report doesn't lie," Price said.

Questions

17-10. Do you think organizations should be allowed to investigate applicants' credit histories in the hiring process? Why or why not?

17-11. Do you think Seamon's Joey Price was within her rights to reject the applicant with the poor credit history? Do you think this candidate's financial problems might be job relevant?

⭐**17-12.** Some employers choose to disclose their reasoning to applicants rejected for poor credit. Says one hiring manager, "If a credit check comes back poor, the potential employee has a week to dispute and correct the errors." What are the advantages and disadvantages of such a policy?

Sources: J. B. Bernerth, S. G. Taylor, H. J. Walker, and D. S. Whitman, "Empirical Investigation of Dispositional Antecedents and Performance-Related Outcomes of Credit Scores," *Journal of Applied Psychology* 97 (2012), pp. 469–478; J. Zappe, "Survey Finds More Companies Credit-Checking Candidates," *ERE. net* (May 16, 2011), downloaded on July 11, 2011, from www.ere.net/2011/; S. Greenhouse, "Hiring Suit Takes on Bias Based on Credit," *The New York Times* (December 22, 2010), pp. B1, B4; J. Fairley, "Employers Face Challenges in Screening Candidates," *Workforce Management* (November 2010), pp. 7–9; and B. Roberts, "Close-Up on Screening," *HR Magazine* (February 2011), p. 23–29.

CASE INCIDENT 1 The End of the Performance Appraisal?

As we discussed in the chapter, organizations measure employee performance for a variety of reasons, including determining which employees need training, who is performing well enough to earn a performance reward, and who deserves a promotion. Performance appraisal information can also help determine where problems lie in the company's overall training and selection systems and defend HR decisions such as firings in court.

In light of these multiple uses, it might surprise you to learn that some companies are moving away from formal appraisal processes. Business scholar Jeffery Pfeffer describes how HR managers at companies like Apple had to bribe managers to complete assigned reviews with free tickets to San Francisco Giants games, and the head of HR at SAS received cheers from employees when he had a bonfire to burn performance appraisal forms. Clearly, appraisals are not popular with the managers asked to perform them. Pfeffer notes that the subjective nature of these reviews is troubling to many managers, leading employees to spend much of their time ingratiating themselves with the boss rather than doing their jobs. Moreover, appraisals put the focus on individual performance rather than on the performance of whole teams. Research conducted by Globoforce found that more than half the 631 survey

respondents believed appraisals did not accurately reflect their performance on the job.

So what is the alternative? Zappos now rates employees not on how well they accomplish tasks, but rather on how well they embody the company's core values. This feedback is delivered much more frequently during the year than the traditional annual performance meeting. Nor are the ratings used for disciplinary actions or promotions, though employees who get low scores are invited to take developmental classes to improve the fit between their behavior and the company culture. Apple has also eliminated annual performance reviews as neither timely nor helpful. Other companies have developed performance management software that automates and streamlines a more continuous performance review, allowing employees to track their performance in real time. The ongoing performance review offers real-time feedback, flexible goals, and frequent rewards.

Questions

⭐**17-13.** Have you ever been through a performance appraisal? Do the reactions to appraisal systems described here match your experience? Why or why not?

17-14. Are there potential drawbacks to eliminating conventional performance appraisal systems? What systems would need to be put in place to replace formal appraisals?

17-15. Would you feel comfortable providing others with performance feedback? What are some of the possible reasons managers often prefer not to give employees critiques of their performance?

Sources: Based on R. Pyrillis, "Is Your Performance Review Underperforming?" *Workforce Management* (May 2011), pp. 20–25; S. A. Culbert and L. Rout, *Get Rid of the Performance Review!* (New York: Business Plus, 2010); M. Lev-Ram, "Performance Reviews Remade," *Fortune* (October 29, 2012), p. 60; and J. Pfeffer, "Low Grades for Performance Reviews," *BusinessWeek* (August 3, 2009), p. 68.

CASE INCIDENT 2 **You May Be Supporting Slavery**

It's your birthday, and you're going out for hors d'oeuvres at the club followed by a celebration at your favorite restaurant. The club staff greets you warmly as always, and your seafood dinner is predictably excellent. You've visited these places many times before, own a stake in the club, and take clients to the restaurant. How did you not know you and your company support slavery?

It may be a case of ignorance being bliss, according to experts. Alberto Pozzi, who manages Miami Shores Country Club, claimed he was unaware the 39 Filipino workers he employed through a staffing agency were slaves. The agency, Quality Staffing Services, charged immigrants fees for food, housing, and utilities that depleted their earnings to near zero and left them perpetually owing the initial $5,000 recruiting fee. Living conditions were awful, medical care was refused, and abuse was common. Workers' visas were withheld, so they couldn't leave. Yet, Pozzi said, "These people never had a word or outward indication that they were unhappy."

We are equally unaware of the slaves used to bring P.F. Chang's signature calamari to the table. New Zealand fisherman with United Fisheries may voice the indignities their enslavement through their staffing agency brings them—no net pay, squalid conditions, debt, 16-hour work days, lack of safety equipment—but no one hears them half a world away, where much of the company's revenue is generated.

The cases of Miami Shores Country Club and United Fisheries are far from unique. There are more than 27 million victims of human trafficking worldwide, and their number is growing with the increasing demand for inexpensive labor, particularly in the United States and other Western democracies. In response, U.S. law now holds companies responsible for violations even when they are not the direct employers. According to the federal Trafficking Victims Protection Act, employers are liable if they are aware of or profit from human trafficking. Individual states are following suit, enacting laws such as the California Transparency in Supply Chains Act, which requires large multinational companies to proactively address slavery throughout their supply chains.

Human resource departments are on the front lines of the unwitting use of slavery, whether slaves are employees in our midst or employees of suppliers. "Just like you've got to know where your raw materials come from, you've got to know where your people come from. I think HR people are just awakening to this," said ManpowerGroup executive vice president Mara Swan. Experts urge human resource professionals to understand the laws that apply to their organizations, build no-tolerance policies, train employees to identify infractions, monitor contractors and suppliers, and join industry groups to share information.

While individuals can help end slavery by refusing to purchase items produced by indentured workers, human resource professionals can play a pivotal role in eliminating the economic feasibility of the violators.

Questions

17-16. What are two ways in which modern-day workers become slaves?

17-17. How might an employer seek to determine whether the individuals hired through agencies are in indentured servitude?

17-18. Once an indentured worker, why might he or she stay?

17-19. What would you do if you discovered a group of your employees were slaves to their placement agencies?

Sources: D. Meinert, "Modern-day Slavery," *HR Magazine* (May 2012), pp. 22–27; and E. B. Skinner, "The Cruelest Catch," *Bloomberg Businessweek* (February 27–March 4, 2012), pp. 70–76.

MyManagementLab

Go to **mymanagementlab.com** for Auto-graded writing questions as well as the following Assisted-graded writing questions:

17-20. From your reading of Case Incident 1, what are some potential advantages of providing employees with more regular developmental feedback than an annual meeting?

17-21. In regard to Case Incident 2, how might an employer seek to determine whether the individuals hired through agencies are in indentured servitude?

17-22. MyManagementLab Only—comprehensive writing assignment for this chapter.

18 Organizational Change and Stress Management

STRESS AND THE WORK-MORE ECONOMY

Melvin Williams, a human resources vice president for Administrative Services Inc., tells a common story. When his company downsized from 400 to 200 employees, his office lost four of its six staff members, even though the workload didn't decrease. Williams is now a member of the work-more economy. "For the past eight months I've been putting in extremely long hours," he said. "I average 60 hours a week." The extra hours have taken a toll on his quality of life, increasing his stress at work and at home. "It's blown the hell out of my relationship. My wife tells me, 'There's no time for us anymore. All you do is work.' I tell my wife we have bills to pay."

Like many survivors of downsizing, Williams is glad to have the job, but not the stress. He is not alone; in fact, 42 percent of workers have reported their responsibilities have increased significantly in the work-more economy. Organizational changes, globalizing, and the omnipresence of smartphones have all of us working harder than we can handle, says David Posen, a Canadian physician and stress specialist. Posen believes the workplace is "generating stress that even the most expert stress manager can't dissipate." Randy Martin of employee assistance provider (EAP) Harris, Rothenberg International Inc. observes a dramatic jump in the number of employee calls for help in coping. "We've seen a fairly significant spike in workplace anxiety and stress," he said. "People are working longer hours. They are grieving colleagues who have lost their jobs. They don't feel any sense of job security."

According to Posen, "This issue is affecting everyone up and down the hierarchy: workers, managers, executives and owners. It's not only a health issue for individuals, it's also a performance/productivity issue for employers. It not only hurts the bottom line, it hammers it!" In answer to the title of his latest book, *Is Work Killing You?*, he said, "It's killing [employees'] family life and their personal life. It's killing their spirit."

Erin Callan, former chief financial officer (CFO) of Lehman Brothers and once one of the most powerful women on Wall Street, gives an account of the high cost of stress in the work-more economy. "I didn't start out with the goal of devoting all of myself to my job," she said. "It crept in over time. Each year that went by, slight modifications became the new normal. First I spent a half-hour on Sunday organizing my e-mail, to-do list and calendar . . . then I was working a few hours on Sunday, then all day. My boundaries slipped away until work was all that was left." The stress mounted. "I'm not sure I was consciously willing to admit it," Callan said. Months before the company went bankrupt, she resigned. Callan was burnt out and has not recovered from the effects of the stress. Since she wrote her manifesto "Is There Life After Work?" for *The New York Times*, declaring "I couldn't just rally and move on" in her career, Callan has opted for a smaller, quieter life in Sanibel, Florida, and is no longer working. "Don't do it like me," she advises others.

LEARNING OBJECTIVES

After studying this chapter, you should be able to:

1 Contrast planned and unplanned change.

2 Describe the sources of resistance to change.

3 Compare the four main approaches to managing organizational change.

4 Demonstrate two ways of creating a culture for change.

5 Identify potential sources of stress.

6 Identify the consequences of stress.

7 Contrast the individual and organizational approaches to managing stress.

Though the work-more economy may be here to stay, Posen believes the resulting stress can be proactively managed to great effect for the employee and the organization. He said, "Everyone in an organization is a stakeholder and everyone can contribute to the solutions. Similarly, everyone will reap the benefits of a healthier, safer workplace. It's time for everyone to step up, admit that workplace stress is real and damaging and take steps to address it."

Sources: E. Callan, "Is There Life After Work?" *The New York Times* (March 9, 2013), www.nytimes .com/2013/03/10/opinion/sunday/is-there-life-after-work.html; S. Jayson, "'Is Work Killing You?' How Downsizing is Upsizing Stress," *USA Today* (April 8, 2013), p. 3D; E. Frauenheim, "Stressed & Pressed," *Workforce Management* (January 2012), pp. 18–22; J. La Roche, "Erin Callan: I Want to Be a Cautionary Tale—Don't 'Lean In' The Way I Did," *Business Insider* (March 15, 2013), www .businessinsider.com/erin-callan-nbc-rock-center-2013-3; D. Posen, "Is Work Killing You? Five Ways to Lower Your Stress," *The Wall Street Journal* (June 11, 2013), http://blogs.wsj.com/speakeasy/ 2013/06/11/five-ways-to-lower-workplace-stress/; and R. Pyrillis, "EAPs: First-Responders in a 'Work-More Economy,'" *Workforce Management* (January 2012), p. 21.

This chapter is about change and stress. We describe environmental forces that require firms to change, why people and organizations often resist change, and how this resistance can be overcome. We review processes for managing organizational change. Then we move to the topic of stress and its sources and consequences. As you can see from the opening discussion, stress is an important topic for organizations to address in strengthening and maintaining talented individuals like Melvin Williams and Erin Callan. In closing, we discuss what individuals and organizations can do to better manage stress levels.

First, see how well you handle change by taking the following self-assessment.

SELF-ASSESSMENT LIBRARY

How Well Do I Respond to Turbulent Change?

In the Self-Assessment Library (available in MyManagementLab), take assessment III.C.1 (How Well Do I Respond to Turbulent Change?), and answer the following questions.

1. How did you score? Are you surprised by your score?
2. During what time of your life have you experienced the most change? How did you deal with it? Would you handle these changes in the same way today? Why or why not?
3. Are there ways you might reduce your resistance to change?

Forces for Change

1   Contrast planned and unplanned change.

No company today is in a particularly stable environment. Even those with dominant market share must change, sometimes radically. The car market, for instance, is particularly volatile. The Toyota Camry and the Honda Accord were market leaders in the midsize division until the 2007 recession hit, but their sales have not been as strong since then, while sales for the Ford Fusion climbed 66 percent in four years, leading Ford to market segment dominance. Meanwhile, the Ford Fiesta debuted to good sales in 2010 but has been eclipsed by the Chevrolet Sonic. In each car market segment, then, producers must continue to change in order to compete.[1]

"Change or die!" is the rallying cry among today's managers worldwide. Exhibit 18-1 summarizes six specific forces stimulating change.

In a number of places in this book, we've discussed the *changing nature of the workforce.* Almost every organization must adjust to a multicultural environment, demographic changes, immigration, and outsourcing. *Technology* is continually changing jobs and organizations. It is not hard to imagine the very idea of an office becoming an antiquated concept in the near future.

The housing and financial sectors recently have experienced extraordinary *economic shocks,* leading to the elimination, bankruptcy, or acquisition of some of the best-known U.S. companies, including Bear Stearns, Merrill Lynch, Lehman Brothers, Countrywide Financial, Washington Mutual, and Ameriquest. Tens of thousands of jobs were lost and may never return. After years of declining numbers of bankruptcies, the global recession caused the bankruptcy of auto manufacturers General Motors and Chrysler, retailers Borders and Sharper Image, and myriad other organizations.

Competition is changing. Competitors are as likely to come from across the ocean as from across town. Successful organizations will be fast on their feet, capable of developing new products rapidly and getting them to market quickly. In other words, they'll be flexible and will require an equally flexible and responsive workforce. Increasingly, in the United States and Europe, the government regulates business practices, including executive pay.

Social trends don't remain static either. Consumers who are otherwise strangers now meet and share product information in chat rooms and blogs.

Exhibit **18-1**	Forces for Change
Force	**Examples**
Nature of the workforce	More cultural diversity
	Aging population
	Increased immigration and outsourcing
Technology	Faster, cheaper, and more mobile computers and handheld devices
	Emergence and growth of social networking sites
	Deciphering of the human genetic code
Economic shocks	Rise and fall of global housing market
	Financial sector collapse
	Global recession
Competition	Global competitors
	Mergers and consolidations
	Increased government regulation of commerce
Social trends	Increased environmental awareness
	Liberalization of attitudes toward gay, lesbian, and transgender employees
	More multitasking and connectivity
World politics	Rising health care costs
	Negative social attitudes toward business and executives
	Opening of markets in China

Companies must continually adjust product and marketing strategies to be sensitive to changing social trends, as Liz Claiborne did when it sold off fashion brands such as Ellen Tracy, deemphasized large vendors such as Macy's, streamlined operations, and cut staff. Consumers, employees, and organizational leaders are increasingly sensitive to environmental concerns. "Green" practices are quickly becoming expected rather than optional.

Not even globalization's strongest proponents could have imagined how *world politics* would change in recent years. We've seen a major set of financial crises that have rocked global markets, a dramatic rise in the power and influence of China, and intense shakeups in governments across the Arab world. Throughout the industrialized world, businesses—particularly in the banking and financial sectors—have come under new scrutiny.

Planned Change

A group of housekeeping employees who work for a small hotel confronted the owner: "It's very hard for most of us to maintain rigid 7-to-4 work hours," said their spokeswoman. "Each of us has significant family and personal responsibilities. And rigid hours don't work for us. We're going to begin looking for someplace else to work if you don't set up flexible work hours." The owner listened thoughtfully to the group's ultimatum and agreed to its request. The next day, a flextime plan for these employees was introduced.

A major automobile manufacturer spent several billion dollars to install state-of-the-art robotics. One area that received the new equipment was quality control, where sophisticated computers significantly improved the company's ability to find and correct defects. Because the new equipment dramatically changed the jobs in the quality-control area, and because management anticipated considerable employee resistance to it, executives developed a program to help people become familiar with it and deal with any anxieties they might be feeling.

change   *Making things different.*

planned change   *Change activities that are intentional and goal oriented.*

Both these scenarios are examples of **change**, or making things different. However, only the second scenario describes **planned change**. Many changes are like the one that occurred at the hotel: They just happen. Some organizations treat all change as an accidental occurrence. In this chapter, we address change as an intentional, goal-oriented activity.

What are the goals of planned change? First, it seeks to improve the ability of the organization to adapt to changes in its environment. Second, it seeks to change employee behavior.

change agents   *Persons who act as catalysts and assume the responsibility for managing change activities.*

Who in organizations is responsible for managing change activities? The answer is **change agents**.[2] They see a future for the organization that others have not identified, and they are able to motivate, invent, and implement this vision. Change agents can be managers or nonmanagers, current or new employees, or outside consultants.

DuPont has two primary change agents in CEO Ellen Kullman and Chief Innovation Officer Thomas Connelly.[3] Taking the reins of the company in 2010, Kullman has pushed the organization toward a higher level of achievement by focusing on a principle Connelly calls "launch hard and ramp fast." This means the organization will seek to derive as much of its revenues from new products as possible. The goal is to move DuPont from a comparatively placid culture to one that focuses on market-driven science and delivers products customers need. The process has not always been easy, but is necessary to keep DuPont ahead in the competitive marketplace. General Motors expects its human resource managers to be change agents and its top human resource executive to set the tone. Experts attribute some of the failed changes at General Motors to Kathleen Barclay's stint as global human resource vice president. General Motors next hired Mary Barra, a manufacturing executive they thought could bring about better changes. Barra seemed like a change agent, but even CEO Dan Akerson said, "It was the worst application of talent I've ever seen." General Motors next selected Cynthia Brinkley, who supposedly has the right combination as a change agent. Yet, she has no HR background.[4]

Many change agents fail because organizational members resist change. In the next section, we discuss resistance to change and what managers can do about it.

Resistance to Change

2 Describe the sources of resistance to change.

Our egos are fragile, and we often see change as threatening. One study showed that even when employees are shown data that suggest they need to change, they latch onto whatever data they can find that suggests they are okay and don't

The State of Perpetual Change: Globalization

It's often said that change brings opportunity. Managers in the midst of organizational change often do acquire new perspectives on how their businesses can run more efficiently. This is never more true than when an organization expands into new global regions and learns from the best practices that each international business culture has to offer.

However, changing first and then seeing what opportunities arise is reactive; companies that expand globally this way often learn by painful trial-and-error. Have you ever considered the converse of the opening statement, that perhaps *opportunity* should bring change? Organizations that have successfully met the opportunity of globalization have embraced the concept of perpetual change. Their managers create an organizational culture of change, plan for overcoming resistance to new initiatives, and address the stress

implications of a constantly evolving, worldwide workforce.

Many of the successful global organizations we have discussed in this book are in a state of perpetual change, from big companies like Amazon and Facebook to small startups like Echo Nest and InterviewStreet. They, and many like them, are committed to the constant changes needed to follow current trends around the world. From their cutting-edge global technology to their virtual collaborations worldwide, these companies rapidly reorganize people and resources to find the best new ideas wherever they are and sell them wherever there is a market. Their organizational cultures champion change agents and challenge the status quo, rewarding individuals who quickly act on new opportunities. For some companies like technology-based Echo Nest and InterviewStreet, this means creating a strategic invitation to potential

customers and employees globally through the Internet. For other companies, particularly those in manufacturing or retailing, this means establishing physical locations for customers and employees worldwide.

There is no one right way to "go global." Experts vary on how to incorporate a new subsidiary into the organization chart, how much to centralize or decentralize leadership and decision making, how to transmit an organizational culture across the Internet, and so forth. But they do agree that the decision to globalize should include a commitment to perpetual change . . . and growth.

Sources: G. Anders, "Solve Puzzle, Get Job," *Forbes* (May 6, 2013), pp. 46–48; M.-G. Seo, M. S. Taylor, N. S. Hill, X. Zhang, P. E. Tesluk, and N. M. Lorinkova, "The Role of Affect and Leadership during Organizational Change," *Personnel Psychology* 65 (2012), pp. 121–165; and K. Wilson and Y. L. Doz, "10 Rules for Managing Global Innovation," *Harvard Business Review* (October 2012), pp. 85–90.

need to change.[5] Employees who have negative feelings about a change cope by not thinking about it, increasing their use of sick time, or quitting. All these reactions can sap the organization of vital energy when it is most needed.[6]

Resistance to change can be positive if it leads to open discussion and debate.[7] These responses are usually preferable to apathy or silence and can indicate that members of the organization are engaged in the process, providing change agents an opportunity to explain the change effort. Change agents can also use resistance to modify the change to fit the preferences of other members of the organization. When they treat resistance only as a threat, rather than a point of view to be discussed, they may increase dysfunctional conflict.

Resistance doesn't necessarily surface in standardized ways. It can be overt, implicit, immediate, or deferred. It's easiest for management to deal with overt and immediate resistance, such as complaints, a work slowdown, or a strike threat. The greater challenge is managing resistance that is implicit or deferred. These responses—loss of loyalty or motivation, increased errors or absenteeism— are more subtle and more difficult to recognize for what they are. Deferred actions also cloud the link between the change and the reaction to it and may surface weeks, months, or even years later. Or a single change of little inherent impact may be the straw that breaks the camel's back because resistance to earlier changes has been deferred and stockpiled.

Exhibit 18-2 summarizes major forces for resistance to change, categorized by their sources. Individual sources reside in human characteristics such as perceptions, personalities, and needs. Organizational sources reside in the structural makeup of organizations themselves.

Exhibit 18-2	Sources of Resistance to Change

Individual Sources

Habit—To cope with life's complexities, we rely on habits or programmed responses. But when confronted with change, this tendency to respond in our accustomed ways becomes a source of resistance.

Security—People with a high need for security are likely to resist change because it threatens their feelings of safety.

Economic factors—Changes in job tasks or established work routines can arouse economic fears if people are concerned that they won't be able to perform the new tasks or routines to their previous standards, especially when pay is closely tied to productivity.

Fear of the unknown—Change substitutes ambiguity and uncertainty for the unknown.

Selective information processing—Individuals are guilty of selectively processing information in order to keep their perceptions intact. They hear what they want to hear, and they ignore information that challenges the world they've created.

Organizational Sources

Structural inertia—Organizations have built-in mechanisms—such as their selection processes and formalized regulations—to produce stability. When an organization is confronted with change, this structural inertia acts as a counterbalance to sustain stability.

Limited focus of change—Organizations consist of a number of interdependent subsystems. One can't be changed without affecting the others. So limited changes in subsystems tend to be nullified by the larger system.

Group inertia—Even if individuals want to change their behavior, group norms may act as a constraint.

Threat to expertise—Changes in organizational patterns may threaten the expertise of specialized groups.

Threat to established power relationships—Any redistribution of decision-making authority can threaten long-established power relationships within the organization.

It's worth noting that not all change is good. Speed can lead to bad decisions, and sometimes those initiating change fail to realize the full magnitude of the effects or their true costs. Rapid, transformational change is risky, and some organizations have collapsed for this reason.[8] Change agents need to carefully think through the full implications.

Overcoming Resistance to Change

Eight tactics can help change agents deal with resistance to change.[9] Let's review them briefly.

Education and Communication Communicating the logic of a change can reduce employee resistance on two levels. First, it fights the effects of misinformation and poor communication: If employees receive the full facts and clear up misunderstandings, resistance should subside. Second, communication can help "sell" the need for change by packaging it properly.[10] A study of German companies revealed changes are most effective when a company communicates a rationale that balances the interests of various stakeholders (shareholders, employees, community, customers) rather than those of shareholders only.[11] Another study of a changing organization in the Philippines found that formal change information sessions decreased employees' anxiety about the change, while providing high-quality information about the change increased their commitment to it.[12]

Participation It's difficult to resist a change decision in which we've participated. Assuming participants have the expertise to make a meaningful contribution, their involvement can reduce resistance, obtain commitment, and increase the quality of the change decision. However, against these advantages are the negatives: potential for a poor solution and great consumption of time.

Building Support and Commitment When employees' fear and anxiety are high, counseling and therapy, new-skills training, or a short paid leave of absence may facilitate adjustment. When managers or employees have low emotional commitment to change, they favor the status quo and resist it.[13] Employees are

Photo 18-1 Participation was an effective tactic for overcoming resistance to change at the Ohio Department of Natural Resources. Faced with the tough task of reducing the use of its time and resources, the cash-strapped department involved employees in a continuous improvement process (shown here) to help find better ways to do their jobs more efficiently.

Source: Kiichiro Sato/ASSOCIATED PRESS.

also more accepting of changes when they are committed to the organization as a whole.[14] So, firing up employees and emphasizing their commitment to the organization overall can also help them emotionally commit to the change rather than embrace the status quo.

Develop Positive Relationships   People are more willing to accept changes if they trust the managers implementing them.[15] One study surveyed 235 employees from a large housing corporation in The Netherlands that was experiencing a merger. Those who had a more positive relationship with their supervisors, and who felt that the work environment supported development, were much more positive about the change process.[16] Another set of studies found that individuals who were dispositionally resistant to change felt more positive about the change if they trusted the change agent.[17] This research suggests that if managers are able to facilitate positive relationships, they may be able to overcome resistance to change even among those who ordinarily don't like changes.

Implementing Changes Fairly   One way organizations can minimize negative impact is to make sure change is implemented fairly. As we saw in Chapter 7, procedural fairness is especially important when employees perceive an outcome as negative, so it's crucial that employees see the reason for the change and perceive its implementation as consistent and fair.[18]

Manipulation and Cooptation   *Manipulation* refers to covert influence attempts. Twisting facts to make them more attractive, withholding information, and creating false rumors to get employees to accept change are all examples of manipulation. If management threatens to close a manufacturing plant whose employees are resisting an across-the-board pay cut, and if the threat is actually untrue, management is using manipulation. *Cooptation,* on the other hand, combines manipulation and participation. It seeks to "buy off" the leaders of a resistance group by giving them a key role, seeking their advice not to find a better solution but to get their endorsement. Both manipulation and cooptation are relatively inexpensive ways to gain the support of adversaries, but they can backfire if the targets become aware they are being tricked or used. Once that's discovered, the change agent's credibility may drop to zero.

Selecting People Who Accept Change   Research suggests the ability to easily accept and adapt to *change* is related to personality—some people simply have more positive attitudes about change than others.[19] Such individuals are open to experience, take a positive attitude toward change, are willing to take risks, and are flexible in their behavior. One study of managers in the United States, Europe, and Asia found those with a positive self-concept and high risk tolerance coped better with organizational change. A study of 258 police officers found those who were higher in growth-needs, internal locus of control, and internal work motivation had more positive attitudes about organizational change efforts.[20] Individuals higher in general mental ability are also better able to learn and adapt to changes in the workplace.[21] In sum, an impressive body of evidence shows organizations can facilitate change by selecting people predisposed to accept it.

Besides selecting individuals who are willing to accept changes, it is also possible to select teams that are more adaptable. Studies have shown that teams that are strongly motivated by learning about and mastering tasks are better able to adapt to changing environments.[22] This research suggests that it may be necessary to consider not just individual motivation, but also group motivation when trying to implement changes.

Coercion   Last on the list of tactics is *coercion,* the application of direct threats or force on the resisters. If management really is determined to close a manufacturing plant whose employees don't acquiesce to a pay cut, the company is using coercion. Other examples are threats of transfer, loss of promotions, negative performance evaluations, and a poor letter of recommendation. The advantages and drawbacks of coercion are approximately the same as for manipulation and cooptation.

The Politics of Change

No discussion of resistance would be complete without a brief mention of the politics of change. Because change invariably threatens the status quo, it inherently implies political activity.

Politics suggests the impetus for change is more likely to come from outside change agents, employees new to the organization (who have less invested in the status quo), or managers slightly removed from the main power structure. Managers who have spent their entire careers with a single organization and achieved a senior position in the hierarchy are often major impediments to change. It is a very real threat to their status and position. Yet they may be expected to implement changes to demonstrate they're not merely caretakers. By acting as change agents, they can convey to stockholders, suppliers, employees, and customers that they are addressing problems and adapting to a dynamic environment. Of course, as you might guess, when forced to introduce change, these longtime power holders tend to implement incremental changes. Radical change is threatening. This explains why boards of directors that recognize the imperative for rapid and radical change frequently turn to outside candidates for new leadership.[23]

Approaches to Managing Organizational Change

3 Compare the four main approaches to managing organizational change.

Now we turn to several approaches to managing change: Lewin's classic three-step model of the change process, Kotter's eight-step plan, action research, and organizational development.

Lewin's Three-Step Model

Kurt Lewin argued that successful change in organizations should follow three steps: **unfreezing** the status quo, **movement** to a desired end state, and **refreezing** the new change to make it permanent[24] (see Exhibit 18-3).

The status quo is an equilibrium state. To move from equilibrium—to overcome the pressures of both individual resistance and group conformity—unfreezing must happen in one of three ways (see Exhibit 18-4). The **driving forces**, which direct behavior away from the status quo, can be increased. The

unfreezing   *Changing to overcome the pressures of both individual resistance and group conformity.*

movement   *A change process that transforms the organization from the status quo to a desired end state.*

refreezing   *Stabilizing a change intervention by balancing driving and restraining forces.*

driving forces   *Forces that direct behavior away from the status quo.*

Exhibit **18-3**   Lewin's Three-Step Change Model

Unfreezing → Movement → Refreezing

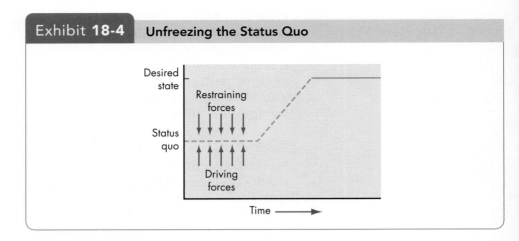

Exhibit **18-4**   Unfreezing the Status Quo

restraining forces   *Forces that hinder movement from the existing equilibrium.*

restraining forces, which hinder movement away from equilibrium, can be decreased. A third alternative is to combine the first two approaches. Companies that have been successful in the past are likely to encounter restraining forces because people question the need for change.[25] Similarly, research shows that companies with strong cultures excel at incremental change but are overcome by restraining forces against radical change.[26]

Consider a large oil company that decided to consolidate its three divisional marketing offices in Seattle, San Francisco, and Los Angeles into a single regional San Francisco office. The decision was made in New York, and the people affected had no say whatsoever in the choice. The reorganization meant transferring more than 150 employees, eliminating some duplicate managerial positions, and instituting a new hierarchy of command.

The oil company's management could expect employee resistance to the consolidation. Those in Seattle or Los Angeles may not want to transfer to another city, pull children out of school, make new friends, adapt to new co-workers, or undergo the reassignment of responsibilities. Positive incentives such as pay increases, liberal moving expenses, and low-cost mortgage funds for new homes in San Francisco might encourage employees to accept the change. Management might also unfreeze acceptance of the status quo by removing restraining forces. It could counsel employees individually, hearing and clarifying each employee's specific concerns and apprehensions. Assuming most are unjustified, the counselor could assure employees there was nothing to fear and offer tangible evidence that restraining forces are unwarranted. If resistance is extremely high, management may have to resort to both reducing resistance and increasing the attractiveness of the alternative if the unfreezing is to be successful.

Research on organizational change has shown that, to be effective, the actual change has to happen quickly.[27] Organizations that build up to change do less well than those that get to and through the movement stage quickly.

Once change has been implemented, to be successful the new situation must be refrozen so it can be sustained over time. Without this last step, change will likely be short-lived, and employees will attempt to revert to the previous equilibrium state. The objective of refreezing, then, is to stabilize the new situation by balancing the driving and restraining forces.

How could the oil company's management refreeze its consolidation change? By systematically replacing temporary forces with permanent ones. Management might impose a permanent upward adjustment of salaries. The formal rules and regulations governing behavior of those affected by the change should also be revised to reinforce the new situation. Over time, of course, the workgroup's norms will evolve to sustain the new equilibrium. But until that point is reached, management will have to rely on more formal mechanisms.

Kotter's Eight-Step Plan for Implementing Change

John Kotter of Harvard Business School built on Lewin's three-step model to create a more detailed approach for implementing change.[28] Kotter began by listing common mistakes managers make when trying to initiate change. They may fail to create a sense of urgency about the need for change, to create a coalition for managing the change process, to have a vision for change and effectively communicate it, to remove obstacles that could impede the vision's achievement, to provide short-term and achievable goals, and/or to anchor the changes into the organization's culture. They may also declare victory too soon.

Kotter then established eight sequential steps to overcome these problems. They're listed in Exhibit 18-5.

Notice how Kotter's first four steps essentially extrapolate Lewin's "unfreezing" stage. Steps 5, 6, and 7 represent "movement," and the final step works on "refreezing." So Kotter's contribution lies in providing managers and change agents with a more detailed guide for successfully implementing change.

Action Research

action research *A change process based on systematic collection of data and then selection of a change action based on what the analyzed data indicate.*

Action research is a change process based on the systematic collection of data and selection of a change action based on what the analyzed data indicate.[29] Its value is in providing a scientific methodology for managing planned change. Action research consists of five steps (note how they closely parallel the scientific method): diagnosis, analysis, feedback, action, and evaluation.

The change agent, often an outside consultant in action research, begins by gathering information about problems, concerns, and needed changes from members of the organization. This *diagnosis* is analogous to the physician's search to find specifically what ails a patient. In action research, the change agent asks questions, reviews records, and interviews employees and listens to their concerns.

Diagnosis is followed by *analysis*. What problems do people key in on? What patterns do these problems seem to take? The change agent synthesizes this information into primary concerns, problem areas, and possible actions.

Exhibit 18-5   Kotter's Eight-Step Plan for Implementing Change

1. Establish a sense of urgency by creating a compelling reason for why change is needed.
2. Form a coalition with enough power to lead the change.
3. Create a new vision to direct the change and strategies for achieving the vision.
4. Communicate the vision throughout the organization.
5. Empower others to act on the vision by removing barriers to change and encouraging risk taking and creative problem solving.
6. Plan for, create, and reward short-term "wins" that move the organization toward the new vision.
7. Consolidate improvements, reassess changes, and make necessary adjustments in the new programs.
8. Reinforce the changes by demonstrating the relationship between new behaviors and organizational success.

Source: Based on M. du Plessis, "Re-implementing an Individual Performance Management System as a Change Intervention at Higher Education Institutions - Overcoming Staff Resistance," *Proceedings of the 7th European Conference on Management Leadership and Governance* (2011), pp. 105–115.

Action research requires the people who will participate in any change program to help identify the problem and determine the solution. So the third step—*feedback*—requires sharing with employees what has been found from the first and second steps. The employees, with the help of the change agent, develop action plans for bringing about any needed change.

Now the *action* part of action research is set in motion. The employees and the change agent carry out the specific actions they have identified to correct the problem.

The final step, consistent with the scientific underpinnings of action research, is *evaluation* of the action plan's effectiveness, using the initial data gathered as a benchmark.

Action research provides at least two specific benefits. First, it's problem focused. The change agent objectively looks for problems, and the type of problem determines the type of change action. Although this may seem intuitively obvious, many change activities are not handled this way. Rather, they're solution centered. The change agent has a favorite solution—for example, implementing flextime, teams, or a process reengineering program—and then seeks out problems that the solution fits.

Second, because action research engages employees so thoroughly in the process, it reduces resistance to change. Once employees have actively participated in the feedback stage, the change process typically takes on a momentum of its own under their sustained pressure to bring it about.

Organizational Development

organizational development (OD) *A collection of planned change interventions, built on humanistic–democratic values, that seeks to improve organizational effectiveness and employee well-being.*

Organizational development (OD) is a collection of change methods that try to improve organizational effectiveness and employee well-being.[30]

OD methods value human and organizational growth, collaborative and participative processes, and a spirit of inquiry.[31] Contemporary OD borrows heavily from postmodern philosophy in placing heavy emphasis on the subjective ways in which people see their environment. The focus is on how individuals make sense of their work environment. The change agent may take the lead in OD, but there is a strong emphasis on collaboration. These are the underlying values in most OD efforts:

1. **Respect for people.** Individuals are perceived as responsible, conscientious, and caring. They should be treated with dignity and respect.
2. **Trust and support.** An effective and healthy organization is characterized by trust, authenticity, openness, and a supportive climate.
3. **Power equalization.** Effective organizations deemphasize hierarchical authority and control.
4. **Confrontation.** Problems should be openly confronted, not swept under the rug.
5. **Participation.** The more engaged in the decisions they are, the more people affected by a change will be committed to implementing them.

What are some OD techniques or interventions for bringing about change? Here are six.

sensitivity training *Training groups that seek to change behavior through unstructured group interaction.*

Sensitivity Training A variety of names—**sensitivity training**, laboratory training, encounter groups, and T-groups (training groups)—all refer to an early method of changing behavior through unstructured group interaction.[32] Members were brought together in a free and open environment in which participants discussed themselves and their interactive processes, loosely directed by a professional behavioral scientist who created the opportunity to express ideas, beliefs, and attitudes without taking any leadership role. The group was process oriented, which means individuals learned through observing and participating rather than being told.

Many participants found these unstructured groups intimidating, chaotic, and damaging to work relationships. Although extremely popular in the 1960s, they diminished in use during the 1970s and have essentially disappeared. However, organizational interventions such as diversity training, executive coaching, and team-building exercises are descendants of this early OD intervention technique.

Survey Feedback   One tool for assessing attitudes held by organizational members, identifying discrepancies among member perceptions, and solving these differences is the **survey feedback** approach.[33]

Everyone in an organization can participate in survey feedback, but of key importance is the organizational "family"—the manager of any given unit and the employees who report directly to him or her. All usually complete a questionnaire about their perceptions and attitudes on a range of topics, including decision-making practices; communication effectiveness; coordination among units; and satisfaction with the organization, job, peers, and immediate supervisor.

Data from this questionnaire are tabulated with data pertaining to an individual's specific "family" and to the entire organization, and then distributed to employees. These data become the springboard for identifying problems and clarifying issues that may be creating difficulties for people. Particular attention is given to encouraging discussion and ensuring it focuses on issues and ideas and not on attacking individuals. For instance, are people listening? Are new ideas being generated? Can decision making, interpersonal relations, or job assignments be improved? Answers should lead the group to commit to various remedies for the problems identified.

The survey feedback approach can be helpful to keep decision makers informed about the attitudes of employees toward the organization. However, individuals are influenced by many factors when they respond to surveys, and a high number of nonresponses may indicate organizational dysfunction or decreased job satisfaction. Managers who use the survey feedback approach should therefore monitor their response rates.

Process Consultation   Managers often sense their unit's performance can be improved but are unable to identify what to improve and how. The purpose of **process consultation (PC)** is for an outside consultant to assist a client, usually a manager, "to perceive, understand, and act upon process events" with which the manager must deal.[34] These events might include workflow, informal relationships among unit members, and formal communication channels.

PC is similar to sensitivity training in assuming we can improve organizational effectiveness by dealing with interpersonal problems and in emphasizing involvement. But PC is more task directed, and consultants are there to "give the client 'insight' into what is going on around him, within him, and between him and other people."[35] They do not solve the organization's problems, but rather guide or coach the client to solve his or her own problems after *jointly* diagnosing what needs improvement. The client develops the skill to analyze processes within his or her unit and can continue to call on it long after the consultant is gone. Because the client actively participates in both the diagnosis and the development of alternatives, he or she arrives at a greater understanding of the process and the remedy and is less resistant to the action plan chosen.

survey feedback   *The use of questionnaires to identify discrepancies among member perceptions; discussion follows, and remedies are suggested.*

process consultation (PC)   *A meeting in which a consultant assists a client in understanding process events with which he or she must deal and identifying processes that need improvement.*

team building *High interaction among team members to increase trust and openness.*

Team Building We've noted throughout this book that organizations increasingly rely on teams to accomplish work tasks. **Team building** uses high-interaction group activities to increase trust and openness among team members, improve coordinative efforts, and increase team performance.[36] Here, we emphasize the intragroup level, meaning organizational families (command groups) as well as committees, project teams, self-managed teams, and task groups.

Team building typically includes goal-setting, development of interpersonal relations among team members, role analysis to clarify each member's role and responsibilities, and team process analysis. It may emphasize or exclude certain activities, depending on the purpose of the development effort and the specific problems with which the team is confronted. Basically, however, team building uses high interaction among members to increase trust and openness.

intergroup development *OD efforts to change the attitudes, stereotypes, and perceptions that groups have of each other.*

Intergroup Development A major area of concern in OD is dysfunctional conflict among groups. **Intergroup development** seeks to change groups' attitudes, stereotypes, and perceptions about each other. Here, training sessions closely resemble diversity training (in fact, diversity training largely evolved from intergroup development in OD), except rather than focusing on demographic differences, they focus on differences among occupations, departments, or divisions within an organization.

In one company, the engineers saw the accounting department as composed of shy and conservative types and the HR department as having a bunch of "ultra-liberals more concerned that some protected group of employees might get their feelings hurt than with the company making a profit." Such stereotypes can have an obvious negative impact on coordination efforts among departments.

Among several approaches for improving intergroup relations, a popular one emphasizes problem solving.[37] Each group meets independently to list its perceptions of itself and of the other group and how it believes the other group perceives it. The groups share their lists, discuss similarities and differences, and look for the causes of disparities. Are the groups' goals at odds?

Photo 18-2 As a sponsor of Habitat for Humanity, ServiceMaster provides employee volunteers and the funds to build homes for needy families. Building homes also serves as a high-interaction team-building activity that increases trust and openness among employees and promotes better communication and cooperation on their regular jobs.

Were perceptions distorted? On what basis were stereotypes formulated? Have some differences been caused by a misunderstanding of intentions? Have words and concepts been defined differently by a each group? Answers to questions like these clarify the exact nature of the conflict.

Once they have identified the causes of the difficulty, the groups move to the integration phase—developing solutions to improve relations between them. Subgroups can be formed of members from each of the conflicting groups to conduct further diagnoses and formulate alternative solutions.

appreciative inquiry (AI) *An approach that seeks to identify the unique qualities and special strengths of an organization, which can then be built on to improve performance.*

Appreciative Inquiry Most OD approaches are problem centered. They identify a problem or set of problems, then look for a solution. **Appreciative inquiry (AI)** instead accentuates the positive.[38] Rather than looking for problems to fix, it seeks to identify the unique qualities and special strengths of an organization, which members can build on to improve performance. That is, AI focuses on an organization's successes rather than its problems.

The AI process consists of four steps—discovery, dreaming, design, and destiny—often played out in a large-group meeting over a 2- or 3-day time period and overseen by a trained change agent. *Discovery* sets out to identify what people think are the organization's strengths. Employees recount times they felt the organization worked best or when they specifically felt most satisfied with their jobs. In *dreaming,* employees use information from the discovery phase to speculate on possible futures, such as what the organization will be like in 5 years. In *design,* participants find a common vision of how the organization will look in the future and agree on its unique qualities. For the fourth step, participants seek to define the organization's *destiny* or how to fulfill their dream, and they typically write action plans and develop implementation strategies.

AI has proven an effective change strategy in organizations such as GTE, Roadway Express, and the U.S. Navy. American Express used AI to revitalize its culture during a lean economy. In workshops, employees described how they already felt proud of working at American Express and were encouraged to create a change vision by describing how it could be better in the future. The efforts led to some very concrete improvements. Senior managers were able to use employees' information to better their methods of making financial forecasts, improve IT investments, and create new performance-management tools for managers. The end result was a renewed culture focused on winning attitudes and behaviors.[39]

Creating a Culture for Change

4 Demonstrate two ways of creating a culture for change.

We've considered how organizations can *adapt* to change. But recently, some OB scholars have focused on a more proactive approach—how organizations can *embrace* change by transforming their cultures. In this section, we review two such approaches: stimulating an innovative culture and creating a learning organization. We also address the issue of organizational change and stress.

Stimulating a Culture of Innovation

How can an organization become more innovative? An excellent model is W. L. Gore, the $2.6-billion-per-year company best known as the maker of Gore-Tex fabric.[40] Gore has developed a reputation as one of the most innovative

U.S. companies by developing a stream of diverse products—including guitar strings, dental floss, medical devices, and fuel cells.

What's the secret of Gore's success? What can other organizations do to duplicate its track record for innovation? Although there is no guaranteed formula, certain characteristics surface repeatedly when researchers study innovative organizations. We consider the characteristics as structural, cultural, and human resources. Change agents should consider introducing these characteristics into their organization to create an innovative climate. Let's start by clarifying what we mean by innovation.

Definition of *Innovation*   We said change refers to making things different. **Innovation**, a more specialized kind of change, is a new idea applied to initiating or improving a product, process, or service.[41] So all innovations imply change, but not all changes necessarily introduce new ideas or lead to significant improvements. Innovations can range from small incremental improvements, such as tablets, to radical breakthroughs, such as Nissan's electric Leaf car.

innovation   *A new idea applied to initiating or improving a product, process, or service.*

Sources of Innovation   *Structural variables* have been the most studied potential source of innovation.[42] A comprehensive review of the structure–innovation relationship leads to the following conclusions:[43]

1. Organic structures positively influence innovation. Because they're lower in vertical differentiation, formalization, and centralization, organic organizations facilitate the flexibility, adaptation, and cross-fertilization that make the adoption of innovations easier.
2. Long tenure in management is associated with innovation. Managerial tenure apparently provides legitimacy and knowledge of how to accomplish tasks and obtain desired outcomes.
3. Innovation is nurtured when there are slack resources. Having an abundance of resources allows an organization to afford to purchase innovations, bear the cost of instituting them, and absorb failures.
4. Interunit communication is high in innovative organizations.[44] These organizations are high users of committees, task forces, cross-functional teams, and other mechanisms that facilitate interaction across departmental lines.

Innovative organizations tend to have similar *cultures*. They encourage experimentation. They reward both successes and failures. They celebrate mistakes. Unfortunately, in too many organizations, people are rewarded for the absence of failures rather than for the presence of successes. Such cultures extinguish risk taking and innovation. People will suggest and try new ideas only when they feel such behaviors exact no penalties. Managers in innovative organizations recognize that failures are a natural by-product of venturing into the unknown.

Within the *human resources* category, innovative organizations actively promote the training and development of their members so they keep current, offer high job security so employees don't fear getting fired for making mistakes, and encourage individuals to become champions of change. Once a new idea is developed, **idea champions** actively and enthusiastically promote it, build support, overcome resistance, and ensure it is implemented.[45] Champions have common personality characteristics: extremely high self-confidence, persistence, energy, and a tendency to take risks. They also display characteristics associated with transformational leadership—they inspire and energize others with their vision of an innovation's potential and their strong personal conviction about their mission. Idea champions are good at gaining the commitment of others, and their jobs provide considerable decision-making discretion; this autonomy helps them introduce and implement innovations.[46]

idea champions   *Individuals who take an innovation and actively and enthusiastically promote the idea, build support, overcome resistance, and ensure that the idea is implemented.*

Photo 18-3 China's Baidu Inc., which made the first search engine that was designed specifically for the Chinese language, has built a culture that fosters innovation. Baidu describes its culture as simple and reliable, where candor and trust are valued, politicking is taboo, and an organic structure promotes the cross-fertilization of ideas.

Do successful idea champions do things differently in different cultures? Yes.[47] People in collectivist cultures prefer appeals for cross-functional support for innovation efforts; people in high power distance cultures prefer champions to work closely with those in authority to approve innovative activities before work is begun; and the higher the uncertainty avoidance of a society, the more champions should work within the organization's rules and procedures to develop the innovation. These findings suggest that effective managers will alter their organization's championing strategies to reflect cultural values. So, for instance, although idea champions in Russia might succeed by ignoring budgetary limitations and working around confining procedures, champions in Austria, Denmark, Germany, or other cultures high in uncertainty avoidance will be more effective by closely following budgets and procedures.

Sergio Marcchione, CEO of Fiat-Chrysler, has acted as idea champion for the single objective of updating the pipeline of vehicles for Chrysler. To facilitate this change, he has radically dismantled the bureaucracy, tearing up Chrysler's organization chart and introducing a flatter structure with himself at the lead. As a result, the company introduced a more innovative line of vehicles and planned to redesign or significantly refresh 75 percent of its lineup in 2010 alone.[48]

Creating a Learning Organization

Another way an organization can proactively manage change is to make continuous growth part of its culture—to become a learning organization.[49]

What's a Learning Organization? Just as individuals learn, so too do organizations. A **learning organization** has developed the continuous capacity to adapt and change. "All organizations learn, whether they consciously choose to or not—it is a fundamental requirement for their sustained existence."[50] Some organizations just do it better than others.

learning organization *An organization that has developed the continuous capacity to adapt and change.*

single-loop learning *A process of correcting errors using past routines and present policies.*

double-loop learning *A process of correcting errors by modifying the organization's objectives, policies, and standard routines.*

Most organizations engage in **single-loop learning**.[51] When they detect errors, their correction process relies on past routines and present policies. In contrast, learning organizations use **double-loop learning**. They correct errors by *modifying* objectives, policies, and standard routines. Double-loop learning challenges deeply rooted assumptions and norms. It provides opportunities for radically different solutions to problems and dramatic jumps in improvement.

Exhibit 18-6 summarizes the five basic characteristics of a learning organization. It's one in which people put aside their old ways of thinking, learn to be open with each other, understand how their organization really works, form a plan or vision everyone can agree on, and work together to achieve that vision.[52]

Proponents of the learning organization envision it as a remedy for three fundamental problems of traditional organizations: fragmentation, competition, and reactiveness.[53] First, *fragmentation* based on specialization creates "walls" and "chimneys" that separate different functions into independent and often warring fiefdoms. Second, an overemphasis on *competition* often undermines collaboration. Managers compete to show who is right, who knows more, or who is more persuasive. Divisions compete when they ought to cooperate and share knowledge. Team leaders compete to show who the best manager is. And third, *reactiveness* misdirects management's attention to problem solving rather than creation. The problem solver tries to make something go away, while a creator tries to bring something new into being. An emphasis on reactiveness pushes out innovation and continuous improvement and, in its place, encourages people to run around "putting out fires."

Managing Learning   What can managers do to make their firms learning organizations? Here are some suggestions:

- **Establish a strategy.**   Management needs to make explicit its commitment to change, innovation, and continuous improvement.
- **Redesign the organization's structure.**   The formal structure can be a serious impediment to learning. Flattening the structure, eliminating or combining departments, and increasing the use of cross-functional teams reinforces interdependence and reduces boundaries.
- **Reshape the organization's culture.**   To become a learning organization, managers must demonstrate by their actions that taking risks and admitting failures are desirable. That means rewarding people who take chances and make mistakes. And management needs to encourage functional conflict. "The key to unlocking real openness at work," says one expert on learning organizations, "is to teach people to give up having

---

Exhibit 18-6   **Characteristics of a Learning Organization**

1. There exists a shared vision that everyone agrees on.
2. People discard their old ways of thinking and the standard routines they use for solving problems or doing their jobs.
3. Members think of all organizational processes, activities, functions, and interactions with the environment as part of a system of interrelationships.
4. People openly communicate with each other (across vertical and horizontal boundaries) without fear of criticism or punishment.
5. People sublimate their personal self-interest and fragmented departmental interests to work together to achieve the organization's shared vision.

Source: Based on P. M. Senge, *The Fifth Discipline: The Art and Practice of The Learning Organization* (New York: Doubleday, 2006).

to be in agreement. We think agreement is so important. Who cares? You have to bring paradoxes, conflicts, and dilemmas out in the open, so collectively we can be more intelligent than we can be individually."[54]

Organizational Change and Stress

Think about the times you have felt stressed during your work life. Look past the everyday stress factors that can spill over to the workplace, like a traffic jam that makes you late for work or a broken coffee machine that keep you from your morning java. What were the more memorable and lasting stressful times? For many people, these were caused by organizational change.

Researchers are increasingly studying the effects of organizational change on employees. We are interested in determining the specific causes and mitigating factors of stress in order to learn how to manage organizational change effectively. The overall findings are that organizational changes incorporating OB knowledge of how people react to stressors may yield more effective results than organizational changes that are only objectively managed through goal-setting.[55] Not surprisingly, the role of leadership is critical. A recent study found that transformational leaders can help shape employee affect so employees stay committed to the change and do not perceive it as stressful.[56] Another study indicated that a positive orientation toward change *before* specific changes are planned will predict how employees deal with new initiatives. A positive change orientation will decrease employees' stress when they go through organizational changes and will increase their positive attitudes. Managers can be continually working to increase employees' self-efficacy, change-related attitudes, and perceived control to create this positive change orientation. For instance, they can use role clarification and continual rewards to increase self-efficacy. They can also enhance employees' perceived control and positive change attitudes by including them from the planning stages through to the application of new processes.[57] Another study added the need for increasing the amount of communication to employees during change, assessing and enhancing the employees' psychological resilience through offering social support, and training employees in emotional self-regulation techniques.[58] Through these methods, managers can help employees keep their stress levels low and their commitment high.

Often, organizational changes are stressful because employees perceive aspects of the changes as threatening. These employees are more likely to quit, partially in reaction to their stress. To reduce the perception of threat, employees need to see the organizational changes as fair. Research indicates that those who have a positive change orientation before changes are planned are less likely to perceive of changes as unfair or threatening.

Work Stress and Its Management

5 Identify potential sources of stress.

Friends say they're stressed from greater workloads and longer hours because of downsizing at their companies. Parents worry about the lack of job stability and reminisce about a time when a job with a large company implied lifetime security. We read surveys in which employees complain about the stress of trying to balance work and family responsibilities.[59] Harris, Rothenberg International, a leading provider of employee assistance programs (EAPs), finds that employees

Exhibit 18-7	Work Is the Biggest Source of Stress for Most

"What area of your life causes you the most stress?"

Area	Causes Most Stress
My job	34%
My finances	30%
Health	17%
Other	19%

Source: Based on 2013 poll of over 2,000 U.K. individuals, www.mind.org.uk/news/8566_work_is_biggest_cause_of_stress_in_peoples_lives, accessed July 31, 2013.

are having mental breakdowns and needing professional help at higher rates than ever.[60] Indeed, as Exhibit 18-7 shows, work is, for most people, the most important source of stress in life. What are the causes and consequences of stress, and what can individuals and organizations do to reduce it?

What Is Stress?

stress *An unpleasant psychological process that occurs in response to environmental pressures.*

Stress is a dynamic condition in which an individual is confronted with an opportunity, demand, or resource related to what the individual desires and for which the outcome is perceived to be both uncertain and important.[61] This is a complicated definition. Let's look at its components more closely.

Although stress is typically discussed in a negative context, it is not necessarily bad in and of itself; it also has a positive value.[62] In response to stress, your nervous system, hypothalamus, pituitary, and adrenal glands supply you with stress hormones to cope. Your heartbeat and breathing accelerate to increase oxygen, while your muscles tense for action.[63] This is an opportunity when it offers potential gain. Consider, for example, the superior performance an athlete or stage performer gives in a "clutch" situation. Such individuals often use stress positively to rise to the occasion and perform at their maximum. Similarly, many professionals see the pressures of heavy workloads and deadlines as positive challenges that enhance the quality of their work and the satisfaction they get from their job. However, when the situation is negative, stress is harmful and may hinder your progress by elevating your blood pressure uncomfortably and creating an erratic heart rhythm as you struggle to speak and think logically.[64]

challenge stressors *Stressors associated with workload, pressure to complete tasks, and time urgency.*

hindrance stressors *Stressors that keep you from reaching your goals (for example, red tape, office politics, confusion over job responsibilities).*

Researchers have argued that **challenge stressors**—or stressors associated with workload, pressure to complete tasks, and time urgency—operate quite differently from **hindrance stressors**—or stressors that keep you from reaching your goals (for example, red tape, office politics, confusion over job responsibilities). Although research is just starting to accumulate, early evidence suggests challenge stressors produce less strain than hindrance stressors.[65]

Researchers have sought to clarify the conditions under which each type of stress exists. It appears that employees who have stronger affective commitment to their organizations can transfer psychological stress into greater focus and higher sales performance, whereas employees with low levels of commitment perform worse under stress.[66] And when challenge stress increases, those with high levels of organizational support have higher role-based performance, but those with low levels of organizational support do not.[67]

demands *Responsibilities, pressures, obligations, and even uncertainties that individuals face in the workplace.*

resources *Things within an individual's control that can be used to resolve demands.*

More typically, stress is associated with **demands** and **resources**. Demands are responsibilities, pressures, obligations, and uncertainties individuals face in the workplace. Resources are things within an individual's control that he or she can use to resolve the demands. Let's discuss what this demands–resources model means.[68]

When you take a test at school or undergo your annual performance review at work, you feel stress because you confront opportunities and performance

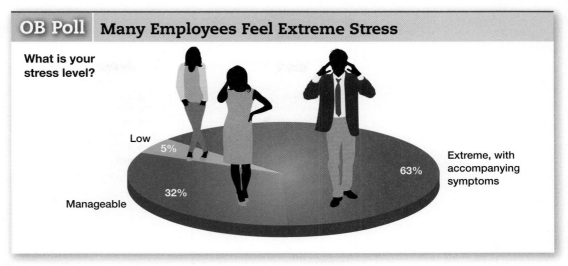

OB Poll | **Many Employees Feel Extreme Stress**

What is your stress level?

Low 5%

Manageable 32%

Extreme, with accompanying symptoms 63%

Note: According to StressPulse survey of 1,880 employees.

Source: Based on "Presenteeism on the Rise as Employees Show Fatigue From a Slow- to No-Hire Economy," ComPsych Corporation press release (October 29, 2012), www.compsych.com/press-room/press-releases-2012/678-october-29-2012.

pressures. A good performance review may lead to a promotion, greater responsibilities, and a higher salary. A poor review may prevent you from getting a promotion. An extremely poor review might even result in your being fired. To the extent you can apply resources to the demands on you—such as being prepared, placing the exam or review in perspective, or obtaining social support—you will feel less stress.

Research suggests adequate resources help reduce the stressful nature of demands when demands and resources match. If emotional demands are stressing you, having emotional resources in the form of social support is especially important. If the demands are cognitive—say, information overload—then job resources in the form of computer support or information are more important. Thus, under the demands–resources perspective, having resources to cope with stress is just as important in offsetting it as demands are in increasing it.[69]

Potential Sources of Stress

What causes stress? As the model in Exhibit 18-8 shows, there are three categories of potential stressors: environmental, organizational, and personal. Let's take a look at each.[70]

Environmental Factors   Just as environmental uncertainty influences the design of an organization's structure, it also influences stress levels among employees in that organization. Indeed, uncertainty is the biggest reason people have trouble coping with organizational changes.[71] There are three main types of environmental uncertainty: economic, political, and technological.

Changes in the business cycle create *economic uncertainties*. When the economy is contracting, for example, people become increasingly anxious about their job security. *Political uncertainties* don't tend to create stress among North Americans as they do for employees in countries such as Haiti or Venezuela. The obvious reason is that the United States and Canada have stable political systems, in which change is typically implemented in an orderly manner. Yet political threats and changes, even in countries such as the United States and Canada, can induce stress. Threats of terrorism in developed and developing nations, for instance, lead to political uncertainty that becomes stressful to people in these countries.[72] Because innovations can make an employee's skills

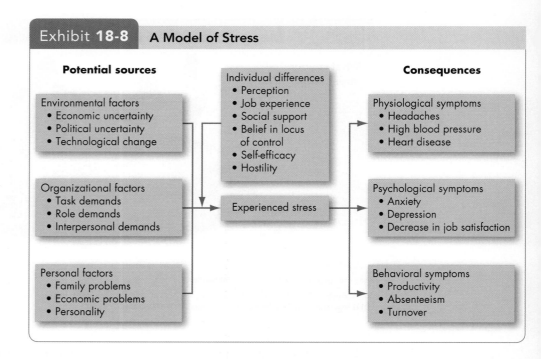

Exhibit 18-8 **A Model of Stress**

Potential sources

Environmental factors
• Economic uncertainty
• Political uncertainty
• Technological change

Organizational factors
• Task demands
• Role demands
• Interpersonal demands

Personal factors
• Family problems
• Economic problems
• Personality

Individual differences
• Perception
• Job experience
• Social support
• Belief in locus
  of control
• Self-efficacy
• Hostility

Experienced stress

Consequences

Physiological symptoms
• Headaches
• High blood pressure
• Heart disease

Psychological symptoms
• Anxiety
• Depression
• Decrease in job satisfaction

Behavioral symptoms
• Productivity
• Absenteeism
• Turnover

and experience obsolete in a very short time, computers, robotics, automation, and similar forms of *technological change* are also a threat to many people and cause them stress.

Organizational Factors   There is no shortage of factors within an organization that can cause stress. Pressures to avoid errors or complete tasks in a limited time, work overload, a demanding and insensitive boss, and unpleasant co-workers are a few examples. We've categorized these factors around task, role, and interpersonal demands.[73]

Task demands relate to a person's job. They include the design of the job (its degrees of autonomy, task variety, degree of automation), working conditions, and the physical work layout. Assembly lines can put pressure on people when they perceive the line's speed to be excessive. Working in an overcrowded room or a visible location where noise and interruptions are constant can increase anxiety and stress.[74] As customer service grows ever more important, emotional labor becomes a source of stress.[75] Imagine being a flight attendant for South-west Airlines or a cashier at Starbucks. Do you think you could put on a happy face when you're having a bad day?

Role demands relate to pressures placed on a person as a function of the particular role he or she plays in the organization. Role conflicts create expectations that may be hard to reconcile or satisfy. Role overload occurs when the employee is expected to do more than time permits. Role ambiguity means role expectations are not clearly understood and the employee is not sure what to do. Individuals who face high situational constraints (such as fixed work hours or demanding job responsibilities) are also less able to engage in the proactive coping behaviors that reduce stress levels.[76] When faced with hassles at work, they will not only have higher levels of distress at the time, but they'll also be less likely to take steps to eliminate stressors in the future.

Interpersonal demands are pressures created by other employees. Lack of social support from colleagues and poor interpersonal relationships can cause stress, especially among employees with a high social need. A rapidly growing body of research has also shown that negative co-worker and supervisor behaviors, including fights, bullying, incivility, racial harassment, and sexual harassment, are especially strongly related to stress at work.[77]

Personal Factors   The typical individual works about 40 to 50 hours a week. But the experiences and problems people encounter in the other 120-plus hours can spill over to the job. Our final category, then, is factors in the employee's personal life: family issues, personal economic problems, and inherent personality characteristics.

National surveys consistently show people hold *family* and personal relationships dear. Marital difficulties, the breaking of a close relationship, and discipline troubles with children create stresses employees often can't leave at the front door when they arrive at work.[78]

Regardless of income level—people who make $100,000 per year seem to have as much trouble handling their finances as those who earn $20,000—some people are poor money managers or have wants that exceed their earning capacity. The *economic* problems of overextended financial resources create stress and siphon attention away from work.

Studies in three diverse organizations found that participants who reported stress symptoms before beginning a job reported most of the same variance in stress symptoms 9 months later.[79] The researchers concluded that some people may have an inherent tendency to accentuate negative aspects of the world. If this is true, then a significant individual factor that influences stress is a person's basic disposition. Subsequent research has suggested that stress symptoms expressed on the job may actually originate in the person's personality.[80]

Stressors Are Additive   When we review stressors individually, it's easy to overlook that stress is an additive phenomenon—it builds up.[81] Each new and persistent stressor adds to an individual's stress level. So a single stressor may be relatively unimportant in and of itself, but if added to an already high level of stress, it can be too much. To appraise the total amount of stress an individual is under, we have to sum up his or her opportunity stresses, constraint stresses, and demand stresses.

Individual Differences

Some people thrive on stressful situations, while others are overwhelmed by them. What differentiates people in terms of their ability to handle stress? What individual variables moderate the relationship between *potential* stressors and *experienced* stress? At least four—perception, job experience, social support, and personality—are relevant.

In Chapter 6, we demonstrated that employees react in response to their perception of reality, rather than to reality itself. *Perception,* therefore, will moderate the relationship between a potential stress condition and an employee's reaction to it. Layoffs may cause one person to fear losing his job, while another sees an opportunity to get a large severance allowance and start her own business. So stress potential doesn't lie in objective conditions; rather, it lies in an employee's interpretation of those conditions.

Experience on the job tends to be negatively related to work stress. Why? Two explanations have been offered.[82] First is selective withdrawal. Voluntary turnover is more probable among people who experience more stress. Therefore, people who remain with an organization longer are those with more stress-resistant traits or those more resistant to the stress characteristics of their organization. Second, people eventually develop coping mechanisms to deal with stress. Because this takes time, senior members of the organization are more likely to be fully adapted and should experience less stress.

Photo 18-4 DentalPlans .com employee Kristen Reineke celebrates after scoring a point while playing foosball in the employee lounge. In giving its employees the opportunity to form collegial relationships with each other by playing games like foosball and Wii, DentalPlans provides them with the social support that can lessen the impact of on-the-job stress.

Social support—collegial relationships with co-workers or supervisors—can buffer the impact of stress.[83] This is among the best-documented relationships in the stress literature. Social support acts as a palliative, mitigating the negative effects of even high-strain jobs.

Perhaps the most widely studied *personality* trait in stress is neuroticism, which we discussed in Chapter 5. As you might expect, neurotic individuals are more prone to experience psychological strain.[84] Evidence suggests that neurotic individuals are more prone to believe there are stressors in their work environments, so part of the problem is that they believe their environments are more threatening. They also tend to select less adaptive coping mechanisms, relying on avoidance as a way of dealing with problems rather than attempting to resolve them.[85]

Workaholism is another personal characteristic related to stress levels. Workaholics are people obsessed with their work; they put in an enormous number of hours, think about work even when not working, and create additional work responsibilities to satisfy an inner compulsion to work more. In some ways, they might seem like ideal employees. That's probably why when most people are asked in interviews what their greatest weakness is, they reflexively say, "I just work too hard." However, there is a difference between working hard and working compulsively. Workaholics are not necessarily more productive than other employees, despite their extreme efforts. The strain of putting in such a high level of work effort eventually begins to wear on the workaholic, leading to higher levels of work–life conflict and psychological burnout.[86]

Cultural Differences

Research suggests the job conditions that cause stress show some differences across cultures. One study revealed that whereas U.S. employees were stressed by a lack of control, Chinese employees were stressed by job evaluations and lack of training. It doesn't appear that personality effects on stress are different across cultures, however. One study of employees in Hungary, Italy, the United Kingdom, Israel, and the United States found Type A personality traits (see Chapter 5) predicted stress equally well across countries.[87] A study of

5,270 managers from 20 countries found individuals from individualistic countries such as the United States, Canada, and the United Kingdom experienced higher levels of stress due to work interfering with family than did individuals from collectivist countries in Asia and Latin America.[88] The authors proposed that this may occur because, in collectivist cultures, working extra hours is seen as a sacrifice to help the family, whereas in individualistic cultures, work is seen as a means to personal achievement that takes away from the family.

Evidence suggests that stressors are associated with perceived stress and strains among employees in different countries. In other words, stress is equally bad for employees of all cultures.[89]

SELF-ASSESSMENT LIBRARY

How Stressful Is My Life?

In the Self-Assessment Library (available in MyManagementLab), take assessment III.C.2 (How Stressful Is My Life?).

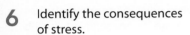

6 Identify the consequences of stress.

Consequences of Stress

Stress shows itself in a number of ways, such as high blood pressure, ulcers, irritability, difficulty making routine decisions, loss of appetite, accident proneness, and the like. These symptoms fit under three general categories: physiological, psychological, and behavioral symptoms.

Physiological Symptoms Most early concern with stress was directed at physiological symptoms because most researchers were specialists in the health and medical sciences. Their work led to the conclusion that stress could create changes in metabolism, increase heart and breathing rates and blood pressure, bring on headaches, and induce heart attacks.

Evidence now clearly suggests stress may have harmful physiological effects. One study linked stressful job demands to increased susceptibility to upper-respiratory illnesses and poor immune system functioning, especially for individuals with low self-efficacy.[90] A long-term study conducted in the United Kingdom found that job strain was associated with higher levels of coronary heart disease.[91] Still another study conducted with Danish human services workers found that higher levels of psychological burnout at the work-unit level were related to significantly higher levels of sickness absence.[92] Many other studies have shown similar results linking work stress to a variety of indicators of poor health.

Psychological Symptoms Job dissatisfaction is an obvious cause of stress. But stress shows itself in other psychological states—for instance, tension, anxiety, irritability, boredom, and procrastination. For example, a study that tracked physiological responses of employees over time found that stress due to high workloads was related to higher blood pressure and lower emotional well-being.[93]

Jobs that make multiple and conflicting demands or that lack clarity about the incumbent's duties, authority, and responsibilities increase both stress and dissatisfaction.[94] Similarly, the less control people have over the pace of their work, the greater their stress and dissatisfaction. Jobs that provide a low level of variety, significance, autonomy, feedback, and identity appear to create stress and reduce satisfaction and involvement in the job.[95] Not everyone reacts to

"When You're Working Hard, Sleep Is Optional"

This is false. Individuals who do not get enough sleep are unable to perform well on the job. A recent study found that sleeplessness costs U.S. employers $63.2 billion per year, almost $2,300 per employee, partially due to decreased productivity and increased safety issues. Sleep deprivation has been cited as a contributing factor in heart disease, obesity, stroke, and cancer. It can also lead to disastrous accidents. For example, U.S. military researchers report that sleep deprivation is one of the top causes of friendly fire (when soldiers mistakenly fire on their own troops), and 20 percent of auto accidents are due to drowsy drivers. More than 160 people on Air India Flight 812 from Dubai to Mangalore were killed when pilot Zlatko Glusica awoke from a nap and, suffering from sleep inertia, overshot the runway in India's third-deadliest air crash.

Sleeplessness is affecting the performance of millions of workers. According to a recent study, one-third of U.S. employees in most industries, and more than one-quarter of workers in the finance and insurance industry, are sleep deprived, getting fewer than 6 hours of sleep per night (7 to 9 are recommended). More than 50 percent of U.S. adults age 19 to 29, 43 percent age 30 to 45, and 38 percent age 46 to 64 report that they rarely or never get a good nightly rest on weekdays.

Research has shown that lack of sleep impairs our ability to learn skills and find solutions, which may be part of the reason law-enforcement organizations, Super Bowl–winning football teams, and half of the *Fortune* 500 companies employ "fatigue management specialists" as performance consultants.

Meanwhile, managers and employees increasingly take prescription sleep aids, attend sleep labs, and consume caffeine in efforts to either sleep better or reduce the effects of sleeplessness on their performance. These methods often backfire. Studies indicate that prescription sleep aids increase sleep time by only 11 minutes and cause short-term memory loss. The effects of sleep labs may not be helpful after the sessions are over. And the diminishing returns of caffeine, perhaps the most popular method of fighting sleep deprivation (74 percent of U.S. adults consume caffeine per day), require the ingestion of increasing amounts to achieve alertness, which can make users jittery before the effect wears off and leave them exhausted.

When you're working hard, it's easy to consider using sleep hours to get the job done, and to think that the stress and adrenaline from working will keep you alert. It's also easy to consider artificial methods in attempts to counteract the negative impact of sleep deprivation. However, research indicates that when it comes to maximizing performance and reducing accidents, we are not even good at assessing our impaired capabilities when we are sleep deprived. In the end, there is no substitute for a solid night's sleep.

Sources: Fatigue Risk Management Science Ltd. Website, www.frmsc.com, accessed June 26, 2013; D. K. Randall, "Decoding the Science of Sleep," *The Wall Street Journal* (August 4–5, 2012), pp. C1–C2; M. Sallinen, J. Onninen, K. Tirkkonen, M.-L. Haavisto, M. Harma, T. Kubo, et al., "Effects of Cumulative Sleep Restriction on Self-Perceptions While Multitasking," *Journal of Sleep Research* (June 2012), pp. 273–281; and P. Walker, "Pilot Was Snoring before Air India Crash," *The Guardian* (November 17, 2010), www.guardian.co.uk/world/2010/nov/17/sleepy-pilot-blamed-air-india-crash.

autonomy in the same way, however. For those with an external locus of control, increased job control increases the tendency to experience stress and exhaustion.[96]

Behavioral Symptoms Research on behavior and stress has been conducted across several countries and over time, and the relationships appear relatively consistent. Behavior-related stress symptoms include reductions in productivity, absence, and turnover, as well as changes in eating habits, increased smoking or consumption of alcohol, rapid speech, fidgeting, and sleep disorders.[97]

A significant amount of research has investigated the stress–performance relationship. The most widely studied pattern of this relationship is the inverted U shown in Exhibit 18-9.[98] The logic underlying the figure is that low to moderate levels of stress stimulate the body and increase its ability to react. Individuals then often perform their tasks better, more intensely, or more rapidly. But too much stress places unattainable demands on a person, which result in lower

Exhibit 18-9	The Proposed Inverted-U Relationship Between Stress and Job Performance

performance. In spite of the popularity and intuitive appeal of the inverted-U model, it doesn't get a lot of empirical support.[99] So we should be careful of assuming it accurately depicts the stress–performance relationship.

As we mentioned earlier, researchers have begun to differentiate challenge and hindrance stressors, showing that these two forms of stress have opposite effects on job behaviors, especially job performance. A meta-analysis of responses from more than 35,000 individuals showed role ambiguity, role conflict, role overload, job insecurity, environmental uncertainty, and situational constraints were all consistently negatively related to job performance.[100] There is also evidence that challenge stress improves job performance in a supportive work environment, whereas hindrance stress reduces job performance in all work environments.[101]

Managing Stress

7 Contrast the individual and organizational approaches to managing stress.

Because low to moderate levels of stress can be functional and lead to higher performance, management may not be concerned when employees experience them. Employees, however, are likely to perceive even low levels of stress as undesirable. It's not unlikely, therefore, for employees and management to have different notions of what constitutes an acceptable level of stress on the job. What management may consider to be "a positive stimulus that keeps the adrenaline running" is very likely to be seen as "excessive pressure" by the employee. Keep this in mind as we discuss individual and organizational approaches toward managing stress.[102]

Individual Approaches   An employee can take personal responsibility for reducing stress levels. Individual strategies that have proven effective include time-management techniques, increased physical exercise, relaxation training, and expanded social support networks.

Many people manage their time poorly. The well-organized employee, like the well-organized student, can often accomplish twice as much as the person who is poorly organized. So an understanding and utilization of basic time-management principles can help individuals better cope with tensions created by job demands.[103] A few of the best-known time-management principles are (1) making daily lists of activities to be accomplished, (2) prioritizing activities by importance and urgency, (3) scheduling activities according to the priorities set, (4) knowing your daily cycle and handling the most demanding parts of your job when you are most alert and productive, and (5) avoiding electronic distractions like frequently checking e-mail, which can limit attention and reduce efficiency.[104] These time-management skills can help minimize procrastination by focusing efforts on immediate goals and boosting motivation even in the face of tasks that are less desirable.[105]

Physicians have recommended noncompetitive *physical exercise*, such as aerobics, walking, jogging, swimming, and riding a bicycle, as a way to deal with excessive stress levels. These activities increase lung capacity, lower the resting heart rate, and provide a mental diversion from work pressures, effectively reducing work-related levels of stress.[106]

Individuals can also teach themselves to reduce tension through *relaxation techniques* such as meditation, hypnosis, and deep breathing. The objective is to

An Ethical Choice

Manager and Employee Stress during Organizational Change

When organizations are in a state of change, employees feel the stress. In fact, a recent study indicated that job pressures, often due to downsizing and other organizational changes, are the second-leading cause of stress. Dealing with that stress has long been in the domain of workers, who could turn to constructive (counselors, health professionals, support networks) or destructive (alcohol, gossip, counterproductive work behaviors) options as coping mechanisms. Employees who couldn't cope with stress suffered job burnout and headed to the unemployment line. But are managers ethically obligated to alleviate employee stress?

Historically, no. Beneficent employers provided employee assistance programs (EAP) through subcontracted counselors or in-house HR departments to counsel employees dealing with stress. Managers simply steered individuals toward these resources when workplace problems indicated a need for intervention. This help often arrived too late to mitigate the negative outcomes of stress such as lost productivity and burnout—and sometimes

too late to save the employee's job. Research suggests that continually occurring job stressors, such as when organizations are in the midst of change, reduce employee engagement because workers are deprived of recovery periods. Employee stress thus needs to be addressed proactively at the manager level if it is to be effective, even before there are negative work outcomes.

On the one hand, managers are responsible for maximizing productivity and realize that organizations increase profitability when fewer employees perform increased work. On the other hand, overwork will increase employee stress, particularly when the organization is in a state of change due to downsizing or growth. Managers who keep head count low and workloads high may find short-term gains from lower workforce costs but long-term losses from negative stress outcomes, such as increased turnover and lowered productivity. Experts recommend that managers consider hiring the workers they need to keep employee workloads reasonable, adding reward programs to keep top employees

engaged, and cutting non-workforce costs to maintain profitability. Smaller methods, such as teaching employees stress reduction techniques and creating a "greenery room" for a nature retreat from the office environment, can also be helpful. Managers must make the ethical choice between spending more money now on labor costs and stress reduction methods versus later on the more hidden but salient costs of employee stress.

As research increasingly indicates, when employees react to stress, they and their organizations suffer the consequences. Managers must, therefore, consider their opportunity to help alleviate the stress before it's too late.

Sources: E. Frauenheim, "Stressed & Pressed," *Workforce Management* (January 2012), pp. 18–22; J. B. Oldroyd and S. S. Morris, "Catching Falling Stars: A Human Resource Responses to Social Capital's Detrimental Effect of Information Overload on Star Employees," *Academy of Management Review* 37 (2012), pp. 396–418; and S. Sonnentag, E. J. Mojza, E. Demerouti, and A. B. Bakker, "Reciprocal Relations Between Recovery and Work Engagement: The Moderating Role of Job Stressors," *Journal of Applied Psychology* 97 (2012), pp. 842–853.

reach a state of deep physical relaxation, in which you focus all your energy on release of muscle tension.[107] Deep relaxation for 15 or 20 minutes a day releases strain and provides a pronounced sense of peacefulness, as well as significant changes in heart rate, blood pressure, and other physiological factors. A growing body of research shows that simply taking breaks from work at routine intervals can facilitate psychological recovery and reduce stress significantly and may improve job performance, and these effects are even greater if relaxation techniques are employed.[108]

As we have noted, friends, family, or work colleagues can provide an outlet when stress levels become excessive. Expanding your *social support network* provides someone to hear your problems and offer a more objective perspective on a stressful situation than your own.

Organizational Approaches   Several organizational factors that cause stress—particularly task and role demands—are controlled by management and thus can be modified or changed. Strategies to consider include improved employee selection and job placement, training, realistic goal-setting, redesign of jobs, increased employee involvement, improved organizational communication, employee sabbaticals, and corporate wellness programs.

Certain jobs are more stressful than others but, as we've seen, individuals differ in their response to stressful situations. We know individuals with little experience or an external locus of control tend to be more prone to stress. *Selection and placement* decisions should take these facts into consideration. Obviously, management shouldn't restrict hiring to only experienced individuals with an internal locus, but such individuals may adapt better to high-stress jobs and perform those jobs more effectively. Similarly, *training* can increase an individual's self-efficacy and thus lessen job strain.

We discussed *goal-setting* in Chapter 7. Individuals perform better when they have specific and challenging goals and receive feedback on their progress toward these goals. Goals can reduce stress as well as provide motivation.[109] Employees who are highly committed to their goals and see purpose in their jobs experience less stress, because they are more likely to perceive stressors as challenges rather than hindrances. Specific goals perceived as attainable clarify performance expectations. In addition, goal feedback reduces uncertainties about actual job performance. The result is less employee frustration, role ambiguity, and stress.

Redesigning jobs to give employees more responsibility, more meaningful work, more autonomy, and increased feedback can reduce stress because these factors give employees greater control over work activities and lessen dependence on others. But as we noted in our discussion of work design, not all employees want enriched jobs. The right redesign for employees with a low need for growth might be less responsibility and increased specialization. If individuals prefer structure and routine, reducing skill variety should also reduce uncertainties and stress levels.

Role stress is detrimental to a large extent because employees feel uncertain about goals, expectations, how they'll be evaluated, and the like. By giving these employees a voice in the decisions that directly affect their job performance, management can increase employee control and reduce role stress. Thus, managers should consider *increasing employee involvement* in decision making because evidence clearly shows that increases in employee empowerment reduce psychological strain.[110]

Increasing formal *organizational communication* with employees reduces uncertainty by lessening role ambiguity and role conflict. Given the importance that perceptions play in moderating the stress–response relationship,

Photo 18-5 Corporate wellness programs are one way organizations can help employees manage stress. As part of its wellness and fitness initiatives, the Fowler White Boggs law firm brings in yoga instructors during employees' lunch hour to lead them in stretching and breathing exercises that help relieve stress and promote a sense of well-being.

Source: ZUMA Press, Inc./Alamy

wellness programs *Organizationally supported programs that focus on the employee's total physical and mental condition.*

management can also use effective communications as a means to shape employee perceptions. Remember that what employees categorize as demands, threats, or opportunities at work is an interpretation and that interpretation can be affected by the symbols and actions communicated by management.

Some employees need an occasional escape from the frenetic pace of their work. Companies including Genentech, American Express, Intel, General Mills, Microsoft, Morningstar, DreamWorks Animation, and Adobe Systems have begun to provide extended voluntary leaves.[111] These *sabbaticals*—ranging in length from a few weeks to several months—allow employees to travel, relax, or pursue personal projects that consume time beyond normal vacations. Proponents say they can revive and rejuvenate workers who might otherwise be headed for burnout.

Our final suggestion is organizationally supported **wellness programs**. These typically provide workshops to help people quit smoking, control alcohol use, lose weight, eat better, and develop a regular exercise program; they focus on the employee's total physical and mental condition.[112] Some help employees improve their psychological health as well. A meta-analysis of 36 programs designed to reduce stress (including wellness programs) showed that interventions to help employees reframe stressful situations and use active coping strategies appreciably reduced stress levels.[113] Most wellness programs assume employees need to take personal responsibility for their physical and mental health and that the organization is merely a means to that end.

Most firms that have introduced wellness programs have found significant benefits. A study of eight Canadian organizations found that every dollar spent on comprehensive wellness programs generated a return of $1.64, and for high-risk employees, such as smokers, the return was nearly $4.00.[114]

Summary

The need for change has been implied throughout this text. For instance, think about attitudes, motivation, work teams, communication, leadership, organizational structures, human resource practices, and organizational cultures. Change was an integral part in our discussion of each. If environments were perfectly static, if employees' skills and abilities were always up to date and incapable of deteriorating, and if tomorrow were always exactly the same as today, organizational change would have little or no relevance to managers. But the real world is turbulent, requiring organizations and their members to undergo dynamic change if they are to perform at competitive levels.

Implications for Managers

- Consider that, as a manager, you are a change agent in your organization. The decisions you make and your role-modeling behaviors will help shape the organization's change culture.
- Your management policies and practices will determine the degree to which the organization learns and adapts to changing environmental factors.
- Some stress is good. Low to moderate amounts of stress enable many people to perform their jobs better by increasing their work intensity, alertness, and ability to react. This is especially true if stress arises due to challenges on the job rather than hindrances that prevent employees from doing their jobs effectively.
- You can help alleviate harmful workplace stress for your employees by accurately matching workloads to employees, providing employees with stress-coping resources, and responding to their concerns.
- You can identify extreme stress in your employees when performance declines, turnover increases, health-related absenteeism increases, and engagement declines. However, by the time these symptoms are visible, it may be too late to be helpful, so stay alert for early indicators and be proactive.

Responsible Managers Relieve Stress for Their Employees

One of the reasons the economic recovery has been sluggish is that employers have been reluctant to replace those they laid off. If you can produce the same amount or provide the same service with fewer employees, that's efficient, of course. But is it a short-sighted way to manage? Evidence suggests that employees are at their breaking point—and employers will pay a price just like the employees they are stressing.

Employees are really stressed. More work is being done with fewer people. Workers wonder whether they will be the "next shoe to fall" in layoffs. In a recent survey of managers, 81 percent agreed worker stress and fatigue is a greater problem than in the past.

Says one Sacramento, California, employee, "I can't remember the last time I went out for lunch. I bring my lunch and eat at my desk," she says. She can't even complain to her husband because he's the same boat—working 10-hour days and "coming home late and exhausted."

Some employers are long-sighted enough to address the problem.

Tony Schwartz, CEO of a consulting firm, decided to institute a program he called "Take Back Your Lunch." He encourages his employees to take a lunch break and even urges them to organize midday gatherings with social networking site Meetup.com.

Another company with progressive management is the accounting firm Ernst & Young. Of the company's 23,000 employees, about 10 percent work under flexible arrangements where they can work less or adopt a more flexible schedule during nonpeak times.

These companies have found that taking the long view and emphasizing balance helps good employees be more productive over the long-term—and more likely to stick around. "We listen to our people and they tell us very consistently that flexibility in incredibly important to them and to their family," said James Turley, Ernst & Young's CEO.

It is not hard to find employees who think they're overworked and underpaid. If a company managed according to worker complaints, the squeakiest wheel would always get the grease. Sure, people might work fewer hours and feel less stressed, but that would compromise an organization's ability to be competitive and to reward its hardest-working and most productive employees.

Labor is often the largest single cost for an employer, which means that if it is to be competitive, the firm needs to earn more revenue per employee. It doesn't take a math genius to realize that one way of accomplishing that is to pay attention to the denominator. It's that magical thing we call "productivity," a central metric by which we can measure the organization's performance. Organizations that are productive today enjoy higher earnings later.

Take Deutsche Bank as an example. The number of front-office employees in Deutsche Bank's investment banking division has fallen 12 percent from pre-crisis levels, while net revenue per employee has increased 20 percent. That sounds like a well-managed company, doesn't it? Yet Deutsche Bank employees probably do feel they're working harder. They are. What would you think of a company if the story instead was, "Net revenue per employee has fallen 20 percent, but employees feel much less stressed at work"? We don't live in a world where companies have the luxury of doing less with more.

Managers shouldn't go out of their way to stress out their employees. Nor should they turn a blind eye toward burnout. But realistically, in today's globally competitive business environment, the organizations that will survive are those that can do more with less. If that means employees are stressed by higher workloads, well, it beats the unemployment line, doesn't it?

Sources: S. Greenhouse, "The Retention Bonus? Time," *The New York Times* (January 8, 2011), pp. B1, B7; M. V. Rafter, "The Yawning of a New Era," *Workforce Management* (December 2010), pp. 3–4; and M. Turner, "Deutsche Says It Does More with Less," *Financial News* (June 2, 2011), downloaded on July 19, 2011, from www.efinancialnews.com/.

END-OF-CHAPTER REVIEW

MyManagementLab   Go to **mymanagementlab.com** to complete the problems marked with this icon. ⭐

QUESTIONS FOR REVIEW

18-1 What is the difference between planned and unplanned change?

18-2 What forces act as sources of resistance to change?

18-3 What are the four main approaches to managing organizational change?

18-4 How can managers create a culture for change?

18-5 What are the possible sources of stress?

18-6 What are the consequences of stress?

18-7 What are the individual and organizational approaches to managing stress?

EXPERIENTIAL EXERCISE Strategizing Change

Objectives

1. To think through the obstacles organizations encounter when they initiate change.

2. To consider solutions to increase the probability of meeting the organization's change goals.

Time

Approximately 20 minutes.

The Situation

TutorMe is a midsize company that employs 45 former teachers as tutors in public and private schools, in the company's branches and corporate headquarters, and at home via phone and Internet. The firm employs a support staff of 15. TutorMe used to be the only such company in the area, but two new tutoring chains recently opened branches nearby. Online tutoring firms have added competition as well.

TutorMe is beginning to struggle because it is no longer the only provider. Its organizational culture could best be described as "lackadaisical" and its business practices as "loose." Although it provides a meaningful service to students, many of its tutors use their own methods instead of following the TutorMe manuals. Tutor pay is low and benefits are near zero. But the tutors are skilled teachers who appreciate the opportunity to use their expertise in a flexible work situation, and turnover is low.

TutorMe's facilities look "tired" and are located in mostly abandoned strip malls far from well-traveled roads. The corporate headquarters is a bit nicer and in a more visible location. But the managers often don't know what the tutors are doing, and billing practices are chaotic. There is no HR department, so the business staff handles both payments and employee issues, mostly by creating further problems that upper management must settle. The pay for the business staff is mid-range for the area with standard benefits, but high staff turnover has been an accepted part of TutorMe's business.

Upper management understands the company needs to change to survive, so its executives hired consultants to diagnose what TutorMe needs. The consultants believe the company should (1) eliminate some of its less-used branches, (2) relocate other branches to more visible locations, (3) train tutors with the TutorMe manuals and insist on standardization of teaching practices, (4) overhaul the organizational culture to reflect a commitment to tutoring excellence, and (5) train and set expectations for the business staff to raise performance levels and tighten accountability.

The consultants have warned TutorMe management that recent studies indicate only 30 to 43 percent of organizations achieve their goals for change initiatives. They have outlined the following specific obstacles and offered to help TutorMe be successful in its transformation:

1. Lack of adoption and commitment from top management.
2. Employee resistance.
3. Manager resistance.
4. Insufficient communication.
5. Budget overages and project delays.
6. Employees and managers who ignore the new policies and procedures.

The Procedure

Break into groups of three to four members. Each group will act as the consultants to guide TutorMe through the change process. Your group will need to come to a consensus, in writing, for each of the following assignments.

18-8. First, gather all you know about TutorMe's current business practices. Write down the reasons tutors stay while staff turnover is high. Decide what is currently working for TutorMe. What is not working and needed change even before competition came in?

18-9. Based on what you determine about TutorMe's business practices, do you agree or disagree with each of the consultants' five recommendations? Why or why not?

18-10. Now consider the six obstacles the consultants have identified, the five recommendations, and your answer to question 18-8. Which of the obstacles do you think will present problems for achieving the five recommendations? How? Make a list.

18-11. From your list in question 18-10, write down your targeted, informed recommendations for overcoming the obstacles. Also consider what further information would you like from the company.

18-12. Bring the class together, and discuss your recommendations from question 18-11.

Sources: D. Meinert, "Communicate Early and Often," *HR Magazine* (November 2012), p. 36; D. Meinert, "Define the Goals," *HR Magazine* (November 2012), pp. 32–33; and D. Meinert, "Wings of Change," *HR Magazine* (November 2012), pp. 30–32.

ETHICAL DILEMMA Changes at WPAC

WPAC—a television station based in Yuma, Arizona—had been experiencing a ratings decline for several years. In 2009, the station switched from a CBS to NBC affiliate. That has explained some of the ratings decline. However, in recent months, the ratings have continued to slide. Eventually, the station manager, Lucien Stone, decided he had to make a change to the local newscast.

After meeting with the programming manager, Stone called a meeting of WPAC employees and announced his intention to "spice things up" during the 5 P.M. and 10 P.M. local news. The 30-minute broadcasts would still include the traditional "top stories," "sports," and "weather" segments. However, on slow news days, more attention-getting material would be used. Stone also indicated some programming decisions would probably be revisited. "The days of *Little House on the Prairie* are over," he said.

Madison Devereaux, 29, had been the chief meteorologist for WPAC since 2010. After receiving her degree in meteorology from the University of Oklahoma in 2007, she

joined WPAC and quickly worked her way up the ranks, impressing viewers and WPAC management alike with her extension knowledge and articulate, professional, mistake-free delivery.

Though she was Christian, Devereaux never was one to go around "thumping Bibles in the newsroom," as she put it. Most of those at WPAC weren't even aware of her religious views.

Devereaux was troubled by the announced changes to WPAC's programming but didn't speak up at the time. One Monday during a pre-production meeting, she learned that on Thursday of that week, WPAC reporter Sam Berkshow would present a segment called "Dancing Around the Economy," which would focus on how local strip clubs were doing well despite the sluggish economy.

Devereaux didn't think it was appropriate to air the segment during the 5 P.M. newscast and asked both her producer and Stone to reconsider the piece, or at least air it in the 10 P.M. time slot. When they refused, she asked whether she could take the day off when the segment aired. Stone again refused. This was "sweeps week" (when ratings are calculated), Stone wanted to air the story, and Devereaux's contract prohibited her from taking time off during sweeps week.

When Devereaux didn't show up for work that Thursday, WPAC fired her, arguing she had breached her contract.

For her part, Devereaux said, "I'm not angry with the station, but I am sorry about the changes that have taken place."

Questions

18-13. Do you think either party behaved unethically in this case? If so, why?

18-14. If you shared Devereaux's views, would you have handled the situation differently? How?

⭐ **18-15.** Drawing on Kotter's eight-step plan for implementing change, how might WPAC have handled its planned change differently?

Sources: Based on C. Edelhart, "Weatherman's Stand Against Story Costs Job," *Californian* (May 16, 2011), downloaded July 7, 2011, from www.bakersfield.com/; and K. T. Phan, "ABC Affiliate Fires Christian over Strip Club Segment," *Fox News* (May 10, 2011), www.nation.foxnews.com.

CASE INCIDENT 1 Starbucks Returns to Its Roots

You are probably so used to seeing Starbucks coffee shops everywhere that you might not realize the company went from just 11 stores in 1987 to 2,600 in the year 2000. This incredibly rapid growth sprang from the company's ability to create a unique experience for customers who wanted to buy its distinct brand of lattes and mochas wherever they found themselves. At Starbucks' core, there was also a culture of treating each customer as a valued guest who should feel comfortable relaxing and taking in the ambience of the store. Whether you were in the company's founding location in Seattle, Washington, or at the other end of the country in Miami, Florida, you knew what to expect when you went to a Starbucks.

This uniform culture was truly put to the test in the face of massive expansion, however, and by 2006 Starbucks' chairman and former CEO Howard Schultz knew something had gone wrong. He noted that "As I visited hundreds of Starbucks stores in cities around the world, the entrepreneurial merchant in me sensed that something intrinsic to Starbucks' brand was missing. An aura. A spirit. The stores were lacking a certain soul." Starbucks' performance had become lackluster, with hundreds of planned store openings being canceled and hundreds more stores being closed.

So, Schultz took the dramatic step of coming back as CEO and engaging in a companywide effort to change the corporate culture back to what it had been before its expansion. All 7,000 Starbucks stores were closed for a single afternoon as part of a training effort of 135,000 baristas. Quality control was a primary mission; baristas were instructed to pour every glass of espresso like honey from

a spoon, to preserve the flavor. This emphasis on quality over speed ran counter to the principles of mass production, but it was just what the company needed to ensure it could retain its culture. Espresso machines that obscured the customers' view were replaced with lower-profile machines that allowed baristas to look directly at guests while making beverages. And "assembly-line production," like making several drinks at once, was discouraged in favor of slowly making each drink for each customer.

Schultz is convinced his efforts to take the culture back to its roots as a neighborhood coffee shop—one entranced with the "romance of coffee" and treating every customer as an old friend—has saved the company. Today, Starbucks earns more than $3.6 billion in quarterly revenue and operates more than 18,000 stores in 60 countries around the globe.

Questions

18-16. What factors are most likely to change when a company grows very rapidly, as Starbucks did? How can these changes threaten the culture of an organization?

18-17. Why might this type of radical change process be easier for Starbucks to implement than it would be for other companies?

⭐ **18-18.** A great deal of the return to an original culture has been credited to Howard Schultz, who acted as an idea champion. Explain how Schultz's efforts to change the Starbucks culture fit with our discussion of culture change earlier in the chapter.

Sources: Associated Press, "High New York Court: Starbucks Baristas Must Share Tips," *CBS New York* (June 26, 2013), http://newyork.cbslocal.com/2013/06/26/high-n-y-court-starbucks-baristas-must-share-tips/; H. Schultz, "How Starbucks Got Its Mojo Back," *Newsweek* (March 21, 2011), www.newsweek .com; A. Ignatius, "We Had to Own the Mistakes," *Harvard Business Review* (July/August 2010), pp. 108–115; and R. Baker, "Starbucks Demonstrates Power of Brand," *Marketing Week* (April 28, 2011), www.marketingweek.co.uk.

CASE INCIDENT 2 When Companies Fail to Change

The Triniton TV, transistor radio, Walkman, and VCR are the stuff of time capsules nowadays, but not long ago they were cutting-edge technology. Japan was at the pinnacle of the home consumer electronics industry from the 1970s to the 1990s, introducing new innovations to the world each year. Now those same Japanese firms are at the back of the pack and struggling to stay in the game. Japanese electronics production has fallen by more than 41 percent, and Japan's global market share of electronics goods and services has decreased by more than half since 2000. Sony, for example, hasn't earned a profit since 2008. What happened?

The simple answer is failure to innovate. While firms outside Japan pioneered digital technology and conquered the Internet, Japanese firms stuck to semiconductors and hardware. But the deeper issue is the refusal of Japanese managers to adapt to the changing global environment and to change their organizations accordingly. For instance, Sony mastered the technology needed for a digital music player years before Apple introduced the iPod in 2001, but its engineers resisted the change. Sony's divisions would not cooperate with one another fast enough to compete in this market or in the new market for flat-screen TVs. Even now, Sony has not managed to change its organization to reflect current global thinking in the industry. For instance, they and other Japanese firms make a larger number of products than most of their global competitors. Former Sony executive Yoshiaki

Sakito said, "Sony makes too many models, and for none of them can they say, 'This contains our best, most cutting-edge technology.' Apple, on the other hand, makes one amazing phone in just two colors and says, 'This is the one.'"

For Japanese electronics companies to survive, they must change. They were once able to structure their organizations around abundant, inexpensive labor to keep costs down and prices competitive, but that's no longer the case. One complicating factor is that Japan is an ancient country of many traditions, with a low birth rate and an aging population. The country's culture will make it even more difficult to realign to globalization. It now must change to foster innovation, which may involve a cultural as much as an organizational transformation.

Questions

18-19. What made the Japanese electronics industry initially successful?

18-20. Why is the Japanese electronics industry no longer a success story?

18-21. What types of organizational changes would you advise Japanese electronics managers to consider?

18-22. How do you think Japanese demographic trends have been a factor in the innovation problem?

Sources: H. Hiyama, "Sony Break-Up Call Shines Light on Electronics Industry Problems," *Japan Today* (June 7, 2013), www.japantoday.com/category/opinions/view/sony-break-up-call-shines-light-on-electronic-industry-problems; R. Katz, "How Japan Blew Its Lead in Electronics," *The Wall Street Journal* (March 23, 2012), p. A15; and H. Tabuchi, "How the Parade Passed Sony By," *The New York Times* (April 15, 2012), pp. B1, B7.

MyManagementLab

Go to **mymanagementlab.com** for Auto-graded writing questions as well as the following Assisted-graded writing questions:

18-23. In considering Case Incident 1 , assume Schultz's change initiative might succeed at another company that values customization and high levels of customer service. How would it need to differ at a firm that emphasizes speed and efficiency of service?

18-24. In regard to Case Incident 2 , only 13 of the top 21 U.S. electronics manufacturers today were in existence in 1970 (and 6 were smaller than *Fortune* 500 firms), while there have been no new top Japanese electronics manufacturers for more than 50 years. How do you think their age affects the ability of Japanese firms to bring about the changes they need to be competitive?

18-25. MyManagementLab Only—comprehensive writing assignment for this chapter.

Appendix   Research in Organizational Behavior

A number of years ago, a friend of mine was excited because he had read about the findings from a research study that finally, once and for all, resolved the question of what it takes to make it to the top in a large corporation. I doubted there was any simple answer to this question but, not wanting to dampen his enthusiasm, I asked him to tell me of what he had read. The answer, according to my friend, was *participation in college athletics*. To say I was skeptical of his claim is a gross understatement, so I asked him to tell me more.

The study encompassed 1,700 successful senior executives at the 500 largest U.S. corporations. The researchers found that half of these executives had played varsity-level college sports.[1] My friend, who happens to be good with statistics, informed me that since fewer than 2 percent of all college students participate in intercollegiate athletics, the probability of this finding occurring by mere chance is less than 1 in 10 million! He concluded his analysis by telling me that, based on this research, I should encourage my management students to get into shape and to make one of the varsity teams.

My friend was somewhat perturbed when I suggested that his conclusions were likely to be flawed. These executives were all males who attended college in the 1940s and 1950s. Would his advice be meaningful to females in the twenty-first century? These executives also weren't your typical college students. For the most part, they had attended elite private colleges such as Princeton and Amherst, where a large proportion of the student body participates in intercollegiate sports. And these "jocks" hadn't necessarily played football or basketball; many had participated in golf, tennis, baseball, cross-country running, crew, rugby, and similar minor sports. Moreover, maybe the researchers had confused the direction of causality. That is, maybe individuals with the motivation and ability to make it to the top of a large corporation are drawn to competitive activities like college athletics.

My friend was guilty of misusing research data. Of course, he is not alone. We are all continually bombarded with reports of experiments that link certain substances to cancer in mice and surveys that show changing attitudes toward sex among college students, for example. Many of these studies are carefully designed, with great caution taken to note the implications and limitations of the findings. But some studies are poorly designed, making their conclusions at best suspect, and at worst meaningless.

Rather than attempting to make you a researcher, the purpose of this appendix is to increase your awareness as a consumer of behavioral research. A knowledge of research methods will allow you to appreciate more fully the care in data collection that underlies the information and conclusions presented in this text. Moreover, an understanding of research methods will make you a more skilled evaluator of the OB studies you will encounter in business and professional journals. So an appreciation of behavioral research is important because (1) it's the foundation on which the theories in this text are built, and (2) it will benefit you in future years when you read reports of research and attempt to assess their value.

Purposes of Research

Research is concerned with the systematic gathering of information. Its purpose is to help us in our search for the truth. Although we will never find ultimate truth—in our case, that would be to know precisely how any person or group would behave in any organizational context—ongoing research adds to our body of OB knowledge by supporting some theories, contradicting others, and suggesting new theories to replace those that fail to gain support.

Research Terminology

Researchers have their own vocabulary for communicating among themselves and with outsiders. The following briefly defines some of the more popular terms you're likely to encounter in behavioral science studies.[2]

Variable

A *variable* is any general characteristic that can be measured and that changes in amplitude, intensity, or both. Some examples of OB variables found in this textbook are job satisfaction, employee productivity, work stress, ability, personality, and group norms.

Hypothesis

A tentative explanation of the relationship between two or more variables is called a *hypothesis*. My friend's statement that participation in college athletics leads to a top executive position in a large corporation is an example of a hypothesis. Until confirmed by empirical research, a hypothesis remains only a tentative explanation.

Dependent Variable

A *dependent variable* is a response that is affected by an independent variable. In terms of the hypothesis, it is the variable that the researcher is interested in explaining. Referring back to our opening example, the dependent variable in my friend's hypothesis was executive succession. In organizational behavior research, the most popular dependent variables are productivity, absenteeism, turnover, job satisfaction, and organizational commitment.[3]

Independent Variable

An *independent variable* is the presumed cause of some change in the dependent variable. Participating in varsity athletics was the independent variable in my friend's hypothesis. Popular independent variables studied by OB researchers include intelligence, personality, job satisfaction, experience, motivation, reinforcement patterns, leadership style, reward allocations, selection methods, and organization design.

You may have noticed we said that job satisfaction is frequently used by OB researchers as both a dependent and an independent variable. This is not an error. It merely reflects that the label given to a variable depends on its place in the hypothesis. In the statement "Increases in job satisfaction lead to reduced turnover," job satisfaction is an independent variable. However, in the statement "Increases in money lead to higher job satisfaction," job satisfaction becomes a dependent variable.

Moderating Variable

A *moderating variable* abates the effect of the independent variable on the dependent variable. It might also be thought of as the contingency variable: If X (independent variable), then Y (dependent variable) will occur, but only under conditions Z (moderating variable). To translate this into a real-life example, we might say that if we increase the amount of direct supervision in the work area (X), then there will be a change in worker productivity (Y), but this effect will be moderated by the complexity of the tasks being performed (Z).

Causality

A hypothesis, by definition, implies a relationship. That is, it implies a presumed cause and effect. This direction of cause and effect is called *causality*. Changes in the independent variable are assumed to cause changes in the dependent variable. However, in behavioral research, it's possible to make an incorrect assumption of causality when relationships are found. For example,

early behavioral scientists found a relationship between employee satisfaction and productivity. They concluded that a happy worker was a productive worker. Follow-up research has supported the relationship, but disconfirmed the direction of the arrow. The evidence more correctly suggests that high productivity leads to satisfaction rather than the other way around.

Correlation Coefficient

It's one thing to know that there is a relationship between two or more variables. It's another to know the *strength* of that relationship. The term *correlation coefficient* is used to indicate that strength, and is expressed as a number between −1.00 (a perfect negative relationship) and +1.00 (a perfect positive correlation).

When two variables vary directly with one another, the correlation will be expressed as a positive number. When they vary inversely—that is, one increases as the other decreases—the correlation will be expressed as a negative number. If the two variables vary independently of each other, we say that the correlation between them is zero.

For example, a researcher might survey a group of employees to determine the satisfaction of each with his or her job. Then, using company absenteeism reports, the researcher could correlate the job satisfaction scores against individual attendance records to determine whether employees who are more satisfied with their jobs have better attendance records than their counterparts who indicated lower job satisfaction. Let's suppose the researcher found a correlation coefficient of +0.50 between satisfaction and attendance. Would that be a strong association? There is, unfortunately, no precise numerical cutoff separating strong and weak relationships. A standard statistical test would need to be applied to determine whether the relationship was a significant one.

A final point needs to be made before we move on: A correlation coefficient measures only the strength of association between two variables. A high value does *not* imply causality. The length of women's skirts and stock market prices, for instance, have long been noted to be highly correlated, but one should be careful not to infer that a causal relationship between the two exists. In this instance, the high correlation is more happenstance than predictive.

Theory

The final term we introduce in this section is *theory*. Theory describes a set of systematically interrelated concepts or hypotheses that purports to explain and predict phenomena. In OB, theories are also frequently referred to as *models*. We use the two terms interchangeably.

There are no shortages of theories in OB. For instance, we have theories to describe what motivates people, the most effective leadership styles, the best way to resolve conflicts, and how people acquire power. In some cases, we have half a dozen or more separate theories that purport to explain and predict a given phenomenon. In such cases, is one right and the others wrong? No! They tend to reflect science at work—researchers testing previous theories, modifying them, and, when appropriate, proposing new models that may prove to have higher explanatory and predictive powers. Multiple theories attempting to explain common phenomena merely attest that OB is an active discipline, still growing and evolving.

Evaluating Research

As a potential consumer of behavioral research, you should follow the dictum of *caveat emptor*—let the buyer beware! In evaluating any research study, you need to ask three questions.[4]

Is it valid? Is the study actually measuring what it claims to be measuring? A number of psychological tests have been discarded by employers in recent years because they have not been found to be valid measures of the applicants' ability to do a given job successfully. But the validity issue is relevant to all research studies. So, if you find a study that links cohesive work teams with higher productivity, you want to know how each of these variables was measured and whether it is actually measuring what it is supposed to be measuring.

Is it reliable? Reliability refers to consistency of measurement. If you were to have your height measured every day with a wooden yardstick, you'd get highly reliable results. On the other hand, if you were measured each day by an elastic tape measure, there would probably be considerable disparity between your height measurements from one day to the next. Your height, of course, doesn't change from day to day. The variability is due to the unreliability of the measuring device. So if a company asked a group of its employees to complete a reliable job satisfaction questionnaire, and then repeat the questionnaire six months later, we'd expect the results to be very similar—provided nothing changed in the interim that might significantly affect employee satisfaction.

Is it generalizable? Are the results of the research study generalizable to groups of individuals other than those who participated in the original study? Be aware, for example, of the limitations that might exist in research that uses college students as subjects. Are the findings in such studies generalizable to full-time employees in real jobs? Similarly, how generalizable to the overall work population are the results from a study that assesses job stress among 10 nuclear power plant engineers in the hamlet of Mahone Bay, Nova Scotia?

Research Design

Doing research is an exercise in trade-offs. Richness of information typically comes with reduced generalizability. The more a researcher seeks to control for confounding variables, the less realistic his or her results are likely to be. High precision, generalizability, and control almost always translate into higher costs. When researchers make choices about whom they'll study, where their research will be done, the methods they'll use to collect data, and so on, they must make some concessions. Good research designs are not perfect, but they do carefully reflect the questions being addressed. Keep these facts in mind as we review the strengths and weaknesses of five popular research designs: case studies, field surveys, laboratory experiments, field experiments, and aggregate quantitative reviews.

Case Study

You pick up a copy of Soichiro Honda's autobiography. In it he describes his impoverished childhood; his decisions to open a small garage, assemble motorcycles, and eventually build automobiles; and how this led to the creation of one of the largest and most successful corporations in the world. Or you're in a business class and the instructor distributes a 50-page handout covering two companies: Walmart and Kmart. The handout details the two firms' histories; describes their corporate strategies, management philosophies, and merchandising plans; and includes copies of their recent balance sheets and income statements. The instructor asks the class members to read the handout, analyze the data, and determine why Walmart has been so much more successful than Kmart in recent years.

Soichiro Honda's autobiography and the Walmart and Kmart handouts are case studies. Drawn from real-life situations, case studies present an in-depth analysis of one setting. They are thorough descriptions, rich in details about an individual, a group, or an organization. The primary source of information in case studies is obtained through observation, occasionally backed up by interviews and a review of records and documents.

Case studies have their drawbacks. They're open to the perceptual bias and subjective interpretations of the observer. The reader of a case is captive to what the observer/case writer chooses to include and exclude. Cases also trade off generalizability for depth of information and richness of detail. Because it's always dangerous to generalize from a sample of one, case studies make it difficult to prove or reject a hypothesis. On the other hand, you can't ignore the in-depth analysis that cases often provide. They are an excellent device for initial exploratory research and for evaluating real-life problems in organizations.

Field Survey

A lengthy questionnaire was created to assess the use of ethics policies, formal ethics structures, formalized activities such as ethics training, and executive involvement in ethics programs among billion-dollar corporations. The public affairs or corporate communications office of all *Fortune* 500 industrial firms and 500 service corporations were contacted to get the name and address of the "officer most responsible for dealing with ethics and conduct issues" in each firm. The questionnaire, with a cover letter explaining the nature of the study, was mailed to these 1,000 officers. Of the total, 254 returned a completed questionnaire, for a response rate just above 25 percent. The results of the survey found, among other things, that 77 percent had formal codes of ethics and 54 percent had a single officer specifically assigned to deal with ethics and conduct issues.[5]

The preceding study illustrates a typical field survey. A sample of respondents (in this case, 1,000 corporate officers in the largest U.S. publicly held corporations) was selected to represent a larger group that was under examination (billion-dollar U.S. business firms). The respondents were then surveyed using a questionnaire or interviewed to collect data on particular characteristics (the content and structure of ethics programs and practices) of interest to the researchers. The standardization of response items allows for data to be easily quantified, analyzed, and summarized, and for the researchers to make inferences from the representative sample about the larger population.

The field survey provides economies for doing research. It's less costly to sample a population than to obtain data from every member of that population. (There are, for instance, more than 5,000 U.S. business firms with sales in excess of a billion dollars; and since some of these are privately held and don't release financial data to the public, they are excluded from the *Fortune* list). Moreover, as the ethics study illustrates, field surveys provide an efficient way to find out how people feel about issues or how they say they behave. These data can then be easily quantified.

But the field survey has a number of potential weaknesses. First, mailed questionnaires rarely obtain 100 percent returns. Low response rates call into question whether conclusions based on respondents' answers are generalizable to nonrespondents. Second, the format is better at tapping respondents' attitudes and perceptions than behaviors. Third, responses can suffer from social desirability; that is, people saying what they think the researcher wants to hear. Fourth, since field surveys are designed to focus on specific issues, they're a relatively poor means of acquiring depth of information. Finally, the quality of the generalizations is largely a factor of the population chosen. Responses from executives at *Fortune* 500 firms, for instance, tell us nothing about small- or medium-sized firms or not-for-profit organizations. In summary, even a well-designed field survey trades off depth of information for breadth, generalizability, and economic efficiencies.

Laboratory Experiment

The following study is a classic example of the laboratory experiment. A researcher, Stanley Milgram, wondered how far individuals would go in following commands. If subjects were placed in the role of a teacher in a learning experiment and told by an experimenter to administer a shock to a learner each time that learner made a mistake, would the subjects follow the commands of the experimenter? Would their willingness to comply decrease as the intensity of the shock was increased?

To test these hypotheses, Milgram hired a set of subjects. Each was led to believe that the experiment was to investigate the effect of punishment on memory. Their job was to act as teachers and administer punishment whenever the learner made a mistake on the learning test.

Punishment was administered by an electric shock. The subject sat in front of a shock generator with 30 levels of shock—beginning at zero and progressing in 15-volt increments to a high of 450 volts. The demarcations of these positions ranged from "Slight Shock" at 15 volts to "Danger: Severe Shock" at 450 volts. To increase the realism of the experiment, the subjects received a sample shock of 45 volts and saw the learner—a pleasant, mild-mannered man about 50 years old—strapped into an "electric chair" in an adjacent room. Of course, the learner was an actor, and the electric shocks were phony, but the subjects didn't know this.

Taking his seat in front of the shock generator, the subject was directed to begin at the lowest shock level and to increase the shock intensity to the next level each time the learner made a mistake or failed to respond.

When the test began, the shock intensity rose rapidly because the learner made many errors. The subject got verbal feedback from the learner: At 75 volts, the learner began to grunt and moan; at 150 volts, he demanded to be released from the experiment; at 180 volts, he cried out that he could no longer stand the pain; and at 300 volts, he insisted that he be let out, yelled about his heart condition, screamed, and then failed to respond to further questions.

Most subjects protested and, fearful they might kill the learner if the increased shocks were to bring on a heart attack, insisted they could not go on with their job. Hesitations or protests by the subject were met by the experimenter's statement, "You have no choice, you must go on! Your job is to punish the learner's mistakes." Of course, the subjects did have a choice. All they had to do was stand up and walk out.

The majority of the subjects dissented. But dissension isn't synonymous with disobedience. Sixty-two percent of the subjects increased the shock level to the maximum of 450 volts. The average level of shock administered by the remaining 38 percent was nearly 370 volts.[6]

In a laboratory experiment such as that conducted by Milgram, an artificial environment is created by the researcher. Then the researcher manipulates an independent variable under controlled conditions. Finally, since all other things are held equal, the researcher is able to conclude that any change in the dependent variable is due to the manipulation or change imposed on the independent variable. Note that, because of the controlled conditions, the researcher is able to imply causation between the independent and dependent variables.

The laboratory experiment trades off realism and generalizability for precision and control. It provides a high degree of control over variables and precise measurement of those variables. But findings from laboratory studies are often difficult to generalize to the real world of work. This is because the artificial laboratory rarely duplicates the intricacies and nuances of real organizations. In addition, many laboratory experiments deal with phenomena that cannot be reproduced or applied to real-life situations.

Field Experiment

The following is an example of a field experiment. The management of a large company is interested in determining the impact that a four-day workweek would have on employee absenteeism. To be more specific, management wants to know if employees working four 10-hour days have lower absence rates than similar employees working the traditional five-day week of 8 hours each day. Because the company is large, it has a number of manufacturing plants that employ essentially similar workforces. Two of these are chosen for the experiment, both located in the greater Cleveland area. Obviously, it would not be appropriate to compare two similar-sized plants if one is in rural Mississippi and the other is in urban Copenhagen because factors such as national culture, transportation, and weather might be more likely to explain any differences found than changes in the number of days worked per week.

In one plant, the experiment was put into place—workers began the four-day week. At the other plant, which became the control group, no changes were made in the employees' five-day week. Absence data were gathered from the company's records at both locations for a period of 18 months. This extended time period lessened the possibility that any results would be distorted by the mere novelty of changes being implemented in the experimental plant. After 18 months, management found that absenteeism had dropped by 40 percent at the experimental plant, and by only 6 percent in the control plant. Because of the design of this study, management believed that the larger drop in absences at the experimental plant was due to the introduction of the compressed workweek.

The field experiment is similar to the laboratory experiment except it is conducted in a real organization. The natural setting is more realistic than the laboratory setting, and this enhances validity but hinders control. In addition, unless control groups are maintained, there can be a loss of control if extraneous forces intervene—for example, an employee strike, a major layoff, or a corporate restructuring. Maybe the greatest concern with field studies has to do with organizational selection bias. Not all organizations are going to allow outside researchers to come in and study their employees and operations. This is especially true of organizations that have serious problems. Therefore, since most published studies in OB are done by outside researchers, the selection bias might work toward the publication of studies conducted almost exclusively at successful and well-managed organizations.

Our general conclusion is that, of the four research designs we've discussed to this point, the field experiment typically provides the most valid and generalizable findings and, except for its high cost, trades off the least to get the most.[7]

Aggregate Quantitative Reviews

What's the overall effect of organizational behavior modification (OB Mod) on task performance? There have been a number of field experiments that have sought to throw light on this question. Unfortunately, the wide range of effects from these various studies makes it hard to generalize.

To try to reconcile these diverse findings, two researchers reviewed all the empirical studies they could find on the impact of OB Mod on task performance over a 20-year period.[8] After discarding reports that had inadequate information, had nonquantitative data, or didn't meet all conditions associated with principles of behavioral modification, the researchers narrowed their set to 19 studies that included data on 2,818 individuals. Using an aggregating technique called *meta-analysis*, the researchers were able to synthesize the studies quantitatively and to conclude that the average person's task performance will rise from the 50th percentile to the 67th percentile after an OB Mod intervention.

The OB Mod–task performance review done by these researchers illustrates the use of meta-analysis, a quantitative form of literature review that enables researchers to look at validity findings from a comprehensive set of individual studies, and then apply a formula to them to determine if they consistently produced similar results.[9] If results prove to be consistent, it allows researchers to conclude more confidently that validity is generalizable. Meta-analysis is a means for overcoming the potentially imprecise interpretations of qualitative reviews and to synthesize variations in quantitative studies. In addition, the technique enables researchers to identify potential moderating variables between an independent and a dependent variable.

In the past 25 years, there's been a surge in the popularity of this research method. Why? It appears to offer a more objective means for doing traditional literature reviews. Although the use of meta-analysis requires researchers to make a number of judgment calls, which can introduce a considerable amount of subjectivity into the process, there is no arguing that meta-analysis reviews have now become widespread in the OB literature.

Ethics in Research

Researchers are not always tactful or candid with subjects when they do their studies. For instance, questions in field surveys may be perceived as embarrassing by respondents or as an invasion of privacy. Also, researchers in laboratory studies have been known to deceive participants about the true purpose of their experiment "because they felt deception was necessary to get honest responses."[10]

The "learning experiments" conducted by Stanley Milgram, which were conducted more than 30 years ago, have been widely criticized by psychologists on ethical grounds. He lied to subjects, telling them his study was investigating learning, when, in fact, he was concerned with obedience. The shock machine he used was a fake. Even the "learner" was an accomplice of Milgram's who had been trained to act as if he were hurt and in pain. Yet ethical lapses continue. For instance, in 2001, a professor of organizational behavior at Columbia University sent out a common letter on university letterhead to 240 New York City restaurants in which he detailed how he had eaten at this restaurant with his wife in celebration of their wedding anniversary, how he had gotten food poisoning, and that he had spent the night in his bathroom throwing up.[11] The letter closed with: "Although it is not my intention to file any reports with the Better Business Bureau or the Department of Health, I want you to understand what I went through in anticipation that you will respond accordingly. I await your response." The fictitious letter was part of the professor's study to determine how restaurants responded to complaints. But it created culinary chaos among many of the restaurant owners, managers, and chefs as they reviewed menus and produce deliveries

for possibly spoiled food, and questioned kitchen workers about possible lapses. A follow-up letter of apology from the university for "an egregious error in judgment by a junior faculty member" did little to offset the distress it created for those affected.

Professional associations like the American Psychological Association, the American Sociological Association, and the Academy of Management have published formal guidelines for the conduct of research. Yet the ethical debate continues. On one side are those who argue that strict ethical controls can damage the scientific validity of an experiment and cripple future research. Deception, for example, is often necessary to avoid contaminating results. Moreover, proponents of minimizing ethical controls note that few subjects have been appreciably harmed by deceptive experiments. Even in Milgram's highly manipulative experiment, only 1.3 percent of the subjects reported negative feelings about their experience. The other side of this debate focuses on the rights of participants. Those favoring strict ethical controls argue that no procedure should ever be emotionally or physically distressing to subjects, and that, as professionals, researchers are obliged to be completely honest with their subjects and to protect the subjects' privacy at all costs.

Summary

The subject of organizational behavior is composed of a large number of theories that are research based. Research studies, when cumulatively integrated, become theories, and theories are proposed and followed by research studies designed to validate them. The concepts that make up OB, therefore, are only as valid as the research that supports them.

The topics and issues in this book are for the most part research-derived. They represent the result of systematic information gathering rather than merely hunch, intuition, or opinion. This doesn't mean, of course, that we have all the answers to OB issues. Many require far more corroborating evidence. The generalizability of others is limited by the research methods used. But new information is being created and published at an accelerated rate. To keep up with the latest findings, we strongly encourage you to regularly review the latest research in organizational behavior. More academic work can be found in journals such as the *Academy of Management Journal, Academy of Management Review, Administrative Science Quarterly, Human Relations, Journal of Applied Psychology, Journal of Management, Journal of Organizational Behavior,* and *Leadership Quarterly.* For more practical interpretations of OB research findings, you may want to read the *Academy of Management Executive, California Management Review, Harvard Business Review, Organizational Dynamics,* and the *Sloan Management Review.*

Comprehensive Cases

Managing Motivation in a Difficult Economy

Learning Goals

In this case, you'll have an opportunity to assess a motivational program designed to reenergize a troubled company's workforce. Acting on behalf of the company's executive board, you'll evaluate the board's current strategy based on survey data. You'll also advise board members about improving the effectiveness of this program based on what you've learned about goal-setting and motivation in organizations.

Major Topic Areas

- Changing nature of work
- Diversity and age
- Goal-setting
- Organizational downsizing
- Organizational justice

The Scenario

Morgan-Moe's drug stores are in trouble. A major regional player in the retail industry, the company has hundreds of stores in the upper Midwest. Unfortunately, a sharp decline in the region's manufacturing economy has put management in a serious financial bind. Revenues have been consistently dwindling. Customers spend less, and the stores have had to switch their focus to very low-margin commodities, such as milk and generic drugs, rather than the high-margin impulse-buy items that used to be the company's bread and butter. The firm has closed quite a few locations, reversing its expansion plans for the first time since it incorporated.

Being that this is uncharted territory for the company, Jim Claussen, vice president for human relations, had been struggling with how to address the issue with employees. As the company's fortunes worsened, he could see that employees were becoming more and more disaffected. Their insecurity about their jobs was taking a toll on attitudes. The company's downsizing was big news, and the employees didn't like what they were hearing.

Media reports of Morgan-Moe's store closings have focused on the lack of advance notice or communication from the company's corporate offices, as well as the lack of severance payments for departing employees. In the absence of official information, rumors and gossip have spread like wildfire among remaining employees. A few angry blogs developed by laid-off employees, like IHateMorganMoe.blogspot.com, have made the morale and public relations picture even worse.

Morgan-Moe is changing in other ways as well. The average age of its workforce is increasing rapidly. A couple of factors have contributed to this shift. First, fewer qualified young people are around because many families have moved away to find jobs. Second, stores have been actively encouraged to hire older workers, such as retirees looking for supplemental income. Managers are very receptive to these older workers because they are more mature, miss fewer days of work, and do not have child care responsibilities. They are also often more qualified than younger workers because they have more experience, sometimes in the managerial or executive ranks.

These older workers have been a great asset to the company in troubled times, but they are especially likely to leave if things get bad. If these older workers start to leave the company, taking their hard-earned experience with them, it seems likely that Morgan-Moe will sink deeper toward bankruptcy.

The System

Claussen wasn't sure how to respond to employees' sense of hopelessness and fear until a friend gave him a book entitled *Man's Search for Meaning*. The book was written by a psychologist named Victor Frankl, who survived the concentration camps at Auschwitz. Frankl found that those who had a clear sense of purpose, a reason to live, were more likely to persevere in the face of nearly unspeakable suffering. Something about this book, and its advocacy of finding meaning and direction as a way to triumph over adversity, really stuck with Claussen. He thought he might be able to apply its lessons to his workforce. He proposed the idea of a new direction for management to the company's executive committee, and they reluctantly agreed to try his suggestions.

Over the last 6 months, stores throughout the company have used a performance management system that, as Claussen says, "gets people to buy into the idea of performing so that they can see some real results in their stores. It's all about seeing that your work serves a broader purpose. I read about how some companies have been sharing store performance information with employees to get them to understand what their jobs really mean and participate in making changes, and I thought that was something we'd be able to do."

The HR team came up with five options for the management system. Corporate allowed individual managers to choose the option they thought would work best with their employees so that managers wouldn't feel too much like a rapid change was being forced on them. Program I is opting out of the new idea, continuing to stay the course and providing employees with little to no information or opportunities for participation. Program II tracks employee absence and sick leave data and shares that information with individual employees, giving them feedback about things they can control. Management takes no further action. Program III tracks sales and inventory replacement rates across shifts. As in Program II, information is shared with employees, but without providing employee feedback about absence and sick leave data. Program IV, the most comprehensive, tracks the same information as Programs II and III. Managers communicate it in weekly brainstorming sessions, during which employees try to determine what they can do better in the future and make suggestions for improving store performance. Program V keeps the idea of brainstorming but doesn't provide employees with information about their behavior or company profits.

Since implementing the system, Claussen has spoken with several managers about what motivated them to choose the program they did. Artie Washington, who chose Program IV, said, "I want to have my employees' input on how to keep the store running smoothly. Everybody worries about their job security in this economy. Letting them know what's going on and giving them ways to change things keeps them involved."

Betty Alvarez couldn't disagree more. She selected Program I. "I would rather have my employees doing their jobs than going to meetings to talk about doing their jobs. That's what management is for." Michael Ostremski, another proponent of Program I, added, "It's okay for the employees to feel a little uncertain—if they think we're in the clear, they'll slack off. If they think we're in trouble, they'll give up."

Cal Martins also questions the need to provide information to the whole team, but he chose Program II. "A person should know where he or she stands in the job, but they don't have to know about everyone else. It creates unnecessary tension."

This is somewhat similar to Cindy Ang's reason for picking Program V. "When we have our brainstorming meetings, I learn what they [the employees] think is most pressing, not what some spreadsheet says. It gives me a better feel for what's going on in my store. Numbers count, of course, but they don't tell you everything. I was also a little worried that employees would be upset if they saw that we aren't performing well."

Results to Date

Claussen is convinced the most elaborate procedure (Program IV) is the most effective, but not everyone in the executive committee is won over by his advocacy. Although they have supported the test implementation of the system because it appears to have relatively low costs, others on the committee want to see results. CEO Jean Masterson has asked for a complete breakdown of the performance of the various stores over the past 4 years. She's especially interested in seeing how sales figures and turnover rates have been affected by the new program.

The company has been collecting data in spreadsheets on sales and turnover rates, and it prepared the following report, which also estimates the dollar cost of staff time taken up in each method. These costs are based on the number of hours employees spend working on the program multiplied by their wage rate. Estimates of turnover, profit, and staff time are collected per store. Profit and turnover data include means and standard deviations across locations; profit is net of the monthly time cost. Turnover information refers to the percentage of employees who either quit or are terminated in a month.

To see if any patterns emerged in managers' selection of programs, the company calculated relationships between program selection and various attributes of the stores. Program I was selected most frequently by the oldest stores and those in the most economically distressed areas. Programs II and III were selected most frequently by stores in urban areas and in areas where the workforce was younger on average. Programs IV and V were selected most frequently in stores in rural areas, and especially where the workforce is older on average.

Program	Methods	Number of Stores	Average Turnover	Weekly Profit per Month	Monthly Staff Time Cost
Program I	Traditional management	83	Mean = 30% SD = 10%	Mean = $5,700 SD = $3,000	None
Program II	Share absence and sick leave	27	Mean = 23% SD = 14%	Mean = $7,000 SD = $5,800	$1,960
Program III	Share sales and inventory	35	Mean = 37% SD = 20%	Mean = $11,000 SD = $2,700	$2,440
Program IV	Share information and brainstorm	67	Mean = 17% SD = 20%	Mean = $13,000 SD = $3,400	$3,420
Program V	Brainstorm without sharing information	87	Mean = 21% SD = 12%	Mean = $14,000 SD = $2,400	$2,750

Your Assignment

Your task is to prepare a report for the company's executive committee on the effectiveness of these programs. Make certain it is in the form of a professional business document. Your audience won't necessarily know about the organizational principles you're describing, so make sure you provide detailed explanations that someone in a real business can understand.

When you write, make sure you touch on the following points:

CC-1. Consider the five management systems as variables in an experiment. Identify the independent and dependent variables, and explain how they are related to one another.

CC-2. Based on the discussion of independent and dependent variables in the textbook, is there anything else you'd like to measure as an outcome?

CC-3. Look over the data and decide which method of management appears most effective in generating revenues and reducing turnover, and why. Which methods appear least effective, and why?

CC-4. Are there any concerns you have about these data?

CC-5. Does a comparison of the number of stores using each method influence your conclusions at all?

CC-6. Does the fact that managers are selecting the specific program to use (including Program I, which continues the status quo) affect the inferences you can draw about program success?

CC-7. What are the advantages of randomly assigning different conditions to the stores instead of using this self-selection process?

CC-8. How does the changing nature of the workforce and the economy, described in your textbook and in the case, affect your conclusions about how to manage retail employees? Does the participation of a more experienced workforce help or hurt these programs? Why might these programs work differently in an economy that isn't doing so poorly?

CC-9. Claussen essentially designed the program on his own, with very little research into goal-setting and motivation. Based on your textbook, how well has he done? Which parts of the program appear to fit well with research evidence on goal-setting? What parts would you change to get more substantial improvements in employee motivation?

CC-10. Describe the feelings employees might have when these systems are implemented that could help or hinder the program's success. What advice would you give managers about how to implement the programs so they match the principles of organizational justice described in your textbook?

Repairing Jobs That Fail to Satisfy

Learning Goals

Companies often divide up work as a way to improve efficiency, but specialization can lead to negative consequences. DrainFlow is a company that has effectively used specialization to reduce costs relative to its competitors' costs for years, but rising customer complaints suggest the firm's strong position may be slipping. After reading the case, you will suggest some ways it can create more interesting work for employees. You'll also tackle the problem of finding people qualified and ready to perform the multiple responsibilities required in these jobs.

Major Topic Areas

- Job design
- Job satisfaction
- Personality
- Emotional labor

The Scenario

DrainFlow is a large residential and commercial plumbing maintenance firm that operates around the United States. It has been a major player in residential plumbing for decades, and its familiar rhyming motto, "When Your Drain Won't Go, Call DrainFlow," has been plastered on billboards since the 1960s.

Lee Reynaldo has been a regional manager at DrainFlow for about 2 years. She used to work for a newer competing chain, Lightning Plumber, that has been drawing more and more customers from DrainFlow. Although her job at DrainFlow pays more, Reynaldo isn't happy with the way things are going. She's noticed the work environment just isn't as vital or energetic as the environment she saw at Lightning.

Reynaldo thinks the problem is that employees aren't motivated to provide the type of customer service Lightning Plumber employees offer. She recently sent surveys to customers to collect information about performance, and the data confirmed her fears. Although 60 percent of respondents said they were satisfied with their experience and would use DrainFlow

again, 40 percent felt their experience was not good, and 30 percent said they would use a competitor the next time they had a plumbing problem.

Reynaldo is wondering whether DrainFlow's job design might be contributing to its problems in retaining customers. DrainFlow has about 2,000 employees in four basic job categories: plumbers, plumber's assistants, order processors, and billing representatives. This structure is designed to keep costs as low as possible. Plumbers make very high wages, whereas plumber's assistants make about one-quarter of what a licensed plumber makes. Using plumber's assistants is therefore a very cost-effective strategy that has enabled DrainFlow to easily undercut the competition when it comes to price. Order processors make even less than assistants but about the same as billing processors. All work is very specialized, but employees are often dependent on another job category to perform at their most efficient level.

Like most plumbing companies, DrainFlow gets business mostly from the Yellow Pages and the Internet. Customers either call in to describe a plumbing problem or submit an online request for plumbing services, receiving a return call with information within 24 hours. In either case, DrainFlow's order processors listen to the customer's description of the problem to determine whether a plumber or a plumber's assistant should make the service call. The job is then assigned accordingly, and a service provider goes to the location. When the job has been completed, via cell phone a billing representative relays the fee to the service rep, who presents a bill to the customer for payment. Billing representatives can take customers' credit card payments by phone or e-mail an invoice for online payment.

The Problem

Although specialization does cut costs significantly, Reynaldo is worried about customer dissatisfaction. According to her survey, about 25 percent of customer contacts ended in no service call because customers were confused by the diagnostic questions the order processors asked and because the order processors did not have sufficient knowledge or skill to explain the situation. That means fully one in four people who call

DrainFlow to hire a plumber are worse than dissatisfied: they aren't customers at all! The remaining 75 percent of calls that did end in a customer service encounter resulted in other problems.

The most frequent complaints Reynaldo found in the customer surveys were about response time and cost, especially when the wrong person was sent to a job. A plumber's assistant cannot complete a more technically complicated job. The appointment has to be rescheduled, and the customer's time and the staff's time have been wasted. The resulting delay often caused customers in these situations to decline further contact with DrainFlow—many of them decided to go with Lightning Plumber.

"When I arrive at a job I can't take care of," says plumber's assistant Jim Larson, "the customer gets ticked off. They thought they were getting a licensed plumber, since they were calling for a plumber. Telling them they have to have someone else come out doesn't go over well."

On the other hand, when a plumber responds to a job easily handled by a plumber's assistant, the customer is still charged at the plumber's higher pay rate. Licensed plumber Luis Berger also does not like being in the position of giving customers bad news. "If I get called out to do something like snake a drain, the customer isn't expecting a hefty bill. I'm caught between a rock and a hard place—I don't set the rates or make the appointments, but I'm the one who gets it from the customer." Plumbers also resent being sent to do such simple work.

Susie McCarty is one of DrainFlow's order processors. She's frustrated too when the wrong person is sent to a job but feels she and the other order processors are doing the best they can. "We have a survey we're supposed to follow with the calls to find out what the problem is and who needs to take the job," she explains. "The customers don't know that we have a standard form, so they think we can answer all their questions. Most of us don't know any more about plumbing than the caller. If they don't use the terms on the survey, we don't understand what they're talking about. A plumber would, but we're not plumbers; we just take the calls."

Customer service issues also involve the billing representatives. They are the ones who have to keep contacting customers about payment. "It's not my fault the wrong guy was sent," says Elizabeth Monty. "If two guys went out, that's two trips. If a plumber did the work, you pay plumber rates. Some of these customers don't get that I didn't take their first call, and so I get yelled at." The billing representatives also complain that they see only the tail end of the process, so they don't know what the original call entailed. The job is fairly impersonal, and much of the work is recording customer complaints. Remember—40 percent of customers aren't satisfied, and it's the billing representatives who take the brunt of their negative reactions on the phone.

As you can probably tell, all employees have to engage in emotional labor, as described in this textbook, and many lack the skills or personality traits to complete the customer interaction component of their jobs. They aren't trained to provide customer service, and they see their work mostly in technical, or mechanical, terms. Quite a few are actually anxious about speaking directly with customers. The office staff (order processors and billing representatives) realize customer service is part of their job, but they also find dealing with negative feedback from customers and co-workers taxing.

A couple of years ago a management consulting company was hired to survey DrainFlow worker attitudes. The results showed they were less satisfied than workers in other comparable jobs. The following table provides a breakdown of respondent satisfaction levels across a number of categories:

	DrainFlow Plumbers	DrainFlow Plumber Assistants	DrainFlow Office Workers	Average Plumber	Average Office Workers
I am satisfied with the work I am asked to do.	3.7	2.5	2.5	4.3	3.5
I am satisfied with my working conditions.	3.8	2.4	3.7	4.1	4.2
I am satisfied with my interactions with co-workers.	3.5	3.2	2.7	3.8	3.9
I am satisfied with my interactions with my supervisor.	2.5	2.3	2.2	3.5	3.4

The information about average plumbers and average office workers is taken from the management consulting company's records of other companies. They aren't exactly surprising, given some of the complaints Drain-Flow employees have made. Top management is worried about these results, but they haven't been able to formulate a solution. The traditional DrainFlow culture has been focused on cost containment, and the "soft stuff" like employee satisfaction hasn't been a major issue.

The Proposed Solution

The company is in trouble, and as revenues shrink and the cost savings that were supposed to be achieved by dividing up work fail to materialize, a change seems to be in order.

Reynaldo is proposing using cash rewards to improve performance among employees. She thinks if employees were paid based on work outcomes, they'd work harder to satisfy customers. Because it's not easy to measure how satisfied people are with the initial call-in, Reynaldo would like to give the order processors a small reward for every 20 calls successfully completed. For the hands-on work, she'd like to have each billing representative collect information about customer satisfaction for each completed call. If no complaints are made and the job is handled promptly, a moderate cash reward would be given to the plumber or plumber's assistant. If the customer indicates real satisfaction with the service, a larger cash reward would be provided.

Reynaldo also wants to find people who are a better fit with the company's new goals. Current hiring procedure relies on unstructured interviews with each location's general manager, and little consistency is found in the way these managers choose employees. Most lack training in customer service and organizational behavior. Reynaldo thinks it would be better if hiring methods were standardized across all branches in her region to help managers identify recruits who can actually succeed in the job.

Your Assignment

Your task is to prepare a report for Reynaldo on the potential effectiveness of her cash reward and structured-interview programs. Make certain it is in the form of a professional business document that you'd actually give to an experienced manager at this level of a fairly large corporation. Reynaldo is very smart when it comes to managing finances and running a plumbing business, but she won't necessarily know about the organizational behavior principles you're describing. Because any new proposals must be passed through top management, you should also address their concerns about cost containment. You'll need to make a strong evidence-based financial case that changing the management style will benefit the company.

When you write, make sure you touch on the following points:

CC-11. Although it's clear employees are not especially satisfied with their work, do you think this is a reason for concern? Does research suggest satisfied workers are actually better at their jobs? Are any other behavioral outcomes associated with job satisfaction?

CC-12. Using job characteristics theory, explain why the present system of job design may be contributing to employee dissatisfaction. Describe some ways you could help employees feel more satisfied with their work by redesigning their jobs.

CC-13. Reynaldo has a somewhat vague idea about how to implement the cash rewards system. Describe some of the specific ways you would make the reward system work better, based on the case.

CC-14. Explain the advantages and disadvantages of using financial incentives in a program of this nature. What, if any, potential problems might arise if people are given money for achieving customer satisfaction goals? What other types of incentives might be considered?

CC-15. Create a specific plan to assess whether the reward system is working. What are the dependent variables that should change if the system works? How will you go about measuring success?

CC-16. What types of hiring recommendations would you make to find people better suited for these jobs? Which Big Five personality traits would be useful for the customer service responsibilities and emotional labor?

CASE
3   Building a Coalition

Learning Goals

Many of the most important organizational behavior challenges require coordinating plans and goals among groups. This case describes a multiorganizational effort, but the same principles of accommodation and compromise also apply when trying to work with multiple divisions within a single organization. You'll create a blueprint for managing a complex development team's progress, steering team members away from negative conflicts and toward productive discussion. You'll also be asked to help create a new message for executives so they can lead effectively.

Major Topic Areas

- Group dynamics
- Maximizing team performance
- Organizational culture
- Integrative bargaining

The Scenario

The Woodson Foundation, a large nonprofit social service agency, is teaming up with the public school system in Washington, D.C., to improve student outcomes. There's ample room for improvement. The schools have problems with truancy, low student performance, and crime. New staff quickly burn out as their initial enthusiasm for helping students is blunted by the harsh realities they encounter in the classroom. Turnover among new teachers is very high, and many of the best and brightest are the most likely to leave for schools that aren't as troubled.

The plan is to create an experimental after-school program that will combine the Woodson Foundation's skill in raising private money and coordinating community leaders with the educational expertise of school staff. Ideally, the system will be financially self-sufficient, which is important because less money is available for schools than in the past. After several months of negotiation, the leaders of the Woodson Foundation and the school system have agreed that the best course is to develop a new agency that will draw on resources from both organizations. The Woodson foundation will provide logistical support and program development and measurement staff; the school system will provide classrooms and teaching staff.

The first stage in bringing this new plan to fruition is the formation of an executive development team. This team will span multiple functional areas and establish the operating plan for improving school performance. Its cross-organizational nature means representatives from both the Woodson Foundation and the school district must participate. The National Coalition for Parental Involvement in Education (NCPIE) is also going to be a major partner in the program, acting as a representative for parents on behalf of the PTA.

Conflict and Agreement in the Development Team

While it would be perfect if all the groups could work together easily to improve student outcomes, there is little doubt some substantive conflicts will arise. Each group has its own interests, and in some cases these are directly opposed to one another.

School district representatives want to ensure the new jobs will be unionized and will operate in a way consistent with current school board policies. They are very concerned that if Woodson assumes too dominant a role, the school board won't be able to control the operations of the new system. The complexity of the school system has led to the development of a highly complex bureaucratic structure over time, and administrators want to make sure their policies and procedures will still hold for teachers in these programs even outside the regular school day. They also worry that jobs going into the new system will take funding from other school district jobs.

Woodson, founded by entrepreneur Theodore Woodson around 1910, still bears the hallmarks of its founder's way of doing business. Woodson emphasized efficiency and experimentation in everything he did. Many of the foundation's charities have won awards for minimizing costs while still providing excellent services. Their focus on using hard data to measure performance for all their initiatives is not consistent with the school district culture.

Finally, the NCPIE is driven by a mission to increase parental control. The organization believes that when communities are able to drive their own educational methods, students and parents are better able to achieve success together. The organization is strongly committed to celebrating diversity along racial, gender, ethnic, and disability status categories. Its members are most interested in the process by which changes are made, ensuring everyone has the ability to weigh in.

Some demographic diversity issues complicate the team's situation. Most of the students served by the Washington, D.C., school district are African American, along with large populations of Caucasians and Hispanics. The NCPIE makeup generally matches the demographic diversity of the areas served by the public schools. The Woodson foundation, based in northern Virginia, is predominantly staffed by Caucasian professionals. There is some concern with the idea that a new group that does not understand the demographic concerns of the community will be so involved in a major change in educational administration. The leadership of the new program will have to be able to present an effective message for generating enthusiasm for the program across diverse stakeholder groups.

Although the groups differ in important ways, it's also worth considering what they have in common. All are interested in meeting the needs of students. All would like to increase student learning. The school system does benefit from anything that increases student test scores. And the Woodson Foundation and NCPIE are united in their desire to see more parents engaged in the system.

Candidates for the Development Team

The development team will consist of three individuals— HR representatives from the Woodson Foundation, the schools, and the NCPIE—who have prepared the following list of potential candidates for consideration.

Victoria Adams is the superintendent of schools for Washington, D.C. She spearheaded the initial communication with the Woodson Foundation and has been building support among teachers and principals. She thinks the schools and the foundation need to have larger roles than the parents and communities. "Of course we want their involvement and support, but as the professionals, we should have more say when it comes to making decisions and implementing programs. We don't want to shut anyone out, but we have to be realistic about what the parents can do."

Duane Hardy has been a principal in the Washington area for more than 15 years. He also thinks the schools should have the most power. "We're the ones who work with these kids every day. I've watched class sizes get bigger, and scores and graduation rates go down. Yes, we need to fix this, but these outside groups can't understand the limitations we're dealing with. We have the community, the politicians, the taxpayers—everyone watching what we're doing, everyone thinking they know what's best. The parents, at least, have more of a stake in this."

"The most important thing is the kids," says second-year teacher Ari Kaufman. He is well liked by his students but doesn't get along well with other faculty members. He's seen as a "squeaky wheel." "The schools need change so badly. And how did they get this way? From too little outside involvement."

Community organizer Mason Dupree doesn't like the level of bureaucracy either. He worries that the school's answer to its problems is to throw more money at them. "I know these kids. I grew up in these neighborhoods. My parents knew every single teacher I had. The schools wanted our involvement then. Now all they want is our money. And I wouldn't mind giving it to them if I thought it would be used responsibly, not spent on raises for people who haven't shown they can get the job done."

Meredith Watson, with the Woodson Foundation, agrees the schools have become less focused on the families. A former teacher, she left the field of education after being in the classroom for 6 years. "There is so much waste in the system," she complains. "Jobs are unnecessarily duplicated, change processes are needlessly convoluted. Unless you're an insider already, you can't get anything done. These parents want to be involved. They know their kids best."

Unlike her NCPIE colleagues, Candace Sharpe thinks the schools are doing the best they can. She is a county social worker, relatively new to the D.C. area. "Parents say they want to be involved but then don't follow through. *We* need to step it up, *we* need to lead the way. Lasting change doesn't come from the outside, it comes from the home."

Victor Martinez has been at the Woodson Foundation for 10 years, starting as an intern straight out of college. "It's sometimes hard to see a situation when you're in the thick of it," he explains. "Nobody likes to be told they're doing something wrong, but sometimes it has to be said. We all know there are flaws in the system. We can't keep the status quo. It just isn't cutting it."

Strategies for the Program Team

Once the basic membership and principles for the development team have been established, the program team would also like to develop a handbook for those who will be running the new program. Ideally, this set of principles can help train new leaders to create an inspirational message that will facilitate success. The actual content of the program and the nature of the message will be hammered out by the development team, but it is still possible to generate some overriding principles for the program team in advance of these decisions.

Your Assignment

The Woodson Foundation, the NCPIE, and the schools have asked you to provide some information about how to form teams effectively. They would like your response to explain what should be done at each step of the way, from the selection of appropriate team members to setting group priorities and goals, setting deadlines, and describing effective methods for resolving conflicts that arise. After this, they'd like you to prepare a brief set of principles for leaders of the newly established program. That means you will have two audiences: the development team, which will receive one report on how it can effectively design the program, and the program team, which will receive one report on how it can effectively lead the new program.

The following points should help you form a comprehensive message for the development team:

CC-17. The development team will be more effective if members have some idea about how groups and teams typically operate. Review the dominant perspectives on team formation and performance from the chapters in the book for the committee so it can know what to expect.

CC-18. Given the profiles of candidates for the development team, provide suggestions for who would likely be a good group member and who might be less effective in this situation. Be sure you are using the research on groups and teams in the textbook to defend your choices.

CC-19. Using principles from the chapters on groups and teams, describe how you will advise the team to manage conflict effectively.

CC-20. Describe how integrative negotiation strategies might achieve joint goals for the development team.

The following points should help you form a message for the program team:

CC-21. Leaders of the new combined organization should have a good idea of the culture of the school district, the NCPIE, and the Woodson Foundation because they will need to manage relationships with all three groups on an ongoing basis. How would you describe the culture of these various stakeholder organizations? Use concepts from the chapter on organizational culture to describe how they differ and how they are similar.

CC-22. Consider how leaders of the new program can generate a transformational message and encourage employee and parent trust. Using material from the chapter on leadership, describe how you would advise leaders to accomplish these ends.

CC-23. Given the potential for demographic fault lines in negotiating these changes, what would you advise as a strategy for managing diversity issues for program leaders?

CASE 4

Boundaryless Organizations

Learning Goals

The multinational organization is an increasingly common and important part of the economy. This case takes you into the world of a cutting-edge music software business seeking success across three very different national and organizational cultures. Its managers need to make important decisions about how to structure work processes so employees can be satisfied and productive doing very different tasks.

Major Topic Areas

- Organizational structure and boundaryless organizations
- Organizational culture
- Human resources
- Organizational socialization

The Scenario

Newskool Grooves is a transnational company developing music software. The software is used to compose music, play recordings in clubs, and produce albums. Founder and CEO Gerd Finger is, understandably, the company's biggest fan. "I started this company from nothing, from just me, my ideas, and my computer. I love music—love playing music, love writing programs for making music, love listening to music—and the money is nice, too." Finger says he never wanted to work for someone else, to give away his ideas and let someone else profit from them. He wanted to keep control over them, and their image. "Newskool Grooves is always ahead of the pack. In this business, if you can't keep up, you're out. And we are the company everyone else must keep up with. Everyone knows when they get something from us, they're getting only the best and the newest."

The company headquarters are in Berlin, the nerve center for the organization, where new products are developed and the organizational strategy is established. Newskool outsources a great deal of its coding work to programmers in Kiev, Ukraine. Its marketing efforts are increasingly based in its Los Angeles offices. This division of labor is at least partially based on technical expertise and cost issues. The German team excels at design and production tasks. Because most of Newskool's customers are English speakers, the Los Angeles office has been the best group to write ads and market products. The Kiev offices are filled with outstanding programmers who don't require the very high rates of compensation you'd find in German or U.S. offices. The combination of high-tech software, rapid reorganization, and outsourcing makes Newskool the very definition of a boundaryless organization.

Finger also makes the final decision on hiring every employee for the company and places a heavy emphasis on independent work styles. "Why would I want to put my company in the hands of people I can't count on?" he asks with a laugh. "They have to believe in what we're doing here, really understand our direction and be able to go with it. I'm not the babysitter, I'm not the school master handing out homework. School time is over. This is the real world."

The Work Culture

Employees want to work at this company because it's cutting edge. Newskool's software is used by a number of dance musicians and DJs, who have been the firm's core market, seeing it as a relatively expensive but very high-quality and innovative brand. Whenever the rest of the market for music software goes in one direction, it seems like Newskool heads in a completely different direction in an effort to keep itself separate from the pack. This strategy has tended to pay off. While competitors develop similar products and therefore need to continually lower their prices to compete with one another, Newskool has kept revenues high by creating completely new types of products that don't face this type of price competition.

Unfortunately, computer piracy has eroded Newskool's ability to make money with just software-based music tools, and it has had to move into the production of hardware, such as drum machines and amplifiers that incorporate its computer technology. Making this massive market change might be challenging for some

companies, but for an organization that reinvents itself every 2 or 3 years like Newskool does, the bigger fight is a constant war against stagnation and rigidity.

The organization has a very decentralized culture. With only 115 employees, the original management philosophy of allowing all employees to participate in decision making and innovation is still the lifeblood of the company's culture. One developer notes, "At Newskool, they want you to be part of the process. If you are a person who wants to do what you're told at work, you're in trouble. Most times, they can't tell you what they want you to do next—they don't even know what comes next! That's why they hire employees who are creative, people who can try to make the next thing happen. It's challenging, but a lot of us think it's very much an exciting environment."

The Boundaryless Environment

Because so much of the work can be performed on computers, Finger decided early to allow employees to work outside the office. The senior management in Berlin and Los Angeles are both quite happy with this arrangement. Because some marketing work does require face-to-face contact, the Los Angeles office has weekly in-person meetings. Employees who like Newskool are happiest when they can work through the night and sleep most of the day, firing up their computers to get work done at the drop of a hat. Project discussions often happen via social networking on the company's intranet.

The Kiev offices have been less eager to work with the boundaryless model. Managers say their computer programmers find working with so little structure rather uncomfortable. They are more used to the idea of a strong leadership structure and well-defined work processes.

"When I started," says one manager, "Gerd said getting in touch with him would be no problem, getting in touch with L.A. would be no problem. We're small, we're family, he said. Well, it is a problem. When I call L.A., they say to wait until their meeting day. I can't always wait until they decide to get together. I call Gerd—he says, 'Figure it out.' Then when I do, he says it isn't right and we have to start again. If he just told me in the first place, we would have done it."

Some recent events have also shaken up the company's usual way of doing business. Developers in the corporate offices had a major communications breakdown about their hardware DJ controller, which required many hours of discussion to resolve. It seems that people who seldom met face to face had all made progress—but had moved in opposite directions.

To test and design the company's hardware products, employees apparently need to do more than send each other code; sometimes they need to collaborate face to face. Some spirited disagreements have been voiced within the organization about how to move forward in this new environment.

The offices are experiencing additional difficulties. Since the shift to newer products, Sandra Pelham in the Los Angeles office has been more critical of the company. "With the software, we were more limited in the kinds of advertising media we could access. So now, with the hardware—real instruments—we finally thought, 'All right, this is something we can work with!' We had a whole slate of musicians and DJs and producers to contact for endorsements, but Gerd said, 'No way.' He didn't want customers who only cared that a celebrity liked us. He scrapped the whole campaign. He says we're all about creativity and doing our own thing— until we don't want to do things his way."

Although the organization is not without problems, there is little question Newskool has been a standout success in the computer music software industry. While many are shuttering their operations, Newskool is using its market power to push forward the next generation of electronic music-making tools. As Gerd Finger puts it, "Once the rest of the industry has gotten together and figured out how they're all going to cope with change, they'll look around and see that we're already three miles ahead of them down the road to the future."

Your Assignment

Finger has asked for your advice on how to keep his organization successful. He wants to have some sort of benchmark for how other boundaryless organizations in the tech sector stay competitive despite the challenges of so many workers heading in so many different directions. You will need to prepare a report for the company's executive committee. Your report should read like a proposal to a corporate executive who has a great deal of knowledge about the technical aspects of his company but might not have much knowledge of organizational behavior.

When you write, make sure you touch on the following points:

CC-24. Identify some of the problems likely to occur in a boundaryless organization like Newskool Grooves. What are the advantages of boundaryless organizations?

CC-25. Consider some of the cultural issues that will affect a company operating in such different parts of the world and whose employees may not be representative of the national cultures of each country. Are the conflicts you observe a function of the different types of work people have to perform?

CC-26. Based on what you know about motivation and personality, what types of people are likely to be satisfied in each area of the company? Use concepts from job characteristics theory and the emerging social relationships perspective on work to describe what might need to change to increase employee satisfaction in all areas.

CC-27. What types of human resources practices need to be implemented in this sort of organization? What principles of selection and hiring are likely to be effective? Which Big Five traits and abilities might Newskool supervisors want to use for selection?

CC-28. What kind of performance measures might you want to see for each office?

CC-29. How can the company establish a socialization program that will maximize employee creativity and independence? Do employees in all its locations need equal levels of creativity?

The Stress of Caring

Learning Goals

One of the most consistent changes in the structure of work over the past few decades has been a shift from a manufacturing economy to a service economy. More workers are now engaged in jobs that include providing care and assistance, especially in education and medicine. This work is satisfying for some people, but it can also be highly stressful. In the following scenario, consider how a company in the nursing care industry is responding to the challenges of the new environment.

Major Topic Areas

- Stress
- Organizational change
- Emotions
- Leadership

The Scenario

Parkway Nursing Care is an organization facing a massive change. The company was founded in 1972 with just two nursing homes in Phoenix, Arizona. The company was very successful, and throughout the 1980s it continued to turn a consistent profit while slowly acquiring or building 30 more units. This low-profile approach changed forever in 1993 when venture capitalist Robert Quine decided to make a major investment in expanding Parkway in return for a portion of its profits over the coming years. The number of nursing homes exploded, and Parkway was operating 180 homes by the year 2000.

The company now has 220 facilities in the southwestern United States, with an average of 115 beds per facility and a total of nearly 30,000 employees. In addition to health care facilities, it also provides skilled in-home nursing care. Parkway is seen as one of the best care facilities in the region, and it has won numerous awards for its achievements in the field.

As members of the Baby Boom generation become senior citizens, the need for skilled care will only increase. Parkway wants to make sure it is in a good position to meet this growing need. This means the company must continue expanding rapidly.

The pressure for growth is one significant challenge, but it's not the only one. The nursing home industry has come under increasing government scrutiny following investigations that turned up widespread patient abuse and billing fraud. Parkway has always had outstanding patient care, and no substantiated claim of abuse or neglect in any of its homes has ever been made, but the need for increased documentation will still affect the company. As the federal government tries to trim Medicare expenses, Parkway may face a reduction in funding.

The Problem

As growth has continued, Parkway has remained committed to providing dignity and health to all residents in its facilities. The board of directors wants to see renewed commitment to the firm's mission and core values, not a diffusion of its culture. Its members are worried there might be problems to address. Interviews with employees suggest there's plenty to worry about.

Shift leader Maxine Vernon has been with Parkway for 15 years. "Now that the government keeps a closer eye on our staffing levels, I've seen management do what it can to keep positions filled, and I don't always agree with who is hired. Some of the basic job skills can be taught, sure, but how to *care* for our patients—a lot of these new kids just don't pick up on that."

"The problem isn't with staff—it's with Parkway's focus on filling the beds," says nurse's aide Bobby Reed. "When I started here, Parkway's reputation was still about the service. Now it's about numbers. No one is intentionally negligent—there just are too many patients to see."

A recent college graduate with a B.A. in psychology, Dalton Manetti is more stressed than he expected he would be. "These aren't the sweet grannies you see in the movies. Our patients are demanding. They complain about everything, even about being called patients, probably because most of them think they shouldn't be here in the first place. A lot of times, their gripes amount to nothing, but we have to log them in anyway."

Carmen Frank has been with Parkway almost a year and is already considering finding a new job. "I knew there were going to be physical parts to this job, and I thought I'd be able to handle that. It's not like I was looking for a desk job, you know? I go home after every shift with aches all over—my back, my arms, my legs. I've never had to take so much time off from a job because I hurt. And then when I come back, I feel like the rest of the staff thinks I'm weak."

Year	Patients	Injuries per Staff Member	Incidents per Patient	Certified Absences per Staff	Other Absence per Staff	Turnover Rate
2000	21,200	3.32	4.98	4.55	3.14	0.31
2001	22,300	3.97	5.37	5.09	3.31	0.29
2002	22,600	4.87	5.92	4.71	3.47	0.28
2003	23,100	4.10	6.36	5.11	3.61	0.35
2004	23,300	4.21	6.87	5.66	4.03	0.31
2005	23,450	5.03	7.36	5.33	3.45	0.28
2006	23,600	5.84	7.88	5.28	4.24	0.36
2007	24,500	5.62	8.35	5.86	4.06	0.33
2008	24,100	7.12	8.84	5.63	3.89	0.35
2009	25,300	6.95	9.34	6.11	4.28	0.35

"I started working here right out of high school because it was the best-paid of the jobs I could get," says Niecey Wilson. "I had no idea what I was getting myself into. Now I really like my job. Next year I'm going to start taking some night classes so I can move into another position. But some of the staff just think of this as any other job. They don't see the patients as people, more like inventory. If they want to work with inventory, they should get a job in retail."

Last month, the company's human resources department pulled the following information from its records at the request of the board of directors. The numbers provide some quantitative support for the concerns voiced by staff.

Injuries to staff occur mostly because of back strain from lifting patients. Patient incidents reflect injuries due to slips, falls, medication errors, or other accidents. Certified absences are days off from work due to medically verified illnesses or injuries. Other absences are days missed that are not due to injuries or illnesses; these are excused absences (unexcused absences are grounds for immediate firing).

Using Organizational Development to Combat Stress and Improve Performance

The company wants to use such organizational development methods as appreciative inquiry (AI) to create change and reenergize its sense of mission. As the chapter on organizational change explains, AI procedures systematically collect employee input and then use this information to create a change message everyone can

support. The human resources department conducted focus groups, asking employees to describe some of their concerns and suggestions for the future. The focus groups highlighted a number of suggestions, although they don't all suggest movement in the same direction.

Many suggestions concerned schedule flexibility. One representative comment was this: "Most of the stress on this job comes because we can't take time off when we need it. The LPNs [licensed practical nurses, who do much of the care] and orderlies can't take time off when they need to, but a lot of them are single parents or primary caregivers for their own children. When they have to leave for child care responsibilities, the work suffers and there's no contingency plan to help smooth things over. Then everyone who is left has to work extra hard. The person who takes time off feels guilty, and there can be fights over taking time off. If we had some way of covering these emergency absences, we'd all be a lot happier, and I think the care would be a lot better."

Other suggestions proposed a better method for communicating information across shifts. Most of the documentation for shift work is done in large spiral notebooks. When a new shift begins, staff members say they don't have much time to check on what happened in the previous shift. Some younger caregivers would like to have a method that lets them document patient outcomes electronically because they type faster than they can write. The older caregivers are more committed to the paper-based process, in part because they think switching systems would require a lot of work. (Government regulations on health care reporting require that any documentation be made in a form that cannot be altered after the fact, to prevent covering up abuse, so specialized software systems must be used for electronic documentation.)

Finally, the nursing care staff believes its perspectives on patient care are seldom given an appropriate hearing. "We're the ones who are with the patients most of the time, but when it comes to doing this the right way, our point of view gets lost. We really could save a lot of money by eliminating some of these unnecessary routines and programs, but it's something management always just says it will consider." Staff members seem to want some way to provide suggestions for improvement, but it isn't clear what method they would prefer.

Your Assignment

Parkway has taken some initial steps toward a new direction, but clearly it has a lot of work left to do. You've been brought in as a change management consultant to help the company change its culture and respond to the stress that employees experience. Remember to create your report as if for the leadership of a major corporation.

When you write your recommendations, make sure you touch on the following points:

CC-30. What do the data on employee injuries, incidents, absences, and turnover suggest to you? Is there reason for concern about the company's direction?

CC-31. The company is going to be making some significant changes based on the AI process, and most change efforts are associated with resistance. What are the most common forms of resistance, and which would you expect to see at Parkway?

CC-32. Given the board of directors' desire to reenergize the workforce, what advice would you provide for creating a leadership strategy? What leader behaviors should nursing home directors and nurse supervisors demonstrate?

CC-33. What are the major sources of job stress at Parkway? What does the research on employee stress suggest you should do to help minimize the experience of psychological strain for employees? Create a plan for how to reduce stress among employees.

CC-34. Based on the information collected in the focus groups, design a survey to hand out to employees. What sort of data should the survey gather? What types of data analysis methods would you like to employ for these data?

Glossary

ability   An individual's capacity to perform the various tasks in a job.

accommodating   The willingness of one party in a conflict to place the opponent's interests above his or her own.

action research   A change process based on systematic collection of data and then selection of a change action based on what the analyzed data indicate.

adjourning stage   The final stage in group development for temporary groups, characterized by concern with wrapping up activities rather than task performance.

affect   A broad range of feelings that people experience.

affect intensity   Individual differences in the strength with which individuals experience their emotions.

affective component   The emotional or feeling segment of an attitude.

affective events theory (AET)   A model that suggests that workplace events cause emotional reactions on the part of employees, which then influence workplace attitudes and behaviors.

agreeableness   A personality dimension that describes someone who is good natured, cooperative, and trusting.

anchoring bias   A tendency to fixate on initial information, from which one then fails to adequately adjust for subsequent information.

anthropology   The study of societies to learn about human beings and their activities.

appreciative inquiry (AI)   An approach that seeks to identify the unique qualities and special strengths of an organization, which can then be built on to improve performance.

approach–avoidance framework   The framework by which individuals react to stimuli, whereby approach motivation is attraction to positive stimuli and avoidance motivation is our aversion to negative stimuli.

arbitrator   A third party to a negotiation who has the authority to dictate an agreement.

assessment centers   A set of performance-simulation tests designed to evaluate a candidate's managerial potential.

attitudes   Evaluations employees make about objects, people, or events.

attribution theory   An attempt to determine whether an individual's behavior is internally or externally caused.

attribution theory of leadership   A leadership theory that says that leadership is merely an attribution that people make about other individuals.

authentic leaders   Leaders who know who they are, know what they believe in and value, and act on those values and beliefs openly and candidly. Their followers would consider them to be ethical people.

authority   The rights inherent in a managerial position to give orders and to expect the orders to be obeyed.

automatic processing   A relatively superficial consideration of evidence and information making use of heuristics.

autonomy   The degree to which a job provides substantial freedom and discretion to the individual in scheduling the work and in determining the procedures to be used in carrying it out.

availability bias   The tendency for people to base their judgments on information that is readily available to them.

avoiding   The desire to withdraw from or suppress a conflict.

BATNA   The **b**est **a**lternative **t**o a **n**egotiated **a**greement; the least the individual should accept.

behavioral component   An intention to behave in a certain way toward someone or something.

behavioral ethics   Analyzing how people actually behave when confronted with ethical dilemmas.

behavioral theories of leadership   Theories proposing that specific behaviors differentiate leaders from nonleaders.

behaviorally anchored rating scales (BARS)   Scales that combine major elements from the critical incident and graphic rating scale approaches. The appraiser rates the employees based on items along a continuum, but the points are examples of actual behavior on the given job rather than general descriptions or traits.

behaviorism   A theory that argues that behavior follows stimuli in a relatively unthinking manner.

Big Five Model   A personality assessment model that taps five basic dimensions.

biographical characteristics   Personal characteristics—such as age, gender, race, and length of tenure—that are objective and easily obtained from personnel records. These characteristics are representative of surface-level diversity.

bonus   A pay plan that rewards employees for recent performance rather than historical performance.

boundaryless organization   An organization that seeks to eliminate the chain of command, have limitless spans of control, and replace departments with empowered teams.

bounded rationality   A process of making decisions by constructing simplified models that extract the essential features from problems without capturing all their complexity.

brainstorming   An idea-generation process that specifically encourages any and all alternatives while withholding any criticism of those alternatives.

bureaucracy   An organization structure with highly routine operating tasks achieved through specialization, very formalized rules and regulations, tasks that are grouped into functional departments, centralized authority, narrow spans of control, and decision making that follows the chain of command.

centralization   The degree to which decision making is concentrated at a single point in an organization.

chain of command   The unbroken line of authority that extends from the top of the organization to the lowest echelon and clarifies who reports to whom.

challenge stressors   Stressors associated with workload, pressure to complete tasks, and time urgency.

change   Making things different.

change agents   Persons who act as catalysts and assume the responsibility for managing change activities.

channel richness   The amount of information that can be transmitted during a communication episode.

charismatic leadership theory   A leadership theory that states that followers make attributions of heroic or extraordinary leadership abilities when they observe certain behaviors.

citizenship   Actions that contribute to the psychological environment of the organization, such as helping others when not required.

citizenship behavior   Discretionary behavior that contributes to the psychological and social environment of the workplace.

coercive power   A power base that is dependent on fear of the negative results from failing to comply.

cognitive component   The opinion or belief segment of an attitude.

cognitive dissonance   Any incompatibility between two or more attitudes or between behavior and attitudes.

cognitive evaluation theory   A version of self-determination theory which holds that allocating extrinsic rewards for behavior that had been previously intrinsically rewarding tends to decrease the overall level of motivation if the rewards are seen as controlling.

cohesiveness   The degree to which group members are attracted to each other and are motivated to stay in the group.

collaborating   A situation in which the parties to a conflict each desire to satisfy fully the concerns of all parties.

collectivism   A national culture attribute that describes a tight social framework in which people expect others in groups of which they are a part to look after them and protect them.

communication   The transfer and understanding of meaning.

communication apprehension   Undue tension and anxiety about oral communication, written communication, or both.

communication process   The steps between a source and a receiver that result in the transfer and understanding of meaning.

competing   A desire to satisfy one's interests, regardless of the impact on the other party to the conflict.

compromising   A situation in which each party to a conflict is willing to give up something.

conceptual skills   The mental ability to analyze and diagnose complex situations.

conciliator   A trusted third party who provides an informal communication link between the negotiator and the opponent.

confirmation bias   The tendency to seek out information that reaffirms past choices and to discount information that contradicts past judgments.

conflict   A process that begins when one party perceives that another party has negatively affected, or is about to negatively affect, something that the first party cares about.

conflict management   The use of resolution and stimulation techniques to achieve the desired level of conflict.

conflict process   A process that has five stages: potential opposition or incompatibility, cognition and personalization, intentions, behavior, and outcomes.

conformity   The adjustment of one's behavior to align with the norms of the group.

conscientiousness   A personality dimension that describes someone who is responsible, dependable, persistent, and organized.

consideration   The extent to which a leader is likely to have job relationships characterized by mutual trust, respect for subordinates' ideas, and regard for their feelings.

contingency variables   Situational factors: variables that moderate the relationship between two or more variables.

contrast effect   Evaluation of a person's characteristics that is affected by comparisons with other people recently encountered who rank higher or lower on the same characteristics.

controlled processing   A detailed consideration of evidence and information relying on facts, figures, and logic.

controlling   Monitoring activities to ensure they are being accomplished as planned and correcting any significant deviations.

core self-evaluation (CSE)   Bottom-line conclusions individuals have about their capabilities, competence, and worth as a person.

core values   The primary or dominant values that are accepted throughout the organization.

cost-minimization strategy   A strategy that emphasizes tight cost controls, avoidance of unnecessary innovation or marketing expenses, and price cutting.

counterproductivity   Actions that actively damage the organization, including stealing, behaving aggressively toward co-workers, or being late or absent.

creativity   The ability to produce novel and useful ideas.

critical incidents   A way of evaluating the behaviors that are key in making the difference between executing a job effectively and executing it ineffectively.

cross-functional teams   Employees from about the same hierarchical level, but from different work areas, who come together to accomplish a task.

Dark Triad   A constellation of negative personality traits consisting of Machiavellianism, narcissism, and psychopathy.

decisions   Choices made from among two or more alternatives.

deep acting   Trying to modify one's true inner feelings based on display rules.

deep-level diversity   Differences in values, personality, and work preferences that become progressively more important for determining similarity as people get to know one another better.

defensive behaviors   Reactive and protective behaviors to avoid action, blame, or change.

demands   Responsibilities, pressures, obligations, and even uncertainties that individuals face in the workplace.

departmentalization   The basis by which jobs in an organization are grouped together.

dependence **B**'s relationship to **A** when **A** possesses something that **B** requires.

deviant workplace behavior Voluntary behavior that violates significant organizational norms and, in so doing, threatens the well-being of the organization or its members. Also called antisocial behavior or workplace incivility.

discrimination Noting of a difference between things; often we refer to unfair discrimination, which means making judgments about individuals based on stereotypes regarding their demographic group.

displayed emotions Emotions that are organizationally required and considered appropriate in a given job.

distributive bargaining Negotiation that seeks to divide up a fixed amount of resources; a win–lose situation.

distributive justice Perceived fairness of the amount and allocation of rewards among individuals.

diversity The extent to which members of a group are similar to, or different from, one another.

diversity management The process and programs by which managers make everyone more aware of and sensitive to the needs and differences of others.

dominant culture A culture that expresses the core values that are shared by a majority of the organization's members.

double-loop learning A process of correcting errors by modifying the organization's objectives, policies, and standard routines.

driving forces Forces that direct behavior away from the status quo.

dyadic conflict Conflict that occurs between two people.

dysfunctional conflict Conflict that hinders group performance.

effectiveness The degree to which an organization meets the needs of its clientele or customers.

efficiency The degree to which an organization can achieve its ends at a low cost.

emotional contagion The process by which peoples' emotions are caused by the emotions of others.

emotional dissonance Inconsistencies between the emotions people feel and the emotions they project.

emotional intelligence (EI) The ability to detect and to manage emotional cues and information.

emotional labor A situation in which an employee expresses organizationally desired emotions during interpersonal transactions at work.

emotional stability A personality dimension that characterizes someone as calm, self-confident, secure (positive) versus nervous, depressed, and insecure (negative).

emotions Intense feelings that are directed at someone or something.

employee engagement An individual's involvement with, satisfaction with, and enthusiasm for the work he or she does.

employee involvement A participative process that uses the input of employees and is intended to increase employee commitment to an organization's success.

employee-oriented leader A leader who emphasizes interpersonal relations, takes a personal interest in the needs of employees, and accepts individual differences among members.

employee stock ownership plan (ESOP) A company-established benefits plan in which employees acquire stock, often at below-market prices, as part of their benefits.

encounter stage The stage in the socialization process in which a new employee sees what the organization is really like and confronts the possibility that expectations and reality may diverge.

environment Institutions or forces outside an organization that potentially affect the organization's performance.

equity theory A theory that says that individuals compare their job inputs and outcomes with those of others and then respond to eliminate any inequities.

escalation of commitment An increased commitment to a previous decision in spite of negative information.

ethical dilemmas and ethical choices Situations in which individuals are required to define right and wrong conduct.

ethical work climate (EWC) The shared concept of right and wrong behavior in the workplace that reflects the true values of the organization and shapes the ethical decision-making of its members.

evidence-based management (EBM) The basing of managerial decisions on the best available scientific evidence.

exit Dissatisfaction expressed through behavior directed toward leaving the organization.

expectancy theory A theory that says that the strength of a tendency to act in a certain way depends on the strength of an expectation that the act will be followed by a given outcome and on the attractiveness of that outcome to the individual.

expert power Influence based on special skills or knowledge.

extraversion A personality dimension describing someone who is sociable, gregarious, and assertive.

faultlines The perceived divisions that split groups into two or more subgroups based on individual differences such as sex, race, age, work experience, and education.

feedback The degree to which carrying out the work activities required by a job results in the individual obtaining direct and clear information about the effectiveness of his or her performance.

felt conflict Emotional involvement in a conflict that creates anxiety, tenseness, frustration, or hostility.

felt emotions An individual's actual emotions.

femininity A national culture attribute that indicates little differentiation between male and female roles; a high rating indicates that women are treated as the equals of men in all aspects of the society.

Fiedler contingency model The theory that effective groups depend on a proper match between a leader's style of interacting with subordinates and the degree to which the situation gives control and influence to the leader.

filtering A sender's manipulation of information so that it will be seen more favorably by the receiver.

five-stage group-development model The five distinct stages groups go through: forming, storming, norming, performing, and adjourning.

fixed pie The belief that there is only a set amount of goods or services to be divvied up between the parties.

flexible benefits A benefits plan that allows each employee to put together a benefits package individually tailored to his or her own needs and situation.

flextime Flexible work hours.

forced comparison Method of performance evaluation where an employee's performance is made in explicit comparison to others (e.g., an employee may rank third out of ten employees in her work unit).

formal channels Communication channels established by an organization to transmit messages related to the professional activities of members.

formal group A designated work group defined by an organization's structure.

formalization The degree to which jobs within an organization are standardized.

forming stage The first stage in group development, characterized by much uncertainty.

functional conflict Conflict that supports the goals of the group and improves its performance.

fundamental attribution error The tendency to underestimate the influence of external factors and overestimate the influence of internal factors when making judgments about the behavior of others.

gainsharing A formula-based group incentive plan.

general mental ability (GMA) An overall factor of intelligence, as suggested by the positive correlations among specific intellectual ability dimensions.

goal-setting theory A theory that says that specific and difficult goals, with feedback, lead to higher performance.

grapevine An organization's informal communication network.

graphic rating scales An evaluation method in which the evaluator rates performance factors on an incremental scale.

group Two or more individuals, interacting and interdependent, who have come together to achieve particular objectives.

group cohesion The extent to which members of a group support and validate one another while at work.

group functioning The quantity and quality of a work group's output.

group order ranking An evaluation method that places employees into a particular classification, such as quartiles.

groupshift A change between a group's decision and an individual decision that a member within the group would make; the shift can be toward either conservatism or greater risk but it generally is toward a more extreme version of the group's original position.

groupthink A phenomenon in which the norm for consensus overrides the realistic appraisal of alternative courses of action.

halo effect The tendency to draw a general impression about an individual on the basis of a single characteristic.

heredity Factors determined at conception; one's biological, physiological, and inherent psychological makeup.

hierarchy of needs Abraham Maslow's hierarchy of five needs—physiological, safety, social, esteem, and self-actualization—in which, as each need is substantially satisfied, the next need becomes dominant.

high-context cultures Cultures that rely heavily on nonverbal and subtle situational cues in communication.

higher-order needs Needs that are satisfied internally, such as social, esteem, and self-actualization needs.

hindrance stressors Stressors that keep you from reaching your goals (for example, red tape, office politics, confusion over job responsibilities).

hindsight bias The tendency to believe falsely, after an outcome of an event is actually known, that one would have accurately predicted that outcome.

human skills The ability to work with, understand, and motivate other people, both individually and in groups.

hygiene factors Factors—such as company policy and administration, supervision, and salary—that, when adequate in a job, placate workers. When these factors are adequate, people will not be dissatisfied.

idea champions Individuals who take an innovation and actively and enthusiastically promote the idea, build support, overcome resistance, and ensure that the idea is implemented.

idea evaluation The process of creative behavior involving the evaluation of potential solutions to problems to identify the best one.

idea generation The process of creative behavior that involves developing possible solutions to a problem from relevant information and knowledge.

identification-based trust Trust based on a mutual understanding of each other's intentions and appreciation of each other's wants and desires.

illusory correlation The tendency of people to associate two events when in reality there is no connection.

imitation strategy A strategy that seeks to move into new products or new markets only after their viability has already been proven.

impression management (IM) The process by which individuals attempt to control the impression others form of them.

individualism A national culture attribute that describes the degree to which people prefer to act as individuals rather than as members of groups.

individual ranking An evaluation method that rank-orders employees from best to worst.

informal channels Communication channels that are created spontaneously and that emerge as responses to individual choices.

informal group A group that is neither formally structured nor organizationally determined; such a group appears in response to the need for social contact.

informational justice The degree to which employees are provided truthful explanations for decisions.

information gathering The stage of creative behavior when possible solutions to a problem incubate in individual's mind.

information overload   A condition in which information inflow exceeds an individual's processing capacity.

ingroup favoritism   Perspective in which we see members of our ingroup as better than other people, and people not in our group as all the same.

initiating structure   The extent to which a leader is likely to define and structure his or her role and those of subordinates in the search for goal attainment.

innovation   A new idea applied to initiating or improving a product, process, or service.

innovation strategy   A strategy that emphasizes the introduction of major new products and services.

input   Variables that lead to processes.

institutionalization   A condition that occurs when an organization takes on a life of its own, apart from any of its members, and acquires immortality.

instrumental values   Preferable modes of behavior or means of achieving one's terminal values.

integrative bargaining   Negotiation that seeks one or more settlements that can create a win–win solution.

intellectual abilities   The capacity to do mental activities—thinking, reasoning, and problem solving.

intentions   Decisions to act in a given way.

interacting groups   Typical groups in which members interact with each other face to face.

interactionist view of conflict   The belief that conflict is not only a positive force in a group but also an absolute necessity for a group to perform effectively.

intergroup conflict   Conflict between different groups or teams.

intergroup development   OD efforts to change the attitudes, stereotypes, and perceptions that groups have of each other.

interpersonal justice   The degree to which employees are treated with dignity and respect.

intragroup conflict   Conflict that occurs within a group or team.

intuition   A gut feeling not necessarily supported by research.

intuitive decision making   An unconscious process created out of distilled experience.

job characteristics model (JCM)   A model that proposes that any job can be described in terms of five core job dimensions: skill variety, task identity, task significance, autonomy, and feedback.

job design   The way the elements in a job are organized.

job engagement   The investment of an employee's physical, cognitive, and emotional energies into job performance.

job enrichment   The vertical expansion of jobs, which increases the degree to which the worker controls the planning, execution, and evaluation of the work.

job involvement   The degree to which a person identifies with a job, actively participates in it, and considers performance important to self-worth.

job rotation   The periodic shifting of an employee from one task to another.

job satisfaction   A positive feeling about one's job resulting from an evaluation of its characteristics.

job sharing   An arrangement that allows two or more individuals to split a traditional 40-hour-a-week job.

leader–member exchange (LMX) theory   A theory that supports leaders' creation of ingroups and outgroups; subordinates with ingroup status will have higher performance ratings, less turnover, and greater job satisfaction.

leader–member relations   The degree of confidence, trust, and respect subordinates have in their leader.

leader-participation model   A leadership theory that provides a set of rules to determine the form and amount of participative decision making in different situations.

leadership   The ability to influence a group toward the achievement of a vision or set of goals.

leading   A function that includes motivating employees, directing others, selecting the most effective communication channels, and resolving conflicts.

learning organization   An organization that has developed the continuous capacity to adapt and change.

least preferred co-worker (LPC) questionnaire   An instrument that purports to measure whether a person is task or relationship oriented.

legitimate power   The power a person receives as a result of his or her position in the formal hierarchy of an organization.

long-term orientation   A national culture attribute that emphasizes the future, thrift, and persistence.

low-context cultures   Cultures that rely heavily on words to convey meaning in communication.

lower-order needs   Needs that are satisfied externally, such as physiological and safety needs.

loyalty   Dissatisfaction expressed by passively waiting for conditions to improve.

Machiavellianism   The degree to which an individual is pragmatic, maintains emotional distance, and believes that ends can justify means.

management by objectives (MBO)   A program that encompasses specific goals, participatively set, for an explicit time period, with feedback on goal progress.

manager   An individual who achieves goals through other people.

masculinity   A national culture attribute that describes the extent to which the culture favors traditional masculine work roles of achievement, power, and control. Societal values are characterized by assertiveness and materialism.

material symbols   What conveys to employees who is important, the degree of egalitarianism top management desires, and the kinds of behavior that are appropriate.

matrix structure   An organization structure that creates dual lines of authority and combines functional and product departmentalization.

McClelland's theory of needs   A theory that states achievement, power, and affiliation are three important needs that help explain motivation.

mechanistic model   A structure characterized by extensive departmentalization, high formalization, a limited information network, and centralization.

mediator A neutral third party who facilitates a negotiated solution by using reasoning, persuasion, and suggestions for alternatives.

mental models Team members' knowledge and beliefs about how the work gets done by the team.

mentor A senior employee who sponsors and supports a less-experienced employee, called a protégé.

merit-based pay plan A pay plan based on performance appraisal ratings.

metamorphosis stage The stage in the socialization process in which a new employee changes and adjusts to the job, work group, and organization.

model An abstraction of reality. A simplified representation of some real-world phenomenon.

moods Feelings that tend to be less intense than emotions and that lack a contextual stimulus.

motivating potential score (MPS) A predictive index that suggests the motivating potential in a job.

motivation The processes that account for an individual's intensity, direction, and persistence of effort toward attaining a goal.

movement A change process that transforms the organization from the status quo to a desired end state.

multiteam system A collection of two or more interdependent teams that share a superordinate goal; a team of teams.

Myers-Briggs Type Indicator (MBTI) A personality test that taps four characteristics and classifies people into 1 of 16 personality types.

narcissism The tendency to be arrogant, have a grandiose sense of self-importance, require excessive admiration, and have a sense of entitlement.

need for achievement (nAch) The drive to excel, to achieve in relationship to a set of standards, and to strive to succeed.

need for affiliation (nAff) The desire for friendly and close interpersonal relationships.

need for power (nPow) The need to make others behave in a way in which they would not have behaved otherwise.

negative affect A mood dimension that consists of emotions such as nervousness, stress, and anxiety at the high end and relaxation, tranquility, and poise at the low end.

neglect Dissatisfaction expressed through allowing conditions to worsen.

negotiation A process in which two or more parties exchange goods or services and attempt to agree on the exchange rate for them.

neutralizers Attributes that make it impossible for leader behavior to make any difference to follower outcomes.

nominal group technique A group decision-making method in which individual members meet face to face to pool their judgments in a systematic but independent fashion.

norming stage The third stage in group development, characterized by close relationships and cohesiveness.

norms Acceptable standards of behavior within a group that are shared by the group's members.

openness to experience A personality dimension that characterizes someone in terms of imagination, sensitivity, and curiosity.

organic model A structure that is flat, uses cross-hierarchical and cross-functional teams, has low formalization, possesses a comprehensive information network, and relies on participative decision making.

organization A consciously coordinated social unit, composed of two or more people, that functions on a relatively continuous basis to achieve a common goal or set of goals.

organizational behavior (OB) A field of study that investigates the impact that individuals, groups, and structure have on behavior within organizations, for the purpose of applying such knowledge toward improving an organization's effectiveness.

organizational climate The shared perceptions organizational members have about their organization and work environment.

organizational commitment The degree to which an employee identifies with a particular organization and its goals and wishes to maintain membership in the organization.

organizational culture A system of shared meaning held by members that distinguishes the organization from other organizations.

organizational demography The degree to which members of a work unit share a common demographic attribute, such as age, sex, race, educational level, or length of service in an organization, and the impact of this attribute on turnover.

organizational development (OD) A collection of planned change interventions, built on humanistic–democratic values, that seeks to improve organizational effectiveness and employee well-being.

organizational justice An overall perception of what is fair in the workplace, composed of distributive, procedural, informational, and interpersonal justice.

organizational structure The way in which job tasks are formally divided, grouped, and coordinated.

organizational survival The degree to which an organization is able to exist and grow over the long term.

organizing Determining what tasks are to be done, who is to do them, how the tasks are to be grouped, who reports to whom, and where decisions are to be made.

outcomes Key factors that are affected by some other variables.

participative management A process in which subordinates share a significant degree of decision-making power with their immediate superiors.

path–goal theory A theory that states that it is the leader's job to assist followers in attaining their goals and to provide the necessary direction and/or support to ensure that their goals are compatible with the overall objectives of the group or organization.

perceived conflict Awareness by one or more parties of the existence of conditions that create opportunities for conflict to arise.

perceived organizational support (POS) The degree to which employees believe an organization values their contribution and cares about their well-being.

perception   A process by which individuals organize and interpret their sensory impressions in order to give meaning to their environment.

performing stage   The fourth stage in group development, during which the group is fully functional.

personality   The sum total of ways in which an individual reacts to and interacts with others.

personality–job fit theory   A theory that identifies six personality types and proposes that the fit between personality type and occupational environment determines satisfaction and turnover.

personality traits   Enduring characteristics that describe an individual's behavior.

physical abilities   The capacity to do tasks that demand stamina, dexterity, strength, and similar characteristics.

piece-rate pay plan   A pay plan in which workers are paid a fixed sum for each unit of production completed.

planned change   Change activities that are intentional and goal oriented.

planning   A process that includes defining goals, establishing strategy, and developing plans to coordinate activities.

political behavior   Activities that are not required as part of a person's formal role in the organization but that influence, or attempt to influence, the distribution of advantages and disadvantages within the organization.

political skill   The ability to influence others in such a way as to enhance one's objectives.

position power   Influence derived from one's formal structural position in the organization; includes power to hire, fire, discipline, promote, and give salary increases.

positive affect   A mood dimension that consists of specific positive emotions such as excitement, self-assurance, and cheerfulness at the high end and boredom, sluggishness, and tiredness at the low end.

positive organizational culture   A culture that emphasizes building on employee strengths, rewards more than punishes, and emphasizes individual vitality and growth.

positive organizational scholarship   An area of OB research that concerns how organizations develop human strength, foster vitality and resilience, and unlock potential.

positivity offset   The tendency of most individuals to experience a mildly positive mood at zero input (when nothing in particular is going on).

power   A capacity that **A** has to influence the behavior of **B** so that **B** acts in accordance with **A**'s wishes.

power distance   A national culture attribute that describes the extent to which a society accepts that power in institutions and organizations is distributed unequally.

power tactics   Ways in which individuals translate power bases into specific actions.

prearrival stage   The period of learning in the socialization process that occurs before a new employee joins the organization.

prevention focus   A self-regulation strategy that involves striving for goals by fulfilling duties and obligations.

proactive personality   People who identify opportunities, show initiative, take action, and persevere until meaningful change occurs.

problem   A discrepancy between the current state of affairs and some desired state.

problem formulation   The stage of creative behavior which involved identifying problem or opportunity that requires a solution that is as yet unknown.

problem-solving teams   Groups of 5 to 12 employees from the same department who meet for a few hours each week to discuss ways of improving quality, efficiency, and the work environment.

procedural justice   The perceived fairness of the process used to determine the distribution of rewards.

process conflict   Conflict over how work gets done.

process consultation (PC)   A meeting in which a consultant assists a client in understanding process events with which he or she must deal and identifying processes that need improvement.

processes   Actions that individuals, groups, and organizations engage in as a result of inputs and that lead to certain outcomes.

production-oriented leader   A leader who emphasizes technical or task aspects of the job.

productivity   The combination of the effectiveness and efficiency of an organization.

profit-sharing plan   An organization-wide program that distributes compensation based on some established formula designed around a company's profitability.

promotion focus   A self-regulation strategy that involves striving for goals through advancement and accomplishment.

psychological contract   An unwritten agreement that sets out what management expects from an employee and vice versa.

psychological empowerment   Employees' belief in the degree to which they affect their work environment, their competence, the meaningfulness of their job, and their perceived autonomy in their work.

psychology   The science that seeks to measure, explain, and sometimes change the behavior of humans and other animals.

psychopathy   The tendency for a lack of concern for others and a lack of guilt or remorse when their actions cause harm.

punctuated-equilibrium model   A set of phases that temporary groups go through that involves transitions between inertia and activity.

randomness error   The tendency of individuals to believe that they can predict the outcome of random events.

rational   Characterized by making consistent, value-maximizing choices within specified constraints.

rational decision-making model   A decision-making model that describes how individuals should behave in order to maximize some outcome.

reference group   A group in which a person is aware of other members, defines himself or herself as a member or would like to be a member, and feels group members are significant to him or her.

referent power   Influence based on identification with a person who has desirable resources or personal traits.

reflexivity   A team characteristic of reflecting on and adjusting the master plan when necessary.

refreezing   Stabilizing a change intervention by balancing driving and restraining forces.

reinforcement theory   A theory that says that behavior is a function of its consequences.

relationship conflict   Conflict based on interpersonal relationships.

representative participation   A system in which workers participate in organizational decision making through a small group of representative employees.

resources   Things within an individual's control that can be used to resolve demands.

restraining forces   Forces that hinder movement from the existing equilibrium.

reward power   Compliance achieved based on the ability to distribute rewards that others view as valuable.

risk aversion   The tendency to prefer a sure gain of a moderate amount over a riskier outcome, even if the riskier outcome might have a higher expected payoff.

rituals   Repetitive sequences of activities that express and reinforce the key values of the organization, which goals are most important, which people are important, and which are expendable.

role   A set of expected behavior patterns attributed to someone occupying a given position in a social unit.

role conflict   A situation in which an individual is confronted by divergent role expectations.

role expectations   How others believe a person should act in a given situation.

role perception   An individual's view of how he or she is supposed to act in a given situation.

selective perception   The tendency to selectively interpret what one sees on the basis of one's interests, background, experience, and attitudes.

self-actualization   The drive to become what a person is capable of becoming.

self-concordance   The degree to which peoples' reasons for pursuing goals are consistent with their interests and core values.

self-determination theory   A theory of motivation that is concerned with the beneficial effects of intrinsic motivation and the harmful effects of extrinsic motivation.

self-efficacy theory   An individual's belief that he or she is capable of performing a task.

self-fulfilling prophecy   A situation in which a person inaccurately perceives a second person, and the resulting expectations cause the second person to behave in ways consistent with the original perception.

self-managed work teams   Groups of 10 to 15 people who take on responsibilities of their former supervisors.

self-monitoring   A personality trait that measures an individual's ability to adjust his or her behavior to external, situational factors.

self-serving bias   The tendency for individuals to attribute their own successes to internal factors and put the blame for failures on external factors.

sensitivity training   Training groups that seek to change behavior through unstructured group interaction.

servant leadership   A leadership style marked by going beyond the leader's own self-interest and instead focusing on opportunities to help followers grow and develop.

sexual harassment   Any unwanted activity of a sexual nature that affects an individual's employment and creates a hostile work environment.

short-term orientation   A national culture attribute that emphasizes the past and present, respect for tradition, and fulfillment of social obligations.

simple structure   An organization structure characterized by a low degree of departmentalization, wide spans of control, authority centralized in a single person, and little formalization.

single-loop learning   A process of correcting errors using past routines and present policies.

situational leadership theory (SLT)   A contingency theory that focuses on followers' readiness.

situation-strength theory   A theory indicating that the way personality translates into behavior depends on the strength of the situation.

skill-based pay   A pay plan that sets pay levels on the basis of how many skills employees have or how many jobs they can do.

skill variety   The degree to which a job requires a variety of different activities.

social identity theory   Perspective that considers when and why individuals consider themselves members of groups.

social-learning theory   The view that we can learn through both observation and direct experience.

socialization   A process that adapts employees to the organization's culture.

socialized charismatic leadership   A leadership concept that states that leaders convey values that are other centered versus self centered and who role-model ethical conduct.

social loafing   The tendency for individuals to expend less effort when working collectively than when working individually.

social psychology   An area of psychology that blends concepts from psychology and sociology and that focuses on the influence of people on one another.

sociology   The study of people in relation to their social environment or culture.

span of control   The number of subordinates a manager can efficiently and effectively direct.

status   A socially defined position or rank given to groups or group members by others.

status characteristics theory   A theory that states that differences in status characteristics create status hierarchies within groups.

stereotyping   Judging someone on the basis of one's perception of the group to which that person belongs.

storming stage   The second stage in group development, characterized by intragroup conflict.

stress   An unpleasant psychological process that occurs in response to environmental pressures.

strong culture   A culture in which the core values are intensely held and widely shared.

subcultures   Minicultures within an organization, typically defined by department designations and geographical separation.

substitutes   Attributes, such as experience and training, that can replace the need for a leader's support or ability to create structure.

surface acting   Hiding one's inner feelings and forgoing emotional expressions in response to display rules.

surface-level diversity   Differences in easily perceived characteristics, such as gender, race, ethnicity, age, or disability, that do not necessarily reflect the ways people think or feel but that may activate certain stereotypes.

survey feedback   The use of questionnaires to identify discrepancies among member perceptions; discussion follows, and remedies are suggested.

systematic study   Looking at relationships, attempting to attribute causes and effects, and drawing conclusions based on scientific evidence.

task conflict   Conflict over content and goals of the work.

task identity   The degree to which a job requires completion of a whole and identifiable piece of work.

task performance   The combination of effectiveness and efficiency at doing your core job tasks.

task significance   The degree to which a job has a substantial impact on the lives or work of other people.

task structure   The degree to which job assignments are procedurized.

team building   High interaction among team members to increase trust and openness.

technical skills   The ability to apply specialized knowledge or expertise.

technology   The way in which an organization transfers its inputs into outputs.

telecommuting   Working from home at least two days a week on a computer that is linked to the employer's office.

terminal values   Desirable end-states of existence; the goals a person would like to achieve during his or her lifetime.

Theory X   The assumption that employees dislike work, are lazy, dislike responsibility, and must be coerced to perform.

Theory Y   The assumption that employees like work, are creative, seek responsibility, and can exercise self-direction.

three-stage model of creativity   The proposition that creativity involves three stages: causes (creative potential and creative environment), creative behavior, and creative outcomes (innovation).

traditional view of conflict   The belief that all conflict is harmful and must be avoided.

trait activation theory (TAT)   A theory that predicts that some situations, events, or interventions "activate" a trait more than others.

trait theories of leadership   Theories that consider personal qualities and characteristics that differentiate leaders from nonleaders.

transactional leaders   Leaders who guide or motivate their followers in the direction of established goals by clarifying role and task requirements.

transformational leaders   Leaders who inspire followers to transcend their own self-interests and who are capable of having a profound and extraordinary effect on followers.

trust   A positive expectation that another will not act opportunistically.

two-factor theory   A theory that relates intrinsic factors to job satisfaction and associates extrinsic factors with dissatisfaction. Also called motivation-hygiene theory.

uncertainty avoidance   A national culture attribute that describes the extent to which a society feels threatened by uncertain and ambiguous situations and tries to avoid them.

unfreezing   Changing to overcome the pressures of both individual resistance and group conformity.

unity of command   The idea that a subordinate should have only one superior to whom he or she is directly responsible.

utilitarianism   A system in which decisions are made to provide the greatest good for the greatest number.

values   Basic convictions that a specific mode of conduct or end-state of existence is personally or socially preferable to an opposite or converse mode of conduct or end-state of existence.

value system   A hierarchy based on a ranking of an individual's values in terms of their intensity.

variable-pay program   A pay plan that bases a portion of an employee's pay on some individual and/or organizational measure of performance.

virtual organization   A small, core organization that outsources major business functions.

virtual teams   Teams that use computer technology to tie together physically dispersed members in order to achieve a common goal.

vision   A long-term strategy for attaining a goal or goals.

vision statement   A formal articulation of an organization's vision or mission.

voice   Dissatisfaction expressed through active and constructive attempts to improve conditions.

wellness programs   Organizationally supported programs that focus on the employee's total physical and mental condition.

whistle-blowers   Individuals who report unethical practices by their employer to outsiders.

withdrawal behavior   The set of actions employee take to separate themselves from the organization.

workforce diversity   The concept that organizations are becoming more heterogeneous in terms of gender, age, race, ethnicity, sexual orientation, and inclusion of other diverse groups.

work group   A group that interacts primarily to share information and to make decisions to help each group member perform within his or her area of responsibility.

workplace spirituality   The recognition that people have an inner life that nourishes and is nourished by meaningful work that takes place in the context of community.

work sample tests   Hands-on simulations of part or all of the work that applicants for routine jobs must perform.

work specialization   The degree to which tasks in an organization are subdivided into separate jobs.

work team   A group whose individual efforts result in performance that is greater than the sum of the individual inputs.

Endnotes

CHAPTER 1

1. Cited in R. Alsop, "Playing Well with Others," *Wall Street Journal* (September 9, 2002).
2. S. E. Humphrey, J. D. Nahrgang, and F. P. Morgeson, "Integrating Motivational, Social, and Contextual Work Design Features: A Meta-Analytic Summary and Theoretical Extension of the Work Design Literature," *Journal of Applied Psychology* 92, no. 5 (2007), pp. 1332–1356.
3. E. R. Burris, "The Risks and Rewards of Speaking Up: Managerial Responses to Employee Voice," *Academy of Management Journal* 55, no. 4 (2012), pp. 851–875.
4. I. S. Fulmer, B. Gerhart, and K. S. Scott, "Are the 100 Best Better? An Empirical Investigation of the Relationship Between Being a 'Great Place to Work' and Firm Performance," *Personnel Psychology* (Winter 2003), pp. 965–993.
5. T. L. Miller, C. L. Wesley II, and D. E. Williams, "Educating the Minds of Caring Hearts: Comparing the Views of Practitioners and Educators on the Importance of Social Entrepreneurship Competencies," *Academy of Management Learning & Education* 2, no. 3 (2012), pp. 349–370.
6. H. Aguinis and A. Glavas, "What We Don't Know About Corporate Social Responsibility: A Review and Research Agenda," *Journal of Management* (July 2012), pp. 932–968.
7. H. Fayol, *Industrial and General Administration* (Paris: Dunod, 1916).
8. A. I. Kraut, P. R. Pedigo, D. D. McKenna, and M. D. Dunnette, "The Role of the Manager: What's Really Important in Different Management Jobs," *Academy of Management Executive* 19, no. 4 (2005), pp. 122–129.
9. H. Mintzberg, *The Nature of Managerial Work* (Upper Saddle River, NJ: Prentice Hall, 1973).
10. R. L. Katz, "Skills of an Effective Administrator," *Harvard Business Review* (September–October 1974), pp. 90–102; D. Bartram, "The Great Eight Competencies: A Criterion-Centric Approach to Validation," *Journal of Applied Psychology* 90, no. 6 (2005), pp. 1185–1203; and S. E. Scullen, M. K. Mount, and T. A. Judge, "Evidence of the Construct Validity of Developmental Ratings of Managerial Performance," *Journal of Applied Psychology* 88, no. 1 (2003), pp. 50–66.
11. F. Luthans, "Successful vs. Effective Real Managers," *Academy of Management Executive* (May 1988), pp. 127–132; and F. Luthans, R. M. Hodgetts, and S. A. Rosenkrantz, *Real Managers* (Cambridge, MA: Ballinger, 1988). See also F. Shipper and J. Davy, "A Model and Investigation of Managerial Skills, Employees' Attitudes, and Managerial Performance," *Leadership Quarterly* 13 (2002), pp. 95–120.
12. P. Wu, M. Foo, and D. B. Turban, "The Role of Personality in Relationship Closeness, Developer Assistance, and Career Success," *Journal of Vocational Behavior* 73, no. 3 (2008), pp. 440–448; and A. M. Konrad, R. Kashlak, I. Yoshioka, R. Waryszak, and N. Toren, "What Do Managers Like to Do? A Five-Country Study," *Group & Organization Management* (December 2001), pp. 401–433.
13. A. S. Tsui, S. J. Ashford, L. St. Clair, and K. R. Xin, "Dealing with Discrepant Expectations: Response Strategies and Managerial Effectiveness," *Academy of Management Journal* (December 1995), pp. 1515–1543.
14. See, for instance, C. Heath and S. B. Sitkin, "Big-B Versus Big-O: What Is *Organizational* about Organizational Behavior?" *Journal of Organizational Behavior* (February 2001), pp. 43–58. For a review of what one eminent researcher believes *should* be included in organizational behavior, based on survey data, see J. B. Miner, "The Rated Importance, Scientific Validity, and Practical Usefulness of Organizational Behavior Theories: A Quantitative Review," *Academy of Management Learning & Education* (September 2003), pp. 250–268.
15. D. M. Rousseau and S. McCarthy, "Educating Managers from an Evidence-Based Perspective," *Academy of Management Learning & Education* 6, no. 1 (2007), pp. 84–101; and S. L. Rynes, T. L. Giluk, and K. G. Brown, "The Very Separate Worlds of Academic and Practitioner Periodicals in Human Resource Management: Implications for Evidence-Based Management," *Academy of Management Journal* 50, no. 5 (2007), pp. 987–1008.
16. J. Surowiecki, "The Fatal-Flaw Myth," *The New Yorker* (July 31, 2006), p. 25.
17. A. McAfee and E. Brynjolfsson, "Big Data: The Management Revolution," *Harvard Business Review* (October 2012), pp. 59–68.
18. N. Bloom, R. Sadun, and J. Van Reenan, "How Three Essential Practices Can Address Even the Most Complex Global Practices," *Harvard Business Review* (November 2012), pp. 77–82.
19. M. J. Mauboussin, "Most Companies Use the Wrong Metrics. Don't Be One of Them," *Harvard Business Review* (October 2012), pp. 46–56.
20. M. Toossi, "A Century of Change: The U.S. Labor Force, 1950–2050," *Bureau of Labor Statistics* (May 2002), www.bls.gov/opub/mlr/2002/05/art2full.pdf.
21. M. Toossi, "Labor Force Projections to 2020: A More Slowly Growing Workforce," *Bureau of Labor Statistics* (January 2012), www.bls.gov/opub/mlr/2012/01/art3full.pdf.
22. See, for instance, M. Workman and W. Bommer, "Redesigning Computer Call Center Work: A Longitudinal Field Experiment," *Journal of Organizational Behavior* (May 2004), pp. 317–337.
23. E. J. Hirst, "Burnout on the Rise," *Chicago Tribune* (October 19, 2012), http://articles.chicagotribune.com/2012-10-29/business/ct-biz-1029-employee-burnout-20121029_1_employee-burnout-herbert-freudenberger-employee-stress.
24. S. Shellenbarger, "Single and Off the Fast Track," *The Wall Street Journal* (May 23, 2012), pp. D1, D3.
25. M. Mithel, "What Women Want," *Business Today* (March 8, 2013), http://businesstoday.intoday.in/story/careers-work-life-balance-women/1/193135.html.
26. D. S. Ones and S. Dilchert, "Environmental Sustainability at Work: A Call to Action," *Industrial and Organizational Psychology* 5 (2012), pp. 444–466.
27. F. Luthans and C. M. Youssef, "Emerging Positive Organizational Behavior," *Journal of Management* (June 2007), pp. 321–349; C. M. Youssef and F. Luthans, "Positive Organizational Behavior in the Workplace: The Impact of Hope, Optimism, and Resilience," *Journal of Management* 33,

no. 5 (2007), pp. 774–800; and J. E. Dutton and S. Sonenshein, "Positive Organizational Scholarship," in C. Cooper and J. Barling (eds.), *Encyclopedia of Positive Psychology* (Thousand Oaks, CA: Sage, 2007).

28. L. M. Roberts, G. Spreitzer, J. Dutton, R. Quinn, E. Heaphy, and B. Barker, "How to Play to Your Strengths," *Harvard Business Review* (January 2005), pp. 1–6; and L. M. Roberts, J. E. Dutton, G. M. Spreitzer, E. D. Heaphy, and R. E. Quinn, "Composing the Reflected Best-Self Portrait: Becoming Extraordinary in Work Organizations," *Academy of Management Review* 30, no. 4 (2005), pp. 712–736.

29. W. Bailey and A. Spicer, "When Does National Identity Matter? Convergence and Divergence in International Business Ethics," *Academy of Management Journal* 50, no. 6 (2007), pp. 1462–1480; and A. B. Oumlil and J. L. Balloun, "Ethical Decision-Making Differences between American and Moroccan Managers," *Journal of Business Ethics* 84, no. 4 (2009), pp. 457–478.

30. J. Merritt, "For MBAs, Soul-Searching 101," *Business Week* (September 16, 2002), pp. 64–66; and S. Greenhouse, "The Mood at Work: Anger and Anxiety," *The New York Times* (October 29, 2002), p. E1.

31. See, for instance, G. R. Weaver, L. K. Trevino, and P. L. Cochran, "Corporate Ethics Practices in the Mid-1990's: An Empirical Study of the Fortune 1000," *Journal of Business Ethics* (February 1999), pp. 283–294; and C. De Mesa Graziano, "Promoting Ethical Conduct: A Review of Corporate Practices," *Strategic Investor Relations* (Fall 2002), pp. 29–35.

32. D. M. Mayer, M. Kuenzi, R. Greenbaum, M. Bardes, and R. Salvador, "How Low Does Ethical Leadership Flow? Test of a Trickle-Down Model," *Organizational Behavior and Human Decision Processes* 108, no. 1 (2009), pp. 1–13; and A. Ardichvili, J. A. Mitchell, and D. Jondle, "Characteristics of Ethical Business Cultures," *Journal of Business Ethics* 85, no. 4 (2009), pp. 445–451.

33. "Unplanned Absence Costs Organizations 8.7 Percent of Payroll, Mercer/Kronos Study" (June 28, 2010), www.mercer.com/press-releases/1383785.

34. W. Hoge, "Sweden's Cradle-to-Grave Welfare Starts to Get Ill," *International Herald Tribune* (September 25, 2002), p. 8.

35. See www.bls.gov/data (May 11, 2005).

36. See, for example, M. C. Sturman and C. O Trevor, "The Implications of Linding the Dynamic Performance and Turnover Literatures," *Journal of Applied Psychology* (August 2001), pp. 684–696.

37. M. Casey-Campbell and M. L. Martens, "Sticking It All Together: A Critical Assessment of the Group Cohesion-Performance Literature," *International Journal of Management Reviews* 11, (2008), pp. 223–246.

38. A. J. Rucci, S. P. Kirn, and R. T. Quinn, "The Employee–Customer–Profit Chain at Sears," *Harvard Business Review* (January–February 1998), pp. 83–97.

CHAPTER 2

1. M. DiNatale and S. Boraas, "The Labor Force Experience of Women from Generation X," *Monthly Labor Review* (March 2002), pp. 1–15.

2. See, for example, F. Welch, "Catching Up: Wages of Black Men," *The American Economic Review* 93, no. 2 (2003), pp. 320–325; A. Sakamoto, H. Wu, and J. M. Tzeng, "The Declining Significance of Race Among American Men During the Latter Half of the Twentieth Century," *Demography* 37 (January 2000), pp. 41–51; and A Sakomoto, K. A. Goyette, and C. Kim, "Socioeconomic Attainments of Asian Americans," *Annual Review of Sociology* 35, (2009), pp. 255–276.

3. J. Schram, *SHRM Workplace Forecast* (Alexandria, VA: Society for Human Resource Management, 2006).

4. D. A. Harrison, K. H. Price, J. H. Gavin, and A. T. Florey, "Time, Teams, and Task Performance: Changing Effects of Surface- and Deep-Level Diversity on Group Functioning," *Academy of Management Journal* 45, no. 5 (2002), pp. 1029–1045; and A. H. Eagly and J. L. Chin, "Are Memberships in Race, Ethnicity, and Gender Categories Merely Surface Characteristics?" *American Psychologist* 65 (2010), pp. 934–935.

5. P. Chattopadhyay, M. Tluchowska, and E. George, "Identifying the Ingroup: A Closer Look at the Influence of Demographic Dissimilarity on Employee Social Identity," *Academy of Management Review* 29, no. 2 (2004), pp. 180–202; and P. Chattopadhyay, "Beyond Direct and Symmetrical Effects: The Influence of Demographic Dissimilarity on Organizational Citizenship Behavior," *Academy of Management Journal* 42, no. 3 (1999), pp. 273–287.

6. L. M. Cortina, "Unseen Injustice: Incivility as Modern Discrimination in Organizations," *Academy of Management Review* 33, no. 1 (2008), pp. 55–75.

7. T. Lytle, "Benefits for Older Workers," *HR Magazine* (March 2012), pp. 53–58.

8. L. Weber, "Americans Rip Up Retirement Plans," *The Wall Street Journal* (January 31, 2013), http://online.wsj.com/article/SB10001424127887323926104578276241741448064.html.

9. K. A. Wrenn and T. J. Maurer, "Beliefs About Older Workers' Learning and Development Behavior in Relation to Beliefs About Malleability of Skills, Age-Related Decline, and Control," *Journal of Applied Social Psychology* 34, no. 2 (2004), pp. 223–242; and R. A. Posthuma and M. A. Campion, "Age Stereotypes in the Workplace: Common Stereotypes, Moderators, and Future Research Directions," *Journal of Management* 35 (2009), pp. 158–188.

10. T. W. H. Ng and D. C. Feldman, "Re-examining the Relationship Between Age and Voluntary Turnover," *Journal of Vocational Behavior* 74 (2009), pp. 283–294.

11. T. W. H. Ng and D. C. Feldman, "The Relationship of Age to Ten Dimensions of Job Performance," *Journal of Applied Psychology* 93 (2008), pp. 392–423.

12. T. W. H. Ng and D. C. Feldman, "Evaluating Six Common Stereotypes about Older Workers with Meta-Analytical Data," *Personnel Psychology* 65 (2012), pp. 821–858.

13. See Ng and Feldman, "The Relationship of Age to Ten Dimensions of Job Performance."

14. T. W. H. Ng and D. C. Feldman, "The Relationship of Age with Job Attitudes: A Meta-Analysis," *Personnel Psychology* 63 (2010), pp. 677–718.

15. F. Kunze, S. A. Boehm, and H. Bruch, "Age Diversity, Age Discrimination Climate and Performance

Consequences—A Cross Organizational Study," *Journal of Organizational Behavior* 32 (2011), pp. 264–290.

16. P. L. Roth, K. L. Purvis, and P. Bobko, "A Meta-Analysis of Gender Group Differences for Measures of Job Performance in Field Studies," *Journal of Management* (March 2012), pp. 719–739.

17. See E. M. Weiss, G. Kemmler, E. A. Deisenhammer, W. W. Fleischhacker, and M. Delazer, "Sex Differences in Cognitive Functions," *Personality and Individual Differences* (September 2003), pp. 863–875; and A. F. Jorm, K. J. Anstey, H. Christensen, and B. Rodgers, "Gender Differences in Cognitive Abilities: The Mediating Role of Health State and Health Habits," *Intelligence* (January 2004), pp. 7–23.

18. S. Kolhatkar, "Emasculation Nation," *Bloomberg Businessweek* (September 17–September 23, 2012), pp. 102–103.

19. R K. Chang, "Bias Persists for Women of Science, A Study Finds," *The New York Times* (September 25, 2012), Science pp. 1, 6.

20. K. Peters, M. Ryan, S. A. Haslam, and H. Fernandes, "To Belong or Not to Belong: Evidence That Women's Occupational Disidentification Is Promoted by Lack of Fit with Masculine Occupational Prototypes," *Journal of Personnel Psychology* 2 (2012), pp. 148–158.

21. R. E. Silverman, "Study Suggests Fix for Gender Bias on the Job," *The Wall Street Journal* (January 9, 2013), p. D4.

22. E. B. King et al., "Benevolent Sexism at Work: Gender Differences in the Distribution of Challenging Developmental Experiences," *Journal of Management* (November 2012), pp. 1835–1866.

23. M. E. Heilman and T. G. Okimoto, "Why Are Women Penalized for Success at Male Tasks? The Implied Communality Deficit," *Journal of Applied Psychology* 92, no. 1 (2007), pp. 81–92.

24. See, for instance, J. Bussey, "How Women Can Get Ahead: Advice from Female CEOs," *The Wall Street Journal* (May 18, 2012), pp. B1–B2; T. Gara, "Sandberg Opens Up on Women and Work," *The Wall Street Journal* (February 6, 2013); and L. Petrecca, "High-Paying Careers Top More Young Women's Lists," *The Wall Street Journal* (April 20, 2012) pp. 1A–2A.

25. D. R. Avery, P. F. McKay, and D. C. Wilson "What Are the Odds? How Demographic Similarity Affects the Prevalence of Perceived Employment Discrimination," *Journal of Applied Psychology* 93 (2008), pp. 235–249.

26. A. Damast, "She Works Hard for Less Money," *Bloomberg Businessweek* (December 24, 2012–January 6, 2013), pp. 31–32.

27. B. Casselman, "Male Nurses Earn More," *The Wall Street Journal* (February 26, 2013), p. A2.

28. M. A. Belliveau, "Engendering Inequity? How Social Accounts Create vs. Merely Explain Unfavorable Pay Outcomes for Women," *Organization Science* (July–August 2012), pp. 1154–1174.

29. A. J. C. Cuddy, "Increasingly, Juries are Taking the Side of Women Who Face Workplace Discrimination," *Harvard Business Review* (September 2012), pp. 95–100.

30. J. L. Raver and L. H. Nishii, "Once, Twice, or Three Times as Harmful? Ethnic Harassment, Gender Harassment, and Generalized Workplace Harassment," *Journal of Applied Psychology* 95 (2010), pp. 236–254.

31. J. I Hancock, D. G. Allen, F. A. Bosco, K. R. McDaniel, and C. A. Pierce, "Meta-Analytic Review of Employee Turnover

as a Predictor of Firm Performance," *Journal of Management* (March 2013), pp. 573–603.

32. D. R. Avery, J. A. Richeson, M R. Hebl, and N. Ambady, "It Does Not Have to Be Uncomfortable: The Role of Behavioral Scripts in Black-White Interracial Interactions," *Journal of Applied Psychology* 94 (2009), pp. 1382–1393.

33. J. M. McCarthy, C. H. Van Iddekinge, and M. A. Campion, "Are Highly Structured Job Interviews Resistant to Demographic Similarity Effects?" *Personnel Psychology* 63 (2010), pp. 325–359; and G. N. Powell and D. A. Butterfield, "Exploring the Influence of Decision Makers' Race and Gender on Actual Promotions to Top Management," *Personnel Psychology* 55, no. 2 (2002), pp. 397–428.

34. D. R. Avery, P F. McKay, and D. C. Wilson "What Are the Odds? How Demographic Similarity Affects the Prevalence of Perceived Employment Discrimination," *Journal of Applied Psychology* 93 (2008), pp. 235–249.

35. J. M. Sacco, C. R. Scheu, A. M. Ryan, and N. Schmitt, "An Investigation of Race and Sex Similarity Effects in Interviews: A Multilevel Approach to Relational Demography," *Journal of Applied Psychology* 88, no. 5 (2003), pp. 852–865; and P. F. McKay and M. A. McDaniel, "A Reexamination of Black-White Mean Differences in Work Performance: More Data, More Moderators," *Journal of Applied Psychology* 91, no. 3 (2006), pp. 538–554.

36. T. Vega, "With Diversity Still Lacking, Industry Focuses on Retention," *The New York Times* (September 4, 2012), p. B3.

37. Avery, McKay, and Wilson, "What Are the Odds? How Demographic Similarity Affects the Prevalence of Perceived Employment Discrimination"; and Raver and Nishii, "Once, Twice, or Three Times as Harmful? Ethnic Harassment, Gender Harassment, and Generalized Workplace Harassment."

38. B. R. Ragins, J. A. Gonzalez, K. Ehrhardt, and R. Singh, "Crossing the Threshold: The Spillover of Community Racial Diversity and Diversity Climate to the Workplace," *Personnel Psychology* 65 (2012), pp. 755–787.

39. P. F. McKay, D. R. Avery, and M. A. Morris, "Mean Racial-Ethnic Differences in Employee Sales Performance: The Moderating Role of Diversity Climate," *Personnel Psychology* 61, no. 2 (2008), pp. 349–374.

40. *Americans with Disabilities Act,* 42 U.S.C. § 12101, et seq. (1990).

41. S. G. Goldberg, M. B. Killeen, and B. O'Day, "The Disclosure Conundrum: How People with Psychiatric Disabilities Navigate Employment," *Psychology, Public Policy, and Law* 11, no. 3 (2005), pp. 463–500; and M. L. Ellison, Z. Russinova, K. L. MacDonald-Wilson, and A. Lyass, "Patterns and Correlates of Workplace Disclosure Among Professionals and Managers with Psychiatric Conditions," *Journal of Vocational Rehabilitation* 18, no. 1 (2003), pp. 3–13.

42. L. R. Ren, R. L. Paetzold, and A. Colella, "A Meta-Analysis of Experimental Studies on the Effects of Disability on Human Resource Judgments," *Human Resource Management Review* 18, no. 3 (2008), pp. 191–203.

43. S. Almond and A. Healey, "Mental Health and Absence from Work: New Evidence from the UK Quarterly Labour Force Survey," *Work, Employment, and Society* 17, no. 4 (2003), pp. 731–742.

44. B. S. Bell and K. J. Klein, "Effect of Disability, Gender, and Job Level on Ratings of Job Applicants," *Rehabilitation Psychology*

46, no. 3 (2001), pp. 229–246; and E. Louvet, "Social Judgment Toward Job Applicants with Disabilities: Perception of Personal Qualities and Competences," *Rehabilitation Psychology* 52, no. 3 (2007), pp. 297–303.

45. T. W. H. Ng and D. C. Feldman, "Organizational Tenure and Job Performance," *Journal of Management* 36, (2010), pp. 1220–1250.

46. I. R. Gellatly, "Individual and Group Determinants of Employee Absenteeism: Test of a Causal Model," *Journal of Organizational Behavior* (September 1995), pp. 469–485.

47. R. W. Griffeth, P. W. Hom, and S. Gaertner, "A Meta-Analysis of Antecedents and Correlates of Employee Turnover: Update, Moderator Tests, and Research Implications for the Next Millennium," *Journal of Management* 26, no. 3 (2000), pp. 463–488.

48. M. R. Barrick and R. D. Zimmerman, "Hiring for Retention and Performance," *Human Resource Management* 48 (2009), pp. 183–206.

49. W. van Breukelen, R. van der Vlist, and H. Steensma, "Voluntary Employee Turnover: Combining Variables from the 'Traditional' Turnover Literature with the Theory of Planned Behavior," *Journal of Organizational Behavior* 25, no. 7 (2004), pp. 893–914.

50. E. B. King and A. S. Ahmad, "An Experimental Field Study of Interpersonal Discrimination Toward Muslim Job Applicants," *Personnel Psychology* 63 (2010), pp. 881–906.

51. A. Tilcsik, "Pride and Prejudice: Employment Discrimination against Openly Gay Men in the United States," *American Journal of Sociology* 117 (2011), pp. 586–626.

52. "Facts about Discrimination in Federal Government Employment Based on Marital Status, Political Affiliation, Status as a Parent, Sexual Orientation, or Transgender (Gender Identity) Status," U.S. Equal Employment Opportunity Commission (2013), www.eeoc.gov/federal/otherprotections.cfm.

53. "Sex-Based Discrimination," U.S. Equal Employment Opportunity Commission (2013), www.eeoc.gov/laws/types/sex.cfm.

54. M. Keisling, "No Longer at Zero: An Update on ENDA," *Huffington Post* (March 13, 2013), www.huffingtonpost.com/mara-keisling/no-longer-at-zero-an-upda_b_2861885.html.

55. C. Burns, "The Costly Business of Discrimination," *Center for American Progress* (March 2012), p. 11, www.scribd.com/doc/81214767/The-Costly-Business-of-Discrimination.

56. Ibid, p. 13.

57. *HRC Corporate Equality Index,* 2013, www.hrc.org/files/assets/resources/CorporateEqualityIndex_2013.pdf.

58. R. Donadio, "Stuck in Recession, Italy Takes on Labor Laws That Divide the Generations," *The New York Times* (March 19, 2012), pp. A4, A6.

59. P. A. Freund and N. Kasten, "How Smart Do You Think You Are? A Meta-Analysis of the Validity of Self-Estimates of Cognitive Ability," *Psychological Bulletin* 138 (2012), pp. 296–321.

60. R. E. Nisbett et al., "Intelligence: New Findings and Theoretical Developments," *American Psychologist* (February–March 2012), pp. 130–159.

61. L. S. Gottfredson, "The Challenge and Promise of Cognitive Career Assessment," *Journal of Career Assessment* 11, no. 2 (2003), pp. 115–135.

62. M. D. Dunnette, "Aptitudes, Abilities, and Skills," in M. D. Dunnette (ed.), *Handbook of Industrial and Organizational Psychology* (Chicago: Rand McNally, 1976), pp. 478–483.

63. J. W. B. Lang, M. Kersting, U. R. Hülscheger, and J. Lang, "General Mental Ability, Narrower Cognitive Abilities, and Job Performance: The Perspective of the Nested-Factors Model of Cognitive Abilities" *Personnel Psychology* 63 (2010), pp. 595–640.

64. N. Barber, "Educational and Ecological Correlates of IQ: A Cross-National Investigation," *Intelligence* (May–June 2005), pp. 273–284.

65. M. E. Beier and F. L. Oswald, "Is Cognitive Ability a Liability? A Critique and Future Research Agenda on Skilled Performance," *Journal of Experimental Psychology: Applied* 18 (2012), pp. 331–345.

66. J. F. Salgado, N. Anderson, S. Moscoso, C. Bertua, F. de Fruyt, and J. P. Rolland, "A Meta-Analytic Study of General Mental Ability Validity for Different Occupations in the European Community," *Journal of Applied Psychology* (December 2003), pp. 1068–1081; and F. L. Schmidt and J. E. Hunter, "Select on Intelligence," in E. A. Locke (ed.), *Handbook of Principles of Organizational Behavior* (Malden, MA: Blackwell, 2004).

67. Y. Ganzach, "Intelligence and Job Satisfaction," *Academy of Management Journal* 41, no. 5 (1998), pp. 526–539; and Y. Ganzach, "Intelligence, Education, and Facets of Job Satisfaction," *Work and Occupations* 30, no. 1 (2003), pp. 97–122.

68. J. J. Caughron, M. D. Mumford, and E. A. Fleishman, "The Fleishman Job Analysis Survey: Development, Validation, and Applications," in M. A. Wilson, W. Bennett Jr., S. G. Gibson, and G. M. Alliger (eds.), *The Handbook of Work Analysis: Methods, Systems, Applications and Science of Work Measurement in Organizations* (New York: Routledge/Taylor & Francis Group, 2012); P. D. Converse, F. L. Oswald, M. A. Gillespie, K. A. Field, and E. B. Bizot, "Matching Individuals to Occupations Using Abilities and the O*Net: Issues and an Application in Career Guidance," *Personnel Psychology* (Summer 2004), pp. 451–487; and E. A. Fleishman, "Evaluating Physical Abilities Required by Jobs," *Personnel Administrator* (June 1979), pp. 82–92.

69. D. R. Avery, "Reactions to Diversity in Recruitment Advertising: Are the Differences Black and White?" *Journal of Applied Psychology* 88, no. 4 (2003), pp. 672–679; P. F. McKay and D. R. Avery, "What Has Race Got to Do with It? Unraveling the Role of Racioethnicity in Job Seekers' Reactions to Site Visits," *Personnel Psychology* 59, no. 2 (2006), pp. 395–429; and D. R. Avery and P. F. McKay, "Target Practice: An Organizational Impression Management Approach to Attracting Minority and Female Job Applicants," *Personnel Psychology* 59, no. 1 (2006), pp. 157–187.

70. C. C. Miller, "Google Search and Replace," *The New York Times* (August 23, 2012), pp. B1, B5.

71. A. Overholt, "More Women Coders," *Fortune* (February 25, 2013), p. 14.

72. L. Kwoh, "McKinsey Tries to Recruit Mothers Who Left the Fold," *The Wall Street Journal* (February 20, 2013), pp. B1, B7.

73. M. R. Buckley, K. A. Jackson, M. C. Bolino, J. G. Veres, and H. S. Field, "The Influence of Relational Demography on

Panel Interview Ratings: A Field Experiment," *Personnel Psychology* 60 (2007), pp. 627–646; J. M. Sacco, C. R. Scheu, A. M. Ryan, and N. Schmitt, "An Investigation of Race and Sex Similarity Effects in Interviews: A Multilevel Approach to Relational Demography," *Journal of Applied Psychology* 88 (2003), pp. 852–865; and J. C. Ziegert and P. J. Hanges, "Employment Discrimination: The Role of Implicit Attitudes, Motivation, and a Climate for Racial Bias," *Journal of Applied Psychology* 90 (2005), pp. 553–562.

74. J. Schaubroeck and S. S. K. Lam, "How Similarity to Peers and Supervisor Influences Organizational Advancement in Different Cultures," *Academy of Management Journal* 45 (2002), pp. 1120–1136.

75. K. Bezrukova, K. A. Jehn, and C. S. Spell, "Reviewing Diversity Training: Where We Have Been and Where We Should Go," *Academy of Management Learning & Education* 2 (2012), pp. 207–227.

76. S. T. Bell, "Deep-Level Composition Variables as Predictors of Team Performance: A Meta–Analysis," *Journal of Applied Psychology* 92, no. 3 (2007), pp. 595–615; S. K. Horwitz and I. B. Horwitz, "The Effects of Team Diversity on Team Outcomes: A Meta-Analytic Review of Team Demography," *Journal of Management* 33, no. 6 (2007), pp. 987–1015; G. L. Stewart, "A Meta-Analytic Review of Relationships Between Team Design Features and Team Performance," *Journal of Management* 32, no. 1 (2006), pp. 29–54; and A. Joshi and H. Roh, "The Role of Context in Work Team Diversity Research: A Meta-Analytic Review," *Academy of Management Journal* 52, no. 3 (2009), pp. 599–627.

77. A. C. Homan, J. R. Hollenbeck, S. E. Humphrey, D. Van Knippenberg, D. R. Ilgen, and G. A. Van Kleef, "Facing Differences with an Open Mind: Openness to Experience, Salience of Intragroup Differences, and Performance of Diverse Work Groups," *Academy of Management Journal* 51, no. 6 (2008), pp. 1204–1222.

78. E. Kearney and D. Gebert, "Managing Diversity and Enhancing Team Outcomes: The Promise of Transformational Leadership," *Journal of Applied Psychology* 94, no. 1 (2009), pp. 77–89.

79. C. L. Holladay and M. A. Quiñones, "The Influence of Training Focus and Trainer Characteristics on Diversity Training Effectiveness," *Academy of Management Learning and Education* 7, no. 3 (2008), pp. 343–354; and R. Anand and M. Winters, "A Retrospective View of Corporate Diversity Training from 1964 to the Present," *Academy of Management Learning and Education* 7, no. 3 (2008), pp. 356–372.

80. Q. M. Roberson and C. K. Stevens, "Making Sense of Diversity in the Workplace: Organizational Justice and Language Abstraction in Employees' Accounts of Diversity-Related Incidents," *Journal of Applied Psychology* 91 (2006), pp. 379–391; and D. A. Harrison, D. A. Kravitz, D. M. Mayer, L. M. Leslie, and D. Lev-Arey, "Understanding Attitudes Toward Affirmative Action Programs in Employment: Summary and Meta-Analysis of 35 Years of Research," *Journal of Applied Psychology* 91 (2006), pp. 1013–1036.

81. A. Kalev, F. Dobbin, and E. Kelly, "Best Practices or Best Guesses? Assessing the Efficacy of Corporate Affirmative Action and Diversity Policies," *American Sociological Review* 71, no. 4 (2006), pp. 589–617.

82. R. J. Crisp and R. N. Turner, "Cognitive Adaptation to the Experience of Social and Cultural Diversity," *Psychological Bulletin* 137 (2011), pp. 242–266.

83. A. Sippola and A. Smale, "The Global Integration of Diversity Management: A Longitudinal Case Study," *International Journal of Human Resource Management* 18, no. 11 (2007), pp. 1895–1916.

CHAPTER 3

1. A. Barsky, S. A. Kaplan, and D. J. Beal, "Just Feelings? The Role of Affect in the Formation of Organizational Fairness Judgments," *Journal of Management* (January 2011), pp. 248–279; S. J. Breckler, "Empirical Validation of Affect, Behavior, and Cognition as Distinct Components of Attitude," *Journal of Personality and Social Psychology* (May 1984), pp. 1191–1205; J. A. Mikels, S. J. Maglio, A. E. Reed, and L. J. Kaplowitz, "Should I Go with My Gut? Investigating the Benefits of Emotion-Focused Decision Making," *Emotion* (August 2011), pp. 743–753; and A. J. Rojas Tejada, O. M. Lozano Rojas, M. Navas Luque, and P. J. Pérez Moreno, "Prejudiced Attitude Measurement Using the Rasch Scale Model," *Psychological Reports* (October 2011), pp. 553–572.

2. A. W. Wicker, "Attitude Versus Action: The Relationship of Verbal and Overt Behavioral Responses to Attitude Objects," *Journal of Social Issues* (Autumn 1969), pp. 41–78.

3. L. Festinger, *A Theory of Cognitive Dissonance* (Stanford, CA: Stanford University Press, 1957).

4. See, for instance, L. R. Fabrigar, R. E. Petty, S. M. Smith, and S. L. Crites, "Understanding Knowledge Effects on Attitude-Behavior Consistency: The Role of Relevance, Complexity, and Amount of Knowledge," *Journal of Personality and Social Psychology* 90, no. 4 (2006), pp. 556–577; and D. J. Schleicher, J. D. Watt, and G. J. Greguras, "Reexamining the Job Satisfaction-Performance Relationship: The Complexity of Attitudes," *Journal of Applied Psychology* 89, no. 1 (2004), pp. 165–177.

5. A. S. McCance, C. D. Nye, L. Wang, K. S. Jones, and C. Chiu, "Alleviating the Burden of Emotional Labor: The Role of Social Sharing," *Journal of Management* (February 2013), pp. 392–415.

6. See L. R. Glasman and D. Albarracín, "Forming Attitudes That Predict Future Behavior: A Meta-Analysis of the Attitude–Behavior Relation," *Psychological Bulletin* (September 2006), pp. 778–822; I. Ajzen, "Nature and Operation of Attitudes," in S. T. Fiske, D. L. Schacter, and C. Zahn-Waxler (eds.), *Annual Review of Psychology*, vol. 52 (Palo Alto, CA: Annual Reviews Inc., 2001), pp. 27–58; and M. Riketta, "The Causal Relation Between Job Attitudes and Performance: A Meta-Analysis of Panel Studies," *Journal of Applied Psychology*, 93, no. 2 (2008), pp. 472–481.

7. Ibid.

8. D. A. Harrison, D. A. Newman, and P. L. Roth, "How Important Are Job Attitudes? Meta-Analytic Comparisons of Integrative Behavioral Outcomes and Time Sequences," *Academy of Management Journal* 49, no. 2 (2006), pp. 305–325.

9. D. P. Moynihan and S. K. Pandey, "Finding Workable Levers Over Work Motivation: Comparing Job Satisfaction, Job Involvement, and Organizational Commitment," *Administration & Society* 39, no. 7 (2007), pp. 803–832.

10. See, for example, J. M. Diefendorff, D. J. Brown, and A. M. Kamin, "Examining the Roles of Job Involvement and Work Centrality in Predicting Organizational Citizenship Behaviors and Job Performance," *Journal of Organizational Behavior* (February 2002), pp. 93–108.

11. Based on G. J. Blau and K. R. Boal, "Conceptualizing How Job Involvement and Organizational Commitment Affect Turnover and Absenteeism," *Academy of Management Review* (April 1987), p. 290.

12. G. Chen and R. J. Klimoski, "The Impact of Expectations on Newcomer Performance in Teams as Mediated by Work Characteristics, Social Exchanges, and Empowerment," *Academy of Management Journal* 46, no. 5 (2003), pp. 591–607; A. Ergeneli, G. Saglam, and S. Metin, "Psychological Empowerment and Its Relationship to Trust in Immediate Managers," *Journal of Business Research* (January 2007), pp. 41–49; and S. E. Seibert, S. R. Silver, and W. A. Randolph, "Taking Empowerment to the Next Level: A Multiple-Level Model of Empowerment, Performance, and Satisfaction," *Academy of Management Journal* 47, no. 3 (2004), pp. 332–349.

13. B. J. Avolio, W. Zhu, W. Koh, and P. Bhatia, "Transformational Leadership and Organizational Commitment: Mediating Role of Psychological Empowerment and Moderating Role of Structural Distance," *Journal of Organizational Behavior* 25, no. 8 (2004), pp. 951–968.

14. M. Singh and A. Sarkar, "The Relationship Between Psychological Empowerment and Innovative Behavior," *Journal of Personnel Psychology* 2 (2012), pp. 127–137.

15. J. M. Diefendorff, D. J. Brown, A. M. Kamin, and R. G. Lord, "Examining the Roles of Job Involvement and Work Centrality in Predicting Organizational Citizenship Behaviors and Job Performance," *Journal of Organizational Behavior* (February 2002), pp. 93–108.

16. O. N. Solinger, W. van Olffen, and R. A. Roe, "Beyond the Three-Component Model of Organizational Commitment," *Journal of Applied Psychology* 93 (2008), pp. 70–83.

17. B. J. Hoffman, C. A. Blair, J. P. Meriac, and D. J. Woehr, "Expanding the Criterion Domain? A Quantitative Review of the OCB Literature," *Journal of Applied Psychology* 92, no. 2 (2007), pp. 555–566.

18. T. A. Wright and D. G. Bonett, "The Moderating Effects of Employee Tenure on the Relation Between Organizational Commitment and Job Performance: A Meta-Analysis," *Journal of Applied Psychology* (December 2002), pp. 1183–1190.

19. T. W. H. Ng, D. C. Feldman, and S. S. K. Lam, "Psychological Contract Breaches, Organizational Commitment, and Innovation-Related Behaviors: A Latent Growth Modeling Approach," *Journal of Applied Psychology* 95 (2010), pp. 744–751.

20. See, for instance, K. Bentein, C. Vandenberghe, R. Vandenberg, and F. Stinglhamber, "The Role of Change in the Relationship between Commitment and Turnover: A Latent Growth Modeling Approach," *Journal of Applied Psychology* 90 (2005), pp. 468–482; and J. D. Kammeyer-Mueller, C. R. Wanberg, T. M. Glomb, and D. Ahlburg, "The Role of Temporal Shifts in Turnover Processes: It's About Time," *Journal of Applied Psychology* 90 (2005), pp. 644–658.

21. J. P. Hausknecht, N. J. Hiller, and R. J. Vance, "Work-Unit Absenteeism: Effects of Satisfaction, Commitment, Labor Market Conditions, and Time," *Academy of Management Journal* 51 (2008), pp. 1223–1245.

22. D. A. Kaplan, "Salesforce's Happy Workforce," *Fortune* (February 6, 2012), pp. 101–112.

23. L. Rhoades, R. Eisenberger, and S. Armeli, "Affective Commitment to the Organization: The Contribution of Perceived Organizational Support," *Journal of Applied Psychology* 86, no. 5 (2001), pp. 825–836.

24. C. Vandenberghe, K. Bentein, R. Michon, J. Chebat, M. Tremblay, and J. Fils, "An Examination of the Role of Perceived Support and Employee Commitment in Employee–Customer Encounters," *Journal of Applied Psychology* 92, no. 4 (2007), pp. 1177–1187; and P. Eder and R. Eisenberger, "Perceived Organizational Support: Reducing the Negative Influence of Coworker Withdrawal Behavior," *Journal of Management* 34, no. 1 (2008), pp. 55–68.

25. J. Farh, R. D. Hackett, and J. Liang, "Individual-Level Cultural Values as Moderators of Perceived Organizational Support—Employee Outcome Relationships in China: Comparing the Effects of Power Distance and Traditionality," *Academy of Management Journal* 50, no. 3 (2007), pp. 715–729.

26. B. L. Rich, J. A. Lepine, and E. R. Crawford, "Job Engagement: Antecedents and Effects on Job Performance," *Academy of Management Journal* 53 (2010), pp. 617–635.

27. J. K. Harter, F. L. Schmidt, and T. L. Hayes, "Business-Unit-Level Relationship Between Employee Satisfaction, Employee Engagement, and Business Outcomes: A Meta-Analysis," *Journal of Applied Psychology* 87, no. 2 (2002), pp. 268–279.

28. N. R. Lockwood, *Leveraging Employee Engagement for Competitive Advantage* (Alexandria, VA: Society for Human Resource Management, 2007); and R. J. Vance, *Employee Engagement and Commitment* (Alexandria, VA: Society for Human Resource Management, 2006).

29. "Employee Engagement," *Workforce Management* (February 2013), p. 19; and "The Cornerstone OnDemand 2013 U.S. Employee Report," *Cornerstone OnDemand* (2013), www.cornerstoneondemand.com/resources/research/survey-2013.

30. W. H. Macey and B. Schneider, "The Meaning of Employee Engagement," *Industrial and Organizational Psychology* 1 (2008), pp. 3–30; and A. Saks, "The Meaning and Bleeding of Employee Engagement: How Muddy Is the Water?" *Industrial and Organizational Psychology* 1 (2008), pp. 40–43.

31. Y. Brunetto, S. T. T. Teo, K. Shacklock, and R. Farr-Wharton, "Emotional Intelligence, Job Satisfaction, Well-being and Engagement: Explaining Organisational Commitment and Turnover Intentions in Policing," *Human Resource Management Journal* (2012), pp. 428–441.

32. P. Petrou, E. Demerouti, M. C. W. Peeters, W. B. Schaufeli, and Jørn Hetland, "Crafting a Job on a Daily Basis: Contextual Correlates and the Link to Work Engagement," *Journal of Organizational Behavior* (November 2012), pp. 1120–1141.

33. P. W. Hom, T. R. Mitchell, T. W. Lee, and R. W. Griffeth, "Reviewing Employee Turnover: Focusing on Proximal Withdrawal States and an Expanded Criterion," *Psychological Bulletin* 138, no. 5 (2012), pp. 831–858.

34. The Wyatt Company's 1989 national Work America study identified 12 dimensions of satisfaction: Work organization, working conditions, communications, job performance

and performance review, co-workers, supervision, company management, pay, benefits, career development and training, job content and satisfaction, and company image and change.

35. See E. Spector, *Job Satisfaction: Application, Assessment, Causes, and Consequences* (Thousand Oaks, CA: Sage, 1997), p. 3.

36. C. L. Dolbier, J. A. Webster, K. T. McCalister, M. W. Mallon, and M. A. Steinhardt, "Reliability and Validity of a Single-Item Measure of Job Satisfaction," *American Journal of Health Promotion* (January–February 2005), pp. 194–198; and J. Wanous, A. E. Reichers, and M. J. Hudy, "Overall Job Satisfaction: How Good Are Single-Item Measures?" *Journal of Applied Psychology* (April 1997), pp. 247–252.

37. N. A. Bowling, M. R. Hoepf, D. M. LaHuis, and L. R. Lepisto, "Mean Job Satisfaction Levels over Time: Are Things Bad and Getting Worse?" *The Industrial-Organizational Psychologist* (April 2013), pp. 57–64.

38. A. F. Chelte, J. Wright, and C. Tausky, "Did Job Satisfaction Really Drop During the 1970s?" *Monthly Labor Review* (November 1982), pp. 33–36; "Job Satisfaction High in America, Says Conference Board Study," *Monthly Labor Review* (February 1985), p. 52; K. Bowman, "Attitudes About Work, Chores, and Leisure in America," *AEI Opinion Studies* (August 25, 2003); and J. Pepitone, "U.S. Job Satisfaction Hits 22-Year Low," *CNNMoney.com* (January 5, 2010).

39. W. K. Balzer, J. A. Kihm, P. C. Smith, J. L. Irwin, P. D. Bachiochi, C. Robie, E. F. Sinar, and L. F. Parra, *Users' Manual for the Job Descriptive Index (JDI; 1997 Revision) and the Job in General Scales* (Bowling Green, OH: Bowling Green State University, 1997).

40. M. J. Gelfand, M. Erez, and Z. Aycan, "Cross-Cultural Organizational Behavior," *Annual Review of Psychology* 58 (2007), pp. 479–514; and A. S. Tsui, S. S. Nifadkar, and A. Y. Ou, "Cross-National, Cross-Cultural Organizational Behavior Research: Advances, Gaps, and Recommendations," *Journal of Management* (June 2007), pp. 426–478.

41. World Business Culture, "Doing Business in South Korea," www.worldbusinessculture.com/Business-in-South-Korea.html, accessed June 24, 2013.

42. Ibid.

43. C. Osborne, "South Korea Hits 100% Mark in Wireless Broadband," *C/NET* (July 23, 2012), www.news.cnet.com/8301-1035_3-57477593-94/south-korea-hits-100-mark-in-wireless-broadband/.

44. J. Barling, E. K. Kelloway, and R. D. Iverson, "High-Quality Work, Job Satisfaction, and Occupational Injuries," *Journal of Applied Psychology* 88, no. 2 (2003), pp. 276–283; and F. W. Bond and D. Bunce, "The Role of Acceptance and Job Control in Mental Health, Job Satisfaction, and Work Performance," *Journal of Applied Psychology* 88, no. 6 (2003), pp. 1057–1067.

45. Y. Georgellis and T. Lange, "Traditional versus Secular Values and the Job-Life Satisfaction Relationship Across Europe," *British Journal of Management* 23 (2012), pp. 437–454.

46. S. E. Humphrey, J. D. Nahrgang, and F. P. Morgeson, "Integrating Motivational, Social, and Contextual Work Design Features: A Meta-Analytic Summary and Theoretical Extension of the Work Design Literature," *Journal of Applied Psychology* 92, no. 5 (2007), pp. 1332–1356; and D. S. Chiaburu and D. A. Harrison, "Do Peers Make the Place? Conceptual Synthesis and Meta-Analysis of Coworker Effect on Perceptions, Attitudes, OCBs, and Performance," *Journal of Applied Psychology* 93, no. 5 (2008), pp. 1082–1103.

47. E. Diener, E. Sandvik, L. Seidlitz, and M. Diener, "The Relationship Between Income and Subjective Well-Being: Relative or Absolute?" *Social Indicators Research* 28 (1993), pp. 195–223.

48. R. E. Silverman, "Work as Labor or Love?" *The Wall Street Journal* (October 18, 2012), p. D3.

49. See D. Farrell, "Exit, Voice, Loyalty, and Neglect as Responses to Job Dissatisfaction: A Multidimensional Scaling Study," *Academy of Management Journal* (December 1983), pp. 596–606; C. E. Rusbult, D. Farrell, G. Rogers, and A. G. Mainous III, "Impact of Exchange Variables on Exit, Voice, Loyalty, and Neglect: An Integrative Model of Responses to Declining Job Satisfaction," *Academy of Management Journal* (September 1988), pp. 599–627; M. J. Withey and W. H. Cooper, "Predicting Exit, Voice, Loyalty, and Neglect," *Administrative Science Quarterly* (December 1989), pp. 521–539; J. Zhou and J. M. George, "When Job Dissatisfaction Leads to Creativity: Encouraging the Expression of Voice," *Academy of Management Journal* (August 2001), pp. 682–696; J. B. Olson-Buchanan and W. R. Boswell, "The Role of Employee Loyalty and Formality in Voicing Discontent," *Journal of Applied Psychology* (December 2002), pp. 1167–1174; and A. Davis-Blake, J. P. Broschak, and E. George, "Happy Together? How Using Nonstandard Workers Affects Exit, Voice, and Loyalty Among Standard Employees," *Academy of Management Journal* 46, no. 4 (2003), pp. 475–485.

50. A. J. Nyberg and R. E. Ployhart, "Context-Emergent Turnover (CET) Theory: A Theory of Collective Turnover," *Academy of Management Review* 38 (2013), pp. 109–131.

51. R. B. Freeman, "Job Satisfaction as an Economic Variable," *American Economic Review* (January 1978), pp. 135–141.

52. T. A. Judge, C. J. Thoresen, J. E. Bono, and G. K. Patton, "The Job Satisfaction–Job Performance Relationship: A Qualitative and Quantitative Review," *Psychological Bulletin* (May 2001), pp. 376–407.

53. C. Ostroff, "The Relationship Between Satisfaction, Attitudes, and Performance: An Organizational Level Analysis," *Journal of Applied Psychology* (December 1992), pp. 963–974; A. M. Ryan, M. J. Schmit, and R. Johnson, "Attitudes and Effectiveness: Examining Relations at an Organizational Level," *Personnel Psychology* (Winter 1996), pp. 853–882; and J. K. Harter, F. L. Schmidt, and T. L. Hayes, "Business-Unit Level Relationship Between Employee Satisfaction, Employee Engagement, and Business Outcomes: A Meta-Analysis," *Journal of Applied Psychology* (April 2002), pp. 268–279.

54. See P. M. Podsakoff, S. B. MacKenzie, J. B. Paine, and D. G. Bachrach, "Organizational Citizenship Behaviors: A Critical Review of the Theoretical and Empirical Literature and Suggestions for Future Research," *Journal of Management* 26, no. 3 (2000), pp. 513–563.

55. B. J. Hoffman, C. A. Blair, J. P. Maeriac, and D. J. Woehr, "Expanding the Criterion Domain? A Quantitative Review of the OCB Literature," *Journal of Applied Psychology* 92, no. 2 (2007), pp. 555–566.

56. S. L. Blader and T. R. Tyler, "Testing and Extending the Group Engagement Model: Linkages Between Social Identity, Procedural Justice, Economic Outcomes, and Extrarole Behavior," *Journal of Applied Psychology* 94, no. 2 (2009), pp. 445–464.

57. D. S. Chiaburu and D. A. Harrison, "Do Peers Make the Place? Conceptual Synthesis and Meta-Analysis of Coworker Effect on Perceptions, Attitudes, OCBs, and Performance," *Journal of Applied Psychology* 93, no. 5 (2008), pp. 1082–1103.

58. R. Ilies, I. S. Fulmer, M. Spitzmuller, and M. D. Johnson, "Personality and Citizenship Behavior: The Mediating Role of Job Satisfaction," *Journal of Applied Psychology* 94 (2009), pp. 945–959.

59. R. Ilies, B. A. Scott, and T. A. Judge, "The Interactive Effects of Personal Traits and Experienced States on Intraindividual Patterns of Citizenship Behavior," *Academy of Management Journal* 49 (2006), pp. 561–575.

60. See, for instance, D. J. Koys, "The Effects of Employee Satisfaction, Organizational Citizenship Behavior, and Turnover on Organizational Effectiveness: A Unit-Level, Longitudinal Study," *Personnel Psychology* (Spring 2001), pp. 101–114; and C. Vandenberghe, K. Bentein, R. Michon, J. Chebat, M. Tremblay, and J. Fils, "An Examination of the Role of Perceived Support and Employee Commitment in Employee-Customer Encounters," *Journal of Applied Psychology* 92, no. 4 (2007), pp. 1177–1187; and M. Schulte, C. Ostroff, S. Shmulyian, and A. Kinicki, "Organizational Climate Configurations: Relationships to Collective Attitudes, Customer Satisfaction, and Financial Performance," *Journal of Applied Psychology* 94 (2009), pp. 618–634.

61. J. M. O'Brien, "Zappos Knows How to Kick It," *Fortune* (February 2, 2009), pp. 55–60.

62. K. D. Scott and G. S. Taylor, "An Examination of Conflicting Findings on the Relationship Between Job Satisfaction and Absenteeism: A Meta-Analysis," *Academy of Management Journal* (September 1985), pp. 599–612; R. P. Steel and J. R. Rentsch, "Influence of Cumulation Strategies on the Long-Range Prediction of Absenteeism," *Academy of Management Journal* (December 1995), pp. 1616–1634; and J. F. Ybema, P. G. W. Smulders, and P. M. Bongers, "Antecedents and Consequences of Employee Absenteeism: A Longitudinal Perspective on the Role of Job Satisfaction and Burnout," *European Journal of Work and Organizational Psychology* 19 (2010), pp. 102–124.

63. J. P. Hausknecht, N. J. Hiller, and R. J. Vance, "Work-Unit Absenteeism: Effects of Satisfaction, Commitment, Labor Market Conditions, and Time," *Academy of Management Journal* 51, no. 6 (2008), pp. 1123–1245.

64. G. Chen, R. E. Ployhart, H. C. Thomas, N. Anderson, and P. D. Bliese, "The Power of Momentum: A New Model of Dynamic Relationships Between Job Satisfaction Change and Turnover Intentions," *Academy of Management Journal* (February 2011), pp. 159–181; R. W. Griffeth, P. W. Hom, and S. Gaertner, "A Meta-Analysis of Antecedents and Correlates of Employee Turnover: Update, Moderator Tests, and Research Implications for the Next Millennium," *Journal of Management* 26, no. 3 (2000), p. 479; and W. Hom and R. W. Griffeth, *Employee Turnover* (Cincinnati, OH: South-Western Publishing, 1995).

65. D. Liu, T. R. Mitchell, T. W. Lee, B. C. Holtom, and T. R. Hinkin, "When Employees Are Out of Step with Coworkers: How Job Satisfaction Trajectory and Dispersion Influence Individual- and Unit-Level Voluntary Turnover," *Academy of Management Journal* 55, no. 6 (2012), pp. 1360–1380.

66. T. H. Lee, B. Gerhart, I. Weller, and C. O. Trevor, "Understanding Voluntary Turnover: Path-Specific Job Satisfaction Effects and the Importance of Unsolicited Job Offers," *Academy of Management Journal* 51, no. 4 (2008), pp. 651–671.

67. K. Jiang, D. Liu, P. F. McKay, T. W. Lee, and T. R. Mitchell, "When and How Is Job Embeddedness Predictive of Turnover? A Meta-Analytic Investigation," *Journal of Applied Psychology* 97 (2012), pp. 1077–1096.

68. P. E. Spector, S. Fox, L. M. Penney, K. Bruursema, A. Goh, and S. Kessler, "The Dimensionality of Counterproductivity: Are All Counterproductive Behaviors Created Equal?" *Journal of Vocational Behavior* 68, no. 3 (2006), pp. 446–460; and D. S. Chiaburu and D. A. Harrison, "Do Peers Make the Place? Conceptual Synthesis and Meta-Analysis of Coworker Effect on Perceptions, Attitudes, OCBs, and Performance," *Journal of Applied Psychology* 93, no. 5 (2008), pp. 1082–1103.

69. K. Holland, "Inside the Minds of Your Employees," *The New York Times* (January 28, 2007), p. B1; "Study Sees Link Between Morale and Stock Price," *Workforce Management* (February 27, 2006), p. 15; and "The Workplace as a Solar System," *The New York Times* (October 28, 2006), p. B5.

70. E. White, "How Surveying Workers Can Pay Off," *The Wall Street Journal* (June 18, 2007), p. B3.

CHAPTER 4

1. See, for instance, C. D. Fisher and N. M. Ashkanasy, "The Emerging Role of Emotions in Work Life: An Introduction," *Journal of Organizational Behavior*, Special Issue 2000, pp. 123–129; N. M. Ashkanasy, C. E. J. Hartel, and W. J. Zerbe (eds.), *Emotions in the Workplace: Research, Theory, and Practice* (Westport, CT: Quorum Books, 2000); N. M. Ashkanasy and C. S. Daus, "Emotion in the Workplace: The New Challenge for Managers," *Academy of Management Executive* (February 2002), pp. 76–86; and N. M. Ashkanasy, C. E. J. Hartel, and C. S. Daus, "Diversity and Emotion: The New Frontiers in Organizational Behavior Research," *Journal of Management* 28, no. 3 (2002), pp. 307–338.

2. See, for example, L. L. Putnam and D. K. Mumby, "Organizations, Emotion and the Myth of Rationality," in S. Fineman (ed.), *Emotion in Organizations* (Thousand Oaks, CA: Sage, 1993), pp. 36–57; and J. Martin, K. Knopoff, and C. Beckman, "An Alternative to Bureaucratic Impersonality and Emotional Labor: Bounded Emotionality at the Body Shop," *Administrative Science Quarterly* (June 1998), pp. 429–469.

3. B. E. Ashforth and R. H. Humphrey, "Emotion in the Workplace: A Reappraisal," *Human Relations* (February 1995), pp. 97–125.

4. S. G. Barsade and D. E. Gibson, "Why Does Affect Matter in Organizations?" *Academy of Management Perspectives* (February 2007), pp. 36–59.

5. See N. H. Frijda, "Moods, Emotion Episodes and Emotions," in M. Lewis and J. M. Haviland (eds.), *Handbook of Emotions* (New York: Guilford Press, 1993), pp. 381–403.

6. H. M. Weiss and R. Cropanzano, "Affective Events Theory: A Theoretical Discussion of the Structure, Causes and Consequences of Affective Experiences at Work," in B. M. Staw and L. L. Cummings (eds.), *Research in Organizational Behavior*, vol. 18 (Greenwich, CT: JAI Press, 1996), pp. 17–19.

7. See P. Ekman and R. J. Davidson (eds.), *The Nature of Emotions: Fundamental Questions* (Oxford, UK: Oxford University Press, 1994).

8. Frijda, "Moods, Emotion Episodes and Emotions," p. 381.

9. See Ekman and Davidson (eds.), *The Nature of Emotions.*

10. See, for example, P. Ekman, "An Argument for Basic Emotions," *Cognition and Emotion* (May/July 1992), pp. 169–200; C. E. Izard, "Basic Emotions, Relations Among Emotions, and Emotion–Cognition Relations," *Psychological Bulletin* (November 1992), pp. 561–565; and J. L. Tracy and R. W. Robins, "Emerging Insights into the Nature and Function of Pride," *Current Directions in Psychological Science* 16, no. 3 (2007), pp. 147–150.

11. R. C. Solomon, "Back to Basics: On the Very Idea of 'Basic Emotions,'" *Journal for the Theory of Social Behaviour* 32, no. 2 (June 2002), pp. 115–144.

12. P. Ekman, *Emotions Revealed: Recognizing Faces and Feelings to Improve Communication and Emotional Life* (New York: Times Books/Henry Holt and Co., 2003).

13. Ashforth and Humphrey, "Emotion in the Workplace," p. 104; B. Plasait, "Accueil des Touristes Dans les Grands Centres de Transit Paris," *Rapport du Bernard Plasait* (October 4, 2004), www.tourisme.gouv.fr/fr/navd/presse/dossiers/att00005767/dp_plasait.pdf; B. Mesquita, "Emotions in Collectivist and Individualist Contexts," *Journal of Personality and Social Psychology* 80, no. 1 (2001), pp. 68–74; and D. Rubin, "Grumpy German Shoppers Distrust the Wal-Mart Style," *Seattle Times* (December 30, 2001), p. A15.

14. Weiss and Cropanzano, "Affective Events Theory," pp. 20–22.

15. Cited in R. D. Woodworth, *Experimental Psychology* (New York: Holt, 1938).

16. D. Watson, L. A. Clark, and A. Tellegen, "Development and Validation of Brief Measures of Positive and Negative Affect: The PANAS Scales," *Journal of Personality and Social Psychology* (1988), pp. 1063–1070.

17. A. Ben-Ze'ev, *The Subtlety of Emotions* (Cambridge, MA: MIT Press, 2000), p. 94.

18. Ibid, p. 99.

19. J. T. Cacioppo and W. L. Gardner, "Emotion," in *Annual Review of Psychology*, vol. 50 (Palo Alto, CA: Annual Reviews, 1999), pp. 191–214.

20. D. Holman, "Call Centres," in D. Holman, T. D. Wall, C. Clegg, P. Sparrow, and A. Howard (eds.), *The Essentials of the New Work Place: A Guide to the Human Impact of Modern Working Practices* (Chichester, UK: Wiley, 2005), pp. 111–132.

21. M. Eid and E. Diener, "Norms for Experiencing Emotions in Different Cultures: Inter- and International Differences," *Journal of Personality & Social Psychology* 81, no. 5 (2001), pp. 869–885.

22. O. Burkeman, "The Power of Negative Thinking," *The New York Times* (August 5, 2012), p. 9.

23. E. Jaffe, "Positively Negative," *Association for Psychological Science* (November 2012), pp. 13–17.

24. Eid and Diener, "Norms for Experiencing Emotions in Different Cultures."

25. L. M. Poverny and S. Picascia, "There Is No Crying in Business," Womensmedia.com, October 20, 2009, www.womensmedia.com/new/Crying-at-Work.shtml.

26. A. R. Damasio, *Descartes' Error: Emotion, Reason, and the Human Brain* (New York: Quill, 1994).

27. M.-A. Reinhard and N. Schwartz, "The Influence of Affective States on the Process of Lie Detection," *Journal of Experimental Psychology* 18 (2012), pp. 377–389.

28. J. Haidt, "The New Synthesis in Moral Psychology," *Science* 316 (May 18, 2007), pp. 998, 1002; I. E. de Hooge, R. M. A. Nelissen, S. M. Breugelmans, and M. Zeelenberg, "What Is Moral about Guilt? Acting 'Prosocially' at the Disadvantage of Others," *Journal of Personality and Social Psychology* 100 (2011), pp. 462–473; and C. A. Hutcherson and J. J. Gross, "The Moral Emotions: A Social-Functionalist Account of Anger, Disgust, and Contempt," *Journal of Personality and Social Psychology* 100 (2011), pp. 719–737.

29. T. Jacobs, "My Morals Are Better Than Yours," *Miller-McCune .com* (March/April 2012), pp. 68–69.

30. B. Darrow, "Lucovsky Moves from Cloud Foundry Back to VMware in Pivotal Shift," Gigaom.com (January 25, 2013), http://gigaom.com/2013/01/25/lucovsky-moves-from-cloud-foundry-back-to-vmware-in-pivotal-shift/.

31. D. C. Rubin, R. M. Hoyle, and M. R. Leary, "Differential Predictability of Four Dimensions of Affect Intensity," *Cognition and Emotion* 26 (2012), pp. 25–41.

32. D. Watson, *Mood and Temperament* (New York: Guilford Press, 2000).

33. B. P. Hasler, M. S. Mehl, R. R. Bootzin, and S. Vazire, "Preliminary Evidence of Diurnal Rhythms in Everyday Behaviors Associated with Positive Affect," *Journal of Research in Personality* 42 (2008), pp. 1537–1546.

34. Watson, *Mood and Temperament.*

35. A. A. Stone, J. E. Schwartz, D. Schkade, N. Schwarz, A. Krueger, and D. Kahneman, "A Population Approach to the Study of Emotion: Diurnal Rhythms of a Working Day Examined with the Day Reconstruction Method," *Emotion* 6 (2006), pp. 139–149.

36. S. A. Golder and M. W. Macy, "Diurnal and Seasonal Mood Vary with Work, Sleep, and Daylength Across Diverse Cultures," *Science* 333, (2011), pp. 1878–1881.

37. S. A. Golder and M. W. Macy, "Diurnal and Seasonal Mood Vary with Work, Sleep, and Daylength Across Diverse Cultures," *Science.*

38. J. J. A. Denissen, L. Butalid, L. Penke, and M. A. G. van Aken, "The Effects of Weather on Daily Mood: A Multilevel Approach," *Emotion* 8, no. 5 (2008), pp. 662–667; M. C. Keller, B. L. Fredrickson, O. Ybarra, S. Côté, K. Johnson, J. Mikels, A. Conway, and T. Wagner, "A Warm Heart and a Clear Head: The Contingent Effects of Weather on Mood and Cognition," *Psychological Science* 16 (2005) pp. 724–731; and Watson, *Mood and Temperament.*

39. Watson, *Mood and Temperament*, p. 100.

40. J. A. Fuller, J. M. Stanton, G. G. Fisher, C. Spitzmüller, S. S. Russell, and P. C. Smith, "A Lengthy Look at the Daily Grind: Time Series Analysis of Events, Mood, Stress, and

Satisfaction," *Journal of Applied Psychology* 88, no. 6 (December 2003), pp. 1019–1033.

41. G. Schaffer, "What's Good, When, and Why?" *Association for Psychological Science* (November 2012), pp. 27–29.

42. A. M. Isen, "Positive Affect as a Source of Human Strength," in L. G. Aspinwall and U. Staudinger (eds.), *The Psychology of Human Strengths* (Washington, DC: American Psychological Association, 2003), pp. 179–195.

43. Watson, *Mood and Temperament.*

44. *Sleep in America Poll* (Washington, DC: National Sleep Foundation, 2005), www.kintera.org/atf/cf/%7Bf6bf2668-a1b4-4fe8-8d1a-a5d39340d9cb%7D/2005_summary_of_find-ings.pdf.

45. D. Meinert, "Sleepless in Seattle . . . and Cincinnati and Syracuse," *HR Magazine* (October 2012), pp. 55–57.

46. E. K. Miller and J. D. Cohen, "An Integrative Theory of Prefrontal Cortex Function," *Annual Review of Neuroscience* 24 (2001), pp. 167–202.

47. B. A. Scott and T. A. Judge, "Insomnia, Emotions, and Job Satisfaction: A Multilevel Study," *Journal of Management* 32, no. 5 (2006), pp. 622–645.

48. P. R. Giacobbi, H. A. Hausenblas, and N. Frye, "A Naturalistic Assessment of the Relationship Between Personality, Daily Life Events, Leisure-Time Exercise, and Mood," *Psychology of Sport & Exercise* 6, no. 1 (January 2005), pp. 67–81.

49. L. L. Carstensen, M. Pasupathi, M. Ulrich, and J. R. Nesselroade, "Emotional Experience in Everyday Life Across the Adult Life Span," *Journal of Personality and Social Psychology* 79, no. 4 (2000), pp. 644–655.

50. M. LaFrance and M. Banaji, "Toward a Reconsideration of the Gender–Emotion Relationship," in M. Clark (ed.), *Review of Personality and Social Psychology,* vol. 14 (Newbury Park, CA: Sage, 1992), pp. 178–197; and A. M. Kring and A. H. Gordon, "Sex Differences in Emotion: Expression, Experience, and Physiology," *Journal of Personality and Social Psychology* (March 1998), pp. 686–703.

51. M. G. Gard and A. M. Kring, "Sex Differences in the Time Course of Emotion," *Emotion* 7, no. 2 (2007), pp. 429–437; M. Jakupcak, K. Salters, K. L. Gratz, and L. Roemer, "Masculinity and Emotionality: An Investigation of Men's Primary and Secondary Emotional Responding," *Sex Roles* 49 (2003), pp. 111–120; and M. Grossman and W. Wood, "Sex Differences in Intensity of Emotional Experience: A Social Role Interpretation," *Journal of Personality and Social Psychology* (November 1992), pp. 1010–1022.

52. A. H. Fischer, P. M. Rodriguez Mosquera, A. E. M. van Vianen, and A. S. R. Manstead, "Gender and Culture Differences in Emotion," *Emotion* 4 (2004), pp. 84–87.

53. L. F. Barrett and E. Bliss-Moreau, "She's Emotional. He's Having a Bad Day: Attributional Explanations for Emotion Stereotypes," *Emotion* 9 (2009), pp. 649–658.

54. D. V. Becker, D. T. Kenrick, S. L. Neuberg, K. C. Blackwell, and D. M. Smith, "The Confounded Nature of Angry Men and Happy Women," *Journal of Personality and Social Psychology* 92 (2007), pp. 179–190.

55. A. R. Hochschild, "Emotion Work, Feeling Rules, and Social Structure," *American Journal of Sociology* (November 1979), pp. 551–575; W.-C. Tsai, "Determinants and Consequences of Employee Displayed Positive Emotions," *Journal of Management* 27, no. 4 (2001), pp. 497–512; M. W. Kramer and

J. A. Hess, "Communication Rules for the Display of Emotions in Organizational Settings," *Management Communication Quarterly* (August 2002), pp. 66–80; and J. M. Diefendorff and E. M. Richard, "Antecedents and Consequences of Emotional Display Rule Perceptions," *Journal of Applied Psychology* (April 2003), pp. 284–294.

56. J. M. Diefendorff and G. J. Greguras, "Contextualizing Emotional Display Rules: Examining the Roles of Targets and Discrete Emotions in Shaping Display Rule Perceptions," *Journal of Management* 35 (2009), pp. 880–898.

57. C. M. Brotheridge and R. T. Lee, "Development and Validation of the Emotional Labour Scale," *Journal of Occupational & Organizational Psychology* 76 (2003), pp. 365–379.

58. U. R. Hulsheger, H. J. E. M. Alberts, A. Feinholdt, and J. W. B. Lang, "Benefits of Mindfulness at Work: The Role of Mindfulness in Emotion Regulation, Emotional Exhaustion, and Job Satisfaction," *Journal of Applied Psychology* (March 2013), pp. 310–325.

59. J. P. Trougakos, D. J. Beal, S. G. Green, and H. M. Weiss, "Making the Break Count: An Episodic Examination of Recovery Activities, Emotional Experiences, and Positive Affective Displays," *Academy of Management Journal* 51 (2008), pp. 131–146.

60. J. M. Diefendorff, R. J. Erickson, A. A. Grandey, and J. J. Dahling, "Emotional Display Rules as Work Unit Norms: A Multilevel Analysis of Emotional Labor among Nurses," *Journal of Occupational Health Psychology* 16 (2011), pp. 170–186.

61. H. M. Weiss and R. Cropanzano, "An Affective Events Approach to Job Satisfaction," *Research in Organizational Behavior* 18 (1996), pp. 1–74.

62. J. Basch and C. D. Fisher, "Affective Events–Emotions Matrix: A Classification of Work Events and Associated Emotions," in N. M. Ashkanasy, C. E. J. Hartel, and W. J. Zerbe (eds.), *Emotions in the Workplace* (Westport, CT: Quorum Books, 2000), pp. 36–48.

63. See, for example, H. M. Weiss and R. Cropanzano, "Affective Events Theory"; and C. D. Fisher, "Antecedents and Consequences of Real-Time Affective Reactions at Work," *Motivation and Emotion* (March 2002), pp. 3–30.

64. Based on Weiss and Cropanzano, "Affective Events Theory," p. 42.

65. D. Ropeik, "Inside the Mind of Worry," *The New York Times* (September 30, 2012), p. 11.

66. N. M. Ashkanasy, C. E. J. Hartel, and C. S. Daus, "Diversity and Emotion: The New Frontiers in Organizational Behavior Research," *Journal of Management* 28, no. 3 (2002), p. 324.

67. Based on D. R. Caruso, J. D. Mayer, and P. Salovey, "Emotional Intelligence and Emotional Leadership," in R. E. Riggio, S. E. Murphy, and F. J. Pirozzolo (eds.), *Multiple Intelligences and Leadership* (Mahwah, NJ: Lawrence Erlbaum, 2002), p. 70.

68. This section is based on Daniel Goleman, *Emotional Intelligence* (New York: Bantam, 1995); P. Salovey and D. Grewal, "The Science of Emotional Intelligence," *Current Directions in Psychological Science* 14, no. 6 (2005), pp. 281–285; M. Davies, L. Stankov, and R. D. Roberts, "Emotional Intelligence: In Search of an Elusive Construct," *Journal of Personality and Social Psychology* (October 1998), pp. 989–1015; D. Geddes and R. R. Callister, "Crossing the Line(s): A Dual Threshold

Model of Anger in Organizations," *Academy of Management Review* 32, no. 3 (2007), pp. 721–746.

69. R. Gilkey, R. Caceda, and C. Kilts, "When Emotional Reasoning Trumps IQ," *Harvard Business Review* (September 2010), p. 27.

70. F. I. Greenstein, *The Presidential Difference: Leadership Style from FDR to Clinton* (Princeton, NJ: Princeton University Press, 2001).

71. M. Seo and L. F. Barrett, "Being Emotional During Decision Making—Good or Bad? An Empirical Investigation," *Academy of Management Journal* 50, no. 4 (2007), pp. 923–940.

72. F. J. Landy, "Some Historical and Scientific Issues Related to Research on Emotional Intelligence," *Journal of Organizational Behavior* 26, no. 4 (June 2005), pp. 411–424.

73. K. S. Law, C.-S. Wong, and L. J. Song, "The Construct and Criterion Validity of Emotional Intelligence and Its Potential Utility for Management Studies," *Journal of Applied Psychology* 89, no. 3 (2004), pp. 483–496.

74. D. L. Joseph and D. A. Newman, "Emotional Intelligence: An Integrative Meta-Analysis and Cascading Model," *Journal of Applied Psychology* 95 (2010), pp. 54–78.

75. R. Bar-On, D. Tranel, N. L. Denburg, and A. Bechara, "Exploring the Neurological Substrate of Emotional and Social Intelligence," *Brain* 126, no. 8 (August 2003), pp. 1790–1800.

76. P. A. Vernon, K. V. Petrides, D. Bratko, and J. A. Schermer, "A Behavioral Genetic Study of Trait Emotional Intelligence," *Emotion* 8, no. 5 (2008), pp. 635–642.

77. E. A. Locke, "Why Emotional Intelligence Is an Invalid Concept," *Journal of Organizational Behavior* 26, no. 4 (June 2005), pp. 425–431.

78. J. D. Mayer, R. D. Roberts, and S. G. Barsade, "Human Abilities: Emotional Intelligence," *Annual Review of Psychology* 59 (2008), pp. 507–536; H. A. Elfenbein, "Emotion in Organizations: A Review and Theoretical Integration," *Academy of Management Annals* 1 (2008), pp. 315–386; and D. L. Joseph and D. A. Newman, "Emotional Intelligence: An Integrative Meta-Analysis and Cascading Model," *Journal of Applied Psychology* 95 (2010), pp. 54–78.

79. J. M. Conte, "A Review and Critique of Emotional Intelligence Measures," *Journal of Organizational Behavior* 26, no. 4 (June 2005), pp. 433–440; and M. Davies, L. Stankov, and R. D. Roberts, "Emotional Intelligence," pp. 989–1015.

80. T. Decker, "Is Emotional Intelligence a Viable Concept?" *Academy of Management Review* 28, no. 2 (April 2003), pp. 433–440; and Davies, Stankov, and Roberts, "Emotional Intelligence."

81. D. L. Joseph and D. A. Newman, "Emotional Intelligence: An Integrative Meta-Analysis and Cascading Model," *Journal of Applied Psychology* 95 (2010), pp. 54–78.

82. S. L. Koole, "The Psychology of Emotion Regulation: An Integrative Review," *Cognition and Emotion* 23 (2009), pp. 4–41; H. A. Wadlinger and D. M. Isaacowitz, "Fixing Our Focus: Training Attention to Regulate Emotion," *Personality and Social Psychology Review* 15 (2011), pp. 75–102.

83. D. H. Kluemper, T. DeGroot, and S. Choi, "Emotion Management Ability: Predicting Task Performance, Citizenship, and Deviance," *Journal of Management* (May 2013), pp. 878–905.

84. B. A. Scott, C. M. Barnes, and D. T. Wagner, "Chameleonic or Consistent? A Multilevel Investigation of Emotional Labor Variability and Self-Monitoring," *Academy of Management Journal* 55, no. 4 (2012), pp. 905–926.

85. T. L. Webb, E. Miles, and P. Sheeran, "Dealing with Feeling: A Meta-Analysis of the Effectiveness of Strategies Derived from the Process Model of Emotion Regulation," *Psychological Bulletin* 138, no. 4 (2012), pp. 775–808; S. Srivastava, M. Tamir, K. M. McGonigal, O. P. John, and J. J. Gross, "The Social Costs of Emotional Suppression: A Prospective Study of the Transition to College," *Journal of Personality and Social Psychology* 96 (2009), pp. 883–897; Y. Liu, L. M. Prati, P. L. Perrewé, and R. A. Brymer, "Individual Differences in Emotion Regulation, Emotional Experiences at Work, and Work-Related Outcomes: A Two-Study Investigation," *Journal of Applied Social Psychology* 40 (2010), pp. 1515–1538; and H. A. Wadlinger and D. M. Isaacowitz, "Fixing our Focus: Training Attention to Regulate Emotion," *Personality and Social Psychology Review* 15 (2011), pp. 75–102.

86. E. Halperin, R. Porat, M. Tamir, and J. J. Gross, "Can Emotion Regulation Change Political Attitudes in Intractable Conflicts? From the Laboratory to the Field," *Psychological Science* (January 2013), pp. 106–111.

87. F. Nils and B. Rimé, "Beyond the Myth of Venting: Social Sharing Modes Determine the Benefits of Emotional Disclosure," *European Journal of Social Psychology* 42 (2012), pp. 672–681; and J. D. Parlamis, "Venting as Emotion Regulation The Influence of Venting Responses and Respondent Identity on Anger and Emotional Tone," *International Journal of Conflict Management* 23 (2012), pp. 77–96.

88. J. V. Wood, S. A. Heimpel, L. A. Manwell, and E. J. Whittington, "This Mood Is Familiar and I Don't Deserve to Feel Better Anyway: Mechanisms Underlying Self-Esteem Differences in Motivation to Repair Sad Moods," *Journal of Personality and Social Psychology* 96 (2009), pp. 363–380.

89. S. L. Koole, "The Psychology of Emotion Regulation: An Integrative Review," *Cognition and Emotion* 23 (2009), pp. 4–41.

90. L. K. Barber, P. G. Bagsby, and D. C. Munz, "Affect Regulation Strategies for Promoting (or Preventing) Flourishing Emotional Health," *Personality and Individual Differences* 49 (2010), pp. 663–666.

91. S.-C. S. Chi and S.-G. Liang, "When Do Subordinates' Emotion-Regulation Strategies Matter? Abusive Supervision, Subordinates' Emotional Exhaustion, and Work Withdrawal," *Leadership Quarterly* (February 2013), pp. 125–137.

92. R. H. Humphrey, "How Do Leaders Use Emotional Labor?" *Journal of Organizational Behavior* (July 2012), pp. 740–744.

93. L. M. J. Spencer, D. C. McClelland, and S. Kelner, *Competency Assessment Methods: History and State of the Art* (Boston: Hay/McBer, 1997).

94. J. Park and M. R. Banaji, "Mood and Heuristics: The Influence of Happy and Sad States on Sensitivity and Bias in Stereotyping," *Journal of Personality and Social Psychology* 78, no. 6 (2000), pp. 1005–1023.

95. See A. M. Isen, "Positive Affect and Decision Making," in M. Lewis and J. M. Haviland-Jones (eds.), *Handbook of Emotions*, 2nd ed. (New York: Guilford, 2000), pp. 261–277.

96. L. B. Alloy and L. Y. Abramson, "Judgment of Contingency in Depressed and Nondepressed Students: Sadder but Wiser?" *Journal of Experimental Psychology: General* 108 (1979), pp. 441–485.

97. N. Ambady and H. M. Gray, "On Being Sad and Mistaken: Mood Effects on the Accuracy of Thin-Slice Judgments," *Journal of Personality and Social Psychology* 83, no. 4 (2002), pp. 947–961.

98. S. Lyubomirsky, L. King, and E. Diener, "The Benefits of Frequent Positive Affect: Does Happiness Lead to Success?" *Psychological Bulletin* 131, no. 6 (2005), pp. 803–855; and M. Baas, C. K. W. De Dreu, and B. A. Nijstad, "A Meta-Analysis of 25 Years of Mood-Creativity Research: Hedonic Tone, Activation, or Regulatory Focus," *Psychological Bulletin* 134 (2008), pp. 779–806.

99. M. J. Grawitch, D. C. Munz, and E. K. Elliott, "Promoting Creativity in Temporary Problem-Solving Groups: The Effects of Positive Mood and Autonomy in Problem Definition on Idea-Generating Performance," *Group Dynamics* 7, no. 3 (September 2003), pp. 200–213.

100. S. Lyubomirsky, L. King, and E. Diener, "The Benefits of Frequent Positive Affect: Does Happiness Lead to Success?" *Psychological Bulletin* 131, no. 6 (2005), pp. 803–855.

101. N. Madjar, G. R. Oldham, and M. G. Pratt, "There's No Place Like Home? The Contributions of Work and Nonwork Creativity Support to Employees' Creative Performance," *Academy of Management Journal* 45, no. 4 (2002), pp. 757–767.

102. J. M. George and J. Zhou, "Understanding When Bad Moods Foster Creativity and Good Ones Don't: The Role of Context and Clarity of Feelings," *Journal of Applied Psychology* 87, no. 4 (August 2002), pp. 687–697; and J. P. Forgas and J. M. George, "Affective Influences on Judgments and Behavior in Organizations: An Information Processing Perspective," *Organizational Behavior and Human Decision Processes* 86, no. 1 (2001), pp. 3–34.

103. C. K. W. De Dreu, M. Baas, and B. A. Nijstad, "Hedonic Tone and Activation Level in the Mood-Creativity Link: Toward a Dual Pathway to Creativity Model," *Journal of Personality and Social Psychology* 94, no. 5 (2008), pp. 739–756; J. M. George and J. Zhou, "Dual Tuning in a Supportive Context: Joint Contributions of Positive Mood, Negative Mood, and Supervisory Behaviors to Employee Creativity," *Academy of Management Journal* 50, no. 3 (2007), pp. 605–622.

104. M. B. Wieth, and R. T. Zacks, "Time of Day Effects on Problem Solving: When the Non-optimal Is Optimal," *Thinking & Reasoning* 17 (2011), pp. 387–401.

105. A. Erez and A. M. Isen, "The Influence of Positive Affect on the Components of Expectancy Motivation," *Journal of Applied Psychology* 87, no. 6 (2002), pp. 1055–1067.

106. R. Ilies and T. A. Judge, "Goal Regulation Across Time: The Effect of Feedback and Affect," *Journal of Applied Psychology* 90, no. 3 (May 2005), pp. 453–467.

107. W. Tsai, C.-C. Chen, and H. Liu, "Test of a Model Linking Employee Positive Moods and Task Performance," *Journal of Applied Psychology* 92, no. 6 (2007), pp. 1570–1583.

108. S. G. Liang and S.-C. S. Chi, "Transformational Leadership and Follower Task Performance: The Role of Susceptibility to Positive Emotions and Follower Positive Emotions," *Journal of Business and Psychology* (March 2013), pp. 17–29.

109. Ashforth and Humphrey, "Emotion in the Workplace," p. 116.

110. J. E. Bono, H. J. Foldes, G. Vinson, and J. P. Muros, "Workplace Emotions: The Role of Supervision and Leadership," *Journal of Applied Psychology* 92, no. 5 (2007), pp. 1357–1367.

111. N. Reynolds, "Whiz-Kids Gamble on TV Channel for Poker," *telegraph.co.uk* (April 16, 2005), www.telegraph.co.uk/news/uknews/1487949/Whiz-kids-gamble-on-TV-channel-for-poker.html.

112. G. A. Van Kleef, C. K. W. De Dreu, and A. S. R. Manstead, "The Interpersonal Effects of Emotions in Negotiations: A Motivated Information Processing Approach," *Journal of Personality and Social Psychology* 87, no. 4 (2004), pp. 510–528; and G. A. Van Kleef, C. K. W. De Dreu, and A. S. R. Manstead, "The Interpersonal Effects of Anger and Happiness in Negotiations," *Journal of Personality and Social Psychology* 86, no. 1 (2004), pp. 57–76.

113. E. van Dijk, G. A. Van Kleef, W. Steinel, and I. van Beest, "A Social Functional Approach to Emotions in Bargaining: When Communicating Anger Pays and When It Backfires," *Journal of Personality and Social Psychology* 94, no. 4 (2008), pp. 600–614.

114. K. M. O'Connor and J. A. Arnold, "Distributive Spirals: Negotiation Impasses and the Moderating Role of Disputant Self-Efficacy," *Organizational Behavior and Human Decision Processes* 84, no. 1 (2001), pp. 148–176.

115. B. Shiv, G. Loewenstein, A. Bechara, H. Damasio, and A. R. Damasio, "Investment Behavior and the Negative Side of Emotion," *Psychological Science* 16, no. 6 (2005), pp. 435–439.

116. W.-C. Tsai and Y.-M. Huang, "Mechanisms Linking Employee Affective Delivery and Customer Behavioral Intentions," *Journal of Applied Psychology* (October 2002), pp. 1001–1008.

117. Grandey, "When 'The Show Must Go On,'" *Academy of Management Journal* 46 (2003), pp. 86–96.

118. See P. B. Barker and A. A. Grandey, "Service with a Smile and Encounter Satisfaction: Emotional Contagion and Appraisal Mechanisms," *Academy of Management Journal* 49, no. 6 (2006), pp. 1229–1238; and S. D. Pugh, "Service with a Smile: Emotional Contagion in the Service Encounter," *Academy of Management Journal* (October 2001), pp. 1018–1027.

119. D. E. Rupp and S. Spencer, "When Customers Lash Out: The Effects of Customer Interactional Injustice on Emotional Labor and the Mediating Role of Emotions, *Journal of Applied Psychology* 91, no. 4 (2006), pp. 971–978; and Tsai and Huang, "Mechanisms Linking Employee Affective Delivery and Customer Behavioral Intentions."

120. R. Ilies and T. A. Judge, "Understanding the Dynamic Relationships Among Personality, Mood, and Job Satisfaction: A Field Experience Sampling Study," *Organizational Behavior and Human Decision Processes* 89 (2002), pp. 1119–1139.

121. R. Rau, "Job Strain or Healthy Work: A Question of Task Design," *Journal of Occupational Health Psychology* 9, no. 4 (October 2004), pp. 322–338; and R. Rau and A. Triemer, "Overtime in Relation to Blood Pressure and Mood During Work, Leisure, and Night Time," *Social Indicators Research* 67, no. 1–2 (June 2004), pp. 51–73.

122. Z. Song, M. Foo, and M. A. Uy, "Mood Spillover and Crossover Among Dual-Earner Couples: A Cell Phone

Event Sampling Study," *Journal of Applied Psychology* 93, no. 2 (2008), pp. 443–452.

123. T. A. Judge and R. Ilies, "Affect and Job Satisfaction: A Study of Their Relationship at Work and at Home," *Journal of Applied Psychology* 89 (2004), pp. 661–673.

124. See R. J. Bennett and S. L. Robinson, "Development of a Measure of Workplace Deviance," *Journal of Applied Psychology*, June 2000, pp. 349–360; see also P. R. Sackett and C. J. DeVore, "Counterproductive Behaviors at Work," in N. Anderson, D. S. Ones, H. K. Sinangil, and C. Viswesvaran (eds.), *Handbook of Industrial, Work & Organizational Psychology*, vol. 1 (Thousand Oaks, CA: Sage, 2001), pp. 145–164.

125. A. G. Bedeian, "Workplace Envy," *Organizational Dynamics* (Spring 1995), p. 54; and Y. Cohen-Charash, "Episodic Envy," *Journal of Applied Social Psychology* (September 2009), pp. 2128–2173.

126. S. C. Douglas, C. Kiewitz, M. Martinko, P. Harvey, Y. Kim, and J. U. Chun, "Cognitions, Emotions, and Evaluations: An Elaboration Likelihood Model for Workplace Aggression," *Academy of Management Review* 33, no. 2 (2008), pp. 425–451.

127. K. Lee and N. J. Allen, "Organizational Citizenship Behavior and Workplace Deviance: The Role of Affect and Cognition," *Journal of Applied Psychology* 87, no. 1 (2002), pp. 131–142; T. A. Judge, B. A. Scott, and R. Ilies, "Hostility, Job Attitudes, and Workplace Deviance: Test of a Multilevel Model," *Journal of Applied Psychology* 91, no. 1 (2006), 126–138; and S. Kaplan, J. C. Bradley, J. N. Luchman, and D. Haynes, "On the Role of Positive and Negative Affectivity in Job Performance: A Meta-Analytic Investigation," *Journal of Applied Psychology* 94, no. 1 (2009), pp. 162–176.

128. A. K Khan, S. Quratulain, and J. R. Crawshaw, "The Mediating Role of Discrete Emotions in the Relationship Between Injustice and Counterproductive Work Behaviors: A Study in Pakistan," *Journal of Business and Psychology* (March 2013), pp. 49–61.

129. R. D. Iverson and P. J. Erwin, "Predicting Occupational Injury: The Role of Affectivity," *Journal of Occupational and Organizational Psychology* 70, no. 2 (1997), pp. 113–128; Kaplan, Bradley, Luchman, and Haynes, "On the Role of Positive and Negative Affectivity in Job Performance: A Meta-Analytic Investigation;" and J. Maiti, "Design for Worksystem Safety Using Employees' Perception About Safety," *Work—A Journal of Prevention Assessment & Rehabilitation* 41 (2012), pp. 3117–3122.

130. A. M. Isen, A. A. Labroo, and P. Durlach, "An Influence of Product and Brand Name on Positive Affect: Implicit and Explicit Measures," *Motivation & Emotion* 28, no. 1 (March 2004), pp. 43–63.

131. T. Sy, S. Côté, and R. Saavedra, "The Contagious Leader: Impact of the Leader's Mood on the Mood of Group Members, Group Affective Tone, and Group Processes," *Journal of Applied Psychology* 90, no. 2 (2005), pp. 295–305.

132. V. A. Visser, D. van Knippenberg, G. van Kleef, and B. Wisse, "How Leader Displays of Happiness and Sadness Influence Follower Performance: Emotional Contagion and Creative versus Analytical Performance," *Leadership Quarterly* (February 2013), pp. 172–188.

133. P. Totterdell, "Catching Moods and Hitting Runs: Mood Linkage and Subjective Performance in Professional Sports Teams," *Journal of Applied Psychology* 85, no. 6 (2000), pp. 848–859.

134. S. Nelton, "Emotions in the Workplace," *Nation's Business* (February 1996), p. 25.

135. Geddes and Kruml, "Catching Fire Without Burning Out," *Management Communication Quarterly* (August 2000), pp. 8–49.

CHAPTER 5

1. G. W. Allport, *Personality: A Psychological Interpretation* (New York: Holt, Rinehart & Winston, 1937), p. 48. For a brief critique of current views on the meaning of personality, see R. T. Hogan and B. W. Roberts, "Introduction: Personality and Industrial and Organizational Psychology," in B. W. Roberts and R. Hogan (eds.), *Personality Psychology in the Workplace* (Washington, DC: American Psychological Association, 2001), pp. 11–12.

2. K. I. van der Zee, J. N. Zaal, and J. Piekstra, "Validation of the Multicultural Personality Questionnaire in the Context of Personnel Selection," *European Journal of Personality* 17, Supl. 1 (2003), pp. S77–S100.

3. S. A. Birkeland, T. M. Manson, J. L. Kisamore, M. T. Brannick, and M. A. Smith, "A Meta-Analytic Investigation of Job Applicant Faking on Personality Measures," *International Journal of Selection and Assessment* 14, no. 14 (2006), pp. 317–335.

4. T. A. Judge, C. A. Higgins, C. J. Thoresen, and M. R. Barrick, "The Big Five Personality Traits, General Mental Ability, and Career Success Across the Life Span," *Personnel Psychology* 52, no. 3 (1999), pp. 621–652; I. Oh, G. Wang, and M. K. Mount, "Validity of Observer Ratings of the Five-Factor Model of Personality Traits: A Meta-Analysis," *Journal of Applied Psychology* 96, no. 4 (2011), pp. 762–773.

5. See R. Illies, R. D. Arvey, and T. J. Bouchard, "Darwinism, Behavioral Genetics, and Organizational Behavior: A Review and Agenda for Future Research," *Journal of Organizational Behavior* 27, no. 2 (2006), pp. 121–141; and W. Johnson, E. Turkheimer, I. I. Gottesman, and T. J. Bouchard, Jr., "Beyond Heritability: Twin Studies in Behavioral Research," *Current Directions in Psychological Science* 18, no. 4 (2009), pp. 217–220.

6. S. Srivastava, O. P. John, and S. D. Gosling, "Development of Personality in Early and Middle Adulthood: Set Like Plaster or Persistent Change?" *Journal of Personality and Social Psychology* 84, no. 5 (2003), pp. 1041–1053; and B. W. Roberts, K. E. Walton, and W. Viechtbauer, "Patterns of Mean-Level Change in Personality Traits Across the Life Course: A Meta-Analysis of Longitudinal Studies," *Psychological Bulletin* 132, no. 1 (2006), pp. 1–25.

7. S. E. Hampson and L. R. Goldberg, "A First Large Cohort Study of Personality Trait Stability Over the 40 Years Between Elementary School and Midlife," *Journal of Personality and Social Psychology* 91, no. 4 (2006), pp. 763–779.

8. See A. H. Buss, "Personality as Traits," *American Psychologist* 44, no. 11 (1989), pp. 1378–1388; R. R. McCrae, "Trait Psychology and the Revival of Personality and Culture Studies," *American Behavioral Scientist* 44, no. 1 (2000), pp. 10–31; and L. R. James and M. D. Mazerolle, *Personality in Work Organizations* (Thousand Oaks, CA: Sage, 2002).

9. See, for instance, G. W. Allport and H. S. Odbert, "Trait Names, A Psycholexical Study," *Psychological Monographs,*

no. 47 (1936); and R. B. Cattell, "Personality Pinned Down," *Psychology Today* (July 1973), pp. 40–46.

10. R. B. Kennedy and D. A. Kennedy, "Using the Myers-Briggs Type Indicator in Career Counseling," *Journal of Employment Counseling* 41, no. 1 (2004), pp. 38–44.

11. See, for instance, D. J. Pittenger, "Cautionary Comments Regarding the Myers-Briggs Type Indicator," *Consulting Psychology Journal: Practice and Research* 57, no. 3 (2005), pp. 10–221; L. Bess and R. J. Harvey, "Bimodal Score Distributions and the Myers-Briggs Type Indicator: Fact or Artifact?" *Journal of Personality Assessment* 78, no. 1 (2002), pp. 176–186; R. M. Capraro and M. M. Capraro, "Myers-Briggs Type Indicator Score Reliability Across Studies: A Meta-Analytic Reliability Generalization Study," *Educational & Psychological Measurement* 62, no. 4 (2002), pp. 590–602; and R. C. Arnau, B. A. Green, D. H. Rosen, D. H. Gleaves, and J. G. Melancon, "Are Jungian Preferences Really Categorical? An Empirical Investigation Using Taxometric Analysis," *Personality & Individual Differences* 34, no. 2 (2003), pp. 233–251.

12. See, for example, Oh, Wang, and Mount, "Validity of Observer Ratings of the Five-Factor Model of Personality Traits: A Meta-Analysis"; and M. R. Barrick and M. K. Mount, "Yes, Personality Matters: Moving On to More Important Matters," *Human Performance* 18, no. 4 (2005), pp. 359–372.

13. W. Fleeson and P. Gallagher, "The Implications of Big Five Standing for the Distribution of Trait Manifestation in Behavior: Fifteen Experience-Sampling Studies and a Meta-Analysis," *Journal of Personality and Social Psychology* 97, no. 6 (2009), pp. 1097–1114.

14. See, for instance, I. Oh and C. M. Berry, "The Five-Factor Model of Personality and Managerial Performance: Validity Gains Through the Use of 360 Degree Performance Ratings," *Journal of Applied Psychology* 94, no. 6 (2009), pp. 1498–1513; G. M. Hurtz and J. J. Donovan, "Personality and Job Performance: The Big Five Revisited," *Journal of Applied Psychology* 85, no. 6 (2000), pp. 869–879; J. Hogan and B. Holland, "Using Theory to Evaluate Personality and Job-Performance Relations: A Socioanalytic Perspective," *Journal of Applied Psychology* 88, no. 1 (2003), pp. 100–112; and M. R. Barrick and M. K. Mount, "Select on Conscientiousness and Emotional Stability," in E. A. Locke (ed.), *Handbook of Principles of Organizational Behavior* (Malden, MA: Blackwell, 2004), pp. 15–28.

15. M. K. Mount, M. R. Barrick, and J. P. Strauss, "Validity of Observer Ratings of the Big Five Personality Factors," *Journal of Applied Psychology* 79, no. 2 (1994), p. 272. Additionally confirmed by Hurtz and Donovan, "Personality and Job Performance: The Big Five Revisited"; and Oh and Berry, "The Five-Factor Model of Personality and Managerial Performance."

16. A. E. Poropat, "A Meta-Analysis of the Five-Factor Model of Personality and Academic Performance," *Psychological Bulletin* 135, no. 2 (2009), pp. 322–338.

17. A. M. Cianci, H. J. Klein, and G. H. Seijts, "The Effect of Negative Feedback on Tension and Subsequent Performance: The Main and Interactive Effects of Goal Content and Conscientiousness," *Journal of Applied Psychology* 95, no. 4 (2010), pp. 618–630.

18. H. Le, I. Oh, S. B. Robbins, R. Ilies, E. Holland, and P. Westrick, "Too Much of a Good Thing: Curvilinear Relationships Between Personality Traits and Job Performance," *Journal of Applied Psychology* 96, no. 1 (2011), pp. 113–133.

19. T. Bogg and B. W. Roberts, "Conscientiousness and Health-Related Behaviors: A Meta-Analysis of the Leading Behavioral Contributors to Mortality," *Psychological Bulletin* 130, no. 6 (2004), pp. 887–919.

20. G. J. Feist, "A Meta-Analysis of Personality in Scientific and Artistic Creativity," *Personality and Social Psychology Review* 2, no. 4 (1998), pp. 290–309; C. Robert and Y. H. Cheung, "An Examination of the Relationship Between Conscientiousness and Group Performance on a Creative Task," *Journal of Research in Personality* 44, no. 2 (2010), pp. 222–231; and M. Batey, T. Chamorro-Premuzic, and A. Furnham, "Individual Differences in Ideational Behavior. Can the Big Five and Psychometric Intelligence Predict Creativity Scores?" *Creativity Research Journal* 22, no. 1 (2010), pp. 90–97.

21. R. J. Foti and M. A. Hauenstein, "Pattern and Variable Approaches in Leadership Emergence and Effectiveness," *Journal of Applied Psychology* 92, no. 2 (2007), pp. 347–355.

22. L. I. Spirling and R. Persaud, "Extraversion as a Risk Factor," *Journal of the American Academy of Child & Adolescent Psychiatry* 42, no. 2 (2003), p. 130.

23. B. Weiss, and R. S. Feldman, "Looking Good and Lying to Do It: Deception as an Impression Management Strategy in Job Interviews," *Journal of Applied Social Psychology* 36, no. 4 (2006), pp. 1070–1086.

24. J. A. LePine, J. A. Colquitt, and A. Erez, "Adaptability to Changing Task Contexts: Effects of General Cognitive Ability, Conscientiousness, and Openness to Experience," *Personnel Psychology* 53, no. 3 (2000), pp. 563–595; S. Clarke and I. Robertson, "An Examination of the Role of Personality in Accidents Using Meta-Analysis," *Applied Psychology: An International Review* 57, no. 1 (2008), pp. 94–108; and M. Baer, "The Strength-of-Weak-Ties Perspective on Creativity: A Comprehensive Examination and Extension," *Journal of Applied Psychology* 95, no. 3 (2010), pp. 592–601.

25. R. Ilies, I. S. Fulmer, M. Spitzmuller, and M. D. Johnson, "Personality and Citizenship Behavior: The Mediating Role of Job Satisfaction," *Journal of Applied Psychology* 94, no. 4 (2009), pp. 945–959.

26. See, for instance, S. Yamagata, A. Suzuki, J. Ando, Y. Ono, K. Yutaka, N. Kijima, et al., "Is the Genetic Structure of Human Personality Universal? A Cross-Cultural Twin Study from North America, Europe, and Asia," *Journal of Personality and Social Psychology* 90, no. 6 (2006), pp. 987–998; H. C. Triandis and E. M. Suh, "Cultural Influences on Personality," *Annual Review of Psychology* 53, no. 1 (2002), pp. 133–160; and R. R. McCrae, P. T. Costa Jr., T. A. Martin, V. E. Oryol, A. A. Rukavishnikov, I. G. Senin, et al., "Consensual Validation of Personality Traits Across Cultures," *Journal of Research in Personality* 38, no. 2 (2004), pp. 179–201.

27. J. F. Rauthmann, "The Dark Triad and Interpersonal Perception: Similarities and Differences in the Social Consequences of Narcissism, Machiavellianism, and Psychopathy," *Social Psychological and Personality Science* 3 (2012), pp. 487–496.

28. P. K. Jonason, S. Slomski, and J. Partyka, "The Dark Triad at Work: How Toxic Employees Get Their Way," *Personality and Individual Differences* 52 (2012), pp. 449–453.

29. E. H. O'Boyle, D. R. Forsyth, G. C. Banks, and M. A. McDaniel, "A Meta-Analysis of the Dark Triad and Work Behavior: A Social Exchange Perspective," *Journal of Applied Psychology* 97 (2012), pp. 557–579.

30. L. Zhang, and M. A. Gowan, "Corporate Social Responsibility, Applicants' Individual Traits, and Organizational Attraction: A Person–Organization Fit Perspective," *Journal of Business and Psychology* 27 (2012), pp. 345–362.

31. D. N. Hartog and F. D. Belschak, "Work Engagement and Machiavellianism in the Ethical Leadership Process," *Journal of Business Ethics* 107 (2012), pp. 35–47.

32. J. J. Sosik, J. U. Chun, and W. Zhu, "Hang On to Your Ego: The Moderating Role of Leader Narcissism on Relationships Between Leader Charisma and Follower Psychological Empowerment and Moral Identity," *Journal of Business Ethics* (February 12, 2013); and B. M. Galvin, D. A. Waldman, and P. Balthazard, "Visionary Communication Qualities as Mediators of the Relationship between Narcissism and Attributions of Leader Charisma," *Personnel Psychology* 63, no. 3 (2010), pp. 509–537.

33. C. Andreassen, H. Ursin, H. Eriksen, S. Pallesen, "The Relationship of Narcissism with Workaholism, Work Engagement, and Professional Position," *Social Behavior and Personality* 40, no. 6 (2012), pp. 881–890.

34. K. A. Byrne and D. A. Worthy, "Do Narcissists Make Better Decisions? An Investigation of Narcissism and Dynamic Decision-Making Performance," *Personality and Individual Differences* (July 2013), pp. 112–117.

35. B. J. Hoffman, S. E. Strang, K. W. Kuhnert, W. K. Campbell, C. L. Kennedy, et al., "Leader Narcissism and Ethical Context: Effects on Ethical Leadership and Leader Effectiveness," *Journal of Leadership & Organizational Studies* 20 (2013), pp. 25–37.

36. M. Maccoby, "Narcissistic Leaders: The Incredible Pros, the Inevitable Cons," *The Harvard Business Review* (January–February 2000), pp. 69–77, www.maccoby.com/Articles/NarLeaders.shtml.

37. A. Chatterjee and D. C. Hambrick, "Executive Personality, Capability Cues, and Risk Taking: How Narcissistic CEOs React to Their Successes and Stumbles," *Administrative Science Quarterly* 56 (2011), pp. 202–237.

38. C. J. Resick, D. S. Whitman, S. M. Weingarden, and N. J. Hiller, "The Bright-Side and Dark-Side of CEO Personality: Examining Core Self-Evaluations, Narcissism, Transformational Leadership, and Strategic Influence," *Journal of Applied Psychology* 94, no. 6 (2009), pp. 1365–1381.

39. C. Carpenter, "Narcissism on Facebook: Self-Promotional and Anti-Social Behavior," *Personality and Individual Differences* 52 (2012), pp. 482–486.

40. L. L. Meier and N. K. Semmer, "Lack of Reciprocity and Strain: Narcissism as a Moderator of the Association Between Feeling Under-benefited and Irritation," *Work & Stress* 26 (2012), pp. 56–67.

41. O'Boyle, Forsyth, Banks, and McDaniel, "A Meta-Analysis of the Dark Triad and Work Behavior: A Social Exchange Perspective," p. 558.

42. B. Wille, F. De Fruyt, and B. De Clercq, "Expanding and Reconceptualizing Aberrant Personality at Work: Validity of Five-Factor Model Aberrant Personality Tendencies to Predict Career Outcomes," *Personnel Psychology* 66 (2013), pp. 173–223.

43. P. K. Jonason, S. Slomski, and J. Partyka, "The Dark Triad at Work: How Toxic Employees Get Their Way," *Personality and Individual Differences* 52 (2012), pp. 449–453; and H. M. Baughman, S. Dearing, E. Giammarco, and P. A. Vernon, "Relationships Between Bullying Behaviours and the Dark Triad: A Study with Adults," *Personality and Individual Differences* 52 (2012), pp. 571–575.

44. J. Concannon, "Mind Matters: Mental Disability and the History and Future of the American with Disabilities Act," *Law & Psychology Review* 36 (2012), pp. 89–114.

45. D. L. Ferris, R. E. Johnson, C. C. Rosen, E. Djurdjevic, C.-H. Chang, et al., "When Is Success Not Satisfying? Integrating Regulatory Focus and Approach/Avoidance Motivation Theories to Explain the Relation Between Core Self-Evaluation and Job Satisfaction," *Journal of Applied Psychology* 98 (2013), pp. 342–353.

46. K. Murayama and A. J. Elliot, "The Competition–Performance Relation: A Meta-Analytic Review and Test of the Opposing Processes Model of Competition and Performance," *Psychological Bulletin* 138 (2012), pp. 1035–1070.

47. S. Nifadkar, A. S. Tsui, and B. E. Ashforth, "The Way You Make Me Feel and Behave: Supervisor-Triggered Newcomer Affect and Approach-Avoidance Behavior," *Academy of Management Journal* 55 (2012), pp. 1146–1168.

48. T. A. Judge and J. E. Bono, "A Rose by Any Other Name . . . Are Self-Esteem, Generalized Self-Efficacy, Neuroticism, and Locus of Control Indicators of a Common Construct?" in B. W. Roberts and R. Hogan (eds.), *Personality Psychology in the Workplace* (Washington, DC: American Psychological Association, 2001), pp. 93–118.

49. A. Erez and T. A. Judge, "Relationship of Core Self-Evaluations to Goal Setting, Motivation, and Performance," *Journal of Applied Psychology* 86, no. 6 (2001), pp. 1270–1279.

50. A. N. Salvaggio, B. Schneider, L. H. Nishi, D. M. Mayer, A. Ramesh, and J. S. Lyon, "Manager Personality, Manager Service Quality Orientation, and Service Climate: Test of a Model," *Journal of Applied Psychology* 92, no. 6 (2007), pp. 1741–1750; B. A. Scott and T. A. Judge, "The Popularity Contest at Work: Who Wins, Why, and What Do They Receive?" *Journal of Applied Psychology* 94, no. 1 (2009), pp. 20–33; and T. A. Judge and C. Hurst, "How the Rich (and Happy) Get Richer (and Happier): Relationship of Core Self-Evaluations to Trajectories in Attaining Work Success," *Journal of Applied Psychology* 93, no. 4 (2008), pp. 849–863.

51. A. M. Grant and A. Wrzesniewksi, "I Won't Let You Down . . . or Will I? Core Self-Evaluations, Other-Orientation, Anticipated Guilt and Gratitude, and Job Performance," *Journal of Applied Psychology* 95, no. 1 (2010), pp. 108–121.

52. U. Malmendier and G. Tate, "CEO Overconfidence and Corporate Investment," *Journal of Finance* 60, no. 6 (2005), pp. 2661–2700.

53. R. Sandomir, "Star Struck," *The New York Times* (January 12, 2007), pp. C10, C14.

54. See M. Snyder, *Public Appearances/Private Realities: The Psychology of Self-Monitoring* (New York: W. H. Freeman, 1987); and S. W. Gangestad and M. Snyder, "Self-Monitoring: Appraisal and Reappraisal," *Psychological Bulletin* 126, no. 4 (2000), pp. 530–555.

55. F. J. Flynn and D. R. Ames, "What's Good for the Goose May Not Be as Good for the Gander: The Benefits of Self-Monitoring

for Men and Women in Task Groups and Dyadic Conflicts," *Journal of Applied Psychology* 91, no. 2 (2006), pp. 272–281; and Snyder, *Public Appearances/Private Realities.*

56. D. V. Day, D. J. Shleicher, A. L. Unckless, and N. J. Hiller, "Self-Monitoring Personality at Work: A Meta-Analytic Investigation of Construct Validity," *Journal of Applied Psychology* 87, no. 2 (2002), pp. 390–401.

57. H. Oh and M. Kilduff, "The Ripple Effect of Personality on Social Structure: Self-Monitoring Origins of Network Brokerage," *Journal of Applied Psychology* 93, no. 5 (2008), pp. 1155–1164; and A. Mehra, M. Kilduff, and D. J. Brass, "The Social Networks of High and Low Self-Monitors: Implications for Workplace Performance," *Administrative Science Quarterly* 46, no. 1 (2001), pp. 121–146.

58. J. M. Crant, "Proactive Behavior in Organizations," *Journal of Management* 26, no. 3 (2000), p. 436.

59. P. D. Converse, Patrick J. Pathak, A. M. DePaul-Haddock, T. Gotlib, and M. Merbedone, "Controlling Your Environment and Yourself: Implications for Career Success," *Journal of Vocational Behavior* 80 (2012), pp. 148-159.

60. G. Van Hoye and H. Lootens, "Coping with Unemployment: Personality, Role Demands, and Time Structure," *Journal of Vocational Behavior* 82 (2013), pp. 85–95.

61. G. Chen, J. Farh, E. M. Campbell-Bush, Z. Wu, and X. Wu, "Teams as Innovative Systems: Multilevel Motivational Antecedents of Innovation in R&D Teams," *Journal of Applied Psychology* (2013).

62. Z. Zhang, M. Wang, J. Shi, Junqi, "Leader-Follower Congruence in Proactive Personality and Work Outcomes: The Mediating Role of Leader-Member Exchange," *Academy of Management Journal* 55 (2012), pp. 111–130.

63. R. D. Meyer, R. S. Dalal, and R. Hermida, "A Review and Synthesis of Situational Strength in the Organizational Sciences," *Journal of Management* 36 (2010), pp. 121–140.

64. A. M. Grant and N. P. Rothbard, "When in Doubt, Seize the Day? Security Values, Prosocial Values, and Proactivity Under Ambiguity," *Journal of Applied Psychology* (2013).

65. A. M. Watson, T. F. Thompson, J. V. Rudolph, T. J. Whelan, T. S. Behrend, et al., "When Big Brother Is Watching: Goal Orientation Shapes Reactions to Electronic Monitoring During Online Training," *Journal of Applied Psychology* (2013).

66. Y. Kim, L. Van Dyne, D. Kamdar, and R. E. Johnson, "Why and When Do Motives Matter? An Integrative Model of Motives, Role Cognitions, and Social Support as Predictors of OCB," *Organizational Behavior and Human Decision Processes* (2013).

67. M. Rokeach, *The Nature of Human Values* (New York: The Free Press, 1973), p. 5.

68. M. Rokeach and S. J. Ball-Rokeach, "Stability and Change in American Value Priorities, 1968–1981," *American Psychologist* 44, no. 5 (1989), pp. 775–784; and A. Bardi, J. A. Lee, N. Hofmann-Towfigh, and G. Soutar, "The Structure of Intraindividual Value Change," *Journal of Personality and Social Psychology* 97, no. 5 (2009), pp. 913–929.

69. S. Roccas, L. Sagiv, S. H. Schwartz, and A. Knafo, "The Big Five Personality Factors and Personal Values," *Personality and Social Psychology Bulletin* 28, no. 6 (2002), pp. 789–801.

70. B. C. Holtz and C. M. Harold, "Interpersonal Justice and Deviance: The Moderating Effects of Interpersonal Justice Values and Justice Orientation," *Journal of Management* (February 2013), pp. 339–365.

71. See, for example, N. R. Lockwood, F. R. Cepero, and S. Williams, *The Multigenerational Workforce* (Alexandria, VA: Society for Human Resource Management, 2009).

72. B. Hite, "Employers Rethink How They Give Feedback," *The Wall Street Journal* (October 13, 2008), p. B5.

73. E. Parry and P. Urwin, "Generational Differences in Work Values: A Review of Theory and Evidence," *International Journal of Management Reviews* 13, no. 1 (2011), pp. 79–96.

74. J. M. Twenge, S. M. Campbell, B. J. Hoffman, and C. E. Lance, "Generational Differences in Work Values: Leisure and Extrinsic Values Increasing, Social and Intrinsic Values Decreasing," *Journal of Management* 36, no. 5 (2010), pp. 1117–1142.

75. J. L. Holland, *Making Vocational Choices: A Theory of Vocational Personalities and Work Environments* (Odessa, FL: Psychological Assessment Resources, 1997).

76. D. A. McKay and D. M. Tokar, "The HEXACO and Five-Factor Models of Personality in Relation to RIASEC Vocational Interests," *Journal of Vocational Behavior* (October 2012), pp. 138–149.

77. See B. Schneider, H. W. Goldstein, and D. B. Smith, "The ASA Framework: An Update," *Personnel Psychology* 48, no. 4 (1995), pp. 747–773; B. Schneider, D. B. Smith, S. Taylor, and J. Fleenor, "Personality and Organizations: A Test of the Homogeneity of Personality Hypothesis," *Journal of Applied Psychology* 83, no. 3 (1998), pp. 462–470; W. Arthur Jr., S. T. Bell, A. J. Villado, and D. Doverspike, "The Use of Person-Organization Fit in Employment Decision-Making: An Assessment of Its Criterion-Related Validity," *Journal of Applied Psychology* 91, no. 4 (2006), pp. 786–801; and J. R. Edwards, D. M. Cable, I. O. Williamson, L. S. Lambert, and A. J. Shipp, "The Phenomenology of Fit: Linking the Person and Environment to the Subjective Experience of Person–Environment Fit," *Journal of Applied Psychology* 91, no. 4 (2006), pp. 802–827.

78. T. A. Judge and D. M. Cable, "Applicant Personality, Organizational Culture, and Organization Attraction," *Personnel Psychology* 50, no. 2 (1997), pp. 359–394; and A. Leung and S. Chaturvedi, "Linking the Fits, Fitting the Links: Connecting Different Types of PO Fit to Attitudinal Outcomes," *Journal of Vocational Behavior* (October 2011), pp. 391–402.

79. M. L. Verquer, T. A. Beehr, and S. E. Wagner, "A Meta-Analysis of Relations Between Person–Organization Fit and Work Attitudes," *Journal of Vocational Behavior* 63, no. 3 (2003), pp. 473–489; and J. C. Carr, A. W. Pearson, M. J. Vest, and S. L. Boyar, "Prior Occupational Experience, Anticipatory Socialization, and Employee Retention," *Journal of Management* 32, no. 32 (2006), pp. 343–359.

80. A. Ramesh and M. J. Gelfand, "Will They Stay or Will They Go? The Role of Job Embeddedness in Predicting Turnover in Individualistic and Collectivistic Cultures," *Journal of Applied Psychology* 95, no. 5 (2010), pp. 807–823.

81. G. Hofstede, *Cultures and Organizations: Software of the Mind* (London: McGraw-Hill, 1991); G. Hofstede, "Cultural Constraints in Management Theories," *Academy of Management Executive* 7, no. 1 (1993), pp. 81–94; G. Hofstede and M. F. Peterson, "National Values and Organizational Practices," in N. M. Ashkanasy, C. M. Wilderom, and M. F. Peterson (eds.), *Handbook of Organizational Culture and*

Climate (Thousand Oaks, CA: Sage, 2000), pp. 401–416; and G. Hofstede, *Culture's Consequences: Comparing Values, Behaviors, Institutions, and Organizations Across Nations*, 2nd ed. (Thousand Oaks, CA: Sage, 2001). For criticism of this research, see B. McSweeney, "Hofstede's Model of National Cultural Differences and Their Consequences: A Triumph of Faith—A Failure of Analysis," *Human Relations* 55, no. 1 (2002), pp. 89–118.

82. V. Taras, B. L. Kirkman, and P. Steel, "Examining the Impact of Culture's Consequences: A Three-Decade, Multilevel, Meta-Analytic Review of Hofstede's Cultural Value Dimensions," *Journal of Applied Psychology* 95, no. 5 (2010), pp. 405–439.

83. M. Javidan and R. J. House, "Cultural Acumen for the Global Manager: Lessons from Project GLOBE," *Organizational Dynamics* 29, no. 4 (2001), pp. 289–305; and R. J. House, P. J. Hanges, M. Javidan, and P. W. Dorfman (eds.), *Leadership, Culture, and Organizations: The GLOBE Study of 62 Societies* (Thousand Oaks, CA: Sage, 2004).

84. J. P. Meyer, D. J. Stanley, T. A. Jackson, K. J. McInnis, E. R. Maltin, et al., "Affective, Normative, and Continuance Commitment Levels Across Cultures: A Meta-Analysis," *Journal of Vocational Behavior* 80 (2012), pp. 225–245.

85. B. Adkins and D. Caldwell, "Firm or Subgroup Culture: Where Does Fitting in Matter Most?" *Journal of Organizational Behavior* 25, no. 8 (2004), pp. 969–978; H. D. Cooper-Thomas, A. van Vianen, and N. Anderson, "Changes in Person–Organization Fit: The Impact of Socialization Tactics on Perceived and Actual P–O Fit," *European Journal of Work & Organizational Psychology* 13, no. 1 (2004), pp. 52–78; and C. A. O'Reilly III, J. Chatman, and D. F. Caldwell, "People and Organizational Culture: A Profile Comparison Approach to Assessing Person–Organization Fit," *Academy of Management Journal* 34, no. 3 (1991), pp. 487–516.

CHAPTER 6

1. H. H. Kelley, "Attribution in Social Interaction," in E. Jones et al. (eds.), *Attribution: Perceiving the Causes of Behavior* (Morristown, NJ: General Learning Press, 1972); and M. J. Martinko, P. Harvey, and M. T. Dasborough, "Attribution Theory in the Organizational Sciences: A Case of Unrealized Potential," *Journal of Organizational Behavior* 32, no. 1 (2011), pp. 144–149.

2. See L. Ross, "The Intuitive Psychologist and His Shortcomings," in L. Berkowitz (ed.), *Advances in Experimental Social Psychology*, vol. 10 (Orlando, FL: Academic Press, 1977), pp. 174–220; and A. G. Miller and T. Lawson, "The Effect of an Informational Option on the Fundamental Attribution Error," *Personality and Social Psychology Bulletin* 15, no. 2 (1989), pp. 194–204.

3. See, for instance, N. Epley and D. Dunning, "Feeling 'Holier Than Thou': Are Self-Serving Assessments Produced by Errors in Self- or Social Prediction?" *Journal of Personality and Social Psychology* 76, no. 6 (2000), pp. 861–875; M. Goerke, J. Moller, S. Schulz-Hardt, U. Napiersky, and D. Frey, "'It's Not My Fault—But Only I Can Change It': Counterfactual and Prefactual Thoughts of Managers," *Journal of Applied Psychology* 89, no. 2 (2004), pp. 279–292; and E. G. Hepper, R. H. Gramzow, and C. Sedikides, "Individual Differences in Self-Enhancement and Self-Protection Strategies: An

Integrative Analysis," *Journal of Personality* 78, no. 2 (2010), pp. 781–814.

4. See D. M. Cain and A. S. Little, "Everyone's a Little Bit Biased (even Physicians)," *JAMA: Journal of the American Medical Association* 299, no. 24 (2008), pp. 2893–2895.

5. See, for instance, A. H. Mezulis, L. Y. Abramson, J. S. Hyde, and B. L. Hankin, "Is There a Universal Positivity Bias in Attributions: A Meta-Analytic Review of Individual, Developmental, and Cultural Differences in the Self-Serving Attributional Bias," *Psychological Bulletin* 130, no. 5 (2004), pp. 711–747; C. F. Falk, S. J. Heine, M. Yuki, and K. Takemura, "Why Do Westerners Self-Enhance More than East Asians?" *European Journal of Personality* 23, no. 3 (2009), pp. 183–203; and F. F. T. Chiang and T. A. Birtch, "Examining the Perceived Causes of Successful Employee Performance: An East–West Comparison," *International Journal of Human Resource Management* 18, no. 2 (2007), pp. 232–248.

6. S. Nam, "Cultural and Managerial Attributions for Group Performance," unpublished doctoral dissertation, University of Oregon. Cited in R. M. Steers, S. J. Bischoff, and L. H. Higgins, "Cross-Cultural Management Research," *Journal of Management Inquiry*, December 1992, pp. 325–326.

7. T. Menon, M. W. Morris, C. Chiu, and Y. Y. Hong, "Culture and the Construal of Agency: Attribution to Individual Versus Group Dispositions," *Journal of Personality and Social Psychology* 76, no. 5 (1999), pp. 701–717; and R. Friedman, W. Liu, C. C. Chen, and S.-C. S. Chi, "Causal Attribution for Interfirm Contract Violation: A Comparative Study of Chinese and American Commercial Arbitrators," *Journal of Applied Psychology* 92, no. 3 (2007), pp. 856–864.

8. J. Spencer-Rodgers, M. J. Williams, D. L. Hamilton, K. Peng, and L. Wang, "Culture and Group Perception: Dispositional and Stereotypic Inferences about Novel and National Groups," *Journal of Personality and Social Psychology* 93, no. 4 (2007), pp. 525–543.

9. J. D. Brown, "Across the (Not So) Great Divide: Cultural Similarities in Self-Evaluative Processes," *Social and Personality Psychology Compass* 4, no. 5 (2010), pp. 318–330.

10. A. Zhang, C. Reyna, Z. Qian, and G. Yu, "Interpersonal Attributions of Responsibility in the Chinese Workplace: A Test of Western Models in a Collectivistic Context," *Journal of Applied Social Psychology* 38, no. 9 (2008), pp. 2361–2377; and A. Zhang, F. Xia, and C. Li, "The Antecedents of Help Giving in Chinese Culture: Attribution, Judgment of Responsibility, Expectation Change and the Reaction of Affect," *Social Behavior and Personality* 35, no. 1 (2007), pp. 135–142.

11. J. Healy and M. M. Grynbaum, "Why Analysts Keep Telling Investors to Buy," *The New York Times* (February 9, 2009), pp. B1, B7.

12. See P. Rosenzweig, *The Halo Effect* (New York: The Free Press, 2007); I. Dennis, "Halo Effects in Grading Student Projects," *Journal of Applied Psychology* 92, no. 4 (2007), pp. 1169–1176; C. E. Naquin and R. O. Tynan, "The Team Halo Effect: Why Teams Are Not Blamed for Their Failures," *Journal of Applied Psychology* 88, no. 2 (2003), pp. 332–340; and T. M. Bechger, G. Maris, and Y. P. Hsiao, "Detecting Halo Effects in Performance-Based Evaluations," *Applied Psychological Measurement* 34, no. 8 (2010), pp. 607–619.

13. S. E. Asch, "Forming Impressions of Personality," *Journal of Abnormal and Social Psychology* 41, no. 3 (1946), pp. 258–290.

14. J. L. Hilton and W. von Hippel, "Stereotypes," *Annual Review of Psychology* 47 (1996), pp. 237–271.

15. See, for example, C. Ostroff and L. E. Atwater, "Does Whom You Work with Matter? Effects of Referent Group Gender and Age Composition on Managers' Compensation," *Journal of Applied Psychology* 88, no. 4 (2003), pp. 725–740; M. E. Heilman, A. S. Wallen, D. Fuchs, and M. M. Tamkins, "Penalties for Success: Reactions to Women Who Succeed at Male Gender-Typed Tasks," *Journal of Applied Psychology* 89, no. 3 (2004), pp. 416–427; V. K. Gupta, D. B. Turban, and N. M. Bhawe, "The Effect of Gender Stereotype Activation on Entrepreneurial Intentions," *Journal of Applied Psychology* 93, no. 5 (2008), pp. 1053–1061; and R. A. Posthuma and M. A. Campion, "Age Stereotypes in the Workplace: Common Stereotypes, Moderators, and Future Research Directions," *Journal of Management* 35, no. 1 (2009), pp. 158–188.

16. See, for example, N. Dasgupta, D. DeSteno, L. A. Williams, and M. Hunsinger, "Fanning the Flames of Prejudice: The Influence of Specific Incidental Emotions on Implicit Prejudice," *Emotion* 9, no. 4 (2009), pp. 585–591; and J. C. Ziegert and P. C. Hanges, "Strong Rebuttal for Weak Criticisms: Reply to Blanton et al. (2009)," *Journal of Applied Psychology* 94, no. 3 (2009), pp. 590–597.

17. J. L. Eberhardt, P. G. Davies, V. J. Purdie-Vaughns, and S. L. Johnson, "Looking Deathworthy: Perceived Stereotypicality of Black Defendants Predicts Capital-Sentencing Outcomes," *Psychological Science* 17, no. 5 (2006), pp. 383–386.

18. A. S. Rosette, G. J. Leonardelli, and K. W. Phillips, "The White Standard: Racial Bias in Leader Categorization," *Journal of Applied Psychology* 93, no. 4 (2008), pp. 758–777.

19. H. G. Heneman III, T. A. Judge, and J. D. Kammeyer-Mueller, *Staffing Organizations* (Middleton, WI: Mendota House, 2012).

20. J. Willis and A. Todorov, "First Impressions: Making Up Your Mind after a 100ms Exposure to a Face," *Psychological Science* 17, no. 7 (2006), pp. 592–598.

21. N. Eisenkraft, "Accurate by Way of Aggregation Should You Trust Your Intuition-based First Impressions?" *Journal of Experimental Social Psychology* (March 2013), pp. 277–279.

22. See, for example, D. B. McNatt, "Ancient Pygmalion Joins Contemporary Management: A Meta-Analysis of the Result," *Journal of Applied Psychology* 85, no. 2 (2000), pp. 314–322; O. B. Davidson and D. Eden, "Remedial Self-Fulfilling Prophecy: Two Field Experiments to Prevent Golem Effects among Disadvantaged Women," *Journal of Applied Psychology* 85, no. 3 (2000), pp. 386–398; and G. Natanovich and D. Eden, "Pygmalion Effects among Outreach Supervisors and Tutors: Extending Sex Generalizability," *Journal of Applied Psychology* 93, no. 6 (2008), pp. 1382–1389.

23. D. Eden and A. B. Shani, "Pygmalion Goes to Boot Camp: Expectancy, Leadership, and Trainee Performance," *Journal of Applied Psychology* (April 1982), pp. 194–199; D. B. McNatt and T. A. Judge, "Boundary Conditions of the Galatea Effect: A Field Experiment and Constructive Replication," *Academy of Management Journal* (August 2004), pp. 550–565; and X. M. Bezuijen, P. T. van den Berg, K. van Dam, and H. Thierry, "Pygmalion and Employee Learning: The Role

of Leader Behaviors," *Journal of Management* 35, (2009), pp. 1248–1267.

24. See, for example, K. F. E. Wong and J. Y. Y. Kwong, "Effects of Rater Goals on Rating Patterns: Evidence from an Experimental Field Study," *Journal of Applied Psychology* 92, no. 2 (2007), pp. 577–585; and S. E. DeVoe and S. S. Iyengar, "Managers' Theories of Subordinates: A Cross-Cultural Examination of Manager Perceptions of Motivation and Appraisal of Performance," *Organizational Behavior and Human Decision Processes* (January 2004), pp. 47–61.

25. R. Sanders, *The Executive Decisionmaking Process: Identifying Problems and Assessing Outcomes* (Westport, CT: Quorum, 1999).

26. See H. A. Simon, "Rationality in Psychology and Economics," *Journal of Business* (October 1986), pp. 209–224; and E. Shafir and R. A. LeBoeuf, "Rationality," *Annual Review of Psychology* 53 (2002), pp. 491–517.

27. For a review of the rational decision-making model, see M. H. Bazerman and D. A. Moore, *Judgment in Managerial Decision Making*, 7th ed. (Hoboken, New Jersey: Wiley, 2008).

28. J. G. March, *A Primer on Decision Making* (New York: The Free Press, 2009); and D. Hardman and C. Harries, "How Rational Are We?" *Psychologist* (February 2002), pp. 76–79.

29. Bazerman and Moore, *Judgment in Managerial Decision Making*.

30. J. E. Russo, K. A. Carlson, and M. G. Meloy, "Choosing an Inferior Alternative," *Psychological Science* 17, no. 10 (2006), pp. 899–904.

31. D. Kahneman, "Maps of Bounded Rationality: Psychology for Behavioral Economics," *The American Economic Review* 93, no. 5 (2003), pp. 1449–1475; and J. Zhang, C. K. Hsee, and Z. Xiao, "The Majority Rule in Individual Decision Making," *Organizational Behavior and Human Decision Processes* 99 (2006), pp. 102–111.

32. See H. A. Simon, *Administrative Behavior*, 4th ed. (New York: The Free Press, 1997); and M. Augier, "Simon Says: Bounded Rationality Matters," *Journal of Management Inquiry* (September 2001), pp. 268–275.

33. G. Gigerenzer, "Why Heuristics Work," *Perspectives on Psychological Science* 3, no. 1 (2008), pp. 20–29; and A. K. Shah and D. M. Oppenheimer, "Heuristics Made Easy: An Effort-Reduction Framework," *Psychological Bulletin* 134, no. 2 (2008), pp. 207–222.

34. See A. W. Kruglanski and G. Gigerenzer, "Intuitive and Deliberate Judgments Are Based on Common Principles," *Psychological Review* 118 (2011), pp. 97–109.

35. E. Dane and M. G. Pratt, "Exploring Intuition and Its Role in Managerial Decision Making," *Academy of Management Review* 32, no. 1 (2007), pp. 33–54; and J. A. Hicks, D. C. Cicero, J. Trent, C. M. Burton, and L. A. King, "Positive Affect, Intuition, and Feelings of Meaning," *Journal of Personality and Social Psychology* 98 (2010), pp. 967–979.

36. C. Akinci and E. Sadler-Smith, "Intuition in Management Research: A Historical Review," *International Journal of Management Reviews* 14 (2012), pp. 104–122.

37. S. P. Robbins, *Decide & Conquer: Making Winning Decisions and Taking Control of Your Life* (Upper Saddle River, NJ: Financial Times/Prentice Hall, 2004), p. 13.

38. S. Ludwig and J. Nafziger, "Beliefs about Overconfidence," *Theory and Decision* (April 2011), pp. 475–500.

39. S. Plous, *The Psychology of Judgment and Decision Making* (New York: McGraw-Hill, 1993), p. 217.

40. C. R. M. McKenzie, M. J. Liersch, and I. Yaniv, "Overconfidence in Interval Estimates: What Does Expertise Buy You," *Organizational Behavior and Human Decision Processes* 107 (2008), pp. 179–191.

41. J. Kruger and D. Dunning, "Unskilled and Unaware of It: How Difficulties in Recognizing One's Own Incompetence Lead to Inflated Self-Assessments," *Journal of Personality and Social Psychology* (November 1999), pp. 1121–1134; and R. P. Larrick, K. A. Burson, and J. B. Soll, "Social Comparison and Confidence: When Thinking You're Better than Average Predicts Overconfidence (and When It Does Not)" *Organizational Behavior and Human Decision Processes* 102 (2007), pp. 76–94.

42. K. M. Hmieleski and R. A. Baron, "Entrepreneurs' Optimism and New Venture Performance: A Social Cognitive Perspective," *Academy of Management Journal* 52, no. 3 (2009), pp. 473–488.

43. R. Frick and A. K. Smith, "Overconfidence Game," *Kiplinger's Personal Finance* 64, no. 3 (2010), p. 23.

44. See, for instance, J. P. Simmons, R. A. LeBoeuf, and L. D. Nelson, "The Effect of Accuracy Motivation on Anchoring and Adjustment: Do People Adjust from Their Provided Anchors?" *Journal of Personality and Social Psychology* 99 (2010), pp. 917–932.

45. J. Bailey, "Dreams Fly Into Reality," *The New York Times* (April 10, 2008), pp. B1, B4.

46. C. Janiszewski and D. Uy, "Precision of the Anchor Influences the Amount of Adjustment," *Psychological Science* 19, no. 2 (2008), pp. 121–127.

47. See E. Jonas, S. Schultz-Hardt, D. Frey, and N. Thelen, "Confirmation Bias in Sequential Information Search after Preliminary Decisions," *Journal of Personality and Social Psychology* (April 2001), pp. 557–571; and W. Hart, D. Albarracín, A. H. Eagly, I. Brechan, M. Lindberg, and L. Merrill, "Feeling Validated Versus Being Correct: A Meta-Analysis of Selective Exposure to Information," *Psychological Bulletin* 135 (2009), pp. 555–588.

48. T. Pachur, R. Hertwig, and F. Steinmann, "How Do People Judge Risks: Availability Heuristic, Affect Heuristic, or Both?" *Journal of Experimental Psychology: Applied* 18 (2012), pp. 314–330; A. Tversky and D. Kahneman, "Availability: A Heuristic for Judging Frequency and Probability," in D. Kahneman, P. Slovic, and A. Tversky (eds.), *Judgment Under Uncertainty: Heuristics and Biases* (Cambridge, U.K.: Cambridge University Press, 1982), pp. 163–178.

49. G. Morgenson, "Debt Watchdogs: Tamed or Caught Napping?" *The New York Times* (December 7, 2009), pp. 1, 32.

50. K. Moser, H.-G. Wolff, and A. Kraft, "The De-escalation of Commitment: Predecisional Accountability and Cognitive Processes," *Journal of Applied Social Psychology* (February 2013), pp. 363–376; and B. M. Staw, "The Escalation of Commitment to a Course of Action," *Academy of Management Review* (October 1981), pp. 577–587.

51. T. Schultze, F. Pfeiffer, and S. Schulz-Hardt, "Biased Information Processing in the Escalation Paradigm: Information Search and Information Evaluation as Potential Mediators of Escalating Commitment," *Journal of Applied Psychology* 97 (2012), pp. 16–32.

52. D. J. Sleesman, D. E. Conlon, G. McNamara, and J. E. Miles, "Cleaning Up the Big Muddy: A Meta-Analytic Review of the Determinants of Escalation of Commitment," *Academy of Management Journal* 55 (2012), pp. 541–562.

53. See, for instance, A. James and A. Wells, "Death Beliefs, Superstitious Beliefs and Health Anxiety," *British Journal of Clinical Psychology* (March 2002), pp. 43–53; and U. Hahn and P. A. Warren, "Perceptions of Randomness: Why Three Heads Are Better than One," *Psychological Review* 116 (2009), pp. 454–461.

54. See, for example, D. J. Keys and B. Schwartz, "Leaky Rationality: How Research on Behavioral Decision Making Challenges Normative Standards of Rationality," *Psychological Science* 2, no. 2 (2007), pp. 162–180; and U. Simonsohn, "Direct Risk Aversion: Evidence from Risky Prospects Valued Below Their Worst Outcome," *Psychological Science* 20, no. 6 (2009), pp. 686–692.

55. J. K. Maner, M. T. Gailliot, D. A. Butz, and B. M. Peruche, "Power, Risk, and the Status Quo: Does Power Promote Riskier or More Conservative Decision Making," *Personality and Social Psychology Bulletin* 33, no. 4 (2007), pp. 451–462.

56. A. Chakraborty, S. Sheikh, and N. Subramanian, "Termination Risk and Managerial Risk Taking," *Journal of Corporate Finance* 13 (2007), pp. 170–188.

57. D. Kahneman and A. Tversky, "Prospect Theory: An Analysis of Decisions Under Risk," *Econometrica* 47, no. 2 (1979), pp. 263–291; and P. Bryant and R. Dunford, "The Influence of Regulatory Focus on Risky Decision-Making," *Applied Psychology: An International Review* 57, no. 2 (2008), pp. 335–359.

58. A. J. Porcelli and M. R. Delgado, "Acute Stress Modulates Risk Taking in Financial Decision Making," *Psychological Science* 20, no. 3 (2009), pp. 278–283.

59. R. L. Guilbault, F. B. Bryant, J. H. Brockway, and E. J. Posavac, "A Meta-Analysis of Research on Hindsight Bias," *Basic and Applied Social Psychology* (September 2004), pp. 103–117; and L. Werth, F. Strack, and J. Foerster, "Certainty and Uncertainty: The Two Faces of the Hindsight Bias," *Organizational Behavior and Human Decision Processes* (March 2002), pp. 323–341.

60. J. Bell, "The Final Cut?" *Oregon Business* 33, no. 5 (2010), p. 27.

61. E. Dash and J. Creswell, "Citigroup Pays for a Rush to Risk," *The New York Times* (November 20, 2008), pp. 1, 28; S. Pulliam, S. Ng, and R. Smith, "Merrill Upped Ante as Boom in Mortgage Bonds Fizzled," *The Wall Street Journal* (April 16, 2008), pp. A1, A14; and M. Gladwell, "Connecting the Dots," *The New Yorker* (March 10, 2003).

62. H. Moon, J. R. Hollenbeck, S. E. Humphrey, and B. Maue, "The Tripartite Model of Neuroticism and the Suppression of Depression and Anxiety within an Escalation of Commitment Dilemma," *Journal of Personality* 71 (2003), pp. 347–368; and H. Moon, "The Two Faces of Conscientiousness: Duty and Achievement Striving in Escalation of Commitment Dilemmas," *Journal of Applied Psychology* 86 (2001), pp. 535–540.

63. J. Musch, "Personality Differences in Hindsight Bias," *Memory* 11 (2003), pp. 473–489.

64. W. K. Campbell and C. Sedikides, "Self-Threat Magnifies the Self-Serving Bias: A Meta-Analytic Integration," *Review of General Psychology* 3 (1999), pp. 23–43.

65. This section is based on S. Nolen-Hoeksema, J. Larson, and C. Grayson, "Explaining the Gender Difference in Depressive Symptoms," *Journal of Personality & Social Psychology* (November 1999), pp. 1061–1072; and J. S. Hyde, A. H. Mezulis, and L. Y. Abramson, "The ABCs of Depression: Integrating Affective, Biological, and Cognitive Models to Explain the Emergence of the Gender Difference in Depression," *Psychological Review* 115, no. 2 (2008), pp. 291–313.

66. H. Connery and K. M. Davidson, "A Survey of Attitudes to Depression in the General Public: A Comparison of Age and Gender Differences," *Journal of Mental Health* 15, no. 2 (April 2006), pp. 179–189.

67. M. Elias, "Thinking It Over, and Over, and Over," *USA Today* (February 6, 2003), p. 10D.

68. K. E. Stanovich and R. F. West, "On the Relative Independence of Thinking Biases and Cognitive Ability," *Journal of Personality and Social Psychology* 94, no. 4 (2008), pp. 672–695.

69. N. J. Adler, *International Dimensions of Organizational Behavior,* 4th ed. (Cincinnati, OH: South-Western Publishing, 2002), pp. 182–189.

70. A. Wildavsky, *The Politics of the Budgetary Process* (Boston: Little, Brown, 1964).

71. G. F. Cavanagh, D. J. Moberg, and M. Valasquez, "The Ethics of Organizational Politics," *Academy of Management Journal* (June 1981), pp. 363–374.

72. L. L. Shu and F. Gino, "Sweeping Dishonesty Under the Rug: How Unethical Actions Lead to Forgetting of Moral Rules," *Journal of Personality and Social Psychology* 102 (2012), pp. 1164-1177.

73. B. C. Gunia, L. Wang, L. Huang, J. Wang, and J. K. Murnighan, "Contemplation and Conversation: Subtle Influences on Moral Decision Making," *Academy of Management Journal* 55 (2012), pp. 13–33.

74. R. F. West, R. J. Meserve, and K. E. Stanovich, "Cognitive Sophistication Does Not Attenuate the Bias Blind Spot," *Journal of Personality and Social Psychology* 103 (2012), pp. 506–519.

75. T. Jackson, "Cultural Values and Management Ethics: A 10-Nation Study," *Human Relations* (October 2001), pp. 1267–1302; see also J. B. Cullen, K. P. Parboteeah, and M. Hoegl, "Cross-National Differences in Managers' Willingness to Justify Ethically Suspect Behaviors: A Test of Institutional Anomie Theory," *Academy of Management Journal* (June 2004), pp. 411–421.

76. "Is Your Art Killing You?" Investorideas.com (May 13, 2013), downloaded May 14, 2013, from www.investorideas.com/news/2013/renewable-energy/05134.asp.

77. G. Anderson, "Three Tips to Foster Creativity at Your Startup," *ArcticStartup* (May 8, 2013), downloaded May 14, 2013, from http://www.arcticstartup.com/.

78. E. Millar, "How Do Finnish Kids Excel without Rote Learning and Standardized Testing?" *The Globe and Mail* (May 9, 2013), downloaded May 14, 2013, from www.theglobeandmail.com/.

79. Z. Harper, "Mark Cuban Wants You to Design the New Dallas Mavericks Uniforms," CBSSports.com (May 13, 2013), downloaded May 14, 2013, from www.cbssports.com/nba/.

80. C. K. W. De Dreu, B. A. Nijstad, M. Baas, I. Wolsink, and M. Roskes, "Working Memory Benefits Creative Insight, Musical Improvisation, and Original Ideation Through Maintained Task-Focused Attention," *Personality and Social Psychology Bulletin* 38 (2012), pp. 656–669.

81. S. M. Wechsler, C. Vendramini, and T. Oakland, "Thinking and Creative Styles: A Validity Study," *Creativity Research Journal* 24 (April 2012), pp. 235–242.

82. Y. Gong, S. Cheung, M. Wang, and J. Huang, "Unfolding the Proactive Processes for Creativity: Integration of the Employee Proactivity, Information Exchange, and Psychological Safety Perspectives," *Journal of Management* 38 (2012), pp. 1611–1633.

83. S. N. de Jesus, C. L. Rus, W. Lens, and S. Imaginário, "Intrinsic Motivation and Creativity Related to Product: A Meta-Analysis of the Studies Published Between 1990–2010," *Creativity Research Journal* 25 (2013), pp. 80–84.

84. L. Sun, Z. Zhang, J. Qi, and Z. X. Chen, "Empowerment and Creativity: A Cross-Level Investigation," *Leadership Quarterly* 23 (2012), pp. 55–65.

85. T. Rinne, D. G. Steel, and J. Fairweather, "The Role of Hofstede's Individualism in National-Level Creativity," *Creativity Research Journal* 25 (2013), pp. 129–136.

86. X. Yi, W. Hu, H. Scheithauer, and W. Niu, "Cultural and Bilingual Influences on Artistic Creativity Performances: Comparison of German and Chinese Students," *Creativity Research Journal* 25 (2013), pp. 97–108.

87. D. Liu, H. Liao, and R. Loi, "The Dark Side of Leadership: A Three-Level Investigation of the Cascading Effect of Abusive Supervision on Employee Creativity," *Academy of Management Journal* 55 (2012), pp. 1187–1212.

88. J. B. Avey, F. L. Richmond, and D. R. Nixon, "Leader Positivity and Follower Creativity: An Experimental Analysis," *Journal of Creative Behavior* 46 (2012), pp. 99–118; and A. Rego, Arménio; F. Sousa, C. Marques, M. E. Cunha, "Authentic Leadership Promoting Employees' Psychological Capital and Creativity," *Journal of Business Research* 65 (2012), pp. 429–437.

89. I. J. Hoever, D. van Knippenberg, W. P. van Ginkel, and H. G. Barkema, "Fostering Team Creativity: Perspective Taking as Key to Unlocking Diversity's Potential," *Journal of Applied Psychology* 97 (2012), pp. 982–996.

90. S. J. Shin, T. Kim, J. Lee, and L. Bian, "Cognitive Team Diversity and Individual Team Member Creativity: A Cross-Level Interaction," *Academy of Management Journal* 55 (2012), pp. 197–212.

91. A. W. Richter, G. Hirst, D. van Knippenberg, and M. Baer, "Creative Self-Efficacy and Individual Creativity in Team Contexts: Cross-Level Interactions with Team Informational Resources," *Journal of Applied Psychology* 97 (2012), pp. 1282–1290.

92. J. S. Mueller, S. Melwani, and J. A. Goncalo, "The Bias against Creativity: Why People Desire but Reject Creative Ideas," *Psychological Science* 23 (2012), pp. 13–17.

93. T. Montag, C. P. Maertz, and M. Baer, "A Critical Analysis of the Workplace Creativity Criterion Space," *Journal of Management* 38 (2012), pp. 1362–1386.

94. M. Baer, "Putting Creativity to Work: The Implementation of Creative Ideas in Organizations," *Academy of Management Journal* 55 (2012), pp. 1102–1119.

95. A. Somech, and A. Drach-Zahavy, "Translating Team Creativity to Innovation Implementation: The Role of Team Composition and Climate for Innovation," *Journal of Management* 39 (2013), pp. 684–708.

CHAPTER 7

1. See, for example, G. P. Latham and C. C. Pinder, "Work Motivation Theory and Research at the Dawn of the Twenty-First Century," *Annual Review of Psychology* 56 (2005), pp. 485–516; and C. C. Pinder, *Work Motivation in Organizational Behavior,* 2nd ed. (London, UK: Psychology Press, 2008).

2. R. Wagner and J. K. Harter, *12: The Elements of Great Managing* (Washington, DC: Gallup Press, 2006).

3. "The 2013 Wasting Time at Work Survey: Everything You've Always Wanted to Know About Wasting Time in the Office, Salary.com (2013), www.salary.com.

4. See, for instance, Pinder, *Work Motivation in Organizational Behavior.*

5. A. Maslow, *Motivation and Personality* (New York: Harper & Row, 1954).

6. G. Hofstede, "Motivation, Leadership, and Organization: Do American Theories Apply Abroad?" *Organizational Dynamics* (Summer 1980), p. 55.

7. See, for example, E. E. Lawler III and J. L. Suttle, "A Causal Correlation Test of the Need Hierarchy Concept," *Organizational Behavior and Human Performance* 7, no. 2 (1972), pp. 265–287; D. T. Hall and K. E. Nougaim, "An Examination of Maslow's Need Hierarchy in an Organizational Setting," *Organizational Behavior and Human Performance* 3, no. 1 (1968), pp. 12–35; and J. Rauschenberger, N. Schmitt, and J. E. Hunter, "A Test of the Need Hierarchy Concept by a Markov Model of Change in Need Strength," *Administrative Science Quarterly* 25, no. 4 (1980), pp. 654–670.

8. D. T. Kenrick, V. Griskevicius, S. L. Neuberg, and M. Schaller, "Renovating the Pyramid of Needs: Contemporary Extensions Built on Ancient Foundations," *Perspectives on Psychological Science* 5, no. 3 (2010), pp. 292–314.

9. D. McGregor, *The Human Side of Enterprise* (New York: McGraw-Hill, 1960). For an updated analysis of Theory X and Theory Y constructs, see R. E. Kopelman, D. J. Prottas, and D. W. Falk, "Construct Validation of a Theory X/Y Behavior Scale," *Leadership and Organization Development Journal* 31, no. 2 (2010), pp. 120–135.

10. F. Herzberg, B. Mausner, and B. Snyderman, *The Motivation to Work* (New York: Wiley, 1959).

11. R. J. House and L. A. Wigdor, "Herzberg's Dual-Factor Theory of Job Satisfaction and Motivations: A Review of the Evidence and Criticism," *Personnel Psychology* 20, no. 4 (1967), pp. 369–389; D. P. Schwab and L. L. Cummings, "Theories of Performance and Satisfaction: A Review," *Industrial Relations* 9, no. 4 (1970), pp. 403–430; and J. Phillipchuk and J. Whittaker, "An Inquiry into the Continuing Relevance of Herzberg's Motivation Theory," *Engineering Management Journal* 8 (1996), pp. 15–20.

12. D. C. McClelland, *The Achieving Society* (New York: Van Nostrand Reinhold, 1961); J. W. Atkinson and J. O. Raynor, *Motivation and Achievement* (Washington, DC: Winston, 1974); D. C. McClelland, *Power: The Inner Experience* (New York: Irvington, 1975); and M. J. Stahl, *Managerial and Technical Motivation: Assessing Needs for Achievement, Power, and Affiliation* (New York: Praeger, 1986).

13. D. C. McClelland and D. G. Winter, *Motivating Economic Achievement* (New York: The Free Press, 1969); and J. B. Miner, N. R. Smith, and J. S. Bracker, "Role of Entrepreneurial Task Motivation in the Growth of Technologically Innovative Firms: Interpretations from Follow-up Data," *Journal of Applied Psychology* 79, no. 4 (1994), pp. 627–630.

14. McClelland, *Power;* D. C. McClelland and D. H. Burnham, "Power Is the Great Motivator," *Harvard Business Review* (March–April 1976), pp. 100–110; and R. E. Boyatzis, "The Need for Close Relationships and the Manager's Job," in D. A. Kolb, I. M. Rubin, and J. M. McIntyre, *Organizational Psychology: Readings on Human Behavior in Organizations,* 4th ed. (Upper Saddle River, NJ: Prentice Hall, 1984), pp. 81–86.

15. D. G. Winter, "The Motivational Dimensions of Leadership: Power, Achievement, and Affiliation," in R. E. Riggio, S. E. Murphy, and F. J. Pirozzolo (eds.), *Multiple Intelligences and Leadership* (Mahwah, NJ: Lawrence Erlbaum, 2002), pp. 119–138.

16. J. B. Miner, *Studies in Management Education* (New York: Springer, 1965).

17. Ibid.

18. E. Deci and R. Ryan (eds.), *Handbook of Self-Determination Research* (Rochester, NY: University of Rochester Press, 2002); R. Ryan and E. Deci, "Self-Determination Theory and the Facilitation of Intrinsic Motivation, Social Development, and Well-Being," *American Psychologist* 55, no. 1 (2000), pp. 68–78; and M. Gagné and E. L. Deci, "Self-Determination Theory and Work Motivation," *Journal of Organizational Behavior* 26, no. 4 (2005), pp. 331–362.

19. See, for example, E. L. Deci, R. Koestner, and R. M. Ryan, "A Meta-Analytic Review of Experiments Examining the Effects of Extrinsic Rewards on Intrinsic Motivation," *Psychological Bulletin* 125, no. 6 (1999), pp. 627–668; G. J. Greguras and J. M. Diefendorff, "Different Fits Satisfy Different Needs: Linking Person-Environment Fit to Employee Commitment and Performance Using Self-Determination Theory," *Journal of Applied Psychology* 94, no. 2 (2009), pp. 465–477; and D. Liu, X. Chen, and X. Yao, "From Autonomy to Creativity: A Multilevel Investigation of the Mediating Role of Harmonious Passion," *Journal of Applied Psychology* 96, no. 2 (2011), pp. 294–309.

20. R. Eisenberger and L. Rhoades, "Incremental Effects of Reward on Creativity," *Journal of Personality and Social Psychology* 81, no. 4 (2001), 728–741; and R. Eisenberger, W. D. Pierce, and J. Cameron, "Effects of Reward on Intrinsic Motivation—Negative, Neutral, and Positive: Comment on Deci, Koestner, and Ryan (1999)," *Psychological Bulletin* 125, no. 6 (1999), pp. 677–691.

21. M. Burgess, M. E. Enzle, and R. Schmaltz, "Defeating the Potentially Deleterious Effects of Externally Imposed Deadlines: Practitioners' Rules-of-Thumb," *Personality and Social Psychology Bulletin* 30, no. 7 (2004), pp. 868–877.

22. K. Byron and S. Khazanchi, "Rewards and Creative Performance: A Meta-Analytic Test of Theoretically Derived Hypotheses," *Psychological Bulletin* 138, no. 4 (2012), pp. 809–830.

23. K. M. Sheldon, A. J. Elliot, and R. M. Ryan, "Self-Concordance and Subjective Well-Being in Four Cultures," *Journal of Cross-Cultural Psychology* 35, no. 2 (2004), pp. 209–223.

24. J. E. Bono and T. A. Judge, "Self-Concordance at Work: Toward Understanding the Motivational Effects of Transformational Leaders," *Academy of Management Journal* 46, no. 5 (2003), pp. 554–571.

25. L. M. Graves, M. N. Ruderman, P. J. Ohlott, and Todd J. Webber, "Driven to Work and Enjoyment of Work: Effects on Managers' Outcomes, "*Journal of Management* 38, no. 5 (2012), pp. 1655–1680.

26. J. P. Meyer, T. E. Becker, and C. Vandenberghe, "Employee Commitment and Motivation: A Conceptual Analysis and Integrative Model," *Journal of Applied Psychology* 89, no. 6 (2004), pp. 991–1007.

27. W. A. Kahn, "Psychological Conditions of Personal Engagement and Disengagement at Work," *Academy of Management Journal* 33, no. 4 (1990), pp. 692–724.

28. www.gallup.com/consulting/52/Employee-Engagement .aspx

29. J. K. Harter, F. L. Schmidt, and T. L. Hayes, "Business-Unit-Level Relationship Between Employee Satisfaction, Employee Engagement, and Business Outcomes: A Meta-Analysis," *Journal of Applied Psychology* 87, no. 2 (2002), pp. 268–279.

30. M. S. Christian, A. S. Garza, and J. E. Slaughter, "Work Engagement: A Quantitative Review and Test of Its Relations with Task and Contextual Performance," *Personnel Psychology* 64, no. 1 (2011), pp. 89–136.

31. W. B. Schaufeli, A. B. Bakker, and W. van Rhenen, "How Changes in Job Demands and Resources Predict Burnout, Work Engagement, and Sickness Absenteeism," *Journal of Organizational Behavior* 30, no. 7 (2009), pp. 893–917; E. R. Crawford, J. A. LePine, and B. L. Rich, "Linking Job Demands and Resources to Employee Engagement and Burnout: A Theoretical Extension and Meta-Analytic Test," *Journal of Applied Psychology* 95, no. 5 (2010), pp. 834–848; and D. Xanthopoulou, A. B. Bakker, E. Demerouti, and W. B. Schaufeli, "Reciprocal Relationships Between job Resources, Personal Resources, and Work Engagement," *Journal of Vocational Behavior* 74, no. 3 (2009), pp. 235–244.

32. B. L. Rich, J. A. LePine, and E. R. Crawford, "Job Engagement: Antecedents and Effects on Job Performance," *Academy of Management Journal* 53, no. 3 (2010), pp. 617–635.

33. M. Tims, A. B. Bakker, and D. Xanthopoulou, "Do Transformational Leaders Enhance Their Followers' Daily Work Engagement?" *Leadership Quarterly* 22, no. 1 (2011), pp. 121–131; and F. O. Walumbwa, P. Wang, H. Wang, J. Schaubroeck, and B. J. Avolio, "Psychological Processes Linking Authentic Leadership to Follower Behaviors," *Leadership Quarterly* 21, no. 5 (2010), pp. 901–914.

34. D. A. Newman and D. A. Harrison, "Been There, Bottled That: Are State and Behavioral Work Engagement New and Useful Construct 'Wines?'" *Industrial and Organizational Psychology* 1, no. 1 (2008), pp. 31–35; and A. J. Wefald and R. G. Downey, "Job Engagement in Organizations: Fad, Fashion, or Folderol," *Journal of Organizational Behavior* 30, no. 1 (2009), pp. 141–145.

35. See, for example, Rich, LePine, and Crawford, "Job Engagement: Antecedents and Effects on Job Performance;" and Christian, Garza, and Slaughter, "Work Engagement: A Quantitative Review and Test of Its Relations with Task and Contextual Performance."

36. J. M. George, "The Wider Context, Costs, and Benefits of Work Engagement," *European Journal of Work and Organizational Psychology* 20, no. 1 (2011), pp. 53–59; and J. R. B. Halbesleben, J. Harvey, and M. C. Bolino, "Too Engaged? A Conservation of Resources View of the Relationship Between Work Engagement and Work Interference with Family," *Journal of Applied Psychology* 94, no. 6 (2009), pp. 1452–1465.

37. E. A. Locke, "Toward a Theory of Task Motivation and Incentives," *Organizational Behavior and Human Performance* 3, no. 2 (1968), pp. 157–189.

38. P. C. Earley, P. Wojnaroski, and W. Prest, "Task Planning and Energy Expended: Exploration of How Goals Influence Performance," *Journal of Applied Psychology* 72, no. 1 (1987), pp. 107–114.

39. See M. E. Tubbs, "Goal Setting: A Meta-Analytic Examination of the Empirical Evidence," *Journal of Applied Psychology* 71, no. 3 (1986), pp. 474–483; and E. A. Locke and G. P. Latham, "New Directions in Goal-Setting Theory," *Current Directions in Psychological Science* 15, no. 5 (2006), pp. 265–268.

40. E. A. Locke and G. P. Latham, "Building a Practically Useful Theory of Goal Setting and Task Motivation," *American Psychologist* 57, no. 2 (2002), pp. 705–717.

41. C. Gabelica, P. Van den Bossche, M. Segers, and W. Gijselaersa, "Feedback, a Powerful Lever in Teams: A Review," *Educational Research Review* (June 2012), pp. 123–144.

42. S. Huang, Y. Zhang, and S. M. Broniarczyk, "So Near and Yet So Far: The Mental Representation of Goal Progress," *Journal of Personality and Social Psychology* 103, no. 2 (2012), pp. 225–241.

43. K. Dewettinck and H. van Dijk, "Linking Belgian Employee Performance Management System Characteristics with Performance Management System Effectiveness: Exploring the Mediating Role of Fairness," *International Journal of Human Resource Management* (February 1, 2013), pp. 806–825; and M. Erez, P. C. Earley, and C. L. Hulin, "The Impact of Participation on Goal Acceptance and Performance: A Two-Step Model," *Academy of Management Journal* 28, no. 1 (1985), pp. 50–66.

44. T. S. Bateman and B. Bruce, "Masters of the Long Haul: Pursuing Long-Term Work Goals," *Journal of Organizational Behavior* (October 2012), pp. 984-1006; and E. A. Locke, "The Motivation to Work: What We Know," *Advances in Motivation and Achievement* 10 (1997), pp. 375–412.

45. Ibid.

46. J. E. Bono and A. E. Colbert, "Understanding Responses to Multi-Source Feedback: The Role of Core Self-evaluations," *Personnel Psychology* 58, no. 1 (2005), pp. 171–203; and S. A. Jeffrey, A. Schulz, and A. Webb, "The Performance Effects of an Ability-Based Approach to Goal Assignment," *Journal of Organizational Behavior Management* 32 (2012), pp. 221–241.

47. A. M. O'Leary-Kelly, J. J. Martocchio, and D. D. Frink, "A Review of the Influence of Group Goals on Group Performance," *Academy of Management Journal* 37, no. 5 (1994), pp. 1285–1301; and T. Tammemagi, D. O'Hora, and K. A. Maglieri, "The Effects of a Goal Setting Intervention on Productivity and Persistence in an Analogue Work Task," *Journal of Organizational Behavior Management* (March 1, 2013), pp. 31–54.

48. K. D. Vohs, J. K. Park, and B. J. Schmeichel, "Self-Affirmation Can Enable Goal Disengagement," *Journal of Personality and Social Psychology* 104, no. 1 (2013), pp. 14–27.

49. D. F. Crown, "The Use of Group and Groupcentric Individual Goals for Culturally Heterogeneous and Homogeneous Task Groups: An Assessment of European Work Teams," *Small Group Research* 38, no. 4 (2007), pp. 489–508; J. Kurman, "Self-Regulation Strategies in Achievement Settings: Culture and Gender Differences," *Journal of Cross-Cultural Psychology* 32, no. 4 (2001), pp. 491–503; and M. Erez and P. C. Earley, "Comparative Analysis of Goal-Setting Strategies Across Cultures," *Journal of Applied Psychology* 72, no. 4 (1987), pp. 658–665.

50. C. Sue-Chan and M. Ong, "Goal Assignment and Performance: Assessing the Mediating Roles of Goal Commitment and Self-Efficacy and the Moderating Role of Power Distance," *Organizational Behavior and Human Decision Processes* 89, no. 2 (2002), pp. 1140–1161.

51. G. P. Latham and E. A. Locke, "Enhancing the Benefits and Overcoming the Pitfalls of Goal Setting," *Organizational Dynamics* 35, no. 6, pp. 332–340; L. D. Ordóñez, M. E. Schweitzer, A. D. Galinsky, and M. H. Bazerman, "Goals Gone Wild: The Systematic Side Effects of Overprescribing Goal Setting," *Academy of Management Perspectives* 23, no. 1 (2009), pp. 6–16; and E. A. Locke and G. P. Latham, "Has Goal Setting Gone Wild, or Have Its Attackers Abandoned Good Scholarship?" *Academy of Management Perspectives* 23, no. 1 (2009), pp. 17–23.

52. S. J. Perry, L. A. Witt, L. M. Penney, and L. Atwater, "The Downside of Goal-Focused Leadership: The Role of Personality in Subordinate Exhaustion," *Journal of Applied Psychology* 95, no. 6 (2010), pp. 1145–1153.

53. K. Lanaj, C. D. Chang, and R. E. Johnson, "Regulatory Focus and Work-Related Outcomes: A Review and Meta-Analysis," *Psychological Bulletin* 138, no. 5 (2012), pp. 998–1034.

54. "KEYGroup Survey Finds Nearly Half of All Employees Have No Set Performance Goals," *IPMA-HR Bulletin* (March 10, 2006), p. 1; S. Hamm, "SAP Dangles a Big, Fat Carrot," *BusinessWeek* (May 22, 2006), pp. 67–68; and "P&G CEO Wields High Expectations but No Whip," *USA Today* (February 19, 2007), p. 3B.

55. See, for instance, S. J. Carroll and H. L. Tosi, *Management by Objectives: Applications and Research* (New York: Macmillan, 1973); and R. Rodgers and J. E. Hunter, "Impact of Management by Objectives on Organizational Productivity," *Journal of Applied Psychology* 76, no. 2 (1991), pp. 322–336.

56. See, for instance, T. H. Poister and G. Streib, "MBO in Municipal Government: Variations on a Traditional Management Tool," *Public Administration Review* (January/February 1995), pp. 48–56; C. Garvey, "Goalsharing Scores," *HRMagazine* (April 2000), pp. 99–106; E. Lindberg and T. L. Wilson, "Management by Objectives: The Swedish Experience in Upper Secondary Schools," *Journal of Educational Administration* 49, no. 1 (2011), pp. 62–75; and A. C. Spaulding, L. D. Gamm, and J. M. Griffith, "Studer Unplugged: Identifying Underlying Managerial Concepts," *Hospital Topics* 88, no. 1 (2010), pp. 1–9.

57. See, for instance, R. Rodgers, J. E. Hunter, and D. L. Rogers, "Influence of Top Management Commitment on Management Program Success," *Journal of Applied*

Psychology 78, no. 1 (1993), pp. 151–155; M. Tanikawa, "Fujitsu Decides to Backtrack on Performance-Based Pay," *New York Times* (March 22, 2001), p. W1; and W. F. Roth, "Is Management by Objectives Obsolete?" *Global Business and Organizational Excellence* 28 (May/June 2009), pp. 36–43.

58. A. Bandura, *Self-Efficacy: The Exercise of Control* (New York: Freeman, 1997).

59. A. D. Stajkovic and F. Luthans, "Self-Efficacy and Work-Related Performance: A Meta-Analysis," *Psychological Bulletin* 124, no. 2 (1998), pp. 240–261; and A. Bandura, "Cultivate Self-Efficacy for Personal and Organizational Effectiveness," in E. Locke (ed.), *Handbook of Principles of Organizational Behavior* (Malden, MA: Blackwell, 2004), pp. 120–136.

60. M. Salanova, S. Llorens, and W. B. Schaufeli, "Yes I Can, I Feel Good, and I Just Do It! On Gain Cycles and Spirals of Efficacy Beliefs, Affect, and Engagement," *Applied Psychology* 60, no. 2 (2011), pp. 255–285.

61. P. Tierney and S. M. Farmer, "Creative Self-Efficacy Development and Creative Performance Over Time," *Journal of Applied Psychology* 96, no. 2 (2011), pp. 277–293.

62. A. Bandura and D. Cervone, "Differential Engagement in Self-Reactive Influences in Cognitively-Based Motivation," *Organizational Behavior and Human Decision Processes* 38, no. 1 (1986), pp. 92–113.

63. Bandura, *Self-Efficacy.*

64. R. C. Rist, "Student Social Class and Teacher Expectations: The Self-Fulfilling Prophecy in Ghetto Education," *Harvard Educational Review* 70, no. 3 (2000), pp. 266–301.

65. D. Eden, "Self-Fulfilling Prophecies in Organizations," in J. Greenberg (ed.), *Organizational Behavior: The State of the Science,* 2nd ed. (Mahwah, NJ: Lawrence Erlbaum, 2003), pp. 91–122.

66. Ibid.

67. C. L. Holladay and M. A. Quiñones, "Practice Variability and Transfer of Training: The Role of Self-Efficacy Generality," *Journal of Applied Psychology* 88, no. 6 (2003), pp. 1094–1103.

68. E. C. Dierdorff, E. A. Surface, and K. G. Brown, "Frame-of-Reference Training Effectiveness: Effects of Goal Orientation and Self-Efficacy on Affective, Cognitive, Skill-Based, and Transfer Outcomes," *Journal of Applied Psychology* 95, no. 6 (2010), pp. 1181–1191; and R. Grossman, and E. Salas, "The Transfer of Training: What Really Matters," *International Journal of Training and Development* 15, no. 2 (2011), pp. 103–120.

69. T. A. Judge, C. L. Jackson, J. C. Shaw, B. Scott, and B. L. Rich, "Self-Efficacy and Work-Related Performance: The Integral Role of Individual Differences," *Journal of Applied Psychology* 92, no. 1 (2007), pp. 107–127.

70. Ibid.

71. K. M. Eddington, C. Majestic, and P. J. Silvia, "Contrasting Regulatory Focus and Reinforcement Sensitivity: A Daily Diary Study of Goal Pursuit and Emotion," *Personality and Individual Differences* (August 2012), pp. 335–340.

72. B. F. Skinner, *Contingencies of Reinforcement* (East Norwalk, CT: Appleton-Century-Crofts, 1971).

73. J. A. Mills, *Control: A History of Behavioral Psychology* (New York: New York University Press, 2000).

74. E. A. Locke, "Latham vs. Komaki: A Tale of Two Paradigms," *Journal of Applied Psychology* 65, no. 1 (1980), pp. 16–23.

75. A. Bandura, *Social Learning Theory* (Upper Saddle River, NJ: Prentice Hall, 1977).

76. J. S. Adams, "Inequity in Social Exchanges," in L. Berkowitz (ed.), *Advances in Experimental Social Psychology* (New York: Academic Press, 1965), pp. 267–300.

77. See, for example, J. Greenberg, "Cognitive Reevaluation of Outcomes in Response to Underpayment Inequity," *Academy of Management Journal*, March 1989, pp. 174–184; and C. Maslach and M. P. Leiter, "Early Predictors of Job Burnout and Engagement, *Journal of Applied Psychology* (May 2008), pp. 498–512.

78. P. S. Goodman and A. Friedman, "An Examination of Adams' Theory of Inequity," *Administrative Science Quarterly* 16, no. 3 (1971), pp. 271–288; R. P. Vecchio, "An Individual-Differences Interpretation of the Conflicting Predictions Generated by Equity Theory and Expectancy Theory," *Journal of Applied Psychology* 66, no. 4 (1981), pp. 470–481; R. T. Mowday, "Equity Theory Predictions of Behavior in Organizations," in R. Steers, L. W. Porter, and G. Bigley (eds.), *Motivation and Work Behavior*, 6th ed. (New York: McGraw-Hill, 1996), pp. 111–131; R. W. Griffeth and S. Gaertner, "A Role for Equity Theory in the Turnover Process: An Empirical Test," *Journal of Applied Social Psychology* 31, no. 5 (2001), pp. 1017–1037; and L. K. Scheer, N. Kumar, and J.-B. E. M. Steenkamp, "Reactions to Perceived Inequity in U.S. and Dutch Interorganizational Relationships," *Academy of Management* 46, no. 3 (2003), pp. 303–316.

79. See, for example, R. C. Huseman, J. D. Hatfield, and E. W. Miles, "A New Perspective on Equity Theory: The Equity Sensitivity Construct," *Academy of Management Journal* 12, no. 2 (1987), pp. 222–234; K. S. Sauley and A. G. Bedeian, "Equity Sensitivity: Construction of a Measure and Examination of Its Psychometric Properties," *Journal of Management* 26, no. 5 (2000), pp. 885–910; and J. A. Colquitt, "Does the Justice of One Interact with the Justice of Many? Reactions to Procedural Justice in Teams," *Journal of Applied Psychology* 89, no. 4 (2004), pp. 633–646.

80. See, for instance, J. A. Colquitt, D. E. Conlon, M. J. Wesson, C. O. L. H. Porter, and K.-Y. Ng, "Justice at the Millennium: A Meta-Analytic Review of the 25 Years of Organizational Justice Research," *Journal of Applied Psychology* 86, no. 3 (2001), pp. 425–445; T. Simons and Q. Roberson, "Why Managers Should Care About Fairness: The Effects of Aggregate Justice Perceptions on Organizational Outcomes," *Journal of Applied Psychology* 88, no. 3 (2003), pp. 432–443; and B. C. Holtz and C. M. Harold, "Fair Today, Fair Tomorrow? A Longitudinal Investigation of Overall Justice Perceptions," *Journal of Applied Psychology* 94, no. 5 (2009), pp. 1185–1199.

81. C. O. Trevor, G. Reilly, and B. Gerhart, "Reconsidering Pay Dispersion's Effect on the Performance of Interdependent Work: Reconciling Sorting and Pay Inequality," *Academy of Management Journal* (June 2012), pp. 585–610.

82. See, for example, R. Cropanzano, J. H. Stein, and T. Nadisic, *Social Justice and the Experience of Emotion* (New York: Routledge/Taylor and Francis Group, 2011).

83. G. S. Leventhal, "What Should Be Done with Equity Theory? New Approaches to the Study of Fairness in Social Relationships," in K. Gergen, M. Greenberg, and R. Willis (eds.), *Social Exchange: Advances in Theory and Research* (New York: Plenum, 1980), pp. 27–55.

84. J. Brockner and B. M. Wiesenfeld, "An Integrative Framework for Examining Reactions to Decisions: Interactive Effects of Outcomes and Procedures," *Psychological Bulletin* 120 (1996), pp. 189–208.

85. R. Folger and D. P. Skarlicki, "Fairness as a Dependent Variable: Why Tough Times Can Lead to Bad Management," in R. Cropanzano (ed.), *Justice in the Workplace: From Theory to Practice* (Mahway, NJ: Erlbaum, 2001), pp. 97–118.

86. C. R. Wanberg, L. W. Bunce, and M. B. Gavin, "Perceived Fairness of Layoffs Among Individuals Who Have Been Laid Off," *Personnel Psychology* 52 (1999), pp. 59–84.

87. J. C. Shaw, E. Wild, and J. A. Colquitt, "To Justify or Excuse? A Meta-Analytic Review of the Effects of Explanations," *Journal of Applied Psychology* 88, no. 3 (2003), pp. 444–458.

88. R. J. Bies, "Are Procedural and Interactional Justice Conceptually Distinct?" in J. Greenberg and J. A. Colquitt (eds.), *Handbook of Organizational Justice* (Mahwah, NJ: Erlbaum, 2005), pp. 85–112; and B. A. Scott, J. A. Colquitt, and E. L. Paddock, "An Actor-Focused Model of Justice Rule Adherence and Violation: The Role of Managerial Motives and Discretion," *Journal of Applied Psychology* 94, no. 3 (2009), pp. 756–769.

89. G. A. Van Kleef, A. C. Homan, B. Beersma, D. V. Knippenberg, B. V. Knippenberg, and F. Damen, "Searing Sentiment or Cold Calculation? The Effects of Leader Emotional Displays on Team Performance Depend on Follower Epistemic Motivation," *Academy of Management Journal* 52, no. 3 (2009), pp. 562–580.

90. "Rutgers Fires Mike Rice," 2013, www.espn.com.

91. J. M. Robbins, M. T. Ford, and L. E. Tetrick, "Perceived Unfairness and Employee Health: A Meta-Analytic Integration," *Journal of Applied Psychology* 97, no. 2 (2012), pp. 235–272.

92. J. A. Colquitt, B. A. Scott, J. B. Rodell, D. M. Long, C. P. Zapata, D. E. Conlon, and M. J. Wesson, "Justice at the Millennium, A Decade Later: A Meta-Analytic Test of Social Exchange and Affect-Based Perspectives," *Journal of Applied Psychology* 98, no. 2 (2013), pp. 199–236.

93. B. A. Scott, J. A. Colquitt, and E. L. Paddock, "An Actor-Focused Model of Justice Rule Adherence and Violation: The Role of Managerial Motives and Discretion," *Journal of Applied Psychology* 94, no. 3 (2009), pp. 756–769.

94. Ibid.

95. K. Leung, K. Tong, and S. S. Ho, "Effects of Interactional Justice on Egocentric Bias in Resource Allocation Decisions," *Journal of Applied Psychology* 89, no. 3 (2004), pp. 405–415; and L. Francis-Gladney, N. R. Manger, and R. B. Welker, "Does Outcome Favorability Affect Procedural Fairness as a Result of Self-Serving Attributions," *Journal of Applied Social Psychology* 40, no. 1 (2010), pp. 182–194.

96. L. J. Barlcay and D. P. Skarlicki, "Healing the Wounds of Organizational Injustice: Examining the Benefits of Expressive Writing," *Journal of Applied Psychology* 94, no. 2 (2009), pp. 511–523.

97. R. Fischer and P. B. Smith, "Reward Allocation and Culture: A Meta-Analysis," *Journal of Cross-Cultural Psychology* 34, no. 3 (2003), pp. 251–268.

98. F. F. T. Chiang and T. Birch, "The Transferability of Management Practices: Examining Cross-National Differences in Reward Preferences," *Human Relations* 60, no. 9 (2007), pp. 1293–1330; A. E. Lind, T. R. Tyler, and Y. J. Huo, "Procedural Context and Culture: Variation in the Antecedents of Procedural Justice Judgments," *Journal of Personality and Social Psychology* 73, no. 4 (1997), pp. 767–780; and M. J. Gelfand, M. Erez, and Z. Aycan, "Cross-Cultural Organizational Behavior," *Annual Review of Psychology* 58 (2007), pp. 479–514.

99. J. K. Giacobbe-Miller, D. J. Miller, and V. I. Victorov, "A Comparison of Russian and U.S. Pay Allocation Decisions, Distributive Justice Judgments, and Productivity Under Different Payment Conditions," *Personnel Psychology* 51, no. 1 (1998), pp. 137–163.

100. M. C. Bolino and W. H. Turnley, "Old Faces, New Places: Equity Theory in Cross-Cultural Contexts," *Journal of Organizational Behavior* 29, no. 1 (2008), pp. 29–50.

101. V. H. Vroom, *Work and Motivation* (New York: Wiley, 1964).

102. For criticism, see H. G. Heneman III and D. P. Schwab, "Evaluation of Research on Expectancy Theory Prediction of Employee Performance," *Psychological Bulletin* 78, no. 1 (1972), pp. 1–9; T. R. Mitchell, "Expectancy Models of Job Satisfaction, Occupational Preference and Effort: A Theoretical, Methodological and Empirical Appraisal," *Psychological Bulletin* 81, no. 12 (1974), pp. 1053–1077; and W. Van Eerde and H. Thierry, "Vroom's Expectancy Models and Work-Related Criteria: A Meta-Analysis," *Journal of Applied Psychology* 81, no. 5 (1996), pp. 575–586. For support, see L. W. Porter and E. E. Lawler III, *Managerial Attitudes and Performance* (Homewood, IL: Irwin, 1968); and J. J. Donovan, "Work Motivation," in N. Anderson et al. (eds.), *Handbook of Industrial, Work & Organizational Psychology*, vol. 2 (Thousand Oaks, CA: Sage, 2001), pp. 56–59.

103. Vroom refers to these three variables as expectancy, instrumentality, and valence, respectively.

104. J. Nocera, "The Anguish of Being an Analyst," *The New York Times* (March 4, 2006), pp. B1, B12.

105. R. J. House, H. J. Shapiro, and M. A. Wahba, "Expectancy Theory as a Predictor of Work Behavior and Attitudes: A Re-evaluation of Empirical Evidence," *Decision Sciences* 5, no. 3 (1974), pp. 481–506.

106. For other examples of models that seek to integrate motivation theories, see H. J. Klein, "An Integrated Control Theory Model of Work Motivation," *Academy of Management Review* 14, no. 2 (1989), pp. 150–172; E. A. Locke, "The Motivation Sequence, the Motivation Hub, and the Motivation Core," *Organizational Behavior and Human Decision Processes* 50, no. 2 (1991), pp. 288–299; and T. R. Mitchell, "Matching Motivational Strategies with Organizational Contexts," pp. 60–62.

CHAPTER 8

1. J. R. Hackman and G. R. Oldham, "Motivation Through the Design of Work: Test of a Theory," *Organizational Behavior and Human Performance* 16, no. 2 (1976), pp. 250–279; and J. R. Hackman and G. R. Oldham, *Work Redesign* (Reading, MA: Addison-Wesley, 1980).

2. J. R. Hackman, "Work Design," in J. R. Hackman and J. L. Suttle (eds.), *Improving Life at Work* (Santa Monica, CA: Goodyear, 1977), p. 129.

3. See B. T. Loher, R. A. Noe, N. L. Moeller, and M. P. Fitzgerald, "A Meta-Analysis of the Relation of Job Characteristics to Job Satisfaction," *Journal of Applied Psychology* 70, no. 2 (1985), pp. 280–289; S. J. Zaccaro and E. F. Stone, "Incremental Validity of an Empirically Based Measure of Job Characteristics," *Journal of Applied Psychology* 73, no. 2 (1988), pp. 245–252; J. R. Rentsch and R. P. Steel, "Testing the Durability of Job Characteristics as Predictors of Absenteeism over a Six-Year Period," *Personnel Psychology* 51, no. 2 (1998), pp. 165–190; S. J. Behson, E. R. Eddy, and S. J. Lorenzet, "The Importance of the Critical Psychological States in the Job Characteristics Model: A Meta-Analytic and Structural Equations Modeling Examination," *Current Research in Social Psychology* 51, no. 12 (2000), pp. 170–189; and S. E. Humphrey, J. D. Nahrgang, and F. P. Morgeson, "Integrating Motivational, Social, and Contextual Work Design Features: A Meta-Analytic Summary and Theoretical Extension of the Work Design Literature," *Journal of Applied Psychology* 92, no. 5 (2007), pp. 1332–1356.

4. B. M. Meglino and A. M. Korsgaard, "The Role of Other Orientation in Reactions to Job Characteristics," *Journal of Management* 33, no. 1 (2007), pp. 57–83.

5. M. F. Peterson and S. A. Ruiz-Quintanilla, "Cultural Socialization as a Source of Intrinsic Work Motivation," *Group & Organization Management* 28, no. 2 (2003), pp. 188–216.

6. Skytrax website review of Singapore Airlines, www.airlinequality.com/Airlines/SQ.htm, accessed May 31, 2013.

7. T. Silver, "Rotate Your Way to Higher Value," *Baseline* (March/April 2010), p. 12; and J. J. Salopek, "Coca-Cola Division Refreshes Its Talent with Diversity Push on Campus," *Workforce Management Online* (March 2011), www.workforce.com.

8. A. Christini and D. Pozzoli, "Workplace Practices and Firm Performance in Manufacturing: A Comparative Study of Italy and Britain," *International Journal of Manpower* 31, no. 7 (2010), pp. 818–842; and K. Kaymaz, "The Effects of Job Rotation Practices on Motivation: A Research on Managers in the Automotive Organizations," *Business and Economics Research Journal* 1, no. 3 (2010), pp. 69–86.

9. Hackman and Oldham, *Work Redesign*.

10. A. M. Grant, J. E. Dutton, and B. D. Rosso, "Giving Commitment: Employee Support Programs and the Prosocial Sensemaking Process," *Academy of Management Journal* 51, no. 5 (2008), pp. 898–918.

11. See, for example, R. W. Griffin, "Effects of Work Redesign on Employee Perceptions, Attitudes, and Behaviors: A Long-Term Investigation," *Academy of Management Journal* 34, no. 2 (1991), pp. 425–435; and M. Subramony, "A Meta-Analytic Investigation of the Relationship between HRM Bundles and Firm Performance," *Human Resource Management* 48, no. 5 (2009), pp. 745–768.

12. R. D. Pritchard, M. M. Harrell, D. DiazGrandos, and M. J. Guzman, "The Productivity Measurement and Enhancement System: A Meta-Analysis," *Journal of Applied Psychology* 93, no. 3 (2008), pp. 540–567.

13. F. P. Morgeson, M. D. Johnson, M. A. Campion, G. J. Medsker, and T. V. Mumford, "Understanding Reactions to Job Redesign: A Quasi-Experimental Investigation of the Moderating Effects of Organizational Contact on Perceptions of Performance Behavior," *Personnel Psychology* 59, no. 2 (2006), pp. 333–363.

14. F. W. Bond, P. E. Flaxman, and D. Bunce, "The Influence of Psychological Flexibility on Work Redesign: Mediated Moderation of a Work Reorganization Intervention," *Journal of Applied Psychology* 93, no. 3 (2008), pp. 645–654.

15. A. M. Grant, "Leading with Meaning: Beneficiary Contact, Prosocial Impact, and the Performance Effects of Transformational Leadership," *Academy of Management Journal,* 55 (2012), pp. 458–476; and A. M. Grant and S. K. Parker, "Redesigning Work Design Theories: The Rise of Relational and Proactive Perspectives," *Annals of the Academy of Management* 3, no. 1 (2009), pp. 317–375.

16. Y. N. Turner, I. Hadas-Halperin, and D. Raveh, "Patient Photos Spur Radiologist Empathy and Eye for Detail." Paper presented at the annual meeting of the Radiological Society of North America (November 2008).

17. A. M. Grant, E. M. Campbell, G. Chen, K. Cottone, D. Lapedis, and K. Lee, "Impact and the Art of Motivation Maintenance: The Effects of Contact with Beneficiaries on Persistence Behavior," *Organizational Behavior and Human Decision Processes* 103, no. 1 (2007), pp. 53–67.

18. A. M. Grant, "The Significance of Task Significance: Job Performance Effects, Relational Mechanisms, and Boundary Conditions," *Journal of Applied Psychology* no. 93 (2008), pp. 108–124.

19. Society for Human Resource Management, *2012 Employee Benefits* (Alexandria, VA: Author, 2012).

20. T. Kato, "Work and Family Practices in Japanese Firms: Their Scope, Nature, and Impact on Employee Turnover," *International Journal of Human Resource Management* 20, no. 2 (2009), pp. 439–456; and P. Mourdoukoutas, "Why Do Women Fare Better in the German World of Work than in the US?" *Forbes* (March 25, 2013), www.forbes.com/sites/panosmourdoukoutas/2013/03/25/why-do-women-fare-better-in-the-german-world-of-work-than-in-the-us/.

21. R. Waring, "Sunday Dialogue: Flexible Work Hours," *The New York Times* (January 19, 2013), www.nytimes.com.

22. S. Westcott, "Beyond Flextime: Trashing the Workweek," *Inc.* (August 2008), p. 30.

23. See, for example, D. A. Ralston and M. F. Flanagan, "The Effect of Flextime on Absenteeism and Turnover for Male and Female Employees," *Journal of Vocational Behavior* 26, no. 2 (1985), pp. 206–217; B. B. Baltes, T. E. Briggs, J. W. Huff, J. A. Wright, and G. A. Neuman, "Flexible and Compressed Workweek Schedules: A Meta-Analysis of Their Effects on Work-Related Criteria," *Journal of Applied Psychology* 84, no. 4 (1999), pp. 496–513; K. M. Shockley, and T. D. Allen, "When Flexibility Helps: Another Look at the Availability of Flexible Work Arrangements and Work–Family Conflict," *Journal of Vocational Behavior* 71, no. 3 (2007), pp. 479–493; J. G. Grzywacz, D. S. Carlson, and S. Shulkin, "Schedule Flexibility and Stress: Linking Formal Flexible Arrangements and Perceived Flexibility to Employee Health." *Community, Work, and Family* 11, no. 2 (2008), pp. 199–214; and L. A. McNall, A. D. Masuda, and J. M. Nicklin "Flexible Work Arrangements, Job Satisfaction, and Turnover Intentions: The Mediating Role of Work-to-Family Enrichment," *Journal of Psychology* 144, no. 1 (2010), pp. 61–81.

24. K. M. Shockley and T. D. Allen, "Investigating the Missing Link in Flexible Work Arrangement Utilization: An Individual Difference Perspective," *Journal of Vocational Behavior* 76, no. 1 (2010), pp. 131–142.

25. J. LaReau, "Ford's 2 Julies Share Devotion—and Job," *Automotive News* (October 25, 2010), p. 4.

26. Society for Human Resource Management, *2012 Employee Benefits.*

27. S. Shellenbarger, "Two People, One Job," *The Wall Street Journal* (December 7, 1994), p. B1.

28. C. B. Mulligan, "What Job Sharing Brings," *Forbes* (May 8, 2013), http://economix.blogs.nytimes.com/2013/05/08/what-job-sharing-brings/.

29. L. Woellert, "U.S. Work Share Program Helps Employers Avoid Layoffs," *Bloomberg Businessweek* (January 24, 2013), www.businessweek.com/articles/2013-01-24/u-dot-s-dot-work-share-program-helps-employers-avoid-layoffs.

30. P. R. Gregory, "Why Obama Cannot Match Germany's Jobs Miracle," *Forbes* (May 5, 2013), www.forbes.com/sites/paulroderickgregory/2013/05/05/why-obama-cannot-match-germanys-jobs-miracle/.

31. See, for example, E. J. Hill, M. Ferris, and V. Martinson, "Does It Matter Where You Work? A Comparison of How Three Work Venues (Traditional Office, Virtual Office, and Home Office) Influence Aspects of Work and Personal/Family Life," *Journal of Vocational Behavior* 63, no. 2 (2003), pp. 220–241; B. Williamson, "Managing Virtual Workers," *Bloomberg Businessweek* (July 16, 2009), www.businessweek.com, and B. A. Lautsch and E. E. Kossek, "Managing a Blended Workforce: Telecommuters and Non-Telecommuters," *Organizational Dynamics* 40, no. 1 (2010), pp. 10–17.

32. B. Belton, "Best Buy Copies Yahoo, Reins in Telecommuting," *USA Today* (March 6, 2013), www.usatoday.com.

33. J. Tozzi, "Home-Based Businesses Increasing," *Bloomberg Businessweek* (January 25, 2010), www.businessweek.com.

34. Society for Human Resource Management, *2012 Employee Benefits.*

35. See, for instance, M. Conlin, "The Easiest Commute of All," *BusinessWeek* (December 12, 2005), p. 78; S. Shellenbarger, "Telework Is on the Rise, but It Isn't Just Done from Home Anymore," *The Wall Street Journal* (January 23, 2001), p. B1; and E. O'Keefe, "Teleworking Grows But Still a Rarity," *The Washington Post* (February 22, 2011), p. B3.

36. Conlin, "The Easiest Commute of All."

37. E. E. Kossek, B. A. Lautsch, S. C. Eaton, "Telecommuting, Control, and Boundary Management: Correlates of Policy Use and Practice, Job Control, and Work-Family Effectiveness," *Journal of Vocational Behavior* 68, no. 2 (2006), pp. 347–367.

38. J. Kotkin, "Marissa Mayer's Misstep and the Unstoppable Rise of Telecommuting," *Forbes* (March 26, 2013).

39. J. M. Stanton and J. L. Barnes-Farrell, "Effects of Electronic Performance Monitoring on Personal Control, Task Satisfaction, and Task Performance," *Journal of Applied Psychology* 81, no. 6 (1996), pp. 738–745; and L. Taskin and F. Bridoux, "Telework: A Challenge to Knowledge Transfer in Organizations," *International Journal of Human Resource Management* 21, no. 13 (2010), pp. 2503–2520.

40. See, for example, P. Brotherton, "For Teleworkers, Less Is Definitely More," *T1D* 65 (March 2011), p. 29; and M. Virick, N. DaSilva, and K. Arrington, "Moderators of the Curvilinear Relation Between Extent of Telecommuting

and Job and Life Satisfaction: The Role of Performance Outcome Orientation and Worker Type," *Human Relations* 63, no. 1 (2010), pp. 137–154.

41. J. Welch and S. Welch, "The Importance of Being There," *BusinessWeek* (April 16, 2007), p. 92; Z. I. Barsness, K. A. Diekmann, and M. L. Seidel, "Motivation and Opportunity: The Role of Remote Work, Demographic Dissimilarity, and Social Network Centrality in Impression Management," *Academy of Management Journal* 48, no. 3 (2005), pp. 401–419.

42. F. P. Morgeson and S. E. Humphrey, "The Work Design Questionnaire (WDQ): Developing and Validating a Comprehensive Measure for Assessing Job Design and the Nature of Work," *Journal of Applied Psychology* 91, no. 6 (2006), pp. 1321–1339; S. E. Humphrey, J. D. Nahrgang, and F. P. Morgeson, "Integrating Motivational, Social, and Contextual Work Design Features: A Meta-Analytic Summary and Theoretical Extension of the Work Design Literature," *Journal of Applied Psychology* 92, no. 5 (2007), pp. 1332–1356; and R. Takeuchi, D. P. Lepak, H. Wang, and K. Takeuchi, "An Empirical Examination of the Mechanisms Mediating Between High-Performance Work Systems and the Performance of Japanese Organizations," *Journal of Applied Psychology* 92, no. 4 (2007), pp. 1069–1083.

43. See, for example, the increasing body of literature on empowerment, such as D. P. Ashmos, D. Duchon, R. R. McDaniel Jr., and J. W. Huonker, "What a Mess! Participation as a Simple Managerial Rule to 'Complexify' Organizations," *Journal of Management Studies* 39, no. 2 (2002), pp. 189–206; S. E. Seibert, S. R. Silver, and W. A. Randolph, "Taking Empowerment to the Next Level: A Multiple-Level Model of Empowerment, Performance, and Satisfaction," *Academy of Management Journal* 47, no. 3 (2004), pp. 332–349; M. M. Butts, R. J. Vandenberg, D. M. DeJoy, B. S. Schaffer, and M. G. Wilson, "Individual Reactions to High Involvement Work Processes: Investigating the Role of Empowerment and Perceived Organizational Support," *Journal of Occupational Health Psychology* 14, no. 2 (2009), pp. 122–136; R. Park, E. Applebaum, and D. Kruse, "Employee Involvement and Group Incentives in Manufacturing Companies: A Multi-Level Analysis," *Human Resource Management Journal* 20, no. 3 (2010), pp. 227–243; D. C. Jones, P. Kalmi, and A. Kauhanen, "How Does Employee Involvement Stack Up? The Effects of Human Resource Management Policies in a Retail Firm," *Industrial Relations* 49, no. 1 (2010), pp. 1–21; and M. T. Maynard, L. L. Gilson, and J. E. Mathieu, "Empowerment— Fad or Fab? A Multilevel Review of the Past Two Decades of Research," *Journal of Management* 38, no. 4 (2012), pp. 1231–1281.

44. See, for instance, A. Sagie and Z. Aycan, "A Cross-Cultural Analysis of Participative Decision-Making in Organizations," *Human Relations* 56, no. 4 (2003), pp. 453–473; and J. Brockner, "Unpacking Country Effects: On the Need to Operationalize the Psychological Determinants of Cross-National Differences," in R. M. Kramer and B. M. Staw (eds.), *Research in Organizational Behavior*, vol. 25 (Oxford, UK: Elsevier, 2003), pp. 336–340.

45. C. Robert, T. M. Probst, J. J. Martocchio, R. Drasgow, and J. J. Lawler, "Empowerment and Continuous Improvement in the United States, Mexico, Poland, and India: Predicting Fit on the Basis of the Dimensions of Power Distance and Individualism," *Journal of Applied Psychology* 85, no. 5 (2000), pp. 643–658.

46. Z. X. Chen and S. Aryee, "Delegation and Employee Work Outcomes: An Examination of the Cultural Context of Mediating Processes in China," *Academy of Management Journal* 50, no. 1 (2007), pp. 226–238.

47. G. Huang, X. Niu, C. Lee, and S. J. Ashford, "Differentiating Cognitive and Affective Job Insecurity: Antecedents and Outcomes," *Journal of Organizational Behavior* 33, no. 6 (2012), pp. 752–769.

48. J. J. Caughron and M. D. Mumford, "Embedded Leadership: How Do a Leader's Superiors Impact Middle-Management Performance?" *Leadership Quarterly* (June 2012), pp. 342–353.

49. See, for instance, K. L. Miller and P. R. Monge, "Participation, Satisfaction, and Productivity: A Meta-Analytic Review," *Academy of Management Journal* (December 1986), pp. 727–753; J. A. Wagner III, "Participation's Effects on Performance and Satisfaction: A Reconsideration of Research Evidence," *Academy of Management Review* 19, no. 2 (1994), pp. 312–330; C. Doucouliagos, "Worker Participation and Productivity in Labor-Managed and Participatory Capitalist Firms: A Meta-Analysis," *Industrial and Labor Relations Review* 49, no. 1 (1995), pp. 58–77; J. A. Wagner III, C. R. Leana, E. A. Locke, and D. M. Schweiger, "Cognitive and Motivational Frameworks in U.S. Research on Participation: A Meta-Analysis of Primary Effects," *Journal of Organizational Behavior* 18, no. 1 (1997), pp. 49–65; A. Pendleton and A. Robinson, "Employee Stock Ownership, Involvement, and Productivity: An Interaction-Based Approach," *Industrial and Labor Relations Review* 64, no. 1 (2010), pp. 3–29.

50. D. K. Datta, J. P. Guthrie, and P. M. Wright, "Human Resource Management and Labor Productivity: Does Industry Matter?" *Academy of Management Journal* 48, no. 1 (2005), pp. 135–145; C. M. Riordan, R. J. Vandenberg, and H. A. Richardson, "Employee Involvement Climate and Organizational Effectiveness." *Human Resource Management* 44, no. 4 (2005), pp. 471–488; and J. Kim, J. P. MacDuffie, and F. K. Pil, "Employee Voice and Organizational Performance: Team Versus Representative Influence," *Human Relations* 63, no. 3 (2010), pp. 371–394.

51. Cotton, *Employee Involvement,* p. 114.

52. See, for example, M. Gilman and P. Marginson, "Negotiating European Works Council: Contours of Constrained Choice," *Industrial Relations Journal* 33, no. 1 (2002), pp. 36–51; J. T. Addison and C. R. Belfield, "What Do We Know About the New European Works Council? Some Preliminary Evidence from Britain," *Scottish Journal of Political Economy* 49, no. 4 (2002), pp. 418–444; and B. Keller, "The European Company Statute: Employee Involvement—and Beyond," *Industrial Relations Journal* 33, no. 5 (2002), pp. 424–445.

53. Cotton, *Employee Involvement,* pp. 129–130, 139–140.

54. Ibid., p. 140.

55. E. White, "Opportunity Knocks, and It Pays a Lot Better," *The Wall Street Journal* (November 13, 2006), p. B3.

56. D. A. McIntyre and S. Weigley, "8 companies That Most Owe Workers a Raise," *USA Today* (May 13, 2013), www.usatoday .com/story/money/business/2013/05/12/8-companies-that-most-owe-workers-a-raise/2144013/.

57. M. Sabramony, N. Krause, J. Norton, and G. N. Burns "The Relationship Between Human Resource Investments and

Organizational Performance: A Firm-Level Examination of Equilibrium Theory," *Journal of Applied Psychology* 93, no. 4 (2008), pp. 778–788.

58. See, for example, B. Martinez, "Teacher Bonuses Emerge in Newark," *The Wall Street Journal* (April 21, 2011), p. A.15; and D. Weber, "Seminole Teachers to Get Bonuses Instead of Raises," *Orlando Sentinel* (January 19, 2011), www.orlandosentinel.com.

59. Based on J. R. Schuster and P. K. Zingheim, "The New Variable Pay: Key Design Issues," *Compensation & Benefits Review* (March–April 1993), p. 28; K. S. Abosch, "Variable Pay: Do We Have the Basics in Place?" *Compensation & Benefits Review* (July–August 1998), pp. 12–22; and K. M. Kuhn and M. D. Yockey, "Variable Pay as a Risky Choice: Determinants of the Relative Attractiveness of Incentive Plans," *Organizational Behavior and Human Decision Processes* 90, no. 2 (2003), pp. 323–341.

60. S. Miller, "Companies Worldwide Rewarding Performance with Variable Pay," *Society for Human Resource Management* (March 1, 2010), www.shrm.org.

61. S. Miller, "Asian Firms Offer More Variable Pay Than Western Firms," *Society for Human Resource Management* (March 28, 2012), www.shrm.org.

62. Hay Group, "Hay Group Research Finds Increased Use of Variable Pay for Employees," *Investment Weekly News*, (July 24, 2010), p. 269.

63. H. Kim, K. L. Sutton, and Y. Gong, "Group-Based Pay-for-Performance Plans and Firm Performance: The Moderating Role of Empowerment Practices," *Asia Pacific Journal of Management* (March 2013), pp. 31–52.

64. B. Wysocki Jr., "Chilling Reality Awaits Even the Employed," *The Wall Street Journal* (November 5, 2001), p. A1; and J. C. Kovac, "Sour Economy Presents Compensation Challenges," *Employee Benefit News* (July 1, 2008), p. 18.

65. G. D. Jenkins Jr., N. Gupta, A. Mitra, and J. D. Shaw, "Are Financial Incentives Related to Performance? A Meta-Analytic Review of Empirical Research," *Journal of Applied Psychology* 83, no. 5 (1998), pp. 777–787; and S. L. Rynes, B. Gerhart, and L. Parks, "Personnel Psychology: Performance Evaluation and Pay for Performance," *Annual Review of Psychology* 56, no. 1 (2005), pp. 571–600.

66. K. Zernike, "Newark Teachers Approve a Contract with Merit Pay," *The New York Times* (November 14, 2012), www.nytimes.com/.

67. "Paying Doctors for Performance," *The New York Times* (January 27, 2013), p. A16.

68. S. Halzack, "Companies Look to Bonuses Instead of Salary Increases in an Uncertain Economy," *Washington Post* (November 6, 2012), http://articles.washingtonpost.com/.

69. C. M. Barnes, J. Reb, and D. Ang, "More Than Just the Mean: Moving to a Dynamic View of Performance-Based Compensation," *Journal of Applied Psychology* 97, no. 3 (2012), pp. 711–718.

70. P. Furman, "Ouch! Top Honchos on Wall Street See Biggest Cuts to Bonuses," *New York Daily News* (February 18, 2013), www.nydailynews.com.

71. E. White, "Employers Increasingly Favor Bonuses to Raises," *The Wall Street Journal* (August 28, 2006), p. B3; and J. S. Lublin, "Boards Tie CEO Pay More Tightly to Performance," *The Wall Street Journal* (February 21, 2006), pp. A1, A14.

72. S. S. Wiltermuth and F. Gino, "I'll Have One of Each": How Separating Rewards into (Meaningless) Categories Increases Motivation," *Journal of Personality and Social Psychology* (January 2013), pp. 1–13.

73. G. E. Ledford Jr., "Paying for the Skills, Knowledge, and Competencies of Knowledge Workers," *Compensation & Benefits Review,* (July–August 1995), pp. 55–62; B. Murray and B. Gerhart, "An Empirical Analysis of a Skill-Based Pay Program and Plant Performance Outcomes," *Academy of Management Journal* 41, no. 1 (1998), pp. 68–78; J. R. Thompson and C. W. LeHew, "Skill-Based Pay as an Organizational Innovation," *Review of Public Personnel Administration* 20, no. 1 (2000), pp. 20–40; and J. D. Shaw, N. Gupta, A. Mitra, and G. E. Ledford, Jr., "Success and Survival of Skill-Based Pay Plans," *Journal of Management* 31, no. 1 (2005), pp. 28–49.

74. A. Mitra, N. Gupta, and J. D. Shaw, "A Comparative Examination of Traditional and Skill-Based Pay Plans," *Journal of Managerial Psychology* 26, no. 4 (2011), pp. 278–296.

75. E. C. Dierdorff and E. A. Surface, "If You Pay for Skills, Will They Learn? Skill Change and Maintenance under a Skill-Based Pay System," *Journal of Management* 34, no. 4 (2008), pp. 721–743.

76. F. Giancola, "Skill-Based Pay—Issues for Consideration," *Benefits and Compensation Digest* 44, no. 5 (2007), pp. 1–15.

77. C. Vanderborg, "Oracle's Larry Ellison Tops List Of Highest Paid CEO's," *International Business Times* (April 8, 2013), www.ibtimes.com/oracles-larry-ellison-tops-list-highest-paid-ceos-photos-1177217.

78. "Mark Zuckerberg Reaped $2.3 Billion on Facebook Stock Options," *Huffington Post* (April 26, 2013), www.huffingtonpost.com.

79. N. Chi and T. Han, "Exploring the Linkages Between Formal Ownership and Psychological Ownership for the Organization: The Mediating Role of Organizational Justice," *Journal of Occupational and Organizational Psychology* 81, no. 4 (2008), pp. 691–711.

80. See, for instance, D. O. Kim, "Determinants of the Survival of Gainsharing Programs," *Industrial & Labor Relations Review* 53, no. 1 (1999), pp. 21–42; "Why Gainsharing Works Even Better Today Than in the Past," *HR Focus* (April 2000), pp. 3–5; L. R. Gomez-Mejia, T. M. Welbourne, and R. M. Wiseman, "The Role of Risk Sharing and Risk Taking Under Gainsharing," *Academy of Management Review* 25, no. 3 (2000), pp. 492–507; M. Reynolds, "A Cost-Reduction Strategy That May Be Back," *Healthcare Financial Management* (January 2002), pp. 58–64; M. R. Dixon, L. J. Hayes, and J. Stack, "Changing Conceptions of Employee Compensation," *Journal of Organizational Behavior Management* 23, no. 2–3 (2003), pp. 95–116; and I. M. Leitman, R. Levin, M. J. Lipp, L. Sivaprasad, C. J. Karalakulasingam, D. S. Bernard, P. Friedmann, and D. J. Shulkin, "Quality and Financial Outcomes from Gainsharing for Inpatient Admissions: A Three-Year Experience," *Journal of Hospital Medicine* 5, no. 9 (2010), pp. 501–517.

81. T. M. Welbourne and C. J. Ferrante, "To Monitor or Not to Monitor: A Study of Individual Outcomes from Monitoring One's Peers under Gainsharing and Merit Pay," *Group & Organization Management* 33, no. 2 (2008), pp. 139–162.

82. National Center for Employee Ownership, *The Employee Ownership 100* (July 2003), www.nceo.org.

83. Cited in K. Frieswick, "ESOPs: Split Personality," *CFO* (July 7, 2003), p. 1.

84. A. A. Buchko, "The Effects of Employee Ownership on Employee Attitudes: A Test of Three Theoretical Perspectives," *Work and Occupations* 19, no. 1 (1992), 59–78; and R. P. Garrett, "Does Employee Ownership Increase Innovation?" *New England Journal of Entrepreneurship* 13, no. 2, (2010), pp. 37–46.

85. D. McCarthy, E. Reeves, and T. Turner, "Can Employee Share-Ownership Improve Employee Attitudes and Behaviour?" *Employee Relations* 32, no. 4 (2010), pp. 382–395.

86. A. Pendleton and A. Robinson, "Employee Stock Ownership, Involvement, and Productivity: An Interaction-Based Approach," *Industrial and Labor Relations Review* 64, no. 1 (2010), pp. 3–29.

87. X. Zhang, K. M. Bartol, K. G. Smith, M. D. Pfarrer, and D. M. Khanin, "CEOs on the Edge: Earnings Manipulation and Stock-Based Incentive Misalignment," *Academy of Management Journal* 51, no. 2 (2008), pp. 241–258.

88. D. D'Art and T. Turner, "Profit Sharing, Firm Performance, and Union Influence in Selected European Countries," *Personnel Review* 33, no. 3 (2004), pp. 335–350; and D. Kruse, R. Freeman, and J. Blasi, *Shared Capitalism at Work: Employee Ownership, Profit and Gain Sharing, and Broad-Based Stock Options* (Chicago: University of Chicago Press, 2010).

89. A. Bayo-Moriones and M. Larraza-Kintana, "Profit-Sharing Plans and Affective Commitment: Does the Context Matter?" *Human Resource Management* 48, no. 2 (2009), pp. 207–226.

90. C. B. Cadsby, F. Song, and F. Tapon, "Sorting and Incentive Effects of Pay for Performance: An Experimental Investigation," *Academy of Management Journal* 50, no. 2 (2007), pp. 387–405.

91. S. C. L. Fong and M. A. Shaffer, "The Dimensionality and Determinants of Pay Satisfaction: A Cross-Cultural Investigation of a Group Incentive Plan," *International Journal of Human Resource Management* 14, no. 4 (2003), pp. 559–580.

92. See, for instance, M. W. Barringer and G. T. Milkovich, "A Theoretical Exploration of the Adoption and Design of Flexible Benefit Plans: A Case of Human Resource Innovation," *Academy of Management Review* 23, no. 2 (1998), pp. 305–324; D. Brown, "Everybody Loves Flex," *Canadian HR Reporter* (November 18, 2002), p. 1; J. Taggart, "Putting Flex Benefits Through Their Paces," *Canadian HR Reporter* (December 2, 2002), p. G3; and N. D. Cole and D. H. Flint, "Perceptions of Distributive and Procedural Justice in Employee Benefits: Flexible Versus Traditional Benefit Plans," *Journal of Managerial Psychology* 19, no. 1 (2004), pp. 19–40.

93. D. A. DeCenzo and S. P. Robbins, *Fundamentals of Human Resource Management,* 10th ed. (New York: Wiley, 2009).

94. P. Stephens, "Flex Plans Gain in Popularity," *CA Magazine* (January/February 2010), p. 10.

95. D. Lovewell, "Flexible Benefits: Benefits on Offer," *Employee Benefits* (March 2010), p. S15.

96. S. E. Markham, K. D. Scott, and G. H. McKee, "Recognizing Good Attendance: A Longitudinal, Quasi-Experimental Field Study," *Personnel Psychology* 55, no. 3 (2002), p. 641; and S. J. Peterson and F. Luthans, "The Impact of Financial and Nonfinancial Incentives on Business Unit Outcomes over Time," *Journal of Applied Psychology* 91, no. 1 (2006), pp. 156–165.

97. A. D. Stajkovic and F. Luthans, "Differential Effects of Incentive Motivators on Work Performance," *Academy of Management Journal* 4, no. 3 (2001), p. 587. See also F. Luthans and A. D. Stajkovic, "Provide Recognition for Performance Improvement," in E. A. Locke (ed.), *Handbook of Principles of Organizational Behavior* (Malden, MA: Blackwell, 2004), pp. 166–180.

98. L. Shepherd, "Special Report on Rewards and Recognition: Getting Personal," *Workforce Management* (September 2010), pp. 24–29.

99. L. Shepherd, "On Recognition, Multinationals Think Globally," *Workforce Management* (September 2010), p. 26.

100. R. J. Long and J. L. Shields, "From Pay to Praise? Non-Case Employee Recognition in Canadian and Australian Firms," *International Journal of Human Resource Management* 21, no. 8 (2010), pp. 1145–1172.

CHAPTER 9

1. B. E. Ashforth and F. Mael, "Social Identity Theory and the Organization," *Academy of Management Review* 14, no. 1 (1989), pp. 20–39; and M. A. Hogg and D. J. Terry, "Social Identity and Self-Categorization Processes in Organizational Contexts," *Academy of Management Review* 25, no. 1 (2000), pp. 121–140.

2. H. Takahashi, M. Kato, M., M. Matsuura, D. Mobbs, T. Suhara, and Y. Okubo, "When Your Gain Is My Pain and Your Pain Is My Gain: Neural Correlates of Envy and Schadenfreude," *Science* 323, no. 5916 (2009), pp. 937–939; and C. W. Leach, R. Spears, N. R. Branscombe, and B. Doosje, "Malicious Pleasure: Schadenfreude at the Suffering of Another Group," *Journal of Personality and Social Psychology* 84, no. 5 (2003), pp. 932–943.

3. O. Yakushko, M. M. Davidson, and E. N. Williams, "Identity Salience Model: A Paradigm for Integrating Multiple Identities in Clinical Practice," *Psychotherapy* 46, no. 2 (2009), pp. 180-192; and S. M. Toh and A. S. Denisi, "Host Country Nationals as Socializing Agents: A Social Identity Approach," *Journal of Organizational Behavior* 28, no. 3 (2007), pp. 281–301.

4. D. M. Cable and D. S. DeRue, "The Convergent and Discriminant Validity of Subjective Fit Perceptions," *Journal of Applied Psychology* 87, no. 5 (2002), pp. 875–884; E. George and P. Chattopadhyay, "One Foot in Each Camp: The Dual Identification of Contract Workers," *Administrative Science Quarterly* 50, no. 1 (2005), pp. 68–99; and D. M. Cable and J. R. Edwards, "Complementary and Supplementary Fit: A Theoretical and Empirical Integration," *Journal of Applied Psychology* 89, no. 5 (2004), pp. 822–834.

5. P. F. McKay and D. R. Avery, "What Has Race Got to Do with It? Unraveling the Role of Racioethnicity in Job Seekers' Reactions to Site Visits," *Personnel Psychology* 59, no. 2 (2006), pp. 395–429; A. S. Leonard, A. Mehra, and R. Katerberg, "The Social Identity and Social Networks of Ethnic Minority Groups in Organizations: A Crucial Test of Distinctiveness Theory," *Journal of Organizational Behavior* 29, no. 5 (2008), pp. 573–589.

6. M. D. Johnson, F. P. Morgeson, D. R. Ilgen, C. J. Meyer, and J. W. Lloyd, "Multiple Professional Identities: Examining Differences in Identification Across Work-Related Targets," *Journal of Applied Psychology* 91, no. 2 (2006), pp. 498–506.

7. K. Mignonac, O. Herrbach, and S. Guerrero, "The Interactive Effects of Perceived External Prestige and Need for Organizational Identification on Turnover Intentions," *Journal of Vocational Behavior* 69, no. 3 (2006), pp. 477–493; A. Carmeli, and A. Shteigman, "Top Management Team Behavioral Integration in Small-Sized Firms: A Social Identity Perspective," *Group Dynamics* 14, no. 4 (2010), pp. 318–331.

8. M. Hogg and D. Abrams, "Towards a Single-Process Uncertainty-Reduction Model of Social Motivation in Groups," In M. Hogg and D. Abrams (eds.), *Group Motivation: Social Psychological Perspectives* (New York: Harvester-Wheatsheaf, 1993), pp. 173–190.

9. D. A. Gioia, K. N. Price, A. L. Hamilton, and J. B. Thomas, "Change Reference to Forging An Identity: An Insider-Outsider Study of Processes Involved in the Formation of Organizational Identity," *Administrative Science Quarterly* 55, no. 1 (2010), pp. 1–46.

10. B. W. Tuckman, "Developmental Sequences in Small Groups," *Psychological Bulletin,* June 1965, pp. 384–399; B. W. Tuckman and M. C. Jensen, "Stages of Small-Group Development Revisited," *Group and Organizational Studies,* December 1977, pp. 419–427; M. F. Maples, "Group Development: Extending Tuckman's Theory," *Journal for Specialists in Group Work* (Fall 1988), pp. 17–23; and K. Vroman and J. Kovacich, "Computer-Mediated Interdisciplinary Teams: Theory and Reality," *Journal of Interprofessional Care* 16, no. 2 (2002), pp. 159–170.

11. J. E. Mathieu and T. L. Rapp, "Laying the Foundation for Successful Team Performance Trajectories: The Roles of Team Charters and Performance Strategies," *Journal of Applied Psychology* 94, no. 1 (2009), pp. 90–103; and E. C. Dierdorff, S. T. Bell, and J. A. Belohlav, "The Power of 'We': Effects of Psychological Collectivism on Team Performance Over Time," *Journal of Applied Psychology* 96, no. 2 (2011), pp. 247–262.

12. C. J. G. Gersick, "Time and Transition in Work Teams: Toward a New Model of Group Development," *Academy of Management Journal* (March 1988), pp. 9–41; C. J. G. Gersick, "Marking Time: Predictable Transitions in Task Groups," *Academy of Management Journal* (June 1989), pp. 274–309; M. J. Waller, J. M. Conte, C. B. Gibson, and M. A. Carpenter, "The Effect of Individual Perceptions of Deadlines on Team Performance," *Academy of Management Review* (October 2001), pp. 586–600; and A. Chang, P. Bordia, and J. Duck, "Punctuated Equilibrium and Linear Progression: Toward a New Understanding of Group Development," *Academy of Management Journal* (February 2003), pp. 106–117.

13. Gersick, "Time and Transition in Work Teams"; and Gersick, "Marking Time."

14. M. M. Kazmer, "Disengaging from a Distributed Research Project: Refining a Model of Group Departures," *Journal of the American Society for Information Science and Technology* (April 2010), pp. 758–771.

15. See D. M. Rousseau, *Psychological Contracts in Organizations: Understanding Written and Unwritten Agreements* (Thousand Oaks, CA: Sage, 1995); E. W. Morrison and S. L. Robinson, "When Employees Feel Betrayed: A Model of How Psychological Contract Violation Develops," *Academy of Management Review* (April 1997), pp. 226–256; L. Sels, M. Janssens, and I. Van den Brande, "Assessing the Nature of Psychological Contracts: A Validation of Six Dimensions," *Journal of Organizational Behavior* (June 2004), pp. 461–488; and C. Hui, C. Lee, and D. M. Rousseau, "Psychological Contract and Organizational Citizenship Behavior in China: Investigating Generalizability and Instrumentality," *Journal of Applied Psychology* (April 2004), pp. 311–321.

16. M. D. Collins, "The Effect of Psychological Contract Fulfillment on Manager Turnover Intentions and Its Role As a Mediator in a Casual, Limited-Service Restaurant Environment," *International Journal of Hospitality Management* 29, no. 4 (2010), pp. 736–742; J. M. Jensen, R. A. Opland, and A. M. Ryan, "Psychological Contracts and Counterproductive Work Behaviors: Employee Responses to Transactional and Relational Breach," *Journal of Business and Psychology* 25, no. 4 (2010), pp. 555–568.

17. D. C. Thomas, S. R. Fitzimmons, E. C. Ravlin, K. Y. Au, B. Z. Ekelund, and C. Barzantny, "Psychological Contracts Across Cultures," *Organization Studies* 31 (2010), pp. 1437–1458.

18. See M. F. Peterson et al., "Role Conflict, Ambiguity, and Overload: A 21-Nation Study," *Academy of Management Journal* (April 1995), pp. 429–452; and I. H. Settles, R. M. Sellers, and A. Damas Jr., "One Role or Two? The Function of Psychological Separation in Role Conflict," *Journal of Applied Psychology* (June 2002), pp. 574–582.

19. See, for example, F. T. Amstad, L. L. Meier, U. Fasel, A. Elfering, and N. K. Semmer, "A Meta-Analysis of Work-Family Conflict and Various Outcomes with a Special Emphasis on Cross-Domain Versus Matching-Domain Relations," *Journal of Occupational Health Psychology* 16, no. 2 (2011), pp. 151–169.

20. M. A. Hogg and D. J. Terry, "Social Identity and Self-Categorization Processes in Organizational Contexts," *Academy of Management Review* 25, no. 1 (2000), pp. 121–140.

21. D. Vora and T. Kostova. "A Model of Dual Organizational Identification in the Context of the Multinational Enterprise," *Journal of Organizational Behavior* 28 (2007), pp. 327–350.

22. C. Reade, "Dual Identification in Multinational Corporations: Local Managers and Their Psychological Attachment to the Subsidiary Versus the Global Organization," *International Journal of Human Resource Management,* 12, no. 3 (2001), pp. 405–424.

23. P. G. Zimbardo, C. Haney, W. C. Banks, and D. Jaffe, "The Mind Is a Formidable Jailer: A Pirandellian Prison," *The New York Times* (April 8, 1973), pp. 38–60; and C. Haney and P. G. Zimbardo, "Social Roles and Role-Playing: Observations from the Stanford Prison Study," *Behavioral and Social Science Teacher* (January 1973), pp. 25–45.

24. S. A. Haslam and S. Reicher, "Stressing the Group: Social Identity and the Unfolding Dynamics of Responses to Stress," *Journal of Applied Psychology* 91, no. 5 (2006), pp. 1037–1052; S. Reicher and S. A. Haslam, "Rethinking the Psychology of Tyranny: The BBC Prison Study," *British Journal of Social Psychology* 45, no. 1 (2006), pp. 1–40; and P. G. Zimbardo, "On Rethinking the Psychology of Tyranny: The BBC Prison

Study," *British Journal of Social Psychology* 45, no. 1 (2006), pp. 47–53.

25. For a review of the research on group norms, see J. R. Hackman, "Group Influences on Individuals in Organizations," in M. D. Dunnette and L. M. Hough (eds.), *Handbook of Industrial & Organizational Psychology,* 2nd ed., vol. 3 (Palo Alto, CA: Consulting Psychologists Press, 1992), pp. 235–250. For a more recent discussion, see M. G. Ehrhart and S. E. Naumann, "Organizational Citizenship Behavior in Work Groups: A Group Norms Approach," *Journal of Applied Psychology* (December 2004), pp. 960–974.

26. Adapted from P. S. Goodman, E. Ravlin, and M. Schminke, "Understanding Groups in Organizations," in L. L. Cummings and B. M. Staw (eds.), *Research in Organizational Behavior,* vol. 9 (Greenwich, CT: JAI Press, 1987), p. 159; and L. Rosh, L. R. Offermann, and R. Van Diest, "Too Close for Comfort? Distinguishing between Team Intimacy and Team Cohesion," *Human Resource Management Review* (June 2012), pp. 116–127.

27. E. Mayo, *The Human Problems of an Industrial Civilization* (New York: Macmillan, 1933); and F. J. Roethlisberger and W. J. Dickson, *Management and the Worker* (Cambridge, MA: Harvard University Press, 1939).

28. C. A. Kiesler and S. B. Kiesler, *Conformity* (Reading, MA: Addison-Wesley, 1969); R. B. Cialdini and N. J. Goldstein, "Social Influence: Compliance and Conformity," *Annual Review of Psychology* 55 (2004), pp. 591–621.

29. S. E. Asch, "Effects of Group Pressure upon the Modification and Distortion of Judgments," in H. Guetzkow (ed.), *Groups, Leadership and Men* (Pittsburgh: Carnegie Press, 1951), pp. 177–190; and S. E. Asch, "Studies of Independence and Conformity: A Minority of One Against a Unanimous Majority," *Psychological Monographs: General and Applied* 70, no. 9 (1956), pp. 1–70.

30. R. Bond and P. B. Smith, "Culture and Conformity: A Meta-Analysis of Studies Using Asch's (1952, 1956) Line Judgment Task," *Psychological Bulletin* (January 1996), pp. 111–137.

31. See S. L. Robinson and A. M. O'Leary-Kelly, "Monkey See, Monkey Do: The Influence of Work Groups on the Antisocial Behavior of Employees," *Academy of Management Journal* (December 1998), pp. 658–672; R. J. Bennett and S. L. Robinson, "The Past, Present, and Future of Workplace Deviance," in J. Greenberg (ed.), *Organizational Behavior: The State of the Science,* 2nd ed. (Mahwah, NJ: Erlbaum, 2003), pp. 237–271; and C. M. Berry, D. S. Ones, and P. R. Sackett, "Interpersonal Deviance, Organizational Deviance, and Their Common Correlates: A Review and Meta-Analysis," *Journal of Applied Psychology* 92, no. 2 (2007), pp. 410–424.

32. C. M. Pearson, L. M. Andersson, and C. L. Porath, "Assessing and Attacking Workplace Civility," *Organizational Dynamics* 29, no. 2 (2000), p. 130; see also C. Pearson, L. M. Andersson, and C. L. Porath, "Workplace Incivility," in S. Fox and P. E. Spector (eds.), *Counterproductive Work Behavior: Investigations of Actors and Targets* (Washington, DC: American Psychological Association, 2005), pp. 177–200.

33. S. Lim, L. M. Cortina, V. J. Magley, "Personal and Workgroup Incivility: Impact on Work and Health Outcomes," *Journal of Applied Psychology* 93, no. 1 (2008), pp. 95–107.

34. M. S. Christian and A. P. J. Ellis, "Examining the Effects of Sleep Deprivation on Workplace Deviance: A Self-Regulatory Perspective," *Academy of Management Journal* 54, no. 5 (2011), pp. 913–934.

35. Robinson and O'Leary-Kelly, "Monkey See, Monkey Do"; and T. M. Glomb and H. Liao, "Interpersonal Aggression in Workgroups: Social Influence, Reciprocal, and Individual Effects," *Academy of Management Journal* 46 (2003), pp. 486–496.

36. P. Bamberger and M. Biron, "Group Norms and Excessive Absenteeism: The Role of Peer Referent Others," *Organizational Behavior and Human Decision Processes* 103, no. 2 (2007), pp. 179–196; and A. Väänänen, N. Tordera, M. Kivimäki, A. Kouvonen, J. Pentti, A. Linna, and J. Vahtera, "The Role of Work Group in Individual Sickness Absence Behavior," *Journal of Health & Human Behavior* 49, no. 4 (2008), pp. 452–467.

37. M. S. Cole, F. Walter, and H. Bruch, "Affective Mechanisms Linking Dysfunctional Behavior to Performance in Work Teams: A Moderated Mediation Study," *Journal of Applied Psychology* 93, no. 5 (2008), pp. 945–958.

38. See J. Berger, M. H. Fisek, R. Z. Norman, and M. Zelditch, *Status Characteristics and Social Interaction: An Expected States Approach* (New York: Elsevier, 1977).

39. Cited in Hackman, "Group Influences on Individuals in Organizations," p. 236.

40. R. R. Callister and J. A. Wall Jr., "Conflict Across Organizational Boundaries: Managed Care Organizations Versus Health Care Providers," *Journal of Applied Psychology* 86, no. 4 (2001), pp. 754–763; and P. Chattopadhyay, W. H. Glick, and G. P. Huber, "Organizational Actions in Response to Threats and Opportunities," *Academy of Management Journal* 44, no. 5 (2001), pp. 937–955.

41. P. F. Hewlin, "Wearing the Cloak: Antecedents and Consequences of Creating Facades of Conformity," *Journal of Applied Psychology* 94, no. 3 (2009), pp. 727–741.

42. B. Groysberg, J. T. Polzer, and H. A. Elfenbein, "Too Many Cooks Spoil the Broth: How High-Status Individuals Decrease Group Effectiveness," *Organization Science* (May–June 2011), pp. 722–737.

43. See J. M. Levine and R. L. Moreland, "Progress in Small Group Research," in J. T. Spence, J. M. Darley, and D. J. Foss (eds.), *Annual Review of Psychology,* vol. 41 (Palo Alto, CA: Annual Reviews, 1990), pp. 585–634; S. D. Silver, B. P. Cohen, and J. H. Crutchfield, "Status Differentiation and Information Exchange in Face-to-Face and Computer-Mediated Idea Generation," *Social Psychology Quarterly* (1994), pp. 108–123; and J. M. Twenge, "Changes in Women's Assertiveness in Response to Status and Roles: A Cross-Temporal Meta-Analysis, 1931–1993," *Journal of Personality and Social Psychology* (July 2001), pp. 133–145.

44. A. M. Christie and J. Barling, "Beyond Status: Relating Status Inequality to Performance and Health in Teams," *Journal of Applied Psychology* 95, no. 5 (2010), pp. 920–934; and L. H. Nishii and D. M. Mayer, "Do Inclusive Leaders Help to Reduce Turnover in Diverse Groups? The Moderating Role of Leader-Member Exchange in the Diversity to Turnover Relationship," *Journal of Applied Psychology* 94, no. 6 (2009), pp. 1412–1426.

45. V. Venkataramani, S. G. Green, and D. J. Schleicher, "Well-Connected Leaders: The Impact of Leaders' Social Network

Ties on LMX and Members' Work Attitudes," *Journal of Applied Psychology* 95, no. 6 (2010), pp. 1071–1084.

46. H. van Dijk and M. L. van Engen, "A Status Perspective on the Consequences of Work Group Diversity," *Journal of Occupational and Organizational Psychology* (June 2013), pp. 223–241.

47. Based on J. B. Pryor, G. D. Reeder, and A. E. Monroe, "The Infection of Bad Company: Stigma by Association," *Journal of Personality and Social Psychology*. 102, no. 2 (2012), pp. 224–241; E. Goffman, *Stigma: Notes on the Management of Spoiled Identity* (Touchstone Digital, 2009); and M. R. Hebl, and L. M. Mannix, "The Weight of Obesity in Evaluating Others: A Mere Proximity Effect," *Personality and Social Psychology Bulletin* 29 (2003), pp. 28–38.

48. M. Kilduff and D. Krackhardt, "Structural Analysis of the Internal Market for Reputation in Organizations," *Academy of Management Journal*, 37 no. 1 (1994), pp. 87–108.

49. See, for instance, D. R. Comer, "A Model of Social Loafing in Real Work Groups," *Human Relations* (June 1995), pp. 647–667; S. M. Murphy, S. J. Wayne, R. C. Liden, and B. Erdogan, "Understanding Social Loafing: The Role of Justice Perceptions and Exchange Relationships," *Human Relations* (January 2003), pp. 61–84; and R. C. Liden, S. J. Wayne, R. A. Jaworski, and N. Bennett, "Social Loafing: A Field Investigation," *Journal of Management* (April 2004), pp. 285–304.

50. W. Moede, "Die Richtlinien der Leistungs-Psychologie," *Industrielle Psychotechnik* 4 (1927), pp. 193–207. See also D. A. Kravitz and B. Martin, "Ringelmann Rediscovered: The Original Article," *Journal of Personality and Social Psychology* (May 1986), pp. 936–941.

51. See, for example, J. A. Shepperd, "Productivity Loss in Performance Groups: A Motivation Analysis," *Psychological Bulletin* (January 1993), pp. 67–81; and S. J. Karau and K. D. Williams, "Social Loafing: A Meta-Analytic Review and Theoretical Integration," *Journal of Personality and Social Psychology* (October 1993), pp. 681–706.

52. A. W. Delton, L. Cosmides, M. Guemo, T. E. Robertson, and J. Tooby, "The Psychosemantics of Free Riding: Dissecting the Architecture of a Moral Concept," *Journal of Personality and Social Psychology* 102, no. 6 (2012), pp. 1252–1270.

53. S. G. Harkins and K. Szymanski, "Social Loafing and Group Evaluation," *Journal of Personality and Social Psychology* (December 1989), pp. 934–941.

54. D. L. Smrt and S. J. Karau, "Protestant Work Ethic Moderates Social Loafing," *Group Dynamics-Theory Research and Practice* (September 2011), pp. 267–274.

55. A. Gunnthorsdottir and A. Rapoport, "Embedding Social Dilemmas in Intergroup Competition Reduces Free-Riding," *Organizational Behavior and Human Decision Processes* 101 (2006), pp. 184–199; and E. M. Stark, J. D. Shaw, and M. K. Duffy, "Preference for Group Work, Winning Orientation, and Social Loafing Behavior in Groups," *Group and Organization Management* 32, no. 6 (2007), pp. 699–723.

56. Ibid.

57. Based on J. L. Gibson, J. M. Ivancevich, and J. H. Donnelly Jr., *Organizations*, 8th ed. (Burr Ridge, IL: Irwin, 1994), p. 323; and L. L. Greer, "Group Cohesion: Then and Now," *Small Group Research* (December 2012), pp. 655–661.

58. D. S. Staples and L. Zhao, "The Effects of Cultural Diversity in Virtual Teams Versus Face-to-Face Teams," *Group Decision and Negotiation* (July 2006), pp. 389–406.

59. N. Chi, Y. Huang, and S. Lin, "A Double-Edged Sword? Exploring the Curvilinear Relationship Between Organizational Tenure Diversity and Team Innovation: The Moderating Role of Team-Oriented HR Practices," *Group and Organization Management* 34, no. 6 (2009), pp. 698–726.

60. K. J. Klein, A. P. Knight, J. C. Ziegert, B. C. Lim, and J. L. Saltz, "When Team Members' Values Differ: The Moderating Role of Team Leadership," *Organizational Behavior and Human Decision Processes* 114, no. 1 (2011), pp. 25–36; and G. Park and R. P. DeShon, "A Multilevel Model of Minority Opinion Expression and Team Decision-Making Effectiveness," *Journal of Applied Psychology* 95, no. 5 (2010), pp. 824–833.

61. M. Rigoglioso, "Diverse Backgrounds and Personalities Can Strengthen Groups," *Stanford Knowledgebase*, (August 15, 2006), www.stanford.edu/group/knowledgebase/.

62. K. W. Phillips and D. L. Loyd, "When Surface and Deep-Level Diversity Collide: The Effects on Dissenting Group Members," *Organizational Behavior and Human Decision Processes* 99 (2006), pp. 143–160; and S. R. Sommers, "On Racial Diversity and Group Decision Making: Identifying Multiple Effects of Racial Composition on Jury Deliberations," *Journal of Personality and Social Psychology* (April 2006), pp. 597–612.

63. E. Mannix and M. A. Neale, "What Differences Make a Difference? The Promise and Reality of Diverse Teams in Organizations," *Psychological Science in the Public Interest* (October 2005), pp. 31–55.

64. See M. B. Thatcher and P. C. Patel, "Group Faultlines: A Review, Integration, and Guide to Future Research," *Journal of Management* 38, no. 4 (2012), pp. 969–1009.

65. K. Bezrukova, S. M. B. Thatcher, K. A. Jehn, and C. S. Spell, "The Effects of Alignments: Examining Group Faultlines, Organizational Cultures, and Performance," *Journal of Applied Psychology* 97, no. 1 (2012), pp. 77–92.

66. R. Rico, M. Sanchez-Manzanares, M. Antino, and D. Lau, "Bridging Team Faultlines by Combining Task Role Assignment and Goal Structure Strategies," *Journal of Applied Psychology* 97, no. 2 (2012), pp. 407–420.

67. See N. R. F. Maier, "Assets and Liabilities in Group Problem Solving: The Need for an Integrative Function," *Psychological Review* (April 1967), pp. 239–249; G. W. Hill, "Group Versus Individual Performance: Are $N + 1$ Heads Better Than One?" *Psychological Bulletin* (May 1982), pp. 517–539; M. D. Johnson and J. R. Hollenbeck, "Collective Wisdom as an Oxymoron: Team-Based Structures as Impediments to Learning," in J. Langan-Fox, C. L. Cooper, and R. J. Klimoski (eds), *Research Companion to the Dysfunctional Workplace: Management Challenges and Symptoms* (Northampton, MA: Edward Elgar Publishing, 2007), pp. 319–331; and R. F. Martell and M. R. Borg, "A Comparison of the Behavioral Rating Accuracy of Groups and Individuals," *Journal of Applied Psychology* (February 1993), pp. 43–50.

68. D. Gigone and R. Hastie, "Proper Analysis of the Accuracy of Group Judgments," *Psychological Bulletin* (January 1997), pp. 149–167; and B. L. Bonner, S. D. Sillito, and M. R. Baumann, "Collective Estimation: Accuracy, Expertise, and Extroversion as Sources of Intra-Group Influence," *Organizational Behavior and Human Decision Processes* 103 (2007), pp. 121–133.

69. See, for example, W. C. Swap and Associates, *Group Decision Making* (Newbury Park, CA: Sage, 1984).

70. I. L. Janis, *Groupthink* (Boston: Houghton Mifflin, 1982); W.-W. Park, "A Review of Research on Groupthink," *Journal of Behavioral Decision Making* (July 1990), pp. 229–245; J. N. Choi and M. U. Kim, "The Organizational Application of Groupthink and Its Limits in Organizations," *Journal of Applied Psychology* (April 1999), pp. 297–306; and W.-W. Park, "A Comprehensive Empirical Investigation of the Relationships Among Variables of the Groupthink Model," *Journal of Organizational Behavior* (December 2000), pp. 873–887.

71. Janis, *Groupthink.*

72. G. Park and R. P. DeShon, "A Multilevel Model of Minority Opinion Expression and Team Decision-Making Effectiveness," *Journal of Applied Psychology* 95, no. 5 (2010), pp. 824–833.

73. R. Benabou, "Groupthink: Collective Delusions in Organizations and Markets," *Review of Economic Studies* (April 2013), pp. 429–462; and M. E. Turner and A. R. Pratkanis, "Mitigating Groupthink by Stimulating Constructive Conflict," in C. K. W. De Dreu and E. Van de Vliert (eds.), *Using Conflict in Organizations* (London: Sage, 1997), pp. 53–71.

74. J. A. Goncalo, E. Polman, and C. Maslach, "Can Confidence Come Too Soon? Collective Efficacy, Conflict, and Group Performance over Time," *Organizational Behavior and Human Decision Processes* 113, no. 1 (2010), pp. 13–24.

75. See N. R. F. Maier, *Principles of Human Relations* (New York: Wiley, 1952); I. L. Janis, *Groupthink: Psychological Studies of Policy Decisions and Fiascoes*, 2nd ed. (Boston: Houghton Mifflin, 1982); N. Richardson Ahlfinger and J. K. Esser, "Testing the Groupthink Model: Effects of Promotional Leadership and Conformity Predisposition," *Social Behavior & Personality* 29, no. 1 (2001), pp. 31–41; and S. Schultz-Hardt, F. C. Brodbeck, A. Mojzisch, R. Kerschreiter, and D. Frey, "Group Decision Making in Hidden Profile Situations: Dissent as a Facilitator for Decision Quality," *Journal of Personality and Social Psychology* 91, no. 6 (2006), pp. 1080–1093.

76. See P. W. Paese, M. Bieser, and M. E. Tubbs, "Framing Effects and Choice Shifts in Group Decision Making," *Organizational Behavior and Human Decision Processes* (October 1993), pp. 149–165; and I. Yaniv, "Group Diversity and Decision Quality: Amplification and Attenuation of the Framing Effect," *International Journal of Forecasting* (January–March 2011), pp. 41–49.

77. R. D. Clark III, "Group-Induced Shift Toward Risk: A Critical Appraisal," *Psychological Bulletin* (October 1971), pp. 251–270; M. Brauer and C. M. Judd, "Group Polarization and Repeated Attitude Expression: A New Take on an Old Topic," *European Review of Social Psychology* 7, (1996), pp. 173–207; and M. P. Brady and S. Y. Wu, "The Aggregation of Preferences in Groups: Identity, Responsibility, and Polarization," *Journal of Economic Psychology* 31, no. 6 (2010), pp. 950–963.

78. Z. Krizan and R. S. Baron, "Group Polarization and Choice-Dilemmas: How Important Is Self-Categorization?" *European Journal of Social Psychology* 37, no. 1 (2007), pp. 191–201.

79. A. F. Osborn, *Applied Imagination: Principles and Procedures of Creative Thinking*, 3rd ed. (New York: Scribner, 1963). See also R. P. McGlynn, D. McGurk, V. S. Effland, N. L. Johll, and D. J. Harding, "Brainstorming and Task Performance in Groups Constrained by Evidence," *Organizational Behavior and Human Decision Processes* (January 2004), pp. 75–87; and R. C. Litchfield, "Brainstorming Reconsidered: A Goal-Based View," *Academy of Management Review* 33, no. 3 (2008), pp. 649–668.

80. N. L. Kerr and R. S. Tindale, "Group Performance and Decision-Making," *Annual Review of Psychology* 55 (2004), pp. 623–655.

81. See A. L. Delbecq, A. H. Van deVen, and D. H. Gustafson, *Group Techniques for Program Planning: A Guide to Nominal and Delphi Processes* (Glenview, IL: Scott Foresman, 1975); and P. B. Paulus and H.-C. Yang, "Idea Generation in Groups: A Basis for Creativity in Organizations," *Organizational Behavior and Human Decision Processing* (May 2000), pp. 76–87.

82. C. Faure, "Beyond Brainstorming: Effects of Different Group Procedures on Selection of Ideas and Satisfaction with the Process," *Journal of Creative Behavior* 38 (2004), pp. 13–34.

83. A. G. Bedeian and A. A. Armenakis, "A Path-Analytic Study of the Consequences of Role Conflict and Ambiguity," *Academy of Management Journal* (June 1981), pp. 417–424; and P. L. Perrewe, K. L. Zellars, G. R. Ferris, A. M. Rossi, C. J. Kacmar, and D. A. Ralston, "Neutralizing Job Stressors: Political Skill as an Antidote to the Dysfunctional Consequences of Role Conflict," *Academy of Management Journal* (February 2004), pp. 141–152.

84. M. E. Shaw, *Group Dynamics: The Psychology of Small Group Behavior*, 3rd ed. (New York: McGraw-Hill, 1981).

CHAPTER 10

1. This section is based on J. R. Katzenbach and D. K. Smith, *The Wisdom of Teams* (Cambridge, MA: Harvard University Press, 1993), pp. 21, 45, 85; and D. C. Kinlaw, *Developing Superior Work Teams* (Lexington, MA: Lexington Books, 1991), pp. 3–21.

2. J. Mathieu, M. T. Maynard, T. Rapp, and L. Gilson, "Team Effectiveness 1997–2007: A Review of Recent Advancements and a Glimpse into the Future," *Journal of Management* 34, no. 3 (2008), pp. 410–476.

3. J. H. Shonk, *Team-Based Organizations* (Homewood, IL: Business One Irwin, 1992); and M. A. Verespej, "When Workers Get New Roles," *IndustryWeek* (February 3, 1992), p. 11.

4. G. Bodinson and R. Bunch, "AQP's National Team Excellence Award: Its Purpose, Value and Process," *The Journal for Quality and Participation* (Spring 2003), pp. 37–42.

5. See, for example, A. Erez, J. A. LePine, and H. Elms, "Effects of Rotated Leadership and Peer Evaluation on the Functioning and Effectiveness of Self-Managed Teams: A Quasi-experiment," *Personnel Psychology* (Winter 2002), pp. 929–948.

6. See, for instance, C. W. Langfred, "Too Much of a Good Thing? Negative Effects of High Trust and Individual Autonomy in Self-Managing Teams," *Academy of Management Journal* (June 2004), pp. 385–399.

7. C. W. Langfred, "The Downside of Self-Management: A Longitudinal Study of the Effects of Conflict on Trust, Autonomy, and Task Interdependence in Self-Managing

Teams," *Academy of Management Journal* 50, no. 4 (2007), pp. 885–900.

8. B. H. Bradley, B. E. Postlethwaite, A. C. Klotz, M. R. Hamdani, and K. G. Brown, "Reaping the Benefits of Task Conflict in Teams: The Critical Role of Team Psychological Safety Climate," *Journal of Applied Psychology,* 97, no. 1 (2012), pp. 151–158.

9. G. L. Stewart, S. H. Courtright, and M. R. Barrick, "Peer-Based Control in Self-Managing Teams: Linking Rational and Normative Influence with Individual and Group Performance," *Journal of Applied Psychology* 97, no. 2 (2012), pp. 435–447.

10. J. Devaro, "The Effects of Self-Managed and Closely Managed Teams on Labor Productivity and Product Quality: An Empirical Analysis of a Cross-Section of Establishments," *Industrial Relations* 47, no. 4 (2008), pp. 659–698.

11. A. Shah, "Starbucks Strives for Instant Gratification with Via Launch," *PRWeek* (December 2009), p. 15.

12. B. Freyer and T. A. Stewart, "Cisco Sees the Future," *Harvard Business Review* (November 2008), pp. 73–79.

13. See, for example, L. L. Martins, L. L. Gilson, and M. T. Maynard, "Virtual Teams: What Do We Know and Where Do We Go from Here?" *Journal of Management* (November 2004), pp. 805–835; and B. Leonard, "Managing Virtual Teams," *HRMagazine* (June 2011), pp. 39–42.

14. R. S. Gajendran and A. Joshi, "Innovation in Globally Distributed Teams: The Role of LMX, Communication Frequency, and Member Influence on Team Decisions, *Journal of Applied Psychology* 97, no. 6 (2012), pp. 1252–1261.

15. J. R. Mesmer-Magnus, L. A. DeChurch, M. Jimenez-Rodriguez, J. Wildman, and M. Shuffler, "A Meta-Analytic Investigation of Virtuality and Information Sharing in Teams," *Organizational Behavior and Human Decision Processes* 115, no. 2 (2011), pp. 214–225.

16. A. Malhotra, A. Majchrzak, and B. Rosen, "Leading Virtual Teams," *Academy of Management Perspectives* (February 2007), pp. 60–70; and J. M. Wilson, S. S. Straus, and B. McEvily, "All in Due Time: The Development of Trust in Computer-Mediated and Face-to-Face Teams," *Organizational Behavior and Human Decision Processes* 19 (2006), pp. 16–33.

17. P. Balkundi and D. A. Harrison, "Ties, Leaders, and Time in Teams: Strong Inference About Network Structure's Effects on Team Viability and Performance," *Academy of Management Journal* 49, no. 1 (2006), pp. 49–68; G. Chen, B. L. Kirkman, R. Kanfer, D. Allen, and B. Rosen, "A Multilevel Study of Leadership, Empowerment, and Performance in Teams," *Journal of Applied Psychology* 92, no. 2 (2007), pp. 331–346; L. A. DeChurch and M. A. Marks, "Leadership in Multiteam Systems," *Journal of Applied Psychology* 91, no. 2 (2006), pp. 311–329; A. Srivastava, K. M. Bartol, and E. A. Locke, "Empowering Leadership in Management Teams: Effects on Knowledge Sharing, Efficacy, and Performance," *Academy of Management Journal* 49, no. 6 (2006), pp. 1239–1251; and J. E. Mathieu, K. K. Gilson, and T. M. Ruddy, "Empowerment and Team Effectiveness: An Empirical Test of an Integrated Model," *Journal of Applied Psychology* 91, no. 1 (2006), pp. 97–108.

18. R. B. Davison, J. R. Hollenbeck, C. M. Barnes, D. J. Sleesman, and D. R. Ilgen, "Coordinated Action in Multiteam Systems," *Journal of Applied Psychology* 97, no. 4 (2012), pp. 808–824.

19. See, for instance, J. R. Hackman, "The Design of Work Teams," in J. W. Lorsch (ed.), *Handbook of Organizational Behavior* (Upper Saddle River, NJ: Prentice Hall, 1987), pp. 315–342; and M. A. Campion, G. J. Medsker, and C. A. Higgs, "Relations Between Work Group Characteristics and Effectiveness: Implications for Designing Effective Work Groups," *Personnel Psychology* (Winter 1993), pp. 823–850.

20. D. E. Hyatt and T. M. Ruddy, "An Examination of the Relationship Between Work Group Characteristics and Performance: Once More into the Breech," *Personnel Psychology* (Autumn 1997), p. 555.

21. This model is based on M. A. Campion, E. M. Papper, and G. J. Medsker, "Relations Between Work Team Characteristics and Effectiveness: A Replication and Extension," *Personnel Psychology* (Summer 1996), pp. 429–452; Hyatt and Ruddy, "An Examination of the Relationship Between Work Group Characteristics and Performance," pp. 553–585; S. G. Cohen and D. E. Bailey, "What Makes Teams Work: Group Effectiveness Research from the Shop Floor to the Executive Suite," *Journal of Management* 23, no. 3 (1997), pp. 239–290; L. Thompson, *Making the Team* (Upper Saddle River, NJ: Prentice Hall, 2000), pp. 18–33; and J. R. Hackman, *Leading Teams: Setting the Stage for Great Performance* (Boston: Harvard Business School Press, 2002).

22. See G. L. Stewart and M. R. Barrick, "Team Structure and Performance: Assessing the Mediating Role of Intrateam Process and the Moderating Role of Task Type," *Academy of Management Journal* (April 2000), pp. 135–148.

23. Hyatt and Ruddy, "An Examination of the Relationship Between Work Group Characteristics and Performance," p. 577.

24. P. Balkundi and D. A. Harrison, "Ties, Leaders, and Time in Teams: Strong Inference About Network Structure's Effects on Team Viability and Performance," *Academy of Management Journal* 49, no. 1 (2006), pp. 49–68; G. Chen, B. L. Kirkman, R. Kanfer, D. Allen, and B. Rosen, "A Multilevel Study of Leadership, Empowerment, and Performance in Teams," *Journal of Applied Psychology* 92, no. 2 (2007), pp. 331–346; L. A. DeChurch and M. A. Marks, "Leadership in Multiteam Systems," *Journal of Applied Psychology* 91, no. 2 (2006), pp. 311–329; A. Srivastava, K. M. Bartol, and E. A. Locke, "Empowering Leadership in Management Teams: Effects on Knowledge Sharing, Efficacy, and Performance," *Academy of Management Journal* 49, no. 6 (2006), pp. 1239–1251; and J. E. Mathieu, K. K. Gilson, and T. M. Ruddy, "Empowerment and Team Effectiveness: An Empirical Test of an Integrated Model," *Journal of Applied Psychology* 91, no. 1 (2006), pp. 97–108.

25. J. B. Carson, P. E. Tesluk, and J. A. Marrone, "Shared Leadership in Teams: An Investigation of Antecedent Conditions and Performance," *Academy of Management Journal* 50, no. 5 (2007), pp. 1217–1234.

26. K. T. Dirks, "Trust in Leadership and Team Performance: Evidence from NCAA Basketball," *Journal of Applied Psychology* (December 2000), pp. 1004–1012; M. Williams, "In Whom We Trust: Group Membership as an Affective Context for Trust Development," *Academy of Management Review* (July 2001), pp. 377–396; and J. Schaubroeck, S. S. K. Lam, and A. C. Peng, "Cognition-Based and Affect-Based Trust as Mediators of Leader Behavior Influences on

Team Performance," *Journal of Applied Psychology,* Online First Publication (February 7, 2011), doi: 10.1037/a0022625.

27. B. A. De Jong, and K. T. Dirks, "Beyond Shared Perceptions of Trust and Monitoring in Teams: Implications of Asymmetry and Dissensus," *Journal of Applied Psychology* 97, no. 2 (2012), pp. 391–406.

28. See F. Aime, C. J. Meyer, and S. E. Humphrey, "Legitimacy of Team Rewards: Analyzing Legitimacy as a Condition for the Effectiveness of Team Incentive Designs," *Journal of Business Research* 63, no. 1 (2010), pp. 60–66; and P. A. Bamberger and R. Levi, "Team-Based Reward Allocation Structures and the Helping Behaviors of Outcome-Interdependent Team Members," *Journal of Managerial Psychology* 24, no. 4 (2009), pp. 300–327; and M. J. Pearsall, M. S. Christian, and A. P. J. Ellis, "Motivating Interdependent Teams: Individual Rewards, Shared Rewards, or Something in Between?" *Journal of Applied Psychology* 95, no. 1 (2010), pp. 183–191.

29. R. R. Hirschfeld, M. H. Jordan, H. S. Feild, W. F. Giles, and A. A. Armenakis, "Becoming Team Players: Team Members' Mastery of Teamwork Knowledge as a Predictor of Team Task Proficiency and Observed Teamwork Effectiveness," *Journal of Applied Psychology* 91, no. 2 (2006), pp. 467–474; and K. R. Randall, C. J. Resick, and L. A. DeChurch, "Building Team Adaptive Capacity: The Roles of Sensegiving and Team Composition," *Journal of Applied Psychology* 96, no. 3 (2011), pp. 525–540.

30. H. Moon, J. R. Hollenbeck, and S. E. Humphrey, "Asymmetric Adaptability: Dynamic Team Structures as One-Way Streets," *Academy of Management Journal* 47, no. 5 (October 2004), pp. 681–695; A. P. J. Ellis, J. R. Hollenbeck, and D. R. Ilgen, "Team Learning: Collectively Connecting the Dots," *Journal of Applied Psychology* 88, no. 5 (October 2003), pp. 821–835; C. L. Jackson and J. A. LePine, "Peer Responses to a Team's Weakest Link: A Test and Extension of LePine and Van Dyne's Model," *Journal of Applied Psychology* 88, no. 3 (June 2003), pp. 459–475; and J. A. LePine, "Team Adaptation and Postchange Performance: Effects of Team Composition in Terms of Members' Cognitive Ability and Personality," *Journal of Applied Psychology* 88, no. 1 (February 2003), pp. 27–39.

31. S. T. Bell, "Deep-Level Composition Variables as Predictors of Team Performance: A Meta-Analysis," *Journal of Applied Psychology* 92, no. 3 (2007), pp. 595–615; and M. R. Barrick, G. L. Stewart, M. J. Neubert, and M. K. Mount, "Relating Member Ability and Personality to Work-Team Processes and Team Effectiveness," *Journal of Applied Psychology* (June 1998), pp. 377–391.

32. T. A. O'Neill and N. J. Allen, "Personality and the Prediction of Team Performance," *European Journal of Personality* 25, no. 1 (2011), pp. 31–42.

33. Ellis, Hollenbeck, and Ilgen, "Team Learning"; C. O. L. H. Porter, J. R. Hollenbeck, and D. R. Ilgen, "Backing Up Behaviors in Teams: The Role of Personality and Legitimacy of Need," *Journal of Applied Psychology* 88, no. 3 (June 2003), pp. 391–403; J. A. Colquitt, J. R. Hollenbeck, and D. R. Ilgen, "Computer-Assisted Communication and Team Decision-Making Performance: The Moderating Effect of Openness to Experience," *Journal of Applied Psychology* 87, no. 2 (April 2002), pp. 402–410; J. A. LePine, J. R. Hollenbeck, D. R. Ilgen, and J. Hedlund, "The Effects of Individual Differences

on the Performance of Hierarchical Decision Making Teams: Much More Than G," *Journal of Applied Psychology* 82 (1997), pp. 803–811; Jackson and LePine, "Peer Responses to a Team's Weakest Link"; and LePine, "Team Adaptation and Postchange Performance."

34. Barrick, Stewart, Neubert, and Mount, "Relating Member Ability and Personality to Work-Team Processes and Team Effectiveness," p. 388; and S. E. Humphrey, J. R. Hollenbeck, C. J. Meyer, and D. R. Ilgen, "Trait Configurations in Self-Managed Teams: A Conceptual Examination of the Use of Seeding for Maximizing and Minimizing Trait Variance in Teams," *Journal of Applied Psychology* 92, no. 3 (2007), pp. 885–892.

35. S. E. Humphrey, F. P. Morgeson, and M. J. Mannor, "Developing a Theory of the Strategic Core of Teams: A Role Composition Model of Team Performance," *Journal of Applied Psychology* 94, no. 1 (2009), pp. 48–61.

36. C. Margerison and D. McCann, *Team Management: Practical New Approaches* (London: Mercury Books, 1990).

37. K. Y. Williams and C. A. O'Reilly III, "Demography and Diversity in Organizations: A Review of 40 Years of Research," in B. M. Staw and L. L. Cummings (eds.), *Research in Organizational Behavior,* vol. 20, (Stamford, CT: Jai Press, 1998) pp. 77–140; and A. Joshi, "The Influence of Organizational Demography on the External Networking Behavior of Teams," *Academy of Management Review* (July 2006), pp. 583–595.

38. A. Joshi and H. Roh, "The Role of Context in Work Team Diversity Research: A Meta-Analytic Review," *Academy of Management Journal* 52, no. 3 (2009), pp. 599–627; S. K. Horwitz and I. B. Horwitz, "The Effects of Team Diversity on Team Outcomes: A Meta-Analytic Review of Team Demography," *Journal of Management* 33, no. 6 (2007), pp. 987–1015; and S. T. Bell, A. J. Villado, M. A. Lukasik, L. Belau, and A. L. Briggs, "Getting Specific about Demographic Diversity Variable and Team Performance Relationships: A Meta-Analysis," *Journal of Management* 37, no. 3 (2011), pp. 709–743.

39. S. J. Shin and J. Zhou, "When Is Educational Specialization Heterogeneity Related to Creativity in Research and Development Teams? Transformational Leadership as a Moderator," *Journal of Applied Psychology* 92, no. 6 (2007), pp. 1709–1721; and K. J. Klein, A. P. Knight, J. C. Ziegert, B. C. Lim, and J. L. Saltz, "When Team Members' Values Differ: The Moderating Role of Team Leadership," *Organizational Behavior and Human Decision Processes* 114, no. 1 (2011), pp. 25–36.

40. S. J. Shin, T. Kim, J. Lee, and L. Bian, "Cognitive Team Diversity and Individual Team Member Creativity: A Cross-Level Interaction," *Academy of Management Journal* 55, no. 1 (2012), pp. 197–212.

41. W. E. Watson, K. Kumar, and L. K. Michaelsen, "Cultural Diversity's Impact on Interaction Process and Performance: Comparing Homogeneous and Diverse Task Groups," *Academy of Management Journal* (June 1993), pp. 590–602; P. C. Earley and E. Mosakowski, "Creating Hybrid Team Cultures: An Empirical Test of Transnational Team Functioning," *Academy of Management Journal* (February 2000), pp. 26–49; and S. Mohammed and L. C. Angell, "Surface- and Deep-Level Diversity in Workgroups: Examining the Moderating Effects

of Team Orientation and Team Process on Relationship Conflict," *Journal of Organizational Behavior* (December 2004), pp. 1015–1039.

42. Watson, Kumar, and Michaelsen, "Cultural Diversity's Impact on Interaction Process and Performance."

43. D. Coutu, "Why Teams Don't Work" *Harvard Business Review* (May 2009), pp. 99–105. The evidence in this section is described in Thompson, *Making the Team*, pp. 65–67. See also L. A. Curral, R. H. Forrester, and J. F. Dawson, "It's What You Do and the Way That You Do It: Team Task, Team Size, and Innovation-Related Group Processes," *European Journal of Work & Organizational Psychology* 10, no. 2 (June 2001), pp. 187–204; R. C. Liden, S. J. Wayne, and R. A. Jaworski, "Social Loafing: A Field Investigation," *Journal of Management* 30, no. 2 (2004), pp. 285–304; and J. A. Wagner, "Studies of Individualism–Collectivism: Effects on Cooperation in Groups," *Academy of Management Journal* 38, no. 1 (February 1995), pp. 152–172.

44. "Is Your Team Too Big? Too Small? What's the Right Number? *Knowledge@Wharton* (June 14, 2006), pp. 1–5; see also A. M. Carton and J. N. Cummings, "A Theory of Subgroups in Work Teams," *Academy of Management Review* 37, no. 3 (2012), pp. 441–470.

45. Hyatt and Ruddy, "An Examination of the Relationship Between Work Group Characteristics and Performance"; J. D. Shaw, M. K. Duffy, and E. M. Stark, "Interdependence and Preference for Group Work: Main and Congruence Effects on the Satisfaction and Performance of Group Members," *Journal of Management* 26, no. 2 (2000), pp. 259–279; and S. A. Kiffin-Peterson and J. L. Cordery, "Trust, Individualism, and Job Characteristics of Employee Preference for Teamwork," *International Journal of Human Resource Management* (February 2003), pp. 93–116.

46. J. A. LePine, R. F. Piccolo, C. L. Jackson, J. E. Mathieu, and J. R. Saul, "A Meta-Analysis of Teamwork Processes: Tests of a Multidimensional Model and Relationships with Team Effectiveness Criteria," *Personnel Psychology* 61 (2008), pp. 273–307.

47. I. D. Steiner, *Group Processes and Productivity* (New York: Academic Press, 1972).

48. J. A. LePine, R. F. Piccolo, C. L. Jackson, J. E. Mathieu, and J. R. Saul, "A Meta-Analysis of Teamwork Processes: Tests of a Multidimensional Model and Relationships with Team Effectiveness Criteria"; and J. E. Mathieu and T. L. Rapp, "Laying the Foundation for Successful Team Performance Trajectories: The Roles of Team Charters and Performance Strategies," *Journal of Applied Psychology* 94, no. 1 (2009), pp. 90–103.

49. J. E. Mathieu and W. Schulze, "The Influence of Team Knowledge and Formal Plans on Episodic Team Process—Performance Relationships," *Academy of Management Journal* 49, no. 3 (2006), pp. 605–619.

50. A. N. Pieterse, D. van Knippenberg, and W. P. van Ginkel, "Diversity in Goal Orientation, Team Reflexivity, and Team Performance," *Organizational Behavior and Human Decision Processes* 114, no. 2 (2011), pp. 153–164.

51. A. Gurtner, F. Tschan, N. K. Semmer, and C. Nagele, "Getting Groups to Develop Good Strategies: Effects of Reflexivity Interventions on Team Process, Team Performance, and Shared Mental Models," *Organizational Behavior and Human Decision Processes* 102 (2007), pp. 127–142; M. C. Schippers, D. N. Den Hartog, and P. L. Koopman, "Reflexivity in Teams: A Measure and Correlates," *Applied Psychology: An International Review* 56, no. 2 (2007), pp. 189–211; and C. S. Burke, K. C. Stagl, E. Salas, L. Pierce, and D. Kendall, "Understanding Team Adaptation: A Conceptual Analysis and Model," *Journal of Applied Psychology* 91, no. 6 (2006), pp. 1189–1207.

52. A. N. Pieterse, D. van Knippenberg, and W. P. van Ginkel, "Diversity in Goal Orientation, Team Reflexivity, and Team Performance," *Organizational Behavior and Human Decision Processes* 114, no. 2 (2011), pp. 153–164.

53. E. Weldon and L. R. Weingart, "Group Goals and Group Performance," *British Journal of Social Psychology* (Spring 1993), pp. 307–334. See also R. P. DeShon, S. W. J. Kozlowski, A. M. Schmidt, K. R. Milner, and D. Wiechmann, "A Multiple-Goal, Multilevel Model of Feedback Effects on the Regulation of Individual and Team Performance," *Journal of Applied Psychology* (December 2004), pp. 1035–1056.

54. K. Tasa, S. Taggar, and G. H. Seijts, "The Development of Collective Efficacy in Teams: A Multilevel and Longitudinal Perspective," *Journal of Applied Psychology* 92, no. 1 (2007), pp. 17–27; D. I. Jung and J. J. Sosik, "Group Potency and Collective Efficacy: Examining Their Predictive Validity, Level of Analysis, and Effects of Performance Feedback on Future Group Performance," *Group & Organization Management* (September 2003), pp. 366–391; and R. R. Hirschfeld and J. B. Bernerth, "Mental Efficacy and Physical Efficacy at the Team Level: Inputs and Outcomes Among Newly Formed Action Teams," *Journal of Applied Psychology* 93, no. 6 (2008), pp. 1429–1437.

55. A. W. Richter, G. Hirst, D. van Knippenberg, and M. Baer, "Creative Self-Efficacy and Individual Creativity in Team Contexts: Cross-Level Interactions with Team Informational Resources," *Journal of Applied Psychology* 97, no. 6 (2012), pp. 1282–1290.

56. S. Mohammed, L. Ferzandi, and K. Hamilton, "Metaphor No More: A 15-Year Review of the Team Mental Model Construct," *Journal of Management* 36, no. 4 (2010), pp. 876–910.

57. A. P. J. Ellis, "System Breakdown: The Role of Mental Models and Transactive Memory on the Relationships Between Acute Stress and Team Performance," *Academy of Management Journal* 49, no. 3 (2006), pp. 576–589.

58. S. W. J. Kozlowski and D. R. Ilgen, "Enhancing the Effectiveness of Work Groups and Teams," *Psychological Science in the Public Interest* (December 2006), pp. 77–124; and B. D. Edwards, E. A. Day, W. Arthur Jr., and S. T. Bell, "Relationships Among Team Ability Composition, Team Mental Models, and Team Performance," *Journal of Applied Psychology* 91, no. 3 (2006), pp. 727–736.

59. L. A. DeChurch and J. R. Mesmer-Magnus, "The Cognitive Underpinnings of Effective Teamwork: A Meta-Analysis," *Journal of Applied Psychology* 95, no. 1 (2010), pp. 32–53.

60. J. Farh, C. Lee, and C. I. C. Farh, "Task Conflict and Team Creativity: A Question of How Much and When," *Journal of Applied Psychology* 95, no. 6 (2010), pp. 1173–1180.

61. K. J. Behfar, R. S. Peterson, E. A. Mannix, and W. M. K. Trochim, "The Critical Role of Conflict Resolution in Teams: A Close Look at the Links Between Conflict Type, Conflict

Management Strategies, and Team Outcomes," *Journal of Applied Psychology* 93, no. 1 (2008), pp. 170–188.

62. K. H. Price, D. A. Harrison, and J. H. Gavin, "Withholding Inputs in Team Contexts: Member Composition, Interaction Processes, Evaluation Structure, and Social Loafing," *Journal of Applied Psychology* 91, no. 6 (2006), pp. 1375–1384.

63. See, for instance, B. L. Kirkman and D. L. Shapiro, "The Impact of Cultural Values on Employee Resistance to Teams: Toward a Model of Globalized Self-Managing Work Team Effectiveness," *Academy of Management Review,* July 1997, pp. 730–757; and B. L. Kirkman, C. B. Gibson, and D. L. Shapiro, "'Exporting' Teams: Enhancing the Implementation and Effectiveness of Work Teams in Global Affiliates," *Organizational Dynamics* 30, no. 1 (2001), pp. 12–29.

64. G. Hertel, U. Konradt, and K. Voss, "Competencies for Virtual Teamwork: Development and Validation of a Web-Based Selection Tool for Members of Distributed Teams," *European Journal of Work and Organizational Psychology* 15, no. 4 (2006), pp. 477–504.

65. T. V. Riper, "The NBA's Most Overpaid Players," *Forbes* (April 5, 2013), downloaded on June 10, 2013, from www.forbes.com.

66. E. Kearney, D. Gebert, and S. C. Voelpel, "When and How Diversity Benefits Teams: The Importance of Team Members' Need for Cognition," *Academy of Management Journal* 52, no. 3 (2009), pp. 581–598.

67. H. M. Guttman, "The New High-Performance Player," *The Hollywood Reporter* (October 27, 2008), www.hollywoodreporter.com.

68. C.-H. Chuang, S. Chen, and C.-W. Chuang, "Human Resource Management Practices and Organizational Social Capital: The Role of Industrial Characteristics," *Journal of Business Research* (May 2013), pp. 678–687; and L. Prusak and D. Cohen, "How to Invest in Social Capital," *Harvard Business Review* (June 2001), pp. 86–93.

69. T. Erickson and L. Gratton, "What It Means to Work Here," *BusinessWeek* (January 10, 2008), www.businessweek.com.

70. M. D. Johnson, J. R. Hollenbeck, S. E. Humphrey, D. R. Ilgen, D. Jundt, and C. J. Meyer, "Cutthroat Cooperation: Asymmetrical Adaptation to Changes in Team Reward Structures," *Academy of Management Journal* 49, no. 1 (2006), pp. 103–119.

71. C. E. Naquin and R. O. Tynan, "The Team Halo Effect: Why Teams Are Not Blamed for Their Failures," *Journal of Applied Psychology,* April 2003, pp. 332–340.

72. E. R. Crawford and J. A. Lepine, "A Configural Theory of Team Processes: Accounting for the Structure of Taskwork and Teamwork," *Academy of Management Review* (January 2013), pp. 32–48; and A. B. Drexler and R. Forrester, "Teamwork—Not Necessarily the Answer," *HR Magazine* (January 1998), pp. 55–58.

CHAPTER 11

1. W. G. Scott and T. R. Mitchell, *Organization Theory: A Structural and Behavioral Analysis* (Homewood, IL: Irwin, 1976).

2. D. K. Berlo, *The Process of Communication* (New York: Holt, Rinehart & Winston, 1960), pp. 30–32; see also K. Byron, "Carrying Too Heavy a Load? The Communication and Miscommunication of Emotion by Email," *Academy of Management Review* 33, no. 2 (2008), pp. 309–327.

3. J. Langan-Fox, "Communication in Organizations: Speed, Diversity, Networks, and Influence on Organizational Effectiveness, Human Health, and Relationships," in N. Anderson, D. S. Ones, H. K. Sinangil, and C. Viswesvaran (eds.), *Handbook of Industrial, Work and Organizational Psychology*, vol. 2 (Thousand Oaks, CA: Sage, 2001), p. 190.

4. R. L. Simpson, "Vertical and Horizontal Communication in Formal Organizations," *Administrative Science Quarterly* (September 1959), pp. 188–196; A. G. Walker and J. W. Smither, "A Five-Year Study of Upward Feedback: What Managers Do with Their Results Matter," *Personnel Psychology* (Summer 1999), pp. 393–424; and J. W. Smither and A. G. Walker, "Are the Characteristics of Narrative Comments Related to Improvement in Multirater Feedback Ratings Over Time?" *Journal of Applied Psychology* 89, no. 3 (June 2004), pp. 575–581.

5. P. Dvorak, "How Understanding the 'Why' of Decisions Matters," *The Wall Street Journal* (March 19, 2007), p. B3.

6. T. Neeley and P. Leonardi, "Effective Managers Say the Same Thing Twice (or More)," *Harvard Business Review* (May 2011), pp. 38–39.

7. H. A. Richardson and S. G. Taylor, "Understanding Input Events: A Model of Employees' Responses to Requests for Their Input," *Academy of Management Review* 37 (2012), pp. 471–491.

8. J. Ewing, "Nokia: Bring on the Employee Rants," *BusinessWeek* (June 22, 2009), p. 50.

9. E. Nichols, "Hyper-Speed Managers," *HR Magazine* (April 2007), pp. 107–110.

10. See, for example, N. B. Kurland and L. H. Pelled, "Passing the Word: Toward a Model of Gossip and Power in the Workplace," *Academy of Management Review* (April 2000), pp. 428–438; and G. Michelson, A. van Iterson, and K. Waddington, "Gossip in Organizations: Contexts, Consequences, and Controversies," *Group and Organization Management* 35, no. 4 (2010), pp. 371–390.

11. G. Van Hoye and F. Lievens, "Tapping the Grapevine: A Closer Look at Word-of-Mouth as a Recruitment Source," *Journal of Applied Psychology* 94, no. 2 (2009), pp. 341–352.

12. R. L. Rosnow and G. A. Fine, *Rumor and Gossip: The Social Psychology of Hearsay* (New York: Elsevier, 1976).

13. J. K. Bosson, A. B. Johnson, K. Niederhoffer, and W. B. Swann Jr., "Interpersonal Chemistry Through Negativity: Bonding by Sharing Negative Attitudes About Others," *Personal Relationships* 13 (2006), pp. 135–150.

14. T. J. Grosser, V. Lopez-Kidwell, and G. Labianca, "A Social Network Analysis of Positive and Negative Gossip in Organizational Life," *Group and Organization Management* 35, no. 2 (2010), pp. 177–212.

15. M. Feinberg, R. Willer, J. Stellar, and D. Keltner, "The Virtues of Gossip: Reputational Information Sharing as Prosocial Behavior," *Journal of Personality and Social Psychology* 102 (2012), pp. 1015–1030.

16. L. Dulye, "Get Out of Your Office," *HR Magazine* (July 2006), pp. 99–101.

17. A. Bryant, "Getting Stuff Done: It's a Goal, and a Rating System," *The New York Times* (March 9, 2013), www.nytimes .com/2013/03/10/business/kris-duggan-of-badgeville-on-the-getting-stuff-done-index.html?pagewanted=all&_r=0.

18. M. Mihelich, "Bit by Bit: Stand-up Comedy as a Team-Building Exercise," *Workforce Management* (February 2013), p. 16.

19. E. Agnvall, "Meetings Go Virtual," *HR Magazine* (January 2009), pp. 74–77.

20. N. Bilton, "Disruptions: Life's Too Short for So Much E-mail," *The New York Times* (July 8, 2012), http://bits.blogs .nytimes.com/2012/07/08/life%E2%80%99s-too-short-for-so-much-e-mail/.

21. R. E. Silverman, "How to Be a Better Boss in 2013," *The Wall Street Journal* (January 2, 2013), pp. B1, B4.

22. B. Gates, "How I Work," *Fortune* (April 17, 2006), money .cnn.com.

23. "Executive Summary," *Messagemind* (2012), www.messagemind .com.

24. G. J. Mark, S. Voida, and A. V. Cardello, "'A Pace Not Dictated by Electrons': An Empirical Study of Work Without Email," *Proceedings of the SIGCHI Conference on Human Factors in Computing Systems* (2012), pp. 555–564.

25. B. Roberts, "Social Media Gets Strategic," *HR Magazine* (October 2012), pp. 30–38.

26. Gartner Inc. website, www.gartner.com/technology/topics/ social-media.jsp, downloaded May 29, 2013.

27. The Associated Press, "Number of Active Users at Facebook Over the Years," *Yahoo! News* (May 1, 2013), http://news .yahoo.com/number-active-users-facebook-over-230449748 .html.

28. "Facebook Quarterly Earnings Slides: Q1 2013," Facebook website, http://files.shareholder.com/downloads/AMDA-NJ5DZ/2462702744x0x659143/b4c0beda-da0a-4f8e-9735-9852ef08adb1/FB_Q113_InvestorDeck_FINAL.pdf.

29. L. Kwoh and M. Korn, "140 Characters of Risk: CEOs on Twitter," *The Wall Street Journal* (September 26, 2012), pp. B1, B8.

30. R. Barnett, "Ex-employee Is Sued over Keeping Work Twitter Account," *USA Today* (February 24, 2012), p. 4A.

31. L. S. Rashotte, "What Does That Smile Mean? The Meaning of Nonverbal Behaviors in Social Interaction," *Social Psychology Quarterly* (March 2002), pp. 92–102.

32. C. K. Goman, "5 Body Language Tips to Increase Your Curb Appeal," *Forbes* (March 4, 2013), www.forbes.com/sites/ carolkinseygoman/2013/03/14/5-body-language-tips-to-increase-your-curb-appeal/.

33. A. Metallinou, A. Katsamanis, and S. Narayanan, "Tracking Continuous Emotional Trends of Participants During Affective Dyadic Interactions using Body Language and Speech Information," *Image and Vision Computing* (February 2013), pp. 137–152.

34. J. Smith, "10 Nonverbal Cues That Convey Confidence at Work," *Forbes* (March 11, 2013), www.forbes.com/sites/ jacquelynsmith/2013/03/11/10-nonverbal-cues-that-convey-confidence-at-work/.

35. See R. L. Daft and R. H. Lengel, "Information Richness: A New Approach to Managerial Behavior and Organization Design," in B. M. Staw and L. L. Cummings (eds.), *Research in Organizational Behavior*, vol. 6 (Greenwich, CT: JAI Press, 1984), pp. 191–233; R. L. Daft and R. H.

Lengel, "Organizational Information Requirements, Media Richness, and Structural Design," *Managerial Science* (May 1986), pp. 554–572; R. E. Rice, "Task Analyzability, Use of New Media, and Effectiveness," *Organization Science* (November 1992), pp. 475–500; S. G. Straus and J. E. McGrath, "Does the Medium Matter? The Interaction of Task Type and Technology on Group Performance and Member Reaction," *Journal of Applied Psychology* (February 1994), pp. 87–97; L. K. Trevino, J. Webster, and E. W. Stein, "Making Connections: Complementary Influences on Communication Media Choices, Attitudes, and Use," *Organization Science* (March–April 2000), pp. 163–182; and N. Kock, "The Psychobiological Model: Towards a New Theory of Computer-Mediated Communication Based on Darwinian Evolution," *Organization Science* 15, no. 3 (May–June 2004), pp. 327–348.

36. E. Frauenheim, "Communicating for Engagement During Tough Times," *Workforce Management Online* (April 2010), www.workforce.com.

37. S. Shellenbarger, "Is This How You Really Talk?" *The Wall Street Journal* (April 24, 2013), pp. D1, D3.

38. D. Brady, "*!#?@ the E-mail. Can We Talk?" *BusinessWeek* (December 4, 2006), p. 109.

39. J. Sancton, "Re: Fwd: URGENT!," *Bloomberg Businessweek* (July 2–8, 2012), p. 69.

40. C. Byron, "Carrying Too Heavy a Load? The Communication and Miscommunication of Emotion by Email," *Academy of Management Review* 33, no. 2 (2008), pp. 309–327.

41. D. Goleman, "Flame First, Think Later: New Clues to E-mail Misbehavior," *The New York Times* (February 20, 2007), p. D5; and E. Krell, "The Unintended Word," *HR Magazine* (August 2006), pp. 50–54.

42. J. E. Hall, M. T. Kobata, and M. Denis, "Employees and E-mail Privacy Rights," *Workforce Management* (June 2010), p. 10.

43. T. Lytle, "Cybersleuthing," *HR Magazine* (January 2012), pp. 55–57.

44. E. Bernstein, "The Miscommunicators," *The Wall Street Journal* (July 3, 2012), pp. D1, D3.

45. B. Giamanco and K. Gregoire, "Tweet Me, Friend Me, Make Me Buy," *Harvard Business Review* (July–August 2012), pp. 88–93.

46. D. Zielinski, "Find Social Media's Value," *HR Magazine* (August 2012), pp. 53–55.

47. B. Roberts, "Social Media Gets Strategic," *HR Magazine* (October 2012), pp. 30–38.

48. T. Lytle, "Cybersleuthing," *HR Magazine* (January 2012), pp. 55–57.

49. J. Segal, "Widening Web of Social Media," *HR Magazine* (June 2012), pp. 117–118.

50. M. V. Rafter, "Falling from a Cloud," *Workforce Management* (February 2013), pp. 22–23.

51. "At Many Companies, Hunt for Leakers Expands Arsenal of Monitoring Tactics," *The Wall Street Journal* (September 11, 2006), pp. B1, B3; and B. J. Alge, G. A. Ballinger, S. Tangirala, and J. L. Oakley, "Information Privacy in Organizations: Empowering Creative and Extrarole Performance," *Journal of Applied Psychology* 91, No. 1 (2006), pp. 221–232.

52. R. E. Petty and P. Briñol, "Persuasion: From Single to Multiple to Metacognitive Processes," *Perspectives on Psychological Science* 3, no. 2 (2008), pp. 137–147; F. A. White, M. A. Charles, and

J. K. Nelson, "The Role of Persuasive Arguments in Changing Affirmative Action Attitudes and Expressed Behavior in Higher Education," *Journal of Applied Psychology* 93, no. 6 (2008), pp. 1271–1286.

53. B. T. Johnson, and A. H. Eagly, "Effects of Involvement on Persuasion: A Meta-Analysis," *Psychological Bulletin* 106, no. 2 (1989), pp. 290–314; and K. L. Blankenship and D. T. Wegener, "Opening the Mind to Close It: Considering a Message in Light of Important Values Increases Message Processing and Later Resistance to Change," *Journal of Personality and Social Psychology* 94, no. 2 (2008), pp. 196–213.

54. See, for example, Y. H. M. See, R. E. Petty, and L. R. Fabrigar, "Affective and Cognitive Meta-Bases of Attitudes: Unique Effects of Information Interest and Persuasion," *Journal of Personality and Social Psychology* 94, no. 6 (2008), pp. 938–955; M. S. Key, J. E. Edlund, B. J. Sagarin, and G. Y. Bizer, "Individual Differences in Susceptibility to Mindlessness," *Personality and Individual Differences* 46, no. 3 (2009), pp. 261–264 and M. Reinhard and M. Messner, "The Effects of Source Likeability and Need for Cognition on Advertising Effectiveness Under Explicit Persuasion," *Journal of Consumer Behavior* 8, no. 4 (2009), pp. 179–191.

55. M. Richtel, "Lost in E-mail, Tech Firms Face Self-Made Beast," *The New York Times* (June 14, 2008), pp. A1, A14; and M. Johnson, "Quelling Distraction," *HR Magazine* (August 2008), pp. 43–46.

56. W. R. Boswell and J. B. Olson-Buchanan, "The Use of Communication Technologies After Hours: The Role of Work-Attitudes and Work-Life Conflict," *Journal of Management* 33, no. 4 (2007), pp. 592–610.

57. P. Briñol, R. E. Petty, and J. Barden, "Happiness Versus Sadness as a Determinant of Thought Confidence in Persuasion: A Self-Validation Analysis," *Journal of Personality and Social Psychology* 93, no. 5 (2007), pp. 711–727.

58. R. C. Sinclair, S. E. Moore, M. M. Mark, A. S. Soldat, and C. A. Lavis, "Incidental Moods, Source Likeability, and Persuasion: Liking Motivates Message Elaboration in Happy People," *Cognition and Emotion* 24, no. 6 (2010), pp. 940–961; and V. Griskevicius, M. N. Shiota, and S. L. Neufeld, "Influence of Different Positive Emotions on Persuasion Processing: A Functional Evolutionary Approach," *Emotion* 10, no. 2 (2010), pp. 190–206.

59. J. Sandberg, "The Jargon Jumble: Kids Have 'Skeds,' Colleagues, 'Needs,' " *The Wall Street Journal* (October 24, 2006), http://online.wsj.com/article/SB116165746415401680 .html.

60. E. W. Morrison and F. J. Milliken, "Organizational Silence: A Barrier to Change and Development in a Pluralistic World," *Academy of Management Review* 25, no. 4 (2000), pp. 706–725; and B. E. Ashforth and V. Anand, "The Normalization of Corruption in Organizations," *Research in Organizational Behavior* 25 (2003), pp. 1–52.

61. F. J. Milliken, E. W. Morrison, and P. F. Hewlin, "An Exploratory Study of Employee Silence: Issues That Employees Don't Communicate Upward and Why," *Journal of Management Studies* 40, no. 6 (2003), pp. 1453–1476.

62. S. Tangirala and R. Ramunujam, "Employee Silence on Critical Work Issues: The Cross-Level Effects of Procedural Justice Climate," *Personnel Psychology* 61, no. 1 (2008), pp. 37–68; and F. Bowen and K. Blackmon, "Spirals of Silence: The Dynamic Effects of Diversity on Organizational Voice," *Journal of Management Studies* 40, no. 6 (2003), pp. 1393–1417.

63. B. R. Schlenker and M. R. Leary, "Social Anxiety and Self-Presentation: A Conceptualization and Model," *Psychological Bulletin* 92 (1982), pp. 641–669; and L. A. Withers, and L. L. Vernon, "To Err Is Human: Embarrassment, Attachment, and Communication Apprehension," *Personality and Individual Differences* 40, no. 1 (2006), pp. 99–110.

64. See, for instance, S. K. Opt and D. A. Loffredo, "Rethinking Communication Apprehension: A Myers-Briggs Perspective," *Journal of Psychology* (September 2000), pp. 556–570; and B. D. Blume, G. F. Dreher, and T. T. Baldwin, "Examining the Effects of Communication Apprehension within Assessment Centres," *Journal of Occupational and Organizational Psychology* 83, no. 3 (2010), pp. 663–671.

65. See, for example, J. A. Daly and J. C. McCroskey, "Occupational Desirability and Choice as a Function of Communication Apprehension," *Journal of Counseling Psychology* 22, no. 4 (1975), pp. 309–313; and T. L. Rodebaugh, "I Might Look OK, But I'm Still Doubtful, Anxious, and Avoidant: The Mixed Effects of Enhanced Video Feedback on Social Anxiety Symptoms," *Behaviour Research & Therapy* 42, no. 12 (December 2004), pp. 1435–1451.

66. B. M. Depaulo, D. A. Kashy, S. E. Kirkendol, M. M. Wyer, and J. A. Epstein, "Lying in Everyday Life," *Journal of Personality and Social Psychology* 70, No. 5 (1996), pp. 979–995; and K. B. Serota, T. R. Levine, and F. J. Boster, "The Prevalence of Lying in America: Three Studies of Self-Reported Lies," *Human Communication Research* 36, no. 1. (2010), pp. 2–25.

67. DePaulo, Kashy, Kirkendol, Wyer, and Epstein, "Lying in Everyday Life"; and C. E. Naguin, T. R. Kurtzberg, and L. Y. Belkin, "The Finer Points of Lying Online: E-Mail Versus Pen and Paper," *Journal of Applied Psychology* 95, no. 2 (2010), pp. 387–394.

68. A. Vrij, P. A. Granhag, and S. Porter, "Pitfalls and Opportunities in Nonverbal and Verbal Lie Detection," *Psychological Science in the Public Interest* 11, no. 3 (2010), pp. 89–121.

69. R. E. Axtell, *Gestures: The Do's and Taboos of Body Language Around the World* (New York: Wiley, 1991); Watson Wyatt Worldwide, "Effective Communication: A Leading Indicator of Financial Performance—2005/2006 Communication ROI Study," www.watsonwyatt.com/research/resrender .asp?id=w-868; and A. Markels, "Turning the Tide at P&G," *U.S. News & World Report* (October 30, 2006), p. 69.

70. See M. Munter, "Cross-Cultural Communication for Managers," *Business Horizons* (May–June 1993), pp. 75–76; and H. Ren and B. Gray, "Repairing Relationship Conflict: How Violation Types and Culture Influence the Effectiveness of Restoration Rituals," *Academy of Management Review* 34, no. 1 (2009), pp. 105–126.

71. See E. T. Hall, *Beyond Culture* (Garden City, NY: Anchor Press/Doubleday, 1976); W. L. Adair, "Integrative Sequences and Negotiation Outcome in Same- and Mixed-Culture Negotiations," *International Journal of Conflict Management* 14, no. 3–4 (2003), pp. 1359–1392; W. L. Adair and J. M. Brett, "The Negotiation Dance: Time, Culture, and Behavioral Sequences in Negotiation," *Organization Science* 16, no. 1 (2005), pp. 33–51; E. Giebels and P. J. Taylor, "Interaction

Patterns in Crisis Negotiations: Persuasive Arguments and Cultural Differences," *Journal of Applied Psychology* 94, no. 1 (2009), pp. 5–19; and M. G. Kittler, D. Rygl, and A. Mackinnon, "Beyond Culture or Beyond Control? Reviewing the Use of Hall's High-/Low-Context Concept," *International Journal of Cross-Cultural Management* 11, no. 1 (2011), pp. 63–82.

72. M. C. Hopson, T. Hart, and G. C. Bell, "Meeting in the Middle: Fred L. Casmir's Contributions to the Field of Intercultural Communication," *International Journal of Intercultural Relations* (November 2012), pp. 789–797.

CHAPTER 12

1. J. G. Geier, "A Trait Approach to the Study of Leadership in Small Groups," *Journal of Communication* (December 1967), pp. 316–323.

2. S. A. Kirkpatrick and E. A. Locke, "Leadership: Do Traits Matter?" *Academy of Management Executive* (May 1991), pp. 48–60; and S. J. Zaccaro, R. J. Foti, and D. A. Kenny, "Self-Monitoring and Trait-Based Variance in Leadership: An Investigation of Leader Flexibility Across Multiple Group Situations," *Journal of Applied Psychology* (April 1991), pp. 308–315.

3. See T. A. Judge, J. E. Bono, R. Ilies, and M. W. Gerhardt, "Personality and Leadership: A Qualitative and Quantitative Review," *Journal of Applied Psychology* (August 2002), pp. 765–780.

4. Ibid.

5. D. R. Ames and F. J. Flynn, "What Breaks a Leader: The Curvilinear Relation Between Assertiveness and Leadership," *Journal of Personality and Social Psychology* 92, no. 2 (2007), pp. 307–324.

6. K.-Y. Ng, S. Ang, and K. Chan, "Personality and Leader Effectiveness: A Moderated Mediation Model of Leadership Self-Efficacy, Job Demands, and Job Autonomy," *Journal of Applied Psychology* 93, no. 4 (2008), pp. 733–743.

7. This section is based on J. M. George, "Emotions and Leadership: The Role of Emotional Intelligence," *Human Relations* (August 2000), pp. 1027–1055; C.-S. Wong and K. S. Law, "The Effects of Leader and Follower Emotional Intelligence on Performance and Attitude: An Exploratory Study," *Leadership Quarterly* (June 2002), pp. 243–274; and J. Antonakis, N. M. Ashkanasy, and M. T. Dasborough, "Does Leadership Need Emotional Intelligence?" *Leadership Quarterly* 20 (2009), pp. 247–261.

8. R. H. Humphrey, J. M. Pollack, and T. H. Hawver, "Leading with Emotional Labor," *Journal of Managerial Psychology* 23 (2008), pp. 151–168.

9. F. Walter, M. S. Cole, and R. H. Humphrey, "Emotional Intelligence: Sine Qua Non of Leadership or Folderol?" *Academy of Management Perspectives* (February 2011), pp. 45–59.

10. S. Côté, P. N. Lopez, P. Salovey, and C. T. H. Miners, "Emotional Intelligence and Leadership Emergence in Small Groups," *Leadership Quarterly* 21 (2010), pp. 496–508.

11. N. Ensari, R. E. Riggio, J. Christian, and G. Carslaw, "Who Emerges as a Leader? Meta-Analyses of Individual Differences as Predictors of Leadership Emergence,"

Personality and Individual Differences (September 2011), pp. 532–536.

12. R. M. Stogdill and A. E. Coons (eds.), *Leader Behavior: Its Description and Measurement,* Research Monograph no. 88 (Columbus: Ohio State University, Bureau of Business Research, 1951). This research is updated in C. A. Schriesheim, C. C. Cogliser, and L. L. Neider, "Is It 'Trustworthy'? A Multiple-Levels-of-Analysis Reexamination of an Ohio State Leadership Study, with Implications for Future Research," *Leadership Quarterly* (Summer 1995), pp. 111–145; and T. A. Judge, R. F. Piccolo, and R. Ilies, "The Forgotten Ones? The Validity of Consideration and Initiating Structure in Leadership Research," *Journal of Applied Psychology* (February 2004), pp. 36–51.

13. D. Akst, "The Rewards of Recognizing a Job Well Done," *The Wall Street Journal* (January 31, 2007), p. D9.

14. Judge, Piccolo, and Ilies, "The Forgotten Ones?"

15. M. Javidan, P. W. Dorfman, M. S. de Luque, and R. J. House, "In the Eye of the Beholder: Cross Cultural Lessons in Leadership from Project GLOBE," *Academy of Management Perspectives* (February 2006), pp. 67–90.

16. F. E. Fiedler, *A Theory of Leadership Effectiveness* (New York: McGraw-Hill, 1967).

17. S. Shiflett, "Is There a Problem with the LPC Score in LEADER MATCH?" *Personnel Psychology* (Winter 1981), pp. 765–769.

18. F. E. Fiedler, M. M. Chemers, and L. Mahar, *Improving Leadership Effectiveness: The Leader Match Concept* (New York: Wiley, 1977).

19. Cited in R. J. House and R. N. Aditya, "The Social Scientific Study of Leadership," *Journal of Management* 23, no. 3 (1997), p. 422.

20. L. H. Peters, D. D. Hartke, and J. T. Pohlmann, "Fiedler's Contingency Theory of Leadership: An Application of the Meta-Analysis Procedures of Schmidt and Hunter," *Psychological Bulletin* (March 1985), pp. 274–285; C. A. Schriesheim, B. J. Tepper, and L. A. Tetrault, "Least Preferred Coworker Score, Situational Control, and Leadership Effectiveness: A Meta-Analysis of Contingency Model Performance Predictions," *Journal of Applied Psychology* (August 1994), pp. 561–573; and R. Ayman, M. M. Chemers, and F. Fiedler, "The Contingency Model of Leadership Effectiveness: Its Levels of Analysis," *Leadership Quarterly* (Summer 1995), pp. 147–167.

21. House and Aditya, "The Social Scientific Study of Leadership."

22. See, for instance, R. W. Rice, "Psychometric Properties of the Esteem for the Least Preferred Coworker (LPC) Scale," *Academy of Management Review* (January 1978), pp. 106–118; C. A. Schriesheim, B. D. Bannister, and W. H. Money, "Psychometric Properties of the LPC Scale: An Extension of Rice's Review," *Academy of Management Review* (April 1979), pp. 287–290; and J. K. Kennedy, J. M. Houston, M. A. Korgaard, and D. D. Gallo, "Construct Space of the Least Preferred Coworker (LPC) Scale," *Educational & Psychological Measurement* (Fall 1987), pp. 807–814.

23. See E. H. Schein, *Organizational Psychology,* 3rd ed. (Upper Saddle River, NJ: Prentice Hall, 1980), pp. 116–117; and B. Kabanoff, "A Critique of Leader Match and Its Implications for Leadership Research," *Personnel Psychology* (Winter 1981), pp. 749–764.

24. See, for instance, Ibid., pp. 67–84; C. L. Graeff, "Evolution of Situational Leadership Theory: A Critical Review," *Leadership Quarterly* 8, no. 2 (1997), pp. 153–170; and R. P. Vecchio and K. J. Boatwright, "Preferences for Idealized Styles of Supervision," *Leadership Quarterly* (August 2002), pp. 327–342.

25. R. J. House, "A Path-Goal Theory of Leader Effectiveness," *Administrative Science Quarterly* (September 1971), pp. 321–338; R. J. House and T. R. Mitchell, "Path-Goal Theory of Leadership," *Journal of Contemporary Business* (Autumn 1974), pp. 81–97; and R. J. House, "Path-Goal Theory of Leadership: Lessons, Legacy, and a Reformulated Theory," *Leadership Quarterly* (Fall 1996), pp. 323–352.

26. A. E. Colbert and L. A. Witt, "The Role of Goal-Focused Leadership in Enabling the Expression of Conscientiousness," *Journal of Applied Psychology* 94, no. 3 (2009), pp. 790–796.

27. S. J. Perry, L. A. Witt, L. M. Penney, and L. Atwater, "The Downside of Goal-Focused Leadership: The Role of Personality in Subordinate Exhaustion," *Journal of Applied Psychology* 95, no. 6 (2010), pp. 1145–1153.

28. See V. H. Vroom and P. W. Yetton, *Leadership and Decision-Making* (Pittsburgh: University of Pittsburgh Press, 1973); and V. H. Vroom and A. G. Jago, "The Role of the Situation in Leadership," *American Psychologist* (January 2007), pp. 17–24.

29. W. Bennis, "The Challenges of Leadership in the Modern World," *American Psychologist* (January 2007), pp. 2–5.

30. X. Zhou and C. A. Schriesheim, "Supervisor–Subordinate Convergence in Descriptions of Leader–Member Exchange (LMX) Quality: Review and Testable Propositions." *Leadership Quarterly* 20, no. 6 (2009), pp. 920–932; G. B. Graen and M. Uhl-Bien, "Relationship-Based Approach to Leadership: Development of Leader–Member Exchange (LMX) Theory of Leadership Over 25 Years: Applying a Multi-Domain Perspective," *Leadership Quarterly* (Summer 1995), pp. 219–247; R. C. Liden, R. T. Sparrowe, and S. J. Wayne, "Leader–Member Exchange Theory: The Past and Potential for the Future," in G. R. Ferris (ed.), *Research in Personnel and Human Resource Management,* vol. 15 (Greenwich, CT: JAI Press, 1997), pp. 47–119; and C. A. Schriesheim, S. L. Castro, X. Zhou, and F. J. Yammarino, "The Folly of Theorizing 'A' but Testing 'B': A Selective Level-of-Analysis Review of the Field and a Detailed Leader–Member Exchange Illustration," *Leadership Quarterly* (Winter 2001), pp. 515–551.

31. B. Erdogan and T. N. Bauer, "Differentiated Leader–Member Exchanges: The Buffering Role of Justice Climate," *Journal of Applied Psychology* 95, no. 6 (2010), pp. 1104–1120; R. C. Liden, S. J. Wayne, and D. Stilwell, "A Longitudinal Study of the Early Development of Leader–Member Exchanges," *Journal of Applied Psychology* (August 1993), pp. 662–674; S. J. Wayne, L. M. Shore, W. H. Bommer, and L. E. Tetrick, "The Role of Fair Treatment and Rewards in Perceptions of Organizational Support and Leader–Member Exchange," *Journal of Applied Psychology* 87, no. 3 (June 2002), pp. 590–598; and S. S. Masterson, K. Lewis, and B. M. Goldman, "Integrating Justice and Social Exchange: The Differing Effects of Fair Procedures and Treatment on Work Relationships," *Academy of Management Journal* 43, no. 4 (August 2000), pp. 738–748.

32. D. Duchon, S. G. Green, and T. D. Taber, "Vertical Dyad Linkage: A Longitudinal Assessment of Antecedents, Measures, and Consequences," *Journal of Applied Psychology* (February 1986), pp. 56–60; Liden, Wayne, and Stilwell, "A Longitudinal Study on the Early Development of Leader–Member Exchanges"; and M. Uhl-Bien, "Relationship Development as a Key Ingredient for Leadership Development," in S. E. Murphy and R. E. Riggio (eds.), *Future of Leadership Development* (Mahwah, NJ: Lawrence Erlbaum, 2003) pp. 129–147.

33. R. Vecchio and D. M. Brazil, "Leadership and Sex-Similarity: A Comparison in a Military Setting," *Personnel Psychology* 60 (2007), pp. 303–335.

34. See, for instance, C. R. Gerstner and D. V. Day, "Meta-Analytic Review of Leader–Member Exchange Theory: Correlates and Construct Issues," *Journal of Applied Psychology* (December 1997), pp. 827–844; R. Ilies, J. D. Nahrgang, and F. P. Morgeson, "Leader–Member Exchange and Citizenship Behaviors: A Meta-Analysis," *Journal of Applied Psychology* 92, no. 1 (2007), pp. 269–277; and Z. Chen, W. Lam, and J. A. Zhong, "Leader–Member Exchange and Member Performance: A New Look at Individual-Level Negative Feedback-Seeking Behavior and Team-Level Empowerment Culture," *Journal of Applied Psychology* 92, no. 1 (2007), pp. 202–212.

35. R. Eisenberger, G. Karagonlar, F. Stinglhamber, P. Neves, T. E. Becker, M. G. Gonzalez-Morales, and M. Steiger-Mueller, "Leader-Member Exchange and Affective Organizational Commitment: The Contribution of Supervisor's Organizational Embodiment," *Journal of Applied Psychology* 95, no. 6 (2010), pp. 1085–1103.

36. B. Erdogan and T. N. Bauer, "Differentiated Leader-Member Exchanges: The Buffering Role of Justice Climate," *Journal of Applied Psychology* 95, no. 6 (2010), pp. 1104–1120.

37. M. Ozer, "Personal and Task-Related Moderators of Leader-Member Exchange Among Software Developers," *Journal of Applied Psychology* 93, no. 5 (2008), pp. 1174–1182.

38. M. Weber, *The Theory of Social and Economic Organization,* A. M. Henderson and T. Parsons (trans.) (New York: The Free Press, 1947).

39. J. A. Conger and R. N. Kanungo, "Behavioral Dimensions of Charismatic Leadership," in J. A. Conger, R. N. Kanungo, and Associates (eds.), *Charismatic Leadership* (San Francisco: Jossey-Bass, 1988), p. 79; and A.-K. Samnani and P. Singh, "When Leaders Victimize: The Role of Charismatic Leaders in Facilitating Group Pressures," *Leadership Quarterly* (pp. 189–202).

40. J. A. Conger and R. N. Kanungo, *Charismatic Leadership in Organizations* (Thousand Oaks, CA: Sage, 1998); and R. Awamleh and W. L. Gardner, "Perceptions of Leader Charisma and Effectiveness: The Effects of Vision Content, Delivery, and Organizational Performance," *Leadership Quarterly* (Fall 1999), pp. 345–373.

41. R. J. House and J. M. Howell, "Personality and Charismatic Leadership," *Leadership Quarterly* 3 (1992), pp. 81–108; D. N. Den Hartog and P. L. Koopman, "Leadership in Organizations," in N. Anderson and D. S. Ones (eds.), *Handbook of Industrial, Work and Organizational Psychology,* vol. 2 (Thousand Oaks, CA: Sage, 2002), pp. 166–187.

42. P. Balkundi, M. Kilduff, and D. A. Harrison, "Centrality and Charisma: Comparing How Leader Networks and Attributions Affect Team Performance," *Journal of Applied Psychology* 96 (2012), pp. 1209–1222.

43. D. N. Den Hartog, A. H. B. De Hoogh, and A. E. Keegan, "The Interactive Effects of Belongingness and Charisma on Helping and Compliance," *Journal of Applied Psychology* 92, no. 4 (2007), pp. 1131–1139.

44. A. Erez, V. F. Misangyi, D. E. Johnson, M. A. LePine, and K. C. Halverson, "Stirring the Hearts of Followers: Charismatic Leadership as the Transferal of Affect," *Journal of Applied Psychology* 93, no. 3 (2008), pp. 602–615. For reviews on the role of vision in leadership, see S. J. Zaccaro, "Visionary and Inspirational Models of Executive Leadership: Empirical Review and Evaluation," in S. J. Zaccaro (ed.), *The Nature of Executive Leadership: A Conceptual and Empirical Analysis of Success* (Washington, DC: American Psychological Association, 2001), pp. 259–278; and M. Hauser and R. J. House, "Lead Through Vision and Values," in E. A. Locke (ed.), *Handbook of Principles of Organizational Behavior* (Malden, MA: Blackwell, 2004), pp. 257–273.

45. A. H. B. de Hoogh, D. N. Den Hartog, P. L. Koopman, H. Thierry, P. T. van den Berg, and J. G. van der Weide, "Charismatic Leadership, Environmental Dynamism, and Performance," *European Journal of Work & Organizational Psychology* (December 2004), pp. 447–471; S. Harvey, M. Martin, and D. Stout, "Instructor's Transformational Leadership: University Student Attitudes and Ratings," *Psychological Reports* (April 2003), pp. 395–402; and D. A. Waldman, M. Javidan, and P. Varella, "Charismatic Leadership at the Strategic Level: A New Application of Upper Echelons Theory," *Leadership Quarterly* (June 2004), pp. 355–380.

46. J. C. Pastor, M. Mayo, and B. Shamir, "Adding Fuel to Fire: The Impact of Followers' Arousal on Ratings of Charisma," *Journal of Applied Psychology* 92, no. 6 (2007), pp. 1584–1596.

47. A. H. B. De Hoogh and D. N. Den Hartog, "Neuroticism and Locus of Control as Moderators of the Relationships of Charismatic and Autocratic Leadership with Burnout," *Journal of Applied Psychology* 94, no. 4 (2009), pp. 1058–1067.

48. F. Cohen, S. Solomon, M. Maxfield, T. Pyszczynski, and J. Greenberg, "Fatal Attraction: The Effects of Mortality Salience on Evaluations of Charismatic, Task-Oriented, and Relationship-Oriented Leaders," *Psychological Sciences* (December 2004), pp. 846–851; and M. G. Ehrhart and K. J. Klein, "Predicting Followers' Preferences for Charismatic Leadership: The Influence of Follower Values and Personality," *Leadership Quarterly* (Summer 2001), pp. 153–179.

49. H. L. Tosi, V. Misangyi, A. Fanelli, D. A. Waldman, and F. J. Yammarino, "CEO Charisma, Compensation, and Firm Performance," *Leadership Quarterly* (June 2004), pp. 405–420.

50. See, for instance, R. Khurana, *Searching for a Corporate Savior: The Irrational Quest for Charismatic CEOs* (Princeton, NJ: Princeton University Press, 2002); and J. A. Raelin, "The Myth of Charismatic Leaders," *Training & Development* (March 2003), pp. 47–54.

51. B. M. Galvin, D. A. Waldman, and P. Balthazard, "Visionary Communication Qualities as Mediators of the Relationship between Narcissism and Attributions of Leader Charisma," *Personnel Psychology* 63, no. 3 (2010), pp. 509–537.

52. See, for instance, B. M. Bass, B. J. Avolio, D. I. Jung, and Y. Berson, "Predicting Unit Performance by Assessing Transformational and Transactional Leadership," *Journal of Applied Psychology* (April 2003), pp. 207–218; and T. A. Judge and R. F. Piccolo, "Transformational and Transactional Leadership: A Meta-Analytic Test of Their Relative Validity," *Journal of Applied Psychology* (October 2004), pp. 755–768.

53. A. M. Grant, "Leading with Meaning: Beneficiary Contact, Prosocial Impact, and the Performance Effects of Transformational Leadership," *Academy of Management Journal* 55 (2012), pp. 458–476.

54. B. M. Bass, "Leadership: Good, Better, Best," *Organizational Dynamics* (Winter 1985), pp. 26–40; and J. Seltzer and B. M. Bass, "Transformational Leadership: Beyond Initiation and Consideration," *Journal of Management* (December 1990), pp. 693–703.

55. T. R. Hinkin and C. A. Schriescheim, "An Examination of 'Nonleadership': From Laissez-Faire Leadership to Leader Reward Omission and Punishment Omission," *Journal of Applied Psychology* 93, no. 6 (2008), pp. 1234–1248.

56. S. J. Shin and J. Zhou, "Transformational Leadership, Conservation, and Creativity: Evidence from Korea," *Academy of Management Journal* (December 2003), pp. 703–714; V. J. García-Morales, F. J. Lloréns-Montes, and A. J. Verdú-Jover, "The Effects of Transformational Leadership on Organizational Performance Through Knowledge and Innovation," *British Journal of Management* 19, no. 4 (2008), pp. 299–313; and S. A. Eisenbeiss, D. van Knippenberg, and S. Boerner, "Transformational Leadership and Team Innovation: Integrating Team Climate Principles," *Journal of Applied Psychology* 93, no. 6 (2008), pp. 1438–1446.

57. Y. Ling, Z. Simsek, M. H. Lubatkin, and J. F. Veiga, "Transformational Leadership's Role in Promoting Corporate Entrepreneurship: Examining the CEO-TMT Interface," *Academy of Management Journal* 51, no. 3 (2008), pp. 557–576.

58. X. Zhang and K. M. Bartol, "Linking Empowering Leadership and Employee Creativity: The Influence of Psychological Empowerment, Intrinsic Motivation, and Creative Process Engagement," *Academy of Management Journal* 53, no. 1 (2010), pp. 107–128.

59. D. Liu, H. Liao, and R. Loi, "The Dark Side of Leadership: A Three-Level Investigation of the Cascading Effect of Abusive Supervision on Employee Creativity," *Academy of Management Journal* 55 (2012), pp. 1187–1212.

60. A. E. Colbert, A. E. Kristof-Brown, B. H. Bradley, and M. R. Barrick, "CEO Transformational Leadership: The Role of Goal Importance Congruence in Top Management Teams," *Academy of Management Journal* 51, no. 1 (2008), pp. 81–96.

61. D. Zohar and O. Tenne-Gazit, "Transformational Leadership and Group Interaction as Climate Antecedents: A Social Network Analysis," *Journal of Applied Psychology* 93, no. 4 (2008), pp. 744–757.

62. F. O. Walumbwa, B. J. Avolio, and W. Zhu, "How Transformational Leadership Weaves Its Influence on Individual Job Performance: The Role of Identification and Efficacy Beliefs," *Personnel Psychology* 61, no. 4 (2008), pp. 793–825.

63. J. E. Bono and T. A. Judge, "Self-Concordance at Work: Toward Understanding the Motivational Effects of Transformational

Leaders," *Academy of Management Journal* (October 2003), pp. 554–571; Y. Berson and B. J. Avolio, "Transformational Leadership and the Dissemination of Organizational Goals: A Case Study of a Telecommunication Firm," *Leadership Quarterly* (October 2004), pp. 625–646; and J. Schaubroeck, S. S. K. Lam, and S. E. Cha, "Embracing Transformational Leadership: Team Values and the Impact of Leader Behavior on Team Performance," *Journal of Applied Psychology* 92, no. 4 (2007), pp. 1020–1030.

64. J. R. Baum, E. A. Locke, and S. A. Kirkpatrick, "A Longitudinal Study of the Relation of Vision and Vision Communication to Venture Growth in Entrepreneurial Firms," *Journal of Applied Psychology* (February 2000), pp. 43–54.

65. R. T. Keller, "Transformational Leadership, Initiating Structure, and Substitutes for Leadership: A Longitudinal Study of Research and Development Project Team Performance," *Journal of Applied Psychology* 91, no. 1 (2006), pp. 202–210.

66. Y. Gong, J. Huang, and J. Farh, "Employee Learning Orientation, Transformational Leadership, and Employee Creativity: The Mediating Role of Employee Creative Self-Efficacy," *Academy of Management Journal* 52, no. 4 (2009), pp. 765–778.

67. G. Wang, I. Oh, S. H. Courtright, and A. E. Colbert, "Transformational Leadership and Performance Across Criteria and Levels: A Meta-Analytic Review of 25 Years of Research," *Group and Organization Management* 36, no. 2 (2011), pp. 223–270.

68. Y. Ling, Z. Simsek, M. H. Lubatkin, and J. F. Veiga, "The Impact of Transformational CEOs on the Performance of Small- to Medium-Sized Firms: Does Organizational Context Matter?" *Journal of Applied Psychology* 93, no. 4 (2008), pp. 923–934.

69. Schaubroeck, Lam, and Cha, "Embracing Transformational Leadership."

70. B. L. Kirkman, G. Chen, J. Farh, Z. X. Chen, and K. B. Lowe, "Individual Power Distance Orientation and Follower Reactions to Transformational Leaders: A Cross-Level, Cross-Cultural Examination," *Academy of Management Journal* 52, no. 4 (2009), pp. 744–764.

71. J. Liu, O. Siu, and K. Shi, "Transformational Leadership and Employee Well-Being: The Mediating Role of Trust in the Leader and Self-Efficacy," *Applied Psychology: An International Review* 59, no. 3 (2010), pp. 454–479.

72. X. Wang and J. M. Howell, "Exploring the Dual-Level Effects of Transformational Leadership on Followers," *Journal of Applied Psychology* 95, no. 6 (2010), pp. 1134–1144.

73. H. Hetland, G. M. Sandal, and T. B. Johnsen, "Burnout in the Information Technology Sector: Does Leadership Matter?" *European Journal of Work and Organizational Psychology* 16, no. 1 (2007), pp. 58–75; and K. B. Lowe, K. G. Kroeck, and N. Sivasubramaniam, "Effectiveness Correlates of Transformational and Transactional Leadership: A Meta-Analytic Review of the MLQ Literature," *Leadership Quarterly* (Fall 1996), pp. 385–425.

74. R. J. House, M. Javidan, P. Hanges, and P. Dorfman, "Understanding Cultures and Implicit Leadership Theories Across the Globe: An Introduction to Project GLOBE," *Journal of World Business* (Spring 2002), pp. 3–10.

75. D. E. Carl and M. Javidan, "Universality of Charismatic Leadership: A Multi-Nation Study," paper presented at the National Academy of Management Conference, Washington, DC (August 2001), p. 29.

76. See B. J. Avolio, W. L. Gardner, F. O. Walumbwa, F. Luthans, and D. R. May, "Unlocking the Mask: A Look at the Process by Which Authentic Leaders Impact Follower Attitudes and Behaviors," *Leadership Quarterly* (December 2004), pp. 801–823; W. L. Gardner and J. R. Schermerhorn Jr., "Performance Gains Through Positive Organizational Behavior and Authentic Leadership," *Organizational Dynamics* (August 2004), pp. 270–281; and M. M. Novicevic, M. G. Harvey, M. R. Buckley, J. A. Brown-Radford, and R. Evans, "Authentic Leadership: A Historical Perspective," *Journal of Leadership and Organizational Behavior* 13, no. 1 (2006), pp. 64–76.

77. C. Tan, "CEO Pinching Penney in a Slowing Economy," *The Wall Street Journal* (January 31, 2008), pp. 1–2; and A. Carter, "Lighting a Fire Under Campbell," *BusinessWeek* (December 4, 2006), pp. 96–101.

78. K. M. Hmieleski, M. S. Cole, and R. A. Baron, "Shared Authentic Leadership and New Venture Performance," *Journal of Management* (September 2012), pp. 1476–1499.

79. R. Ilies, F. P. Morgeson, and J. D. Nahrgang, "Authentic Leadership and Eudaemonic Well-Being: Understanding Leader-follower Outcomes," *Leadership Quarterly* 16 (2005), pp. 373–394; B. Levin, "Raj Rajaratnam Did Not Appreciate Rajat Gupta's Attempt to Leave The Goldman Board, Join 'The Billionaire circle,'" *NetNet with John Carney* (March 14, 2011), downloaded July 26, 2011, from www.cnbc.com/.

80. This section is based on E. P. Hollander, "Ethical Challenges in the Leader–Follower Relationship," *Business Ethics Quarterly* (January 1995), pp. 55–65; J. C. Rost, "Leadership: A Discussion About Ethics," *Business Ethics Quarterly* (January 1995), pp. 129–142; L. K. Treviño, M. Brown, and L. P. Hartman, "A Qualitative Investigation of Perceived Executive Ethical Leadership: Perceptions from Inside and Outside the Executive Suite," *Human Relations* (January 2003), pp. 5–37; and R. M. Fulmer, "The Challenge of Ethical Leadership," *Organizational Dynamics* 33, no. 3 (2004), pp. 307–317.

81. J. Stouten, M. van Dijke, and D. De Cremer, "Ethical Leadership: An Overview and Future Perspectives," *Journal of Personnel Psychology* 11 (2012), pp. 1–6.

82. J. M. Schaubroeck, S. T. Hannah, B. J. Avolio, S. W. J. Kozlowski, et al., "Embedding Ethical Leadership within and Across Organization Levels," *Academy of Management Journal* 55 (2012), pp. 1053–1078.

83. D. van Knippenberg, D. De Cremer, and B. van Knippenberg, "Leadership and Fairness: The State of the Art," *European Journal of Work and Organizational Psychology* 16, no. 2 (2007), pp. 113–140.

84. B. P. Owens and D. R. Hekman, "Modeling How to Grow: An Inductive Examination of Humble Leader Behaviors, Contingencies, and Outcomes," *Academy of Management Journal* 55 (2012), pp. 787–818.

85. K. M. Kacmar, D. G. Bachrach, K. J. Harris, and S. Zivnuska, "Fostering Good Citizenship Through Ethical Leadership: Exploring the Moderating Role of Gender and Organizational Politics," *Journal of Applied Psychology*, 96, no. 3 (May 2011), pp. 633–642; and

F. O. Walumbwa and J. Schaubroeck, "Leader Personality Traits and Employee Voice Behavior: Mediating Roles of Ethical Leadership and Work Group Psychological Safety," *Journal of Applied Psychology* 94, no. 5 (2009), pp. 1275–1286.

86. D. M. Mayer, K. Aquino, R. L. Greenbaum, and M. Kuenzi, "Who Displays Ethical Leadership, and Why Does It Matter? An Examination of Antecedents and Consequences of Ethical Leadership," *Academy of Management Journal* 55 (2012), pp. 151–171.

87. S. A. Eisenbeiss and S. R. Giessner, "The Emergence and Maintenance of Ethical Leadership in Organizations," *Journal of Personnel Psychology* 11 (2012), pp. 7–19.

88. J. Antonakis, M. Fenley, and S. Liechti, "Learning Charisma," *Harvard Business Review* (June 2012), pp. 127–130.

89. M. E. Brown and L. K. Treviño, "Socialized Charismatic Leadership, Values Congruence, and Deviance in Work Groups," *Journal of Applied Psychology* 91, no. 4 (2006), pp. 954–962.

90. M. E. Brown and L. K. Treviño, "Leader-Follower Values Congruence: Are Socialized Charismatic Leaders Better Able to Achieve It?" *Journal of Applied Psychology* 94, no. 2 (2009), pp. 478–490.

91. D. van Dierendonck, "Servant Leadership: A Review and Synthesis," *Journal of Management* 37, no. 4 (2011), pp. 1228–1261.

92. S. J. Peterson, F. M. Galvin, and D. Lange, "CEO Servant Leadership: Exploring Executive Characteristics and Firm Performance," *Personnel Psychology* 65 (2012), pp. 565–596.

93. F. Walumbwa, C. A. Hartnell, and A. Oke, "Servant Leadership, Procedural Justice Climate, Service Climate, Employee Attitudes, and Organizational Citizenship Behavior: A Cross-Level Investigation," *Journal of Applied Psychology* 95, no. 3 (2010), pp. 517–529.

94. D. De Cremer, D. M. Mayer, M. van Dijke, B. C. Schouten, and M. Bardes, "When Does Self-Sacrificial Leadership Motivate Prosocial Behavior? It Depends on Followers' Prevention Focus," *Journal of Applied Psychology* 2009, no. 4 (2009), pp. 887–899.

95. J. Hu and R. C. Liden, "Antecedents of Team Potency and Team Effectiveness: An Examination of Goal and Process Clarity and Servant Leadership," *Journal of Applied Psychology*, 96, no. 4 (July 2011), pp. 851–862.

96. M. J. Neubert, K. M. Kacmar, D. S. Carlson, L. B. Chonko, and J. A. Roberts, "Regulatory Focus as a Mediator of the Influence of Initiating Structure and Servant Leadership on Employee Behavior," *Journal of Applied Psychology* 93, no. 6 (2008), pp. 1220–1233.

97. T. Menon, J. Sim, J. Ho-Ying Fu, C. Chiu, and Y. Hong, "Blazing the Trail Versus Trailing the Group: Culture and Perceptions of the Leader's Position," *Organizational Behavior and Human Decision Processes* 113, no. 1 (2010), pp. 51–61.

98. D. M. Rousseau, S. B. Sitkin, R. S. Burt, and C. Camerer, "Not So Different After All: A Cross-Discipline View of Trust," *Academy of Management Review* (July 1998), pp. 393–404; and J. A. Simpson, "Psychological Foundations of Trust," *Current Directions in Psychological Science* 16, no. 5 (2007), pp. 264–268.

99. See, for instance, K. T. Dirks and D. L. Ferrin, "Trust in Leadership: Meta-Analytic Findings and Implications for Research and Practice," *Journal of Applied Psychology* 87, no. 4, (2002), pp. 611–628; D. I. Jung and B. J. Avolio, "Opening the Black Box: An Experimental Investigation of the Mediating Effects of Trust and Value Congruence on Transformational and Transactional Leadership," *Journal of Organizational Behavior* (December 2000), pp. 949–964; and A. Zacharatos, J. Barling, and R. D. Iverson, "High-Performance Work Systems and Occupational Safety," *Journal of Applied Psychology* (January 2005), pp. 77–93.

100. Based on L. T. Hosmer, "Trust: The Connecting Link Between Organizational Theory and Philosophical Ethics," *Academy of Management Review* (April 1995), p. 393; R. C. Mayer, J. H. Davis, and F. D. Schoorman, "An Integrative Model of Organizational Trust," *Academy of Management Review* (July 1995), pp. 709–734; and F. D. Schoorman, R. C. Mayer, and J. H. Davis, "An Integrative Model of Organizational Trust: Past, Present, and Future," *Academy of Management Review* 32, no. 2 (2007), pp. 344–354.

101. J. Schaubroeck, S. S. K. Lam, and A. C. Peng, "Cognition-Based and Affect-Based Trust as Mediators of Leader Behavior Influences on Team Performance." *Journal of Applied Psychology,* 96, no. 4 (July 2011), pp. 863–871.

102. Mayer, Davis, and Schoorman, "An Integrative Model of Organizational Trust"; and J. A. Colquitt, B. A. Scott, and J. A. LePine, "Trust, Trustworthiness, and Trust Propensity: A Meta-Analytic Test of Their Unique Relationships with Risk Taking and Job Performance," *Journal of Applied Psychology* 92, no. 4 (2007), pp. 909–927.

103. Cited in D. Jones, "Do You Trust Your CEO?" *USA Today* (February 12, 2003), p. 7B.

104. R. C. Mayer and J. H. Davis, "The Effect of the Performance Appraisal System on Trust for Management: A Quasi-Experiment," *Journal of Applied Psychology* 84, no. 1 (1999), pp. 123–136; and R. C. Mayer and M. B. Gavin, "Trust in Management and Performance: Who Minds the Shop While the Employees Watch the Boss?" *Academy of Management Journal* 38 (2005), pp. 874–888.

105. J. A. Simpson, "Foundations of Interpersonal Trust," in A. W. Kruglanski and E. T. Higgins (eds.), *Social Psychology: Handbook of Basic Principles,* 2nd ed. (New York: Guilford, 2007), pp. 587–607.

106. Ibid.

107. B. Groysberg and M. Slind, "Leadership Is a Conversation," *Harvard Business Review* (June 2012), pp. 76–84.

108. H. Zhao, S. J. Wayne, B. C. Glibkowski, and J. Bravo, "The Impact of Psychological Contract Breach on Work-Related Outcomes: A Meta-Analysis," *Personnel Psychology* 60 (2007), pp. 647–680.

109. D. L. Shapiro, A. D. Boss, S. Salas, S. Tangirala, and M. A. Von Glinow, "When Are Transgressing *Leaders* Punitively Judged? An Empirical Test," *Journal of Applied Psychology* 96, no. 2 (2011), pp. 412–422.

110. D. L. Ferrin, P. H. Kim, C. D. Cooper, and K. T. Dirks, "Silence Speaks Volumes: The Effectiveness of Reticence in Comparison to Apology and Denial for Responding to Integrity- and Competence-Based Trust Violations," *Journal of Applied Psychology* 92, no. 4 (2007), pp. 893–908.

111. M. E. Schweitzer, J. C. Hershey, and E. T. Bradlow, "Promises and Lies: Restoring Violated Trust," *Organizational Behavior and Human Decision Processes* 101, no. 1 (2006), pp. 1–19.

112. J. R. Detert and E. R. Burris, "Leadership Behavior and Employee Voice: Is the Door Really Open?" *Academy of Management Journal* 50, no. 4 (2007), pp. 869–884.

113. Colquitt, Scott, and LePine, "Trust, Trustworthiness, and Trust Propensity."

114. See, for example, M. Murray, *Beyond the Myths and Magic of Mentoring: How to Facilitate an Effective Mentoring Process*, rev. ed. (New York: Wiley, 2001); K. E. Kram, "Phases of the Mentor Relationship," *Academy of Management Journal* (December 1983), pp. 608–625; R. A. Noe, "An Investigation of the Determinants of Successful Assigned Mentoring Relationships," *Personnel Psychology* (Fall 1988), pp. 559–580; and L. Eby, M. Buits, and A. Lockwood, "Protégés' Negative Mentoring Experiences: Construct Development and Nomological Validation," *Personnel Psychology* (Summer 2004), pp. 411–447.

115. B. R. Ragins and J. L. Cotton, "Easier Said than Done: Gender Differences in Perceived Barriers to Gaining a Mentor," *Academy of Management Journal* 34, no. 4 (1993), pp. 939–951; C. R. Wanberg, E. T. Welsh, and S. A. Hezlett, "Mentoring Research: A Review and Dynamic Process Model," in G. R. Ferris and J. J. Martocchio (eds.), *Research in Personnel and Human Resources Management,* vol. 22 (Greenwich, CT: Elsevier Science, 2003), pp. 39–124; and T. D. Allen, "Protégé Selection by Mentors: Contributing Individual and Organizational Factors," *Journal of Vocational Behavior* 65, no. 3 (2004), pp. 469–483.

116. T. D. Allen, M. L. Poteet, J. E. A. Russell, and G. H. Dobbins, "A Field Study of Factors Related to Supervisors' Willingness to Mentor Others," *Journal of Vocational Behavior* 50, no. 1 (1997), pp. 1–22; S. Aryee, Y. W. Chay, and J. Chew, "The Motivation to Mentor Among Managerial Employees in the Maintenance Career Stage: An Interactionist Perspective," *Group and Organization Management* 21, no. 3 (1996), pp. 261–277; L. T. Eby, A. L. Lockwood, and M. Butts, "Perceived Support for Mentoring: A Multiple Perspectives Approach," *Journal of Vocational Behavior* 68, no. 2 (2006), pp. 267–291; and T. D. Allen, E. Lentz, and R. Day, "Career Success Outcomes Associated with Mentoring Others: A Comparison of Mentors and Nonmentors," *Journal of Career Development* 32, no. 3 (2006), pp. 272–285.

117. See, for example, K. E. Kram and D. T. Hall, "Mentoring in a Context of Diversity and Turbulence," in E. E. Kossek and S. A. Lobel (eds.), *Managing Diversity* (Cambridge, MA: Blackwell, 1996), pp. 108–136; B. R. Ragins and J. L. Cotton, "Mentor Functions and Outcomes: A Comparison of Men and Women in Formal and Informal Mentoring Relationships," *Journal of Applied Psychology* (August 1999), pp. 529–550; and D. B. Turban, T. W. Dougherty, and F. K. Lee, "Gender, Race, and Perceived Similarity Effects in Developmental Relationships: The Moderating Role of Relationship Duration," *Journal of Vocational Behavior* (October 2002), pp. 240–262.

118. J. U. Chun, J. J. Sosik, and N. Y. Yun, "A Longitudinal Study of Mentor and Protégé Outcomes in Formal Mentoring Relationships," *Journal of Organizational Behavior* (November 12, 2012), pp. 35–49.

119. Ragins and Cotton, "Mentor Functions and Outcomes"; and C. M. Underhill, "The Effectiveness of Mentoring Programs in Corporate Settings: A Meta-Analytical Review of the Literature," *Journal of Vocational Behavior* 68, no. 2 (2006), pp. 292–307.

120. T. D. Allen, E. T. Eby, and E. Lentz, "The Relationship Between Formal Mentoring Program Characteristics and Perceived Program Effectiveness," *Personnel Psychology* 59 (2006), pp. 125–153; T. D. Allen, L. T. Eby, and E. Lentz, "Mentorship Behaviors and Mentorship Quality Associated with Formal Mentoring Programs: Closing the Gap Between Research and Practice," *Journal of Applied Psychology* 91, no. 3 (2006), pp. 567–578; and M. R. Parise and M. L. Forret, "Formal Mentoring Programs: The Relationship of Program Design and Support to Mentors' Perceptions of Benefits and Costs," *Journal of Vocational Behavior* 72, no. 2 (2008), pp. 225–240.

121. L. T. Eby and A. Lockwood, "Protégés' and Mentors' Reactions to Participating in Formal Mentoring Programs: A Qualitative Investigation," *Journal of Vocational Behavior* 67, no. 3 (2005), pp. 441–458; G. T. Chao, "Formal Mentoring: Lessons Learned from Past Practice," *Professional Psychology: Research and Practice* 40, no. 3 (2009), pp. 314–320; and C. R. Wanberg, J. D. Kammeyer-Mueller, and M. Marchese, "Mentor and Protégé Predictors and Outcomes of Mentoring in a Formal Mentoring Program," *Journal of Vocational Behavior* 69 (2006), pp. 410–423.

122. M. K. Feeney and B. Bozeman, "Mentoring and Network Ties," *Human Relations* 61, no. 12 (2008), pp. 1651–1676; N. Bozionelos, "Intra-Organizational Network Resources: How They Relate to Career Success and Organizational Commitment," *Personnel Review* 37, no. 3 (2008), pp. 249–263; and S. A. Hezlett and S. K. Gibson, "Linking Mentoring and Social Capital: Implications for Career and Organization Development," *Advances in Developing Human Resources* 9, no. 3 (2007), pp. 384–412.

123. Comment by Jim Collins, cited in J. Useem, "Conquering Vertical Limits," *Fortune* (February 19, 2001), p. 94.

124. See, for instance, J. R. Meindl, "The Romance of Leadership as a Follower-Centric Theory: A Social Constructionist Approach," *Leadership Quarterly* (Fall 1995), pp. 329–341; and B. Schyns, J. Felfe, and H. Blank, "Is Charisma Hyper-Romanticism? Empirical Evidence from New Data and a Meta-Analysis," *Applied Psychology: An International Review* 56, no. 4 (2007), pp. 505–527.

125. M. J. Martinko, P. Harvey, D. Sikora, and S. C. Douglas, "Perceptions of Abusive Supervision: The Role of Subordinates' Attribution Styles," *Leadership Quarterly* (August 2011), pp. 751–764.

126. J. R. Meindl, S. B. Ehrlich, and J. M. Dukerich, "The Romance of Leadership," *Administrative Science Quarterly* (March 1985), pp. 78–102; and M. C. Bligh, J. C. Kohles, C. L. Pearce, J. E. Justin, and J. F. Stovall, "When the Romance Is Over: Follower Perspectives of Aversive Leadership," *Applied Psychology: An International Review* 56, no. 4 (2007), pp. 528–557.

127. B. R. Agle, N. J. Nagarajan, J. A. Sonnenfeld, and D. Srinivasan, "Does CEO Charisma Matter?" *Academy of Management Journal* 49, no. 1 (2006), pp. 161–174.

128. Bligh, Kohles, Pearce, Justin, and Stovall, "When the Romance Is Over."

129. Schyns, Felfe, and Blank, "Is Charisma Hyper-Romanticism?"

130. J. Cassidy, "Subprime Suspect: The Rise and Fall of Wall Street's First Black C.E.O.," *The New Yorker* (March 31, 2008), pp. 78–91.

131. A. S. Rosette, G. J. Leonardelli, and K. W. Phillips, "The White Standard: Racial Bias in Leader Categorization," *Journal of Applied Psychology* 93, no. 4 (2008), pp. 758–777.

132. A. M. Koenig, A. H. Eagly, A. A. Mitchell, and T. Ristikari, "Are Leader Stereotypes Masculine? A Meta-Analysis of Three Research Paradigms," *Psychological Bulletin* 137, no. 4 (2011), pp. 616–642.

133. M. Van Vugt and B. R. Spisak, "Sex Differences in the Emergence of Leadership During Competitions Within and Between Groups," *Psychological Science* 19, no. 9 (2008), pp. 854–858.

134. Ibid.

135. R. E. Silverman, "Who's the Boss? There Isn't One," *The Wall Street Journal* (June 20, 2012), pp. B 1, B8.

136. S. D. Dionne, F. J. Yammarino, L. E. Atwater, and L. R. James, "Neutralizing Substitutes for Leadership Theory: Leadership Effects and Common-Source Bias," *Journal of Applied Psychology,* 87 (2002), pp. 454–464; and J. R. Villa, J. P. Howell, P. W. Dorfman, and D. L. Daniel, "Problems with Detecting Moderators in Leadership Research Using Moderated Multiple Regression," *Leadership Quarterly* 14 (2002), pp. 3–23.

137. L. A. Hambley, T. A. O'Neill, and T. J. B. Kline, "Virtual Team Leadership: The Effects of Leadership Style and Communication Medium on Team Interaction Styles and Outcomes," *Organizational Behavior and Human Decision Processes* 103 (2007), pp. 1–20; and B. J. Avolio and S. S. Kahai, "Adding the 'E' to E-Leadership: How It May Impact Your Leadership," *Organizational Dynamics* 31, no. 4 (2003), pp. 325–338.

138. S. J. Zaccaro and P. Bader, "E-Leadership and the Challenges of Leading E-Teams: Minimizing the Bad and Maximizing the Good," *Organizational Dynamics* 31, no. 4 (2003), pp. 381–385.

139. C. E. Naquin and G. D. Paulson, "Online Bargaining and Interpersonal Trust," *Journal of Applied Psychology* (February 2003), pp. 113–120.

140. B. M. Bass, "Cognitive, Social, and Emotional Intelligence of Transformational Leaders," in R. E. Riggio, S. E. Murphy, and F. J. Pirozzolo (eds.), *Multiple Intelligences and Leadership* (Mahwah, NJ: Lawrence Erlbaum, 2002), pp. 113–114.

141. See, for instance, P. Dvorak, "M.B.A. Programs Hone 'Soft Skills,'" *The Wall Street Journal* (February 12, 2007), p. B3.

142. J. Weber, "The Leadership Factor," *BusinessWeek* (June 12, 2006), pp. 60–64.

143. D. Brady, "The Rising Star of CEO Consulting," *Bloomberg Businessweek* (November 24, 2010), www.businessweek.com.

144. D. S. DeRue, J. D. Nahrgang, J. R. Hollenbeck, and K. Workman, "A Quasi-Experimental Study of After-Event Reviews and Leadership Development," *Journal of Applied Psychology* 97 (2012), pp. 997–1015.

145. Dvir, Eden, and Avolio, "Impact of Transformational Leadership on Follower Development and Performance"; B. J. Avolio and B. M. Bass, *Developing Potential Across a Full Range of Leadership: Cases on Transactional and Transformational Leadership* (Mahwah, NJ: Lawrence Erlbaum, 2002); A. J. Towler, "Effects of Charismatic Influence Training on Attitudes, Behavior, and Performance," *Personnel Psychology* (Summer 2003), pp. 363–381; and Barling, Weber, and Kelloway, "Effects of Transformational Leadership Training on Attitudinal and Financial Outcomes."

CHAPTER 13

1. R. M. Kanter, "Power Failure in Management Circuits," *Harvard Business Review* (July–August 1979), p. 65.

2. J. Pfeffer, "Understanding Power in Organizations," *California Management Review* (Winter 1992), p. 35.

3. Based on B. M. Bass, *Bass & Stogdill's Handbook of Leadership,* 3rd ed. (New York: The Free Press, 1990).

4. M. Gongloff, "Steve Cohen, Super-Rich and Secretive Trader, Faces Possible SEC Investigation," *Huffington Post* (November 28, 2012), downloaded May 24, 2013, from www.huffingtonpost.com/.

5. J. R. P. French Jr. and B. Raven, "The Bases of Social Power," in D. Cartwright (ed.), *Studies in Social Power* (Ann Arbor, MI: University of Michigan, Institute for Social Research, 1959), pp. 150–167; B. H. Raven, "The Bases of Power: Origins and Recent Developments," *Journal of Social Issues* (Winter 1993), pp. 227–251; and G. Yukl, "Use Power Effectively," in E. A. Locke (ed.), *Handbook of Principles of Organizational Behavior* (Malden, MA: Blackwell, 2004), pp. 242–247.

6. E. A. Ward, "Social Power Bases of Managers: Emergence of a New Factor," *Journal of Social Psychology* (February 2001), pp. 144–147.

7. S. R. Giessner and T. W. Schubert, "High in the Hierarchy: How Vertical Location and Judgments of Leaders' Power Are Interrelated," *Organizational Behavior and Human Decision Processes* 104, no. 1 (2007), pp. 30–44.

8. P. M. Podsakoff and C. A. Schriesheim, "Field Studies of French and Raven's Bases of Power: Critique, Reanalysis, and Suggestions for Future Research," *Psychological Bulletin* (May 1985), pp. 387–411; T. R. Hinkin and C. A. Schriesheim, "Development and Application of New Scales to Measure the French and Raven (1959) Bases of Social Power," *Journal of Applied Psychology* (August 1989), pp. 561–567; and P. P. Carson, K. D. Carson, and C. W. Roe, "Social Power Bases: A Meta-Analytic Examination of Interrelationships and Outcomes," *Journal of Applied Social Psychology* 23, no. 14 (1993), pp. 1150–1169.

9. S. Perman, "Translation Advertising: Where Shop Meets Hip Hop," *Time* (August 30, 2010), www.time.com.

10. R. E. Emerson, "Power–Dependence Relations," *American Sociological Review* (February 1962), pp. 31–41.

11. H. Mintzberg, *Power In and Around Organizations* (Upper Saddle River, NJ: Prentice Hall, 1983), p. 24.

12. R. M. Cyert and J. G. March, *A Behavioral Theory of the Firm* (Upper Saddle River, NJ: Prentice Hall, 1963).

13. C. Perrow, "Departmental Power and Perspective in Industrial Firms," in M. N. Zald (ed.), *Power in Organizations* (Nashville, TN: Vanderbilt University Press, 1970).

14. N. Foulkes, "Tractor Boy," *High Life* (October 2002), p. 90.

15. See, for example, D. Kipnis and S. M. Schmidt, "Upward-Influence Styles: Relationship with Performance Evaluations, Salary, and Stress," *Administrative Science Quarterly* (December 1988), pp. 528–542; G. Yukl and J. B. Tracey, "Consequences of Influence Tactics Used with Subordinates, Peers, and the Boss," *Journal of Applied Psychology* (August 1992), pp. 525–535; G. Blickle, "Influence Tactics Used by Subordinates: An Empirical Analysis of the Kipnis and Schmidt Subscales," *Psychological Reports* (February 2000), pp. 143–154; and G. Yukl, "Use Power Effectively," pp. 249–252.

16. G. Yukl, *Leadership in Organizations,* 5th ed. (Upper Saddle River, NJ: Prentice Hall, 2002), pp. 141–174; G. R. Ferris, W. A. Hochwarter, C. Douglas, F. R. Blass, R. W. Kolodinksy, and D. C. Treadway, "Social Influence Processes in Organizations and Human Resource Systems," in G. R. Ferris and J. J. Martocchio (eds.), *Research in Personnel and Human Resources Management,* vol. 21 (Oxford, UK: JAI Press/Elsevier, 2003), pp. 65–127; and C. A. Higgins, T. A. Judge, and G. R. Ferris, "Influence Tactics and Work Outcomes: A Meta-Analysis," *Journal of Organizational Behavior* (March 2003), pp. 89–106.

17. C. M. Falbe and G. Yukl, "Consequences for Managers of Using Single Influence Tactics and Combinations of Tactics," *Academy of Management Journal* (July 1992), pp. 638–653.

18. R. E. Petty and P. Briñol, "Persuasion: From Single to Multiple to Metacognitive Processes," *Perspectives on Psychological Science* 3, no. 2 (2008), pp. 137–147.

19. J. Badal, "Getting a Raise from the Boss," *The Wall Street Journal* (July 8, 2006), pp. B1, B5.

20. Yukl, *Leadership in Organizations.*

21. Ibid.

22. Falbe and Yukl, "Consequences for Managers of Using Single Influence Tactics and Combinations of Tactics."

23. A. W. Kruglanski, A. Pierro, and E. T. Higgins, "Regulatory Mode and Preferred Leadership Styles: How Fit Increases Job Satisfaction," *Basic and Applied Social Psychology* 29, no. 2 (2007), pp. 137–149; and A. Pierro, L. Cicero, and B. H. Raven, "Motivated Compliance with Bases of Social Power," *Journal of Applied Social Psychology* 38, no. 7 (2008), pp. 1921–1944.

24. P. P. Fu and G. Yukl, "Perceived Effectiveness of Influence Tactics in the United States and China," *Leadership Quarterly* (Summer 2000), pp. 251–266; O. Branzei, "Cultural Explanations of Individual Preferences for Influence Tactics in Cross-Cultural Encounters," *International Journal of Cross Cultural Management* (August 2002), pp. 203–218; G. Yukl, P. P. Fu, and R. McDonald, "Cross-Cultural Differences in Perceived Effectiveness of Influence Tactics for Initiating or Resisting Change," *Applied Psychology: An International Review* (January 2003), pp. 66–82; and P. P. Fu, T. K. Peng, J. C. Kennedy, and G. Yukl, "Examining the Preferences of Influence Tactics in Chinese Societies: A Comparison of Chinese Managers in Hong Kong, Taiwan, and Mainland China," *Organizational Dynamics* 33, no. 1 (2004), pp. 32–46.

25. C. J. Torelli and S. Shavitt, "Culture and Concepts of Power," *Journal of Personality and Social Psychology* 99, no. 4 (2010), pp. 703–723.

26. Fu and Yukl, "Perceived Effectiveness of Influence Tactics in the United States and China."

27. S. J. Heine, "Making Sense of East Asian Self-Enhancement," *Journal of Cross-Cultural Psychology* (September 2003), pp. 596–602.

28. G. R. Ferris, D. C. Treadway, P. L. Perrewé, R. L. Brouer, C. Douglas, and S. Lux, "Political Skill in Organizations," *Journal of Management* (June 2007), pp. 290–320; K. J. Harris, K. M. Kacmar, S. Zivnuska, and J. D. Shaw, "The Impact of Political Skill on Impression Management Effectiveness," *Journal of Applied Psychology* 92, no. 1 (2007), pp. 278–285; W. A. Hochwarter, G. R. Ferris, M. B. Gavin, P. L. Perrewé, A. T. Hall, and D. D. Frink, "Political Skill as Neutralizer of Felt Accountability–Job Tension Effects on Job Performance Ratings: A Longitudinal Investigation," *Organizational Behavior and Human Decision Processes* 102 (2007), pp. 226–239; and D. C. Treadway, G. R. Ferris, A. B. Duke, G. L. Adams, and J. B. Tatcher, "The Moderating Role of Subordinate Political Skill on Supervisors' Impressions of Subordinate Ingratiation and Ratings of Subordinate Interpersonal Facilitation," *Journal of Applied Psychology* 92, no. 3 (2007), pp. 848–855.

29. M. C. Andrews, K. M. Kacmar, and K. J. Harris, "Got Political Skill? The Impact of Justice on the Importance of Political Skills for Job Performance." *Journal of Applied Psychology* 94, no. 6 (2009), pp. 1427–1437.

30. C. Anderson, S. E. Spataro, and F. J. Flynn, "Personality and Organizational Culture as Determinants of Influence," *Journal of Applied Psychology* 93, no. 3 (2008), pp. 702–710.

31. Y. Cho and N. J. Fast, "Power, Defensive Denigration, and the Assuaging Effect of Gratitude Expression," *Journal of Experimental Social Psychology* 48, 2012, pp. 778–782.

32. M. Pitesa and S. Thau, "Masters of the Universe: How Power and Accountability Influence Self-Serving Decisions under Moral Hazard," *Journal of Applied Psychology* 98 (2013), pp. 550–558; and N. J. Fast, N. Sivanathan, D. D. Mayer, and A. D. Galinsky, "Power and Overconfident Decision-Making," *Organizational Behavior and Human Decision Processes* 117, 2012, pp. 249–260.

33. A. Grant, "Yes, Power Corrupts, But Power Also Reveals," *Government Executive* (May 23, 2013), downloaded May 23, 2013, from www.govexec.com/.

34. J. K. Maner, M. T. Gaillot, A. J. Menzel, and J. W. Kunstman, "Dispositional Anxiety Blocks the Psychological Effects of Power," *Personality and Social Psychology Bulletin* 38 (2012), pp. 1383–1395.

35. N. J. Fast, N. Halevy, and A. D. Galinsky, "The Destructive Nature of Power Without Status," *Journal of Experimental Social Psychology* 48 (2012), pp. 391–394.

36. T. Seppälä, J. Lipponen, A. Bardi, and A. Pirttilä-Backman, Change-Oriented Organizational Citizenship Behaviour: An Interactive Product of Openness to Change Values, Work Unit Identification, and Sense of Power," *Journal of Occupational and Organizational Psychology* 85 (2012), pp. 136–155.

37. K. A. DeCelles, D. S. DeRue, J. D. Margolis, and T. L. Ceranic, "Does Power Corrupt or Enable? When and Why Power Facilitates Self-Interested Behavior," *Journal of Applied Psychology* 97 (2012), pp. 681–689.

38. S. Stecklow, "Sexual-Harassment Cases Plague U.N.," *The Wall Street Journal* (May 21, 2009), p. A1.

39. N. Bode, "Flushing Hospital Nurse Gets $15 Million Award in Sexual Harassment Suit," *New York Daily News* (February 23, 2009), www.nydailynews.com.

40. A. M. Dionisi, J. Barling, and K. E. Dupré, "Revisiting the Comparative Outcomes of Workplace Aggression and Sexual Harassment," *Journal of Occupational Health Psychology* 17 (2012), pp. 398–408.

41. M. B. Nielsen and S. Einarsen, "Prospective Relationships between Workplace Sexual Harassment and Psychological Distress," *Occupational Medicine* 62 (2012), pp. 226–228.

42. S. Silverstein and S. Christian, "Harassment Ruling Raises Free-Speech Issues," *Los Angeles Times* (November 11, 1993), p. D2.

43. R. Ilies, N. Hauserman, S. Schwochau, and J. Stibal, "Reported Incidence Rates of Work-Related Sexual Harassment in the United States: Using Meta-Analysis to Explain Reported Rate Disparities," *Personnel Psychology* (Fall 2003), pp. 607–631.

44. "Sexual Harassment Charges," Equal Employment Opportunity Commission, downloaded May 15, 2013, from www.eeoc.gov/eeoc/statistics/.

45. "Study Details Rates of Sexual Harassment, Assault in Military," *The Daily Report* (January 3, 2013), downloaded May 24, 2013, from www.nationalpartnership.org/.

46. R. L. Weiner, R. Reiter-Palmon, R. J. Winter, E. Richter, A. Humke, and E. Maeder, "Complainant Behavioral Tone, Ambivalent Sexism, and Perceptions of Sexual Harassment," *Psychology, Public Policy, and Law* 16, no. 1 (2010), pp. 56–84.

47. Ilies, Hauserman, Schwochau, and Stibal, "Reported Incidence Rates of Work-Related Sexual Harassment in the United States; A. B. Malamut and L. R. Offermann, "Coping with Sexual Harassment: Personal, Environmental, and Cognitive Determinants," *Journal of Applied Psychology* (December 2001), pp. 1152–1166; L. M. Cortina and S. A. Wasti, "Profiles in Coping: Responses to Sexual Harassment Across Persons, Organizations, and Cultures," *Journal of Applied Psychology* (February 2005), pp. 182–192; and J. W. Kunstman, "Sexual Overperception: Power, Mating Motives, and Biases in Social Judgment," *Journal of Personality and Social Psychology* 100, no. 2 (2011), pp. 282–294.

48. F. Krings and S. Facchin, "Organizational Justice and Men's Likelihood to Sexually Harass: The Moderating Role of Sexism and Personality," *Journal of Applied Psychology* 94, no. 2 (2009), pp. 501–510.

49. Mintzberg, *Power In and Around Organizations*, p. 26. See also K. M. Kacmar and R. A. Baron, "Organizational Politics: The State of the Field, Links to Related Processes, and an Agenda for Future Research," in G. R. Ferris (ed.), *Research in Personnel and Human Resources Management*, vol. 17 (Greenwich, CT: JAI Press, 1999), pp. 1–39; and G. R. Ferris, D. C. Treadway, R. W. Kolokinsky, W. A. Hochwarter, C. J. Kacmar, and D. D. Frink, "Development and Validation of the Political Skill Inventory," *Journal of Management* (February 2005), pp. 126–152.

50. S. B. Bacharach and E. J. Lawler, "Political Alignments in Organizations," in R. M. Kramer and M. A. Neale (eds.), *Power and Influence in Organizations* (Thousand Oaks, CA: Sage, 1998), pp. 68–69.

51. A. Drory and T. Romm, "The Definition of Organizational Politics: A Review," *Human Relations* (November 1990), pp. 1133–1154; and R. S. Cropanzano, K. M. Kacmar, and D. P. Bozeman, "Organizational Politics, Justice, and Support: Their Differences and Similarities," in R. Cropanzano and K. M. Kacmar (eds.), *Organizational Politics, Justice and Support: Managing Social Climate at Work* (Westport, CT: Quorum Books, 1995), pp. 1–18; and G. R. Ferris and W. A. Hochwarter, "Organizational Politics," in S. Zedeck (ed.), *APA Handbook of Industrial and Organizational Psychology*, vol. 3 (Washington, DC: American Psychological Association, 2011), pp. 435–459.

52. D. A. Buchanan, "You Stab My Back, I'll Stab Yours: Management Experience and Perceptions of Organization Political Behavior," *British Journal of Management* 19, no. 1 (2008), pp. 49–64.

53. J. Pfeffer, *Power: Why Some People Have It—And Others Don't* (New York: Harper Collins, 2010).

54. Drory and Romm, "The Definition of Organizational Politics."

55. S. M. Rioux and L. A. Penner, "The Causes of Organizational Citizenship Behavior: A Motivational Analysis," *Journal of Applied Psychology* (December 2001), pp. 1306–1314; M. A. Finkelstein and L. A. Penner, "Predicting Organizational Citizenship Behavior: Integrating the Functional and Role Identity Approaches," *Social Behavior & Personality* 32, no. 4 (2004), pp. 383–398; and J. Schwarzwald, M. Koslowsky, and M. Allouf, "Group Membership, Status, and Social Power Preference," *Journal of Applied Social Psychology* 35, no. 3 (2005), pp. 644–665.

56. See, for example, G. R. Ferris, G. S. Russ, and P. M. Fandt, "Politics in Organizations," in R. A. Giacalone and P. Rosenfeld (eds.), *Impression Management in the Organization* (Hillsdale, NJ: Lawrence Erlbaum, 1989), pp. 155–156; and W. E. O'Connor and T. G. Morrison, "A Comparison of Situational and Dispositional Predictors of Perceptions of Organizational Politics," *Journal of Psychology* (May 2001), pp. 301–312.

57. D. Farrell and J. C. Petersen, "Patterns of Political Behavior in Organizations," *Academy of Management Review* 7, no. 3 (1982), pp. 403–412.

58. G. R. Ferris and K. M. Kacmar, "Perceptions of Organizational Politics," *Journal of Management* (March 1992), pp. 93–116.

59. See, for example, P. M. Fandt and G. R. Ferris, "The Management of Information and Impressions: When Employees Behave Opportunistically," *Organizational Behavior and Human Decision Processes* (February 1990), pp. 140–158; Ferris, Russ, and Fandt, "Politics in Organizations," p. 147; and J. M. L. Poon, "Situational Antecedents and Outcomes of Organizational Politics Perceptions," *Journal of Managerial Psychology* 18, no. 2 (2003), pp. 138–155.

60. Ferris and Hochwarter, "Organizational Politics."

61. W. A. Hochwarter, C. Kiewitz, S. L. Castro, P. L. Perrewe, and G. R. Ferris, "Positive Affectivity and Collective Efficacy as Moderators of the Relationship Between Perceived Politics and Job Satisfaction," *Journal of Applied Social Psychology* (May 2003), pp. 1009–1035; and C. C. Rosen, P. E. Levy, and R. J. Hall, "Placing Perceptions of Politics in the

Context of Feedback Environment, Employee Attitudes, and Job Performance," *Journal of Applied Psychology* 91, no. 1 (2006), pp. 211–230.

62. G. R. Ferris, D. D. Frink, M. C. Galang, J. Zhou, K. M. Kacmar, and J. L. Howard, "Perceptions of Organizational Politics: Prediction, Stress-Related Implications, and Outcomes," *Human Relations* (February 1996), pp. 233–266; and E. Vigoda, "Stress-Related Aftermaths to Workplace Politics: The Relationships Among Politics, Job Distress, and Aggressive Behavior in Organizations," *Journal of Organizational Behavior* (August 2002), pp. 571–591.

63. S. Aryee, Z. Chen, and P. S. Budhwar, "Exchange Fairness and Employee Performance: An Examination of the Relationship Between Organizational Politics and Procedural Justice," *Organizational Behavior & Human Decision Processes* (May 2004), pp. 1–14; and K. M. Kacmar, D. P. Bozeman, D. S. Carlson, and W. P. Anthony, "An Examination of the Perceptions of Organizational Politics Model," *Human Relations* 52, no. 3 (1999), pp. 383–416.

64. C. Kiewitz, W. A. Hochwarter, G. R. Ferris, and S. L. Castro, "The Role of Psychological Climate in Neutralizing the Effects of Organizational Politics on Work Outcomes," *Journal of Applied Social Psychology* (June 2002), pp. 1189–1207; and M. C. Andrews, L. A. Witt, and K. M. Kacmar, "The Interactive Effects of Organizational Politics and Exchange Ideology on Manager Ratings of Retention," *Journal of Vocational Behavior* (April 2003), pp. 357–369.

65. O. J. Labedo, "Perceptions of Organisational Politics: Examination of the Situational Antecedent and Consequences Among Nigeria's Extension Personnel," *Applied Psychology: An International Review* 55, no. 2 (2006), pp. 255–281.

66. Kacmar, Bozeman, Carlson, and Anthony, "An Examination of the Perceptions of Organizational Politics Model," p. 389.

67. Ibid., p. 409.

68. K. M. Kacmar, D. G. Bachrach, K. J. Harris, and S. Zivnuska, "Fostering Good Citizenship Through Ethical Leadership: Exploring the Moderating Role of Gender and Organizational Politics," *Journal of Applied Psychology* 96 (2011), pp. 633–642.

69. B. E. Ashforth and R. T. Lee, "Defensive Behavior in Organizations: A Preliminary Model," *Human Relations* (July 1990), pp. 621–648.

70. M. Valle and P. L. Perrewe, "Do Politics Perceptions Relate to Political Behaviors? Tests of an Implicit Assumption and Expanded Model," *Human Relations* (March 2000), pp. 359–386.

71. See, for instance, W. L. Gardner and M. J. Martinko, "Impression Management in Organizations," *Journal of Management* (June 1988), pp. 321–338; M. C. Bolino and W. H. Turnley, "More Than One Way to Make an Impression: Exploring Profiles of Impression Management," *Journal of Management* 29, no. 2 (2003), pp. 141–160; S. Zivnuska, K. M. Kacmar, L. A. Witt, D. S. Carlson, and V. K. Bratton, "Interactive Effects of Impression Management and Organizational Politics on Job Performance," *Journal of Organizational Behavior* (August 2004), pp. 627–640; and M. C. Bolino, K. M. Kacmar, W. H. Turnley, and J. B. Gilstrap, "A Multi-Level Review of Impression Management Motives

and Behaviors," *Journal of Management* 34, no. 6 (2008), pp. 1080–1109.

72. M. Snyder and J. Copeland, "Self-Monitoring Processes in Organizational Settings," in R. A. Giacalone and P. Rosenfeld (eds.), *Impression Management in the Organization* (Hillsdale, NJ: Lawrence Erlbaum, 1989), p. 11; Bolino and Turnley, "More Than One Way to Make an Impression"; and W. H. Turnley and M. C. Bolino, "Achieved Desired Images While Avoiding Undesired Images: Exploring the Role of Self-Monitoring in Impression Management," *Journal of Applied Psychology* (April 2001), pp. 351–360.

73. M. R. Leary and R. M. Kowalski, "Impression Management: A Literature Review and Two-Component Model." *Psychological Bulletin* (January 1990), pp. 34–47.

74. J. Ham and R. Vonk, "Impressions of Impression Management: Evidence of Spontaneous Suspicion of Ulterior Motivation," *Journal of Experimental Social Psychology* 47, no. 2 (2011), pp. 466–471; and W. M. Bowler, J. R. B. Halbesleben, and J. R. B. Paul, "If You're Close with the Leader, You Must Be a Brownnose: The Role of Leader–Member Relationships in Follower, Leader, and Coworker Attributions of Organizational Citizenship Behavior Motives," *Human Resource Management Review* 20, no. 4 (2010), pp. 309–316.

75. C. Lebherz, K. Jonas, and B. Tomljenovic, "Are We Known by the Company We Keep? Effects of Name Dropping on First Impressions," *Social Influence* 4, no. 1 (2009), pp. 62–79.

76. J. R. B. Halbesleben, W. M. Bowler, M. C. Bolino, and W. H Turnley, "Organizational Concern, Prosocial Values, or Impression Management? How Supervisors Attribute Motives to Organizational Citizenship Behavior," *Journal of Applied Social Psychology* 40, no. 6 (2010), pp. 1450–1489.

77. C. K. Stevens and A. L. Kristof, "Making the Right Impression: A Field Study of Applicant Impression Management During Job Interviews," *Journal of Applied Psychology* 80 (1995), pp. 587– 606; L. A. McFarland, A. M. Ryan, and S. D. Kriska, "Impression Management Use and Effectiveness Across Assessment Methods," *Journal of Management* 29, no. 5 (2003), pp. 641–661; C. A. Higgins and T. A. Judge, "The Effect of Applicant Influence Tactics on Recruiter Perceptions of Fit and Hiring Recommendations: A Field Study," *Journal of Applied Psychology* 89, no. 4 (2004), pp. 622–632; and W. C. Tsai, C.-C. Chen, and S. F. Chiu, "Exploring Boundaries of the Effects of Applicant Impression Management Tactics in Job Interviews," *Journal of Management* (February 2005), pp. 108–125.

78. D. C. Gilmore and G. R. Ferris, "The Effects of Applicant Impression Management Tactics on Interviewer Judgments," *Journal of Management* 15, no. 4 (1989), pp. 557–564.

79. Stevens and Kristof, "Making the Right Impression."

80. C. A. Higgins, T. A. Judge, and G. R. Ferris, "Influence Tactics and Work Outcomes: A Meta-Analysis," *Journal of Organizational Behavior* (March 2003), pp. 89–106.

81. Ibid.

82. K. J. Harris, K. M. Kacmar, S. Zivnuska, and J. D. Shaw, "The Impact of Political Skill on Impression Management Effectiveness," *Journal of Applied Psychology* 92, no. 1 (2007), pp. 278–285; and D. C. Treadway, G. R. Ferris, A. B. Duke, G. L. Adams, and J. B. Thatcher, "The Moderating Role of Subordinate Political Skill on Supervisors' Impressions

of Subordinate Ingratiation and Ratings of Subordinate Interpersonal Facilitation," *Journal of Applied Psychology* 92, no. 3 (2007), pp. 848–855.

83. J. D. Westphal and I. Stern, "Flattery Will Get You Everywhere (Especially if You Are a Male Caucasian): How Ingratiation, Boardroom Behavior, and Demographic Minority Status Affect Additional Board Appointments of U.S. Companies," *Academy of Management Journal* 50, no. 2 (2007), pp. 267–288.

84. See T. Romm and A. Drory, "Political Behavior in Organizations: A Cross-Cultural Comparison," *International Journal of Value Based Management* 1 (1988), pp. 97–113; and E. Vigoda, "Reactions to Organizational Politics: A Cross-Cultural Examination in Israel and Britain," *Human Relations* (November 2001), pp. 1483–1518.

85. J. L. T. Leong, M. H. Bond, and P. P. Fu, "Perceived Effectiveness of Influence Strategies in the United States and Three Chinese Societies," *International Journal of Cross Cultural Management* (May 2006), pp. 101–120.

86. Y. Miyamoto and B. Wilken, "Culturally Contingent Situated Cognition: Influencing Other People Fosters Analytic Perception in the United States but Not in Japan," *Psychological Science* 21, no. 11 (2010), pp. 1616–1622.

87. Vigoda, "Reactions to Organizational Politics," p. 1512.

88. Ibid., p. 1510.

89. D. Clark, "A Campaign Strategy for Your Career," *Harvard Business Review* (November 2012), pp. 131–134.

CHAPTER 14

1. See, for instance, D. Tjosvold, "Defining Conflict and Making Choices About Its Management: Lighting the Dark Side of Organizational Life," *International Journal of Conflict Management* 17, no. 2 (2006), pp. 87–95; and M. A. Korsgaard, S. S. Jeong, D. M. Mahony, and A. H. Pitariu, "A Multilevel View of Intragroup Conflict," *Journal of Management* 34, no. 6 (2008), pp. 1222–1252.

2. K. W. Thomas, "Conflict and Negotiation Processes in Organizations," in M. D. Dunnette and L. M. Hough (eds.), *Handbook of Industrial and Organizational Psychology*, 2nd ed., vol. 3 (Palo Alto, CA: Consulting Psychologists Press, 1992), pp. 651–717.

3. For a comprehensive review of the interactionist approach, see C. K. W. De Dreu and E. Van de Vliert (eds.), *Using Conflict in Organizations* (London: Sage, 1997).

4. J. Yang and K. W. Mossholder, "Decoupling Task and Relationship Conflict: The Role of Intragroup Emotional Processing," *Journal of Organizational Behavior* 25, no. 5 (August 2004), pp. 589–605; and N. Gamero, V. González-Romá, and J. M. Peiró, "The Influence of Intra-Team Conflict on Work Teams' Affective Climate: A Longitudinal Study," *Journal of Occupational and Organizational Psychology* 81, no. 1 (2008), pp. 47–69.

5. N. Halevy, E. Y. Chou, and A. D. Galinsky, "Exhausting or Exhilarating? Conflict as Threat to Interests, Relationships and Identities," *Journal of Experimental Social Psychology* 48 (2012), pp. 530–537.

6. F. R. C. de Wit, L. L. Greer, and K. A. Jehn, "The Paradox of Intragroup Conflict: A Meta-Analysis," *Journal of Applied Psychology* 97 (2012), pp. 360–390.

7. J. Farh, C. Lee, and C. I. C. Farh, "Task Conflict and Team Creativity: A Question of How Much and When," *Journal of Applied Psychology* 95, no. 6 (2010), pp. 1173–1180.

8. B. H. Bradley, A. C. Klotz, B. F. Postlethwaite, and K. G. Brown, "Ready to Rumble: How Team Personality Composition and Task Conflict Interact to Improve Performance," *Journal of Applied Psychology* 98 (2013), pp. 385–392.

9. B. H. Bradley, B. F. Postlethwaite, A. C. Klotz, M. R. Hamdani, and K. G. Brown, "Reaping the Benefits of Task Conflict in Teams: The Critical Role of Team Psychological Safety Climate," *Journal of Applied Psychology* 97 (2012), pp. 151–158.

10. G. A. Van Kleef, W. Steinel, and A. C. Homan, "On Being Peripheral and Paying Attention: Prototypicality and Information Processing in Intergroup Conflict," *Journal of Applied Psychology* 98 (2013), pp. 63–79.

11. S. Benard, "Cohesion from Conflict: Does Intergroup Conflict Motivate Intragroup Norm Enforcement and Support for Centralized Leadership?" *Social Psychology Quarterly* 75 (2012), pp. 107–130.

12. R. S. Peterson and K. J. Behfar, "The Dynamic Relationship Between Performance Feedback, Trust, and Conflict in Groups: A Longitudinal Study," *Organizational Behavior & Human Decision Processes* (September–November 2003), pp. 102–112.

13. T. M. Glomb and H. Liao, "Interpersonal Aggression in Work Groups: Social Influence, Reciprocal, and Individual Effects," *Academy of Management Journal* 46, no. 4 (2003), pp. 486–496; and V. Venkataramani and R. S. Dalal, "Who Helps and Harms Whom? Relational Aspects of Interpersonal Helping and Harming in Organizations," *Journal of Applied Psychology* 92, no. 4 (2007), pp. 952–966.

14. R. Friedman, C. Anderson, J. Brett, M. Olekalns, N. Goates, and C. C. Lisco, "The Positive and Negative Effects of Anger on Dispute Resolution: Evidence from Electronically Mediated Disputes," *Journal of Applied Psychology* (April 2004), pp. 369–376.

15. L. R. Pondy, "Organizational Conflict: Concepts and Models," *Administrative Science Quarterly* (September 1967), p. 302.

16. See, for instance, J. R. Curhan, "What Do People Value When They Negotiate? Mapping the Domain of Subjective Value in Negotiation," *Journal of Personality and Social Psychology* (September 2006), pp. 117–126; R. L. Pinkley, "Dimensions of Conflict Frame: Disputant Interpretations of Conflict," *Journal of Applied Psychology* (April 1990), pp. 117–126; and R. L. Pinkley and G. B. Northcraft, "Conflict Frames of Reference: Implications for Dispute Processes and Outcomes," *Academy of Management Journal* (February 1994), pp. 193–205.

17. A. M. Isen, A. A. Labroo, and P. Durlach, "An Influence of Product and Brand Name on Positive Affect: Implicit and Explicit Measures," *Motivation & Emotion* (March 2004), pp. 43–63.

18. Ibid.

19. P. J. D. Carnevale and A. M. Isen, "The Influence of Positive Affect and Visual Access on the Discovery of Integrative Solutions in Bilateral Negotiations," *Organizational Behavior and Human Decision Processes* (February 1986), pp. 1–13; and

C. Montes, D. Rodriguez, and G. Serrano, "Affective Choice of Conflict Management Styles," *International Journal of Conflict Management* 23 (2012), pp. 6–18.

20. Thomas, "Conflict and Negotiation Processes in Organizations."

21. Ibid.

22. Ibid.

23. B. A. Nijstad and S. C. Kaps, "Taking the Easy Way Out: Preference Diversity, Decision Strategies, and Decision Refusal in Groups," *Journal of Personality and Social Psychology* 94, no. 5 (2008), pp. 860–870.

24. M. E. Zellmer-Bruhn, M. M. Maloney, A. D. Bhappu, and R. Salvador, "When and How Do Differences Matter? An Exploration of Perceived Similarity in Teams," *Organizational Behavior and Human Decision Processes* 107, no. 1 (2008), pp. 41–59.

25. See T. H. Cox, S. A. Lobel, and P. L. McLeod, "Effects of Ethnic Group Cultural Differences on Cooperative Behavior on a Group Task," *Academy of Management Journal* (December 1991), pp. 827–847; and D. van Knippenberg, C. K. W. De Dreu, and A. C. Homan, "Work Group Diversity and Group Performance: An Integrative Model and Research Agenda," *Journal of Applied Psychology* (December 2004), pp. 1008–1022.

26. For example, see J. A. Wall Jr. and R. R. Callister, "Conflict and Its Management," *Journal of Management* 21, no. 3 (1995) pp. 523–526, for evidence supporting the argument that conflict is almost uniformly dysfunctional. See also P. J. Hinds and D. E. Bailey, "Out of Sight, Out of Sync: Understanding Conflict in Distributed Teams," *Organization Science* (November–December 2003), pp. 615–632.

27. K. A. Jehn, L. Greer, S. Levine, and G. Szulanski, "The Effects of Conflict Types, Dimensions, and Emergent States on Group Outcomes," *Group Decision and Negotiation* 17, no. 6 (2005), pp. 777–796.

28. Zellmer-Bruhn, Maloney, Bhappu, and Salvador, "When and How Do Differences Matter?"

29. K. B. Dahlin, L. R. Weingart, and P. J. Hinds, "Team Diversity and Information Use," *Academy of Management Journal* 48, no. 6 (2005), pp. 1107–1123; and M. J. Pearsall, A. P. J. Ellis, and J. M. Evans, "Unlocking the Effects of Gender Faultlines on Team Creativity: Is Activation the Key?" *Journal of Applied Psychology* 93, no. 1 (2008), pp. 225–234.

30. J. Fried, "I Know You Are, But What Am I?" *Inc.* (July/August 2010), pp. 39–40.

31. K. J. Behfar, R. S. Peterson, E. A. Mannix, and W. M. K. Trochim, "The Critical Role of Conflict Resolution in Teams: A Close Look at the Links Between Conflict Type, Conflict Management Strategies, and Team Outcomes," *Journal of Applied Psychology* 93, no. 1 (2008), pp. 170–188; A. G. Tekleab, N. R. Quigley, and P. E. Tesluk, "A Longitudinal Study of Team Conflict, Conflict Management, Cohesion, and Team Effectiveness," *Group and Organization Management* 34, no. 2 (2009), pp. 170–205; and E. Van de Vliert, M. C. Euwema, and S. E. Huismans, "Managing Conflict with a Subordinate or a Superior: Effectiveness of Conglomerated Behavior," *Journal of Applied Psychology* 80 (1995), pp. 271–281.

32. A. Somech, H. S. Desivilya, and H. Lidogoster, "Team Conflict Management and Team Effectiveness: The Effects of Task Interdependence and Team Identification," *Journal of Organizational Behavior* 30, no. 3 (2009), pp. 359–378.

33. H. R. Markus and S. Kitayama, "Culture and the Self: Implications for Cognition, Emotion, and Motivation," *Psychological Review* 98, no. 2 (1991), pp. 224–253; and H. Ren and B. Gray, "Repairing Relationship Conflict: How Violation Types and Culture Influence the Effectiveness of Restoration Rituals," *Academy of Management Review* 34, no. 1 (2009), pp. 105–126.

34. M. J. Gelfand, M. Higgins, L. H. Nishii, J. L. Raver, A. Dominguez, F. Murakami, S. Yamaguchi, and M. Toyama, "Culture and Egocentric Perceptions of Fairness in Conflict and Negotiation," *Journal of Applied Psychology* (October 2002), pp. 833–845; and Z. Ma, "Chinese Conflict Management Styles and Negotiation Behaviours: An Empirical Test," *International Journal of Cross Cultural Management* (April 2007), pp. 101–119.

35. P. P. Fu, X. H. Yan, Y. Li, E. Wang, and S. Peng, "Examining Conflict-Handling Approaches by Chinese Top Management Teams in IT Firms," *International Journal of Conflict Management* 19, no. 3 (2008), pp. 188–209.

36. M. H. Bazerman, J. R. Curhan, D. A. Moore, and K. L. Valley, "Negotiation," *Annual Review of Psychology* 51 (2000), pp. 279–314.

37. See, for example, D. R. Ames, "Assertiveness Expectancies: How Hard People Push Depends on the Consequences They Predict," *Journal of Personality and Social Psychology* 95, no. 6 (2008), pp. 1541–1557; and J. R. Curhan, H. A. Elfenbein, and H. Xu, "What Do People Value When They Negotiate? Mapping the Domain of Subjective Value in Negotiation," *Journal of Personality and Social Psychology* 91, no. 3 (2006), pp. 493–512.

38. R. Lewicki, D. Saunders, and B. Barry, *Negotiation,* 6th ed. (New York: McGraw-Hill/Irwin, 2009).

39. J. C. Magee, A. D. Galinsky, and D. H. Gruenfeld, "Power, Propensity to Negotiate, and Moving First in Competitive Interactions," *Personality and Social Psychology Bulletin* (February 2007), pp. 200–212.

40. H. R. Bowles, L. Babcock, and L. Lei, "Social Incentives for Gender Differences in the Propensity to Initiative Negotiations: Sometimes It Does Hurt to Ask," *Organizational Behavior and Human Decision Processes* 103 (2007), pp. 84–103.

41. D. A. Moore, "Myopic Prediction, Self-Destructive Secrecy, and the Unexpected Benefits of Revealing Final Deadlines in Negotiation," *Organizational Behavior & Human Decision Processes* (July 2004), pp. 125–139.

42. E. Wilson, "The Trouble with Jake," *The New York Times* (July 15, 2009), www.nytimes.com.

43. J. R. Curhan, H. A. Elfenbein, and H. Xu, "What Do People Value When They Negotiate? Mapping the Domain of Subjective Value in Negotiation," *Journal of Personality and Social Psychology* 91, no. 3 (2006), pp. 493–512.

44. Thomas, "Conflict and Negotiation Processes in Organizations."

45. P. M. Morgan and R. S. Tindale, "Group vs. Individual Performance in Mixed-Motive Situations: Exploring an Inconsistency," *Organizational Behavior & Human Decision Processes* (January 2002), pp. 44–65.

46. C. E. Naquin, "The Agony of Opportunity in Negotiation: Number of Negotiable Issues, Counterfactual Thinking, and Feelings of Satisfaction," *Organizational Behavior & Human Decision Processes* (May 2003), pp. 97–107.

47. M. Giacomantonio, C. K. W. De Dreu, and L. Mannetti, "Now You See It, Now You Don't: Interests, Issues, and Psychological Distance in Integrative Negotiation," *Journal of Personality and Social Psychology* 98, no. 5 (2010), pp. 761–774.

48. F. S. Ten Velden, B. Beersma, and C. K. W. De Dreu, "It Takes One to Tango: The Effect of Dyads' Epistemic Motivation Composition in Negotiation," *Personality and Social Psychology Bulletin* 36, no. 11 (2010), pp. 1454–1466.

49. C. K. W. De Dreu, L. R. Weingart, and S. Kwon, "Influence of Social Motives on Integrative Negotiation: A Meta-Analytic Review and Test of Two Theories," *Journal of Personality & Social Psychology* (May 2000), pp. 889–905.

50. This model is based on R. J. Lewicki, "Bargaining and Negotiation," *Exchange: The Organizational Behavior Teaching Journal* 6, no. 2 (1981), pp. 39–40.

51. J. R. Curhan, H. A. Elfenbein, and G. J. Kilduff, "Getting Off on the Right Foot: Subjective Value Versus Economic Value in Predicting Longitudinal Job Outcomes from Job Offer Negotiations," *Journal of Applied Psychology* 94, no. 2 (2009), pp. 524–534.

52. M. H. Bazerman and M. A. Neale, *Negotiating Rationally* (New York: The Free Press, 1992), pp. 67–68.

53. R. P. Larrick and G. Wu, "Claiming a Large Slice of a Small Pie: Asymmetric Disconfirmation in Negotiation," *Journal of Personality and Social Psychology* 93, no. 2 (2007), pp. 212–233.

54. T. A. Judge, B. A. Livingston, and C. Hurst, "Do Nice Guys—and Gals—Really Finish Last? The Joint Effects of Sex and Agreeableness on Income," *Journal of Personality and Social Psychology* 102 (2012), pp. 390–407.

55. N. Dimotakis, D. E. Conlon, and R. Ilies, "The Mind and Heart (Literally) of the Negotiator: Personality and Contextual Determinants of Experiential Reactions and Economic Outcomes in Negotiation," *Journal of Applied Psychology* 97 (2012), pp. 183–193.

56. E. T. Amanatullah, M. W. Morris, and J. R. Curhan, "Negotiators Who Give Too Much: Unmitigated Communion, Relational Anxieties, and Economic Costs in Distributive and Integrative Bargaining," *Journal of Personality and Social Psychology* 95, no. 3 (2008), pp. 723–738; and D. S. DeRue, D. E. Conlon, H. Moon, and H. W. Willaby, "When Is Straightforwardness a Liability in Negotiations? The Role of Integrative Potential and Structural Power," *Journal of Applied Psychology* 94, no. 4 (2009), pp. 1032–1047.

57. B. Barry and R. A. Friedman, "Bargainer Characteristics in Distributive and Integrative Negotiation," *Journal of Personality & Social Psychology* (February 1998), pp. 345–359; and H. A. Elfenbein, J. R. Curhan, N. Eisenkraft, A. Shirako, and L. Baccaro, "Are Some Negotiators Better than Others? Individual Differences in Bargaining Outcomes," *Journal of Research in Personality* (December 2008), pp. 1463–1475.

58. A. Zerres, J. Hüffmeier, P. A. Freund, K. Backhaus, and G. Hertel, "Does It Take Two to Tango? Longitudinal Effects of Unilaterial and Bilateral Integrative Negotiation Training," *Journal of Applied Psychology* 98 (2013), pp. 478–491.

59. G. Lelieveld, E. Van Dijk, I. Van Beest, and G. A. Van Kleef, "Why Anger and Disappointment Affect Other's Bargaining Behavior Differently: The Moderating Role of Power and the Mediating Role of Reciprocal Complementary Emotions," *Personality and Social Psychology Bulletin* 38 (2012), pp. 1209–1221.

60. S. Côté, I. Hideg, and G. A. van Kleef, "The Consequences of Faking Anger in Negotiations," *Journal of Experimental Social Psychology* 49 (2013), pp. 453–463.

61. G. A. Van Kleef and C. K. W. De Dreu, "Longer-Term Consequences of Anger Expression in Negotiation: Retaliation or Spillover?" *Journal of Experimental Social Psychology* 46, no. 5 (2010), pp. 753–760.

62. H. Adam and A. Shirako, "Not All Anger Is Created Equal: The Impact of the Expresser's Culture on the Social Effects of Anger in Negotiations," *Journal of Applied Psychology* (2013).

63. Lelieveld, Van Dijk, Van Beest, and Van Kleef, "Why Anger and Disappointment Affect Other's Bargaining Behavior Differently."

64. M. Olekalns and P. L Smith, "Mutually Dependent: Power, Trust, Affect, and the Use of Deception in Negotiation," *Journal of Business Ethics* 85, no. 3 (2009), pp. 347–365.

65. A. W. Brooks and M. E. Schweitzer, "Can Nervous Nellie Negotiate? How Anxiety Causes Negotiators to Make Low First Offers, Exit Early, and Earn Less Profit," *Organizational Behavior and Human Decision Processes* 115, no. 1 (2011), pp. 43–54.

66. M. Sinaceur, H. Adam, G. A. Van Kleef, and A. D. Galinsky, "The Advantages of Being Unpredictable: How Emotional Inconsistency Extracts Concessions in Negotiation," *Journal of Experimental Social Psychology* 49 (2013), pp. 498–508.

67. K. Leary, J. Pillemer, and M. Wheeler, "Negotiating with Emotion," *Harvard Business Review* (January–February 2013), pp. 96–103.

68. L. A. Liu, R. Friedman, B. Barry, M. J. Gelfand, and Z. Zhang, "The Dynamics of Consensus Building in Intracultural and Intercultural Negotiations," *Administrative Science Quarterly* 57 (2012), pp. 269–304.

69. M. Liu, "The Intrapersonal and Interpersonal Effects of Anger on Negotiation Strategies: A Cross-Cultural Investigation," *Human Communication Research* 35, no. 1 (2009), pp. 148–169; and H. Adam, A. Shirako, and W. W. Maddux, "Cultural Variance in the Interpersonal Effects of Anger in Negotiations," *Psychological Science* 21, no. 6 (2010), pp. 882–889.

70. P. D. Trapnell and D. L. Paulhus, "Agentic and Communal Values: Their Scope and Measurement," *Journal of Personality Assessment* 94 (2012), pp. 39–52.

71. C. T. Kulik and M. Olekalns, "Negotiating the Gender Divide: Lessons from the Negotiation and Organizational Behavior Literatures," *Journal of Management* 38 (2012), pp. 1387–1415.

72. C. Suddath, "The Art of Haggling," *Bloomberg Businessweek* (November 26, 2012), p. 98.

73. Kulik and Olekalns, "Negotiating the Gender Divide," p. 1390.

74. A. Tugend, "Tips for Putting a Price on Your Work," *The New York Times* (January 28, 2012), p. B5.

75. L. J. Kray, C. C. Locke, and A B. Van Zant, "Feminine Charm: An Experimental Analysis of its Costs and Benefits

in Negotiations," *Personality and Social Psychology Bulletin* 38 (2012), pp. 1343–1357.

76. S. de Lemus, R. Spears, M. Bukowski, M. Moya, and J. Lupiáñez, "Reversing Implicit Gender Stereotype Activation as a Function of Exposure to Traditional Gender Roles," *Social Psychology* 44 (2013), pp. 109–116.

77. D. A. Small, M. Gelfand, L. Babcock, and H. Gettman, "Who Goes to the Bargaining Table? The Influence of Gender and Framing on the Initiation of Negotiation," *Journal of Personality and Social Psychology* 93, no. 4 (2007), pp. 600–613.

78. E. T. Amanatullah and M. W. Morris, "Negotiating Gender Roles: Gender Differences in Assertive Negotiating Are Mediated by Women's Fear of Backlash and Attenuated When Negotiating on Behalf of Others," *Journal of Personality and Social Psychology* 98, no. 2 (2010), pp. 256–267.

CHAPTER 15

1. L. Garicano and Y. Wu, "Knowledge, Communication, and Organizational Capabilities," *Organization Science* (September–October 2012), pp. 1382–1397.

2. See, for instance, R. L. Daft, *Organization Theory and Design,* 10th ed. (Cincinnati, OH: South-Western Publishing, 2010).

3. T. W. Malone, R. J. Laubacher, and T. Johns, "The Age of Hyperspecialization," *Harvard Business Review* (July–August 2011), pp. 56–65.

4. J. G. Miller, "The Real Women's Issue: Time," *The Wall Street Journal* (March 9–10, 2013), p. C3.

5. J. Schramm, "A Cloud of Workers," *HR Magazine* (March 2013), p. 80.

6. C. Woodyard, "Toyota Brass Shakeup Aims to Give Regions More Control," *USA Today* (March 6, 2013), www .usatoday.com/story/money/cars/2013/03/06/toyota-shakeup/1966489/.

7. C. Hymowitz, "Managers Suddenly Have to Answer to a Crowd of Bosses," *The Wall Street Journal* (August 12, 2003), p. B1.

8. See, for instance, "How Hierarchy Can Hurt Strategy Execution," *Harvard Business Review* (July–August 2010), pp. 74–75.

9. See, for instance, J. H. Gittell, "Supervisory Span, Relational Coordination, and Flight Departure Performance: A Reassessment of Postbureaucracy Theory," *Organization Science* (July–August 2001), pp. 468–483.

10. F. A. Csascar, "Organizational Structure as a Determinant of Performance: Evidence from Mutual Funds," *Strategic Management Journal* (June 2013), pp. 611–632.

11. B. Brown and S. D. Anthony, "How P&G Tripled Its Innovation Success Rate," *Harvard Business Review* (June 2011), pp. 64–72.

12. A. Leiponen and C. E. Helfat, "Location, Decentralization, and Knowledge Sources for Innovation," *Organization Science* 22, no. 3 (2011), pp. 641–658.

13. K. Parks, "HSBC Unit Charged in Argentine Tax Case," *The Wall Street Journal* (March 19, 2013), p. C2.

14. P. Hempel, Z.-X. Zhang, and Y. Han, "Team Empowerment and the Organizational Context: Decentralization and the

15. H. Mintzberg, *Structure in Fives: Designing Effective Organizations* (Upper Saddle River, NJ: Prentice Hall, 1983), p. 157.

16. A. Murray, "Built Not to Last," *The Wall Street Journal* (March 18, 2013), p. A11.

17. W. M. Bulkeley, "Back from the Brink," *The Wall Street Journal* (April 24, 2006), pp. B1, B3.

18. L. R. Burns and D. R. Wholey, "Adoption and Abandonment of Matrix Management Programs: Effects of Organizational Characteristics and Interorganizational Networks," *Academy of Management Journal* (February 1993), pp. 106–138; J. R. Galbraith, *Designing Matrix Organizations That Actually Work: How IBM, Procter & Gamble, and Others Design for Success* (San Francisco: Jossey Bass, 2009); and E. Krell, "Managing the Matrix," *HRMagazine* (April 2011), pp. 69–71.

19. See, for instance, M. Bidwell, "Politics and Firm Boundaries: How Organizational Structure, Group Interests, and Resources Affect Outsourcing," *Organization Science* (November–December 2012), pp. 1622–1642.

20. See, for instance, T. Sy and L. S. D'Annunzio, "Challenges and Strategies of Matrix Organizations: Top-Level and Mid-Level Managers' Perspectives," *Human Resource Planning* 28, no. 1 (2005), pp. 39–48; and T. Sy and S. Cote, "Emotional Intelligence: A Key Ability to Succeed in the Matrix Organization," *Journal of Management Development* 23, no. 5 (2004), pp. 437–455.

21. N. Anand and R. L. Daft, "What Is the Right Organization Design?" *Organizational Dynamics* 36, no. 4 (2007), pp. 329–344.

22. See, for instance, R. E. Miles and C. C. Snow, "The New Network Firm: A Spherical Structure Built on Human Investment Philosophy," *Organizational Dynamics* (Spring 1995), pp. 5–18; D. Pescovitz, "The Company Where Everybody's a Temp," *New York Times Magazine* (June 11, 2000), pp. 94–96; B. Hedberg, G. Dahlgren, J. Hansson, and N. Olve, *Virtual Organizations and Beyond* (New York: Wiley, 2001); N. S. Contractor, S. Wasserman, and K. Faust, "Testing Multitheoretical, Multilevel Hypotheses About Organizational Networks: An Analytic Framework and Empirical Example," *Academy of Management Review* 31, no. 3 (2006) pp. 681–703; and Y. Shin, "A Person-Environment Fit Model for Virtual Organizations," *Journal of Management* (October 2004), pp. 725–743.

23. J. Bates, "Making Movies and Moving On," *Los Angeles Times* (January 19, 1998), p. A1.

24. D. Dahl, "Want a Job? Let the Bidding Begin," *Inc.* (March 2011), pp. 94–96.

25. J. Schramm, "At Work in a Virtual World," *HR Magazine* (June 2010), p. 152.

26. C. B. Gibson and J. L. Gibbs, "Unpacking the Concept of Virtuality: The Effects of Geographic Dispersion, Electronic Dependence, Dynamic Structure, and National Diversity on Team Innovation," *Administrative Science Quarterly* 51, no. 3 (2006), pp. 451–495; H. M. Latapie and V. N. Tran, "Subculture Formation, Evolution, and Conflict Between Regional Teams in Virtual Organizations," *The Business Review* (Summer 2007), pp. 189–193; and S. Davenport and U. Daellenbach, "'Belonging' to a Virtual

Research Center: Exploring the Influence of Social Capital Formation Processes on Member Identification in a Virtual Organization" *British Journal of Management* 22, no. 1 (2011), pp. 54–76.

27. A. Poon and K. Tally, "Yoga-Pants Supplier Says Lululemon Stretches Truth," *The Wall Street Journal* (March 20, 2013), p. B1.

28. "GE: Just Your Average Everyday $60 Billion Family Grocery Store," *IndustryWeek* (May 2, 1994), pp. 13–18.

29. General Electric Company Annual Financials, MarketWatch, *The Wall Street Journal* (April 9, 2013), www.marketwatch.com/investing/stock/ge/financials.

30. J. Scheck, L. Moloney, and A. Flynn, "Eni, CNPC Link Up in Mozambique," *The Wall Street Journal* (March 15, 2013), p. B3.

31. See, for example, U. Wassmer, "Alliance Portfolios: A Review and Research Agenda," *Journal of Management* 36, no. 1 (2010), pp. 141–171; A. M. Hess and F. T. Rothaemel, "When Are Assets Complementary? Star Scientists, Strategic Alliances, and Innovation in the Pharmaceutical Industry," *Strategic Management Journal* 32, no. 8 (2011), pp. 895–909; and J. A. Adegbesan and M. J. Higgins, "The Intra-Alliance Division of Value Created through Collaboration," *Strategic Management Journal* 32, no. 2 (2011), pp. 187–211.

32. Z. Yao, Z. Yang, G. Fisher, C. Ma, and E. Fang, "Knowledge Complementarity, Knowledge Absorption Effectiveness, and New Product Performance: The Exploration of International Joint Ventures in China," *International Business Review* (February 2013), pp. 216–227.

33. S. Constable, "Google's Motorola Starts Layoffs," *The Wall Street Journal* (March 8, 2013), video broadcast with George Stahl, http://online.wsj.com/article/B5AAEF65-2F62-487E-AE7E-EDBD4E0D20F8.html#!B5AAEF65-2F62-487E-AE7E-EDBD4E0D20F8; and R. Yu, "Google's Motorola Mobility to Cut Additional 1,200 Jobs," *USA Today* (March 8, 2013), www.usatoday.com/story/tech/2013/03/08/googles-motorola-mobility-to-cut-jobs/1973007/.

34. S. Brady, "American Express Kicks Off 2013 With Biggest Layoffs in Four Years," *Brand Channel* (January 10, 2013), www.brandchannel.com/home/post/American-Express-Layoffs-011013.aspx; and R. Sidel and A. R. Johnson, "Travel Cuts at AmEx Point to End of Era," *The Wall Street Journal* (January 13, 2013), http://online.wsj.com/article/SB10001424127887324595704578239493843399684.html#articleTabs%3Darticle.

35. "Starbucks Reports 13% Rise in Profit," *The New York Times* (January 24, 2013), www.nytimes.com/2013/01/25/business/starbucks-earnings-increased-13-in-latest-quarter.html?_r=0.

36. See J. P. Guthrie and D. K. Datta, "Dumb and Dumber: The Impact of Downsizing on Firm Performance as Moderated by Industry Conditions," *Organization Science* 19, no. 1 (2008), pp. 108–123; and K. P. De Meuse, T. J. Bergmann, P. A. Vanderheiden, and C. E. Roraff, "New Evidence Regarding Organizational Downsizing and a Firm's Financial Performance: A Long-Term Analysis," *Journal of Managerial Issues* 16, no. 2 (2004), pp. 155–177.

37. L. Alpert, "Can Imported CEO Fix Russian Cars?" *The Wall Street Journal* (March 20, 2013), p. B1.

38. See, for example, C. O. Trevor and A. J. Nyberg, "Keeping Your Headcount When All About You Are Losing Theirs: Downsizing, Voluntary Turnover Rates, and the Moderating Role of HR Practices," *Academy of Management Journal* 51, no. 2 (2008), pp. 259–276; T. M. Probst, S. M. Stewart, M. L. Gruys, and B. W. Tierney, "Productivity, Counterproductivity and Creativity: The Ups and Downs of Job Insecurity," *Journal of Occupational and Organizational Psychology* 80, no. 3 (2007), pp. 479–497; and C. P. Maertz, J. W. Wiley, C. LeRouge, and M. A. Campion, "Downsizing Effects on Survivors: Layoffs, Offshoring, and Outsourcing," *Industrial Relations* 49, no. 2 (2010), pp. 275–285.

39. C. D. Zatzick, and R. D. Iverson, "High-Involvement Management and Workforce Reduction: Competitive Advantage or Disadvantage?" *Academy of Management Journal* 49, no. 5 (2006), pp. 999–1015; A. Travaglione, and B. Cross, "Diminishing the Social Network in Organizations: Does There Need to Be Such a Phenomenon as 'Survivor Syndrome' After Downsizing?" *Strategic Change* 15, no. 1 (2006), pp. 1–13; and J. D. Kammeyer-Mueller, H. Liao, and R. D. Arvey, "Downsizing and Organizational Performance: A Review of the Literature from a Stakeholder Perspective," *Research in Personnel and Human Resources Management* 20 (2001), pp. 269–329.

40. T. Burns and G. M. Stalker, *The Management of Innovation* (London: Tavistock, 1961); and J. A. Courtright, G. T. Fairhurst, and L. E. Rogers, "Interaction Patterns in Organic and Mechanistic Systems," *Academy of Management Journal* (December 1989), pp. 773–802.

41. This analysis is referred to as a contingency approach to organization design. See, for instance, J. M. Pennings, "Structural Contingency Theory: A Reappraisal," in B. M. Staw and L. L. Cummings (eds.), *Research in Organizational Behavior*, vol. 14 (Greenwich, CT: JAI Press, 1992), pp. 267–309; J. R. Hollenbeck, H. Moon, A. P. J. Ellis, B. J. West, D. R. Ilgen, L. Sheppard, C. O. L. H. Porter, and J. A. Wagner III, "Structural Contingency Theory and Individual Differences: Examination of External and Internal Person-Team Fit," *Journal of Applied Psychology* (June 2002), pp. 599–606; and A. Drach-Zahavy and A. Freund, "Team Effectiveness Under Stress: A Structural Contingency Approach," *Journal of Organizational Behavior* 28, no. 4 (2007), pp. 423–450.

42. The strategy–structure thesis was originally proposed in A. D. Chandler Jr., *Strategy and Structure: Chapters in the History of the Industrial Enterprise* (Cambridge, MA: MIT Press, 1962). For an updated analysis, see T. L. Amburgey and T. Dacin, "As the Left Foot Follows the Right? The Dynamics of Strategic and Structural Change," *Academy of Management Journal* (December 1994), pp. 1427–1452.

43. See R. E. Miles and C. C. Snow, *Organizational Strategy, Structure, and Process* (New York: McGraw-Hill, 1978); D. C. Galunic and K. M. Eisenhardt, "Renewing the Strategy–Structure–Performance Paradigm," in B. M. Staw and L. L. Cummings (eds.), *Research in Organizational Behavior*, vol. 16 (Greenwich, CT: JAI Press, 1994), pp. 215–255; and S. M. Toh, F. P. Morgeson, and M. A. Campion, "Human Resource Configurations: Investigating Fit with the Organizational Context," *Journal of Applied Psychology* 93, no. 4 (2008), pp. 864–882.

44. M. Mesco, "Moleskine Tests Appetite for IPOs," *The Wall Street Journal* (March 19, 2013), p. B8.

45. See C. Perrow, "A Framework for the Comparative Analysis of Organizations," *American Sociological Review* (April 1967), pp. 194–208; J. Hage and M. Aiken, "Routine Technology,

Social Structure, and Organizational Goals," *Administrative Science Quarterly* (September 1969), pp. 366–377; C. C. Miller, W. H. Glick, Y. Wang, and G. P. Huber, "Understanding Technology-Structure Relationships: Theory Development and Meta-Analytic Theory Testing," *Academy of Management Journal* (June 1991), pp. 370–399; and W. D. Sine, H. Mitsuhashi, and D. A. Kirsch, "Revisiting Burns and Stalker: Formal Structure and New Venture Performance in Emerging Economic Sectors," *Academy of Management Journal* 49, no. 1 (2006), pp. 121–132.

46. G. G. Dess and D. W. Beard, "Dimensions of Organizational Task Environments," *Administrative Science Quarterly* (March 1984), pp. 52–73; E. A. Gerloff, N. K. Muir, and W. D. Bodensteiner, "Three Components of Perceived Environmental Uncertainty: An Exploratory Analysis of the Effects of Aggregation," *Journal of Management* (December 1991), pp. 749–768; and O. Shenkar, N. Aranya, and T. Almor, "Construct Dimensions in the Contingency Model: An Analysis Comparing Metric and Non-metric Multivariate Instruments," *Human Relations* (May 1995), pp. 559–580.

47. C. S. Spell and T. J. Arnold, "A Multi-Level Analysis of Organizational Justice and Climate, Structure, and Employee Mental Health," *Journal of Management* 33, no. 5 (2007), pp. 724–751; and M. L. Ambrose and M. Schminke, "Organization Structure as a Moderator of the Relationship Between Procedural Justice, Interactional Justice, Perceived Organizational Support, and Supervisory Trust," *Journal of Applied Psychology* 88, no. 2 (2003), pp. 295–305.

48. See, for instance, Spell and Arnold, "A Multi-Level Analysis of Organizational Justice Climate, Structure, and Employee Mental Health"; J. D. Shaw and N. Gupta, "Job Complexity, Performance, and Well-Being: When Does Supplies-Values Fit Matter? *Personnel Psychology* 57, no. 4 (2004), 847–879; and C. Anderson and C. E. Brown, "The Functions and Dysfunctions of Hierarchy," *Research in Organizational Behavior* 30 (2010), pp. 55–89.

49. T. Martin, "Pharmacies Feel More Heat," *The Wall Street Journal* (March 16–17, 2013), p. A3.

50. See, for instance, R. E. Ployhart, J. A. Weekley, and K. Baughman, "The Structure and Function of Human Capital Emergence: A Multilevel Examination of the Attraction-Selection-Attrition Model," *Academy of Management Journal* 49, no. 4 (2006), pp. 661–677.

51. J. B. Stewart, "A Place to Play for Google Staff," *The New York Times* (March 16, 2013), p. B1.

52. See, for instance, B. K. Park, J. A. Choi, M. Koo, et al., "Culture, Self, and Preference Structure: Transitivity and Context Independence Are Violated More by Interdependent People," *Social Cognition* (February 2013), pp. 106–118.

53. J. Hassard, J. Morris, and L. McCann, "'My Brilliant Career'? New Organizational Forms and Changing Managerial Careers in Japan, the UK, and USA," *Journal of Management Studies* (May 2012), pp. 571–599.

CHAPTER 16

1. See, for example, E. H. Schein, "Culture: The Missing Concept in Organization Studies," *Administrative Science Quarterly* 41, no. 2 (1996), pp. 229–240.

2. This seven-item description is based on C. A. O'Reilly III, J. Chatman, and D. F. Caldwell, "People and Organizational Culture: A Profile Comparison Approach to Assessing Person-Organization Fit," *Academy of Management Journal* (September 1991), pp. 487–516; and J. A. Chatman and K. A. Jehn, "Assessing the Relationship Between Industry Characteristics and Organizational Culture: How Different Can You Be?" *Academy of Management Journal* (June 1994), pp. 522–553.

3. K. S. Cameron, R. E. Quinn, J. DeGraff, and A. V. Thakor, *Competing Values Leadership: Creating Value in Organizations* (Cheltenham, UK and Northampton, MA: Edward Elgar, 2006).

4. C. A. Hartnell, A. Y. Ou, and A. Kinicki, "Organizational Culture and Organizational Effectiveness: A Meta-Analytic Investigation of the Competing Values Framework's Theoretical Suppositions," *Journal of Applied Psychology,* Online first publication (January 17, 2011), doi: 10.1037/a0021987.

5. The view that there will be consistency among perceptions of organizational culture has been called the "integration" perspective. For a review of this perspective and conflicting approaches, see D. Meyerson and J. Martin, "Cultural Change: An Integration of Three Different Views," *Journal of Management Studies* (November 1987), pp. 623–647; and P. J. Frost, L. F. Moore, M. R. Louis, C. C. Lundberg, and J. Martin (eds.), *Reframing Organizational Culture* (Newbury Park, CA: Sage, 1991).

6. See J. M. Jermier, J. W. Slocum Jr., L. W. Fry, and J. Gaines, "Organizational Subcultures in a Soft Bureaucracy: Resistance Behind the Myth and Facade of an Official Culture," *Organization Science* (May 1991), pp. 170–194; and P. Lok, R. Westwood, and J. Crawford, 'Perceptions of Organisational Subculture and their Significance for Organisational Commitment,' *Applied Psychology: An International Review* 54, no. 4 (2005), pp. 490–514.

7. D. A. Hoffman and L. M. Jones, "Leadership, Collective Personality, and Performance," *Journal of Applied Psychology* 90, no. 3 (2005), pp. 509–522.

8. T. Hsieh, "Zappos's CEO on Going to Extremes for Customers," *Harvard Business Review* (July/August 2010), pp. 41–45.

9. See, for example, G. G. Gordon and N. DiTomaso, "Predicting Corporate Performance from Organizational Culture," *Journal of Management Studies* (November 1992), pp. 793–798; J. B. Sorensen, "The Strength of Corporate Culture and the Reliability of Firm Performance," *Administrative Science Quarterly* (March 2002), pp. 70–91; and J. Rosenthal and M. A. Masarech, "High-Performance Cultures: How Values Can Drive Business Results," *Journal of Organizational Excellence* (Spring 2003), pp. 3–18.

10. Y. Wiener, "Forms of Value Systems: A Focus on Organizational Effectiveness and Cultural Change and Maintenance," *Academy of Management Review* (October 1988), p. 536; and B. Schneider, A. N. Salvaggio, and M. Subirats, "Climate Strength: A New Direction for Climate Research," *Journal of Applied Psychology* 87 (2002), pp. 220–229.

11. R. T. Mowday, L. W. Porter, and R. M. Steers, *Employee Linkages: The Psychology of Commitment, Absenteeism,*

and Turnover (New York: Academic Press, 1982); C. Vandenberghe, "Organizational Culture, Person-Culture Fit, and Turnover: A Replication in the Health Care Industry," *Journal of Organizational Behavior* (March 1999), pp. 175–184; and M. Schulte, C. Ostroff, S. Shmulyian, and A. Kinicki, "Organizational Climate Configurations: Relationships to Collective Attitudes, Customer Satisfaction, and Financial Performance," *Journal of Applied Psychology* 94, no. 3 (2009), pp. 618–634.

12. J. W. Grizzle, A. R. Zablah, T. J. Brown, J. C. Mowen, and J. M. Lee, "Employee Customer Orientation in Context: How the Environment Moderates the Influence of Customer Orientation on Performance Outcomes," *Journal of Applied Psychology* 94, no. 5 (2009), pp. 1227–1242.

13. M. R. Bashshur, A. Hernández, and V. González-Romá, "When Managers and Their Teams Disagree: A Longitudinal Look at the Consequences of Differences in Perceptions of Organizational Support," *Journal of Applied Psychology* 96, no. 3 (2011), pp. 558–573.

14. S. L. Dolan and S. Garcia, "Managing by Values: Cultural Redesign for Strategic Organizational Change at the Dawn of the Twenty-First Century," *Journal of Management Development* 21, no. 2 (2002), pp. 101–117.

15. See C. A. O'Reilly and J. A. Chatman, "Culture as Social Control: Corporations, Cults, and Commitment," in B. M. Staw and L. L. Cummings (eds.), *Research in Organizational Behavior*, vol. 18 (Greenwich, CT: JAI Press, 1996), pp. 157–200. See also M. Pinae Cunha, "The 'Best Place to Be': Managing Control and Employee Loyalty in a Knowledge-Intensive Company," *Journal of Applied Behavioral Science* (December 2002), pp. 481–495.

16. Y. Ling, Z. Simsek, M. H. Lubatkin, and J. F. Veiga, "Transformational Leadership's Role in Promoting Corporate Entrepreneurship: Examining the CEO-TMT Interface," *Academy of Management Journal* 51, no. 3 (2008), pp. 557–576; and A. Malhotra, A. Majchrzak, and B. Rosen, Benson, "Leading Virtual Teams," *Academy of Management Perspectives* 21, no. 1 (2007), pp. 60–70.

17. D. Denison, "What Is the Difference Between Organizational Culture and Organizational Climate? A Native's Point of View on a Decade of Paradigm Wars," *Academy of Management Review* 21 (1996) pp. 519–654; and L. R. James, C. C. Choi, C. E. Ko, P. K. McNeil, M. K. Minton, M. A. Wright, and K. Kim, "Organizational and Psychological Climate: A Review of Theory and Research," *European Journal of Work and Organizational Psychology* 17, no. 1 (2008), pp. 5–32.

18. J. Z. Carr, A. M. Schmidt, J. K. Ford, and R. P. DeShon, "Climate Perceptions Matter: A Meta-Analytic Path Analysis Relating Molar Climate, Cognitive and Affective States, and Individual Level Work Outcomes," *Journal of Applied Psychology* 88, no. (2003), pp. 605–619.

19. Schulte, Ostroff, Shmulyian, and Kinicki, "Organizational Climate Configurations."

20. S. D. Pugh, J. Dietz, A. P. Brief, and J. W. Wiley, "Looking Inside and Out: The Impact of Employee and Community Demographic Composition on Organizational Diversity Climate," *Journal of Applied Psychology* 93, no. 6 (2008), pp. 1422–1428; K. H. Ehrhart, L. A. Witt, B. Schneider, and S. J. Perry, "Service Employees Give as They Get: Internal Service as a Moderator of the Service Climate-Service Outcomes Link," *Journal of Applied Psychology* 96, no. 2 (2011), pp. 423–431; and A. Simha and J. B. Cullen, "Ethical Climates and Their Effects on Organizational Outcomes: Implications from the Past and Prophecies for the Future," *Academy of Management Perspectives* (November 2011), pp. 20–34.

21. J. C. Wallace, P. D. Johnson, K. Mathe, and J. Paul, "Structural and Psychological Empowerment Climates, Performance, and the Moderating Role of Shared Felt Accountability: A Managerial Perspective," *Journal of Applied Psychology* 96, no. 3 (2011), pp. 840–850.

22. J. M. Beus, S. C. Payne, M. E. Bergman, and W. Arthur, "Safety Climate and Injuries: An Examination of Theoretical and Empirical Relationships," *Journal of Applied Psychology* 95, no. 4 (2010), pp. 713–727.

23. A. Simha and J. B. Cullen, "Ethical Climates and Their Effects on Organizational Outcomes: Implications from the Past and Prophecies for the Future," *Academy of Management* (November 2012), pp. 20–34.

24. Ibid.

25. Simha and Cullen, "Ethical Climates and Their Effects on Organizational Outcomes."

26. A. Arnaud, "Conceptualizing and Measuring Ethical Work Climate Development and Validation of the Ethical Climate Index," *Business & Society* (June 2010), pp. 345–458.

27. A. Arnaud and M. Schminke, "The Ethical Climate and Context of Organizations: A Comprehensive Model," *Organization Science* (November–December 2012), pp. 1767–1780.

28. J. P. Kotter, "Change Management: Accelerate!" *Harvard Business Review* (November 2012), pp. 44–58.

29. R. Walker, "Behind the Music," *Fortune* (October 29, 2012), pp. 57–58.

30. M. Herper, "Niche Pharma," *Forbes* (September 24, 2012), pp. 80–89.

31. R. Pyrillis, "2012 Optimas Award Winners: ChildNet," *Workforce Management* (November 2012), pp. 24–26.

32. C. Hannan, "Management Secrets from the Meanest Company in America," *Bloomberg Businessweek* (January 2, 2013), pp. 46–51.

33. Ibid.

34. J. Bandler and D. Burke, "How HP Lost Its Way," *Fortune* (May 21, 2012), pp. 147–164.

35. R. L. Jepperson, "Institutions, Institutional Effects, and Institutionalism," in W. W. Powell and P. J. DiMaggio (eds.), *The New Institutionalism in Organizational Analysis* (Chicago: University of Chicago Press, 1991), pp. 143–163; G. F. Lanzara and G. Patriotta, "The Institutionalization of Knowledge in an Automotive Factory: Templates, Inscriptions, and the Problems of Durability," *Organization Studies* 28, no. 5 (2007), pp. 635–660; and T. B. Lawrence, M. K. Mauws, B. Dyck, and R. F. Kleysen, "The Politics of Organizational Learning: Integrating Power into the 4I Framework," *Academy of Management Review* (January 2005), pp. 180–191.

36. J. B. Sorensen, "The Strength of Corporate Culture and the Reliability of Firm Performance," *Administrative Science Quarterly* (March 2002), pp. 70–91.

37. See T. Cox Jr., *Cultural Diversity in Organizations: Theory, Research & Practice* (San Francisco: Berrett-Koehler, 1993),

pp. 162–170; L. Grensing-Pophal, "Hiring to Fit Your Corporate Culture," *HRMagazine* (August 1999), pp. 50–54; and D. L. Stone, E. F. Stone-Romero, and K. M. Lukaszewski, "The Impact of Cultural Values on the Acceptance and Effectiveness of Human Resource Management Policies and Practices," *Human Resource Management Review* 17, no. 2 (2007), pp. 152–165.

38. S. Cartwright and C. L. Cooper, "The Role of Culture Compatibility in Successful Organizational Marriages," *Academy of Management Executive* (May 1993), pp. 57–70; R. A. Weber and C. F. Camerer, "Cultural Conflict and Merger Failure: An Experimental Approach," *Management Science* (April 2003), pp. 400–412; and I. H. Gleibs, A. Mummendey, and P. Noack, "Predictors of Change in Postmerger Identification During a Merger Process: A Longitudinal Study," *Journal of Personality and Social Psychology* 95, no. 5 (2008), pp. 1095–1112.

39. P. Gumbel, "Return of the Urge to Merge," *Time Europe Magazine* (July 13, 2003), www.time.com/time/europe/magazine/article/0,13005,901030721-464418,00.html.

40. E. H. Schein, "The Role of the Founder in Creating Organizational Culture," *Organizational Dynamics* (Summer 1983), pp. 13–28; and Y. L. Zhao, O. H. Erekson, T. Wang, and M. Song, "Pioneering Advantages and Entrepreneurs' First-Mover Decisions: An Empirical Investigation for the United States and China," *Journal of Product Innovation Management* (December 2012), pp. 190–210.

41. E. H. Schein, "Leadership and Organizational Culture," in F. Hesselbein, M. Goldsmith, and R. Beckhard (eds.), *The Leader of the Future* (San Francisco: Jossey-Bass, 1996), pp. 61–62.

42. See, for example, J. R. Harrison and G. R. Carroll, "Keeping the Faith: A Model of Cultural Transmission in Formal Organizations," *Administrative Science Quarterly* (December 1991), pp. 552–582; and D. E. Bowen and C. Ostroff, "The 'Strength' of the HRM System, Organizational Climate Formation, and Firm Performance," *Academy of Management Review* 29 (2004), pp. 203–221.

43. B. Schneider, H. W. Goldstein, and D. B. Smith, "The ASA Framework: An Update," *Personnel Psychology* (Winter 1995), pp. 747–773; D. M. Cable and T. A. Judge, "Interviewers' Perceptions of Person-Organization Fit and Organizational Selection Decisions," *Journal of Applied Psychology* (August 1997), pp. 546–561; M. L. Verquer, T. A. Beehr, and S. H. Wagner, "A Meta-Analysis of Relations Between Person-Organization Fit and Work Attitudes," *Journal of Vocational Behavior* (December 2003), pp. 473–489; and W. Li, Y. Wang, P. Taylor, K. Shi, and D. He, "The Influence of Organizational Culture on Work-Related Personality Requirement Ratings: A Multilevel Analysis," *International Journal of Selection and Assessment* 16, no. 4 (2008), pp. 366–384.

44. R. Levering and M. Moskowitz, "And the Winners Are . . .," *Fortune* (January 20, 2011), http://money.cnn.com/magazines/fortune/bestcompanies/2011/full_list/.

45. D. C. Hambrick and P. A. Mason, "Upper Echelons: The Organization as a Reflection of Its Top Managers," *Academy of Management Review* (April 1984), pp. 193–206; M. A. Carpenter, M. A. Geletkanycz, and W. G. Sanders, "Upper Echelons Research Revisited: Antecedents, Elements, and Consequences of Top Management Team Composition," *Journal of Management* 30, no. 6 (2004), pp. 749–778, and H. Wang, A. S. Tsui, and K. R. Xin, "CEO Leadership Behaviors, Organizational Performance, and Employees' Attitudes," *The Leadership Quarterly* 22, no. 1 (2011), pp. 92–105.

46. "100 Best Companies to Work For," *Fortune* (2013), http://money.cnn.com/magazines/fortune/best-companies/2013/snapshots/5.html, accessed June 28, 2013.

47. See, for instance, J. P. Wanous, *Organizational Entry*, 2nd ed. (New York: Addison-Wesley, 1992); D. M. Cable and C. K. Parsons, "Socialization Tactics and Person-Organization Fit," *Personnel Psychology* (Spring 2001), pp. 1–23; and T. N. Bauer, T. Bodner, B. Erdogan, D. M. Truxillo, and J. S. Tucker, "Newcomer Adjustment During Organizational Socialization: A Meta-Analytic Review of Antecedents, Outcomes, and Methods," *Journal of Applied Psychology* 92, no. 3 (2007), pp. 707–721.

48. G. Kranz, "Training That Starts Before the Job Begins," *Workforce Management Online* (July 2009), www.workforce.com.

49. R. E. Silverman, "Companies Try to Make the First Day for New Hires More Fun," *The Wall Street Journal* (May 28, 2013), http://online.wsj.com/article/SB10001424127887323336104578501631475934850.html.

50. D. C. Feldman, "The Multiple Socialization of Organization Members," *Academy of Management Review* (April 1981), p. 310.

51. C. J. Collins, "The Interactive Effects of Recruitment Practices and Product Awareness on Job Seekers' Employer Knowledge and Application Behaviors," *Journal of Applied Psychology* 92, no. 1 (2007), pp. 180–190.

52. J. D. Kammeyer-Mueller and C. R. Wanberg, "Unwrapping the Organizational Entry Process: Disentangling Multiple Antecedents and Their Pathways to Adjustment," *Journal of Applied Psychology* 88 (2003), pp. 779–794; E. W. Morrison, "Longitudinal Study of the Effects of Information Seeking on Newcomer Socialization," *Journal of Applied Psychology* 78 (2003), pp. 173–183; and M. Wangm Y. Zhan, E. McCune, and D. Truxillo, "Understanding Newcomers' Adaptability and Work-Related Outcomes: Testing the Mediating Roles of Perceived P-E Fit Variables," *Personnel Psychology* 64, no. 1 (2011), pp. 163–189.

53. E. W. Morrison, "Newcomers' Relationships: The Role of Social Network Ties During Socialization," *Academy of Management Journal* 45 (2002), pp. 1149–1160.

54. T. N. Bauer, T. Bodner, B. Erdogan, D. M. Truxillo, and J. S. Tucker, "Newcomer Adjustment During Organizational Socialization: A Meta-Analytic Review of Antecedents, Outcomes, and Methods," *Journal of Applied Psychology* 92, no. 3 (2007), pp. 707–721.

55. W. R. Boswell, A. J. Shipp, S. C., Payne, and S. S. Culbertson, "Changes in Newcomer Job Satisfaction Over Time: Examining the Pattern of Honeymoons and Hangovers," *Journal of Applied Psychology* 94, no. 4 (2009), pp. 844–858.

56. C Vandenberghe, A. Panaccio, K. Bentein, K. Mignonac, and P. Roussel, "Assessing Longitudinal Change of and Dynamic Relationships Among Role Stressors, Job Attitudes, Turnover Intention, and Well-Being in Neophyte Newcomers," *Journal of Organizational Behavior* 32, no. 4 (2011), pp. 652–671.

57. E. Ransdell, "The Nike Story? Just Tell It!" *Fast Company* (January–February 2000), pp. 44–46; and A. Muccino, "Exclusive Interview with Chuck Eichten," *Liquid Brand Summit Blog*, (February 4, 2011), http://blog.liquidbrand-summit.com/.

58. D. M. Boje, "The Storytelling Organization: A Study of Story Performance in an Office-Supply Firm," *Administrative Science Quarterly* (March 1991), pp. 106–126; and M. Ricketts and J. G. Seiling, "Language, Metaphors, and Stories: Catalysts for Meaning Making in Organizations," *Organization Development Journal* (Winter 2003), pp. 33–43l.

59. A. J. Shipp and K. J. Jansen, "Reinterpreting Time in Fit Theory: Crafting and Recrafting Narratives of Fit in Medias Res," *Academy of Management Review* 36, no. 1 (2011), pp. 76–101.

60. See G. Islam and M. J. Zyphur, "Rituals in Organizations: A Review and Expansion of Current Theory," *Group and Organization Management* 34, no. 1 (2009), pp. 114–139.

61. M. Moskowitz and F. Levering, "The 100 Best Companies to Work For," *Fortune* (February 6, 2012), p. 120.

62. A. Bryant, "Take the Bus, and Watch the Ideas Flow," *The New York Times* (September 16, 2012), p. 2.

63. M. G. Pratt and A. Rafaeli "Artifacts and Organizations: Understanding Our Objective Reality," in A. Rafaeli and M. G. Pratt, *Artifacts and Organizations: Beyond Mere Symbolism* (Mahwah, NJ: Lawrence Erlbaum, 2006), pp. 279–288.

64. B. Gruley, "Relaxed Fit," *Bloomberg Businessweek* (September 17–23, 2012), pp. 98–99.

65. M. Moskowitz and R. Levering, "The 100 Best Companies to Work For," *Fortune* (February 6, 2012), pp. 117–124.

66. See B. Victor and J. B. Cullen, "The Organizational Bases of Ethical Work Climates," *Administrative Science Quarterly* (March 1988), pp. 101–125; R. L. Dufresne, "An Action Learning Perspective on Effective Implementation of Academic Honor Codes," *Group & Organization Management* (April 2004), pp. 201–218; and A. Ardichvilli, J. A. Mitchell, and D. Jondle, "Characteristics of Ethical Business Cultures," *Journal of Business Ethics* 85, no. 4 (2009), pp. 445–451.

67. K. Lynn, "National Security Agency," Universum Top 100 IT, www.universumglobal.com, accessed June 27, 2013.

68. J. P. Mulki, J. F. Jaramillo, and W. B. Locander, "Critical Role of Leadership on Ethical Climate and Salesperson Behaviors," *Journal of Business Ethics* 86, no. 2 (2009), pp. 125–141; M. Schminke, M. L. Ambrose, and D. O. Neubaum, "The Effect of Leader Moral Development on Ethical Climate and Employee Attitudes," *Organizational Behavior and Human Decision Processes* 97, no. 2 (2005), pp. 135–151; and M. E. Brown, L. K. Treviño, and D. A. Harrison, "Ethical Leadership: A Social Learning Perspective for Construct Development and Testing," *Organizational Behavior and Human Decision Processes* 97, no. 2 (2005), pp. 117–134.

69. D. M. Mayer, M. Kuenzi, R. Greenbaum, M. Bardes, and S. Salvador, "How Low Does Ethical Leadership Flow? Test of a Trickle-Down Model," *Organizational Behavior and Human Decision Processes* 108, no. 1 (2009), pp. 1–13.

70. B. Sweeney, D. Arnold, and B. Pierce, "The Impact of Perceived Ethical Culture of the Firm and Demographic Variables on Auditors' Ethical Evaluation and Intention to Act Decisions," *Journal of Business Ethics* 93, no. 4 (2010), pp. 531–551.

71. M. L. Gruys, S. M. Stewart, J. Goodstein, M. N. Bing, and A. C. Wicks, "Values Enactment in Organizations: A Multi-Level Examination," *Journal of Management* 34, no. 4 (2008), pp. 806–843.

72. D. L. Nelson and C. L. Cooper (eds.), *Positive Organizational Behavior* (London: Sage, 2007); K. S. Cameron, J. E. Dutton, and R. E. Quinn (eds.), *Positive Organizational Scholarship: Foundations of a New Discipline* (San Francisco: Berrett-Koehler, 2003); and F. Luthans and C. M. Youssef, "Emerging Positive Organizational Behavior," *Journal of Management* (June 2007), pp. 321–349.

73. J. Robison, "Great Leadership Under Fire," *Gallup Leadership Journal* (March 8, 2007), pp. 1–3.

74. R. Wagner and J. K. Harter, *12: The Elements of Great Managing* (New York: Gallup Press, 2006).

75. M. Mihelich, "2012 Optimas Award Winners: Safelite AutoGlass," *Workforce Management* (November 2012), p. 27.

76. R. Wagner and J. K. Harter, "Performance Reviews Without the Anxiety," *Gallup Leadership Journal* (July 12, 2007), pp. 1–4; and Wagner and Harter, *12: The Elements of Great Managing*.

77. S. Fineman, "On Being Positive: Concerns and Counterpoints," *Academy of Management Review* 31, no. 2 (2006), pp. 270–291.

78. D. P. Ashmos and D. Duchon, "Spirituality at Work: A Conceptualization and Measure," *Journal of Management Inquiry* (June 2000), p. 139; and E. Poole, "Organisational Spirituality: A Literature Review," *Journal of Business Ethics* 84, no. 4 (2009), pp. 577–588.

79. L. W. Fry and J. W. Slocum, "Managing the Triple Bottom Line Through Spiritual Leadership," *Organizational Dynamics* 37, no. 1 (2008), pp. 86–96.

80. This section is based on I. A. Mitroff and E. A. Denton, *A Spiritual Audit of Corporate America: A Hard Look at Spirituality, Religion, and Values in the Workplace* (San Francisco: Jossey-Bass, 1999); E. H. Burack, "Spirituality in the Workplace," *Journal of Organizational Change Management* 12, no. 3 (1999), pp. 280–291; and C. L. Jurkiewicz and R. A. Giacalone, "A Values Framework for Measuring the Impact of Workplace Spirituality on Organizational Performance," *Journal of Business Ethics* 49, no. 2 (2004), pp. 129–142.

81. See, for example, B. S. Pawar, "Workplace Spirituality Facilitation: A Comprehensive Model," *Journal of Business Ethics* 90, no. 3 (2009), pp. 375–386; and L. Lambert, *Spirituality Inc.: Religion in the American Workplace* (New York: New York University Press, 2009).

82. M Oppenheimer, "The Rise of the Corporate Chaplain," *Bloomberg Businessweek* (August 23, 2012), pp. 58–61.

83. M. Lips-Miersma, K. L. Dean, and C. J. Fornaciari, "Theorizing the Dark Side of the Workplace Spirituality Movement," *Journal of Management Inquiry* 18, no. 4 (2009), pp. 288–300.

84. J.-C. Garcia-Zamor, "Workplace Spirituality and Organizational Performance," *Public Administration Review* (May–June 2003), pp. 355–363; and L. W. Fry, S. T. Hannah, M. Noel, and F. O. Walumbwa, "Impact of Spiritual Leadership on Unit Performance," *Leadership Quarterly* 22, no. 2 (2011), pp. 259–270.

85. A. Rego and M. Pina e Cunha, "Workplace Spirituality and Organizational Commitment: An Empirical Study," *Journal of Organizational Change Management* 21, no. 1 (2008), pp. 53–75; and R. W. Kolodinsky, R. A. Giacalone, and C. L. Jurkiewicz, "Workplace Values and Outcomes: Exploring Personal, Organizational, and Interactive Workplace Spirituality," *Journal of Business Ethics* 81, no. 2 (2008), pp. 465–480.

86. J. Nicas, "American, US Airways Face Challenges in Integration," *The Wall Street Journal* (February 14, 2013), http://online.wsj.com/article/SB10001424127887324432 00457830419216293 1544.html.

87. D. J. McCarthy and S. M. Puffer, "Interpreting the Ethicality of Corporate Governance Decision in Russia: Utilizing Integrative Social Contracts Theory to Evaluate the Relevance of Agency Theory Norms," *Academy of Management Review* 33, no. 1 (2008), pp. 11–31.

88. P. Dvorak, "A Firm's Culture Can Get Lost in Translation," *The Wall Street Journal* (April 3, 2006), pp. B1, B3; K. Kranhold, "The Immelt Era, Five Years Old, Transforms GE," *The Wall Street Journal* (September 11, 2006), pp. B1, B3; and S. McCartney, "Teaching Americans How to Behave Abroad," *The Wall Street Journal* (April 11, 2006), pp. D1, D4.

89. R. Vesely, "Seven Seas Change," *Workforce Management* (September 2012), pp. 20–21.

CHAPTER 17

1. See B. Becker and B. Gerhart, "The Impact of Human Resource Management on Organizational Performance: Progress and Prospects," *Academy of Management Journal* (August 1996), pp. 779–801; M. A. Huselid, S. E. Jackson, and R. S. Schuler, "Technical and Strategic Human Resource Management Effectiveness as Determinants of Firm Performance," *Academy of Management Journal* (February 1997), pp. 171–188; C. J. Collins, and K. D. Clark, "Strategic Human Resource Practices, Top Management Team Social Networks, and Firm Performance: The Role of Human Resource Practices in Creating Organizational Competitive Advantage," *Academy of Management Journal* (December 2003), pp. 740–751; D. E. Bowen and C. Ostroff, "Understanding HRM–Firm Performance Linkages: The Role of the 'Strength' of the HRM System," *Academy of Management Review* (April 2004), pp. 203–221; and K. Birdi, C. Clegg, M. Patterson, A. Robinson, C. B. Stride, T. D. Wall, and S. J. Wood, "The Impact of Human Resource and Operational Management Practices on Company Productivity: A Longitudinal Study," *Personnel Psychology* 61, no. 3 (2008), pp. 467–501.

2. M. Diamond and A. W. Boyd, "Manufacturers Search for Workers to Sustain Revival," *USA Today* (May 7, 2012), http://usatoday30.usatoday.com/money/industries/manufacturing/story/2012-05-03/manufacturing-jobs-economy/54813582/1; and L. Weber, "On the Hunt for Tech Hires," *The Wall Street Journal* (April 11, 2012), p. B6.

3. C. Hymowitz and J. Green, "Executive Headhunters Squeezed by In-House Recruiters," *Bloomberg Businessweek* (January 17, 2013), www.businessweek.com/articles/2013-01-17/executive-headhunters-squeezed-by-in-house-recruiters.

4. D. Zielinski, "Get to the Source," *HR Magazine* (November 2012), pp. 67–70.

5. G. Anders, "Solve Puzzle, Get Job," *Forbes* (May 6, 2013), pp. 46–48; and S. Sengupta, "Waiting and Waiting for Green Cards," *The Wall Street Journal* (April 12, 2013), pp. B1, B6.

6. See, for instance, A. L. Kristof-Brown, R. D. Zimmerman, and E. C. Johnson, "Consequences of Individual's Fit at Work: A Meta-Analysis of Person-Job, Person-Organization, Person-Group, and Person-Supervisor Fit," *Personnel Psychology* 58, no. 2 (2005), pp. 281–342; and D. S. DeRue and F. P. Morgeson, "Stability and Change in Person-Team and Person-Role Fit over Time: The Effects of Growth Satisfaction, Performance, and General Self-Efficacy," *Journal of Applied Psychology* 92, no. 5 (2007), pp. 1242–1253.

7. L. Weber, "Seeking Software Fix for Job-Search Game," *The Wall Street Journal* (June 6, 2012), p. B8.

8. L. Hill, "Only BFFs Need Apply," *Bloomberg Businessweek* (January 7–13, 2013), pp. 63–65; and L. Petrecca, "Entrepreneurs Hire Close to Home: Their Moms," *USA Today* (August 20, 2012), p. 4B.

9. H. Husock, "From Prison to a Paycheck," *The Wall Street Journal* (August 4, 2012), p. C3; E. Krell, "Criminal Background," *HR Magazine* (February 2012), pp. 45–54; and M. Waldo, "Second Chances: Employing Convicted Felons," *HR Magazine* (March 2012), pp. 36–41.

10. A. M. F. Hiemstra, E. Derous, A. W. Serlie, and M. P. Born, "Fairness Perceptions of Video Résumés among Ethnically Diverse Applicants," *International Journal of Selection and Assessment* (December 2012), pp. 423–433.

11. K. Gray, "Facial-Recognition Technology Might Get Employers in Trouble," *HR Magazine* (April 2012), p. 17.

12. C. L. Wilkin and C. E. Connelly, "Do I Look Like Someone Who Cares? Recruiters' Ratings of Applicants' Paid and Volunteer Experience," *International Journal of Selection and Assessment* (September 2012), pp. 308–316.

13. M. M. Breslin, "Can You Handle Rejection?" *Workforce Management* (October 2012), pp. 32–36.

14. C. Suddath, "Imaginary Friends," *Bloomberg Businessweek* (January 21–27, 2013), p. 68.

15. M. Goodman, "Reference Checks Go Tech," *Workforce Management* (May 2012), pp. 26–28.

16. L. Kwoh, "Workplace Crystal Ball, Courtesy of Facebook," *The Wall Street Journal* (February 21, 2012), p. B8.

17. J. B. Bernerth, S. G. Taylor, H. J. Walker, and D. S. Whitman, "An Empirical Investigation of Dispositional Antecedents and Performance-Related Outcomes of Credit Scores," *Journal of Applied Psychology* 97 (2012), pp. 469–478.

18. H. B. Bernerth, "Demographic Variables and Credit Scores: An Empirical Study of a Controversial Selection Tool," *International Journal of Selection and Assessment* (June 2012), pp. 242–250.

19. H. O'Neill, "Thinking Outside the Box," *Workforce Management* (January 2012), pp. 24–26.

20. L. Weber, "Didn't Get the Job? You'll Never Know Why," *The Wall Street Journal* (June 4, 2013), www.online.wsj.com/article/SB10001424127887324423904578523683173841190.html?mod=wsj_valettop_email; and D. Meinert, "Search and Verify," *HR Magazine* (December 2012), pp. 37–41.

21. E. J. Hirst, "Business Risks Rise in Criminal History Discrimination," *The Chicago Tribune* (October 21, 2012),

http://articles.chicagotribune.com/2012-10-21/business/ct-biz-1021-eeoc-felony-20121021_1_criminal-records-eeocs-chicago-district-office-court-case.

22. C. Lachnit, "The Cost of Not Doing Background Checks," *Workforce Management*, www.workforce.com.

23. Cited in J. H. Prager, "Nasty or Nice: 56-Question Quiz," *The Wall Street Journal* (February 22, 2000), p. A4; see also H. Wessel, "Personality Tests Grow Popular," *Seattle Post–Intelligencer* (August 3, 2003), p. G1; and E. Frauenheim, "Personality Tests Adapt to the Times," *Workforce Management* (February 2010), p. 4.

24. E. Maltby, "To Find Best Hires, Firms Become Creative," *The Wall Street Journal* (November 17, 2009), p. B6.

25. J. P. Hausknecht, D. V. Day, and S. C. Thomas, "Applicant Reactions to Selection Procedures: An Updated Model and Meta-Analysis," *Personnel Psychology* (September 2004), pp. 639–683.

26. J. E. Hunter, "Cognitive Ability, Cognitive Aptitudes, Job Knowledge, and Job Performance," *Journal of Vocational Behavior* 29, no. 3 (1986), pp. 340–362; and F. L. Schmidt, "Cognitive Tests Used in Selection Can Have Content Validity as Well as Criterion Validity: A Broader Research Review and Implications for Practice," *International Journal of Selection and Assessment* (March 2012), pp. 1–13.

27. F. L. Schmidt, and J. Hunter, "General Mental Ability in the World of Work: Occupational Attainment and Job Performance," *Journal of Personality and Social Psychology* 86, no. 1 (2004), pp. 162–173; and F. L. Schmidt, J. A. Shaffer, and I. Oh, "Increased Accuracy for Range Restriction Corrections: Implications for the Role of Personality and General Mental Ability in Job and Training Performance," *Personnel Psychology* 61, no. 4 (2008), pp. 827–868.

28. J. F. Salgado, N. Anderson, S. Moscoso, C. Bertua, F. de Fruyt, and J. P. Rolland, "A Meta-Analytic Study of General Mental Ability Validity for Different Occupations in the European Community," *Journal of Applied Psychology* (December 2003), pp. 1068–1081.

29. W. Poundstone, "The Google Cheat Sheet," *Bloomberg Businessweek* (January 9–15, 2012), p. 79.

30. M. R. Barrick, M. K. Mount, and T. A. Judge, "Personality and Performance at the Beginning of the New Millennium: What Do We Know and Where Do We Go Next?" *International Journal of Selection & Assessment* (March–June 2001), pp. 9–30; M. R. Barrick, G. L. Stewart, and M. Piotrowski, "Personality and Job Performance: Test of the Mediating Effects of Motivation Among Sales Representatives," *Journal of Applied Psychology* (February 2002), pp. 43–51; and C. J. Thoresen, J. C. Bradley, P. D. Bliese, and J. D. Thoresen, "The Big Five Personality Traits and Individual Job Performance and Growth Trajectories in Maintenance and Transitional Job Stages," *Journal of Applied Psychology* (October 2004), pp. 835–853.

31. C. J. König, A.-S. Merz, and N. Trauffer, "What Is in Applicants' Minds When They Fill Out a Personality Test? Insights from a Qualitative Study," *International Journal of Selection and Assessment* (December 2012), pp. 442–450; R. N. Landers, P. R. Sackett, and K. A. Tuzinski, "Retesting after Initial Failure, Coaching Rumors, and Warnings against Faking in Online Personality Measures for Selection," *Journal of Applied Psychology* 96, no. 1 (2011), pp. 202–210; and

J. P. Hausknecht, "Candidate Persistence and Personality Test Practice Effects: Implications for Staffing System Management," *Personnel Psychology* 63, no. 2 (2010), pp. 299–324.

32. Z. Galic, Z. Jerneic, and M. P. Kovacic, "Do Applicants Fake Their Personality Questionnaire Responses and How Successful Are Their Attempts? A Case of Military Pilot Cadent Selection," *International Journal of Selection and Assessment* (June 2012), pp. 229–241.

33. J. Fan, D. Gao, S. A. Carroll, F. J. Lopen, T. S. Tian, and H. Meng, "Testing the Efficacy of a New Procedure for Reducing Faking on Personality Tests Within Selection Contexts," *Journal of Applied Psychology* 97 (2012), pp. 866–880.

34. I. Oh, G. Wang, and M. K. Mount, "Validity of Observer Ratings of the Five-Factor Model of Personality Traits: A Meta-Analysis," *Journal of Applied Psychology* 96, no. 4 (2011), pp. 762–773; and B. S. Connelly and D. S. Ones, "An Other Perspective on Personality: Meta-Analytic Integration of Observers' Accuracy and Predictive Validity," *Psychological Bulletin* 136, no. 6 (2010), pp. 1092–1122.

35. D. S. Ones, C. Viswesvaran, and F. L. Schmidt, "Comprehensive Meta-Analysis of Integrity Test Validities: Findings and Implications for Personnel Selection and Theories of Job Performance," *Journal of Applied Psychology* (August 1993), pp. 679–703; D. S. Ones, C. Viswesvaran, and F. L. Schmidt, "Personality and Absenteeism: A Meta-Analysis of Integrity Tests," *European Journal of Personality* (March–April 2003), Supplement 1, pp. S19–S38; and C. M. Berry, P. R. Sackett, and S. Wiemann, "A Review of Recent Developments in Integrity Test Research," *Personnel Psychology* 60, no. 2 (2007), pp. 271–301.

36. C. H. Van Iddekinge, P. L. Roth, P. H. Raymark, and H. N. Odle-Dusseau, "The Criterion-Related Validity of Integrity Tests: An Updated Meta-Analysis," *Journal of Applied Psychology* 97 (2012), pp. 499–530.

37. P. L. Roth, P. Bobko, and L. A. McFarland, "A Meta-Analysis of Work Sample Test Validity: Updating and Integrating Some Classic Literature," *Personnel Psychology* 58, no. 4 (2005), pp. 1009–1037.

38. See, for instance, A. C. Spychalski, M. A. Quinones, B. B. Gaugler, and K. Pohley, "A Survey of Assessment Center Practices in Organizations in the United States, *Personnel Psychology* (Spring 1997), pp. 71–90; C. Woodruffe, *Development and Assessment Centres: Identifying and Assessing Competence* (London: Institute of Personnel and Development, 2000); and J. Schettler, "Building Bench Strength," *Training* (June 2002), pp. 55–58.

39. F. Lievens, H. Peeters, and E. Schollaert, "Situational Judgment Tests: A Review of Recent Research," *Personnel Review* 37, no. 4 (2008), pp. 426–441.

40. F. Lievens, T. Buyse, P. R. Sackett, and B. S. Connelly, "The Effects of Coaching on Situational Judgment Tests in High-Stakes Selection," *International Journal of Selection and Assessment* (September 2012), pp. 272–282.

41. F. Lievens, and F. Patterson, "The Validity and Incremental Validity of Knowledge Tests, Low-Fidelity Simulations, and High-Fidelity Simulations for Predicting Job Performance in Advanced-Level High-Stakes Selection," *Journal of Applied Psychology*, Online First Publication (April 11, 2011), doi: 10.1037/a0023496.

42. M. A. Tucker, "Show and Tell," *HR Magazine* (January 2012), pp. 51–53.

43. J. Alsever, "How to Get a Job: Show, Don't Tell," *Fortune* (March 19, 2012), pp. 29–31.

44. B. K. Griepentrog, C. M. Harold, B. C. Holtz, R. J. Kimoski, and S. M. Marsh, "Integrating Social Identity and the Theory of Planned Behavior: Predicting Withdrawal from an Organizational Recruitment Process," *Personnel Psychology* 65 (2012), pp. 723–753.

45. R. A. Posthuma, F. P. Moregeson, and M. A. Campion, "Beyond Employment Interview Validity: A Comprehensive Narrative Review of Recent Research and Trend Over Time," *Personnel Psychology* (Spring 2002), p. 1; and S. L. Wilk and P. Cappelli, "Understanding the Determinants of Employer Use of Selection Methods," *Personnel Psychology* (Spring 2003), p. 111.

46. B. W. Swider, M. R. Barrick, T. B. Harris, and A. C. Stoverink, "Managing and Creating an Image in the Interview; The Role of Interviewee Initial Impressions," *Journal of Applied Psychology*, Online First Publication, (May 30, 2011), doi: 10.1037/a0024005.

47. J. M. Madera and M. R. Hebl, "Discrimination Against Facially Stigmatized Applicants in Interviews: An Eye-Tracking and Face-to-Face Investigation," *Journal of Applied Psychology* 97 (2012), pp. 317–330.

48. K. I. van der Zee, A. B. Bakker, and P. Bakker, "Why Are Structured Interviews So Rarely Used in Personnel Selection?" *Journal of Applied Psychology* (February 2002), pp. 176–184.

49. See M. A. McDaniel, D. L. Whetzel, F. L. Schmidt, and S. D. Maurer, "The Validity of Employment Interviews: A Comprehensive Review and Meta-Analysis," *Journal of Applied Psychology* (August 1994), pp. 599–616; M. A. Campion, D. K. Palmer, and J. E. Campion, "A Review of Structure in the Selection Interview," *Personnel Psychology* (Autumn 1997), pp. 655–702; A. I. Huffcutt and D. J. Woehr, "Further Analysis of Employment Interview Validity: A Quantitative Evaluation of Interviewer-Related Structuring Methods," *Journal of Organizational Behavior* (July 1999), pp. 549–560; and M. Ziegler, E. Dietl, E. Danay, M. Vogel, and M. Bühner, "Predicting Training Success with General Mental Ability, Specific Ability Tests, and (Un)Structured Interviews: A Meta-Analysis with Unique Samples," *International Journal of Selection and Assessment* 19, no. 2 (2011), pp. 170–182.

50. van der Zee, Bakker, and Bakker, "Why Are Structured Interviews So Rarely Used in Personnel Selection?"

51. A. Bryant, "You Can't Find the Future in the Archives," *The New York Times* (January 29, 2012), p. 2.

52. T. W. Dougherty, D. B. Turban, and J. C. Callender, "Confirming First Impressions in the Employment Interview: A Field Study of Interviewer Behavior," *Journal of Applied Psychology* (October 1994), pp. 659–665; and M. R. Barrick, B. W. Swider, and G. L. Stewart, "Initial Evaluations in the Interview: Relationships with Subsequent Interviewer Evaluations and Employment Offers," *Journal of Applied Psychology* 95, no. 6 (2010), pp. 1163–1172.

53. K. G. Melchers, N. Lienhardt, M. von Aarburg, and M. Kleinmann, "Is More Structure Really Better? A Comparison of Frame-of-Reference Training and Descriptively Anchored Rating Scales to Improve Interviewers' Rating Quality," *Personnel Psychology* 64, no. 1 (2011), pp. 53–87.

54. F. L. Schmidt and R. D. Zimmerman, "A Counterintuitive Hypothesis About Employment Interview Validity and Some Supporting Evidence," *Journal of Applied Psychology* 89, no. 3 (2004), pp. 553–561.

55. See G. A. Adams, T. C. Elacqua, and S. M. Colarelli, "The Employment Interview as a Sociometric Selection Technique," *Journal of Group Psychotherapy* (Fall 1994), pp. 99–113; R. L. Dipboye, "Structured and Unstructured Selection Interviews: Beyond the Job-Fit Model," *Research in Personnel Human Resource Management* 12 (1994), pp. 79–123; B. Schneider, D. B. Smith, S. Taylor, and J. Fleenor, "Personality and Organizations: A Test of the Homogeneity of Personality Hypothesis," *Journal of Applied Psychology* (June 1998), pp. 462–470; and M. Burke, "Funny Business," *Forbes* (June 9, 2003), p. 173.

56. N. Anderson and C. Witvliet, "Fairness Reactions to Personnel Selection Methods: An International Comparison Between the Netherlands, the United States, France, Spain, Portugal, and Singapore," *International Journal of Selection and Assessment* 16, no. 1 (2008), pp. 1–13.

57. American Society for Training and Development, *2010 State of the Industry Report*, www.astd.org/content/research.

58. T. Minton-Eversole and K. Gurchiek, "New Workers Not Ready for Prime Time," *HR Magazine* (December 2006), pp. 28–34.

59. P. Galagan, "Bridging the Skills Gap: New Factors Compound the Growing Skills Shortage," *T1D*, (February 2010), pp. 44–49.

60. M. Smulian, "England Fails on Numeracy and Literacy," *Public Finance* (February 6, 2009), p. 13; E. K. Sharma, "Growing a New Crop of Talent: India Inc. Is Increasingly Going Rural," *Business Today* (June 28, 2009), http://businesstoday.intoday.in/; and G. Paton, "Almost Half of Employers Forced to Teach Teenagers Basic Literacy and Numeracy Skills," *Telegraph* (May 9, 2011), www.telegraph.com.

61. D. Baynton, "America's $60 Billion Problem," *Training*, (May 2001) p. 52.

62. G. Anand, "India Graduates Millions, But Few Are Fit to Hire," *The Wall Street Journal* (April 5, 2011), www.online.wsj.com.

63. J. Barbarian, "Mark Spear: Director of Management and Organizational Development, Miller Brewing Co.," *Training* (October 2001), pp. 34–38.

64. See, for example, P. J. Taylor, D. F. Russ-Eft, and H. Taylor, "Transfer of Management Training from Alternative Perspectives," *Journal of Applied Psychology* 94, no. 1 (2009), pp. 104–121.

65. See, for example, S. Lim and A. Lee, "Work and Nonwork Outcomes of Workplace Incivility: Does Family Support Help?" *Journal of Occupational Health Psychology* 16, no. 1 (2011), pp. 95–111; C. L. Porath and C. M. Pearson, "The Cost of Bad Behavior," *Organizational Dynamics* 39, no. 1 (2010), pp. 64–71; and B. Estes and J. Wang, "Workplace Incivility: Impacts on Individual and Organizational Performance," *Human Resource Development Review* 7, no. 2 (2008), pp. 218–240.

66. M. P. Leiter, H. K. S. Laschinger, A. Day, and D. G. Oore, "The Impact of Civility Interventions on Employee Social

Behavior, Distress, and Attitudes," *Journal of Applied Psychology*, Advance online publication (July 11, 2011), doi: 10.1037/a0024442.

67. G. R. Weaver, L. K. Trevino, and P. L. Cochran, "Corporate Ethics Practices in the Mid-1990's: An Empirical Study of the Fortune 1000," *Journal of Business Ethics* (February 1999), pp. 283–294.

68. M. B. Wood, *Business Ethics in Uncertain Times* (Upper Saddle River, NJ: Prentice Hall, 2004), p. 61.

69. See, for example, D. Seligman, "Oxymoron 101," *Forbes* (October 28, 2002), pp. 160–164; and R. B. Schmitt, "Companies Add Ethics Training; Will It Work?" *The Wall Street Journal* (November 4, 2002), p. B1; A. Becker, "Can You Teach Ethics to MBAs?" *BNet* (October 19, 2009), www.bnet .com.

70. W. R. Allen, P. Bacdayan, K. B. Kowalski, and M. H. Roy, "Examining the Impact of Ethics Training on Business Student Values," *Education and Training* 47, no. 3 (2005), pp. 170–182; A. Lämsä, M. Vehkaperä, T. Puttonen, and H. Pesonen, "Effect of Business Education on Women and Men Students' Attitudes on Corporate Responsibility in Society," *Journal of Business Ethics* 82, no. 1 (2008), pp. 45–58; and K. M. Sheldon and L. S. Krieger, "Understanding the Negative Effects of Legal Education on Law Students: A Longitudinal Test of Self-Determination Theory," *Personality and Social Psychology Bulletin* 33, no. 6 (2007), pp. 883–897.

71. S. Valentine and G. Fleischman, "Ethics Programs, Perceived Corporate Social Responsibility, and Job Satisfaction," *Journal of Business Ethics* 77, no. 2 (2008), pp. 159–172.

72. L. Weber and L. Kwoh, "Co-Workers Change Places," *The Wall Street Journal* (February 21, 2012), p. B8.

73. K. Tyler, "A New U," *HR Magazine* (April 2012), pp. 27–34.

74. See, for instance, R. E. Derouin, B. A. Fritzsche, and E. Salas, "E-Learning in Organizations," *Journal of Management* 31, no. 3 (2005), pp. 920–940; and K. A. Orvis, S. L. Fisher, and M. E. Wasserman, "Power to the People: Using Learner Control to Improve Trainee Reactions and Learning in Web-Based Instructional Environments," *Journal of Applied Psychology* 94, no 4 (2009), pp. 960–971.

75. T. Sitzmann, K. Kraiger, D. Stewart, and R. Wisher, "The Comparative Effectiveness of Web-Based and Classroom Instruction: A Meta-Analysis," *Personnel Psychology* 59, no. 3 (2006), pp. 623–664.

76. T. Sitzmann, B. S. Bell, K. Kraiger, and A. M. Kanar, "A Multilevel Analysis of the Effect of Prompting Self-Regulation in Technology-Delivered Instruction," *Personnel Psychology* 62 no. 4 (2009), pp. 697–734.

77. B. Roberts, "From E-Learning to Mobile Learning," *HR Magazine* (August 2012), pp. 61–65.

78. E. A. Ensher, T. R. Nielson, and E. Grant-Vallone, "Tales from the Hiring Line: Effects of the Internet and Technology on HR Processes," *Organizational Dynamics* 31, no. 3 (2002), pp. 232–233; and J. B. Arbaugh, "Do Undergraduates and MBAs Differ Online? Initial Conclusions from the Literature," *Journal of Leadership and Organizational Studies* 17, no. 2 (2010), pp. 129–142.

79. G. M. Alliger, S. I. Tannenbaum, W. Bennett, H. Traver, and A. Shotland, "A Meta-Analysis of the Relations Among Training Criteria," *Personnel Psychology* 50, no. 2 (1997),

pp. 341–358; and T. Sitzmann, K. G. Brown, W. J. Casper, K. Ely, and R. D. Zimmerman, "A Review and Meta-Analysis of the Nomological Network of Trainee Reactions," *Journal of Applied Psychology* 93, no. 2 (2008), pp. 280–295.

80. J. A. Colquitt, J. A. LePine, and R. A. Noe, "Toward an Integrative Theory of Training Motivation: A Meta-Analytic Path Analysis of 20 Years of Research," *Journal of Applied Psychology* (October 2000), pp. 678–707.

81. See L. A. Burke and H. S. Hutchins, "Training Transfer: An Integrative Literature Review," *Human Resource Development Review* 6 (2007), pp. 263–296; and D. S. Chiaburu and S. V. Marinova, "What Predicts Skill Transfer? An Exploratory Study of Goal Orientation, Training Self-Efficacy, and Organizational Supports," *International Journal of Training and Development* 9, no. 2 (2005), pp. 110–123.

82. M. Rotundo and P. R. Sackett, "The Relative Importance of Task, Citizenship, and Counterproductive Performance to Global Ratings of Job Performance: A Policy Capturing Approach," *Journal of Applied Psychology* 87, no. 1 (2002), pp. 66–80; and S. W. Whiting, P. M. Podsakoff, and J. R. Pierce, "Effects of Task Performance, Helping, Voice, and Organizational Loyalty on Performance Appraisal Ratings," *Journal of Applied Psychology* 93, no. 1 (2008), pp. 125–139.

83. W. F. Cascio and H. Aguinis, *Applied Psychology in Human Resource Management,* 7th ed. (Upper Saddle River, NJ: Prentice Hall, 2010).

84. A. H. Locher and K. S. Teel, "Appraisal Trends," *Personnel Journal* (September 1988), pp. 139–145.

85. Cited in S. Armour, "Job Reviews Take on Added Significance in Down Times," *USA Today* (July 23, 2003), p. 4B.

86. D. J. Woehr, M. K. Sheehan, and W. Bennett, "Assessing Measurement Equivalence Across Rating Sources: A Multitrait-Multirater Approach," *Journal of Applied Psychology* 90, no. 3 (2005), pp. 592–600; and H. Heidemeier and K. Moser, "Self–Other Agreement in Job Performance Ratings: A Meta-Analytic Test of a Process Model," *Journal of Applied Psychology* 94, no. 2 (March 2009), pp. 353–370.

87. See, for instance, J. D. Facteau and S. B. Craig, "Are Performance Appraisal Ratings from Different Rating Sources Compatible?" *Journal of Applied Psychology* (April 2001), pp. 215–227; J. F. Brett and L. E. Atwater, "360-Degree Feedback: Accuracy, Reactions, and Perceptions of Usefulness," *Journal of Applied Psychology* (October 2001), pp. 930–942; F. Luthans and S. J. Peterson, "360 Degree Feedback with Systematic Coaching: Empirical Analysis Suggests a Winning Combination," *Human Resource Management* (Fall 2003), pp. 243–256; and B. I. J. M. van der Heijden and A. H. J. Nijhof, "The Value of Subjectivity: Problems and Prospects for 360-Degree Appraisal Systems," *International Journal of Human Resource Management* (May 2004), pp. 493–511.

88. M. K. Mount and S. E. Scullen, "Multisource Feedback Ratings: What Do They Really Measure?" in M. London (Ed.), *How People Evaluate Others in Organizations* (Mahwah, NJ: Lawrence Erlbaum, 2001), pp. 155–176; and K.-Y. Ng, C. Koh, S. Ang, J. C. Kennedy, and K. Chan, "Rating Leniency and Halo in Multisource Feedback Ratings: Testing Cultural Assumptions of Power Distance and Individualism-Collectivism," *Journal of Applied Psychology*,

Online First Publication (April 11, 2011), doi: 10.1037/a0023368.

89. C. Rampbell, "A History of College Grade Inflation," *The New York Times* (July 14, 2011), accessed at http://economix.blogs.nytimes.com/2011/07/14/the-history-of-college-grade-inflation/?scp51&sq5grade%20inflation&st5cse.

90. X. M. Wang, K. F. E. Wong, and J. Y. Y. Kwong, "The Roles of Rater Goals and Ratee Performance Levels in the Distortion of Performance Ratings," *Journal of Applied Psychology* 95, no. 3 (2010), pp. 546–561; J. R. Spence and L. M. Keeping, "The Impact of Non-Performance Information on Ratings of Job Performance: A Policy-Capturing Approach," *Journal of Organizational Behavior* 31 (2010), pp. 587–608; and J. R Spence and L. Keeping, "Conscious Rating Distortion in Performance Appraisal: A Review, Commentary, and Proposed Framework for Research," *Human Resource Management Review* 21, no. 2 (2011), pp. 85–95.

91. L. E. Atwater, J. F. Brett, and A. C. Charles, "Multisource Feedback: Lessons Learned and Implications for Practice," *Human Resource Management* 46, no. 2 (2007), pp. 285–307; and R. Hensel, F. Meijers, R. van der Leeden, and J. Kessels, "360 Degree Feedback: How Many Raters Are Needed for Reliable Ratings on the Capacity to Develop Competences, with Personal Qualities as Developmental Goals?" *International Journal of Human Resource Management* 21, no. 15 (2010), pp. 2813–2830.

92. See, for instance, J. W. Hedge and W. C. Borman, "Changing Conceptions and Practices in Performance Appraisal," in A. Howard (ed.), *The Changing Nature of Work* (San Francisco, CA: Jossey-Bass, 1995), pp. 453–459.

93. See, for instance, K. L. Uggerslev and L. M. Sulsky, "Using Frame-of-Reference Training to Understand the Implications of Rater Idiosyncrasy for Rating Accuracy," *Journal of Applied Psychology* 93, no. 3 (2008), pp. 711–719; and R. F. Martell and D. P. Evans, "Source-Monitoring Training: Toward Reducing Rater Expectancy Effects in Behavioral Measurement," *Journal of Applied Psychology* 90, no. 5 (2005), pp. 956–963.

94. B. Erdogan, "Antecedents and Consequences of Justice Perceptions in Performance Appraisals," *Human Resource Management Review* 12, no. 4 (2002), pp. 555–578; and I. M. Jawahar, "The Mediating Role of Appraisal Feedback Reactions on the Relationship Between Rater Feedback-Related Behaviors and Ratee Performance," *Group and Organization Management* 35, no. 4 (2010), pp. 494–526.

95. S. C. Payne, M. T. Horner, W. R. Boswell, A. N. Schroeder, and K. J. Stine-Cheyne, "Comparison of Online and Traditional Performance Appraisal Systems," *Journal of Managerial Psychology* 24, no. 6 (2009), pp. 526–544.

96. B. D. Cawley, L. M. Keeping, and P. E. Levy, "Participation in the Performance Appraisal Process and Employee Reactions: A Meta-Analytic Review of Field Investigations," *Journal of Applied Psychology* (August 1998), pp. 615–633; and P. E. Levy and J. R. Williams, "The Social Context of Performance Appraisal: A Review and Framework for the Future," *Journal of Management* 30, no. 6 (2004), pp. 881–905.

97. F. Gino and M. E. Schweitzer, "Blinded by Anger or Feeling the Love: How Emotions Influence Advice Taking," *Journal of Applied Psychology* 93, no. 3 (2008), pp. 1165–1173.

98. Heidemeier and Moser, "Self–Other Agreement in Job Performance Ratings."

99. J. Han, "Does Performance-Based Salary System Suit Korea?" *The Korea Times* (January 15, 2008), www.korea-times.co.kr.

100. F. F. T. Chiang and T. A. Birtch, "Appraising Performance across Borders: An Empirical Examination of the Purposes and Practices of Performance Appraisal in a Multi-Country Context," *Journal of Management Studies* 47, no. 7 (2010), pp. 1365–1393.

101. K.-Y. Ng, C. Koh, S. Ang, J. C. Kennedy, and K. Chan, "Rating Leniency and Halo in Multisource Feedback Ratings: Testing Cultural Assumptions of Power Distance and Individualism-Collectivism," *Journal of Applied Psychology*, Online First Publication (April 11, 2011), doi: 10.1037/a0023368.

102. J. Camps and R. Luna-Arocas, "A Matter of Learning: How Human Resources Affect Organizational Performance," *British Journal of Management* 23 (2012), pp. 1–21.

103. R. R. Kehoe and P. M. Wright, "The Impact of High-Performance Human Resource Practices on Employees' Attitudes and Behaviors," *Journal of Management* (February 2013), pp. 366–391.

104. K. Van De Voorde, J. Paauwe, and M. Van Veldhoven, "Employee Well-Being and the HRM-Organizational Performance Relationship: A Review of Quantitative Studies," *International Journal of Management Reviews* 14 (2012), pp. 391–407.

105. M. Heller, "Title VII Protections Debated in 'Great Texas Lactation Case'," *Workforce Management* (October 2012), p. 6.

106. S. Greenhouse, "With Jobs Few, Internships Lure More Graduates to Unpaid Work," *The New York Times* (May 6, 2012), pp. 1, 4.

107. J.-A. B. Casuga, "Judge Rules Fox Searchlight Interns Are FLSA Employees, Certifies Class Action," *Bloomberg BNA* (June 19, 2013), http://www.bna.com/judge-rules-fox-n17179874627/.

108. See, for instance, *Harvard Business Review on Work and Life Balance* (Boston: Harvard Business School Press, 2000); R. Rapoport, L. Bailyn, J. K. Fletcher, and B. H. Pruitt, *Beyond Work-Family Balance* (San Francisco: Jossey-Bass, 2002); and E. E. Kossek, S. Pichler, T. Bodner, and L. B. Hammer, "Workplace Social Support and Work-Family Conflict: A Meta-Analysis Clarifying the Influence of General and Work-Family Specific Supervisor and Organizational Support," *Personnel Psychology* 64, no. 2 (2011), pp. 289–313.

109. B. Harrington, F. Van Deusen, and B. Humberd, *The New Dad: Caring Committed and Conflicted.* (Boston: Boston College Center for Work and Family, 2011).

110. A. Grant, "Top 25 Companies for Work-Life Balance," *US News and World Report* (May 11, 2011), www.money.usnews.com.

111. C. P. Maertz and S. L. Boyar, "Work-Family Conflict, Enrichment, and Balance Under 'Levels' and 'Episodes' Approaches," *Journal of Management* 37, no. 1 (2011), pp. 68–98.

112. L. M. Lapierre and T. D. Allen, "Control at Work, Control at Home, and Planning Behavior: Implications for Work-Family Conflict," *Journal of Management* (September 2012), pp. 1500–1516.

113. J. S. Michel and M. B. Hargis, "Linking Mechanisms of Work-Family Conflict and Segmentation," *Journal of Vocational Behavior* 73, no. 3 (2008), pp. 509–522; G. E. Kreiner, "Consequences of Work-Home Segmentation or Integration: A Person-Environment Fit Perspective," *Journal of Organizational Behavior* 27, no. 4 (2006), pp. 485–507; and C. A. Bulger, R. A. Matthews, and M. E. Hoffman, "Work and Personal Life Boundary Management: Boundary Strength, Work/Personal Life Balance, and the Segmentation-Integration Continuum," *Journal of Occupational Health Psychology* 12, no. 4 (2007), pp. 365–375.

114. D. Catanzaro, H. Moore, and T. R. Marshall, "The Impact of Organizational Culture on Attraction and Recruitment of Job Applicants," *Journal of Business and Psychology* 25 (2010), pp. 649–662.

115. E. O'Regan, "Spain Hampered by Rigid Labor Laws," *The Wall Street Journal* (June 11, 2012), p. 4A.

116. D. Meinert, "Layoff Victims Won't Hold a Grudge If Treated Fairly," *HR Magazine* (November 2012), p. 24.

117. D. van Dierendonck and G. Jacobs, "Survivors and Victims, a Meta-analytical Review of Fairness and Organizational Commitment after Downsizing," *British Journal of Management* 23 (2012), pp. 96–109.

CHAPTER 18

1. J. Muller, "Why Ford Should Worry," *Forbes* (February 13, 2012), pp. 34–40.

2. See, for instance, J. Birkinshaw, G. Hamel, and M. J. Mol, "Management Innovation," *Academy of Management Review* 33, no. 4 (2008), pp. 825–845; and J. Welch and S. Welch, "What Change Agents Are Made Of," *BusinessWeek* (October 20, 2008), p. 96.

3. C. J. Loomis and D. Burke, "Can Ellen Kullman Make DuPont Great Again?" *Fortune* (May 3, 2010), pp. 156–163.

4. R. J. Grossman, "Accelerating Change at GM," *HR Magazine* (June 2012), pp. 58–64.

5. P. G. Audia and S. Brion, "Reluctant to Change: Self-Enhancing Responses to Diverging Performance Measures," *Organizational Behavior and Human Decision Processes* 102 (2007), pp. 255–269.

6. M. Fugate, A. J. Kinicki, and G. E. Prussia, "Employee Coping with Organizational Change: An Examination of Alternative Theoretical Perspectives and Models," *Personnel Psychology* 61, no. 1 (2008), pp. 1–36.

7. J. D. Ford, L. W. Ford, and A. D'Amelio, "Resistance to Change: The Rest of the Story," *Academy of Management Review* 33, no. 2 (2008), pp. 362–377.

8. M. T. Hannan, L. Pólos, and G. R. Carroll, "The Fog of Change: Opacity and Asperity in Organizations," *Administrative Science Quarterly* (September 2003), pp. 399–432.

9. J. P. Kotter and L. A. Schlesinger, "Choosing Strategies for Change," *Harvard Business Review* (March–April 1979), pp. 106–114; and R. K. Smollan, "The Multi-Dimensional Nature of Resistance to Change," *Journal of Management & Organization* (November 2011), pp. 828–849.

10. J. E. Dutton, S. J. Ashford, R. M. O'Neill, and K. A. Lawrence, "Moves That Matter: Issue Selling and Organizational Change," *Academy of Management Journal* (August 2001), pp. 716–736.

11. P. C. Fiss and E. J. Zajac, "The Symbolic Management of Strategic Change: Sensegiving via Framing and Decoupling," *Academy of Management Journal* 49, no. 6 (2006), pp. 1173–1193.

12. A. E. Rafferty and S. L. D. Restubog, "The Impact of Change Process and Context on Change Reactions and Turnover During a Merger," *Journal of Management* 36, no. 5 (2010), pp. 1309–1338.

13. Q. N. Huy, "Emotional Balancing of Organizational Continuity and Radical Change: The Contribution of Middle Managers," *Administrative Science Quarterly* (March 2002), pp. 31–69; D. M. Herold, D. B. Fedor, and S. D. Caldwell, "Beyond Change Management: A Multilevel Investigation of Contextual and Personal Influences on Employees' Commitment to Change," *Journal of Applied Psychology* 92, no. 4 (2007), pp. 942–951; and G. B. Cunningham, "The Relationships Among Commitment to Change, Coping with Change, and Turnover Intentions," *European Journal of Work and Organizational Psychology* 15, no. 1 (2006), pp. 29–45.

14. R. Peccei, A. Giangreco, and A. Sebastiano, "The Role of Organizational Commitment in the Analysis of Resistance to Change: Co-predictor and Moderator Effects," *Personnel Review* 40, no. 2 (2011), pp. 185–204.

15. J. P. Kotter, "Leading Change: Why Transformational Efforts Fail," *Harvard Business Review* 85 (January 2007), p. 96–103.

16. K. van Dam, S. Oreg, and B. Schyns, "Daily Work Contexts and Resistance to Organisational Change: The Role of Leader-Member Exchange, Development Climate, and Change Process Characteristics," *Applied Psychology: An International Review* 57, no. 2 (2008), pp. 313–334.

17. S. Oreg and N. Sverdlik, "Ambivalence toward Imposed Change: The Conflict between Dispositional Resistance to Change and the Orientation toward the Change Agent," *Journal of Applied Psychology* 96, no. 2 (2011), pp. 337–349.

18. D. B. Fedor, S. Caldwell, and D. M. Herold, "The Effects of Organizational Changes on Employee Commitment: A Multilevel Investigation," *Personnel Psychology* 59 (2006), pp. 1–29; and R. D. Foster, "Resistance, Justice, and Commitment to Change," *Human Resource Development Quarterly* 21, no. 1 (2010), pp. 3–39.

19. S. Oreg, "Personality, Context, and Resistance to Organizational Change," *European Journal of Work and Organizational Psychology* 15, no. 1 (2006), pp. 73–101.

20. S. M. Elias, "Employee Commitment in Times of Change: Assessing the Importance of Attitudes Toward Organizational Change," *Journal of Management* 35, no. 1 (2009), pp. 37–55.

21. J. W. B. Lang and P. D. Bliese, "General Mental Ability and Two Types of Adaptation to Unforeseen Change: Applying Discontinuous Growth Models to the Task-Change Paradigm," *Journal of Applied Psychology* 94, no. 2 (2009), pp. 411–428.

22. C. O. L. H. Porter, J. W. Webb, and C. I. Gogus, "When Goal Orientations Collide: Effects of Learning and Performance Orientation on Team Adaptability in Response to Workload Imbalance," *Journal of Applied Psychology* 95, no. 5 (2010), pp. 935–943.

23. See, for instance, A. Karaevli, "Performance Consequences for New CEO 'Outsiderness': Moderating Effects of Pre- and Post-Succession Contexts," *Strategic Management Journal* 28, no. 7 (2007), pp. 681–706.

24. K. Lewin, *Field Theory in Social Science* (New York: Harper & Row, 1951).

25. P. G. Audia, E. A. Locke, and K. G. Smith, "The Paradox of Success: An Archival and a Laboratory Study of Strategic Persistence Following Radical Environmental Change," *Academy of Management Journal* (October 2000), pp. 837–853; and P. G. Audia and S. Brion, "Reluctant to Change: Self-Enhancing Responses to Diverging Performance Measures," *Organizational Behavior and Human Decision Processes* 102, no. 2 (2007), pp. 255–269.

26. J. B. Sorensen, "The Strength of Corporate Culture and the Reliability of Firm Performance," *Administrative Science Quarterly* (March 2002), pp. 70–91.

27. J. Amis, T. Slack, and C. R. Hinings, "The Pace, Sequence, and Linearity of Radical Change," *Academy of Management Journal* (February 2004), pp. 15–39; and E. Autio, H. J. Sapienza, and J. G. Almeida, "Effects of Age at Entry, Knowledge Intensity, and Imitability on International Growth," *Academy of Management Journal* (October 2000), pp. 909–924.

28. J. P. Kotter, "Leading Changes: Why Transformation Efforts Fail," *Harvard Business Review* (March–April 1995), pp. 59–67; and J. P. Kotter, *Leading Change* (Harvard Business School Press, 1996).

29. See, for example, C. Eden and C. Huxham, "Action Research for the Study of Organizations," in S. R. Clegg, C. Hardy, and W. R. Nord (eds.), *Handbook of Organization Studies* (London: Sage, 1996); and L. S. Lüscher and M. W. Lewis, "Organizational Change and Managerial Sensemaking: Working Through Paradox," *Academy of Management Journal* 51, no. 2 (2008), pp. 221–240.

30. For a sampling of various OD definitions, see H. K. Sinangil and F. Avallone, "Organizational Development and Change," in N. Anderson, D. S. Ones, H. K. Sinangil, and C. Viswesvaran (eds.), *Handbook of Industrial, Work and Organizational Psychology*, vol. 2 (Thousand Oaks, CA: Sage, 2001), pp. 332–335; and R. J. Marshak and D. Grant, "Organizational Discourse and New Organization Development Practices," *British Journal of Management* 19, no. 1 (2008), pp. S7–S19.

31. See, for instance, R. Lines, "Influence of Participation in Strategic Change: Resistance, Organizational Commitment and Change Goal Achievement," *Journal of Change Management* (September 2004), pp. 193–215.

32. S. Highhouse, "A History of the T-Group and Its Early Application in Management Development," *Group Dynamics: Theory, Research, & Practice* (December 2002), pp. 277–290.

33. J. E. Edwards and M. D. Thomas, "The Organizational Survey Process: General Steps and Practical Considerations," in P. Rosenfeld, J. E. Edwards, and M. D. Thomas (eds.), *Improving Organizational Surveys: New Directions, Methods, and Applications* (Newbury Park, CA: Sage, 1993), pp. 3–28; and T. Fauth, K. Hattrub, K. Mueller, and B. Roberts, "Nonresponse in Employee Attitude Surveys: A Group-Level Analysis," *Journal of Business and Psychology* (March 2013), pp. 1–16.

34. F. J. Lambrechts, R. Bouwen, S. Grieten, J. P. Huybrechts, and E. H. Schein, "Learning to Help Through Humble Inquiry and Implications for Management Research, Practice, and Education: An Interview with Edgar H. Schein," *Academy of Management Learning & Education* (March 2011), pp. 131–148; E. H. Schein, *Process Consultation: Its Role in Organizational Development*, 2nd ed. (Reading, MA: Addison-Wesley, 1988), p. 9; and E. H. Schein, *Process Consultation Revisited: Building Helpful Relationships* (Reading, MA: Addison-Wesley, 1999).

35. Schein, *Process Consultation*.

36. W. W. G. Dyer, W. G. Dyer, and J. H. Dyer, *Team Building: Proven Strategies for Improving Team Performance* (Hoboken, NJ: Jossey-Bass, 2007).

37. U. Wagner, L. Tropp, G. Finchilescu, and C. Tredoux (eds.), *Improving Intergroup Relations* (New York: Wiley-Blackwell, 2008).

38. See, for example, R. Fry, F. Barrett, J. Seiling, and D. Whitney (eds.), *Appreciative Inquiry & Organizational Transformation: Reports from the Field* (Westport, CT: Quorum, 2002); J. K. Barge and C. Oliver, "Working with Appreciation in Managerial Practice," *Academy of Management Review* (January 2003), pp. 124–142; and D. van der Haar and D. M. Hosking, "Evaluating Appreciative Inquiry: A Relational Constructionist Perspective," *Human Relations* (August 2004), pp. 1017–1036.

39. G. Giglio, S. Michalcova, and C. Yates, "Instilling a Culture of Winning at American Express," *Organization Development Journal* 25, no. 4 (2007), pp. P33–P37.

40. A. Harrington, "Who's Afraid of a New Product?" *Fortune* (November 10, 2003), pp. 189–192; and C. C. Manz, F. Shipper, and G. L. Stewart, "Everyone a Team Leader: Shared Influence at W. L. Gore and Associates," *Organizational Dynamics* 38, no. 3 (2009), pp. 239–244.

41. See, for instance, R. M. Kanter, "When a Thousand Flowers Bloom: Structural, Collective and Social Conditions for Innovation in Organizations," in B. M. Staw and L. L. Cummings (eds.), *Research in Organizational Behavior*, vol. 10 (Greenwich, CT: JAI Press, 1988), pp. 169–211.

42. F. Damanpour, "Organizational Innovation: A Meta-Analysis of Effects of Determinants and Moderators," *Academy of Management Journal* (September 1991), p. 557; and H. W. Volberda, F. A. J. Van den Bosch, and C. V. Heij, "Management Innovation: Management as Fertile Ground for Innovation," *European Management Review* (Spring 2013), pp. 1–15.

43. Damanpour, "Organizational Innovation," pp. 555–590; and G. Westerman, F. W. McFarlan, and M. Iansiti, "Organization Design and Effectiveness over the Innovation Life Cycle," *Organization Science* 17, no. 2 (2006), pp. 230–238.

44. See P. R. Monge, M. D. Cozzens, and N. S. Contractor, "Communication and Motivational Predictors of the Dynamics of Organizational Innovation," *Organization Science* (May 1992), pp. 250–274; P. Schepers and P. T. van den Berg, "Social factors of work-environment creativity," *Journal of Business and Psychology* 21, no. 3 (2007), pp. 407–428.

45. D. L. Day, "Raising Radicals: Different Processes for Championing Innovative Corporate Ventures," *Organization Science* (May 1994), pp. 148–172; and M. E. Mullins, S. W. J. Kozlowski, N. Schmitt, and A. W. Howell, "The Role of the Idea Champion in Innovation: The Case of the

Internet in the Mid-1990s," *Computers in Human Behavior* 24, no. 2 (2008), pp. 451–467.

46. J. M. Howell and C. A. Higgins, "Champions of Change: Identifying, Understanding, and Supporting Champions of Technological Innovations," *Organizational Dynamics* 19, (1990), pp. 40–55; and S. C. Parker, "Intrapreneurship or Entrepreneurship?" *Journal of Business Venturing* (January 2011), pp. 19–34.

47. M. Cerne, M. Jaklic, and M. Skerlavaj, "Decoupling Management and Technological Innovations: Resolving the Individualism-Collectivism Controversy," *Journal of International Management* (June 2013), pp. 103–117; and S. Shane, S. Venkataraman, and I. MacMillan, "Cultural Differences in Innovation Championing Strategies," *Journal of Management* 21, no. 5 (1995), pp. 931–952.

48. A. Taylor, "Chrysler's Speed Merchant," *Fortune* (September 6, 2010), pp. 77–82.

49. See, for example, T. B. Lawrence, M. K. Mauws, B. Dyck, and R. F. Kleysen, "The Politics of Organizational Learning: Integrating Power into the 4I Framework," *Academy of Management Review* (January 2005), pp. 180–191.

50. D. H. Kim, "The Link Between Individual and Organizational Learning," *Sloan Management Review* (Fall 1993), p. 37.

51. C. Argyris and D. A. Schon, *Organizational Learning* (Reading, MA: Addison-Wesley, 1978).

52. L. Berghman, P. Matthyssens, S. Streukens, and K. Vandenbempt, "Deliberate Learning Mechanisms for Stimulating Strategic Innovation Capacity," *Long Range Planning* (February–April 2013), pp. 39–71; and B. Dumaine, "Mr. Learning Organization," *Fortune* (October 17, 1994), p. 148.

53. F. Kofman and P. M. Senge, "Communities of Commitment: The Heart of Learning Organizations," *Organizational Dynamics* (Autumn 1993), pp. 5–23.

54. Dumaine, "Mr. Learning Organization," p. 154.

55. D. Meinert, "Wings of Change," *HR Magazine* (November 2012), pp. 30–36.

56. M.-G. Seo, M. S. Taylor, N. S. Hill, X. Zhang, P. E. Tesluk, and N. M. Lorinkova, "The Role of Affect and Leadership During Organizational Change," *Personnel Psychology* 65 (2012), pp. 121–165.

57. M. Fugate, G. E. Prussia, and A. J. Kinicki, "Managing Employee Withdrawal During Organizational Change: The Role of Threat Appraisal," *Journal of Management* (May 2012), pp. 890–914.

58. J. Shin, M. S. Taylor, and M.-G. Seo, "Resources for Change: The Relationships of Organizational Inducements and Psychological Resilience to Employees' Attitudes and Behaviors toward Organizational Change," *Academy of Management Journal* 55 (2012), pp. 727–748.

59. See, for instance, S. Armour, "Rising Job Stress Could Affect Bottom Line," *USA Today* (July 29, 2003), p. 1B; and J. Schramm, "Work/Life on Hold," *HR Magazine* 53 (October 2008), p. 120.

60. B. Mirza, "Workplace Stress Hits Three-Year High," *HR Magazine* (April 2012), p. 15.

61. Adapted from R. S. Schuler, "Definition and Conceptualization of Stress in Organizations," *Organizational Behavior and Human Performance* (April 1980), p. 189.

For an updated review of definitions, see C. L. Cooper, P. J. Dewe, and M. P. O'Driscoll, *Organizational Stress: A Review and Critique of Theory, Research, and Applications* (Thousand Oaks, CA: Sage, 2002).

62. See, for instance, M. A. Cavanaugh, W. R. Boswell, M. V. Roehling, and J. W. Boudreau, "An Empirical Examination of Self-Reported Work Stress Among U.S. Managers," *Journal of Applied Psychology* (February 2000), pp. 65–74.

63. S. Shellenbarger, "When Stress Is Good for You," *The Wall Street Journal* (January 24, 2012), pp. D1, D5.

64. Ibid.

65. N. P. Podsakoff, J. A. LePine, and M. A. LePine, "Differential Challenge-Hindrance Stressor Relationships with Job Attitudes, Turnover Intentions, Turnover, and Withdrawal Behavior: A Meta-Analysis," *Journal of Applied Psychology* 92, no. 2 (2007), pp. 438–454; and J. A. LePine, M. A. LePine, and C. L. Jackson, "Challenge and Hindrance Stress: Relationships with Exhaustion, Motivation to Learn, and Learning Performance," *Journal of Applied Psychology* (October 2004), pp. 883–891.

66. L. W. Hunter and S. M. B. Thatcher, "Feeling the Heat: Effects of Stress, Commitment, and Job Experience on Job Performance," *Academy of Management Journal* 50, no. 4 (2007), pp. 953–968.

67. J. C. Wallace, B. D. Edwards, T. Arnold, M. L. Frazier, and D. M. Finch, "Work Stressors, Role-Based Performance, and the Moderating Influence of Organizational Support," *Journal of Applied Psychology* 94, no. 1 (2009), pp. 254–262.

68. N. W. Van Yperen and O. Janssen, "Fatigued and Dissatisfied or Fatigued but Satisfied? Goal Orientations and Responses to High Job Demands," *Academy of Management Journal* (December 2002), pp. 1161–1171; and N. W. Van Yperen and M. Hagedoorn, "Do High Job Demands Increase Intrinsic Motivation or Fatigue or Both? The Role of Job Control and Job Social Support," *Academy of Management Journal* (June 2003), pp. 339–348.

69. J. de Jonge and C. Dormann, "Stressors, Resources, and Strain at Work: A Longitudinal Test of the Triple-Match Principle," *Journal of Applied Psychology* 91, no. 5 (2006), pp. 1359–1374.

70. This section is adapted from C. L. Cooper and R. Payne, *Stress at Work* (London: Wiley, 1978); S. Parasuraman and J. A. Alutto, "Sources and Outcomes of Stress in Organizational Settings: Toward the Development of a Structural Model," *Academy of Management Journal* 27, no. 2 (June 1984), pp. 330–350; and P. M. Hart and C. L. Cooper, "Occupational Stress: Toward a More Integrated Framework," in N. Anderson, D. S. Ones, H. K. Sinangil, and C. Viswesvaran (eds.), *Handbook of Industrial, Work and Organizational Psychology*, vol. 2 (London: Sage, 2001), pp. 93–114.

71. A. E. Rafferty and M. A. Griffin, "Perceptions of Organizational Change: A Stress and Coping Perspective," *Journal of Applied Psychology* 71, no. 5 (2007), pp. 1154–1162.

72. H. Garst, M. Frese, and P. C. M. Molenaar, "The Temporal Factor of Change in Stressor-Strain Relationships: A Growth Curve Model on a Longitudinal Study in East Germany," *Journal of Applied Psychology* (June 2000), pp. 417–438.

73. See, for example, M. L. Fox, D. J. Dwyer, and D. C. Ganster, "Effects of Stressful Job Demands and Control

of Physiological and Attitudinal Outcomes in a Hospital Setting," *Academy of Management Journal* (April 1993), pp. 289–318; and R. Ilies, N. Dimotakis, and I. E. De Pater, "Psychological and Physiological Reactions to High Workloads: Implications for Well-Being," *Personnel Psychology* (Summer 2010), pp. 407–436.

74. T. L. Smith-Jackson and K. W. Klein, "Open-Plan Offices: Task Performance and Mental Workload," *Journal of Environmental Psychology* 29, no. 2 (2009), pp. 279–289.

75. T. M. Glomb, J. D. Kammeyer-Mueller, and M. Rotundo, "Emotional Labor Demands and Compensating Wage Differentials," *Journal of Applied Psychology* (August 2004), pp. 700–714; and A. A. Grandey, "When 'The Show Must Go On': Surface Acting and Deep Acting as Determinants of Emotional Exhaustion and Peer-Rated Service Delivery," *Academy of Management Journal* (February 2003), pp. 86–96.

76. C. Fritz and S. Sonnentag, "Antecedents of Day-Level Proactive Behavior: A Look at Job Stressors and Positive Affect During the Workday," *Journal of Management* 35, no. 1 (2009), pp. 94–111.

77. S. Lim, L. M. Cortina, and V. J. Magley, "Personal and Workgroup Incivility: Impact on Work and Health Outcomes," *Journal of Applied Psychology* 93, no. 1 (2008), pp. 95–107; N. T. Buchanan, and L. F. Fitzgerald, "Effects of Racial and Sexual Harassment on Work and the Psychological Well-Being of African American Women," *Journal of Occupational Health Psychology* 13, no. 2 (2008), pp. 137–151; C. R. Willness, P. Steel, and K. Lee, "A Meta-Analysis of the Antecedents and Consequences of Workplace Sexual Harassment," *Personnel Psychology* 60, no. 1 (2007), pp. 127–162; and B. Moreno-Jiménez, A. Rodríguez-Muñoz, J. C. Pastor, A. I. Sanz-Vergel, and E. Garrosa, "The Moderating Effects of Psychological Detachment and Thoughts of Revenge in Workplace Bullying," *Personality and Individual Differences* 46, no. 3 (2009), pp. 359–364.

78. V. S. Major, K. J. Klein, and M. G. Ehrhart, "Work Time, Work Interference with Family, and Psychological Distress," *Journal of Applied Psychology* (June 2002), pp. 427–436. See also P. E. Spector, C. L. Cooper, S. Poelmans, T. D. Allen, M. O'Driscoll, J. I. Sanchez, et al., "A Cross-National Comparative Study of Work-Family Stressors, Working Hours, and Well-Being: China and Latin America Versus the Anglo World," *Personnel Psychology* (Spring 2004), pp. 119–142.

79. D. L. Nelson and C. Sutton, "Chronic Work Stress and Coping: A Longitudinal Study and Suggested New Directions," *Academy of Management Journal* (December 1990), pp. 859–869.

80. J. B. Avey, F. Luthans, and S. M. Jensen, "Psychological Capital: A Positive Resource for Combating Employee Stress and Turnover," *Human Resource Management* (September–October 2009), pp. 677–693.

81. H. Selye, *The Stress of Life,* rev. ed. (New York: McGraw-Hill, 1976); and Q. Hu, W. B. Schaufeli, and T. W. Taris, "The Job Demands–Resources Model: An Analysis of Additive and Joint Effects of Demands and Resources," *Journal of Vocational Behavior* 79, no. 1 (2011), pp. 181–190.

82. S. J. Motowidlo, J. S. Packard, and M. R. Manning, "Occupational Stress: Its Causes and Consequences for Job Performance," *Journal of Applied Psychology* (November

1987), pp. 619–620; and E. R. Crawford, J. A. LePine, and B. L. Rich, "Linking Job Demands and Resources to Employee Engagement and Burnout: A Theoretical Extension and Meta-Analytic test," *Journal of Applied Psychology* 95, no. 5 (2010), pp. 834–848.

83. See J. B. Halbesleben, "Sources of Social Support and Burnout: A Meta-Analytic Test of the Conservation of Resources Model," *Journal of Applied Psychology* 91, no. 5 (2006), pp. 1134–1145; N. Bolger and D. Amarel, "Effects of Social Support Visibility on Adjustment to Stress: Experimental Evidence," *Journal of Applied Psychology* 92, no. 3 (2007), pp. 458–475; and C. Fernet, M. Gagné and S. Austin, "When Does Quality of Relationships with Coworkers Predict Burnout over Time? The Moderating Role of Work Motivation" *Journal of Organizational Behavior* 31 (2010), pp. 1163–1180.

84. See, for example, C. M. Middeldorp, D. C. Cath, A. L. Beem, G. Willemsen, and D. I. Boomsma, "Life Events, Anxious Depression, and Personality: A Prospective and Genetic Study," *Psychological Medicine* 38, no. 11 (2008), pp. 1557–1565; A. A. Uliaszek, R. E. Zinbarg, S. Mineka, M. G. Craske, J. M. Sutton, J. W. Griffith, R. Rose, A. Waters, and C. Hammen, "The Role of Neuroticism and Extraversion in the Stress-Anxiety and Stress-Depression Relationships," *Anxiety, Stress, and Coping* 23, no. 4 (2010), pp. 363–381.

85. J. D. Kammeyer-Mueller, T. A. Judge, and B. A. Scott, "The Role of Core Self-Evaluations in the Coping Process," *Journal of Applied Psychology* 94, no. 1 (2009), pp. 177–195.

86. R. J. Burke, A. M. Richardson, and M. Mortinussen, "Workaholism Among Norwegian Managers: Work and Well-Being Outcomes," *Journal of Organizational Change Management* 7 (2004), pp. 459–470; and W. B. Schaufeli, T. W. Taris, and W. van Rhenen, "Workaholism, Burnout, and Work Engagement: Three of a Kind or Three Different Kinds of Employee Well-Being," *Applied Psychology: An International Review* 57, no. 2 (2008), pp. 173–203.

87. J. Chen, C. Silverthorne, and J. Hung, "Organization Communication, Job Stress, Organizational Commitment, and Job Performance of Accounting Professionals in Taiwan and America," *Leadership & Organization Development Journal* 27, no. 4 (2006), pp. 242–249; and C. Liu, P. E. Spector, and L. Shi, "Cross-National Job Stress: A Quantitative and Qualitative Study," *Journal of Organizational Behavior* (February 2007), pp. 209–239.

88. P. E. Spector, T. D. Allen, S. A. Y. Poelmans, L. M. Lapierre, C. L. Cooper, M. O'Driscoll, et al., "Cross National Differences in Relationships of Work Demands, Job Satisfaction, and Turnover Intention with Work-Family Conflict," *Personnel Psychology* 60, no. 4 (2007), pp. 805–835.

89. H. M. Addae and X. Wang, "Stress at Work: Linear and Curvilinear Effects of Psychological-, Job-, and Organization-Related Factors: An Exploratory Study of Trinidad and Tobago," *International Journal of Stress Management* (November 2006), pp. 476–493.

90. J. Schaubroeck, J. R. Jones, and J. L. Xie, "Individual Differences in Utilizing Control to Cope with Job Demands: Effects on Susceptibility to Infectious Disease," *Journal of Applied Psychology* (April 2001), pp. 265–278.

91. M. Kivimäki, J. Head, J. E. Ferrie, E. Brunner, M. G. Marmot, J. Vahtera, and M. J. Shipley, "Why Is Evidence

on Job Strain and Coronary Heart Disease Mixed? An Illustration of Measurement Challenges in the Whitehall II Study," *Psychosomatic Medicine* 68, no. 3 (2006), pp. 398–401.

92. M. Borritz, K. B. Christensen, U. Bültmann, R. Rugulies, T. Lund, I Andersen, E. Villadsen, F. Didreichsen, and T. S. Krisensen, "Impact on Burnout and Psychosocial Work Characteristics on Future Long-Term Sickness Absence, Prospective Results of the Danish PUMA Study Among Human Service Workers," *Journal of Occupational and Environmental Medicine* 52, no. 10 (2010), pp. 964–970.

93. R. Ilies, N. Dimotakis, and I. E. DePater, "Psychological and Physiological Reactions to High Workloads: Implications for Well-Being," *Personnel Psychology* 63, no. 2 (2010), pp. 407–463.

94. D. Örtqvist and J. Wincent, "Prominent Consequences of Role Stress: A Meta-Analytic Review," *International Journal of Stress Management*, 13, no. 4 (2006), pp. 399–422.

95. J. R. Hackman and G. R. Oldham, "Development of the Job Diagnostic Survey," *Journal of Applied Psychology* (April 1975), pp. 159–170; J. J. Hakanen, A. B. Bakker, and M. Jokisaari, "A 35-Year Follow-Up Study on Burnout Among Finnish Employees," *Journal of Occupational Health Psychology* 16, no. 3 (2011), pp. 345–360; Crawford, LePine, and Rich, "Linking Job Demands and Resources to Employee Engagement and Burnout; and G. A. Chung-Yan, "The Nonlinear Effects of Job Complexity and Autonomy on Job Satisfaction, Turnover, and Psychological Well-Being," *Journal of Occupational Health Psychology* 15, no. 3 (2010), pp. 237–251.

96. L. L. Meier, N. K. Semmer, A. Elfering, and N. Jacobshagen, "The Double Meaning of Control: Three-Way Interactions Between Internal Resources, Job Control, and Stressors at Work," *Journal of Occupational Health Psychology* 13, no. 3 (2008), pp. 244–258.

97. E. M. de Croon, J. K. Sluiter, R. W. B. Blonk, J. P. J. Broersen, and M. H. W. Frings-Dresen, "Stressful Work, Psychological Job Strain, and Turnover: A 2-Year Prospective Cohort Study of Truck Drivers," *Journal of Applied Psychology* (June 2004), pp. 442–454; R. Cropanzano, D. E. Rupp, and Z. S. Byrne, "The Relationship of Emotional Exhaustion to Work Attitudes, Job Performance, and Organizational Citizenship Behaviors," *Journal of Applied Psychology* (February 2003), pp. 160–169; and S. Diestel and K. Schmidt, "Costs of Simultaneous Coping with Emotional Dissonance and Self-Control Demands at Work: Results from Two German Samples," *Journal of Applied Psychology* 96, no. 3 (2011), pp. 643–653.

98. See, for instance, S. Zivnuska, C. Kiewitz, W. A. Hochwarter, P. L. Perrewe, and K. L. Zellars, "What Is Too Much or Too Little? The Curvilinear Effects of Job Tension on Turnover Intent, Value Attainment, and Job Satisfaction," *Journal of Applied Social Psychology* (July 2002), pp. 1344–1360.

99. L. A. Muse, S. G. Harris, and H. S. Field, "Has the Inverted-U Theory of Stress and Job Performance Had a Fair Test?" *Human Performance* 16, no. 4 (2003), pp. 349–364.

100. S. Gilboa, A. Shirom, Y. Fried, and C. L. Cooper, "A Meta-Analysis of Work Demand Stressors and Job Performance: Examining Main and Moderating Effects," *Personnel Psychology* 61, no. 2 (2008), pp. 227–271.

101. J. C. Wallace, B. D. Edwards, T. Arnold, M. L. Frazier, and D. M. Finch, "Work Stressors, Role-Based Performance, and the Moderating Influence of Organizational Support," *Journal of Applied Psychology* 94, no. 1 (2009), pp. 254–262.

102. The following discussion has been influenced J. M. Ivancevich, M. T. Matteson, S. M. Freedman, and J. S. Phillips, "Worksite Stress Management Interventions," *American Psychologist* (February 1990), pp. 252–261; R. Schwarzer, "Manage Stress at Work Through Preventive and Proactive Coping," in E. A. Locke (ed.), *Handbook of Principles of Organizational Behavior* (Malden, MA: Blackwell, 2004), pp. 342–355; and K. M. Richardson and H. R. Rothstein, "Effects of Occupational Stress Management Intervention Programs: A Meta-Analysis," *Journal of Occupational Health Psychology* 13, no. 1 (2008), pp. 69–93.

103. T. H. Macan, "Time Management: Test of a Process Model," *Journal of Applied Psychology* (June 1994), pp. 381–391; and B. J. C. Claessens, W. Van Eerde, C. G. Rutte, and R. A. Roe, "Planning Behavior and Perceived Control of Time at Work," *Journal of Organizational Behavior* (December 2004), pp. 937–950.

104. See, for example, G. Lawrence-Ell, *The Invisible Clock: A Practical Revolution in Finding Time for Everyone and Everything* (Seaside Park, NJ: Kingsland Hall, 2002); and B. Tracy, *Time Power* (New York: AMACOM, 2004).

105. R. W. Renn, D. G. Allen, and T. M. Huning, "Empirical Examination of Individual-Level Personality-Based Theory of Self-Management Failure," *Journal of Organizational Behavior* 32, no. 1 (2011), pp. 25–43; and P. Gröpel and P. Steel, "A Mega-Trial Investigation of Goal Setting, Interest Enhancement, and Energy on Procrastination," *Personality and Individual Differences* 45, no. 5 (2008), pp. 406–411.

106. P. Salmon, "Effects of Physical Exercise on Anxiety, Depression, and Sensitivity to Stress: A Unifying Theory," *Clinical Psychology Review* 21, no. 1 (2001), pp. 33–61.

107. K. M. Richardson and H. R. Rothstein, "Effects of Occupational Stress Management Intervention Programs: A Meta-Analysis," *Journal of Occupational Health Psychology* 13, no. 1 (2008), pp. 69–93.

108. V. C. Hahn, C. Binnewies, S. Sonnentag, and E. J. Mojza, "Learning How to Recover From Job Stress: Effects of a Recovery Training Program on Recovery, Recovery-Related Self-Efficacy, and Well-Being," *Journal of Occupational Health Psychology* 16, no. 2 (2011), pp. 202–216; and C. Binnewies, S. Sonnentag, and E. J. Mojza, "Recovery During the Weekend and Fluctuations in Weekly Job Performance: A Week-Level Study Examining Intra-Individual Relationships," *Journal of Occupational and Organizational Psychology* 83, no. 2 (2010), pp. 419–441.

109. E. R. Greenglass and L. Fiksenbaum, "Proactive Coping, Positive Affect, and Well-Being: Testing for Mediation Using Path Analysis," *European Psychologist* 14, no. 1 (2009), pp. 29–39; and P. Miquelon and R. J. Vallerand, "Goal Motives, Well-Being, and Physical Health: Happiness and Self-Realization as Psychological Resources under Challenge," *Motivation and Emotion* 30, no. 4 (2006), pp. 259–272.

110. M. M. Butts, R. J. Vandenberg, D. M. DeJoy, B. S. Schaffer, and M. G. Wilson, "Individual Reactions to High Involvement Work Processes: Investigating the Role of Empowerment and Perceived Organizational Support," *Journal of Occupational Health Psychology* 14, no. 2 (2009), pp. 122–136.

111. "100 Best Companies to Work For," *Fortune* (August 17, 2011), http://money.cnn.com/magazines/fortune.

112. L. Blue, "Making Good Health Easy," *Time* (November 12, 2009), www.time.com; and M. Andrews, "Americas Best Health Plans," *US News and World Report* (November 5, 2007), pp. 54–60.

113. K. M. Richardson and H. R. Rothstein, "Effects of Occupational Stress Management Intervention Programs: A Meta-Analysis," *Journal of Occupational Health Psychology* 13, no. 1 (2008), pp. 69–93.

114. D. Brown, "Wellness Programs Bring Healthy Bottom Line," *Canadian HR Reporter* (December 17, 2001), pp. 1ff.

APPENDIX

1. J. A. Byrne, "Executive Sweat," *Forbes* (May 20), 1985, pp. 198–200.

2. See D. P. Schwab, *Research Methods for Organizational Behavior* (Mahwah, NJ: Lawrence Erlbaum Associates, 1999); and S. G. Rogelberg (ed.), *Blackwell Handbook of Research Methods in Industrial and Organizational Psychology* (Malden, MA: Blackwell, 2002).

3. B. M. Staw and G. R. Oldham, "Reconsidering Our Dependent Variables: A Critique and Empirical Study," *Academy of Management Journal* (December 1978), pp. 539–559; and B. M. Staw, "Organizational Behavior: A Review and Reformulation of the Field's Outcome Variables," in M. R. Rosenzweig and L. W. Porter (eds.), *Annual Review of Psychology,* vol. 35 (Palo Alto, CA: Annual Reviews, 1984), pp. 627–666.

4. R. S. Blackburn, "Experimental Design in Organizational Settings," in J. W. Lorsch (ed.), *Handbook of Organizational Behavior* (Upper Saddle River, NJ: Prentice Hall, 1987), pp. 127–128; and F. L. Schmidt, C. Viswesvaran, D. S. Ones, "Reliability Is Not Validity and Validity Is Not Reliability," *Personnel Psychology* (Winter 2000), pp. 901–912.

5. G. R. Weaver, L. K. Trevino, and P. L. Cochran, "Corporate Ethics Practices in the Mid-1990's: An Empirical Study of the Fortune 1000," *Journal of Business Ethics* (February 1999), pp. 283–294.

6. S. Milgram, *Obedience to Authority* (New York: Harper & Row, 1974). For a critique of this research, see T. Blass, "Understanding Behavior in the Milgram Obedience Experiment: The Role of Personality, Situations, and Their Interactions," *Journal of Personality and Social Psychology* (March 1991), pp. 398–413.

7. See, for example, W. N. Kaghan, A. L. Strauss, S. R. Barley, M. Y. Brannen, and R. J. Thomas, "The Practice and Uses of Field Research in the 21st Century Organization," *Journal of Management Inquiry* (March 1999), pp. 67–81.

8. A. D. Stajkovic and F. Luthans, "A Meta-Analysis of the Effects of Organizational Behavior Modification on Task Performance, 1975–1995," *Academy of Management Journal* (October 1997), pp. 1122–1149.

9. See, for example, K. Zakzanis, "The Reliability of Meta Analytic Review," *Psychological Reports* (August 1998), pp. 215–222; C. Ostroff and D. A. Harrison, "Meta-Analysis, Level of Analysis, and Best Estimates of Population Correlations: Cautions for Interpreting Meta-Analytic Results in Organizational Behavior," *Journal of Applied Psychology* (April 1999), pp. 260–270; R. Rosenthal and M. R. DiMatteo, "Meta-Analysis: Recent Developments in Quantitative Methods for Literature Reviews," in S. T. Fiske, D. L. Schacter, and C. Zahn-Wacher (eds.), *Annual Review of Psychology,* vol. 52 (Palo Alto, CA: Annual Reviews, 2001), pp. 59–82; and F. L. Schmidt and J. E. Hunter, "Meta-Analysis," in N. Anderson, D. S. Ones, H. K. Sinangil, and C. Viswesvaran (eds.), *Handbook of Industrial, Work & Organizational Psychology,* vol. 1 (Thousand Oaks, CA: Sage, 2001), pp. 51–70.

10. For more on ethical issues in research, see T. L. Beauchamp, R. R. Faden, R. J. Wallace, Jr., and L. Walters (eds.), *Ethical Issues in Social Science Research* (Baltimore, MD: Johns Hopkins University Press, 1982); and J. G. Adair, "Ethics of Psychological Research: New Policies, Continuing Issues, New Concerns," *Canadian Psychology* (February 2001), pp. 25–37.

11. J. Kifner, "Scholar Sets Off Gastronomic False Alarm," *New York Times* (September 8), 2001, p. A1.

Name Index

Organizations Index

Subject Index